Introduction to Data Structures and Algorithm Analysis with C++

Introduction to Data Structures and Algorithm Analysis with C++

George J. Pothering
College of Charleston

Thomas L. Naps
Lawrence University

West Publishing Company
Minneapolis/St. Paul   New York   San Francisco   Los Angeles

WEST'S COMMITMENT TO THE ENVIRONMENT

In 1906, West Publishing Company began recycling materials left over from the production of books. This began a tradition of efficient and responsible use of resources. Today, up to 95 percent of our legal books and 70 percent of our college and school texts are printed on recycled, acid-free stock. West also recycles nearly 22 million pounds of scrap paper annually—the equivalent of 181,717 trees. Since the 1960s, West has devised ways to capture and recycle waste inks, solvents, oils, and vapors created in the printing process. We also recycle plastics of all kinds, wood, glass, corrugated cardboard, and batteries, and have eliminated the use of Styrofoam book packaging. We at West are proud of the longevity and the scope of our commitment to the environment.

Production, Prepress, Printing and Binding by West Publishing Company.

British Library Cataloguing-in-Publication Data. A catalogue record for this book is available from the British Library.

Production Credits:
Copyediting: Lorretta Palagi
Interior Text Design: John Rokusek
Composition: Publication Services
Art: Publication Services
Indexing: Publication Services
Cover Photograph: Gregory MacNicol

Printed in the United States of America
02 01 00 99 98 97 96   8 7 6 5 4 3 2 1

Library of Congress Cataloging-in-Publication Data

Pothering, George.
Introduction to data structures and algorithm analysis with C++/ George J. Pothering, Thomas L. Naps.
p. cm.
Includes index.
ISBN 0-314-04574-0
1. C++ (Computer program language) 2. Data structures (Computer science) 3. Computer algorithms. I. Naps, Thomas L. II. Title.
QA76.73.C153P684 1995
005.7'3–dc20   94-44364
CIP

To our teachers, especially:

Dr. Alan Huckleberry

Dr. Henry Gordon

G.J.P.

Dr. Lee Rice

Dr. Robert Mullins

T.L.N.

Preface

Background and Objectives

In March 1991, the Joint Curriculum Task Force of the Association for Computing Machinery (ACM) and the Institute of Electrical and Electronic Engineers—Computer Society (IEEE—CS) issued its report, *Computing Curricula 1991.* Central to this report and the curricular recommendations it makes are the recurring themes of theory, abstraction, and design in all areas of computer science. Earlier editions of the authors' data structures textbooks (Naps, *Introduction to Data Structures and Algorithm Analysis* (2nd edition), West Publishing Company, 1992; and Naps and Pothering, *Introduction to Data Structures and Algorithm Analysis with Pascal* (2nd edition), West Publishing Company, 1992) reflected these themes by incorporating formal definitions of all data structures as abstract data types (ADTs). Each ADT included a set of operations that was specified in formal pre- and postcondition style. These strict definitions replaced the more intuitive approach that was often used in earlier editions. After an ADT had been defined, various implementations of it were studied, making the theory and abstraction mesh with the design theme. In developing this book we wished to continue this approach, but to take it one step further by implementing our algorithms and data structures using an object-oriented language to enforce the maxim that access to the data structures of an ADT should only be possible through ADT operations. We have chosen the language C++ for such implementations because of the support it provides, by means of its class construct, for such restricted access to data structures, and because of its increasingly widespread availability.

Different implementations of an ADT illustrate different design perspectives. These perspectives are reflected in the time and space efficiency of a particular implementation. Each implementation of an ADT that we present is accompanied by an efficiency analysis. Sometimes it's a run-time efficiency we analyze, sometimes a space efficiency, and sometimes both. Such analyses typically combine mathematical theory with the empirical observation paradigm of the natural sciences.

The design theme in computer science runs much deeper than mere consideration of how to implement ADTs. Given an ADT and its implementation, students must recognize the role of that ADT in realistic, large-scale applications. This will help prepare them for future careers in software engineering. For instance, to study queues without gaining some insight into how queues are used in scheduling and simulation applications would seriously shortchange the design theme. It is important that students see how to use complex data structures in other areas of computer science. In this respect, we maintain an emphasis on applications of data structures, which are viewed as an integrated component in the entire discipline of computer science.

Organization and Coverage of Topics

The text's organization makes it appropriate for several types of courses. It could be used for a student's second course in computer science (the "CS2" course), assuming the student has completed a rigorous first course based on a procedural high-level language such as Pascal, Ada, or given the orientation of this textbook, C or C++. Ideally, the student has also completed a discrete mathematics course. With such a background, the early chapters of the text would be covered thoroughly, and selected advanced topics from later chapters could be skipped as described in the figure on page vii. Although we assume a familiarity with C, for students unfamiliar with this language we also include a brief introduction in Appendix C. We do not assume familiarity with the object-oriented extensions that C++ adds to C.

The text could also be used for a more advanced course in data structures and algorithms, assuming a previous course that included a survey of elementary data structures such as stacks, queues, linked lists, and binary trees. For this more advanced course, some early chapters of the text could be covered quickly, allowing appropriate time for later treatment of advanced topics. The figure on page viii provides a possible sequencing of topics for such an advanced course.

Possible Sequence of Topics for CS2 Course

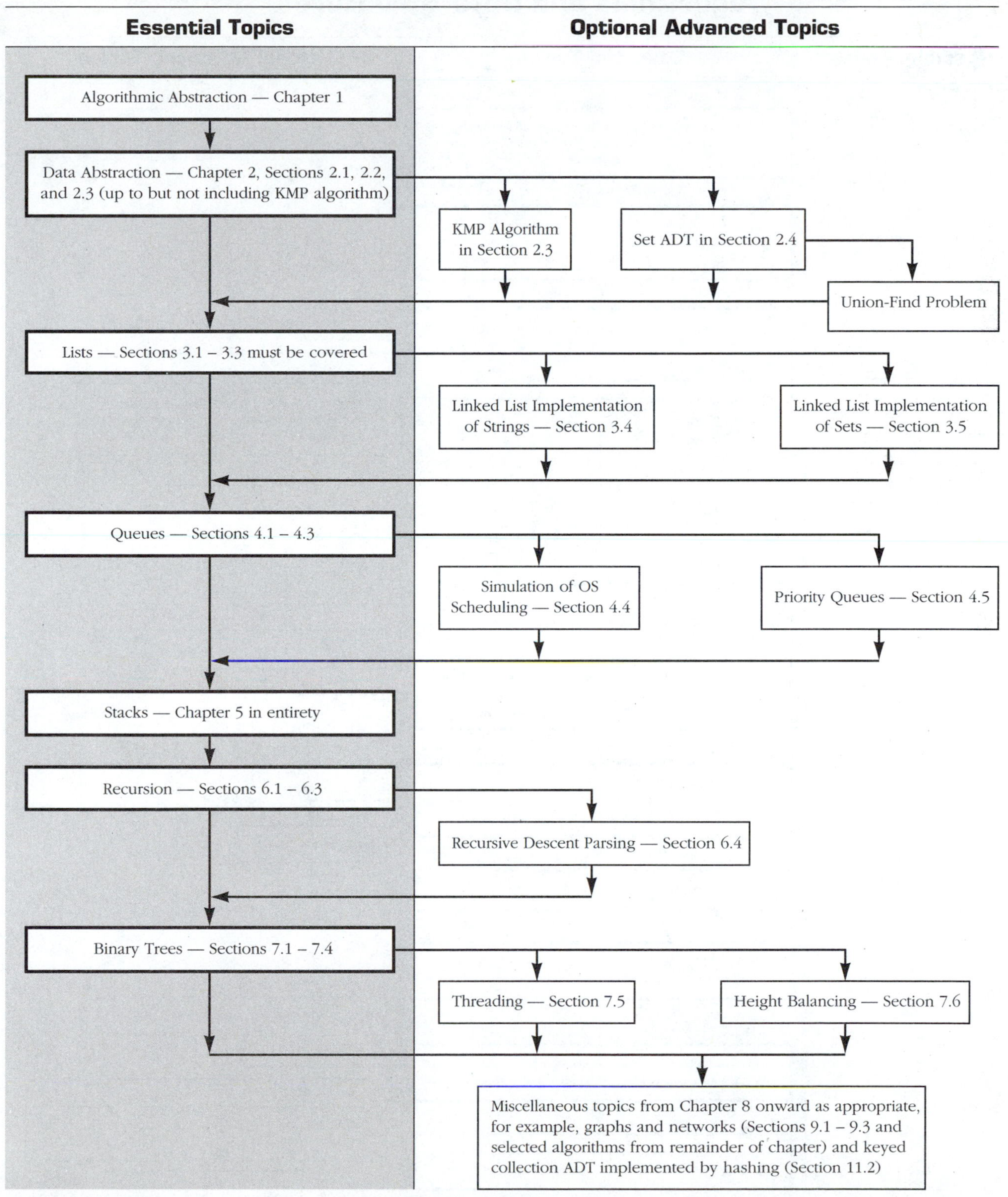
Essential Topics
Optional Advanced Topics
Algorithmic Abstraction — Chapter 1
Data Abstraction — Chapter 2, Sections 2.1, 2.2, and 2.3 (up to but not including KMP algorithm)
KMP Algorithm in Section 2.3
Set ADT in Section 2.4
Union-Find Problem
Lists — Sections 3.1 – 3.3 must be covered
Linked List Implementation of Strings — Section 3.4
Linked List Implementation of Sets — Section 3.5
Queues — Sections 4.1 – 4.3
Simulation of OS Scheduling — Section 4.4
Priority Queues — Section 4.5
Stacks — Chapter 5 in entirety
Recursion — Sections 6.1 – 6.3
Recursive Descent Parsing — Section 6.4
Binary Trees — Sections 7.1 – 7.4
Threading — Section 7.5
Height Balancing — Section 7.6
Miscellaneous topics from Chapter 8 onward as appropriate, for example, graphs and networks (Sections 9.1 – 9.3 and selected algorithms from remainder of chapter) and keyed collection ADT implemented by hashing (Section 11.2)

Possible Sequence of Topics for More Advanced Course on Algorithms and Data Structures

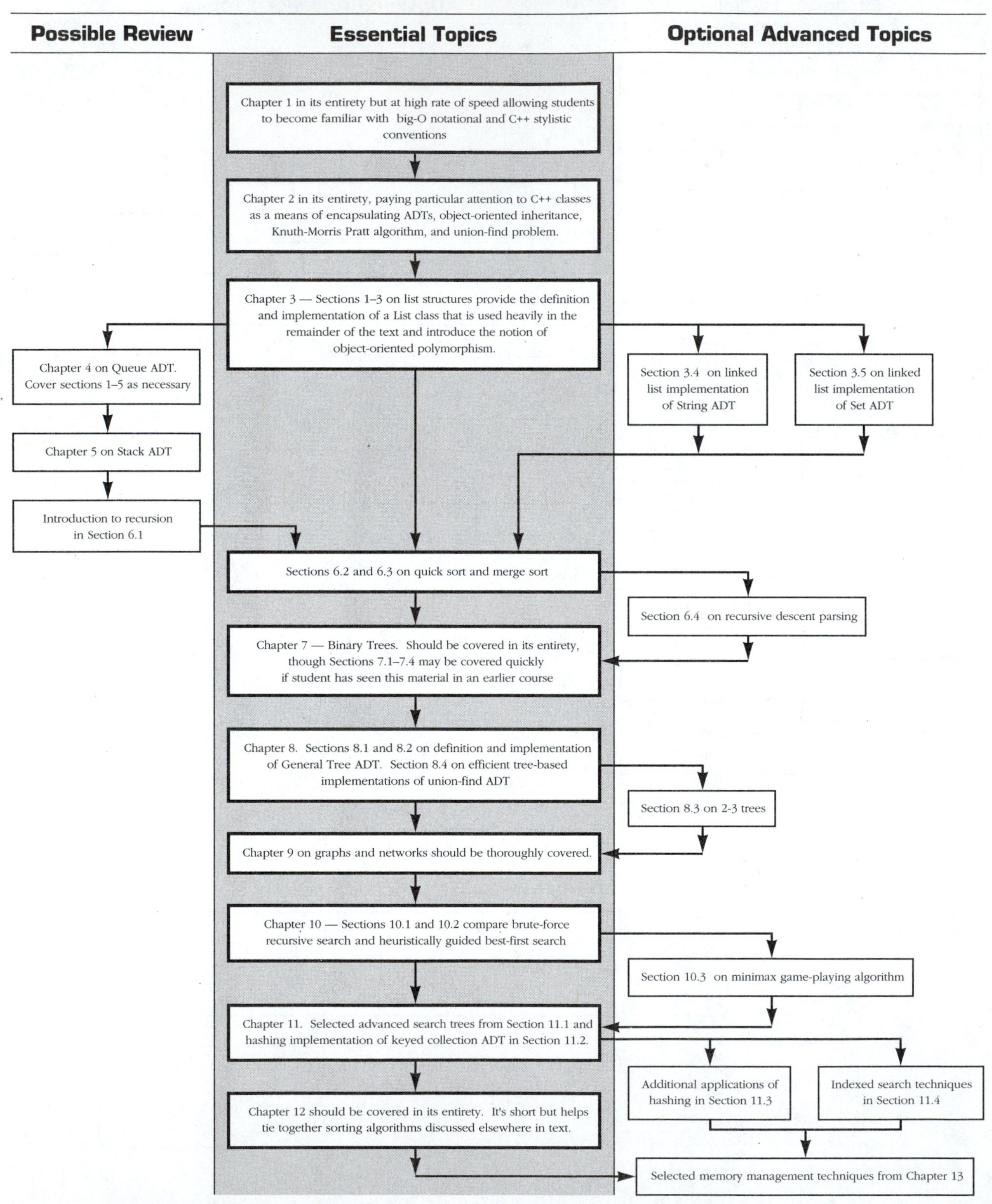

Possible Review
Essential Topics
Optional Advanced Topics
Chapter 1 in its entirety but at high rate of speed allowing students to become familiar with big-O notational and C++ stylistic conventions
Chapter 2 in its entirety, paying particular attention to C++ classes as a means of encapsulating ADTs, object-oriented inheritance, Knuth-Morris Pratt algorithm, and union-find problem.
Chapter 3 — Sections 1–3 on list structures provide the definition and implementation of a List class that is used heavily in the remainder of the text and introduce the notion of object-oriented polymorphism.
Chapter 4 on Queue ADT. Cover sections 1–5 as necessary
Chapter 5 on Stack ADT
Introduction to recursion in Section 6.1
Section 3.4 on linked list implementation of String ADT
Section 3.5 on linked list implementation of Set ADT
Sections 6.2 and 6.3 on quick sort and merge sort
Section 6.4 on recursive descent parsing
Chapter 7 — Binary Trees. Should be covered in its entirety, though Sections 7.1–7.4 may be covered quickly if student has seen this material in an earlier course
Chapter 8. Sections 8.1 and 8.2 on definition and implementation of General Tree ADT. Section 8.4 on efficient tree-based implementations of union-find ADT
Section 8.3 on 2-3 trees
Chapter 9 on graphs and networks should be thoroughly covered.
Chapter 10 — Sections 10.1 and 10.2 compare brute-force recursive search and heuristically guided best-first search
Section 10.3 on minimax game-playing algorithm
Chapter 11. Selected advanced search trees from Section 11.1 and hashing implementation of keyed collection ADT in Section 11.2.
Additional applications of hashing in Section 11.3
Indexed search techniques in Section 11.4
Chapter 12 should be covered in its entirety. It's short but helps tie together sorting algorithms discussed elsewhere in text.
Selected memory management techniques from Chapter 13

In terms of content, Chapters 1 and 2 of the text set the stage for the abstraction theme that will be emphasized throughout the rest of the text. The focus in Chapter 1 is on algorithmic abstraction. We review C as the base language for implementing our algorithms and establish a standard for documenting such implementations that emphasizes the formal specification of an algorithm in terms of its pre- and postconditions. Students who have already had an introductory course in C or C++ will be able to move quickly through this material. Those students who are receiving their initial exposure to C will have to use supplementary materials (such as in Appendix C) to bring themselves up to speed in C programming. Our approach also encourages the use of parameters that are functions as a means of increasing the degree of generality of an algorithm's interface. Students who have not previously used parameters that are functions should thoroughly master this technique. Chapter 1 also establishes the mathematical framework for analyzing the efficiency of algorithms and applies it to the analysis of various sorting algorithms.

In Chapter 2 the emphasis switches to data abstraction. A formalism for specifying ADTs is established. The formalism is thoroughly illustrated by presenting definitions of the array, string, and set ADTs. The latter two ADTs will recur throughout the remainder of the text as we study more sophisticated ways of implementing them. Our discussion of the array ADT illustrates how one can take a data type with limited support in the base language, in this case a C/C++ array that permits only integer indices starting from 0 and lacks range checking (long a source of stress for C/C++ programmers), and remove these limitations while at the same time preserving the original array indexing syntax. The implementation of the array ADT also provides us with our first exposure to the class construct of C++ that is so critical in enforcing our objective of binding data structures to the operations that access and manipulate them. We also see our first instance of operator overloading when we overload the indexing operator [ ]. In Section 2.2 we show how we can endow an existing ADT with additional properties by extending the definition of an array to that of a sortable array, that is a type of array in which having a (user-specified) precedence relationship among its elements is regarded as an integral part of its definition. This affords a smooth transition to the concept of class inheritance.

Having the array ADT available also makes for a smoother transition to the implementation of the string ADT in Section 2.3 where the ability to use arrays indexed from 1 and strengthened with range-checking makes for a more natural and secure implementation of strings. Note, while the material in Section 2.3 on the Knuth-Morris-Pratt implementation of the string operation will be particularly appropriate for more advanced students, if this book is a student's initial exposure to ADTs, this material could be skipped without loss of continuity.

Section 2.4 defines the set ADT and again affords us the opportunity to use our enhanced array capabilities to provide a simpler and clearer implementation of sets than would be possible using only the built-in array capabilities of C and C++. We also introduce the union-find problem, recasting it into a definition of an ADT. The union-find ADT is the first of several ADTs that we shall revisit as we progress through the text and develop additional, and possibly more effective structures to use in the implementations of these earlier ADTs.

Chapter 3 establishes an ADT definition for a list type, the unordered list. Linked lists and physically ordered arrays are compared as two implementation strategies for the list ADT. Once again our treatment builds upon our earlier foundation by using our array ADT instead of the built-in array type of C++. We also introduce the concept of polymorphism in Section 3.1. Applications discussed in Chapter 3 include sparse matrices, strings, sets, and the union-find problem.

Chapters 4 and 5 treat specialized lists: queues, priority queues, and stacks. Since these ADTs are conceptually simple to define, the emphasis in these two chapters is on applications. The radix sort algorithm and scheduling users of a shared resource are examined as applications of a queue. At the same time, the latter application allows us to further explore the power of abstract data typing as we define additional ADTs—the semaphore ADT and the shared resource ADT—to facilitate our solution to shared resource scheduling. Parsing and evaluation of expressions are the stack applications. It is necessary to cover queues before stacks since the parsing application that involves stacks also assumes knowledge of the queue ADT.

Chapter 6 examines recursion in depth. A student who has already been introduced to recursion in a prior course may skim Section 6.1. Recurrence relations and recursive call trees are introduced as a means of analyzing recursive algorithms. Applications of recursion covered in later sections of the chapter include quick sort, merge sort, and recursive descent parsing. The section on recursive descent parsing could be skipped without loss of continuity.

Chapters 7 and 8 provide in-depth coverage of trees. Chapter 7 focuses on the binary tree ADT. Because of the variety of hierarchical relationships that can underlie the structure of a binary tree it is impossible to provide appropriate algorithms for all of the operations we associate with this ADT, so we identify those operations for which general implementations are feasible and defer the implementation of other operations to more specialized ADTs such as the binary search tree ADT and the heap ADT. This requires that we introduce the concept of an abstract base class in Section 7.2. Sections 7.3 and 7.4 examine applications of binary trees in the heap sort algorithm and in implementing ordered lists and priority queues. Sections 7.5 and 7.6 describe threading and height balancing as ways of enhancing the efficiency of a binary tree implementation of an ordered list.

Chapter 8 defines the general tree as an ADT and then investigates applications of it in the implementation of ordered lists via 2-3 trees and in the union-find problem. Advanced search strategies using trees are covered in Section 11.1. The material in that section could be covered after completing Chapter 8.

Chapters 9 and 10 focus on graphs and networks. In Chapter 9, ADT definitions are provided for these structures. Algorithms for traversing graphs and networks (depth-first and breadth-first algorithms), finding paths (Dijkstra, Floyd, and Warshall algorithms), constructing minimum spanning trees (Prim and Kruskal algorithms), and sorting topologically are explored. Chapter 10 scrutinizes path finding from a slightly different perspective. The notion of a conceptual network is introduced, and heuristically guided search techniques are studied. Since such techniques are particularly relevant in artificial intelligence, the chapter concludes with a discussion of the minimax algorithm in searching game trees.

Search and sort algorithms that have not fit into earlier chapters are covered in Chapters 11 and 12, respectively. Chapter 11 investigates additional search strategies, including variations on trees (Section 11.1), hashing (Section 11.2), and indexing for file structures (Section 11.4). The applications described in Section 11.3 (implementation of ordered lists, implementation of sparse matrices, and Rabin-Karp string search) are all dependent only on hashing. Hence Sections 11.1 and 11.4 could readily be skipped if time does not allow coverage of them. Since the material in Section 11.1 examines the use of a variety of tree structures (splay trees, 2-3-4 trees, and red-black trees) in developing search algorithms, this section could be covered anytime after the presentation of 2-3 trees in section 8.3.

Chapter 12 is relatively short because internal sorting algorithms are covered earlier in the text. It summarizes the sorting methods that have been previously studied and establishes an $n \log_2 n$ limit on the efficiency of comparison-based sorting algorithms. In Section 12.2 external sorting algorithms are discussed in relation to the stream ADT; these algorithms could be skipped without loss of continuity.

Chapter 13 illustrates the use of data structures in several memory management applications. From an operating systems perspective, the fragmentation problem and buddy systems are studied as approaches for implementing operations for the memory ADT, an abstraction of a computer storage system such as main memory, disk storage, or tape storage. From a programming language perspective, heap management for implementations of pointer variables is investigated.

Features of the Text

Topical coverage alone is certainly not enough in a text. Such coverage must be couched in a style that integrates quality pedagogical features with sound principals of software engineering. Toward these ends we have integrated many unique features into the text:

1. *Presentation of all ADTs by formal specification of their operations.* This specification takes the form of function interfaces that combine a high degree of generality with a unique and consistent style of documentation. The documentation style incorporates the pre- and postconditions for the operation into the protocol for the corresponding function. Students thus view the definition of pre- and postconditions as an indispensable component of the function interface. They are encouraged from the outset to develop ADT operations that are reusable in a variety of contexts.
2. *A selective use of C++ constructs that promotes simple and clear coding and does not overwhelm the student with syntax.* We want to emphasize at the outset that while C++ is the language chosen to implement our ADTs, it has never been our intention to make this book a primer on object-oriented programming or a comprehensive textbook on programming in C++. This allows us to be selective in the features of C++ that we choose to employ and those that we choose to omit. For instance, we do not extensively cover operations of the C++ IOstream support library (although modest coverage of this library is given in

Appendix D). Also, while we feel that exception handling is an important facet of all software design, we find the use of the assert macro suitable for our purposes and employ it instead of the richer (but currently less widely implemented) throw-try-catch constructs. On the other hand because of the greater flexibility they provide we make generous use of parameters that are functions and regard templates as an indispensable construct for promoting clearer and simpler implementations of our ADTs.

3. *Extensive use of figures and graphic documentation.* This allows students to visualize the effect of algorithms on data structures. Algorithms are pictorially traced in a way that will bring them to life in the students' minds. It is our feeling that this visualization of data structures and algorithms represents true data abstraction, allowing students to understand at the conceptual level while also seeing the implementation of the algorithm in C++ code.
4. *Relevant issues.* These asides provide glimpses of how the topic under discussion in a particular chapter finds application in a more advanced area of computer science, and some of them discuss the potential societal impact of such an application.
5. *Exercises at the end of each section.* The exercises tend to be thought provoking and relatively short. They require the student to trace an algorithm studied in the chapter, provide a brief essay answer to a conceptual question, write a short algorithm to accomplish a specific task, or analyze the efficiency of an algorithm.
6. *An extensive set of programming problems and projects at the end of each chapter.* Solutions to some of these should be implemented by the students.
7. *Appendices.* These provide hints and solutions to many odd-numbered exercises, random number algorithms that can be used in a variety of the experimentation-based problems, a review of important recurrence relations used in the analysis of recursive algorithms, and overviews of C and the IOstream libraries.

Ancillaries

Ancillary materials for the text include the following:

1. An Instructor's Manual, which provides solutions to most exercises that are not solved in the previously cited appendix.
2. Transparency masters, which can be used to illustrate key concepts, are available to adopters from the publisher. A list of figures from the text available as transparency masters is in the Instructor's Manual.
3. Software disk containing the ADT interfaces and all other source code presented in the text. Additionally, complete implementations of virtually all classes discussed in the text are available via anonymous ftp. Instructions for downloading these class libraries are provided in the Instructor's Manual. Because of the text's heavy emphasis on reusable code, these software libraries can save instructors and students from having to "reinvent the wheel."
4. A lab manual will be available for use in conjunction with this text. The manual contains collections of lab exercises coordinated with the algorithms and data structures presented in the text. Each exercise centers around a program that implements the algorithm being studied. The student initially uses the program to discover and explore the nuances of the algorithm. The student then modifies the program to see how the performance of the algorithm is affected. Often the goal of such a modification is to make the algorithm more efficient. The programs produce output that allows the student to monitor this efficiency. For each exercise there is a series of questions the student must answer. Initial questions reinforce the student's understanding of the basic algorithm. Later questions have the student write up the results of his or her experimentation and exploration with the algorithm.
5. Related to the exercises in the lab manual, we are happy to make available a public domain algorithm visualization system called GAIGS (Generalized Algorithm Illustration through Graphical Software). Work on the GAIGS project has been led by Tom Naps and was originally funded through grants to Lawrence University from the NSF Instrumentation and Laboratory Improvement Program (NSF grant #88-51781) and Cray Research. In its present form, GAIGS runs under Microsoft Windows 3.1. It uses the graphical capabilities of the Windows environment to visualize in real time many of the algorithms that are explored in the lab manual. Instructions for downloading GAIGS via anonymous ftp are provided in the lab manual.

Acknowledgments

All textbooks of this nature require countless hours of dedication and hard work from a multitude of individuals. Never have so few owed so much to so many. The encouragement of our senior editor, Jerry Westby, was vital for getting this project underway as was the patient support of Jerry and our developmental editor Dean DeChambeau. The production staff, including Peter Krall at West and Jan Fisher, Trisha Noffsinger, and Scott Schriefer at Publication Services battled a variety of obstacles to keep the project on schedule and to ensure a relentless stream of documents to look over. If all the paper we used gets recycled the timberlands should be safe for generations to come. From the College of Charleston, Jimmy Wilkinson offered many helpful suggestions and corrections for the manuscripts while the other members of the Computer Science Department are to be thanked for their patience while the department's phone and photocopying budget was being sacked. We greatly appreciate the efforts of Jeremy Stenglein of Lawrence University for assisting with the solutions and to Andy Whitsitt of the University of Wisconsin-Madison for helping with the code. As we revised and revised, the wisdom of many reviewers has woven itself into the text. They are

Hamid R. Arabnia
University of Georgia
Daniel Falabella
Albright College
Habib Kashani
Vancouver Community College
Kenneth A. Lambert
Washington & Lee University
Kathleen Neuman
UCLA
James M. Slack
Mankato State University
Jeff Slomka
Southwest Texas State University
David B. Teague
Western Carolina University
Jerry Weltman
Louisiana State University
Judith C. Williams
William Penn College

To our families, of course, goes our greatest expression of appreciation as they once again shared the highs and lows of husbands and fathers seeing a textbook through the seemingly endless process from conception to publication. Without their support it would have been an impossible process. Finally, we would each like to express our mutual gratitude to our co-author not only for the insight, wisdom, and dedication he demonstrated throughout this project, but for the sheer pleasure it brought us to work with each other. What's next?

Contents

CHAPTER 1 Algorithms—Abstraction and Efficiency

'Where shall I begin, please your Majesty?' he asked. 'Begin at the beginning,' the King said, gravely, 'and go on till you come to the end: then stop.'
Lewis Carroll

Chapter Outline:

Perhaps the most important factor in successful problem-solving is *abstraction*. Webster's defines abstraction as something that is "dissociated from any specific instance," or "the process of identifying certain properties or characteristics of a material entity and using them to specify a new entity that represents a simplification of the entity from which it was derived." This "new entity" of course is an abstraction as given in the first sense of the definition.

To understand the role of abstraction in problem-solving, consider the following instance from our earliest childhood problem-solving experiences.

Problem Jane had five apples and Jim had three apples. How many apples did they have altogether? Figure 1.1 illustrates several methods by which this problem could be solved. Each of the problem-solvers in this figure manipulated different abstractions of the information in the problem to answer the question posed.

Consider now this somewhat more complex problem from your high school days.

Problem A laboratory technician needs 50 ml of a 30% sulfuric acid solution, but only has solutions of concentrations 10% and 40% available. How much of each of these concentrations should be mixed to obtain what is needed? Figure 1.2 illustrates some of the methods by which this problem could be solved. Here again, we see several different abstractions of the problem being manipulated in order to answer the question.

Finally, consider the following problem.

Figure 1.1
Solving a problem at different levels of abstraction.

Problem As a prize for being the fifth caller to a radio call-in contest, a person was given the chance to select prizes from various categories. All items from category A have a value of $15 and are packaged in containers of volume 0.5 cubic feet. All items of category B have a value of $25 and are packaged in containers of volume 1.25 cubic feet. Finally all items from category C have a value of $40 and are packaged in containers of volume 1.75 cubic feet. If the total volume of prizes the contestant can choose cannot exceed 15 cubic feet, how many prizes from each category should this person choose to maximize the total value of the

Figure 1.2
Solving a harder problem at different levels of abstraction.

Figure 1.3
Solving an even harder problem.

(a)

(b)

prizes received? Figure 1.3 illustrates some methods by which this problem could be solved.

In Figure 1.3(b) we are assuming, of course, that the problem-solver has written a computer program to solve the problem and is submitting it for execution on the computer. In this case we have several degrees of abstraction at work. On the one hand, some of the program's variables, or perhaps the elements of an array, are being used to represent the containers of the problem description. At the same time, these and other variables also represent abstractions of storage areas in the computer's primary memory, while the program's statements represent abstractions of the computer's machine language instructions.

In this book we wish to take the abstractions suggested in Figure 1.3(b) one step further by considering abstractions beyond those given in the programs of a certain high-level language, transcending the constraints on data types and program statements imposed by such a language. In particular, the abstractions we deal with are *algorithms* and *data structures* and a merging of these into a still higher level abstraction known as an *abstract data type*. Soon we will define these terms more precisely, but for now we may regard an algorithm as an abstraction of a program, a data structure as an abstraction of a collection of similarly typed variables in a program, and an abstract data type as an abstraction that prevents one from using a data structure inappropriately. An abstract data type prevents inappropriate use of a data structure in much the same way that a programming language, or even the central processing unit itself, prevents variables of certain types from being manipulated inappropriately by certain operations (for example, comparing two records, negating a character string, subtracting a character variable from a real variable, and so forth).

Our objective in this book is to explore the work that computer scientists have carried out with abstractions. Our primary emphases are on providing thorough, understandable definitions that are paramount in data structures and algorithms, and on examining their application in a variety of areas. Once a concept is understood at an abstract level, implementations of that concept—that is, realizations of it using the tools provided by a particular programming language—will also be explored. We will see that an abstraction may have many implementations in a single programming language. Furthermore, when compared according to efficiency considerations, some of these implementations will be seen as better or worse than others, independent of the implementation language.

1.1 Algorithms, Data Structures, and Abstract Data Types

There are as many different definitions of the term *algorithm* as there are authors who write about them. Underlying all of these definitions, however, are some common premises:

- An algorithm is a sequence of instructions for solving a problem.
- The problem to be solved has specific goal conditions that, when met, stop the execution of the algorithm and allow one to categorize the problem as having been "solved" in accordance with a set of specific initial conditions. Furthermore, the goal conditions must be attainable from the initial conditions in a finite amount of time.
- The intent of each instruction in the algorithm must be apparent to and within the capabilities of the agent that will be carrying out the instruction.
- As soon as one instruction in the algorithm has been carried out, the next instruction to be performed is uniquely determined by the instruction just completed and the current status of the solution.

Assimilating these assumptions into our own definition, we define an algorithm as an *unambiguous sequence of clear instructions that will solve a given problem in a finite amount of time and then halt.*

Although the term *algorithm* is now closely linked with computer science, algorithms have been a part of our lives since the first time one person explained to another person how to do something. People use algorithms when they follow recipes in a cookbook or instructions for assembling a child's toy or when they program a VCR. Scientists publish algorithms describing experiments they have carried out so that other scientists can duplicate their work and confirm their results. Space agencies follow elaborate algorithms—countdowns—for launching rockets. Considered in this light, all of us have had frustrations at one time or another when dealing with algorithms that were ambiguous or beyond our capabilities. One can therefore understand the need for clarity in an algorithm when the agent carrying out the instructions of the algorithm will be a computer—which is incapable of the ingenious improvisations that often allow human agents to deal effectively and appropriately with unexpected circumstances.

Data Structures

As we noted in our opening remarks, a data structure represents an abstraction of the data types provided by a language. *Elementary data types* are characterized by the fact that the values they admit are *atomic;* that is, they admit no further decomposition. Integer, floating-point, and character data types are among the elementary data types supported in most programming languages. If the values of a data type do admit a decomposition into several components, however, then the data type is referred to as *structured* instead of elementary, and the organization of each component and the relationships among components constitute what is known as a *data structure.* Arrays and records are two examples of data structures that enjoy direct support in many programming languages and are suitable for effectively handling the representation of information in a great many applications. Computer scientists and insightful programmers have developed data structures other than arrays and records that are better suited to other applications. The primary goal of this book is to describe some of these data structures and to show how they can be realized in object-oriented languages such as C++.

Abstract Data Types

In recent years an additional emphasis has been added to the study of data structures and algorithms. If they are to be realistic abstractions of the data types and operations found in programming languages, then not only are the organization and interrelationships among the components of their values important, but the operations permitted on these values must also be considered. Although arithmetic operations and order comparisons are among the operations one normally expects to be associated with numeric data values, one does not normally associate these operations with Boolean values. Similarly, one does not expect arithmetic or comparison operations to be provided for record types. Consequently, when considering data types that go beyond those found in a high-level language, the abstraction would be incomplete if one discussed only the structure of the values of these types without also considering the operations to be performed on data objects that can assume these values. Furthermore, once a set of operations for a data structure has been identified, restraints must be imposed so that a programmer manipulates the data structure only with these explicitly specified operations. At one time, the programmer was responsible for exercising this restraint. Lately, however, many programming languages (such as C++) have incorporated features that permit this responsibility to be shifted from the programmer to the language support system.

The term *abstract data type* (ADT) is used to define those data abstractions that require not only a specification of the structure of the values for this new data type, but also a specification of the complete set of operations that can be performed on data objects of this type. The approach we have adopted in this book is to introduce all data structures as abstract data types. As we will see, this approach is particularly well suited to object-oriented languages. We then use algorithms to describe how these operations can be carried out for given implementations of these abstract data types.

Algorithms and Languages—C and C++

If an algorithm is a sequence of *instructions,* then a *language* must be used to express the algorithm's semantics with adequate precision and freedom from ambiguity. This requires us to use a language that is sufficiently formal to avoid the imprecision inherent in a natural language. Beyond this, we want our language to be sufficiently concise and compact to facilitate verification of an algorithm's correctness. This verification can take the form of mathematical proofs of correctness or, more often, of observations of the performance of the algorithm with a carefully selected set of test cases. These test cases should attempt to cover all of the exceptional circumstances likely to be encountered by the algorithm. Just what these exceptional circumstances are will depend on the structures being used to represent and manipulate the data. However, certain generic circumstances must be verified for all algorithms manipulating data structures:

- Does the algorithm work when the data structure is empty? For instance, does the logic of the algorithm correctly allow data to be added to a structure that currently contains no data? Is an attempt to delete data from such a structure appropriately trapped?
- Does the algorithm work when the data structure is full? Is an attempt to add data to such a structure appropriately trapped?
- Does the algorithm work for the range of possibilities that can occur between an empty structure and a full structure?

The need for conciseness in algorithms becomes obvious when one considers the problem of verifying their correctness. The more an algorithm attempts to do, the more possibilities must be considered in its verification. Hence, we take the view that *an algorithm should concern itself with one specific problem*. Each algorithm is a logical *module* designed to perform a particular operation on a data item or structure. Once defined and verified, such a module represents an abstraction in that it can be used by other algorithms, which need not be concerned with the details underlying the module's implementation. These other algorithms need only understand what the module does and how to call on the module.

In this book we use the object-oriented language C++ to specify our abstract data types, to define the data structures used in their implementations, and to express algorithms for implementing their operations. Our approach assumes that you are familiar with at least one block-oriented, procedural language that uses type-checking (C, Pascal, Ada, and Modula-2 are examples of such languages), and that you can use this background to become familiar quickly with the basic syntax and semantics of C. If you are not already familiar with C, we provide a brief introduction to it in Appendix C. As necessary, we introduce those object-oriented features of C++ that facilitate our discussions of algorithms, data structures, and abstract data types.

Throughout, we emphasize that this is first and foremost a text on algorithms, data structures, and abstract data types, not a treatise on object-oriented programming in C++. To set the stage for our future explorations, we briefly summarize those features of C with which we assume familiarity and begin to demonstrate how extensions offered by C++ allow a greater degree of abstraction than is possible in traditional C.

Traditional C Data Types For unstructured data we use the following C data types:

int
float
char
enum
pointer

together with the standard arithmetic, logical, and relational operations that go with these types. We will add to this collection a specific **enum** type called BOOLEAN, defined as follows:

```
typedef enum boolean
  {FALSE, TRUE } BOOLEAN;
```

To enhance the readability of our algorithms, the BOOLEAN data type will be used in situations that require a variable to signal whether a logical condition is true or false. We will not explicitly provide the **typedef** for BOOLEAN in those situations but rather will assume that this **typedef** has been appropriately included from a header (.h) file.

Initially the structured types we use are the array and the **struct,** although in Chapter 2 we introduce the notion of a structured **class** and then use that extensively throughout the remainder of the text.

Traditional C Control Constructs For specifying the order of execution of statements (also known as *flow of control*) we use the following C constructs:

decisional constructs:
- **if** statement
- **if-else** statement
- **switch** statement

iterative constructs:
- **for** statement
- **while** statement
- **do-while** statement

Modules in Traditional C—Functions No language structure is more critical to encouraging the success of abstraction than the program *module.* In traditional C, the function is the means by which such program modules are developed. Ideally, a module should be a structure that can be written and compiled apart from a program that uses it and whose specific task can be understood and activated solely through an interface, without requiring knowledge of its internal details. Three important objectives should be kept in mind when developing modules.

First, a module should be *functionally cohesive;* that is, it should be focused on solving one particular aspect of a problem. Because modules are typically used in concert with higher level modules, no unforeseen side effects should result when a module is called. It solves the problem it is designed to solve and does nothing else. In particular, a module must not alter any data items or structures other than those that, according to the definition of the problem, it is required to alter.

Second, when viewed as a name applied to a collection of instructions designed to solve a particular problem, a module encourages the abstract approach we emphasized at the beginning of the chapter. Once we have a module called **sort,** which sorts a collection of values, we will be able to work at a higher level of abstraction—a level that views sorting as a given primitive operation.

Third, because one module typically solves a problem so that other modules at a higher level can be shielded from the details of that particular problem's solution, it is important that a module have an *interface*. This interface represents the lines of communication between a module and those that use it. For instance, a module that sorts a collection of values must be given access to those values. The interface to a module includes its formal parameters. The skillful use of parameters can greatly enhance a module's degree of abstraction by making the module usable in more contexts and by hiding the details of the underlying algorithm.

Although functions in traditional C provide some support for developing modules with these three objectives, this support is not ideal, nor are there universally accepted conventions for using C functions. Consequently, we devote a disproportionately larger amount of time to discussing C functions than to other control constructs in the language. We review those features that traditional C does supply, introduce our own documentation standards to establish consistency in module interfaces, and begin to introduce those features offered by C++ that enhance a function's ability to capture the power of full-fledged data abstraction.

The general forms of a C function prototype are the following:

```
return-type  function-name ( parameter list )
```

or

```
void  function-name ( parameter list )
```

where **void** is used in place of a **return-type** for a function that does not return an explicit value through its name. For example,

```
void swap(int *x, int *y)
```

is one prototype for a function to swap two **int** locations.

Prototypes and their parameter lists must be described in more detail. Ideally, a prototype embodies the preconditions and postconditions for the algorithm implemented in the module. A *precondition* is a condition that exists before the algorithm executes. A *postcondition* is a condition that arises as a result of executing the algorithm. Hence, preconditions represent what the algorithm is given and postconditions what it returns. For example, in a module that sorts an array of integers, one might have as preconditions the array, a parameter or parameters indicating a subrange of array indices over which to perform the sort, and perhaps a parameter indicating the ordering criterion to be used in the sort. The postcondition would be a modified version of the original array in which the elements within the specified subrange have been arranged according to the ordering criterion. Or, as in the following example, in a module to swap the values of two storage locations, the preconditions would be the locations whose values are to be swapped, whereas the postconditions would be those same two locations, but with each holding what was formerly the other's value.

Although the prototype embodies these pre- and postconditions in its parameters, there is nothing in the prototype itself that clearly defines the pre- and postconditions. Our convention is that the definition of a module's pre- and postconditions is to occur in a documentation block immediately preceding the prototype for the module. The preconditions are defined as what the module is *given*, whereas the postconditions specify what the module *returns*. The interface to a module is the combination of a documentation block defining its pre- and postconditions and a prototype that establishes order and type of parameters. Such an interface introduces the following function, which exchanges the contents of two **int** locations. (We use the double slash comment indicator of C++ to signal that everything following "//" on the current line is to be regarded as a comment.)

```
//-----------------------------------------------------------------------
// Interface for function swap
// GIVEN:   x and y -- references to integer locations to be swapped
// RETURN: x and y -- integers referenced by x and y have been
//                    exchanged
// RETURN as value of function: void

void swap(int *x, int *y)
{
  int temp;

  temp = *x;
  *x = *y;
  *y = temp;
}
```

We follow this convention for defining module interfaces throughout the text. A module without a documentation block defining its pre- and postconditions is, for our purposes, an incomplete module.

Reference Parameters and Function Templates in C++

Although the preceding **swap** module is unambiguously defined, two complaints can be registered against it. First, since the intended usage of the **swap** function is to exchange the values of two variables, it is inelegant at best—and seems unnatural at worst—to force one to use pointers to pass a parameter by reference. This is a complaint that has long been lodged against traditional C—that one must learn about the intricacies of pointers before one can understand the notion of a reference parameter. To correct this shortcoming, C++ offers a more direct type of reference parameter denoted by the ampersand operator, &. A reference parameter signaled by this notation need not have the * dereference operator applied to it to access the data it references. To illustrate, consider the **swap** module recast with C++ reference parameters.

```
//---------------------------------------------------------------------------
// Interface for function swap
// GIVEN:   x and y -- integer locations whose data values are to be swapped
// RETURN:  x and y -- data in locations x and y have been exchanged
// RETURN as value of function:  void

void swap(int &x, int &y)     // Note use of C++ reference parameters
{
  int temp;

  temp = x;     // x and y no longer must be explicitly dereferenced
  x = y;
  y = temp;
}
```

Moreover, when calling on a function with such reference parameters, it is not necessary to pass an explicit address for the parameter. Rather the address is passed implicitly by the C++ compiler. To illustrate, consider the following call to **swap** that will interchange **int** locations a and b:

```
int a, b;
.
.
.
swap(a, b);   // Note that the addresses of a and b need not
              // be made explicit with the & operator
              // as in traditional C
```

The second complaint against our **swap** module is that it can only be used to swap locations containing **ints,** even though logically swapping other data types such as complex **structs** uses precisely the same algorithm. That is, to swap two **floats** or two **structs,** we would have to clone our preceding function into one that was exactly the same *except* that it was named differently and received two pointers to data items of the type we wanted to swap. It seems terribly awkward that we must write separate, although almost identical, functions to swap **ints, floats,** and other more complicated structures.

To overcome this awkwardness, C++ has introduced the notion of a *function template* (but only since version 2.0 of C++; templates were not in C++ originally). Such a template simply allows one to write a function in terms of a generic data type. When the function is called with specific data items, the compiler generates the code appropriate for the particular type of the actual parameter. To illustrate, we develop our previous swap module as a function template. The main differences in the actual C++ code from our previous version are the **template** line that precedes the function's protocol and the use of the generic type **ElementType** instead of the specific type **int** throughout the coding of the function.

```
//-------------------------------------------------------------
// Interface for function swap
// GIVEN:    x and y -- ElementType locations to be swapped
// RETURN:   x and y -- data in locations x and y have been
//                      exchanged
// RETURN as value of function:  void

template <class ElementType>
void swap(ElementType &x, ElementType &y)
{
  ElementType temp;

  temp = x;
  x = y;
  y = temp;
}
```

Here the line **template <class ElementType>** declares that the function that follows will be written in terms of a generic data type (called a *class* by C++) identified as **ElementType**. The keywords **template** and **class** and the angle brackets are reserved for this purpose in C++; at the discretion of the programmer the name **ElementType** can be replaced with a more appropriate identifier. You should think of the definition of **swap** as being written for the generic data type **ElementType.** If we call on **swap** with two **ints,** as in,

```
int a, b;
swap(a, b);
```

then the C++ compiler will generate the code necessary to swap two **ints.** The net effect is that the actual type **int** is substituted for the generic type **ElementType.** Similarly, if we were to define a more complex type **CustomerRec** with the following **struct**

```
struct CustomerRec
{
  int IDnumber;
  float balance;
};
```

we could then exchange customer records **p** and **q** with the function call

```
CustomerRec p, q;
swap(p, q);
```

The C++ compiler will generate the code to swap **struct**s of type **CustomerRec;** that is, the template to swap data of type **ElementType** is "filled in" with the specific data type **CustomerRec.**

We consider the C++ reference parameters and function templates to be substantial improvements over the traditional C constructs and hereafter use them as appropriate. We also frequently use the C++ notion of a *constant reference parameter*. To illustrate this usage of a reference parameter, consider the following specification for the function **betterCustomer,** which compares two customer records to determine which is the "better" customer.

```
//-----------------------------------------------------------------
// Interface for function betterCustomer
// GIVEN:    c1 and c2 -- customer records to compare
// RETURN as value of function:
//           TRUE      if c1 has a larger balance than c2;
//           FALSE     if c1 and c2 have equal balances, or
//                     if c2 has a larger balance than c1
```

In traditional C, the two customer records would be passed to this function by value since the function should not alter either of these records.

```
BOOLEAN betterCustomer(CustomerRec c1, CustomerRec c2)
// customer records c1 and c2 are passed by value

{
  if (c1.balance > c2.balance)
    return(TRUE);
  else
    return(FALSE);
}
```

However, this version of the function entails the overhead of making copies of both customer record arguments since that is the C mechanism for passing by value. If the customer records incorporated a large amount of information, this copying of customer records could result in a substantial inefficiency. From an efficiency perspective, it would be better to pass the records by reference even though the function will not alter the records. This is where the C++ constant reference parameter can be used. It declares that an argument will be passed by reference but that the argument is not to be altered by the function. Hence it combines the efficiency of passing by reference with the safety of enforcing a function's inability to alter an argument. Coded with constant reference parameters, the **betterCustomer** function would appear as follows:

```
BOOLEAN betterCustomer(const CustomerRec &c1, const CustomerRec &c2)
// c1 and c2 are now constant reference args. In the function,
// we refer to them just as we would value parameters.

{
  if (c1.balance > c2.balance)
    return(TRUE);
  else
    return(FALSE);
}
```

Functions as Parameters in C and C++

Both C and C++ allow the arguments of a function to contain other functions as parameters, although a discussion of this feature is often omitted in introductory courses. This feature can be a powerful tool for developing functions with a higher degree of generality than would otherwise be possible. To illustrate, consider first the following function, which returns the index position of the smallest ("champion") value in a prescribed subrange of an array:

```
//-------------------------------------------------------------------
// Interface for function findChampionIndex
// GIVEN:    a -- an array of ElementType values;
//           lo and hi -- a subrange of array indices.
// RETURN as value of function:
//            The index of the "champion" (here "smallest") value among
//            a[lo]...a[hi]. If the champion value occurs more than once,
//            the index returned is that of the first occurrence.

template <class ElementType>
int findChampionIndex(ElementType a[], int lo, int hi)
{
  int i, tentative;

  tentative = lo;
  for (i = lo+1; i <= hi; ++i)
    if (a[i] < a[tentative])
      tentative = i;
  return(tentative);
}
```

In this algorithm we viewed the smallest entry as the "champion." Clearly the same algorithm would work to find the index of the largest as "champion," but we would have to code a new function with ">" replacing "<". Moreover, the same algorithm should work for finding the position of the "champion" in a subrange of an array of **floats** or any other data type on which we can define a "better than" comparison between two elements (such as our earlier example of customer records). That is, the current version of **findChampionIndex** is not as abstract as we would like because it ties what should be a general algorithm to a particular data type and order relation. However, if we provide **findChampionIndex** with a **betterThan** relation to apply to two data items of type **ElementType,** we succeed in stating a more generalized algorithm. To provide **findChampionIndex** with a **betterThan** relation, we pass it as a function parameter. The syntax for doing this is illustrated in the following version of the function. In particular, note that function **findChampionIndex** receives as a new third argument a pointer to a function **betterThan** whose protocol is given directly within the argument list of **findChampionIndex.**

```
//----------------------------------------------------------------
// Interface for function findChampionIndex
// GIVEN:    a -- an array of ElementType values;
//           lo and hi -- a subrange of array indices;
//           betterThan -- a function to compare ElementType values
//             GIVEN:    x and y -- values to compare
//             RETURN as value of function:
//                       TRUE     if x is "better than" y;
//                       FALSE    if x and y are equal, or
//                                if y is "better than" x
// RETURN as value of function:
//             The index of the "best" value among a[lo]...a[hi].
//             If the best value occurs more than once, the index
//             returned is that of the first occurrence.

template <class ElementType>
int findChampionIndex (ElementType a[], int lo, int hi,
        BOOLEAN (*betterThan)(const ElementType &x, const ElementType &y))
{
  int i, tentative;

  tentative = lo;
  for (i = lo+1; i <= hi; ++i)
    if (betterThan(a[i], a[tentative]))
      tentative = i;
  return(tentative);
}
```

Note the function parameter declaration

Note the use of the function parameter

If we now want **findChampionIndex** to return the position of the largest entry in a subrange of an array **xval** of **floats** (instead of the smallest entry within an array of **ints**), we merely declare

```
int lo, hi;
float xval[100];
```

and define an appropriate **greaterThan** function for **floats:**

```
BOOLEAN greaterThan(const float &x, const float &y)
{
  if (x > y)
    return(TRUE);
  else
    return(FALSE);
}
```

A sample call to **findChampionIndex** then appears as

```
findChampionIndex(xval, lo, hi, greaterThan);
```

The preceding example illustrates that the syntax for a formal parameter that is a function must have that function's protocol appearing in the formal parameter list along with a pointer reference (the * operator) to the formal name of the function. Then, when an actual function parameter is passed into the function, *only the name* of the function is furnished—*not* the name along with parameters or the address-of (&) operator. Although this syntax may not be particularly elegant, it is what C++ demands, and, because of its effectiveness in generalizing the applicability of a function, we use it frequently.

Example 1.1

Using the struct **CustomerRec** and function **betterCustomer** that were introduced earlier, indicate how the **findChampionIndex** function could be used to find the index position of the customer with the largest balance.

The **betterCustomer** function defines the relationship that we want to impose on the data in an array of customer records. Hence we merely declare an array of such structs:

```
const int NUMBEROFCUSTOMERS = 2000;
CustomerRec customers[NUMBEROFCUSTOMERS];
```

and then call on **findChampionIndex** with

```
findChampionIndex(customers, 0, NUMBEROFCUSTOMERS - 1,
                  betterCustomer);
```

There is one further (pedagogic) note we wish to make about the **findChampionIndex** function. The commentary appearing to the right of the brace next to **betterThan** in the parameter list and in the code for **findChampionIndex** is illustrative of a technique called *graphic documentation,* which we will frequently use to clarify C++ algorithms when purely textual commentary is not enough.

This completes our review of C and brief introduction to C++, the language we will use to describe all of the algorithms in the text.

Exercises 1.1

1. Write a C++ function that will invert the order of elements in an array.
2. Write a C++ function that receives three values and returns them arranged with the "best" value first and "worst" value last. Here "best-worst" is determined by a parameter given to the function.
3. Write a C++ function that will accumulate the entries in an array. To "accumulate" could mean to form a sum or a product. The caller of the function should be able to pass in the specified operation. Be sure to specify any assumptions in your preconditions for the function to allow for this generality.

1.2 Algorithm Efficiency and the Sorting Problem

As we pointed out in the opening paragraphs of this chapter, from a practical perspective a measure of the efficiency of an algorithm is achieved by analyzing the efficiency with which its implementation utilizes a computer's time and space. By space efficiency, we mean the amount of memory an algorithm consumes when it runs. As for time efficiency, at first glance one would expect this to mean the amount of time it takes the algorithm to execute; however, there are several reasons why such an absolute measure is not appropriate:

- The execution time of an algorithm is sensitive to the amount of data that it must manipulate and typically grows as the amount of data increases.
- The execution times for an algorithm when run with the same data set on two different computers may differ because of the execution speeds of the processors.
- Depending on how an algorithm is implemented on a particular computer (choice of programming language, use of a compiler or interpreter, and so forth), one implementation of an algorithm may run faster than another, even on the same computer and with the same data set.

In our opening remarks we observed that an algorithm is one of the *abstractions* that a computer scientist studies. Consequently, in assessing the efficiency of an algorithm's run time we want to remove all implementation considerations from our analysis and focus on those aspects of the algorithm that most critically affect this execution time. We noted that one of these is the number of data items the algorithm manipulates. Typically, the rest of the analysis consists of trying to determine how often a critical operation (e.g., a comparison, data interchange, or addition or multiplication of values) or sequence of such operations gets performed in manipulating these data items. This count, expressed as a function of a variable **n** that provides an indicator of the size of the set of data items, is what represents the "running time" of the algorithm.

Consider the following two examples of nested loops intended to sum each of the rows of an **n** × **n** array **a,** storing the row sums in a one-dimensional array **sum** and the overall total in **grandTotal.**

Version 1

```
grandTotal = 0;
for (k = 0; k < n; ++k)
{
   sum[k] = 0;
   for (j = 0; j < n; ++j)
   {
      sum[k] = sum[k] + a[k][j];
      grandTotal = grandTotal + a[k][j];
   }
}
```

Version 2

```
grandTotal = 0;
for (k = 0; k < n; ++k)
{
   sum[k] = 0;
   for (j = 0; j < n; ++j)
      sum[k] = sum[k] + a[k][j];
   grandTotal = grandTotal + sum[k];
}
```

If we analyze the number of addition operations required by these two versions, we see that Version 2 is better in this respect. Because Version 1 incorporates the accumulation of **grandTotal** into its inner loop, it requires $2\mathbf{n}^2$ additions. That is, the additions **sum[k] + a[k][j]** and **grandTotal + a[k][j]** are each executed $\mathbf{n}^2$ times, for a total of $2\mathbf{n}^2$. Version 2, on the other hand, accumulates **grandTotal** after the inner loop; hence it requires only $\mathbf{n}^2 + \mathbf{n}$ additions, which is less than $2\mathbf{n}^2$ for any **n** greater than 1. Version 2 is apparently guaranteed to execute faster than Version 1 for any nontrivial value of **n.** As a final observation, we point out that the variable **n** being used in our analysis is merely an indicator of the number of data items being manipulated (namely, $\mathbf{n}^2$) rather than giving the actual number of data items.

Note also that "faster" here may not have much significance in the real world of computing. If we assume a hypothetical computer that allows us to store a 1000 × 1000 array and that executes at a microsecond per instruction, Version 1 would require two seconds to perform its addition; Version 2 would require just over one second. On a 100,000 × 100,000 array, Version 1 would crunch numbers for slightly under six hours and Version 2 would take about three hours. Although Version 2 is certainly better from an aesthetic perspective, it may not be good enough to be appreciably different from a user's perspective. That is, in situations where one version will respond within seconds, so will the other. Conversely, when one is annoyingly slow, the other will be also. For the 1000 × 1000 array, both versions would be fast enough to allow their use in an interactive environment. For the 100,000 × 100,000 array, both versions would dictate an overnight run in batch mode since an interactive user will be no more willing to wait three hours than six hours for a response.

In terms of the *order of magnitude* of run time involved, these versions should not be considered significantly different. Order of magnitude is an expression used by scientists to loosely compare two values. Traditionally, two positive values A and B are of the same order of magnitude if the ratio of the larger to the smaller is less than 10 : 1. On the other hand, value A would be k orders of magnitude greater than value B if the ratio of A to B is between 10^k : 1 and 10^{k+1} : 1. However, the reliance on powers of 10 for determining the ranges for these ratios is frequently relaxed and other ranges used instead. For example, for time measurements, seconds, minutes, hours, days, months, and years could be used to assess orders of magnitude. Under this progression, an hour would be two orders of magnitude above a second rather than the three orders the traditional method would yield.

Considerations such as these have led computer scientists to use a method of algorithm classification that makes more precise the notion of order of magnitude as it applies to time and space considerations. This method of classification, typically referred to as *big-O notation* (in reference to "on the order of"), hinges on the definition given in the following section.

Big-O Analysis

Suppose there exists a function $f(n)$ defined on the nonnegative integers such that the number of operations required by an algorithm for an input of size n, say $T(n)$, is less than some constant C times $f(n)$ for all sufficiently large values of n. That is, there is a positive integer M and a constant C such that for all $n \geq M$ we have $T(n) \leq Cf(n)$. Such an algorithm is said to be an $O(f(n))$ algorithm relative to the number of operations it requires to execute. Similarly, we could classify an algorithm as $O(f(n))$ relative to the number of memory locations it requires to execute. The constant C is known as the *constant of proportionality* of the order relationship.

Consider the algorithms discussed earlier for summing the elements of the $n \times n$ array. For the Version 1 algorithm we calculated its run time to be $T(n) = 2n^2$ for all n; hence, with $C = 2$ in the definition of big-O, we see that $T(n)$ is $O(n^2)$. For the Version 2 algorithm, whose run time we calculated as $n^2 + n$, we note when $n \geq 1$, we have $n \leq n^2$, so that $n^2 + n \leq n^2 + n^2 = 2n^2$. Thus, this algorithm is also $O(n^2)$.

Essentially, the definition of $O(f(n))$ as applied to the run time of an algorithm states that, up to a constant factor, the function $f(n)$ gives an upper bound on how the algorithm is performing for large n; saying in effect that as n gets larger, the growth in execution time will be no worse than that shown by $f(n)$. What the definition does not say is how good this upper bound is. For example, although the Version 1 and Version 2 algorithms just analyzed were both $O(n^2)$, we could just as well have said they were $O(n^3)$, since when $n \geq 2$ we have $2n^2 \leq n^3$; similarly they are $O(n^4)$, or $O(n^2\log_2 n)$, and so forth. If the statement "$T(n)$ is $O(f(n))$" is to be meaningful, it must be understood that f is the "smallest" such function that can be used. In practice, the manner in which f is determined in the analysis of an algorithm often ensures this minimality, but there are algorithms for which such minimal functions are currently unavailable (see the discussion of the Shell sort in Section 1.4).

Two questions merit further discussion at this stage.

How well does big-O analysis provide a way of classifying algorithms from a real-world perspective? To answer this question, consider Table 1.1. This table presents some of the typical $f(n)$ functions we will use to classify algorithms and their order of magnitude run time for an input of size 10^5 on our hypothetical computer. From this table, we can see that an $O(n^2)$ algorithm will take hours to execute for an input of size 10^5—just how many hours depends on the constant of proportionality in the definition of the big-O notation. Regardless of the value of this constant of proportionality, however, a categorization of an algorithm as an $O(n^2)$ algorithm has achieved a very practical goal: We now know that, for an input of size 10^5, we cannot expect an immediate response for such an algorithm. Moreover, we

TABLE 1.1
Some typical $f(n)$ functions and their associated run times.

$f(n)$	Order of magnitude run time for input of size 10^5 (assuming proportionality constant $k = 1$ and one operation per microsecond)	
$\log_2 n$	2×10^{-5}	second
n	0.1	second
$n \log_2 n$	2	seconds
n^2	3	hours
n^3	32	years
2^n	*many*	centuries

know that, for a reasonably small constant of proportionality, we have an algorithm for which submission as an overnight job would be practical. That is, unlike an $O(n^3)$ algorithm, we could expect the computer to finish executing our algorithm in a time frame that would be acceptable, if it could be scheduled so as not to interfere with other uses of the machine. On the other hand, an $O(n^3)$ algorithm applied to a data set of this size would be completely impractical.

Two other observations on using big-O notation to classify algorithms should be mentioned. The first pertains to the use of the phrase "for all sufficiently large values of n" in our definition of big-O. This highlights the fact that there is usually little difference in the choice of an algorithm if n is reasonably small. For example, almost any sorting algorithm would sort 100 integers quickly. Second, the constant of proportionality used to establish that an algorithm's run-time efficiency is $O(f(n))$ is crucial only for comparing algorithms that share the same function $f(n)$; it makes almost no difference when comparing algorithms whose $f(n)$'s are of different magnitudes. It is therefore appropriate to say that the function $f(n)$ dominates the run-time performance of an algorithm and characterizes it in its big-O analysis. The following example should help clarify this situation.

Consider two algorithms L_1 and L_2 with run times equal to $2n^2$ and n^2, respectively. The constants of proportionality of L_1 and L_2 are 2 and 1, respectively. The dominating function $f(n)$ for both of these algorithms is n^2, but L_2 runs twice as fast as L_1 for a data set of n values. The different sizes of the two constants of proportionality indicate that L_2 is faster than L_1. Now suppose that the function $f(n)$ for L_2 is n^3. Then, even though its constant of proportionality is half of what it is for L_1, L_2 will be frustratingly slower than L_1 for large n. This latter comparison is shown in Figure 1.4.

How does one determine the function $f(n)$ that categorizes a particular algorithm? We will give an overview of that process here and later illustrate it more fully by doing actual analyses for two sorting algorithms. In general, the run-time behavior of an algorithm is dominated by its behavior in any loops it contains. Hence, by analyzing the loop structures of an algorithm, we can estimate the number of run-time operations required by the algorithm as a sum of several terms, each dependent on n, the indicator of the number of items being processed by the algorithm. That is, we are typically able to express the number of run-time operations (and, for that matter, the amount of memory) as a sum of the form

$$f_1(n) + f_2(n) + \cdots + f_k(n)$$

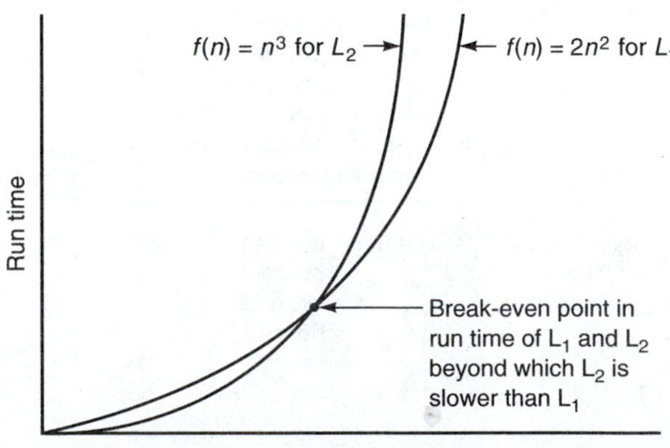

Figure 1.4
Graphical comparison of two run times.

It is also typical that we identify one of the terms in this expression as the *dominant* term. A dominant term is one that, for bigger values of n, becomes so large that it allows us to ignore all the other terms, from a big-O perspective. For instance, suppose that we had an expression involving two terms, such as $n^2 + 6n$. The n^2 term dominates the $6n$ term since, for $6 \leq n$, we have $6n \leq n^2$, whence

$$n^2 + 6n \leq n^2 + n^2 = 2n^2$$

Thus, $n^2 + 6n$ would lead to an $O(n^2)$ categorization because of the dominance of the n^2 term. In general, the problem of big-O categorization can be reduced to one of finding the dominant term in an expression representing the number of operations (or amount of memory) required by an algorithm.

Example 1.2

Use big-O analysis to determine the time efficiency of the following C++ fragment in terms of the integer **n**:

```
for (k = 0; k < n/2; ++k)
{
   .
   .
   .
   for (j = 0; j < n*n; ++j)
   {
      .
      .
      .
   }
}
```

Because these loops are nested, the critical operations for this analysis will be those within the innermost loop—they are the ones that will execute most often. Operations within the innermost loop will each execute n^2 times whenever the innermost loop executes. We see in fact that this innermost loop will execute $n/2$ times. Consequently, the critical operations for this algorithm will execute $(n/2)(n^2)$, or $n^3/2$, times. It follows then that the run-time efficiency of this algorithm is $O(n^3)$ in big-O terms, with a constant of proportionality equal to $1/2$.

Example 1.3

Use big-O analysis to determine the time efficiency of the following C++ fragment in terms of the integer **n**:

```
for (k = 0; k < n/2; ++k)
{
   .
   .
   .
}
for (j = 0; j < n*n; ++j)
{
   .
   .
   .
}
```

Since one loop follows the other, the number of operations executed by both of them is the sum of the individual loop efficiencies. Hence, the efficiency is $n/2+n^2$, or $O(n^2)$ in big-O terms.

Example 1.4 Use big-O analysis to determine the time efficiency of the following C++ fragment in terms of the integer **n:**

```
k = n;
while (k > 1)
{
   .
   .
   .
   k /= 2;      // integer division; equivalent to k = k/2;
}
```

Since the loop control variable is cut in half each time through the loop, the number of times that statements inside the loop will be executed is measured by $\log_2 n$. For instance, if n is 64, then the loop will be executed for the following values of k:

64
32
16
8
4
2

Note that this yields six loop iterations, that is, $\log_2 64$. For values of n that are not precisely a power of 2, the number of loop iterations will be the smallest integer greater than $\log_2 n$. In any case, the run-time efficiency of this algorithm is $O(\log_2 n)$.

Table 1.2, which lists frequently occurring dominant terms, will prove helpful in our future big-O analyses of algorithms. It is worthwhile to characterize briefly some of the classes of algorithms that arise from the dominant terms listed in Table 1.2. Algorithms with an efficiency function that is dominated by the $\log_a n$ term—and hence are categorized as $O(\log_a n)$—are often called *logarithmic algorithms*. Since $\log_a n$ will increase more slowly than n itself, logarithmic algorithms are generally very efficient. Algorithms with an efficiency function that can be expressed in terms of a polynomial of the form

$$a_m n^m + a_{m-1} n^{m-1} + \cdots + a_2 n^2 + a_1 n + a_0$$

are called *polynomial algorithms*. Since the highest power of n will dominate such a polynomial, these algorithms are $O(n^m)$. The only polynomial algorithms we will discuss in this book have $m = 1$, 2, or 3; they are called *linear, quadratic,* and *cubic* algorithms, respectively.

Algorithms with an efficiency function that is dominated by a term of the form a^n are called *exponential algorithms*. These algorithms are of more theoretical than practical interest because for moderate or large values of n they cannot reasonably be run on typical computers. We will not encounter algorithms in the exponential

TABLE 1.2
Common dominant terms in expressions for algorithmic efficiency based on the variable n.

n dominates $\log_a n$; a is often 2
$n \log_a n$ dominates n; a is often 2
n^m dominates n^k when $m > k$
a^n dominates n^m for any values of a and m greater than 1

and $n \log_a n$ categories until we study recursion in Chapter 6. At that time, we will develop some additional principles for analyzing such algorithms. The relationships between all of these various classes of algorithms are graphically summarized in Figure 1.5.

The Sorting Problem

Stated generally, the sorting problem requires that one take a given sequence of items (perhaps presented in an array or a sequential file) and reorder them so that an item and its successor satisfy a prescribed ordering relationship (for example, greater than or less than). Here we apply the concepts of big-O analysis to determine the efficiency of two sorting algorithms.

For the purposes of discussion, we can use the following C++ interface to specify the pre- and postconditions for the sorting problem when the items to be sorted appear in an array.

Figure 1.5
Relationships in run time between commonly occurring classes of algorithms.

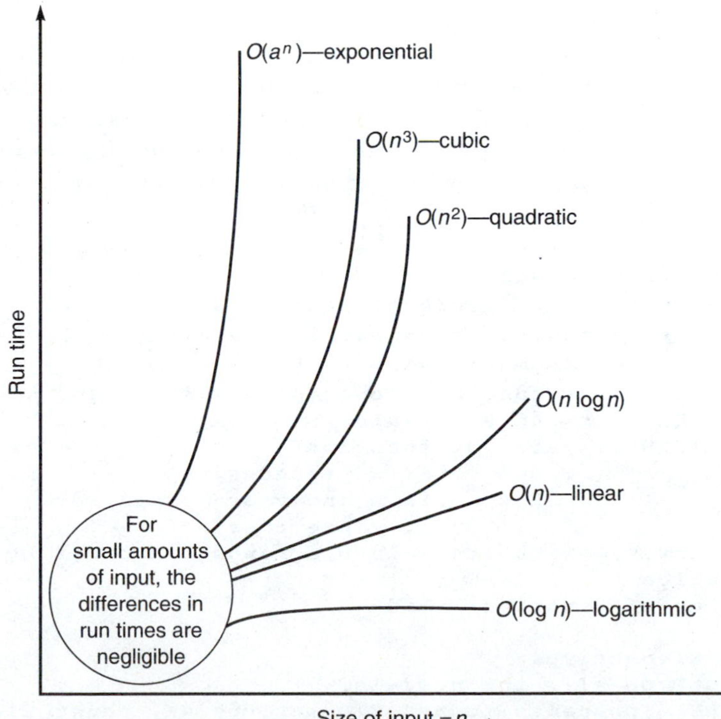

```
//-------------------------------------------------------------------
// Interface for function sort
// GIVEN:    a -- an array of ElementType values;
//           numvals -- number of values in the array,
//                      assume numvals >= 0;
//           precedes -- a function to compare ElementType values:
//             GIVEN:   x and y -- values of type ElementType to
//                                 compare
//             RETURN as value of function:
//                      TRUE    if x precedes y;
//                      FALSE   if x and y are equal, or
//                              if y precedes x
// RETURN:   The array a with its values arranged in order by the
//           precedes relation
// RETURN as value of function: void

template <class ElementType>
void sort(ElementType a[], int numvals,
          BOOLEAN (*precedes)(const ElementType &x, const ElementType &y))
```

Selection Sort

A simple solution to the sorting problem just specified is the *selection sort* algorithm. This algorithm repeatedly finds the position of the entry that should come first from among array positions **k**, **k** + 1, . . . , **numvals** − 1. This entry is then exchanged with the entry in position **k.** Hence, as **k** runs from 0 to **numvals** − 2, we *select* the entry that belongs in index zero and swap it there, then the entry which belongs in index 1 and swap it there, and so on (thus the name *selection sort*). The action of this sorting algorithm on a small array is illustrated in Figure 1.6. In this figure we assume that the *precedes* relation is the usual *less than* relation between integers. Hence, the five-element array is arranged in ascending numerical order after four passes.

It is apparent from Figure 1.6 that sorting an array of **numvals** elements will require **numvals** − 1 passes through the array, with one less comparison needed to select the appropriate entry on each successive pass. We may bury the internal logic of each pass in a call to the function **findChampionIndex** discussed in Section 1.2, thereby enhancing the function's degree of abstraction.

```
//-------------------------------------------------------------------
// Interface for function sort
// GIVEN:    a -- an array of ElementType values;
//           numvals -- number of values in the array,
//                      assume numvals >= 0
//           precedes -- a function to compare ElementType values:
//             GIVEN:   x and y -- values to compare
//             RETURN as value of function:
//                      TRUE      if x precedes y;
//                      FALSE     if x and y are equal, or
//                                if y precedes x
// RETURN:   The array a with its values arranged in order by the precedes
//           relation
// RETURN as value of function: void

template <class ElementType>
void sort(ElementType a[], int numvals,
          BOOLEAN (*precedes)(const ElementType &x, const ElementType &y))
```

```
{
  int k, firstAmongRest;

  for (k = 0; k < numvals-1; ++k)
  {
    firstAmongRest = findChampionIndex(a, k, numvals-1, precedes);
    swap(a[k], a[firstAmongRest]);
  }
}
```

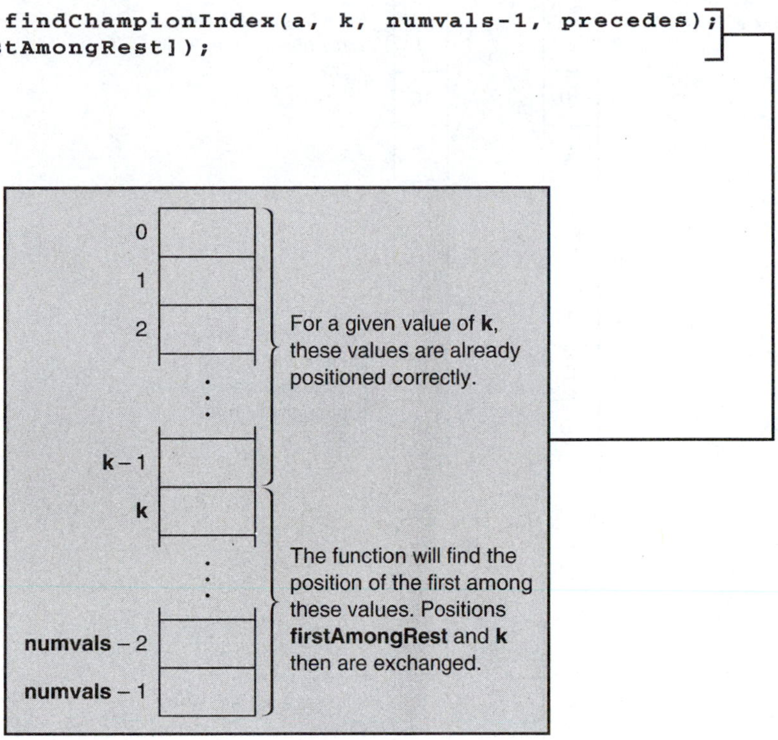

0
1
2
...
k − 1
k
...
numvals − 2
numvals − 1

For a given value of **k**, these values are already positioned correctly.

The function will find the position of the first among these values. Positions **firstAmongRest** and **k** then are exchanged.

Insertion Sort

Selection sort is blind to the original order of the array being sorted. That is, the number of comparisons required to sort the array will be the same whether the array's initial state is sorted, almost sorted, randomized, or completely reversed. This property of selection sort is attributable to its use of fixed iteration loops in both the **sort** function and the subordinate **findChampionIndex** function. Hence, neither of these loops can be short-circuited (that is, terminated normally, but earlier than expected) when an array or a portion of an array is already ordered.

Insertion sort attempts to overcome this deficiency using logic similar to that used in arranging a hand of playing cards dealt one card at a time. Given that we are holding **k** cards already arranged in order and are dealt a new card, we scan the cards in our hand, seeking the position to insert the new card. This process is illustrated in Figure 1.7. With some luck we may not have to examine all (or even a significant portion) of the cards in our hand before finding the insertion slot for the new card. This will potentially reduce the number of comparisons made by insertion sort vis-à-vis selection sort. The action of insertion sort on the array of numbers from Figure 1.6 is portrayed in Figure 1.8. Here we scan the sorted portions of the array from bottom to top.

Note that only one comparison is made on the first, second, and third passes in Figure 1.8. Only in the final pass would the number being inserted have to be compared to all previous values in the array. This dependency of the number of comparisons on the original order of the data is reflected in the inner **while** loop of the following C++ function for insertion sort:

Figure 1.6
Action of selection sort on five-entry array. During pass **k** the smallest value between index **k** and the last entry is exchanged with the entry at index **k.**

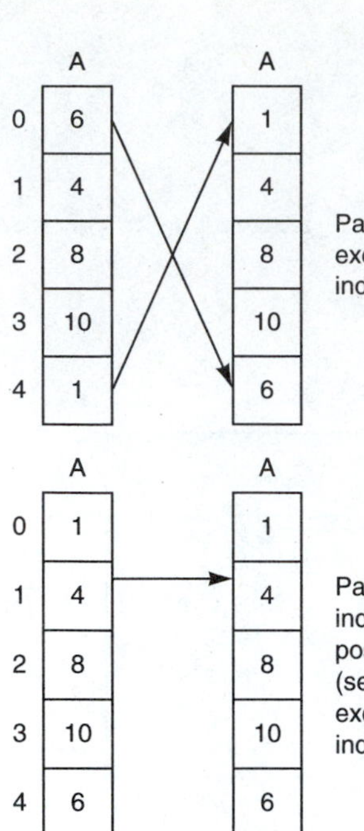

Pass 1: starts at index 1, smallest entry in positions 1 through 4 (second smallest overall) exchanged with entry in index 1

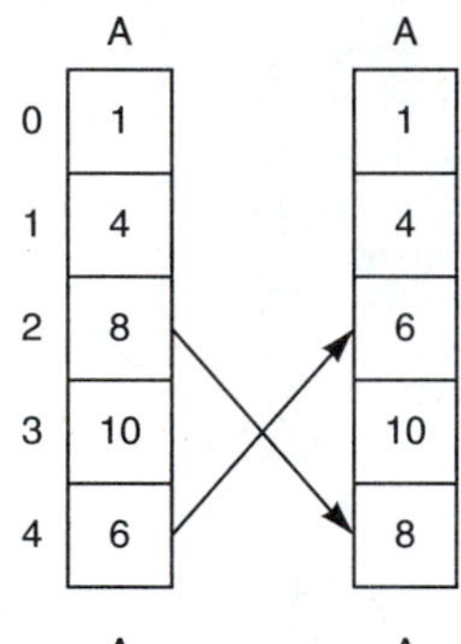

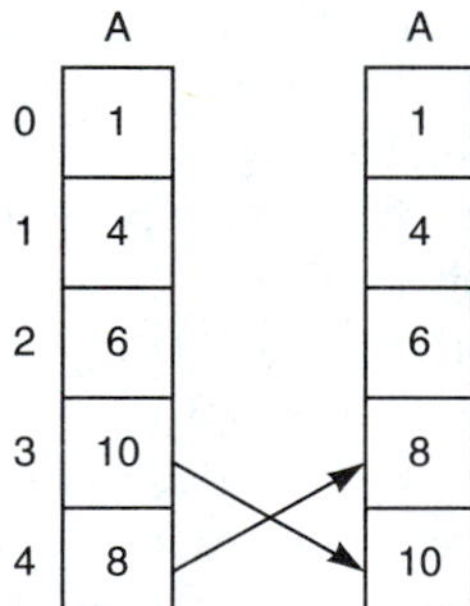


```
//-----------------------------------------------------------------
// Interface for function sort
// GIVEN:    a -- an array of ElementType values;
//           numvals -- number of values in the array,
//                      assume numvals >= 0
//           precedes -- a function to compare ElementType values:
//             GIVEN:   x and y -- values to compare
//             RETURN as value of function:
//                      TRUE       if x precedes y;
//                      FALSE      if x and y are equal, or
//                                 if y precedes x
```

Figure 1.7
Insertion sort logic in arranging playing cards.

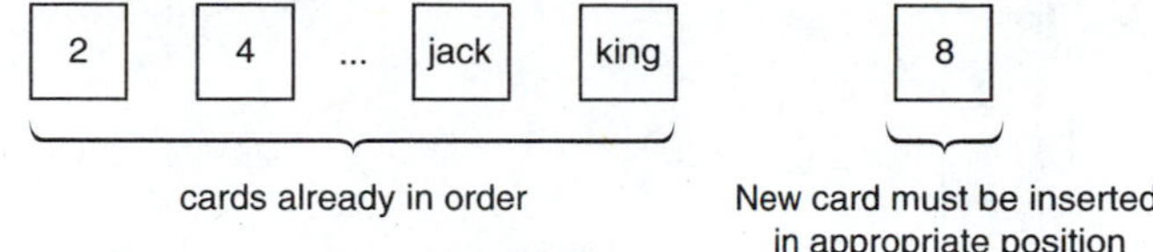


```
// RETURN:  The array a with its values arranged in order by the
//          precedes relation
// RETURN as value of function: void

template <class ElementType>
void sort(ElementType a[], int numvals,
          BOOLEAN (*precedes)(const ElementType &x, const ElementType &y))
{
  int k,j;
  BOOLEAN done;

  for (k = 1; k < numvals; ++k)   // On pass k, insert entry from
  {                               // index k
    j = k;
    done = FALSE;

    // When (j-1)th element precedes jth element, it is appropriately
    // positioned
    while ((j >= 1) && !done)
      if (precedes(a[j], a[j-1]))
      {
        swap(a[j], a[j-1]);
        --j;
      }
      else                 // Know array now sorted in indices 0...k
        done = TRUE;
  }
}
```

Array at beginning of the **k**th stage

0 1 2 ··· **k**−1 **k**

Sorted

Unsorted

element from index **k** inserted in its rightful place among indices 0 . . . **k**

Big-O Analysis of Selection Sort Recall that the loop structure of the selection sort algorithm was given by

```
for (k = 0; k < numvals-1; ++k)
{
  firstAmongRest = findChampionIndex(a, k, numvals-1, precedes);
  swap(a[k], a[firstAmongRest]);
}
```

Figure 1.8
Tracing the action of insertion sort. During pass **k** the number from index **k** is inserted into its correct position relative to indices 0 . . . **k**.

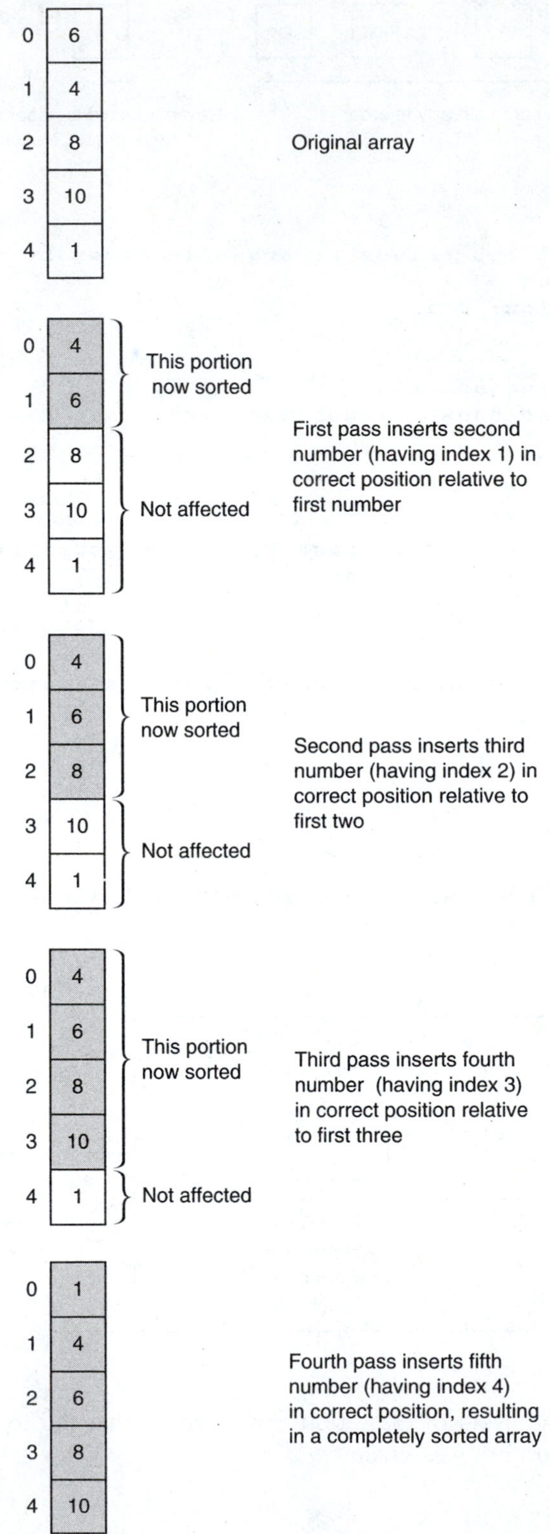
0 6
1 4
2 8
3 10
4 1
Original array
0 4
1 6
2 8
3 10
4 1
This portion now sorted
Not affected
First pass inserts second number (having index 1) in correct position relative to first number
0 4
1 6
2 8
3 10
4 1
This portion now sorted
Not affected
Second pass inserts third number (having index 2) in correct position relative to first two
0 4
1 6
2 8
3 10
4 1
This portion now sorted
Not affected
Third pass inserts fourth number (having index 3) in correct position relative to first three
0 1
1 4
2 6
3 8
4 10
Fourth pass inserts fifth number (having index 4) in correct position, resulting in a completely sorted array

where **numvals** represents the number of values being sorted. Observe that the first time **findChampionIndex** is executed, the comparison in the **if** statement of this subordinate function will be made **numvals** − 1 times. Then it will be made **numvals** − 2 times, **numvals** − 3 times, and, finally, just one time. Hence, the number of comparisons will be the sum of the sequence of numbers

numvals − 1
numvals − 2
⋮
1

A well-known formula from algebra shows this sum to be

$$\textbf{numvals} \times (\textbf{numvals} - 1)/2$$

Thus we conclude that selection sort is an $O(\textbf{numvals}^2)$ algorithm, in terms of the number of comparisons it must make.

Although selection sort is $O(\textbf{numvals}^2)$, we note that it is $O(\textbf{numvals})$ in the number of times it must swap data items because they are not swapped until after the internal loop of **findChampionIndex** is executed. This minimization of data interchanges is one of selection sort's strengths and can be particularly important when the cost of an interchange is high vis-à-vis the cost of a comparison. For instance, this would be the case if we were sorting an array of large records and the **precedes** relationship was determined by comparing integer key fields within two records. The integer comparison would be a very fast operation on all computers, but interchanging two large records would actually result in a machine language loop whose cost would not be apparent in the high-level, algorithmic language. This illustrates how the choice of an algorithm for an actual application should be tied to the realities of the machine on which the algorithm will eventually run.

Big-O Analysis of Insertion Sort Because selection sort is blind to the original order of data in an array, it is always $O(\textbf{numvals}^2)$ in the number of comparisons it makes, where **numvals** is the number of values being sorted. Insertion sort, on the other hand, may occasionally fare better because its inner **while** loop may result in an early exit. That is, for insertion sort, we expect different levels of performance for different original orderings of the array being sorted. Hence, an efficiency discussion of insertion sort should really analyze the behavior of the algorithm from three perspectives—the worst case, the best case, and the average case.

For insertion sort, it is evident that the worst case is an array that is completely reversed in its original order. Under these circumstances, the Boolean variable **done,** which controls insertion sort's inner loop, is never set to TRUE. Hence, on the first pass through the inner loop one comparison is made, on the next pass two comparisons, then three, until **numvals** − 1 comparisons are made on the last pass. The sum of the numbers of comparisons is precisely the same as for selection sort, and we conclude that insertion sort is $O(\textbf{numvals}^2)$ in its worst case.

In its best case, insertion sort receives an array that is ordered at the start. Under these circumstances, the inner loop is always exited after one comparison. Hence only **numvals** − 1 comparisons are necessary to verify the sorted array, and the algorithm is determined to be $O(\textbf{numvals})$ in this case.

However, the best and worst cases represent extremes. Perhaps a more relevant question is how we can expect insertion sort to behave on the average. An exact analysis of this case requires the use of probability theory; however, a satisfactory intuitive analysis can be achieved by starting with the quite reasonable expectation that on average an item being inserted would have to be compared to half of the already sorted items before finding its niche. This means that the number of comparisons in this average case is half of the number in the worst case. Since the average case is proportional to the worst case, we conclude that insertion sort is $O(\mathbf{numvals}^2)$ in its average performance.

Our big-O analysis of the selection and insertion sort algorithms has thus led us to the conclusion that, overall, there is no order-of-magnitude difference between the two algorithms. However, during the course of this analysis, we have also identified some relatively significant differences in the algorithms. These differences are summarized in Table 1.3.

TABLE 1.3

Comparison of time efficiencies: selection sort and insertion sort.

Selection	Insertion sort
Always performs $O(n^2)$ comparisons.	In its average case, $O(n^2)$ comparisons. However, its constant of proportionality is roughly half that of selection sort.
No best case; that is, no difference among cases.	$O(n)$ comparisons and interchanges in its best case.
No worst case; that is, no difference among cases.	Equivalent to selection sort in the worst-case number of comparisons, plus considerably more data interchanges.
Always $O(n)$ data interchanges.	$O(n^2)$ data interchanges in worst and average cases.

Exercises 1.2

1. Trace the contents of the array

18	90	40	9	3	92	6

as the selection sort algorithm would manipulate it into ascending order. To "trace" means to show the contents of the array each time two values are interchanged.

2. Repeat Exercise 1.2.1 for the insertion sort algorithm.
3. An improved insertion sort algorithm can be obtained if, instead of employing element "swaps," one employs element "moves." In this latter case, one inserts the value of index **k** into its proper position with respect to the previous indices by starting at index **k** − 1 and copying it and the values of each of its predecessors into their respective succeeding elements until one encounters an element, say at index **j,** whose value precedes that of the original value at index **k.** One then copies the original value at index **k** into index **j** + 1. Write a C++ algorithm for this version of the insertion sort and do a big-O efficiency analysis as we did for the version of insertion sort that uses element swaps.
4. The *bubble sort* is another sorting algorithm typically covered in introductory computer science courses. The general idea behind the bubble sort is to make repeated passes through the array and on each pass compare the value of each element in the array with that of its

successor. If the two values are not in the proper order relative to each other, they are swapped. The array will be completely sorted when no swaps are made during a pass. Write a C++ version of this algorithm. Then subject your algorithm to a big-O efficiency analysis as we did for the selection and insertion sorts. Compare bubble sort's best, average, and worst case performance to those of the other two algorithms.

5. Do a big-O analysis for those statements inside each of the following nested loop constructs.

a.
```
for (k = 0; k < n; ++k)
  for (j = 6; j < n; ++j)
  {
    ...
  }
```

b.
```
for (k = 0; k < n; ++k)
{
  j = n;
  while (j > 0)
  {
    ...
    j /= 2;      // integer division
  }
}
```

c.
```
k = 1;
do
{
  j = 1;
  do
  {
    ...
    j *= 2;
  }
  while (j < n);
  ++k;
}
while (k < n);
```

6. An algorithm has an efficiency $O(n^2|\sin(n)|)$. Is it any better than $O(n^2)$ for large integer n? Explain why, or why not.

7. Suppose that each of the following expressions represents the number of logical operations in an algorithm as a function of n, the number of data items being manipulated. For each expression, determine the dominant term and then classify the algorithm in big-O terms.

a. $n^3 + n^2 \log_2 n + n^3 \log_2 n$

b. $n + 4n^2 + 4^n$

c. $48n^4 + 16n^2 + \log_8 n + 2n$

8. Consider the following nested loop construct. Categorize its efficiency in terms of the variable ***n*** using big-O notation. Suppose the statements represented by the ellipsis require four main memory accesses (each requiring one microsecond) and two disk file accesses (each requiring one millisecond). Express in milliseconds the amount of time this construct would require to execute if ***n*** were 1000.

```
x = 1;
do
{
  y = n;
  while (y > 0)
  {
    ...
    --y;
  }
  x *= 2;
}
while (x < n*n);
```

9. A sorting algorithm is called *stable* if it does not change the relative order of array elements that are equal. For example, a stable sorting algorithm will not place 13_1 after 13_2 in the array

18	13	6	12	13	9

Are insertion sort and selection sort stable? If not, provide an example of an array with at least two equal elements that change in their order relative to each other.

■ 1.3 Algorithm Efficiency—The Search Problem

In the previous section, we introduced big-O notation and used it to analyze two algorithmic solutions to the sorting problem. In this section we examine a general strategy for solving the search problem—finding a particular value in an ordered array. As in Section 1.2, we may state this problem more formally as a C++ interface expressed in precondition/postcondition form.

```
//------------------------------------------------------------
// Interface for function search:
// GIVEN:    a -- an array of values of type ElementType arranged
//               in order by precedes function;
//           numvals -- number of values in the array,
//                      assume numvals >= 0
//           target -- value being sought in the array;
//           precedes -- a function to compare ElementType values:
//             GIVEN:   x and y -- values to compare
//             RETURN as value of function:
//                        TRUE       if x precedes y,
//                        FALSE      if x and y are equal, or
//                                   if y precedes x
//           split -- a function to determine how the array
//                    should be split
//             GIVEN: lo and hi, integer values with
//                    0 <= lo <= hi <= numvals-1 for numvals > 0
//             RETURN as value of function:
//                        An integer between 0 and numvals-1 inclusive
// RETURN: place -- If the return value is TRUE, place contains the
//                  index position of target in a; otherwise,
//                  place is unreliable.
// RETURN as value of function:
//            TRUE    if target can be found in the array a;
//            FALSE   otherwise

template <class ElementType>
BOOLEAN search(ElementType a[], int numvals, const ElementType &target,
               BOOLEAN (*precedes)(const ElementType &x, const ElementType &y),
               int (*split)(int lo, int hi), int &place)
```

The **precedes** and **split** parameters in the **search** interface require some explanation. If we do not assume that the array being searched is ordered, these two parameters are not needed. However, we prefer to work under that assumption because it allows us to develop search strategies that are more efficient than a sequential search strategy. Recall that such a strategy merely examines successive locations (starting with the first) until it finds the **target** or advances beyond index **numvals** − 1.

By assuming an array that is ordered according to the **precedes** relationship, we may develop a *divide-and-conquer* search strategy similar to that used when searching for a name in a phone book. We do not search for "Smith, Sam" in a phone book by starting with the first page and examining successive pages. Rather, because the phone book is alphabetically ordered, we make a guess that the location of "Smith, Sam" will be roughly three-quarters of the way into the phone book. We open to the page designated by this guess. If "Smith, Sam" appears on this page, we are done. If the names on this page precede "Smith, Sam," we iterate this process with the portion of the phone book that follows. If the names on the page follow "Smith, Sam," we iterate with the front portion of the book. This divide-and-conquer strategy is highlighted in Figure 1.9. The **split** function parameter that appears in our **search** function interface represents the method on which our divide-and-conquer guess is based.

In the code for **search** you will see that we use the C++ operator "==" to test for equality as the way to determine whether **target** appears in the array **a** or not. While this may be appropriate for certain data types (especially **int, char,** or **enum**)

Figure 1.9
Divide-and-conquer search strategy.

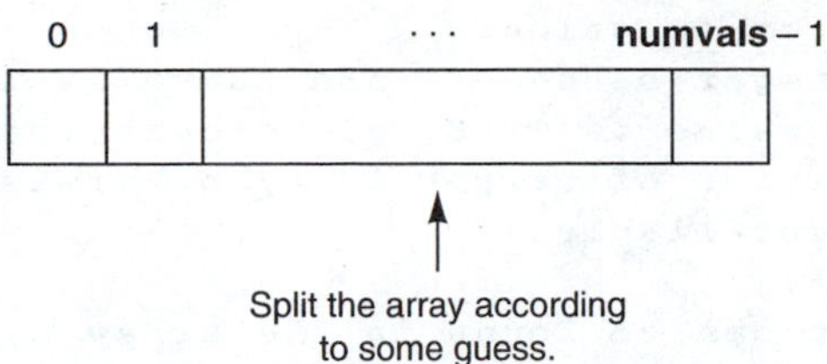

If the **target** follows the data at the splitting location, work with the portion to the right of the splitting.

If the **target** precedes the data at the splitting location, work with the portion to the left of the splitting.

it may not be appropriate for others. For example, even though in our discussion in the previous paragraph we use "Smith, Sam" as a target value, C++ does not permit us to use == to compare two string values; hence, our search function would not work in this case. On the other hand, suppose the array **a** stored values of the following structured type:

```
struct RecType
{
   int ID;
   int age;
   float height;
};
```

Here we could not just search for an array entry with the value of 1234 for its **ID** component; we would have to have matching values for **age** and **height** as well. As we shall see in Chapter 2, C++ allows us to (re)define the meaning of the "==" operator for a data type; thus we could get our **search** function to work as desired for the data types described here. For now, however, we must assume that "==" is meaningfully defined for whatever representative of ElementType we use.

With these explanations behind us, we now give the complete C++ function for the divide-and-conquer search.

```
//---------------------------------------------------------------
// Interface for function search
// GIVEN:   a -- an array of values of type ElementType arranged
//               in order according to the relationship given by
//               the precedes function;
//          numvals -- number of values in the array,
//                     assume numvals >= 0;
//          target -- value being sought in the array;
//          precedes -- a function to compare ElementType values:
//            GIVEN:   x and y -- values to compare
//            RETURN as value of function:
//                      TRUE      if x precedes y,
//                      FALSE     if x and y are equal, or
//                                if y precedes x;
//          split -- a function to determine how the array
//                   should be split
//            GIVEN: lo and hi, integer values with
//                   0 <= lo <= hi <= numvals - 1, numvals > 0
```

```
//              RETURN as value of function:
//                        An integer between 0 and numvals -1 inclusive
// RETURN: place -- if return value is TRUE, place contains the
//                  index position of target in a; otherwise,
//                  place is unreliable
// RETURN as value of function:
//             TRUE     if target can be found in the array a;
//             FALSE    otherwise

template <class ElementType>
BOOLEAN search(ElementType a[], int numvals, const ElementType &target,
               BOOLEAN (*precedes) (const ElementType &x, const ElementType &y),
               int (*split)(int lo, int hi), int &place)
{
  int hi, lo, guess;
  BOOLEAN found;

  hi = numvals - 1;
  lo = 0;
  found = FALSE;
  while (!found && (lo <= hi))
  {
    guess = split(lo, hi);
    if (a[guess] == target)
    {
      place = guess;
      found = TRUE;
    }
    else
      if (precedes(a[guess], target))
        lo = guess + 1;
      else
        hi = guess - 1;
  }
  return(found);
}
```

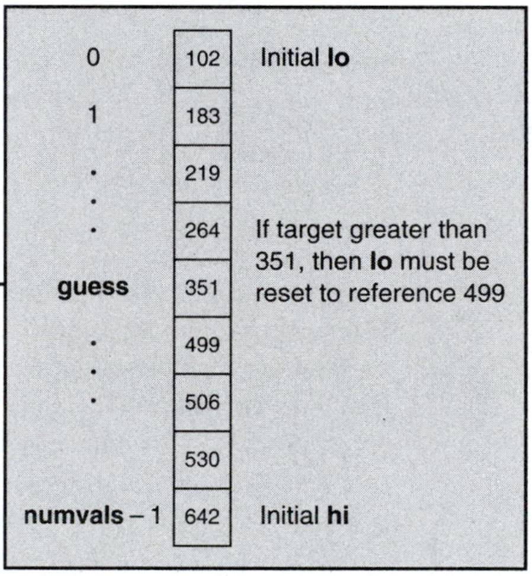

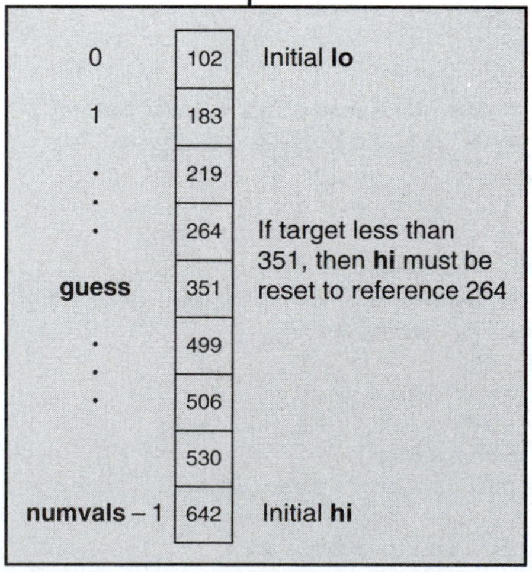

0	102	Initial **lo**
1	183	
·	219	
·	264	If target greater than 351, then **lo** must be reset to reference 499
guess	351	
·	499	
·	506	
·	530	
numvals – 1	642	Initial **hi**

0	102	Initial **lo**
1	183	
·	219	
·	264	If target less than 351, then **hi** must be reset to reference 264
guess	351	
·	499	
·	506	
·	530	
numvals – 1	642	Initial **hi**

Big-O Analysis of the Divide-and-Conquer Search Strategy

Clearly the time efficiency of this search strategy is dependent on how well the **split** function zeros in on the **target** being sought. One particular **split** function that lends itself to an easy analysis is

```
return((lo + hi)/2);      // integer division
```

This particular choice for a **split** function is interesting because it doesn't make a truly guided guess at the location of **target** but merely splits the array in half. The search algorithm that results from this choice of a **split** function is called a *binary search*. From our discussion in Example 1.4, we know that such a repeated halving strategy will yield a worst case efficiency of $O(\log_2$ **numvals**$)$, where **numvals** represents the number of values in the array being searched. As you will discover in the Exercises 1.3, an $O(\log_2$ **numvals**$)$ search algorithm will execute very quickly. This raises a question about whether other divide-and-conquer strategies, which make a "better" guess based on the particular relationship between **a[lo], target,** and **a[hi],** will actually outperform the binary search. Such strategies are called *interpolative*. Because these other strategies are highly dependent on the distribution of values in the array, a comparison between them and the binary search requires more than formal big-O analysis. In the exercises you will explore some other possibilities for the **split** function. The discussion in Section 1.4 will then provide you with means for analyzing these other schemes in comparison with the binary search.

Exercises 1.3

1. Suppose that you have a large database with 4 million items in an ordered array. How many probes into the array will the binary search require before finding its target or concluding that it cannot be found? Assuming it takes 1 microsecond to access an item, estimate the execution time of the binary search.
2. Why is it unrealistic to assume that the 4 million data items of Exercise 1.3.1 would be stored in an array? More likely such a large number of data items would have to reside in external storage, such as a random access disk file for which access times are much slower. Compute the execution time for the binary search if the data items of Exercise 1.3.1 are stored in a random access file for which the time to access one record is 50 milliseconds.
3. Suppose the **split** function for our search function is

   ```
   return(lo);
   ```

   Describe the search strategy that results. What is its big-O time efficiency?
4. Develop a **split** function that actually interpolates for an array of numerical data. That is, it should take into account the range of values between **a[lo]** and **a[hi]** and split the array at a distance from **lo** that is proportional to the relative distance between **a[lo]** and **target**.
5. Develop a **split** function that actually interpolates for an array of alphanumeric data. That is, it should take into account the range of values between **a[lo]** and **a[hi]** and split the array at a distance from **lo** that is proportional to the relative distance between **a[lo]** and **target**.
6. The *Fibonacci sequence* of numbers starts with two 1's. Thereafter, each number in the sequence is the sum of the preceding two numbers. Hence, the first seven terms of the Fibonacci sequence are

   $$1, 1, 2, 3, 5, 8, 13, \ldots$$

   If we suppose that the number of records **numvals** in the array being searched has the property that **numvals** + 1 is the kth Fibonacci number F_k for some k, then the array may be split at the (F_{k-1})th record, dividing the array into sub arrays of $F_{k-1} - 1$ and $F_{k-2} - 1$ records. For example, given an array of **numvals** = 7 records, we note that

   `numvals + 1 = 8 =` F_6

   whence we choose the F_5 = 5th record for our splitting point

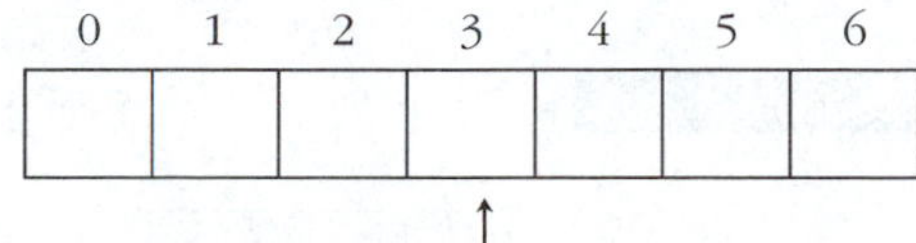

Choose this as a splitting point

Notice that such a splitting strategy will result in two subarrays (index ranges 0...3 and 5...6), each of which also has the property that the number of elements in the subarray plus one is a Fibonacci number. That is, if we iterate this choice of a splitting point, **hi** and **lo** from function **search** will have the property that **hi** − **lo** + 2 is always a Fibonacci number. The motivation for this splitting strategy is the hope that this iteration of splitting points will choose the smaller, right half of the array often enough to converge to the **target** faster than a plain binary search. The resulting search is called a *Fibonacci search*. Discuss an appropriate initialization to ensure that the Fibonacci search works even when **numvals** + 1 is not a Fibonacci number, and then write the **split** function necessary for this search.

1.4 Empirical Efficiency Analysis of Algorithms

The insertion sort, selection sort, and binary search algorithms of the preceding two sections have lent themselves to a straightforward big-O analysis. Such analysis has been sufficient to categorize completely the behavior of these algorithms. However, as we study more complex algorithms, the results of merely doing a big-O analysis may not give us a sufficiently precise handle on predicting an algorithm's performance for the vast variety of data sets it will encounter. In such situations, our inability to package data sets conveniently into best case, worst case, and average case categories may necessitate that we empirically observe the performance of the algorithm. For instance, strategies for developing interpolative **split** functions for the **search** function of the preceding section would have to be observed under actual run-time conditions to determine if they result in search times significantly faster than the binary search.

A sorting algorithm that similarly defies big-O analysis is the *Shell sort* algorithm. Originally conceived by D. L. Shell (*Communications of the Association of Computing Machinery,* 2, July 1959, pp. 30–32), this algorithm is inspired by the insertion sort's ability to work very fast on an array that is almost in order originally.

Instead of sorting the entire array at once, Shell sort first divides the array into smaller, noncontiguous segments, which are then separately sorted using the insertion sort. The advantage of doing this is twofold. First, whenever a comparison dictates a swap of two data items in a segment, this swap within a noncontiguous segment of the array moves an item a greater distance within the overall array than the swap of adjacent array entries in the usual insertion sort. This means that one swap is more likely to place an element closer to its final location in the array when using Shell sort than when using the simple insertion sort. For instance, a large-valued entry that appears near the front of the array will more quickly move to the back because each swap moves it a greater distance in the array. The second advantage of dividing the array into segments is tied to the first. That is, because early passes tend to move elements closer to their final destination than in a straight insertion sort, the array readily becomes partially sorted. The fact that the array is likely to become partially sorted earlier thus allows the embedded insertion sort logic to make more frequent use of its early loop exit. (Recall that this potential early exit makes the insertion sort particularly efficient for partially sorted arrays.) An example will help clarify this rationale behind Shell sort.

Example 1.5 Suppose we have an array **a** containing the following integers:

80	93	60	12	42	30	68	85	10

We first divide this into three segments of three elements each:

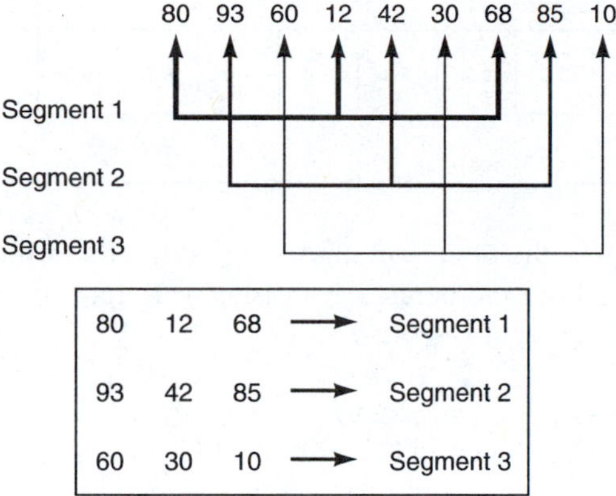

and sort each of the segments:

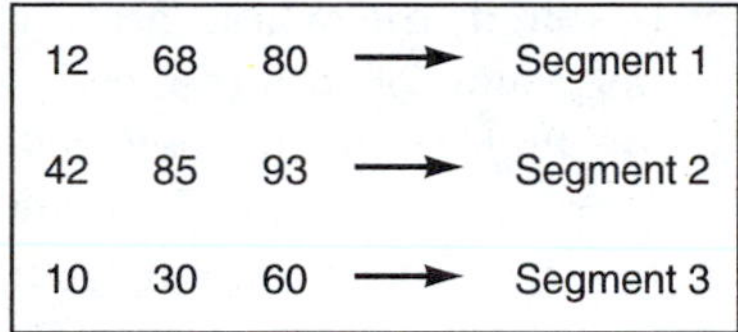

The original array, partially sorted, now appears as

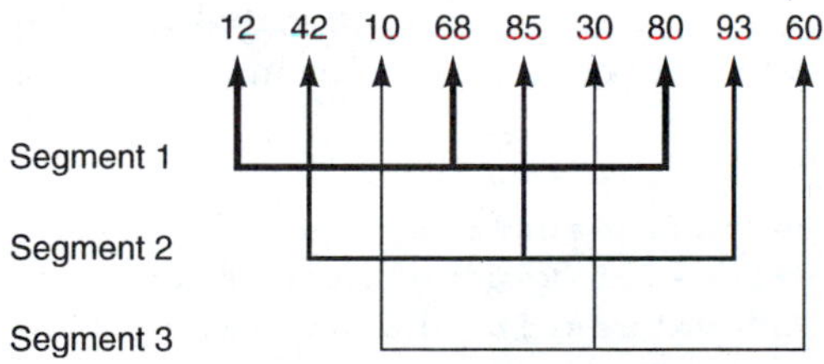

We next divide this partially sorted array into two segments:

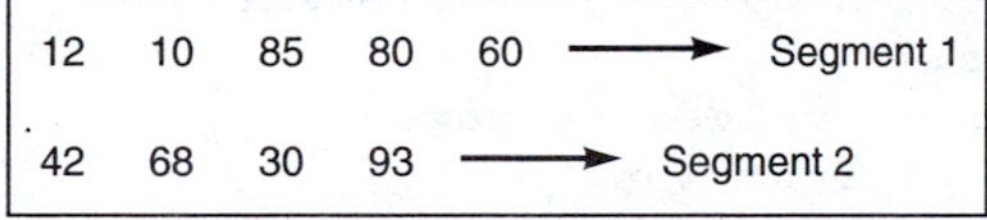

These segments are then sorted and array **a** takes the form

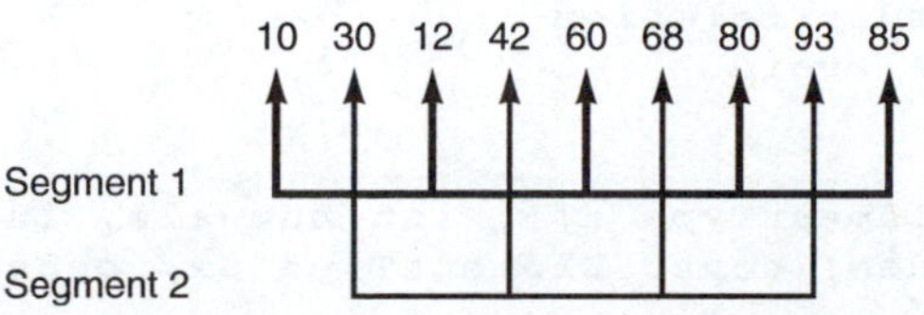

Finally, this array is sorted as one segment; 12 and 30, and then 93 and 85 are swapped to give us the following sorted array:

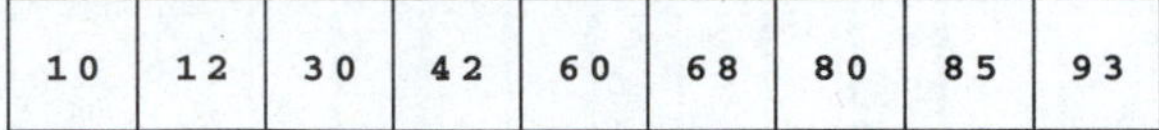

10	12	30	42	60	68	80	85	93

The key to the Shell sort algorithm is that the whole array is first fragmented into segments whose elements are a distance **k** apart for some number **k**. There will be **k** of these segments

```
a[0], a[k], a[2 * k],  . . .
a[1], a[k + 1], a[2 * k + 1],  . . .
.
.
.
a[k - 1], a[2 * k - 1], a[3 * k - 1],  . . .
```

Because each segment is sorted, the whole array is partially sorted after the first pass. For the next pass, the value of **k** is reduced, which increases the number of elements in each segment. Preferably, the next value of **k** is also chosen so that it is relatively prime to its previous value. (Two integers are said to be *relatively prime* to each other if they have no common factor greater than 1.) The process is finally repeated with **k** = 1, at which point the array is sorted. As the insertion sort is applied to each segment, later applications of the insertion sort become very efficient, dramatically increasing the overall efficiency of the Shell sort.

To emphasize the fashion in which the Shell sort algorithm relies on the logic of insertion sort, we present a **segmentedInsertionSort** function, which arranges segments with distance **k** between elements in an array into ascending order.

```
//------------------------------------------------------------
// Interface for function segmentedInsertionSort
// GIVEN:    a -- an array of values of type ElementType;
//           numvals -- number of values in the array,
//                      assume numvals >= 0;
//           k -- distance between elements of the same segment
//                within the array a.  The ith segment consists
//                of a[i], a[i+k], a[i+2*k], and so on;
//           precedes -- a function to compare ElementType
//                       values:
//             GIVEN:    x and y -- values to compare
//             RETURN as value of function:
//                       TRUE      if x precedes y,
//                       FALSE     if x and y are equal, or
//                                 if y precedes x
// RETURN:   The array a with each of its k segments arranged in
//           order by the precedes relation
// RETURN as value of function: void

template <class ElementType>
void segmentedInsertionSort(ElementType a[], int numvals, int k,
             BOOLEAN (*precedes)(const ElementType &x, const ElementType &y))
```

```
{
  int j, m;
  BOOLEAN done;

  // Insert element from index m in appropriate slot in its segment

  for (m = k; m < numvals; ++m)
  {
    j = m;
    done = FALSE;

    // When (j-k)th element precedes jth element, jth is appropriately
    // positioned in its segment

    while ((j >= k) && !done)
      if (precedes(a[j], a[j-k]))
      {
        swap(a[j], a[j-k]);
        j -= k;
      }
      else
        done = TRUE;
  }
}
```

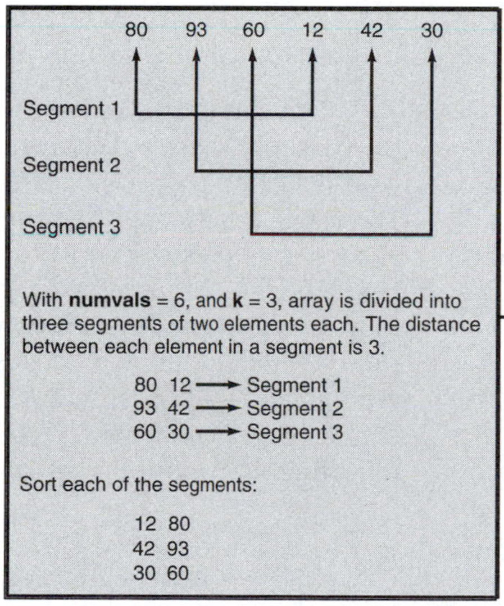

80 93 60 12 42 30

Segment 1

Segment 2

Segment 3

With **numvals** = 6, and **k** = 3, array is divided into three segments of two elements each. The distance between each element in a segment is 3.

80 12 ⟶ Segment 1
93 42 ⟶ Segment 2
60 30 ⟶ Segment 3

Sort each of the segments:

12 80
42 93
30 60

Given the **segmentedInsertionSort** function, we now merely call on this with values of **k** that become successively smaller. Eventually, **segmentedInsertionSort** must be called with **k** = 1 to guarantee that the array, viewed as one segment, is completely sorted.

The following function for Shell sort illustrates these successive calls to **segmentedInsertionSort** for values of **k** that are repeatedly halved:

```
//-------------------------------------------------------------
// Interface for function sort
// GIVEN:   a -- an array of values of type ElementType;
```

```
//          numvals -- number of values in the array,
//                     assume numvals >= 0;
//          precedes -- a function to compare ElementType
//                      values:
//            GIVEN:    x and y -- values to compare
//            RETURN as value of function:
//                      TRUE       if x precedes y,
//                      FALSE      if x and y are equal, or
//                                 if y precedes x
// RETURN:  The array a arranged in order by precedes relation
// RETURN as value of function: void

template <class ElementType>
void sort (ElementType a[], int numvals,
           BOOLEAN (*precedes)(const ElementType &x, const ElementType &y))
{
  int eledist;            // eledist is the distance between elements of the same
                          // segment
  eledist = numvals / 2;
  while (eledist > 0)
  {
    segmentedInsertionSort(a, numvals, eledist, precedes);
    eledist /= 2;     // Halve the distance between elements
  }
}
```

Efficiency of the Shell Sort

The Shell sort is also called the *diminishing increment sort* because the value of **k** (the distance between elements of a segment) continually decreases. The sort will work with any decreasing sequence of values of **k,** as long as the last value of **k** is 1. There will clearly be $\log_2$ **numvals** repetitions of **segmentedInsertionSort** for the version of Shell sort that we have presented here. Within each of these repetitions, big-O analysis of the efficiency of **segmentedInsertionSort** is difficult. The outer loop of **segmentedInsertionSort** is clearly O(**numvals**), but the inner loop defies such a precise analysis because it is so dependent on the order of data within the segment—an order that we hope is closer to sorted as we progress through the diminishing increments. Thus, a big-O analysis of Shell sort is complicated by the following triple-nested loop structure.

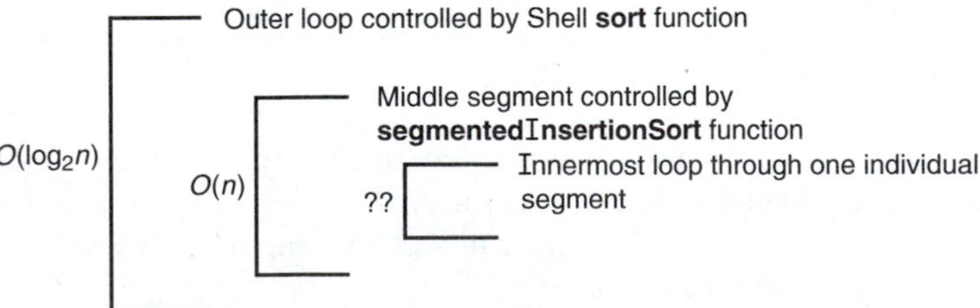

We can only conclude that the number of comparisons required by Shell sort is

$$O(A \times \textbf{numvals} \times \log_2 \textbf{numvals})$$

where A is some unknown factor, possibly dependent on **numvals.**

TABLE 1.4
Results of Shell sort experimentation.

Size of randomly generated data set	**Average number of comparisons**	**Number of comparisons expressed in terms of $n \times (\log_2 n)^2$**	**Number of comparisons expressed in terms of $n^{(3/2)}$**
1000	14,702	$0.148 \times n \times (\log_2 n)^2$	$0.465 \times n^{(3/2)}$
3000	57,958	$0.145 \times n \times (\log_2 n)^2$	$0.353 \times n^{(3/2)}$
5000	109,065	$0.144 \times n \times (\log_2 n)^2$	$0.309 \times n^{(3/2)}$

Experimentation with an algorithm can often be used to augment a purely formal mathematical analysis. By observing how an algorithm performs on a variety of data sets, we may be able to draw some statistical conclusions concerning its behavior. For instance, in the case of Shell sort, we counted the number of comparisons made by the algorithm for a variety of randomly generated data sets of 1000, 3000, and 5000 items. We then averaged the number of comparisons required for data sets of each of these three sizes. Table 1.4 summarizes our results.

Although such results do not have the clout of a mathematical proof, they certainly lend credence to a claim that $O(\textbf{numvals} \times (\log_2 \textbf{numvals})^2)$ and $O(\textbf{numvals}^{3/2})$ are reasonable estimates of the average case behavior of Shell sort. Our results are consistent with those of many larger studies that have been done on Shell sort. [See Donald E. Knuth, *Searching and Sorting,* Vol. 3 of *The Art of Computer Programming* (Menlo Park, CA: Addison-Wesley, 1973).]

An important observation arises from the preceding discussion: Computer science is *science* in the sense that sometimes a complex situation will arise whose analysis defies a mathematical model. Here we often hypothesize a solution to a problem and prove or disprove that hypothesis through experimental observation. Not all solutions can yet be verified by purely formal mathematical arguments. The exercises and programming problems/projects in this book will often encourage you to perform such exploratory analyses.

In the spirit of such exploration, we should note that the particular sequence of diminishing increments that we have chosen for our implementation of Shell sort may not be the best possible because many values within the entire array will never be compared to each other until the increment size reaches 1. This phenomenon is illustrated in Figure 1.10. In an attempt to make a greater variety of comparisons when the increment size is large (and hence array elements move a great distance), Knuth suggests choosing a sequence of diminishing increments in which successive values are relatively prime to each other. For instance, Knuth suggests a sequence of diminishing values such as $\ldots 31, 15, 7, 3, 1$. You will experiment with this and other possible sequences in the exercises and programming problems that follow.

Figure 1.10
An inefficiency in the present sequence of diminishing increments: 4, 2, 1. Many values within the array will not be compared to each other until the increment size reaches 1.

1	2	3	4	5	6	7	8
80	70	60	50	40	30	20	10

As we attempt to sort into ascending order, none of [80, 60, 40, 20] is compared to any value in [70, 50, 30, 10] until the final pass

Exercises 1.4

1. Consider the Shell sort function given in this section. Suppose that we sort into ascending order and trace the contents of the array being sorted after each call to the function **segmentedInsertionSort**. What would we see as output if we called Shell sort with the following array?

60	12	90	30	64	8	6

2. Repeat Exercise 1.4.1 for a six-element array that initially contains

1	8	2	7	3	6

3. Why is the Shell sort called by that name?
4. Why is the Shell sort more efficient when the original data are in an almost-sorted order?
5. What advantage do the relatively prime values of the increments have over other values in a Shell sort?
6. What property must the sequence of diminishing increments in the Shell sort have to ensure that the method will work?
7. Provide examples of best case and worst case data sets for the Shell sort algorithm presented in this section.
8. Repeat Exercise 1.4.1 for the following sequence of diminishing increments: 5, 3, 1. Compare the performance of the algorithm for this sequence to that of the halving sequence used in this section.
9. Consider the eight-element array

80	70	60	50	40	30	20	10

Suppose that we wish to sort this array into ascending order. Count the number of comparisons required to do this by insertion sort, by Shell sort with the halving sequence of diminishing increments given in this section, and by Shell sort with 5, 3, 1 as the sequence of diminishing increments.

10. Repeat Exercise 1.4.1 for the array

8	5	2	6	3	7	4	1

using the sequence of diminishing increments 5, 3, 1.

11. Rewrite the Shell sort function of this section so that it works with the following sequences of diminishing increments:

    a. 1, 3, 5, 9, . . . (reverse order)

    b. 1, 3, 7, 15, . . .

    c. 1, 3, 5, 11, 21, . . .

    d. 1, 4, 13, 40, . . .

12. A sorting algorithm is called *stable* if it does not change the relative order of array elements that are equal. For example, a stable sorting algorithm will not place 13_1 after 13_2 in the array

18	13	6	12	13	9

Is Shell sort stable? If not, provide an example of an array with at least two equal elements that change in their order relative to each other.

Chapter Summary

In this chapter we introduced the concepts that will be the foundation for the rest of our work in this book—abstraction, algorithms, data structures, abstract data types, and efficiency. *Abstraction* is the process of identifying certain properties of an object and then using these properties to specify a new object, which represents a simplification of the object from which it was derived. An *algorithm* is an abstraction of a computer program. It specifies a sequence of instructions for solving a problem in a way that is free from the constraints imposed by the architecture of any given computer. The instructions must be clear and unambiguous, must solve the problem in a finite amount of time, and must conclude when the problem has been solved.

A *data structure* is an abstraction of the data types supported by a language. Whereas the values of elementary data types are atomic, those of data structures are composites of values of both elementary data types and previously defined data structures. The definition of a data structure requires a specification of the organization of its composite values as well as any relationships that may exist between the components. An *abstract data type* (ADT) results when, in addition to specifying the organization and intercomponent relationships of a data structure, one specifies the complete set of operations that can be performed among objects admitting values with this structure.

The concepts of algorithms, data structures, and abstract data types come together when *implementing* an abstract data type; that is, in moving from the specification of the data type to a realization of it on a computer via the data types and instructions of a programming language for that computer. Choices must be made concerning which of the language's data types to use in representing the components of the data structure, how to represent the relationships among these components, and which algorithms to use for the operations associated with the abstract data type. To provide a means by which different implementations may be compared, *efficiency analysis,* in terms of the run time and memory utilizations of algorithms and structures, is introduced. Classifications of efficiency, in terms of the *big-O analysis,* are described.

C++ has been chosen as the language in which the algorithms and data structures discussed in this book are described, so this chapter provided a review of the traditional C constructs that we will need and introduced some new features of the object-oriented C++ language. Finally, algorithms for solving the sorting problem and the searching problem were given, together with a big-O analysis of each algorithm.

Keywords

abstract data type
abstraction
algorithm
big-O notation
binary search
constant of proportionality
constant reference parameter
data structure
divide-and-conquer
exponential algorithms
functionally cohesive
implementation
insertion sort
interface
logarithmic algorithms
module
order of magnitude
polynomial algorithms
reference parameter
selection sort
Shell sort
template

Programming Problems/Projects

1. Consider a collection of records for students at a university. Each record includes fields for student name, credits taken, credits earned, and total grade points. Write a program that, based on a user's request, will sort the records in ascending or descending order keying on one of the four fields within the record. For instance, the user might specify that the sort should proceed in descending order according to credits earned. As much as possible, try to refrain from having to write a separate sort function for each particular ordering and field. Experiment by developing different functions based on each of the three sorting strategies discussed in this chapter.

2. Consider the same collection of records as in Problem 1. Now write a function to sort the records in descending order by credits earned. Records having the same number of credits earned should be arranged in descending order by total grade points. Those with the same number of credits earned and total grade points should be arranged alphabetically by name. Incorporate this function into the complete program that you wrote for Problem 1. Experiment by developing different functions based on each of the three sorting strategies discussed in this chapter.

For any or all of Problems 3 through 7, design a program to answer the question posed. Then analyze the time efficiency of your program in big-O terms. Run your program to try to see the relationship between big-O classification and actual run time as measured by a clock.

3. In the first century A.D., numbers were separated into "abundant" (such as 12, whose divisors have a sum greater than 12), "deficient" (such as 9, whose divisors have a sum less than 9), and "perfect" (such as 6, whose divisors add up to 6). In all cases, the number itself is not included. For example, the only numbers that divide evenly into 6 are 1, 2, 3, and 6; and 6 = 1 + 2 + 3.

Write a program to list all numbers between 2 and *N* and classify each as abundant, deficient, or perfect. Keep track of the numbers in each class.

4. In the first century A.D., Nicomachus wrote a book entitled *Introduction Arithmetica*. In it the question "How can the cubes be represented in terms of the natural numbers?" was answered by the statement: "Cubical numbers are always equal to the sum of successive odd numbers and can be represented this way." For example,

$$1^3 = 1 = 1$$
$$2^3 = 8 = 3 + 5$$
$$3^3 = 27 = 7 + 9 + 11$$
$$4^3 = 64 = 13 + 15 + 17 + 19$$

Write a program to find the successive odd numbers whose sum equals K^3 for K having the values from 1 to N, where N is a user-supplied integer.

5. A conjecture, first made by the mathematician Goldbach, a proof of which has defied all attempts, is that "every even number larger than two can be written as the sum of two prime numbers." For example,

$$4 = 2 + 2$$
$$6 = 3 + 3$$
$$8 = 3 + 5$$
$$10 = 3 + 7$$
$$100 = 89 + 11$$

Write a program that determines for every even integer N with $2 < N$ two prime numbers P and Q such that $N = P + Q$.

6. A pair of numbers M and N are called "friendly" (or they are referred to as an "amicable pair") if the sum of all the divisors of M (excluding M) is equal to the number N and the sum of all the divisors of the number N (excluding N) is equal to M ($M \neq N$). For example, the numbers 220 and 284 are an amicable pair because the only numbers that divide evenly into 220 (1, 2, 4, 5, 10, 11, 20, 22, 44, 55, and 110) add up to 284, and the only numbers that divide evenly into 284 (1, 2, 4, 71, and 142) add up to 220.

Write a program to find at least one other pair of amicable numbers. Be prepared to let your program search for some time.

7. A consequence of a famous theorem (of the mathematician Fermat) is the fact that

$$2^{(P-1)} \textbf{ mod } P = 1$$

for every odd prime number P. An odd positive integer K satisfying

$$2^{(K-1)} \textbf{ mod } K = 1$$

is called a *pseudoprime*. Write a program to determine a table of pseudoprimes and primes between 2 and N. How many pseudoprimes occur that are not prime numbers?

8. Design a program that allows you to experiment with the various **split** functions discussed in Section 1.3. Your program should allow you to

a. Enter an array interactively,

b. Load an array from a text file, or

c. Randomly generate data for an array.

Sort the array so that the **search** function of Section 1.3 applies. Then the program should allow you to search for specific **target** values using the binary **split** function, the Fibonacci **split** function (see Exercise 1.3.6), and other interpolative **split** functions (see Exercises 1.3.4 and 1.3.5; you may have to add the array as a parameter for the **split** function). As the search is conducted, your program should count the number of comparisons necessary to find the **target** or it should conclude that the **target** is not in the array.

Use the program to conduct an empirical comparative analysis between the various **split** functions. Present the results of this analysis, which should include a statistical table and a writeup in which you state your conclusions regarding the relative efficiencies of the methods. Save your program so that it can be extended as we discuss other solutions to the search problem in future chapters.

9. Design a program that allows you to experiment with the selection, insertion, and Shell sort functions described in this chapter. The program should allow you to

a. Enter an array interactively,

b. Load an array from a text file, or

c. Randomly generate an array.

You should be able to enter the method(s) by which the array should be sorted. If Shell sort is one of the methods chosen, allow entry of the sequence of diminishing increments. The program should then sort the array for each of the methods chosen and count the number of comparisons and data interchanges required for each method. Use the program to conduct an empirical comparative analysis that includes a statistical table and writeup in which you state your conclusions regarding the relative efficiencies of the algorithms. Pay particular attention to various sequences of diminishing increments for the Shell sort.

10. In Exercise 1.2.4, you developed a function to implement the bubble sort algorithm. The logic of this algorithm allows for an early loop exit as soon as the array under consideration falls into sorted order. Because of this, Shell sort may also be implemented using array segments that are sorted by bubble sort instead of insertion sort.

Develop a version of Shell sort that uses an underlying bubble sort function on array segments. Run this version of Shell sort against that based on insertion sort for a variety of data sets, counting the number of operations performed by each version of the algorithm. Write a statement, backed by your empirical findings, in which you summarize the relative performance of the two algorithms. If one algorithm seems to perform better than the other, be sure to explain why.

CHAPTER 2

Data: Abstraction and Implementation

Does it contain any abstract reasoning concerning quantity or number? No. Does it contain any experimental reasoning, concerning matter of fact and existence? No. Commit it then to the flames: for it can contain nothing but sophistry and illusion.
David Hume

Chapter Outline:

In the first chapter we emphasized an abstract approach to describing algorithms and how this approach increases the potential for an algorithm to be applicable in a variety of contexts. The question we raise in this chapter is the following: Can an abstract approach in describing data yield a similar benefit? As an initial step in answering this question, in Section 2.1 we reexamine the concept of an abstract data type (ADT), which we introduced in Section 1.1. Examples of abstract data types—arrays, sortable arrays, strings, and sets—are discussed in Sections 2.1, 2.2, 2.3, and 2.4 respectively. For each of these examples, we show how to define that data type in a way that will allow many alternative implementations. Some of these implementations are discussed in this chapter. Other more efficient implementations are developed in subsequent chapters as we study more advanced techniques. It is critical to realize, however, that whatever implementation we use, it must fit the original definition of the particular abstract data type. We also introduce the notion of a class as a feature of C++ that enforces the distinction between a data type as an abstraction and the implementation of such an abstraction as it is ultimately used by programmers.

2.1 Abstract Data Types

In this age of increasing dependence on computer software, it is important that we design software systems that are reliable, flexible, expandable, efficient, and verifiable. How can we have a reasonable chance of attaining these goals? One answer to this question indicates how far the still young discipline of computer science has progressed. In the late 1950s and early 1960s there was a widely held belief that designing effective software systems was something akin to an occult art. That is, those who succeeded in designing such systems did so for reasons that could not always be explained—similar to the spark of unfathomable inspiration that separates a great painter from a doodler.

Software Engineering

This view of successful software designers began to change in the latter part of the 1960s. We discovered that such designers seemed to use a methodology similar to an engineer's approach to problem-solving. What characterizes this engineering approach? Consider the various phases involved in the successful development of a complex structure such as a bridge. First, the engineer meets with the people (often laypersons) who want the bridge built and learns about its intended function: Is it to be part of a heavily traveled urban freeway or a one-lane country road? From such meetings, the engineer develops a conceptual picture of the bridge. This picture is an abstract entity in the engineer's mind or perhaps exists in very rough form on paper. At this stage the engineer is working with ideas and ignoring most physical construction details.

The next steps allow the engineer to come successively closer to the tangible implementation of the bridge. A miniature prototype of the bridge is built that allows the engineer to come face to face with many potential construction problems. It also provides a way to check whether the bridge will serve the needs specified by those who originally wanted it built. This prototype is followed by the development of detailed plans in blueprint form. Again, this represents a step away from the purely abstract bridge toward its actual implementation. These blueprints provide the essential details to the contractor, and the contractor completes the entire process by implementing the engineer's plans in the physical structure of the bridge.

As we review the engineering approach, three important points should be made:

1. The entire process that culminates in the building of the bridge is a series of refinements from an abstract view of the bridge to its tangible implementation. This process parallels closely the phases in the development of a successful software system, beginning with a purely conceptual view of the problem and culminating with the implementation of a solution in program code.
2. This engineering approach truly places the emphasis on design issues. The design process is a very creative endeavor. During the design process, engineers typically try various combinations of possible options and frequently change their minds about many significant aspects of the overall design. The opportunity for such experimentation exists when the design is still in abstract form and when such creative considerations are possible—even encouraged—because of the openness of the conceptual model. As the model draws nearer to actual implementation, myriad details specific to the chosen implementation make similar "what-if" reasoning expensive and often impossible.
3. The engineering approach encourages prototyping—quickly building systems that, from outward appearances, appear to be finished. To facilitate rapid and inexpensive development of a prototype, we may rely on underlying modules that perform a task in some relatively inefficient way. However, a prototype has the advantage of allowing prospective users to interact with the system and to voice their opinions about it. This provides the engineer with some early

feedback on the system, which is critical in the overall design process. If users are pleased with the prototype, the engineer can then concentrate on replacing the quickly developed, inefficient modules with modules that optimize the overall performance of the system. Essential in this fine-tuning phase is the ability to "plug in" a new module for a particular function in a way that doesn't require tampering with the rest of the system.

As early software developers analyzed frequent programming failures, they looked to the already established field of engineering for a paradigm. The engineering methodology of successively refining abstract models toward an eventual implementation made sense as an approach to developing complete data structures. A system designer who decides too quickly how to implement a data structure in the code of a particular computer language is analogous to an engineer who allows construction of a bridge to begin before adequate planning has been done. Both are heading for final results that are inelegant and riddled with serious flaws. The solution seemed obvious: Attempt to apply a similarly rigorous methodology to the discipline of computer science. Hence, software engineering has developed into an important area of study within computer science. It represents an attempt to apply the disciplined methods of engineering to software development. Its goal is to ensure that software is produced in a way that is cost-effective and sufficiently reliable to deserve the increasing trust we are placing in it.

Abstract Data Types—Concepts and the Array ADT

To approach the development of a complex data structure as an engineer would approach the development of a bridge, we must initially view the data from an abstract perspective. We want to specify the data types apart from considerations regarding their implementation. This separation of a data type's specification from declarations that implement the data type in a particular language is the essence of data abstraction. It turns out that some abstract data types will have very easy implementations in your favorite language. For others, their implementations will be much less direct. At this stage of our problem analysis, we don't want language considerations to influence our solution to the problem. Such considerations should come later, after we have accurately described the problem. The *specification* of an abstract data type involves three factors:

1. A description of the elements that compose the data type
2. A description of the relationships between the individual components in the data type
3. A description of the operations that we wish to perform on the components of the data type.

Note that all three factors are language independent. An abstract data type is a formal description of data elements and relationships as envisioned by the software engineer; it is thus a conceptual model. Ultimately this model must be implemented in an appropriate computer language via declarations for the elements and relationships and via instructions (often in the form of function calls) for the operations. At an even deeper level, the implementation is translated by the compiler into a representation in an assembler language. An assembler then translates this representation into a physical, electronic representation on a particular computer.

This hierarchy of levels of abstraction is illustrated in Figure 2.1. Each level in this hierarchy should be shielded as much as possible from details of the levels

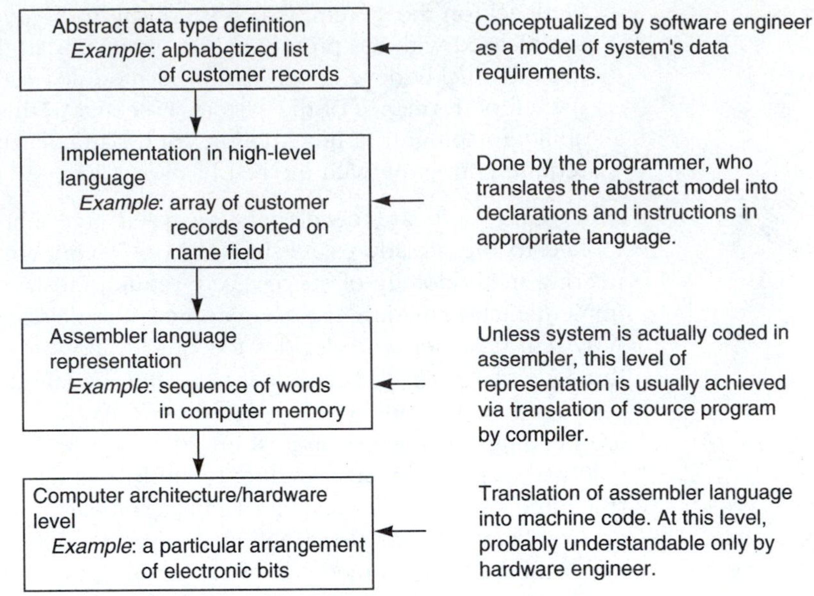

Figure 2.1
Levels of abstraction in specifying data.

that appear below it. Consider, for instance, the separation between the definition of an abstract data type and its implementation in a computer language. There may be several ways to implement a given abstract data type. Each implementation will carry its own collection of declarations, instructions, and, possibly, limitations. This collection should form a cohesive package that meets all the specifications in the definition of the abstract data type. From the perspective of the abstract data type, we are not concerned with the details of how the data relationships and instructions are implemented in this package; we are concerned only that they meet the specification of the definition. Indeed, keeping the implementation details of an abstract data type out of its specification as much as possible (a practice known as *information hiding*) makes it relatively easy to interchange one package of declarations and instructions with another package implementing the same abstract data type. Such interchangeability is desirable when we want to evaluate and compare the performance characteristics of several implementation strategies for a given abstract data type. Similarly, in situations where a prototype system has been developed quickly to obtain user feedback, interchangeability is critical as the prototype is transformed into an efficient system based on more complex implementations of the critical data structures. Thus, *information hiding* describes the ability of a package to meet the specifications of an abstract data type in a self-contained fashion, which allows us to use the package without having to know how it is implemented.

To illustrate the separation between the specification of an ADT and its implementations, we consider the familiar notion of an array.

Definition: The ADT *Array* is an association between an index range and a collection of identically typed data items. An index range is a finite collection of consecutive enumerated values such as integers or characters. The association between the index range and the data items allows us to designate the first value in the array as the datum associated with the first index and, in general, the *i*th value in the array as the datum associated with the *i*th index. The operations performed on an array are:

Construct Operation

Preconditions: An uninitialized Array object.
Postconditions: The Array object has been allocated sufficient storage to store its associated data items, though no specific values have been stored in the Array.

Destroy Operation

Preconditions: An Array object that has been previously constructed.
Postconditions: All storage allocated to the Array object is deallocated; that is, returned to an available space pool for allocation to other objects.

Retrieve Operation

Preconditions: An Array object that has been previously created;
i—a valid index.
Postconditions: The value associated with index *i* in the Array object is returned.

Assign Operation

Preconditions: An Array object that has been previously created;
i—a valid index;
val—a specified value for an Array datum.
Postconditions: The Array object has *val* associated with index *i*. We say that "*val* is stored at index *i* in the Array object."

Figure 2.2 provides a conceptual picture of an array and shows the effect of the *Retrieve* and *Assign* operations. Observe that the three factors involved in an ADT's definition have all been carefully specified for the Array ADT:

- *Description of elements:* The only restriction is that all elements be of the same type.
- *Relationships between individual components:* Specified as a position determined by the index.

Figure 2.2
Array with index range −5 to 5 and its operations.

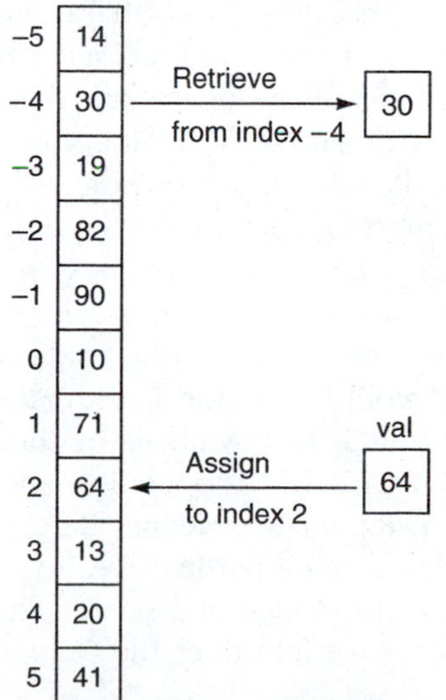

- *Operations:* Specified as a set of pre- and postconditions.

All ADT definitions should appear in this three-factor format.

The preceding definition and Figure 2.2 should not surprise you; you are familiar with the notion of an array from your previous work in computer science. It is important to note, however, that our definition of an array as an ADT is not identical to the notion of an array in traditional C. Arrays in C can only be indexed by integers, beginning with index 0. The Array ADT allows indices to come from an ordinal type such as **int**, **char**, or **enum**. Arrays in C do not respect the restriction that the value of an index must remain within the valid index range. (C's failure to check the bounds of an array index has cost virtually every C programmer many sleepless nights spent in debugging mode.) The preconditions for the Retrieve and Assign operations of the Array ADT do not allow the index value to be outside of the index range. Keep in mind the distinction between the formal definition of an ADT and a structured data type in C (or any other programming language). The ADT definition specifies a purely conceptual notion. C's structured data types are harsh realities imposed on us by the implementors of the language.

The Array ADT definition also introduces some vocabulary that will be important throughout the remainder of this text. First, the Construct and Destroy operations cite the need to allocate and deallocate storage in memory. That an operation is responsible for allocating storage implies that this allocation takes place when the operation is invoked, that is, during execution of a program. This is in contrast to space being allocated to an array at the time a program is compiled. This operation allows us to construct an Array object using variables to establish its size. An array whose size is determined at run time is not directly supported in traditional C nor in many other popular languages such as Pascal. The space in memory where storage for objects can be allocated and then deallocated when no longer needed is called the *free store* (or *heap*). The allocation of space in the free store at run time is called *dynamic allocation*, as opposed to the *static allocation* of storage, which is done at compile time. Soon we describe special C++ operators, **new** and **delete**, that can be used to allocate and deallocate space in the free store.

Second, the Array ADT definition continually mentions an Array *object*. This is in reference to the *object-oriented* paradigm on which C++ is based. We refine the notion of an object in later sections, so for now you should think of an object as an instance of an ADT. In other words, an Array object is an instance of the Array ADT just as, in the animal kingdom, a dog object (that is, an actual dog) is an instance of the class of animals categorized as a dog. In object-oriented terminology, an object is considered to be the owner of the operations that characterize its ADT, that is, that characterize the class of objects to which it belongs. This ownership perspective means that an object invokes an operation, or, as object-oriented purists would say, an object is "sent a message" to invoke a particular operation. For instance, the Array object **x** could be sent a Retrieve message with an index value **i**. This particular message should result in the return of the value stored at index **i** in object **x**. This is a different perspective from traditional programming languages. The traditional languages would view the Retrieve operation as a function that is given two arguments—**x** and **i**. In the object-oriented perspective, each instance of the class Array has its own Retrieve operation and this operation requires only one argument, the index **i**. Rather than telling Retrieve which array to operate on (the traditional approach), we tell a particular Array object that we want to use its Retrieve operation (the object-oriented approach). Though subtle, this difference is important to keep in mind as we introduce the C++ class concept.

A *class* could be regarded as the C++ synonym for the term abstract data type. The class feature of C++ syntax allows us to encapsulate an ADT in a wrapper, exposing to higher level *client programs* only that information needed to use the ADT. Details of how the ADT is implemented are considered to be "hidden" by this wrapper. That is, they are regarded as being inaccessible to anything outside of the wrapper. There are typically two components to a class—the class declaration that defines the interface to the ADT, and the implementation of the operations defined in the class declaration. Although in C++ it is possible to provide code for implementing operations within the class declaration itself, we usually refrain from doing this to emphasize the distinction between a class's definition and its implementation. We illustrate classes by examining one possible class declaration for the Array ADT. This definition precedes the implementations of the various Array operations and is specified in a header file, say, array.h. Do not be concerned about any unfamiliar syntax (for example, **private**, **public**, ~**Array**, etc.) at this time; it will be explained in the paragraphs immediately following the definitions.

```
// HEADER   : array.h
// PURPOSE  : Define the Array ADT.
// We assume IndexType is a finite collection of consecutively
// enumerated values such as integers, characters, or enum values,
// and that BaseData is any type or class.

template <class IndexType, class BaseData>
class Array
{
  private:
    BaseData *arrayData;                   // Points to array data
    int loIndex, hiIndex;                  // Store index range
    BOOLEAN outOfRange(IndexType i);       // Used for internal range
                                           // checking
  public:

//-----------------------------------------------------------------
// Interface for Array constructor
// GIVEN:     An uninitialized Array object;
//            lo and hi -- values of type IndexType, with lo <= hi,
//                         that define an allowable index range
//                         for an Array object.
// RETURN:    Array object with space allocated for it, but with no
//            values assigned to array indices.

    Array(IndexType lo, IndexType hi);

//-----------------------------------------------------------------
// Interface for Array destructor
// GIVEN:     A previously allocated Array object.
// RETURN:    Array object deallocated; that is, all storage
//            allocated to the Array object is returned to an
//            available space pool for reallocation.

    ~Array();

//-----------------------------------------------------------------
// Interface for assign operator
// GIVEN:     An Array object;
//            i -- an index within the index range defined when
//                 the Array was constructed;
```

```
//          val -- the value to be assigned to index i of
//                 the Array.
// RETURN:     Array object with val assigned to index i.  If
//             index i is erroneously outside the index range
//             for the Array, an error message is generated and
//             program execution is not allowed to continue.
// RETURN as value of function: void

   void assign(IndexType i, const BaseData &val);

//-----------------------------------------------------------
// Interface for retrieve operator
// GIVEN:      An Array object,
//             i -- an index within the index range defined when
//                  the Array was constructed.
// RETURN as value of function:
//             The Array value at index i.  If index i is
//             erroneously outside the allowable index range for
//             the Array, an error message is generated and
//             program execution is not allowed to continue.

   BaseData retrieve(IndexType i);
};
```

The class declaration provides an interface to the **Array** class and its operations. The declaration section of the file contains all the information that a client program (that is, a program that uses the **Array** class) must know to use this ADT. Consequently, such a client program may use the Array ADT merely by including its header file using the directive:

```
#include "array.h"
```

Note that the class definition given above uses a **template**—as did some of the functions introduced in Chapter 1. Here the **template** declares that the **Array** class is defined in terms of two other generic classes—**IndexType**, which defines the type of the index range, and **BaseData**, which defines the type of data in each array location. Within the class, we see that there is a **private** portion and a **public** portion to the **Array** class. The private portion should be ignored for the time being because it relates to the implementation of the ADT and is *completely inaccessible* to any client program that uses the Array ADT. The public portion of the class definition is where the interface to the class is truly established. For the Array ADT, we see that this public interface consists of four functions—corresponding to the four operations already defined for the Array ADT. Unlike a traditional C **struct**, a class definition contains both data declarations and functions, not just data declarations. These functions are typically called *member functions* because they belong to the class being defined. This ability of a class to encapsulate functions as well as data is one of the hallmarks of an object-oriented language.

The first member function is the **Array** constructor—a function whose name is the same as the class itself. Calling the constructor function in an application that uses the Array ADT corresponds to invoking the conceptual construct operation in the definition of the Array ADT. For instance, to construct an array **z** with index range 'A' to 'Z' whose **BaseData** type is **float**, we declare:

```
Array<char, float> z('A','Z');
```

The angle brackets here are required to instantiate with **char** and **float**, respectively, the generic **IndexType** and **BaseData** classes for the **template** in the class definition. As another example, consider the following array **y**, which is indexed by an enumeration type **MARITAL_STATUS** and has base data type **char**:

```
typedef enum MARITAL_STATUS
  {single, married, divorced, widowed };

Array<MARITAL_STATUS, char> y(single, widowed);
```

Note that the syntax for using a C++ constructor closely parallels that of a traditional C declaration. You can think of it as a declaration, but be aware that there is an executable function being called here, namely, the **constructor** function written by the implementor of the class.

The second function in the public portion of the Array header file is the destructor. It appears as ~ **Array**—the class name preceded by the tilde (~) character. It corresponds to the Destroy operation of the ADT definition. Destructors are rarely called explicitly in C++ programs. Instead, they are invoked automatically when a class variable goes out of scope, that is, when program execution exits the curly braces {} in which the array variable is declared. They may also be involved when the **delete** operator is used (**delete** is described later in this section). This essentially means that client programs need not worry about destructors. A destructor works in totally silent fashion.

The **assign** and **retrieve** functions in the header file correspond to the two similarly named operations in the ADT definition. The unusual aspect of these functions for a traditional C programmer is the fashion in which they are invoked. Remember our earlier discussion about characterizing objects as instances of a class—instances that possess the operations defined for that class. Hence the arrays **z** and **y** defined earlier represent **Array** objects. To assign a value to index 'M' of **z**, we must send an **assign** message to **z**; that is, send a message to **x** telling it to invoke its **assign** operator. The syntax for doing this is:

```
z.assign('M',14.6);        // Assign 14.6 to index 'M' of z
```

Similarly, we could assign 'X' to the **married** index of **y**:

```
y.assign(married, 'X');
```

Before proceeding, we summarize the syntax of class definitions and their use by client programs:

1. The syntax of a class definition is:

```
template <class generic1 , class generic2 , ...>
class class-name
{
  private:
    Data members and interfaces for member functions used in
    implementing the class. Anything in the private portion of
    a class definition is completely inaccessible to any client
    program that uses the class.
  public:
    Interfaces for member functions used by client programs to
```

```
      perform operations on instances of the class that are
      "declared" as variables by the client program. At least
      one constructor should be provided as a means of allowing
      client programs to declare such instance variables.
};
```

2. The **template** in item 1 can be omitted if no generic types are used in defining the class.
3. The semicolon at the end of the class definition is required. If forgotten, it can cause immense debugging agony.
4. Client programs invoke a constructor using a syntax that resembles a traditional C variable declaration:

   class-name < type1, type2,... > instance-variable(arg1, arg2,...);

5. Client programs rarely make explicit reference to destructors. We therefore omit the syntax for doing so.
6. To invoke an operation other than a constructor, we send a message to an instance variable that owns such an operation with the following C++ syntax:

   instance-variable.operation-name(arg1,arg2,...);

Example 2.1 Consider the following main program that declares some Arrays of varying types and sizes, assigns values to their index positions, and then verifies by retrieving and printing all of the assigned values. Note the use of C++'s **iostream** library for input and output (see Appendix D).

```
void main()
{
   typedef enum MARITAL_STATUS
     {single, married, divorced, widowed };

   MARITAL_STATUS m;
   int i, n;
   char c;

   // Declare three arrays of varying types

   Array<int, float> x1(100,103);
   Array<MARITAL_STATUS, char> y(single, widowed);
   Array<char, int> z('A','C');

   // Assign values to them

   x1.assign(100,3.2);
   x1.assign(101,7.8);
   x1.assign(102,2.1);
   x1.assign(103,19.4);
   y.assign(single, 'S');
   y.assign(married, 'M');
   y.assign(divorced,'D');
   y.assign(widowed, 'W');
   z.assign('A', 14);
   z.assign('B', 34);
   z.assign('C', 9);
```

```
  // Use a variable to dimension one array

  cout << "How many locations to allocate for float array x2? ";
  cin >> n;
  Array<int, float> x2(1,n);

  // Enter values interactively

  for (i = 1; i <= n; ++i)
  {
    float x;

    cout << "Enter value ";
    cin >> x;
    x2.assign(i,x);
  }

  // Verify all values

  cout << "x1 contains:" << endl;
  for (i = 100; i <= 103; ++i)
    cout << x1.retrieve(i) << endl;

  cout << "y contains:" << endl;
  for (m = single; m <= widowed; ++m)
    cout << y.retrieve(m) << endl;

  cout << "z contains:" << endl;
  for (c = 'A'; c <= 'C'; ++c)
    cout << z.retrieve(c) << endl;

  cout << "x2 contains:" << endl;
  for (i = 1; i <= n; ++i)
    cout << x2.retrieve(i) << endl;

  // Note the next assignment isn't valid, so it will
  // generate an error message and cause the program to
  // terminate (abnormally).

  x1.assign(50,6.7);
  cout << "All done" << endl;
}
```

Sample output for this program appears below. Note how the attempted assignment to index 50 of array **x1** at the end of the program results in a warning message that the index violates the index range. This is consistent with the ADT specification that indices provided to the **assign** and **retrieve** operations must remain within the bounds of the index range.

```
Output from sample run:
 How many locations to allocate for float array x2? 4
 Enter value 40
 Enter value 30
 Enter value 20
 Enter value 10
 x1 contains:
 3.2
 7.8
 2.1
 19.4
```

```
y contains:
S
M
D
W
z contains:
14
34
9
x2 contains:
40
30
20
10
Index 50 out of range
Assertion failed: !outOfRange(i), file ARRAY.H, line 96
Abnormal program termination
```

This example illustrates an important point about abstract data types. It is entirely possible to discuss an application that uses abstract data types without ever knowing anything about how those ADTs are implemented. This is the essence of information hiding—complete separation of the use of an ADT from its implementation. This separation is so critical that we specify the following rule:

ADT Use Rule
Applications that use an ADT may access variables of that type only through the operations provided in the ADT definition.

Compliance with this rule ensures that the application can use any implementation of the ADT because implementations must obey a corresponding rule:

ADT Implementation Rule
An implementation of an ADT must provide an interface that is entirely consistent with the operations specified in the ADT's definition.

Implementing a C++ Class

Thus far our discussion of the C++ class construct has focused on that portion of the class that is available to users of the ADT, that is, the abstract operations that are provided as public member functions. We now turn our attention to the issues involved in implementing these member functions. When templates are used, this implementation is most conveniently located after the class declaration in the header file. The implementor of a class has full access to all private members from the class declaration. These include data members that store information necessary for the implementation and private member functions that perform subordinate tasks of which only the implementor need be cognizant. Examination of the **private** portion of our **Array** class shows three data members:

- A pointer **arrayData** to a traditional C array of items of the generic type **BaseData**
- Two **ints**, **loIndex** and **hiIndex**.

These private data members expose our strategy for implementing the abstract **Array** class. We store the data in a traditional C array and use **loIndex** and **hiIndex** to keep track of the index range specified by the client program. Whenever the client program

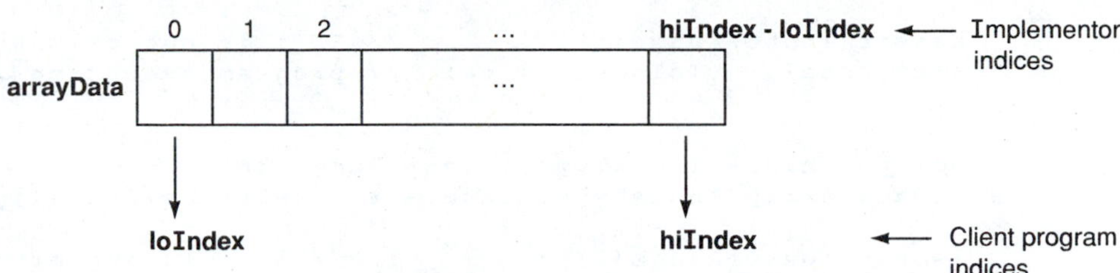

Figure 2.3
Implementation of the Array class.

accesses the array through the **assign** or **retrieve** operations, we will use **loIndex** to translate from the client program's index value to the index in the hidden array **arrayData**. Also, **loIndex** and **hiIndex** will be checked each time the array is accessed to ensure that the index value is within the specified index range. This implementation strategy is depicted in Figure 2.3.

Given this strategy for implementing an **Array** class, we must now provide the detailed C++ code to carry it out. This code appears after the class declaration in our header file. The graphical documentation and comments that follow will help to clarify our implementation.

Scope resolution operator :: qualifies the class to which this operation belongs

```
// Implementations of operations for the Array class

#include <assert.h>  // error handling done with assert macro

template <class IndexType, class BaseData>
Array<IndexType, BaseData>::Array(IndexType lo, IndexType hi)
{
  arrayData = new BaseData[hi - lo + 1];
  assert(arrayData != 0);
  // if there was no storage for arrayData, terminate execution

  loIndex = lo;
  hiIndex = hi;
}
```

new allocates space in the free store

```
template <class IndexType, class BaseData>
Array<IndexType, BaseData>::~Array()
{
  delete [] arrayData;
}
```

delete returns space to the free store

```
template <class IndexType, class BaseData>
BOOLEAN Array<IndexType, BaseData>::outOfRange(IndexType i)
{
  if ((i < loIndex) || (i > hiIndex))
  {
    cerr << "Index " << i << " out of range" << endl;
    return(TRUE);
  }
  else
    return(FALSE);
}

template <class IndexType, class BaseData>
void Array<IndexType, BaseData>::assign(IndexType i, const BaseData &val)
{
```

```
  assert(!outOfRange(i));        // If i is out of range abort
  arrayData[i - loIndex] = val;  // program execution
}

template <class IndexType, class BaseData>
BaseData Array<IndexType, BaseData>::retrieve(IndexType i)
{
  assert(!outOfRange(i));                // If i is out of range abort
  return(arrayData[i - loIndex]);        // program execution
}
```

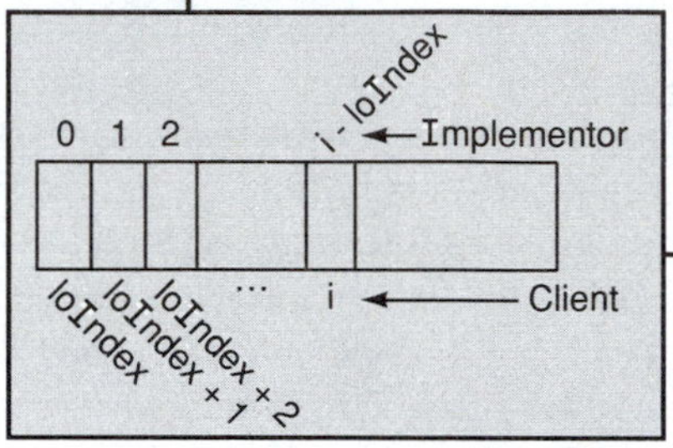

The implementations illustrate some C++ syntax with which you may not be familiar. The double colon (::) separating class and operation identifiers is officially called the *scope resolution operator.* Its purpose is to indicate the class to which the function belongs. In our simple example it is obvious the function belongs to the **Array** class; however, in more complex situations the scope resolution operator would allow us to define, in the same file, an operation called **assign** for two different classes. The C++ compiler would need the scope resolution operator to resolve ambiguity regarding the class to which a particular **assign** belonged. Like it or not, the scope resolution operator is *always* required when implementing a class member function outside of the class declaration. Thus, the syntax for implementing a class operation can be summarized as follows:

```
template <class generic1 , class generic2, ... >
return-type class-name <generic1, generic2, ... >::member-func(arg1, ...)
{
    Instructions to execute the operation
}
```

If no generic types are used in defining the protocol for the operation in the class declaration, then the **template** may be omitted from this schema.

The implementation of the constructor and destructor for the **Array** class requires that we introduce the **new** and **delete** operators of C++. The **new** operator is given a data type and returns a pointer to a storage location in the free store that is capable of storing a datum of the given type. How this space in memory is obtained is not of concern to us. Suffice it to say that the memory management system of C++ ensures that an appropriate pointer is returned. (However, the value 0 is returned if the free store has run out of space.) For example, the following code would ensure that **p** is pointing at a location capable of storing an **int**:

```
int *p;
p = new int;
```

In the case of our Array constructor, the statement

```
arrayData = new BaseData[hi - lo + 1];
```

ensures that the pointer **arrayData** declared in the **private** portion of the **Array** class references a free store location capable of storing **hi − lo + 1** items of type **BaseData**. The constructor then sets the private data members **loIndex** and **hiIndex** to the **lo** and **hi** arguments that are passed to it when called by a client program.

Following the **new** statement is an **assert** statement. This has been inserted to provide a degree of error handling for our code. In particular, if there is sufficient memory in the program's free store to satisfy the request of the **new** statement then, as indicated earlier, a nonzero pointer to this memory is returned by **new**. We can have **assert** test for such a condition. If the condition holds, then control passes to the next statement, otherwise an error message is generated (typically it gives the condition that failed, and the file and line number in that file where the **assert** was located) and the program *terminates abnormally*. To use the **assert** function, one must precede its first use by including the standard header file <assert.h>.

Although primitive, the degree of error handling provided by **assert** will be sufficient for our purposes. If you are interested in using more extensive error handling methods you should investigate the **try-throw-catch** constructs proposed by Bjarne Stroustrup and Andrew Koenig ("Exception Handling for C++ (revised)," published in the *Proceedings of the USENIX C++ Conference,* San Francisco, April 1990). These have been included in ANSI version 3.0 of C++. Be warned, however, that at the time this book was published version 3.0 was still not widely implemented.

The destructor, ~**Array**, is responsible for deallocating the storage currently being used by an **Array** object. For this purpose C++ provides the **delete** operator. The **delete** operator is given a pointer to an object and interacts with the memory management system of C++ to restore that space referenced by the pointer to the free store. To return all of the storage that was allocated dynamically to an array, one alters the invocation of the **delete** operator to **delete []**, followed by the name of the array. Hence, to implement the destructor, we need only one line of code:

```
delete [] arrayData;
```

This will deallocate the free store space currently being referenced by **arrayData**, the private pointer within the **Array** class.

Once the constructor has taken care of allocating the array, the implementation of the **outOfRange**, **assign**, and **retrieve** functions is relatively straightforward. The operators **assign** and **retrieve** merely translate the index provided by the client program as indicated in Figure 2.3. Both call on the private function **outOfRange** to ensure that no array bounds violation has occurred. Note that there is no syntactical difference in the way a **private** function (such as **outOfRange**) is implemented versus the way a **public** function (such as **assign** or **retrieve**) is implemented. The only difference between public and private functions is in their accessibility. A client program can only access public member functions. The implementor of a class can access anything defined within the class—public or private.

Operator Overloading

Although we have developed an **Array** class that is more versatile and safer to use than that provided by traditional C, one might argue that it is more difficult to use because it does not use the index (subscript) operator [] to which C programmers are so accustomed. Instead of being able to assign to an array component by a normal assignment statement such as

```
z[c] = 14;
```

we are forced into the less natural notation

```
z.assign(c,14);
```

Fortunately, C++ also provides a means of overcoming this objection. The technique is called *operator overloading*, and it allows us to view the index operator [] as a function that we will redefine for this new notion of an array. C++ syntax for an overloaded operator prototype is as follows:

return-type **operator** *operator-symbol (arg1, arg2, ...);*

where *return-type* is the type of data returned by the operation; *operator-symbol* is the operator symbol being overloaded; and *arg1, arg2, ...* represent the arguments to the operation. It is important to remember that, as a member function of a class definition, the owner of the operation is always an implied argument that does not appear in the formal parameter list. Consider, for example, the following class declaration for an array that uses the overloaded index [] operator instead of separate **assign** and **retrieve** operations:

```
// HEADER   : array.h
// PURPOSE : Provides an alternative definition of the Array ADT.
// We assume IndexType is a finite collection of consecutively
// enumerated values such as integers, characters, or enum values,
// and that BaseData is any type or class.

template <class IndexType, class BaseData>
class Array
{
  private:
    BaseData *arrayData;                    // Points to array data
    int loIndex, hiIndex;                   // Store index range for internal
    BOOLEAN outOfRange(IndexType i);        // range checking

  public:

//----------------------------------------------------------------
// Interface for Array constructor
// GIVEN:    An uninitialized Array object;
//           lo and hi -- values of type IndexType, with lo <= hi, that define
//                        an allowable index range for an Array object.
// RETURN:   The array object with space allocated for it, but with
//           no values assigned to Array indices

    Array(IndexType lo, IndexType hi);

//----------------------------------------------------------------
// Interface for Array destructor
// GIVEN:    A previously allocated Array object.
// RETURN:   Array object deallocated; that is, all storage
//           allocated to the Array object is returned to an
//           available space pool for reallocation.

    ~Array();
```

```
//-------------------------------------------------------------
// Interface for Array index operator
// GIVEN:    An Array object;
//           i -- an index within the index range defined when the
//                Array was constructed.
// RETURN as value of function:
//            A reference to the Array value at index i that can be
//            used as an lvalue, that is, appear on the left side
//            of = to allow assignment of a value to that index
//            position. If i is (erroneously) not within the index
//            range for the Array,  an error message is generated
//            and program execution is not allowed to continue.

    BaseData& operator[](IndexType i);
};
```

As a member function of the **Array** class, the index operator [] is owned by an Array. Moreover, it takes one additional argument, **i**, which is of generic type **IndexType**. Finally, we are informed that the index operator [] will return a reference to **BaseData**. It is imperative that it return a reference to **BaseData** so that we may use it on the left side of the assignment operator "=". For example, given an Array **xval** declared by

```
Array<int, float> xval(100,200);
```

we could assign *pi* to the 150th index by:

```
xval[150] = 3.14159;
```

Similarly, we could retrieve the value in the 150th index of **xval** for use in a more complicated expression:

```
area = x[150] * radius * radius;
```

Example 2.2

Write a client program equivalent to that of Example 2.1 except that it uses the **Array** class with the overloaded [] operator.

```
void main()
{
  typedef enum MARITAL_STATUS
    {single, married, divorced, widowed };

  MARITAL_STATUS m;
  int i, n;
  char c;

  // Declare three Arrays of varying types

  Array<int, float> x1(100,103);
  Array<MARITAL_STATUS, char> y(single, widowed);
  Array<char, int> z('A','C');

  // Assign values to them

  x1[100] = 3.2;
  x1[101] = 7.8;
  x1[102] = 2.1;
  x1[103] = 19.4;
```

```
    y[single] = 'S';
    y[married] = 'M';
    y[divorced] = 'D';
    y[widowed] = 'W';
    z['A'] = 14;
    z['B'] = 34;
    z['C'] = 9;

    // Use a variable to dimension one array

    cout << "How many locations to allocate for float Array x2? ";
    cin >> n;
    Array<int, float> x2(1,n);

    // Enter values interactively

    for (i = 1; i <= n; ++i)
    {
      cout << "Enter value ";
      cin >> x2[i];
    }

    // Verify all values

    cout << "x1 contains:" << endl;
    for (i = 100; i <= 103; ++i)
      cout << x1[i] << endl;

    cout << "y contains:" << endl;
    for (m = single; m <= widowed; ++m)
      cout << y[m] << endl;

    cout << "z contains:" << endl;
    for ( c = 'A'; c <= 'C'; ++c)
      cout << z[c] << endl;

    cout << "x2 contains:" << endl;
    for (i = 1; i <= n; ++i)
      cout << x2[i] << endl;

    // Note the next assignment isn't valid, so it will generate
    // an abnormal program termination

    x1[50] = 6.7;
    cout << "All done" << endl;
}
```

The implementation of the overloaded [] operator in this alternate **Array** class is straightforward. Just as we implemented **assign** and **retrieve** in the initial **Array** class, we use **loIndex** to adjust the index received by the function to the corresponding offset in the hidden member **arrayData**:

```
template <class IndexType, class BaseData>
BaseData& Array<IndexType, BaseData>::operator [] (IndexType i)
{
  assert(!outOfRange(i));
  return(arrayData[i - loIndex]);
}
```

Overloaded operators represent a major convenience offered by C++. Although it is possible to use only conventional member functions, in many cases the readability of high-level code can be greatly enhanced by employing overloaded operators. Throughout the remainder of this text, whenever we use our **Array** class, we will assume it is the version that defines an overloaded index [] operator. As we develop more ADTs, we will see numerous examples of overloading other operators such as +, −, *, !!, &&, and so forth.

Exercises 2.1

1. Explain the meaning of the term *information hiding*. In what sense do the **Array** classes discussed in this section hide information?
2. Consider the following general statement: *Data members of a class (as opposed to function members) should never be public*. Do you agree or disagree? Explain why.
3. Write a client program that reads characters one at a time from a file. The program should count how many times each letter of the alphabet occurs in the file. Use an appropriately constructed Array to store these 26 counters.
4. A text file contains sales information for a company that has been in business since 1950. Each line of the file contains two numbers—a four-digit year and a **float** that represents the amount of sales registered by a regional office during that year. Write a C++ client program that reads this file and then does the following:

   a. Accumulates total company sales (the sum of the sales of each regional office) for each year since 1950.

   b. Determines the average and standard deviation of annual total sales since 1950.

   Use an appropriately declared **Array** to maintain these annual totals.
5. The eight departments at a local company are identified by the letters 'A' through 'H'. For each department the company keeps track of the number of employees in the department and the accumulated total of all salaries of that department. Design an appropriate C++ **struct** or **class** to keep track of each department's information. Then declare a single Array that appropriately stores the records of all departments. Finally, write a client program to accumulate the information in this Array by reading from a text file where each line of the text file contains one of the departmental letters 'A' through 'H' followed by a **float** that represents the salary of one employee in that department. After reading the file, have your program determine the departments that have the most employees and highest total of salaries.
6. The *Matrix* ADT is essentially a two-dimensional array. Develop a complete definition for the Matrix ADT that allows different index ranges for rows and columns. Formulate your definition first as a conceptual ADT with operations specified by pre- and postconditions. Then provide a C++ class declaration with public interfaces for each Matrix operation. Discuss a strategy for implementing the Matrix class and write C++ implementations of each operation. (*Hint:* You must overload two index operators, using one for rows and one for columns.)
7. A *sparse array* is an array in which most of the values stored in the array equal some default value. For example, such a default value might be zero for arrays of **int** or **float** data. Sparse arrays can be very space inefficient if all these occurrences of the default value are actually stored. Develop an implementation of the **Array** class that is space efficient for storing sparse arrays. You may want to develop a new constructor that allows the default value to be specified as an argument at the time the array is constructed. Finally, write a report in which you analyze the space and time efficiency of your implementation and discuss how it could be extended to an implementation of the Matrix ADT as you defined it for Exercise 2.1.6. We call such an implementation a *sparse matrix*.

2.2 Extending ADTs by Inheritance

In Section 2.1 we learned that the C++ **class** construct provides us with the ability to encapsulate all the components—data and functions—of an ADT. Moreover, by using **private** and **public** we can control which components of that ADT are available to client programs. Such *encapsulation* is one key ingredient of an object-oriented language. Yet, to fully qualify as object oriented, a language must also exhibit two additional properties: *inheritance* and *polymorphism*. We discuss inheritance in this section and delay our treatment of polymorphism until we encounter lists in Chapter 3.

Inheritance is that aspect of an object-oriented language that lets us build new, more complex abstractions from existing ones. For instance, we've already defined one ADT—the Array. Now suppose that we'd like to extend the notion of an array to that of a *sortable array*. Intuitively, a sortable array is an array that can be sorted because an order relationship can be defined on its elements. More specifically, we provide the following formal definition of a sortable array as an ADT.

Definition: The *sortable array* ADT is an array for which we define an order relationship among its components. The operations performed on a sortable array are:

`Construct Operation`

Preconditions: An uninitialized sortable array object ;
precedes—a relationship that defines an ordering between any two possible array components.

Postconditions: The sortable array object has been allocated sufficient storage to store its associated data items, although no specific values have been stored in the array. The function *precedes* is established as the order relationship between array components.

`Sort Operation`

Preconditions: A sortable array object that has been previously constructed. Beginning with the first index of the array, *numvals* consecutive locations in the array have been assigned well-defined values.

Postconditions: The first *numvals* locations in the array have been arranged in order according to the *precedes* relationship.

By layering one abstraction upon another, we've been able to define the more complex notion of a sortable array with much less work than we originally encountered in defining an array. This is because we are allowed to assume everything that we've previously defined for an array. For instance, we don't redefine the Destroy or the [] (index) operations for a sortable array because these operations are exactly the same for sortable arrays as they are for ordinary arrays. What distinguishes a sortable array from an ordinary array? First, the Construct operation is slightly more complicated because it is given an ordering relationship to use on array elements. Second, a sortable array possesses a new operation, *Sort*, that makes use of this ordering relationship.

Ideally a programming language should allow new, more complex ADTs to be built from previous ones without forcing us to recode completely those operations that don't change in the new ADT. Many traditional languages, however, would require that we recode everything, perhaps making some mechanical textual changes along the way. Fortunately, object-oriented languages allow inheritance, and this will enable us to specify conveniently that "a sortable array is an array with the following changes and extensions." We illustrate inheritance in C++ by providing and then commenting on a **Sort Array** class declaration for the sortable array ADT.

```
// HEADER  : sortarray.h
// PURPOSE : Provides the definition for the sortable array ADT.

#include "array.h"     // Sortable arrays must know about Arrays

// We assume IndexType is a finite collection of consecutively enumerated values
// such as integers, characters, or enum values, and that BaseData is any
// type or class.
```

```
template <class IndexType, class BaseData>
class SortArray : public Array<IndexType, BaseData>
{
  protected:
    BOOLEAN (*compare)(const BaseData &x, const BaseData &y);
    // Comparison function for prescribing the ordering relationship
    // among array elements in a sortable array

    void swap(BaseData &x, BaseData &y);    // Swapping function

  public:

//------------------------------------------------------------------
// Interface for SortArray constructor
// GIVEN:     An uninitialized SortArray object;
//            lo and hi -- defining allowable index range for
//                         array object;
//            precedes -- a function to compare BaseData values:
//              GIVEN:   x and y -- values to compare
//              RETURN as value of function:
//                  TRUE    if x precedes y,
//                  FALSE   if x and y are equal, or
//                          if y precedes x
// RETURN:    SortArray object with space allocated for it and a
//            precedence relation between elements, but with no
//            values assigned to array indices.

    SortArray(IndexType lo, IndexType hi,
              BOOLEAN (*precedes)(const BaseData &x, const BaseData &y));


//------------------------------------------------------------------
// Interface for sort operation
// GIVEN:    A SortArray object;
//           numvals -- logical size of the array, assuming values
//                      are stored consecutively from lowest index.
// RETURN:   SortArray object arranged in order by its precedes relation
// RETURN as value of function: void

    void sort(int numvals);
};
```

In using inheritance, we say that one class is *derived* from another. For instance, the initial portion of the preceding declaration, namely,

```
template <class IndexType, class BaseData>
class SortArray : public Array<IndexType, BaseData>
```

declares that the class **SortArray** is derived from the class **Array**. We also say that **Array** is the *parent* class of **SortArray**. The appearance of **public** in front of **Array** declares that all those operations that are public in the **Array** class are also to be considered public for objects that are instances of the class **SortArray**. The alternative to **public** in this context would be **private**, in which case an object of type **SortArray** would only be able to use the operations that are declared public in **SortArray**. Those operations that are public for objects of type **Array** would be private, and therefore inaccessible, to objects of type **SortArray**. Figure 2.4 depicts these differences in accessibility between a derived class and its parent class.

The next segment of our **SortArray** class definition defines a new category of member accessibility: **protected**.

Figure 2.4
Accessibility of operations in parent class by object that is instance of derived class.

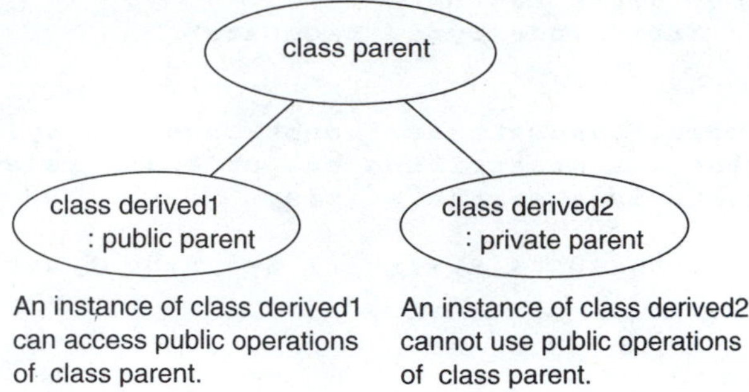

An instance of class derived1 can access public operations of class parent.

An instance of class derived2 cannot use public operations of class parent.

```
protected:
  BOOLEAN (*compare)(const BaseData &x, const BaseData &y);
  // Comparison function for prescribing the ordering
  // relationship among array elements in a sortable array

  void swap(BaseData &x, BaseData &y); // Swapping function
```

Those data and function members of a class that are **protected** are accessible to a derived class but not to a client program that uses the class. Thus, in the preceding declarations, we have prepared ourselves for the possibility of deriving another class from the **SortArray** class. Another implication of inheritance is that, if the class **SortArray** is to access the members **arrayData**, **loIndex**, **hiIndex**, and **outOfRange** from the **Array** class defined in Section 2.1, these members must be declared **protected**, not **private**, in the definition of the **Array** class. *We will proceed under the assumption that this change has been made in the Array class;* it is the *only* change in the **Array** class that is necessary to allow **SortArray** to be successfully derived from it. It also follows from this discussion that, if

FIGURE 2.5
Accessibility of **private**, **protected**, and **public** class members.

```
class parent
{
  private:
      -------        These members are accessible only to
      -------        the implementor of class parent.
      -------
      -------

  protected:
      -------        These members are accessible to implementors of
      -------        class parent and implementors of classes derived
      -------        from parent but not accessible to client programs
      -------        that use class parent or its derived classes.

  public:
      -------        These members are accessible to implementors of
      -------        parent class, implementors of classes that
      -------        derive from parent, and to client programs that
      -------        use parent directly.  Whether these members are
                     accessible to client programs of classes derived
                     from parent depends on whether such derivation
                     is public or private in the sense of Figure 2.4.

};
```

you anticipate a class may become the parent class of another class, it is wise to use the **protected** level of accessibility instead of **private**. Figure 2.5 depicts these differences in accessibility between private, protected, and public. For the moment we defer a more detailed discussion of the **protected** members of the **SortArray** class since these details are related to the implementation of the class.

The final segment of the class definition for **SortArray** defines those operations that are public and therefore available to client programs that declare an object of this type.

```
//-------------------------------------------------------------------
// Interface for SortArray constructor
// GIVEN:     An uninitialized SortArray object;
//            lo and hi -- defining allowable index range for array
//            precedes -- a function to compare BaseData values:
//              GIVEN:    x and y -- values to compare
//              RETURN as value of function:
//                  TRUE     if x precedes y;
//                  FALSE    if x and y are equal, or if y precedes x
// RETURN:    SortArray object with space allocated for it and a
//            precedence relation between elements, but with no
//            values assigned to array indices.

    SortArray(IndexType lo, IndexType hi,
              BOOLEAN (*precedes)(const BaseData &x, const BaseData &y));

//-------------------------------------------------------------------
// Interface for sort operation
// GIVEN:    a SortArray object;
//           numvals -- logical size of the array, assuming values
//                      are stored consecutively from lowest index
// RETURN:   SortArray object arranged in order by its precedes relation
// RETURN as value of function: void

    void sort(int numvals);
```

Only two public operations are provided for **SortArray**—a constructor that has a different interface than that of an ordinary **Array** and a **sort** operation. Note, however, that because **SortArray** is derived as **public** from **Array**, a client program that uses **SortArray** also has access to the destructor and the overloaded index operator [] for the **Array** class.

Example 2.3 Assuming that we employ the **Array** class with an overloaded [] operator, consider the following client program that invokes operation **sort** for **SortArrays** with various kinds of data.

```
//****************************************************************
// Client program to demonstrate SortArray class

#include "sortarray.h"

// Define an order relationship for ints - needed to sort int array

BOOLEAN lessThanInt(const int &x, const int &y)
{
  if (x < y)
    return(TRUE);
```

```
  else
    return(FALSE);
}

// Define an order relationship for chars - needed to sort char array

BOOLEAN lessThanChar(const char &x, const char &y)
{
  if (x < y)
    return(TRUE);
  else
    return(FALSE);
}

// Define an order relationship for floats - needed to sort float array

BOOLEAN lessThanFloat(const float &x, const float &y)
{
  if (x < y)
    return(TRUE);
  else
    return(FALSE);
}

// The main program will invoke sort on three different kinds of SortArrays

void main()
{
  typedef enum MARITAL_STATUS
    {single, married, divorced, widowed };

  MARITAL_STATUS m;
  int i;
  char c;

  // An array of floats indexed by ints with ascending order relationship

  SortArray<int, float> x(100,103, lessThanFloat);

  // An array of chars indexed by MARITAL_STATUS with alphabetical ordering

  SortArray<MARITAL_STATUS, char> y(single, widowed, lessThanChar);

  // An array of ints indexed by chars with ascending order relationship

  SortArray<char, int> z('A','Z', lessThanInt);

  // Assign values to the arrays; note the use of the index
  // operator inherited from Array

  x[100] = 3.2;
  x[101] = 7.8;
  x[102] = 2.1;
  x[103] = 19.4;
  y[single] = 'S';
  y[married] = 'M';
  y[divorced] = 'D';
  y[widowed] = 'W';
```

```
    // Note only three of 26 locations in z are assigned

    z['A'] = 14;
    z['B'] = 34;
    z['C'] = 9;

    // Sort all the arrays

    x.sort(4);
    y.sort(4);
    z.sort(3);

    // Verify the data

    for (i = 100; i <= 103; ++i)
      cout << x[i] << endl;
    for (m = single; m <= widowed; ++m)
      cout << y[m] << endl;
    for ( c = 'A'; c <= 'C'; ++c)
      cout << z[c] << endl;
}
```

```
Output from sample run:

2.1
3.2
7.8
19.4
D
M
S
W
9
14
34
```

As indicated in Example 2.3, the constructor for a **SortArray** requires passing a function argument that determines the order relationship for the **Array**. Once this order relationship is established upon construction of the **SortArray**, it remains bound to that **SortArray** for the duration of the program. That is, **sort** will always sort the array according to this order relationship. You will explore other options for defining a **SortArray** class in the exercises.

Implementing the SortArray class

To implement the **SortArray** class, we will use our earlier stated assumption that the **private** members of the **Array** class in Section 2.1 have been changed to **protected**. Hence, the **Array** data members **arrayData**, **loIndex**, and **hiIndex** are available to us in our implementation. Additionally, **SortArray** extends the protected members inherited from the **Array** class by adding its own members **compare** and **swap**. The **compare** member references the function that is used to compare two items in the array. The function **swap** is a subordinate function that will be needed to implement the **sort** operation by the insertion sort algorithm that we studied in

Figure 2.6
SortArray extends the **protected** members of the **Array** class.

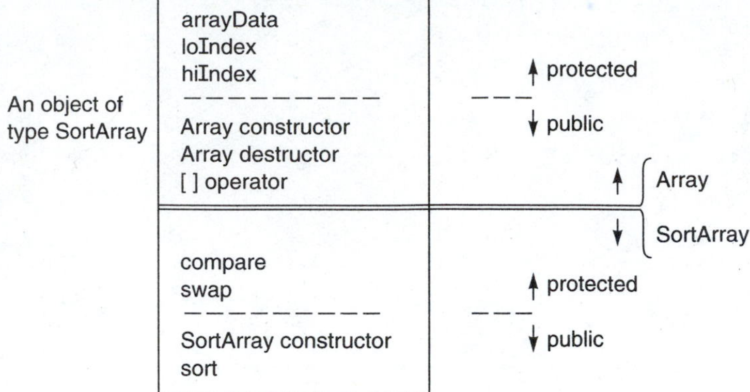

Section 1.2. Figure 2.6 summarizes how the **protected** members of the **Array** class are extended by **SortArray**.

As with our implementation of the **Array** class, the implementation of the operations for the **SortArray** class would follow the class declaration in the header file sortarray.h. These implementations appear next. The graphic documentation and discussion that follow will help clarify how the pieces fit together.

```
template <class IndexType, class BaseData>
SortArray<IndexType,BaseData>::SortArray(IndexType lo,IndexType hi,
          BOOLEAN(*precedes)(const BaseData &x, const BaseData &y))
              : Array<IndexType, BaseData>(lo, hi)
{
  compare = precedes;
}
```

This specifies that the **sortArray** constructor calls on **Array** constructor

The protected **compare** member is set to the precedes argument

```
template <class IndexType, class BaseData>
void SortArray<IndexType,BaseData>::swap(BaseData &x, BaseData &y)
{
  BaseData temp;

  temp = x;
  x = y;
  y = temp;
}

template <class IndexType, class BaseData>
void SortArray<IndexType, BaseData>::sort(int numvals)
// Use insertion sort algorithm
{
  int k,j;
  BOOLEAN done;

  for (k = 1; k < numvals; ++k)
  // On pass k, insert (k+1)th element
  {
    j = k;
    done = FALSE;

    // When (j-1)th element precedes jth element, we know it is
    // appropriately positioned.

    while (j >= 1 && !done)
```

```
        if (compare(arrayData[j], arrayData[j-1]))
        {
          swap(arrayData[j], arrayData[j-1]);
          --j;
        }
        else
          done = TRUE;
    }
}
```

The **SortArray** constructor does not have much to do. Given three arguments **lo**, **hi**, and **precedes**, it must merely pass the first two on to the constructor for the **Array** class and then set **compare** to the function that is passed in as **precedes**. *In an inheritance relationship among classes, constructors are always invoked from parent class to derived class.* As easy as this sounds, the C++ syntax for specifying it is ugly. Invoking the **Array** constructor with **lo** and **hi** is achieved by the following segment of the **SortArray** constructor:

```
template <class IndexType, class BaseData>
SortArray<IndexType,BaseData>::SortArray(IndexType lo,IndexType hi,
         BOOLEAN (*precedes)(const BaseData &x, const BaseData &y))
             : Array<IndexType, BaseData>(lo, hi)
```

Note that this entire segment precedes the executable code for the function. Think of the line above that starts with a colon (:) as saying "when you construct a **SortArray**, first invoke the constructor for **Array** using the **lo** and **hi** arguments from the **SortArray** constructor." After this parent constructor has been invoked, the executable code for the **SortArray** constructor requires only one line to assign **precedes** to the **compare** member of the derived **SortArray** class.

Although no specific destructor appears for the **SortArray** class, you should nonetheless be aware that the destructor for the parent **Array** class will automatically be called when a **SortArray** goes out of scope. The policy for destructors is just the opposite of that for constructors. That is, when a destructor is invoked upon an object's going out of scope, the destructor for the derived class is invoked first, then the destructor for the parent class, then that for the parent of the parent, and so forth.

Given our discussion of the insertion sort algorithm in Section 1.2, the implementations of the **sort** and **swap** functions earlier should be clear. The function **swap** is merely a subordinate function that will exchange two objects of type **BaseData**. The function **sort** has access to operate directly with the array pointer **arrayData**, which is a protected member of the parent class. Because of this access, this algorithm appears almost exactly as it did in Section 1.2. The only difference is that **arrayData** and **compare** are now data members of the class instead of arguments to the **sort** function. Clearly, any other sorting algorithm could also be used to implement the **sort** operation for this class. Moreover, such substitution of different sorting algorithms could be done in a way that would not affect at all the logic of a client program using the **SortArray** class. The only apparent difference in the client program would be the speed with which it executes when a different algorithm is employed.

Object-oriented inheritance is a technique that we will employ frequently in the remainder of this text. Strategic utilization of inheritance can allow a programmer to realize fully the power of abstraction.

Exercises 2.2

1. Detail the changes that would have to be made in the code of Example 2.3 to allow the Array of **floats** to be sorted in descending order.
2. Does the **SortArray** class allow for a single array of **floats** to be sorted in both ascending and descending order in the same client program? If so, write a client program that achieves this. If not, explain why not.
3. In the sorting algorithms we studied in Chapter 1, the ordering relation is passed as a function parameter to the **sort** function. In the **SortArray** class of this section, the ordering relation is passed as a function parameter to the **SortArray** constructor. What is the advantage of passing the ordering relation as a parameter to the **sort** function? Rewrite the **SortArray** class such that it also achieves this advantage. Then demonstrate the use of your new **SortArray** class in a client program that takes advantage of the new feature.
4. Use a **struct** or **class** to define a customer record type in which each customer has an **int** identification number and a **float** balance owed amount. Then write a client program that establishes a **SortArray** of such customer records. Use the client program to sort the customer records by identification number. Can you sort the customer records by balance owed in the same program? If so, do it. If not, explain why.
5. Design an ADT called a *searchable array*—an array that can be searched for a particular target value. First develop a formal ADT definition. Then establish a C++ interface in which you derive a searchable array from the basic **Array** class. Finally demonstrate the use of this new class in a client program.

2.3 The String ADT

In the previous section we considered the Array ADT—a data type with few operations and for which most programming languages provide a complete implementation. We now consider an ADT with a more complex set of operations that programming languages provide in varying styles and degrees. This is the String ADT, defined as follows.

Definition: A *String* is a sequence of characters. The characters in a String are related in linear fashion with an identifiable first character, second character, and so on. The operations associated with the String ADT are:

`Construct Operation (Alternative 1)`

Preconditions: An uninitialized String object.
Postconditions: The String object is initialized to the empty string.

`Construct Operation (Alternative 2)`

Preconditions: An uninitialized String object;
initstr—a "quoted" constant string.
Postconditions: The String object is initialized to *initstr*.

`Construct Operation (Alternative 3)`

Preconditions: An uninitialized String object;
initstr—a String object that was previously constructed.
Postconditions: The String object is initialized to *initstr*.

`Destroy Operation`

Preconditions: A String object that has been previously constructed.
Postconditions: The String object is deallocated, with the contents of the String object unreliable.

`ReadString` Operation

Preconditions: A String object that has been previously constructed.
Postconditions: The String object contains characters read from a standard input source.

`WriteString` Operation

Preconditions: A String object that has been previously constructed.
Postconditions: The String object is unchanged but its characters have been written to standard output.

`Assign` Operation

Preconditions: A String object that has been previously constructed;
source—a second String object.
Postconditions: The contents of *source* have been copied to the String object that owns the operation.

`Length` Operation

Preconditions: A String object that has been previously constructed.
Postconditions: The number of characters in the string is returned, leaving the string unchanged.

`Concatenate` Operation

Preconditions: A String object that has been previously constructed;
t—a second String object.
Postconditions: The contents of *t* have been appended to the owner of the operation. String *t* is unchanged.

`Substring` Operation

Preconditions: A String object has been previously constructed;
start—an integer between 1 and the length of the String object;
len—the length of substring to be returned.
Postconditions: A substring of the String object beginning at *start* and ending at *start* + *len* − *1* is returned. If *start* + *len* − *1* exceeds the length of the String object that owns the operation, then the substring returned stops at the last character in the String object. If (erroneously) *start* exceeds the length of the String object or *len* is zero, then the substring returned is empty.

`Search` Operation

Preconditions: A previously constructed String object that is considered the *master* String;
sub—a string to be searched for in the given (master) String;
start—an integer representing a character position in the *master* String. The *master* String is to be searched from this position onward.
Postconditions: The position of the first occurrence of *sub* in the *master* String object is returned, beginning at position *start* or after. Zero is returned if *sub* is not found in the *master* String.

`Insert` Operation

Preconditions: A String object that has been previously constructed;
t—a string to be inserted in the String object that owns the operation;

place—an integer representing a character position in the String object. The string *t* is to be inserted in the String object at this position.

Postconditions: The String object has *t* inserted at *place*. If *place* exceeds the length of the String object, the String object is left unchanged.

Remove Operation

Preconditions: A String object that has been previously constructed;
start—a starting position in the String object;
number—the number of characters to delete from the String object, beginning at *start*.

Postconditions: The String object has the appropriate characters deleted. If the number of characters specified extends beyond the length of the String object, deletion occurs only through the end of the string.

Precedes Operation

Preconditions: A String object that has been previously constructed;
t—a second String object to compare, alphabetically, to the owner of the object.

Postconditions: A Boolean value is returned indicating the alphabetic (lexicographic) relationship between the owner of the operation and *t*: TRUE if owner precedes *t*; and FALSE if owner and *t* are equal, or if *t* precedes owner

Equality Operation

Preconditions: A String object that has been previously constructed;
t—a second String object to compare, character-by-character, to the given object.

Postconditions: Returns TRUE if the String object and *t* match each other character-for-character (are equal), and returns FALSE otherwise.

FIGURE 2.7
Examples of String operations.

concatenate: Appends the contents of String *t* to the String object s.

	t	yields	
"BIRD"	"DOG"	⟶	"BIRDDOG"

substring: Returns the five characters of String object s between locations three and seven.

	start	*len*	yields	
"TALE OF TWO CITIES"	3	5	⟶	"LE OF"

search: Returns the position of the first occurrence of the String *sub* in *master* string, at position *start* or after.

master	*sub*	*start*	yields	
"MODERN BASEBALL HISTORY"	"BASEBALL"	1	⟶	8

insert: Inserts the contents of String *t* into String object s, starting at location 5.

	t	*place*	yields	
"SALT PEPPER"	" AND"	5	⟶	"SALT AND PEPPER"

remove: Removes nine characters from String object s, starting with the fifth character

	start	*number*	yields	
"SALT AND PEPPER"	5	9	⟶	"SALTER"

Figure 2.7 portrays examples of some of the operations specified for strings. Strings find widespread applications in such diverse areas as text editing, computer-assisted instruction, and language processing.

As we did with Arrays, we must migrate from the conceptual definition of the String ADT to a class definition that provides a starting point for C++ implementations of the String class. Such a class definition is provided at the beginning of the following header file. As you read these C++ specifications, you will become aware of a dilemma often faced by implementors of an ADT. That is, as we pass from a conceptual definition to the realities of a programming language, we often start to make concessions. These concessions are an admission of the limitations of programming languages to implement abstract concepts in a perfect way. In particular, realizing that an array of **char** might be one possibility for implementing the String ADT, we allow the String constructor to be given a maximum length for the string being constructed. This maximum length limitation also restricts other operations, as indicated in the documentation that accompanies the class definition. In the exercises at the end of this section, you will explore whether some of these restrictions can be relaxed or perhaps even eliminated.

```
// HEADER  : string.h
// PURPOSE : This file provides the definition for the String ADT.

#include "array.h"
class String : public Array<int,char>
{
  protected:
    int currentLength;        // Stores length of string
    int maximumLength;        // Stores maximum length of string

  public:

//-------------------------------------------------------------------
// Interface for first String constructor
// GIVEN:    An uninitialized String object;
//           maxLength -- an integer that defines the maximum length
//                        for this String.
// RETURN:   The String object is initialized to the empty string
//           with space allocated for up to maxLength characters.

    String(int maxLength);

//-------------------------------------------------------------------
// Interface for second String constructor
// GIVEN:    An uninitialized String object;
//           maxLength -- defines maximum length for this String;
//           initstr -- a pointer to a traditional C array of
//                      characters.
// RETURN:   The String object initialized to initsr with space
//           allocated for up to maxLength characters.

    String(int maxLength, char *initstr);

//-------------------------------------------------------------------
// Interface for third String constructor
// GIVEN:    An uninitialized String object;
//           initstr -- a previously constructed String object.
// RETURN:   The String object initialized to initstr.  The maximum
//           number of characters that can be stored is the same
//           as that for initstr.
```

```
    String(String &initstr);

//------------------------------------------------------------------
// Interface for String destructor
// GIVEN:     A previously constructed String object.
// RETURN:    The String object deallocated; the contents of the
//            String object are unreliable.

    ~String();

//------------------------------------------------------------------
// Interface for readString operation
// GIVEN:     A previously constructed String object.
// RETURN:    The String object contains characters read from
//            standard input and terminated by delimiting end of
//            line (\n). The end of line is not stored as part of
//            the String. If the number of characters read exceeds
//            the maxLength for which the String was constructed,
//            only the first maxLength characters are stored.
// RETURN as value of function: void

    void readString();

//------------------------------------------------------------------
// Interface for writeString operation
// GIVEN:     A previously constructed String object.
// RETURN:    The String object is unchanged but its characters
//            have been written to standard output.
// RETURN as value of function: void

    void writeString();

//------------------------------------------------------------------
// Interface for String assign (=) operator
// GIVEN:     A previously constructed String object;
//            source -- a second String object.
// RETURN:    The contents of source have been copied to the
//            String object that owns the operation.  If this
//            assignment exceeds the maxLength for which the owner
//            was constructed, the extra characters are truncated.
// RETURN as value of function: void

    void operator = (const String &source);

//------------------------------------------------------------------
// Interface for length operation
// GIVEN:     A previously constructed String object.
// RETURN as value of function:
//            The number of characters in the String.

    int length();

//------------------------------------------------------------------
// Interface for concatenate operation
// GIVEN:     A previously constructed String object;
//            t -- a second String object.
// RETURN:    The contents of t have been appended to the owner of
//            the operation. The string t is unchanged.  If the
//            result of appending exceeds the maxLength for which
//            the owner was constructed, the extra characters are
//            truncated.
```

```
// RETURN as value of function: void

    void concatenate(const String &t);

//-------------------------------------------------------------------
// Interface for substring operation
// GIVEN:     A previously constructed String object;
//            start -- an integer between 1 and the length of the
//                     String object;
//            len -- the length of substring to be returned.
// RETURN as value of function:
//            A substring of the String object beginning at start
//            and ending at start + len - 1.  If start + len - 1
//            exceeds the length of the String object that owns
//            the operation, then the substring returned stops at
//            the last character in the String object. If
//            (erroneously) start exceeds the length of the String
//            object or len is zero, then the substring returned
//            is empty.

    String substring(int start, int len);

//-------------------------------------------------------------------
// Interface for search operation
// GIVEN:     A previously constructed String object that is
//            considered the master string to be searched for a
//            substring;
//            sub -- a string to search for in the master string;
//            start -- a character position in the master String
//                     object. The master string is to be searched from
//                     this position onward
// RETURN as value of function:
//            The position of the first occurrence of sub in the
//            master String object, beginning at position start or
//            after. Zero is returned if sub is not found in the
//            master string.

    int search(const String &sub, int start);

//-------------------------------------------------------------------
// Interface for insert operation
// GIVEN:     A previously constructed String object;
//            t -- a string to be inserted in the String object
//                 that owns the operation;
//            place -- a character position in the String object.
//                     t is to be inserted in the String object at
//                     this position.
// RETURN:    The String object with t inserted at place. If the
//            length of the String object after this insertion
//            exceeds  the maxLength for which it was originally
//            constructed, characters are truncated. If place
//            exceeds the length of the String object, the String
//            object is left unchanged.
// RETURN as value of function: void

    void insert(const String &t, int place);

//-------------------------------------------------------------------
// Interface for remove operation
// GIVEN:     A previously constructed String object;
```

```
//             start -- a starting position in the String object;
//             number -- the number of characters to delete from the
//                       String object, beginning at start.
// RETURN:     The String object has the appropriate characters
//             deleted. If the number of characters specified
//             extends beyond the length of the String object,
//             delete only through the end of the String.
// RETURN as value of function: void

    void remove(int start, int number);

//------------------------------------------------------------------
// Interface for precedes operation
// GIVEN:      A previously constructed String object;
//             t -- a second String object to compare,
//                  alphabetically, to the owner of the operation.
// RETURN as value of function:
//             TRUE    if owner precedes t,
//             FALSE   if owner and t are equal, or if t precedes owner

    BOOLEAN precedes(const String &t);

//------------------------------------------------------------------
// Interface for equality (==) operation
// GIVEN:      A previously constructed String object;
//             t -- a second String object to compare, alphabetically,
//                  to the owner of the operation.
// RETURN as value of function:
//             TRUE    if owner and t are equal,
//             FALSE   otherwise

    BOOLEAN operator == (const String &t);
};
```

A RELEVANT ISSUE Instruction Sets for Computers—What's All This About RISC?

The dilemma faced by software designers about which operations to include in the specification of an abstract data type is not unlike that faced by the designers of computer processors, who must decide what types of instructions to put in the machine language instruction set of the processor. In the early days of electronic computers, the need to keep hardware size and cost under control forced computer architects to use small instruction sets with simple instructions. Beginning in the 1960s, however, advances in technology, primarily the use of integrated circuitry, caused the costs of hardware to decline and allowed machine language instructions sets to increase, both in size and in the functional complexity of their instructions. One of the motivations for this increase in complexity was to provide more efficient support for high-level languages; ideally, to provide individual machine language instructions that correspond with high-level language statements. Thus, we see the inclusion of instructions for handling such high-level constructs as **case** statements, or new addressing modes to facilitate handling data structures such as arrays, records, and strings. The accumulated effects of these and other considerations were as follows:

- The machine language instruction sets became larger, with instruction sets of at least 100 instructions being common and extending beyond 200 instructions in some cases.
- To handle complex data structures, instruction sets sought more and more to operate on data in memory rather than in registers.
- The number of addressing modes increased.
- Some functionally complex instructions were added to the instruction set.
- Instruction formats of different lengths were introduced.

As a result, to implement these complex instructions sets, the direct, "hard-wired" approach to CPU design was abandoned in favor of microprogramming, which uses a "processor-within-a-processor" to interpret each machine language instruction. One consequence of this shift to microprogramming was that in accommodating the more complex, but less frequently used instructions, the execution times of simpler, more commonly used instructions also increased.

In the late 1970s interest was rekindled in designing processors whose architecture employed simpler instruction sets. Named RISC (for *reduced instruction set computer*) architectures, the aim of these architectures was to improve the execution speed of processors by offering an instruction set with the following features:

- A relatively small number of instructions
- Instructions that relied primarily on registers for data manipulations, with memory operations limited mostly to load and store instructions
- A small number of addressing modes
- Fixed-length instructions to facilitate instruction decoding
- Instructions that are implemented with a hard-wired control unit rather than a micro-programmed control unit

Some of the motivation for a RISC architecture, rather than the prevailing CISC (*complex instruction set computer*) architecture, came from studies conducted in the 1970s that showed that 85% of the instructions in high-level programs consisted of assignments, **if** statements, and procedure calls; that 80% of all assignment statements were "simple assignments" that assigned to one location a constant value, a value of a variable, or a value of an array or record element; and that another 15% of all assignments used an expression on the right-hand side of the assignment that involved only one operator. In other words, the complex instructions that were put into the instruction set to make the implementation of high-level languages easier (at the expense of slowing the execution time of other instructions) were being used infrequently, if at all.

Which is better, RISC or CISC? Unfortunately, there is no clear answer to this question, since there is not even agreement as to what "better" means. Programs whose characteristics play into the hands of RISC architectures can certainly be expected to execute faster on a RISC machine, but how about programs with complicated floating-point operations, for which RISC machines usually require additional support hardware? Or, will a RISC machine run a typical Lisp program as effectively as it runs a typical C program? Also, each architecture has advantages and disadvantages for compiler writers that influence the ease with which efficient object code can be produced, transferring some responsibility for effectiveness from hardware to software. The RISC/CISC debate is likely to continue as new processors are developed, some RISC, some CISC. It is unlikely, however, that any one architecture will emerge that can successfully address all diverse requirements that computing requires.

Notice that in this class we have three constructor operations—one to initialize the string to the empty (or null) string, a second to initialize the string to the value of a traditional C string, and a third to initialize the string to the current value and length of another **String** object. The third constructor is a specific case for the **String** class of a constructor often defined for classes—the *copy constructor*.

Why the interest in a copy constructor? To appreciate the answer, let us consider three cases where a copy of an object needs to be made, but where at first glance the need for copying may not be obvious to a programmer:

- When the object is an actual parameter for a function whose corresponding formal parameter is call-by-value
- When the object is the return value of a function call
- When the object is a temporary value such as one that might be needed in the evaluation of an expression.

Although the programmer may not always be aware of when a copy of an object needs to be made, compiler designers are, and in the absence of alternative directions, they institute copying by means of *memberwise copying* (that is, making a bit-by-bit copy of each data member of the class). This form of copying can present a problem when the object being copied uses dynamically allocated storage that is accessed via a pointer variable because what will be copied will be the value of the variable (that is, an address) not the data item to which the pointer variable is referring. This means that both the original object and its copy will point to the same area of dynamically allocated storage. This may lead to unforeseen side effects if one object alters this storage (see Exercise 2.3.4).

Fortunately, by supplying a copy constructor, the programmer can override the default memberwise copying and institute complete copying of the member data values, including, if desired, the values in dynamically allocated storage. The function prototype for the copy constructor for a class **ClassName** and source object **source** is

```
ClassName (ClassName &source);
```

The use of a reference parameter in the formal parameter list is critical here. If we omit the ampersand, and thus use pass-by-value rather than pass-by-reference, we can get into a theoretically endless chain of calls to the copy constructor since each time the actual parameter is passed a copy needs to be made, which requires a call to the copy constructor, which requires a copy of the actual parameter, which requires a call to the copy constructor, and so forth.

We will return to the copy constructor when we discuss the implementation of the String class. First, however, we examine how to use the String ADT independent of its implementation.

Example 2.4

To give some idea of how the String ADT and its operations could be used in a program, consider an application in which a user enters a master string and a target string, and the program prints the master string with *all* occurrences of the target string removed. Hence, if the master string were "BAA-BAA BLACK SHEEP" and the target string were "BAA", the program should respond with "- BLACK SHEEP". A client program that uses String operations to achieve this is given by the following:

```
void main()
{
  String master(80);
  String sub(80);
  int pos = 1;

  master.readString();
  sub.readString();
  pos = master.search(sub, pos);
  while (pos)
  {
    master.remove(pos, target.length());
    pos = master.search(sub, pos);
  }
  master.writeString();
}
```

Embedded-Length Array Implementation of the String ADT

A glimpse at the protected members of the **String** class indicates an initial strategy for implementation:

```
class String : public Array<int, char>
{
  protected:
    int currentLength;     // Stores length of string
    int maximumLength;     // Stores maximum length of string
```

We begin by taking advantage of the **Array** class already developed. A string will be implemented as an array of **char** indexed from 1 to a **maxLength** parameter that is specified (either explicitly or implicitly) in all **String** constructors. Additionally we extend the **Array** class by adding protected members **currentLength** and **maximumLength**. These data members will always maintain the current number of characters and maximum possible number of characters in the string, respectively. Because we embed the string length as a protected data member of the class, this string implementation is called the *embedded-length array implementation* of the String ADT. This approach makes it almost trivial to write the first **String** constructor (to initialize to an empty string). It must merely call on the **Array** constructor with 1 and **maxLength** as actual arguments and then set the **currentLength** member to zero and **maximumLength** to the value of the **maxLength** parameter.

```
String::String(int maxLength) : Array<int, char>(1,maxLength)
{
  maximumLength = maxLength;
  currentLength = 0;
}
```

The **length** operation is also made trivial by this implementation strategy since it need only return the **currentLength** member:

```
int String::length()
{
  return(currentLength);
}
```

You will see in the exercises that other implementation strategies for the **String** class can make the length operation much more costly to compute.

The second **String** constructor offers a bit more of a challenge. We want to be able to initialize a String variable to a given quoted string, as in:

```
// Construct a string able to hold up to 80
// characters, initially  containing DICKENS
String author(80, "DICKENS");
```

Implementing this introduces two complications. First, we must move through the **initstr** argument of the second constructor on a character-by-character basis, assigning each character in **initstr** to the **Array** underlying the **String** object. To do this, we must know when we've reached the end of **initstr**. In traditional C such **char*** arrays (including quoted strings) are terminated with the *null character* (represented by '\0' in C code), so our code must check for this character.

A second complication entails referencing the **Array** that underlies the **String** class as a class derived from **Array**. We could certainly access the protected **arrayData** member of the **Array** class, but this would force us to use zero-based indexing in developing our algorithms. We prefer to use indexing that starts at 1 since this more naturally fits the conceptual definition of a string. The problem is that, in order to use the overloaded index operator for **Array** objects, we need a way to adapt this use of the index to C++'s requirement that the owner of an operator (in this case []) be known so the proper implementation of the operator can be used. We can't merely write [*indexvalue*] without an accompanying array since there is no way for the C++ compiler to know whether it is supposed to treat [] as the index operator for a C++ built-in array, or treat it as the **Array** index operator, or perhaps treat it as an operator from some other class with an overloaded [] operator. The solution to this dilemma is provided by a pointer that C++ makes implicitly available in the implementation of any operation, the **this** pointer. The pointer **this** references the current object; in particular, it references the owner of any operation in whose code it appears. This means we can access the object that owns an operation by dereferencing the **this** pointer via the notation ***this**. Having accessed that object, we can now access any of that object's member data or functions using the usual C++ syntax. In particular, in the case of a current **String** object, we can apply the inherited **Array** operator [] to it using the notation **(*this) [indexvalue]**. Note how this technique is used in the implementation of the second **String** constructor given here:

```
String::String(int maxLength, char *initstr) : Array<int, char>(1, maxLength)
{
  int c = 0;

  maximumLength = maxLength;
  currentLength = 0;
  while(initstr[c] != '\0')    // Proceed until null character is
                               // encountered
    // The current object, (*this), is an Array; so we can use its
    // index operator, []. Note we also move to next character in initstr
    (*this)[++currentLength] = initstr[c++];

  // On exit, currentLength has correctly counted string length
}
```

Following up on what we learned in implementing this constructor, the implementation of the third (copy) constructor is similar.

```
String::String(String &initstr) :
Array<int, char>(1, initstr.maximumLength)
{
  maximumLength = initstr.maximumLength;
  currentLength = initstr.currentLength;
  for (int el = 1; el <= currentLength; ++el)
    (*this)[el] = source[el];
    //The current object, (*this), and source are both Arrays, so each can
    //use its index  operator, []
}
```

Array-Based Strings and the Substring and Search Operations

You will explore writing most of the operations for the embedded-length and other array-based implementations of strings in the exercises. The **substring** and **search** operations, however, merit some special discussion—the **substring** operation because it illustrates the (implicit) use of the copy constructor, and the **search** operation because it has spawned several interesting algorithms.

We begin with the **substring** operation. The only complication that arises here is in handling the case where the length and starting position of the desired substring are incompatible with the current length of the **String** object from which the substring is to be extracted:

```
String String::substring(int start, int len)
{
  String substr(len);     // Using first String constructor
  int subLength;

  if ((start > currentLength) || (len == 0))
    substr.currentLength = 0;
  else
    // Check to see if length of desired substring extends past end of
    // String object
    if (start+len-1 <= currentLength)
      subLength = len;
    else
      subLength = currentLength - start + 1;

  // Copy characters of the substring to substr
  for (int index = 1; index <= subLength; ++index)
    substr[index] = (*this)[start+index-1];
  substr.currentLength = subLength;

  return(substr);     // Implicit use of copy constructor
}
```

We now turn our attention to the **search** operation. We first consider a straightforward algorithm to solve this problem and then examine how we can dramatically improve its worst case efficiency.

Straightforward String Search

The general flavor of the algorithms we discuss is given by the following loop structure:

Initially, align the string sub against leftmost portion of the string master;
do
  Perform a character-by-character comparison of sub against master, stopping when you can conclude match or no match;
  if *no match*
    realign sub to the right against a new portion of master
while ((*no match has been found*) **and** (*a match remains possible*));

Before refining this statement of the algorithm, we use Figure 2.8 to trace its execution for the straightforward approach. In this figure, we are searching the master string "KOKOMO" for the substring "KOM." Aligning "KOM" against the leftmost portion of **master**, we realize that they do not match after three individual character comparisons. Realignment in the straightforward approach means simply sliding the string **sub** one position to the right in the **master** string. This is done in the second snapshot of Figure 2.8. We compare "OKO" from **master** with "KOM" and realize that they do not match after one individual character comparison. Once more **sub** is realigned one position to the right in **master**, and this time a match is found.

The complete C++ code for this straightforward approach is

```
int String::search(const String &sub, int start)
// Straightforward algorithm
{
```

```
  int m, s;

  m = start;
  s = 1;
  while ((s <= sub.length()) && (sub.length() <= length() - start + 1))
    if ((*this)[m] == sub[s])        // Current characters match
    {
      ++m;
      ++s;
    }
    else                             // No match, so realign
    {
      m = ++start;
      s = 1;
    }
  if (s > sub.length())              // A match was found
    return(start);
  else
    return(0);
}
```

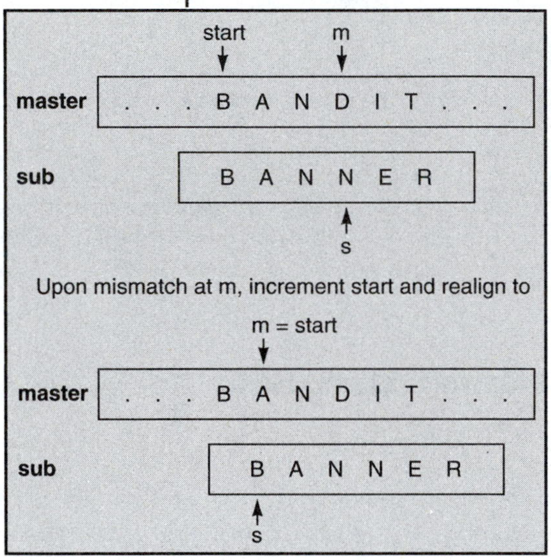

Figure 2.8
master.search(sub,1) where **master** is KOKOMO and **sub** is KOM. If after a character-by-character comparison of **sub** against its current alignment in **master** a mismatch occurs, **sub** is realigned by moving it one position to the right in **master**. This is repeated until a complete match occurs (here, beginning at position three in **master**) or until we conclude that no match is possible.

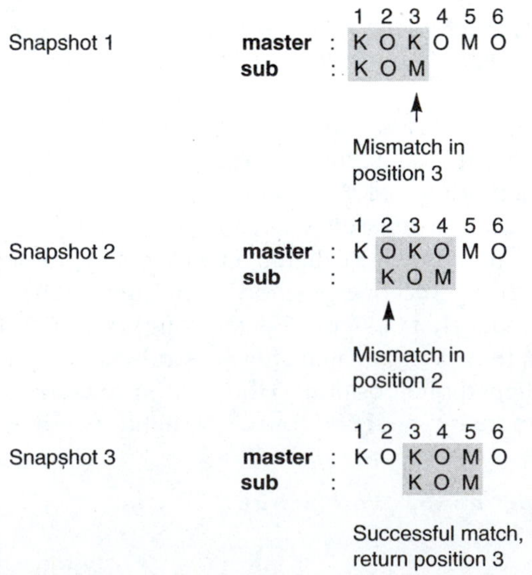

Figure 2.9
Worst case for straightforward search.

```
master : AAAAAAAAAAAAH
sub    : AAAAAAH
```

We must repeatedly compare characters all the way to H before realigning

Analysis of Straightforward Search The average performance of the straightforward search is highly dependent on the nature of the text being processed. In normal English text, we would not expect to proceed too far into **sub** before determining that realignment was necessary. However, in the worst case, we may have to proceed all the way to the last character of **sub** before determining that realignment is necessary. This would require **sub.length()** comparisons. This worst case is illustrated in Figure 2.9. Here we would make **sub.length()** comparisons for each of the **master.length()** − **sub.length()** + 1 alignments of **sub** against **master**, for a total of

$$master.length() \times sub.length() - (sub.length())^2 + sub.length()$$

comparisons. Since **master.length()** > **sub.length()**, the term **master.length()** × **sub.length()** dominates this expression, and we therefore conclude that in the worst case the efficiency of search for the straightforward implementation is $O(master.length() \times sub.length())$.

Knuth-Morris-Pratt Search Algorithm (Optional)

The worst case for the straightforward string search illustrates a drawback. Namely, after it realigns the string **sub** it may make many comparisons whose outcome was really determined in a previous alignment of **sub**. To see why it makes these unnecessary comparisons, trace the action of the straightforward approach in Figure 2.10. In Snapshot 3 of this figure, we see that five of the six comparisons that match A against A are in a sense unnecessary, since we know that we have

Figure 2.10
Action of straightforward search for data of Figure 2.9.

Snapshot 1

```
master : AAAAAAAAAAAAH
sub    : AAAAAAH
```

The first pass through **sub** ends here with a mismatch of A and H

Snapshot 2

```
master : AAAAAAAAAAAAH
sub    :  AAAAAAH
```

The second pass through **sub** starts here

Snapshot 3

```
master : AAAAAAAAAAAAH
sub    :  AAAAAAH
```

The second pass ends here after six matches of the A character followed by a mismatch of A and H

matched the five A's preceding H during the first pass through **sub** in Snapshot 1. This phenomenon is highlighted in Figure 2.11. According to this figure, the character comparison of **sub** against **master** could actually start at the point of the mismatch in **master** from the previous alignment. The reason for this is that the five-character pattern immediately preceding H in **sub** matches the five-character pattern that starts **sub**. Since that five-character pattern preceding H matched positions 2 through 6 in **master** before the mismatch at H was detected, it will certainly match again when we shift **sub** one position to the right in its alignment and compare the leading five characters in **sub** against positions 2 through 6 in **master**.

We now illustrate that this ability to use a partial match from the preceding alignment can be generalized apart from the worst case scenario. Suppose we invoke the String **search** operation with

```
String master(20, "KOKOKOMO");
String sub(20, "KOKOMO");
master.search(sub, 1);
```

Figure 2.12 portrays how this search would proceed. This figure indicates that when a mismatch occurs in a particular alignment at index **p** of **sub**, then we must look to the character matches that occurred in the portion of **sub** preceding index **p**. We are seeking a substring of **sub** in the portion of **sub** immediately prior to index **p** that matches a leading substring of **sub**. Once found, **sub** may be realigned so that this leading substring overlays what had been the matching substring immediately prior to index **p**. The character-by-character comparison can then proceed from the position of the prior mismatch. Figure 2.13 illustrates this concept in its most general setting.

This apparently more efficient string search algorithm was discovered in the 1970s by D. E. Knuth, J. H. Morris, and V. R. Pratt. Consequently, it is known as the Knuth-Morris-Pratt (KMP) algorithm. Its use requires an initial pass through the string **sub** to determine the appropriate amount of realignment when a mismatch occurs at position **p** in **sub**. Note that this determination is dependent only on **sub**, not at all on **master**. In effect, for each index **p**, we seek the longest sequence

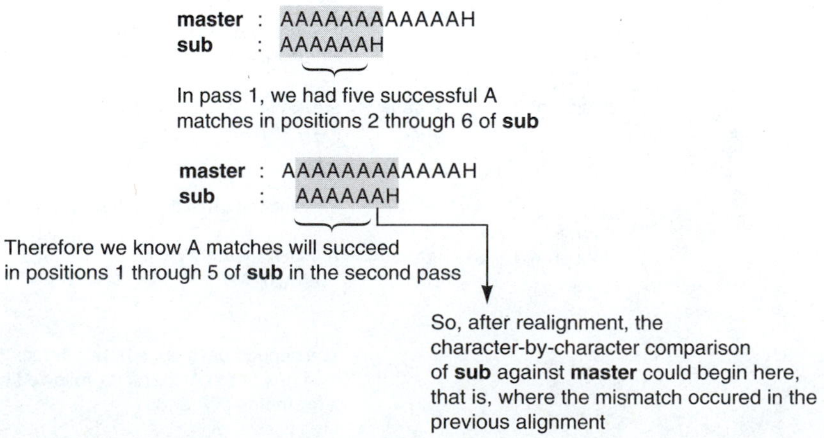

Figure 2.11
Unnecessary comparisons in straightforward search of Figure 2.10. By failing to observe that the five A's preceding H in **sub** match the first five A's of **sub**, the straightforward search algorithm will make five unnecessary comparisons with each realignment against **master**.

Figure 2.12
In performing **master.search (sub, 1)** with **sub** = "KOKOMO" and **master** = "KOKOKOMO" we observe that there is a substring of **sub** (the second "KO") leading up to a point of mismatch with **master** that will match a leading substring of **sub** (the first "KO"). This tells us that **sub** may be realigned with **master** so that this leading substring will automatically match a substring in **master** immediately preceding the position of the prior mismatch.

Snapshot 1
master : K O K O K O M O
sub : K O K O M O
In first alignment, first mismatch occurs here, at index p of **sub**
Snapshot 2
master : K O K O K O M O
sub : K O K O M O
Because the two characters preceding the mismatch in Snapshot 1 match the first two characters of **sub**, we can align the first K in **sub** against the third K in **master** and begin making character-by-character comparisons from the point of the previous mismatch

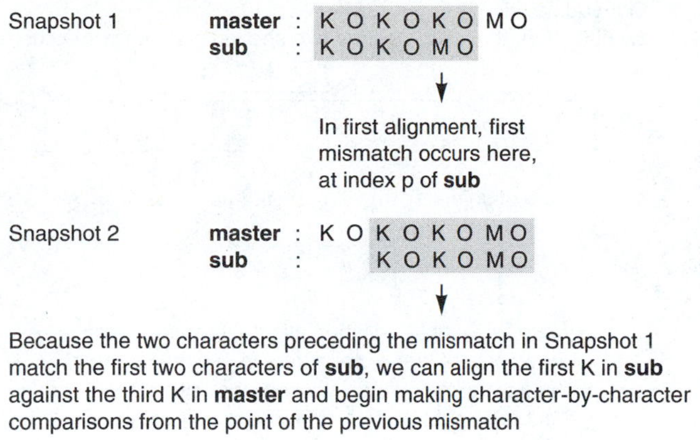

of characters immediately preceding position **p** that matches a sequence at the beginning of **sub**. We must qualify this slightly to avoid problems in the degenerate case, in which all characters preceding position **p** are the same. When this occurs (as exemplified in Figure 2.11), we restart the matching pass through **sub** at position **p** − 1. In other words, we specifically seek the maximum sequence of characters immediately preceding index **p** *with length less than* **p** − 1 such that this sequence matches a sequence at the beginning of **sub**.

Figure 2.13
Method for realigning more efficiently. By observing when a substring of **sub** immediately prior to a point of mismatch is the same as a leading substring of **sub**, a realignment can be made that will allow the next sequence of character-by-character comparisons to begin at the prior point of mismatch.

master:
sub :
Suppose mismatch occurs here in given alignment
Suppose also that the two shaded portions of **sub** match
New alignment
master:
sub :
Character-by-character comparison continues from position of previous mismatch

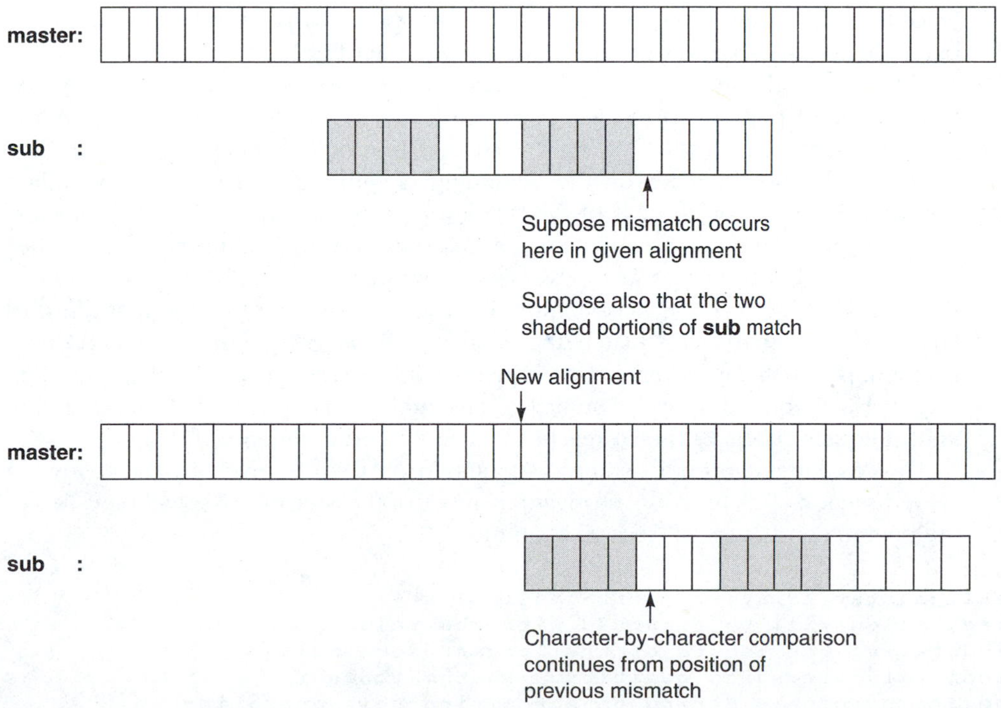

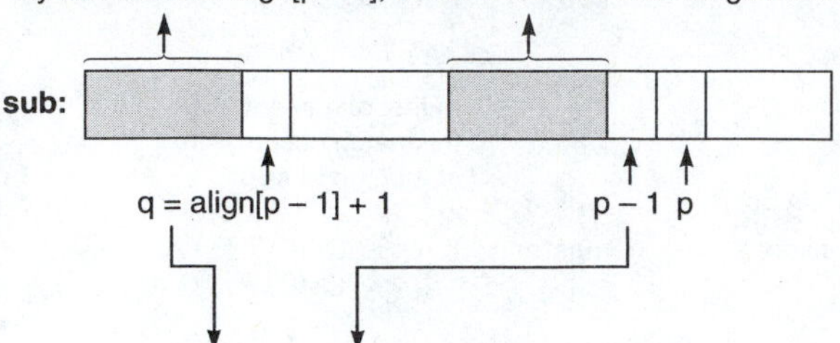
General case:
By definition of align[p – 1], the two shaded substrings match.
sub:
q = align[p – 1] + 1
p – 1 p
If sub [q] = sub[p – 1] then align[p] is q since we know that the first q characters in sub match the q characters immediately preceding position p.
If sub[q]! = sub[p – 1], further checking is required.

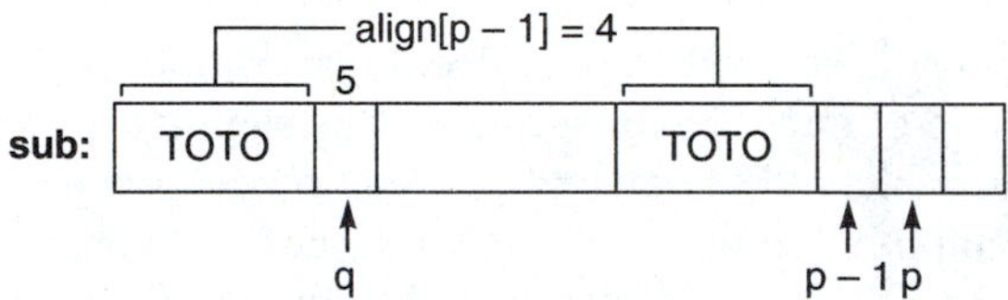
Specific example:
align[p – 1] = 4
5
sub:
TOTO
TOTO
q
p – 1 p
If sub[5] = sub[p – 1] then align[p] will be 5. Otherwise, more checking must be done before we can determine align[p]

Figure 2.14
Initial attempt at computing **align[p]** for **p** ≥ 3. In the lower figure, the substring "TOTO" appears in the first four positions of **sub** and in the four positions preceding position **p** − 1. This substring represents the contents of the two shaded areas of **sub** appearing in the upper figure.

We will store, for each index **p**, the length of such a sequence in an Array called **align**. Since **align[p]** must be less than **p** − 1, we start by initializing **align[1]** to −1 and **align[2]** to 0. Figure 2.14 illustrates that for **p** ≥ 3 we can initially try to determine **align[p]** by comparing **sub[p − 1]** to **sub[q]** where **q** = **align[p − 1]**+1. Since the **align** array is computed for successive values of **p**, **align[p − 1]** will have been computed by the time we attempt to compute **align[p].**

If the test indicated in Figure 2.14 fails, we will then seek a leading substring of the shaded portion on the left of Figure 2.14 that matches a substring ending at position **p** − 1. Working within the shaded portion on the left of Figure 2.14 (that is, with the characters at the beginning of **sub**) we know that the leading **align[q]** characters on the left of this shaded portion exactly match the characters in the **align[q]** positions preceding **q**. This follows from the definition of the values already stored in the **align** array. We also know that the two shaded substrings in Figure 2.14 must match. Combining these facts, we conclude that the first **align[q]** characters in **sub** exactly match the sequence of **align[q]** characters preceding position **p** − 1 in Figure 2.14. Consequently, if we reset **q** to **align[q]** + 1, then **align[p]** will equal **q** *provided* **sub[q]** equals **sub[p − 1]**. This logic is iterated until **sub[q]** equals **sub[p − 1]** or **q** reaches 0, as indicated in Figure 2.15.

The resulting algorithm for the computation of **align** is given by the following C++ function. This function, a private member of the **String** class, will be called at the beginning of the KMP search algorithm.

```
void String::computeAlignArray(Array<int, int> &align)
// Initially undefined, align will be returned with the value at
// each position p indicating the length of the longest sequence
// of characters immediately preceding position p that matches a
// sequence at the beginning of the String object owning this operation
{
```

Figure 2.15
Continuation of logic from Figure 2.14.

General case:

Since the larger shaded substrings in Figure 2.14 match these smaller substrings must match also.

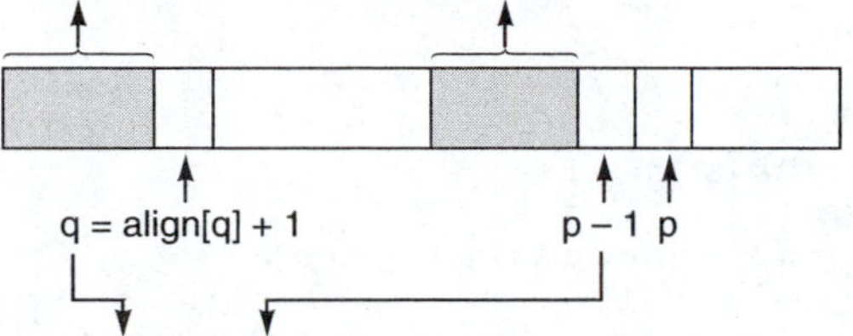

If sub [q] = sub[p – 1] we have determined align[p] to be q.

Otherwise continue reassigning q = align[q] + 1 to work with a similar leading sequence of characters.

Specific example:

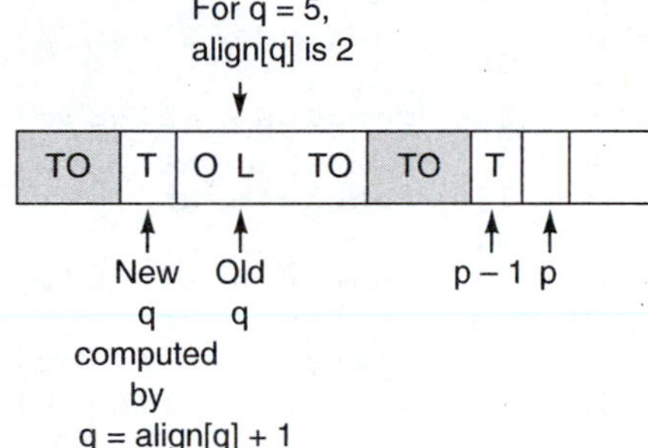

Since sub[q] = sub[p – 1], align[p] is determined to be 3.

If sub[q] were different from sub[p – 1], q would have to be reduced again.

```
  int p, q;

  align[1] = -1;
  align[2] = 0;
  for (p = 3; p <= length(); ++p)
  {
    q = align[p-1] + 1;
    while ((q > 0) && ((*this)[q] != (*this)[p-1]))
      q = align[q] + 1;
    align[p] = q;
  }
}
```

q = align[q] + 1
p–1 p
align(q)
align(q)
If initial test fails, reset q and test these two characters

q
p–1 p
align[p–1]
align[p–1]
Initially test if these characters match

The computation of the **align** array is quite tricky. The following example should help to clarify its logic.

Example 2.5 Trace the computation of the **align** array for the string "AHAHHAHAHAA".

```
          p
          ↓
align [1]  : -1 by definition.
align [2]  : 0 by definition.
align [3]  : Set q = align[2] + 1 = 1.
             Since sub[q] != sub[p - 1],
               reset q = align[1] + 1 = 0,
               exit while loop and conclude align[p] = 0.
align [4]  : Set q = align[3] + 1 = 1.
             Since sub[q] = sub[p - 1], conclude align[p] = 1.
align [5]  : Set q = align[4] + 1 = 2.
             Since sub[q] = sub[p - 1],  conclude align[p] = 2.
align [6]  : Set q = align[5] + 1 = 3.
             Since sub[q] != sub[p - 1], reset q = align[3] + 1 = 1.
             Since sub[q] != sub[p - 1], reset q = align[1] + 1 = 0,
               exit while loop and conclude align[p] = 0.
align [7]  : Set q = align[6] + 1 = 1.
             Since sub[q] = sub[p - 1], conclude align[p] = 1.
align [8]  : Set q = align[7] + 1 = 2.
             Since sub[q] = sub[p - 1], conclude align[p] = 2.
align [9]  : Set q = align[8] + 1 = 3.
             Since sub[q] = sub[p - 1], conclude align[p] = 3.
align [10] : Set q = align[9] + 1 = 4.
             Since sub[q] = sub[p - 1], conclude align[p] = 4.
align [11] : Set q = align[10] + 1 = 5.
             Since sub[q] != sub[p - 1], reset q = align[5] + 1 = 3.
             Since sub[q] = sub[p - 1], conclude align[p] = 3.
```

We are now prepared to provide a complete C++ implementation of the String **search** operation using the KMP algorithm. The **search** function declares a local **align** array, which is computed by the private function that we have just developed.

```
int String::search(const String &sub, int start)
// Implemented by KMP algorithm
{
  int m, s;
  BOOLEAN stillChance;
  Array<int,int> align(1, sub.length());

  // Call on function developed earlier. It would be hidden
  // as a private member of String class in this implementation.
  sub.computeAlignArray(align);
  m = start;
  s = 1;
  if (sub.length() - s <= length() - m)
    stillChance = TRUE;
  else
    stillChance = FALSE;
  while ((s <= sub.length()) && stillChance)
    if ((*this)[m] == sub[s])    // sub and master still match
    {                            // so move on to next characters
      ++m;
      ++s;
    }
    else
    {
```

```
      if (s == 1)       // Mismatch at 1st character is special case
        ++m;
      else
        s = align[s] + 1;     // Realign sub with master using align
      if (sub.length() - s <= length() - m)
        stillChance = TRUE;
      else
        stillChance = FALSE;
    }
  if (s > sub.length())
    return(m - sub.length());
  else
    return(0);
}
```

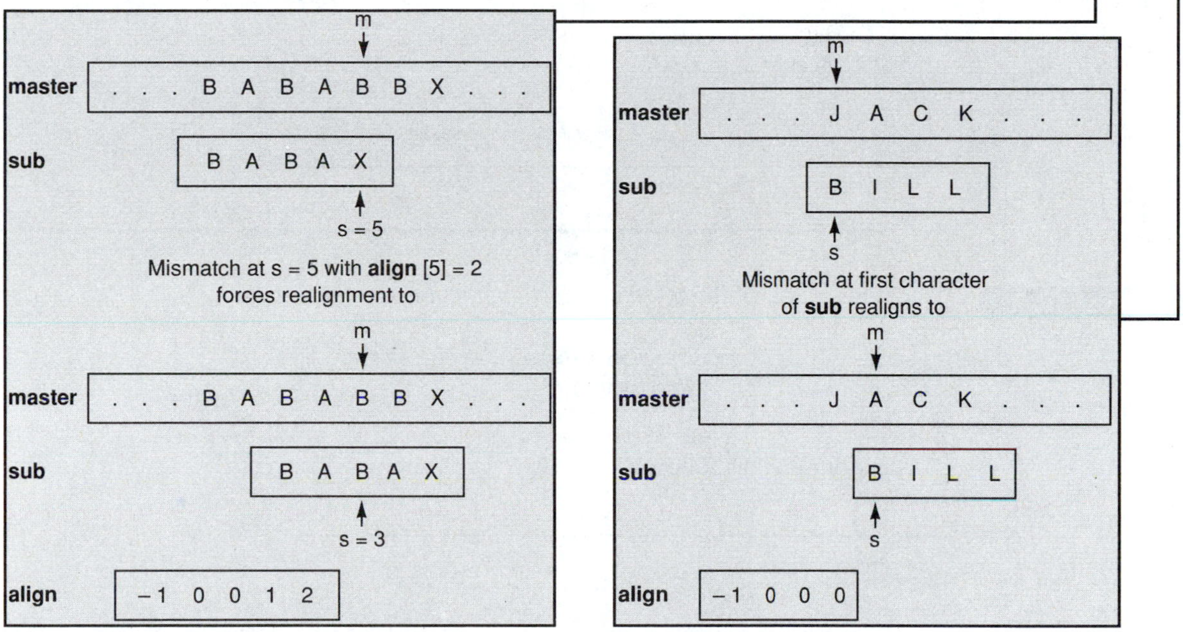

master . . . B A B A B B X . . .

sub B A B A X

s = 5

Mismatch at s = 5 with **align** [5] = 2 forces realignment to

master . . . B A B A B B X . . .

sub B A B A X

s = 3

align −1 0 0 1 2

master . . . J A C K . . .

sub B I L L

s

Mismatch at first character of **sub** realigns to

master . . . J A C K . . .

sub B I L L

s

align −1 0 0 0

Example 2.6 Trace the action of the KMP string search algorithm for the call

```
String master(20,"KOKOKOMO");
String sub(20, "KOKOMO");
master.search(sub,1);
```

This is portrayed as follows:

---

align −1 0 0 1 2 0

m = 1

Start of first pass through **sub**: **master** : K O K O K O M O

sub : K O K O M O

s = 1

```
                          m = 5
                            ↓
End of first       master : K O K O K O M O
pass through sub:  sub    : K O K O M O
                            ↑
                          s = 5

                          m = 5
                            ↓
Start of second    master : K O K O K O M O
pass through sub:  sub    :     K O K O M O
                            ↑
                          s = 3
Since align[5] = 2, s is reset to 2 + 1
and m does not change

                                  m = 9
                                    ↓
End of second      master : K O K O K O M O
pass through sub:  sub    :     K O K O M O
                                    ↑
                                  s = 7
Return m − sub.length() = 3
```

Example 2.7

Trace the action of the KMP string search algorithm for the call

```
String master(80,"AAAAAAAH");
String sub(80, "AAAAAH");
master.search(sub, 1);
```

This is portrayed as follows:

```
align | -1 0 0 1 2 3 4 |

                          m = 1
                            ↓
Start of first     master : A A A A A A A H
pass through sub:  sub    : A A A A A H
                            ↑
                          s = 1
                                  m = 6
                                    ↓
End of first       master : A A A A A A A H
pass through sub:  sub    : A A A A A H
                                    ↑
                                  s = 6

                                  m = 6
                                    ↓
Start of second    master : A A A A A A A H
pass through sub:  sub    :   A A A A A H
                                    ↑
                                  s = 5
(Since align[6] = 4)

                                    m = 7
                                      ↓
End of second      master : A A A A A A A H
pass through sub:  sub    :   A A A A A H
                                      ↑
                                    s = 6
```

```
                                          m = 7
                                            ↓
Start of third        master  : A A A A A A A H
pass through sub:     sub     :     A A A A A H
                                            ↑
                                          s = 5
                      (Since align[6] = 4)

                                              m = 9
                                                ↓
End of third          master  : A A A A A A A H
pass through sub:     sub     :     A A A A A H
                                                ↑
                                              s = 7
                      Return m - sub.length() = 3
```

Keeping track of the movements of the pointers in the KMP algorithm can be confusing; the following guide may help you remember when pointers move ahead in the KMP algorithm.

1. When does the master string pointer move ahead?
  a. When characters in the master and substring match, in which case the substring pointer also moves ahead, OR
  b. When there is a nonmatch at the first character of the substring, in which case the substring pointer remains fixed.

2. When does the substring pointer move ahead?
  a. When there is a mismatch at a position other than the first character of the substring, in which case the substring pointer is reset to the align array value and the master string pointer remains fixed, OR
  b. 1.a above.

Analysis of KMP String Search Intuition tells us that the KMP algorithm becomes more efficient for substrings that contain frequently recurring patterns. In such cases, comparisons between characters in **sub** and a portion of **master** are quite likely to proceed a considerable distance into **sub** before a mismatch occurs. The **align** array may then allow a substantial leap forward in the realignment of **sub** against **master**—a leap bypassing many comparisons made by the straightforward implementation of **search**.

A more formal analysis of KMP's efficiency hinges on the fact that we never back up in the **master** string. Examining the **while** loop in the C++ version of the algorithm, we see that **m**, the index for **master**, either advances or remains fixed each time through the loop. When it remains fixed, we set **s** back to **align[s]** + 1. However, as Figure 2.16 shows, the resetting of **s** in this fashion implies that we have a sequence of matching characters in **master** and **sub** prior to reaching position **m**. In particular, the length of this preceding sequence of matches (during which **m** advanced) will be at least as great as the number of times **s** must be reset via **align** values while we are stuck at the current value of **m**. Hence, although for some index positions the character at position **m** in **master** may have to be compared to numerous characters in **sub**, this will always be offset

Figure 2.16
Preceding matching characters offset the backup of **s** in **sub**. The worst case occurs when all the characters preceding **s** and matching characters in **master** are the same, but do not match the character at location **m** of **master**. **s** will have to back up as many times as there are characters that precede **s**, while **m** stays fixed. Sometimes, however, **s** may have to back up only once, such as when the lack of matching substrings prior to location **s** causes **s** to be reset to the beginning of **sub**.

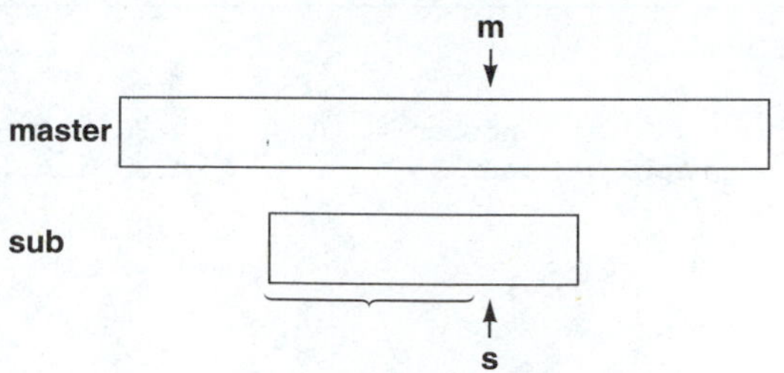

The number of characters that immediately matched values prior to position **m** is at least as great as the number of times **s** will have to be reset via **align** owing to a mismatch at the current position.

by other positions **m** that had to be compared to only one character in **sub**. Due to this balancing, the overall number of comparisons in the **while** loop of KMP **search** must be *O(master.length())*. A similar argument shows that the number of comparisons in **computeAlignArray** will be *O(sub.length())*. Hence, the overall efficiency of KMP search will be *O(master.length() + sub.length())*—a considerable improvement over the *O(master.length() × sub.length())* worst case efficiency of the straightforward approach.

For searching in normal English text, the KMP algorithm is not likely to improve much on the straightforward algorithm because the worst case for the straightforward method rarely occurs in English text; usually a mismatch in characters between **master** and **sub** occurs before we have progressed very far into the strings. Another algorithm, known as the *Boyer-Moore search* algorithm, will generally be more effective on normal English text. You will explore this algorithm in the exercises.

The KMP algorithm is particularly well suited to strings consisting of relatively few different characters—such as binary strings. In such strings, the recurring patterns that heighten the efficiency of KMP are more likely to occur. Because the KMP algorithm never has to back up in the **master** string, it is also the method of choice for applications in which the **master** string is a text file being read one character at a time.

Exercises 2.3

1. Modify the definition of the Array ADT to include a second constructor operation—a copy constructor. Now incorporate such a copy constructor into the interface for the Array class and then provide an implementation for it.
2. In this section we have presented implementations of three String constructors, the **length** function, the **substring** function, and the **search** function for the embedded length array implementation of the String ADT. Formulate C++ functions for each of the other String operations using this implementation.
3. Consider an implementation of the String ADT that uses an array terminated with a null character instead of embedding the current string length as a protected data member of the class. This null character can then be used to determine string length. Rewrite the constructors, the **length** function, and any other operations whose logic would change in this new implementation.
4. This exercise will illustrate possible side effects that may arise when, in the absence of a copy constructor, a compiler invokes memberwise copying by default.
   a. Using the implementation of the String ADT you developed in Exercise 2.3.2, enter and run the following code:

```
#include "string.h"
// string.h is the name of the interface
// file  for the string ADT.

void chString(String inString)
{
```

```
    inString.remove(2,2);
    cout << "String as altered in
      chString" << endl;
    instring.writeString();
    cout << endl;
  }

  void main()
  {
    String master(80);
    cout << "Enter a string of at least four
      characters" << endl;
    master.readString();
    cout << "Input String" << endl;
    master.writeString();
    cout << endl;
    chString(master);
    cout << "Input string after call to
      chString" << endl;
    master.writeString();
  }
```

b. In the interface and implementation file(s) for the **String** class, comment out the specification and code for the copy constructor; if you completed Exercise 2.3.1 comment out the specification and code for the **Array** copy constructor also. Now re-run the code from part a. above and compare the output from each run.

c. If you completed Exercise 2.3.1 re-do part b above but leave the specification and code for the **Array** copy constructor in place. Now re-run the code from part a. and compare the output from both runs.

Don't forget to restore the specification and code for the **Array** and **String** copy constructors when you have completed this exercise.

5. In both the straightforward and KMP search algorithms presented in this section, the **length** function for a string is called quite often. For the implementation of the **length** function given in this section, do these calls to **length** add appreciably to the time efficiency of the search algorithm? Explain. Suppose now the alternate string implementation of Exercise 2.3.3 is used; do the calls to **length** add appreciably to the time efficiency of the search algorithm? Once again, justify your answer.

6. In the style of Example 2.5, trace the computation of the KMP **align** array for each of the following strings:

a. ABBADABBADOO

b. ABRACADABRA

c. UMBOMUMBOJUMBO

7. In the **align** array of the KMP search algorithm

$$0 \leq \textbf{align[p]} < \textbf{p} - 1$$

for $1 < p \leq$ **sub.length()**. Is the KMP algorithm most efficient when the **align[p]** values tend to be close to **p** − 1 or when they tend to be close to 0? Justify your answer with a written explanation.

8. In the style of Examples 2.6 and 2.7, trace the action of both the straightforward and KMP string searches for the following invocations of the operation:

a.
```
String master(80,"ABBADABBADOO");
String sub(80, "ADO");
master.search(sub, 1);
```

b.
```
String master(80,"AAAHAAAHAAHAHAAA");
String sub(80, "HAHA");
master.search(sub, 1);
```

c.
```
String master(80,"PHILS FROM PHILADELPHIA");
String sub(80, "PHILADELPHIA");
master.search(sub, 1);
```

d.
```
String master(80,"IFFIFFIFFIFFFIIIF");
String sub(80, "IFFIFFF");
master.search(sub, 1);
```

9. Suppose that in a particular application you know that **master** and **sub** strings will consist only of combinations of two letters. Explain how computation of the **align** array under these conditions could be altered to make the resulting KMP search slightly more efficient.

10. Provide an argument that the computation of the **align** array for the KMP search algorithm is *O(sub.length())*. [*Hint:* Apply logic similar to that used in our argument that the **while** loop in KMP **search** is *O(master.length())*.]

11. In a particular application, suppose that the KMP **search** function is likely to be called often with the same string for the **sub** argument. In that case the present version of KMP **search** will continually recompute the **align** array for this particular value of **sub**. Specify a way to avoid this in a fashion that does not violate the ADT use and implementation rules formulated in Section 2.1. Rewrite all the **String** operations from Exercise 2.3.1 in a fashion consistent with the method you have specified to solve this problem.

12. *(Boyer-Moore String Search Algorithm)* Like the KMP algorithm, a string search algorithm developed by Boyer and Moore in 1977 initially examines the structure of the string **sub** to see if it can be realigned a considerable distance to the right, when a mismatch occurs. Unlike the KMP algorithm, the *Boyer-Moore algorithm* compares the characters of the string **sub** to that of the **master** string in a right-to-left fashion. The hope is that this will allow realignments of considerable magnitude when a mismatch occurs early in the comparison of **sub** against a portion of **master**. For instance, suppose that, at the beginning of a right-to-left scan of **sub** aligned against a portion of **master**, we find the character "L" in **master** and some other nonmatching character in the rightmost position of **sub**. Then, if "L" does not occur anywhere else in **sub**, **sub** may be realigned **sub.length()** characters to the right. (Why?) Analogously, if the first "L" to the left of the final position occurs at position **i** of **sub,** then **sub** may be realigned **(sub.length() − i)** characters to the right. (Why?) Thus, when a mismatch occurs at the rightmost (that is, the first examined) position of **sub**, the character in **master** that caused the mismatch can be used to tell us how much **sub** can be realigned to the right. A preprocessing pass through **sub** could be used to determine the amount of realignment for any possible character that could occur in **master**. This information could then be used in a fashion similar to the **align** array in the KMP algorithm. (The full-blown version of the Boyer-Moore algorithm actually takes into account possible realignments when the mismatched character does not occur at the rightmost position of **sub**. We omit the details of such a refinement here.)

a. Write a C++ function to compute the **align** array for the Boyer-Moore algorithm.

b. Using your answer to part a, write a C++ version of the Boyer-Moore search algorithm.

c. Would you expect the Boyer-Moore or KMP algorithm to perform better on typical English text? Explain why.

d. Would you use Boyer-Moore or KMP when the **master** string is a text file being read one character at a time? Explain why.

13. The embedded-length array implementation of a string as developed in this section introduces many limitations on string operations because of the **maxLength** argument that must be specified when a string is constructed. Develop and discuss an implementation strategy using dynamically sized arrays that would remove these **maxLength** limitations. Show the specifics of your strategy by writing complete code for an operation such as assign, concatenate, or insert.

2.4 THE SET ADT

The ADT we introduce in this section—the Set—is similar to the String ADT in that there are a variety of ways to implement it. We discuss one implementation of the set in this section and later examine numerous other implementations that may be more effective for other applications. As with strings, the key factor to remember in developing any implementation of sets is to keep the interface to your implementation completely compatible with the specifications for operations on the ADT. That is, you must obey the use and implementation rules for ADTs presented earlier in this chapter. The definition of a set as an ADT is a direct consequence of the way sets are typically used in the disciplines of mathematics and logic.

Definition: A *Set* is a collection of objects with values from some specified type Universe. The objects in a set are not necessarily ordered by any relationship. The operations we can perform on sets are the following:

`Construct Operation (Alternative 1)`

Preconditions: An uninitialized Set object.
Postconditions: The Set object is initialized to the empty set.

`Construct Operation (Copy Constructor)`

Preconditions: An uninitialized Set object;
initset—a Set object that was previously constructed.
Postconditions: The Set object is returned initialized according to initSet.

`Destroy Operation`

Preconditions: A previously constructed Set object.
Postconditions: Set object deallocated, that is, the contents of the Set object are unreliable.

`Element-of Operation`

Preconditions: A previously constructed Set object;
element—a value of type Universe.

Postconditions: Return TRUE if *element* is an element of the Set object and FALSE otherwise.

`Assign Operation`

Preconditions: A previously constructed Set object;
source—a second Set object with the same Universe.

Postconditions: The contents of *source* have been copied to the Set object that owns the operation.

`Empty Operation`

Preconditions: A previously constructed Set object.

Postconditions: Return TRUE if the Set object is empty and FALSE otherwise.

`Equality Operation`

Preconditions: A previously constructed Set object;
t—a second Set object with the same Universe.

Postconditions: Return TRUE if the Set object and t are equal as sets, that is, they have precisely the same elements; and FALSE otherwise.

`Subset Operator`

Preconditions: A previously constructed Set object;
t—a second Set object with the same Universe.

Postconditions: Return TRUE if the Set object is a subset of t, that is, if every element of the Set object is also an element of t. Return FALSE otherwise.

`Union Operator`

Preconditions: A previously constructed Set object;
t—a second Set object with the same Universe.

Postconditions: Return a new Set object that is the union of the given Set object and t, that is, the set whose members are those members of the Universe that are in the Set object or in t.

`Intersection Operator`

Preconditions: A previously constructed Set object;
t—a second Set object with the same Universe.

Postconditions: Return a new Set object that is the intersection of the given Set object and t, that is, the set whose members are those members of the Universe that are in the Set object and in t.

`Difference Operator`

Preconditions: A previously constructed Set object;
t—a second Set object with the same Universe.

Postconditions: Return a new Set object that is the difference of the Set object and t, that is, the set whose members are those members of the Universe that are in the Set object but not in t.

`Add Operation`

Preconditions: A previously constructed Set object;
element—a member of the Universe.

Postconditions: The Set object with *element* added to it. If *element* is already a member of the Set, the Set is unaffected.

Remove Operation

Preconditions: A previously constructed Set object;
element—a member of the Universe.

Postconditions: The Set object with *element* removed from it. If *element* was not a member of the Set, the Set is unaffected.

As was the case for the String ADT, we will introduce some limitations on the Set ADT as we move toward a C++ class declaration for it. In particular, these limitations focus on the universe from which elements are drawn. We specify that for now the Universe data type must be an ordinal type with an identifiable first element and last element. The reason for this restriction is that our initial implementation of the Set type relies upon Arrays and the Universe type must also be capable of serving as the index range for an Array. Keep this constraint in mind as you examine the public portion of the following class definition.

```
// We assume Universe is a finite collection of consecutively
// enumerated values with an identifiable first element and last
// element.

template <class Universe>
class Set
{
  protected:
    Array<Universe,BOOLEAN> *elements;  // Represents the presence
                                        // or absence of an element
                                        // from Universe in the Set
    Universe loElement, hiElement;      // Hold the lower and upper
                                        // bound of Universe values
  public:

//--------------------------------------------------------------------
// Interface for Set constructor
// GIVEN:     An uninitialized Set object;
//            loElement -- the least element in the Set's universe;
//            hiElement -- the greatest element in the Set's universe
// RETURN:    An empty set capable of containing any value between
//            loElement and hiElement

    Set(Universe loElement, Universe hiElement);

//--------------------------------------------------------------------
// Interface for Set copy constructor
// GIVEN:     An uninitialized Set object;
//            initset -- the Set object to be used to initialize
//                       the Set being constructed.
// RETURN:    A Set object with the same universe, number of
//            elements, and elements as initSet.

    Set(Set<Universe> &initSet);

//--------------------------------------------------------------------
// Interface for Set destructor
// GIVEN:     A previously constructed Set object.
// RETURN:    Set object deallocated, the contents of Set object
//            are unreliable.
    ~Set();
```

```
//------------------------------------------------------------------
// Interface for Set element-of ([]) operator
// GIVEN:    A previously constructed Set object;
//           element -- an element of the Universe (between
//                      loElement and hiElement) from which the
//                      Set object was constructed.
// RETURN as value of function:
//           TRUE    if element is an element of the Set object;
//           FALSE   otherwise.

    BOOLEAN operator [] (Universe element);

//------------------------------------------------------------------
// Interface for Set assign = operator
// GIVEN:    A previously constructed Set object;
//           source -- a second Set object that must have been
//                     constructed with the same Universe (between
//                     loElement and hiElement) as the owner of the
//                     assign operation.
// RETURN:   The contents of source have been copied to the Set
//           object that owns the operation.
// RETURN as value of function: void

    void operator = (const Set<Universe> &source);

//------------------------------------------------------------------
// Interface for Set empty operation
// GIVEN:    A previously constructed Set object.
// RETURN as value of function:
//           TRUE    if the Set object is empty;
//           FALSE   otherwise

    BOOLEAN empty();

//------------------------------------------------------------------
// Interface for Set equality == operator
// GIVEN:    A previously constructed Set object;
//           t -- a second Set object that must have been constructed
//                with the same Universe (between loElement and
//                hiElement) as the owner of the equal operation.
// RETURN as value of function:
//           TRUE    if the Set object and t are equal as sets, that is,
//                   have precisely the same elements;
//           FALSE   otherwise.

    BOOLEAN operator == (const Set<Universe> &t);

//------------------------------------------------------------------
// Interface for Set subset <= operator
// GIVEN:    A previously constructed Set object;
//           t -- a second Set object that must have been constructed
//                with the same Universe (between loElement and
//                hiElement) as the owner of the subset operation.
// RETURN as value of function:
//           TRUE    if the Set object is a subset of t, that is,
//                   every element of the Set object is also an element of t;
//           FALSE   otherwise.

    BOOLEAN operator <= (const Set<Universe> &t);
```

```
//-----------------------------------------------------------------
// Interface for Set union || operator
// GIVEN:     A previously constructed Set object;
//            t -- a second Set object that must have been constructed
//                 with the same Universe (between loElement and
//                 hiElement) as the owner of the union operation.
// RETURN as value of function:
//            A Set that is the union of the Set object and t, that is,
//            the set whose members are those members of the Universe
//            that are in the Set object or in t.

   Set operator || (const Set<Universe> &t);

//-----------------------------------------------------------------
// Interface for Set intersection && operator
// GIVEN:     A previously constructed Set object;
//            t -- a second Set object that must have been constructed
//                 with the same Universe (between loElement and
//                 hiElement) as the owner of the intersection operation.
// RETURN as value of function:
//            A Set that is the intersection of the Set object and t,
//            that is, the set whose members are those members of the
//            Universe that are in the Set object and in t.

   Set operator && (const Set<Universe> &t);

//-----------------------------------------------------------------
// Interface for Set difference - operator
// GIVEN:     A previously constructed Set object;
//            t -- a second Set object that must have been constructed
//                 with the same Universe (between loElement and
//                 hiElement) as the owner of the difference operation.
// RETURN as value of function:
//            A Set that is the difference of the Set object and t,
//            that is, the set whose members are those members of the
//            Universe that are in the Set object but not in t.

   Set operator - (const Set<Universe> &t);

//-----------------------------------------------------------------
// Interface for Set add operation
// GIVEN:     A previously constructed Set object;
//            element -- an element of the Universe (between
//                       loElement and hiElement) from which the Set
//                       object was constructed.
// RETURN:    The Set object with element added to it.  If element
//            was already a member of the Set, the Set is unaffected.
// RETURN as value of function: void

   void add(Universe element);

//-----------------------------------------------------------------
// Interface for Set remove operation
// GIVEN:     A previously constructed Set object;
//            element -- an element of the Universe (between
//                       loElement and hiElement) from which the Set
//                       object was constructed.
// RETURN:    The Set object with element removed from it.  If
//            element was not a member of the Set, the Set is unaffected.
```

```
// RETURN as value of function: void

    void remove(Universe element);
};
```

Note the extensive use that is made of overloaded operators in defining Set operations. To illustrate the use of these operations, consider the following example.

Example 2.8 Develop a client program to form the union of the set {1, 4, 7} and {2, 8} drawn from the Universe {1, 2, 3, 4, 5, 6, 7, 8, 9, 10}.

```
void main()
{
  Set<int> s1(1,10);        // Will become 1,4,7
  Set<int> s2(1,10);        // Will become 2,8
  Set<int> s3(1,10);        // Will become union of s1 and s2
  int i;

  s1.add(1);
  s1.add(4);
  s1.add(7);
  s2.add(2);
  s2.add(8);

  s3 = s1 || s2;     // Form the union

  // Verify result by writing out all elements in the set
  cout << "S3" << endl;
  for (i = 1; i <= 10; ++i)
    if (s3[i])
      cout << i << endl;
}
```

Implementation of Sets by Boolean Arrays

As noted earlier, in this implementation of Sets we must place some restrictions on the universe of elements from which set members are drawn. In particular, we specify that the universe must be a finite subrange of some ordinal data type. We call the first element in that subrange **loElement** and the last element **hiElement**. Thus, we do not allow sets whose elements are reals or values of a structured data type. This restriction allows us to view the members of the universe as indices for an Array **elements** of BOOLEANs. Each set will be implemented by such an Array. The criterion for whether or not a value **x** is in the set **s** is whether the value of the **x** index in the **element** Array for **s** is TRUE or FALSE, respectively. In practice, these Boolean values are ideally represented by a bit so that the set requires the minimal possible storage. If you are experienced with using C's bitwise operators, you will have a chance to develop such a space efficient representation in the problems at the end of the chapter.

Example 2.9 Write the first constructor for this implementation of sets.

```
template <class Universe>
Set<Universe>::Set(Universe loElement, Universe hiElement)
```

```
{
  this->loElement = loElement;
  this->hiElement = hiElement;
  elements = new Array<Universe,BOOLEAN>(loElement,hiElement);
  assert (elements != 0);
  for (Universe element=loElement; element <= hiElement; ++element)
    (*elements)[element] = FALSE;
}
```

Apart from constructing the ***elements** array with index range **loElement** to **hiElement**, this Set constructor must ensure that a newly constructed Set is empty by setting all indices to FALSE. Note also the use of the **this** pointer to distingush between the member data **loElement** and **hiElement** of the Set object and the parameters **loElement** and **hiElement**.

Example 2.10

Write the **element-of** function (overloaded as []) for this implementation of sets.

```
template <class Universe>
BOOLEAN Set<Universe>::operator [] (Universe element)
{
  return((*elements)[element])
}
```

We note here the use of the overloaded index operator [] from the **Array** class in defining a different use for the symbol [] when it is applied to sets.

Example 2.11

Write the Union operation (that is, the || overloaded operator) for this implementation of sets.

```
template <class Universe>
Set<Universe> Set<Universe>::operator || (const Set<Universe> &t)
{
  Set<Universe> unionSet(loElement, hiElement);

  for (Universe el = loElement; el <= hiElement; ++el)
    if ((*this)[el] || t[el])
      unionSet.add(el);
  return(unionSet);
}
```

You will explore writing the rest of the operations for this implementation of Sets in the exercises at the end of this section.

The Union-Find Problem

Before closing this chapter, we examine one more problem derived from the Set ADT. It is called the *union-find* problem and can be thought of as a problem that might arise in a large, complex transportation network. In such a network, we could group cities into sets according to whether or not a route exists between

Figure 2.17
Partitioning of Universe of cities for union-find problem. Each set of the partition represents a group of cities between which routes exist in a transportation network. Since Boise is the only member of its set, no routes exist between it and the other cities.

them. Thus, in Figure 2.17, Atlanta, Orlando, and Birmingham would be in one set; New York, Washington, Philadelphia, and Boston in a second set; Milwaukee and Chicago in a third set; Phoenix, Sacramento, San Francisco, and Los Angeles in a fourth set; and Boise in a fifth set by itself. In effect, the sets divide the 14 members of this universe into disjoint groups. This is one of the preconditions for the union-find problem—the members of the universe must be partitioned into sets such that each member is in one and only one set. The two operations we require in such a situation are the following:

1. *The Find operation:* Given X and Y in the universe, determine whether or not there is a route between them. That is, are they in the same set?
2. *The Union operation:* Given X and Y in the universe, link them by a direct route. That is, form the union of the sets that contain X and Y.

Interestingly, we may actually formulate the union-find problem as an abstract data type.

Definition of the Union-Find ADT: Consider objects in a finite universe. At all times these objects are partitioned into disjoint subsets. Each subset is an instance of the Set ADT, and the collection of disjoint subsets is called a *partition*. The operations we perform on these objects and the disjoint subsets into which they are partitioned are:

`Construct Operation`

Preconditions: An uninitialized union-find object.
Postconditions: The union-find partition object initialized to collection of disjoint sets in which each member of the universe is a member of a one-element set, that is, a partition of the universe into sets with only one element each.

`Destroy Operation`

Preconditions: A previously constructed union-find partition object.
Postconditions: The union-find object deallocated, with contents now unreliable.

Find Operation

Preconditions: A previously constructed union-find partition object; x and y—two members of the universe.

Postconditions: Return TRUE if x and y are members of the same set in the union-find partition object and FALSE otherwise.

Union Operation

Preconditions: A previously constructed union-find partition object; x and y—two members of the universe.

Postconditions: The union of the sets containing x and y in the partition is formed. If the union is different from the original sets containing x and y, the union is added to the partition and the original sets removed from the partition. Otherwise the partition is unaffected.

As with sets, our C++ class definition for the union-find ADT will place some constraints on the universe from which set members are drawn. Also, in implementing the Find and Union operations, we cannot use "union" for the name of the union operator, since this term has another meaning in C/C++ and is a reserved word. Instead, we shall use **ufUnion** and, for the sake of consistency, **ufFind**.

```
// We assume Universe is a finite collection of consecutively
// enumerated values with an identifiable first element and last element.

template <class Universe>
class UnionFind
{
  public:

//-------------------------------------------------------------------
// Interface for union-find constructor
// GIVEN:     An uninitialized union-find object;
//            loElement -- the least element in the union-find universe;
//            hiElement -- the greatest element in the union-find universe.
// RETURN:    A union-find partition object is initialized to a collection
//            of disjoint sets in which each member of the Universe
//            is a member of a one-element set, that is, a partition
//            of the Universe into sets with only one element each.

    UnionFind(Universe loElement, Universe hiElement);

//-------------------------------------------------------------------
// Interface for union-find destructor
// GIVEN:     A previously constructed union-find partition object.
// RETURN:    The union-find object deallocated, with contents now
//            unreliable.

    ~UnionFind();

//-------------------------------------------------------------------
// Interface for ufFind operation
// GIVEN:     A previously constructed union-find partition object;
//            x and y -- two elements of the Universe (between
```

```
//                        loElement and hiElement, inclusive) from
//                        which the union-find object was constructed.
// RETURN as value of function:
//          TRUE         if x and y are members of the same set in the
//                       union-find object;
//          FALSE        otherwise

    BOOLEAN ufFind(Universe x, Universe y);

//------------------------------------------------------------------
// Interface for ufUnion operation
// GIVEN:    A previously constructed union-find partition object;
//           x and y -- two elements of the Universe (between
//                        loElement and hiElement, inclusive) from
//                        which the union-find object was constructed.
// RETURN:   The union of the sets containing x and y in the
//           partition is formed.  If the union is different from
//           the original sets containing x and y, the union is
//           added to the partition and the original sets removed.
// RETURN as value of function: void

    BOOLEAN ufUnion(Universe x, Universe y);
};
```

Example 2.12 To illustrate the union-find operations, suppose that our universe consists of six integer objects 1, 2, 3, 4, 5, and 6. Consider the following sequence of union-find operations and their results.

1. UnionFind<int> p(1,6);
   p returned as {{1}, {2}, {3}, {4}, {5}, {6}}
2. p.ufUnion(1,4);
   p returned as {{1, 4}, {2}, {3}, {5}, {6}}
3. p.ufUnion(4,6);
   p returned as {{1, 4, 6}, {2}, {3}, {5}}
4. p.ufUnion(2,5);
   p returned as {{1, 4, 6}, {2, 5}, {3}}
5. p.ufFind(1,6);
   Returns TRUE since 1 and 6 are in same set.
6. p.ufFind(5,3);
   Returns FALSE since 5 and 3 are in different sets.

The union-find problem and its associated ADT form a classic problem in computer science. Although it is possible to develop an implementation for it using the tools we have presented in this chapter, such an implementation will not be highly efficient. We leave it for you to fathom such an implementation in the exercises. We will frequently return to this problem in future chapters to discuss more efficient implementation strategies.

One other interesting aspect of the union-find problem is that it illustrates some of the complexity surrounding ADTs. The union-find ADT is an ADT that requires another ADT, the Set, for its definition. Hence, implementations of the union-find ADT will be highly dependent on the implementation of Sets being used.

Exercises 2.4

1. Example 2.10 provided the element-of ([]) operation for the Boolean array implementation of the Set ADT, and Example 2.11 did the same for the Union (||) operation. Write C++ functions for each of the other Set operations under this implementation.
2. Using big-O notation, analyze the time efficiency of each of the Set ADT operations you implemented in Exercise 2.4.1.
3. Suppose we add a protected data member to the **Set** class that keeps track of the number of elements currently in a set. Explain how this data member could be used to make certain operations more efficient than indicated in your answer to Exercise 2.4.2. What operations would become less efficient? Explain why.
4. Discuss the space efficiency of the Boolean array implementation of sets. Can you identify conditions under which this implementation would be highly space inefficient? Highly space efficient?
5. Discuss how the Boolean array implementation of sets could be extended to sets of strings. What restrictions would you put on the strings?
6. Describe a strategy for implementing the union-find ADT that uses only the ideas presented in this chapter.
7. Write C++ versions of the union-find Construct, Destroy, Find, and Union operations for the implementation you devised in Exercise 2.4.6.
8. The **Set** class, as implemented in this section, uses an **Array** object as a data member to keep track of the elements in a set. An alternative approach would be to treat the **Set** class as a private derived class of the (parent) **Array** class.
   a. Discuss the advantages and disadvantages of this approach.
   b. As you may have observed in your answer to part (a), one effect of deriving the **Set** class from the **Array** class is to make the overloaded [] operator for Arrays inaccessible to client programs that use the **Set** class. Do you agree that this operator should be inaccessible to client programs? If so, explain why. If not, explain why you don't agree and how the **Set** class should be declared to make the overloaded [] operator accessible to clients of the **Set** class.
   c. Implement the Set ADT as a private derived class of the Array ADT. Incorporate your conclusion in part (b) into this implementation.
9. Write a client program that establishes a set whose universe is the letters of the alphabet. The program should then allow a user to add and remove elements interactively from this set. Finally, the program should print all the letters in the set.

Chapter Summary

We have expanded on the notion of an ADT and its implementation. An ADT is specified by describing its elements, the relationships between them, and the operations that can be performed on them. These operations can be conceptually described in pre- and postcondition form. Such a conceptual definition can then be transcribed into a C++ class declaration, although some language-specific constraints might be introduced. Any implementation of an ADT must provide a function for each operation. Moreover, the implementation's functions must closely follow the interfaces established in the formal definition of the ADT. This makes it painless to switch from one implementation to another in a given application.

In particular, we have defined the array, sortable array, string, set, and union-find ADTs in this chapter. We have discussed some simple implementations for these ADTs. We will look at applications and more efficient implementations in future chapters.

Key Terms

abstract data type
Array
Boyer-Moore algorithm
copy constructor
derived class
encapsulate
information hiding
inheritance
Knuth-Morris-Pratt algorithm
matrix
overloaded operator
parent class
Set
Sortable Array
sparse array
sparse matrix
String
union-find problem

Programming Problems/Projects

1. Extend the definition of the Matrix ADT from that developed in Exercise 2.1.6 to include the usual linear algebra operations on matrices of reals—for example, matrix sum, matrix product, transpose, determinant, and inversion. Write appropriate interfaces for each of these operations in a C++ class declaration. Finally develop your implementation of these operations by using the assign and retrieve operations for the matrices you developed in Exercise 2.1.6.
2. Due to factors such as type of airplane, amount of pilot experience, and pilot geographic location, each of the pilots employed by the Wing-and-a-Prayer Airline Company qualifies to fly on only a relatively small percentage of flights offered by this growing company. The information concerning which flights a given pilot is qualified to fly could be stored as a large Boolean array.

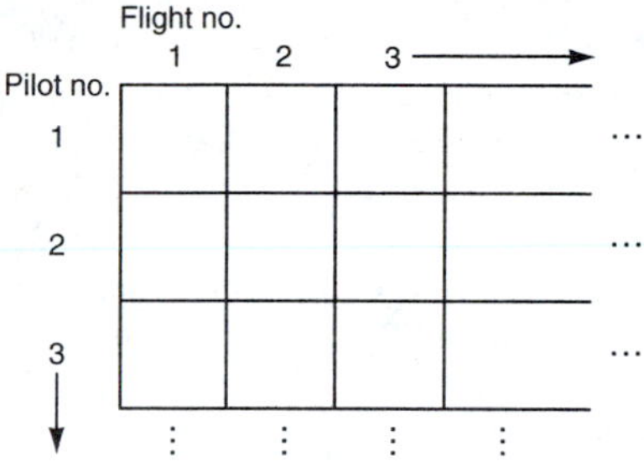

Help Wing-and-a-Prayer by developing a program that will accept as input a flight or pilot number and then print all pilots or flights, respectively, that correspond to the input. Because a given pilot qualifies for only a small percentage of flights, a sparse array technique should be used to store the data. (*Hint:* First work through Exercises 2.1.6 and 2.1.7.)
3. Provide a complete solution to the problem for which a main program is given in Example 2.4. Provide string operations for this program in such a way that the implementation of the **String** class could be changed without changing the main program *at all.*
4. *The Game of Life* was invented by mathematician John H. Conway (*Scientific American*, October 1970, p. 120). This game models the growth and changes in a complex collection of living organisms. The model can be interpreted as applying to a collection of microorganisms, an ecologically closed system of animals or plants, or an urban development.

Start with an $N \times N$ checkerboard on which "counters" are to be placed. Each location that is not on a border has eight neighbors. The counters are born, survive, or die during a "generation" according to the following rules:

Survival: Counters with two or three neighboring counters survive to the next generation.

Death: Counters with four or more neighbors die from overcrowding and are removed for the next generation. Counters with zero or one neighbor die from isolation and are removed for the next generation.

Birth: Each empty location that has exactly three counters in the eight neighboring locations is a birth location. A counter is placed in the location for the next generation. For example, on a 6×6 space, the pattern on the left would look like the one on the right in the next generation:

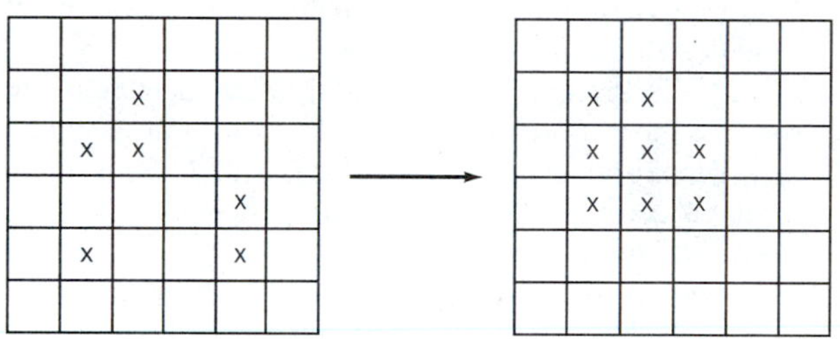

Certain patterns are stable:

Other patterns repeat a sequence:

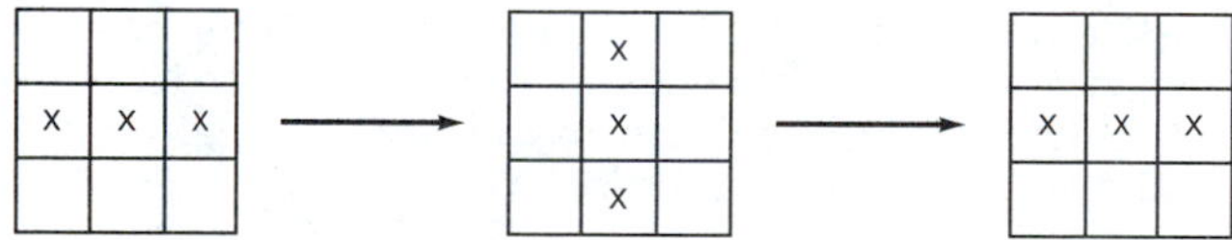

Because two $N \times N$ matrices are required to implement *The Game of Life*, it is clear that memory limitations could easily become a problem for a large N.

After initializing the first generation, print it. Then calculate the next generation in another array and print this too. Repeat for a specified number of generations. Your output should be an "X" for live cells and a blank otherwise.

Develop the high-level logic of your program by employing the fundamental Assign/Retrieve operations for matrices that you developed in Exercise 2.1.6. First use your compiler's implementation of these operations. Then switch to your own implementation of sparse

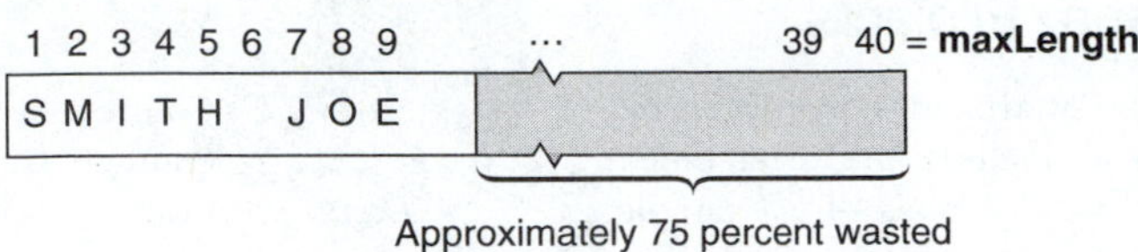

Figure 2.18
Example of wasted memory with array-based implementation of strings that impose a maximum string length at time of construction.

matrices, employing a generalization of the strategy you described in Exercise 2.1.7. Your high-level logic should not need to change at all. In a written statement, describe the performance differences you observe with these two implementations. Explain why these differences occur.

5. Write a program that allows a user to enter a target string to be searched for in a file of text. Your program should then count the number of occurrences of this target string in the file. Your program should make absolutely no assumptions about the line structure of the file; that is, do not assume that all lines in the file are shorter than some specified maximum length.
6. Provide a complete array-based implementation of strings. Then use this implementation to write a high-level program that is a small-scale text editor. Your high-level program should access strings only through the provided operations.
7. Although array-based representations of strings are very easy to implement, they lead to two potential problems. First, what about the string longer than the maximum length for which a string is constructed? Array-based methods simply cannot accommodate such a string. Second, since most strings will be considerably shorter than the maximum length for which a string is constructed, array-based methods will waste a sizeable amount of memory. This memory waste is shown in Figure 2.18.

The alternative implementation method we propose here is known as the *workspace-index method.* We look at another possible implementation for strings in the next chapter, when we discuss linked lists. The idea behind the workspace-index method is that one large memory workspace is allocated to storing all strings. Additionally, an index table of structs with two fields for each string is maintained. One field contains the address in the workspace at which a particular string starts, and the other contains the length of each string. This principle is illustrated in Figure 2.19.

Suppose now that we add a third string to the collection in Figure 2.19. All we need to know is where the free portion of the workspace begins (in this case, it begins at location 10). We place the string starting at that location, add appropriate entries to our index table, and adjust the pointer to the beginning of the free memory. This threefold process is illustrated in Figure 2.20 for the addition of the string CREAM.

The storage advantages of the workspace-index method should be evident. By associating two indexing integers with each string, we are trading off the storage required for two integers against the potentially large number of wasted characters that pad strings in methods that impose a maximum string length at time of construction. Moreover, the only restraint on maxi-

Figure 2.19
Workspace-index method of handling strings. One large region of memory, the workspace, is allocated to storing all strings. An index table maintains the starting address in the work-space of each string that has been stored as well as the length of the string. In this figure the first string stored was "COFFEE" and the second string stored was "TEA". When a third string is stored, its first character will go in location 10.

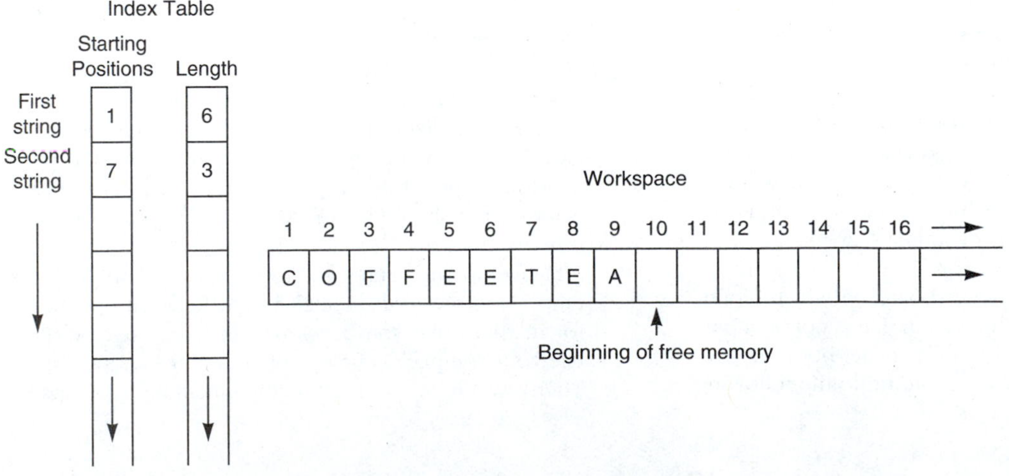

Figure 2.20
String CREAM added to work-space-index storage of Figure 2.19.

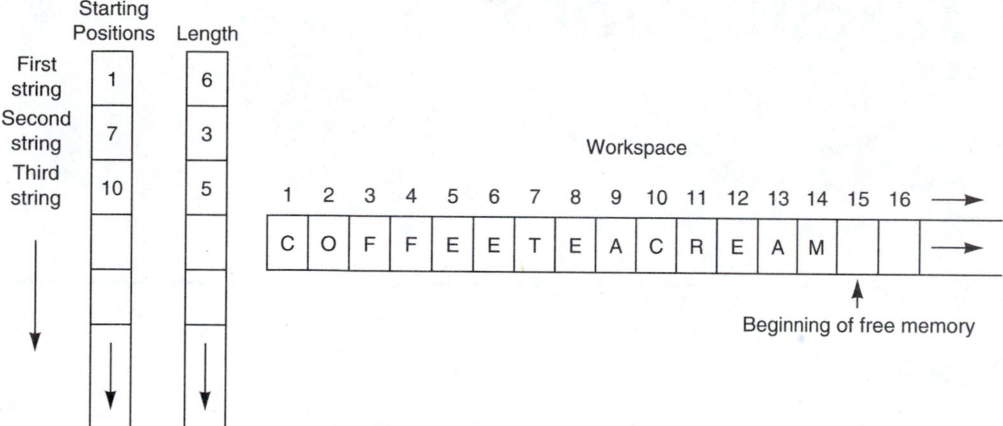

mum string length is the amount of storage left in the workspace.

Begin your work on this problem by developing a workspace-index implementation of all string operations. Then, plug this new implementation into the high-level text editor you wrote for the previous problem.

(*Note:* This is a good problem for working in teams of three. One person should develop the high-level text editor, another the array-based string implementation, and a third the workspace-index implementation. If you obey the use and implementation rules for ADTs given earlier, no changes to the high-level text editor should be required when an alternate implementation is used.)

8. Write a program that allows a user to enter a string. The program should then output the following:

a. All letters that appear in this string (letters as distinguished from other possible characters)

b. A count of how many letters appear in the string.

For example, suppose the input string is

```
The numbers  -2, 5, 20, and symbols
"?", ":" should be ignored.
```

Output from your program should be

```
The letters in this line are
T a b d e g h i l m n o r s u y
There are 16 letters in this sentence.
```

Your program should use a Boolean array implementation of sets to keep track of the sets of all uppercase and lowercase letters and the set of letters that actually occur in the string. Access these sets only through the provided operations so that it will be easy to change the implementation of sets in the future.

9. Write a program that allows input of a string **master** and a string **sub** to be sought in the master. Your program should then use both the straightforward and KMP search algorithms to locate **sub** in **master**. Add statements to these functions that count the number of comparisons made by each method.

Once your program is developed, use it to conduct an experiment. Run it for a variety of strings—strings entered interactively, strings generated randomly, strings from famous passages of English prose, strings composed from a reduced number of letters, and long bit strings composed of random patterns of 0's and 1's. In a separate writeup, summarize the results of your findings. Include charts, tables, and graphs as appropriate.

10. Add the Boyer-Moore string search (Exercise 2.3.12) to your work from the previous problem.

11. Exercises 2.4.6 and 2.4.7 suggest an implementation for the union-find ADT. Develop this implementation by writing functions for each of the union-find operations. Now, use your functions in a high-level program that allows a user to manipulate cities in a transportation network in the fashion described in Section 2.4. Assume the cities are identified by a single letter.

12. If you are familiar with the bitwise operations that are available in C, use these to develop a space-efficient implementation of the **Set** class in which each element of the universe is represented by a single bit instead of by the enumerated BOOLEAN type. Test your implementation with a client program that solves Exercise 8 above.

13. Fully implement the searchable array ADT that you defined in Exercise 2.2.5. Then design a client program to exercise all of the operations provided with this class. Finally, in a written report, analyze the time efficiency of your implementation of each operation.

CHAPTER 3

Lists—Operations, Implementations, and Applications

List, list, O, list!
Shakespeare, *Hamlet*

Chapter Outline:

How many times have you had a request directed at you that began along the lines of "Make a list of . . ."? The variety of uses for lists is mind-boggling. From the records of students in a university class, to the items we need on our weekly trip to the grocery store, to a weekly accounting of popular songs, we organize data into lists. Sometimes the order in which the items appear in a list is determined by some property associated with the values in the list. For example, the list of names of students in a class at a university would most likely be in alphabetical order, or the list of the week's most popular songs might be based on numbers of records sold. We call such lists *ordered lists* since the positions of the various items in the list are usually determined by an ordering relation that exists between consecutive items in the list (for example, one name alphabetically precedes another name, or one song sold more records than its successor). In other cases, the order of items in a list might have no apparent relation to the data being stored, but might merely represent the order in which the items were inserted on the list. For example, unless you are an incredibly organized person, your weekly shopping list of grocery items is probably not ordered by any inherent property of the items; rather the item first on the list is there simply because you thought of it first. We refer to such a list as an *unordered list,* or simply a *list.* As we will see throughout this book, lists are applied widely in computer science. In Section 3.1 we focus our attention on the unordered list, and define it more precisely as an abstract data type (ADT). You will be asked to explore ordered lists in the exercises.

In Section 3.2, we consider two different implementations of lists: an implementation based on the Array ADT defined in Chapter 2, and an implementation based on the concept of a linked list. Several variations on the basic linked-list theme are studied in Section 3.3. A discussion of two applications of lists closes the chapter: strings in Section 3.4, and sets, including the union-find problem, in Section 3.5.

3.1 Definition of the List ADT

To introduce our definition of a list, consider the problem faced by the manager of a baseball team. Prior to each game, the manager must put together a line-up representing the order in which the starting players will bat. This order normally represents the manager's assessment as to the one that will produce the greatest number of runs during the game, but there is seldom an apparent ordering relation between consecutive players in the line-up. The manager will also want to keep track of players who have not yet entered the game in order to determine who is eligible as a substitute. During the course of a game the manager must keep track of who the current batter is and, if the game is close, the manager will usually make several changes to the line-up, replacing players in the current line-up with available substitutes. A player who is removed from the line-up is not eligible to reenter the game, but a substitute who never officially enters the game (perhaps because an inning ended before he or she came to bat) remains eligible.

One way the manager might keep track of the line-up and available substitutes is to use a list for each. An example of such a pair of lists is shown in Figure 3.1.

Now consider the operations the manager will want to perform on each list:

- Nine starting players will be added, one at a time, to an originally empty line-up; the remaining players on the team's roster will be kept in a list of substitutes.
- When the manager wants to make a substitution, a player will be removed from the list of substitutes and that player inserted in the line-up in the place of the player he or she is replacing.
- If a substitute never officially enters the game, he or she may be reinserted anywhere in the list of substitutes, and a correction made to the line-up (the original player may be returned since he or she never officially left the game, or another substitution may be made).

Some of these list operations are highlighted in Figures 3.2 through 3.6. They form part of the motivation for the following definition of a list as an ADT.

Figure 3.1
Line-up and currently available substitutes for a baseball team, represented as lists.

	Line-up		Substitutes
1	Bernard	1	Hopper
2	Chapin	2	Lovelace
3	Ferguson	3	Babbage
4	Pascal	4	von Neumann
5	Church	5	Byron
6	Keane	6	Hollerith
7	Nunes	7	Mauchley
8	Turing		
9	Euler		

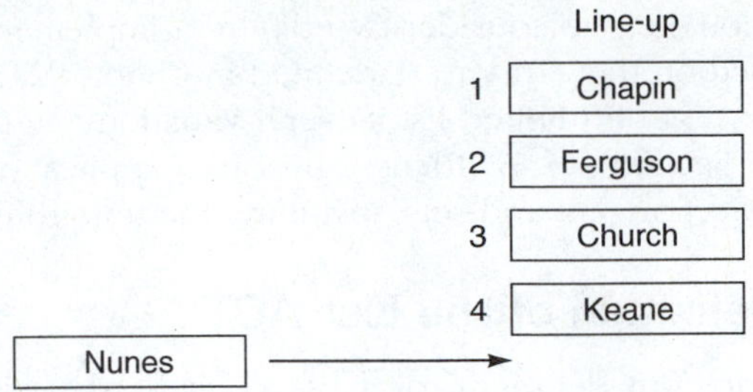

Figure 3.2
Portion of the Line-up from Figure 3.1 while it was being developed. Here "Nunes" is to be **insert**ed into the Line-up **after** "Keane."

Definition: A *List* is a collection of elements, called *nodes,* arranged in a linear sequence. (That is, for a nonempty list the nodes are arranged such that there is a first node, a second node, and so forth up to the last node in the list; an empty list has no nodes.) Assuming each node stores data of type *Basedata,* the following operations are provided for the ADT List:

`Construct Operation`

Preconditions: An uninitialized List object.
Postconditions: The List object is initialized to the empty List.

`Copy Constructor Operation`

Preconditions: An uninitialized List object;
initlist — a List object that was previously constructed.
Postconditions: The List object is initialized to *initlist.*

`Destroy Operation`

Preconditions: A List object that currently exists.
Postconditions: All storage allocated to the List object is deallocated; that is, returned to an available space pool for allocation to other objects.

`Assign Operation`

Preconditions: A previously constructed List object
source — a second List object that uses the same data type as the owner of the operation.
Postconditions: The contents of *source* have been copied to the List object that owns the operation.

`First Operation`

Preconditions: A nonempty List object.
Postconditions: The first node in the List is made the current node.

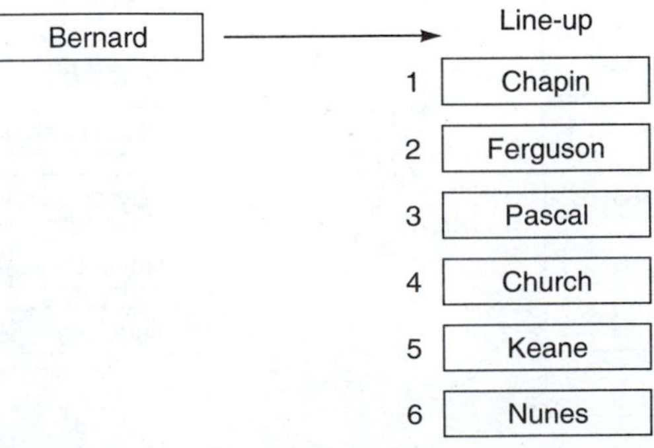

Figure 3.3
Continuation of the development of the Line-up of Figures 3.1 and 3.2 (note a subsequent insertion of "Pascal" after "Ferguson"). It was decided that "Bernard" should be **insert**ed into the Line-up **before** "Chapin."

Figure 3.4
Line-up and Substitutes lists representing an early game situation; **currentNode** for Line-up indicates that "Pascal" is the current batter.

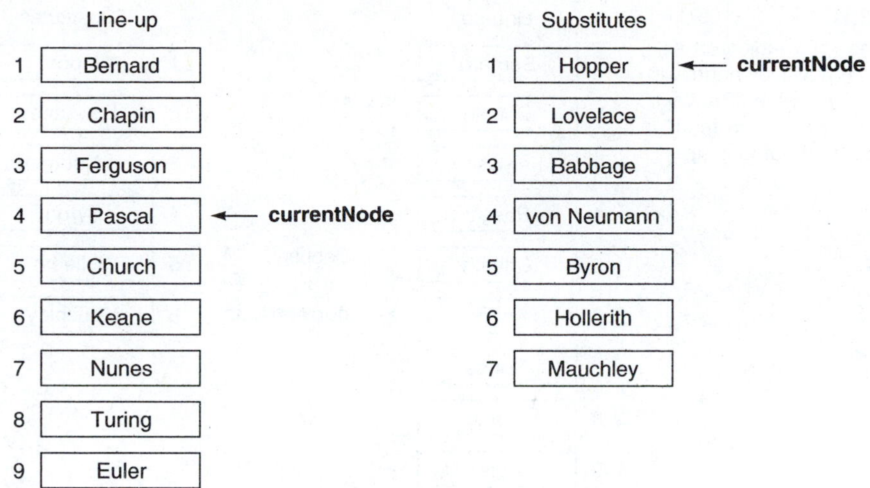

Last Operation

Preconditions: A nonempty List object.
Postconditions: The last node in the List is made the current node.

Makecurrent Operation

Preconditions: A nonempty List object;
pos — an integer between 1 and the number of nodes in the List.
Postconditions: The node at position *pos* in the List is made the current node. If *pos* is out of range, then the "current" operation will return a value of 0 and all else about current should be regarded as unreliable.

Prev Operation

Preconditions: A nonempty List object.
Postconditions: The node immediately preceding the current node becomes the new current node. If the first node is the existing current node, then the "current" operation will return a value of 0 and all else about current should be regarded as unreliable.

Figure 3.5
"Babbage" is to be **remove**d from Substitutes list with the intention of replacing Keane in the Line-up.

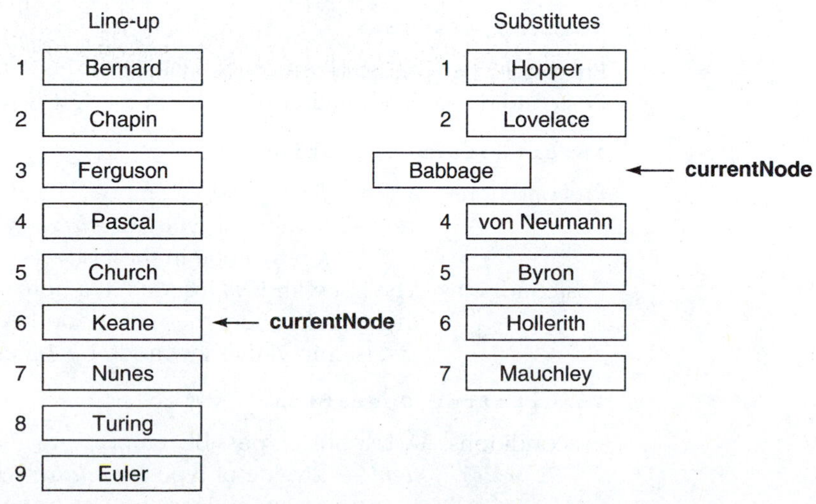

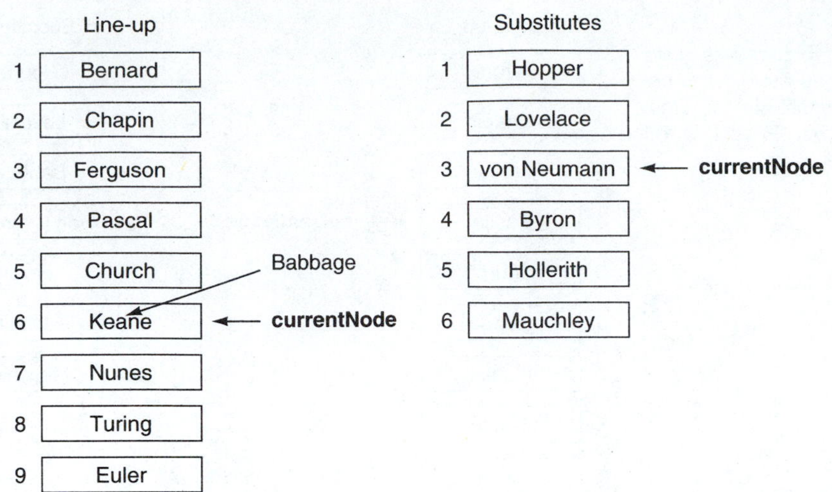

Figure 3.6
Substitutes list readjusted as a result of removal of node with Babbage. The value "Babbage" will **replace** that of "Keane" in the current node of Line-up.

Next Operation

Preconditions: A nonempty List object.
Postconditions: The node immediately following the current node becomes the new current node. If the last node is the existing current node, then the "current" operation will return a value of 0 and all else about current should be regarded as unreliable.

Current Operation

Preconditions: A List object.
Postconditions: The position of a node distinguished as the List's "current node" is returned. If the List is empty or if the current node is made unreliable by a Makecurrent, Prev, or Next operation, the position zero is returned.

Examine Operation

Preconditions: A nonempty List object.
Postconditions: The data of type *Basedata* being stored at the current node is returned.

Count Operation

Preconditions: A List object, possibly empty.
Postconditions: The number of nodes in the List is returned.

Insertbefore Operation

Preconditions: A List object, possibly empty;
item — a value of type *Basedata,* which is to become the value of a new node in the List.
Postconditions: The List with *item* inserted in a new node that immediately precedes the current node; the new node becomes the current node. If the List is empty, the new node becomes the first node in the List.

Insertafter Operation

Preconditions: A List object, possibly empty;
item — a value of type *Basedata,* which is to become the value of a new node in the List.

Postconditions: The List with *item* inserted in a new node that immediately follows the current node; the new node becomes the current node. If the List is empty, the new node becomes the first node in the List.

`Remove Operation`

Preconditions: A nonempty List object.
Postconditions: The List with current node removed. If there is more than one node in the List, the node immediately following the node removed becomes the current node, unless the node removed is the last node. In this case the node immediately preceding the node removed will be the new current node.

`Replace Operation`

Preconditions: A nonempty List object;
item — a value of type *Basedata*.
Postconditions: The List with the current node having its value replaced by that of *item*.

We now rewrite this specification of the List ADT in the form of a C++ header file. For the time being, however, we omit "protected" details from our specification because these are implementation dependent, something we wish to defer until Section 3.2. Instead we just focus on the specification of the List ADT's operations, which are, after all, the *sine qua non* of any abstract data type.

```
// HEADER   : list.h
// PURPOSE : This file provides the definition for the List ADT.

// BaseData is either a C++ built-in type, or a C++ class that has
// an assignment operation that overloads the "=" operator.

template <class BaseData>
class List
{
  protected:
  // data structure(s), protected data, and possibly some
  // functions, used in a particular implementation of the
  // List ADT.

  public:
//------------------------------------------------------------------
// Interface for List constructor
// GIVEN:     An uninitialized List object.
// RETURN:    The List object initialized to an empty List.

    List();

//------------------------------------------------------------------
// Interface for List copy constructor
// GIVEN:     An uninitialized List object;
//            initlist -- a List object
// RETURN:    The List object initialized with the node values and
//            number of nodes of initlist, but with the current
//            node being the first node.

    List(List<BaseData> &initlist);

//------------------------------------------------------------------
// Interface for List destructor
// GIVEN:     A previously allocated List object.
```

```
// RETURN:    The List object deallocated.

    ~List();

//----------------------------------------------------------------
// Interface for List assign = operator
// GIVEN:     A previously constructed List object;
//            source -- a second List object that must have been
//                      constructed with the same BaseData type as
//                      the owner of the assign operator.
// RETURN:    The contents of source have been copied to the List
//            object that owns the operation.
// RETURN as value of function: void

    void operator = (const List<BaseData> &source);

//----------------------------------------------------------------
// Interface for first operation
// GIVEN:     A nonempty List object.
// RETURN:    The List object with the first node as the current
//            node.
// RETURN as value of function: void

    void first();

//----------------------------------------------------------------
// Interface for last operation
// GIVEN:     A nonempty List object.
// RETURN:    The List object with the last node as the current
//            node.
// RETURN as value of function: void

    void last();

//----------------------------------------------------------------
// Interface for makeCurrent operation
// GIVEN:     A nonempty List object,
//            position -- an integer value between 1 and the number
//                        of elements in the List.
// RETURN:    The List object with the "position"th node as the
//            current node.  If the position given is out of range,
//            then the current operation will return a value of 0
//            and all else about current should be regarded as
//            unreliable.
// RETURN as value of function: void

    void makeCurrent(int position);

//----------------------------------------------------------------
// Interface for prev operation
// GIVEN:     A nonempty List object.
// RETURN:    The List object with the node immediately preceding
//            the existing current node as the new current node.  If
//            the first node is the existing current node, then
//            the "current" operation will return a value of 0 and
//            and all else about current should be regarded as
//            unreliable.
// RETURN as value of function: void

    void prev();
```

```
//--------------------------------------------------------------------
// Interface for next operation
// GIVEN:     A nonempty List object.
// RETURN:    The List object with the node immediately following
//            the existing current node as the new current node. If
//            the last node is the existing current node, then the
//            "current" operation will return a value of 0 and all
//            else about current should be regarded as unreliable.
// RETURN as value of function: void

   void next();

//--------------------------------------------------------------------
// Interface for examine operation
// GIVEN:     A nonempty List object.
// RETURN as value of function:
//            The data of type BaseData being stored at the current
//            node.

   BaseData examine();

//--------------------------------------------------------------------
// Interface for current operation
// GIVEN:     A List object.
// RETURN as value of function: The position of the node
//            identified as the current node.  If the List is empty
//            or a makeCurrent, Next, or Prev operation has
//            rendered the current node unreliable,  the value
//            zero is returned.

   int current();

//--------------------------------------------------------------------
// Interface for count operation
// GIVEN:     A  List object.
// RETURN as value of function:
//            The number of nodes currently in the List.

   int count();

//--------------------------------------------------------------------
// Interface for insertBefore operation
// GIVEN:     A List object;
//            item -- a data item to be inserted into the List.
// RETURN:    The List with item inserted in a node immediately
//            before the current node in the List, with the newly
//            inserted node becoming the current node. If the
//            List is empty, item becomes the first node in
//            the List.
// RETURN as value of function: void

   void insertBefore(const BaseData &item);

//--------------------------------------------------------------------
// Interface for insertAfter operation
// GIVEN:     A List object;
//            item -- a data item to be inserted into the List.
// RETURN:    The List with item inserted in a node immediately
//            after the current item in the List, with the newly
//            inserted node becoming the current node.  If the List
//            is empty, item becomes the first node in the List.
```

```
// RETURN as value of function: void

   void insertAfter(const BaseData &item);

//------------------------------------------------------------------
// Interface for remove operation
// GIVEN:     A nonempty List object,
// RETURN:    The List with current node removed. If there is more
//            than one node in the List, the node immediately
//            following the node removed will become the current
//            node, unless the current node is the last node, in
//            which case the node immediately before the current
//            node becomes the new current node.
// RETURN as value of function: void

   void remove();

//------------------------------------------------------------------
// Interface for replace operation
// GIVEN:     A nonempty List object;
//            item -- a data item to replace that of the current
//                    node.
// RETURN:    The List with the value item replacing that of the
//            current node.
// RETURN as value of function: void

   void replace(const BaseData &item);
};
```

Example 3.1

Assuming that the starting line-up list, **lineup**, and substitutes list, **subs**, of Figure 3.1 both use the class **BallPlayer** as *BaseData,* write a C++ function **pinchhit** that will substitute the current player of **subs** for the batter immediately following the current player in **lineup**.

```
template <class BallPlayer>
void pinchhit(List<BallPlayer> &lineup, List<BallPlayer> &subs);

{
  int currentPos;
  currentPos = lineup.current();  // Save position of current node in line-up

  // Change the current node in lineup to the one for the
  // substitution.  If at the end of the line-up, that is,
  // position 9 in the line-up, then substitute for the
  // first player in the line-up.

  if (currentPos == 9)
    lineup.first();
  else
    lineup.next();
  lineup.replace(subs.examine());   // Make substitution.
  lineup.makeCurrent(currentPos);   // Reset current node in
                                    // lineup to original value.
  subs.remove();                    // Remove substitute from
                                    // subs list.
}
```

Example 3.2

Assuming the same line-up list as in the previous example, write a C++ function, **showLineup**, that will display the current lineup, one name per line, starting with the first player. Assume the class **BallPlayer** has both an operation **display()** that writes data about a player object to standard output, and an assignment operator that overloads the symbol "=".

```
template <class BallPlayer>
void showLineup(List<BallPlayer> lineUp);    // Use List copy contructor
                                             // implicitly in passing by value
{
  BallPlayer player;

  lineup.first();
  while (lineup.current() != 0)
  {
    player = lineup.examine();
    player.display();
    cout << endl;
    lineup.next();
  {
```

Example 3.3

In our previous two examples we saw how algorithms involving lists can be developed without concern for how the List ADT is implemented. In this example we show how the ideas of inheritance and derived classes introduced in Chapter 2 can be combined with the idea of a list to produce a heterogeneous list, that is, a list whose nodes may contain one of several different possible types of data values.

Returning to our baseball example, suppose that the public relations director of a baseball team is responsible for arranging the appearance of the team's players at various public functions. As part of her preparation for each event, the director keeps a list of each player appearing at the function and current statistical information on each player. She must be sure, however, that she provides the proper information on each player—for pitchers, besides personal data (name, age, position, and hometown) she will want to keep track of the number of innings pitched, wins, losses, walks, strikeouts, and earned run average. For everyone else (classified as hitters) besides the same personal data, she will want to keep track of at-bats, runs scored, hits, home runs, runs batted in, stolen bases, and batting average. In this example we show how we can easily maintain both sets of data in the same list and then display the information on each node in the list, giving the appropriate information on each player depending on whether he or she is a pitcher or hitter.

We begin by defining a parent class, **BaseballPlayer**, that contains a protected section including the following data structures:

```
String *name;
int age;
int position;    // 1-pitcher, 2-catcher, 3-first base, ...,
                 // 9-right-field; these codes are the
                 // usual convention used by scorekeepers
String *hometown;
```

Being protected, these structures will be inherited by all classes derived from **BaseballPlayer**. We do not specify the **BaseballPlayer** class completely, but assume it has constructor and destructor operations and an operation for assigning values for these data structures. We also assume it has a **display** operation for displaying these values in a predetermined format on standard output, say

```
virtual void BaseballPlayer::display()
// "virtual" will be explained shortly
{
  cout << "Name: ";
  (*name).writeString();
  cout << endl;
  cout << "Position: ";
  switch(position)
  {
    case 1: cout << "Pitcher" << endl;
            break;
    case 2: cout << "Catcher" << endl;
            break;
    case 3: cout << "First Base" << endl;
            break;
    case 4: cout << "Second Base" << endl;
            break;
    case 5: cout << "Third Base" << endl;
            break;
    case 6: cout << "Shortstop" << endl;
            break;
    case 7: cout << "Left Field" << endl;
            break;
    case 8: cout << "Center Field" << endl;
            break;
    case 9: cout << "Right Field" << endl;
            break;
  }
  cout << "Age: " << age << endl;
  cout << "Hometown: ";
  (*hometown).writeString();
  cout << endl;
}
```

From the parent class, **BaseballPlayer**, we derive two other classes, **Pitcher** and **Hitter**, as follows:

```
class Pitcher: public BaseballPlayer
{
  protected:
    int innings, wins, losses, walks, strikeOuts;
    float era;
  public:
    // Various operations, including one for assigning values.  Since we are
    // adding only one operation we implement it inside the class interface.

    void display();
    {
      BaseballPlayer::display();
      cout << "Innings: " << innings << endl;
      cout << "Won: " << wins << " Lost: " << losses << endl;
      cout << "Walks: " << walks <  " Struck Out: " << strikeOuts << endl;
      cout << "ERA: " << era << endl;
    }
};

class Hitter: public BaseballPlayer
{
```

```
  protected:
    int atBats, runs, hits, homeruns, rbis, stolenBases;
    float average;
  public:
    // various operations, including one for assigning values
    // as well as the following display operation.

    void display();
    {
      BaseballPlayer::display();
      cout << "At Bats: " << atBats << " Runs: " << runs;
      cout << " Hits: " << hits << endl;
      cout << " HR: " << homeRuns << " RBI: " << rbis;
      cout << " SB: " << stolenBases << endl;
      cout << "Average: " << average << endl;
    }
};
```

Finally, using the List ADT itself as a parent class, and assuming that the class of data stored in each node admits a **display** operation, we define another ADT, the **DisplayableList** ADT as follows:

```
// BaseDataPtr must be a pointer to a class that has a public
// display() operation.

template <class BaseDataPtr>
class DisplayableList: public List<BaseDataPtr>    // A list of pointers
                                                   // to BaseData
{
  public:
    // display is a method invoked to display all items referenced
    // by pointers in the list of pointers
    void display()
    {
      BaseDataPtr dataPtr;
      int currpos;

      currpos = current();
      first();
      while (current() != 0)
      {
        dataPtr = examine();
        dataPtr->display();
        next();
      }
      makeCurrent(currPos);
    }
};
```

We now give an outline for a main driver program to load and display a list of player information, assuming the **BaseballPlayer**, **Pitcher**, and **Hitter** classes were defined in a file **players.h**. We assume the availability of an operation for inserting information in the list.

```
// Main driver for displaying a list of player information
#include "list.h"
#include "players.h"

void main()
```

```
{
  DisplayableList<Baseballplayer *> players;  // players is a list of pointers

  // Code for inserting player information in a list appears here.

  players.display();     // Now display the list
}
```

Polymorphism and Virtual Functions

In Example 3.3 we examined four different uses of an operation **display**: one for **BaseballPlayer**, one for **Pitcher**, one for **Hitter**, and one for **DisplayableList**. This illustrates an important feature of object-oriented languages known as *polymorphism* (from the Greek for "many shapes"). With polymorphism a user is allowed to decide on a name for a type of operation that is appropriate for an assortment of classes and to leave it to each of those classes to decide how it wants to interpret what that name means. In Example 3.3 we decided we wanted to use an operation **display** to specify a means for displaying information on standard output: common information about all baseball players, special information appropriate for pitchers, and special information appropriate for hitters. Finally, we also use this in the broader context of displaying the data of each node in a list on standard output. Notice that when it came to displaying the information about all nodes in the list we used one statement in the main driver,

```
players.display();
```

whereas in **DisplayableList::display()** we used the statement

```
dataPtr->display();
```

In the latter case the understanding is that if a particular ballplayer is a pitcher, one set of information will be displayed whereas if the ballplayer is a hitter, a different set of information will be displayed. Looking at the statement

```
players.display();
```

and noting that **players** is of type **DisplayableList**, we immediately know that we have to use the **display** operation specified for a **DisplayableList**. This is an example of what is known as *static* (or *early*) *binding*. In static binding, the class to which a polymorphic operator applies can be determined at compilation time. On the other hand, in the statement

```
dataPtr->display();
```

we want to leave it up to the C++ run-time system to determine which implementation of **display** to use, depending on whether the data retrieved by the preceding **examine** operation is a pointer to an object of class **Pitcher** or a pointer to an object of of class **Hitter**. This is an example of *dynamic* (or *late*) *binding*, in which the class to which a polymorphic operator applies must be determined during program execution.

In specifying operators to which polymorphism with dynamic binding can be applied, C++ uses the notion of a *virtual function*. A virtual function is only defined in a parent class and should be applied only to those operations where one might expect one or more derived classes to overload the virtual function with their own implementation of it. The syntax for designating a virtual function is straightforward:

```
virtual returntype name (parameter list)
{
  definition of the function
}
```

For example,

```
class ParentClass
{
  protected:
    char classId;

  public:
    ParentClass()
    {
      classId = 'P';
    }

    virtual void display()
    {
      cout << "ClassId: " << classId << endl;
    }
};
```

To see how to affect dynamic binding, consider the following two classes, which are derived from **ParentClass**:

```
class Derived1: public ParentClass
{
  protected:
    int derivedId;

  public:
    Derived1()
    {
      classId = 'D';
      derivedId = 1;
    }

    void display()
    {
      cout << "ClassId: " << classId << endl;
      cout << "Derived Class " << derivedId << endl;
    }
};

class Derived2: public ParentClass
{
  protected:
    char derivedChar;

  public:
    Derived2()
    {
```

```
      classId = 'D';
      derivedChar = 'X';
    }

    void display()
    {
      cout << "ClassId: " << classId << endl;
      cout << "Derived Char " << derivedChar << endl;
    }
};
```

Suppose now we have the following declaration;

```
ParentClass *p;
Derived1 *d1;
Derived2 *d2;
```

and the statements

```
p = new ParentClass;
p->display();
```

Then one would expect to see as output the line

```
ClassId: P
```

since the pointer **p** is a pointer to an object of type **ParentClass**; hence it should invoke the **display** operation appropriate for **ParentClass**. On the other hand, if we had the statements

```
d1 = new Derived1;
d2 = new Derived2;

p = d1;
p->display();
p = d2;
p->display();
```

then the impact of our declaration of **display** in **ParentClass** as a virtual function is to defer binding of **display** to a class until execution time. In the case of the first statement

```
p->display();
```

at the time this statement is executed, **p** is pointing to an object of class **Derived1**, and so **Derived1::display()** is invoked, and

```
ClassId: D
DerivedClass 1
```

is produced as output. When we get to the second statement

```
p->display();
```

p has been changed to point to an object of class **Derived2**, whence **Derived2::display()** would be invoked, and

```
ClassId: D
DerivedChar X
```

is produced as output. Note that had we not declared **display** as a virtual function in the definition of **ParentClass**, then static binding would have occurred and **Parentclass::display()** would have been invoked in all cases since at compile time **p** was associated with **ParentClass**. This use of pointers to objects and the "->" operator that we have seen in this discussion is the foundation for all dynamic binding of operations in C++.

In the next section we consider implementations of the List ADT. Before moving on, however, we wish to make some final comments concerning our definition of this ADT. First, it is important to note that Examples 3.1, 3.2, and 3.3 have used the operations provided by both the List ADT and the String ADT without making any assumptions about how either ADT has been implemented. This is consistent with the ADT use rule formulated in Section 2.1. Accessing an ADT only through its provided operations allows us to discuss algorithms involving that ADT before ever considering how it is implemented.

Second, the ADT approach we are emphasizing allows a large degree of creativity and flexibility in defining the operations associated with an ADT. It would be a gross overstatement to maintain that the operations we have provided for the List ADT in this section will be sufficient for all applications; nor will there be universal agreement that the operations we have chosen were an optimal choice. One could easily argue that the most important decision a software designer can make, besides deciding to use ADTs in the first place, is deciding on the operations that will characterize each ADT he or she will use. Should one think of every conceivable operation that a user may want and incorporate each into the ADT's specification, possibly resulting in an ADT that is so loaded with operations that a novice user of the ADT may despair of using it effectively? Or should the designer of the ADT concentrate instead on a "leaner" ADT whose set of operations is smaller and more basic? It would then be up to users of the ADT to implement more application-specific operations from these, possibly using inheritance to derive a more specialized ADT whose operations match the needs of the user. In the exercises you will explore ways of extending and altering our collection of operations that might provide a better List ADT for certain situations. Afterwards it should be apparent that specifying the operations for a complex ADT is an endeavor that truly tests the creative abilities of any computer scientist.

Exercises 3.1

1. At the beginning of this section we described the concept of an *ordered list* ADT whose nodes are arranged in a linear sequence according to some ordering criterion between data in the nodes. In other words, the first node on the list is placed there because according to some ordering criterion, its associated data value "precedes" that of all other items in the list. Likewise, the second node in the list is there because its data value precedes all other item in the list, except the first, and so on. Write a complete ADT specification for an ordered list. The operation by which nodes are to be inserted should accept as a parameter a Boolean function **precedes** that accepts two parameters of type **BaseData** and returns a value indicating whether the ordering relation is satisfied between these parameters. After a node has been inserted, of course, the list should still be ordered according to the ordering relation. For node deletions and modifications of node values, you should assume that the underlying data type **BaseData** has an overloaded equality operator (==) that can be used to determine whether two items match each other in accordance with some criterion appropriate for that type.

2. a. Write a C++ function **append** that accepts two Lists as parameters. The function should return with the second List having a copy of the first List appearing after its original last node. The nodes designated as the current nodes in each List should remain so.

   b. Write a C++ function **precede** that accepts two Lists as parameters. The function should return with the second List having a copy of the first List preceding its original first node. The nodes designated as the current nodes in each List should remain so.

   c. Write a C++ function **cut** that accepts as parameters a List and two (positive) integers representing positions between the first and last node of the List, inclusive. The function should return with the given List having the nodes between the indicated positions removed. The function should do all appropriate error checking and take some proper action if an error is detected.

   d. This exercise is similar to that of part (c), but instead of a List and two positive integers, the function should accept as parameters a List and an integer, the latter representing a displacement from the current node. The function should remove the current node and all nodes between it and the one specified by the displacement (inclusive). If the integer parameter is negative, the nodes removed precede the current one; if it is positive, the nodes removed follow the current node. Again, handle all error checking and identify corrective actions.

3. Assume a data type **BaseData** that has an associated **processItem** operation as well as an assignment operation that overloads the "=" symbol. Write a C++ function **processAllItems** that accepts a List as a parameter and traverses the List from first node through last, invoking the **processItem** operation for the data item of type **BaseData** associated with each node.

4. In our discussion of polymorphism we described a class **DisplayableList** that was derived from the **List** class and used a **display** operation polymorphically. Assuming that **DisplayableList** has nodes that store values of type **BaseData** and that **BaseData** has its own **display** operation as well as an assignment operation that overloads the "=" symbol, formulate a more complete definition of the **DisplayableList** class that includes a **load** operation for adding standard input data sequentially to the List, prompting the user each time before inserting another node. Also include additional operations that you think may be appropriate.

5. The List ADT defined in this section could be called a "position-oriented" unordered list because nonsequential designations of the current node are done by specifying the position in the list for a new current node. Alternatively, we can define a "data-oriented" unordered list in which designations for a current node are done not by its position, but by its data. Thus, instead of providing an integer **pos** as its parameter, the **makeCurrent** operation might accept a Boolean-valued function **condition** as a parameter, where **condition** itself accepts a two parameters of type **BaseData**, the same type as the data values of the nodes of the list. Starting from the current node, the first node after the current node for which **condition** evaluates to true becomes the new current node. (Note: We shall assume that any operations, such as comparisons, used by condition are supported in **BaseData** if necessary.) Give a detailed specification of a data-oriented list that includes this operation and any others you feel are appropriate.

6. Define a parent class **Employee** together with derived classes **SalariedEmployee**, **HourlyEmployee**, and **TemporaryEmployee**. The class **Employee** will keep general information about each employee; **SalariedEmployee** will record an employee's yearly salary; **HourlyEmployee** will record an employee's hourly wage; and **TemporaryEmployee** will record that person's hourly wage and length of contract (in weeks). Now write a driver program that will create a list of employee records using keyboard input and then display the list using a format and information appropriate for the data being stored in each node.

7. Write a function **sum** to sum the values (integer or real) in a nonempty List of numeric values. The sum should be returned as a real value.

8. Write a function **reverse** that accepts a List as a parameter and reverses the List; that is, it makes the value in the first node that of the last node and the value of the last node that of the first; it makes the value of the second node that of the second-to-last node and the value of the second-to-last node that of the second node; and so on. The node identified as the current node should remain so.

3.2 Implementations of the List ADT

In the previous section we developed algorithms that used the List ADT. Consequently, it is now imperative that we implement this ADT by strictly adhering to the ADT implementation rule of Section 2.1. This will ensure that the List algorithms we have already developed will not have to be altered to fit our implementations. We discuss two implementations of a List: one based on the Array ADT and one based on the concept of a linked list.

Array Implementation

The techniques behind this implementation should be familiar to you. We will merely maintain the data values in an Array indexed from one up to a predetermined size **maxListSize** such that the first value of the List is stored in the node in the component of the Array with index 1, the second value in the List is stored in the component of the Array with index 2, and so on. This Array will then be encapsulated with a counter that keeps track of the number of nodes currently in the List, up to the maximum of **maxListSize**. Hence, the List ADT will be implemented using the following as its interface file:

```
// HEADER   : list.h
// PURPOSE : This file provides the definition for the List ADT.

#define maxListSize 200 // or some appropriately sized integer

// BaseData is either a C++ built-in type, or a C++ class that has
// an assignment operation that overleads the "=" operator.

template <class BaseData>
class List
{
  protected:
    Array<int, BaseData> *listArray;   // Storage for list data
    int numnodes;                      // Store current size of list
    int currentNode;                   // Store index of current node

  public:
//------------------------------------------------------------------
// Interface for List constructor
// GIVEN:     An uninitialized List object.
// RETURN:    The List object is initialized to an empty List.

    List();

//------------------------------------------------------------------
// Interface for List copy constructor
// GIVEN:    An uninitialized List object;
//           initlist -- a List object.
// RETURN:   The List object initialized with the node values and
//           number of nodes of initlist, but with the current node
//           being the first node.

    List(List<BaseData> &initlist);

//------------------------------------------------------------------
// Interface for List destructor
// GIVEN:     A previously allocated List object.
// RETURN:    The List object deallocated.

     ~List();
```

```
//------------------------------------------------------------------
// Interface for List assign = operator
// GIVEN:     A previously constructed List object;
//            source -- a second List object that must have been
//                      constructed with the same BaseData type as
//                      the owner of the assign operator.
// RETURN:    The contents of source have been copied to the List
//            object that owns the operation.
// RETURN as value of function: void

   void operator = (const List<BaseData> &source);

//------------------------------------------------------------------
// Interface for first operation
// GIVEN:     A nonempty List object;
// RETURN:    The List object with the first node as the current node.
// RETURN as value of function: void

   void first();

//------------------------------------------------------------------
// Interface for last operation
// GIVEN:     A nonempty List object.
// RETURN:    The List object with the last node as the current node.
// RETURN as value of function: void

   void last();

//------------------------------------------------------------------
// Interface for makeCurrent operation

// GIVEN:     A nonempty List object;
//            position -- an integer value between 1 and the number
//                        of elements in the List.
// RETURN:    The List object with the "position"th node as the
//            current node.  If the position given is out of range,
//            then the current operation will return a value of 0
//            and all else about current should be regarded as
//            unreliable.
// RETURN as value of function: void

   void makeCurrent(int position);

//------------------------------------------------------------------
// Interface for prev operation
// GIVEN:     A nonempty List object.
// RETURN:    The List object with the node immediately preceding
//            the existing current node as the new current node. If
//            the first node is the existing current node, then the
//            "current" operation will return a value of 0 and all
//            else about current should be regarded as unreliable.
// RETURN as value of function: void

   void prev();

//------------------------------------------------------------------
// Interface for next operation
// GIVEN:     A nonempty List object.
// RETURN:    The List object with the node immediately following
//            the existing current node as the new current node.
```

```
//           If the last node is the existing current node, then
//           the "current" operation will return a value of 0 and
//           all else about current should be regarded as
//           unreliable.
// RETURN as value of function: void

   void next();

//-----------------------------------------------------------------
// Interface for List examine operation
// GIVEN:    A nonempty List object.
// RETURN as value of function:
//           The data of type BaseData being stored at the current
//           node.

   BaseData examine();

//-----------------------------------------------------------------
// Interface for current operation
// GIVEN:    A List object.
// RETURN as value of function:
//           The position of the node identified as the current
//           node.  If the List is empty or a makeCurrent, next,
//           or prev operation has rendered the current node
//           unreliable,  the value zero is returned.

   int current();

//-----------------------------------------------------------------
// Interface for count operation
// GIVEN:    A List object.
// RETURN as value of function:
//           The number of nodes currently in the List.

   int count();

//-----------------------------------------------------------------
// Interface for insertBefore operation
// GIVEN:    A List object;
//           item -- a data item to be inserted into the list.
// RETURN:   The List with item inserted in a node immediately
//           before the current node in the List, with the
//           newly inserted node becoming the current node.
//           If the List is empty, item becomes the first node in
//           the List.
// RETURN as value of function: void

   void insertBefore(const BaseData &item);

//-----------------------------------------------------------------
// Interface for insertAfter operation
// GIVEN:    A List object;
//           item -- a data item to be inserted into the list.
// RETURN:   The List with item inserted in a node immediately
//           after the current item in the List, with the newly
//           inserted node becoming the current node.  If the List
//           is empty, item becomes the first node in the List.
// RETURN as value of function: void

   void insertAfter(const BaseData &item);
```

```
//-----------------------------------------------------------------
// Interface for remove operation
// GIVEN:     A nonempty List object.
// RETURN:    The List with current node removed. If there is more
//            than one node in the List, the node immediately
//            following the node removed will become the current
//            node, unless the current node is the last node, in
//            which case the node immediately before the current
//            node becomes the new current node.
// RETURN as value of function: void

    void remove();

//-----------------------------------------------------------------
// Interface for replace operation
// GIVEN:     A nonempty List object;
//            item -- a data item to replace that of the current
//                    node.
// RETURN:    The List with the value item replacing that of the
//            current node.
// RETURN as value of function: void

    void replace(const BaseData &item);
};
```

As usual, the implementations of individual operations would follow the **List** class declaration in the header file **list.h**. We do some of these as examples and leave the rest for the exercises.

Example 3.4 Implement the **List** constructor operation.

```
template <class BaseData>
List<BaseData>::List()
{
  listArray = new Array<int, BaseData>(1, maxListSize);
  assert(listArray !=0);
  numnodes = 0;
  currentNode = 0;
}
```

Example 3.5 Implement the **insertBefore** operation of the **List** class.

```
template <class BaseData>
List<BaseData>::insertBefore(const BaseData &item)
{
  if (numnodes >= maxListSize)
  {
    cerr << "INSUFFICIENT STORAGE TO ADD A NEW NODE TO A LIST" << endl;
    assert(numnodes < maxListSize);
  }
  else
  {
    if (numnodes > 0)
```

```
      // List is not empty so move nodes down one position
      // to make room for new node
      for (int k = numnodes+1; k > currentNode; --k)
        (*listArray)[k] = (*listArray)[k-1];
    else
      currentNode = 1;
    (*listArray)[currentNode] = item;
    ++numnodes;
  }
}
```

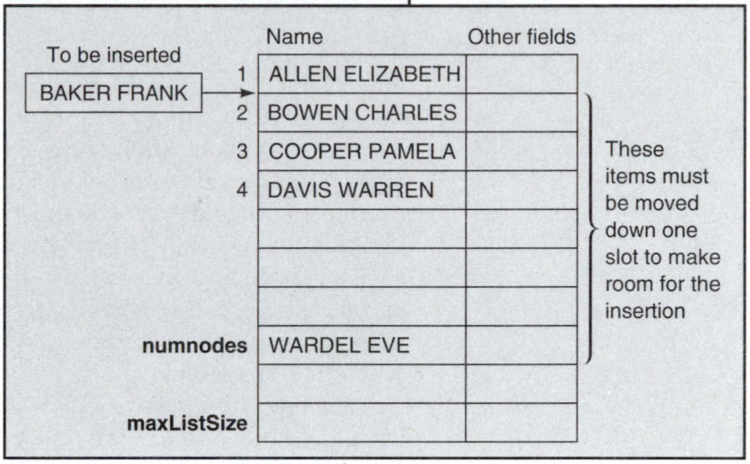

Completion of the other operations for the List ADT are left for the exercises. Note that the efficiency for inserting or removing a node for this implementation can be quickly grasped by examining the graphic documentation accompanying **insertBefore**. Here we see that this implementation of **insertBefore** may require an extensive amount of data movement. For instance, the addition of BAKER FRANK, as indicated in the graphic documentation, will force all nodes beginning at the second index to be moved down one slot. In a realistic situation where your database may have 10,000 records, each consisting of 500 bytes, this will mean shuffling 5,000,000 bytes of data around in computer storage.

An analogous problem occurs when a node in one of the first few positions of the list is deleted. All the nodes following it must move up one slot to maintain the physical order. Thus, the implementation we are proposing here will not fare especially well with respect to all of the operations defined for the List ADT. In particular, this implementation is well suited only for those lists that are *nonvolatile*, that is, not undergoing frequent additions and deletions.

Linked List

The linked-list implementation of the List ADT addresses the shortcomings of the previous implementation by not requiring that a node's physical position in the list match its logical position. That is, the area of storage allocated for the nth node in a list implemented via a linked list will not necessarily be contiguous with the storage allocated for node $n - 1$ or for node $n + 1$. The central motivation behind the linked-list data structure is to eliminate the data movement associated with insertions into and deletions from the middle of the list. Of course, we might suspect that efficiency in eliminating such data movement can only come by trading off other efficiency factors. One of the crucial questions to ask yourself as we study linked lists is, "What price are we paying to handle additions and deletions

Figure 3.7
Rankings and hiding places for a child's gifts.

Ranking	Gift	Hiding place
least desirable	pair of socks	under bed
↓	box of candy	kitchen drawer
	video game	basement cabinet
most desirable	bicycle	garage

effectively?" One way of conceptually understanding a linked list is to think of the game some parents use to make the opening of the holiday gifts particularly exciting for their children. One feature of the game, which helps to build children's anticipation, ensures that minor gifts are opened first, gradually building up to the most substantial gift. (Recall from your own childhood experience the partial letdown that occurred when you opened a gift package containing a mere pair of socks after having already unwrapped something significantly more exciting, such as a baseball glove or new doll!) Thus, the premises of this gift-giving game are that gifts may be ranked according to their desirability and that the game is more fun when the most desirable gifts are opened last.

To achieve this end, parents will hide a child's wrapped gifts at various locations throughout the home. For instance, let us suppose a scenario in which parents have four gifts for their child, ranked and hidden as indicated in Figure 3.7.

The parents will then tell the child *only* the location of the least desirable gift; for instance, they would give instructions to look under a bed for the first gift. Upon opening that gift, the child will find the uninspiring pair of socks plus a more intriguing note with the information that the next gift is in a kitchen drawer. The pattern should now be obvious. From the box of candy, the child follows an informational pointer to a basement cabinet, where the video game is discovered along with a similar informational link to the garage as a location where something bigger and better may be found. The now eager child will uncover a bike along with a final (and no doubt disappointing) note indicating that the end of the chain of gifts has been reached.

A conceptual picture of this chain of gifts is presented in Figure 3.8. This same picture applies to the *linked-list* data structure we are about to study. In this figure, the arrows connecting packages represent the informational note in each package, telling us the location of the next package. Conceptually, the form taken by this informational pointer is not important. However, it is crucial that we have a reliable pointer to the leading gift (often called a *head pointer*) and, thereafter, a reliable pointer in each package to the next package. Should any pointer be flawed, the remaining gifts on the chain become essentially inaccessible (much to the dismay of the child who desperately wanted that bike).

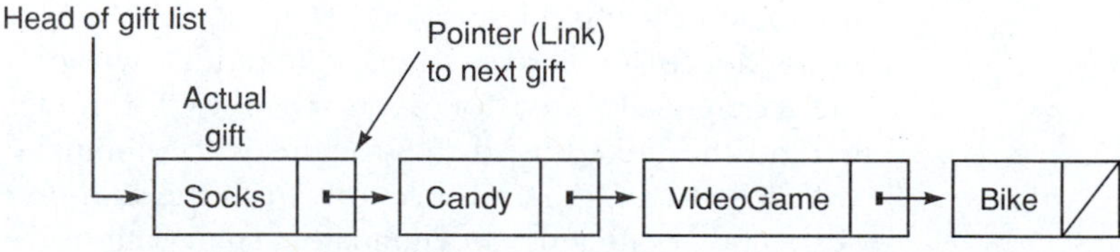

Figure 3.8
Linked chain of gifts. The pointers represent information stored with each gift telling us the location of the next gift. The *head* pointer tells us where to find the first gift, while the pointer with the value / (NULL) tells us (alas) that there are no more gifts.

In addition to introducing us to much of the vernacular that comes with linked lists, this review of a simple childhood game can also give us a hint of the ease with which such a linked chain of nodes can handle additions and deletions. For instance, suppose that a sudden windfall allows the parents to buy a baseball glove in addition to the four gifts already purchased. Assuming that this new gift is ranked between the video game and the bicycle in desirability, consider what must be done to link it into the gift chain. We must do as follows:

1. Find a place to hide it—for example, the attic.
2. Take the informational linking note from the video game package and put it in the baseball glove package. (Why?)
3. Insert a new informational pointer in the video game package, indicating the attic as the location of the next node. (Why?)

The important aspect to note in this series of moves is that no gift had to be moved from its current hiding place to accommodate adding the new gift. From a conceptual perspective, this is the reason linked lists are able to avoid the movement of data associated with an insertion into an array.

Along the same lines, let us now suppose that our shameless parents devour all of their child's candy before the holiday arrives. Clearly they must remove this package from the chain to hide this disgusting behavior from their child. Convince yourself that the following steps will accomplish this deletion:

1. Remove the now empty candy package from the kitchen drawer.
2. Before throwing away the empty package, remove the linking note from it and put this note in the package containing the socks.
3. Dispose of the incriminating candy container and the linking note that originally was in the package with the socks.

It is important to note again that no package remaining on the chain had to be physically moved to a new location: a situation much different from what happened when we removed a name from an array-implemented list. A *formalization* of this intuitive notion of a linked list is the following: A *linked list* is a collection of nodes, each containing a data portion and a pointer. The data portion of each node is of the same type. The pointer in a given node contains the location of the node that logically follows the given node in the ordering of the list. The entire list is referenced by a separate head pointer to the first element in the linear ordering.

According to our definition of a linked list, a linked list with four nodes could be logically viewed as shown in Figure 3.9. The operations of inserting a node in and deleting a node from such a list may also be conveniently represented in such a schematic form. In fact, you will soon discover that the best way to conceive algorithms that manipulate linked lists is to draw what you want to happen via such logical pictures. Once you understand the concept from such a graphic representation, it is usually a straightforward matter to implement it.

For instance, we now wish to add a node containing GRAPE to the list shown in Figure 3.9; all we need to do is to store GRAPE in an available memory location outside the list, such as the one pointed to by **p** in Figure 3.10. We then reset the pointer link of the node containing GRAPE to point to the node containing

Figure 3.9
Linked list with four nodes.

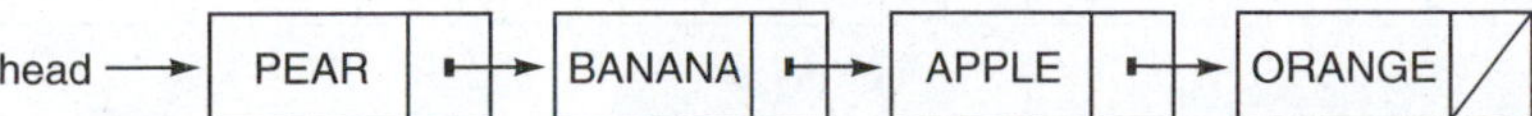

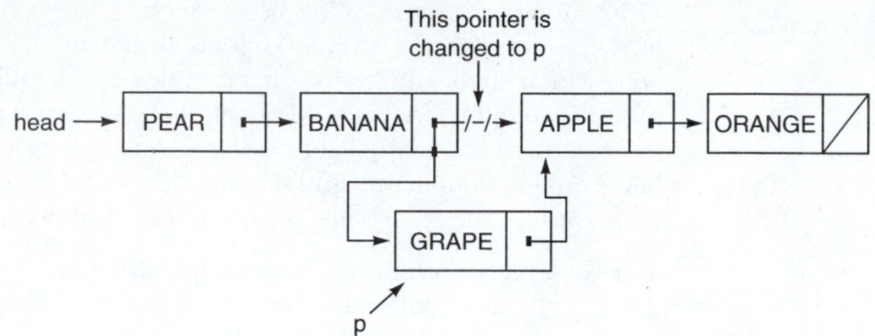

Figure 3.10
Insertion of node containing GRAPE into linked list of Figure 3.9. The pointer field of the new node has been set to the node referenced by the pointer of BANANA's node. The pointer of the node containing the data BANANA has been reset to point to the new node, containing the data GRAPE.

APPLE, and the pointer link of the node containing BANANA to point to the node containing GRAPE. Note that we did not physically move (that is, move to another storage area) any of the existing nodes.

Similarly, should you then wish to remove an existing node from the linked list, a graphic representation of the list can again indicate how the pointers should be altered to reflect such a change. For example, given the list of Figure 3.10, the diagram of Figure 3.11 pictorially outlines what must be done to delete the node containing BANANA. Notice in this figure that, as was the case for insertion, only pointers must be changed to delete a node. Again, no movement of data occurs.

To implement these schematics, we assume that our nodes will store data of the type **BaseData**, and we use the following structure:

```
template <class BaseData>
class ListNode
{
  public:
    BaseData listData;
    ListNode *link;
};
```

Suppose that we are given variables **p** and **q** declared by

```
    ListNode<BaseData> *p, *q;
```

and that we want to "aim" the link field in the node referenced by **p** to another node referenced by **q**, as indicated in Figure 3.12. The statement

Figure 3.11
Deletion of node containing BANANA from linked list of 3.10. The pointer of the node preceding that of BANANA has been reset to bypass BANANA's node, and instead to point to the node following BANANA's in the list. Had BANANA's node been last in the list, the pointer field of PEAR's node would have been given the special value NULL, here represented by the symbol /.

head → PEAR → BANANA → GRAPE → APPLE → ORANGE

This pointer
must be altered

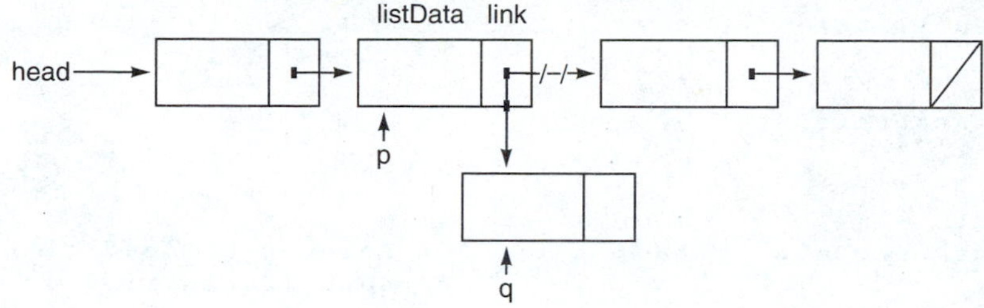

Figure 3.12
Aiming link field in node **p** at node **q**.

```
p->link = q;
```

will achieve this. Similarly, if we wish to advance **p** from one node to the next, the statement

```
p = p->link;
```

is required. This action is highlighted in Figure 3.13.

We are now prepared to write code for a linked-list implementation of the **insertBefore** and **remove** operations. For both of these operations, it is important to note the following two points:

1. A linked list **l** is initialized to the empty list by setting **l** to the **NULL** pointer value. This can be done in our **List** constructor operation.
2. Both the **insertBefore** and **remove** operations require a pointer to the node that precedes the node to be inserted or removed. As Figures 3.10 and 3.11 indicate, the link field in this preceding node must be altered. We agree to keep a protected pointer **previous**, which indicates the node immediately preceding the current node. The only exception to this occurs when the node being inserted or removed is located at the head of the list. We will signal this special case in our functions by having the pointer to the previous node set to **NULL**.

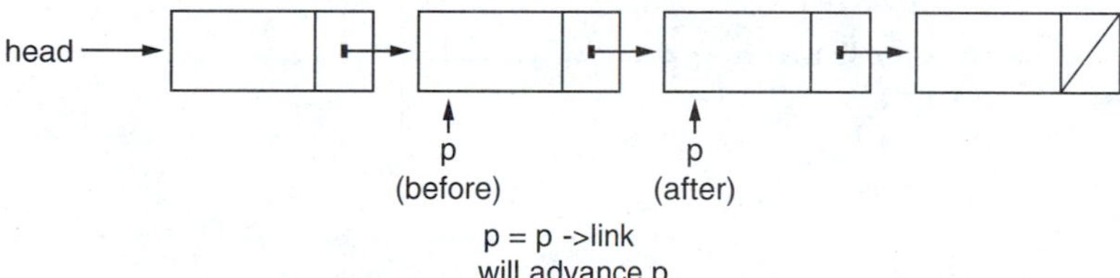

Figure 3.13
Advancing a pointer **p** through a linked list.

Example 3.6 Given the following portion of the interface of the List ADT and the implementation of its constructor:

```
// BaseData is either a C++ built-in type, or a C++ class that has
// an assignment operation that overloads the "=" operator.

template <class BaseData>
class ListNode
{
  public:
    BaseData listData;
```

```
    ListNode *link;
};

template<class BaseData>
class List
{
  protected:
    ListNode<BaseData> *head;          // Pointer to head of List; will be
                                       // NULL if the List is empty.
    ListNode<BaseData> *currentNode;   // Pointer to current node in List.
    ListNode<BaseData> *previous;      // Pointer to node immediately preceding
                                       // currentNode; will be Null if
                                       // currentNode points to the first node
                                       // in the List or if the List is empty.
    int numnodes;     // Gives the number of nodes currently in the List.
    int currentPos:   // Gives the position in the List of currentNode.
  public:
    .
    .
    .
    // Public interface remains as defined earlier
    .
    .
    .
};
```

We may now implement the **insertBefore** operation as follows:

```
template <class BaseData>
void List<BaseData>::insertBefore(const BaseData &item)
{
  ListNode<BaseData> *p;

  p = new ListNode<BaseData>;
  p->listData = item;
  if (currentPos <= 1)
  {
```

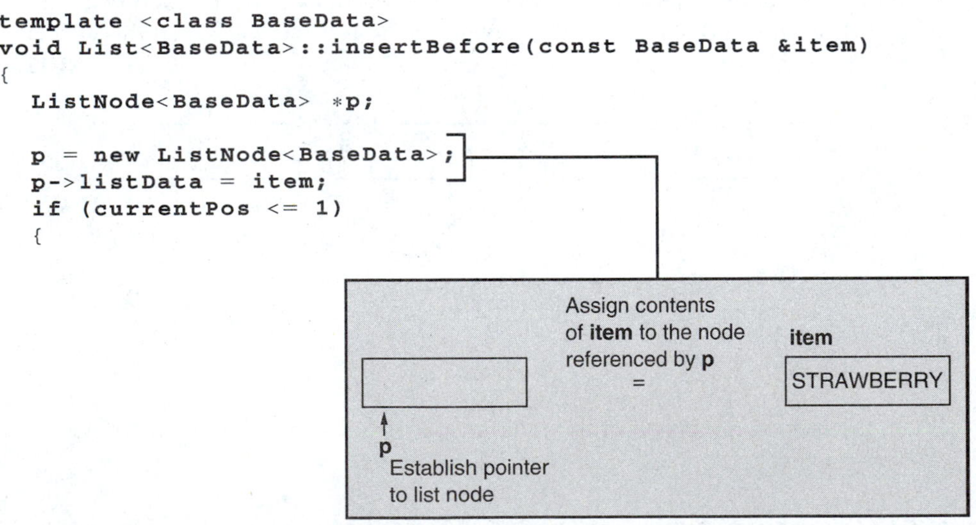

```
    head = p;
    currentPos = 1;
    if (numnodes == 0)
      p->link = NULL;
    else
      p->link = currentNode;
  }
  else
  {
    p->link = currentNode;
    previous->link = p;
  }
  ++numnodes;
  currentNode = p;
}
```

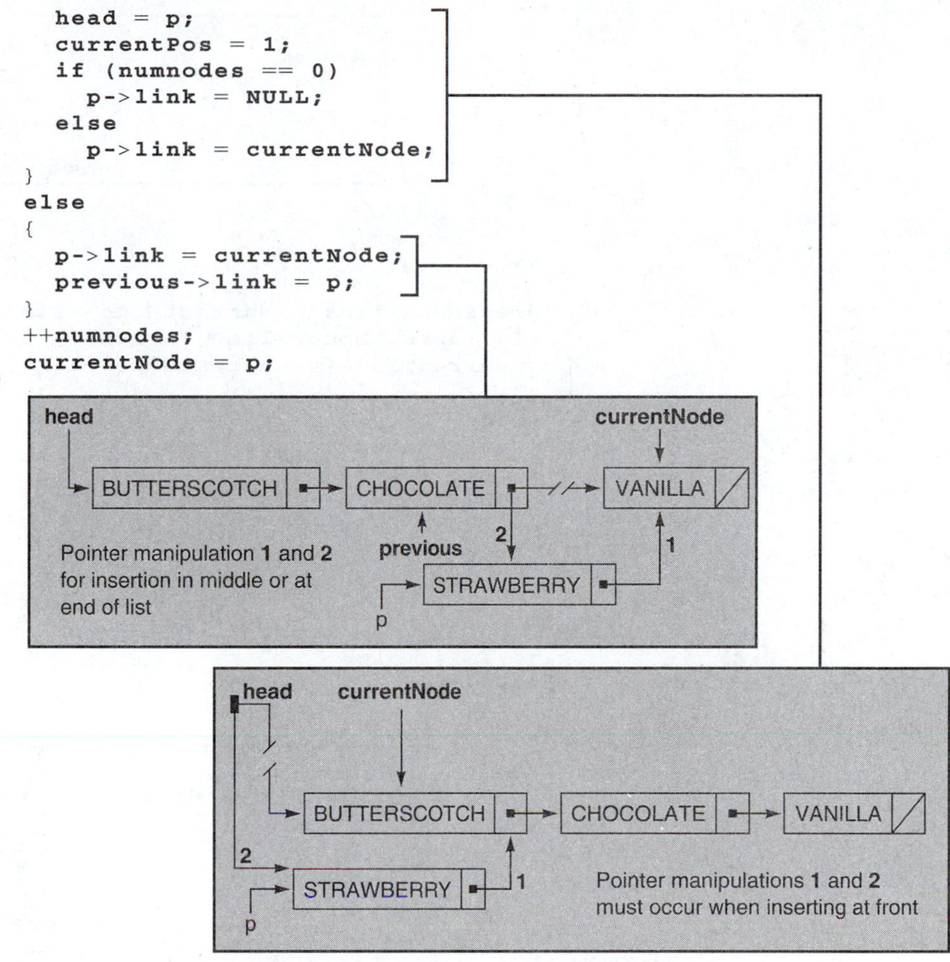

Example 3.7

Using the protected structures of Example 3.6 give a linked list implementation of the **remove** operation.

head

APPLE CRAY DEC IBM

currentNode

```
template <class BaseData>
void List<BaseData>::remove()
{
  ListNode<BaseData> *p, *temp;

  p = currentNode;
  if (currentPos == 1)
  {
    head = currentNode->link;
    currentNode = head;
  }
```

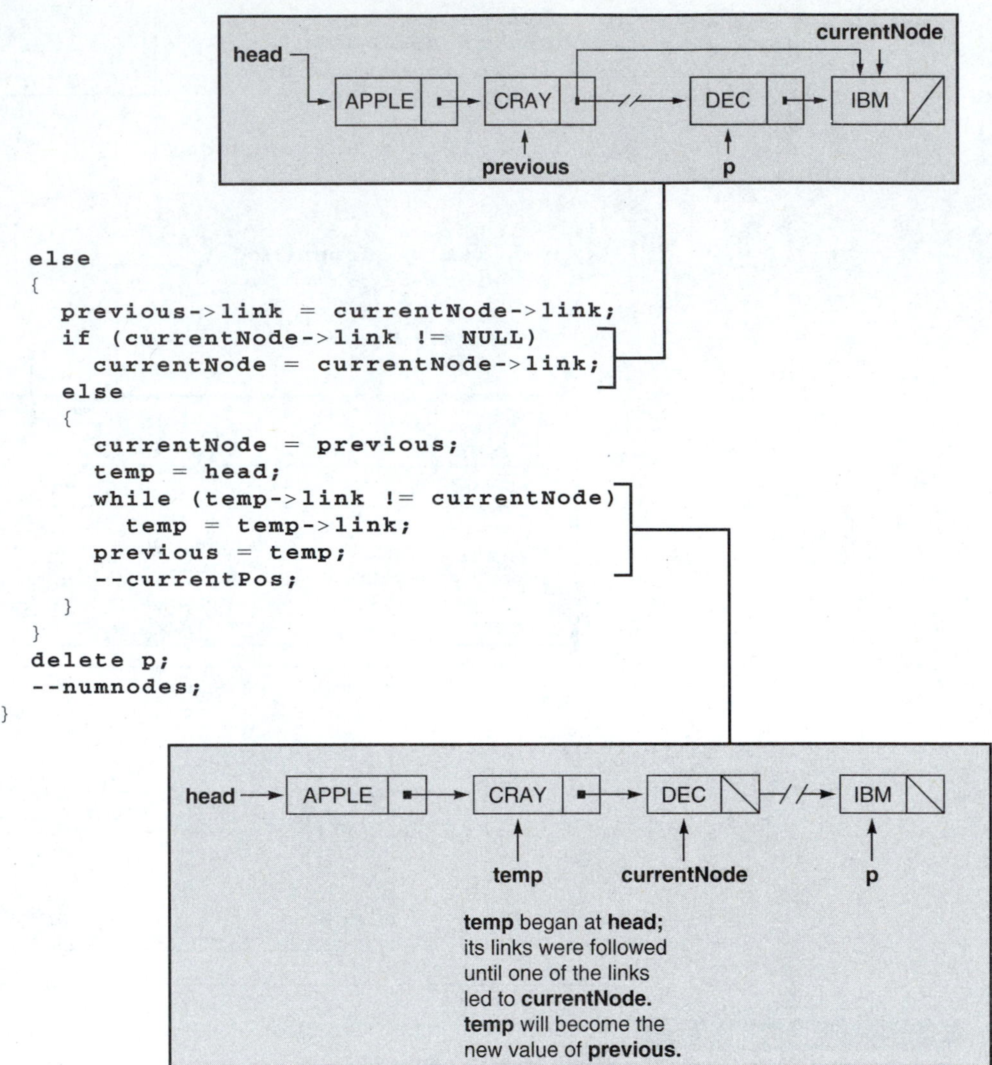


```
  else
  {
    previous->link = currentNode->link;
    if (currentNode->link != NULL)
      currentNode = currentNode->link;
    else
    {
      currentNode = previous;
      temp = head;
      while (temp->link != currentNode)
        temp = temp->link;
      previous = temp;
      --currentPos;
    }
  }
  delete p;
  --numnodes;
}
```

The details of linked-list implementations for the rest of the operations in the List ADT will be left for you to do in the exercises.

Comparison of Efficiencies for the Two Implementations

Considerations regarding the insertion and removal of nodes from a List might make a linked list an attractive alternative to an array implementation of the List ADT. Figures 3.10 and 3.11 indicate that insertions and removals merely require the exchange of two pointers, an $O(1)$ operation that requires the same amount of time to execute no matter how many nodes are in the List. Since pointers are merely locations of other nodes, this means that we are usually manipulating mere integers or similarly simple data in doing such pointer operations. Hence, for linked lists, both insertions and removals would appear to be $O(1)$ operations in terms of data movement.

This compares very favorably to the massive movement of data items forced by an insertion or removal on an array implementation of a List. On the other hand, in general, the **remove** operation will require $O(n)$ pointer comparisons to maintain a correct value for **previous**. This is an important observation because it tells us that the run-time efficiency of **remove**, while still constant in terms of data movement, will still not be $O(1)$ overall.

In general, in an array implementation, insertion and removal operations will be $O(n)$ in terms of data movement. Despite this substantive advantage in favor of linked lists, you should proceed cautiously and not be too quick to adopt the linked list as a cure-all for the ills involved with list-oriented systems. Your experience should make you suspicious that there must be a trade-off involved to get this superior efficiency for insertion and removal operations. The price we pay is giving up *easy random access* to the nodes via the **makeCurrent** operation. For example, to access the fourth node, instead of simply changing the value of **currentNode** to 4, we must follow the head pointer to the first node, the first node's pointer to the second, and so on, until we reach the fourth node.

Linked lists can be used to tremendous advantage when implementing lists that are highly volatile, that is, those that frequently undergo insertions and removals. If the number of these operations is sufficiently great in relation to the number of requests for retrieving and updating data in the nodes, then the linked implementation will probably pay off.

A RELEVANT ISSUE Storage of Disk Files and Computer Security

Operating systems typically grant their users disk storage in units called *blocks*. On the magnetic disk itself, a block is a contiguous area capable of storing a fixed amount of data. For example, a block in DEC's well-known VAX/VMS time-sharing system is 512 bytes. As a user enters data into a disk file, the system must grant additional blocks of storage as they are needed. In such a time-sharing environment, although each block represents physically contiguous storage area on the disk, it may not be possible for the operating system to give a user blocks that are physically next to each other. Instead, when a user needs an additional storage block, the operating system may put information into the current block about where the next block is located. In effect, a link is established from the current block to the next block. By the time a naive user has completed entering a four-block file, it may be scattered over the entire disk surface, as indicated in the following diagram.

Although this may seem like an ingenious way of extending files indefinitely, one pays in several ways for such scattered blocks. Namely, the read-write head that seeks and puts data on the disk surface is forced to move greater distances, thereby slowing system performance. To combat such inefficiencies, shrewd users can often take advantage of options that allow them to preallocate the contiguous disk storage that will be required for a file. Also, blocks may be released to users in clusters of contiguous blocks—similar to the way in which we describe, in Section 3.4, clusters of characters for a linked list representation of strings. In the event that file access remains sluggish in spite of such measures, systems managers may occasionally shut down the entire system to rebuild disks, a process that entails copying all files that are presently scattered over the disk onto a new disk in physically contiguous form.

Yet another more serious price that may be paid for storing disk files in this fashion revolves around the issue of data security and what the operating system does with blocks that are no longer needed by a user. Disk blocks used to store a file are returned to some type of available block list when a user deletes that file from his or her directory. When these blocks are returned to that available space list, the data in them may remain intact until another user's request to extend a file results in the block being reallocated to that new user. This means that, if clever users ("hackers") know

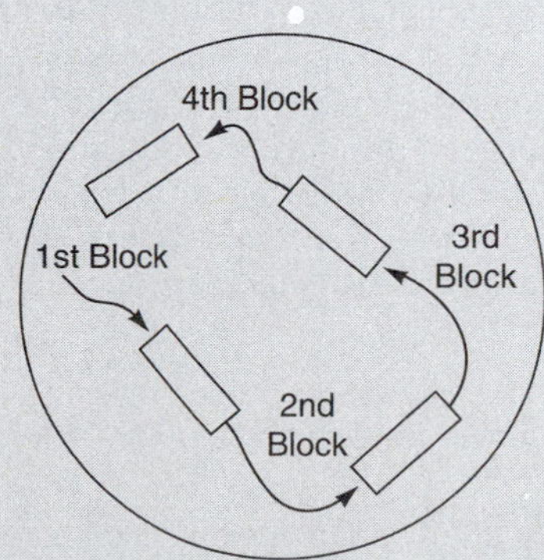

how to access the available space list, they may be able to scavenge through data that other users once owned and then released (assuming it was not destroyed on being released).

One of the authors was actually involved in an incident in which a clever student was able to "find" old versions of a test that a professor had typed in on the computer and then discarded to this available block list. Needless to say, the professor whose tests were being explored by the student was somewhat alarmed on discovering what had happened. As a protection against this type of scavenging, many operating systems will, by default or as an option, actually destroy data returned to the available block list.

Exercises 3.2

1. The definition of the List ADT in Section 3.1 involves 16 operations: constructor, copy constructor, destroy, **assign (=), first, last, makeCurrent, prev, next, examine, current, count, insertBefore, insertAfter, remove,** and **replace**. For the array implementation of this ADT, only the constructor and **insertBefore** operations were actually implemented in C++. Provide C++ code implementations for the other 14 operations.

2. For each of the List operations you implemented in Exercise 3.2.1, give a big-O analysis of its run-time efficiency.

3. a. In Exercise 3.1.1, you were asked to define an ordered list ADT. Implement this ADT using the Array ADT of Chapter 2. You should also give a big-O analysis of the run-time efficiency of each of the operations you implemented.

b. In Exercise 3.1.5, we described a data-oriented (unordered) list and suggested including in its specification a **makeCurrent** operation that, starting after the first node from the current node, identifies as the current node the first node that satisfies a functional parameter **condition**. If you have not already done so in Exercise 3.1.1 and part (a) of this exercise, incorporate such an operation into your definition of the ordered list ADT, implement it using arrays, and give a big-O analysis of its run-time behavior.

c. A special case of the **makeCurrent** operation described in part (b) is that where the functional parameter **condition** is true when there is a match between the values of its parameters. In this case, it would appear to be better to define a separate operation **search** and employ a binary search algorithm to improve the efficiency of this operation. However, **search** and **makeCurrent** with such a match function for its **condition** parameter will sometimes differ as to the node they select to make the current node. Why?

d. Implement the **search** function described in part (c) for an Array implementation of the data-oriented list ADT.

4. Repeat Exercise 3.2.1 for a linked-list implementation of a List.

5. For each of the List operations you implemented in Exercise 3.2.4, give a big-O analysis of its run-time efficiency.

6. Repeat Exercise 3.2.3, but use a linked-list implementation for the ordered list ADT. Again, you should also provide a big-O analysis of the run-time efficiency of each of the operations you implemented.

7. Consider the linked list pictured next. What would be the output of the following loop?

```
p = head;
while (p->link != NULL)
{
   cout << p->listData;
   p = p->link;
}
```

head → Broccoli → Corn → Lima Beans → Peas → Spinach /

8. For a linked-list implementation of the **assign** (overloaded =) operation, consider the following strategy: Merely assign the head pointer for the **source** List to the head pointer of the object owning the operation. Is this a foolproof, $O(1)$ method for achieving this end? If not, explain why. (*Hint*: Consider the consequences of a **replace** operation following such an assignment.)

9. Summarize the advantages and disadvantages of a linked-list implementation of a List compared to an array implementation.

10. a. As part of the definition of a List ADT, implement in C++ a **reverse** operation for the List, assuming a linked-list implementation. Give a big-O analysis of its run-time behavior.

b. In Exercise 3.1.8, you also had to implement a **reverse** operation, but at that time you had to work only with the operations specified for the List ADT defined earlier in the section. Using your results from Exercise 3.2.5, give a big-O analysis of the run-time efficiency of that implementation. Suppose you subsequently learned that a linked-list implementation was used. How does this compare with your analysis in part (a) of this exercise?

3.3 Variations on Linked-List Structures

Linked lists provide a tremendously useful tool in situations where a highly volatile list must be maintained in some prescribed logical order. Their widespread use has led to the development of several "tricks of the trade" suitable in certain applications. These are ways of fine-tuning the basic linked-list structure to meet the needs of particular situations. Four such variations on the linked list are presented in this section: dummy headers, circular lists, doubly linked lists, and multilinked lists.

Dummy Headers

Adding a *dummy header* node in the list before the first actual data node can offer a distinct advantage over not using one. If the list becomes empty and a dummy header node is not used, then the **head** pointer for the list must be set to **NULL**. If the dummy header node is present, however, then the **head** pointer never needs to be changed to **NULL** because it always points to this dummy header. That is, the empty list is only empty in a logical sense. Physically, it still contains the dummy header. Figure 3.14 illustrates this concept. This convention can serve to simplify the coding involved in functions **insertBefore**, **insertAfter**, and **remove** by eliminating the special handling previously required for insertions and removals at the beginning of the list. (You will write these simplified functions as an exercise at the end of this section.) This convenience factor alone provides substantial practical motivation for always using dummy headers. Moreover, in real-world applications, you will find that you can almost always use the extra data space in the dummy header to store some valuable items of information.

Linked Circular Lists

Although linked lists are satisfactory in many instances, the presence of a **NULL** value at the end of the list makes this structure most efficient only if the entire list is to be processed. The efficiency of such list-processing algorithms decreases when the linked list is to be processed beginning at an arbitrary point in the list. In such situations, it would be desirable to be able to enter the list anywhere and process it efficiently independent of the entry point. In other words, we need a linked list that has no beginning or end.

Linked circular lists are precisely such data structures. A *singly linked circular list* is a linked list in which the last node of the list points to the first node in the list. Notice that in circular list structures there are no **NULL** values. Figure 3.15 depicts a singly linked circular list.

As an example of the utility of such a circular list in the area of operating systems, suppose the nodes in Figure 3.15 represent current users on a time-sharing

Figure 3.14
Linked list with dummy header. By using a dummy header, the pointer **head** never needs to be changed to NULL, even if the list becomes empty.

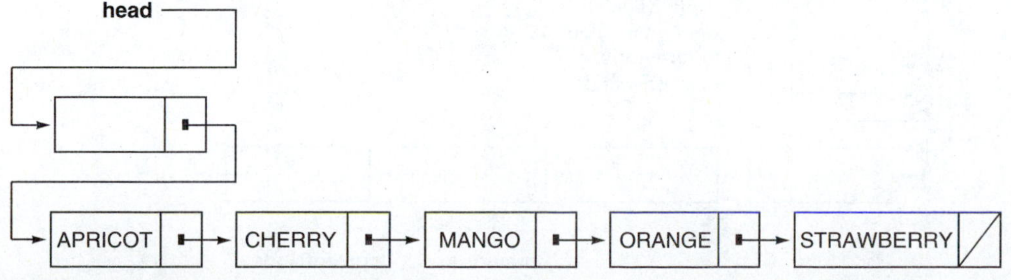

Figure 3.15
Singly linked circular list with dummy header.

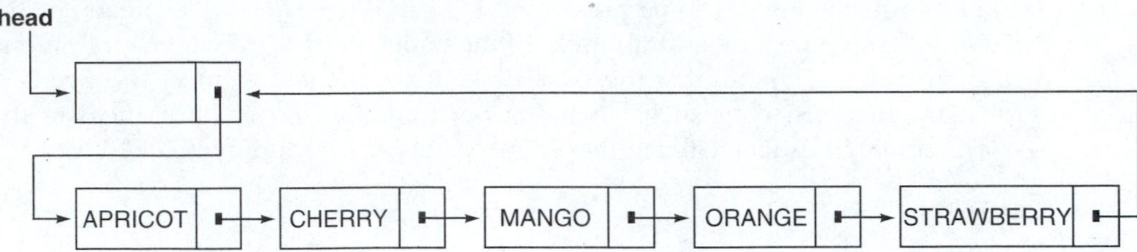

computer. In such an environment, the operating system schedules each user for a small time slice on the central processing unit (CPU) and then proceeds to devote its momentary attention to the next user. When the final user has completed her time slice, ownership of the CPU must again revert to the first user, and the scheduling cycle starts again. Because of the speed of the CPU, this cyclic scheduling creates the illusion for each user that the computer is dedicated to her particular process. Clearly, a circular linked list is made to order for this type of scheduling. The circularity ensures that no unnecessary interruptions occur when restarting the scheduling cycle as the end of the user list is reached. The linked nature of the structure enables the operating system to process quickly new users who log on and users who complete their work and log off.

Doubly Linked Circular Lists

In the previously developed operation **remove** (as well as the **prev** operation), we note that, when implemented using a singly linked list, to update properly the value of the protected variable **previous** we must search the list for the node immediately preceding the one referenced by **currentNode**—an inefficient algorithm in that the list must be searched sequentially. This is illustrated in Figure 3.16. A satisfactory way of getting around this inefficiency is to use a *doubly linked circular list*, in which each node has two pointers: a forward link and a backward link. The forward link is a pointer to the next node in the list; the backward link points to the preceding node. The circular nature of the list, along with a special dummy header node, can be used to avoid special conditional checking when adding to or deleting from the beginning or end of the list.

Figure 3.17 illustrates a doubly linked circular list. This list has five nodes (plus a dummy header), each having a forward link (**flink**) and a backward link (**blink**). The pointer **flink** points to the successor node, whereas **blink** points to the predecessor node. Because the list is circular, **blink** of the header node must point

Figure 3.16
In a singly linked list, removing node A or executing the **prev** operation requires updating the **previous** pointer. This requires a time-consuming, sequential search.

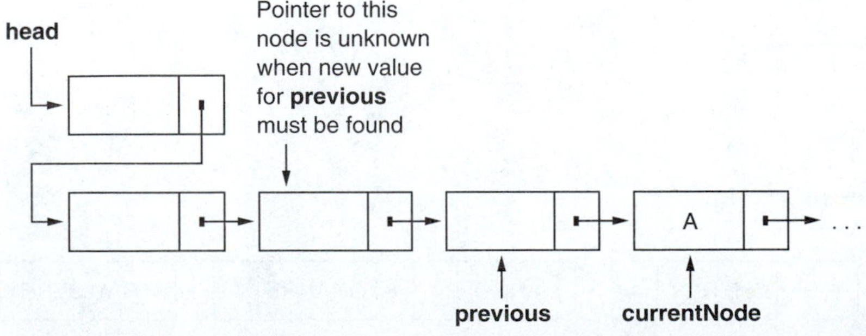

Figure 3.17
Doubly linked circular list. Removing a node is faster than for singly linked lists because we do not need to search sequentially from **head** to find the preceding node.

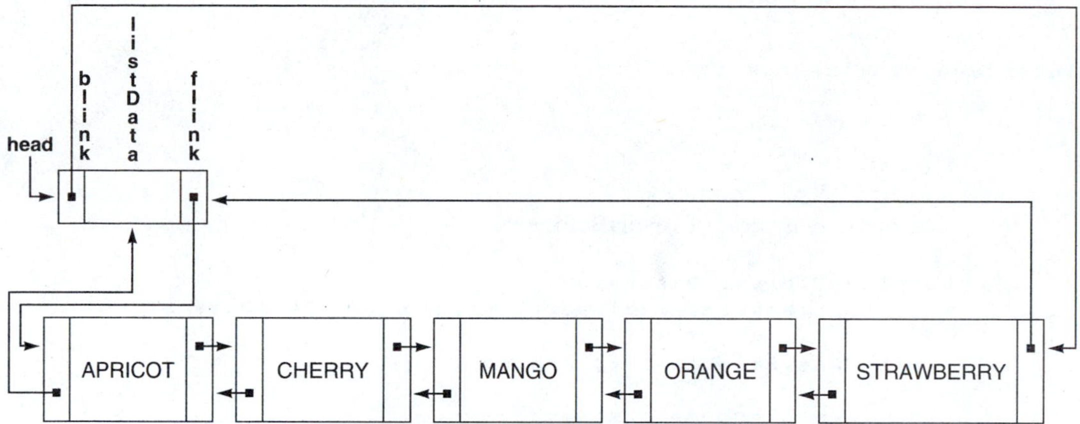

to the last node, and **flink** of the last node must point to the header node. Inserting a node into a doubly linked list, or removing one from it, is potentially a much easier task because we do not need a separate pointer to a preceding node. Hence, by using a doubly linked circular list we may dispense with the protected variable **previous**, and thereby be able to avoid the time inefficiency inherent in updating its value as we had to do in implementing the **remove** operation on a singly linked list. In an empty list represented by a doubly linked circular list, **currentNode** refers to the header node.

The following implementation of **insertBefore** inserts a node, pointed to by **p** into a doubly linked circular list with a dummy header. The node is inserted just before the node pointed to by **currentNode**. Here we assume the following data structures were defined in a List definition file **list.h**.

```
// BaseData is either a C++ built-in type, or a C++ class that has
// an assignment operation that overloads the "=" operator.

template <class BaseData>
class ListNode
{
  public:
    BaseData listData;
    ListNode *flink;
    ListNode *blink;
};

template <class BaseData>
class List
{
  protected:
    ListNode<BaseData> *head;          // Pointer to head of list; forward
                                       // and backward links will point to
                                       // itself if the list is empty.
    ListNode<BaseData> *currentNode;   // Pointer to current node in list;
                                       // will point to head if the list
                                       // is empty.
    int numnodes;                      // Gives the number of nodes currently
                                       // in the list.
```

```
    int currentPos;                    // Gives the position of the node presently
                                       // identified as the current node.
  public:
    .
    .
    .
    // public interface remains the same
    .
    .
    .
};
```

The implementation of **insertBefore** can now be done as follows:

```
template <class BaseData>
void List<BaseData>::insertBefore(const BaseData &item)
{
  ListNode<BaseData> *p, *prev;

  p = new ListNode<BaseData>;
  p->listData = item;
  prev = currentNode->blink;
  p->flink = currentNode;
  p->blink = prev;
  prev->flink = p;
  currentNode->blink = p
  if (currentPos == 0)
    currentPos = 1;
  ++numnodes;
  currentNode = p;
}
```

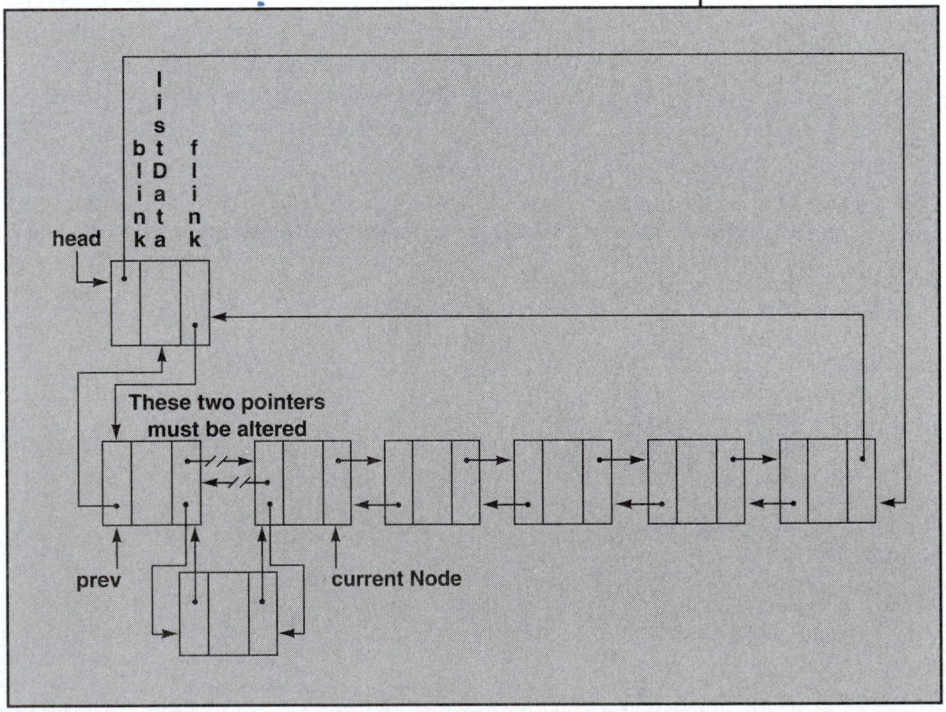

Note that this implementation of **insertBefore** illustrates how streamlined the insert operations become when a dummy header is used. In particular, because the empty List appears as follows:

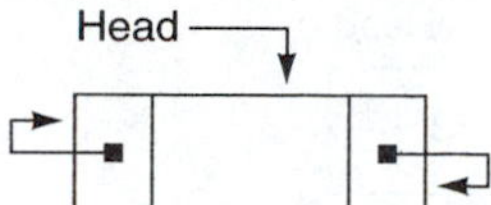

the implementation can proceed without any awkward checking of whether the List is empty or whether the insertion is being made at the front of the List. Clearly a dummy header simplifies the implementation in this situation.

The following code implements the **remove** operation for the List ADT:

```
template <class BaseData>
void List<BaseData>::remove()
{
  ListNode<BaseData> *save, *p;

  p = currentNode;
  save = currentNode->blink;
  save->flink = currentNode->flink;
  save = currentNode->flink;
  save->blink = currentNode->blink;

  if (currentPos == numnodes)          // Is currentNode the last node?
  {
    currentNode = currentNode->blink;  // If so, its predecessor is
    --currentPos;                      // the new current node.
  }
  else
    currentNode = currentNode->flink;  // Otherwise its successor is
                                       // the new current node.
  delete p;
  --numnodes;
  }
```

Multilinked Lists

We end this discussion of variations on the linked-list theme by noting that a doubly linked list is a special case of a structure known as a *multilinked list.* Because each link field determines an order in which the nodes of a list are to be processed, we can in fact establish a different link field for every different order in which we wish to process the nodes in a list. Figure 3.18 illustrates such a multilinked list. By following the IDLink fields, we traverse the list in IDNumber order; by following the NameLink fields, we traverse the list in alphabetical order by Name.

Exercises 3.3

1. What coding advantage does a dummy header node provide in linked lists?
2. What main convenience does a doubly linked list offer in comparison with a singly linked list as a means for implementing the List ADT?
3. Assuming a linked-list implementation in which a dummy header is used, write a complete C++ implementation of the List ADT defined in Section 3.1.
4. Repeat Exercise 3.3.3 assuming the implementation is a doubly linked circular list.

Figure 3.18
Link fields for processing nodes. By following the IDLink pointers, we traverse the list in IDNumber order; by following the NameLink pointers, we traverse the list in alphabetical order by Name.

IDHead: 4

nameHead: 3

	Name	IDNumber	NameLink	IDLink
1	PEMBROOK	8316	4	**NULL**
2	DOUGLAS	4212	5	5
3	ATWATER	6490	2	1
4	WITHERS	1330	**NULL**	2
5	LAYTON	5560	1	3

Multilinked List

3.4 Application: Strings

In Section 2.3 we introduced the String ADT and examined two implementations of it: the fixed-length implementation and, in the programming problems, the workspace-index implementation (see Programming Problem 7 in Chapter 2). Both of these implementations allow highly efficient versions of the string search operation. Moreover, the workspace-index method gracefully solves the problem of having to declare a maximum possible string length and then wasting memory when strings are shorter than that length. However, neither of these methods adequately solves the problem of having to move a tremendous amount of data when insertions and removals occur on a larger scale. This is similar to the situation we saw in Section 3.2 when we implemented the List ADT with an array. We now show how the String ADT can be implemented as a derived class of the List ADT. While the overall efficiency of the string operations will then be tied to those of the underlying List operations, from our discussion in Sections 3.2 and 3.3 we know that there are various linked-list representations that handle insertions and removals more effectively than an Array representation. We reexamine the efficiency of the String operations in this light. Of course, as we have now come to expect in this world of trade-offs, we will see that this approach is not without its own set of problems.

Let us view each String as a special type of List as defined in Section 3.1. Figure 3.19 represents each of the three strings "COFFEE", "TEA", and "CREAM", by a doubly linked circular list with a dummy header. Not shown are variables **currentLength**, one for each string, to keep track of the length of the string stored in the list.

Although the **String (int maxLength)** constructor allows one to allocate storage for a String up to length **maxLength**, since insertions into a doubly linked List implementation of a List are more efficient than insertions into an array implementation (for which **maxLength** was introduced), we ignore this potentially wasteful preallocation of nodes and simply create an empty String. Thus, when represented by a doubly linked list, the List contains the same number of nodes as there are characters in the String.

Let us consider how the String operations we have specified would be performed in such an implementation. The assignment of one String to another could be achieved in very slick and efficient (though perhaps somewhat deceptive) fashion. That is, instead of physically creating two identical Strings, we can simply have two separate pointers referencing the same String. This particular strategy does have some potential repercussions that might have to be avoided in certain applications (as we will see in the exercises at the end of this section). String searching, as defined in the ADT operations, presents no real problem other than a potential reduction in efficiency. This is examined in an exercise at the end of the chapter.

Figure 3.19
Representation of the strings "COFFEE", "TEA", and "CREAM", each in a circular doubly linked list. The encapsulating class for each string has a **currentLength** field storing the length of the string to which it points. Using a linked structure allows insertions and removals to be made in the strings without moving large amounts of data.

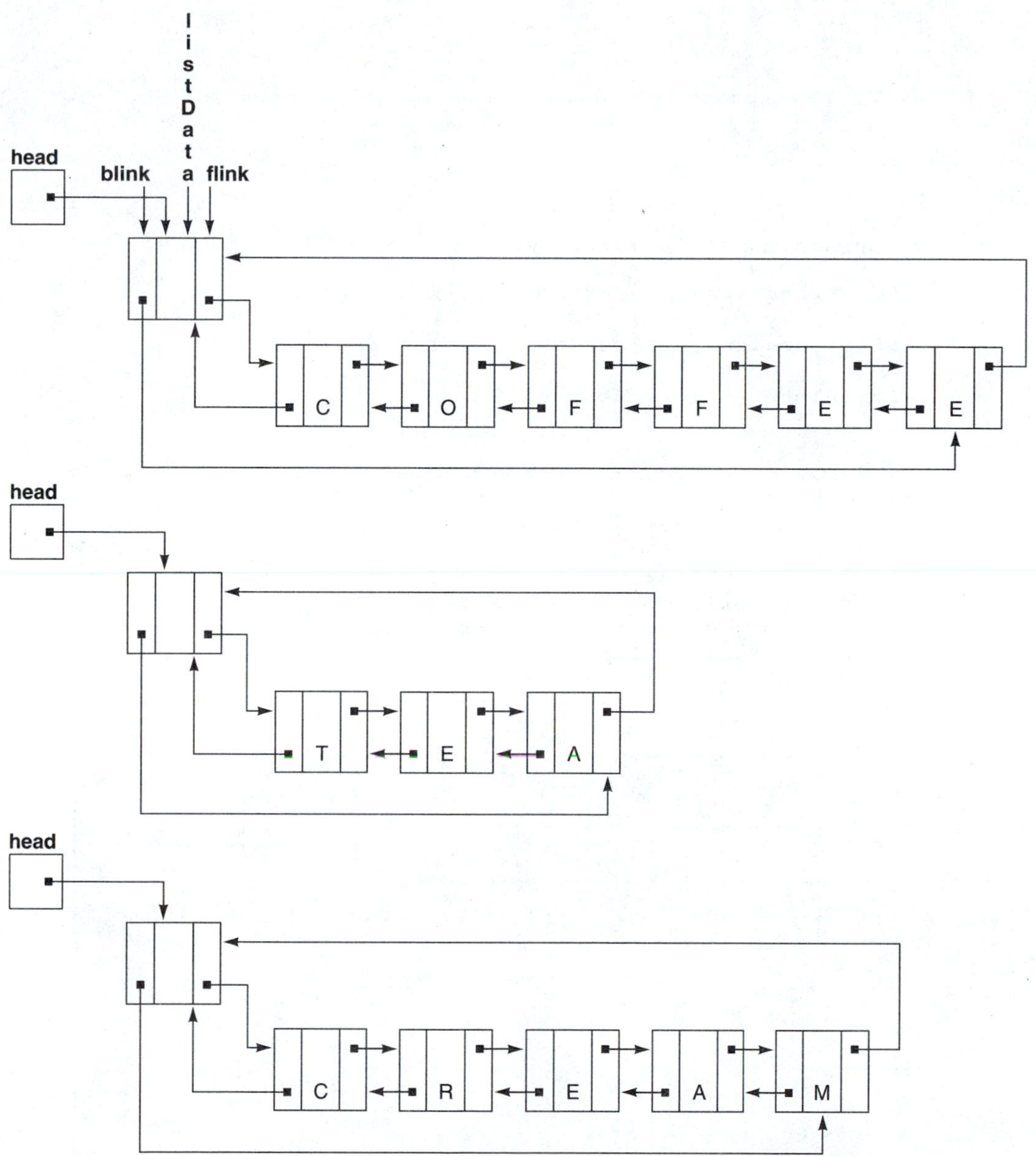

Substring operations do present a problem and are discussed in detail later in this section. Insertion, removal, and concatenation (which may be viewed as a special case of insertion) can be handled elegantly using lists and can be efficient if the lists are implemented by a doubly linked structure.

Example 3.8

The following protected structure, derived from the class **list**, can be used for a List implementation of the **String** class. Here we assume the **List** class is implemented as a doubly linked list.

```
class String: private List<char>
{
  protected:
    int currentLength;             // Stores length of string

  public:
      .
      .
      .
     // Rest of string definition as in Section 2.3
      .
      .
      .
};
```

We can implement the **insert** operation for the String ADT as follows:

```
void String::insert (String &t, int place)
{
  ListNode<char> *firstInT, *lastInT;

  if (place <= currentLength)
  {
    t.first();
    firstInT = t.currentNode;
    t.last();
    lastInT = t.currentNode;
    makeCurrent(place);
    firstInT->blink = currentNode->blink;
    lastInT->flink = currentNode;
    (currentNode->blink)->flink = firstInT;
    currentNode->blink = lastInT;
    currentLength += t.currentLength;
  }
}
```

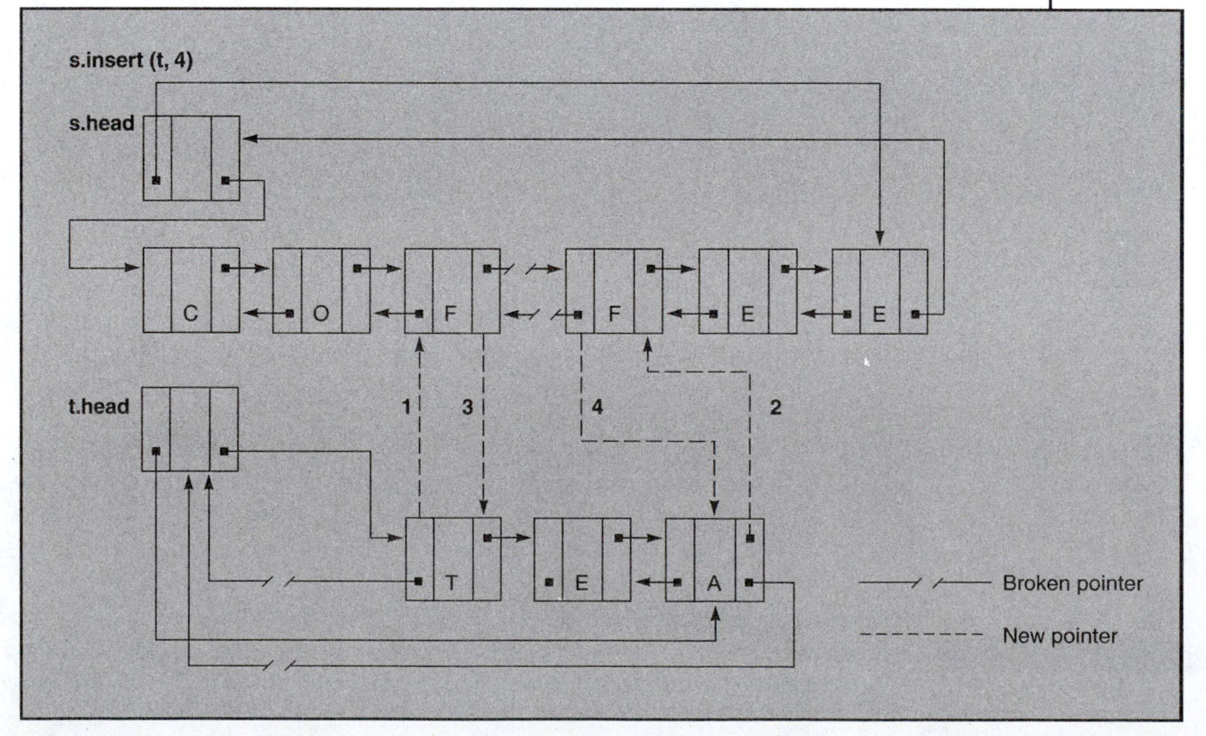

Note that this implementation is doing a slightly more complicated task than our previous insertion algorithm for a linked list. Earlier, we were concerned only with inserting one node. As the graphic documentation in the preceding code fragment indicates, here we are inserting an entire collection of nodes; we are inserting one linked list within another. This is done with relative ease because our implementation of a doubly linked list gives us convenient pointers to both the first and last nodes in the list. Hence, our linked-list implementation of Strings has provided a rather neat illustration of the utility of double linking. Note also that because our algorithm changed some of the pointer fields in the String **t** it was necessary to change the interface for **insert** from that given in the definition in Section 2.3 by dropping the **const** qualifier for the parameter **t**.

Efficiency Considerations for the Linked-List Method

In this string-handling application, we have seen that the linked-list method allows dynamic string allocation with no practical limit on string length. In addition, because insertion and removal operations for doubly linked lists are extrememly efficient, we are able to expand this efficiency to cover operations involving insertions into or removals from a string. However, the linked-list method is not a cure-all, for use in all applications.

Three general problem areas exist. First, you may have already noticed that, although the **insert** operation in Example 3.8 achieves a very efficient insertion, it renders the String **t** thereafter inaccessible as a separate entity. This happens because the pointers within **t** had to be altered to chain it into the String object that owns the **insert** operation. (See the graphic documentation for Example 3.8.)

Second, consider an application in which operating with subtrings is of more importance than insertion and removal. With both the fixed-length and workspace-index table methods, the substring consisting of the *j*th through the *k*th characters could be directly accessed because the characters within any given string are physically next to each other. Accessing the same substring via the linked-list implementation requires beginning at the initial character in the string and traversing the entire string until the *j*th character is reached. Our implementation of a string as a doubly linked list allows this process to be somewhat more efficient. In particular, the length of the string from which we want to extract a substring could be checked to determine if the substring occurs in the front or back half. If in the back half, the pointer to the last character in the string could be used to begin a traversal from the rear of the list that stops when we reach the desired substring. However, this would still require sequential processing of the list until the desired substring is found. Hence, for substring operations, the linked-list method does not stack up to either of the other two methods.

A third problem arises in the efficiency of memory utilization for the linked-list method as we have described it. If the data portion of a node in the linked list contains only one character, then the two pointers associated with that node could require four to eight times more memory than the data. That is, only 11% to 20% of memory is being utilized to store the data in which we are really interested; the rest of the memory is storing data about data.

This memory utilization problem may be alleviated by making the data portion of a node a cluster of characters. Suppose, for instance, we choose a cluster size of four characters. Then the same strings given in Figure 3.19 would appear as shown

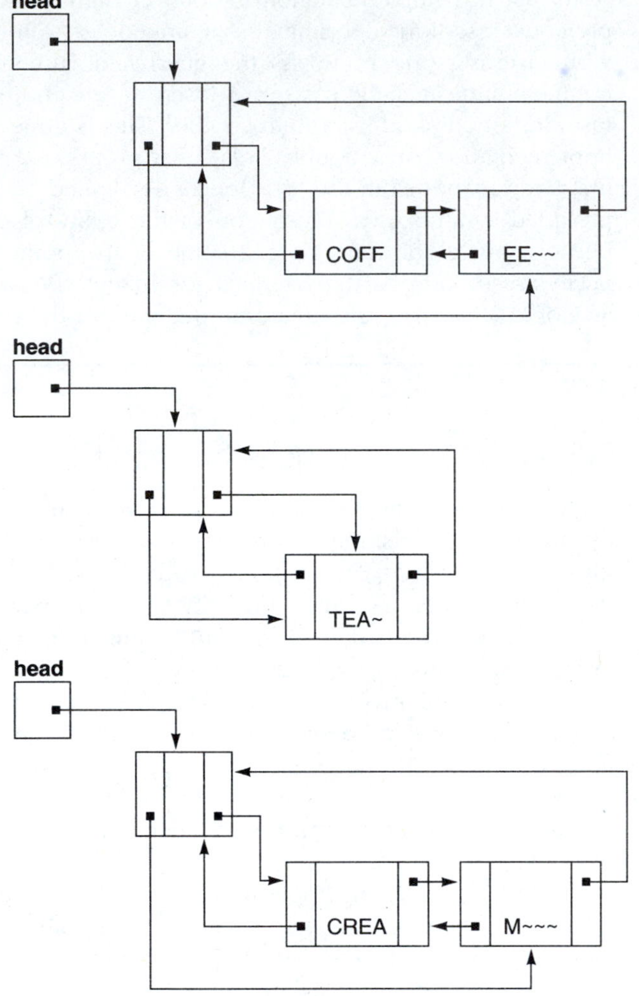

Figure 3.20
Strings from Figure 3.19 with a cluster size of four. By storing a cluster of characters in each node, the amount of memory used can be decreased because fewer pointers have to be used.

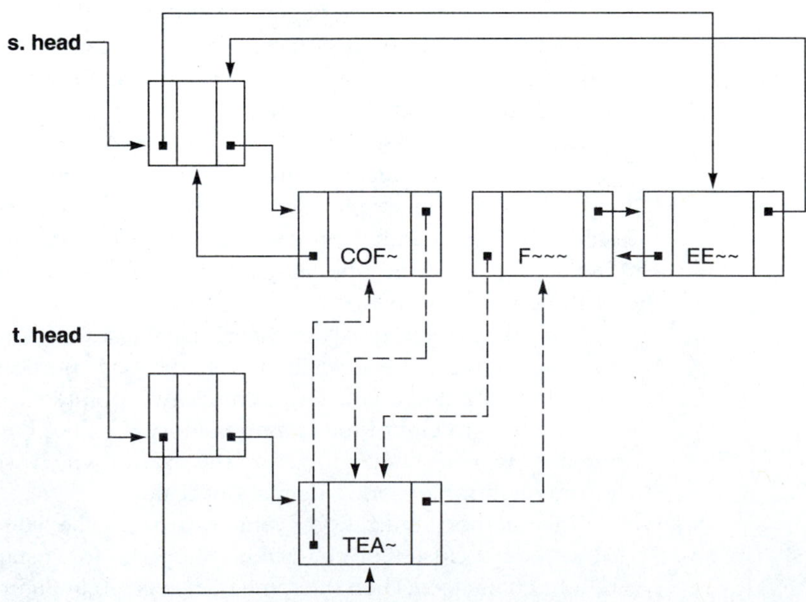

Figure 3.21
Insertion of string **t** into **s** beginning at position 4. The node containing the characters COFF from COFFEE's representation in Figure 3.20 had to be split into two nodes—"COFF~" and "F~~~"— to achieve the insertion.

in Figure 3.20. Here we have used the symbol ~ to represent a null character, one that is always ignored when the string is processed.

Notice that, although this technique has enabled us to devote a greater percentage of memory for storage of data, a significant complication has been added: Our code must now always account for null characters. For example, if we wish to insert the second string from Figure 3.20 in the first string beginning at position 4, the scheme pictured in Figure 3.21 emerges. Here the node containing "COFF" had to be split into the two nodes "COF~" and "F~~~" in order to achieve an effective insertion. As you might expect, we had to trade off one feature for another. To gain more effective memory utilization, we had to make our program code more cumbersome and less efficient in its execution time.

Exercises 3.4

1. Example 3.8 provides C++ code for the String ADT **insert** operation using a doubly linked list implementation of the String ADT. Complete the package of String operations for this implementation. That is, provide C++ versions for each of the other operations in the String ADT definition appearing in Section 2.3.

2. Use big-O notation to analyze the time efficiency of each of the operations you implemented in Exercise 3.4.1. In your analysis, include both the number of comparisons and the number of character interchanges.

3. Discuss some of the potential unsuspected results that might occur if the string assignment strategy discussed in this section were actually used. In particular, consider what might happen in the following situation:

```
string1 = "COFFEE";
string2 = string1;
string1 = "TEA";
string2.writeString();
```

4. Two techniques of storing strings are the workspace-index method (see Programming Problem 7 in Chapter 2) and the doubly linked list (with dummy header) of character clusters. With these techniques in mind, provide answers to the following:

a. For each method, develop a formula that expresses the percentage of memory devoted to storing overhead data (as opposed to actual character data). Each of these formulas should be expressed as a function of the following general parameters:

P–the number of bytes to store a pointer/integer
S–the number of bytes to store one character (usually S = 1)
C–the cluster size
A–the average string length in your application

For each formula you develop, explain how you derived it.

b. Your answer to part (a) should indicate that the workspace-index method is generally more space efficient than the doubly linked list. However, suppose your application calls for frequently inserting one string in another. For this application, the doubly linked list method is more time efficient. Explain why. If it will help, include diagrams in your explanation. Your explanation should also make it evident why a doubly linked list with a dummy header is a more effective structure for this type of application than a singly linked list.

5. Refine the C++ code of Example 3.8 to remedy the side effect that string **t** is rendered useless after invoking **insert.** What is the cost in efficiency of your remedy?

6. In Section 2.3, two sophisticated string search algorithms were discussed: the Knuth-Morris-Pratt algorithm and the Boyer-Moore algorithm (see Exercise 2.3.12). Which of these algorithms is more readily adaptable to a doubly linked list implementation of the String ADT? Explain why. Then provide C++ code for this algorithm adapted to the doubly linked list implementation. Finally, discuss whether the algorithm remains as efficient for the doubly linked list implementation as it was for the array-based implementation of strings.

3.5 Application: Sets

Just as we have in the preceding two sections, we again return to Chapter 2 for a final application of linked ists. In Section 2.4 we introduced the Set ADT and discussed an implementation of it that used Boolean arrays. We remarked that a

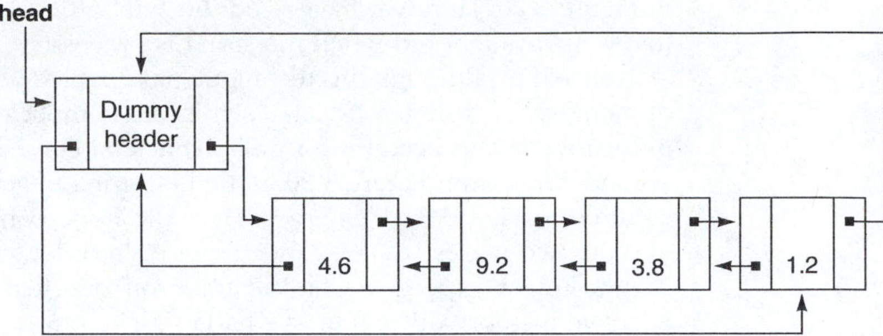

Figure 3.22 Set of floats {4.6, 9.2, 3.8, 1.2} and a corresponding (doubly) linked list implementation.

shortcoming of the Boolean array implementation is that it is limited to sets drawn from a universe that is a finite subrange of some ordinal data type. We now develop an alternative implementation for sets that removes this shortcoming by using a linked list.

Linked-List Implementation of Sets

In this implementation, a set is represented simply as a list of its elements in arbitrary order. This is illustrated in Figure 3.22, where a doubly linked implementation of the list using a dummy header is pictured. For space efficiency we insist that no element appear more than once in such a list. This requires the data type of the elements of the sets to admit an equality test that overloads the "= =" operator. By using a list to represent the elements rather than a Boolean array indexed by the elements, we no longer need the restriction that the universe for the set be a subrange between values **loElement** and **hiElement.** In fact, with a list representation we could have a set of arrays, or even a set of sets. This latter type of set will prove extremely useful when we reexamine the union-find problem at the end of this section.

As we did with our implementation of the String ADT in Section 3.4, we also assume here that the Set ADT is derived from the List ADT, under the assumption that the List ADT was implemented as a doubly linked list with dummy header.

Example 3.9

Implement the **union** (overloaded as ||) operation for the doubly linked list representation of Sets of elements of type **Universe.** We assume that the class **Set<Universe>** has been derived from the **List** class and that **Universe** has an assignment operator that overloads the "=" operator (this is required by the list operation **replace**) and an equality test that overloads the "= =" operator. We also assume that the **elementOf** (overloaded as [ ]), **add,** and **assign** (overloaded as =) operations described in Section 2.4 have already been implemented.

```
// Universe is a class that has an assignment operator that
// overloads the "="operator and an equality test operator that
// overloads the "==" operator.
template <class Universe>
Set<Universe> Set<Universe>::operator || (const Set<Universe> &t)
{
  Set<Universe> temp;
  Universe element;
  int origpos, k;

  // First add to temp the elements in the Set that owns the union operation
```

```
    origpos = current();
    first();
    for (int k = 1; k <= numnodes, ++k)
    {
      element = examine();
      temp.add(element);
      next();
    }
    makeCurrent(origpos);
    // Then add to temp those elements in t that are not also in
    // the Set that owns the operation
    origpos = t.current();
    t.first();
    for (int k = 1; k <= t.numnodes, ++k)
    {
      element = t.examine();
      if (!(*this)[element])
        temp.add(element);
      t.next();
    }
    t.makeCurrent(origpos);
    return(temp);
}
```

Efficiency Considerations for the Linked List Implementation

Specific coding for additional Set operations is left for the exercises. However, some conclusions on the efficiency of the operations are evident. Because we can add any element as the first element of the list, the **add** operation is $O(1)$. On the other hand, because of the requirement that no element appear twice in the list corresponding to a Set, when implementing the **union** operation we have to search **t,** using **elementOf([])**, for each element of the Set that owns the **union** operation (or vice versa). Consequently, the efficiency of this operations is $O(n_{\text{owner}} \times n_t)$. A hidden cost in all of the Set operations accrues when **Universe** itself involves structured data elements. In such a case, determining equality between elements may be a nontrivial operation whose efficiency depends on the complexity and size of the elements.

The Union-Find Problem Revisited

The implementation of sets by a list gives us a convenient way to represent the information needed in the union-find problem, which we introduced in Section 2.4. Consider again the partitioning of cities given in Figure 2.17. Each disjoint subset in this partition may be represented by a linked list as indicated in Figure 3.23. The partition itself, which is nothing but a set of disjoint sets, may be similarly represented via a linked list. The only difference is that the nodes in this linked list do not contain cities but rather pointers to linked lists of cities as indicated in Figure 3.24. That is, since a partition is a set of sets, a representation of sets by linked lists results in a partition being a linked list of linked lists!

Given this implementation, the algorithm for the **ufFind** operation (see Section 2.4) requires that each disjoint set be searched for the pair of cities given to **ufFind.**

Figure 3.23
Representation of sets of cities from Figure 2.17.

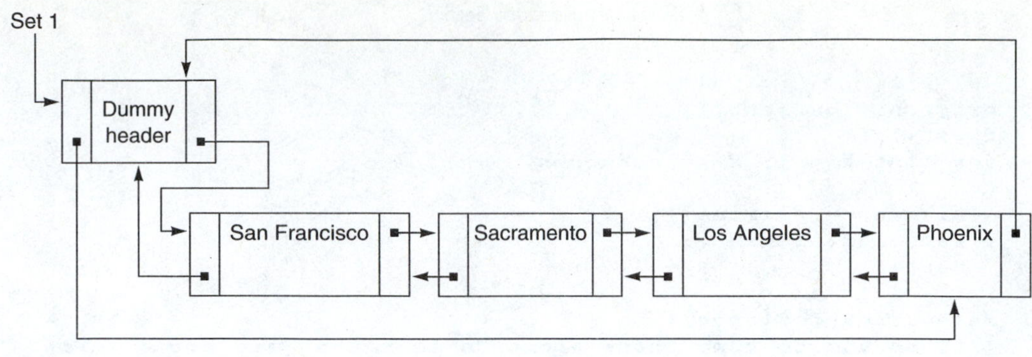

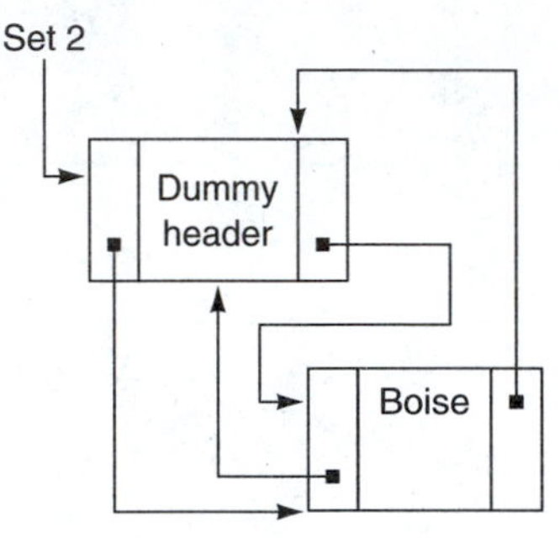

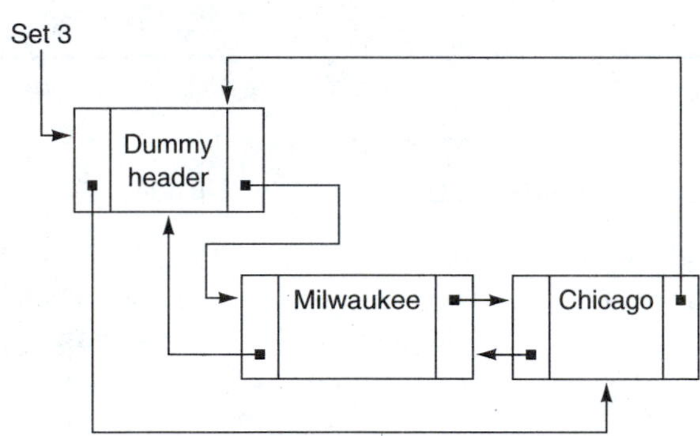

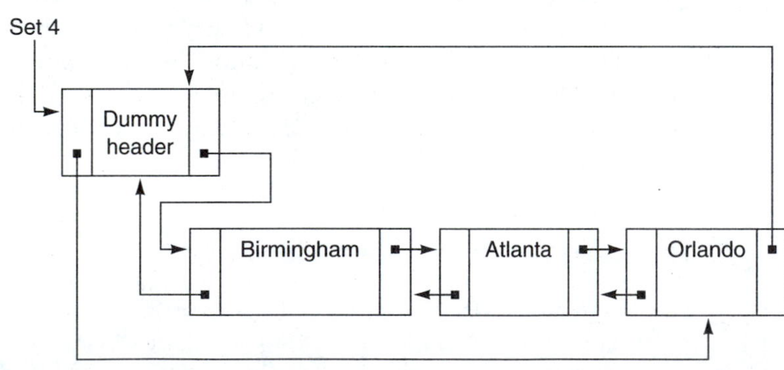

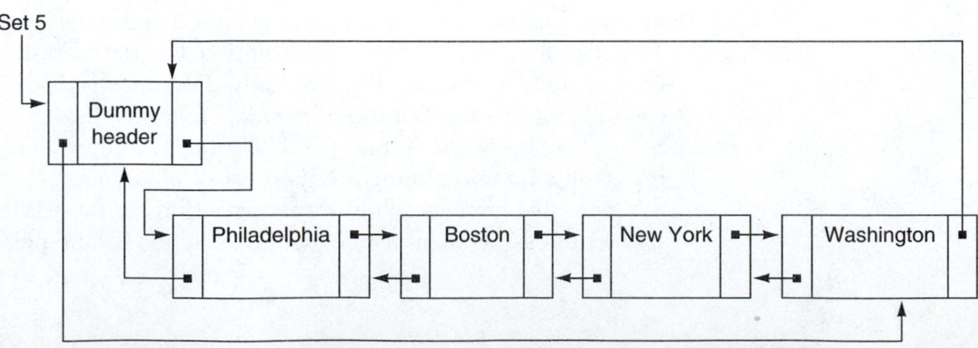

Figure 3.24
Representation of partition **p** of disjoint sets of Figures 2.17 and 3.23.

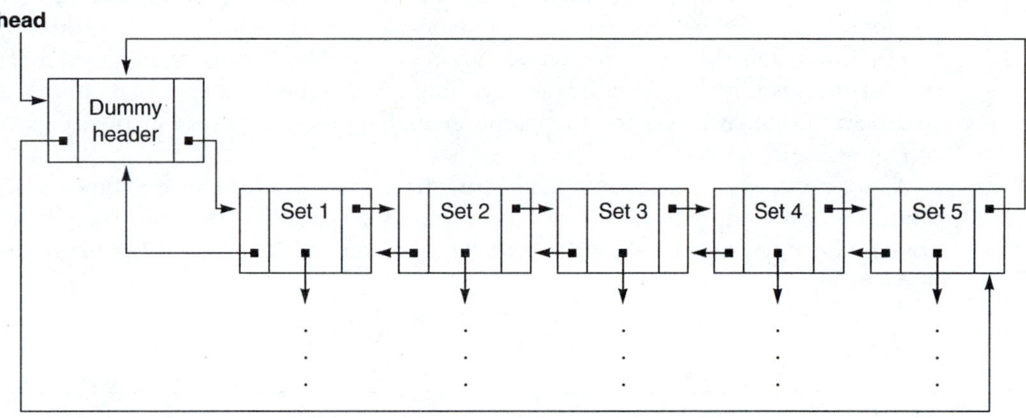

Figure 3.25
Partition **p** from Figures 3.23 and 3.24 after **ufUnion** (Boise, Atlanta).

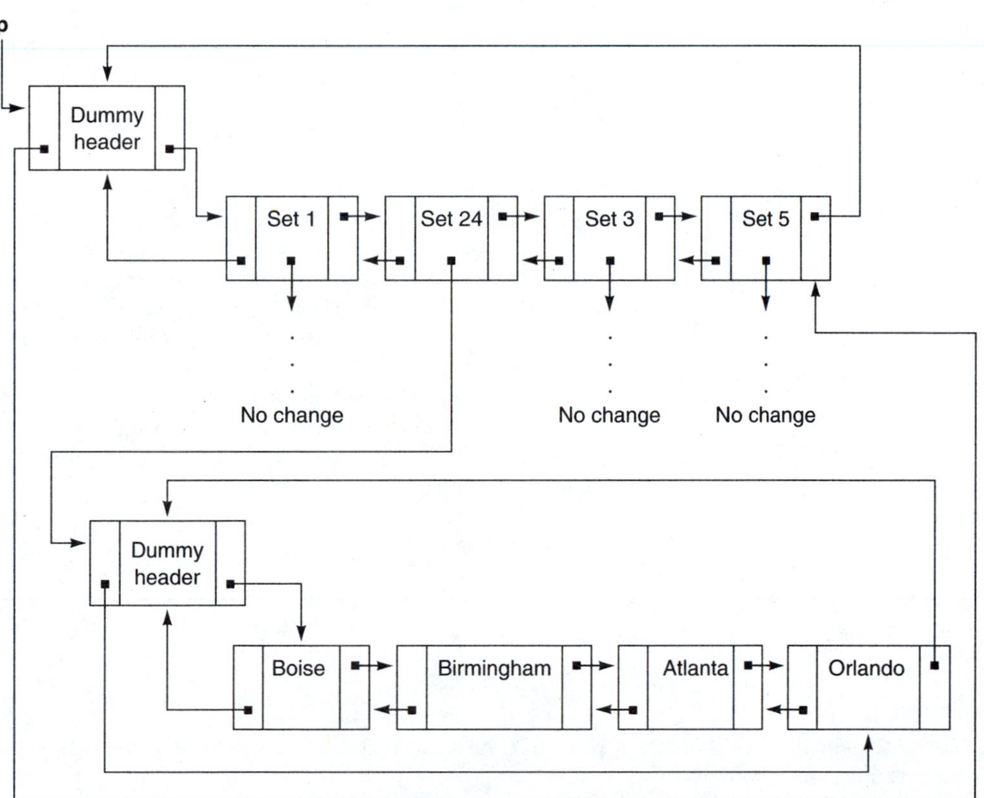

Clearly this will be $O(n)$ (where n is the number of elements in the universe) in both its worst and average efficiency.

The algorithm for the **ufUnion** operation will be $O(n)$ in its number of comparisons since the pair of cities it is given, X and Y, must first be found in the partition. Once found, the actual union of the two sets containing elements X and Y, respectively, can be achieved in $O(1)$ time. For instance, a call to **ufUnion** (Boise, Atlanta) for the partition in Figure 3.24 results in the partition of Figure 3.25.

As we proceed in our study of data structures, we will return several times to the union-find problem. We will see that, by using more sophisticated implementations, we significantly enhance the $O(n)$ efficiency of the **ufFind** and **ufUnion** operations.

Exercises 3.5

1. Example 3.9 provided C++ code for the Union operation (overloaded as ||) under a doubly linked list implementation of sets. Provide C++ code for each of the other Set operations (as defined in Section 2.4) under this implementation.

2. Use big-O notation to analyze the time efficiency of each operation from Exercise 3.5.1.

3. **a.** In the exercises of Section 3.2 we defined the notion of an ordered list. What assumptions must we make about the **Universe** class in order to implement Sets using an ordered linked list?

b. Provide C++ code for each Set operation (as defined in Section 2.4) under an ordered linked-list implementation of sets.

4. **a.** Use big-O notation to analyze the time efficiency of each operation from Exercise 3.5.3.

b. Under what conditions might you choose to use an ordered linked-list implementation for Sets rather than an unordered linked-list representation?

5. Assume we have a collection of cities such as that appearing in Figure 2.17.

a. Provide a C++ definition for a set of such cities using an unordered linked-list implementation of Sets.

b. Given your definition in part (a), provide a C++ definition of a partition as required in the union-find problem.

c. Given your type definitions in parts (a) and (b), provide C++ code for the Union-Find ADT operations as defined in Section 2.4.

6. Suppose that the set of cities you defined in Exercise 3.5.5(a) were implemented as an ordered linked list (see Exercise 3.5.1) instead of unordered. What would be gained by such an implementation? What would be lost?

7. In discussing the unordered list implementation of Sets in this section, we stated that the efficiency of the **union** (overloaded ||) operation would be $O(n_X \times n_Y)$ where n_X and n_Y represent the number of elements in the sets X and Y respectively. Then, in discussing the unordered list implementation of sets for the union-find problem, we stated that the efficiency of the **ufUnion** operation would be $O(1)$. Does this contradict our earlier claim of $O(n_X \times n_Y)$? Explain. (*Hint:* What do we know about sets in the union-find problem that makes the **ufunion** operation "easier" for this problem?)

Chapter Summary

In this chapter we discussed the List ADT, which is based on a data structure known as an unordered list. An unordered list is a collection of data nodes arranged in a linear sequence. Two implementations for the List ADT are given: an implementation using the Array ADT and an implementation using a linked list. As applications of the List ADT, we give alternative implementations for the String ADT, the Set ADT, and the Union-Find ADT, which were introduced in Chapter 2.

The widespread use of linked lists has led to the development of several variations suitable in certain applications. Four such variations presented in this chapter were linked lists with dummy headers, circular lists, doubly linked lists, and multilinked lists.

Keywords

circular linked list	dummy header	linked list	ordered list	unordered list
doubly linked list	head pointer	multilinked list	polymorphism	virtual function

Programming Problems/Projects

1. Wing-and-a-Prayer Airlines maintains four scheduled flights per day, identified by the numbers 1, 2, 3, and 4. For each of these flights, they keep a list of passengers. The database for the entire airline could hence be viewed as four linked lists. Write a program that sets up and maintains this database by handling commands of the following form:

Command	Add
Flight number	3
Passenger name	BROWN
Command	Delete
Flight number	1
Passenger name	JONES
Command	List
Flight number	2

   (List all passengers for the specified flight.)

   Use an appropriate string storage strategy for the passenger names.
2. To take care of their growing business, the Fly-by-Night credit card company would like to update their customer data base. Write a program that sets up a doubly linked list into which a record is:
   a. Inserted in order according to the social security number of the customer.
   b. Updated if the customer record exists.
   c. Deleted if the customer no longer wishes to patronize the company.
3. As a struggling professional football team, the Bay Area Brawlers have a highly volatile player roster. Write a program that allows the team to maintain its roster as a linked list. Data items stored for each player are the following:

   Name
   Height
   Weight
   Age
   University affiliation

   As an added option, allow your program to access players by descending order of weight or by age.
4. Develop a line-oriented text editor that assigns a number to each line of text and then maintains the lines in a linked list in line number order (similar to the way in which BASIC programs are maintained on many systems). See Exercise 3.1.1 on ordered lists for maintaining lists by an ordering criterion. Your program should be able to process the following commands:

   I line number 'text'
   (instruction to insert text at specified number)
   L line1-line2
   (instruction to list line1 through line2)
   D line1-line2
   (instruction to delete line1 through line2)

   If you feel really ambitious, incorporate into your program a string storage strategy that will allow the user to perform editing operations such as inserting and deleting characters within a given line.
5. Write a program that, given a file of text, will add to an index those words in the text that are marked by special delimiting brackets [ ]. The words in the index will be printed after the text itself has been formatted and printed. Words in this index should be listed alphabetically and should have a page-number reference for each page of text on which they are delimited by the special brackets. Note that this program would be part of a word processing system an author could use when developing a book with an index of terms.
6. A data structure sometimes used to facilitate searching a list of values is that of a *self-organizing list*. The idea here is that the list is searched sequentially for a given data item. If the data item does not appear in the list, then a node with the data item is inserted at the beginning of the list; otherwise, after the data item has been found, its node is moved from its current position to the beginning of the list.

   This structure could be useful for situations in which the data items involved exhibit a phenomenon known as *locality of reference*. This is characterized by situations wherein a data item is referenced frequently for a while; then over time it exhibits less and less usage, only to reappear again frequently for a while, and so on. References to identifiers of variables in a program are one example of items that exhibit such locality of reference.

   For this problem you are to specify a self-organizing list as an abstract data type with the usual List operations, but with a modified **examine** operation that causes the list to function in the self-organizing manner just described. Now write a program that accepts a stream of strings (perhaps representing program identifiers) as input and displays the entire list each time the order of the nodes in the list changes. You should use an appropriate string storage strategy for the input strings.

7. Write a program that allows input of an arbitrary number of polynomials as coefficient and exponent pairs. Store each polynomial as a linked list of coefficient-exponent pairs. Your program should then evaluate each of the polynomials for an arbitrary argument X. Be sure that your program works for all "unusual" polynomials such as the zero polynomial, polynomials of degree one, and constant polynomials.
8. Extend the polynomial evaluation program you developed for Problem 7 to perform polynomial arithmetic. That is, develop procedures to perform polynomial addition, subtraction, multiplication, and division.
9. Consider the following memorandum from the registrar at the renowned Lowcountry University.

MEMORANDUM
Lowcountry University
TO: Director of Data Processing
FROM: Head Registrar
DATE: November 18, 1995
RE: Automation of record keeping on students
Records for students at our school consist of a university identification number, a last name, a first name, a middle initial, a Social Security number, a list of courses the student has taken along with the grade received in each course, and a list of extracurricular activities in which the student has indicated an interest. A university identification number for a student consists of a six-digit number: the first two digits represent the year a student entered the university. The remaining four digits are simply assigned on a sequential basis as students are admitted to the school. For instance, the student with ID number 930023 is the twenty-third student admitted in the class that entered L.U. in 1993.

Given this database, we frequently need to work with it in the following ways:

- Find and display all data for a particular student, as identified by university ID number.
- Add and delete student records from the database.
- Print records for all students in Social Security number order, starting with the most recent class and working back.
- Add, change, or delete the information in a course for a particular student. For instance, change the grade received by student 930023 in CompSci2 from C to B.
- Find all students with an extracurricular interest that matches a particular target interest. Students' extracurricular interests are viewed as arbitrarily long strings. These strings are entered into our records directly from information provided by students on their registration forms. For instance, a given student may have indicated PLAYING BASKETBALL and GOING TO PLAYS as her two interests. We would want to be able to find this student (as well as students who indicated an interest such as WATCHING BASKETBALL or SHOOTING BASKETBALLS) if we were to search our data base for students who had an interest matching BASKETBALL.

In what sense could the overall database described in this memo be viewed as a list? As lists embedded within another list? As a two-dimensional matrix (see Exercise 2.1.6)? As a list embedded within a two-dimensional matrix?

Finally, implement a solution based on linked lists for the system requested by the registrar at L.U.

10. Consider the following problem—often referred to as the *Josephus problem*. Imagine that a class of N students decided to choose one from among themselves to approach a curmudgeonly professor about postponing for a week an upcoming examination. They elect to arrange themselves in a circle and excuse the Mth person around the circle—with the size of the circle being reduced by one each time a person is excused. The problem is to find out which person will be the last remaining, or more generally, to find the order in which the people are excused. For example, if $N = 9$ and $M = 5$, then the people are excused in the order 5 1 7 4 3 6 9 2. Hence the eighth person is left to face the professor. To solve the Josephus problem, write a program that inserts persons 1 through N into a list and then appropriately deletes them from the list until only one is left.
11. Computers can only store and do arithmetic with integers of limited size. When integers surpass that limiting value, overflow occurs and the results will either be unreliable or cause your program to die with a runtime error. However, by altering the implementation of an integer, you can develop algorithms to do virtually limitless integer arithmetic. The basis of such an implementation is to store each digit of an integer in a list; that is, to represent an integer as a list of digits. Then develop algorithms to do integer arithmetic operations on a digit-by-digit basis, taking carries, borrows, and so forth into account as you do when performing these operations by hand. After carefully considering which list implementation best suits the problem, develop functions to perform extended integer addition, subtraction, multiplication, and division (quotient and remainder).
12. Incorporate the functions you developed for the union-find problem in the exercises of Section 3.5 into a complete program that allows a user to manipulate cities in a transportation network in the manner described in Section 2.4. Unlike Problem 11 in Chapter 2, you should no longer assume that the cities are identified by a single letter.
13. Write a text editor program as described in the Problem 6 of Chapter 2, but use a linked list implementation of strings. If you did the problem in Chapter 2, formulate in writing a performance comparison of the two string implementations for this text editing application.

CHAPTER 4 Queues

What we call the beginning is often the end. And to make an end is to make a beginning. The end is where we start from.

T. S. Eliot

Chapter Outline:

In Chapter 3 we introduced the linked list as a data structure specifically designed to handle conveniently the insertion and deletion of entries in a list. In this chapter, we discuss another data structure, called a *queue*, which is a special type of list. In particular, a queue is a list with restrictions imposed on the way in which entries are inserted and removed. Another name for a queue is a *first-in, first-out* (FIFO) list. This latter name comes close to completely characterizing the restricted types of insertions and removals that can be performed on a queue. Insertions are limited to one end of the list, and removals can occur only at the other end. Thus an item cannot be deleted from a queue until all items previously placed in the queue have been deleted. Conceptually, a queue resembles a waiting line; for example, jobs waiting to be serviced by a computer, or cars forming a long line at a busy tollbooth. As highlights of this chapter we will use the queue structure to implement a new sorting algorithm, the radix sort, and then explore the application of queues in the scheduling of processes in a time-sharing environment.

4.1 The Queue ADT

The following definition specifies the queue as an abstract data type.

Definition: A *Queue* is a restricted form of a list. In particular, all additions to a queue occur at one end, the *rear*, and all removals occur at the other end, the *front*. Assuming each node of the queue stores data of type *Basedata*, the following operations are provided for the Queue ADT.

`Construct Operation (first form)`

Precondition: An uninitialized Queue object.
Postcondition: The Queue object is initialized to an empty Queue.

`Construct Operation (second form)`

Precondition: An uninitialized Queue object;
size—a positive integer.
Postcondition: The Queue object initialized to an empty Queue, but with storage allocated for *size* nodes.

`Construct Operation (Copy Constructor)`

Precondition: An uninitialized Queue object;
initqueue—a Queue object that was previously constructed.
Postcondition: The Queue object is initialized to *initqueue*.

`Destroy Operation`

Precondition: A Queue object that currently exists.
Postcondition: All storage allocated to the Queue object is deallocated, that is, returned to an available space pool for allocation to other objects.

`Front Operation`

Precondition: A nonempty Queue object.
Postcondition: The data of type *Basedata* that are being stored in the front node of the Queue are returned.

`Empty Operation`

Precondition: A Queue object.
Postcondition: If no removals can be made from the Queue, the operation returns the value TRUE; otherwise it returns the value FALSE.

`Full Operation`

Precondition: A Queue object.
Postcondition: If no additions can be made to the Queue, the operation returns the value TRUE; otherwise it returns the value FALSE.

`Enqueue Operation`

Precondition: A Queue object that is not full;
item—having type *Basedata* is to become the value of a new node in the Queue.
Postcondition: *item* is inserted at the rear of the Queue.

`Dequeue Operation`

Precondition: A nonempty Queue object.
Postcondition: The front node is removed from the Queue.

The effect of the restrictions on insertions and removals is to ensure that the earlier an item enters a queue, the earlier it will leave the queue. That is, items are processed on a first-in, first-out basis. The conceptual picture that emerges from this definition is given in Figure 4.1.

In assigning operations to the Queue ADT, some authors incorporate our Front operation into the Dequeue operation, with the result that Dequeue not only removes a node from the front of the queue but returns the value removed as

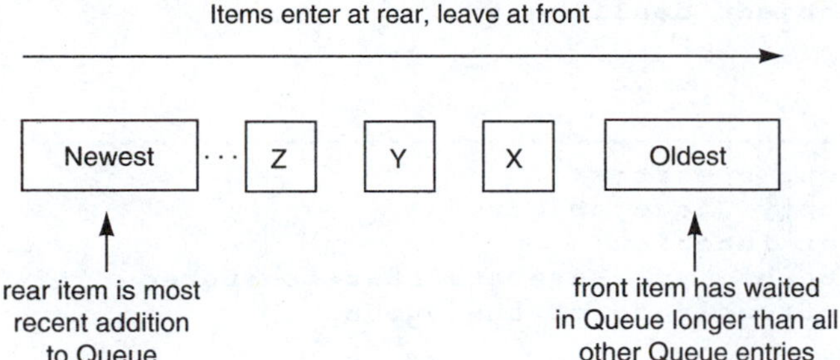

Figure 4.1 Abstract data type Queue as computer embodiment of waiting line.

well. We have chosen to separate the two operations in order to strengthen the *cohesion* of each of the operations. Cohesion is a term used in software design to describe the degree to which a module's responsibilities are interrelated. This can range from *coincidental cohesion*, where the assigned responsibilities seem to have no apparent relationship to one another (resulting in the least desirable level of cohesion) to *functional cohesion*, where all responsibilities are directed toward the accomplishment of a single function (resulting in the most desirable level of cohesion).

Having provided a formal conceptual definition of the Queue ADT, we may now translate the definition into a C++ interface.

```
//   BaseData is either a C++ built-in type, or a C++ class that has an
//   assignment operation that overloads the "=" operator.
template <class BaseData>
class Queue
{
  public:

//-------------------------------------------------------------------------
// Interface for first Queue constructor
// GIVEN:     An uninitialized Queue object.
// RETURN:    The Queue object is initialized to an empty Queue.

    Queue();

//-------------------------------------------------------------------------
// Interface for second Queue constructor
// GIVEN:     An uninitialized Queue object;
//            size -- a positive integer.
// RETURN:    The Queue object is initialized to an empty Queue, but with storage
//            allocated for size nodes.

    Queue(int size);

//-------------------------------------------------------------------------
// Interface for Queue copy constructor
// GIVEN:     An uninitialized Queue object;
//            initqueue -- a Queue object that was previously constructed.
// RETURN:    The Queue object initialized with the node values and number of
//            nodes of initqueue.

    Queue(Queue &initqueue);

//-------------------------------------------------------------------------
// Interface for Queue destructor
// GIVEN:     A previously allocated Queue object.
```

```
// RETURN:    Queue object deallocated.

     ~Queue();

//-------------------------------------------------------------------------------
// Interface for front operator
// GIVEN:     A nonempty Queue object.
// RETURN as value of function:
//            The data of type BaseData that is stored
//            at the front node of the Queue.

     BaseData front();

//-------------------------------------------------------------------------------
// Interface for empty operator
// GIVEN:     A Queue object.
// RETURN as value of function:
//            TRUE if no removals can be made from the Queue; FALSE otherwise.

     BOOLEAN empty();

//-------------------------------------------------------------------------------
// Interface for full operator
// GIVEN:     A Queue object.
// RETURN as value of function:
//            TRUE if no additions can be made to the Queue; FALSE otherwise.

     BOOLEAN full();

//-------------------------------------------------------------------------------
// Interface for enqueue operator
// GIVEN:     A Queue object that is not full.
//            item -- a data item to inserted into the Queue.
// RETURN:    The Queue with item inserted at the rear of the Queue.
// RETURN as value of function: void

     void enqueue (const BaseData &item);

//-------------------------------------------------------------------------------
// Interface for dequeue operator
// GIVEN:     A nonempty Queue object.
// RETURN:    The Queue with the front node removed.
// RETURN as value of function: void

     void dequeue();
};
```

Exercises 4.1

1. Suppose that you are given a queue that is known to contain only positive integers. Using only the fundamental Queue operations, write a routine, **substitute**, having the interface

```
void substitute(Queue<int> &q, int oldValue,
                int newValue)
```

that modifies the Queue **q** by replacing all occurrences of the value **oldValue** in nodes of **q** by the value **newValue**. Other than the replacement of **oldValue** by **newValue**, the Queue **q** is to remain unchanged. Avoid passing through the queue more than once.

2. Suppose that you are given a queue of real numbers. Using only the fundamental Queue operations, write a function that returns the average value of the entries in the queue.

3. **a.** As we noted in the text, some prefer to define a Dequeue operation that removes a node from a queue and also returns the value stored in the node. Rework Exercise 1 above assuming a definition of the Queue ADT that adopts this definition of Dequeue, discarding our Front operation.

   b. Same as part (a) except rework Exercise 2 above.

c. From your answers to parts (a) and (b) you might conclude that combining the responsibilities of the Front and Dequeue operations into one operation affords more elegant solutions to problems involving queues. Can you think of situations where this may not be the case? If so, describe them.

4.2 Implementations of the Queue ADT

In this section we discuss methods for implementing the Queue ADT. We begin by implementing the Queue ADT as a derived class from the List ADT. The efficiency of this implementation is dependent on the efficiency of the underlying List operations. We then compare this efficiency to that obtained when one uses arrays or linked lists to implement directly the Queue ADT rather than deriving the Queue ADT from the List ADT.

Derivation of the Queue ADT from the List ADT

We can specify the Queue ADT as a derived class from the List ADT by means of the following interface:

```
// BaseData is either a C++ built-in type, or a C++ class that has an
// assignment operation that overloads the "=" operator.

template <class BaseData>
class Queue: private List<BaseData>
{
  public:

//--------------------------------------------------------------------------------
// Interface for first Queue constructor
// GIVEN:     An uninitialized Queue object.
// RETURN:    The Queue object is initialized to an empty Queue.

    Queue();

//--------------------------------------------------------------------------------
// Interface for second Queue constructor
// GIVEN:     An uninitialized Queue object;
//            size -- a positive integer.
// RETURN:    The Queue object is initialized to an empty Queue, but with storage
            allocated for size nodes.

     Queue(int size);

//--------------------------------------------------------------------------------
// Interface for Queue copy constructor
// GIVEN:     An uninitialized Queue object;
//            initqueue -- a Queue object that was previously constructed.
// RETURN:    The Queue object initialized with the node values and number of
//            nodes of initqueue.

    Queue (Queue &initqueue);

//--------------------------------------------------------------------------------
// Interface for Queue destructor
// GIVEN:     A previously allocated Queue object.
// RETURN:    Queue object deallocated.

    ~Queue();
```

```
//-----------------------------------------------------------------------
// Interface for front operator
// GIVEN:    A nonempty Queue object.
// RETURN as value of function:
//           The data of type BaseData that is being stored
//           at the front node of the Queue.

    BaseData front();

//-----------------------------------------------------------------------
// Interface for empty operator
// GIVEN:    A Queue object.
// RETURN as value of function:
//           TRUE if no removals can be made from the Queue;
//           FALSE otherwise.

    BOOLEAN empty();

//-----------------------------------------------------------------------
// Interface for full operator
// GIVEN:    A Queue object.
// RETURN as value of function:
//           TRUE if no additions can be made to the Queue;
//           FALSE otherwise.

    BOOLEAN full();

//-----------------------------------------------------------------------
// Interface for enqueue operator
// GIVEN:    A Queue object that is not full;
//           item -- a data item to inserted into the Queue.
// RETURN:   The Queue with item inserted at the rear of the Queue.
// RETURN as value of function: void

    void enqueue (const BaseData &item);

//-----------------------------------------------------------------------
// Interface for dequeue operator
// GIVEN:    A nonempty Queue object.
// RETURN:   The Queue with the front node removed.
// RETURN as value of function: void

    void dequeue();
};
```

Note the use of the qualifier *private* in the header:

```
class Queue: private List<BaseData>
```

This use of **private** ensures that the public and protected data structures and operations of the **List** class remain available to the **Queue** class, but are not available to any routines or classes that use **Queue** objects. This forces these latter routines or classes to manipulate **Queue** objects only through the public operations of the **Queue** class, enforcing the ADT use rule of Chapter 2.

Example 4.1

Given the specification of the class **Queue** as a derived class from the class **List,** the first constructor operation for **Queue** can be derived from the **List** constructor as follows:

```
template <class BaseData>
Queue<BaseData>:: Queue()
  :List<BaseData>()          // Constructor for List is called
{
}
```

Since we are treating a **Queue** as a special type of **List,** it is sufficient to use just the base class constructor for **Lists** as the constructor for the **Queue** constructor. No additional initialization code is needed for a **Queue.**

Example 4.2

Implement the **Queue** operation **dequeue** using only the operations derived from those of the **List** class.

```
template <class BaseData>
void  Queue<BaseData>::dequeue()
{
  assert(!empty());
  first();
  remove();
}
```

Recall that one of our preconditions for **dequeue** is that the **Queue** object is nonempty; hence, we use the **assert** macro to check for this condition prior to removing a node from the Queue. If the Queue is empty, **assert** ensures that a consistent form of program termination is reached.

You will implement the other **Queue** operations in the exercises.

Efficiency of the Implementation of the Queue ADT as a Derived Class

Clearly the efficiency of the implementation of the data structures and operations of the Queue ADT is directly related to the efficiency of the implementation of the List ADT from which it is derived. In the array implementation of the List ADT we saw that the **remove** operation was $O(n)$ in terms of data movement. This means our **dequeue** operation is $O(n)$ in terms of data movement. On the other hand, we saw that for a linked list implementation of the List ADT the **remove** operation was $O(1)$ in terms of data movement. On further analysis of the **remove** operation for a singly linked implementation of the List ADT, however, we noted that in general it would be $O(n)$ in terms of pointer comparisons because of the need to update properly the value of the **previous** pointer. For a queue, however, the constraint that all removals occur at the front of the queue results in **remove**'s actually being $O(1)$ in pointer comparisons. Hence, when using a linked-list implementation of a List, the derived **remove** operation for the Queue will be $O(1)$ in its execution.

It is important to note here that, although we have attempted to analyze the efficiency of the Queue ADT vis-a-vis the implementation of the **List** class from which the **Queue** class is derived, a person who harbors strong concerns about the efficiency of the implementation of the parent class should probably not use a derived class implementation. Anytime information hiding is employed, the potential user of a module whose implementation details are hidden must be willing to sacrifice some concern for efficiency before using that class. Instead such a user must be willing to trust that the implementor of the class exercised appropriate concern for efficiency (and correctness!!) when she implemented the class. In return the user will realize a time savings in coding each time this ready-made class is used in another application. Likewise, a programmer who works in an environment where the use and implementation of classes are separate should also be aware of her own responsibilities to exercise appropriate concern for the efficiency and correctness of the class implementation that she writes.

We now discuss two other implementations of a queue—an array implementation and a circular array implementation. We leave the discussion of linked-list implementations for the exercises. In Section 4.5 we discuss a variation of a queue, known as a *priority queue,* and suggest possible implementations for it.

Array Implementation of the Queue ADT

Let us begin by considering how computer jobs are scheduled in a batch processing environment, a good example of a queue in use. Suppose further that jobs are scheduled strictly in the order in which they arrive. An array and two pointers can then be used to implement the scheduling queue. Assuming the interface for the **Array** class from Section 2.1 is included in the file **array.h,** an interface file for the **Queue** class based on an array implementation can be defined as follows:

```
#include "array.h"

template <class BaseData>
class Queue
{
  private:
    int maxQueueSize;
    Array<int,BaseData> *nodes;
    int frontInd, rearInd; // Indices of front and rear nodes in the array

  public:
  :
  // Public interface remains as defined earlier
  :
};
```

Here **maxQueueSize** stores a value representing the maximum number of entries that the array storing a queue's values can contain. We will see, however, that normally this value is larger than the actual number of entries the queue contains at a given time in processing. Also, note that we use a pointer **nodes** to an array of data values in our protected data members for the class. The array pointed to will use the **Array** class defined in Chapter 2 and will be indexed from 1 to **maxQueueSize.** We must use a pointer to an **Array** object rather than an explicitly declared **Array** to allow the **Array** constructor to be called as part of the constructor code for a **Queue.** The **Array** object can thus be dynamically sized.

The protected members **frontInd** and **rearInd** will store the indices of the front and rear nodes of the queue and are set to 1 and 0, respectively (the state of the queue before any insertions or removals). This situation is illustrated in Figure 4.2. Here the value **rearInd** indicates the location in the **Array** object referenced by **nodes** that was last occupied, not the one where the next addition will take place.

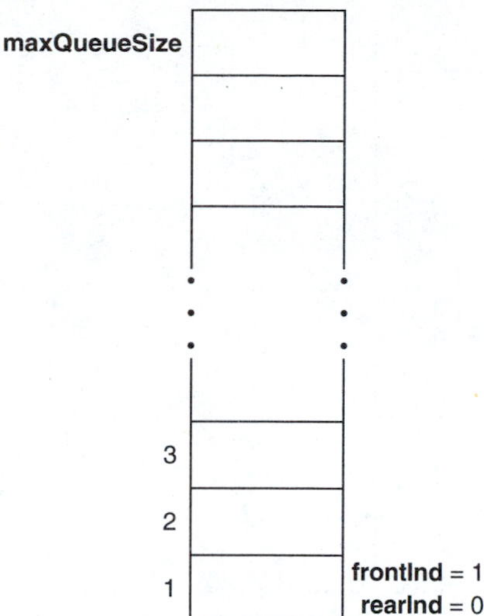

Figure 4.2
Empty queue.

The value **frontInd,** on the other hand, points at the location from which the next removal will take place.

Example 4.3

Implement the second **Queue** constructor operation using the interface given earlier.

```
template <class BaseData>
Queue<BaseData>:: Queue(int size)   // Constructor
{
  maxQueueSize = size;
  nodes = new Array<int, BaseData>(1, maxQueueSize);
  frontInd = 1;
  rearInd = 0;
}
```

As additions are made to the queue, the value of **rearInd** will first match and then exceed the value of **frontInd**. To understand this, suppose that in the queue of Figure 4.2 the job NEWTON arrives to be processed. The queue then changes to the state pictured in Figure 4.3. If job NEWTON is followed by job PAYROLL,

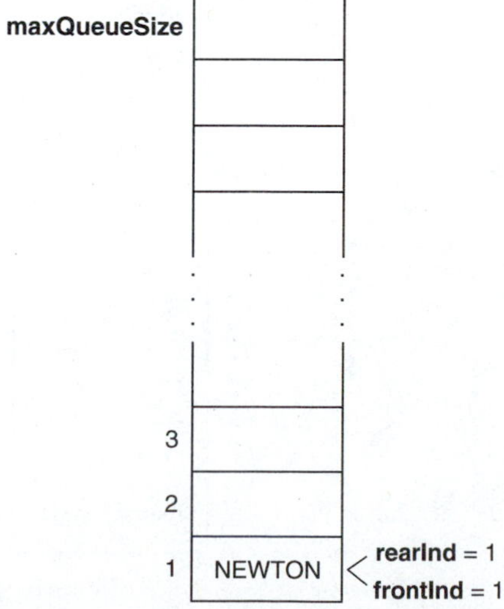

Figure 4.3
NEWTON added to the rear of the queue. **rearInd** points to the location last occupied, **frontInd** points to the location from which the next removal will take place.

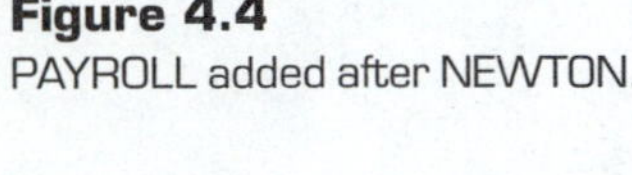

Figure 4.4
PAYROLL added after NEWTON.

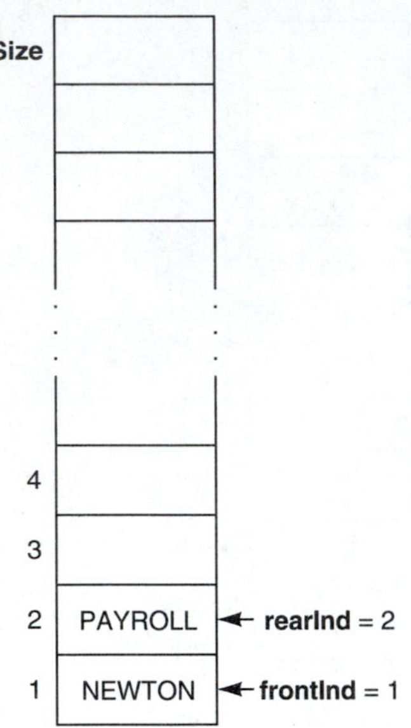

the queue's status changes to that of Figure 4.4. These illustrations show that the addition of any **item** (of type **BaseData**) to the queue requires two steps:

```
++rearInd;
(*nodes)[rearInd] = item;
```

If the system is now ready to process NEWTON in the queue of Figure 4.5, the front entry is returned by the instruction

```
return((*nodes)[frontInd]);
```

Figure 4.5
(a) NEWTON accessed via **(*nodes)[frontInd]**. (b) NEWTON then removed (logically) via ++**frontInd**.

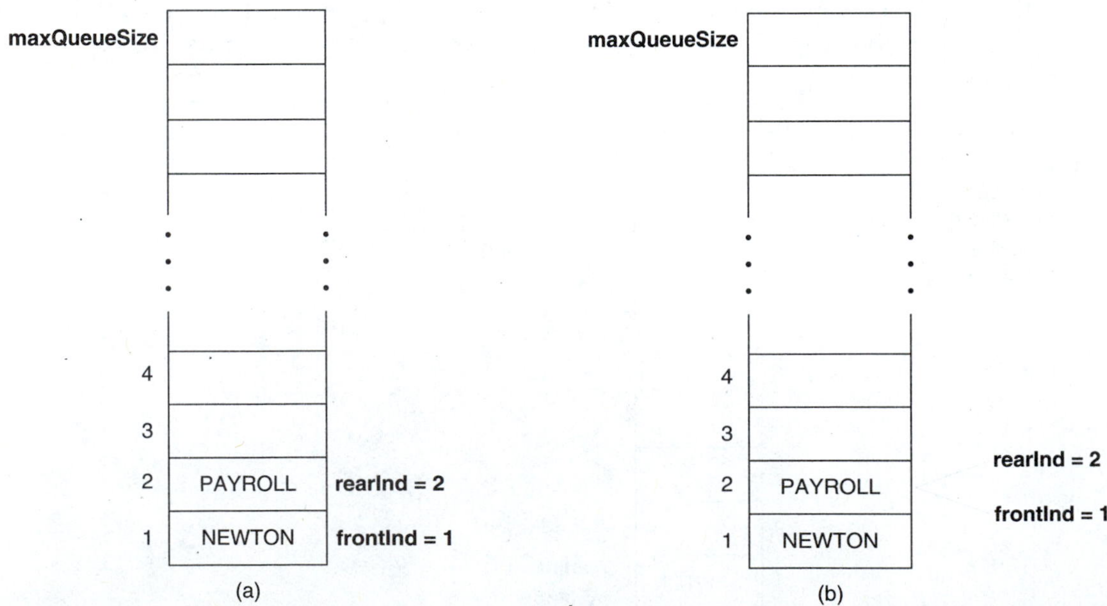

TABLE 4.1
Boundary condition checks for array implementation of queue.

Condition	Special situation
rearInd < frontInd	Empty queue
frontInd = rearInd	One-entry queue
rearInd = maxQueueSize	No more entries may be added to queue

Then, if the front entry must be removed from the queue in Figure 4.5, the instruction

```
++frontInd;
```

achieves the desired effect.

The conditions in Table 4.1 signal the associated boundary conditions for an array implementation of a Queue. The conditions allow us to develop our brief sequences for adding and removing data values into full-fledged routines. These in turn assume the existence of the Boolean-valued functions **empty** and **full** to check whether or not the **dequeue** and **enqueue** operations are possible. In Example 4.4 we give the code to implement the **dequeue** operation. In the exercises, you will be asked to write the **empty, full, front,** and **enqueue** operations.

Example 4.4

Implement the **dequeue** operation using the preceding interface for an array implementation.

```
template <class BaseData>
void Queue<BaseData>::dequeue()
{
  assert(!empty());
  ++frontInd;
}
```

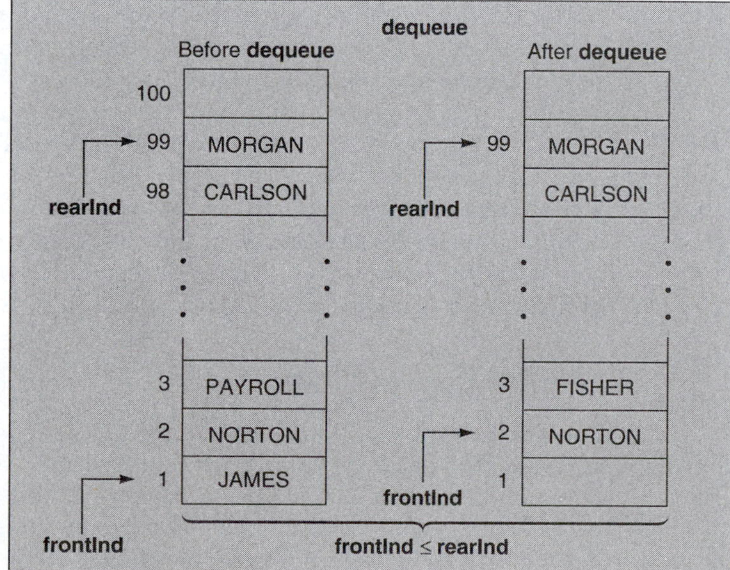

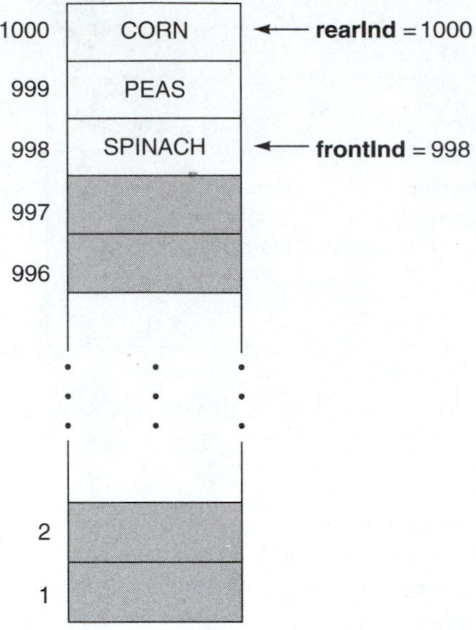

Figure 4.6
A full queue. The shaded region represents slots that were once used but no longer contain data items currently in the queue.

As it now stands, our implementation of a queue as a scheduling structure for jobs in a batch environment functions effectively until **rearInd** matches **maxQueueSize.** Then a call to **enqueue** fails, even though only a small percentage of slots in the array might actually contain data items currently in the queue structure. In fact, given the queue pictured in Figure 4.6, we should be able to use slots 1–997 again. This is not necessarily undesirable. For example, it may be that the mode of operation in a given batch environment is to process 1000 jobs, then print a statistical report on these 1000 jobs, and finally clear the queue to start another group of 1000 jobs. In this case, the queue in Figure 4.6 is the ideal structure because data about jobs are not lost, even after they have left the queue. However, if the goal of a computer installation were to provide continuous scheduling of batch jobs, without interruption after 1000 jobs, then the queue of Figure 4.6 would not be effective. One strategy that could be employed to correct this situation is to move the active queue down the array whenever the value of **rearInd** equals that of **maxQueueSize,** as illustrated in Figure 4.7.

If the queue contains a large number of items, however, this strategy would not be satisfactory because it would require moving all of the individual data items. Two strategies that allow the queue to operate in a continuous and efficient fashion are a *circular implementation* and a *linked-list implementation*. We discuss the circular array implementation next. Since the details of a linked-list implementation are similar to those used in Chapter 3 to implement a list, we leave a consideration of this implementation for the exercises.

Circular Implementation

The circular implementation essentially allows the queue to wrap around upon reaching the end of the array. This transformation is illustrated by the addition of the item UPDATE to the queue in Figure 4.8. The technique is called a *circular* implementation of a queue because if we redraw the right-hand array of Figure 4.8 in order to place position 1 immediately after the position **maxQueueSize** as well as before position 2, then we get the circular arrangement shown in Figure 4.9.

Figure 4.7
Active queue moved down. The shifting of the queue to the lower indexed positions in the array was triggered on reaching the condition **rearInd** = **maxQueueSize** (here, **maxQueueSize** = 1000).

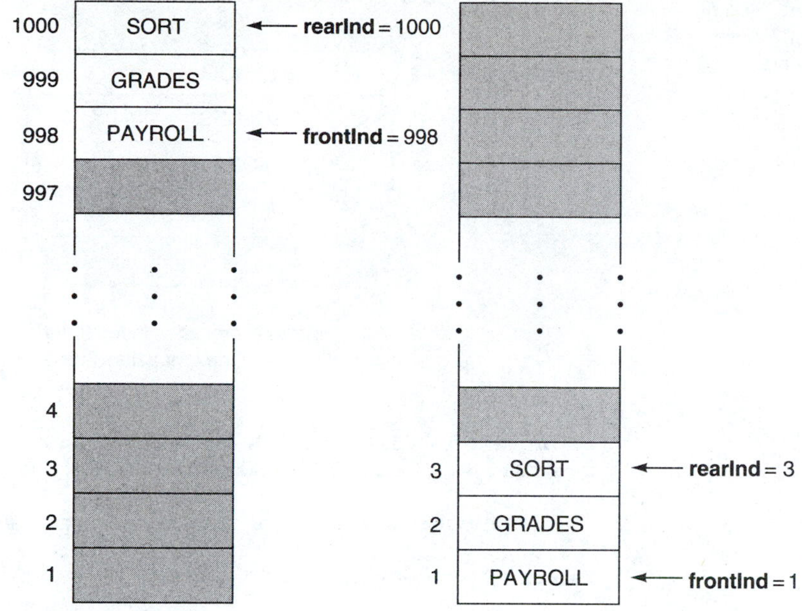

To handle the index arithmetic necessary for such an implementation of a queue, we must make the **frontInd** and **rearInd** indices behave analogously to an odometer in a car that has exceeded its mileage capacity. A convenient way to do this is to use the remainder operator for integer arithmetic. In C++ one uses the symbol "%" to invoke the remainder operator between two integer values (for example, 5 % 3 = 2, and 10 % 7 = 3). Instead of merely incrementing **frontInd** and **rearInd** using the ++ operator, we now advance these indices by the statements:

Figure 4.8
Circular implementation of a queue. Queue wraps around when UPDATE is added.

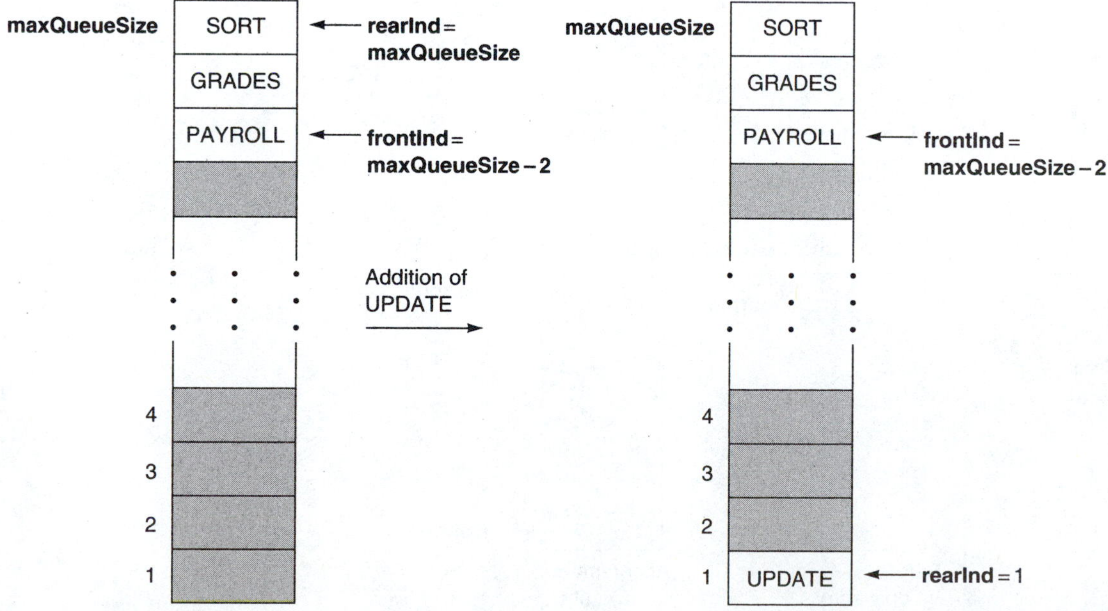

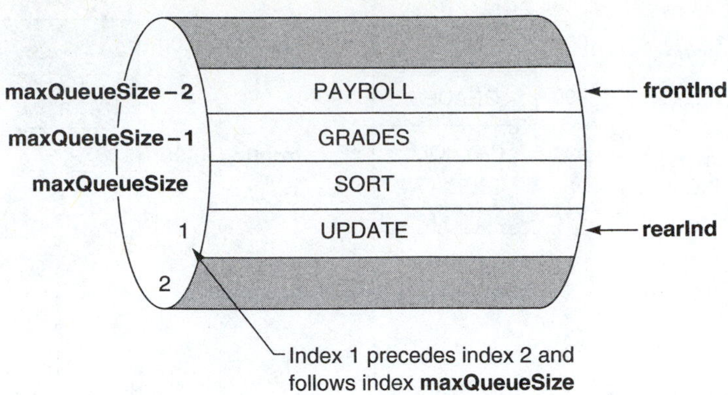

Figure 4.9
Reillustration of Figure 4.8 to show wrap-around.

```
frontInd = (frontInd % maxQueueSize) + 1;
rearInd = (rearInd % maxQueueSize) + 1;
```

An immediate consequence of taking this approach is that the condition

```
rearInd < frontInd
```

will no longer suffice as a condition to signal an empty queue. To derive the empty queue condition, consider what remains after we remove an item from the queue that has only one item in it. There are two possible situations, as illustrated in Figure 4.10.

Case 1: **frontInd** = **rearInd** < **maxQueueSize**

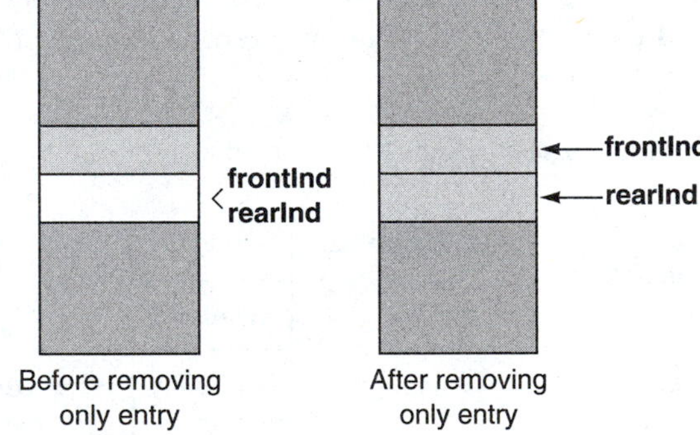

Case 2: **frontInd** = **rearInd** = **maxQueueSize**

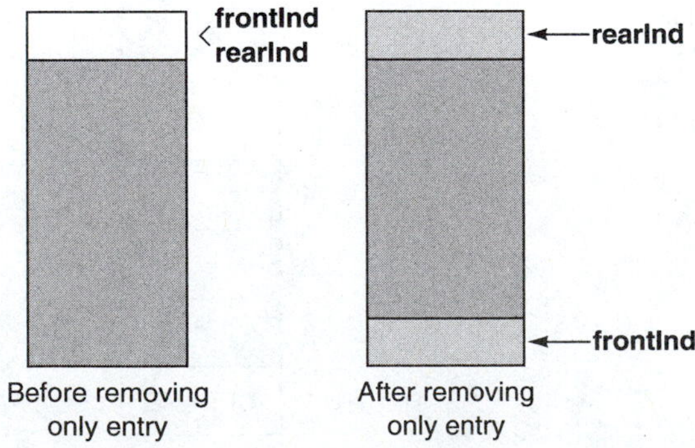

Figure 4.10
Removing from one-entry queue. Since the queue is being represented circularly in the array, deleting a single node at **maxQueueSize** presents a special case.

TABLE 4.2
Boundary condition checks for a circular queue, at most **maxQueueSize** − 1 entries.

Condition	Special situation
frontInd = **rearInd**	One-entry queue
(**rearInd** % **maxQueueSize**) + 1 = **frontInd**	Empty queue
((**rearInd** + 1) % **maxQueueSize**) + 1 = **frontInd**	Full queue

An inspection of both cases reveals that after the lone entry has been removed, the relationship

```
(rearInd % maxQueueSize) + 1 == frontInd
```

holds between the pointers. There is a problem, however, with immediately adopting this as a check for an empty queue. If we allow all slots in the array to be occupied at any one time, this same relationship between pointers also exists when the queue is full. The apparent contradiction can be avoided easily if one memory slot is sacrificed; that is, if we view a queue with **maxQueueSize** − 1 entries as a full queue. Then the test for fullness is met when the **rearInd** pointer lags two behind **frontInd** (including considerations for wrapping around). These results are summarized in Table 4.2.

Example 4.5

Explain why the check for a full queue in Table 4.2 cannot be replaced by the condition

```
(rearInd + 2) % maxQueueSize == frontInd
```

This condition would work for all but one special case of a full queue. In particular, it would fail when **rearInd** is **maxQueueSize** − 2 and **frontInd** is **maxQueueSize.** In that instance, the condition's value would be FALSE even though the queue is full.

Example 4.6

Explain why the check for a full queue in Table 4.2 cannot be replaced by the condition

```
(rearInd % maxQueueSize) + 2 == frontInd
```

This condition would work for all but one special case of a full queue. In particular, it would fail when **rearInd** is **maxQueueSize** − 1 and **frontInd** is 1. In that instance, the condition's value would be FALSE even though the queue is full.

Exercises 4.2

1. In Examples 4.1 and 4.2 we implemented two of the operations of the Queue ADT—the first constructor and **dequeue**—using an implementation where the class **Queue** is derived from the class **List.** Implement the remaining Queue operations—the second constructor, the copy constructor, the destructor, **front, empty, full,** and **enqueue**—using this approach.

2. Consider a circular array implementation of a **Queue** in which the array is declared to have **maxQueueSize** = 5. Trace the status of the array and the **frontInd** and **rearInd** pointers after each of the following successive operations:

   enqueue SMITH
   enqueue JONES

enqueue GREER
dequeue
enqueue CARSON
dequeue
enqueue BAKER
enqueue CHARLES
enqueue BENSON
dequeue
enqueue MILLER

3. Given the discussion of circular queues presented in this section, determine a valid initial setting for the **frontInd** and **rearInd** pointers in a circular queue.
4. In the array implementation of a circular queue as described in this section, what are the conditions to be satisfied by the indices **rearInd** and **frontInd** for a full queue, an empty queue, and a one-entry queue?
5. For a circular queue implemented by a linked list, it is necessary to maintain a pointer to only one queue node—which one: the front or rear? Justify your answer, using a drawing to help.
6. Suppose that we adopt the following conventions for the **frontInd** and **rearInd** indices associated with an array implementation of a **Queue**. **frontInd** is to refer to the next item to be removed from the queue. **rearInd** is to refer to the first available location, that is, the next location to be filled. Explain how this change in convention would affect the constructors and the **empty** and **full** operations for
   a. A noncircular array implementation
   b. A circular array implementation.
7. Explain how a continuously maintained count of the number of elements (instead of checking the relationship between **frontInd** and **rearInd**) in a circular queue could be used to implement the constructors as well as the **empty** and **full** operations. Write a C++ class definition structure for the data members of such a queue and then implement each of the **Queue** operations.
8. Implement the constructors, destructor, **empty, full, enqueue,** and **front** operations for a noncircular array implementation of a **Queue.**
9. Implement all of the **Queue** operations for a circular array implementation of a **Queue.**
10. Implement all of the **Queue** operations for a linked-list implementation of a **Queue.**
11. Consider all of the **Queue** implementations suggested in Exercises 4.2.6 through 4.2.10. Would any operation for any of these implementations have a time efficiency that is not $O(1)$? If so, which operation for which implementation? What would be the efficiency of these operations?

4.3 Application: Radix Sort

The *radix sort* algorithm is also called the *bin sort,* a name derived from its origin as a technique used on (now obsolete) machines called card sorters. These machines would sort a deck of key-punched cards by shuffling the cards into small bins, then collecting the cards from the bins into a newly arranged deck, and repeating this shuffling-collection process until the deck was magically sorted. There was, as we shall see, a very clever algorithm behind this rapid shuffling.

For integer data, the repeated passes of a radix sort focus on the one's digit of each number, then on the ten's digit, the hundred's digit, and so on until the highest order digit of the largest number is reached. For string data, the first pass hinges on the rightmost character in each string with successive passes always shifting attention one character position to the left. To illustrate the algorithm, we will trace it on the following list of nine integers:

459 254 472 534 649 239 432 654 477

On each pass through these data, radix sort will arrange it into 10 sublists (bins), one sublist for each of the digits, 0 through 9. Hence, on the first pass, all the numbers with the one's digit equal to 0 are grouped in one sublist, all those with the one's digit equal to 1 are grouped into another sublist, and so on. The resulting sublists follow:

First pass of radix sort

Digit	Sublist
0	
1	
2	472 432
3	
4	254 534 654
5	
6	
7	477
8	
9	459 649 239

The sublists are then collected into a single large list with the numbers in the sublist for 0 coming first, then those in the sublist for 1, and so on up to the sublist for 9. Hence, we would have a newly arranged list:

472 432 254 534 654 477 459 649 239

This new list is again partitioned into sublists, this time keying on the ten's digit. The result is shown here:

Second pass of radix sort

Digit	Sublist
0	
1	
2	
3	432 534 239
4	649
5	654 254 459
6	
7	472 477
8	
9	

Note that in each sublist the data are arranged in order by their last two digits. The sublists would now be collected in a new master list:

432 534 239 649 654 254 459 472 477

Now focusing on the hundred's digit, the master list would be classified into 10 sublists one more time. These final sublists are shown at the top of the following page. When the sublists are collected from this final partitioning, the data are arranged in ascending order. The final order for the list is

239 254 432 459 472 477 534 649 654

Third (final) pass of radix sort

Digit	Sublist
0	
1	
2	239 254
3	
4	432 459 472 477
5	534
6	649 654
7	
8	
9	

A rough, top-level statement of the radix sort algorithm follows:

```
Begin with the current digit as the one's digit;
while there is still a digit on which to classify data
{
  for each number in the master list
    Add that number to the appropriate sublist, keying on the current digit;
  for each sublist (from 0 through 9)
    for each number in the sublist
      Remove the number from the sublist and append it to a newly arranged
        master list;
  Advance the current digit one place to the left;
}
```

If the radix sort is being applied to character strings instead of integers, this algorithm would have to proceed from the rightmost character to the leftmost character instead of from the one's digit to the highest order digit.

At this point, you may be asking yourself what the radix sort has to do with the subject of this chapter, that is, queues. For the answer to this question, look at the nature of the master list and sublists manipulated by this algorithm. They are all first-in, first-out lists. In other words, queues are the ideal "bins" into which we categorize numbers by digits for the radix sort. In terms of queues, the preceding rough pseudocode statement of the algorithm can be refined to:

```
void radixSort(Queue<int> *masterList) // A pointer to a list/queue of integers
                                       // to be arranged in ascending order
{
  Queue<int> *subList[10];     // A pointer to a sublist for each possible digit

  int k, value, binNumber;
  int digit = 1;           // Represents digit position within number, 1 for
                           // one's digit, 10 for ten's digit, etc.
  for (k = 0; k < 10; ++k)
  {
    subList[k] = new Queue<int>;
```

```
    assert (subList[k] != 0);
  }
  while (stillNonZero(digit))    // Assume existence of a test to determine if
                                 // there is still a nonzero digit to sort on
  {
    while (!masterList->empty())
    {
      value = masterList->front();
      masterList->dequeue();
      binNumber = isolate(value, digit);    // Assume the existence of
                                            // a function that returns the
                                            // appropriate isolated digit
      subList[binNumber]->enqueue(value);
    }
```

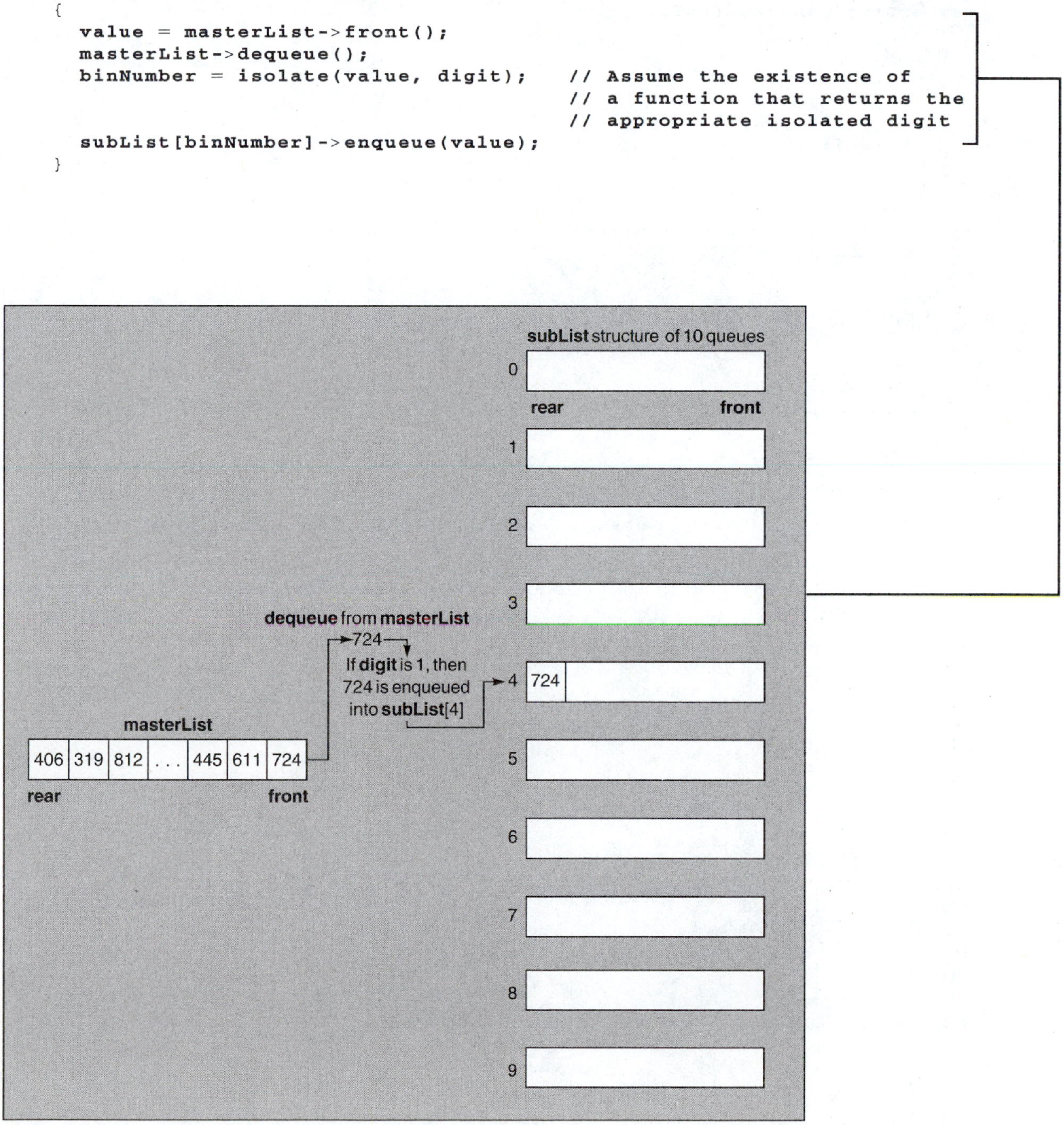

subList structure of 10 queues

0 rear front
1
2
3
4 724
5
6
7
8
9

dequeue from masterList
724
If digit is 1, then 724 is enqueued into subList[4]

masterList

406	319	812	. . .	445	611	724

rear front

```
    for (k = 0; k < 10; ++k)
    {
      while (!subList[k]->empty())
      {
        value = subList[k]->front();
        subList[k]->dequeue();
        masterList->enqueue(value);
      }
    }
    digit *= 10;
  }
  for (k = 0; k < 10; ++k)
    delete subList[k];
}
```

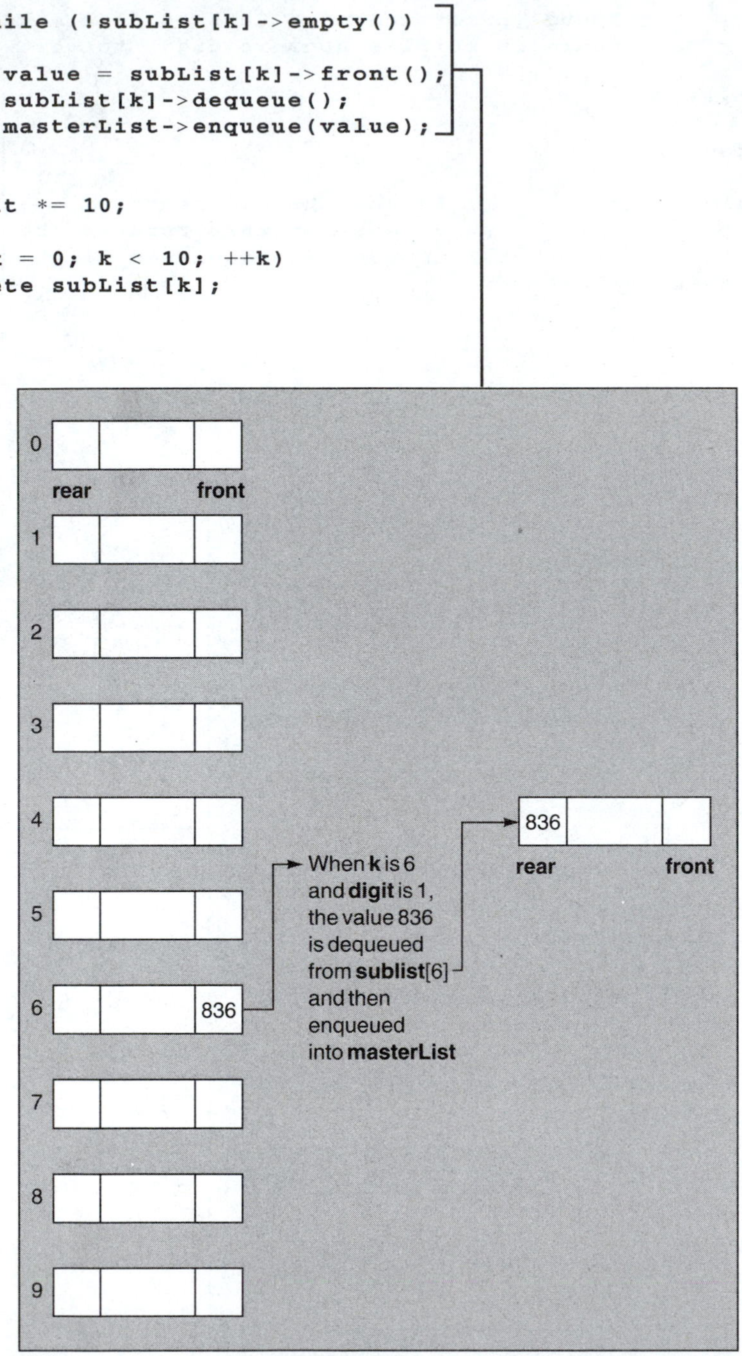

Efficiency of Radix Sort

An examination of the loop structure in the preceding C++ code for the radix sort indicates that, for each pass through the outer **while** loop, $O(n)$ operations must be performed. These $O(n)$ operations consist of the arithmetic necessary to isolate a particular digit within a number and the data swap necessary to attach it to the proper sublist and then collect it again into a new master list. The outer **while** loop will execute C times where C is the number of digits (or characters) in the integer (or string), making radix sort an $O(Cn)$ algorithm. If no duplicate values are permitted among those being sorted, then we must have $\log_{10} n \le C$ in the case of nonnegative integers, or $\log_s n \le C$, in the case of strings, where s is the size of the set from which the characters used in the strings may be chosen. At the same time, practicality will dictate that there be an upper bound on the size of C (for example, rare is the application that requires one to sort 20-digit integers or 1000-character strings); hence, one can find a constant H so that $C \le H \log_{10} n$ (or $C \le H \log_s n$). Consequently, where unique values are being sorted, radix sort is $O(n \log n)$. If duplicate values are allowed, on the other hand, then the C times that the outer **while** loop executes is independent of n, so that in this case radix sort has an $O(n)$ run-time efficiency.

On the surface, our analysis of the radix sort would so far seem to make it a significantly faster and better choice for sorting than the methods we studied in Chapter 1 and a choice comparable to, if not significantly better than, the more sophisticated methods we will study in Chapters 6 and 7. However, caution is urged. There is an old computer adage: You get nothing for nothing. We must examine the trade-offs before we jump too quickly on the radix-sort bandwagon. With the radix sort, these trade-offs include the following:

1. Although the radix sort may qualify as an $O(n)$ algorithm in some cases, remember this merely means that the number of operations can be bounded by $k \times n$ for some constant k. With the radix sort, this constant k can often be large enough that the radix sort will be less efficient than $O(n(\log_2 n)^2)$ and $O(n \log_2 n)$ algorithms for reasonable values of n. How large k is depends to some degree on the efficiency of the methods you use to implement some of the operations within the outer **while** loop of the algorithm—operations such as the fundamental queue operations, checking if there are any numbers in the list that still have a nonzero digit left to sort on, and isolating the current digit within a given value. You will explore some of these ways to enhance the algorithm's efficiency in the exercises and problems.
2. Since you must keep track of the sublists as well as the master list, there is the potential that this algorithm will be much less space efficient than sorting algorithms that directly manipulate a single array. How much less space efficient is again dependent on your implementation techniques and will be explored in the exercises.
3. To a degree, the algorithm is more dependent on the type of data being sorted than other sorting algorithms. Hence, it is more difficult to write a general-purpose version of the radix sort—that is, a version that will work for integers, strings, reals, and even more complex objects that can be compared. The reason for this is simple—the radix sort does not make any comparisons between values in the list being sorted. Hence, we cannot pass it a comparison parameter as we did to add generality to the sorting algorithms studied in Chapter 1. In a sense, this puts the radix sort in a class by itself among sorting algorithms—a fact that is alluded to in our discussion on the inherent limits of sort efficiencies in Chapter 12.

Exercises 4.3

1. Consider the data set given below. How many passes would be made through the outer **while** loop of the radix sort algorithm for these data? Trace the contents of the list after each of these passes.

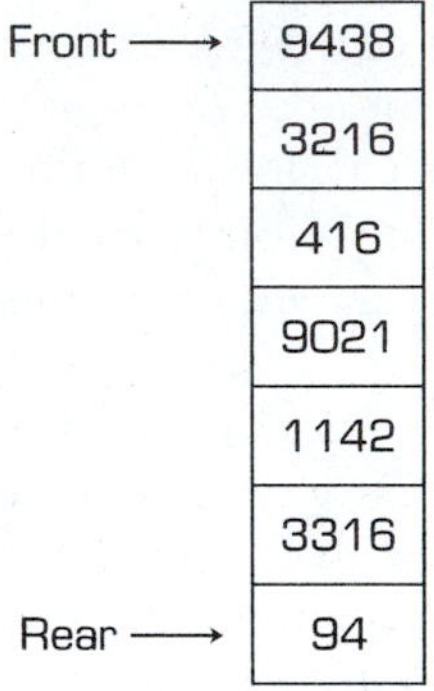

2. Consider the following list of strings:

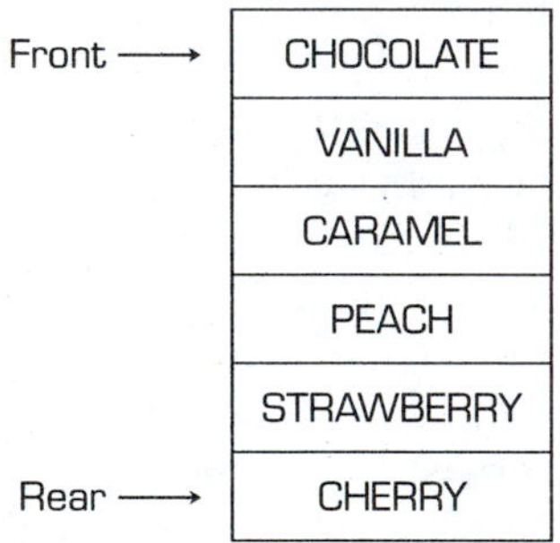

   How many passes would be made through the outer **while** loop of the radix sort algorithm for these data? Trace the contents of the list after each of these passes.

3. In the C++ version of the **radixSort** function presented in this section, we assume the existence of a test to check if any value in the list still has a nonzero digit left to sort on. Describe how you would implement this test, modifying the C++ code for **radixSort** or developing a subordinate function as appropriate. Then describe how the implementation you have chosen would affect the time efficiency of the radix sort for integers. Be as explicit as possible in this description. That is, we know that the radix sort should remain an $O(n)$ algorithm, but what effect will your implementation have on the constant k, which bounds the number of radix sort operations by $k \times n$?

4. In the C++ version of the **radixSort** function presented in this section, we assume the existence of a function that will isolate a specific digit within an integer. Describe how you would implement this function, modifying the C++ code for **radixSort** or developing a subordinate function as appropriate. Then describe how the implementation you have chosen would affect the time efficiency of the radix sort for integers. Be as explicit as possible in this description. That is, we know that radix sort should remain an $O(n)$ algorithm, but what effect will your implementation have on the constant k, which bounds the number of radix sort operations by $k \times n$?

5. The radix sort as presented in this section uses the Queue ADT. What implementation would you choose for the Queue ADT in this algorithm? Explain why.

6. The version of the radix sort presented in this section accesses queues only by the provided ADT operations. Given your answer to Exercise 4.3.5, could you make the radix sort more time efficient by accessing the queue implementation directly? If so, modify the radix sort in this fashion and describe the degree to which this enhances the time efficiency of the algorithm.

7. Suppose you have 1000 records to be sorted. Would the run-time efficiency of an $O(n^2)$ sort algorithm increase significantly if the 1000 records were broken into four groups, each group sorted, and then appended together as one large sorted array instead of sorting the initial unsegmented array? Why or why not?

8. Write a C++ function to implement the radix sort algorithm for a queue of strings.

9. Can you write a radix sort function to sort a queue of reals? If so, do it. If not, explain why.

10. A multiple key sort will sort a list of records giving highest priority to one field, secondary priority according to another field, and so on. For instance, to sort a list of dates in the form

```
struct
{
  int month;
  int day;
  int year;
}
```

   we would view **year** as the primary field, **month** as the secondary field, and **day** as the tertiary field. Explain how you would adapt the radix sort algorithm to sort a list of records that include a date in the above form. Then implement your explanation in a complete C++ function.

4.4 Application: Scheduling Users of a Shared Resource

Queues find extensive application in operating system software for multiuser, time-sharing environments. Consider the situation pictured in Figure 4.11—multiple point-of-sale terminals accessing a common inventory file. Suppose that point-of-sale terminal 1 records a sale of four items with ItemID 36481 at the same time that point-of-sale terminal 2 records a sale of six items with ItemID 36481. Suppose also that, prior to these two sales, the quantity in inventory of item 36481 is 640. Then, if we assume that the sale at point-of-sale terminal 1 occurs momentarily before that at terminal 2, the scenario pictured in Figure 4.12 could occur.

The flaw in this scenario is obvious. After all updates are completed, the inventory record for ItemID 36481 shows a quantity of 634 instead of the correct value of 630. What has caused this error? The two processes associated with terminal 1 and terminal 2, respectively, are allowed simultaneous access to the file record belonging to ItemID 36481. Consequently, the actions of process 2 inadvertently negate the work already done by process 1.

One solution to this problem often used by operating system designers is simply to block any other process from accessing the record associated with ItemID 36481 while that record is being worked with by process 1. In their access to a particular record from the inventory file, any two processes associated with point-of-sale terminals are said to be *mutually exclusive*—one process cannot access this resource (for updating) while it is being used by another. The method for implementing this solution in a time-sharing system is from Dijkstra (Dijkstra, E. W., "Cooperating Sequential Processes," Technological University, Eindhoven, Netherlands, 1965; reprinted in F. Genys (Ed.), *Programming Languages*, New York: Academic Press, 1968). The method employs queues and a special flagging variable known as a *semaphore.*

To understand Dijkstra's solution, we must first define the behavior of processes in a time-sharing environment. In such an environment, the central processor dedicates a small *time slice* to each process before moving on to the next process. The ideal ADT to schedule processes in this fashion is a Queue. In the simplest of scenarios, the processor accesses a process from the queue, dequeues it, and then dedicates a time slice in which to execute this process. If the time slice expires before the process completes, that process will be enqueued again before another process is accessed and dequeued. However, once mutually exclusive processes

Figure 4.11
Point-of-sale terminals sharing an inventory file.

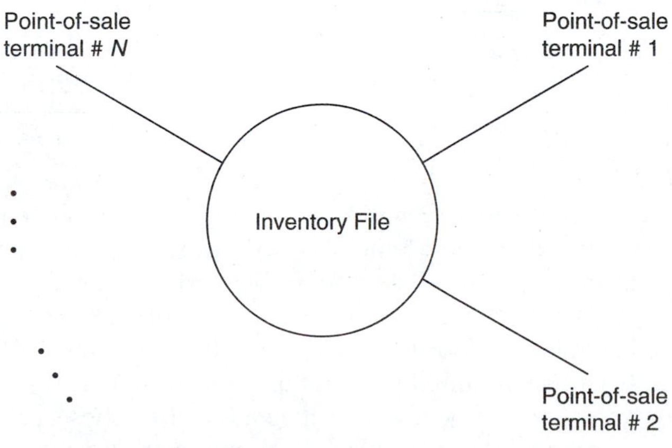

Figure 4.12
Possible scenario of events arising from Figure 4.11.

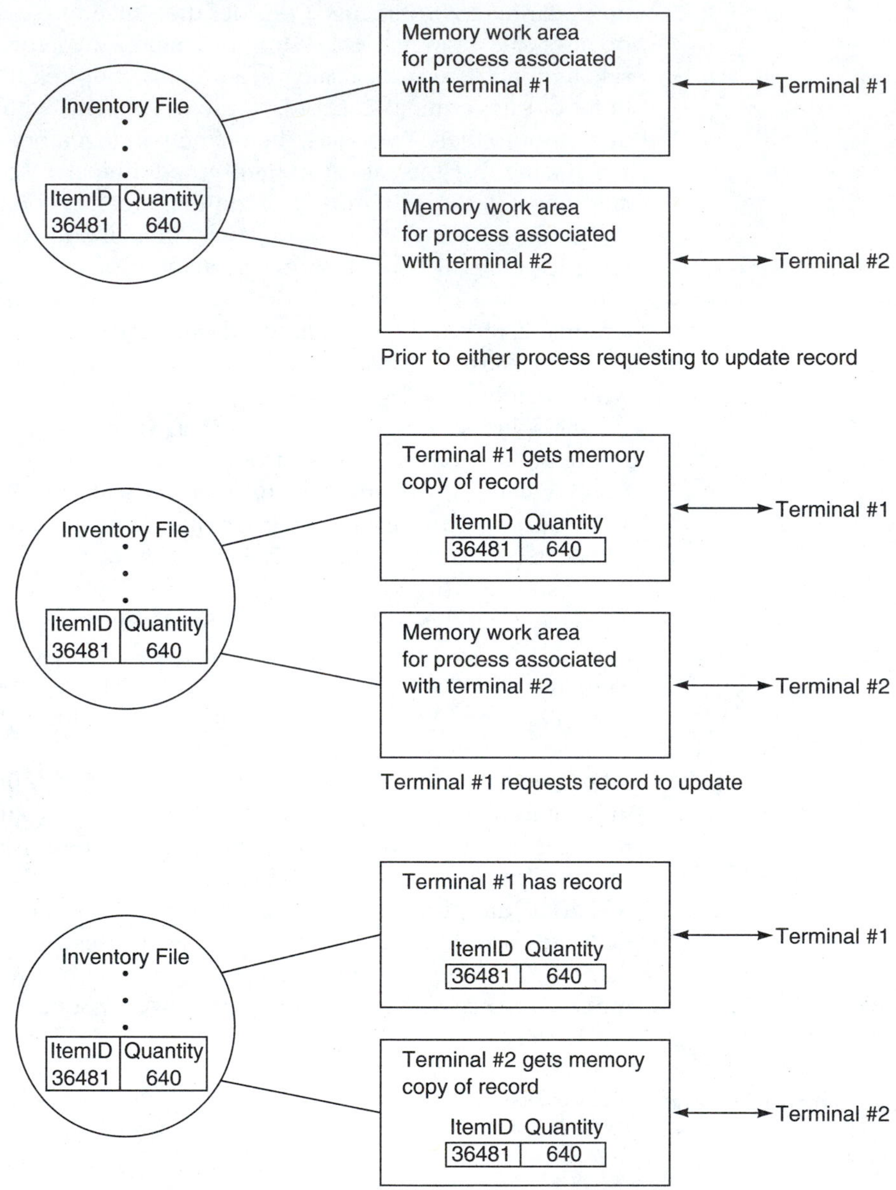

enter into this scenario, it becomes a bit more complicated. Now the processor cannot dedicate a time slice to a process unless that process has access to all the shared resources (such as file records) it currently needs for execution. Thus we shall restrict this notion of a queue of processes waiting to be serviced by the central processor to contain only those processes that currently have access to all resources required to continue execution. Because every process in this queue has access to every resource it needs, all of these processes are "ready" to execute. Consequently, this queue is known as the *ready queue* of processes. It may turn out that sometime during its time slice an executing process may need a resource it did not need at the beginning of the time slice. In this case, the process must cease

Figure 4.12
(continued)

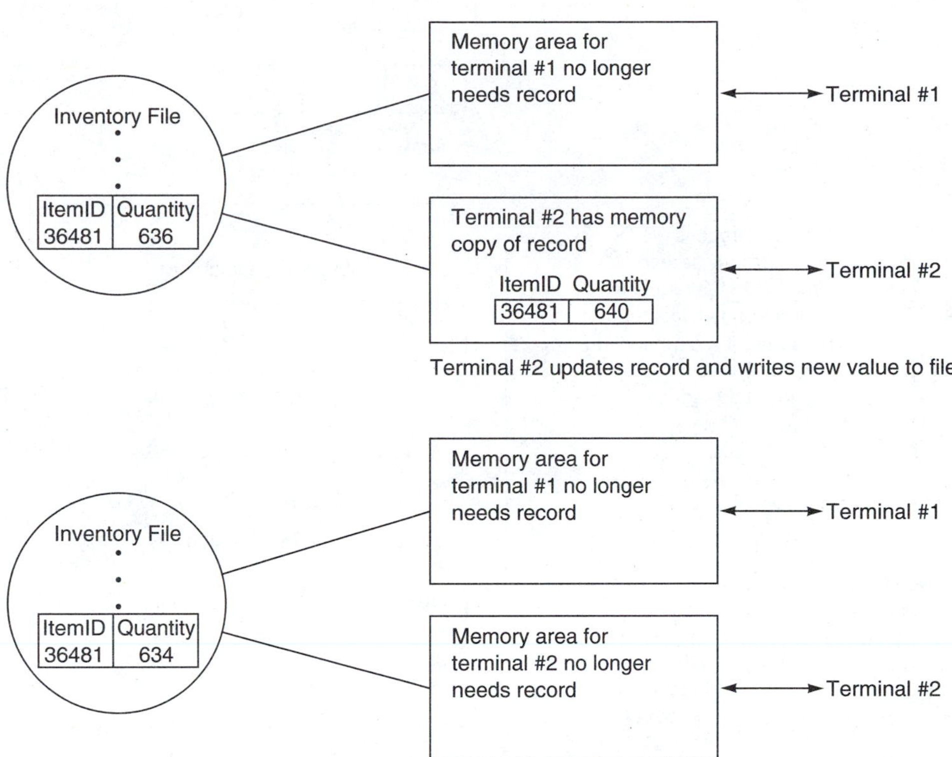

executing, request and acquire the resource, and then await its turn in the ready queue until it is once again assigned a (new) time slice.

Returning to the second snapshot in the scenario of Figure 4.12, suppose the processor grants the process associated with terminal 1 exclusive access to the inventory record ItemID 36481. If process 1 does not finish updating this record before its time slice runs to completion, when process 2 is accessed, dequeued and then requests this record, the processor must in effect say, "Sorry, you cannot have that resource, it is currently dedicated to another process." At this point, process 2 should not be returned to the ready queue because it does not have access to all the resources it needs to run. Process 2 is to be considered *blocked* (from access to a resource it needs) and will be enqueued in a *blocked queue* of processes that are waiting to access this record (or perhaps this file). Hence, every process in the blocked queue for the record with ItemID 36481 has requested access to that record and has been told by the processor that another process already owns it. The multiqueue picture is shown in Figure 4.13.

Traditionally, a *semaphore* is a special Boolean variable used to control enqueuing/dequeuing for queues associated with shared resources such as those in Figure 4.13. A semaphore has the value TRUE when its associated resource is available and FALSE otherwise. Moreover, the semaphore is to be accessed only through two special operations—the **pause** operation and the **signal** operation (called the P and V operations by Dijkstra, from the first letters of the Dutch words *proberen,* "to test" and *verhogen,* "to increment," respectively). As such, semaphores are prime candidates to be an ADT that uses the following C++ definition.

Figure 4.13
Ready and blocked queues for scheduling processes.

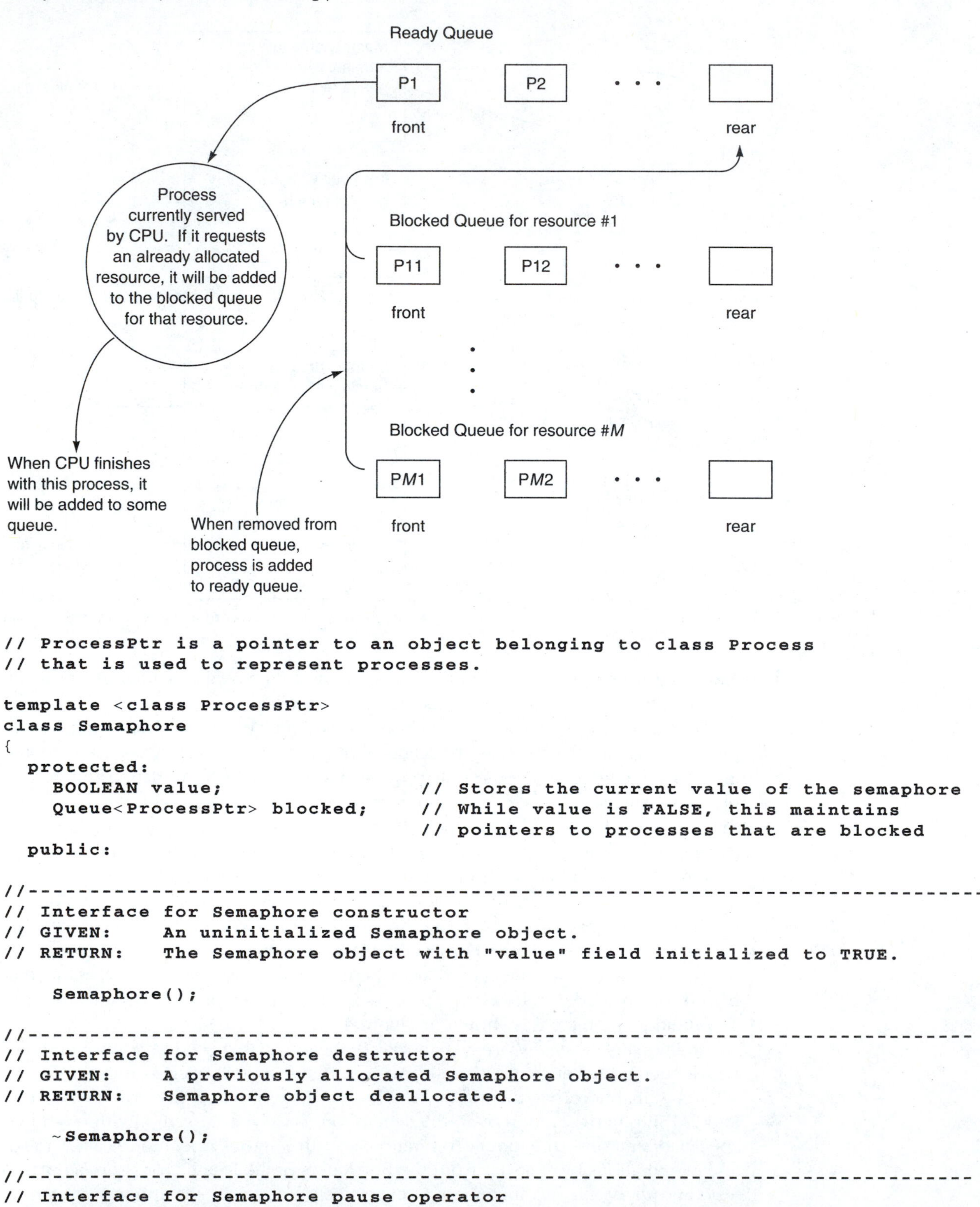


```
// ProcessPtr is a pointer to an object belonging to class Process
// that is used to represent processes.

template <class ProcessPtr>
class Semaphore
{
  protected:
    BOOLEAN value;                  // Stores the current value of the semaphore
    Queue<ProcessPtr> blocked;      // While value is FALSE, this maintains
                                    // pointers to processes that are blocked
  public:

//------------------------------------------------------------------------------
// Interface for Semaphore constructor
// GIVEN:    An uninitialized Semaphore object.
// RETURN:   The Semaphore object with "value" field initialized to TRUE.

    Semaphore();

//------------------------------------------------------------------------------
// Interface for Semaphore destructor
// GIVEN:    A previously allocated Semaphore object.
// RETURN:   Semaphore object deallocated.

    ~Semaphore();

//------------------------------------------------------------------------------
// Interface for Semaphore pause operator
// GIVEN:    A Semaphore object.
```

```
//          procptr -- a pointer to a process.
// RETURN:  If current value of the Semaphore object is TRUE, value will be
//          changed to FALSE; otherwise value will remain FALSE and the process
//          referenced by pointer procptr will be blocked.
// RETURN as value of function:
//          The value of the Semaphore at the time pause was invoked.

   BOOLEAN pause(ProcessPtr procptr);

//------------------------------------------------------------------------------
// Interface for Semaphore signal operator
// GIVEN:   A Semaphore object.
// RETURN:  If the Semaphore's value is TRUE, the Semaphore remains as it is;
//          if the value is FALSE and no (pointers to) processes are blocked,
//          then the value is set to TRUE, while if there are blocked processes,
//          value remains as FALSE and a process pointer is unblocked.
// RETURN as value of function:
//          NULL if Semaphore value is TRUE or Semaphore value is FALSE and
//          no processes are blocked; otherwise return a pointer to the
//          process unblocked.

   ProcessPtr signal();
};
```

Relating these operations to Figure 4.13, the **pause** operation is invoked when the process currently served by the CPU requests resource R. At that point, one of two possibilities occurs. If resource R is available, the operating system allocates it to the currently running process. Otherwise, this process cannot continue since it cannot be granted access to a resource (namely, R) that it needs. Consequently, the operating system will enqueue the process on the blocked queue of processes waiting for resource R.

The **signal** operation is invoked when the process currently serviced by the CPU finishes using a shared resource R. When this occurs, the operating system must check the blocked queue for resource R. If there is a process waiting in this queue, it can be accessed, dequeued, granted access to the resource R, and then enqueued on the ready queue. If the blocked queue for R is empty, the operating system need merely set the semaphore to TRUE so that the resource will be viewed as available when it is next requested.

In our discussion of the role of **pause** and **signal** in granting or denying access to resource R, we delegated the task of these operations to the operating system. The operating system will also need to keep track of which process has been assigned to R. Since each shared resource will need to have its own semaphore as well as a data structure for recording information about the process to which it is currently allocated, and since the operating system will have to use the same protocol for requesting that a process be associated with or released from that resource, it is natural to encapsulate these structures and protocols into an ADT, each of whose instances will represent a shared system resource. A possible C++ definition for such an ADT, which we call the **SharedResource** class, is as follows:

```
template <class ProcessPtr>
class SharedResource
{
  protected:
    ProcessPtr assignedTo;          // Pointer to a Process object representing the
                                    // process currently allocated the shared
                                    // resource.
```

```
    Semaphore<ProcessPtr> access; // Semaphore for controlling access to the
                                  // shared resource object.
  public:

//----------------------------------------------------------------------------
// Interface for SharedResource constructor
// GIVEN:     An uninitialized SharedResource object.
// RETURN:    SharedResource object with no currently associated process,
//            that is, with its assignedTo pointer initialized to NULL.

    SharedResource();

//----------------------------------------------------------------------------
// Interface for SharedResource destructor
// GIVEN:     A previously allocated SharedResource object.
// RETURN:    SharedResource object deallocated.

    ~SharedResource();

//----------------------------------------------------------------------------
// Interface for SharedResource request operator
// GIVEN:     A SharedResource object;
//            proc -- a pointer to a process requesting access to the shared
//                    resource.
// RETURN:    If proc is permitted to access the SharedResource object, proc
//            will be assigned to the resource; otherwise proc will be blocked
//            until it can be assigned to the shared resource.
// RETURN as value of function: void

    void request(ProcessPtr proc);

//----------------------------------------------------------------------------
// Interface for SharedResource grantedTo operator
// GIVEN:     A SharedResource object.
// RETURN as value of function:
//            A pointer to the process currently assigned to the SharedResource;
//            if no process is currently assigned, NULL is returned.

    ProcessPtr grantedTo();

//----------------------------------------------------------------------------
// Interface for SharedResource release operator
// GIVEN:     A SharedResource object.
// RETURN:    Reassigns the shared resource to the next blocked process; if
//            there are no blocked processes, the value NULL is assigned.
// RETURN as value of function: void

    void release();
};
```

Simulation of Mutually Exclusive Processes Sharing a Resource

One of the ways in which queues find frequent application is in the simulation, or modeling, of activities. Such simulation allows us to "experiment in the abstract." That is, we can introduce situations that could be very costly (or dangerous) to create in real life and then use a computer model to predict how such situations affect the critical parameters by which we monitor the activity being observed. For instance, with respect to mutually exclusive processes sharing a resource, it would be useful to explore the relationship between given input conditions such as the following:

- The likelihood that a new process will be enqueued on the ready queue in a given time slice
- The average number of time slices required by a new process to complete its task(s) before logging off
- The likelihood that the currently running process will request a shared resource
- The average amount of time that the shared resource is held by the process to which it is allocated.

We should also explore the effect of these inputs on monitoring parameters such as the following:

- The average length of the blocked queue for that resource
- The average amount of time a process must spend in the blocked queue waiting for the resource it requests.

We now develop the top-level logic in C++ for such a simulation. We begin by assuming that the data associated with a process is encapsulated in a **Process** class, the definition of which might include the following:

```
class Process
{
  protected:
    int processID;          // An integer used to identify a given process. For
                            // the present simulation, this is the only data
                            // associated with a process.  You may add other data
                            // members for the exercises and problems.
  public:

//-----------------------------------------------------------------------------
// Interface for Process constructor
// GIVEN:    An uninitialized Process object;
//           pid -- a previously determined Process identifier (an
//                  integer) to be assigned to the Process object.
// RETURN:   The Process object that has been assigned the designated
//           Process identifier.

    Process(int pid);

//-----------------------------------------------------------------------------
// Interface for Process destructor
// GIVEN:    A previously allocated Process object.
// RETURN:   Process object deallocated.

    ~Process();

//-----------------------------------------------------------------------------
// Interface for Process getPid operator
// GIVEN:    A previously allocated Process object.
// RETURN as value of function:
//           The value of the Process identifier of the Process object.

    int getPid();
};
```

In our logic we treat both an unspecified resource **shResource** as well as the CPU itself as two resources to which processes must be granted mutually exclusive access. The simulation will run for **lengthOfSimulation** time slices. The simulation begins by creating a special process **idleProc** that will "occupy" the CPU when no other processes have CPU requests pending. After this idling process is created, we must, in each time slice of the simulation, do the following:

- Determine if a new process logs on to the CPU in this time slice. The probability of such a logon in any given time slice is determined by a defined constant LOGON.
- When a regular process (that is, one other than the idling process) occupies the CPU, determine if that process:

  a. Is finished with the CPU. This determination is based on a probability established by the defined constant FINISHEDCPU.

  b. If not finished with the CPU, does the current process own the shared resource and, if so, is it now done with the shared resource? This determination is based on a probability established by the defined constant FINISHEDRESOURCE.

  c. If not the owner of the shared resource, does the current process request the shared resource in the current time slice? This determination is based on a probability established by the defined constant RESOURCE.

As you study the following C++ code for the mainline simulation note that all of the probabilistic determinations just described rely on a function **determine,** whose protocol is specified by

```
BOOLEAN determine(float probability)
```

and which abides by the following preconditions and postconditions:

```
//---------------------------------------------------------------------------------
// Interface for determine function
// GIVEN:    probability, a real value between 0 and 1 (noninclusive).
// RETURN as function value:
//           Over a large number of invocations, will return the value TRUE in
//           proportion to the value of probability.
```

In the exercises and problems that follow the main line code below, you will be asked to complete the implementation of this simulation by completing the implementations of the classes used here—the **Semaphore, SharedResource,** and **Process** classes. In addition you will be asked to implement the routine **determine.** This routine requires the use of a random number generator and probability distributions. If you are not familiar with random number generation, this topic is discussed, along with its use in generating events according to specified probabilities, in Appendix A.

```
// Mainline code for shared resource simulation

void main()
{
  const int LENGTHOFSIM = 100;    // The value 100 may be replaced by another
                                  // value.
```

```
const float LOGON = 0.3;           // The probability that a process will logon
                                   // in a given time interval.

const float FINISHEDCPU = 0.3; // The probability that a process has
                                   // finished executing in a given time slice.

const float RESOURCE = 0.3;        // The probability that a process requests the
                                   // shared resource in a given time slice.

const float FINISHEDRESOURCE = 0.3; // The probability that a process has
                                    // finished with the shared resource in
                                    // a given time slice.

const int IDLEID = -1          // The process id for the special process that
                               // runs on the CPU when no other processes have
                               // CPU requests pending.

Process *proc, *idleproc, *currentProc;
SharedResource<Process *> cpu, shResource;
int pid = 1;
char ch;

idleProc = new Process(IDLEID);   // Create a special process idleproc that
                                  // will run the CPU when no other processes
                                  // have CPU requests pending

cpu.request(idleProc);
currentProc = idleProc;
for (int timeSlice = 1; timeSlice <= LENGTHOFSIM; ++timeslice)
{
  if (determine(LOGON))     // Will a process logon in this time interval?
  {
    proc = new Process(pid++);    // Create a process with designated pid;
                                  // increment pid for next process
    cpu.request(proc);            // Schedule proc for execution on CPU
  } // end of logic for LOGON
  if (currentProc != idleProc)    // Is the system currently running a
  {                               // regular (i.e., not the idle) process?
    if (determine(FINISHEDCPU))   // If so, does the current process finish
    {                             // executing in this time slice?
      if (shResource.grantedTo() == currentProc)
                                  // Check to see if currentProc was also
                                  // assigned shResource, and if it was,
      {                           // release shResource.
         shResource.release();
         proc = shResource.grantedTo();
         if (proc != NULL)        // If other processes were awaiting
                                  // shResource, one of them acquires it
                                  // and is scheduled for the CPU.
           cpu.request(proc);     // Another proc assigned resource
      } // End of logic for currentProc assigned resource
    } // End of logic for FINISHEDCPU()
    else        // Current process still needs the CPU, but will have to be
    {           // rescheduled for it
      if (shResource.grantedTo() == currentProc) // Does current Proc have
      {                                          // shResource?
        if (determine(FINISHEDRESOURCE))   // If so, is it finished with it?
        {
          shResource.release();   // currentProc is finished with
                                  // shResource, so release it
          proc = shResource.grantedTo(); // see who gets shResource next
```

```
        if (proc != NULL)                // If other processes were awaiting
                                         // shRs, one of them acquires
                                         // it and is scheduled for CPU.
          cpu.request(proc);
      } // end of logic for FINISHEDRESOURCE
      cpu.request(currentProc);
    }
    else      // Current process does not have shResource; does
              // it request shResource in this time slice?
      if (determine(RESOURCE))
      {
        shResource.request(currentProc);
        if (currentProc == shResource.grantedTo()) // If currentProc acquires
                                                    // shResource, reschedule
                                                    // for CPU; otherwise current
                                                    // process is blocked for
                                                    // shResource
          cpu.request(currentProc);
      } //end of logic for RESOURCE
      else
        cpu.request(currentProc);
   } // End of logic for !FINISHEDCPU
  } // End of logic for currentProc != idlePproc
  cpu.release();                    // Remove current process from the CPU
  currentProc = cpu.grantedTo();    // See which process gets CPU next
  if (currentProc == NULL)          // If no processes are awaiting the CPU,
  {                                 // restart the idle process
    cpu.request(idleProc);
    currentProc = idleProc;
  }
 } // end of for loop logic
}
```

Exercises 4.4

1. Suppose we have the following sequence of events in the first 10 time slices of the simulation discussed in this section:

   Time slice

   1: Process A logs on to system, with a job that will ultimately require six CPU time slices.

   2: Process B logs on to system, with a job that will require four CPU time slices.

   3: Current process requests shared resource for three CPU time slices.

   4: Process C logs on to system, with job that will require six CPU time slices.

   5–10: No new activity except each process that does not own the shared resource requests it for two time slices in its first time slice during this period.

   Trace the status of the ready and blocked queues in each of the first 10 time slices. Also, indicate when the **pause** and **signal** semaphores would be executed during this period of the simulation.

2. Explain how the top-level logic for the simulation discussed in this section would change if the likelihood that a process would request a shared resource were process dependent. That is, instead of this likelihood being a probability that applied to all processes, it would be a potentially different probability for each process. This is more characteristic of a true multiuser operating system environment, where many users would not request a particular shared resource at all, but others would have a very high probability of requesting the resource.
3. Suppose that we had more than one of a particular shared resource; that is, we have a pool of $n > 1$ identical resources. This situation would occur for such shared resources as line printers, tape drives, or memory buffers. Explain how you could extend the notion of a semaphore to apply to such a shared resource. Your explanation should include an appropriate rewrite of the **pause** and **signal** operations.

4. Define an appropriate process-like ADT and design top-level logic for the simulation of
   - **a.** Airplanes arriving at and departing from an airport with multiple runways.
   - **b.** Customers waiting for service at an auto bank with multiple service windows.

   What are the similarities and differences between each of these simulations and the scheduling of computer users as discussed in this section?

A RELEVANT ISSUE Mutually Exclusive Processes Sharing More Than One Resource

In this chapter we have seen how a semaphore and blocked queue can be used effectively to control mutually exclusive processes sharing a single resource. However, this solution is not without complications of its own, as the following example shows.

Suppose that we have two separate shared resources—Resource A and Resource B. Note that A and B are not identical copies of the same resource in the sense of Exercise 3 in Section 4.4. Suppose also that both these resources are presently available and that we have two processes—Process 1 and Process 2—that might potentially request both of these resources. During its time slice, Process 1 requests Resource A. Since Resource A is available, Process 1 receives access to this resource and is placed on the ready queue when Process 2 begins it time slice. Process 2 requests Resource B and is similarly granted access to it. Now Process 1 starts its time slice again, and it requests Resource B in addition to Resource A, which it already owns. Since Process 2 owns Resource B, Process A must be put on the blocked queue for Resource B. Process 2 begins execution during its time slice and finds that it needs Resource A in addition to Resource B, which it already owns. Since Resource A is owned by Process 1, Process 2 must be put on the blocked queue for Resource A.

The dilemma in which we find ourselves is highlighted in Figure 4.14. Both Process 1 and Process 2 are stymied in blocked queues, waiting for a resource owned by the other process. Since neither process can run, neither can complete what it must do with the resource it already owns. The processes are hung in a situation known as *deadlock*, or *fatal embrace*.

Hence, solving one problem—mutually exclusive processes accessing a shared resource—has led to another. The deadlock problem is dreaded by all operating system designers. For a discussion of strategies for coping with it, see Andrew S. Tanenbaum's *Modern Operating Systems* (Englewood Cliffs, N.J.: Prentice-Hall, 1992).

4.5 Priority Queues

Many multiuser operating systems attach priorities to processes that run on the system. Assume that processes with a higher priority will always be serviced before those with a lower priority. Then an appropriate structure for scheduling processes in such an environment is the *priority queue* abstract data type. We may think of a priority queue as a collection of "mini-queues"—one such mini-queue for each priority value of an item in the queue. When an item is added to a priority queue, it is added at the end of the mini-queue associated with that item's priority value. When an item is removed from a priority queue, it is removed from the mini-queue belonging to those items that have the highest priority among all items in the priority queue. This concept is illustrated in Figure 4.15. In this figure, we have a priority queue containing eight processes waiting to be serviced by the CPU of a computer system. STATS, PRINT, and BANK are the priority 3 (highest) jobs awaiting service; COPY and CHECK the priority 2 jobs; and UPDATE, AVERAGE, and TEST the priority 1 (lowest) jobs. If a new priority 3 job PROB1 arrived for service, it would be inserted at the end of the priority 3 queue, between BANK and COPY. Because jobs can be serviced only by leaving the front of the queue, PROB1 would be processed before any of the priority 2 or priority 1 jobs.

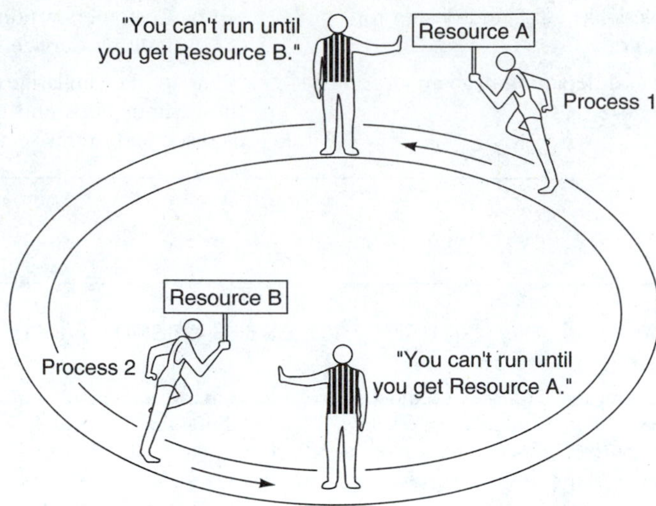

Figure 4.14
Two processes in a deadlock situation.

A formal definition of the priority queue ADT is given in the following, along with preconditions and postconditions for priority queue operations:

Definition: A *priority queue* is a restricted list of items of type *Basedata* arranged according to a priority value associated with each item. When an item is removed from a priority queue, it must be an item having the highest priority value of all items in the priority queue. If there is more than one such item, then the item of highest priority value that has been in the priority queue for the longest time is the item removed.

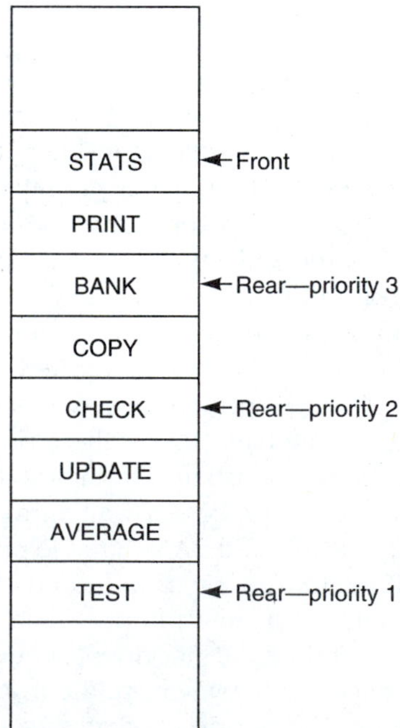

Figure 4.15
A priority queue with eight jobs at three priority levels.

Construct Operation (First Form)

Preconditions: An uninitialized priority queue object;
priority—an integer-valued function that will be used to assign priorities to items of type Basedata.

Postconditions: The priority queue object is initialized to an empty priority queue. New items will be added to the priority queue in accordance with the priority function.

Construct Operation (Copy Constructor)

Preconditions: An uninitialized priority queue object;
initpq—a priority queue object that was previously constructed.

Postconditions: The priority queue object is initialized to *initpq*.

Destroy Operation

Precondition: A priority queue object that currently exists.

Postcondition: Priority queue object deallocated.

Front Operation

Precondition: A nonempty priority queue object.

Postcondition: The data of type *Basedata* that has the highest priority of those being stored in the priority queue is returned. If there is more than one such item, then the item that has been in the queue the longest among those with the highest priority value is returned.

Empty Operation

Precondition: A priority queue object.

Postcondition: If no removals can be made from the priority queue, the operation returns the value TRUE; otherwise it returns the value FALSE.

Full Operation

Precondition: A priority queue object.

Postcondition: If no additions can be made to the priority queue, the operation returns the value TRUE; otherwise it returns the value FALSE.

Enqueue Operation

Precondition: A priority queue object that is not full;
item—a value of type Basedata that is to become the value of a new node in the priority queue.

Postcondition: *item* is inserted in the priority queue in accordance with the previously designated priority function.

Dequeue Operation

Precondition: A nonempty priority queue object.

Postcondition: The highest priority node is removed. If there is more than one such node, then the node that has been in the queue the longest among those with the highest priority value is removed.

Implementation Strategies for Priority Queues

A skeleton C++ interface for specifying the priority queue ADT based on an array implementation can be defined as follows:

```
// BaseData is either a C++ built-in type, or a C++ class that has an assignment
// operation that overloads the "=" operator.

template <class BaseData>
class PriorityQueue
{
  public:

//---------------------------------------------------------------------------------
// Interface for priority queue constructor
// GIVEN:    An uninitialized priority queue object;
//           priority -- an integer-valued function that will be used to
//                       prioritize items in the queue.
// RETURN:   The priority queue object is initialized to an empty priority queue
//           with priority as its underlying priority function.

    PriorityQueue(int (*priority)(const BaseData &item));

//---------------------------------------------------------------------------------
// Interface for priority queue copy constructor
// GIVEN:    An uninitialized priority queue object;
//           initpq -- a priority queue object.
// RETURN:   The given priority queue object is initialized with the node
//           values and priority function of initpq.

    PriorityQueue(Queue &initpq);

//---------------------------------------------------------------------------------
// Interface for priority queue destructor
// GIVEN:    A previously allocated priority queue object
// RETURN:   Priority queue object deallocated.

    ~PriorityQueue();

//---------------------------------------------------------------------------------
// Interface for front operator
// GIVEN:    A nonempty priority queue object.
// RETURN as value of function:
//           The data of type BaseData that is being stored at the front node
//           of the queue. The front node of the queue is the node with the
//           highest priority value.  If there is more than one node with this
//           value, the front node is the one among all such nodes that has
//           been in the queue for  the longest time.

    BaseData front();

//---------------------------------------------------------------------------------
// Interface for empty operator
// GIVEN:    A priority queue object.
// RETURN as value of function:
//           TRUE if no removals can be made from the queue; FALSE otherwise.

    BOOLEAN empty();

//---------------------------------------------------------------------------------
// Interface for full operator
// GIVEN:    A priority queue object.
// RETURN as value of function:
//           TRUE if no additions can be made to the queue; FALSE otherwise.

    BOOLEAN full();
```

```
//---------------------------------------------------------------------------
// Interface for enqueue operator
// GIVEN:   A priority queue object that is not full;
//          item -- a data item to inserted into the queue.
// RETURN:  The priority queue object with item inserted in its proper place
//          as determined by item's priority.
// RETURN as value of function: void

    void enqueue(const Basedata &item);

//---------------------------------------------------------------------------
// Interface for dequeue operator:
// GIVEN:    A nonempty queue object.
// RETURN:   The priority queue with the front node removed. The front node
//           of the priority queue is the node with the highest priority value.
//           If there is more than one node with this value, the front node is
//           the one among all such nodes that has been in the queue for the
//           longest time.
//  RETURN as value of function: void

    void dequeue();
];
```

The priority queue presents some interesting implementation options. We will discuss these options conceptually and leave the details of each suggested implementation, along with its efficiency analysis, to the exercises.

Option 1: Store the priority queue as a circular array, ordered by priority of items. Removal of an item is now easy and quick, but insertion could be costly.

Option 2: Store the priority queue as an unordered circular array. This implementation reverses the pluses and minuses of option 1. Removing an item now becomes quite costly.

Option 3: Store the priority queue as an ordered linked list or variation thereof. Think about whether double linking or maintaining special pointers to nodes within the list could be used to enhance the efficiency of the priority queue operations for this implementation.

Option 4: Store the priority queue as an unordered linked list, or variation thereof. Again consider how double linking or maintaining auxiliary pointers could enhance efficiencies.

Option 5: If the priority function associated with the priority queue can only take on a finite number of values, the priority queue may be stored as a list of subordinate queues—one for each value assumed by the priority function. This would allow one to incorporate both the List and the Queue ADTs into an implementation of the priority queue. This concept is illustrated in Figure 4.16.

The priority queue is a tremendously versatile ADT—one that we have just begun to explore. We return to this ADT in Chapter 7, where we will discuss a more efficient implementation of it, and in Chapter 10, where we use it to guide some sophisticated search techniques.

Figure 4.16
Using an implementation of queues to build an implementation of priority queues.

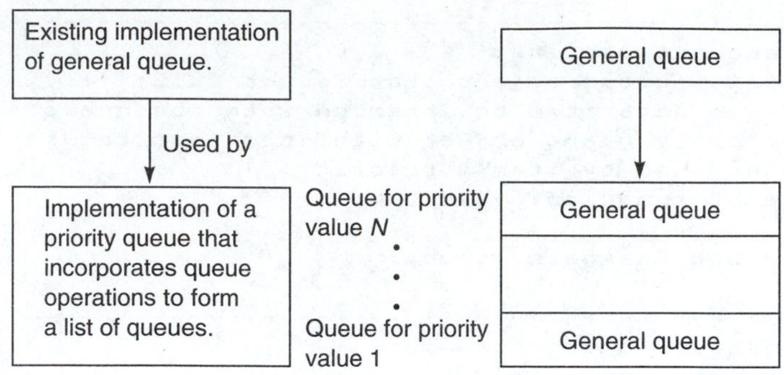

Exercises 4.5

1. Using the suggestion in option 1, which was just given in this section, develop a complete implementation for the priority queue ADT. Then analyze the efficiency of the operations for your implementation.
2. Repeat Exercise 4.5.1 for the suggestion offered in Option 2 of this section.
3. Repeat Exercise 4.5.1 for the suggestion offered in Option 3 of this section.
4. Repeat Exercise 4.5.1 for the suggestion offered in Option 4 of this section.
5. Repeat Exercise 4.5.1 for the suggestion offered in Option 5 of this section.
6. For each of the implementations in Exercises 4.5.1 through 4.5.5, discuss how the number of possible values taken on by the priority function affects the time and space efficiency of the implementation.
7. Suppose that the priority function associated with a priority queue were real-valued instead of integer-valued. How does this complicate the implementation of a priority queue? Does it render impossible any of the implementations you developed in Exercises 4.5.1 through 4.5.5? If so, explain why. If not, convert that implementation so that it appropriately handles a real-valued priority function.
8. In scheduling prioritized processes that share time on a multiuser operating system, it may not be desirable to let a higher priority process always have the CPU before a lower priority process. We might wish simply to give higher priority processes proportionally more time slices than lower priority process. For instance, we may wish to give a priority 4 process four time slices of CPU time for each time slice dedicated to a priority 1 process and, in general, a priority N process processes N time slices for each time slice dedicated to a priority 1 process. Can a priority queue still be used to schedule processes in such an arrangement? If so, provide a detailed explanation of how it would be done. If not, explain why not.

Chapter Summary

Chapter 4 introduced the first of two special types of general lists—the *queue*. A queue is a list with restrictions imposed on the way in which entries may be inserted and removed. In particular, insertions may be made only from one end of the queue, known as the *rear,* while deletions are limited to the other end of the queue, called the *front.* The resulting behavior imposed on a queue by these restrictions gives rise to another name for queues—first-in, first-out (FIFO) lists.

Four methods for implementing a queue were discussed. The first, recognizing a queue as a special type of list, implements the Queue ADT as a derived class from the List ADT; other implementations are those based on arrays, circular lists, and linked lists. The circular implementation is a variation on the array-based implementation and avoids a situation where insertions and deletions cause the indices referencing the rear and front of the queue to move strictly toward the upper index end of the array. This prevents an array location from being used for more than one insertion. By going to a circular implementation, the front and rear indices can wrap around the array, allowing a reuse of locations.

Two applications for queues were given—the *radix sort,* and the scheduling of users of a shared resource. In certain circumstances, the radix sort qualifies as an $O(n)$ algorithm, although implementations of some of the operations it uses may degrade this efficiency significantly. Queues find extensive application in multiuser, time-sharing operating systems, especially through their association with *semaphores,* which are special Boolean variables that control enqueuing and dequeuing for a corresponding queue. They are used to block or grant access to a resource being shared among several processes. This is examined via a simulation of several simultaneously executing processes that must be given mutually exclusive access to a shared resource.

The chapter concluded with an introduction of a *priority queue,* which is a restricted list of items arranged by priority values. Several options for implementing priority queues were described, with analyses left for exercises.

Key Words

blocked queue	front	radix sort	semaphore
circular queue	priority queue	ready queue	simulation
first-in, first-out list	queue	rear	

Programming Problems/Projects

1. Implement fully the simulation of mutually exclusive processes sharing a resource, as described in Section 4.4.
2. In Exercise 4.4.3 you discussed a strategy for extending semaphores to control shared resources of which there is a pool of $n > 1$ identical resources. Add this feature to the simulation you developed for Programming Problem 1.
3. In Exercise 4.5.8 you discussed a strategy that would allow users in a time-sharing environment to have their processes scheduled according to a priority system. Add this feature to the simulation you developed for Programming Problem 1.
4. A *deque* (double-ended queue) is a queue in which insertions and deletions can occur at either end. Write a definition for a *Deque* ADT. Now write an interface for an associated *Deque* class and give an implementation that uses a circular array. Analyze the efficiency of each operation in this implementation.
5. Write an implementation of the Deque ADT (see Programming Problem 4) that uses a linked list. Analyze the efficiency of each operation in this implementation.
6. Develop a program that sorts an array of records on multiple keys using the method you described in your answer to Exercise 4.3.10.
7. In your answer to Exercise 4.3.6 you described how the radix sort could be made more efficient if it were to access the implementation of a queue directly, instead of accessing the queue only via the provided ADT operations. Now develop a program that empirically tests how much more efficient this technique would be. Implement the radix sort by both methods and time the two implementations under comparable conditions with identical data sets. In a written report, summarize the results of your experimentation.
8. Develop a program that empirically races the radix sort against the Shell sort algorithm, discussed in Chapter 1. Have your program sort data by both methods, keeping track of the number of data interchanges, comparisons (for the Shell sort), and determinations of an appropriate bin (for the radix sort). Use your program for experimentation. Race the two sorting methods on a variety of data. Recall that, although the radix sort is $O(n)$, the constant of proportionality in determining its $O(n)$ efficiency can be quite large. How large does n have to be for various kinds of data (for example, integers and strings) before the radix sort actually becomes faster than the $O(n(\log_2 n)^2)$ efficiency of the Shell sort? Summarize the results of your experimentation in a written report.
9. A bank has asked you to develop a program to simulate the arrival of customers in a waiting line at the bank. Factors to consider are the average time it takes to service one customer, the average number of customers that arrive in a given time period, and the number of service windows maintained by the bank. Statistics such as the length of time the average customer has to spend in the waiting line could be very helpful in the bank's future planning.
10. Here is a problem typically encountered in text formatting applications. Given a file of text, any text enclosed in brackets is to be considered a footnote. Footnotes, when encountered, are not to be printed as normal text but are instead stored in a footnote queue. Then, when the special symbol # is encountered, all footnotes currently in the queue are printed and the queue should be returned to an empty state. What you learn in solving this problem will allow you to make good use of string storage techniques discussed in earlier chapters.
11. To improve their services, the Fly-by-Night credit card company has decided to give incentives to their customers for prompt payment. Customers who pay their bill two weeks before the due date receive top priority and a 5% discount. Customers who pay their bills within one week of the due date receive next priority and a 1%

discount. Third priority is given to customers who pay their bills on or within two days after the due date. The customers who pay their bills thereafter are assigned the lowest priority. Write a program to set up a priority queue that accesses customer records accordingly.

12. The Bay Area Brawlers professional football team has been so successful in recent weeks that team management is considering the addition of several ticket windows at the team's stadium. However, before investing a sizable amount of money in such an improvement, they would like to simulate the operation of ticket sales with a variety of ticket window configurations. Develop a computer program that allows input of data such as number of ticket windows, average number of fans arriving each hour as game time approaches, and average length of time to process a ticket sale. Output from your program should include statistics such as the average waiting-line length each hour as game time approaches and the amount of time the average fan has to wait in line. Use queues to represent each of the waiting lines.

13. The management of a grocery store is thinking about expanding the number of checkout lanes in their store (currently there are three). To help them decide what to do, they hire you to write a program to simulate the current activity of their checkout lanes as well as the activity that would ensue if they added a fourth lane. Currently, none of their checkout lanes is an "express" lane, so they would like your simulation to account for two possible setups for the additional lane—either exclusively as an express lane or general patronage.

For this project you are to write a C++ program that produces at least the following statistics for the store's current and potential checkout arrangements (that is, three-lane, four-lane, and three-lane plus express):

- The mean number of people served per hour for each lane
- The mean number of items processed per hour by each lane
- The mean number of customers at a lane each time a new customer comes to that lane
- The maximum number of customers who were at a given lane when a customer came to that lane.

You may add any additional statistics that you feel might be useful to the store managers. Your program should take into account the following patterns:

- The intervals between the arrivals of customers at the checkout area
- The service times required for each customer at a register
- The number of items each customer brings to the checkout area
- The choice of checkout lanes for a customer (assume the express lane limit will be strictly enforced).

A suggestion for implementing the checkout behavior would be to use a uniform random number generator to generate the next arrival time and number of items for a customer and to determine the service time as a function of the number of items. Limits for the ranges of random numbers to be generated for arrival times and number of items can be entered as input, as can express lane limits and coefficients needed to calculate service times. For choosing a checkout lane, assume a customer will go to the lane that offers the shortest overall waiting time; in case of a tie, choose the lowest numbered lane (assume the lanes are numbered 1, 2, 3, and 4).

CHAPTER 5 Stacks

Ah well! I am their leader, I really ought to follow them!
Alexandre Auguste Ledru-Rollin
(From *Histoire Contemporaine No. 79*)

Chapter Outline:

Although a first-in, first-out structure such as a queue seems to be the obvious way of storing items that must wait to be processed, there are many natural instances in which a last-in, first-out (LIFO) strategy is more appropriate. Consider, for example, the order in which a smart traveler will pack a suitcase. To minimize shuffling, the first item to be worn should be the last item packed. Another familiar example of such a storage strategy is that of the pop-up mechanism used to store trays for a cafeteria line. The trays that were loaded into the mechanism first may be stored a long time before they are picked up by a passing diner.

A list of data items processed via a LIFO scheduling strategy is called a *stack*. As we will see in this chapter, stacks are an extremely useful data structure. They find extensive application in the processing of function calls and in the syntactical checking and translation of programming languages by compilers. In Chapter 6, we will see that the Stack ADT supports the powerful programming technique called *recursion*.

5.1 The Stack ADT

The Queue ADT presented in the previous chapter is a special type of list in which all data processing activity occurs at the two ends: the front and the rear. A stack may also be viewed as such a specialized list. However, a stack is even more restricted in that all activity occurs at one designated end called the *top*.

Definition: A *stack* is a restricted list in which entries are added to and removed from one designated end called the *top*. Assuming each node of the stack stores data of type *Basedata*, the following operations are provided for the Stack ADT.

`Construct Operation (First Form)`

Precondition: An uninitialized Stack object.
Postcondition: The Stack object is initialized to an empty Stack.

`Construct Operation (Second Form)`

Precondition: An uninitialized Stack object;
size—a positive integer.
Postcondition: The Stack object is initialized to an empty Stack, but with storage allocated for *size* nodes.

`Construct Operation (Copy Constructor)`

Preconditions: An uninitialized Stack object;
initstack—a Stack object that was previously constructed.
Postconditions: The Stack object is initialized to *initstack.*

`Destroy Operation`

Precondition: A Stack object that currently exists.
Postcondition: All storage allocated to the Stack object is deallocated; that is, returned to an available space pool for allocation to other objects.

`Assign Operation`

Preconditions: A previously constructed Stack object;
source—a second Stack object that uses the same *Basedata* type.
Postconditions: The contents of *source* have been copied to the Stack object that owns the operation.

`Top Operation`

Precondition: A nonempty Stack object.
Postcondition: The data of type *Basedata* that is stored in the top node of the Stack is returned.

`Empty Operation`

Precondition: A Stack object.
Postcondition: If no removals can be made from the Stack, the operation returns the value TRUE; otherwise it returns the value FALSE.

`Full Operation`

Precondition: A Stack object.
Postcondition: If no additions can be made to the Stack, the operation returns the value TRUE; otherwise it returns the value FALSE.

`Push Operation`

Precondition: A Stack object that is not full;
item—having type *Basedata,* is to become the value of a new node in the Stack.
Postcondition: The Stack with *item* inserted at the top.

`Pop Operation`

Precondition: A nonempty Stack object.
Postcondition: The top node is removed from the Stack.

Figure 5.1
Pushing onto and popping from a stack.

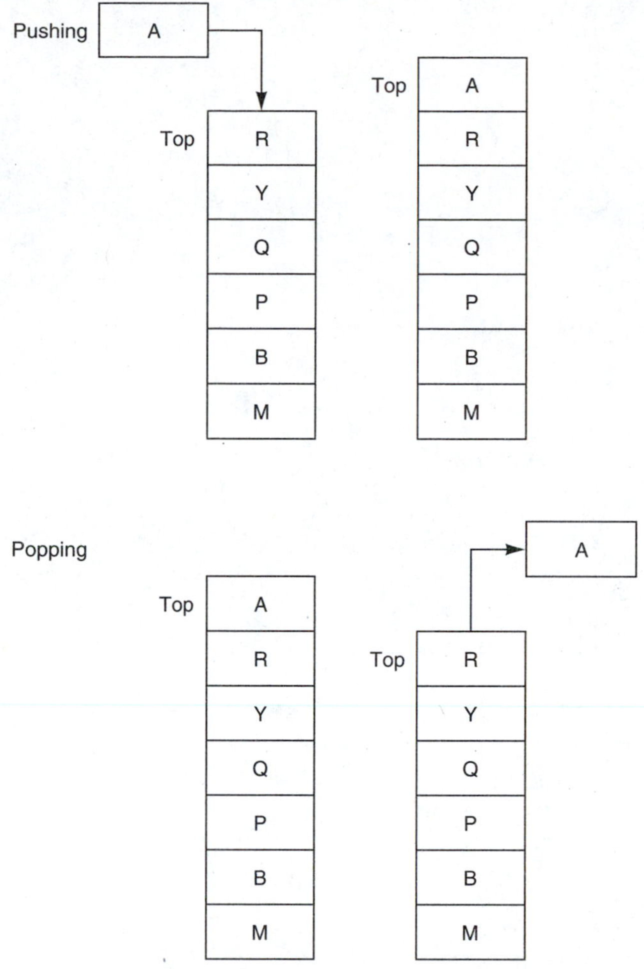

Conceptually, it is easiest to develop a mental image of the Push and Pop operations if you picture a stack as a vertical list with the first entry at the bottom and the last at the top. Then, as indicated in Figure 5.1, adding to the stack—that is, pushing—essentially makes this stack become taller and removing from the stack—that is, popping—results in a shorter stack.

Stacks and Function Calls

Before we discuss methods of implementing a stack, we want to give you some hint of their importance in the processing of function calls. Of key importance to the processing of function in any language is that the return from a function must be to the instruction immediately following the call that originally transferred control to the function. For example, in the partial coding that follows:

```
void  sub3()
{
   .
   .
   .

}
```

```
void sub2()
{
    .
    .
    .
    sub3();
    p -= q;
    .
    .
    .
}

void sub1()
{
    .
    .
    .
    sub2();
    a += b;
    .
    .
    .
}

void main()
{
    .
    .
    .
    sub1();
    cout << q;
    .
    .
    .
}
```

the order of operations would be

1. Leave **main** and transfer to **sub1.**
2. Leave **sub1** and transfer to **sub2.**
3. Leave **sub2** and transfer to **sub3.**
4. Return from **sub3** to the instruction **p −= q** in **sub2.**
5. Return from **sub2** to the instruction **a += b** in **sub1.**
6. Return from **sub1** to the instruction **cout** << **q** in **main**.
7. End of **main.**

Each time a call is made, the machine must remember where to return on completion of that procedure.

A stack is precisely the structure capable of storing the data necessary to handle calls and returns in this sequence. Hence, the preceding code would generate a stack that develops as illustrated in Figure 5.2. (The numbers in the figure correspond to the order of operations in the list just given.) Each time a call to a function is made, a return address is pushed on top of the stack. Each time a function is completed, the top item on the stack is examined and then popped to determine the memory address to which the return operation should be made. The nature of the leave-return sequence for functions makes it crucial that the first return address accessed be the last one that was remembered by the computer. Because

Figure 5.2
Memory stack generated by previous partial coding. Each time a function is called, a return address is pushed onto the stack. When the function completes, the top of the stack is examined to obtain a return address and then popped.

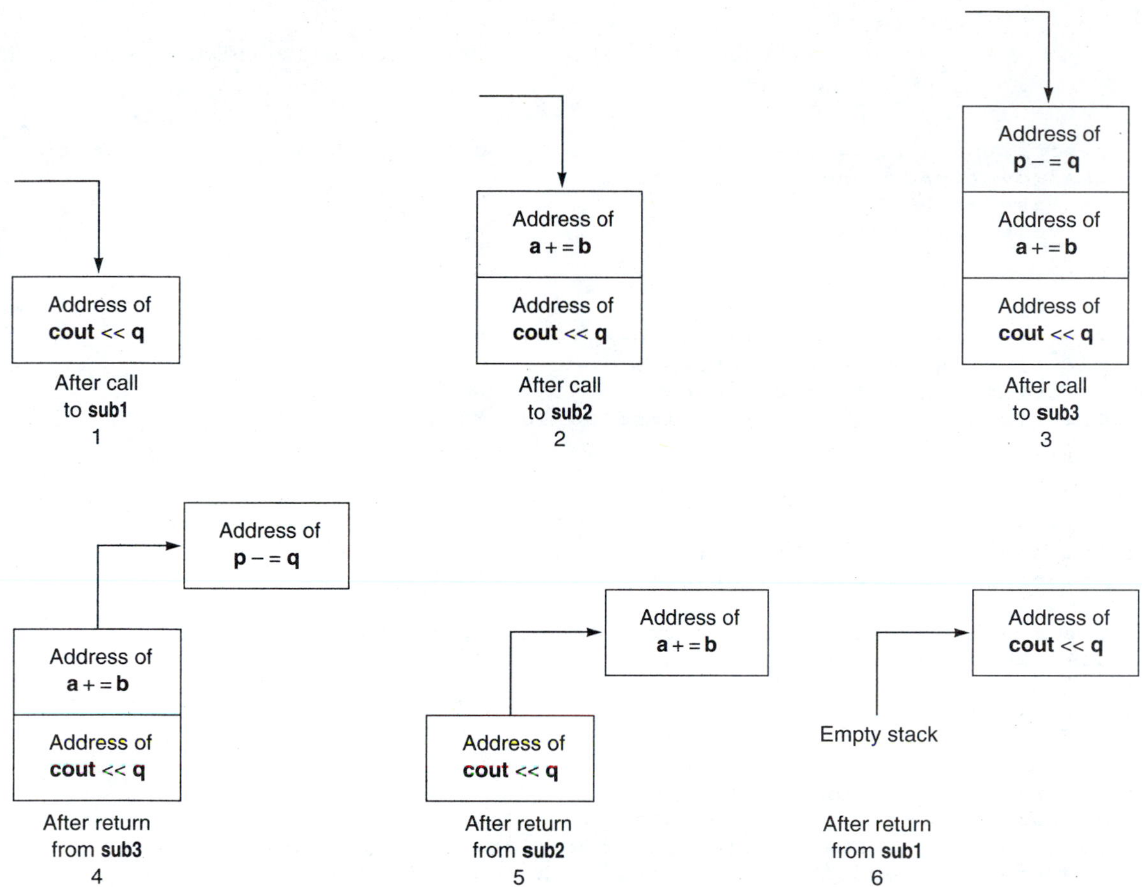

there is only one point, the top, at which data may enter or exit a stack, it is the ideal data structure to be used for this "last-stored, first-recalled" type of operation.

This description of the method by which a compiler actually implements function calls is just one illustration of the utility of stacks. In the next chapter we discuss a different type of function usage called *recursion* and examine in detail the role of the stack in handling such a recursive call. In the next section, however, we will consider two ways of implementing a stack.

Exercises 5.1

1. What is a stack structure?
2. Explain the role of a stack in processing function calls.
3. Explain how the stack used in processing function calls could also be used as memory space for the parameters and local variables of a function.

5.2 Implementations of a Stack

We discuss only the implementation of the Stack ADT as a derived class of the List ADT of Chapter 3. Implementations of the Stack ADT using arrays or linked lists are similar to the implementations of Lists and Queues discussed in Chapters 3 and 4, respectively, and are left for the exercises.

We can specify the Stack ADT as a derived class from the List ADT by means of the following interface:

```
// BaseData is either a C++ built-in type, or a C++ class that has an assignment
// operation that overloads the "=" operator.
template <class BaseData>
class Stack: private List<BaseData>
{
  public:

//------------------------------------------------------------------------------
// Interface for first stack constructor
// GIVEN:     An uninitialized Stack object.
// RETURN:    The Stack object is initialized to an empty stack.

    Stack();

//------------------------------------------------------------------------------
// Interface for second stack constructor
// GIVEN:     An uninitialized Stack object;
//            size -- a nonnegative integer.
// RETURN:    The Stack object is initialized to an empty stack, but with storage
//            allocated for size nodes.

    Stack(int size);

//------------------------------------------------------------------------------
// Interface for Stack copy constructor
// GIVEN:     An uninitialized Stack object;
//            initstack -- a Stack object that was previously constructed.
// RETURN:    The Stack object is initialized with the node values and number of
//            nodes of initstack.

    Stack(Stack<BaseData> &initstack);

//------------------------------------------------------------------------------
// Interface for stack destructor
// GIVEN:     A previously allocated Stack object.
// RETURN:    The Stack object deallocated.

    ~Stack();

//------------------------------------------------------------------------------
// Interface for Stack assign = operator
// GIVEN:     A previously constructed Stack object;
//            source -- a second Stack object that must have been constructed
//                      with the same BaseData type as the owner of the assign
//                      operator.
// RETURN:    The contents of source have been copied to the Stack object that
//            owns the operation.
// RETURN as value of function: void

    void operator = (const Stack<BaseData> &source);
```

```
//----------------------------------------------------------------------------
// Interface for top operation
// GIVEN:     A nonempty Stack object.
// RETURN as value of function:
//            The data of type BaseData that is stored in the top node of the Stack.

   BaseData top();

//----------------------------------------------------------------------------
// Interface for empty operation
// GIVEN:     A Stack object.
// RETURN as value of function:
//            TRUE if no removals can be made from the Stack; FALSE otherwise.

   BOOLEAN empty();

//----------------------------------------------------------------------------
// Interface for full operation
// GIVEN:     A Stack object.
// RETURN as value of function:
//            TRUE if no additions can be made to the Stack; FALSE otherwise.

   BOOLEAN full();

//----------------------------------------------------------------------------
// Interface for push operation
// GIVEN:     A Stack object that is not full;
//            item -- a data item to be inserted into the Stack.
// RETURN:    The Stack with item inserted at the top.
// RETURN as value of function: void

   void push(const BaseData &item);

//----------------------------------------------------------------------------
// Interface for pop operation
// GIVEN:     An nonempty Stack object.
// RETURN:    The Stack with the top node removed.
// RETURN as value of function: void

   void pop();
};
```

The implementations of these operations for the **Stack** class using operations from the parent **List** class would then proceed in a fashion analogous to our derivation of the **Queue** class from the **List** class in Chapter 4. See Examples 4.1 and 4.2 for details.

Exercises 5.2

1. Complete the C++ implementation of the **Stack** class as a derived class of the **List** class.
2. Define the interface and complete the implementations of all operations for a C++ class that implements the Stack ADT using an array.
3. Define the interface and complete the implementation of all operations for a C++ class that implements the Stack ADT using a linked list.
4. Design and implement an algorithm that utilizes a Stack to print a line of text in reverse order.
5. Design and implement an algorithm that utilizes a Stack to check whether an arithmetic expression such as

$$(5/(3 - 2 * (4 + 3) - (8/2)))$$

has appropriately balanced left and right parentheses.

5.3 An Application of Stacks: Parsing and Evaluating Arithmetic Expressions

Often the logic of problems for which a stack is a suitable data structure involves the necessity to backtrack, that is, to return to a previous state. For instance, consider the problem of finding your way out of a maze. One approach to take would be to probe a given path in the maze as deeply as possible. On finding a dead-end, you would need to backtrack to previously visited maze locations in order to try other paths. Such backtracking would require recalling these previous locations in the reverse order from which you visited them.

Not many of us need to find our way out of a maze. However, the designers of compilers are faced with an analogous backtracking situation in the evaluation of arithmetic expressions. As you scan the expression

$$a + b/c + d$$

from left to right, it is impossible to tell on initially encountering the plus sign whether or not you should apply the indicated addition operation to **a** and the immediately following operand. Instead, you must probe further into the expression to determine whether an operation with a higher priority occurs. While you undertake this probing of the expression, you must stack previously encountered operation symbols until you are certain of the operands to which they can be applied.

Compounding the backtracking problem just described is the fact that many different ways are used to represent the same algebraic expression. For example, the assignment statements

$$z = a * b/c + d;$$
$$z = (a * b)/c + d;$$
$$z = ((a * b)/c) + d;$$

should all result in the same order of arithmetic operations even though the expressions involved are written in distinctly different forms. The process of checking the syntax of such an expression and representing it uniquely is called *parsing* the expression. One frequently used method of parsing relies heavily on stacks.

Infix, Postfix, and Prefix Notation

Normal algebraic notation is often termed *infix* notation since the arithmetic operator appears between the two operands to which it is being applied. Infix notation may require parentheses to specify a desired order of operations. For example, in the expression **a/b + c**, the division will occur first. If we want the addition to occur first, the expression must be parenthesized as **a/(b + c)**.

Using *postfix* notation (also called *reverse Polish* notation after the nationality of its originator, the Polish logician Jan Lukasiewicz), the need for parentheses is eliminated because the operator is placed directly after the two operands to which it applies. Hence, **a/b + c** would be written as **ab/c+** in postfix form, which says

1. Apply the division operator to **a** and **b**.
2. To that result, add **c**.

The infix expression **a/(b + c)** would be written as **abc+/** in postfix notation. Reading this postfix expression from left to right, we are told to

1. Apply the addition operator to **b** and **c**.
2. Then divide that result into **a**.

Although relatively short expressions such as the preceding ones can be converted from infix to postfix via an intuitive process, a more systematic method is required for complicated expressions. We propose the following algorithm for humans (and will soon consider a different one for computers):

1. Completely parenthesize the infix expression to specify the order of all operations.
2. Move each operator to the space held by its corresponding right (i.e., closing) parenthesis.
3. Remove all parentheses.

Consider this three-step method as it applies to the following expression in which ^ is used to indicate exponentiation:

```
a / b ^ c + d * e - a * c
```

Completely parenthesizing this expression yields

```
(((a / (b ^ c)) + (d * e)) - (a * c))
```

Moving each operator to its corresponding right parenthesis,

```
(((a / b ^ c)) + (d * e)) - (a * c))
```

and removing all parentheses, we are left with

```
abc^/de*+ac*-
```

Had we started out with

```
a / b ^ c - (d * e - a * c)
```

our three-step procedure would have resulted in

```
((a /(b ^ c)) - ((d * e) - (a * c)))
```

Removing the parentheses would then yield

```
abc^/de*ac*--
```

In a similar way, an expression can be converted into *prefix* form, in which an operator immediately precedes its two operands. The conversion algorithm for infix to prefix specifies that, after completely parenthesizing the infix expression according to order of priority, we move each operator to its corresponding left (that is, opening) parenthesis. Applying the method to

a / b ^ c + d * e − a * c

gives us

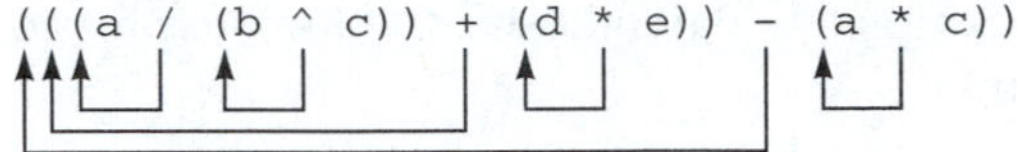

and finally the prefix form

− +/a^bc*de*ac

The importance of postfix and prefix notation in parsing arithmetic expressions is that these notations are completely free of parentheses. Consequently, an expression in postfix (or prefix) form is unique. In the design of compilers, this parsing into postfix form is crucial because having a unique form for an expression greatly simplifies its eventual evaluation. Thus, in handling an assignment statement, a compiler must perform the following actions:

1. Parse the expression on the right-hand side into postfix form.
2. Apply an evaluation algorithm to the postfix form.

We limit our discussion here to postfix notation. The techniques we cover are easily adaptable to the functionally equivalent prefix form.

Converting Infix Expressions to Postfix

First consider the problem of parsing an expression from infix to postfix form. Our three-step procedure is not easily adaptable to machine code. Instead, we will use an algorithm that has as its essential data structures the following:

1. A Queue object, **infix,** representing the infix expression. This expression consists of basic syntactic units known as *tokens.* Tokens can be subdivided into the following categories:
   a. Operator tokens, represented by symbols such as +, −, *, and /. We will assume the existence of a function **validOperator**, which when applied to a token returns TRUE if that token represents a valid operator for the expressions we are considering, and FALSE otherwise.
   b. Operand tokens: These may be thought of as the symbols representing variables and constants defined according to the rules of a particular language. We will assume the existence of a function **validOperand,** which when applied to a token returns TRUE if that token represents a valid operand, and FALSE otherwise.
   c. Left parenthesis and right parenthesis tokens, denoted by **leftParen** and **rightParen,** respectively.
   d. A special token, **endToken,** which represents a symbol that delimits the end of the infix expression.
2. A Stack object, **operatorStack,** which may contain operator tokens, **leftParen, rightParen,** or **endToken.**

3. A Queue object, **postfix,** which represents the final postfix expression.

For the moment, we will consider only expressions that involve the operands +, −, /, and *. In the exercises and programming problems, you will consider some variations introduced by allowing additional operators. Furthermore, we shall assume that the identification of the tokens appearing in the **infix** queue was accomplished in an earlier phase of the parsing problem known as the *lexical analysis* phase, and that the tokens were placed in the **infix** queue in the order in which they were recognized. For us, therefore, the parsing algorithm begins with a queue of tokens representing an infix expression. We leave unspecified the precise manner in which the tokens appearing in this queue were identified.

The description of the algorithm is as follows:

1. Define a function **infixPriority,** which when applied to an operator token, parenthesis token, or **endToken** returns an integer as specified here:

Token	*	/	+	–	leftParen	rightParen	endToken
Returned value	2	2	1	1	3	0	0

This function reflects the relative position of an operator in the arithmetic hierarchy and is used with the function **stackPriority** (defined in step 2) to determine how long an operator waits in the stack before being enqueued on the postfix expression.

2. Define another function **stackPriority,** which when applied to the same possibilities of token values returns an integer as specified here:

Token	*	/	+	–	leftParen	rightParen	endToken
Returned value	2	2	1	1	0	undefined	0

This function is applied to operators in the operator stack and returns their priority in the arithmetic hierarchy—a value that is to be compared to the infix priorities of incoming operators from the *infix* queue. The result of this comparison determines whether or not an operator waits in the stack or is enqueued on the postfix expression.

3. Initialize **operatorStack** by pushing **endToken.**

4. Examine and dequeue the next **token** from the **infix** expression.

5. Test **token** and

5.1 If **token** is an operand, enqueue it on the **postfix** expression.

5.2 If **token** is a **rightParen,** then examine and pop entries from **operatorStack** and enqueue them on **postfix** until a matching **leftParen** is examined and popped. This process ensures that operators within a parenthesized portion of an infix expression will be applied first, regardless of their priority in the usual arithmetic hierarchy. When the process is completed discard both left and right parentheses.

  5.3 If **token** is **endToken,** transfer all entries that remain on the stack to the **postfix** queue.
  5.4 Otherwise, examine and pop from the stack and enqueue on the **postfix** queue those operators whose **stackPriority** is greater than or equal to the **infixPriority** of **token.** This comparison, keying on the priority of **token** from the **infix** queue and operators that have previously been pushed onto the **operatorStack,** ensures that operators are applied in the right order in the resulting **postfix** queue. After popping these operators, push **token** onto the **operatorStack.**

6. Repeat steps 4 and 5 until **token** is the delimiting **endToken.**

The key to the algorithm is the use of the stack to hold operators from the infix expression that appear to the left of another given operator even though that latter operator must be applied first. The defined functions **infixPriority** and **stackPriority** are used to specify this priority of operators and the associated pushing and popping operations. This entire process is best understood by carefully tracing through an example.

Example 5.1

Parse the infix expression

```
a * b + (c - d / e)#
```

into its equivalent postfix form. Trace the contents of the operator stack and the postfix queue as each token is processed. Here the symbol # is used for **endToken.** The solution to this problem is presented in Table 5.1. In this table, the parenthesized numbers in the commentary column refer to subcases of step 5 in the preceding algorithm. We only show the content of a data structure when it changes.

We now develop a C++ implementation of this algorithm. Reviewing our narrative of the parsing process, we can readily identify three classes we can use: **Queue** (for the **infix** and **postfix** queues), **Stack** (for the **operatorStack**), and a new **Token** class (for tokens of various sorts—operator, operand, left parenthesis, right parenthesis, and end token). As part of our definition of the **Token** class, we include operations to identify the type of token represented by each instance of **Token,** as well as an assortment of so-called *occurrence* operations related to the creation, destruction, and manipulation of a **Token.** For example we shall include operations to **get** a token symbol from standard input, to **show** (that is, display) a token symbol on standard output, and to associate the value of a (numeric) type **ValueType** with a token. The latter is useful when we want to associate the values 3 and 4 with the token symbols 'b' and 'c', respectively, and then to use these values in calculating the value of the expression **b + c**.

We now give C++ specifications for the **Token** class discussed above. In our discussion, for the sake of simplicity, we assume the **Token** symbols are of type **char.** You will explore other possibilities in the exercises, especially using classes **CharToken** and **StringToken** as subclasses of **Token** (see Exercise 5.3.12).

```
// ValueType is a numeric type
template <class ValueType>
class Token
{
  protected:
    char symbol;   // For simplicity assume Token symbols are of type char
```

TABLE 5.1
Parsing of infix expression a * b + (c − d/e)#.

token	operatorStack	postfix	Commentary
	#		Push #
a		a	Examine and dequeue token Enqueue token on postfix (5.1)
*	* #		Examine and dequeue token Push token (5.4)
b		ab	Examine and dequeue token Enqueue token on postfix (5.1)
+	+ #	ab*	Examine and dequeue token Examine and pop *, enqueue * on postfix, push token (5.4)
(	(+ #		Examine and dequeue token Push token (5.4)
c		ab*c	Examine and dequeue token Enqueue token on postfix (5.1)
−	− (+ #		Examine and dequeue token Push token (5.4)
d		ab*cd	Examine and dequeue token Enqueue token on postfix (5.1)
/	/ − (+ #		Examine and dequeue token Push token (5.4)
e		ab*cde	Examine and dequeue token Enqueue token on postfix (5.1)
)	+ #	ab*cde/−	Examine and dequeue token Examine/pop from operatorStack and enqueue on postfix until leftParen reached (5.2)
#		ab*cde/−+#	Examine and dequeue token Transfer rest of stack to postfix (5.3)

```
    ValueType val;

  public:

//-----------------------------------------------------------------------------
// Interface for Token constructor
// GIVEN:     An uninitialized Token object.
// RETURN:    The Token object is initialized as an appropriate null symbol.

    Token();

//-----------------------------------------------------------------------------
// Interface for Token destructor
// GIVEN:     A previously allocated Token object.
// RETURN:    The Token object deallocated.

    ~Token();

//-----------------------------------------------------------------------------
// Interface for Token assign = operator
// GIVEN:     A previously constructed Token object;
//            source -- a second Token object that must have been constructed
//                      with the same ValueType type as the owner of the assign
//                      operator.
// RETURN:    The contents of source have been copied to the Token object that
//            owns the operation.
// RETURN as value of function: void

    void operator = (const Token<ValueType> &source);

// ----------------------------------------------------------------------------
// Interface for Token get operation
// GIVEN:     A previously allocated Token object.
// RETURN:    The Token object is assigned the next symbol value taken from
//            standard input.
// RETURN as value of function: void

    void get();

// ----------------------------------------------------------------------------
// Interface for Token show operation
// GIVEN:     A previously allocated Token object.
// RETURN:    The Token object unaltered, but with its symbol value having been
//            written to standard output.
// RETURN as value of function: void

    void show();

// ----------------------------------------------------------------------------
// Interface for Token assignValue operation
// GIVEN:     A previously allocated Token object;
//            newval -- a value of type ValueType.
// RETURN:    The Token object with newval as its associated token value.
// RETURN as value of function: void

    void assignValue(ValueType newval);

// ----------------------------------------------------------------------------
// Interface for Token valueOf operation
// GIVEN:     A previously allocated Token object.
// RETURN as value of function:
```

```
//            The value of type ValueType associated with the token.

    ValueType valueOf();

// ------------------------------------------------------------------------
// Interface for Token stackPriority operation
// GIVEN:     A Token object that is either an operator token, left parenthesis,
//            or the end token.
// RETURN as value of function:
//            An integer reflecting a relative position of the Token in an
//            arithmetic hierarchy; used in converting an arithmetic expression
//            from infix to postfix. Determines whether a token that is in the
//            stack is popped and appended to a postfix expression.

    int stackPriority();

// ------------------------------------------------------------------------
// Interface for token infixPriority operation
// GIVEN:     A Token object that is either an operator token, left parenthesis,
//            right parenthesis, or the end token.
// RETURN as value of function:
//            An integer reflecting a relative position of the Token in
//            an arithmetic hierarchy; used in converting an arithmetic
//            expression from infix to postfix. Determines whether a Token from
//            the infix expression is pushed on top of a Token examined from
//            the stack.

    int infixPriority();

// ------------------------------------------------------------------------
// Interface for Token validOperator operation
// GIVEN:     A previously allocated Token object.
// RETURN as value of function:
//            Returns TRUE if the Token represents a valid operator
//            for an arithmetic expression; FALSE otherwise.

    BOOLEAN validOperator();

// ------------------------------------------------------------------------
// Interface for Token validOperand operation
// GIVEN:     A previously allocated Token object.
// RETURN as value of function:
//            Returns TRUE if the Token represents a valid operand
//            for an arithmetic expression; FALSE otherwise.

    BOOLEAN validOperand();

// ------------------------------------------------------------------------
// Interface for Token endToken operation
// GIVEN:     A previously allocated Token object.
// RETURN as value of function:
//            Returns TRUE if the Token represents the end token
//            for an arithmetic expression; FALSE otherwise.

    BOOLEAN endToken();

// ------------------------------------------------------------------------
// Interface for Token assignEndToken operation
// GIVEN:     A previously constructed Token object.
// RETURN:    The Token object is assigned the value of the end token for an
//            arithmetic expression
```

```
// RETURN as value of function: void

   void assignEndToken();

// ---------------------------------------------------------------------------
// Interface for Token leftParen operation
// GIVEN:    A previously allocated Token object.
// RETURN as value of function:
//           Returns TRUE if the Token represents a left parenthesis;
//           FALSE otherwise.

   BOOLEAN leftParen();

// ---------------------------------------------------------------------------
// Interface for Token rightParen operation
// GIVEN:    A previously allocated Token object.
// RETURN as value of function:
//           Returns TRUE if the Token represents a right parenthesis;
//           FALSE otherwise.

   BOOLEAN rightParen();
};
```

Our implementation of a parsing algorithm will need more than the **Queue, Stack,** and **Token** classes, however. Because we are concerned with the parsing and evaluation of "arithmetic expressions," we need to define a C++ class **ArithExpression** as the embodiment of such expressions and derive from it subclasses **InfixExpression** and **PosfixExpression.** Associated with the **ArithExpression** class will be useful operations **get** and **show** that can be used for input and output of all derived classes. The **PostfixExpression** class will add the operation **evaluate,** which, using the value associated with each operand token, will return a value of type **ValueType** that represents the computed value of the expression. Finally, we associate an operation **parseToPost** with the **InfixExpression** class. This operation is owned by an object representing an infix expression and yields a **PostfixExpression** object that represents the postfix equivalent of the infix expression. C++ specifications for the **ArithExpression** class and its derived classes, **InfixExpression** and **PostfixExpression,** are given next.

```
// TokenType is a class representing various operator, operand, and
// special tokens used in arithmetic expressions, together with operations
// to identify the type of token and an assortment of occurrence operations.
// ValueType is a numeric type.

template <class TokenType, class ValueType>
class ArithExpression
{
  protected:
    Queue<TokenType> expression;   // A queue is used to store expressions.

  public:

//---------------------------------------------------------------------------
// Interface for ArithExpression constructor
// GIVEN:    An uninitialized ArithExpression object.
// RETURN:   ArithExpression is initialized to an empty (null) expression.

    ArithExpression();
```

```
//---------------------------------------------------------------------------
// Interface for ArithExpression destructor
// GIVEN:    A previously allocated ArithExpression object.
// RETURN:   ArithExpression object deallocated.

    ~ArithExpression();

// --------------------------------------------------------------------------
// Interface for ArithExpression get operation
// GIVEN:    A previously allocated ArithExpression object.
// RETURN:   The ArithExpression object with associated tokens, taken from
//           standard input, representing an arithmetic expression. The
//           expression will be terminated by a token representing the
//           endToken.
// RETURN as value of function: void

    void get();

// --------------------------------------------------------------------------
// Interface for ArithExpression show operation
// GIVEN:    A previously allocated ArithExpression object.
// RETURN:   The ArithExpression object unaltered, but with its tokens having
//           been written to standard output.
// RETURN as value of function: void

    void show();
};
```

The following derived **PostfixExpression** and **InfixExpression** classes each add a critical function to the **ArithExpression** class. The **PostfixExpression** class provides an **evaluate** function since the evaluation of expressions typically occurs after the expression has been parsed into postfix form. The **InfixExpression** class provides a **parseToPost** function that is called to parse the infix expression into a postfix expression. Because of the interaction between the **PostfixExpression** and **InfixExpression** classes that is required by the **parseToPost** function, the **PostfixExpression** class must declare the **InfixExpression** class to be a **friend**. The effect of the **friend** declaration, which occurs at the very beginning of the **PostfixExpression** class, is to grant the implementor of the class declared to be a **friend** (in this case **InfixExpression**) full access to all private and protected members of the class making the declaration (in this case **PostfixExpression**).

```
template <class TokenType, class ValueType>
class PostfixExpression : public ArithExpression <TokenType, ValueType>
{
  friend InfixExpression<TokenType, ValueType>;

  public:

// --------------------------------------------------------------------------
// Interface for PostfixExpression constructor
// GIVEN:    An uninitialized PostfixExpression object.
// RETURN:   The PostfixExpression object will be constructed using the
             ArithExpression constructor

    PostfixExpression();
```

```
// -----------------------------------------------------------------------
// Interface for PostfixExpression evaluate operation
// GIVEN:    A previously allocated PostfixExpression object.
// RETURN as value of function:
//           A value of type ValueType representing the calculated value of the
//           postfix expression. The calculation is performed using values of type
//           ValueType that are associated with the expression's operand tokens.

    ValueType evaluate();
};

template <class TokenType, class ValueType>
class InfixExpression : public ArithExpression <TokenType, ValueType>
{
  public:

// -----------------------------------------------------------------------
// Interface for InfixExpression constructor
// GIVEN:    An uninitialized InfixExpression object.
// RETURN:   The InfixExpression object will be constructed using the
//           ArithExpression constructor.

    InfixExpression();

// -----------------------------------------------------------------------
// Interface for parseToPost operation
// GIVEN:    An InfixExpression object;
//           postexp -- an uninitialized PostfixExpression object.
// RETURN:   If the function returns the value TRUE, then postexp will be the
//           postfix equivalent of the infix expression represented by the
//           InfixExpression object; otherwise postexp will be unreliable.
// RETURN as value of function:
//           TRUE if the infix expression was successfully represented
//           in postfix form; FALSE otherwise.

    BOOLEAN parseToPost(PostfixExpression<TokenType, ValueType> &postexp);
};
```

In Examples 5.2 through 5.5, we implement a variety of the operations that have been defined above for the **Token** and **ArithExpression** classes. You will complete the implementation of operations for these classes in the exercises.

Example 5.2 Implement the **validOperator** operation for the **Token** class, assuming token symbols are of type **char.**

```
template <class ValueType>
BOOLEAN Token<ValueType>::validOperator()
{
  if (leftParen() || rightParen() || endToken())
    return(TRUE);
  else
    switch(symbol)
    {
      case '*': return(TRUE);
      case '/': return(TRUE);
      case '+': return(TRUE);
```

```
      case '-': return(TRUE);
      default : return(FALSE);
    }
}
```

Example 5.3

Implement the **stackPriority** operation for the **Token** class, assuming token symbols of type **char** and the priority values given on page 207.

```
template <class ValueType>
int Token<ValueType>::stackPriority()
{
  if (leftParen() || endToken())
    return(0);
  else
    switch(symbol)
    {
      case '*': return(2);
      case '/': return(2);
      case '+': return(1);
      case '-': return(1);
    }
}
```

Example 5.4

Implement the **get** operation for the **ArithExpression** class.

```
template <class TokenType class ValueType>
void ArithExpression<TokenType, ValueType>::get()
{
  Token<ValueType> tok;
  Queue<TokenType> tempq;

  do
  {
    tok.get();
    tempq.enqueue(tok)
  }
  while (!tok.endToken());
  expression = tempq;
}
```

Example 5.5

Implement the **parseToPost** operator for the subclass **InfixExpression.**

```
template <class TokenType, class ValueType>
BOOLEAN InfixExpression<TokenType, ValueType>::
  parseToPost(PostfixExpression<TokenType, ValueType> &postexp)
{
  Queue<TokenType> tempq, postq;
  Stack<TokenType> opstack;
  TokenType newToken, item;
  BOOLEAN parseResult;

  tempq = expression;
  parseResult = TRUE;
```

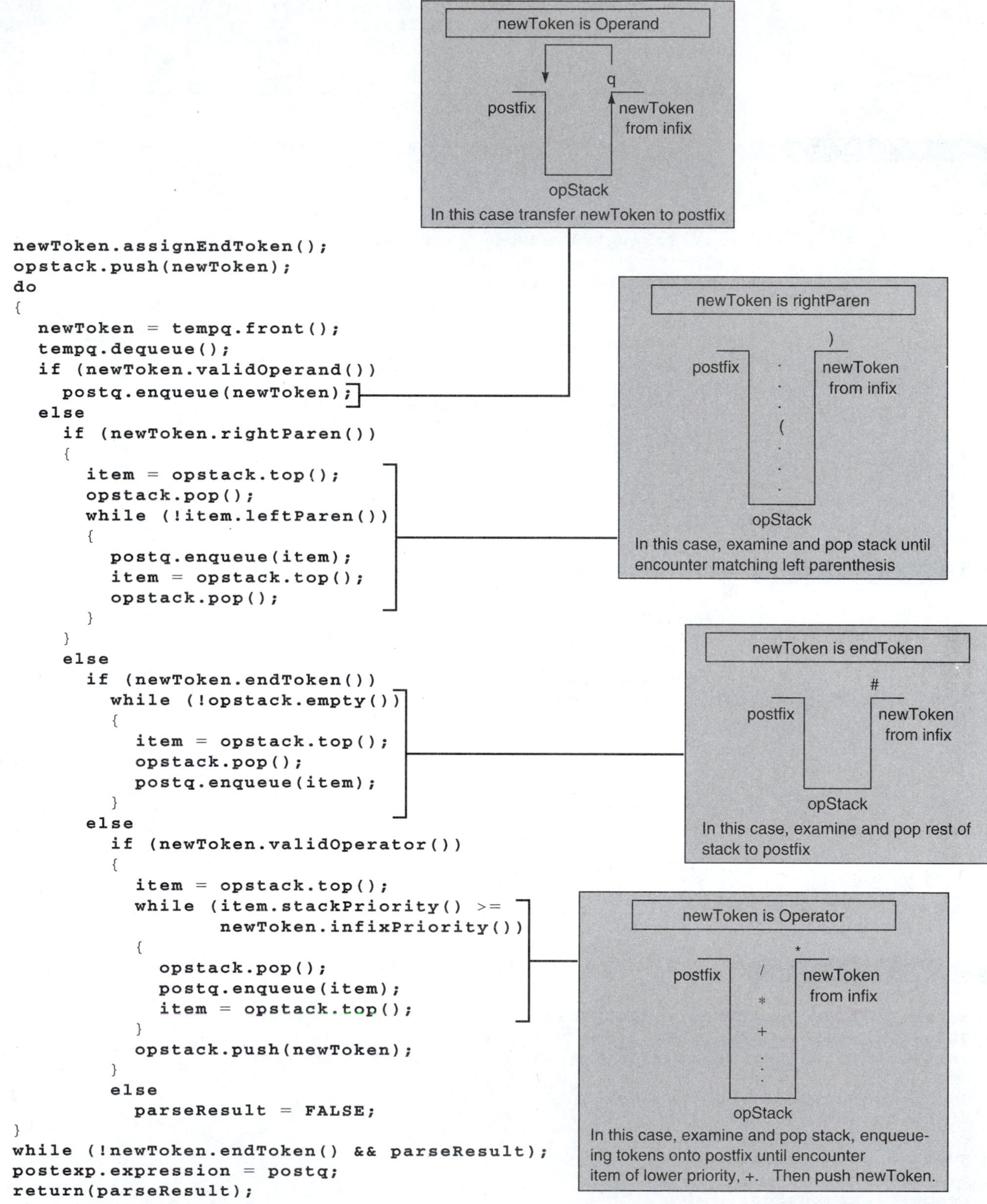

```
    newToken.assignEndToken();
    opstack.push(newToken);
    do
    {
      newToken = tempq.front();
      tempq.dequeue();
      if (newToken.validOperand())
        postq.enqueue(newToken);
      else
        if (newToken.rightParen())
        {
          item = opstack.top();
          opstack.pop();
          while (!item.leftParen())
          {
            postq.enqueue(item);
            item = opstack.top();
            opstack.pop();
          }
        }
        else
          if (newToken.endToken())
            while (!opstack.empty())
            {
              item = opstack.top();
              opstack.pop();
              postq.enqueue(item);
            }
          else
            if (newToken.validOperator())
            {
              item = opstack.top();
              while (item.stackPriority() >=
                         newToken.infixPriority())
              {
                opstack.pop();
                postq.enqueue(item);
                item = opstack.top();
              }
              opstack.push(newToken);
            }
            else
              parseResult = FALSE;
    }
    while (!newToken.endToken() && parseResult);
    postexp.expression = postq;
    return(parseResult);
}
```

newToken is Operand
q
postfix
newToken
from infix
opStack
In this case transfer newToken to postfix
newToken is rightParen
)
postfix
newToken
from infix
(
opStack
In this case, examine and pop stack until encounter matching left parenthesis
newToken is endToken
#
postfix
newToken
from infix
opStack
In this case, examine and pop rest of stack to postfix
newToken is Operator
*
postfix
/
*
+
newToken
from infix
opStack
In this case, examine and pop stack, enqueue-ing tokens onto postfix until encounter item of lower priority, +. Then push newToken.

Note the elegant generality of the conversion algorithm used in Example 5.5. The types of expressions it parses and how it parses them is controlled completely by the **Token** operations, especially the operations **validOperator, validOperand, infixPriority,** and **stackPriority.** By redefining these operations in the **Token** class, you can guide the parse in a variety of directions without ever altering the code in the **parseToPost** operator of the **InfixExpression class.** Thus, the algorithm again illustrates the power of both abstraction and its realization via C++ classes—we are able to apply a technique in many situations by merely changing the **Token** class operations that are used in the algorithm's logic.

A RELEVANT ISSUE Automating the Writing of Compilers

To a certain extent, programming language compilers view the entire source program they are translating as a large expression to be parsed and transformed into a suitable data structure (such as postfix notation). For instance, a **while** control structure could be thought of as a two-operand expression: one operand being the conditional test following **while** and the other operand being the sequence of statements to be executed as long as the first operand is true. Similarly, an **if-else** statement could be viewed as an expression requiring three operands: a conditional test following the **if,** a sequence of statements following this conditional test, and a sequence of statements following **else.**

Although the generation of machine code from such expressions is certainly a more complicated algorithm than the evaluation of algebraic expressions as discussed in this chapter, there are, nonetheless, many similarities between the two tasks. One such similarity is that, like our parsing algorithm for algebraic expressions, many compilers use a generic technique that applies to any source language provided that suitable "priority functions" are available to the algorithm. This technique, known as *LR parsing,* relies on another program called a *parser generator* to compute the appropriate priority tables for a given language. Such a parser generator is thus a program that takes as input the formal definition of a programming language's syntax and then computes the priority information necessary to drive the generic LR parser algorithm. One of the primary advantages of the LR algorithm is that, given the correct priority values for the language being parsed, it is guaranteed to work—just as our infix-to-postfix algorithm is *guaranteed* to work if the correct priority functions are supplied to it.

In the next chapter, we explore formal grammars as a means of precisely describing the syntax of a programming language. A more complete treatment of grammars, LR parsing, and parser generators can be found in *Crafting a Compiler* by Charles N. Fischer and Richard J. LeBlanc (Menlo Park, CA: Benjamin Cummings, 1988).

Evaluating Postfix Expressions

Once an expression has been parsed and represented in postfix form, another stack plays an essential role in its final evaluation. As an example, consider the postfix expression from Example 5.1:

```
ab*cde/-+
```

Let us suppose that the symbols **a, b, c, d,** and **e** had associated with them the following values:

Symbol	Value
a	5
b	3
c	6
d	8
e	2

Figure 5.3
Evaluation of ab $*$ cde/ $-$ $+\#$. If a token taken from the postfix expression is an operand, its value is pushed onto a stack. If the token is an operator, two values are retrieved and popped, the operator applied to them, and the result pushed onto the stack.

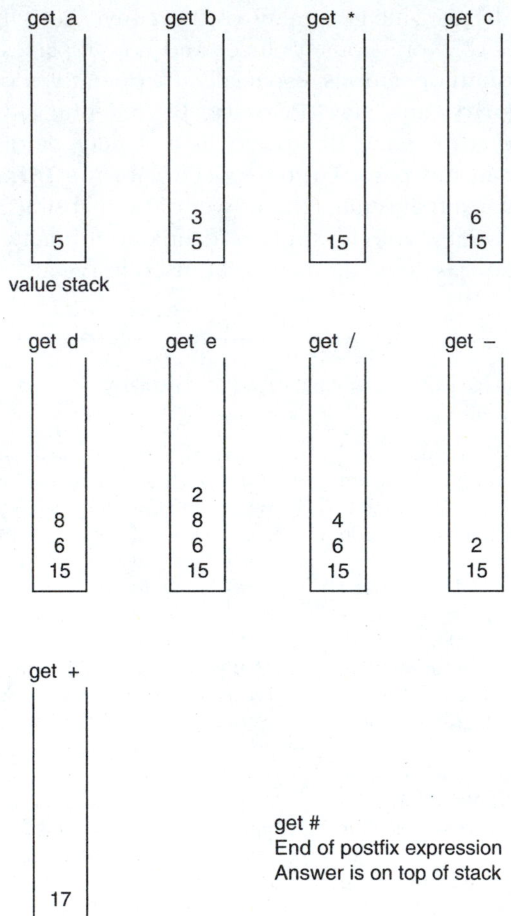

To evaluate such an expression, we repeatedly fetch tokens from the postfix expression. If the token is an operand, we push the value associated with it onto the stack. If it is an operator, we retrieve and pop two values from the stack, apply the operator to them, and push the result back onto the stack. The technique is illustrated for our postfix expression in Figure 5.3.

In the following example, we give a C++ version of the algorithm suggested earlier for evaluating a postfix expression. We assume the existence of an additional **Token** class operation **eval** that is applicable only to operator tokens. This **eval** operation will return the result of applying the arithmetic operator it represents to two operands of (numeric) type **ValueType.**

Example 5.6

Implement the **evaluate** operation for the class **PostfixExpression.**

```
template <class TokenType, class ValueType>
ValueType PostfixExpression<TokenType, ValueType>:: evaluate()
{

   Stack<ValueType> valueStack;
   ValueType value1, value2;
   TokenType<ValueType> tok;
```

```
    tok = expression.front();
    expression.dequeue();

    while (!tok.endToken())
    {
      if (tok.validOperand())
        valueStack.push(tok.valueOf());
      else  // tok must be an operator token
      {
        value2 = valueStack.top();
        valueStack.pop();
        value1 = valueStack.top();
        valueStack.pop();
        valueStack.push(tok.eval(value1,value2));
      }
      tok = expression.front();
      expression.dequeue();
    }
    return(valueStack.top());
}
```

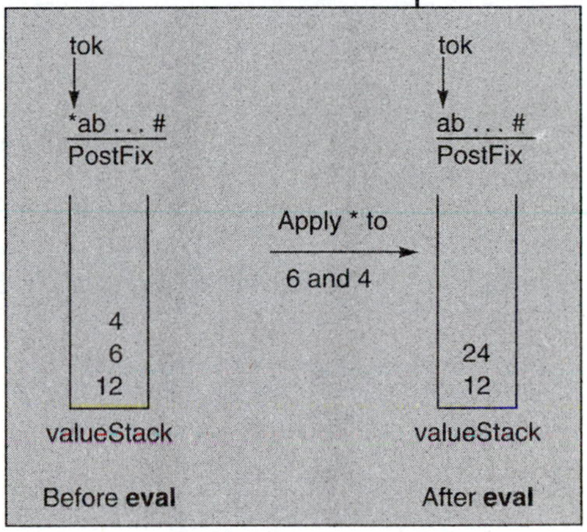

When we explore symbol table methods in Chapters 7 and 11, we shall see how compilers handle expressions with operands far more complex than those involving the mere one-character "variables" we have traced in our examples. However, because of the generality of the operations we have developed in this chapter, the conversion of such expressions to postfix notation and their resulting evaluation will require only that we redefine the **validOperator, validOperand, stackPriority,** and **infixPriority** operations prior to using them in our existing **parseToPost** and **evaluate** routines.

Exercises 5.3

1. What are the infix, postfix, and prefix forms of the following expression?

   `a + b * (c - d) / (p - r)`

2. Trace the contents of the stack as the postfix form of the expression in Exercise 5.3.1 is evaluated. Assume that

   a = 6, **b** = 4, **c** = 3, **d** = 1, **p** = 12, and **r** = 11.

3. Consider the expression with the infix notation

   `p + (q - f) / y`

   Using the algorithm discussed in this section to transform this into a postfix expression, trace the state of both the operator stack and postfix queue as each token of the infix expression is processed.

	Operator Stack Bottom ⟶ Top	Postfix Queue
After 1st token		
After 2nd token		
After 3rd token		
After 4th token		
After 5th token		
After 6th token		
After 7th token		
After 8th token		
After 9th token		

4. Using the postfix expression obtained in Exercise 5.3.3, trace the stack of numeric values that would develop as the postfix expression is evaluated. You should indicate the numeric values on the stack as each token in the postfix expression is processed. Assume the values **p** = 10, **q** = 18, **f** = 4, and **y** = 2.
5. Parse the infix expression

```
p * (q / y) + a - b + d * y
```

using the following definitions of **infixPriority** and **stackPriority:**

Priority	*	/	+	-	leftParen	rightParen	endToken
Infix	2	2	4	4	5	0	0
Stack	1	1	3	3	0	undefined	0

Trace this parsing operation by filling in the table below to indicate the contents of the operator stack and postfix queue after each character is read in.

	Operator Stack Bottom ⟶ Top	Postfix Queue
After 1st token		
After 2nd token		
After 3rd token		
After 4th token		
After 5th token		
After 6th token		
After 7th token		
After 8th token		
After 9th token		
After 10th token		
After 11th token		
After 12th token		
After 13th token		
After 14th token		
After 15th token		
After 16th token		

6. Using the postfix expression you obtained in Exercise 5.3.5, trace the stack of numeric values that would develop as the postfix expression is evaluated. You should indicate the value of the stack as each token in the postfix expression is processed. Assume the values **a** = 4, **b** = 3, **d** = 2, **p** = 1, **q** = 4, and **y** = 2.
7. Explain how the relationship between the stack priorities and infix priorities of *, /, +, −, **leftParen, rightParen,** and **endToken** controls the parsing of an infix expression.
8. Using the rationale you developed in Exercise 5.3.7, explain how the **infixPriority** and **stackPriority** functions would be extended to allow the exponentiation operator ^. Remember that the laws of algebra typically dictate that

```
3^2^3
```

evaluates to 6561, not 729.
9. Based on your work in Exercise 5.3.8, write a paragraph explaining why two priority functions are needed: one for operators in the infix expression and another for operators on the stack.
10. Complete the implementations of the **Token, ArithExpression, PostfixExpression** and **InfixExpression** classes. Your implementation should include the code for the **eval** operation used in Example 5.6.
11. In our C++ implementation of the algorithms for converting an infix expression into postfix form, we assumed that the class **Token** admitted symbols of type **char.** For this exercise you are to implement the class **Token** assuming symbols of type **String** and using the **String** class defined in Chapter 2. Your implementation should include the code for the **eval** operation used in Example 5.6.
12. Rather than assume that Token symbols are exclusively of type **char** as we did in our discussion, or of type **String** as in Exercise 5.3.11, omit the symbol field from the definition of **Token** and define subclasses **CharToken** and **StringToken** of class **Token** and use these subclasses in the implementation of the algorithms for converting infix expressions to postfix form.
13. Discuss how the **parseToPost** and **evaluate** operations of this section would have to be modified to allow expressions to contain unary minus (that is, the negative of a single number) and trigonometric, logarithmic, and exponential functions. Implement these changes.
14. Discuss how the functions **infixPriority** and **stackPriority** could be extended to include the operators <, >, <=, >=, ==, !=, &&, ||, and !.

Chapter Summary

Although a first-in, first-out structure such as a queue seems to be the obvious way of storing items that must wait to be processed, there are many natural instances in which a last-in, first-out (LIFO) strategy is more appropriate. A list of data items that enforces such a last-in, first-out strategy is called a stack. More specifically, a stack is a restricted list in which additions or deletions are permitted only from one designated end, called the top. The importance of stacks is emphasized by first considering the role they play in the processing of subroutine calls. Three methods for implementing stacks are noted, one that derives a Stack from the List class of Chapter 3, another that uses arrays, and a third that uses linked lists. Only the first of these is considered in detail.

Following a discussion of the infix, prefix, and postfix notations for algebraic expressions, stacks are used in parsing expressions from infix to postfix form and for evaluating postfix expressions.

Key Words

friend	parsing	prefix	tokens
infix	postfix	stack	top
last-in, first-out			

Programming Projects/Problems

1. Write C++ code that will parse infix expressions into prefix form.
2. In the programming problems for Chapter 3, you developed a passenger list processing system for the various flights of Wing-and-a-Prayer Airlines. Wing-and-a-Prayer management would now like you to extend this system so that it processes logical combinations of flight numbers. For example, the command

   ```
   LIST 1 OR 2
   ```

   should list all passengers whose names appear on the flight 1 or the flight 2 lists. Your program should also accept the logical operators **AND** and **NOT** and allow parenthesized logical expressions obeying the standard logical hierarchy

   ```
   NOT
   AND
   OR
   ```

3. A tax form can be considered as a sequence of items, each of which is either a number or defined by an arbitrary mathematical formula involving other items in the sequence. To assist them in their tax-planning strategy, top management at the Fly-by-Night Credit Card Company desires a program that would allow them to enter interactively numbers or formulas associated with given lines of a tax form. Once all such lines have been defined, users of the program may redefine the number or formula associated with a particular line, and all other lines dependent on that one should be appropriately updated. Note that, since formulas may be entered interactively, your program will have to use a stack to evaluate them. In effect, you will have written a small-scale spreadsheet program.
4. Write a program that will accept commands of the following form:
   - **INPUT** *variable name*
   - *variable name* = infix expression involving variable names and arithmetic operators +, −, *, /
   - **PRINT** *variable name*
   - **GO**

   These commands are to be stored in an array of strings until the **GO** command is entered. Once **GO** is entered, your program should execute the previously stored commands. "Execute" here means the following:
   - *For an* **INPUT** *command:* Send a question mark to standard output and allow the user to enter a real number; this real number is then stored in *variable name.*
   - *For an assignment statement:* Parse the expression into postfix form and then evaluate it, storing the results in the *variable name* on the left of the equality sign.
   - *For a* **PRINT** *instruction:* Write to standard output the numerical contents of the specified *variable name.*

   To make things relatively easy you may assume a syntax that
   - Allows only one variable name following **INPUT** or **PRINT**
   - Allows one blank space after the keywords **INPUT** and **PRINT** and no blank spaces anywhere else.

   For an additional challenge, enable your program to handle successfully the exponentiation operator within assignment statement expressions. The following example should illustrate the need for care in handling this exponentiation operator:

```
3^2^3 = 3^8,    not  9^3
```

5. This problem is an extension of Problem 4 to a "compiler" for a primitive programming language. Write a program that will accept commands of the following form:

- **INPUT** *variable name*
- **PRINT** *variable name*
- *variable name* = infix arithmetic expression involving variable names and arithmetic operators +, −, *, /, ^
- **GOTO** *line* { **ALWAYS,** or **IF** *infix logical expression* involving variable names and operators +, −, *, /, ^, & (for AND), | (for OR), ! (for NOT), <, >, = }
- **STOP**
- **RUN**

These commands are to be stored in an array of strings until the **RUN** command is entered. On encountering **RUN,** your program should execute the previously stored commands. "Execute" here means the following:

- *For an* **INPUT** *command:* Send a question mark to standard output and allow the user to enter a real number, which is stored in *variable name.*
- *For a* **PRINT** *command:* Write to standard output the numerical contents of the specified *variable name.*
- *For an assignment command:* Parse the expression into postfix form and then evaluate it. Store the result in the *variable name* on the left of the equality sign.
- *For a* **GOTO** *command:* Branch to the line number specified when **ALWAYS** follows the line number or when the infix expression that follows the **IF** evaluates to true. Here "line number" refers to the relative position of the line in the sequence of lines that were entered prior to the **RUN** command. The first line number in this sequence is "00."
- *For a* **STOP** *command:* Halt execution.

To make things relatively easy, you may assume a syntax that

- Ensures that one and only one blank space follows **INPUT, PRINT, GOTO,** and line number. No other blanks appear anywhere.
- Allows only one variable name to follow **INPUT** or **PRINT.**
- Only allows variable names consisting of one uppercase alphabetical character.
- Only allows line numbers consisting of two digits: 00 through 99. The usual hierarchy for operators is assumed.

6. If you are familiar with the concept of integration from calculus, design and implement a program that will evaluate the integral of a function $f(x)$. The left and right endpoints of the interval over which integration is to occur and the definition of the function $f(x)$ should be entered interactively by the user. In particular, interactive entry of the function definition (in infix notation) will require you to parse the function into postfix form for later evaluation of $f(x)$ with various values of x. Approximate the integral by summing up the areas of a suitable number of rectangles bounded by the graph of the function between the endpoints entered by the user. Recall that the formal definition of the integral is nothing more than the limit of this sum of rectangular areas as the number of rectangles approaches infinity.

7. In propositional logic, elementary propositions may be combined by five logical connectives:

p ↔ **q** : **p** if and only if **q**
p → **q** : **p** implies **q**, that is, if **p** then **q**
p ∧ **q** : **p** and **q**
p ∨ **p** : **p** or **q**
~ **p** : not **p**

The truth tables for each of these logical connectives are given by

p	q	p↔q	p→q	p∧q	p∨q	~ p
T	T	T	T	T	T	F
T	F	F	F	F	T	F
F	T	F	T	F	T	T
F	F	T	T	F	F	T

Logical expressions involving these connectives may combine many connectives applied according to the following conventions:

all ~ connectives are applied first
then all ∧ connectives
then all ∨ connectives
then all → connectives
finally, all ↔ connectives

Of course, parentheses may be used to override this hierarchy of operations.

A *tautology* is a logical proposition that is always true, regardless of the truth values of its elementary components. For instance, the proposition

```
(p →q)  ↔  (~p ∨ q)
```

is a tautology since it is always true—for any possible combination of true/false values of **p** and **q.** Write a program that allows a logician to enter interactively a logical proposition and then reports whether or not the proposition is a tautology. You may assume that all elementary propositions are represented by one of the letters **p, q, r, s,** or **t.**

8. A maze may be represented by a two-dimensional Boolean matrix in the form illustrated in the following figure. Those cells marked by *false* are blocked; those cells marked by *true* are open. When exploring a maze, you may move north, south, east, or west from a given cell—provided that the cell in the direction you choose is open. Hence, the line in the following figure represents one possible path from the entrance to the exit.

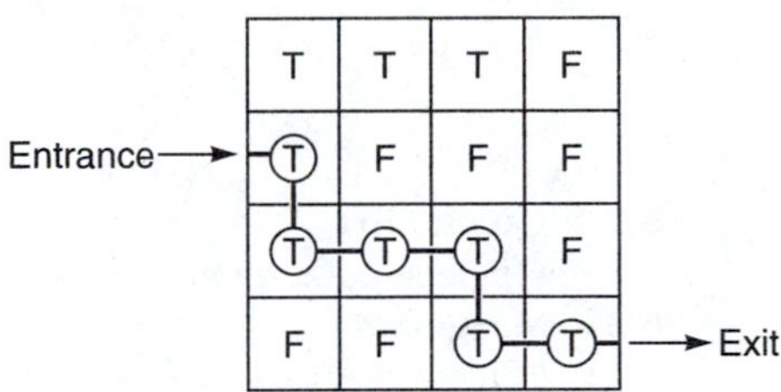

Representation of a maze by a Boolean matrix. Cells marked as false (F) are blocked; those marked as true (T) are open.

Write a program that allows a user to enter a maze interactively and that then searches for a path through the maze. Guide this search by pushing a record of each move made onto a stack. Whenever the search algorithm reaches a dead-end, it can return to the previous position by popping the stack of prior moves and trying an alternative direction from that previous position. Eventually, your algorithm will either find a path to the exit or try all possibilities and find that none of them leads to such a path. In the latter case, have your program report that the maze is impossible to solve.

CHAPTER 6

Recursion

Simple style is like white light. It is complex, but its complexity is not obvious.
Anatole France

Chapter Outline:

In the *Pascal User Manual and Report* (Berlin: Springer-Verlag, 1974), Kathleen Jensen and Niklaus Wirth made famous a graphic way of representing the syntax of a programming language. By way of example, a syntax diagram that defines a C++ statement is presented in Figure 6.1. One interesting feature to note about this diagram is that the term *statement* is used nine times in defining statement. Yet this definition is not ambiguous or circular since, ultimately, a statement must resolve to one of the following:

- expression
- if
- if-else
- switch
- while
- do-while
- for
- goto
- continue
- break
- return

Such a language definition illustrates beautifully the expressive power of *recursion*—defining the solution to a problem in terms of a simpler version of the same problem. To avoid circularity, such a self-referential solution must eventually end in a version so simple that we can declare the solution "trivial" and immediately return an answer through the preceding levels of recursive logic. At each of these levels, the returned answer will often be involved in computations resulting in a yet more complex answer to be returned to a different logical level. Finally, an answer is returned to the level at which the problem was originally posed.

Recursive formulations of problems and their solutions are often so elegant and compact that they give the appearance of magic. In this chapter we explore the basics of recursive algorithms. We will see that there is no magic involved but rather that the implementation of recursive algorithms is based on intricate manipulations of a stack used in processing procedure and function calls. In Section 6.1 we explore in detail the role of this stack in recursive programming. Through introductory examples, we will begin to develop the notions of recurrence relations

FIGURE 6.1
Recursive definition of a C++ statement.

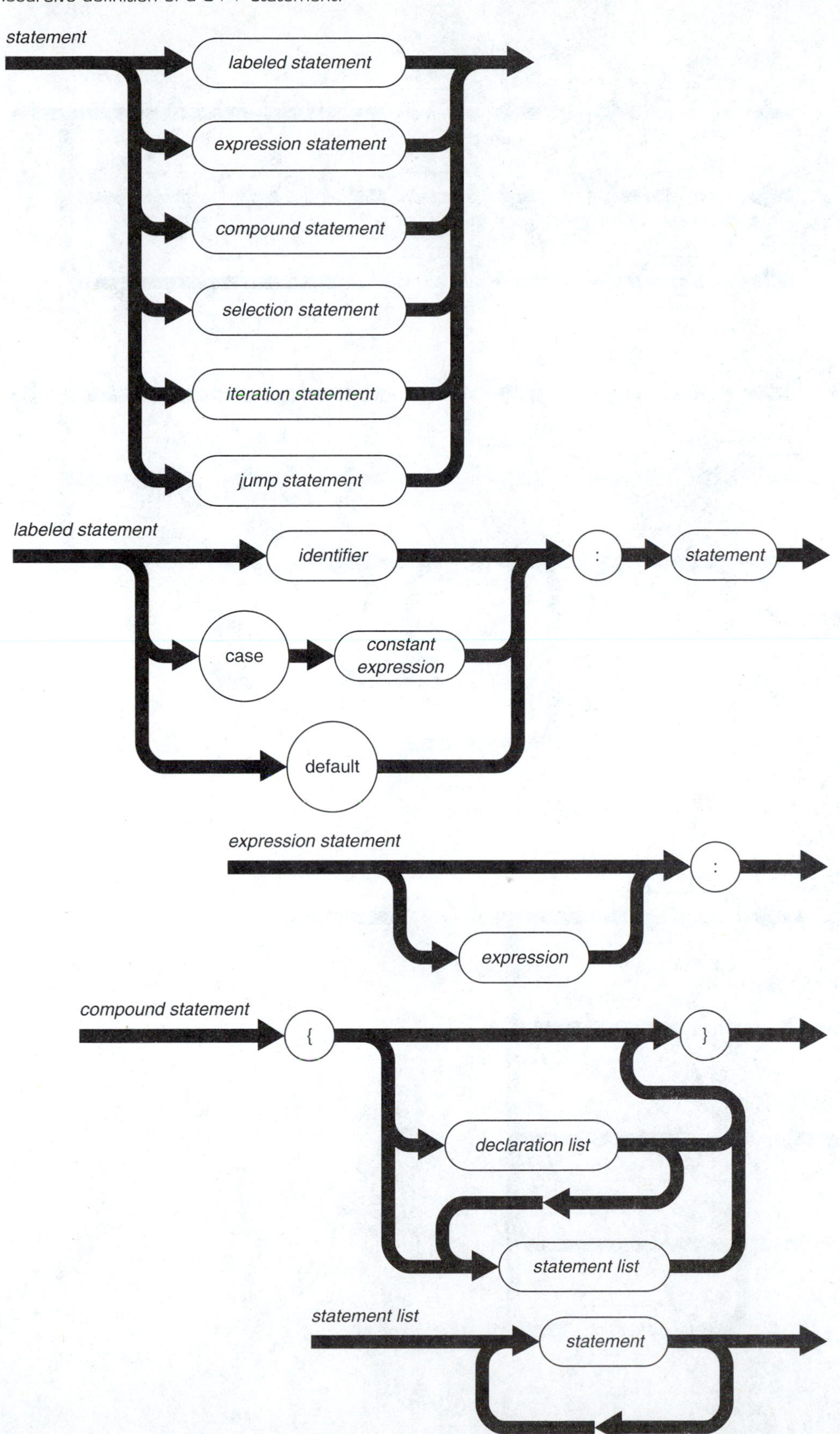

FIGURE 6.1
(*continued*)

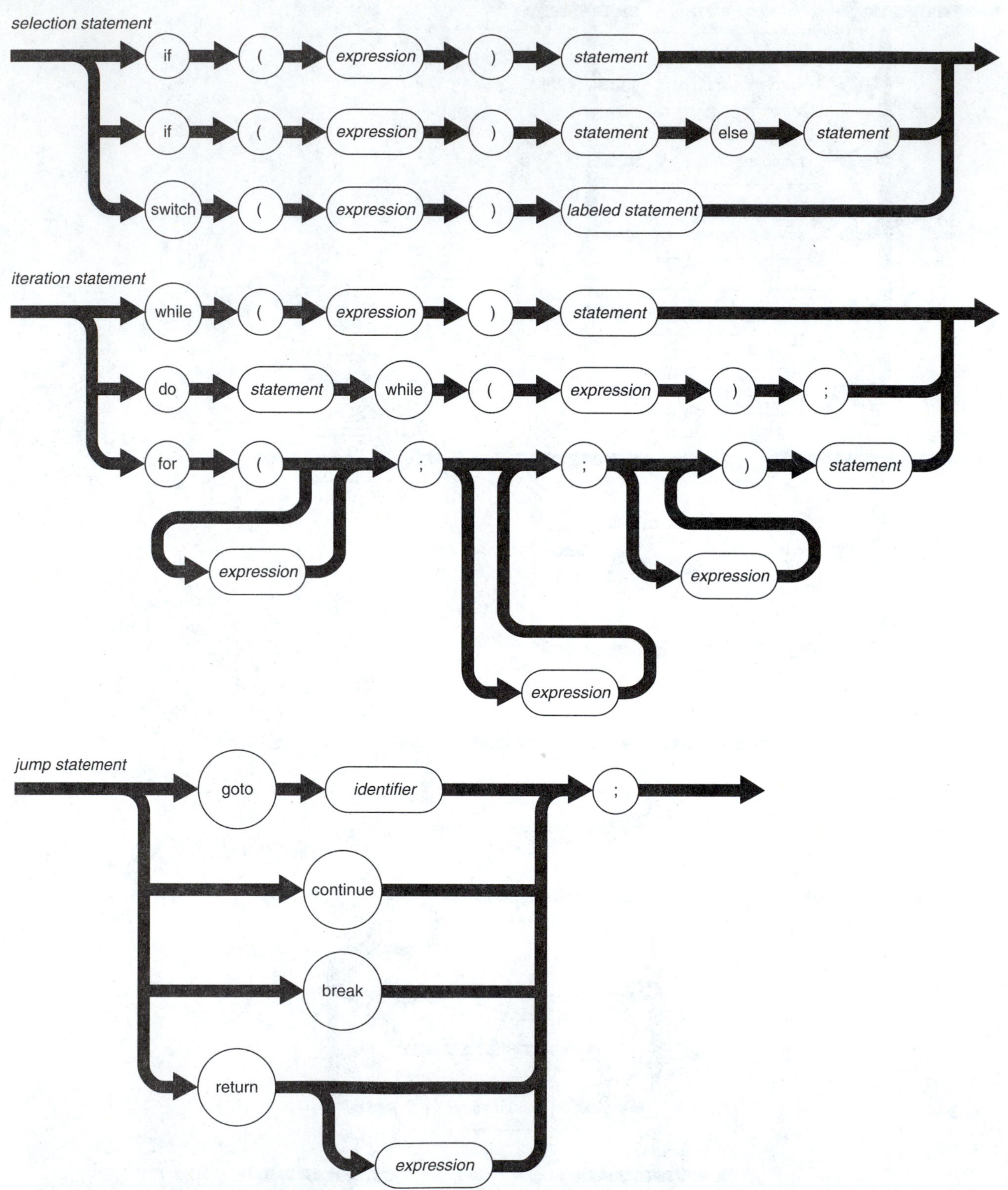

and recursive call trees as ways of analyzing the efficiency of recursive algorithms. In Sections 6.2 and 6.3 two recursive and highly efficient sorting algorithms—merge sort and quick sort—are examined. Finally, in Section 6.4, we demonstrate the expressive power of recursion by examining a parsing technique known as *recursive descent* parsing. This technique offers an alternative implementation to the stack-based, priority function parsing algorithm discussed in Chapter 5.

6.1 Introductory Examples

The Search Problem Revisited

The divide-and-conquer search algorithm we developed in Section 1.3 can be neatly formulated via recursive logic. We illustrate this by defining a new **SearchArray** class derived from the **SortArray** class introduced in Section 2.2. The **SearchArray** class admits a constructor that allows one to specify an index range, a precedence relationship between elements, and a splitting function to provide the basis for a divide-and-conquer **search** operation. We will implement this **search** operation with recursive logic.

```
// We assume IndexType is a finite collection of consecutively enumerated
// values such as integers, characters, or enum values, and that
// BaseData is any type or class that has an assign (overloaded =)
// operator and that admits an order relationship among its elements.
template <class IndexType, class BaseData>
class SearchArray : public SortArray<IndexType, BaseData>
{
  public:

//--------------------------------------------------------------------------------
// Interface for SearchArray constructor
// GIVEN:     An uninitialized SearchArray object;
//            min and max -- defining allowable index range for the array object;
//            precedes -- a function to compare BaseData values:
//              GIVEN:   x and y -- values to compare
//              RETURN as value of function:
//                       TRUE    if x precedes y,
//                       FALSE   if x and y are equal, or if y precedes x.
//            splitFunc -- a function to split the array:
//              GIVEN:   lo and hi - indices within the range of active values
//                       in the array, lo <= hi
//              RETURN as value of function:
//                       An index value between lo and hi inclusive.
// RETURN:    Array object with space allocated for it, a precedence relation between
//            elements, and a splitting function to use for divide-and-conquer
//            search, but with no values assigned to array indices.

    SearchArray (IndexType min, IndexType max,
                 BOOLEAN (*precedes)(const BaseData &x, const BaseData &y),
                 IndexType (*splitFunc)(IndexType lo, IndexType hi));

//--------------------------------------------------------------------------------
// Interface for search operation
// GIVEN:    A SearchArray object;
//           numvals -- logical size of the array object, assuming values are
//                      stored consecutively in ascending order starting at lowest
//                      index in array;
//           target -- containing value to search for.
// RETURN:   place -- If target was found, place contains the index position of
//                    target in array; if target was not found, place is unreliable.
```

```
// RETURN as value of function:
//            TRUE if target was found and FALSE otherwise.

   BOOLEAN search(int numvals, const BaseData &target, IndexType &place);
};
```

If we assume that **lo** is initialized to the first array index and that **hi** is initialized to the last array index containing data, then a high-level, recursive statement of the divide-and-conquer algorithm is as follows:

```
if (lo > hi)
  the target cannot be located between lo and hi inclusive, so return FALSE
else
{
  compute guess index to be split point of lo and hi
  if (a[guess] == target)
    the target has been located, so return TRUE, with guess as the location of
        the match
  else
    if (precedes(a[guess], target))
      (recursively) invoke same logic except now use guess+1 as the new lo
    else
      (recursively) invoke same logic except now use guess-1 as the new hi
}
```

The essence of the recursive paradigm is to recognize that the solution to a problem may be stated in terms of the solution to the same problem at a simpler level. For the divide-and-conquer search, Figure 6.2 indicates that this search-within-a-search uses a continually smaller index range within which **target** may be found. Equally important to the recursive paradigm is recognizing that this problem-within-a-problem theme cannot recur infinitely. Ultimately, conditions must exist that allow us to leave the recursion and return an answer. For the divide-and-conquer search, these termination conditions are either

the target has been located (success)

or

further narrowing of the index range is impossible (failure).

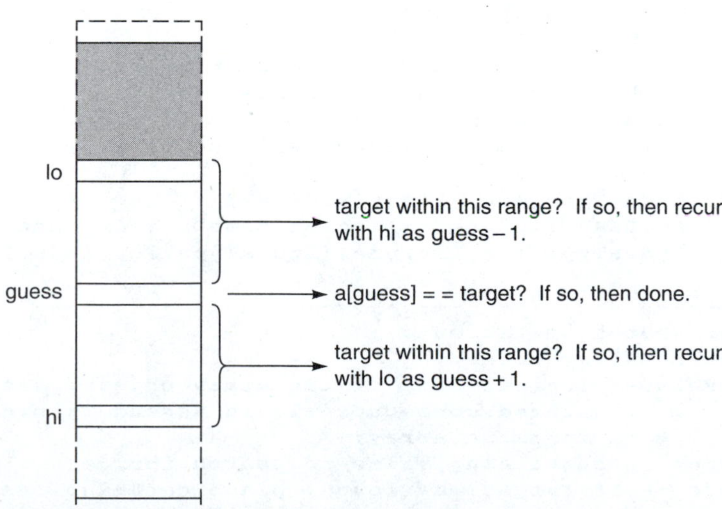

FIGURE 6.2
Recurring search with narrowing index range.

As you gain experience with recursion, you will acquire a feel for the type of problem that lends itself to a recursive expression. Usually you will recognize the problem-within-a-problem phenomenon first and then develop the specific conditions that allow the recursion to halt.

To incorporate a recursive search into our **SearchArray** class, we must add two protected members to the class.

```
protected:
  IndexType (*split)(IndexType lo, IndexType hi);      // Splitting function

  BOOLEAN recSearch(IndexType lo, IndexType hi, const BaseData &target,
                    IndexType &place);
  // Recursive search between lo and hi
```

The first of these members, **split,** is a pointer to the splitting function that a client program uses in the construction of a particular **SearchArray** object. For instance, to establish an array of integers **b** indexed over a subrange of the integers, on which a binary splitting function would be used, the client problem would declare:

```
int binarySplit(int lo, int hi)
{
  return ((lo + hi)/2);
}

BOOLEAN lessThan(const int &x, const int &y)
{
  if (x < y)
    return(TRUE);
  else
    return(FALSE);
}

SearchArray<int,int> b(1, 200, lessThan, binarySplit);
```

The implementation of the **SearchArray** constructor must invoke the constructor for the parent **SortArray** class and then assign the client program's splitting function to the protected member **split.**

```
template <class IndexType, class BaseData>
SearchArray<IndexType, BaseData>::SearchArray (IndexType min, IndexType max,
      BOOLEAN (*precedes)(const BaseData &x, const BaseData &y),
      IndexType (*splitFunc)(IndexType lo, IndexType hi))
  : SortArray<IndexType,BaseData>(min, max, precedes)
{
  split = splitFunc;
}
```

A recursive implementation of the divide-and-conquer search algorithm requires two parameters—one for each of the **lo** and **hi** indices. Since these two indices would disrupt the interface of the **search** operation to client programs, we incorporate the recursive logic into the protected **recSearch** member of the class. The **search** function itself acts merely as a front-end function that sends appropriate initial values for the **lo** and **hi** parameters to the recursive workhorse.

```
template <class IndexType, class BaseData>
BOOLEAN SearchArray<IndexType, BaseData>::
  search(int numvals, const BaseData &target, IndexType &place)
{
  return (recSearch (loIndex, loIndex + numvals - 1, target, place));
}

// Recursive search workhorse
template <class IndexType, class BaseData>
BOOLEAN SearchArray<IndexType, BaseData>::recSearch(IndexType lo, IndexType hi,
                                     const BaseData &target, IndexType &place)
{
  IndexType guess;

  if (lo > hi)
  {
    return(FALSE);
  }
  else
  {
    guess = split(lo, hi);
    if ((*this)[guess] == target)
    {
      place = guess;
      return(TRUE);
    }
    else
      if (precedes((*this[guess], target))
        return(recSearch(guess+1, hi, target, place));
      else
          return(recSearch(lo, guess-1, target, place));
  }
}
```

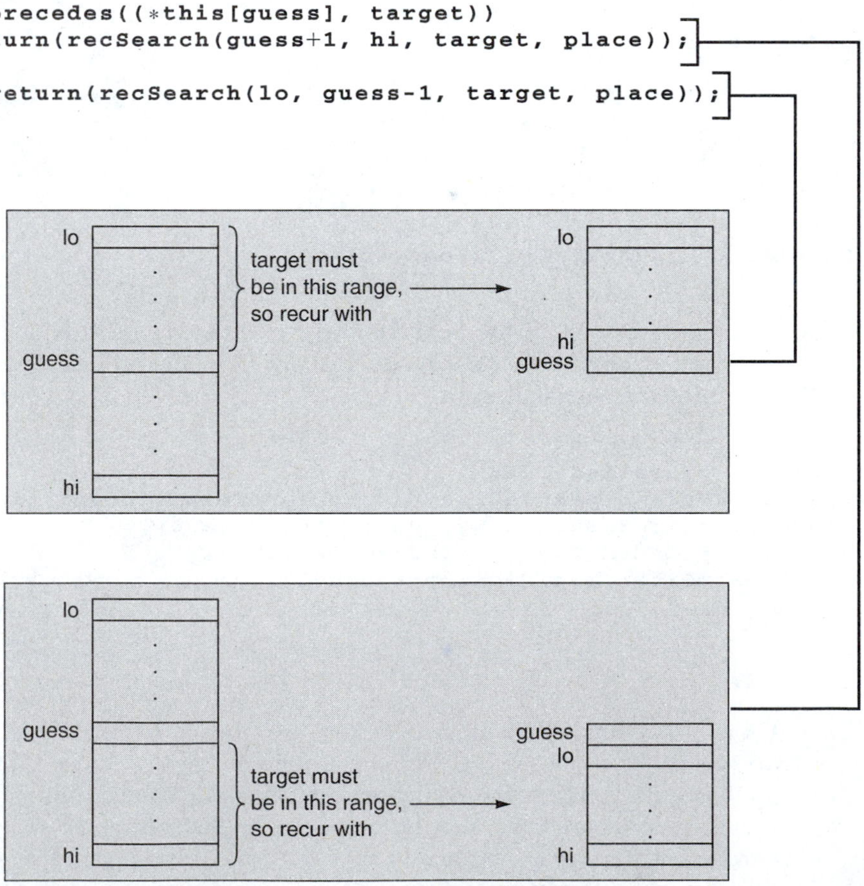

Traversals for General Lists

Recall from Section 3.1 the iterative logic we developed for traversing a list of pointers to objects of class **Ballplayer,** each of which owned a **display** operation.

```
template <class Ballplayer>
void showLineup(List<Ballplayer> lineup)
{
   Ballplayer *player;
   lineup.first();
   while (lineup.current() != 0)
   {
      player = lineup.examine();
      player->display();
      lineup.next();
   }
}
```

Now consider how we could achieve the same traversal using recursive logic. Here the function **showLineup** becomes a front-end function that prepares the list to be traversed for the auxiliary recursive function **showLineupAux.**

```
template <class Ballplayer>
void showLineup(List<Ballplayer> lineup)
{
   lineup.first();              // Make current node first node
   showLineupAux(lineup);       // Call auxiliary recursive routine
}

template <class Ballplayer>
void showLineupAux(List<Ballplayer> lineup)
{
   Ballplayer *player;

   // If there is a current player, display her and recur down the list

   if (lineup.current() != 0)
   {
      player = lineup.examine();
      player->display();
      lineup.next();
      showLineupAux(lineup);    // Recursively display the next player
   }
}
```

Note that if **lineup.current()** is zero, then the call **showLineupAux(lineup)** simply returns, having done nothing.

Suppose now that we wish to modify our traversal algorithm to process the list in the reverse order, that is, starting at the last node in the list and stopping after the first node has been processed. Here again, we can use a recursively defined implementation.

```
template <class Ballplayer>
void showLineupAuxRev(List<Ballplayer> lineup)
{
  Ballplayer *player;

  if (lineup.current() != 0)
  {
    player = lineup.examine();
    lineup.next();
    showLineupAuxRev(lineup);   // Recur to next player before displaying
    player->display ();         // this one
  }
}
```

As before, if **lineup.current()** is zero, then the call **showLineupAuxRev (lineup)** simply returns, without doing anything. What the algorithm says at each node is "put off processing this node until the rest of the list has been processed or until **lineup.current()** is zero (in which case, consider the node as having been processed)." A moment's reflection should be sufficient to convince you that such a sequence of deferred processing of each node does in fact yield the desired order of processing.

Writing and Verifying Recursive Algorithms

For many programmers, it takes some time until they acquire the insight for recognizing problems that might admit a recursive solution, that is, recognizing problems whose solutions can be expressed using a "simpler" version of the original. Often this insight comes when programmers simply remind themselves to *think recursively* while pondering a solution to a problem.

After having recognized the potential for a recursive solution, the programmer must ensure the following conditions when coding the solution as a C++ function:

1. There must be at least one simple (or base) case of the problem being solved that does not require recursion. Such cases will normally lead directly to a completion of the function's task and a return to the point at which it was invoked.

   In our divide-and-conquer solution to the searching problem, the two cases **hi < lo** and **a[guess] == target** are sufficient to deduce that we should return the values **FALSE** and **TRUE,** respectively—no further calls to **recSearch** are needed. In **showLineupAux** and **showLineupAuxRev,** the case **lineup.current() ==** 0 serves as the base case, requiring simply that nothing further be done.
2. Any recursive use of the function must move the problem closer to one of the base cases.

   In our divide-and-conquer solution to the searching problem, the recursive call depends on the outcome of the conditional test **precedes((*this)[guess], target).** Either the recursive call **recSearch(guess + 1, hi, target, place)** will be made, or the call **recSearch (lo, guess − 1, target, place)** will be made. In either case, the parameter **lo** used by **recSearch** will be at least one value closer to **hi** (or one value beyond it if **lo** = **hi** when **recSearch** was called), thereby taking us at least one step closer to the base case **hi < lo.** At the same time, a new value for **guess** will be calculated, which, if **target** is in the array, will move us closer to the position where **target** will be found.

In **showLineupAux** and **showLineupAuxRev,** the recursive calls are made with the current node closer to the last node of the list, which eventually results in **lineup.current()** returning zero for our base case.

Verifying the correctness of a recursive function now becomes a matter of verifying that the following conditions have been satisfied:

1. That the function contains the requisite base cases and that they work
2. That all recursive calls of the function involve a case of the problem that is closer to one of the base cases
3. That, under the assumption that all recursive invocations do indeed solve the "simpler" cases represented in their invocation, the use made of the results of those invocations correctly solves the general problem with which the function is concerned.

Let us see how we can verify the correctness of the recursive search algorithm.

1. **recSearch** has two base cases:
   a. **hi < lo:** Here the assumed precondition **lo ≤ hi,** which specifies the index range within which to search, will be violated, allowing us to conclude that there is no value for **place** such that **lo ≤ place ≤ hi,** and the return value must be **FALSE**. Note also that following the assignment associated with the success of the test **hi < lo**, we go immediately to the end of the function, and hence return to the statement after the point of invocation.
   b. **a[guess] == target:** Here, of course, the sought-after target value has been found; hence, the return value and **place** are the values **TRUE** and **guess,** and we again go immediately to the end of the function, thus returning to the statement after the point of invocation.
2. **recSearch** uses two recursive calls:
   a. **recSearch(guess + 1, hi, target, place):** This case solves a simpler case of the given problem because the range of indices has been reduced from **lo..hi** to **guess + 1..hi.** The value of **guess** was calculated by the function **split,** which by assumption returns a value in the range **lo..hi**. (Verifying that **split** works correctly is a separate problem.)
   b. **recSearch(lo, guess − 1, target, place):** This case solves a simpler case of the given problem because the range of indices has been reduced from **lo..hi** to **lo..guess − 1,** where once again the value of **guess** was calculated by the function **split,** and is assumed to be in the range **lo..hi**.
3. The search problem for a value **target** among the elements of an array having indices in the range **lo..hi** can be broken down into four mutually exclusive cases:
   a. **hi < lo**
   b. **lo ≤ hi** and **(*this)[guess] == target** for some index **guess** dependent on **lo** and **hi** and in the subrange **lo..hi**
   c. **lo ≤ hi** and **precedes((*this)[guess], target) is TRUE**
   d. **lo ≤ hi** and **precedes((*this)[guess], target) is FALSE.**

   The **recSearch** algorithm tests for each case and takes an action that properly solves the search problem since the first two involve base cases that were already verified and the last two cases involve the recursive calls of condition 2 above, which we assume correctly solves the search problem for their simpler cases.

Why Does Recursion Work?

We have thus far approached recursion as an intuitive concept well suited to expressing solutions for certain kinds of problems. We now turn our attention to the question of how recursive function calls are implemented by programming languages. Such a discussion will serve two purposes. First, it will enhance our understanding of recursion as a problem-solving paradigm, thereby enabling us to approach more complex recursive problems with confidence. Second, a thorough understanding of how recursion works is necessary if we are to perform detailed time/space efficiency analyses of recursive algorithms.

In Section 5.1 we alluded to the existence of a general system stack onto which return addresses are pushed each time a function call is made. Let us now explain the role of that stack more fully. Each time a function call is made, an item called a *stack frame* will be pushed onto the system stack. The data in this stack frame consist of the return address (that is, the place where program execution is to resume after the function is completed) and a copy of each local variable for the function.

Figure 6.3 illustrates how stack frames are pushed and popped from the system stack when the function **recSearch** is invoked from the front-end function **search,** with the **split** function computed by (**lo** + **hi**) / 2 on an array indexed from 1 to 15. We can see from this example that a recursive call creates an entirely new collection of variables that a function can manipulate. These variables exist in the stack frame allocated for the current call to the function. While work is done in this topmost stack frame, the values of variables in prior, unfinished levels of recursive calls are protected within the stack. When the current level of recursion is completed, the return address in the topmost stack frame is examined to determine where processing is to resume. Then this stack frame is popped, in effect uncovering the values of variables that had existed at a prior recursive level.

The notion of *levels* is critical in recursive problem-solving and, consequently, in recursive programming. Each recursive invocation of a function involves a view that is one degree simpler than the view at an earlier level. The fact that new space is allocated in the stack frame for parameters and other local variables can make recursion a space-inefficient technique. For those parameters that are passed by value to a function, space to store a complete copy of the parameter must be allocated. For those parameters that passed by reference, the function must receive the address of the actual argument. This is the reason the assignment of **TRUE** as the return value and 6 to **place** in the top stack frame of Figure 6.3 affects the values of the return value and **place** in prior levels that are buried deeper in the stack.

An analysis of the time and space efficiency of a recursive algorithm is dependent on two factors. The first of these is the depth of the calls, that is, the number of levels to which recursive calls are made before reaching the condition that triggers a return without making another recursive call. Clearly, the greater the depth, the greater the number of stack frames that must be allocated and the less space-efficient the algorithm becomes. It is also clear that recursive calls to a greater depth will consume more computer time. The second factor affecting the efficiency analyses (particularly time efficiency) of recursive algorithms is the amount of resource (time or space) consumed at any given recursive level. Figure 6.4 highlights this notion of recursive programs as a hierarchy of potential recursive calls through successively deeper levels. A hierarchy of recursive calls such as that appearing in Figure 6.4 is called a *tree of potential recursive calls*. We will use such trees often in analyzing recursive algorithms. Because a stack frame must be allocated at each level, the space efficiency of a recursive algorithm will be proportional to the deepest level

FIGURE 6.3
Sequence of pushes and pops required by **recSearch** when called by **search** to locate 37 in an array indexed from 1 to 15 and using **split** function (**lo** + **hi**) / 2.

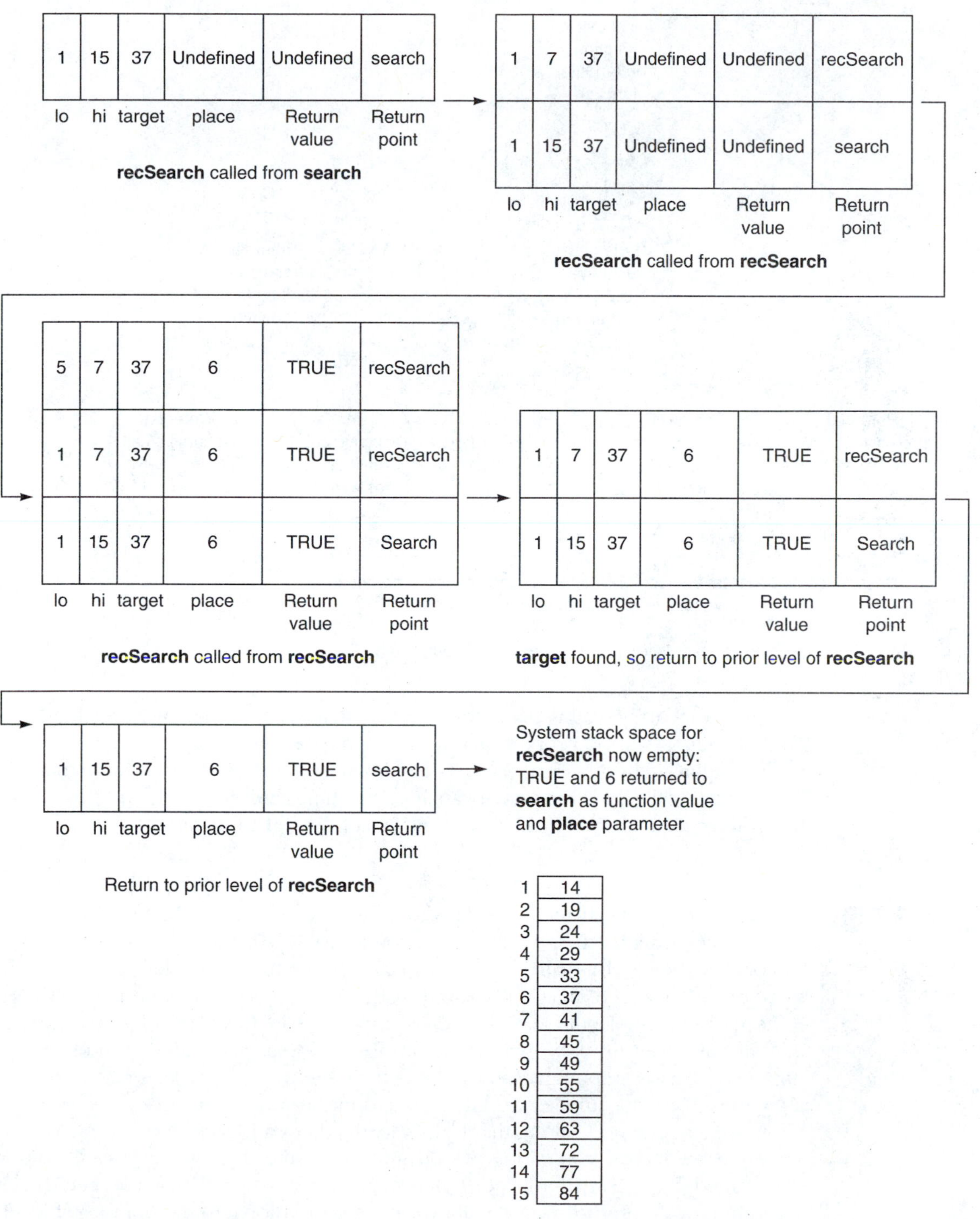

FIGURE 6.4
Generalized tree of potential recursive calls.

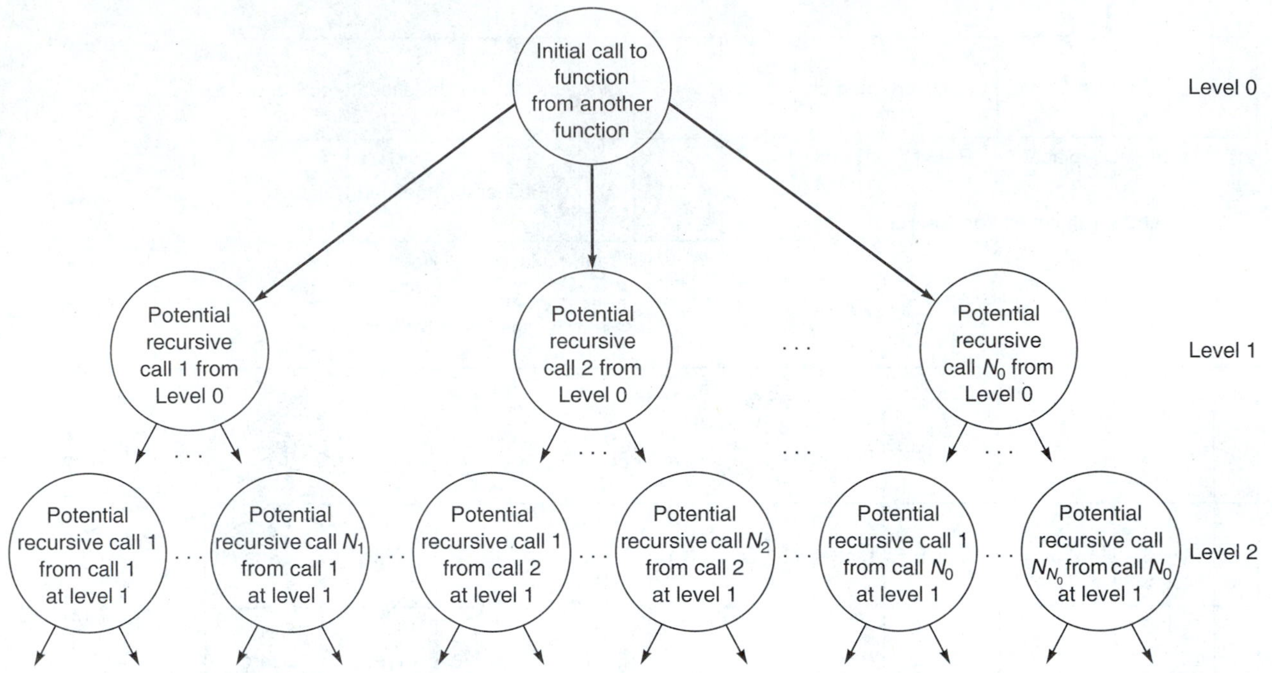

at which a recursive call is made for a particular set of given parameter values. The time efficiency will be proportional to the sum, over all levels, of the times spent processing at each individual level. The following examples clarify how such a tree of recursive calls can be used to analyze the time and space efficiencies of the function **recSearch** for two different choices of the **split** function.

Example 6.1

Use a tree of potential recursive calls to analyze the space and time efficiency of function **recSearch** when the **split** function is (**lo** + **hi**) / 2.

For this choice of a **split** function, we have the tree of potential recursive calls that appears in Figure 6.5. For an array with 15 data items, this tree stops at level 3, as indicated in Figure 6.6. The OR's appearing in these two figures indicate that, at any given level, we will make at most one recursive call or the other, but not both. This is important (and, as we shall see, not the case for all recursive algorithms) since it implies that the work done at any given level is simply the work done at one node along that level. Clearly, the work done at any node is $O(1)$ since we are merely comparing the **target** item to the data at the **guess** position determined by the **split** function. Hence, the time efficiency of the **recSearch** algorithm for this **split** function will merely be proportional to the number of levels in the recursive call tree for an array with N items. From Figures 6.5 and 6.6 it is evident that doubling the number of items in the array will merely add one level to the recursive call tree. That is, the number of levels in the recursive call tree is

FIGURE 6.5
Tree of potential recursive calls for **recSearch** with **split** function (**lo** + **hi**) / 2.

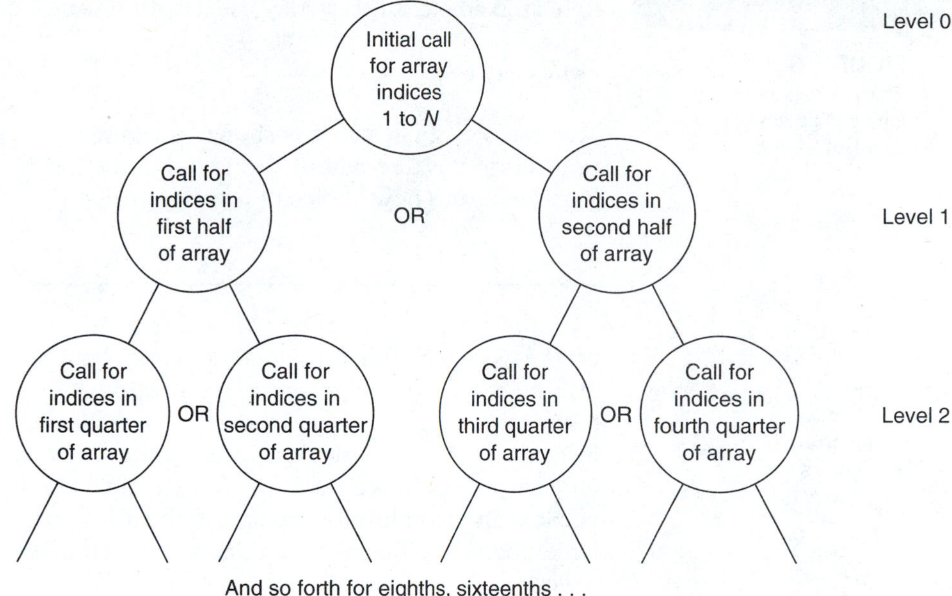

$\log_2 N + 1$ (truncated). With the $O(1)$ work done at each level, we can thus conclude that the time efficiency of **recSearch** for this **split** function is $O(\log_2 N)$. Similarly, since a stack frame will be allocated for each recursive level, the additional space requirements of the algorithm (beyond the array itself) are $O(\log_2 N)$.

FIGURE 6.6
Tree of Figure 6.5 for an array with 15 data items.

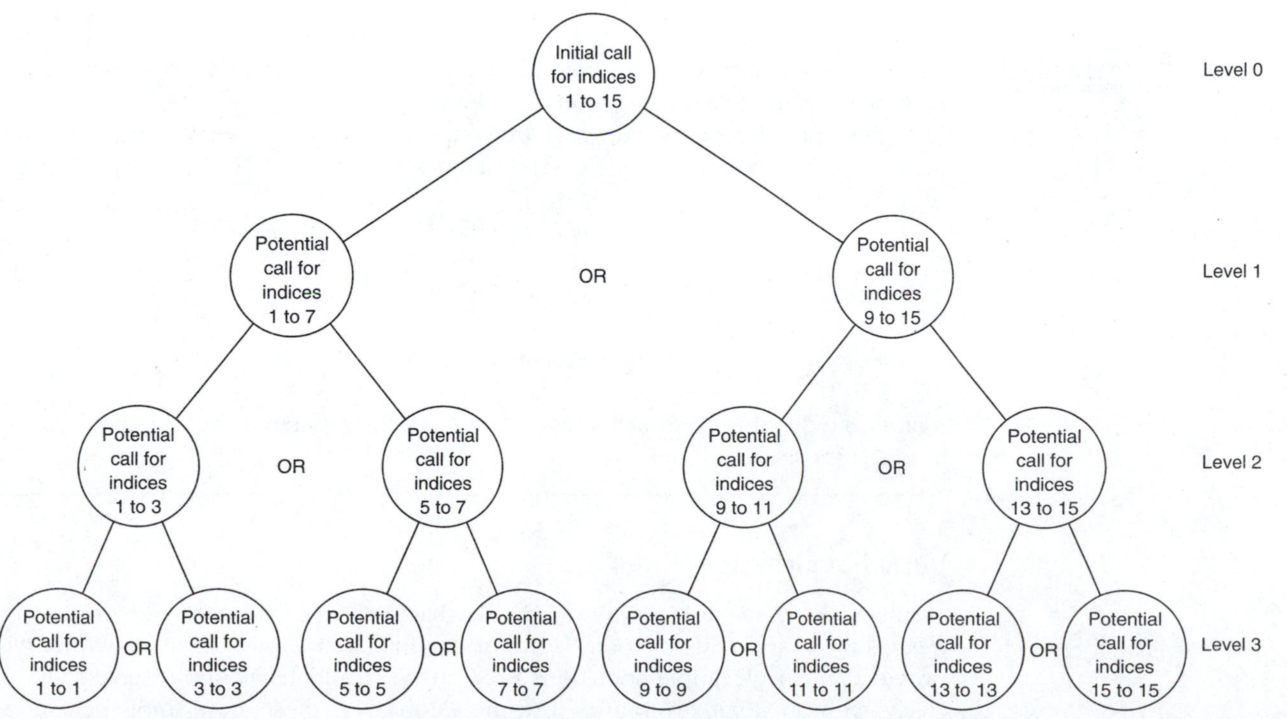

Example 6.2

Repeat Example 6.1, but now use a **split** function defined by

```
return(lo);
```

The tree of recursive calls is shown in Figure 6.7. Note that, potentially, the number of levels in this tree will be N instead of the $\log_2 N$ value that emerged in Example 6.1. Hence, this new choice of a **split** function generates time and space efficiencies of $O(N)$.

FIGURE 6.7
Tree of recursive calls for **recSearch** with **return(lo).**

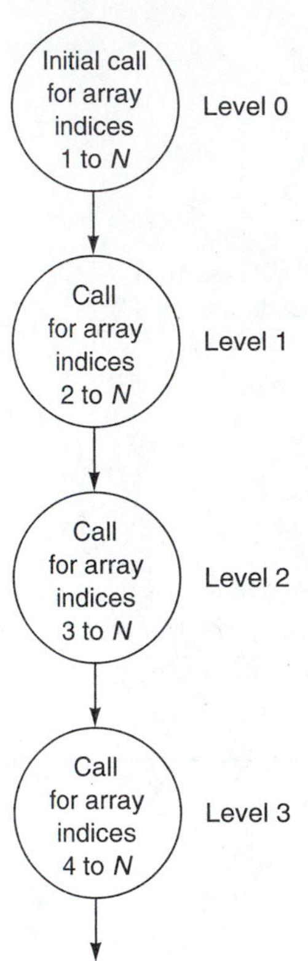

The algorithm efficiency analyses carried out in the two preceding examples can also be achieved using *recurrence relations*. A recurrence relation is an equation that expresses the time or space efficiency of an algorithm for a data set of size N in terms of the efficiency of the algorithm on a smaller data set. For instance, the efficiency analysis we performed in Example 6.1 reported that the efficiency of the **recSearch** algorithm for the specified **split** function on a data set of size N was 1 larger than the efficiency on a data set of half that size. In terms of an equation, we have

$$\text{Efficiency}(N) = \text{Efficiency}(N/2) + 1$$

Using techniques to solve explicitly such a recurrence relation, you can establish that Efficiency(N) is proportional to $\log_2 N$ from the above equation—exactly the result that we obtained by our analysis of the recursive call tree. The techniques to solve explicitly such recurrence relations are covered briefly in Appendix B. We will not cover such techniques here, but we will use results arising from such techniques as needed.

Example 6.3

Develop a recurrence relation to describe the time and space efficiencies for **recSearch** with the **split** function described in Example 6.2.

In this example, the recursive call tree implied that the efficiency of the algorithm on a data set of N items is one greater than on a data set of $N - 1$ items. That is,

$$\text{Efficiency}(N) = \text{Efficiency}(N - 1) + 1$$

Explicitly solving this recurrence relation yields the result

$$\text{Efficiency}(N) = N$$

Again note that this approach is consistent with the efficiency we obtained directly from the recursive call tree.

Why Recursion?

At this point you could argue effectively that we have not achieved much with recursion so far in this chapter. Why? In our initial examples, at least, we merely provided recursive implementations of what we could have implemented just as easily with an iterative control structure. Moreover, these new implementations are less efficient than our previous implementations because they consume stack space without providing any savings in time. Such objections are well taken. Recursion, as an alternative to straightforward iteration, is not a wise choice for an implementation strategy. What we have gained, however, by our treatment of a recursive version of the divide-and-conquer search and the list traversal algorithm is an initial understanding of how recursion works and how to analyze a recursive algorithm.

We now embark on a discussion of some algorithms for which an ordinary iterative control structure would not be sufficient. These algorithms employ a recursive pattern that generates an intricate mix of calls and returns instead of an uninterrupted sequence of calls followed by their associated returns. In examining how such algorithms interact with the system stack, we will observe a subtle ebb and flow as frames are pushed and popped for each recursive level. In effect, such algorithms are using recursion to gain access to the system stack operations that are associated with function calls and returns. In doing so, they often provide a compact and elegantly stated solution to a very complex problem.

There is an additional argument that can be made for recursion that relates to the costs of hardware and software development. In the early days of computing, the hardware was expensive, processing was slow, and computer memory was expensive and scarce. Consequently, when programmers wrote programs they did so with an inclination toward using algorithms that stressed speed of execution and economy of storage utilization over simplicity and clarity of code. Thanks to astounding advances in technology and manufacturing since those early times, the costs of hardware have continually dropped and processing rates have dramatically increased. Computers having tens of megabytes of primary memory have become commonplace—even in personal computers and workstations. At the same time, however, the human costs associated with using these computing resources (including the costs of writing, debugging, and maintaining programs) have increased to the point that they typically outweigh the costs of the hardware. One consequence of the convergence of these two economic trends was that algorithms placing a premium on execution speed and storage utilization at the expense of clarity, simplicity, maintainability, and ease of verification are not as prized as they once were. It should not be surprising therefore that recursion is now seen as an important programming technique and that virtually every modern programming language supports the use of recursion.

The Towers of Hanoi Problem

The solution to the Towers of Hanoi problem represents a classic recursive algorithm. We discuss it now to illustrate the more intricate stack manipulations that arise in a nontrivial recursive function. According to legend, there existed in ancient Hanoi a monastery where the monks had the painstaking task of moving a collection of N stone disks from one pillar, designated as pillar A, to another, designated as pillar C. Moreover, the relative ordering of the disks on pillar A had to be maintained as they were moved to pillar C. That is, as illustrated in Figure 6.8, the disks were to be stacked from largest to smallest, beginning from the bottom. Additionally, the monks were to observe the following rules in moving disks:

- Only one disk could be moved at a time.
- No larger disk could ever be placed on a pillar on top of a smaller disk.
- A third pillar B could be used as an intermediate to store one or more disks as they were being moved from their original source A to their destination C.

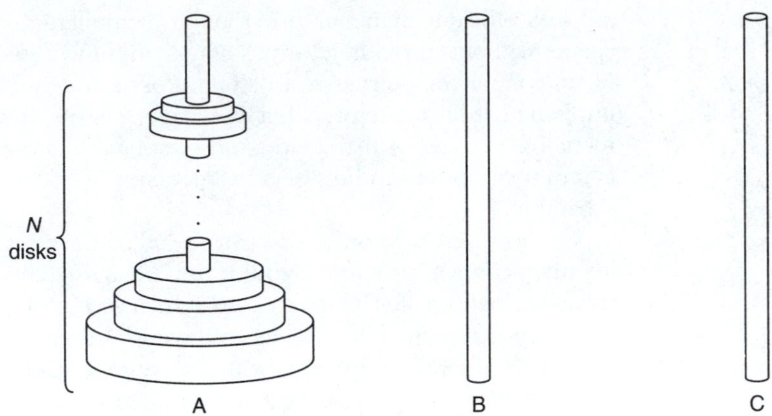

FIGURE 6.8
Towers of Hanoi.

Consider the following recursive solution to this problem:

1. If $N = 1$, merely move the disk from A to C.
2. If $N = 2$, move first disk from A to B. Then move second disk from A to C. Then move first disk from B to C.
3. If $N = 3$, call on the technique already established in step 2 to move the first two disks from A to B, using C as an intermediate. Then move the third disk from A to C. Then use the technique in step 2 to move the first disks from B to C, using A as an intermediate.

⋮

N. For general N, use the technique in the previous step to move $N - 1$ disks from A to B, using C as an intermediate. Then move one disk from A to C. Then use the technique in the previous step to move $N - 1$ disks from B to C, using A as an intermediate.

Notice that the technique described here calls itself but switches the order of parameters in so doing. This can be formalized in the following C++ function. The return-point labels in the function are included only for later discussion purposes.

```
//------------------------------------------------------------
// Interface for function hanoi
// GIVEN:    n -- the number of disks to be moved;
//           source -- the pillar that the disks are being moved from;
//           destination -- the pillar the disks are being moved to;
//           intermediate -- the pillar being used for temporary storage.
// RETURN:   As output, a listing of the individual disk moves necessary to achieve
//           the overall transfer of n disks.
// RETURN as value of function: void

void hanoi(int n, char source, char destination, char intermediate)
{
  if (n == 1)
    cout << "Move disk from " << source << " to " << destination << endl;
  else
  {
    // In every recursive call hanoi works with a value of n less one
```

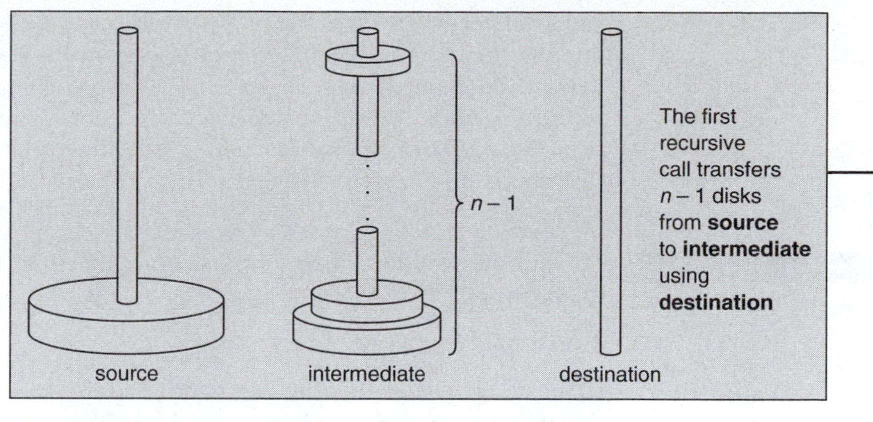
n – 1
The first recursive call transfers n – 1 disks from **source** to **intermediate** using **destination**
source
intermediate
destination

```
    hanoi(n - 1, source, intermediate, destination);
    // Return Point 1

    cout << "Move disk from " << source << " to " << destination  << endl;
    hanoi(n - 1, intermediate, destination, source);
    //  Return Point 2
  }
}
```

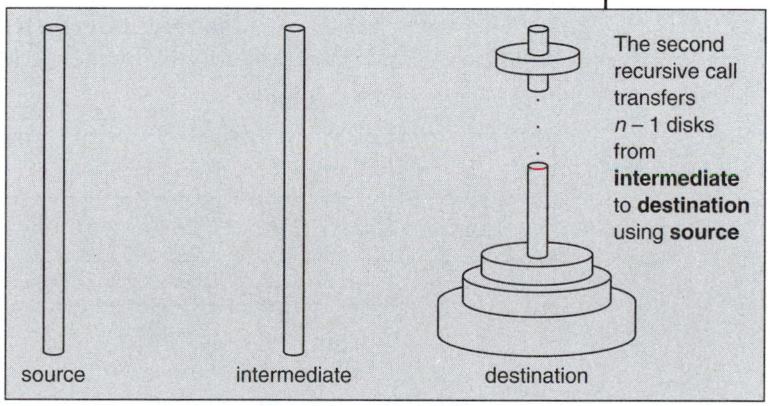
The second recursive call transfers n – 1 disks from **intermediate** to **destination** using **source**
source
intermediate
destination

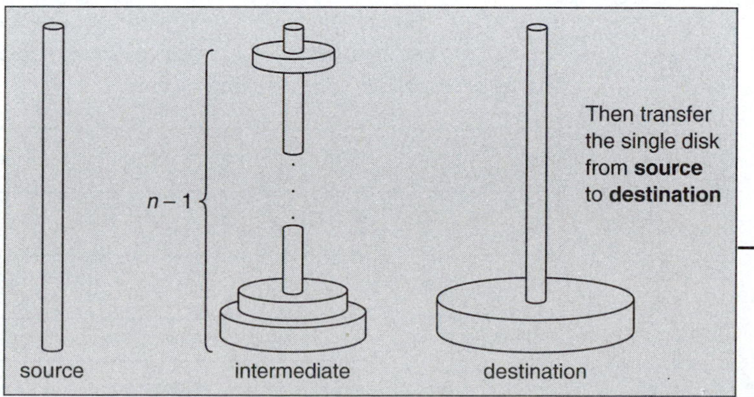
n – 1
Then transfer the single disk from **source** to **destination**
source
intermediate
destination

Unlike the **recSearch** function, in which only one recursive call was made each time the function was invoked, function **hanoi** will reinvoke itself twice each time it is called nontrivially. The result is a more complicated algorithm that cannot be implemented by using mere iterative control structures. Implicitly, through its recursive calls, the **hanoi** function is weaving an intricate pattern of push and pop operations on the system stack.

Example 6.4

To illustrate, we trace through the actions affecting the system stack when a call of the form

```
hanoi(3, 'A', 'C', 'B');
```

is initiated. The values in the return-address portion of the stack refer to the documentary statement labels in our **hanoi** function.

1. We enter **hanoi** with the following stack frame: **n** is not 1, so the condition in the **if** statement is false.

Return	n	source	destination	intermediate
Original call	3	A	C	B

Parameters (n, source, destination, intermediate)

Stack Frame

2. We encounter **hanoi(n−1, source, intermediate, destination)** with A, B, and C as second, third, and fourth arguments. Because this represents a recursive call, some stacking must be done:

Return	n	source	destination	intermediate
1	2	A	B	C
Original call	3	A	C	B

Parameters (n, source, destination, intermediate)

Stack Frames

3. Reenter **hanoi.** Notice that as we enter this time, the view of the parameters is **n** = 2, **source** = A, **destination** = B, and **intermediate** = C. Because **n** is not 1, the condition in the **if** statement is false.
4. We encounter **hanoi(n − 1, source, intermediate, destination).** Because this is a recursive call, stacking occurs.

Return	n	source	destination	intermediate
1	1	A	C	B
1	2	A	B	C
Original call	3	A	C	B

Parameters (n, source, destination, intermediate)

Stack Frames

5. We reenter **hanoi** with **n** = 1, **source** = A, **destination** = C, and **intermediate** = B. Because **n** = 1, the condition in the **if** statement is **TRUE**.
6. Hence,

```
Move disk from A to C
```

is printed and a return triggers an examining and popping of a return address (1) and four parameters, leaving the system stack as pictured here:

Return	n	source	destination	intermediate
1	2	A	B	C
Original call	3	A	C	B

Parameters (n, source, destination, intermediate)

Stack Frames

7. Because the return address examined was 1, we return to the **cout** instruction that triggers the following output:

```
Move disk from A to B
```

Next

```
hanoi(n - 1, intermediate, destination, source);
```

is encountered with **n** = 2, **source** = A, **destination** = B, and **intermediate** = C.
8. The call pushes a return address and four parameters onto the stack system.

Return	n	source	destination	intermediate
2	1	C	B	A
1	2	A	B	C
Original call	3	A	C	B

Parameters (n, source, destination, intermediate)

Stack Frames

9. We reenter **hanoi**, this time with **n** = 1, **source** = C, **destination** = B, and **intermediate** = A.
10. Because **n** = 1, the **if** statement generates the output

```
Move disk from C to B
```

and a return.
11. The return pops a frame from the system stack and we return to the statement labeled by 2 with **n** = 2, **source** = A, **destination** = B, and **intermediate** = C.
12. But statement 2 is the end of the function and triggers a return itself, so a stack frame is popped again and we return to statement 1 with **n** = 3, **source** = A, **destination** = C, **intermediate** = B.

13. Statement 1 triggers the output

```
Move disk from A to C
```

and we are immediately at another call:

```
hanoi(n - 1, intermediate, destination, source);
```

Hence, the status of the system stack is changed to

Return	n	source	destination	intermediate
2	2	B	C	A
Original call	3	A	C	B

Parameters (n, source, destination, intermediate)

Stack Frames

14. We reenter **hanoi** with **n** = 2, **source** = B, **destination** = C, and **intermediate** = A. Because **n** is not 1, another call is executed and more values are stacked.

Return	n	source	destination	intermediate
1	1	B	A	C
2	2	B	C	A
Original call	3	A	C	B

Parameters (n, source, destination, intermediate)

Stack Frames

15. Reenter **hanoi**, with **n** = 1, **source** = B, **destination** = A, and **intermediate** = C. Because **n** = 1, we print

```
Move disk from B to A
```

and return.

16. The return prompts the examining and popping of the system stack. The return address examined is the statement labeled 1. Statement 1 causes output

```
Move disk from B to C
```

with the stack frames left at

Return	n	source	destination	intermediate
2	2	B	C	A
Original call	3	A	C	B

Parameters (n, source, destination, intermediate)

Stack Frames

17. The output from statement 1 is followed by

```
hanoi(n - 1, intermediate, destination, source);
```

Hence, pushed onto the stack is

Return	n	source	destination	intermediate
2	1	A	C	B
2	2	B	C	A
Original call	3	A	C	B

Parameters (n, source, destination, intermediate)

Stack Frames

18. Reenter (for the last time) **hanoi**, with **n** = 1, **source** = A, **destination** = C, and **intermediate** = B. Because **n** = 1, output

```
Move disk from A to C
```

and return.

19. But now the return examines and pops return-address 2 from the stack, so return to statement 2 with the system stack given by

Return	n	source	destination	intermediate
2	2	B	C	A
Original call	3	A	C	B

Parameters (n, source, destination, intermediate)

Stack Frames

20. Statement 2 is another return, so examine and pop the stack again. The return address popped is 2, the same return statement. But this time the return will transfer control back to the original calling location and *we are done!*

Long-winded as this example is, you must understand it. Recursive functions are crucial to many of the algorithms used in computer science, and you can acquire the necessary familiarity with recursion only by convincing yourself that it really works. If you have some doubt or are not sure you understand, we recommend that you trace through the **hanoi** function with **n** = 4 (and be prepared to go through a lot of paper).

The analysis carried out in the next example demonstrates that the **hanoi** algorithm falls into the class of exponential algorithms defined in Section 1.2. This is the first exponential algorithm we have encountered. Recall from our discussion of algorithm efficiency in Section 1.2 that such algorithms are impractical to run for even moderate values of N. We will return to a consideration of exponential algorithms in Chapter 10, where we will explore attempts at using *heuristics* to transform such algorithms into nonexponential $O(N^k)$ algorithms for a reasonable choice of k.

FIGURE 6.9
Tree of recursive calls for **hanoi** function with **n** originally 4 (numbers in parentheses indicate order of recursive calls).

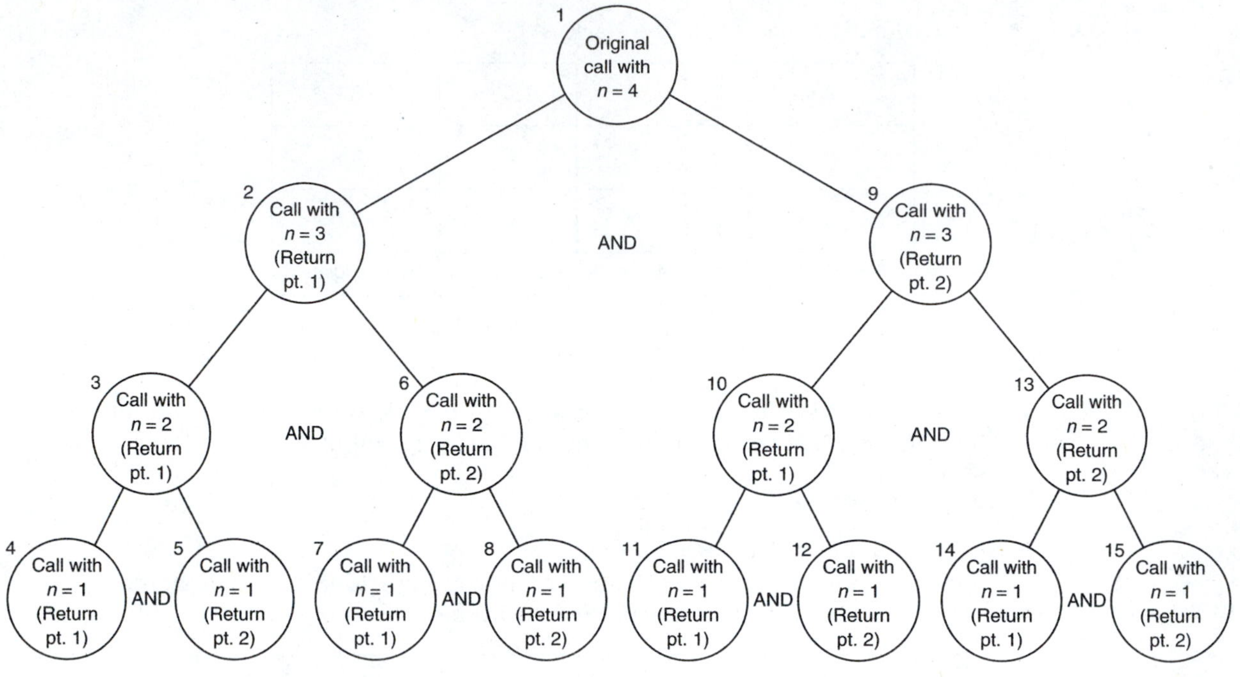

Example 6.5

Use the tree of recursive calls generated by the **hanoi** function to analyze the time and space efficiency of the algorithm.

A graphic of this tree is given in Figure 6.9. The most important difference between this tree and those used to analyze **recSearch** in Figures 6.5 and 6.6 is that the two nodes (representing calls) descending from each node are linked by an AND instead of an OR. This is to emphasize that, when **n** is not 1, *both* recursive calls will be made instead of just one, as was the case with **recSearch**. This difference has a rather dramatic effect on the time efficiency of the algorithm. In particular, calling **hanoi** initially with **n** = 4 results in a total of 15 calls in the recursive call tree. The numbers outside the circles in Figure 6.9 indicate the order in which these 15 call are made. Increasing to **n** = 5 would add a level with 16 nodes to the recursive call tree. In general, adding one disk adds only one level to the recursive call tree but doubles (plus 1) the number of nodes in the tree. This implies that the space efficiency of **hanoi** relative to the system stack is $O(n)$, but, since *every* call in the recursive call tree will be made, the time efficiency is $O(2^n)$.

The recurrence relation to express the time efficiency of the **hanoi** algorithm is

$$\text{Efficiency}(n) = 2 \times \text{Efficiency}(n-1) + 1$$

An explicit solution of this relation with Efficiency (1) = 1 is $2^n - 1$. As in Example 6.3, observe that explicitly solving a recurrence relation yields an efficiency result consistent with that obtained by examining the recursive call tree.

In this section, our primary goal has been to establish a high degree of confidence in recursion as a problem-solving technique. As such, our examples have not been chosen with practical application in mind but rather to illustrate, in detail, how recursion works. We have also discussed how recursive call trees or, alternately, recurrence relations may be used to analyze the efficiency of recursive algorithms. Given the foundation established in this section, we now examine applications of recursion to sorting and parsing in the remainder of the chapter.

Exercises 6.1

1. In the **SearchArray** class the **split** function is passed to the constructor. Explain how the **split** function could be passed to the **search** operation instead of the constructor. Discuss the advantages and disadvantages of doing this.
2. Consider the following two versions of the parameterless function **forever.** Provide implementations of both versions of **forever** in your favorite programming language. Then call on each version from a program that you run on your system. Do you observe any differences in run-time behavior of the two versions? Explain your observations in a written statement.
   Version 1

```
void forever()
{
  while (TRUE)
}
```

   Version 2

```
void forever()
{
  forever();
}
```

3. Consider the following recursive function and associated top-level call. Comments of the form *Return Pt N* label possible return points from recursive calls. What would a stack frame for this function contain? By means of a series of stack "snapshots," show how the stack would be manipulated for the calls indicated. Finally, provide the recursive call tree and output that would be generated as this function was called from the top level.

```
int weird(int m, int n)
{
  cout << m << n << endl;
  if (m == 0)
    return(n + 1);
  else
    if (n == 0)
      return(weird(m - 1, 1));
             // Return Pt 1
    else
      return(weird(m - 1,    weird(m, n - 1)));
             // Return Pt 2 // Return Pt 3
}
```

   Top-level call: `cout << weird(1, 3);`
4. Write a recursive C++ function that reads characters from an input line and prints the characters reversed from their order of entry.
5. Write a recursive version of the insertion sort algorithm.
6. The *Fibonacci sequence* is a sequence of integers, starting with two 1's, such that each member of the sequence is the sum of the two previous numbers. Thus, the first seven terms in the Fibonacci sequence are

   1 1 2 3 5 8 13 . . .

   Use a tree of recursive calls to analyze the time and space efficiency of the following function to compute the Nth Fibonacci number. What is the recurrence relation that describes this efficiency? Try to solve this recurrence relation explicitly (provided that you have studied techniques to solve recurrence relations in a discrete mathematics course).

```
//-----------------------------------------------
// Interface for fibonacci function
// GIVEN:      n -- a positive integer.
// RETURN as value of the function:
//         nth number in Fibonacci sequence.

  int fibonacci(int n)
  {
    if ((n ==1) || (n == 2))
      return(1);
    else
      return(fibonacci(n-1) + fibonacci(n-2));
  }
```

7. Write a *recursive* function to compute the Nth Fibonacci number in a fashion that is significantly more time-efficient than the function provided in the preceding exercise. Analyze the time and space efficiency of your function.
8. Euclid devised a clever algorithm for computing the greatest common divisor of two integers. According to Euclid's algorithm,

$$\gcd(m, n) = \begin{cases} \gcd(n, m) & \text{if } n > m \\ m & \text{if } n = 0 \\ \gcd(n, m \% n) & \text{if } n > 0 \end{cases}$$

   Write a recursive function to compute greatest common divisors via Euclid's method. Analyze the time and space efficiency of your algorithm.
9. Using the operations for the **String** class discussed in Section 2.2, write a recursive function that is given a **String s** and returns the reversal of **s**. For example, given **s** = "PEACH", your function should return the string "HCAEP". Analyze the time and space efficiency of your function.

6.2 Quick Sort

In Section 1.3 we introduced the divide-and-conquer technique and applied it in searching an ordered array. Then, in Section 6.1, we saw how that same divide-and-conquer search strategy could be implemented recursively. With searching, the recursive implementation proved to be less efficient than a straightforward iterative implementation. However, we are now ready to take a recursive leap. We shall see that by considering divide-and-conquer strategies for sorting we can break the $O(n^2)$ and $O(n(\log_2 n)^2)$ barriers we encountered when studying the insertion, selection, and Shell sort algorithms in Chapter 1. Moreover, because such divide-and-conquer techniques applied to sorting are considerably more complex than their searching counterparts, there is no choice other than to implement them recursively. (Actually, any recursive algorithm can be converted to a nonrecursive implementation using your own stack and the technique discussed in Problem 15 at the end of this chapter. However, essentially, such nonrecursive versions replace the system stack with a programmer-implemented stack and consequently achieve no real savings in time or space efficiency.)

The first such divide-and-conquer sorting algorithm we will examine is *quick sort.* The essence of the quick sort algorithm is to rely on a subordinate algorithm to partition the array. The process of partitioning involves moving a data item, called the *pivot,* in the correct direction just enough for it to reach its final place in the array. The partitioning process, therefore, reduces unnecessary interchanges and potentially moves the pivot a great distance in the array without forcing it to be swapped into intermediate locations.

Once the pivot item is chosen, moves are made so that data items to the left of the pivot are less than (or equal to) it; whereas those to the right are greater (or equal). The pivot item is thus in its correct position. The quick sort algorithm then recursively applies the partitioning process to the two parts of the array on either side of the pivot until the entire array is sorted. In the next example, we illustrate the mechanics of this partitioning logic by applying it to an array of numbers.

Example 6.6

Suppose an array **a**, indexed from 1, contains integers initially arranged as

15 20 5 8 95 12 80 17 9 55

Figure 6.10 shows a partition pass applied to this array. The following steps are involved:

FIGURE 6.10
Each call to recursive quick sort algorithm partitions an array segment. The asterisk indicates the pivot value (here 15), and the dashed arrows indicate the starting place for a scan and the range of the scan. The parentheses indicate where a value will be placed following a scan.

Pivot 15

Line number	a[1]	a[2]	a[3]	a[4]	a[5]	a[6]	a[7]	a[8]	a[9]	a[10]
1	15*	20	5	8	95	12	80	17	9	55
2	9	20	5	8	95	12	80	17	( )	55
3	9	( )	5	8	95	12	80	17	20	55
4	9	12	5	8	95	( )	80	17	20	55
5	9	12	5	8	( )	95	80	17	20	55
6	9	12	5	8	15	95	80	17	20	55

1. Remove the first data item, 15, as the pivot, mark its position, and scan the array from right to left, comparing data item values with 15. When you find the first smaller value, remove it from its current position and put it in position **a[1]**. (This is shown in line 2.)
2. Scan line 2 from left to right beginning with position **a[2],** comparing data item values with 15. When you find the first value greater than 15, extract it and store it in the position marked by parentheses in line 2. (This is shown in line 3.)
3. Begin the right-to-left scan of line 3 with position **a[8]** and look for a value smaller than 15. When you find it, extract it and store it in the position marked by the parentheses in line 3. (This is shown in line 4.)
4. Begin scanning line 4 from left to right at position **a[3].** Find a value greater than 15, remove it, mark its position, and store it inside the parentheses in line 4. (This is shown in line 5.)
5. Now, when you scan line 5 from right to left beginning at position **a[5],** you immediately come to a parenthesized position—**a[5].** This is the location to put the first data item, 15. (This is shown in line 6.) At this stage, 15 is in its correct place relative to the final sorted array.

Notice that all values to the left of 15 are less than 15, and all values to the right of 15 are greater than 15. The method will still work if two values are the same. The process can now be applied recursively to the two segments of the array on the left and right of 15.

Notice that these recursive calls eventually result in the sorting of the entire array. The result of any one call to the quick sort algorithm is merely to partition a segment of the array so that the pivotal item is positioned with everything to its left being less than or equal to it and everything to its right being greater than or equal.

To obtain a completely general version of the quick sort algorithm, we implement it within the framework of the SortArray class that was introduced in Section 2.2.

```
// We assume IndexType is a finite collection of consecutively enumerated
// values such as integers, characters, or enum values, and that
// BaseData is either a C++ built-in-type, or a C++ class that has
// an assignment operation that overloads the "=" operator.
template <class IndexType, class BaseData>
class SortArray : public Array<IndexType, BaseData>
{
  protected:
    BOOLEAN (*precedes)(const BaseData &x, const BaseData &y);
    // Comparison function

//----------------------------------------------------------------------------
// Interface for protected partition algorithm used by quick sort:
// GIVEN:     lo and hi -- indices within Array object, lo <= hi.
// RETURN:    Array object partitioned between indices lo and hi, using the entry
//            originally in index lo as the pivot.
// RETURN as value of function:
//            The index where pivot element is placed

    IndexType partition(IndexType lo, IndexType hi);
```

```
//------------------------------------------------------------------------
// Interface for protected qsRecursive implementation of quick sort
// GIVEN:     lo and hi -- indices within Array object, lo <= hi.
// RETURN:    Array object sorted by quick sort between indices lo and hi.
// RETURN as value of function: void

   void qsRecursive(IndexType lo, IndexType hi);

  public:

//------------------------------------------------------------------------
// Interface for SortArray constructor
// GIVEN:     An uninitialized SortArray object;
//            lo and hi -- define an allowable index range for SortArray object;
//            precedes -- a function to compare BaseData values:
//              GIVEN:   x and y -- values to compare
//              RETURN as value of function:
//                       TRUE     if x precedes y;
//                       FALSE    if x and y are equal, or if y precedes x.
// RETURN:    SortArray object with space allocated for it and a precedence relation
//            between elements, but with no values assigned to array indices

   SortArray(IndexType lo, IndexType hi,
             BOOLEAN (*precedes)(const BaseData &x, const BaseData &y));

//------------------------------------------------------------------------
// Interface for sort operation
// GIVEN:   a SortArray object;
//          numvals -- logical size of the Array, assuming values are stored
//                     consecutively from lowest index.
// RETURN:  Array object arranged in order by its precedes relation.
// RETURN as value of function: void

   void sort(int numvals);
};
```

Three methods within this class require description. First, the public **sort** method is not quick sort itself, but rather just prepares parameters to send to the protected recursive function **qsRecursive.** This is the same technique we used with the recursive divide-and-conquer search, allowing us to preserve the public interface to the **sort** operation. The **qsRecursive** function must call on the protected **partition** function and then use the return value as the pivot point to decide whether or not recursive calls are necessary to perform more refined partitioning of the segments to the left and right of this pivot point. The critical **partition** function uses pointers **lo** and **hi** that move left and right, respectively, until they meet in the appropriate location for the **pivot.** The pivotal value is initially chosen to be **(*this)[lo],** that is, the value in the **lo** index of the **Array** object underlying the **SortArray** object. Later we will discuss the possible implications of choosing a different pivotal value. Note that it is crucial for **partition** to return as a pivot point the position where the pivotal value was finally inserted. This information will allow the **qsRecursive** function to determine whether or not a base case has been reached.

```
template <class IndexType, class BaseData>
void SortArray<IndexType, BaseData>::sort(int numvals)
{
  qsRecursive(loIndex, loIndex + numvals - 1);
}
```

```
template <class IndexType, class BaseData>
void SortArray<IndexType, BaseData>::qsRecursive(IndexType lo, IndexType hi)
{
  IndexType pivotPoint;

  pivotPoint = partition(lo, hi);
  if (lo < pivotPoint)
    qsRecursive(lo, pivotPoint - 1);
  if (pivotPoint < hi)
    qsRecursive(pivotPoint + 1, hi);
}

template <class IndexType, class BaseData>
IndexType SortArray<IndexType, BaseData>::partition(IndexType lo, IndexType hi)
{
  BaseData pivot;

  pivot = (*this)[lo];
  while (lo < hi)
  {
    // Begin right-to-left scan

    while ((precedes(pivot,(*this)[hi])) && (lo < hi))
      --hi;
    if (hi != lo) // move entry indexed by hi to left side of partition
      (*this)[lo++] = (*this)[hi];
    // Begin left-to-right scan
    while ((precedes((*this)[lo],pivot)) && (lo < hi))
      ++lo;
    if (hi != lo) // move entry indexed by lo to right side of partition
      (*this)[hi--] = (*this)[lo];
  }
  (*this)[hi] = pivot;
  return(hi);
}
```

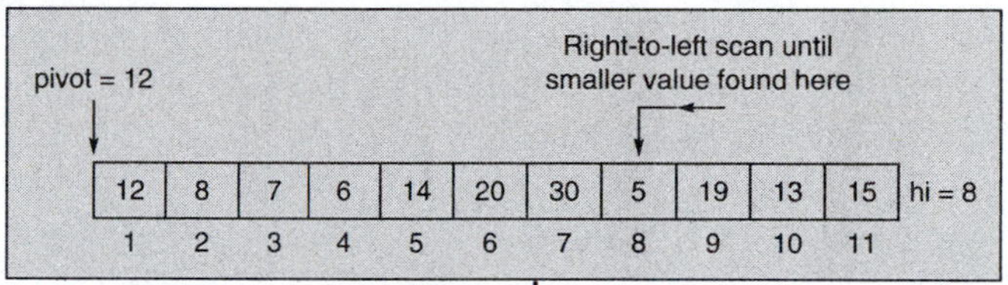

pivot = 12
Right-to-left scan until smaller value found here

12	8	7	6	14	20	30	5	19	13	15	hi = 8
1	2	3	4	5	6	7	8	9	10	11	

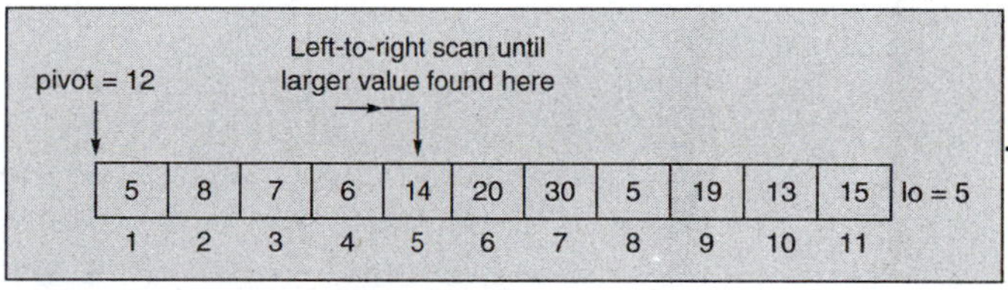

pivot = 12
Left-to-right scan until larger value found here

5	8	7	6	14	20	30	5	19	13	15	lo = 5
1	2	3	4	5	6	7	8	9	10	11	

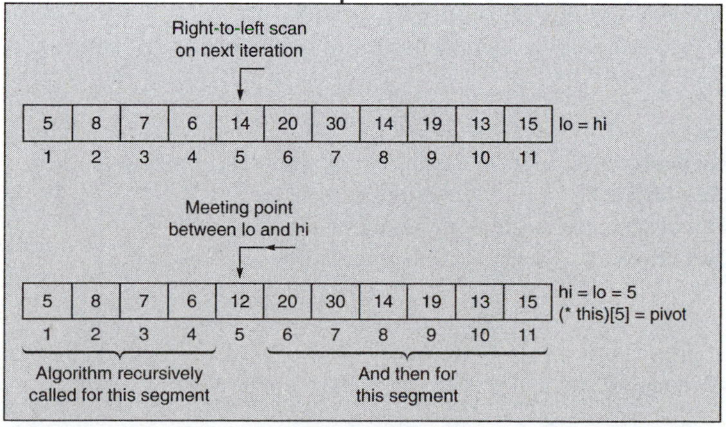

Right-to-left scan on next iteration

5	8	7	6	14	20	30	14	19	13	15	lo = hi
1	2	3	4	5	6	7	8	9	10	11	

Meeting point between lo and hi

5	8	7	6	12	20	30	14	19	13	15	hi = lo = 5 (* this)[5] = pivot
1	2	3	4	5	6	7	8	9	10	11	

Algorithm recursively called for this segment (1–4)
And then for this segment (6–11)

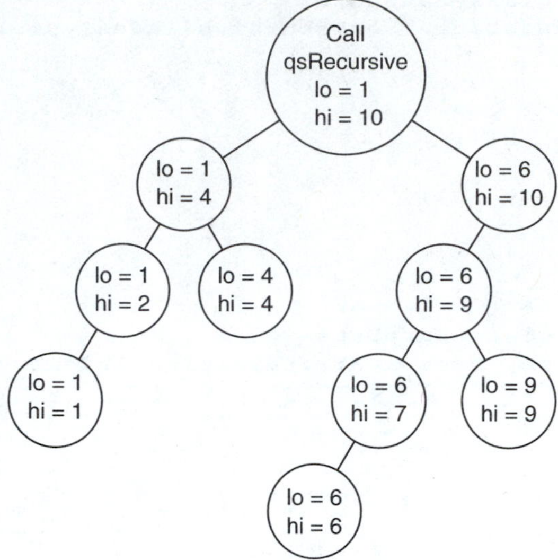

FIGURE 6.11
Tree of (recursive) calls to **qsRecursive** for data in Figure 6.10.

For instance, after the first call to **qsRecursive** for a partitioning pass on the data in Figure 6.10, we would then recursively call on **qsRecursive** with **lo** = 1 and **hi** = 4. This would trigger deeper-level recursive calls from which we would ultimately return, knowing that the segment of the array between indices 1 and 5 is now sorted. This return would be followed by a recursive call to **qsRecursive** with **lo** = 6 and **hi** = 10.

The entire tree of recursive calls to **qsRecursive** for the data of Figure 6.10 is given in Figure 6.11. Trace through the execution of the function to verify this call-return pattern.

Efficiency of the Quick Sort

The average run-time efficiency of the quick sort is $O(n \log_2 n)$. In Chapter 12, we will demonstrate that, in a sense, no sort can do better than this. In the best case, it is quite easy to provide a rationale for this $O(n \log_2 n)$ figure. This best case occurs when each array segment recursively passed to **qsRecursive** partitions at its midpoint; that is, the appropriate location for each pivotal value in the series of recursive calls is the midpoint of the segment being partitioned. In this case,

1 call to **qsRecursive** (the first) is made with a segment of size n.
2 calls to **qsRecursive** are made with segments of size $n/2$.
4 calls to **qsRecursive** are made with segments of size $n/4$.
8 calls to **qsRecursive** are made with segments of size $n/8$.
.
.
.
n calls to **qsRecursive** are made with segments of size 1.

(overall $\log_2 n$ levels)

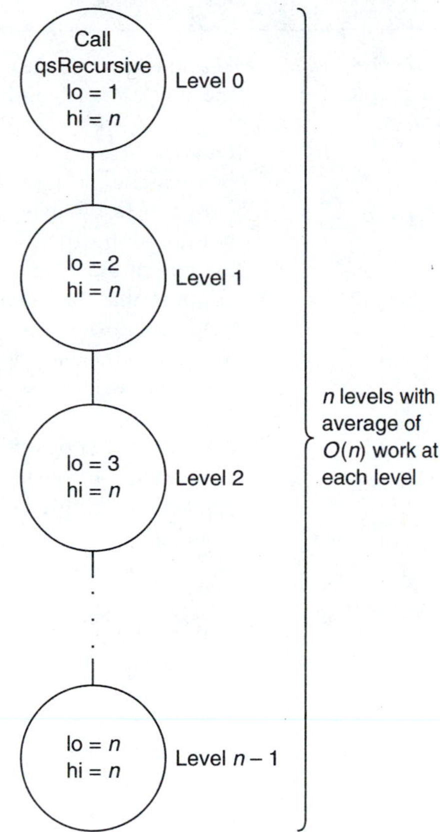

FIGURE 6.12
Recursive call tree for the quick sort's worst case.

Since each call with a segment of size m requires $O(m)$ comparisons, it is clear that k calls with segments of size n/k will require $O(n)$ comparisons. Hence, the total number of comparisons resulting from the preceding sequence of calls will be $O(n \log_2 n)$.

If segments partition away from the midpoint, the efficiency of quick sort begins to deteriorate. In the worst-case situation, when the array is already sorted, the efficiency of the quick sort may drop down to $O(n^2)$ owing to the continuous right-to-left scan all the way to the last left boundary. That is, the recursive call tree will appear as in Figure 6.12. In the exercises at the end of the section, you will explore how the worst-case situation is affected by your choice of the pivotal element.

The recurrence relation that expresses the best-case efficiency is

$$\text{Efficiency}(n) = 2 \times \text{Efficiency}(n/2) + n$$

That is, to quick sort n values when they partition at the midpoint, we must make n comparisons during a partitioning pass and then (recursively) quick sort two segments of size $n/2$. An explicit solution of this recurrence relation yields an $O(n \log_2 n)$ result—consistent with the analysis we obtained from the recursive call tree.

Exercises 6.2

1. Consider the **qsRecursive** function given in this section. Suppose we were to insert the following tracer output immediately at the beginning of this function.

```
cout << lo << hi << endl;
for (k = lo; k <= hi; ++k)
  cout << (*this)[k];
```

What would we see as output from these tracers if we were to call on **qsRecursive** with the array initially containing the following seven entries?

60 12 90 30 64 8 6

Draw the tree of recursive calls that results from this particular data.

2. Repeat Exercise 1 for a six-element array that initially contains

1 8 2 7 3 6

3. When is insertion sort better than quick sort as presented in this section?
4. When is selection sort better than quick sort as presented in this section?
5. Under what circumstances would you not use the quick sort from this section?
6. How does the choice of the pivotal value affect the efficiency of the quick sort algorithm? Suppose that the middle value or the last value in a segment to be partitioned were chosen as the pivotal value. How would this alter the nature of best case and worst case data sets? Give examples to illustrate your answer.
7. Develop trees of function calls to **qsRecursive** for a variety of test data sets (analogous to what was done in Figure 6.11). Use these trees to analyze the efficiency of the quick sort algorithm. What types of data sets yield $O(n \log_2 n)$ efficiency? What types yield $O(n^2)$ efficiency? Can you reach a conclusion about how "far" from the best case a data set may wander before it becomes closer to $O(n^2)$ than $O(n \log_2 n)$? You will explore this last question experimentally in the problems/projects at the end of the chapter.
8. Suppose that the index for the pivot value is chosen at random between **lo** and **hi,** inclusive. How does this affect the efficiency of the quick sort algorithm? Do best case and worst case data sets exist for this strategy? Explain.
9. A sorting method is called *stable* if two data items of the same value are guaranteed not to be rearranged with respect to each other as the algorithm progresses. For example, in the four-element array

$60 \quad 42_1 \quad 80 \quad 42_2$

a stable sorting method would guarantee a final order of

$42_1 \quad 42_2 \quad 60 \quad 80$

Classify each of the insertion, selection, radix, Shell, and quick sort algorithms as to their stability. If you claim that a particular algorithm is not stable, be sure to provide an example data set to justify your claim. (To see why stability may be important, see Programming Problems 4 and 5 at the end of the chapter.)

10. Using trees of recursive calls, analyze the best and worst case space efficiency of the quick sort algorithm presented in this section.

6.3 Merge Sort

Another recursive sorting algorithm is *merge* sort. Unlike quick sort, merge sort can guarantee $O(n \log_2 n)$ efficiency. However, in its average run time, it is usually somewhat slower than quick sort. Moreover, as we shall see, it is considerably less space-efficient than quick sort.

The essential idea behind *merge sort* is to make repeated use of an algorithm that merges two sequences, each already in ascending order, into a third sequence, also arranged in ascending order. The merge algorithm itself only requires access to the values in the order in which they appear in the sequence. Its logic is similar to the method you would use if you were merging two sorted piles of index cards into a third pile. That is, start with the first card from each pile. Compare them to see which one comes first, transfer that one over to the third pile, and advance to the next card in that pile. Repeat the comparison, transfer, and advance operations until one of the piles runs out of cards. At that point, merely move what is left of the remaining pile over to the third merged pile.

To implement a merge sort within the context of our general **SortArray** class, we will incorporate the merge algorithm just described in a protected member function **merge**. The interface for **merge** is:

```
protected:    // Within the SortArray class

//-------------------------------------------------------------------------
// Interface for the merge function
// GIVEN:      lo, mid, hi -- indices within the array source,
//                           where lo <= mid <= hi;
//             source -- a SortArray arranged such that data items between indices
//                       lo and mid are in ascending order and data between indices
//                       indices mid+1 and hi are also in ascending order.
// RETURN:     dest -- a SortArray with data from source merged into ascending
//                     order starting with index lo.
// RETURN as value of function: void

    void merge(IndexType lo, IndexType mid, IndexType hi,
               SortArray<IndexType,BaseData> &source,
               SortArray<IndexType,BaseData> &dest);
```

For reasons that will become apparent when we use **merge** in a full sorting function, this version of the function begins with the two sorted lists stored in one array. The first list runs from subscript **lo** to **mid** of array **source.** The second runs from subscript **mid** + 1 to **hi** of the same array. The merging of the two lists is generated in a second array **dest**. The implementation of the **merge** function follows:

```
template <class IndexType, class BaseData>
void SortArray<IndexType, BaseData>::merge(IndexType lo, IndexType mid,
      IndexType hi, SortArray<IndexType,BaseData> &source,
      SortArray<IndexType,BaseData> &dest)
{
  IndexType s1 = lo;          // Pointer into lower half of source
  IndexType s2 = mid + 1;     // Pointer into upper half of source
  IndexType d = lo;           // Pointer into dest array

  while ((s1 <= mid) && (s2 <= hi))   // Compare current item from each list
    if (precedes(source[s1],source[s2]))  // Then s1 item comes first
      dest[d++] = source[s1++];
    else                                  // s2 item comes first
      dest[d++] = source[s2++];
  // Move what is left of remaining list
  if (s1 > mid)
    while (s2 <= hi)
      dest[d++] = source[s2++];
  else
    while (s1 <= mid)
      dest[d++] = source[s1++];
}
```

Clearly, **merge** is an $O(n)$ algorithm where n is the number of items in the two sequences to be merged. A question remains: How can **merge** be used to actually sort an entire array? To answer this we need another function called **msRecursive** that will take the values in indices **lo** through **hi** of an array **source** and arrange them in ascending order in subscripts **lo** through **hi** of another array called **dest.** Notice that **msRecursive** is itself almost a sorting algorithm except that it produces a sorted sequence in a second array instead of actually transforming the array it originally receives. Our recursive use of **msRecursive** will be to obtain two sorted half-length sequences from our original array.

Then we will use the **merge** function we have already developed to merge the two sorted half-length sequences back into the original array. Of course, this merely defers our original question of how to use **merge** to sort, because now we are faced with the question of how the **msRecursive** function will be able to produce two sorted half-length sequences. This is where recursion enters the picture. To produce a sorted half-length sequence, we use **msRecursive** to produce two sorted quarter-length sequences and apply **merge** to the results. Similarly, the quarter-length sequences are produced by calling on **msRecursive** to produce sorted eighth-length sequences and apply **merge** to the results. The terminating condition for this descent into shorter and shorter ordered sequences is reached when **msRecursive** receives a sequence of length 1.

```
protected:              // Within the SortArray class

//------------------------------------------------------------------------------
// Interface for the protected msRecursive function
// GIVEN:     lo, hi -- indices within the Array source, where lo <= hi;
//            source -- a SortArray of items of type BaseData.
// RETURN:    dest -- a SortArray containing items from source arranged in
//                    ascending order.
// RETURN as value of function: void

    void msRecursive(IndexType lo, IndexType hi,
                     SortArray<IndexType,BaseData> &source,
                     SortArray<IndexType,BaseData> &dest);

// Implementation of msRecursive for SortArray class

template <class IndexType, class BaseData>
void SortArray<IndexType, BaseData>::msRecursive(IndexType lo, IndexType hi,
        SortArray<IndexType,BaseData> &source, SortArray<IndexType,BaseData> &dest)
{
  if (lo != hi)    // Then length of source is more than one
  {
    IndexType mid = (lo + hi)/2;
    msRecursive(lo, mid, dest, source);
    msRecursive(mid + 1, hi, dest, source);
    merge(lo, mid, hi, source, dest);
  }
}
```

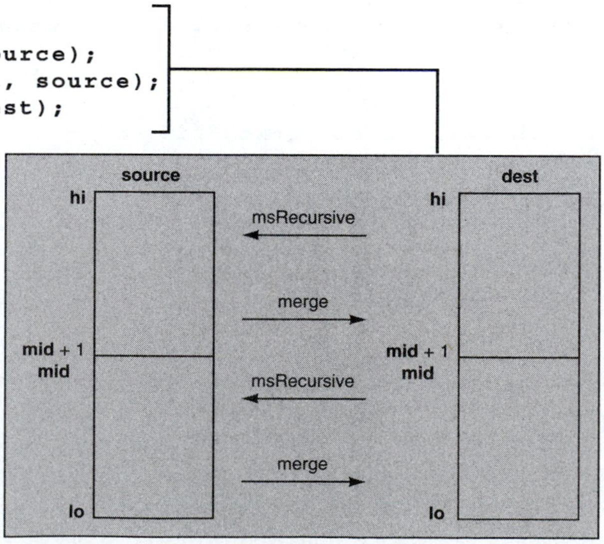

FIGURE 6.13
Tree of function calls to **msRecursive** and **merge**.

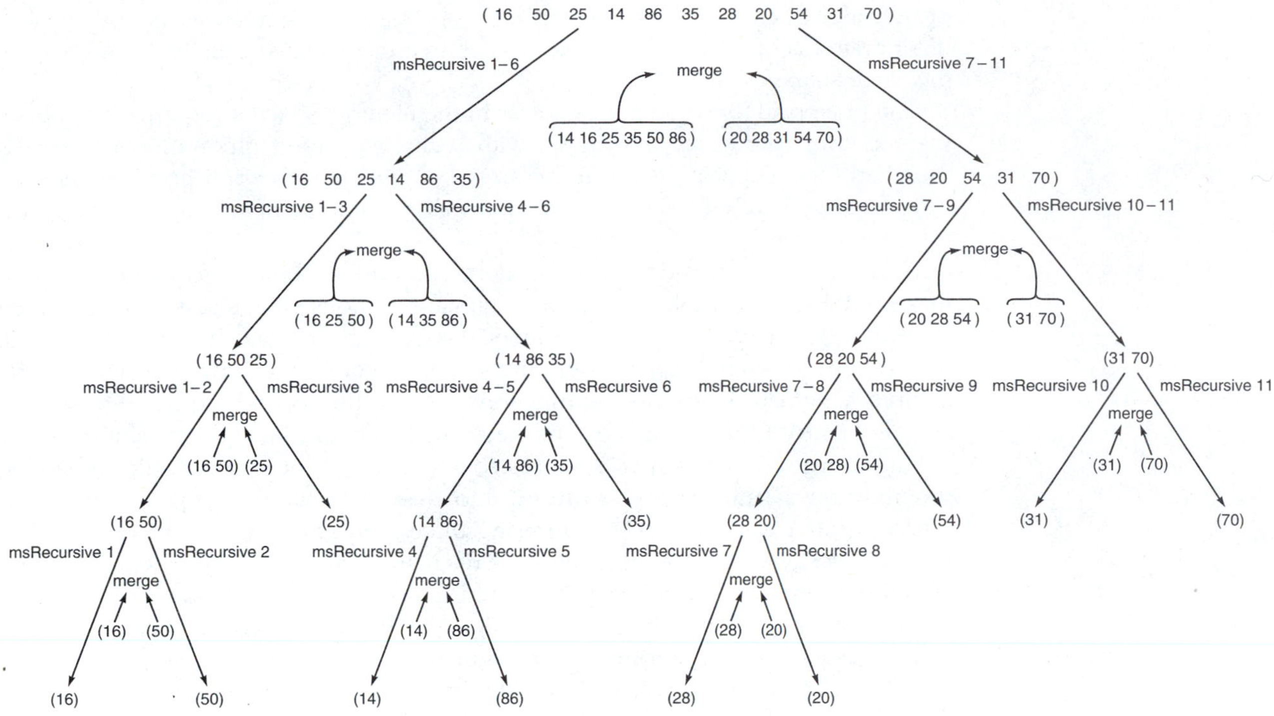

Given the crucial **msRecursive** function, the **sort** function itself is almost trivial. It need merely create a copy of the array to be sorted and then call on **msRecursive** to sort the elements of the copy into the original. Note that because **msRecursive** continually calls on **merge** and **merge** cannot do its work within one array, the need to create a copy of the original array is unavoidable.

```
// Implementation of sort method from SortArray class

template <class IndexType, class BaseData>
void SortArray<IndexType, BaseData>::sort(int numvals)
{
  // Use copy constructor for SortArray to obtain a copy of current object
  SortArray<IndexType,BaseData> copy(*this);

  // Call recursive workhorse
  msRecursive(loIndex, loIndex+numvals-1, copy, *this);
}
```

The tree of function calls in Figure 6.13 highlights the interaction between **msRecursive** and **merge** triggered by calling **sort** with a simple array of size **numvals** = 11. The leaf nodes in this tree represent the recursive termination condition reached when **lo** = **hi.**

Efficiency Analysis of Merge Sort

From a tree of function calls such as that appearing in Figure 6.13, it is quite easy to deduce that merge sort requires $O(n \log_2 n)$ comparisons. The reasoning required for this deduction is as follows. All the **merge** operations across any given level of the tree will require $O(n)$ comparisons. There are $O(\log_2 n)$ levels to the tree of function calls. Hence, the overall efficiency is the product $O(n \log_2 n)$. Notice that, unlike the quick sort, the merge sort can guarantee this efficiency regardless of the original data. That is, there is no worst case that can cause its efficiency to deteriorate (as there is for quick sort). The tree of recursive calls will always have the same shape.

The price paid for using merge sort is in the memory space it requires. Of course, there is the stack space associated with recursion. More important, however, is the need for a duplicate copy of the array being sorted. In applications where the original array barely fits in memory, this space requirement will make merge sort totally impractical.

As steep as the memory price is, there is an added benefit to merge sort that makes it the only possible choice for certain applications: Merge sort may be written in a way that necessitates only sequential access to the data being manipulated. As we have presented it here, random access is required at only one point in the algorithm, namely, in the **merge** function to access the second sequence beginning at index (**mid** + 1) of **source.** The need for this could have been eliminated by having **merge** work with two separate source arrays. That is, we would merge the ordered arrays **source1** and **source2** into **dest.** This would be very costly with arrays because it would necessitate using three arrays to sort one array. However, it is less costly when the sequences being manipulated are implemented not by arrays but rather by dynamically allocated linked lists or sequential files. In both of these latter situations, the need to use sequential access would make the merge sort strategy the only appropriate sorting method. In the programming problems at the end of the chapter, you will be asked to adapt the merge sort algorithm to a linked list. For situations in which the data values exist in a file instead of main memory, the sorting method employed is said to be an *external sort* (as opposed to the *internal sorts* we have studied in this chapter). We will return to strategies for external sorting in Chapter 12.

Exercises 6.3

1. Consider the **msRecursive** function given in this section. Suppose that we were to insert the following tracer output at the beginning of this function:

```
cout << lo << hi << endl;
for (k = lo; k <= hi; ++k)
  cout << source[k];
```

What would we see as output from these tracers if we were to call on **msRecursive** with an array that initially contained the following?

60 12 90 30 64 8 6

Provide the tree of recursive calls for this data set.

2. Repeat Exercise 6.3.1 for a six-element array that initially contains

1 8 2 7 3 6

3. Identify and give an example of best case and worst case data sets for the merge sort algorithm.
4. Exercise 6.2.9 defined the notion of a stable sorting method. Is merge sort a stable sorting method? Justify your answer.
5. You are to sort an array in a program in which the following considerations are to be taken into account. First, there is a large amount of data to be sorted. The amount of data to be sorted is so large that frequent $O(n^2)$ run times will prove unsatisfactory. The amount of data will also make it impossible to use a large amount of overhead data (for example, stack space) to make the sort efficient in its run time because the overhead data would potentially take up space needed by the array. Second, you are told that the array to be sorted is often nearly in order to start with. For each of the six sorting methods listed, specify whether or not that method would be appropriate for this application and, in a brief statement, explain why your answer is correct.

   a. Insertion sort

   b. Selection sort

   c. Shell sort

   d. Quick sort

   e. Radix sort

   f. Merge sort

6.4 Recursive Descent Parsing

In Section 5.3 we studied the parsing of infix algebraic expressions by the use of a stack and appropriate infix and stack priority functions. However, that parsing algorithm emphasized the conversion of the infix expression into a postfix expression. A problem equally important in parsing is the detection of syntax errors in the expression to be processed. One method of parsing with error detection, called *recursive descent parsing,* relies heavily on recursion. The inspiration for such use of recursion comes from the linguistic concept of a *context-free grammar,* which provides a rigorous formalism for defining the syntax of expressions and other programming-language constructs, a formalism similar to that found in the syntax diagram of Figure 6.1. The scope of context-free grammars goes far beyond what we will cover in one section of this text. If your interest is aroused by the following discussion, we encourage you to consult *Crafting a Compiler with C* by Charles N. Fischer and Richard J. LeBlanc, Benjamin Cummings, Menlo Park, CA, 1991.

A context-free grammar is composed of the following three elements.

1. A set of *terminals.* These terminals represent the *tokens*—characters, or groups of characters that logically belong together, such as operator symbols, delimiters, keywords, variable names—that ultimately compose the expression being parsed. In the case of infix algebraic expressions, the terminals would be variables, numeric constants, parentheses, and the various operators that are allowed.
2. A set of *nonterminals.* These nonterminals represent the various grammatical constructs within the language we are parsing. In particular, one nonterminal is designated as the *start symbol* for the grammar.
3. A set of *productions.* The productions are formal rules defining the syntactical composition of the nonterminals from point 2. The productions take the form:

   Nonterminal → String of terminals and/or nonterminals

   We say that the nonterminal on the left of such a production *derives* the string on the right.

An example of a context-free grammar should help to clarify this three-part definition.

Example 6.7

Provide a context-free grammar for infix algebraic expressions involving addition and multiplication and show how the particular expression A + B * C is derived from it.

1. Set of terminals:

   { '+', '*', '(', ')', identifier, number }

2. Set of nonterminals:

   { <expression>, <factor>, <add-factor>, <mult-factor>, <primary> }

   where <expression> is designated as the start symbol. Note that, by convention, nonterminals are enclosed in angle brackets to distinguish them from terminals.

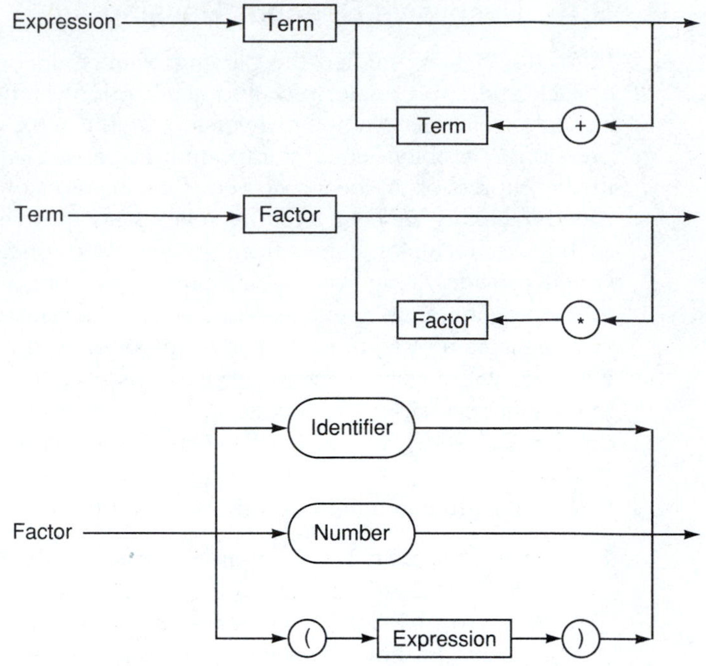

FIGURE 6.14
Expressions defined by the grammar of Example 6.7 depicted with syntax diagrams and based on a different set of productions.

3. Set of productions:

a. <expression> → <factor><add-factor>
b. <factor> → <primary><mult-factor>
c. <add-factor> → '+' <factor><add-factor>
d. <add-factor> → NULL
e. <mult-factor> → '*' <primary><mult-factor>
f. <mult-factor> → NULL
g. <primary> → identifier
h. <primary> → number
i. <primary> → '(' <expression> ')'

The symbol NULL is used here to indicate the empty string. In effect, this implies that one defining option for <add-factor> and <mult-factor> is the empty string. We shall see why this is necessary in the derivation of A + B * C, which follows. As shown in Figure 6.14, these infix algebraic expressions could also have been presented using syntax diagrams and could have been based on a different set of productions.

To derive a particular infix expression, we begin with the start symbol <expression>. The production that defines <expression> says that <expression> must be <factor> followed by <add-factor>. Hence, we must now try to derive these two nonterminals. This process of involving nonterminals in the definition of other nonterminals continues until we finally reach those nonterminals that are defined by the terminals in the infix expression being parsed. Thus, a formal derivation of A + B * C is given by

<expression>	→ <factor><add-factor>	By production a
	→ <primary><mult-factor><add-factor>	By production b
	→ A <mult-factor><add-factor>	By production g
	→ A <add-factor>	By production f
	→ A + <factor><add-factor>	By production c

→ A + <primary><mult-factor><add-factor>	By production b
→ A + B <mult-factor><add-factor>	By production g
→ A + B * <primary><mult-factor><add-factor>	By production e
→ A + B * C <mult-factor><add-factor>	By production g
→ A + B * C	By productions d and f

Note that there is a hint of recursion in the grammar of Example 6.7 in that some of the productions defining <add-factor> and <mult-factor> use these same nonterminals in their definitional pattern on the right of the production being defined. As the next example shows, it is this recursive portion of the definition that allows us to add arbitrarily many identifiers in one expression. That is, by the recursive appearance of <add-factor> and <mult-factor> in productions 3 and 5, respectively, we are able to keep introducing '+' and '*' into the expression being parsed.

Example 6.8

Provide a derivation of the infix expression A + B + C.

<expression> → <factor><add-factor>
→ <primary><mult-factor><add-factor>
→ A <mult-factor><add-factor>
→ A <add-factor>
→ A + <factor><add-factor>
→ A + <primary><mult-factor><add-factor>
→ A + B <mult-factor><add-factor>
→ A + B <add-factor>
→ A + B + <factor><add-factor>
→ A + B + <primary><mult-factor><add-factor>
→ A + B + C <mult-factor><add-factor>
→ A + B + C <add-factor>
→ A + B + C

You are encouraged to justify each step in the derivation by determining the production applied.

Just as we were able to illustrate recursive processing with a tree of recursive calls, the formal derivation of an expression via the productions of a grammar can be represented by a diagram called a *parse tree*. (Parse trees for the derivation in Examples 6.7 and 6.8 are given in Figures 6.15 and 6.16, respectively.) Note that implicit in these parse trees is the order of operations in the algebraic expressions. That is, these parse trees are constructed, top-down, starting at each nonterminal within the tree and, from that nonterminal, descending to those nodes containing the terminals and nonterminals from the right side of the production applied in the derivation of the original nonterminal. Eventually, as we descend deeper into the tree, only terminals are left, and no nodes descend deeper from these terminals. In Figure 6.15, since the <factor> node on Level 2 of the tree encompasses all of B * C below it, we have an indication that B * C must be first evaluated as a <factor> and then added to A. On the other hand, in the parse tree of Figure 6.16, the <factor> node at Level 2 encompasses only the B term. Hence, B is to be added to A, with C (below the <factor> node at Level 3) then added to that result. In the exercises

FIGURE 6.15
Parse tree for A + B * C reflects that B * C is evaluated first.

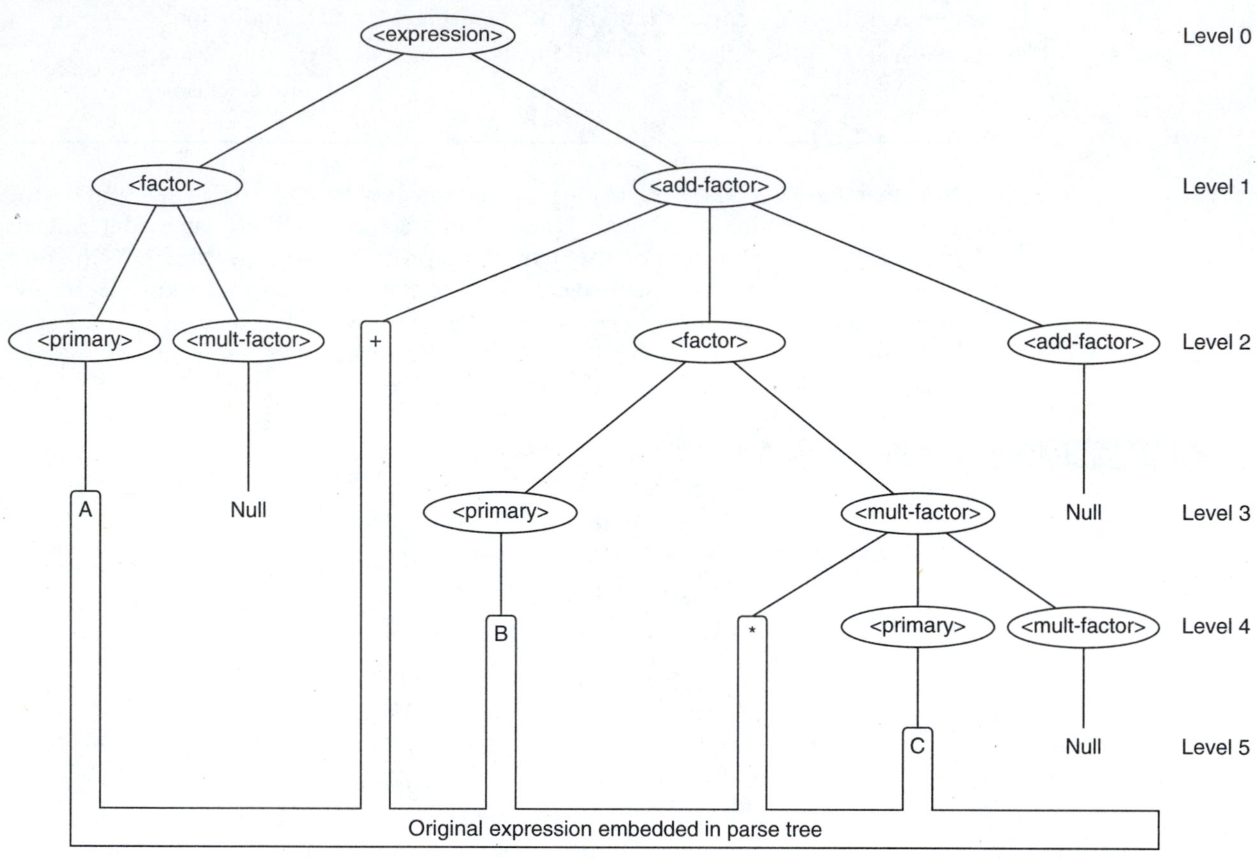

and problems, you will continue to explore the relationships between context-free grammars, derivations, parse trees, and orders of evaluation in infix expressions.

We now turn our attention to the problem of transforming the formal grammar that specifies the syntax of a language into a program that determines whether or not the tokens stored in an incoming queue constitute a valid string. The process is surprisingly easy. It begins with a front-end function called from an external module. This front-end function will eventually return an error flag indicating the success or failure of the parse. To do so, it performs necessary initializations and then calls on the first in a suite of "verifying" functions. We write a separate verifying function for each nonterminal in the grammar. The responsibility of each function is simply to verify the particular grammatical construction after which it is named. The subordinate functions called on by a given function are dictated by the right sides of productions defining that function's associated nonterminal in the context-free grammar. Since typically many of these productions will have the terminal being defined on the left reappearing on the right, many of the associated functions will be recursive in nature. Consequently, the general algorithmic technique is termed *recursive descent parsing*. The tree of recursive calls will parallel the parse tree for the expression.

We illustrate the method by developing a suite of functions to parse infix arithmetic expressions, as defined by the grammar of Example 6.7. These functions are presented in the context of the **Token** and **InfixExpression** classes developed

FIGURE 6.16
Parse tree for A + B + C reflects that B is added to A before addition of C.

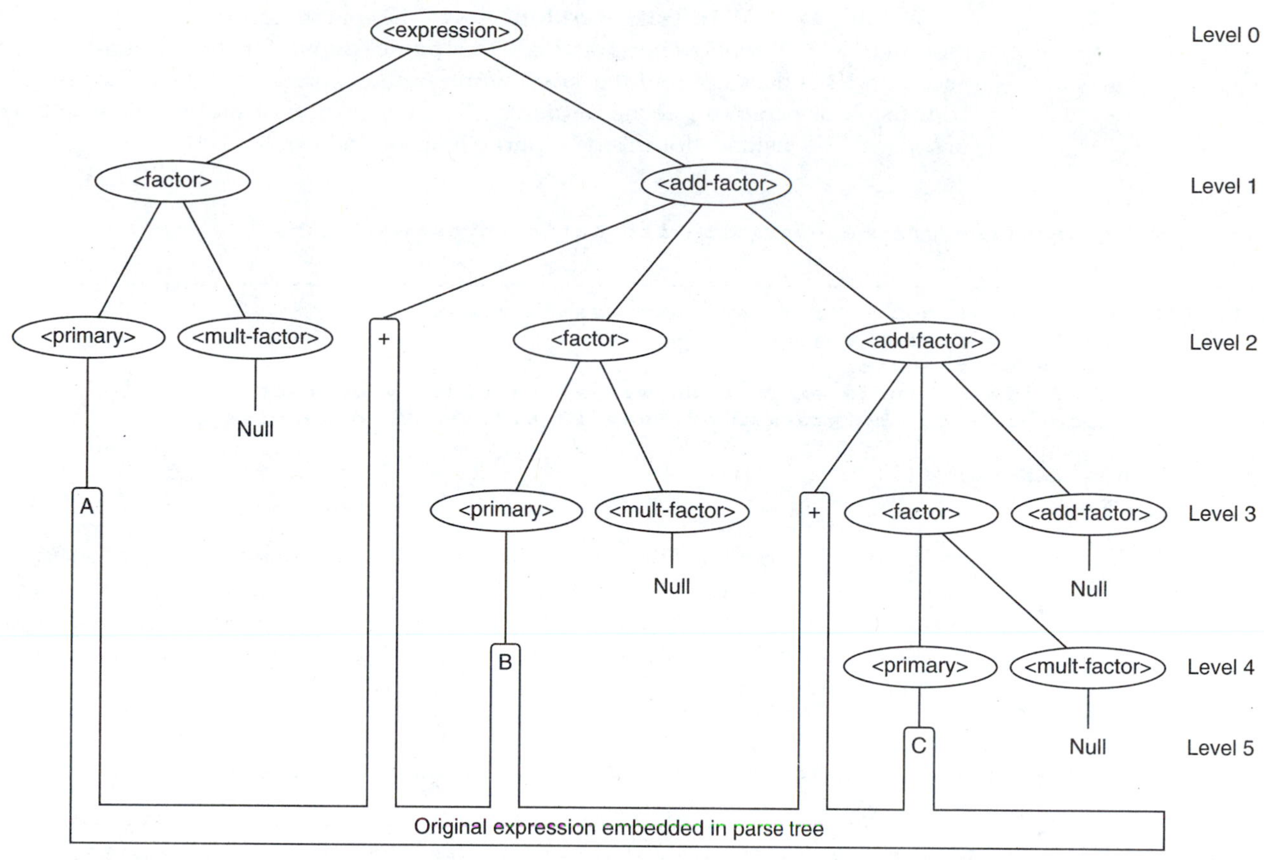

in Section 5.3. In particular, we need to add to the **Token** class of section 5.3 two public methods, **addOperator** and **multOperator**, which will allow us to determine whether a particular token is an addition or multiplication operator, respectively. The interfaces for these functions are as follows:

```
public:       // Additional operations for Token class of Section 5.3

// ---------------------------------------------------------------------------
// Interface for Token class addOperator function
// GIVEN: A previously allocated Token object.
// RETURN as value of function:
//          TRUE if the Token represents a valid addition
//          operator for an infix expression; FALSE otherwise.

    BOOLEAN addOperator();

// ---------------------------------------------------------------------------
// Interface for Token class multOperator function
// GIVEN: A previously allocated Token object.
// RETURN as value of function:
//          TRUE if the Token represents a valid multiplication
//          operator for an infix expression; FALSE otherwise.

    BOOLEAN multOperator();
```

Working from the **InfixExpression** class of Section 5.3, we alter slightly the interface to the parsing operation. Instead of the **parseToPost** function that returned a postfix representation of the infix expression, we simply provide a **parse** function for members of the **InfixExpression** class. The **parse** function does a more thorough job of syntax-checking than the **parseToPost** function described in Section 5.3 but does not return a postfix form of the expression. You will consider conversion of **parse** to a recursive descent implementation of **parseToPost** in the problems. The interface for this new **parse** function follows:

```
public:     // Redefined parse operation for InfixExpression class

// -----------------------------------------------------------------------
// Interface to parse function for InfixExpression class
// GIVEN: An InfixExpression object.
// RETURN as value of function:
//            TRUE if the infix expression was syntactically correct
//            according to the grammar of Example 6.7; FALSE otherwise.

   virtual BOOLEAN parse();
```

The public **parse** function is really just a front-end function that initiates a series of recursive calls to deeper level, protected functions that are also added to the **infixExpression** class. These functions correspond to the "verifying" functions described earlier. There is one such function for each of the nonterminals in our grammar. The interfaces to these verifying functions follow.

```
protected:    // Added as function members of the InfixExpression class

// -----------------------------------------------------------------------
// Interface to parseExpression function for infixExpression class
// GIVEN:     An infixExpression object;
//            currentToken --- the current token from the infix expression.
// RETURN:    An indication as to whether the current token initiates a sequence
//            of tokens that satisfies the definition of an expression,
//            according to the grammar of Example 6.7, and possibly a new current
//            token from the InfixExpression.
// RETURN as value of function:
//            TRUE if an expression was successfully parsed, beginning
//            with the current token; FALSE otherwise.

   BOOLEAN parseExpression(TokenType &currentToken);

// -----------------------------------------------------------------------
// Interface to parseFactor function for InfixExpression class
// GIVEN:     An InfixExpression object;
//            currentToken --- the current token from the infix expression.
// RETURN:    An indication as to whether the current token initiates a sequence
//            of tokens that satisfies the definition of a factor, according to
//            the grammar of Example 6.7, and possibly a new current token
//            from the InfixExpression.
// RETURN as value of function:
//            TRUE if a factor was successfully parsed, beginning with the
//            current token; FALSE otherwise.

   BOOLEAN parseFactor(TokenType &currentToken);
```

```
// -----------------------------------------------------------------------
// Interface to parseAddFactor function for InfixExpression class
// GIVEN:     An InfixExpression object;
//            currentToken ---  the current token from the infix expression.
// RETURN:    An indication as to whether the current token initiates a sequence
//            of tokens that satisfies the definition of an add-factor, according
//            to the grammar of Example 6.7, and possible a new current token
//            from the InfixExpression.
// RETURN as value of function:
//            TRUE if an add-factor was successfully parsed, beginning with the
//            current token; FALSE otherwise.

   BOOLEAN parseAddFactor(TokenType &currentToken);

// -----------------------------------------------------------------------
// Interface to the parseMultFactor function for InfixExpression class
// GIVEN:     An InfixExpression object;
//            currentToken --- the current token from the infix expression.
// RETURN:    An indication as to whether the current token initiates a sequence
//            of tokens that satisfies the definition of a mult-factor, according
//            to the grammar of Example 6.7, and possibly a new current token
//            from the InfixExpression.
// RETURN as value of function:
//            TRUE if a mult-factor was successfully parsed, beginning
//            with the current token; FALSE otherwise.

   BOOLEAN parseMultFactor(TokenType &currentToken);

// -----------------------------------------------------------------------
// Interface to parsePrimary function for InfixExpression class
// GIVEN:     An InfixExpression object;
//            currentToken --- the current token from the infix expression.
// RETURN:    An indication as to whether the current token initiates a sequence
//            of tokens that satisfies the definition of a primary, according
//            to the grammar of Example 6.7, and possibly a new current token
//            from the InfixExpression.
// RETURN as value of function:
//            TRUE if a primary was successfully parsed, beginning with the
//            current token; FALSE otherwise.

   BOOLEAN parsePrimary(TokenType &currentToken);
```

The function **parse** represents the call that a client program would make to have an **InfixExpression** object parsed. For instance, to read an expression whose tokens represent values of type **float,** we would have:

```
InfixExpression<Token<float>, float> exp;

exp.get();
if (exp.parse())
  cout << "expression OK" << endl;
else
  cout << "Invalid Expression" << endl;
```

The interface to **parse** remains the same regardless of the underlying grammar. The structure of the underlying, protected functions that verify each nonterminal is dependent on the grammar. Presented below are implementations of all of the functions for the grammar of Example 6.7.

```
template <class TokenType, class ValueType>
BOOLEAN InfixExpression<TokenType, ValueType>:: parse()
{
  TokenType currentToken;

  if (expression.empty())
    return(FALSE);
  else
  {
    currentToken = expression.front();
    expression.dequeue();
    if (parseExpression(currentToken))
      return(expression.empty());
    else
      return(FALSE);
  }
}

template <class TokenType, class ValueType>
BOOLEAN InfixExpression<TokenType, ValueType>::
        parseExpression(TokenType &currentToken)
{
  if (parseFactor(currentToken))
    return(parseAddFactor(currentToken));
  else
    return(FALSE);
}
```

<expression> → <factor><add-factor>

```
template <class TokenType, class ValueType>
BOOLEAN InfixExpression<TokenType, ValueType>::
        parseFactor(TokenType &currentToken)
{
  if (parsePrimary(currentToken))
    return(parseMultFactor(currentToken)):
  else
    return(FALSE);
}
```

<factor> → <primary><mult-factor>

```
template <class TokenType, class ValueType>
BOOLEAN InfixExpression<TokenType, ValueType>::
        parseAddFactor(TokenType &currentToken)
{
  if (!currenToken.addOperator())    // NULL production is satisfied
    return(TRUE);
  else
    if (expression.empty())          // Something should follow add operator
      return(FALSE);
    else
    {
      currentToken = expression.front();
      expression.dequeue();
      if (parseFactor(currentToken))
        return(parseAddFactor(currentToken));
      else
        return(FALSE);
    }
}
```

<add-factor> → '+' <factor><add-factor>

```
template <class TokenType, class ValueType>
BOOLEAN InfixExpression<TokenType, ValueType>::
        parseMultFactor(TokenType &currentToken)
{
```

```
   if (!currentToken.multOperator())    // NULL production is satisfied
     return(TRUE);
   else
     if (expression.empty())          // Something should follow mult operator
       return(FALSE);
     else
     {
       currentToken = expression.front();
       expression.dequeue();
       if (parseFactor(currentToken))
         return(parseMultFactor(currentToken));
       else
         return(FALSE);
     }
}
```

<mult-factor> → '*' <factor><mult-factor>

```
template <class TokenType, class ValueType>
BOOLEAN InfixExpression<TokenType, ValueType>::
        parsePrimary(TokenType &currentToken)
{
   if (currentToken.validOperand())
   {
     if (!expression.empty())
     {
       currentToken = expression.front();
       expression.dequeue();
     }
     return(TRUE);
   }
   else
     if (!currentToken.leftParen())
       return(FALSE);
     else                        // Must have parenthesized expression
       if (expression.empty())
         return(FALSE);
       else
       {
         currentToken = expression.front());
         expression.dequeue();
         if (parseExpression(currentToken))
           if (currentToken.rightParen())
           {
             if (!expression.empty())
             {
               currentToken = expression.front();
               expression.dequeue();
             }
             return(TRUE);
           }
           else
             return(FALSE);
         else
           return(FALSE);
       }
}
```

<primary> → identifier
<primary> → number

<primary> → '(' expression ')'

The large amount of code in this suite of functions belies the ease with which each function can be written, provided that we start with a sound grammatical description of the expressions being parsed. As indicated by the graphic documentation, each verifying function merely calls on subordinate verifying functions in the order dictated by the right side of a production in the context-free grammar. For nonterminals that have more than one defining production, the **currentToken** parameter is examined to determine which production to follow.

As easy as the process seems, there are some negatives to the recursive descent parsing method. First, it applies only for context-free grammars that have their productions in a suitable form. The productions from Example 6.7 are in that form, but in the exercises you will explore context-free grammars that are not appropriate for the recursive descent method. Thus, to use recursive descent parsing, you must learn to write "correct" grammars. A second negative is the rigidity of a recursive descent parser once it has been implemented. Should you have a change of heart about the syntactical rules of the language being parsed, the resulting changes in productions may lead to widespread and dramatic changes in the code for the parser itself because the code is directly tied to the productions. Hence, maintainability of the code in a recursive descent parser can be a problem. This places a real premium on getting the grammar right the first time, before you begin generating code from it. Compare this to the ease with which one can alter a parse by changing the priority functions in the parsing method discussed in Section 5.3.

A RELEVANT ISSUE Recursion, Lisp, and the Practicality of Artificial Intelligence

Artificial intelligence, the science of implementing on computers the problem-solving methods used by human beings, is one of the most rapidly expanding fields within computer science. Research in this field includes enabling computers to play games of strategy, to understand natural languages, to prove theorems in logic and mathematics, and to mimic the reasoning of human experts in fields such as medical diagnosis. Only recently has artificial intelligence become a commercially viable area of application, capable of solving some real-life problems apart from the idealized setting of a pure research environment. More and more, we are seeing artificial intelligence systems that perform such practical functions as aiding business executives in their decision-making processes and providing a near-English user-interface language for data base management software.

What has sparked the emergence of artificial intelligence? Why was it not possible to produce commercially feasible programs in this field until recently? One of the primary answers to these questions is tied to the language in which most artificial intelligence programming is done. This language is called Lisp (for LISt Processor). Interestingly, the control structures of Lisp are based almost entirely on recursion. What a Pascal, C++, or Modula-2 programmer would view as normal iterative control structures (for example, **while**, **repeat**, and **for** loops) appear in various versions of Lisp only as infrequently used extensions to the language.

One of the reasons that a recursively based language such as Lisp is so ideally suited to this field is that most problem-solving methods in artificial intelligence involve developing rules for solving a complex problem. These rules formally describe the reasoning process used by humans when they solve such a problem. Frequently these rules are formulated in what is called a *production system*—a formalism analogous to the productions that are part of a context-free grammar. Just as a recursive descent parser tracks through productions as it tries to successfully parse an expression, so an artificial intelligence program in Lisp will (recursively) track through the rules in its production system as it attempts to find a solution to a problem.

The complexity of problems studied in artificial intelligence leads to recursive call trees of enormous size. Historically, Lisp has been available as a recursive language ideally suited to such tree searches. It is one of the oldest high-level programming languages, having been first developed by John McCarthy in the late 1950s. Researchers who work in artificial intelligence have long realized that Lisp's ability to process general data structures recursively was, on a theoretical basis, exactly what they needed. The problem through the years has been that, because of the very high overhead associated with recursion (and some other features built into Lisp), computer hardware has not been fast enough to run Lisp programs in practical applications. Thus, researchers were restricted not by Lisp itself but rather by the ability of computer hardware to execute Lisp programs in reasonable times. One of the major reasons for the recent expansion in the study of artificial intelligence has been the increase in speed of computer hardware and the decrease in cost of this same hardware. This has made it possible for users to have dedicated computer resources capable of meeting the demands of Lisp's recursive style. As hardware continues to improve, so will applications in Lisp, and artificial intelligence will become increasingly sophisticated.

Exercises 6.4

1. Using the context-free grammar of Example 6.7, provide formal derivations and parse trees for the following expressions:
   a. A * B * C * D + E
   b. A + B * C * (D + E)
   c. ((A + B) * C) * (D + E)
2. Extend the grammar of Example 6.7 to the following:
   a. Allow minus (−) and division (/) as algebraic operators.
   b. Allow exponentiation (^) as an algebraic operator. Be sure that your grammar yields parse trees that imply that the order of consecutive exponentiations is right-to-left instead of left-to-right (as it is with other operators).
   c. Allow **or** (|), **and** (&), and **not** (~) as logical operators so that Boolean as well as algebraic expressions are allowed by the grammar.
3. Consider the following alternative, context-free grammar for the expressions defined by the grammar of Example 6.7:

   <expression> → <mult-factor>
   <expression> → <mult-factor> '+' <expression>
   <mult-factor> → <primary>
   <mult-factor> → <primary> '*' <mult-factor>
   <primary> → identifier
   <primary> → number
   <primary> → '(' <expression> ')'

   a. Does this grammar allow the same set of expressions as that in Example 6.7?
   b. Provide parse trees for any of the expressions in Exercise 6.4.1 that are accepted by the preceding grammar.
   c. What are differences in the parse trees produced by this grammar versus those produced by the grammar of Example 6.7?
   d. How would the differences you described in part **c** affect the order in which operators are applied?
   e. Which grammar—that of Example 6.7 or the one defined in this exercise—more accurately reflects the order of operations in standard programming languages?
4. (Left-Recursive Grammar) Consider the following alternative, context-free grammar for the expressions defined by the grammar of Example 6.7:

   <expression> → <mult-factor>
   <expression> → <expression> '+' <mult-factor>
   <mult-factor> → <primary>
   <mult-factor> → <mult-factor> '*' <primary>
   <primary> → identifier
   <primary> → number
   <primary> → '(' <expression> ')'

   This grammar is an example of a *left-recursive grammar*—one that admits a derivation of the form.

   $$<a> \rightarrow <a> X$$

   where <a> is a nonterminal and X is a string of terminals and/or nonterminals. For the grammar of this exercise, productions associated with the nonterminals <expression> and <mult-factor> fit this criterion, so the grammar is left-recursive.
   a. Does this grammar allow the same set of expressions as that of Example 6.7?
   b. Provide parse trees for any of the expressions in Exercise 6.4.1 that are accepted by the preceding grammar.
   c. What are differences in the parse trees produced by this grammar versus those produced by the grammars of Example 6.7 and Exercise 6.4.3?
   d. How do the differences you described in part **c** affect the order in which operators are applied?
   e. What is the difficulty arising when you attempt to implement a recursive descent parser that reflects directly the grammar given in this exercise?
5. Provide a context-free grammar for the **if** and **if-else** structures of a conventional programming language like C. Assume that nonterminals <condition> and <statement> are suitably defined elsewhere and, hence, can be used as primitives in your grammar. How many parse trees will your grammar allow for the following C statement?

```
if (a < b)
  if (c < d)
    a = d;
  else
    b = c;
```

   Which, if any, of your parse trees correspond to the fashion in which standard C interprets this statement?
6. The programming language Lisp works with *S-expressions*. They may be defined as follows:
   i. NIL is a special S-expression denoting the empty S-expression.
   ii. Any string composed of letters and/or digits with no other embedded characters is an S-expression.
   iii. If $L_1, L_2, \ldots, L_k$ are S-expressions for $k \geq 0$, then $(L_1\ L_2 \cdots L_k)$ is an S-expression.

   Construct a context-free grammar for S-expressions. Then draw parse trees for the following S-expressions.
   a. ((GLARP))
   b. (GLARP (GLARP) (((GLARP GLARP))) ( ))
   c. (((GLARP GLARP) NIL ( )) GLARP)

Chapter Summary

In this chapter we explored the basics of recursive algorithms, which are algorithms that define a solution to a problem in terms of a simpler version of the same problem. In Section 6.1 we introduced recursive algorithms by revisiting the divide-and-conquer search algorithm from Chapter 1 and by examining an implementation of the list traversal operations (introduced in Chapter 3). We also saw in this section that the implementation of recursive algorithms is based on intricate manipulations of a stack used in processing function calls. We began to develop the notions of recurrence relations and recursive call trees as a means of analyzing the efficiency of recursive algorithms. Having first argued that nothing much was gained by a recursive divide-and-conquer algorithm over an iterative version, we then examined the run-time costs versus programmer costs of using recursion and followed this with a discussion of the Towers of Hanoi problem. Towers of Hanoi provided an example of a problem with a nontrivial recursive solution that could not be implemented merely by using iterative control structures. It also provided us with our first example of an exponential algorithm.

In Sections 6.2 and 6.3 we showed that by considering divide-and-conquer solutions to the sorting problem, namely quick sort in 6.2 and merge sort in 6.3, we can improve on the $O(n^2)$ and $O(n(\log_2 n)^2)$ sorting efficiencies of the insertion, selection and Shell sorts, respectively.

Finally, in Section 6.4 we followed up on our discussion of parsing from Chapter 5 by examining the problem of detecting syntax errors in an expression being parsed. Following an introduction to context-free grammars, we examined the technique of recursive descent parsing for transforming a formal grammar that specifies the syntax of a language into a program that determines whether or not a given set of tokens, submitted to the parser as a queue, constitutes a valid string.

Keyterms

context-free grammar	parsing	recurrence relations	stack frame
merge sort	pivot	recursion	terminals
nonterminals	productions	recursive descent parsing	token
parse tree	quick sort		tree of recursive calls

Programming Problems/Projects

1. Write a program to call for input of a decimal number and convert it to its binary equivalent using the method described in the following flow-chart.

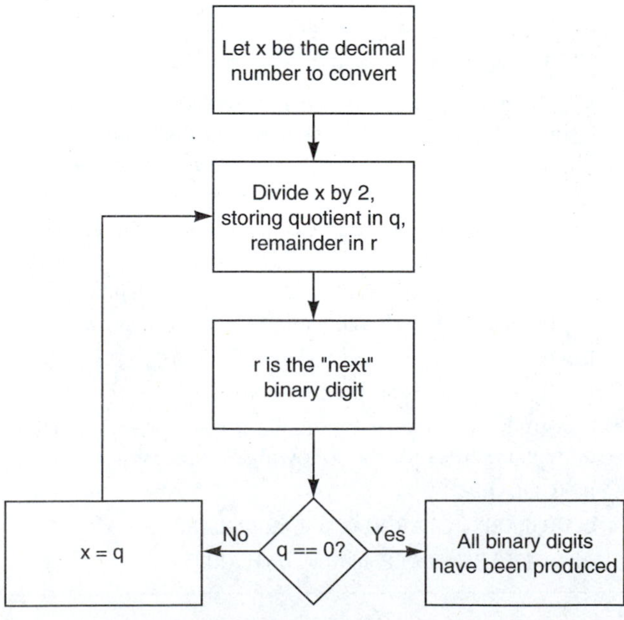

Note that this method produces the binary digits for the given number in reverse order. One strategy for printing out the digits in the correct order would be to store them in an array as they are produced and then print the array. However, this strategy would have the drawbacks of allocating unnecessary storage for an array and limiting the size of the binary number to the size of the array. Your program is not to employ this strategy. Instead call for input of the decimal number in your main program and then immediately transfer control to a function that in turn is called recursively, stacking the binary digits as they are produced. Once division by 2 yields 0, the succession of returns can be used to print the digits one by one as they are examined and popped from the system stack.

2. Suppose that you have N thousand dollars and can use it to buy a combination of Orange computers (which cost \$1000 each), HAL computers (which cost \$2000 each), or MAX computers (which cost \$4000 each). How many different combinations of Orange, HAL, and MAX computers could be bought with your N thousand dollars?

   Write a program that receives N as input and responds with the number of possible combinations. *Hint:* If N were 100, then the number of combinations is

The number of combinations totaling \$100,000
and involving Orange and HAL computers only
plus
The number of combinations totaling \$96,000
and involving potentially all three brands

Think about this hint for a while and extend it to a recursive function that answers this question.

3. Write a *recursive* version of a Fibonacci function that is *significantly* faster than that given in Exercise 6.1.6.
4. The Bay Area Brawlers professional football team has stored the records of all the players who have played on the team throughout its history. One player's record consists of

   Name
   Total points scored
   Number of touchdowns
   Number of field goals
   Number of safeties
   Number of extra points

   Write a program that lists players in order from the highest scorer in the team's history down to the lowest. Those players who have scored the same number of points should then be arranged in alphabetical order. Perform two sorts to achieve this—one sort by points scored and one sort by name. (Which one should be done first?) At least one of your sorts should be implemented as a quick sort or merge sort. Can they both be quick or merge sorts? (*Hint:* Think about your answers to Exercise 6.2.9 and Exercise 6.3.4.)
5. Consider a sequence of records, each containing four fields.

   Name
   Month of birth
   Day of birth
   Year of birth

   Write a program to sort this sequence in oldest-to-youngest order as fast as possible. People with the same birth date should be arranged alphabetically. One strategy you could employ would be to concatenate strategically the four fields into one—sorting just that one field. Another strategy would be to sort the values four times, each time by a different field. (Think carefully about which field to sort first.) Which of the strategies would require that you choose a stable sorting algorithm? (See Exercises 6.2.9 and 6.3.4.)
6. Modify the merge sort algorithm so that it will sort a linked list instead of an array.
7. Add statements to quick sort that count the number of comparisons made by the algorithm. Then run your program on a variety of randomly generated data sets, printing out N^2, $N \times \log_2 N$, and the number of comparisons made by your program for each data set. Observe the results of your program's runs and write a report in which you make conclusions about the average run-time efficiency of quick sort. Be sure to back up your conclusions by citing the empirical results of your program's runs.
8. Repeat Problem 7, making modifications in how the pivot is chosen. See the exercises in Section 6.2 for some suggestions. Also, try selecting the pivot as the median of three values—the first, last, and middle values in the segment of the array being partitioned.
9. Repeat Problem 8, but use insertion sort when the array segment becomes "sufficiently small" to avoid the overhead of recursion as the array becomes nearly sorted. Experiment with a suitable choice of an index range to find the optimal value for "sufficiently small." Be sure to include the results of your experimentation in your report.
10. Design a program that allows you to experiment with any or all of the sorting methods we have studied so far (selection, insertion, Shell, radix, quick, and merge). The program should allow you to do any or all of the following:
    a. Enter an array interactively.
    b. Load an array from a text file.
    c. Randomly generate an array.

    You should be able to enter the method(s) by which the array is to be sorted. If Shell sort is one of the methods chosen, allow entry of the sequence of diminishing increments. If quick sort is chosen, provide some options in terms of how the pivot should be chosen and whether a nonrecursive method should be invoked when the array segment becomes sufficiently small. Your program should then sort the array for each of the methods chosen and count the number of comparisons and data interchanges required for each method. Use the program to conduct an empirical comparative analysis among the various sorting methods. Present the results of this analysis in a statistical table and a write-up in which you state your conclusions regarding the relative efficiencies of the algorithms.
11. Extend the recursive descent parser from Section 6.4 by
    a. Providing descriptive error messages when a syntax error is encountered.
    b. Converting function **parse** to **parseToPost,** which returns a queue of tokens representing the postfix form of the expression.
    c. Allowing any or all of the additional operators suggested in Exercise 6.4.2.
12. Repeat Problem 11, but develop the recursive descent parser from the context-free grammar in Exercise 6.4.3.
13. Develop a recursive descent parser for the S-expression grammar you provided as an answer to Exercise 6.4.6
14. (Removal of Tail Recursion via Iteration) An algorithm is said to be *tail-recursive* if the only recursion takes place in the algorithm's last step. The recursive divide-and-conquer search and list traversal algorithms given in Section 6.1 are both tail-recursive. The recursion can easily be removed from tail-recursive algorithms and replaced by an iterative control structure that yields a more time- and space-efficient algorithm. The key to the removal of the tail recursion is the simple observation that since the recursive call takes place as the last step

in the algorithm, its effect is the same as looping back to the beginning of the algorithm and going through it again—this time, however, with new parameter values. In the iterative rewrite of the algorithm the looping back to the beginning of the algorithm can be controlled by a **while** statement, and local variables can assume the role of formal parameters. A model for such a rewrite can be found by comparing the **recSearch** function of Section 6.1 with its iterative-version search in Section 1.3.

a. Apply the techniques outlined here to rewrite the list traversal function of Section 6.1 so that it uses a nonrecursive algorithm.

b. Write a nonrecursive algorithm based on Euclid's method (see Exercise 6.1.8) to find the GCD of two positive integers.

15. (Recursion Removal via System Stack Simulation) Implement the following strategy to remove recursion from a recursive algorithm. Simulate the system stack by declaring your own stack structure. Each time a recursive call is made in the algorithm, push the necessary information (including some form of return address) onto your stack. When you complete processing at this deeper level, examine and pop the simulated stack frame and continue processing in the higher level at the point dictated by the return address obtained from the stack. In languages that have a **goto** statement, the label following the **goto** can be used to direct processing to continue at a return address. In languages without a **goto**, the return addresses can be specific labels in a **switch** control structure. This **switch** structure is then nested in an iterative control structure that loops until there are no return addresses left on the stack.

Use the strategy to write a nonrecursive version of quick sort or the function defined in Problem 2.

16. A variation of the merge sort is called the *natural merge sort*. This algorithm looks for natural "runs" of ordered data within the original array. For instance, the following array of 16 items shows eight natural runs (indicated by brackets):

```
 0  [503]
 1  ┌ 87┐
 2  └512┘
 3  ┌ 61┐
 4  └908┘
 5  ┌170┐
 6  └897┘
 7  ┌275┐
 8  └653┘
 9  [426]
10  ┌154┐
11  │509│
12  │612│
13  │677│
14  └765┘
15  [703]
```

These eight runs are arranged in a new array with the first run positioned at the top of the new array, the second run reversed and moved to the bottom of the array, the third run positioned after the original first run, the fourth run reversed and positioned above the original second run, and so forth. The pattern in this new array is indicated here:

```
 0  [503]  ←— Original 1st run
 1  ┌ 61┐  ←— Original 3rd run
 2  └908┘
 3  ┌275┐  ←— Original 5th run
 4  └653┘
 5  ┌154┐
 6  │509│
 7  │612│  ←— Original 7th run
 8  │677│
 9  └765┘
10  [703]  ←— Original 8th run reversed
11  [426]  ←— Original 6th run reversed
12  ┌897┐  ←— Original 4th run reversed
13  └170┘
14  ┌512┐  ←— Original 2nd run reversed
15  └ 87┘
```

The runs in this new array are now merged back into the original array, resulting in the pattern of data indicated as follows:

```
 0  ┌ 87┐
 1  │503│  ←— Merged data from original 1st and 2nd runs.
 2  └512┘
 3  ┌275┐
 4  │426│  ←— Merged data from original 5th and 6th runs.
 5  └653┘
 6  ┌765┐
 7  │703│
 8  │677│
 9  │612│  ←— Merged data from original 7th and 8th runs.
10  │509│
11  └154┘
12  ┌908┐
13  │897│
14  │170│  ←— Merged data from original 3rd and 4th runs.
15  └ 61┘
```

This merging pattern then cascades back and forth between the original and new array until only one run remains. Discover this merging pattern and implement the natural merge sort using the **SortArray** class. Describe circumstances under which the natural merge algorithm is likely to perform better and worse than the merge sort algorithm described in Section 6.3.

CHAPTER 7

Binary Trees

A fool sees not the same tree that a wise man sees.
William Blake

Chapter Outline:

In Chapter 6 we used two types of diagrams called trees—a tree of recursive calls to analyze a recursive program's execution and a parse tree to analyze the syntactical structure of an expression. Both of these diagrammatic techniques were hierarchical in nature. That is, a node at level $n + 1$ in some sense belonged to or descended from a node at level n. From the opposite perspective, a node at level n of the tree diagram in some sense owned or controlled all nodes connected to it at levels deeper than n.

Our use of a hierarchical scheme to describe recursion and parsing is not surprising. Human beings organize much of the world around them in hierarchies. For instance, an industrial or governmental body functions effectively only by defining a collection of supervisor-subordinate relationships among its participants.

Figure 7.1
Tree structure representing a student record.

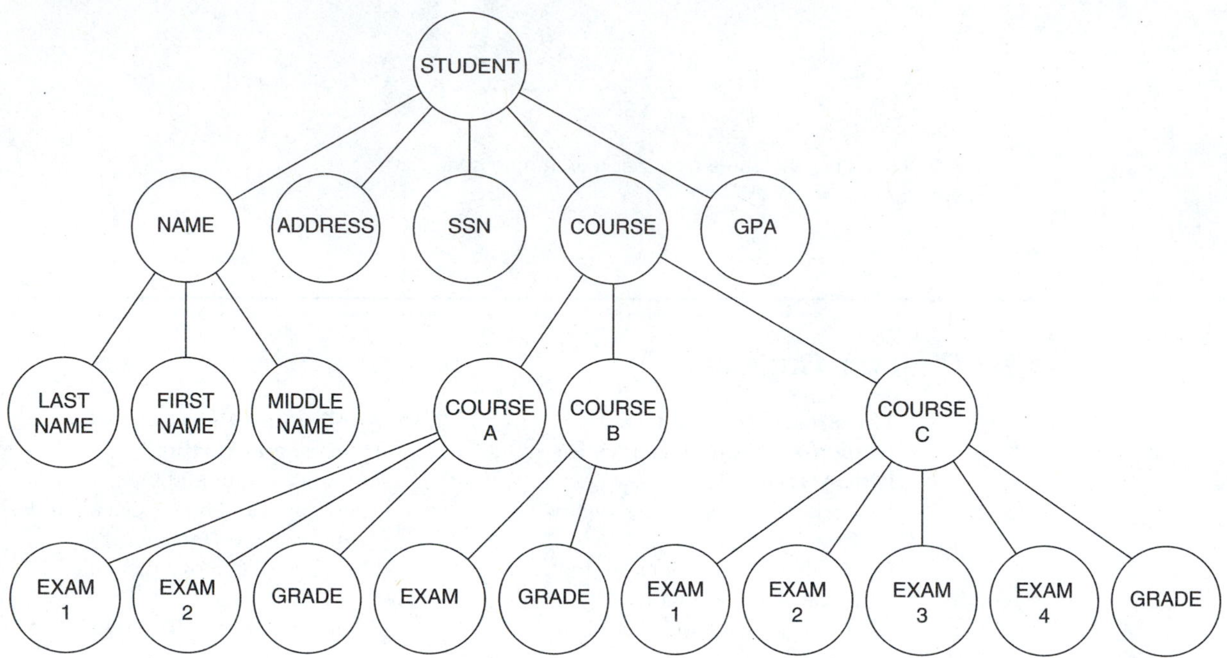

Computer scientists design a software system by breaking it down into modules and defining hierarchical boss-worker relationships among those modules. Parent-child relationships allow a natural categorization of a family's history with the use of a genealogical tree. In computer science, a *tree* is a data structure that represents such hierarchical relationships between data items.

To introduce some of the terminology of tree structures, consider the record of a student at a typical university. In addition to the usual statistical background information such as social security number, name, and address, a student record might contain listings for a number of courses, exams, and final grades in each course, overall grade point average, and other data relating to the student's performance. Figure 7.1 is a tree structure representing such a student record. As in genealogical trees, at the highest *level* (0) of a tree is its *root* (also called the *root node*). Here STUDENT is the root node. The nodes NAME, ADDRESS, SSN, COURSE, and GPA, which are directly connected to the root node, are the *child nodes* of the *parent node* STUDENT. The child nodes of a given parent constitute a set of *siblings*. Thus NAME, ADDRESS, SSN, COURSE, and GPA are siblings. In the hierarchy represented by a tree, the child nodes of a parent are one level lower than the parent node. Thus NAME, ADDRESS, SSN, COURSE, and GPA are at level 1 in Figure 7.1.

A link between a parent and its child is called a *branch*. Each node in a tree except the root must descend from a parent node via a branch. Thus LASTNAME, FIRSTNAME, and MIDDLENAME descend from the parent node NAME. The root of the tree is the *ancestor* of all nodes in the tree. Each node may be the parent of any number of nodes in the tree. A node with no children is called a *leaf node*. In Figure 7.1, GPA is a leaf node. LASTNAME, FIRSTNAME, MIDDLENAME, EXAM1, and EXAM2 also are leaf nodes.

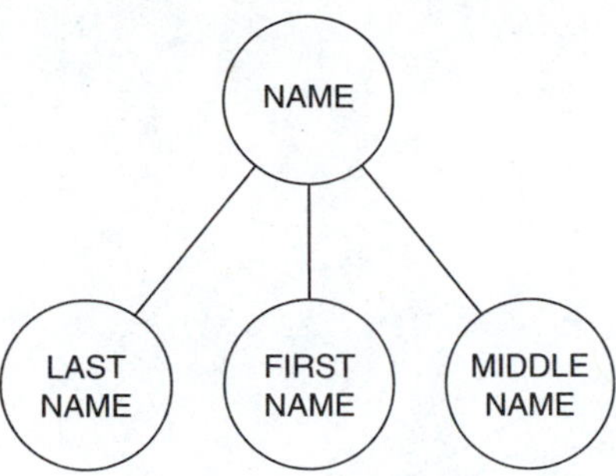

Figure 7.2
A subtree of Figure 7.1.

A *subtree* is a subset of a tree that is itself a tree; the tree in Figure 7.2 is a subtree of the tree in Figure 7.1. This subtree has the root node NAME. Similarly, the tree in Figure 7.3 is another subtree of the tree in Figure 7.1. Notice that the tree in Figure 7.3 is a subtree of the tree in Figure 7.1 and of the tree in Figure 7.4.

7.1 The Binary Tree ADT

It is evident from the preceding discussion that a tree has the following interesting property: Any given node within a tree is itself the root node of a completely analogous tree structure. That is, a tree is composed of a collection of substructures, each of which also meets the criteria for being a tree. This sounds dangerously circular, and, to formally describe a tree in this fashion, we must be sure to give ourselves a terminating condition for the recursion. This is done via the following partial definition of a tree as an abstract data type.

Definition (Partial) of Tree: A *general tree* is a set of nodes that is either empty (the recursive termination condition) or has a designated node, called the root, from which zero or more subtrees (hierarchically) descend. Each subtree itself satisfies the definition of a tree.

At the moment, we will refrain from providing a set of operations for the general tree ADT. Temporarily, we will restrict ourselves to a more limiting definition that will be easier to work with and, at the same time, will provide a surprisingly vast spectrum of applications. The primary restriction of this limited tree ADT is that any node in the tree will have exactly two subtrees. Consequently, it is called a binary tree.

Definition of Binary Tree: A *binary tree* is a tree in which each node has exactly two subtrees, designated the *left subtree* and *right subtree*, either or both of which may be empty. The operations to be performed on a binary tree are shown in terms of the following pre- and postconditions.

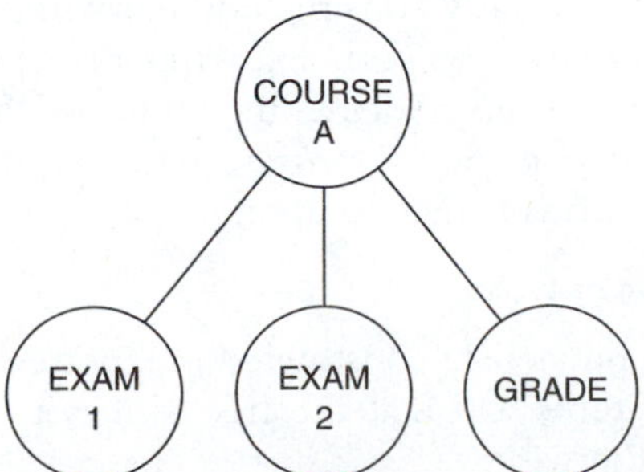

Figure 7.3
Another subtree of Figure 7.1.

Figure 7.4
Another subtree of Figure 7.1.

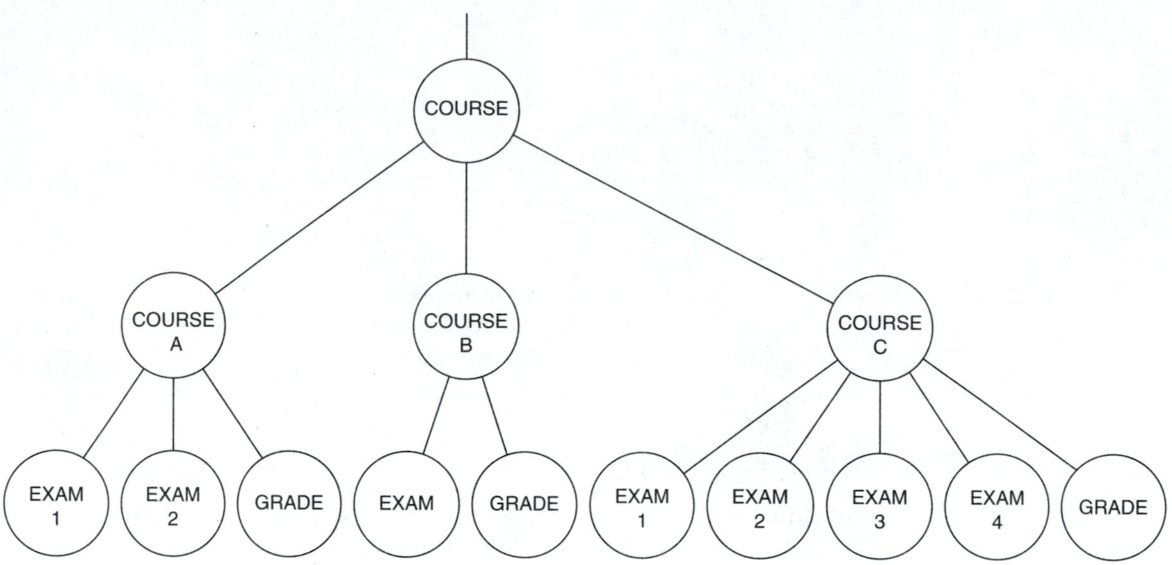

Construct Operation (First Form)

Preconditions: An uninitialized binary tree object.
Postconditions: The binary tree object is initialized to the empty binary tree.

Construct Operation (Copy Constructor)

Preconditions: An uninitialized binary tree object;
initbintree—a binary tree object that was previously contructed.
Postconditions: The binary tree object is initialized to *initbintree*.

Destroy Operation

Preconditions: A previously constructed binary tree object.
Postconditions: All storage associated with the binary tree object is deallocated.

Empty Operation

Preconditions: A previously constructed binary tree object.
Postconditions: Returns TRUE if the tree is empty, FALSE otherwise.

Assign Operation

Preconditions: A previously constructed binary tree object;
source—a second binary tree object that uses the same data type in its nodes as the owner of the operation.
Postconditions: The contents of *source* have been copied to the binary tree object that owns the operation.

NoRoomLeft Operation

Preconditions: A previously constructed binary tree object.
Postconditions: Returns TRUE if the tree will not allow further additions, FALSE otherwise.

Add Operation

Preconditions: A previously constructed binary tree object based on a particular hierarchical property;
item—a value to be inserted in the binary tree.

Postconditions: If the tree is incapable of accepting another node, *item* is not inserted and the binary tree is left unaltered. Otherwise *item* is added to the binary tree in a way that maintains the tree's hierarchical property.

Preorder Traversal Operation

Preconditions: A previously constructed binary tree object;
processnode—an algorithmic process that can be applied to each node in the binary tree.

Postconditions: Each node of the binary tree is visited in the following order: root of the binary tree first, then recursively all nodes in left subtree, then recursively all nodes in right subtree. As each node is visited, *processnode* is applied to it.

Inorder Traversal Operation

Preconditions: A previously constructed binary tree object;
processnode—an algorithmic process that can be applied to each node in the binary tree.

Postconditions: Each node of the binary tree is visited in the following order: first visit recursively all nodes in left subtree, then visit the root, then visit recursively all nodes in right subtree. As each node is visited, *processnode* is applied to it.

Postorder Traversal Operation

Preconditions: A previously constructed binary tree object;
processnode—an algorithmic process that can be applied to each node in the binary tree.

Postconditions: Each node of the binary tree is visited in the following order: first visit recursively all nodes in left subtree, then visit recursively all nodes in right subtree, then visit the root. As each node is visited, *processnode* is applied to it.

Our definition of the Add operation for the binary tree ADT is intentionally vague. How a node is inserted into a binary tree is dependent on the hierarchical organization of the tree. Because of this, it is impossible to view the binary tree ADT as a specification that provides a complete package for every application. Rather, the binary tree ADT represents a generic starting point from which other more specific ADTs may be developed. We will soon see that the notion of an incompletely specified operation for an ADT is handled very nicely by the inheritance capabilities of C++. First, however, we give three examples that will illustrate some of the hierarchical properties that commonly underlie binary trees. The second and third examples will also serve to clarify the various traversal operations that are defined for the binary tree ADT.

Example 7.1

The tree of Figure 7.5 is a binary tree. Each node of this tree has two subtrees (empty or nonempty), designated as left and right. The particular hierarchy for this tree dictates that the datum in any given node is greater than or equal to all the data

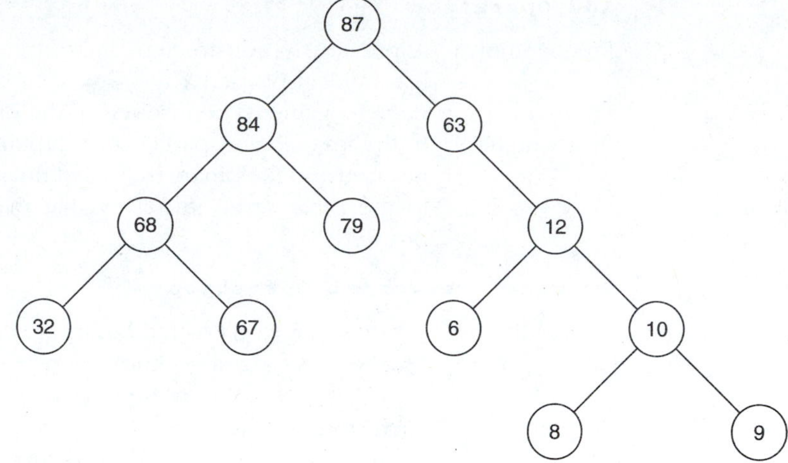

Figure 7.5
Binary tree with the heap property. The data in any given node are greater than or equal to the data in its left and right subtrees.

in its left and right subtrees. A tree with this property is said to be a *heap* and to have the *heap property*. A heap will prove particularly important in our discussion of a nonrecursive, $O(n \log_2 n)$ sorting method in Section 7.4. We will also see how a heap may be used to implement the priority queue ADT introduced in Chapter 4. The heap property is an example of a hierarchical relationship for a tree and is a property that must be preserved when the Add operation is performed on the tree.

Example 7.2

A second example of a hierarchical relationship underlying a binary tree structure is shown in Figure 7.6. This binary tree exhibits the *ordering property:* The datum in each node of the tree is greater than all of the data in that node's left subtree and less than or equal to all the data in the right subtree. We will see in Section 7.3 the importance of trees possessing this property when we explore binary trees as a means of implementing an ordered list in which searches can be performed efficiently.

We can also use this tree to illustrate the effect of the inorder traversal operation. Since the inorder traversal is recursively applied on the left subtree before applying

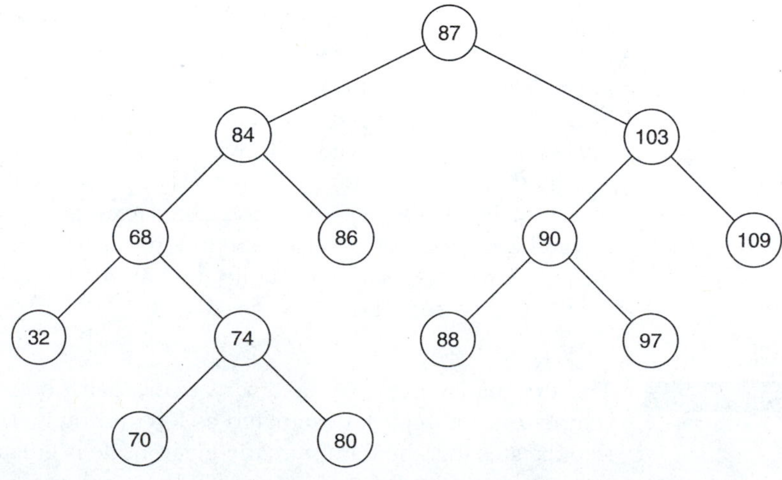

Figure 7.6
Binary tree with the ordering property. The data in each node are greater than the data in its left subtree and less than or equal to the data in its right subtree.

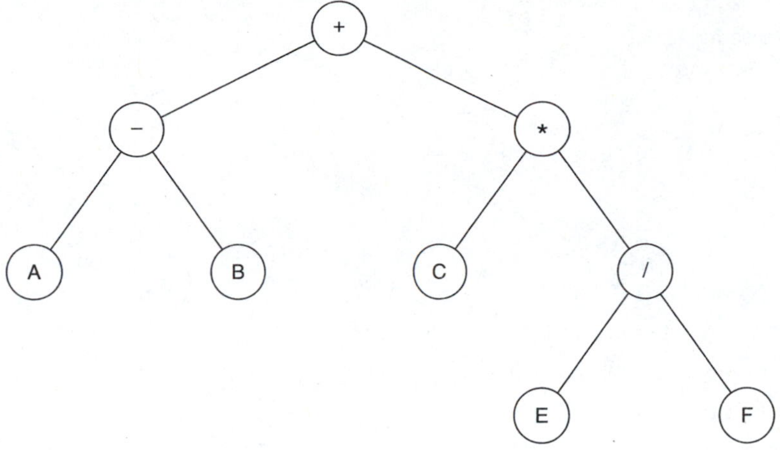

Figure 7.7
Binary expression tree for (A – B) + C * (E/F). The hierarchical relationship of parent to child is that of an algebraic operator to its two operands.

processNode to the root or recursively visiting the right subtree, 32 will be the first node affected by the processNode function. Thereafter, processNode will be applied to 68, that is, the root of the subtree having 32 as its left subtree. After processing 68, the right subtree of 68, rooted at 74, will be visited in the order 70 74 80. Overall, you should confirm that the order in which nodes are visited by the inorder traversal operation is

32 68 70 74 80 84 86 87 88 90 97 103 109

Note that an inorder traversal of a binary tree with the ordering property will visit the nodes of the tree in ascending order with respect to their data values.

Example 7.3

As a final example of a hierarchical relationship that can determine the arrangement of data in a binary tree, consider Figure 7.7. Here we have a binary tree representation of the infix algebraic expression

$$(A - B) + C * (E / F)$$

The hierarchical relationship of parent to children in this tree is that of algebraic operator to its two operands. Note that an operand may itself be an expression (that is, a subtree) that must be evaluated before the operator in the parent node can be applied. Note also that if the order of evaluation in the expression changes to

$$(A - B) + C * E / F$$

then the corresponding binary expression tree must also change, as reflected in Figure 7.8.

Using the tree of Figure 7.7, you should confirm that a postorder traversal (applied recursively on the left subtree, then the right subtree, and finally the root) will visit nodes in the order

$$A\ B\ -\ C\ E\ F\ /\ *\ +$$

This is exactly the postfix representation of the expression. Similarly, a preorder traversal yields the prefix form of the expression

$$+\ -\ A\ B\ *\ C\ /\ E\ F$$

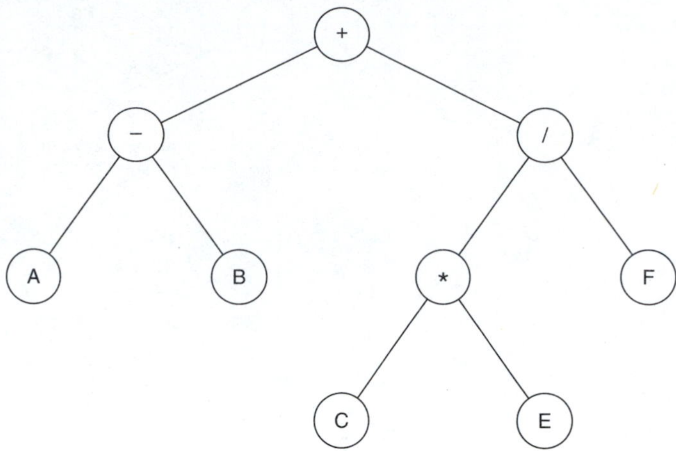

Figure 7.8
Binary expression tree for (A − B) + C * E / F.

Not surprisingly, the link between these traversals and standard forms of representing expressions makes the expression tree an important data structure in contemporary compilers. You will explore the binary expression tree more in the exercises and problems of this chapter.

These three examples indicate that the binary tree ADT is really just a starting point for an entire collection of ADTs. Each of these more specific ADTs in effect inherits the general properties and operations of the binary tree ADT and then extends these by providing operations unique to its hierarchical relationship. This inheritance phenomenon is highlighted in Figure 7.9.

C++ allows the designer of a class library to specify a pattern of inheritance by declaring a class to be an *abstract base class*. An abstract base class is a class in which one or more member functions are *pure virtual*. This means that the designer of the class elects to defer an implementation of these functions to a subclass, where the additional information necessary for a meaningful implementation is available.

The value of an abstract base class lies in the fact that it establishes prototypes for certain operations. As we noted, a class that is derived from an abstract base class must ultimately provide implementations of the pure virtual functions that adhere to the prototypes defined in the abstract base class. Thus, an abstract base class plays a precedent-setting role. Rather than provide a full library of operations, it merely establishes guidelines that derived classes must obey. Since a complete implementation of an abstract data class is lacking, no objects can be instantiated from such a class. In the particular case of the **BinTree** class for binary trees given below, we are told that, although **BinTree** provides constructors, a destructor, an

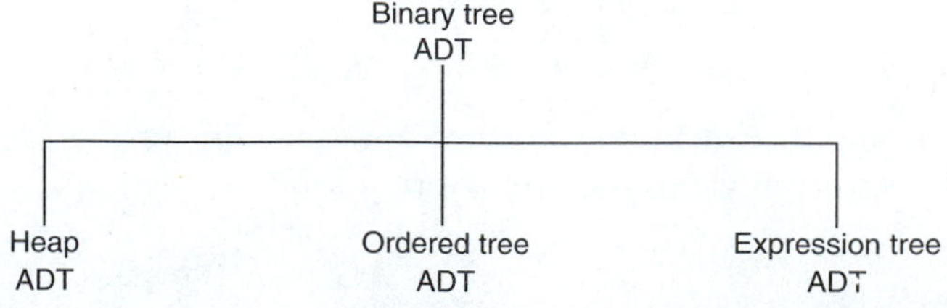

Figure 7.9
A hierarchy of ADTs all inheriting generic properties of the binary tree.

assignment operator, and traversal operations for derived classes, the derived class must provide an **add** operation before it becomes a completely functional class.

Note also that a class inheriting a pure virtual function is not required to provide an implementation for it, but rather can leave it as a pure virtual function. This makes the derived class an abstract class as well, which means that no objects can be instantiated from that class either.

The syntax for declaring a pure virtual function must include "= 0" after the function's prototype in the class definition. This is illustrated in the declaration of the **add** function in the following interface for the **BinTree** class:

```
// BaseData is either a C++ built-in type, or a C++ class that has
// an assignment operation that overloads the "=" operator.
template <class BaseData>
class BinTree
{
  public:
// ---------------------------------------------------------------------------
// Interface for BinTree constructor
// GIVEN:   An uninitialized BinTree object.
// RETURN:  The BinTree object is initialized to the empty tree.

    BinTree();

// ---------------------------------------------------------------------------
// Interface for alternate BinTree constructor
// GIVEN:   An uninitialized BinTree object;
//          maxNodes -- a positive integer.
// RETURN:  The BinTree object is initialized to an empty tree with the
//          capacity to store maxNodes nodes.
    BinTree(int maxNodes);

//--------------------------------------------------------------------------
// Interface for BinTree copy constructor
// GIVEN:   An uninitialized BinTree object;
//          initbintree -- a BinTree object that was previously constructed.
// RETURN:  The BinTree object is initialized with the node values and
//          number of nodes of initbintree.

    BinTree(BinTree<BaseData> &initbintree);

// ---------------------------------------------------------------------------
// Interface for BinTree destructor
// GIVEN:   A previously constructed BinTree object.
// RETURN:  All storage associated with the binary tree is deallocated.

     ~BinTree();

// ---------------------------------------------------------------------------
// Interface for BinTree assign = operator
// GIVEN:   A previously constructed BinTree object;
//          source -- a second BinTree object that must have been
//                    constructed with the same BaseData type as the
//                    owner of the assign operator.
// RETURN:  The contents of source have been copied to the BinTree
//          object that owns the operation.
// RETURN as value of function: void

    void operator = (const BinTree<BaseData> &source);
```

```
// ---------------------------------------------------------------------------
// Interface for empty operation
// GIVEN:   A previously initialized BinTree object.
// RETURN as value of function:
//          TRUE if the binary tree is empty, FALSE otherwise.

   BOOLEAN empty();

// ---------------------------------------------------------------------------
// Interface for noRoomLeft operation
// GIVEN:   A previously initialized BinTree object.
// RETURN as value of function:
//          TRUE if the binary tree will allow no further additions,
//          FALSE otherwise.

   BOOLEAN noRoomLeft();

// ---------------------------------------------------------------------------
// Interface for pure virtual add operation
// GIVEN:   A BinTree object;
//          item -- a value of type BaseData.
// RETURN:  item is added to the binary tree according to the hierarchical
//          property that defines the tree.
// RETURN as value of function: void
// NOTE:    This is a "pure virtual" function that must be overridden.

   virtual void add(const BaseData &item) = 0;

// ---------------------------------------------------------------------------
// Interface to preorder traversal operation
// GIVEN:   A BinTree object;
//          processNode -- a pointer to a function that can act
//                         on each node in the tree.
// RETURN:  All nodes in the tree are visited in a preorder traversal (root,
//          left subtree, right subtree), applying processNode to each node
//          as it is visited.
// RETURN as value of function: void

   void preorderTrav(void (*processNode)(BaseData &item));

// ---------------------------------------------------------------------------
// Interface to postorder traversal operation
// GIVEN:   A BinTree object;
//          processNode -- a pointer to a function that can act
//                         on each node in the tree.
// RETURN:  All nodes in the tree are visited in a postorder
//          traversal (left subtree, right subtree, root),
//          applying processNode to each node as it is visited.
// RETURN as value of function: void

   void postorderTrav(void (*processNode)(BaseData &item));

// ---------------------------------------------------------------------------
// Interface to inorder traversal operation
// GIVEN:   A BinTree object;
//          processNode -- a pointer to a function that can act
//                         on each node in the tree.
// RETURN:  All nodes in the tree are visited in an inorder
//          traversal (left subtree, root, right subtree),
//          applying processNode to each node as it is visited.
// RETURN as value of function: void

   void inorderTrav(void (*processNode)(BaseData &item));
};
```

Example 7.4 To illustrate how the traversal operations of the **BinTree** class would be used, suppose that a class **ParticularTree** has been derived from **BinTree**. Show how to declare a **ParticularTree** of integers and then how to print the integers in the tree via a postorder traversal.

```
void printInt(int &num)                     // This will be the "processNode"
{                                           // function to print one integer
  cout << num << endl;
}

// Declare a particular tree tr, with int for BaseData
ParticularTree<int> tr;

// Then, after inserting values into the tree by a still-to-be-developed add
// function, print the integer values using a postorder traversal.

tr.postorderTrav(printInt);
```

A RELEVANT ISSUE Abstract Base Classes in Application Frameworks

The definition of the **BinTree** class in Section 7.1 introduced the notion of an abstract base class and pure virtual methods in C++. These concepts have some implications for software development that range far beyond tree structures. Many times software developers want to develop applications that have a "look and feel" consistent with other applications for a particular system. This notion was first made popular on Macintosh systems, in which most Macintosh programs looked exactly alike in terms of their user interface. More recently, this idea has been extended to applications running under Microsoft Windows. One of the difficulties in developing programs that have a Macintosh or Windows look and feel is that a tremendous amount of time must be spent developing the highly professional interface—*if* it is developed from scratch. If developers had to implement such interfaces from scratch for each application, it would be totally impractical. Instead, they typically work through an *application framework*. In one sense, an application framework could be thought of as an abstract base class from which all programs can inherit a huge amount of complex user interface routines. They also inherit a pure virtual protocol for writing a specific application that can take advantage of those user interface routines.

For example, the application framework will have routines to detect various types of user interface events—such as particular keys being struck or the mouse being triggered in certain way. These routines have already been coded for anyone using the application framework and they belong to a base class. Let's say that this base class is called *GenericApplication*. In addition to these user interface routines, the *GenericApplication* class will also include a method that a particular derived application must call to run within the application framework. Let's say that this method is called *execute*. The code for *execute* might look like the following:

```
void GenericApplication::execute();
{
   EventType event;

   initializeMenu (menuBar);
   do
   {
     getEvent (event);
     handleEvent (event);
   }
   while ( !endStatus );
}
```

The particulars of this *execute* method are of little concern to a derived application other than to notice that *execute* invokes two other methods—*initializeMenu* and *handleEvent*. Here is where the notion of inheritance from a pure virtual method comes into play. The functions *initializeMenu* and *handleEvent* are pure virtual. That is, the *GenericApplication* class establishes their protocol, but it is the responsibility of a derived application to actually implement them in the context of what that application wants. Hence, if you were writing a word processor application, you would write *initializeMenu* and *handleEvent* so that menus were initialized and user-triggered events were handled in a fashion appropriate for a word processor. Similarly, a spreadsheet (or any other) application could be plugged into this framework merely by writing its own *initializeMenu* and *handleEvent* methods.

Though this brief description has certainly been an oversimplification of the use of application frameworks, it nonetheless indicates the relative ease with which a software developer can write highly professional applications by merely working within the object hierarchy of the application framework that she chooses. Little wonder that the proponents of object-oriented programming claim that it will result in a quantum leap in the speed with which complex applications are developed!

In the sections that follow you will see how this notion of an abstract base class plays itself out. In Section 7.2 we discuss implementation strategies for the abstract base class **BinTree** and show how the traversal operations may be developed for each of these strategies. Then, in Sections 7.3 and 7.4, we examine how the pure virtual **add** operation may be implemented by subclasses for binary trees that have the ordering and heap properties, respectively.

Exercises 7.1

1. Draw a binary tree for the following expression:

   $$A * B - (C + D) * (P / Q)$$

2. Write a C++ code segment that will add 1 to each node in a binary tree of integers.
3. Declare a struct capable of storing a student's name, total credits, and total grade points earned. Then, assuming the existence of a binary tree variable **studentTree** that has the ordering property with respect to alphabetical ordering of names, write a code segment that will use the appropriate traversal to print an alphabetical listing of all students and their grade point averages.
4. Indicate which of the following are binary trees with the ordering property. Explain what is wrong with those that are not.

   a.

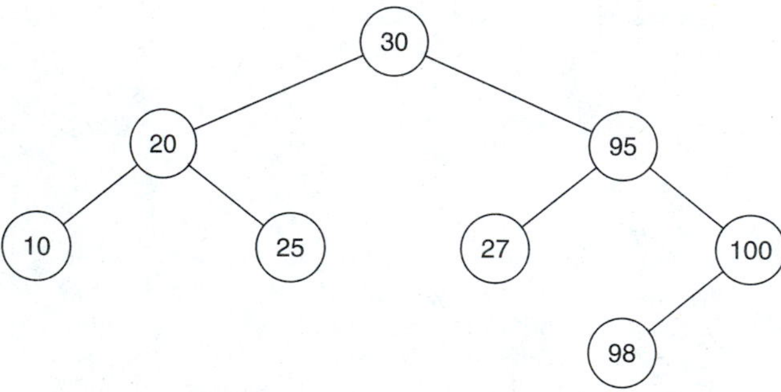

   b.

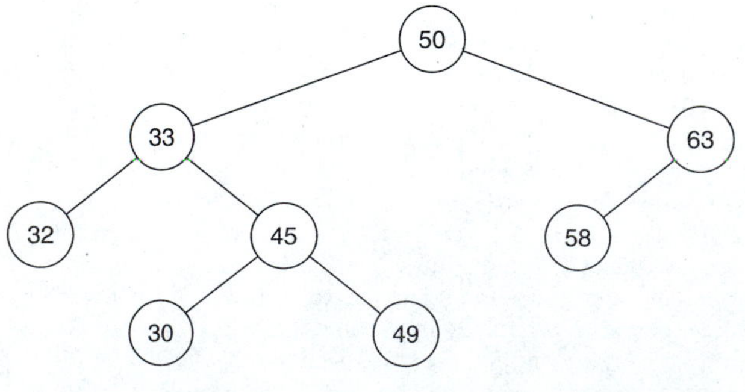

   c.

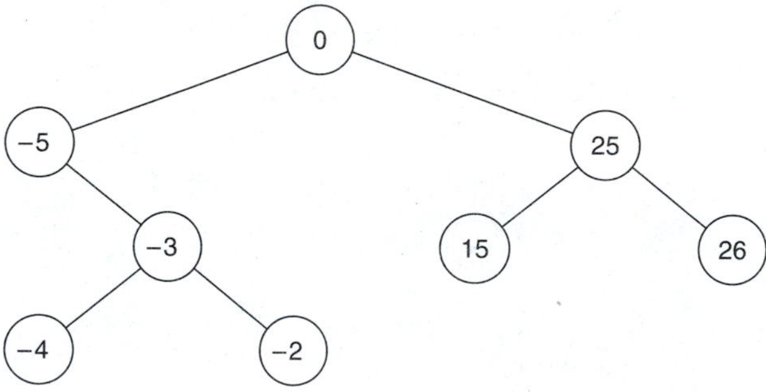

   d.

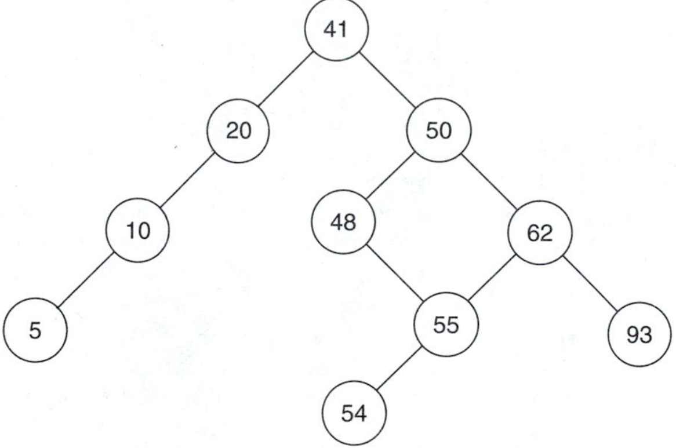

5. Indicate which of the following binary trees are heaps. Explain what is wrong with those that are not.

   a.

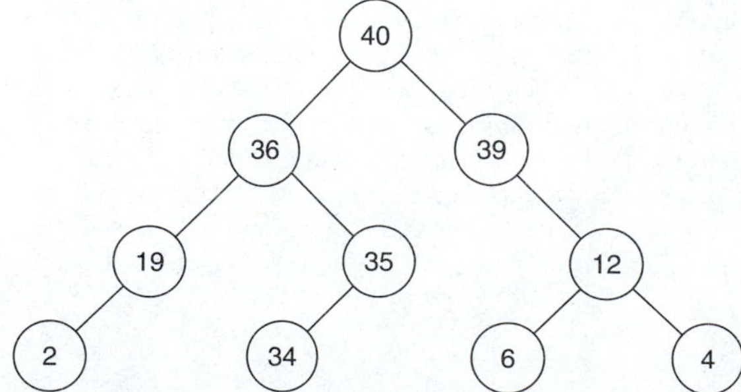

b.

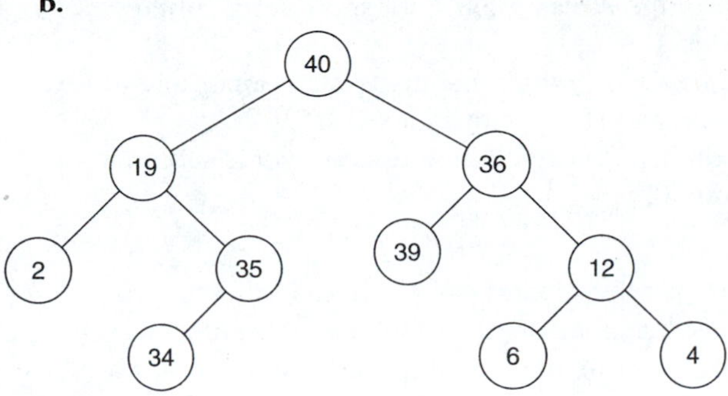

c.

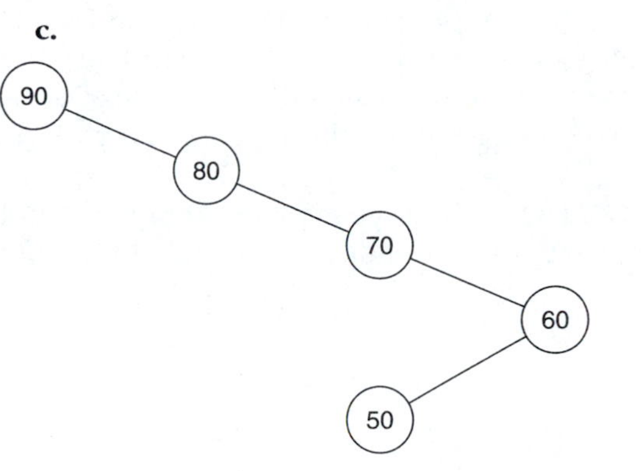

6. Indicate the order in which nodes would be visited by preorder, postorder, and inorder traversals for each of the trees in Exercise 7.1.5.
7. Explain the relationship between parent and children for each of the specific types of binary trees in Figure 7.9 on page 280.
8. Using one of the binary tree traversal operations, write functions
   a. To count the number of nodes in a binary tree
   b. To find the largest value in a binary tree that contains numeric data

7.2 Implementation Strategies for Binary Trees

Consistent with the way in which we have studied other data structures, we now have a very good idea of *what* a tree is without any consideration of *how* we implement it. This latter issue must now be explored. There are two common methods for implementing binary trees. One method, which does not require the overhead of maintaining pointers, is called a *linear* representation; the other, known as a *linked* representation, uses pointers.

Linear Representation of a Binary Tree

The linear representation method of implementing a binary tree uses a one-dimensional array of size $2^{d+1} - 1$ where d is the depth of the tree, that is, the maximum level of any node in the tree. In the tree of Figure 7.7 on page 279, the root + is at the level 0, the nodes − and * are at level 1, and so on. The deepest level in this tree is the level of E and F, level 3. Therefore, $d = 3$ and this tree will require an array of size $2^{3+1} - 1 = 15$.

Once the size of the array has been determined, the following method is used to represent the tree:

1. Store the root in the first location of the array.
2. If a node is in the nth location of the array, store its left child in the $2n$th location and its right child in the $(2n + 1)$th location.

Several natural options are available for implementing a binary tree using an array:

1. Use an object instantiated from the **Array** class, indexed over a subrange of the integers starting with index 1.
2. Use the array type provided by C++, which means it is automatically indexed over a subrange of the integers and starts with index 0.
3. Use an object instantiated from the **Array** class, indexed over a subrange of the integers starting with index 0.

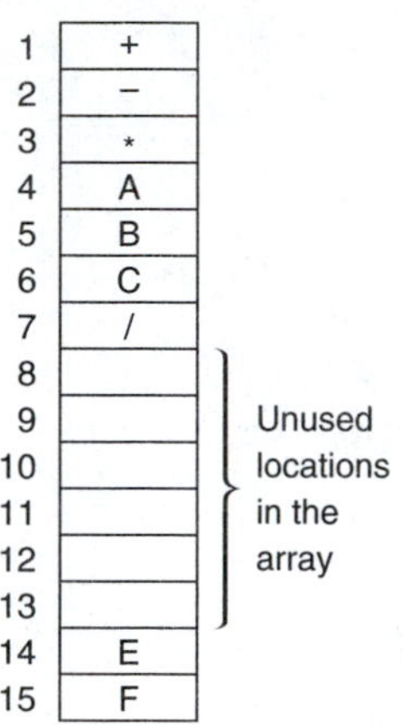

Figure 7.10
Tree of Figure 7.7 stored in a linear representation using an **Array** object indexed over a subrange of the integers starting with index 1. The root is stored in index 1. If a node is at index n, its left child is at index $2n$ and its right child is at index $2n + 1$.

An advantage of the third option over the second is the run-time safety it provides by range-checking; a disadvantage is its higher overhead in execution time and storage utilization. Although recognizing that this may be important in some applications, we will fall back on the maxim of "clarity and safety over cycles and cells," which we have been advocating, and opt for the advantage of using an **Array** object. Having settled on this, we now choose the first option over both the second and third because it permits a more direct implementation of the method of representation as we have described it. This is also our rationale for using this type of **Array** object in other situations.

With the aid of this scheme, the tree of Figure 7.7 is stored in an **Array** object of size 15, as shown in Figure 7.10. The locations with indices 8 through 13 are not used.

Efficiency Considerations for the Linear Representation

The main advantages of this method lie in its simplicity and the fact that, given a child node, its parent node can be determined immediately. If a child node is at location n in the array, then its parent node is at location $n/2$.

In spite of its simplicity and ease of implementation, the linear representation method has all the overhead that comes with physically ordering items. Insertion or deletion of a node in a fashion that maintains the hierarchical relationships within the tree may cause considerable data movement up and down the array and, hence, use a considerable amount of processing time. Also, memory locations (such as locations with indices 8 through 13 in our example) are usually wasted because the tree is only partially filled. Nonetheless, for certain applications, such as maintaining a heap (Section 7.4), the linear representation is highly efficient.

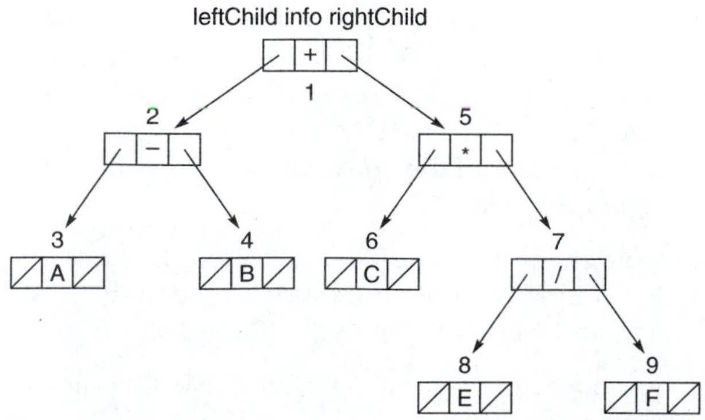

Figure 7.11
Linked representation of the binary expression tree of Figure 7.7. (The numbers on top of the cells represent addresses used in the leftChild and rightChild members in Figure 7.12.)

Figure 7.12
Implementation of Figure 7.11 using an **Array** of **structs** with indexing starting at 1.

Location	info	leftChild	rightChild
1	+	2	5
2	–	3	4
3	A	NULL	NULL
4	B	NULL	NULL
5	*	6	7
6	C	NULL	NULL
7	/	8	9
8	E	NULL	NULL
9	F	NULL	NULL

Linked Representation of a Binary Tree

Because each node in a binary tree may have two child nodes, a node in a linked representation has two pointer fields, one for each child, and one or more data fields. When a node has no children, the corresponding pointer fields are NULL. Figure 7.11 is a linked representation of the binary expression tree of Figure 7.7. The **leftChild** and **rightChild** fields are pointers to (that is, memory addresses of) the left child and the right child of a node.

For the moment, we will consider a detailed description of the linked representation of the binary tree of Figure 7.7 using an **Array** of **structs** with indexing starting at 1. By doing this, we will be able to trace the values of the pointers. Once the concept is thoroughly understood, we return to using C++ pointer variables for the actual implementation of binary trees. For example, we can implement the tree of Figure 7.11 as shown in Figure 7.12, using the strategy of building the left subtree for each node before considering the right subtree. The numbers on top of the cells in Figure 7.11 represent the addresses given in the **leftChild** and **rightChild** fields.

In the linked representation, insertions and deletions involve no data movement except the rearrangement of pointers. Suppose we wish to modify the tree in Figure 7.7 to that of Figure 7.13. (This change might be required by some recent

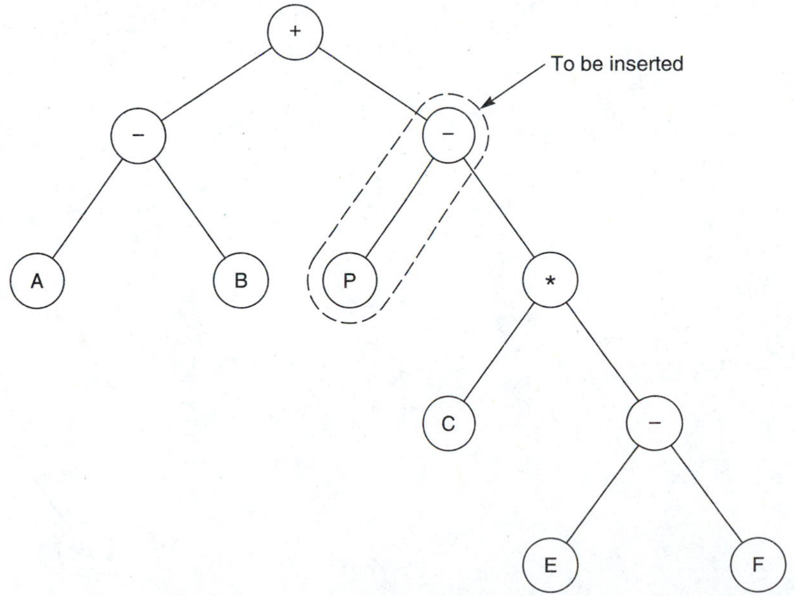

Figure 7.13
Desired modification of Figure 7.7.

Figure 7.14
Modification of Figure 7.12 by insertions into the tree of Figure 7.7. Values that are boxed represent changes from Figure 7.12.

Location	info	leftChild	rightChild
1	+	2	[10]
2	–	3	4
3	A	NULL	NULL
4	B	NULL	NULL
5	*	6	7
6	C	NULL	NULL
7	/	8	9
8	E	NULL	NULL
9	F	NULL	NULL
10	–	[11]	[5]
11	P	[NULL]	[NULL]

modification in the expression represented by Figure 7.7.) For instance, the insertion of nodes containing – and P into the tree structure can easily be achieved by simply inserting the nodes containing – and P in the next available spaces in the array and adjusting the corresponding pointers.

For the implementation of the tree shown in Figure 7.12, the effect of this insertion is given by Figure 7.14. The adjusted pointers have been enclosed in a box. Notice that the change in the **rightChild** of location 1 and the use of locations 10 and 11 are all that is necessary. No data were moved.

Similarly, if we wish to shorten the tree in Figure 7.7 by deleting the nodes * and C, then all we must do is rearrange the pointers to obtain the altered tree, as shown in Figure 7.15. The effect of this deletion is given in Figure 7.16. As before, the adjusted pointers have been boxed.

A more formal statement of an algorithm underlying such insertions and deletions is given later in this chapter, when we discuss algorithms for maintaining a binary tree. Now that we have explained the linked representation of a binary tree by using an **Array** to contain pointer values that can be explicitly traced, we will use the following general class description with C++ pointers to implement this structure in the remainder of the chapter.

Figure 7.15
Another modification of Figure 7.7.

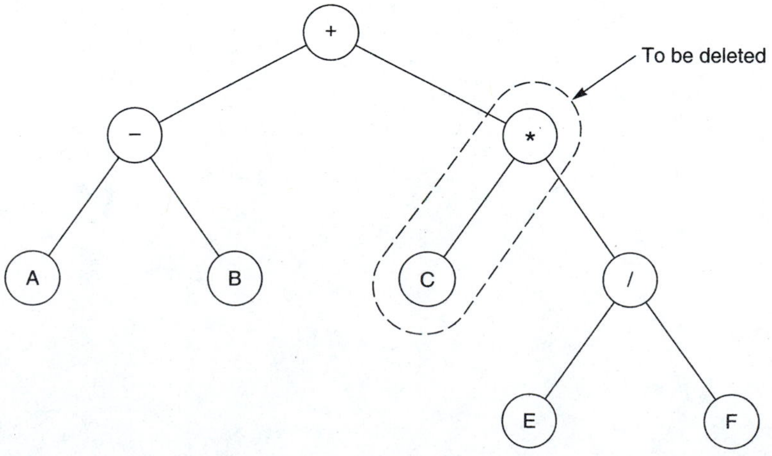

Figure 7.16
Modification of Figure 7.12 by deletions from the tree of Figure 7.7.

Location	info	leftChild	rightChild	Modified tree
1	+	2	7	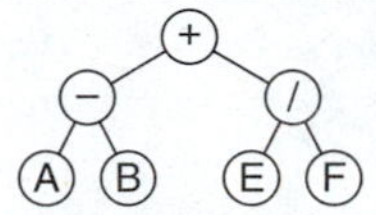
2	−	3	4	
3	A	NULL	NULL	
4	B	NULL	NULL	
5	*			unused space after
6	C			deletion of * and C
7	/	8	9	
8	E	NULL	NULL	
9	F	NULL	NULL	


```
template <class BaseData>
class BtNode
{
  public:
    BaseData info;                     // The data in the node
    BtNode *leftChild, *rightChild;    // Pointers to left and right subtrees
};
```

The **BtNode** class is not needed by clients of the **BinTree** class. Rather the **BinTree** class itself needs a pointer to a node of this type representing the root of the binary tree. That is, we must add the following **protected** data member to the **BinTree** class definition whose public interface was given in Section 7.1.

```
protected:
  BtNode *root; // Member of BinTree class pointing to root of tree
```

A binary tree is constructed by simply initializing its **root** pointer to NULL. Hence the code for the first constructor is given by:

```
template <class BaseData>
BinTree<BaseData>::BinTree()
{
  root = NULL;
}
```

Efficiency Considerations for the Linked Representation

As far as processing efficiency is concerned, the linked representation seems to be more efficient, particularly if frequent insertions and deletions are required. Although for most purposes the linked representation of a binary tree is very efficient, it does have certain disadvantages, namely:

1. Wasted memory space in NULL pointers. For instance, the representation in Figure 7.11 has 10 NULL pointers.
2. Given a node, it is difficult to determine its parent.

The first disadvantage can be offset by "threading" the tree, a technique discussed in Section 7.5. The second drawback can be easily overcome, at the expense of more memory, by adding a pointer field to the parent of each node.

Implementation of Binary Tree Traversals

As noted in our definition of a binary tree as an abstract data structure, a *tree traversal* requires an algorithm that visits (and processes) each node of a tree exactly once. Just as the only way into a linked list is through the head node, the only way into a tree is through the root. However, any attempt to draw an analogy between traversing a singly linked list and traversing a binary tree is limited to the preceding statement. Although both structures have only one entry point, from any given node in a linked list there is no choice about where to proceed. After entering a binary tree, we are faced with a threefold predicament at each node:

1. Do we process the data contained in the node at which we are currently located?
2. Do we remember the location of the current node (so that we can return to process it) and visit (and process) all nodes in its left subtree?
3. Do we remember the location of the current node (so that we can return to process it) and visit (and process) all nodes in its right subtree?

Here the generic term *process* applies to whatever operation is to be performed on the data at a given node—for example, print it or update it. What is actually done to the data is not as relevant to our discussion as the order in which the nodes are visited. Each of the three preceding choices represents a valid choice. The route chosen out of the threefold predicament dictates the order in which the nodes are visited and processed.

Although various arrangements of these three choices allow for many different traversals, three particular traversal techniques have come to be regarded as standard and hence are included in our ADT definition of the binary tree. They are the preorder traversal, the inorder traversal, and the postorder traversal. As alluded to in Examples 7.2 and 7.3, these three traversals correspond to visiting all nodes in ascending order for trees with the ordering property (inorder traversal) and to obtaining prefix and postfix representations of binary expression trees (preorder and postorder traversals, respectively). However, it is important to realize that the three traversals apply broadly to all binary trees, regardless of the hierarchical relationship underlying their structure.

Preorder Traversal

In a *preorder traversal,* the three options are combined in the following order:

1. First, visit and process the root node.
2. Then, recursively traverse (and visit all nodes in) the left subtree.
3. Finally, recursively traverse (and visit all nodes in) the right subtree.

These three ordered steps are recursive. Once the root of the tree is visited and processed, we go to the root of the left subtree, and then to the root of the left subtree of the left subtree, and so on until we can go no farther. Following these three steps, the preorder traversal of the tree of Figure 7.7 would visit and process nodes in the order

$$+ - A B * C / E F$$

which is the prefix form of the expression

$$(A - B) + C * (E / F)$$

Hence, we conclude that, if processing a node means printing it, then a preorder traversal of a binary expression tree would output the prefix form of the expression.

The preorder traversal of an existing binary tree implemented via a linked representation requires that we add a **private** auxiliary function to the **BinTree** class.

```
//--------------------------------------------------------------------------
// Interface for auxiliary preordAux function
// GIVEN:    rt -- the pointer to the root of a binary tree;
//           processNode -- a pointer to a function that can act
//                          on each node in the tree.
// RETURN:   All nodes in the tree are visited in a preorder traversal
//           (root, left subtree, right subtree), applying processNode
//           to each node as it is visited.
// RETURN as value of function: void

    void preordAux(BtNode<BaseData> *rt, void (*processNode)(BaseData &item));
```

This auxiliary function does the real recursive work for the traversal algorithm.

```
// Implementation of preordAux
template <class BaseData>
void BinTree<BaseData>::preordAux(BtNode<BaseData> *rt,
                                  void (*processNode)(BaseData &item))
{
  if (rt != NULL)
  {
    processNode(rt->info);
    preordAux(rt->leftChild, processNode);
    preordAux(rt->rightChild, processNode);
  }
}
```

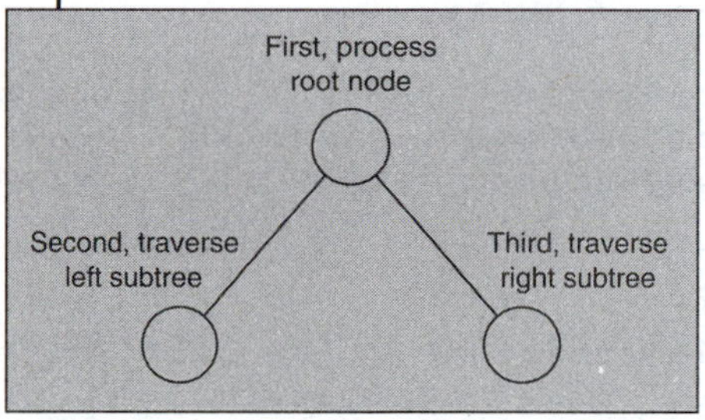

The **public** preorder traversal function must merely pass the **root** pointer for the tree to the auxiliary function. As in Chapter 6, we employ the technique that retains the public interface to an operation by making the function corresponding to that operation a trivial front-end function that merely passes critical parameters to an auxiliary recursive function. This auxiliary function is hidden from clients of the class in a **private** declaration.

```
// Implementation of preorderTrav
template <class BaseData>
void BinTree<BaseData>::preorderTrav(void (*processNode)(BaseData &item))
{
  preordAux(root, processNode);
}
```

Inorder Traversal

The inorder traversal of a binary tree proceeds as outlined in the following three ordered steps:

1. First, recursively traverse (and visit all nodes in) the left subtree.
2. Then, visit and process the root node.
3. Finally, recursively traverse (and visit all nodes in) the right subtree.

By carefully following these steps for the tree of Figure 7.7 and assuming that "process" means "print," we obtain the readily recognizable infix expression

$$A - B + C * E / F$$

Unless we add parentheses, this infix expression is not algebraically equivalent to the order of operations reflected in the tree of Figure 7.7. The fact that prefix and postfix notations do not require parentheses to avoid such ambiguities makes them distinctly superior to infix notation for evaluation purposes.

A more formal statement of the recursive algorithm for an inorder traversal is given in the following pair of functions used with a linked representation of a binary tree:

```
private:
  // A private auxiliary function for implementing the inorder traversal
  void inordAux (BtNode<BaseData> *rt, void (*processNode)(BaseData &item));
.
.
.
// Implementation of inordAux
template <class BaseData>
void BinTree<BaseData>::inordAux(BtNode<BaseData> *rt,
                                 void (*processNode)(BaseData &item))
{
  if (rt != NULL)
  {
    inordAux(rt->leftChild, processNode);
    processNode(rt->info);
    inordAux(rt->rightChild, processNode);
  }
}

// Implementation of the public inorderTrav function
template <class BaseData>
void BinTree<BaseData>::inorderTrav(void (*processNode)(BaseData &item))
{
  inordAux(root, processNode);
}
```

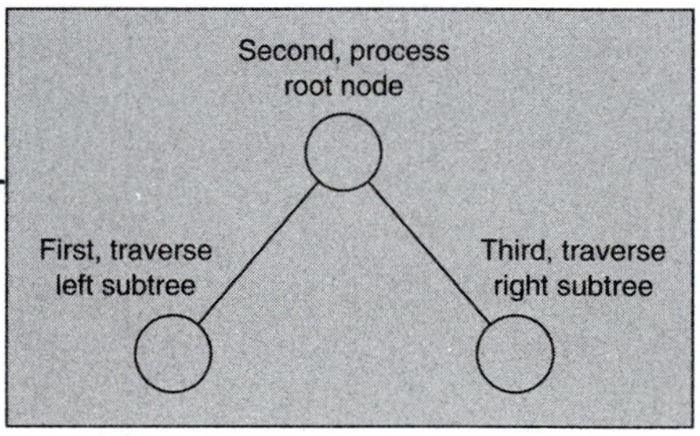

Postorder Traversal

The third standard traversal of a binary tree, the *postorder traversal,* entails an arrangement of options that postpones processing the root node until last.

1. First, recursively traverse (and visit all nodes in) the left subtree of the root node.
2. Then, recursively traverse (and visit all nodes in) the right subtree of the root node.
3. Finally, visit and process the root node.

You will carry out the implementation of the postorder traversal in the exercises.

Although here we have illustrated the three traversal algorithms using binary expression trees, we emphasize that the traversals apply in general to *any* binary tree. Indeed, as we shall see in the next section, when used in combination with a tree exhibiting the hierarchical ordering property, the inorder traversal will neatly allow us to implement an ordered list using a binary tree.

Exercises 7.2

1. You are writing a program that uses a binary tree. To make it easy to trace its structure, you implement pointers using an **Array** of **structs** indexed from 1. Consider the following binary tree:

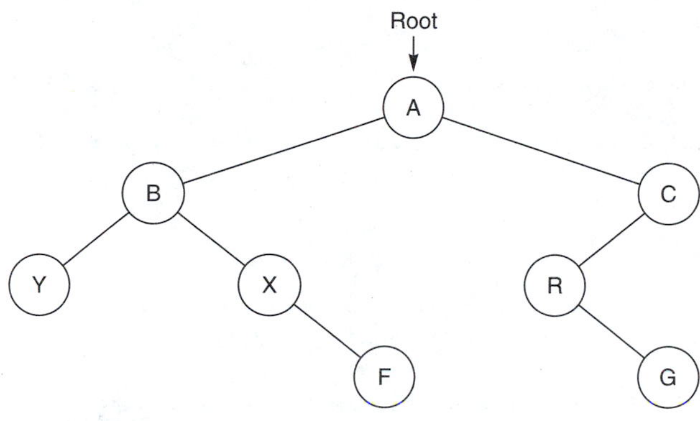

   a. Indicate the contents of **root** and **avail** pointers and **leftChild** and **rightChild** fields in the Array **tree** that follows:

Array tree

Location	info	leftChild	rightChild
1	C		
2	R		
3	G		
4	F		
5	X		
6	Y		
7	B		
8	A		
9			

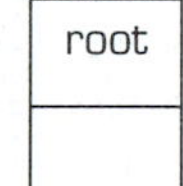

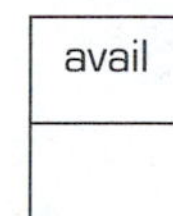

   b. Show the contents of **root** and **avail** pointers and **leftChild** and **rightChild** fields after a node containing J has been inserted as the left child of X and then after R has been deleted with G becoming the left child of C.

2. How is a linked representation of a binary tree an improvement over its linear representation? In what ways could the linked representation be less efficient?
3. Suppose that we add the following **treeWalk** operation and its associated auxiliary function to the **BinTree** class. What output would be produced for the tree pictured below?

```
// Interface for a new public function in the
// BinTree class

void treeWalk();

// Interface for an auxiliary function to
// implement the treeWalk function

void treeWalkAux(BtNode<BaseData> *rt);

// Implementation of the public function
template <class BaseData>
void Bintree<BaseData>::treeWalk()
{
  treeWalkAux(root);
}

// Implementation of treeWalkAux
template <class BaseData>
void BinTree<BaseData>::treeWalkAux
      (BtNode<BaseData> *rt)
{
  if (rt == NULL)
    cout << "OOPS" << endl;
  else
  {
    treeWalkAux(rt->rightChild);
    treeWalkAux(rt->leftChild);
    cout << rt->info << endl;
  }
}
```

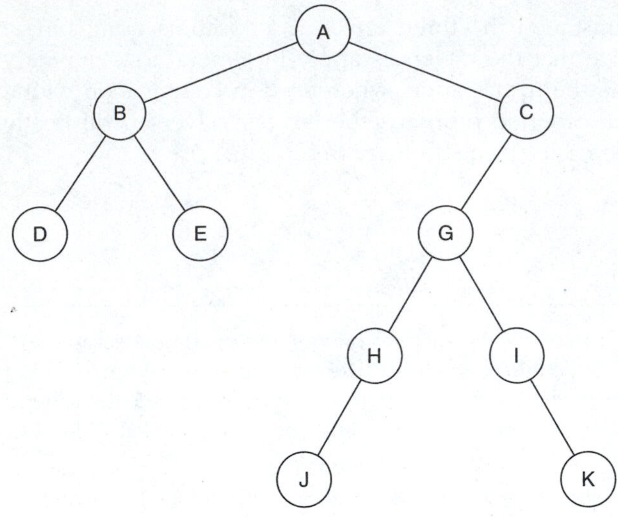

4. How does the output from Exercise 7.2.3 change if the second **cout** instruction is moved ahead of the recursive calls to **treeWalkAux**?
5. How does the output from Exercise 7.2.3 change if the second **cout** instruction is located between the recursive calls to **treeWalkAux**?
6. Repeat Exercises 3, 4, and 5 of this section for the following tree:

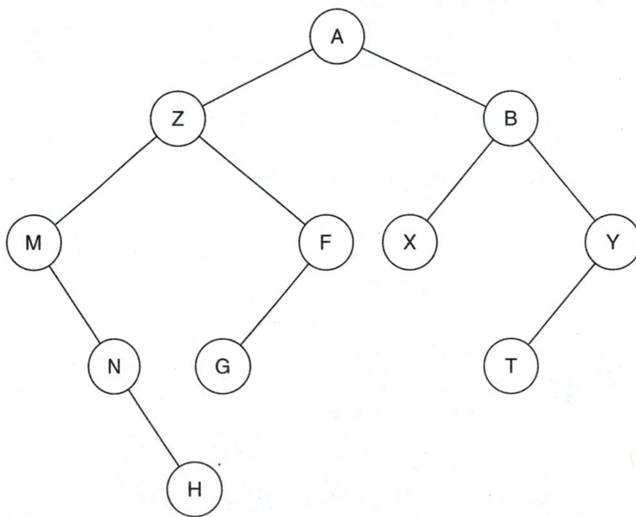

7. Given the following postorder and inorder traversals of a binary tree, draw the tree

   Postorder: A B C D E F I K J G H
   Inorder: C B A E D F H I G K J

   Attempt to deduce your answer in a systematic (and recursive) fashion, not by trial-and-error methods.
8. How could the inorder traversal of a binary tree be used to sort data?
9. A *ternary tree* is a tree in which each node has a left, middle, and right subtree. Suppose that we have **TernaryNode** and **TernaryTree** classes analogous to the **BtNode** and **BinTree** classes, with each **TernaryNode** having a **middleChild** pointer as well as **leftChild** and **rightChild** pointers. Consider the following **treeWalk** method and its associated auxiliary function. What output would be produced for the tree pictured below?

```
// Interface for a public function in the
// TernaryTree class

void treeWalk();

// Interface for an auxiliary function to
// implement the treeWalk function

  void treeWalkAux(ternaryNode<BaseData> *rt);

// Implementation of the public function
template <class BaseData>
void TernaryTree<BaseData>::treeWalk()
{
  treeWalkAux(root);
}

// Implementation of treeWalkAux
template <class BaseData>
void TernaryTree<BaseData>::treeWalkAux
      (TernaryNode<BaseData> *rt)
{
  if (rt == NULL)
    cout << "NULL" << endl;
  else
  {
    cout << rt->info << endl;
    treeWalkAux(rt->leftChild);
    treeWalkAux(rt->middleChild);
    treeWalkAux(rt->rightChild);
  }
}
```

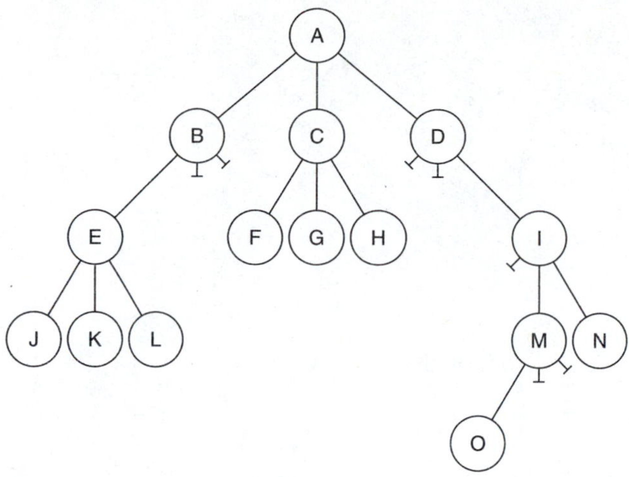

10. Given a linked implementation of a binary tree as described in this section, provide C++ code to implement the following binary tree operations:
    a. BinTree copy constructor
    b. ~BinTree
    c. BinTree assignment (overloaded =) operator
    d. empty
    e. noRoomLeft
    f. postorderTrav
11. Provide the class data members for a linear representation of a binary tree. Then, using your definition, write C++ code for the following binary tree operations.
    a. BinTree constructor (choose appropriate one)
    b. BinTree copy constructor
    c. ~BinTree
    d. BinTree assignment (overloaded =) operator
    e. empty
    f. noRoomLeft
    g. preorderTrav
    h. postorderTrav
    i. inorderTrav
12. Given a linked implementation of a binary tree, analyze the time and space efficiencies of the traversal algorithms developed in this section. On what factors do these efficiencies depend?

7.3 Binary Search Trees

The data structures we have studied so far offer two strategies for implementing a list of records that is maintained in order by some key field such as a name or an ID number. Storing the records in an array would allow the fast inspection of records via the binary search algorithm but would also necessitate excessive data movement when records are added to or deleted from the list. Storage of the records in an ordered linked list would handle additions and deletions nicely but presents us with an undesirable $O(n)$ search efficiency due to the lack of random access, which forces a sequential search strategy. In this section, we will see that by implementing an ordered list using a binary tree, we can achieve efficiency in both searching and adding or deleting while keeping the list in order. Moreover, we do not have to pay too great a price in other trade-offs to achieve this best of both worlds.

The particular kind of binary tree used in this application is known as a *binary search tree* and is organized via the hierarchical ordering property discussed in Example 7.2. Recall that this ordering property stipulates the following:

> For any given data item X in the tree, every node in the left subtree of X contains only items that are less than X with respect to a particular type of ordering. Every node in the right subtree of X contains only items that are greater than or equal to X with respect to the same ordering.

For instance, the tree of Figure 7.17 illustrates this property with respect to alphabetical ordering. You can verify quickly that an inorder traversal of this tree (in which the processing of each node consists merely of printing its contents) leads to the following alphabetized list:

Figure 7.17
Ordering property with respect to alphabetical ordering.

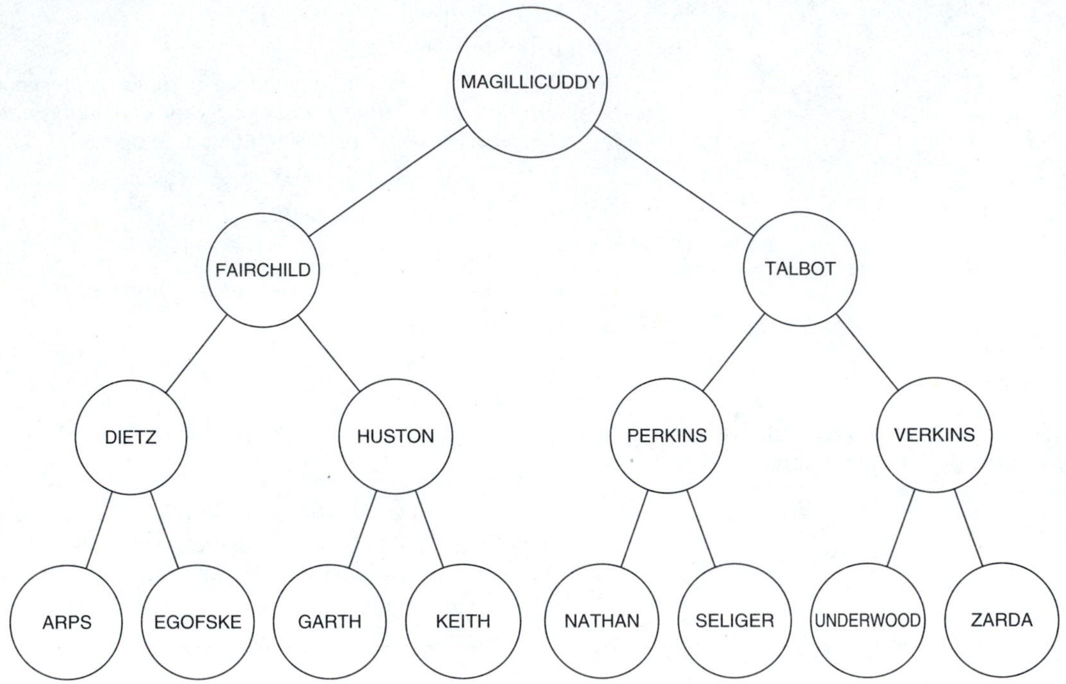

ARPS
DIETZ
EGOFSKE
FAIRCHILD
GARTH
HUSTON
KEITH
MAGILLICUDDY
NATHAN
PERKINS
SELIGER
TALBOT
UNDERWOOD
VERKINS
ZARDA

This reinforces the important conclusion of Example 7.2. That is, an inorder traversal of a binary tree that has the ordering property will visit nodes in ascending order with respect to their data values. Hence, such a tree may be viewed as an ordered list. The first list element is the first node visited by the inorder traversal. More generally, the *n*th node visited by the inorder traversal corresponds precisely to the *n*th element in the list. Given this view of a binary search tree as an implementation of an ordered list, we now consider the operations of adding, deleting, and finding nodes in the list.

Figure 7.18
Tree in Figure 7.17 with the insertion SEFTON.

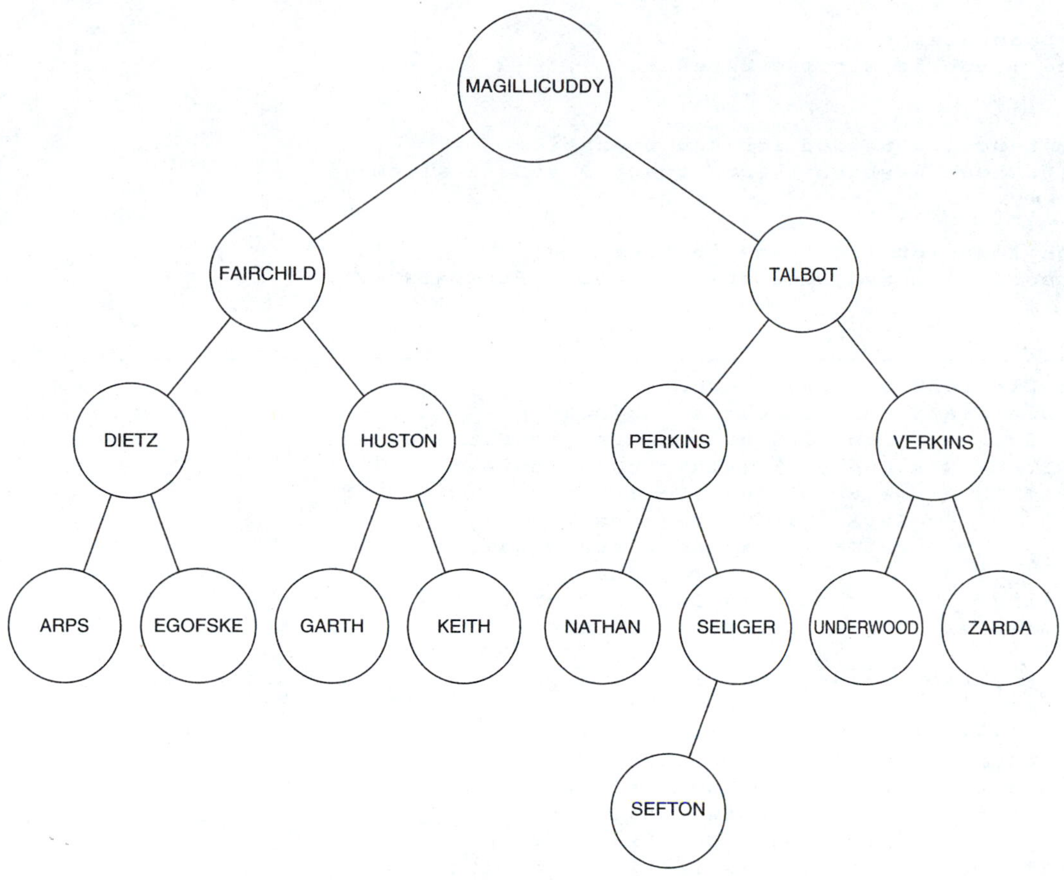

Adding Nodes to a Binary Search Tree

Insertion of a new string into the binary search tree of Figure 7.17 is a fairly easy process that may well require significantly fewer comparisons than insertion into a linked list. Consider, for example, the steps necessary to insert the string SEFTON into this tree in a way that maintains the ordering property. We must

1. Compare SEFTON to MAGILLICUDDY. Because SEFTON is greater than MAGILLICUDDY, follow the **rightChild** pointer to TALBOT.
2. Compare SEFTON to TALBOT. Because SEFTON is less than TALBOT, follow the **leftChild** pointer to PERKINS.
3. SEFTON is greater than PERKINS. Hence, follow the **rightChild** pointer to SELIGER.
4. SELIGER is a leaf node, so SEFTON may be added as one of its children. The **leftChild** is chosen because SEFTON is less than SELIGER.

The resulting tree for this insertion is given in Figure 7.18.

Example 7.5

In this example we extend the abstract base class **BinTree** defined in Section 7.1 to a binary search tree class. To carry out this task, we will first derive a class **BinSrchTree** from the **BinTree** class.

```
// BaseData is either a C++ built-in type, or a C++ class that has
// an assignment operation that overloads the "=" operator and an
// equality test that overloads the "==" operator.

template <class BaseData>
class BinSrchTree : public BinTree<BaseData>
{
  private:
    // Auxiliary function needed for add operation
    void addAux(BtNode<BaseData> *&rt, const BaseData &item);

  protected:
    // Comparison function for items in tree
    BOOLEAN (*precedes)(const BaseData &x, const BaseData &y);

  public:
// ---------------------------------------------------------------------------
// Interface for BinSrchTree constructor
// GIVEN:   An uninitialized BinSrchTree object;
//          precedes -- a function to compare BaseData values:
//             GIVEN:   x and y -- values to compare
//             RETURN as value of function:
//                        TRUE   if x precedes y,
//                        FALSE  if x and y are equal, or
//                               if y precedes x.
// RETURN:  The BinSrchTree object is initialized to the empty tree, with
//          precedes establishing the hierarchical ordering of the tree.

    BinSrchTree (BOOLEAN (*precedes)(const BaseData &x, const BaseData &y));

// ---------------------------------------------------------------------------
// Interface for BinSrchTree copy contructor
// GIVEN:   An uninitialized BinSrchTree object;
//          initbstree -- a BinSrchTree object that was
//                        previously constructed.
// RETURN:  The BinSrchTree object is initialized with the node values,
//          precedes function, and number of nodes of initbstree.

    BinSrchTree(BinSrchTree<BaseData> &initbstree);

// ---------------------------------------------------------------------------
// Interface for BinSrchTree assign = operator
// GIVEN:    A previously constructed BinSrchTree object;
//           source -- a second BinSrchTree object that must have
//                     been constructed with the same BaseData type as
//                     the owner of the assign operator.
// RETURN:   The contents of source have been copied to the BinSrchTree
//           object that owns the operation.
// RETURN as value of function: void

    void operator = (const BinSrchTree<BaseData> &source);

// ---------------------------------------------------------------------------
// Interface for add operation
// GIVEN:   A BinSrchTree object;
//          item -- a value of type BaseData.
// RETURN:  item is added to the binary search tree in fashion that
//          retains the ordering property of the tree.
// RETURN as value of function: void

    virtual void add (const BaseData &item);
};
```

Implementing the **BinSrchTree** class requires the coding of five functions, three of which we discuss in detail—the constructor, the **add** function, and a recursive auxiliary function **addAux** that is needed by **add**. The **BinSrchTree** constructor must merely invoke the constructor of the base class and then set the protected **precedes** function to the **precedes** parameter that it receives.

```
template<class BaseData>
BinSrchTree<BaseData>::
  BinSrchTree(BOOLEAN (*precedes)(const BaseData &x, const BaseData &y))
  : BinTree<BaseData>()
{
  this->precedes = precedes;
}
```

The **add** and **addAux** functions work together as front-end and associated recursive workhorses, respectively. The function **add** passes the **root** pointer to **addAux**, which recurses down a path in the tree until it comes to a NULL pointer. When it does, it sets that NULL pointer to reference the new node that is being added.

```
template<class BaseData>
void BinSrchTree<BaseData>::add(const BaseData &item)
{
  addAux(root, item);
}

template<class BaseData>
void BinSrchTree<BaseData>::addAux(BtNode<BaseData> *&rt, const BaseData &item)
// Note that since the pointer rt will be altered by this function,
// it must be passed by reference.
{
  if (rt == NULL)
  {
    rt = new BtNode<BaseData>;
    rt->info = item;
    rt->leftChild = NULL;
    rt->rightChild = NULL;
  }
```

40
item = 52
30
50
25
35
45
55
When rt is the leftChild pointer of the 55 node, 52 can be inserted here.

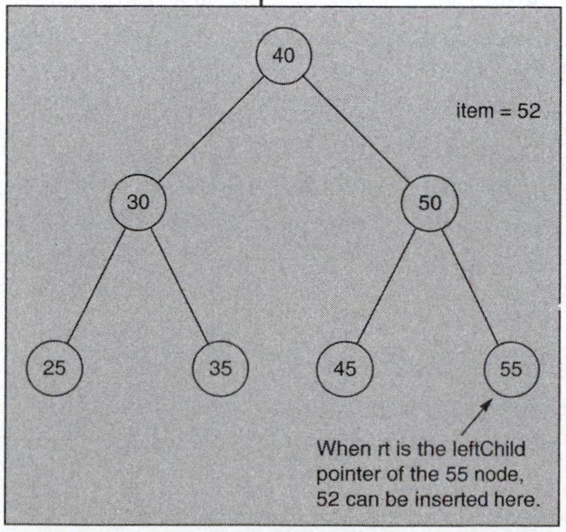

```
  else
    if (precedes(item, rt->info))
      addAux(rt->leftChild, item);
    else
      addAux(rt->rightChild, item);
}
```

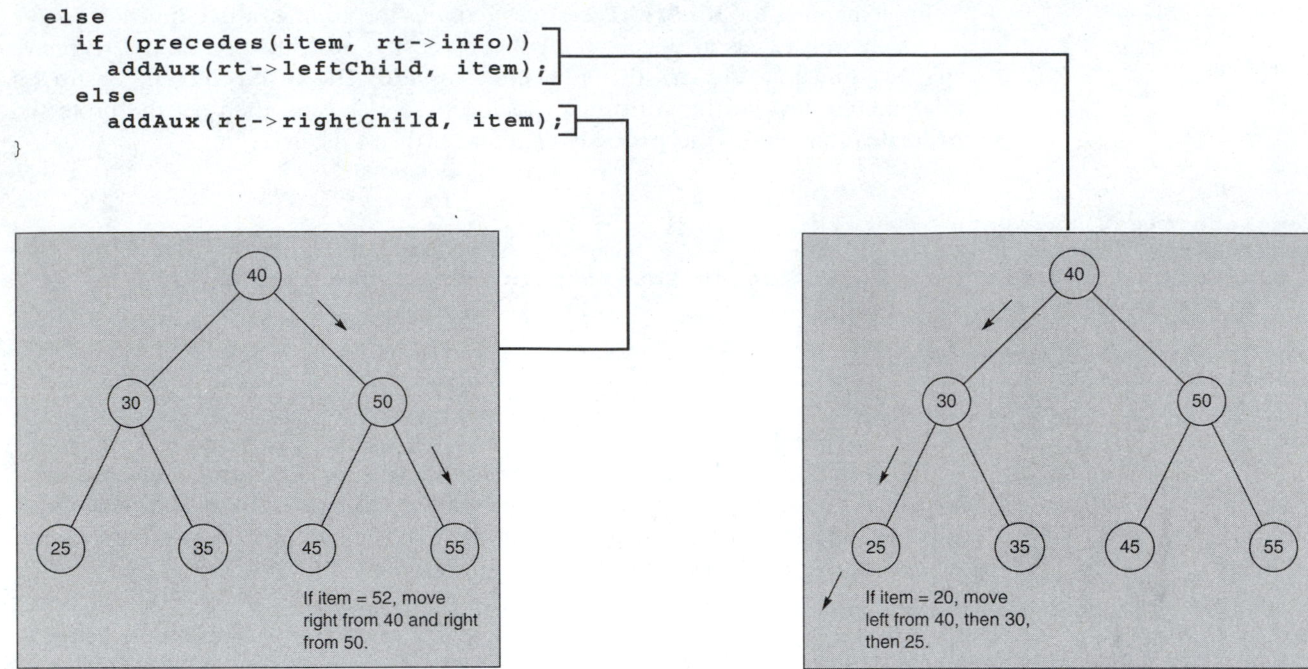

The result of applying the **add** and **addAux** functions to the succession of items given by

JEPHTHAH
GILLIAN
ALMA
LETITIA
PERCY
TYBALT
DUNSTAN
HEDWIG
KASPAR

is the binary tree of Figure 7.19.

The algorithm of Example 7.5 implies that the insertion of new nodes will always occur at the leaf nodes of a tree. As with insertion into a linked list, no data are moved; only pointers are manipulated. However, unlike the steps required for insertion into an ordered linked list, we do not have to traverse the list sequentially to determine where a new node belongs. Instead, using the *insertion rule*—if less than, go left; otherwise, go right—we need merely traverse one branch of the tree to determine the position for a new node. Provided that the tree maintains a full shape, the number of nodes on a given branch will be at most

$$\log_2 n + 1$$

where n is the total number of nodes in the tree. By *full* we mean that all nodes with fewer than two children must occur at level m or $m - 1$ where m is the deepest level in the tree. In other words, all nodes above level $m - 1$ must have exactly two children. Hence, adding ROBERTS to the tree of Figure 7.18 by the insertion rule would destroy its fullness.

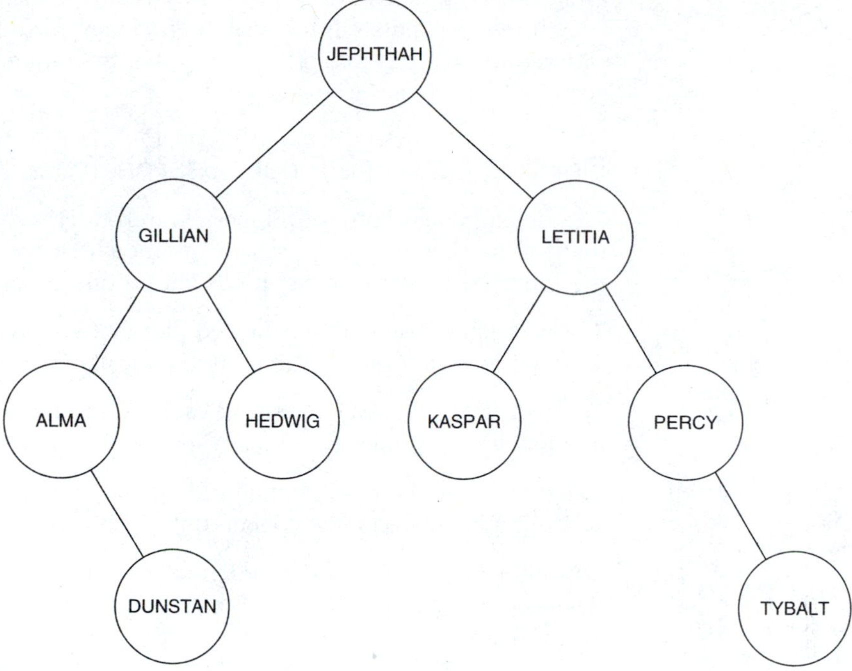

Figure 7.19
Binary tree resulting from **add** and **addAux** functions with sample data from Example 7.5.

Given this definition of full, the $(\log_2 n + 1)$ figure for the maximum number of nodes on a branch emerges immediately upon inspection or, more formally, using a proof by mathematical induction. Our purpose, however, is not to give the details of such a proof but rather to emphasize that a binary search tree presents an alternative to a linked list structure for the type of processing involved in maintaining ordered lists. Moreover, it is a particularly attractive alternative when the tree is full, because substantially fewer comparisons are needed to locate where in the structure an insertion is to be made. For instance, if n is 1024, the linked list may require as many as 1024 comparisons to make an insertion. Because $\log_2 1024$ is 10, the full binary search tree will require at most 11 comparisons. This difference becomes even more dramatic as n gets larger. For an ordered list with 1,000,000 entries, a linked list may require up to 1,000,000 comparisons, but the full binary search tree requires at most 21 comparisons.

What happens when the tree is not full? We comment on that situation at the end of this section, when we discuss the overall efficiency considerations for a binary search tree. Before that, however, we consider the operations of finding and deleting data in a binary search tree.

Searching for Data in a Binary Search Tree

The insertion rule also dictates the search path followed through a binary search tree when we are attempting to find a given data item. Interestingly, if we trace the nodes visited on such a search path for a full binary search tree, we will probe exactly the same items that we would in conducting a binary search on a physically ordered array containing the same data. For instance, if we are searching for SMITH in the tree of Figure 7.17, we will have to probe MAGILLICUDDY, TALBOT, and PERKINS. These are precisely the items that would be probed if the binary search algorithm were applied to the physically ordered array associated with Figure 7.17.

Our analysis of such a tree has allowed us to conclude that, as long as the binary search tree remains full, the search efficiency for this method of implementing an ordered list matches that of the ordered array implementation. That is, the best case search efficiency is $O(\log_2 n)$.

Deleting Data in a Binary Search Tree

The deletion algorithm for a binary search tree is conceptually more complex than that for a linked list. Suppose, for instance, that we wish to remove TALBOT from the binary search tree of Figure 7.17. Two questions arise.

1. Can such a deletion be achieved merely by manipulating pointers?
2. If so, what does the resulting tree look like?

To answer these questions, begin by recalling that the only property that must be continually maintained in a binary search tree is that, for each node in the tree,

1. The left subtree must contain only items less than that node.
2. The right subtree must contain only items greater than or equal to that node.

With the preservation of this ordering property as the primary goal in processing a deletion, one acceptable way of restructuring the tree of Figure 7.17 after deleting TALBOT appears in Figure 7.20; essentially, SELIGER moves up to replace TALBOT in the tree. The choice of SELIGER to replace TALBOT is made because SELIGER represents the greatest data item in the left subtree of the node containing TALBOT. As long as we choose this greatest item in the left subtree to replace the item being deleted, we guarantee preservation of the crucial ordering property that enables the tree to accurately represent an ordered list.

Figure 7.20
Restructuring the tree in Figure 7.17 after deleting TALBOT.

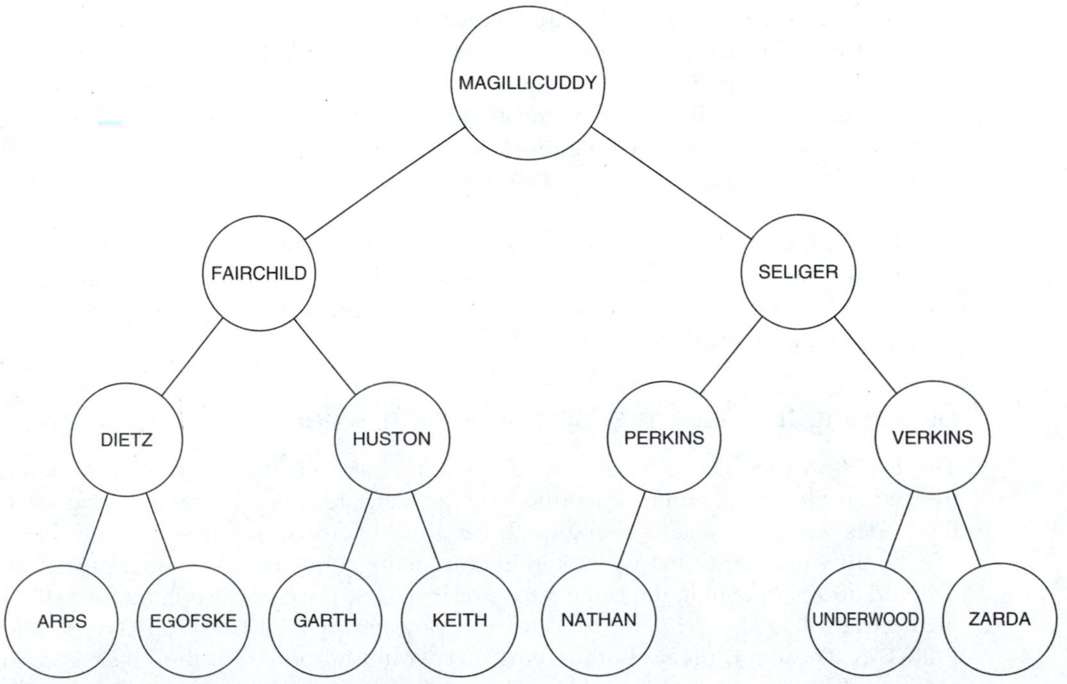

Figure 7.21
Three possibilities for the pointer **p**, representing a node to be deleted.

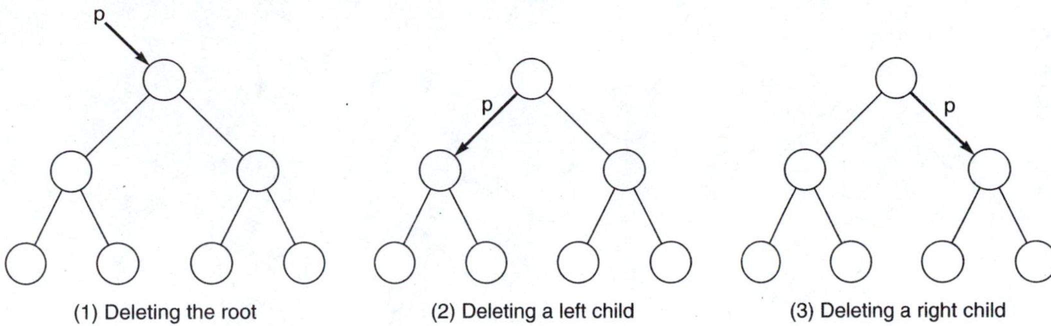

Given this general motivation for choosing a node to replace the one being deleted, let us now outline a case-by-case analysis of the deletion algorithm. Throughout this analysis, we assume that we have a pointer **p** to the item that we wish to delete. The pointer **p** may be one of the following:

1. The root pointer for the entire tree.
2. The left child pointer of the parent of the node to be deleted.
3. The right child pointer of the parent of the node to be deleted.

Figure 7.21 highlights these three possibilities; the algorithm applies whether 1, 2, or 3 holds. We now examine three cases of node deletion on a binary search tree.

1. The node to be deleted has a left child.
2. The node to be deleted has a right child but no left child.
3. The node to be deleted has no children.

Case 1 The node pointed to by **p**, that is, the node to be deleted, has a left child. In Figure 7.22, node M is to be deleted and has left-child K. In this case, because

Figure 7.22
Case 1 with **p->leftChild** (node K) having no right children.

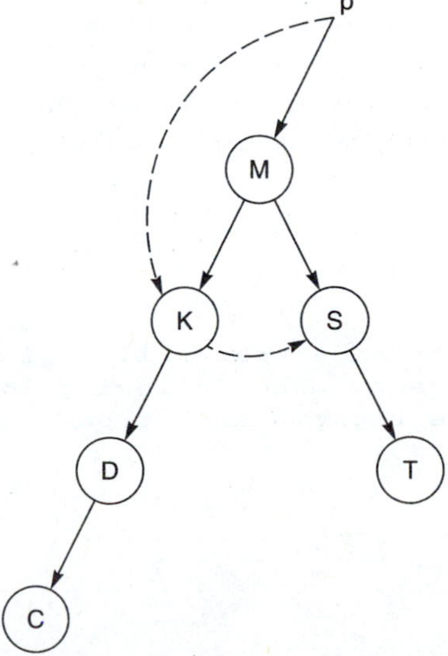

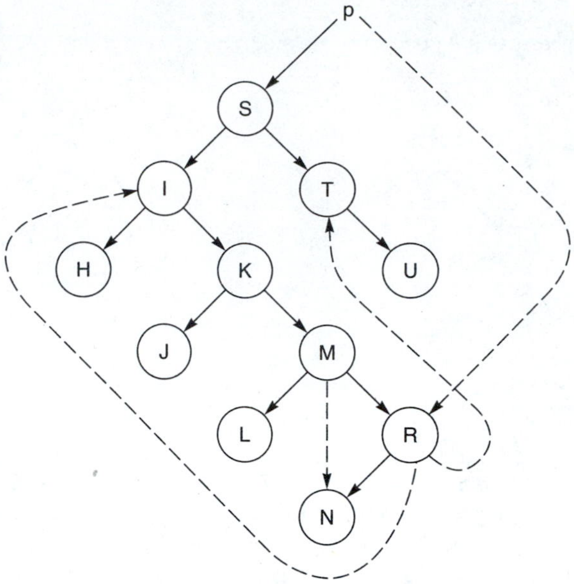

Figure 7.23
Case 1 with **p– >leftChild** having a right child.

we have a nonempty left subtree of the node to be deleted, our previous discussion indicates that we must find the greatest node in that left subtree. If the node pointed to by **p–>leftChild** (node K in the figure) has no right child, then the greatest node in the left subtree of **p** is **p–>leftChild** itself. Figure 7.22 pictorially describes this situation; the dotted lines indicate new pointer values.

The partial coding to achieve this pointer manipulation is given by

```
x = p;
p = x->leftChild;
p->rightChild = x->rightChild;
delete x;
```

If the node pointed to by **p–>leftChild** does have a right child, then to find the greatest node in the left subtree of **p** we must follow the right branch leading from **p–>leftChild** as deeply as possible into the tree. In Figure 7.23, node R is the one chosen to replace the deleted node. This figure gives the schematic representation, with the pointer changes necessary to complete the deletion. The coding necessary for this slightly more complicated version of Case 1 follows:

```
x = p;
q = x->leftChild->rightChild;
qParent = x->leftChild;

//  q will eventually point to the node that will replace p.
//  qParent will point to q's parent.  The following loop forces q
//  as deep as possible along the right branch from p->leftChild

while (q->rightChild != NULL)
{
  qParent = q;
  q = q->rightChild;
}
```

```
// Having found the node q to replace p, adjust pointers to
// appropriately link it into the tree

q->rightChild = x->rightChild;
p = q;
qParent->rightChild = q->leftChild;
q->leftChild = x->leftChild;
delete x;
```

Figure 7.24
In Case 2 the node pointed to by **p** has a right child but no left child.

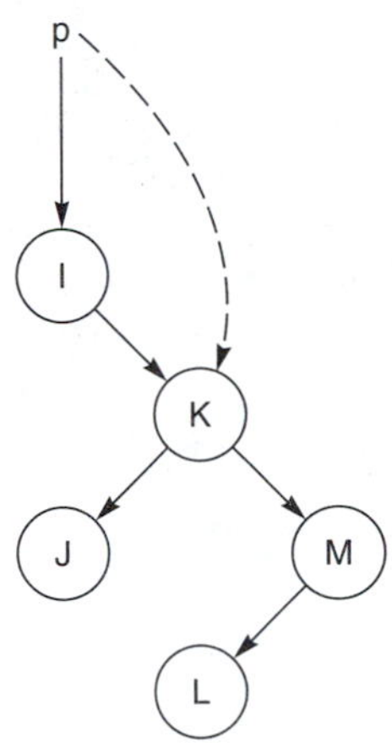

Case 2 The node pointed to by **p**, that is, the node to be deleted, has a right child but no left child. This case is substantially easier than Case 1 and is described in Figure 7.24. The node to be deleted is merely replaced by its right child. The necessary code is

```
x = p;
p = x->rightChild;
delete x;
```

Case 3 The node pointed to by **p**, that is, the node to be deleted, has no children. This is the easiest of all the cases. It can be compactly handled by the same coding used for Case 2 or, more directly, by

```
x = p;
p = NULL;
delete x;
```

Efficiency Considerations for Binary Search Trees

It is important to note that, in all three cases, the deletion of a node from the tree involved only pointer manipulation and no actual data movement. Hence, in an ordered list maintained with a binary search tree, we are able to process both insertions and deletions by the same pure pointer manipulation that makes linked lists so desirable. Moreover, the binary search tree approach apparently allows us to locate data for inspection, insertion, or deletion much faster than a linked-list representation would. However, there are aspects of the binary tree method that tarnish its performance in comparison to an ordered linked list:

- The binary tree implementation requires more memory in two respects. First, each node has two pointers instead of the one required in a singly linked list. This proliferation of pointers is particularly wasteful because many of the pointers may be NULL. Second, we presently can traverse the tree inorder only by using recursive techniques. Even in a language that allows recursion, a substantial amount of overhead is needed to maintain the stack used by recursive calls.
- The $O(\log_2 n)$ efficiency of the binary search tree method is only an optimal, not a guaranteed, efficiency. It is contingent on the tree remaining nearly full. Whether or not the tree remains full is in turn contingent on the order in which data are added and deleted. In the worst case, data entering the tree in the wrong order can cause the tree to degenerate into a glorified linked list, with a corresponding $O(n)$ efficiency. (The exercises at the end of this section have you explore this relationship between the order in which data arrive for insertion and the resulting search efficiency of the ordered binary tree.)

Both of these drawbacks can be overcome. We will see in Section 7.5 that we can actually avoid the overhead associated with recursion if we use a technique known as *threading,* which puts to good use the pointers that are otherwise wasted as NULL.

By using a technique known as *height balancing,* the binary search tree may be maintained in a fashion that approaches fullness at all times, regardless of the order in which data arrive for entry. We examine this technique in Section 7.6. However, be forewarned that both threading and height balancing add a considerable measure of complexity to the algorithms that manipulate binary search trees. Consequently, we will first turn our attention to the somewhat easier topic of binary trees with the heap property.

Exercises 7.3

1. Suppose that integers arrive in the following order for insertion into a binary search tree:

100 90 80 70 60 50 40 30 20 10

Draw the resulting tree, discuss its fullness, and categorize its search efficiency in big-O terms.

2. Repeat Exercise 7.3.1 but assume that the numbers arrive in the following order:

60 80 30 90 70 100 40 20 50 10

3. Repeat Exercise 7.3.1 but assume that the numbers arrive in the following order:

60 50 70 40 80 30 90 20 100 10

4. Describe a full binary search tree.

5. Discuss the relative merits of maintaining an ordered list by a binary search tree, a singly linked list, and a doubly linked list.

6. Discuss how the order in which data are entered into a binary search tree affects the fullness of the tree. Identify the best and worst possible cases.

7. Extend the **BinSrchTree** class by defining and implementing a recursive **retrieve** function to search for a target value in a binary search tree. Follow the style of Example 7.5.

8. Repeat Exercise 7.3.7 except write the function in a nonrecursive fashion.

9. Extend the **BinSrchTree** class by defining and implementing a **remove** function for a binary search tree. This operation should appropriately delete from the tree the node associated with a particular target value. Follow the style of Example 7.5. For an added challenge, use the "mirror image" of the three cases discussed in this section.

10. Write a nonrecursive version of the **add** function from Example 7.5.

11. Provide C++ code for the **add, retrieve,** and **remove** operations assuming that the linear representation of a binary search tree is used (see Section 7.2 and Exercises 7.3.7 and 7.3.9).

12. Suppose that you are given an array of data arranged in increasing order. Develop a function that will load the data from this array into an optimal binary search tree.

13. Suppose that we change the definition of the ordering property for a binary search tree to stipulate that nodes that are equal in value to a given node may appear in either the left or right subtree of the given node. Is this change acceptable or does it cause unreasonable complications? Explain your answer.

7.4 Applications: Heaps, Priority Queues, and Sorting

Recall from Example 7.1 that we defined a heap as a binary tree in which each node's value was greater than or equal to the values of all items in its left and right subtrees. For generality, we assume that "greater than" is relative to some precedence relationship that the heap constructor receives as a parameter. Moreover, the heaps we discuss in this section and later in the text also have the property that they are full binary trees of level m such that

1. All nodes with two children at level $m - 1$ appear to the left of any node with only one child at level $m - 1$.
2. Any node with only one child at level $m - 1$ appears to the left of all nodes with no children at level $m - 1$.
3. There is at most one node with only one child at level $m - 1$.

Figure 7.25
The difference between fullness and denseness.

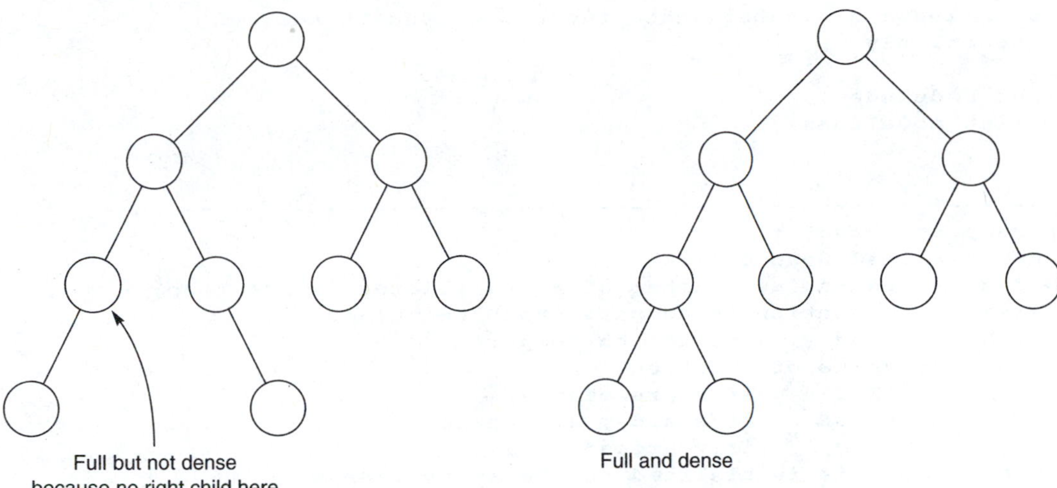

Let us call this property *denseness.* Note that the heap in Example 7.1 is not dense, nor, in general, will a full tree necessarily be dense. Figure 7.25 illustrates two full trees with nine nodes; the one on the left is not dense, but the one on the right is. By maintaining the denseness of the heaps we manipulate, we can embed them in an array using the linear representation strategy described in Section 7.2 and not pay any price in wasted storage.

Our implementation of a heap will rely on the following class hierarchy, with the **Heap** class derived from the **BinTree** class.

```
// BaseData is either a C++ built-in type, or a C++ class that has
// an assignment operation that overloads the "=" operator.

template <class BaseData>
class BinTree
{
  // The following data members allow a linear array implementation of a tree
  protected:
    int maxAllowed;                // Maximum number of nodes allowed in heap
    int numNodes;                  // Number of nodes currently in the heap
    Array<int, BaseData> *nodes;   // Array of data nodes

  public:   // The public operations of BinTree do not change
  :

};

template <class BaseData>
class Heap : public BinTree<BaseData>
{
  protected:
```

```
    // Comparison function for items in tree
    BOOLEAN (*precedes)(const BaseData &x, const BaseData &y);

    // walkUp and walkDown are subordinate functions used by add and
    // remove, respectively

    void walkUp(int nodeIndex);
    void walkDown(int nodeIndex);

  public:
//-----------------------------------------------------------------------
// Interface for Heap constructor
// GIVEN:    An uninitialized Heap object;
//           maxNodes -- the maximum number of nodes allowed in the heap;
//           precedes -- a function to compare BaseData values.
//              GIVEN:   x and y -- values to compare
//              RETURN as value of function:
//                        TRUE     if x precedes y,
//                        FALSE    if x and y are equal, or
//                                 if y precedes x.
// RETURN:   The Heap object is initialized to the empty tree with
//           the capacity to store maxNodes data nodes and with
//           precedes establishing the hierarchical ordering of the
//           tree.

    Heap(int maxNodes,
         BOOLEAN (*precedes)(const BaseData &x, const BaseData &y));

//-----------------------------------------------------------------------
// Interface for Heap copy contructor
// GIVEN:    An uninitialized Heap object;
//           initheap -- a Heap object that was previously constructed.
// RETURN:   The Heap object is initialized with the node values,
//           precedes function, and number of nodes of initheap.

     Heap(Heap<BaseData> &initheap);

//-----------------------------------------------------------------------
// Interface for Heap assign = operator
// GIVEN:    A previously constructed Heap object;
//           source -- a second Heap object that must have been
//                     constructed with the same BaseData type as
//                     the owner of the assign operator.
// RETURN:   The contents of source have been copied to the Heap
//           object that owns the operation.
// RETURN as value of function: void

    void operator = (const Heap<BaseData> &source);

//-----------------------------------------------------------------------
// Interface for add operation
// GIVEN:   A Heap object;
//          item -- a value of type BaseData.
// RETURN:  item is added to the heap in fashion that
//          retains the heap property of the tree.
// RETURN as value of function: void

    virtual void add(const BaseData &item);
```

```
//------------------------------------------------------------------------
// Interface for remove operation
// GIVEN:    A nonempty Heap object.
// RETURN:   The node with the largest value in the heap is removed, and the
//           tree is reshaped into a heap.
// RETURN as value of function:
//            The value of the node that was removed from the heap.

     virtual BaseData remove();
};
```

Note that the **Heap** constructor requires that we specify the maximum number of nodes for the heap as well as a precedence relationship to establish the hierarchical ordering of the heap. Also, note that a **Heap** includes a **remove** operation in addition to the pure virtual **add** operation that any usable binary tree must implement. In the course of developing the **add** and **remove** functions, we need two subordinate functions—**walkUp** and **walkDown**. The algorithm behind the second of these functions will also prove to be valuable in implementing a nonrecursive, $O(n \log_2 n)$ sort algorithm known as *heap sort*. Before elaborating on **walkUp** and **walkDown**, we must first implement the constructor for the **Heap** and its parent **BinTree** classes.

```
// BinTree and Heap constructors
template <class BaseData>
BinTree<BaseData>::BinTree(int maxNodes)
{
  numNodes = 0;                                  // Currently no nodes in tree
  maxAllowed = maxNodes;                         // No more than maxNodes allowed
  nodes = new Array<int,BaseData>(1,maxNodes);   // Allocate array with
                                                 // maxNodes nodes
}

template <class BaseData>
Heap<BaseData>::Heap(int maxNodes,
                     BOOLEAN (*precedes)(const BaseData &x, const BaseData &y))
                     : BinTree<BaseData>(maxNodes)
{
  this->precedes = precedes; // Set precedes to precedence relationship for tree
}
```

The protected member function **walkUp** is needed to add an item to the heap. The essence of **walkUp** relies on your viewing an array of **numNodes** values as having a dense binary tree embedded in it. Clearly, such an interpretation can be placed on any array of **numNodes** items under the relationships

Left child of node at index K is at index $2 \times K$
Right child of node at index K is at index $2 \times K + 1$

which were introduced in Section 3.2. Given this perspective, **walkUp** takes a given node in the underlying binary tree and "walks it up" the path leading to it until its parent on that path is greater than or equal to it.

Figure 7.26
Transformation affected by the **walkUp** function on a binary tree of 10 nodes, with the ninth node (at index 9, having value 40) being "walked up." Numbers outside circles indicate array index positions.

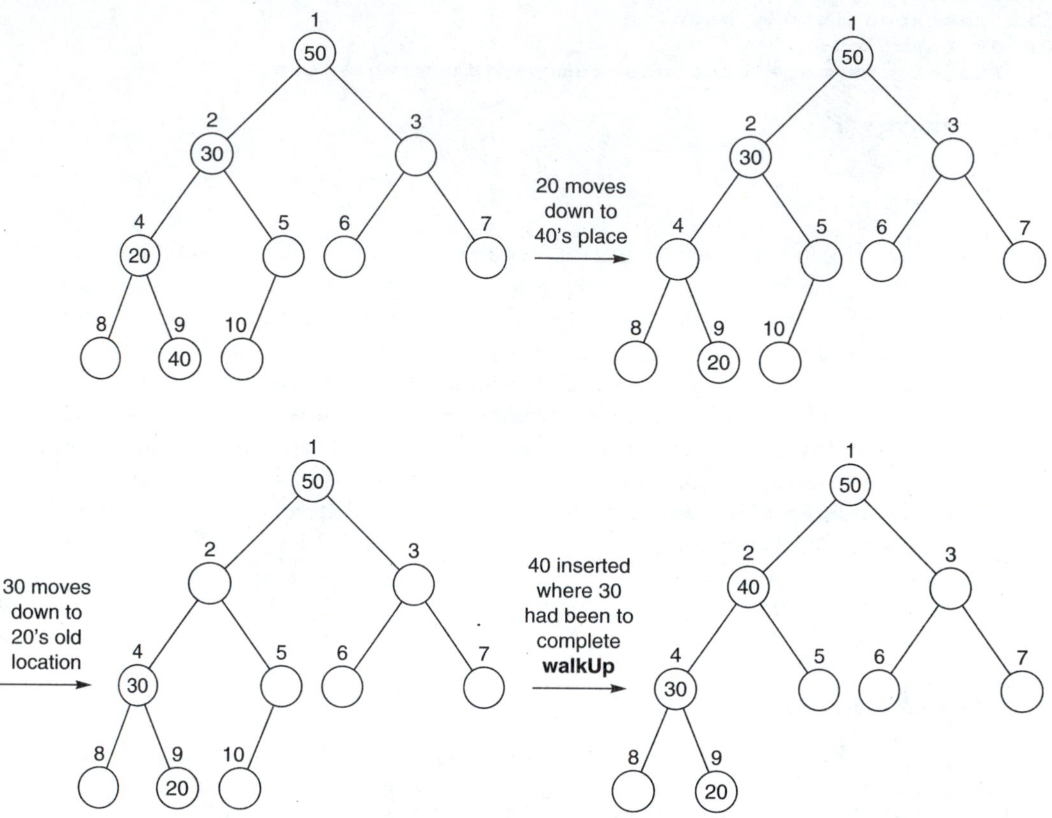

Figure 7.26 illustrates this transformation on a binary tree of 10 nodes with the ninth node designated as the node to be "walked up." Note that, if the node walked up is the only node that is out of place with respect to the heap property, then the tree will be a heap after the **walkUp** operation is performed. Because of this, **walkUp** will play a critical subordinate role in adding a new element to our heap structure.

```
//---------------------------------------------------------------------------
// Interface for walkUp function
// The nodes array is viewed as a dense binary tree, with all indices between
// 1 and numNodes containing tree data.  The nodes array is modified so
// that data originally at nodeIndex is "walked up" a path in the tree; that
// is, this data is repeatedly exchanged with its parent until it is less
// than its parent according to the precedence relation for the tree.

template <class BaseData>
void Heap<BaseData>::walkUp(int nodeIndex)
{
  int j,k;
  BaseData key;

  j = nodeIndex;
  key = (*nodes)[j];  // Key compared to values along appropriate path in tree
  k = j / 2;          // Initially k references parent of key
```

```
  // Continually try new parents for key
  while (k > 0)
    if (precedes((*nodes)[k], key))
    {
      (*nodes)[j] = (*nodes)[k];
      j = k;
      k = j / 2;
    }
    else
      break;
  (*nodes)[j] = key;
}
```

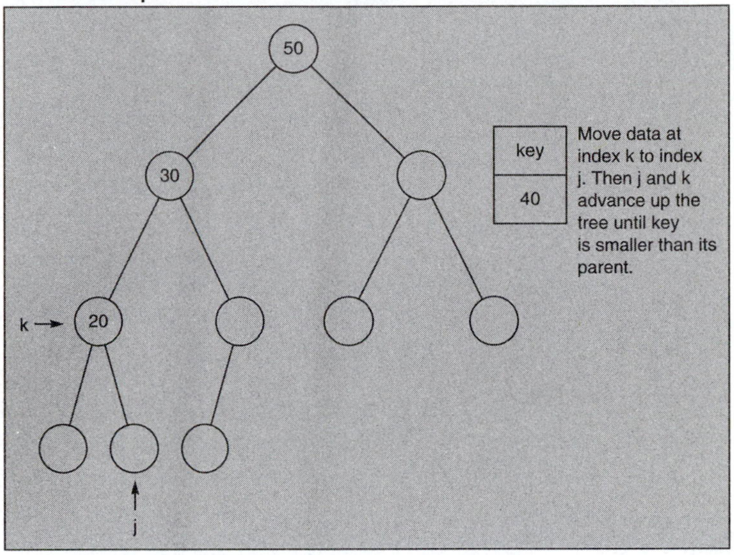

We can now use **walkUp** to make short work of the **add** operation for a binary tree that is to be maintained as a heap. Given a heap with **numNodes** nodes and a new datum **item** to add, we will temporarily attach **item** to the end of the array, that is, in the location following those nodes that have been arranged previously as a heap. Then, merely calling on **walkUp** for the new node will shift the entire tree into a heap. Hence, the **add** operation is implemented as follows:

```
template <class BaseData>
void Heap<BaseData>::add(const BaseData &item)
{
  if (numNodes < maxAllowed)
  {
    (*nodes)[++numNodes] = item;
    walkUp(numNodes);
  }
}
```

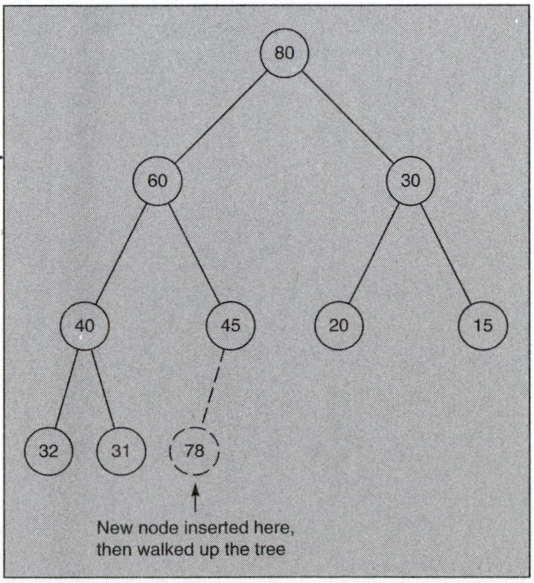

Efficiency of the Add Operation

The number of comparisons required to add a node to this implementation of a heap is clearly proportional to the length of the path that the new item travels as it is "walked up." But, since the tree is dense, our previous discussion of the number of levels in a full binary tree implies that this path length is $O(\log_2 n)$ for a tree with n nodes. Hence, we conclude that the efficiency of the **add** operation is also $O(\log_2 n)$.

The Heap as a Priority Queue and the Remove Operation

To implement the **remove** operation for a binary tree that is a heap, we are not concerned with finding a particular item to remove. If this were a concern, we should be using a binary tree with the ordering property for better search efficiency. Instead, we choose to view the heap as a means of implementing a priority queue (Section 4.5). Since removal from a priority queue always implies removing the item of highest priority, removal from a heap simply means removing the item at the root (the item of greatest value) and then shuffling the remaining tree nodes back into a heap.

To achieve this shuffling, we use a subordinate function called **walkDown**, which does the opposite of **walkUp**. That is, **walkDown** takes a node in the binary tree embedded in the array and walks that node down an appropriate path in the tree until it is greater than both of its children. Figure 7.27 illustrates the tree

Figure 7.27
Transformation affected by **walkDown** function on data 30 at index 1.

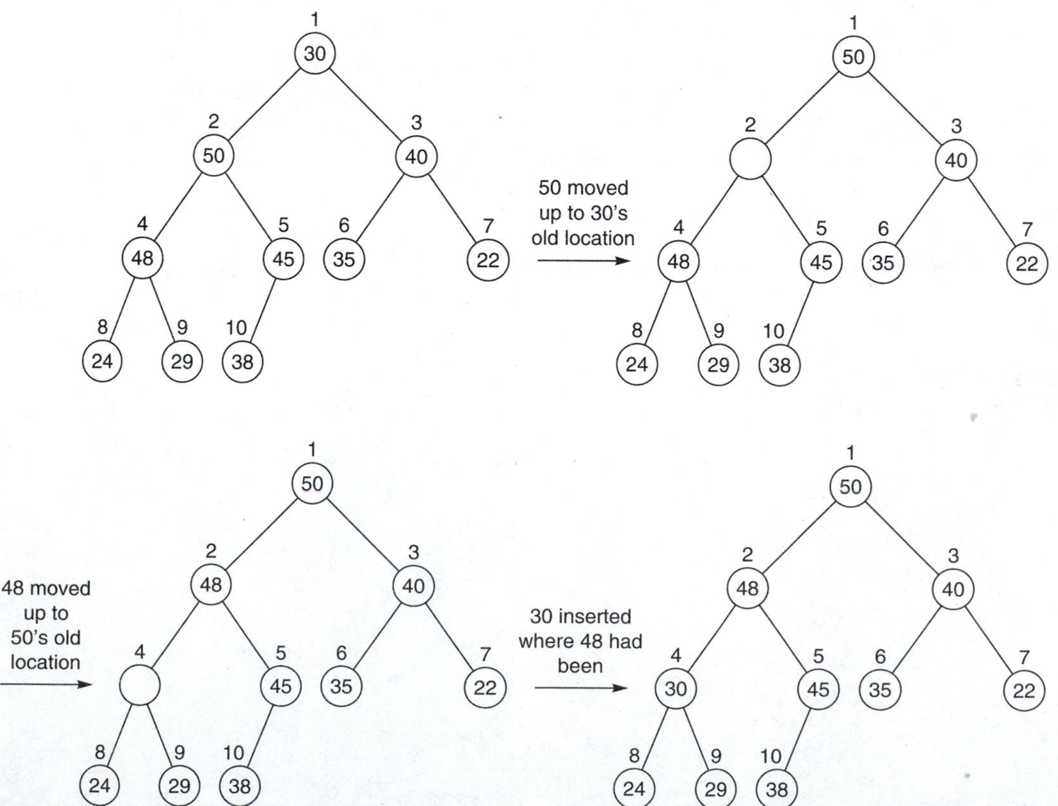

transformation affected by **walkDown**. As with the **walkUp** function, if **walkDown** is applied to the only node in a tree that is out of place with respect to the heap property, then the tree will be a heap after the **walkDown** operation is performed. The following C++ version of **walkDown**, with a small modification, can also be reused conveniently when we turn our attention to sorting via heaps.

```
//-------------------------------------------------------------------
// Interface for walkDown function
// The nodes array is viewed as a dense binary tree, with all indices
// between 1 and numNodes containing tree data.  The nodes array is
// modified so that data originally at nodeIndex is "walked down" a
// path in the tree; that is, repeatedly exchanged with the larger of
// its children until it is greater than its children according to the
// precedence relation for the tree.

template <class BaseData>
void Heap<BaseData>::walkDown(int nodeIndex)
{
  int j,k;
  BaseData key;

  j = nodeIndex;
  key = (*nodes)[j];// Key compared to values along appropriate path in tree
  k = 2*j;           // Initially k references left child
  while (k <= numNodes)
  {
    if (k < numNodes)   // Have k reference largest child
      if (precedes((*nodes)[k], (*nodes)[k+1]))
        ++k;
    if (precedes(key, (*nodes)[k])) // Then child must move up
    {
      (*nodes)[j] = (*nodes)[k];
      j = k;
      k = 2*j;
    }
    else       // Appropriate spot has been found
      break;
  }
  (*nodes)[j] = key;
}
```

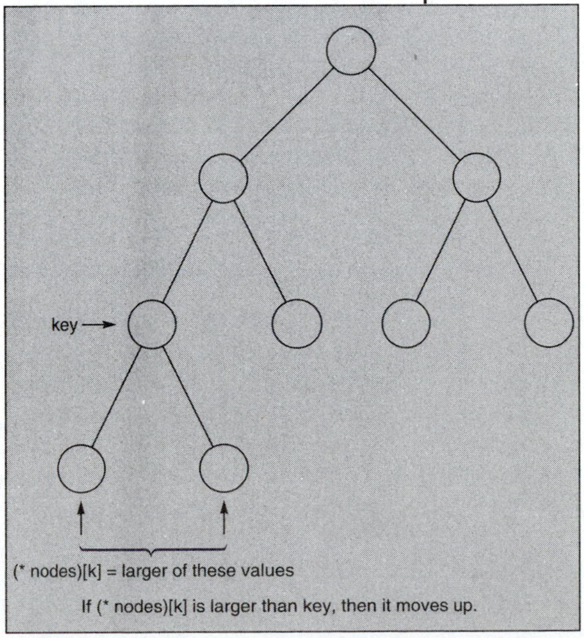

key →

(* nodes)[k] = larger of these values

If (* nodes)[k] is larger than key, then it moves up.

We can now remove a node from a heap (priority queue) by

1. Removing the root (the item of greatest priority).
2. Moving the last item temporarily to the root position.
3. Walking the new root item down the remaining tree until the tree is reformed as a heap.

The complete **remove** function, which invokes **walkDown**, follows:

```
template <class BaseData>
BaseData Heap<BaseData>::remove()
{
  BaseData temp;

   assert (numNodes > 0); // Verify precondition that heap is nonempty
   temp = (*nodes)[1];
   (*nodes)[1] = (*nodes)[numNodes--];
   walkDown(1);
   return(temp);
}
```

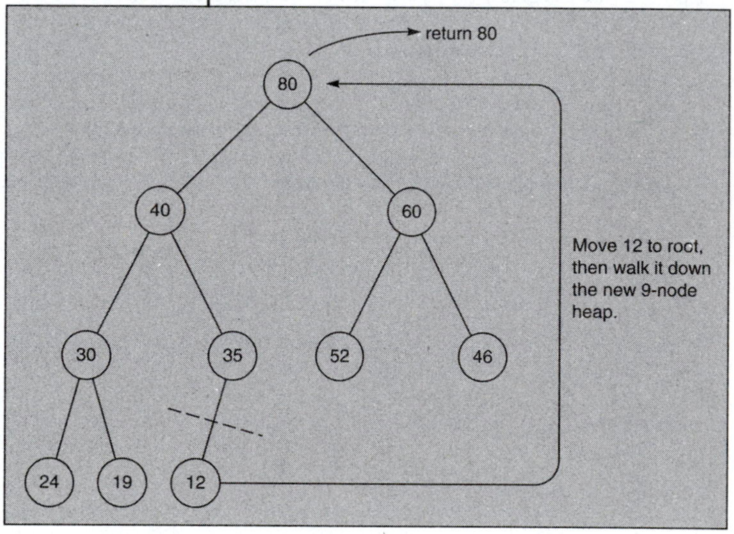

Efficiency of Remove Operation for a Heap

Since the **walkDown** function, like **walkUp**, performs comparisons limited to one path within a dense binary tree, deleting a node is an $O(\log_2 n)$ operation.

Sorting via Heaps—The Heap Sort Algorithm

We have just seen that a heap, embedded in an array via the linear representation for a binary tree, becomes a very efficient priority queue. The utility of heaps does not end here, however. We now see that viewing an array of n items as a binary tree that can be transformed into a heap provides the inspiration for a sorting algorithm that does the following:

Figure 7.28
Full binary tree corresponding to array.

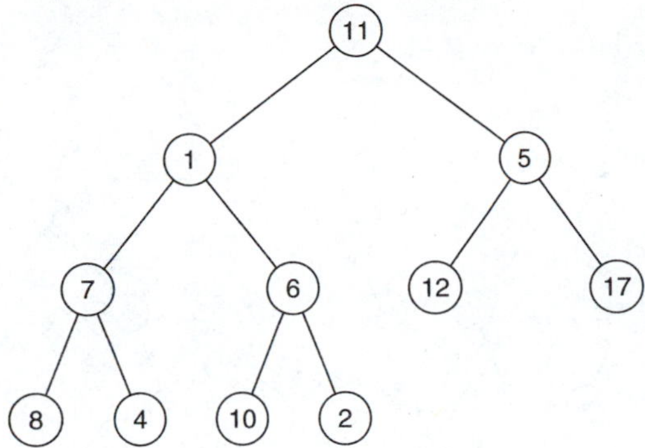

- Guarantees $O(n \log_2 n)$ efficiency (hence, putting it in the same big-O class as the merge and quick sort algorithms).
- Avoids the overhead associated with recursion (unlike merge and quick sorts).
- Sorts the array in place, not requiring an extra copy of the values (unlike merge sort).

These features make the *heap sort* algorithm an attractive alternative when space is at a premium or when your programming language does not support recursion. The method, originally described by R. W. Floyd, has two phases. (If you want to read Floyd's description of this method, see his article, "Algorithm 245: Tree Sort 3," *Communications of the ACM,* 7, December 1964, p. 701.) In the first phase, the array containing the n data items is transformed into a linear heap. As an example, suppose we wish to sort the following array:

11	1	5	7	6	12	17	8	4	10	2

The tree now appears as shown in Figure 7.28. In phase 1, to transform the embedded tree structure into a heap, we take the following steps:

1. Process the node that is the parent of the rightmost node on the lowest level. Call the **walkDown** algorithm with this node.
2. Move left on the same level. Again call the **walkDown** algorithm for this new node.
3. When the left end of this level is reached, move up a level, and, beginning with the rightmost parent node, repeat step 2. That is, call **walkDown** with this node and then move left along the same level.
4. Repeat step 3 until the root node has been processed.

Figure 7.29 shows these steps applied to the data in Figure 7.28.

Phase 2 of the heap sort finds the node with the largest value in the tree and cuts it from the tree. This is then repeated to find the second largest value, which is also removed from the tree. Then process continues until only two nodes are left in the tree; they are then exchanged if necessary. The precise steps for phase 2 are as follows:

1. Swap the root node with the bottom rightmost child, and sever this new bottom rightmost child from the tree. This is the largest value.

Figure 7.29
Phase 1 of heap sort applied to the binary tree in Figure 7.28.

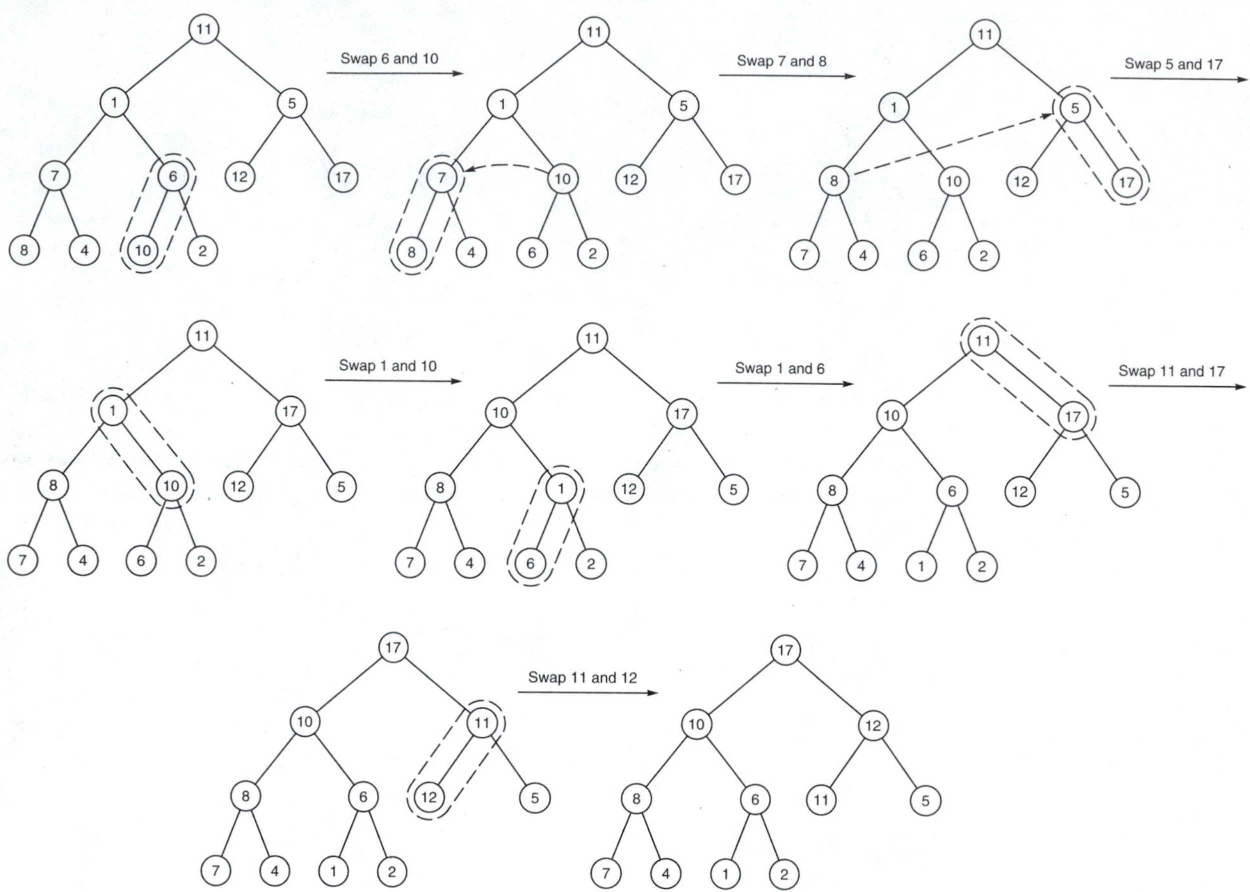

2. Call **walkDown** on the new root value. That is, the tree is being restored to a heap.
3. Repeat steps 1 and 2 until only one element is left.

Phase 2 of the heap sort begun in Figure 7.29 is shown in Figure 7.30 for the three highest values.

The **walkDown** algorithm we developed earlier in this section is clearly a critical subalgorithm in both phases. Don't forget that each time we call on **walkDown** we are performing an $O(\log_2 n)$ operation. Given the **walkDown** logic, phases 1 and 2 of heap sort may now be developed easily. The loop for phase 1 repeatedly calls on **walkDown** to form the tree into a heap. Then a loop for phase 2 repeatedly swaps the root of the tree with the last child and calls on **walkDown** to allow this new root to find an appropriate position in the heap. To implement the heap sort in the context of the **SortArray** class from Chapter 2, we must introduce **walkDown** as a protected function of the class. Also, this version of **walkDown** requires an additional parameter—the number of values in the array to be sorted.

Figure 7.30
Phase 2 of heap sort for three values.

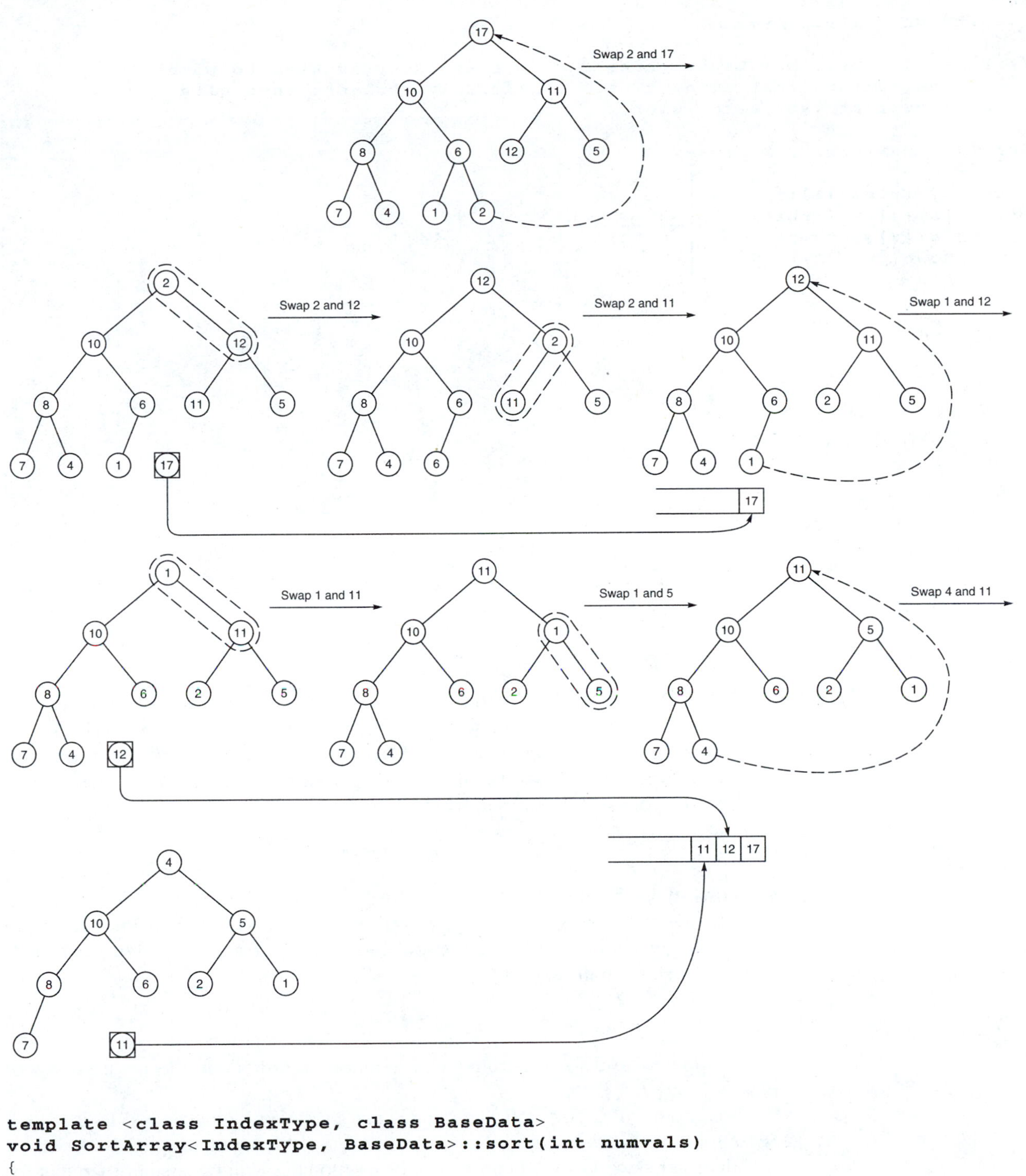


```
template <class IndexType, class BaseData>
void SortArray<IndexType, BaseData>::sort(int numvals)
{
  int y;
  BaseData temp;

  // First, phase 1 arranges the tree into a heap.
  // y starts at the last node to have a child.  Then repeatedly
```

```
  // call walkDown for index y on an array with numvals elements.

  for (y = numvals/2; y > 0; --y)
    walkDown(numvals, y);

  // Phase 1 done.  Now begin phase 2.  In phase 2, y is used to point
  // at the current last array slot.  Continually exchange root with
  // this current last array slot

  for (y = numvals; y > 1; --y)
  {
    temp = (*this)[1];
    (*this)[1] = (*this)[y];
    (*this)[y] = temp;
    walkDown(y-1, 1);
  }
}
```

Swap these two, remove leaf node from further consideration, and walk down new root.

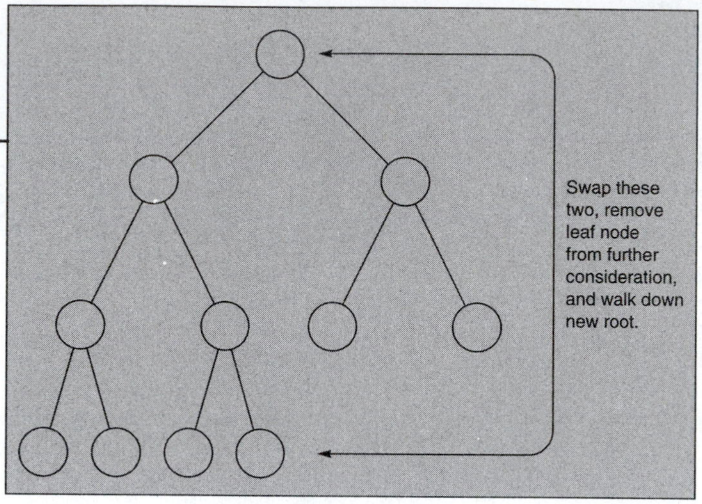

Efficiency of the Heap Sort

It is relatively easy to deduce that the heap sort requires $O(n \log_2 n)$ comparisons. To see this, note that the phase 1 loop in the preceding function will execute $n/2$ times. Inside this loop we call **walkDown**, which in turn has a loop that will execute at most $\log_2 n$ times (because it merely follows a path down a dense binary tree). Hence, phase 1 requires at most

$$(n/2) \log_2 n$$

iterations at its deepest level. Phase 2 may be similarly analyzed. The phase 2 loop iterates n times. Within each iteration, **walkDown** is called, again resulting in at most $\log_2 n$ operations. Thus, phase 2 requires at most $n \log_2 n$ iterations at its deepest level. Overall, we get

$$1.5n \log_2 n$$

as an upper bound for the number of iterations required by the combination of phases 1 and 2.

Thus, both quick sort and heap sort yield $O(n \log_2 n)$ efficiencies. In his book *Searching and Sorting,* Knuth has shown that, on the average, quick sort will be slightly faster since its big-O constant of proportionality will be smaller than that for heap sort. However, heap sort offers the advantage of guaranteeing an $O(n \log_2 n)$ efficiency regardless of the data being sorted. As we have already noted for quick sort in Chapter 6, worst case data can cause its performance to deteriorate to $O(n^2)$.

Exercises 7.4

1. Given the heap implementation described in this section, trace the status of the heap as each of the following operations is processed:

```
add 14
add 40
add 26
add 32
add 12
add 45
add 28
add 9
add 8
add 16
remove
remove
```

2. Repeat Exercise 7.4.1 using the following operations:

```
add 5
add 10
add 20
add 30
add 40
add 50
add 60
add 70
add 80
add 90
remove
remove
```

3. Consider the following heap:

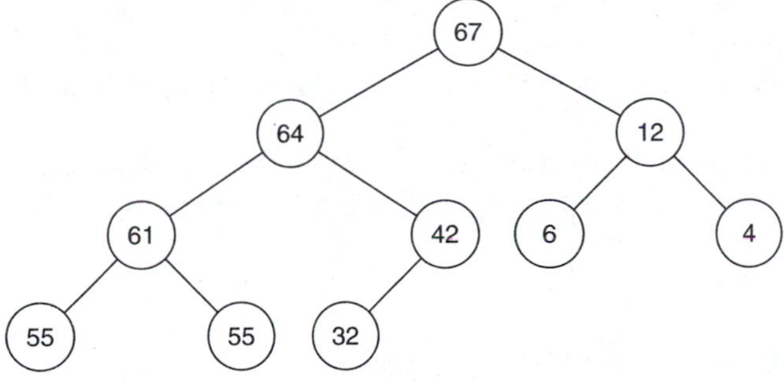

Specify an order in which these values could have arrived for insertion into this heap assuming the implementation described in this section.

4. One of the drawbacks of the linear array representation of a heap is that it places a static bound on the size of the heap. To avoid this, suppose that you decide to implement a heap using dynamically allocated pointers. Provide a class record description for such an implementation and then write C++ code for each heap operation. (*Hint:* Include a parent pointer in each node of the binary tree.)
5. The **walkDown** function used by the heap sort function in this section has a slightly different interface than the **walkDown** function used by a heap's **remove** function. Write a complete version of heap sort's **walkDown** function in the context of the **SortArray** class from Section 2.2.
6. Consider the heap sort function given in this section. Note that **walkDown** is called at two points in the function: once in phase 1 and again in phase 2. Suppose that we were to trace the contents of the array being sorted after each call to **walkDown**. What would we see as output if we called heap sort with an array that initially contained the following?

   60 12 90 30 64 8 6

7. Repeat Exercise 7.4.6 for a six-element array that initially contains the following:

   1 8 2 7 3 6

8. Is heap sort always better than quick sort? If not, when not?
9. What is the worst case and average case efficiency of the heap sort?
10. Give examples of arrays that generate the best and worst performances for the heap sort algorithm.
11. In Exercise 6.3.5, you evaluated the appropriateness of a collection of sorting algorithms for a particular application. Now evaluate the appropriateness of heap sort for that same application.
12. In Exercise 6.2.9, the notion of a stable sorting algorithm is defined. Is heap sort stable? If so, explain why. If not, provide an example of a data set that demonstrates its instability.

7.5 Threading a Tree to Eliminate Recursion

We have seen that a binary search tree can present an efficient alternative to ordered arrays and linked lists as a means of implementing an ordered list. One potential drawback to this strategy is that the algorithms to process binary trees are apparently recursive. This means that you must work in a language that supports

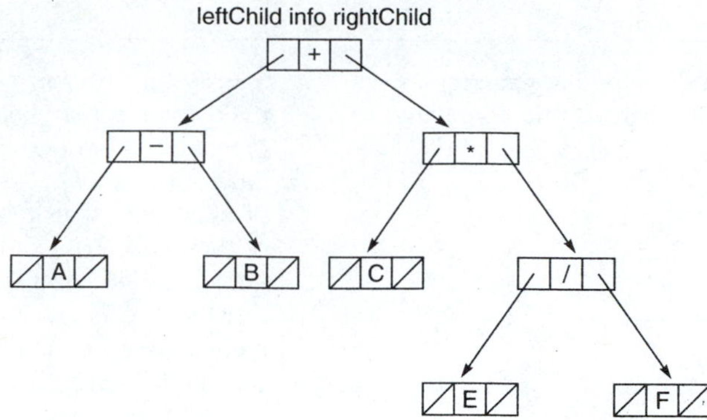

Figure 7.31
Example of binary expression tree to be threaded.

recursion and that sufficient stack space must be allocated to support the recursive calling sequence. However, the results of Exercises 7.3.8, 7.3.9, and 7.3.10 imply that nonrecursive algorithms exist for the **add**, **retrieve**, and **remove** operations on a binary search tree. In this section, we examine a technique called *threading* to eliminate the recursion from our inorder traversal algorithm. Hence, for a binary search tree, *all* frequently used operations may be implemented in a nonrecursive fashion.

Threading eliminates recursion at a very small price because it merely utilizes leaf node pointers that would otherwise be NULL. Consider the linked representation of a binary tree in Figure 7.31. There are ten wasted fields taken up by NULL pointers. These could be effectively used to point to significant nodes chosen according to a traversal scheme for the tree. For the inorder traversal of the binary tree in Figure 7.31, note that node A comes before − and that node B is preceded by − but followed by the root node +. With an inorder traversal, we could therefore adjust the **rightChild** pointer field of the node containing B (presently, NULL) to point to the node containing +, and the **leftChild** pointer field of the node containing B to point to its predecessor node (−). The inorder traversal of this tree yields the expression A − B + C ∗ E / F. Notice that B comes after − but before +. Similarly, because E is preceded by ∗ but followed by /, the NULL left link of the node containing E should, in our scheme, point to ∗. The NULL right link of E should point to /.

Because we are arranging pointers to the inorder predecessor and successor of a leaf node, we call the pointers *inorder threads*. Following a thread pointer allows

Figure 7.32
Threaded version of binary tree in Figure 7.31. Threads (indicated by a dashed line) that take the place of a left child pointer indicate the inorder predecessor, while threads that take the place of a right child pointer indicate the inorder successor.

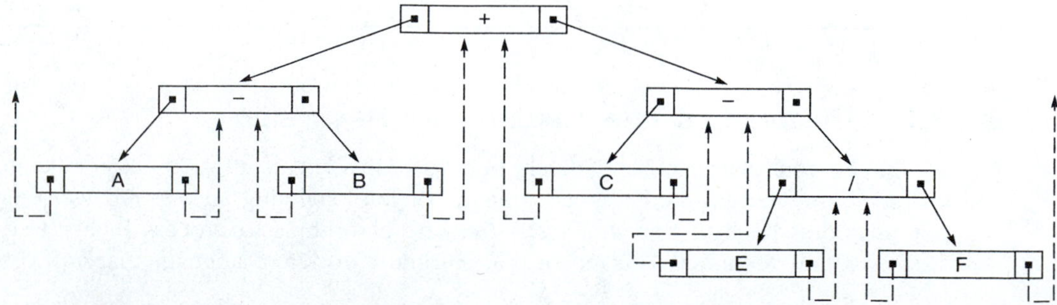

Figure 7.33
An empty, threaded binary tree. By using a dummy root node, initialized as shown, we can avoid treating the empty tree as a special case in our algorithm.

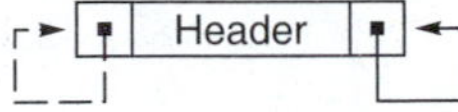

us to ascend strategically one or more appropriate levels in the tree without relying on recursion. Figure 7.32 is the transformed version of Figure 7.31 with threads indicated by dashed lines. Threads that take the place of a left child pointer indicate the inorder predecessor, whereas those that take the place of a right child pointer lead to the inorder successor.

The two threads on the far left and right of Figure 7.32 are the only loose threads at this stage. To correct this situation, we assume that a threaded binary tree is the left subtree of a dummy root node whose right child pointer points to itself. An empty, threaded binary tree drawn according to this convention is shown in Figure 7.33. This choice of a dummy root node for a threaded binary tree is similar to the strategy of using a dummy header for a linked list to eliminate consideration of special cases (see Section 3.3). By initially setting the pointers as indicated in Figure 7.33, we avoid having to treat the empty tree as a special case in our algorithm.

To keep track of which pointers are threads, we include two additional Boolean members of each node. One of these members, **leftThread**, indicates whether the left link of the node is an actual pointer or a thread. **rightThread** is used analogously for the right link. Let **p** be a pointer to a node. We follow the convention that, if **p–>leftThread** is FALSE, then **p–>leftChild** is a normal pointer. Similarly, **p–>leftThread** being TRUE means that the left link of the node pointed to by **p** is a thread pointer. Similar interpretations hold for **p–>rightThread**.

The purpose of this Boolean information as a means of identifying various pointers is only to facilitate writing algorithms for different modes of traversing the tree. When we incorporate the header and Boolean information into the tree of Figure 7.32, it takes the form of Figure 7.34.

To achieve an inorder traversal of the tree in Figure 7.34, we must proceed from each given node to its inorder successor. The inorder successor of a node is determined by one of two methods, depending on whether or not the right child pointer of the node in question is a thread or a normal pointer. If it is a thread, then it leads us directly to the inorder successor. If it is not a thread, then we must follow the right child pointer to the node it references and, from there, follow left child pointers until we encounter a left thread.

To convince yourself of this last step, consider the threaded tree given in Figure 7.35. In this tree, to get the inorder successor of the node containing M, we must

Figure 7.34
Threaded tree of Figure 7.32 with header and Boolean information.

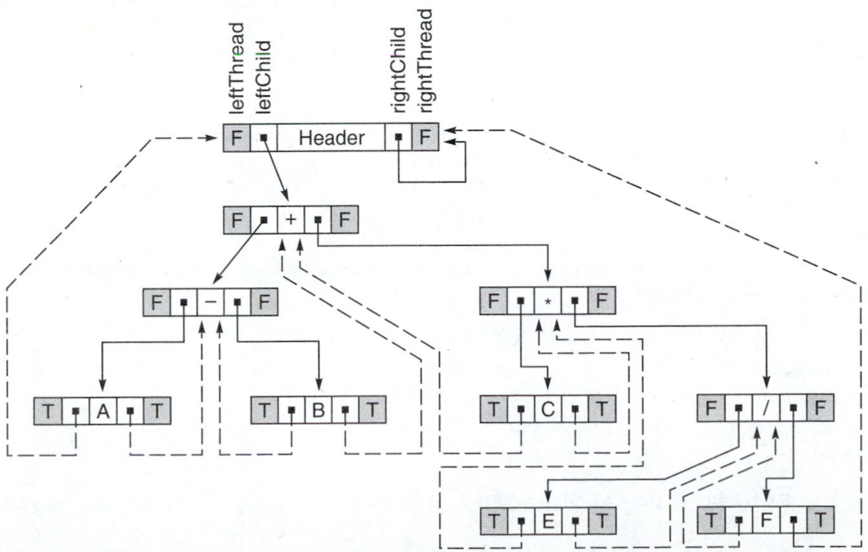

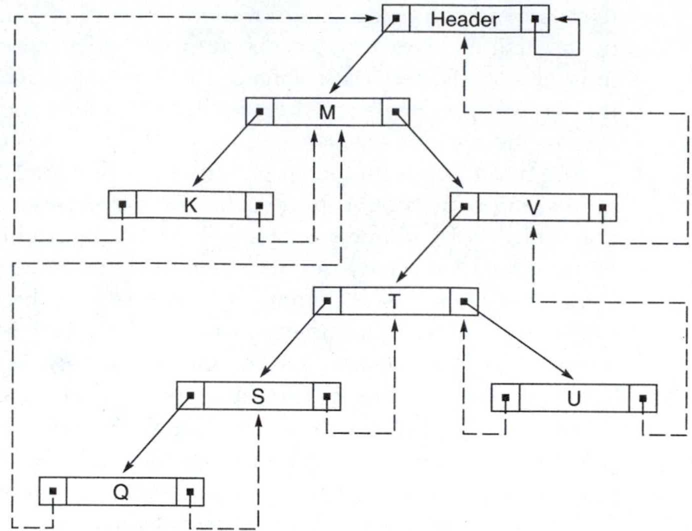

Figure 7.35
Threaded tree. To get the inorder successor of the node containing M, we must follow the right child pointer from M to V and then go left as deeply as possible in the tree, finally arriving at Q.

first follow the right child pointer from M to V and then go left as deeply as possible in the tree, finally arriving at the node containing Q. Note that this general strategy of proceeding one to the right, then left as deeply as possible, in combination with the initial setting of the right child pointer to the header node, ensures that the inorder traversal begins with the proper node. Trace the process shown in Figure 7.35 to find Q as the inorder successor of M.

Example 7.6

The following C++ class and function definitions implement the constructor and the inorder traversal operations for a binary search tree that uses the threaded strategy just discussed.

```
// BaseData is either a C++ built-in type, or a C++ class that has
// an assignment operation that overloads the "=" operator and an
// equality test that overloads the "==" operator.

//-----------------Node structure used by binary trees------------------
template <class BaseData>
class BtNode
{
  public:
    BaseData info;      // The data in the node
    BtNode *leftChild, *rightChild;
    BOOLEAN leftThread, rightThread;
};

//-----------------BinTree abstract base class for binary trees------------
template <class BaseData>
class BinTree
{
  protected:
    BtNode<BaseData> *root;

  public:
    :
    :  // Public operations for BinTree class remain as defined in Section 7.1
};
```

```
//-----------------BinSrchTree class definition derived from BinTree------
template <class BaseData>
class BinSrchTree : public BinTree<BaseData>
{
  protected:
    // Comparison function for items in tree
    BOOLEAN (*precedes)(const BaseData &x, const BaseData &y);

  public:
  :
  :    // Public operations for BinSrchTree class remain as defined in Section 7.3
};

//--------------Implementation of the constructor for the base class BinTree
template <class BaseData>
BinTree<BaseData>::BinTree()
{
  root = new BtNode<BaseData>;
  root->rightChild = root;
  root->rightThread = FALSE;
  root->leftChild = root;
  root->leftThread = TRUE;
}

//--------------Implementation of BinTree threaded inorder traversal
template <class BaseData>
void BinTree<BaseData>::inorderTrav(void (*processNode)(BaseData &item))
{
  BtNode<BaseData> *p;

  p = root;
  do
  {
    if (p->rightThread)
      p = p->rightChild;
    else
    {
      p = p->rightChild;
      while (!p->leftThread)
        p = p->leftChild;
    }
    if (p != root)
      processNode(p->info);
  }
  while (p != root);
}
```

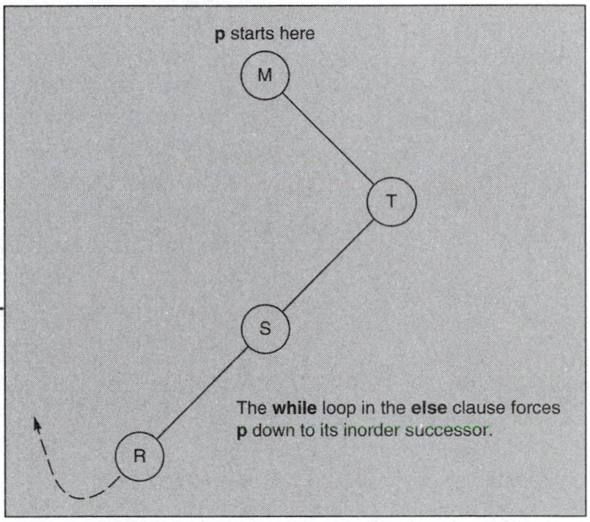

p starts here

M

T

S

R

The **while** loop in the **else** clause forces **p** down to its inorder successor.

```
//--------------Implementation of constructor for BinSrchTree class
template <class BaseData>
BinSrchTree<BaseData>::BinSrchTree
    (BOOLEAN (*precedes)(const BaseData &x, const BaseData &y))
    : BinTree<BaseData>()
{
  this->precedes = precedes;
}
```

We encourage you to trace carefully through the algorithm of Example 7.6 using the tree appearing in Figure 7.35. You should also verify that the function gracefully prints nothing when the **root** pointer refers to an empty tree.

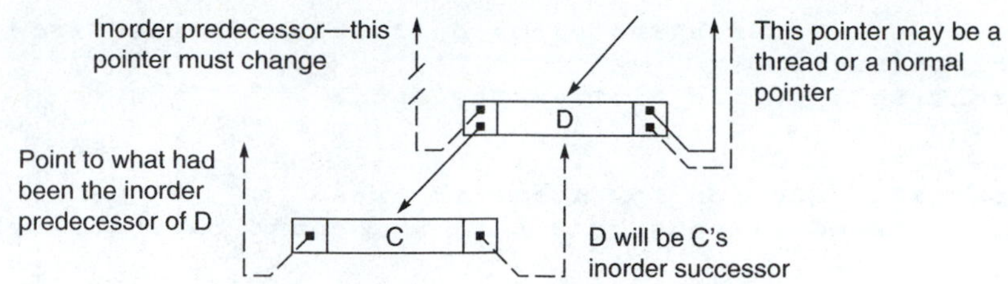

Figure 7.36
Pointer manipulations required to insert C as left child of leaf node D.

A few minor modifications to the function yield a new one that employs the predecessor threads to perform a reverse inorder traversal. Note that, if a given application required only forward traversing of the tree, there would be no need to maintain these predecessor threads. In that case, the left child pointers of the leaf nodes could remain NULL or perhaps even thread the tree for a preorder traversal. (See the exercises at the end of this section.)

A valid question at this stage is: Where do the threads come from? In our examples so far, they have merely been drawn as dashed-line pointers in the context of an already existing tree. However, we stress that, in practice, threads cannot exist unless they are continually maintained while nodes are added to and deleted from the tree.

In the following discussion, we develop the function to insert a node into a threaded binary search tree. In performing insertions, we preserve the ordering property cited in Section 7.3. For any given node (with the exception of the dummy header), its left subtree contains only data less than it, whereas its right subtree contains only data greater than or equal to it.

Given this criterion, insertion requires that the node to be inserted travel down a branch of the tree following the insertion rule (that we saw in Section 7.3): less than, go left; greater than, go right. On reaching a thread (that is, where a NULL pointer would be in an unthreaded tree), the new node is inserted appropriately as the left or right child. Figures 7.36 and 7.37 illustrate the pointer manipulations that must occur in each of these cases.

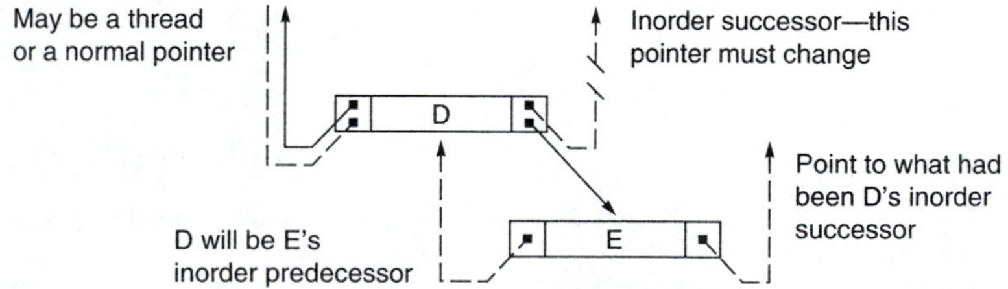

Figure 7.37
Pointer manipulations required to insert E as right child of leaf node D.

Example 7.7

The pointer manipulations just described are achieved by the following function **add** for a threaded implementation of a binary search tree. As is essential to any efficient insertion algorithm, no actual data are moved within the tree.

```
//--------------Implementation of threaded add operation for BinSrchTree class
template <class BaseData>
void BinSrchTree<BaseData>::add(const BaseData &item)
```

```
{
  BtNode<BaseData> *q, *p, *parentq;
  BOOLEAN left, done;

  p = new BtNode<BaseData>;
  p->info = item;

  // Prepare for the while test by following the left child pointer
  // from the dummy header
  parentq = root;
  q = root->leftChild;
  left = TRUE;
  done = parentq->leftThread;
  while (!done)
    // Now allow q and its parent to travel down an appropriate branch until
    // an insertion spot is found
    if (precedes(item, q->info))
    {
      parentq = q;
      q = q->leftChild;
      left = TRUE;
      done = parentq->leftThread;
    }
    else
    {
      parentq = q;
      q = q->rightChild;
      left = FALSE;
      done = parentq->rightThread;
    }

  // Now insert p as the left or right child of parentq
  p->leftThread = TRUE;
  p->rightThread = TRUE;
  if (left)
  {
    p->leftChild = parentq->leftChild;
    p->rightChild = parentq;
    parentq->leftChild = p;
    parentq->leftThread = FALSE;
  }
  else
  {
    p->rightChild = parentq->rightChild;
    p->leftChild = parentq;
    parentq->rightChild = p;
    parentq->rightThread = FALSE;
  }
}
```

Controlling **while** iteration:
parentq
Leaf node may be reached by following left thread from **parentq**
or
Leaf node may be reached by following right thread from **parentq**
parentq

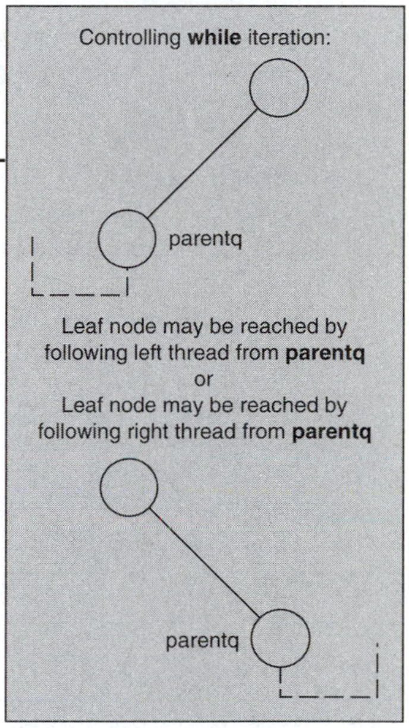

Efficiency Considerations for Threading a Tree

Removal of a node from a threaded tree may be handled by considering the same cases discussed in Section 7.3. The only additional consideration is the maintenance of the Boolean thread indicators. The only new fields required are the threads. Moreover, in practice, if space limitations are severe, the thread indicators may be incorporated into a bit of the left and right child pointers. Thus, threading represents a true bargain. By spending very little, one eliminates both the time and stack space required for recursion.

Exercises 7.5

1. Consider the representation of a binary tree via an array of **structs** as pictured in the table below (with zero indicating a NULL pointer).
   a. Draw the binary tree represented by this implementation.
   b. By filling in the spaces in the table to the right show the full memory representation for this tree with a header node and right threads (for an inorder traversal) added. Also indicate a new value for the root pointer.
2. Redraw the tree in Figure 7.38 as a threaded binary tree. Show the dummy header, inorder predecessor threads, and inorder successor threads in your drawing.
3. Explain why it is not possible to thread a tree for a postorder traversal.
4. Write a function that uses the predecessor pointers in a threaded binary tree to generate a reverse inorder traversal.

Binary Tree

Location	leftChild	info	rightChild
1	3	A	5
2	7	B	11
3	6	C	0
4	0	D	0
5	8	E	10
6	4	F	2
7	0	G	0
8	0	H	0
9	0	K	0
10	0	L	9
11	0	I	0

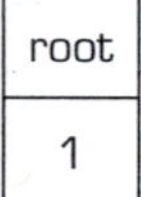

Location	leftChild	info	rightChild	rightThread
1		A		
2		B		
3		C		
4		D		
5		E		
6		F		
7		G		
8		H		
9		K		
10		L		
11		I		
12				

root

5. Write a function to remove a node from a threaded binary search tree.
6. If the inorder predecessor pointers appearing in Figure 7.34 were not maintained, that is, if NULL pointers were stored in their place, it would still be possible to complete a threaded inorder traversal. Indeed, we would only lose the ability to complete a threaded reverse inorder traversal. How would this section's function for threaded inorder traversal and the **add** operation need to be modified if no predecessor threads were maintained?
7. Redraw the threads in Figure 7.34 to indicate a preorder traversal of the tree.
8. Write a C++ function for the preorder traversal diagram suggested in Exercise 7.5.7.
9. Explain why the removal of recursion from the inorder traversal operation would be particularly critical for a large binary search tree whose search efficiency was $O(n)$ instead of the optimal $O(\log_2 n)$.

7.6 Height-Balanced Trees

Height-balanced binary trees represent an alternative that often may *not* be worth the additional storage space and developmental complexities introduced for the sake of increasing speed. After describing the method, we shall cite some statistics

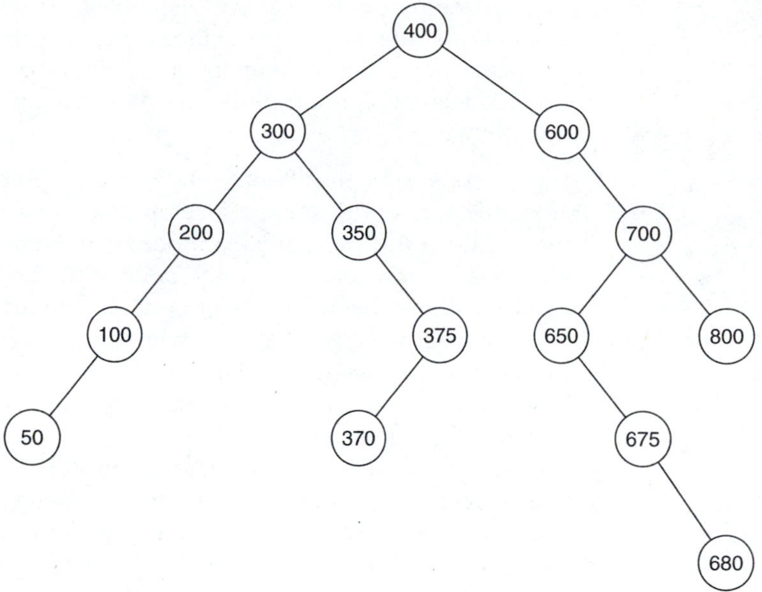

Figure 7.38
Tree for Exercise 7.5.2.

that may help you decide whether or not to height-balance a tree in a particular application. The height-balancing technique was developed in 1962 by researchers G. M. Adelson-Velskii and Y. M. Landis (Adelson-Velskii, G. M., and Y. M. Landis, "An Algorithm for the Organization of Information," *Dokl. Acad. Nauk SSSR,* 146, 1962, pp. 263–66). In credit to their work, height-balanced trees are also referred to as *AVL trees*. The AVL method represents an attempt to maintain binary search trees in a form close to fullness, thereby ensuring rapid insertions and searches. One of the costs involved in doing this is that each node of the tree must store an additional item called its *balance factor,* which is defined to be the difference between the height of its left subtree and the height of its right subtree. In this context, the *height* of a tree is the number of nodes visited in traversing a branch that leads to a leaf node at the deepest level of the tree. An example of a tree with computed balance factors for each node is given in Figure 7.39.

A tree is said to be *height-balanced* if all of its nodes have a balance factor of 1, 0, or −1. Hence, the tree appearing in Figure 7.39 is not height-balanced. Note

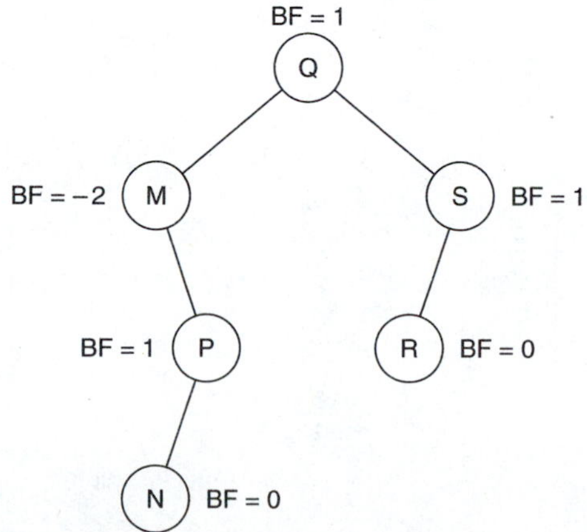

Figure 7.39
A tree with computed balance factors. A balance factor is the difference between the height of a node's left subtree and the height of its right subtree.

that every tree that is full is also height-balanced. However, the converse of this statement is not true (you can convince yourself of this by constructing an example). The AVL technique used to keep a tree in height-balance requires that each time an insertion is made according to the insertion rule specified in Section 7.3 one must do the following:

1. Let the node to be inserted travel down the appropriate branch, keeping track along the way of the deepest level node on that branch that has a balance factor of +1 or −1. (This particular node is called the *pivot node* for reasons that will soon be apparent.) Insert the node at the appropriate point.
2. Inclusive of and below the pivot node, recompute all balance factors along the insertion path traced in step 1. It will be shown that no nodes other than these can possibly change their balance factors using the AVL method.
3. Determine whether the absolute value of the pivot node's balance factor switched from 1 to 2.
4. If there was such a switch as indicated in step 3, perform a manipulation of tree pointers centered at the pivot node to bring the tree back into height-balance. Since the visual effect of this pointer manipulation will be to "rotate" the subtree whose root is the pivot node, the operation is frequently referred to as an *AVL-rotation*.

We will cover these steps in reverse order because, until one fully understands the nature of the AVL-rotation, it is not apparent why the pivot node is chosen as specified in step 1.

AVL-Rotations

In the following discussion we assume that steps 1, 2, and 3 from the preceding list have all been completed and that we have a pointer, **pivot**, to the deepest level node whose balance factor has switched from an absolute value of 1 to 2. In practice, **pivot** may be the root pointer for the entire tree or the child pointer

Figure 7.40

Case 1: The insertion occurred in the left subtree of the left child of the pivot node.

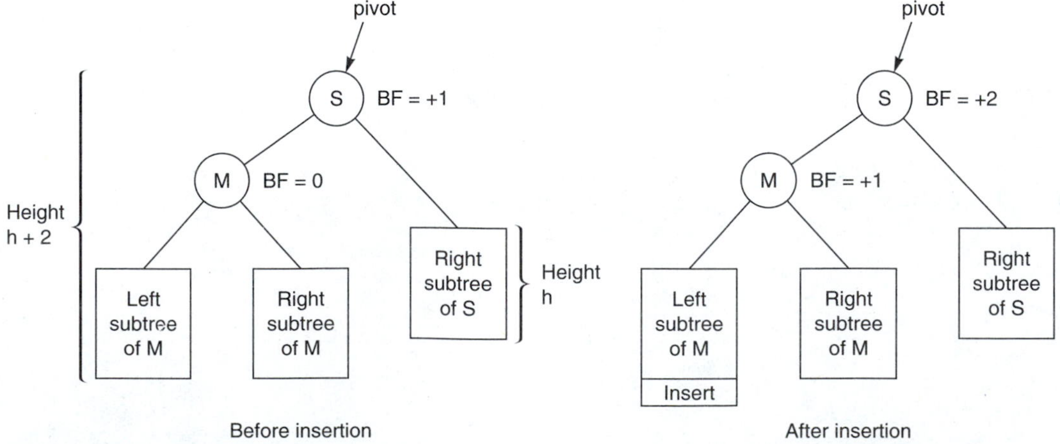

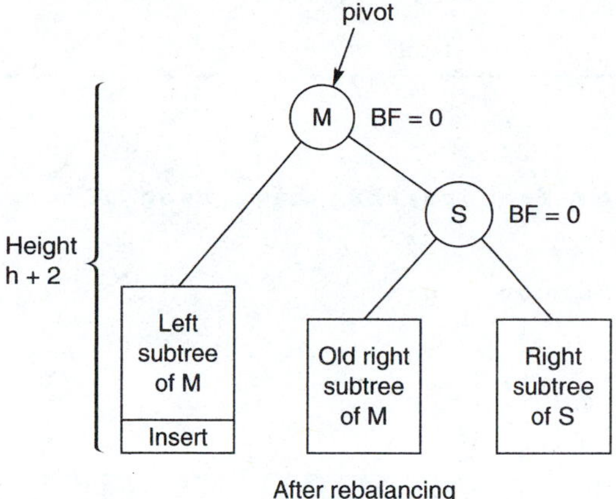

Figure 7.41
Case 1 after rebalancing with a **leftOfLeft** rotation.

of a parent node inside the tree. The pointer manipulations required to rebalance the tree necessitate division into four cases distinguished by the direction of the "guilty" insertion relative to the pivot node.

Case I The insertion that unbalanced the tree occurred in the left subtree of the left child of the pivot node. In this case, the situation pictured in Figure 7.40 must have occurred. Our only criterion for rebalancing the tree is the preservation of the ordering property for binary trees. Hence, if we could force a rotation (merely through changes in pointers) that made the tree pointed to by **pivot** appear as in Figure 7.41, the rebalancing would be complete. The function to achieve this rotation in the context of our **BinSrchTree** class is given next:

```
template <class BaseData>
class BtNode
{
  public:
    BaseData info;              // The data in the node
    BtNode *leftChild, *rightChild;
    short balanceFactor;        // <-- Add a balanceFactor field to BtNode
};

//---------------------------------------------------------------
// Interface for leftOfLeft function - a private member of BinSrchTree class
// GIVEN:   pivot -- a pointer a to pivot node in a tree.
// RETURN:  The subtree pointed to by pivot is altered by performing the AVL
//          rotation for the "left of left" case
// RETURN as value of function: void

template <class BaseData>
void BinSrchTree<BaseData>::leftOfLeft(BtNode<BaseData> *&pivot)
{
  BtNode<BaseData> *p, *q;

  // Begin by altering the necessary pointers
```

```
    p = pivot->leftChild;
    q = p->rightChild;
    p->rightChild = pivot;
    pivot->leftChild = q;
    pivot = p;

    // Then readjust the balance factors that have been affected

    pivot->balanceFactor = 0;
    pivot->rightChild->balanceFactor = 0;
}
```

Figure 7.42

Case 2: The insertion occurred in the right subtree of the right child of the pivot node.

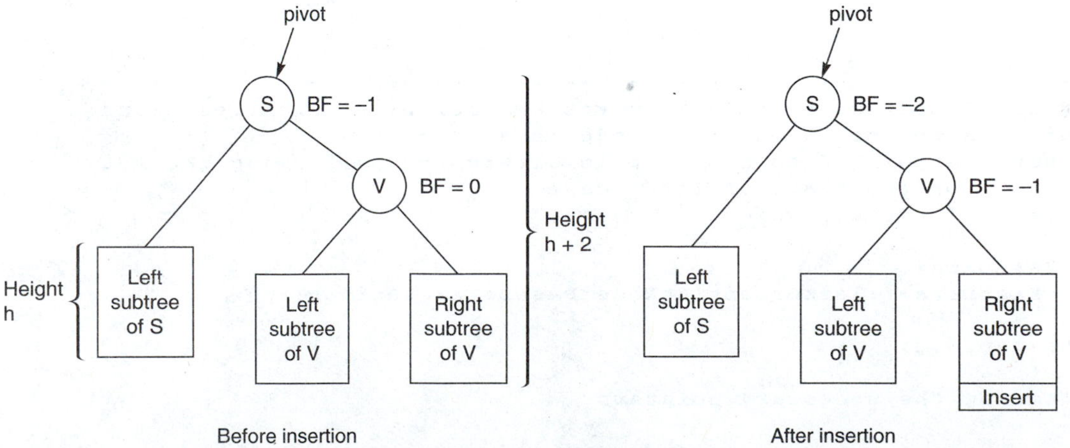

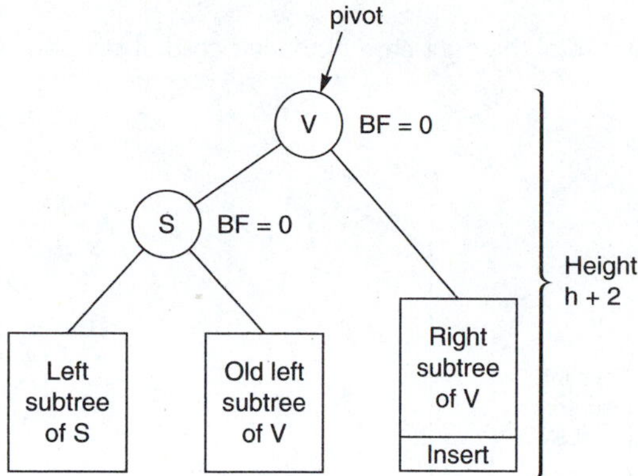

Figure 7.43
Case 2 after rebalancing with a **rightOfRight** rotation.

Case 2 The insertion that unbalanced the tree occurred in the right subtree of the right child of the pivot node. In this case, the situation pictured in Figure 7.42 must have occurred. Figure 7.43 indicates the rebalancing that should occur. Again, the idea is to rotate the tree around the pivot node, except that this time the rotation must occur in the opposite direction. The function **rightOfRight**, necessary to achieve this rotation, remains as an exercise; it is essentially a mirror image of the **leftOfLeft** function.

Case 3 The insertion causing the imbalance occurred in the right subtree of the left child of the pivot node. In this case, the function to perform the pointer manipulations necessary to rebalance the tree will require subdivision into three subcases, portrayed in diagrammatic form in Figures 7.44, 7.45, and 7.46, respectively.

At first glance, the need for splitting case 3 into three subcases may not be apparent. Indeed, all three subcases require nearly identical pointer changes.

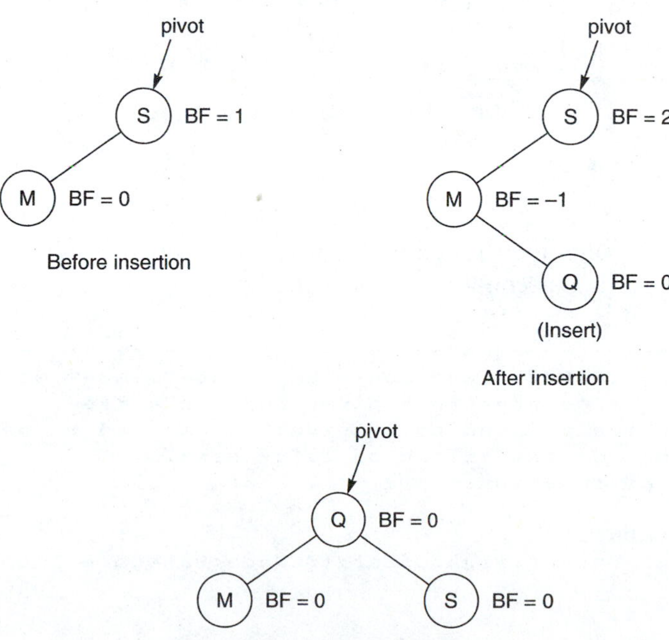

Figure 7.44
Case 3, subcase 1: Neither the pivot node nor its left child has a right child. Insertion occurs as the right child of the left child of the pivot node.

Figure 7.45
Case 3, subcase 2: Insertion is in the left subtree of the right child of the left child of the pivot.

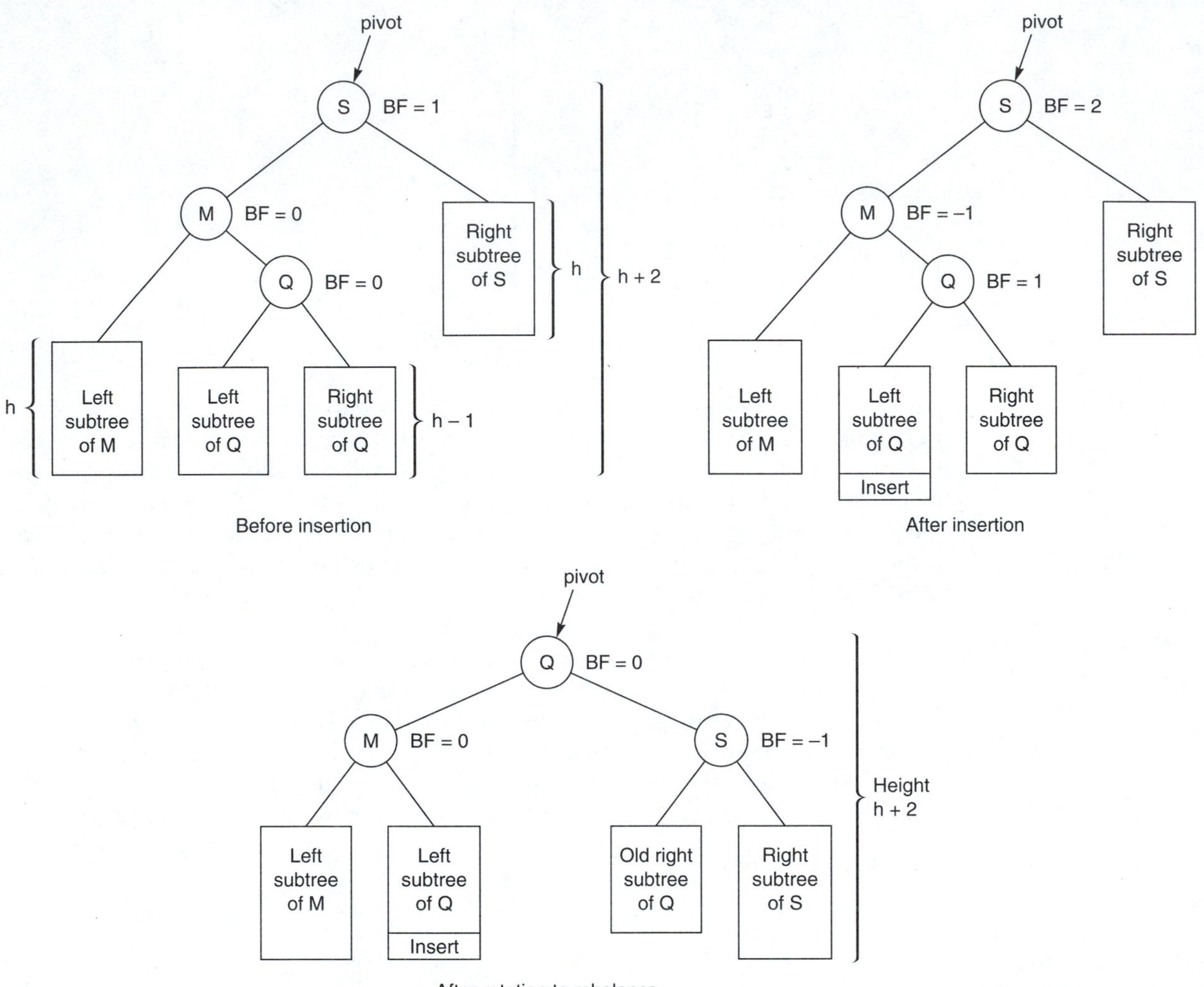

However, the subtle point of differentiation lies in how the balance factors are reset after the rotation has occurred. This subtlety is illustrated in the figures and is taken into account in the following function.

```
//-----------------------------------------------------------------------
// Interface for rightOfLeft function - a private member of BinSrchTree class
// GIVEN:    pivot -- a pointer to a pivot node in a tree.
// RETURN:   The subtree pointed to by pivot is altered by performing the AVL
//           rotation for the "right of left" case.
// RETURN as value of function: void

template <class BaseData>
void BinSrchTree<BaseData>::rightOfLeft(BtNode<BaseData> *&pivot)
{
  BtNode<BaseData> *x, *y;

  // First adjust pointers to perform AVL rotation
```

```
    x = pivot->leftChild;
    y = x->rightChild;
    pivot->leftChild = y->rightChild;
    x->rightChild = y->leftChild;
    y->leftChild = x;
    y->rightChild = pivot;
    pivot = y;

    // Then reset the balance factors according to the subcase

    if (pivot->balanceFactor == 0)
    { // subcase #1
      pivot->leftChild->balanceFactor = 0;
      pivot->rightChild->balanceFactor = 0;
    }
    else
      if (pivot->balanceFactor == 1)
      { // subcase #2
        pivot->balanceFactor = 0;
        pivot->leftChild->balanceFactor = 0;
        pivot->rightChild->balanceFactor = -1;
      }
      else
      { // subcase #3
        pivot->balanceFactor = 0;
        pivot->leftChild->balanceFactor = 1;
        pivot->rightChild->balanceFactor = 0;
      }
}
```

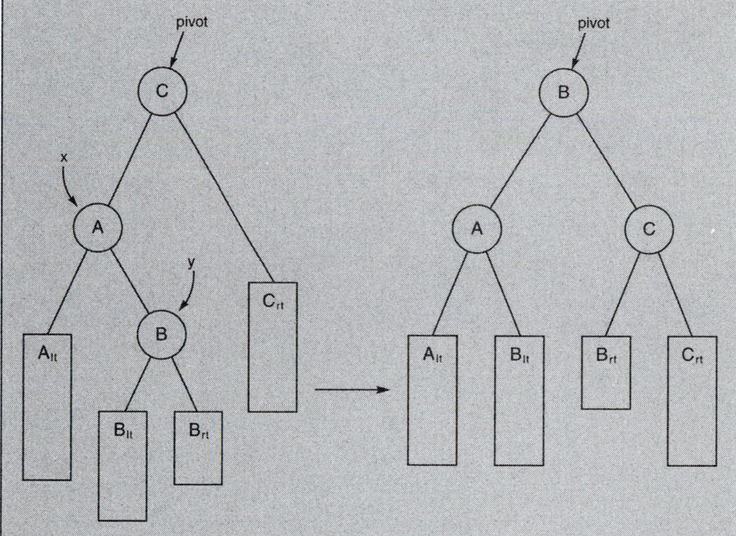

Case 4 The insertion that causes the imbalance in the tree is made in the left subtree of the right child of the pivot node. Case 4 is to case 3 as case 2 is to case 1; it remains as an exercise to write the function **leftOfRight**.

Why Does the AVL Height-Balancing Technique Work?

On first studying the AVL algorithm, it is often not apparent why the pivot node must be the *deepest* node having a balance factor of +1 or −1 along the path of insertion. After all, it would seem that Figures 7.42 through 7.46 work equally well

Figure 7.46
Case 3, subcase 3: Insertion occurs in the right subtree of the right child of the left child of the pivot.

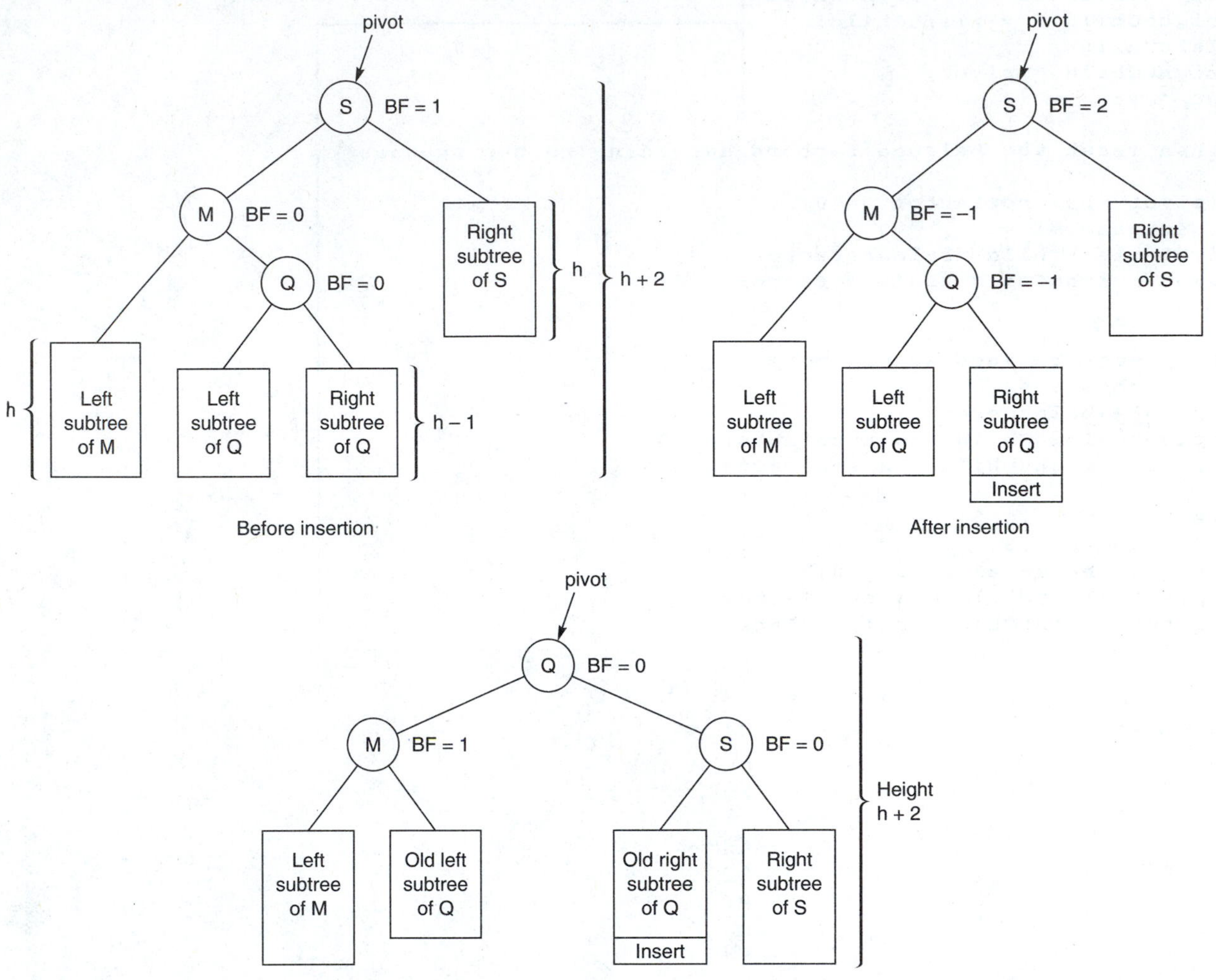

as long as **pivot** points to any node along the insertion path that has a change in the magnitude of its balance factor from 1 to 2. However, three subtle reasons are involved in not allowing the pivot node to be *just any* node of balance factor +1 or −1 along the insertion path but the deepest such node.

First, it is quite evident that we must choose a node whose original balance factor is +1 or −1 as the pivot node. Such nodes are the only candidates for points at which the tree can go out of height-balance. Any node with balance factor zero can, at worst, change to +1 or −1 after insertion, therefore not requiring any rotation at all.

Second, whether a rotation takes place or not, *the only balance factors in the entire tree that will be affected are those of nodes inclusive of and below the pivot node along the insertion path*. In situations where a rotation does occur, this is evident from Figures 7.42 through 7.46. In all four cases of AVL-rotations, the overall height of the subtree pointed to by **pivot** is the same after the rotation as it was before. In situations where no rotation occurs, the balance factor of the pivot node must change from either 1 to 0 or from −1 to 0; it cannot remain what it

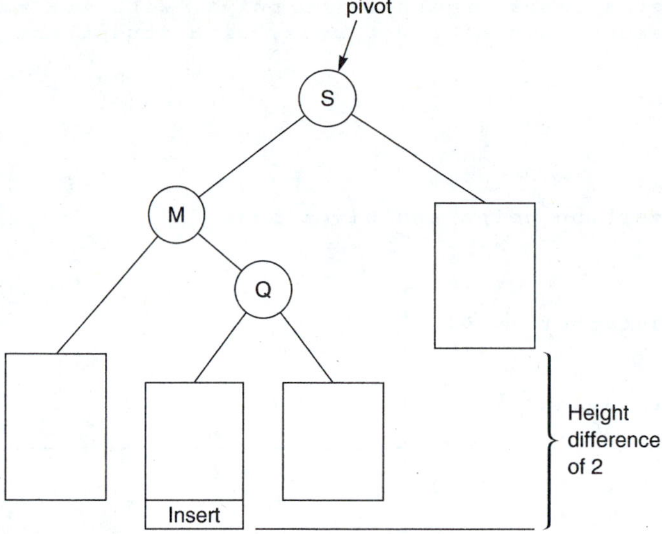

Figure 7.47
Case 3 incorrectly handled by not choosing proper pivot. AVL-rotation only partially rebalances the tree.

originally was. The reason is that every node below it on the insertion path must have an original balance factor of 0. Consequently, there is no way that an insertion may "hide" and not affect the balance factor of the pivot node. However, the fact that the pivot node changes to a zero balance factor in such situations again means that the rest of the tree above the pivot node is unaffected by the insertion.

Third, if we do not choose the deepest level node with balance factor equal to +1 or −1, we run the risk of having an AVL-rotation that only partially rebalances the tree. Figure 7.47 indicates how this could occur. In this figure, if we choose a pivot node above that labeled S, that portion of the tree rooted at S will remain out of balance.

With this rationale in mind, we can now convincingly present a complete implementation of the algorithm to process an insertion into a height-balanced tree, recompute all affected balance factors, and perform an AVL-rotation if necessary.

```
//-------------Implementation of public add operation for BinSrchTree
//-------------class using height-balancing technique

template <class BaseData>
void BinSrchTree<BaseData>::add(const BaseData &item)
{
  BtNode<BaseData> *p, *piv, *pivParent, *inp, *inParent, *q;

  p = new BtNode<BaseData>;
  p->info = item;
  p->leftChild = NULL;
  p->rightChild = NULL;
  p->balanceFactor = 0;

  if (root == NULL)
  {
    root = p;
    return;
  }
```

```
// Pointer inp keeps track of insertion point, with its parent inParent.
// Pointer piv keeps track of pivot node, with its parent pivParent.

inp = root;
piv = root;
inParent = NULL;
pivParent = NULL;

// Search for insertion point and pivot node

do
{
  if (inp->balanceFactor != 0)
  {
    piv = inp;
    pivParent = inParent;
  }
  inParent = inp;
  if (precedes(item, inp->info))
    inp = inp->leftChild;
  else
    inp = inp->rightChild;
}
while (inp != NULL);

// Insert the node as the left or right child
// of inParent

if (precedes(item, inParent->info))
  inParent->leftChild = p;
else
  inParent->rightChild = p;

// Now recompute the balance factors between piv and inParent.
// By definition of a pivot node, all these balance factors must
// change by 1 in the direction of the insertion.

q = piv;
do
{
  if (precedes(item, q->info))
  {
    q->balanceFactor++;
    q = q->leftChild;
  }
  else
  {
    q->balanceFactor--;
    q = q->rightChild;
  }
}
while (q != p);

// Need to rotate?  If not, then we're done!

if (-1 <= piv->balanceFactor && piv->balanceFactor <= 1)
  return;

// An AVL rotation is necessary.  Call on the appropriate
// function, passing one of root, pivParent->leftChild, or
// pivParent->rightChild as the pointer to the pivot node.
```

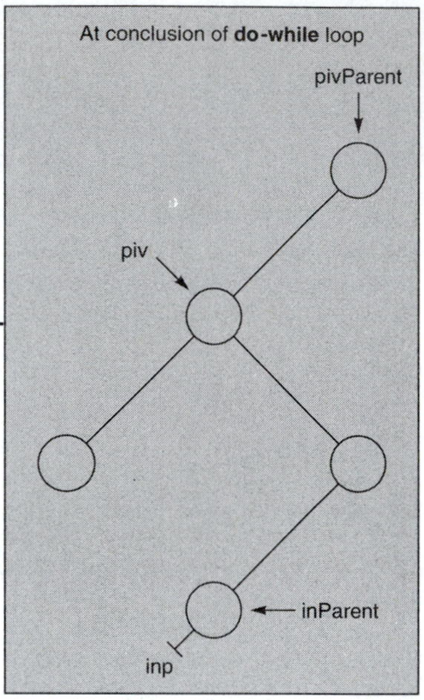

At conclusion of **do-while** loop

pivParent

piv

inParent

inp

```
    if (precedes(item, piv->info))
      if (precedes(item, piv->leftChild->info))
        if (piv == root)
          leftOfLeft(root);
        else
          if (piv == pivParent->leftChild)
            leftOfLeft(pivParent->leftChild);
          else
            leftOfLeft(pivParent->rightChild);
      else
        if (piv == root)
          rightOfLeft(root);
        else
          if (piv == pivParent->leftChild)
            rightOfLeft(pivParent->leftChild);
          else
            rightOfLeft(pivParent->rightChild);
    else
      if (!precedes(item, piv->rightChild->info))
        if (piv == root)
          rightOfRight(root);
        else
          if (piv == pivParent->leftChild)
            rightOfRight(pivParent->leftChild);
          else
            rightOfRight(pivParent->rightChild);
      else
        if (piv == root)
          leftOfRight(root);
        else
          if (piv == pivParent->leftChild)
            leftOfRight(pivParent->leftChild);
          else
            leftOfRight(pivParent->rightChild);
}
```

A subtle question that arises from this function is the following. Namely, consider the segment:

```
if (piv == root)
  leftOfLeft(root);
else
  if (piv == pivParent->leftChild)
    leftOfLeft(pivParent->leftChild);
  else
    leftOfLeft(pivParent->rightChild);
```

Why couldn't this lengthy segment from the function **add** be replaced by the single function call **leftOfLeft(piv)**? The answer lies in the fact that the function **leftOfLeft** alters the argument sent to it. It is for this reason that the argument to **leftOfLeft** must be passed by reference. What we wish to alter in the preceding segment above is *not* the pointer **piv** but rather one of the pointers **root**, **pivParent–>leftChild**, or **pivParent–>rightChild**. The simple function call **leftOfLeft(piv)** would leave the variables we really wish to change unaffected.

Height-Balancing—Is It Worth It?

This is clearly a nontrivial algorithm. Moreover, the algorithm to remove a node from a height-balanced tree is no easier and is left for an exercise. In their paper, Adelson-Velskii and Landis were able to demonstrate that their method would guarantee a maximum branch length proportional to $\log_2 n$ where n is the number of nodes in the tree. In particular, they determined a constant of proportionality between 1.4 and 1.5. This means that the insertion efficiency for a height-balanced tree will be, in terms of orders of magnitude, roughly equivalent to that for a full tree. Compared to the worst case efficiency of $O(n)$ for a nonbalanced tree, it is clear that the AVL method can make a difference. However, one critical question is whether it is likely that random data will generate such worst case performance in a nonbalanced tree. This is a question you can explore empirically in the programming problems at the end of this chapter.

Whether the difference made by height-balancing is worth the added developmental costs is, as always, a consideration tied to a particular application. The real problem in this regard, however, is that it is often impossible to obtain a realistic appraisal during software design of how height-balancing will influence overall run-time efficiency. Consequently, if one does employ height-balancing and it then turns out that system performance would have been adequate without it, a considerable amount of development time may have been wasted. We recommend a rather empirical approach to this dilemma. Unless the need for height-balancing is obvious, design and write the application without height-balancing. After empirically testing the performance of your application without height-balancing, make the decision whether or not to rewrite functions to incorporate height-balancing. If you've adhered to the public interfaces of the **BinSrchTree** class, your AVL functions should be "plug-compatible" with the ones they are replacing.

Exercises 7.6

1. Convince yourself that a height-balanced tree is not necessarily full by constructing an example of a tree that is height-balanced but not full.
2. Repeat Exercise 7.3.1 for a height-balanced tree.
3. Repeat Exercise 7.3.2 for a height-balanced tree.
4. Repeat Exercise 7.3.3 for a height-balanced tree.
5. Complete the functions **rightOfRight** and **leftOfRight** for insertion into a height-balanced tree.
6. Write a C++ function to remove a node from a height-balanced tree. Provide an enumeration of the cases you must consider for such a function.
7. Write a C++ function to add a node to a binary search tree that is *both* threaded and height-balanced.
8. Consider the following alphabetical binary search tree. Draw the tree after the data item A has been inserted and the tree has been height-balanced.

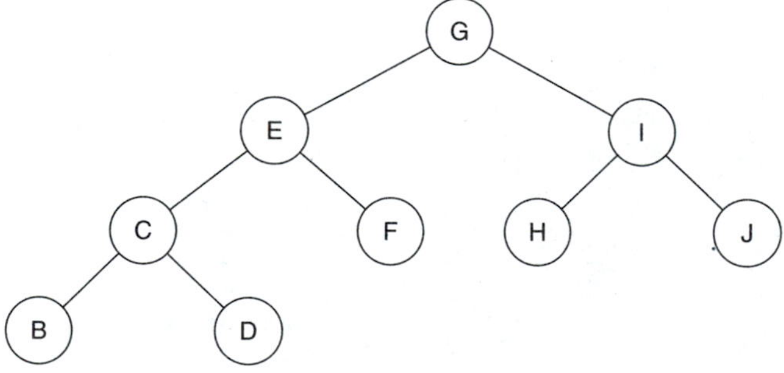

9. Repeat Exercise 7.6.8 for the insertion of the data item D and the corresponding height-balancing of the following tree.

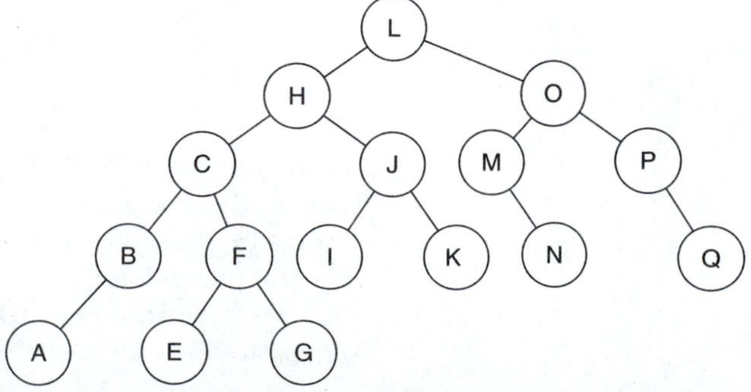

Chapter Summary

In this chapter we introduce some of the basic terminology of trees and define the *binary tree* ADT, where a binary tree is one whose nodes have two subtrees designated as the right and left subtrees. Section 7.3 shows how a binary search tree can be used to implement an ordered list, together with a consideration of its efficiency. Both linear and linked representations for binary trees are considered and the storage efficiencies of each analyzed. Preorder, inorder, and postorder traversals are among the operations contained in the definition of the binary tree ADT, and an implementation for each is given.

Another type of binary tree examined is a heap, which is a binary tree in which each node's value is greater than or equal to the values of all items in its left and right subtrees. Add and remove operations for heaps are developed. In doing the latter we are not concerned with finding a particular item to remove, but instead we view the heap as a means of implementing a priority queue (priority queues were introduced in Chapter 4; only the item of highest priority is removed). Therefore, removal from a heap simply means removing the item at the root and reshuffling the remaining tree nodes back into a heap. This approach is justified on the grounds that if the removal of a particular node is a concern, then a binary tree with the *ordering property* (the data in each node of the tree are greater than all the data in the left subtree and less than or equal to all the data in the right subtree) would be more suitable because of the improved search efficiency it would provide. Heaps are then used as the basis for a nonrecursive sorting algorithm—the heap sort—which sorts an array and guarantees $O(n \log_2 n)$ efficiency, making it an attractive alternative when space is at a premium or when the language used does not support recursion.

The notion of threading is introduced in Section 7.5 as a way to eliminate recursion from the inorder traversal algorithm for binary search trees, allowing all necessary operations for this type of tree to be implemented nonrecursively. Finally, AVL trees are introduced to increase the speed of insertions and searches for ordered trees, and important issues are outlined for determining whether the added complexity of AVL trees makes it worthwhile to implement them.

Keywords

abstract base class
AVL-rotation
AVL trees
balance factor
binary search tree
binary tree
branch
child node
dense tree
full tree
general tree
heap
heap property
heap sort
height-balanced
inorder threads
inorder traversal
insertion rule
leaf node
left subtree
level
ordering property
parent node
pivot node
postorder traversal
preorder traversal
pure virtual operation
right subtree
root node
sibling
subtree
threading
tree traversal

Programming Problems/Projects

1. In Problem 11 of Chapter 4, you developed a program to store customer records for the Fly-by-Night credit card company in a priority queue based on the promptness with which a customer pays his or her bill. Revise that program, using a heap to implement the priority queue.
2. In previous chapters we developed parsers for algebraic expressions—a stack-based parser with priority functions in Section 5.3 and a recursive descent parser in Section 6.4. Extend either or both of these parsers so that a binary expression tree is returned from the parser for a valid infix expression. Then write a function that traverses the tree and evaluates the expression represented by the tree.
3. In Problem 10 of Chapter 6 you developed a program that would allow you to empirically compare the sorting methods we had studied to that point. Extend this program by adding heap sort to the methods that can be chosen. Use your new program to empirically compare heap sort to other "fast" sorting methods such as Shell, quick, and merge sorts. In a written report, summarize your findings on the performance of heap sort compared to those other methods.
4. Develop a program to empirically test the search efficiency of a binary tree with the ordering property. Your program should load such a binary search tree with either

   a. a specific data set designed by the user, or

   b. a randomly generated data set for a user-specified number of values.

Your program should then compute the average length of a search path required to find an item in the tree. This average search efficiency should then be output along with the theoretical upper and lower bounds on the search efficiency, that is, n and $\log_2 n$. Finally, have your program destroy the current tree before it iterates and allows the user to create another.

Use your program to design an experiment that allows you to determine the likelihood of a given data set approaching the worst case $O(n)$ behavior. What kind of properties must a data set have before it seems to cross the line from $O(\log_2 n)$ to $O(n)$ behavior? Write your conclusions in a report in which you use the results from your program to back up your findings.

5. Extend your program from the previous problem so that it loads a given data set into a height-balanced tree as well as a regular binary search tree. Have your program output comparative statistics for the average search efficiency for the two implementations.

Use your program to design an experiment that allows you to reach some general conclusions regarding the difference in search efficiencies for these two implementations on specific kinds of data sets. Write your conclusions in a report using statistics from your program to back up your findings. Your report should also address the concerns addressed at the end of Section 7.6. That is, for what types of applications might the additional design and implementation time required for height-balancing be worthwhile for achieving a significant gain in performance in the resulting system?

6. The definition given in Section 7.1 for the binary tree ADT should not be considered the only definition possible for this ADT. For instance, it is possible to define the binary tree ADT without traversal operations if a collection of more primitive operations is provided that allows you to write your own traversals. For instance, you could maintain a *current node* and **moveLeft**, **moveRight**, **moveToParent**, and **moveToRoot** operations that are always performed relative to the current node. Write a complete ADT definition that employs such an alternate perspective. Then implement the ADT in a C++ class. Finally, use your new binary tree library to solve any of the programming problems presented here.

7. Modify the airline reservation system you developed for Wing-and-a-Prayer Airlines in Problem 1 of Chapter 3 so that the alphabetized lists are maintained with binary search trees instead of linked lists.

8. Write a program that sorts the records of the Fly-by-Night credit card company file (Problem 2, Chapter 3) in alphabetical order by the last name and then the first name of the customer. Use a binary tree and its inorder traversal to accomplish the sort.

9. Recall the roster maintenance system that you wrote for the Bay Area Brawlers in the programming problems for Chapter 3. The system has been so successful that the league office would like to expand the system to include all the players in the league. Again the goal is to maintain the list of players in alphabetical order, allowing for frequent insertions and removals as players are cut, picked up, and traded among teams. In addition to storing each player's height, weight, age, and university affiliation, the record for each player should be expanded to include team affiliation, years in league, and annual salary. Because the database for the entire league is many times larger than that for just one team, maintain this list as a binary search tree to increase efficiency.

10. Write a program that reads an expression in its prefix form and builds the binary tree corresponding to that expression. Then write functions to print the infix and postfix forms of the expression using inorder and postorder traversals of this tree. Then see if you can extend the program to evaluate the expression represented by the tree.

11. Given a file containing some arbitrary text, determine how many times each word appears in the file. Your program should print in alphabetical order the words that appear in the file, with their frequency counts. For an added challenge, do not assume any maximum word length; this will enable you to combine trees with the string handling methods you have already learned.

12. Here is a problem you will encounter if you write statistical analysis software. Given an arbitrarily long list of unordered numbers with an arbitrary number of different values appearing in it, determine and print the marginal distribution for this list of numbers. That is, count how many times each different value appears in the list and then print out each value along with its count (frequency). The final output should be arranged from smallest to largest value. This problem can be solved elegantly using trees.

An example of such output as produced by the COSAP (Conversationally Oriented Statistical Analysis Package) of Lawrence University follows:

```
                Outagamie County Criminal Cases

                     MARGINAL FREQUENCIES

Variable Judge          JUDGE BEFORE WHOM CASE
                        BROUGHT (2)

Value label      Value    Absolute     Relative
                          frequency    frequency
SMITH              1         677         80.8%
JONES              2          88         10.5%
DAVIS              3          26          3.1%
MILLER             5          47          5.6%

838 Valid    0 Missing   838 Total Observations
```

Here the data file contained 838 occurences of the values 1, 2, 3, and 5. Each value was a code number assigned to a particular judge.

13. Many compilers offer the services of a cross-referencing program to aid in debugging. Such a program will list in alphabetical order all the identifiers that appear in a program and the various lines of the program that reference them. Write such a cross-referencer for your favorite language using a binary search tree to maintain the list of identifiers that are encountered.

14. A relatively easy game to implement with a binary tree is to have the computer try to guess an animal about which the user is thinking by asking the user a series of questions that can be answered by *yes* or *no*. A node in the binary tree to play this game could be viewed as

YES/NO pointers leading to

1. Another question.
2. The name of the animal.
3. NULL.

If NULL, have your program surrender and then ask the user for a new question that uniquely defines the animal. Then add this new question to the growing binary tree data base.

15. For this problem, you are to write a program that will differentiate expressions in the variable X. The input to this program will be a series of strings, each representing an infix expression to be differentiated. Each such expression is to be viewed as a stream of tokens. Valid tokens are integers, the variable X, the binary operators (+, −, *, /, ^), and parentheses. To make scanning for tokens easy, you may assume that each token is followed by exactly one space, with the exception of the final token, which is followed by an end-of-line.

First your program will have to scan the infix expression, building up an appropriate binary tree representation of it. For this you should be able to borrow significantly from the work you did with parsing expressions in Chapters 5 and 6. The major difference here is that the end result of this parse is to be a binary tree instead of a postfix string.

Once the binary expression tree is built, traverse it, building up another binary expression tree that represents the derivative of the original expression. The following differentiation rules should be used in this process.

Suppose C is a constant, and S and T are expressions in X:

```
Diff(C) = 0
Diff(X) = 1
Diff(S + T) = Diff(S) + Diff(T)
Diff(S - T) = Diff(S) - Diff(T)
Diff(S * T) = S * Diff(T) + T * Diff(S)
Diff(S / T) = ((T * Diff(S)) -
              (S * Diff(T))) / (T ^ 2)
Diff(S ^ C) = (C * S ^ (C - 1)) * Diff(S)
 (the infamous chain rule)
```

Finally, once the binary expression tree for the derivative has been built, print the expression. Print it in completely parenthesized infix notation to avoid ambiguity.

Note that there are three distinct phases to this problem:

- Parsing of the original infix expression into a binary tree representation.
- Building a binary tree representation of the derivative.
- Printing the derivative in completely parenthesized infix notation.

For an added challenge, simplify the derivative before printing it. Simplify the expression for the derivative according to the following rules:

```
S + 0 = S
0 + S = S
S - 0 = S
S * 0 = 0
0 * S = 0
S * 1 = S
1 * S = S
0 / S = 0
S ^ 0 = 1
S ^ 1 = S
S - S = 0
S / S = 1
S / 0 = 'DIVISION BY ZERO'
0 / 0 = 'UNDEFINED'
```

16. A *mobile* is an object of a specified weight or a beam of a specified weight with a submobile attached to each end. Mobiles must be *balanced;* that is, submobiles suspended from opposite ends of each beam in the mobile should be equal in weight. Using the **BinTree** class, write a function that receives a potential mobile and returns a negative flagging value if the potential mobile is not balanced. If the mobile is balanced, your function should return the overall weight of the mobile. Test your function in an appropriate driver program.

17. Add a *level-order* traversal to the binary tree class. In such a traversal, the root is processed first. Then all level 1 nodes are processed, followed by all level 2 nodes, level 3 nodes, and so forth. Use the **Queue** class from chapter 4 to implement this new traversal operation. Finally, test your implementation in a driver main program.

CHAPTER 8

More General Tree Structures

A tree's a tree. How many more do you need to look at?
Ronald Reagan

Chapter Outline:

We began the last chapter with a discussion of the many ways in which hierarchical structures are used to organize information around us. We then quickly imposed a "birth control" dictate of at most two children, which focused all of our attention on the seemingly restricted case of the binary tree. But what about all those applications requiring a hierarchy in which a parent may have an unrestricted number of children? In this chapter we examine techniques to implement those more general tree structures. In Sections 8.3 and 8.4, we look at two applications of such general trees. The first of these applications, the 2-3 tree, leads to a very efficient implementation of the ordered-list ADT we introduced in Chapter 3. The second application consists of a series of refinements that use general trees to achieve an increasingly efficient implementation of the Union-Find ADT (Sections 2.4 and 3.5).

8.1 The General Tree ADT

In trying to provide a complete definition of a general tree as an abstract data type, we find ourselves in the same predicament as with binary trees. That is, the applications of general trees are so varied in nature that it is impossible to provide a set of abstract operations that proves suitable for all situations. As with binary trees, we will take the approach of including only a small set of generic operations in our basic definition. Then, as we look at specific applications, ways of extending and tailoring these operations to optimize efficiency will be examined.

Definition: A *general tree* is a set of nodes that is either empty (the recursive terminating condition) or has a designated node, called the *root*, from which zero or more subtrees descend. Each subtree itself satisfies the definition of a tree. Moreover, the collection of subtrees of the root is ordered in that there is a first subtree, second subtree, and so forth. The operations to be performed on a general tree are shown in terms of the following pre- and postconditions.

`Construct Operation (First Form)`

Preconditions: An uninitialized general tree object.
Postconditions: The general tree object is initialized to the empty general tree.

`Construct Operation (Copy Constructor)`

Preconditions: An uninitialized general tree object;
inittree—a general tree object that was previously constructed.
Postconditions: The general tree object is initialized to *inittree*.

`Destroy Operation`

Preconditions: A previously constructed general tree object.
Postconditions: All storage associated with the general tree object is deallocated.

`Assign Operation`

Preconditions: A previously constructed general tree object;
source—a second general tree object that uses the same data type as the owner of the operation.
Postconditions: The contents of *source* have been copied to the general tree object that owns the operation.

`Empty Operation`

Preconditions: A previously constructed general tree object.
Postconditions: Returns TRUE if the tree is empty, FALSE otherwise.

`NoRoomLeft Operation`

Preconditions: A previously constructed general tree object.
Postconditions: Returns TRUE if the tree will not allow further additions, FALSE otherwise.

`Preorder Traversal Operation`

Preconditions: A previously constructed general tree object;
processnode—an algorithmic process that can be applied to each node in the general tree.
Postconditions: Each node of the general tree is visited in the following order: root of the general tree first, then recursively all nodes in first subtree, then recursively all nodes in second subtree, then all nodes in the third subtree, and so forth. As each node is visited, *processnode* is applied to it.

`Postorder Traversal Operation`

Preconditions: A previously constructed general tree object;
processnode—an algorithmic process that can be applied to each node in the tree.

Postconditions: Each node of the general tree is visited in the following order: first visit recursively all nodes in first subtree, then visit recursively all nodes in second subtree, then visit all nodes in third subtree, and so forth. After all the nodes in each of the subtrees have been visited, finally visit the root. As each node is visited, *processnode* is applied to it.

These pre- and postconditions translate into the following C++ class interface.

```
// BaseData is either a C++ built-in type, or a C++ class that has
// an assignment operation that overloads the "=" operator.

template <class BaseData>
class GenTree
{
  public:
// ------------------------------------------------------------------------
// Interface for GenTree constructor
// GIVEN:   An uninitialized GenTree object.
// RETURN:  The GenTree object is initialized to the empty tree.

    GenTree();

// ------------------------------------------------------------------------
// Interface for GenTree copy constructor
// GIVEN:    An uninitialized GenTree object;
//           inittree -- a GenTree object that was previously constructed.
// RETURN:   The GenTree object is initialized with the node values and number of
//           nodes of initree.

    GenTree(GenTree &inittree);

// ------------------------------------------------------------------------
// Interface for GenTree destructor
// GIVEN:   A previously initialized GenTree object.
// RETURN:  All storage associated with the GenTree object is deallocated.

    ~GenTree();

// ------------------------------------------------------------------------
// Interface for GenTree assign = operator
// GIVEN:    A previously constructed GenTree object;
//           source -- a second GenTree object that must have been constructed
//                     with the same BaseData type as the owner of the assign
//                     operator.
// RETURN:   The contents of source have been copied to the GenTree object
//           that owns the operation.
// RETURN as value of function: void

    void operator = (const GenTree<BaseData> &source);

// ------------------------------------------------------------------------
// Interface for empty operation
// GIVEN:   A previously initialized GenTree object.
// RETURN as value of function:
//          TRUE if the GenTree object is empty, FALSE otherwise.

    BOOLEAN empty();
```

```
// ----------------------------------------------------------------------------
// Interface for noRoomLeft operation
// GIVEN:    A previously initialized GenTree object.
// RETURN as value of function:
//           TRUE if the GenTree object has no room for additional nodes;
//           FALSE otherwise.

    BOOLEAN noRoomLeft();

// ----------------------------------------------------------------------------
// Interface to preorder traversal operation
// GIVEN:   A GenTree object;
//          processNode---a pointer to a function that can act
//                        on each node in the tree.
// RETURN:  All nodes in the tree are visited in a preorder traversal
//          (root, first subtree, second subtree, third subtree, and so forth),
//          applying processNode to each node as it is visited.
// RETURN as value of function: void

    void preorderTrav(void (*processNode)(BaseData &item));

// ----------------------------------------------------------------------------
// Interface to postorder traversal operation
// GIVEN:   A GenTree object;
//          processNode---a pointer to a function that can act
//                        on each node in the tree.
// RETURN:  All nodes in the tree are visited in a postorder traversal
//          (first subtree, second subtree, third subtree, and so forth,
//          finally the root after all subtrees), applying processNode
//          to each node as it is visited.
// RETURN as value of function: void

    void postorderTrav(void (*processNode)(BaseData &item));
};
```

Notice that we have intentionally omitted defining an **add** operation for the general tree ADT. This is because the variety of possible interfaces for such an operation is literally overwhelming. Rather than define **add** as a pure virtual operation at the base class level (as we did for binary trees), it is better for each application to define its own interface for an **add** operation in a fashion that is most appropriate for that application. We examine two possibilities for the **add** operation in the next section.

Another difference from our interface for the binary tree ADT is that the general tree class provides only two traversal operations. Only the preorder and postorder traversals make sense for a general tree. Because a node may have more than two subtrees, the inorder operation that we defined for binary trees would be ambiguous for general trees. The following two examples indicate the action taken by pre- and postorder traversals for a general tree.

Example 8.1

Given the genealogical tree for the JONES family in Figure 8.1, indicate the order that nodes would be processed in a preorder traversal.

Since a preorder traversal processes the parent first and then, recursively, all the children, we would have

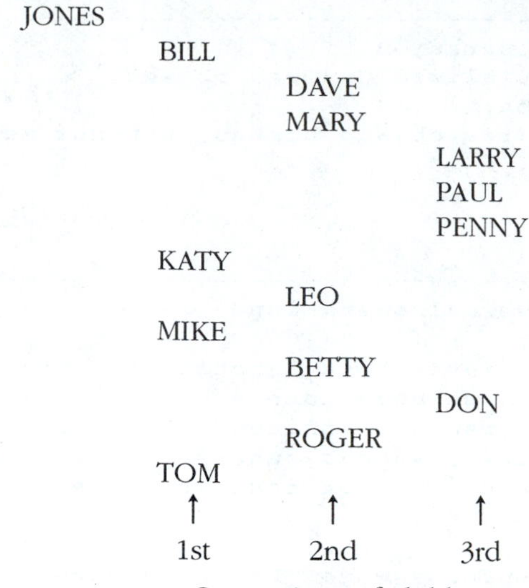

The indentation here has been added to highlight the fact that the preorder traversal will

- Process a parent node, and then
- Recursively process the child nodes from left to right.

Relative to the general tree pictured in Figure 8.1, we see that the effect of the preorder traversal is to fix on a node at one level of the tree and then run through all of that node's children before progressing to the next node at the same level (the sibling). There is a hint here of a generalized nested-loop situation, which has some interesting applications, described in Chapter 10.

Example 8.2

Indicate the order that nodes in the tree of Figure 8.1 would be processed by a postorder traversal.

In general, the postorder traversal works its way up from the leaf nodes of a tree, ensuring that no given node is processed until all nodes in the subtree below it have been processed. Moreover, the subtrees of a given node are processed

Figure 8.1
A genealogical tree.

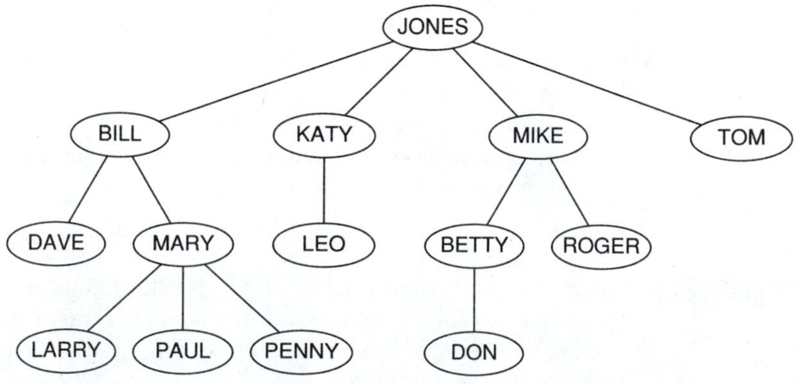

in first-to-last, that is, left-to-right, fashion. Hence, a postorder traversal yields the following listing:

DAVE
LARRY
PAUL
PENNY
MARY
BILL
LEO
KATY
DON
BETTY
ROGER
MIKE
TOM
JONES

Exercises 8.1

1. Indicate the order that nodes would be processed by a preorder traversal of the following general tree:

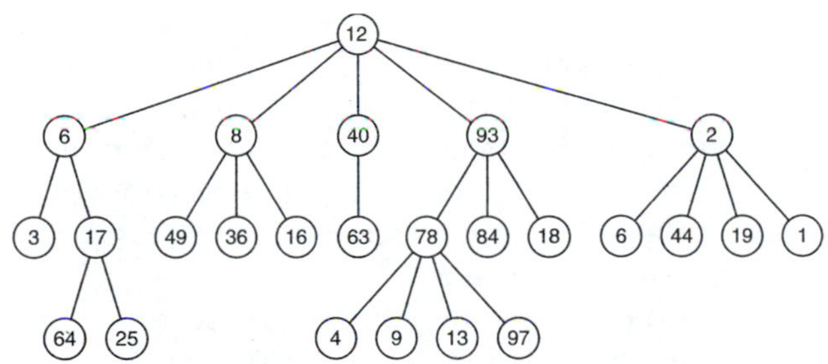

2. Indicate the order that nodes would be processed in a postorder traversal of the tree in Exercise 8.1.1.
3. Explain why an inorder traversal is not an applicable operation for a general tree.
4. Assuming the existence of the **preorderTrav** function, write a C++ algorithm that would print the preorder traversal of a tree in the indented format appearing in Example 8.1.
5. Assuming the existence of the **preorderTrav** function, write a C++ algorithm to count the number of nodes in a general tree.
6. There are certainly alternative methods for defining the general tree ADT. One such method is to not provide explicit traversal operations but rather to provide operations that allow you to "navigate" your position within the tree from a continually changing "current node." For example, you could provide operations that allow you to do the following:
   a. Move to the root of thetree, that is, establish the root as the current node.
   b. Move to the *K*th child of the current node, where *K* would be a parameter for the operation.
   c. Move to the parent of the current node.

   Provide an ADT definition of a general tree based on this approach. Then, using the operations from your definition, write preorder and postorder traversal algorithms.

8.2 Implementations of General Trees

Because, in a general tree, a node may have any number of children, the implementation of a general tree is more complex than that of a binary tree. One alternative is to use a maximum but fixed number of children for each node. This strategy,

Figure 8.2
Binary tree representation of the genealogical tree in Figure 8.1.

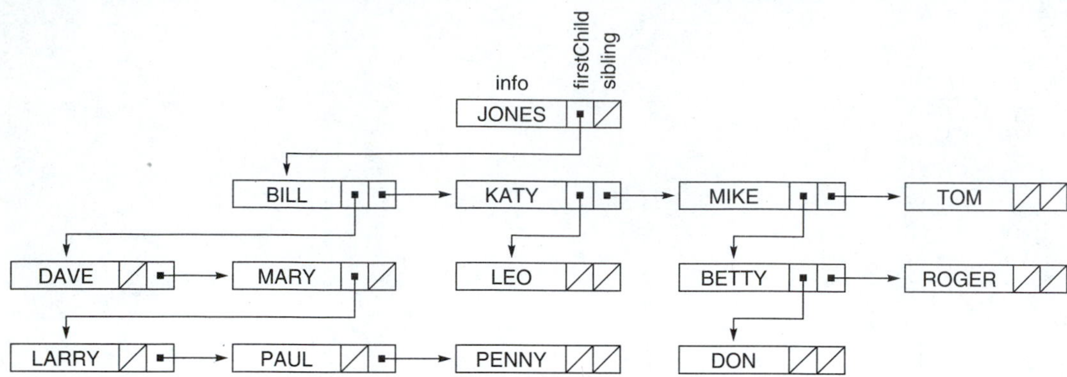

however, has the disadvantage of being very wasteful of memory space taken up by NULL nodes. Hence, it is only effective in applications where you have prior knowledge regarding a realistic limit on the number of children a tree node may have (such as the application we will encounter in Section 8.3).

Binary Tree Representation of General Trees

A more practical way of implementing a completely general tree is to use a binary representation. This requires that each node have only two pointer fields. The first pointer points to the leftmost (that is, first) child of the node, and the second pointer identifies the next sibling to the right of the node under consideration. Since the children form an ordered set of nodes in this context, we can regard the leftmost child of a node as **firstChild** and the sibling to the right of this node as **sibling**. We will henceforth adopt this terminology for the two link fields involved with the binary tree representation of a general tree. Figure 8.2 gives the binary representation of the genealogical tree shown in Figure 8.1.

To implement the **GenTree** class in C++ using this strategy, we need to define a **GtNode** class and then add a protected **root** pointer to the **GenTree** itself.

```
template <class BaseData>
class GtNode
{
  public:
    BaseData info;                      // The data in the node
    GtNode *firstChild, *sibling;
};

template <class BaseData>
class GenTree
{
  protected:
    GtNode<BaseData> *root;

  public:
  :
```

```
   // Interfaces as defined in Section 8.1
      :
};
```

Traversal of a General Tree Implemented via a Binary Tree

Because the binary scheme for a general tree is nothing more than a special interpretation of a binary tree, a traversal for a general tree can be established using any of the binary tree traversals. A more relevant question than the mere existence of a traversal, however, is the significance of the order in which the nodes of a general tree are visited when its representative binary tree is traversed. Of particular interest in this regard are the preorder and postorder traversals.

You should verify using Figure 8.2 that a preorder traversal of the underlying binary tree (assuming that **firstChild** and **sibling** play the roles of **leftChild** and **rightChild**, respectively) yields precisely the order of the general tree preorder traversal that we specified in Example 8.1. However, we are not as fortunate in the case of a postorder traversal. Here the binary tree postorder traversal from Figure 8.2 yields the listing

PENNY
PAUL
LARRY
MARY
DAVE
LEO
DON
ROGER
BETTY
TOM
MIKE
KATY
BILL
JONES

This is *not* the general tree postorder traversal we obtained in Example 8.2. We will leave as a creative exercise the problem of generating a postorder traversal for a binary tree implementation of a general tree.

Adding Nodes to a General Tree that Is Implemented by a Binary Tree

Each application will have the need to add nodes to a tree in its own particular way. For instance, sometimes it may be most convenient to add a node to a tree by specifying what the parent of the node should be. In such situations, the node to be added will have to work its way down from the root of the tree, with comparisons being made to existing tree nodes until the appropriate parent is found. The derived class **TopDownTree** provides an interface for a general tree in which nodes are added in such top-down fashion.

```
// BaseData is either a C++ built-in type, or a C++ class that has an assignment
// operation that overloads the "=" operator and an equality test that overloads
```

```
// the "==" operator.
template <class BaseData>
class TopDownTree : public GenTree<BaseData>
{
  public:
//--------------------------------------------------------------------------------
// Interface for TopDownTree constructor
// GIVEN:   An uninitialized TopDownTree object;
// RETURN:  The TopDownTree object is initialized to the empty tree.

    TopDownTree();

//--------------------------------------------------------------------------------
// Interface for add operation
// GIVEN:   A TopDownTree object;
//          parent -- a value of type BaseData;
//          item -- a value of type BaseData;
//          childnum -- an integer greater than or equal to 1.
// RETURN:  item is added to the TopDownTree as child number childnum of the
//          node containing parent as its data.  If there is more than one node
//          that contains parent as its data, item is added as a child of the
//          first such node found in a preorder traversal.  If childnum exceeds
//          the current number of children of the parent by more than one, item
//          is added as the last child of the parent.  If the parent does not
//          occur in the tree, then the tree is left unaffected unless it is
//          empty, in which case item is added as the root node of the tree.
// RETURN as value of function:
//           TRUE if item is added to the tree, FALSE if item is not added.

    BOOLEAN add(const BaseData &parent, const BaseData &item, int childnum);
};
```

Figure 8.3 indicates how this **add** operation could be used by a client program to build a five-node tree of integers.

Figure 8.3
Adding nodes to a TopDownTree object.

Operation	Resulting trees
1. TopDownTree<int> t();	t is empty
2. t.add(1,1,1);	1
3. t.add(1,2,1);	 1 — 2
4. t.add(1,3,2);	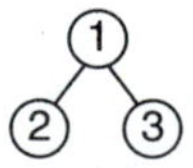 1 — 2, 3
5. t.add(3,4,1);	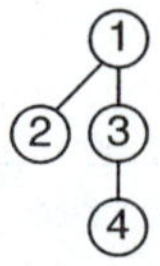 1 — 2, 3; 3 — 4
6. t.add(1,5,3);	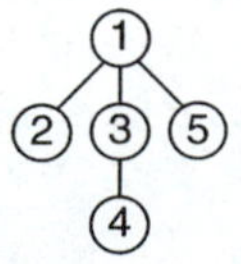 1 — 2, 3, 5; 3 — 4

For other applications, it may be more convenient to build a tree in a bottom-up fashion, with existing subtrees being attached to a root node. For such applications, the derived class **BottomUpTree** is appropriate.

```
// BaseData is either a C++ built-in type, or a C++ class that has an assignment
// operation that overloads the "=" operator.
template <class BaseData>
class BottomUpTree : public GenTree<BaseData>
{
  public:
//--------------------------------------------------------------------------------
// Interface for BottomUpTree constructor
// GIVEN:   An uninitialized BottomUpTree object;
//          item -- a value of type BaseData.
// RETURN:  The BottomUpTree object is initialized to a one-node tree
//          containing item as its root.
//
    BottomUpTree(const BaseData &item);

//--------------------------------------------------------------------------------
// Interface for add operation
// GIVEN:   A nonempty BottomUpTree object;
//          subtree -- another BottomUpTree object;
//          childnum -- an integer greater than or equal to 1.
// RETURN:  subtree is added to the BottomUpTree object as child number
//          childnum.  If childnum exceeds the current number of children of
//          the tree by more than one, item is added as the last child of
//          the tree.

    void add(BottomUpTree<BaseData> subtree, int childnum);
};
```

Figure 8.4 indicates how the same five-node tree of Figure 8.3 would be built using the **add** operation for the **BottomUpTree** class.

Figure 8.4
Building the tree of Figure 8.3 as a BottomUpTree object.

Operation	Resulting trees
1. BottomUpTree<int> t(1);	1
2. BottomUpTree<int> s(2); t.add(s,1);	1 — 2
3. BottomUpTree<int> s(3); BottomUpTree<int> r(4); s.add(r,1);	1 — 2; 3 — 4
4. t.add(s,2);	1 (2, 3 — 4)
5. BottomUpTree<int> s(5); t.add(s,3);	1 (2, 3 — 4, 5)

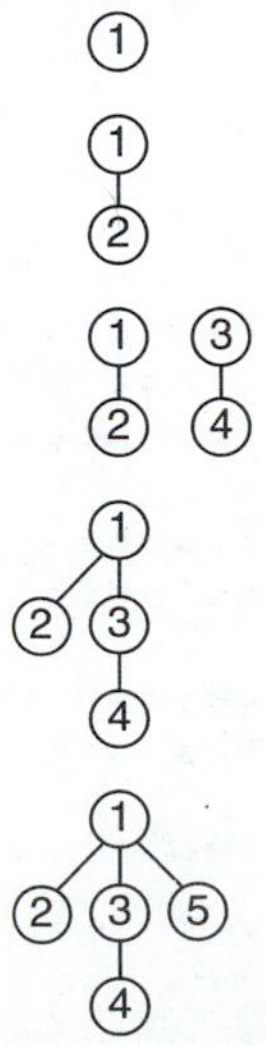

Implementation of the TopDownTree Class

The implementations of the constructor and the **add** operation for the **TopDownTree** and **BottomUpTree** derived classes differ considerably. The constructor for the **TopDownTree** class need do nothing but call on the constructor for the parent **GenTree** class.

```
// Implementation of the TopDownTree constructor
template <class BaseData>
TopDownTree<BaseData>::TopDownTree()
          : GenTree<BaseData>()  // Call on parent constructor
{ // And do nothing else
}
```

The **add** operation for the **TopDownTree** assumes that we can make an equality comparison on items of type **BaseData** using the == operator. The implementation of the **add** operation uses this equality comparison to traverse the tree and detect when the appropriate parent node has been found. This traversal is achieved by having the **add** function itself serve as mere go-between that passes the **root** pointer for the tree to a private auxillary function. This auxiliary function, called **addAux** in the following code, is the real recursive workhorse for the operation.

```
// BaseData is either a C++ built-in type, or a C++ class that has
// an assignment operation that overloads the "=" operator and an
// equality test that overloads the "==" operator.
template <class BaseData>
class TopDownTree : public GenTree<BaseData>
{
:

  private:
//------------------------------------------------------------------------
// Interface for auxiliary addAux function
// GIVEN:    rt -- root pointer for a general TopDownTree;
//           parent -- a value of type BaseData;
//           item -- a value of type BaseData;
//           childnum -- an int greater than or equal to 1.
// RETURN:   item is added to the TopDownTree as child number childnum
//           of the node containing parent as its data.  If there is
//           more than one node that contains parent as its data, item
//           is added as a child of the first such node found in a
//           preorder traversal. If childnum exceeds the current number
//           of children of the parent by more than one, item is added
//           as the last child of the parent.  If the parent does not
//           occur in the tree, then the tree is left unaffected unless
//           it is empty, in which case it is added as the root node of
//           the tree.
// RETURN as value of function:
//           TRUE if item is added to the tree, FALSE if item is not added.

    BOOLEAN addAux(GtNode<BaseData> *rt, const BaseData &parent,
                   const BaseData &item, int childnum);

:
};
```

```
// Implementation of public add and private addAux functions
template <class BaseData>
BOOLEAN TopDownTree<BaseData>::add(const BaseData &parent, const BaseData &item,
                                   int childnum)
{
  if (root == NULL)        // Empty tree is a special case
  {
    root = new GtNode<BaseData>;
    root->info = item;
    root->firstChild = NULL;
    root->sibling = NULL;
    return(TRUE);
  }
  else                     // Call on the auxiliary function
    return(addAux(root, parent, item, childnum));
}

template <class BaseData>
BOOLEAN TopDownTree<BaseData>::addAux(GtNode<BaseData> *rt, const BaseData &parent,
                                      const BaseData &item, int childnum)
{
  GtNode<BaseData> *temp;
  GtNode<BaseData> *prev;
  int c;

  if (rt != NULL)
    if (parent == rt->info)    // We've found the right parent!
    {
      temp = new GtNode<BaseData>;
      temp->info = item;
      temp->firstChild = NULL;
      // First check if we're inserting item as first child of parent
      if (childnum == 1 || rt->firstChild == NULL)
      {
        temp->sibling = rt->firstChild;
        rt->firstChild = temp;
      }
      else  // Advance prev pointer to predecessor of item
      {
```

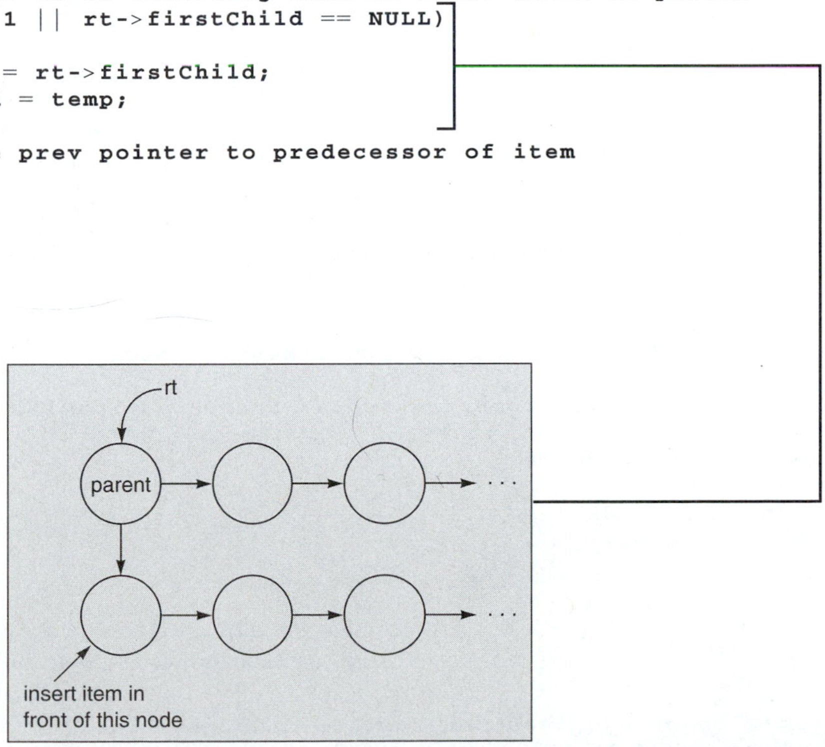

```
      for (c = 2, prev = rt->firstChild; (c < childnum && prev != NULL);
           ++c, prev = prev->sibling);
      temp->sibling = prev->sibling;
      prev->sibling = temp;
    }
    return(TRUE);
  }
  // Look for parent -- first in tree below rt, then in sibling of rt
  else
    if (!addAux(rt->firstChild, parent, item, childnum))
      return(addAux(rt->sibling, parent, item, childnum));
    else
      return(TRUE);
else      // rt is NULL, so parent was not found
  return(FALSE);
}
```

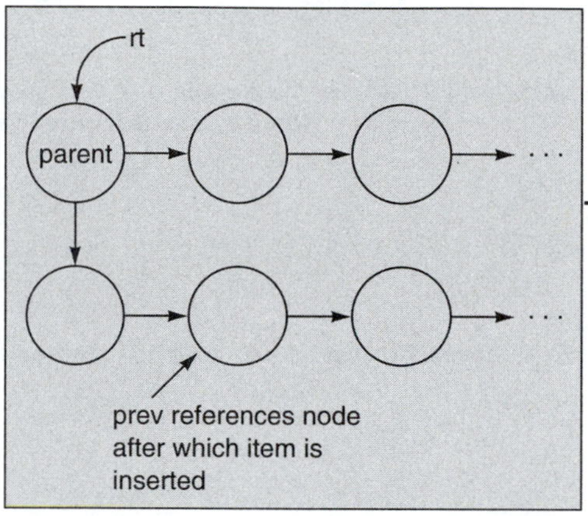

rt
parent
prev references node after which item is inserted

Implementation of the BottomUpTree Class

Because addition of nodes to a **BottomUpTree** is not keyed by searching for a particular parent node, an equality comparison is not needed in the implementation. Instead we provide a constructor that initializes one-node trees to contain a particular data item. This allows us to build larger trees via the construction of many one-node trees as illustrated in Figure 8.4. The implementation of this one-node tree constructor appears as follows:

```
// Implementation of constructor for BottomUpTree class
template <class BaseData>
BottomUpTree<BaseData>::BottomUpTree(const BaseData &item): GenTree<BaseData>()
{
  root = new GtNode<BaseData>;
  root->info = item;
  root->firstChild = NULL;
  root->sibling = NULL;
}
```

Because it is not recursive, the **add** operation for the **BottomUpTree** class does not require a protected auxiliary function for its implementation.

```
// Implementation of add function for BottomUpTree class
template <class BaseData>
```

```
void BottomUpTree<BaseData>::add(BottomUpTree<BaseData> subtree, int childnum)
{
  int c;
  GtNode<BaseData> *prev;

  if (childnum == 1 || root->firstChild == NULL)
  { // Subtree is first child
    subtree.root->sibling = root->firstChild;
    root->firstChild = subtree.root;
  }
  else                                                    // Insert after first child
  {
    for (c = 2, prev = root->firstChild; (c < childnum && prev != NULL);
         ++c, prev = prev->sibling);
    subtree.root->sibling = prev->sibling;
    prev->sibling = subtree.root;
  }
}
```

root of owner of operation

prev references node after which subtree is inserted

root of owner of operation

insert subtree in front of this node

Exercises 8.2

1. Consider the following abstract graphical representation of a general tree. Draw a specific picture of how this tree would actually be stored using the binary tree implementation.

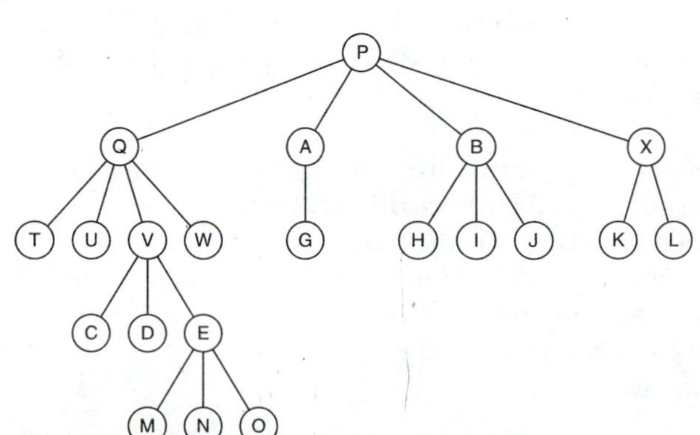

2. Indicate the order in which nodes would be visited by a preorder traversal of the general tree in Exercise 8.2.1.
3. Indicate the order in which nodes would be visited by a postorder traversal of the general tree in Exercise 8.2.1.
4. Write a C++ version of the postorder traversal operation for a general tree using the binary tree implementation.
5. Implement the destructor and **empty** operations for a binary tree representation of a general tree.
6. In Section 3.1 the List ADT was defined. Discuss in general terms how the corresponding **List** class could be used to implement a general tree. Then carry out this implementation by writing C++ code for each of the general tree operations.

7. Extend the list-based implementation of a general tree that you developed in Exercise 8.2.6 to an implementation of the derived **TopDownTree** class.
8. Extend the list-based implementation of a general tree that you developed in Exercise 8.2.6 to an implementation of the derived **BottomUpTree** class.
9. In Exercise 8.1.6, you developed an alternative version of the ADT definition for a general tree. Now provide a complete C++ function for each of the operations in your definition under the assumption that a binary tree implementation of the general tree is used.
10. Repeat Exercise 8.2.9, but now use the list-based implementation that you described in Exercise 8.2.6.
11. A *forest* is defined as a collection of general trees. A preorder traversal of a forest is a preorder traversal of the first tree in the forest, followed by a preorder traversal of the second, and so forth. Explain how a binary tree or list could be used to implement a forest. Then, for one of these implementations, provide the C++ version of a preorder forest traversal.

8.3 Application: 2-3 Trees

We have seen in Section 7.3 that an ordered binary search tree can be used to implement an ordered list. The primary drawback of such an implementation is that, though the search efficiency may be as good as $O(\log_2 n)$, this fast search efficiency cannot be guaranteed. It depends on the order in which data arrive for insertion into the tree. In Section 7.6, we examined height-balancing as an implementation strategy for guaranteeing an $O(\log_2 n)$ search efficiency. We also noted that the constant of proportionality involved in this big-O efficiency figure is approximately 1.5.

In this section we examine another tree-based technique for implementing an ordered list. Called a *2-3 tree*, this technique can improve on the efficiency of a height-balanced tree by guaranteeing a search path that never exceeds $\log_2 n + 1$. That is, it matches the efficiency of a full binary tree. The price paid for this efficiency is space—a price we will analyze more fully after examining the technique. Formally, we can define a 2-3 tree as follows.

Definition: A *2-3 tree* consists of a general tree and a precedence relationship **precedes** with the following properties.

1. Every node in the 2-3 tree has room to store two informational fields. Call these informational fields **firstInfo** and **secondInfo**. Typically, these informational fields can represent two full-fledged data records.
2. Every node in the 2-3 tree has room for three pointers to other nodes. Call these pointers **firstChild, secondChild,** and **thirdChild**.
3. Every node in the 2-3 tree has either
   a. **firstInfo** with active data and **secondInfo** with an empty flag, or
   b. the data in **firstInfo** preceding that in **secondInfo** according to the **precedes** relationship for the tree.
4. In any given nonleaf node:
   a. All data in the subtree referenced by **firstChild** must precede **firstInfo,** and all data in the subtree referenced by **secondChild** must follow **firstInfo** in the **precedes** relationship for the tree.
   b. If **secondInfo** has active data, then all data in the subtree referenced by **secondChild** must precede **secondInfo,** and all data in the subtree referenced by **thirdChild** must follow **secondInfo**.
5. All leaf nodes are on the same level.

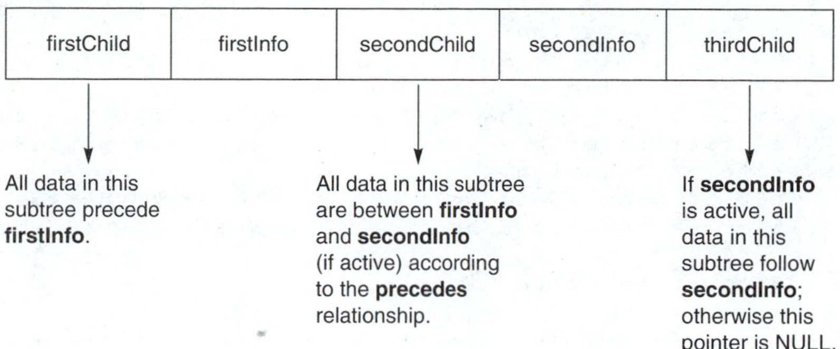

Figure 8.5
2-3 tree node.

According to this definition, we can think of a 2-3 tree node that is *not* at leaf level as the structure in Figure 8.5. An example of a three-level 2-3 tree with integer informational keys appears in Figure 8.6. Those nodes in which the **secondInfo** field is not active appear simply as data nodes with only one integer in them.

A minimal public interface for the 2-3 tree as an ADT is provided in the following class definition. In addition to a constructor that specifies the **precedes** relation for the tree, the class provides operations to add and search for nodes in the tree.

Figure 8.6
A 2-3 tree with integer data. Nodes with only one integer have a **secondInfo** field that is not active.

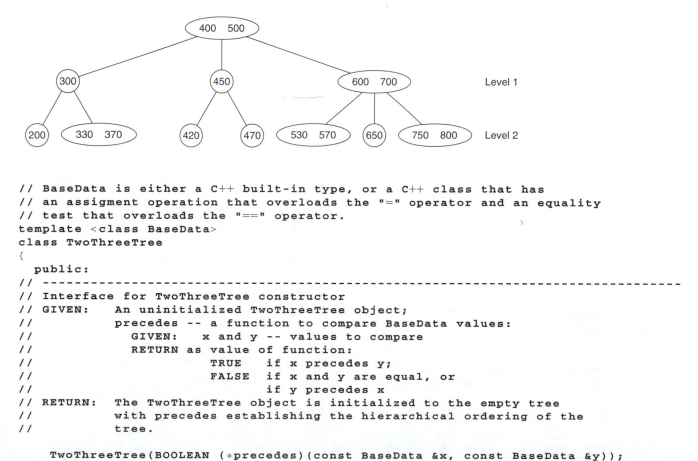

```
// BaseData is either a C++ built-in type, or a C++ class that has
// an assigment operation that overloads the "=" operator and an equality
// test that overloads the "==" operator.
template <class BaseData>
class TwoThreeTree
{
  public:
// ---------------------------------------------------------------------------
// Interface for TwoThreeTree constructor
// GIVEN:    An uninitialized TwoThreeTree object;
//           precedes -- a function to compare BaseData values:
//             GIVEN:    x and y -- values to compare
//             RETURN as value of function:
//                       TRUE    if x precedes y;
//                       FALSE   if x and y are equal, or
//                               if y precedes x
// RETURN:   The TwoThreeTree object is initialized to the empty tree
//           with precedes establishing the hierarchical ordering of the
//           tree.

    TwoThreeTree(BOOLEAN (*precedes)(const BaseData &x, const BaseData &y));
```

```
// ----------------------------------------------------------------------------
// Interface for add operation
// GIVEN:   A TwoThreeTree object;
//          item -- a value of type BaseData.
// RETURN:  item is added to the TwoThreeTree in a fashion that retains
//          the ordering of the tree according to its precedes relation.
// RETURN as value of function:
//           TRUE if item could be added to the TwoThreeTree;  FALSE if
//           item was not added because it was already in the tree.

    BOOLEAN add(const BaseData &item);

// ----------------------------------------------------------------------------
// Interface for search operation
// GIVEN:   A TwoThreeTree object;
//          target -- a value of type BaseData that contains, perhaps in a special
//                    key field, a value to be searched for using the equality test
//                    for BaseData.
// RETURN:  item -- a value of type BaseData. If target can be found in the tree,
//                  item contains the entire contents of the tree node (key value and
//                  all associated data) that matches target.
// RETURN as value of function:
//           TRUE if target could be found in the TwoThreeTree;  FALSE if
//           target is not in the tree.

    BOOLEAN search(const BaseData &target, BaseData &item);
};
```

To implement the **TwoThreeTree** class, we first need to provide a **TwoThreeNode** class.

```
template <class BaseData>
class TwoThreeNode
{
  public:
    BaseData firstInfo, secondInfo;   // The data in the nodes
    TwoThreeNode *firstChild, *secondChild, *thirdChild;
    TwoThreeNode *parent;          // Parent pointer facilitates moving up tree
};
```

We then include two protected members in the **TwoThreeTree** class definition—a root pointer for the tree and a **precedes** function. The constructor merely sets the root pointer to NULL and its **precedes** function to the **precedes** parameter that it receives.

```
template <class BaseData>
class TwoThreeTree
{
  protected:
    TwoThreeNode<BaseData> *root;
    BOOLEAN (*precedes)(const BaseData &x, const BaseData &y);
  :
  :  // Other members specified as before
};

// Implementation of the TwoThreeTree constructor
template <class BaseData>
```

```
TwoThreeTree<BaseData>::TwoThreeTree(BOOLEAN (*precedes)(const BaseData &x,
                                                         const BaseData &y))
{
  root = NULL;
  this->precedes = precedes;
}
```

Search Algorithm

The search algorithm for 2-3 trees is similar to that for a binary search tree. That is, we start at the root of the tree. A comparison of the **target** item to the informational fields indicates whether the **target** is in the current node or, based on the relationship of the **target** to **firstInfo** and **secondInfo**, which child pointer to follow. For instance, to find 650 in the tree of Figure 8.6, you should verify that

1. We follow the **thirdChild** pointer from the root, because 650 follows 500.
2. From the level 1 node containing 600 and 700 we follow the **secondChild** pointer, because 650 is between 600 and 700.
3. At level 2 we find the **target**.

This algorithm is formalized in the following implementation of the **search** function from the **TwoThreeTree** class definition. Following what has become a common trick in implementing recursive tree-based algorithms, the **search** function itself merely serves as a front-end function that passes the root pointer for the tree to the real recursive function. Here that recursive workhorse is called **privSearch** and is declared as a private function member of the **TwoThreeTree** class. As the following documentation indicates, the **privSearch** function does a bit more than needed in merely searching the tree. In particular, when the **target** is not found, it will return a pointer to the leaf node where it expected the **target** to be. This additional information will later allow us to use **privSearch** in the implementation of the **add** operation.

In addition to the **privSearch** function, we need to add another private subordinate function called **leafNode** to our class definition. This function simply tests whether a given tree node is a leaf node. Finally, we must establish a convention for determining if the informational members of a **TwoThreeNode** contain active data or an empty flag. The convention we adapt is to store NULL as the value for an empty flag. By type casting, we can then compare **BaseData** variables to NULL in checking for the empty flag.

```
// Augmenting the TwoThreeTree class definition with appropriate private
// functions for implementing the add operation

template <class BaseData>
class TwoThreeTree
{
  private:                          // Internal auxiliary functions

// ---------------------------------------------------------------------------
// Interface for privSearch function
// GIVEN:    rt -- a pointer to the root of a TwoThreeTree;
//           target -- a value of type BaseData that contains, perhaps in a
//                     special key field, a value to be searched for using the
//                     equality test for BaseData.
// RETURN:   item -- a value of type BaseData. If target can be found in the
//                   tree, item contains the entire contents of the tree node
//                   (key value and all associated data) that matches target,
```

```
//                      and the pointer where references the node where target is
//                      located.  If target is not found, item is unreliable, and
//                      the where pointer references the leaf node where target
//                      would have been located if it were in the tree.
// RETURN as value of function:
//             TRUE if target could be found in the TwoThreeTree;  FALSE if
//             target is not in the tree.
    BOOLEAN privSearch(TwoThreeNode<BaseData> *rt, const BaseData &target,
                       BaseData &item, TwoThreeNode<BaseData> *&where);

// -----------------------------------------------------------------------------
// Interface for leafNode function
// GIVEN:   t -- a pointer to a TwoThreeNode within a TwoThreeTree.
// RETURN as value of function:
//             TRUE if t references a leaf node within the TwoThreeTree and FALSE
//             otherwise.

    BOOLEAN leafNode(TwoThreeNode<BaseData> *t);

  :
  :   // Other class members declared as before
};

// Implementation of search, privSearch, and leafNode operations
template <class BaseData>
BOOLEAN TwoThreeTree<BaseData>::search(const BaseData &target, BaseData &item)
{
  TwoThreeNode<BaseData> *where;

  // Just pass the root pointer to the recursive workhorse
  return(privSearch(root, target, item, where));
}

template <class BaseData>
BOOLEAN TwoThreeTree<BaseData>::
  privSearch(TwoThreeNode<BaseData> *rt, const BaseData &target, BaseData &item,
             TwoThreeNode<BaseData> *&where)
{
  BOOLEAN found, atLeastOneItem, twoItems;

  if (rt == NULL)       // target will not be found in the empty tree
  {
    where = NULL;
    return(FALSE);
  }
  found = FALSE;
  // NULL is used as an empty flag in informational field.
  // Type casting allows comparison of BaseData variable to NULL.
  if (((int)(rt->firstInfo)) != NULL)
    atLeastOneItem = TRUE;
  else
    atLeastOneItem = FALSE;
  if (((int)(rt->secondInfo)) != NULL)
    twoItems = TRUE;
  else
    twoItems = FALSE;
  if (atLeastOneItem)
    if (rt->firstInfo == target)        // Check first key
    {
      found = TRUE;
      item = rt->firstInfo;
    }
```

```
    else
      if (twoItems)
        if (rt->secondInfo == target)    // Check second key
        {
          found = TRUE;
          item = rt->secondInfo;
        }

  // If target was found at rt or rt references a leafnode, return where as rt
  if (found || leafNode(rt))
  {
    where = rt;
    return(found);
  }

  // If reach this point, there must be at least one item in the node, so
  // make recursive call(s) to search appropriate subtree(s)
  if (precedes(target, rt->firstInfo))
    return(privSearch(rt->firstChild, target, item, where));
  if (!twoitems)
    return(privSearch(rt->secondChild, target, item, where));
  if (precedes(target, rt->secondInfo))
    return(privSearch(rt->secondChild, target, item, where));
  else
    return(privSearch(rt->thirdChild, target, item, where));
}

template <class BaseData>
BOOLEAN TwoThreeTree<BaseData>::leafNode(TwoThreeNode<BaseData> *t)
{
  if ((t->firstChild == NULL) && (t->secondChild == NULL) &&
      (t->thirdChild == NULL))
    return(TRUE);
  else
    return(FALSE);
}
```

firstInfo
secondInfo
Call recursively with this tree if **target** precedes **firstInfo**
Call recursively with this tree if **secondInfo** is empty or **target** precedes **secondInfo**
Call recursively with this tree if **secondInfo** precedes **target**

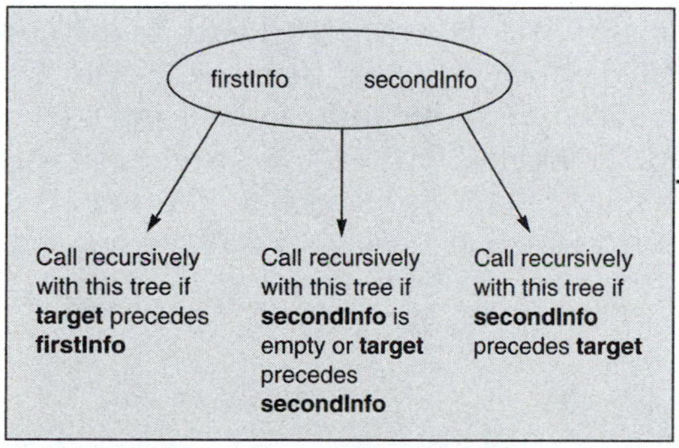

Search Efficiency

Stipulation 5 in our definition of a 2-3 tree is critical in an analysis of search efficiency for this data structure. By its guarantee that all leaf nodes are at the same level, it assures us that a 2-3 tree with N information items will have a maximal search path no longer than that in a *full* binary search tree with the same N items. From our earlier analysis of binary search trees, we know that this maximal path length is $\log_2 N + 1$.

Hence, provided we can develop **add** and **remove** operations that maintain a tree in a fashion dictated by the five stipulations in our definition of a 2-3 tree, we have a scheme for implementing ordered lists that is evidently on a par with full binary search trees and slightly better than height-balanced trees. What price have we paid? As usual, the trade-off is space. Here, we run the risk of having numerous **secondInfo** fields filled with the empty flag. (You will explore how many such fields can be wasted in the exercises and problems for this chapter.) If these fields are actually large data records, you may decide the wasted space is not worth the relatively minor gain in speed over height-balanced trees.

Add Algorithm

To ensure that stipulation 5 of the definition is met, 2-3 trees exhibit the rather curious behavior of adding a new level to the tree by sprouting a new root instead of a leaf at a deeper level. We can illustrate this phenomenon and the algorithm that controls it by making a few insertions on the tree of Figure 8.6.

Example 8.3

Insert 250 as an informational item in the tree of Figure 8.6 on page 357.

Here a search algorithm would dictate that, if 250 were in the tree, it should have been found in the same node as 200. Since there is room for another informational field in the node containing 200, the place to insert 250 is obvious—as the **secondInfo** field in that same node. The resulting tree is shown in Figure 8.7.

Example 8.4

Add 850 to the 2-3 tree of Figure 8.7.

The situation in this example is a bit more complex. As in Example 8.3, the search algorithm tells us that 850 should have been in the level-2 node containing 750 and 800 if it were in the tree. But it cannot fit there since we already have two data items. So, we will look at the tree items 750, 800, and 850; choose the middle one (800) to pass back up to the parent node; and then create two nodes containing one item each (for 750 and 850). Item 800 and the one-node tree containing 850 will then be passed back to the node containing 600 and 700. This is illustrated in Figure 8.8. If there were only one informational item here, 800 could be added as the **secondInfo** field and the node containing 850 added as the **thirdChild.** Unfortunately, there is not enough room, so the splitting process must be repeated with 600, 700, and 800. This time 700 is chosen as the middle value with two subtrees rooted at 600 and 800 also created. This is highlighted in Figure 8.9.

Figure 8.7
2-3 tree of Figure 8.6 with 250 inserted.

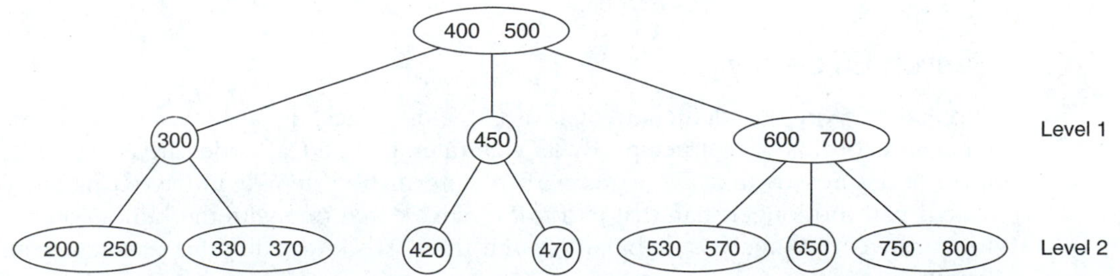

Figure 8.8
As leaf-level nodes become crowded, they are split with data being passed back up the tree to parent node.

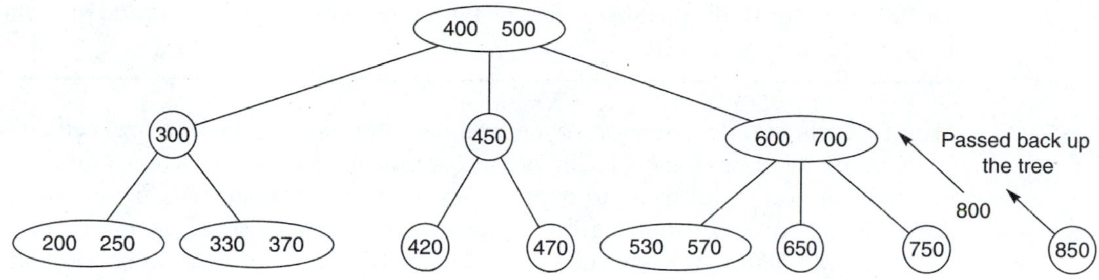

Figure 8.9
Splitting with transfer back up the tree must occur until we find a node with room to expand.

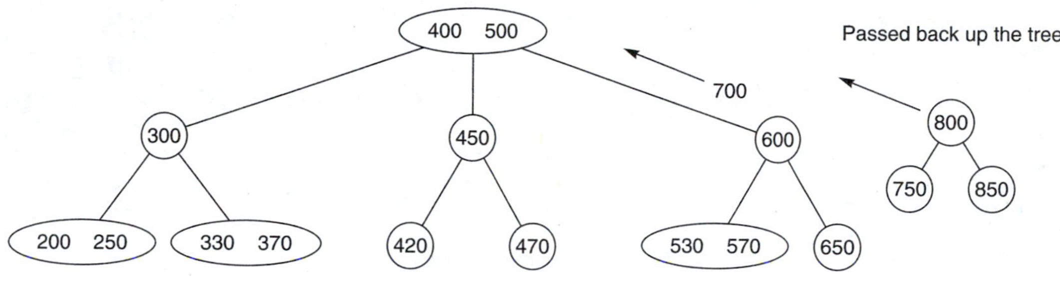

Figure 8.10
Final configuration of tree from Figure 8.7 after adding 850.

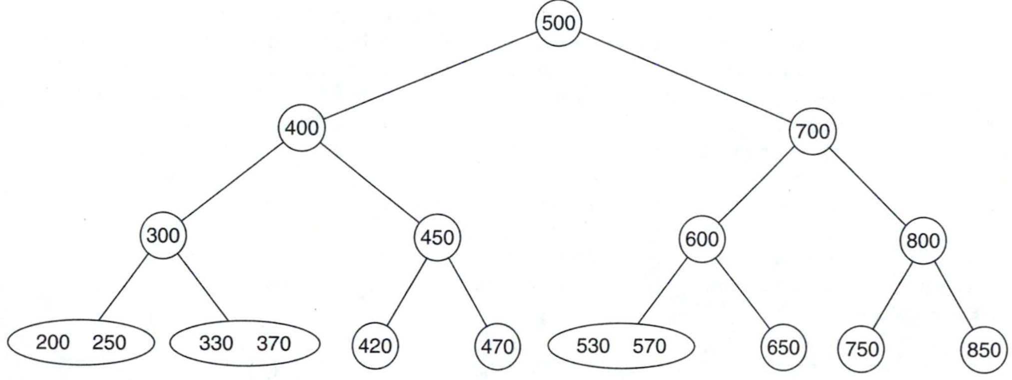

Item 700 is then passed back up the tree along with the subtree rooted at 800 for an encore of the splitting phenomenon. At the root, 400, 500, and 700 are compared. We split at 500, forming subtrees rooted at 400 and 700 and creating a new root with 500 as its **firstInfo** data item. The resulting tree, now with a level added at the top, is shown in Figure 8.10.

The following implementation of the **add** operation for the **TwoThreeTree** class considers the two possibilities illustrated in Examples 8.3 and 8.4, that is, adding an item in a leaf node with room to expand or forcing a split with data being passed recursively up the tree until we find a node with room to store additional data. The details of splitting a node (perhaps recursively) are deferred to a subordinate function called **split.** Finally, as a third possibility, the **add** function must consider the insertion of the first item in an empty tree as a special case.

```
// Augmenting the TwoThreeTree class definition with subordinate functions,
// in addition to privSearch, that are needed in implementing the add operation

template <class BaseData>
class TwoThreeTree
{
  private:                             // Internal auxiliary functions

// ------------------------------------------------------------------------------
// Interface for split function
// GIVEN:    t -- a pointer to the root of an entire TwoThreeTree containing
//                a node to be split;
//           tree -- a pointer to the root of current subtree that must be
//                   split to add the data parameter;
//           branch -- a pointer to a subtree to be added to the node
//                     referenced by tree if the addBranch parameter is TRUE.
//                     If addBranch is FALSE, branch has no well-defined value.
//           data -- the data item forcing the split of the current root
//                   referenced by tree.
//           addBranch -- a BOOLEAN value that is TRUE if a branch must be added
//                        to the splitting node in addition to the data item.
//                        addBranch is FALSE when a leaf node is being split and
//                        TRUE when an interior node is being split.
// RETURN:   t will become a pointer to a new root for the entire TwoThreeTree
//           if the tree parameter is without a parent node.  Otherwise t is
//           unchanged.  The node referenced by tree will be split based on the
//           value in the data parameter.  The node will contain just one
//           informational item and have a new sibling to its right.

    void split (TwoThreeNode<BaseData> *&t, TwoThreeNode<BaseData> *tree,
                TwoThreeNode<BaseData> *branch, const BaseData &data,
                BOOLEAN addBranch);

// ------------------------------------------------------------------------------
// Interface for makeTreeNode function
// GIVEN:    No preconditions.
// RETURN as value of function: A pointer to a TwoThreeNode initialized with all
//           informational fields set to the empty flag and all parent and child
//           pointers set to NULL.

    TwoThreeNode<BaseData> *makeTreeNode();

  :   // Other class members declared as before
};
```

```
// Implementation of the add, split, and makeTreeNode functions
template <class BaseData>
BOOLEAN TwoThreeTree<BaseData>::add(const BaseData &item)
{
  BaseData info;
  BOOLEAN found;
  TwoThreeNode<BaseData> *leaf;

  found = privSearch(root, item, info, leaf);    // Find leaf node for key
  if (leaf == NULL)                              // Make initial root
  {
    root = makeTreeNode();
    root->firstInfo = item;
    return(TRUE);
  }
  if (found)                                     // Item already in tree
    return(FALSE);
  // Add item if it will fit in leaf.  Otherwise call split to split leaf
  if ((int)(leaf->secondInfo) != NULL)
    // Then there are two items
    split(root, leaf, leaf, item, FALSE);
  else
    if (precedes(leaf->firstInfo, item))
      leaf->secondInfo = item;
    else
    {
      leaf->secondInfo = leaf->firstInfo;
      leaf->firstInfo = item;
    }
  return(TRUE);
}

template <class BaseData>
void TwoThreeTree<BaseData>::split(TwoThreeNode<BaseData> *&t,
                                   TwoThreeNode<BaseData> *tree,
                                   TwoThreeNode<BaseData> *branch,
                                   const BaseData &data, BOOLEAN addBranch)
{
  TwoThreeNode<BaseData> *parent, *sibling;
  BaseData key, middle;

  if (tree == t)
  { // Node referenced by tree is root, so make new parent (root) node
```

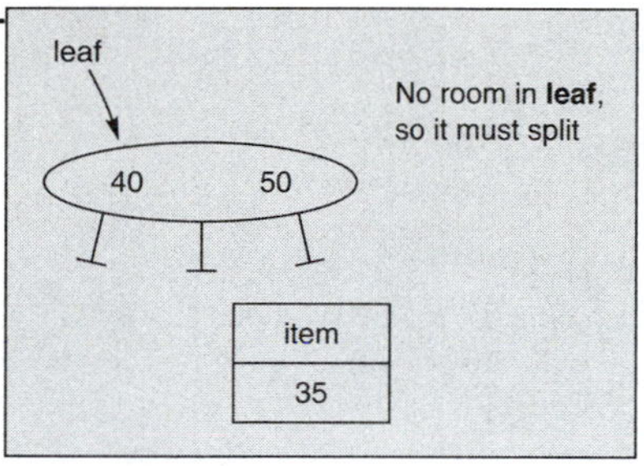

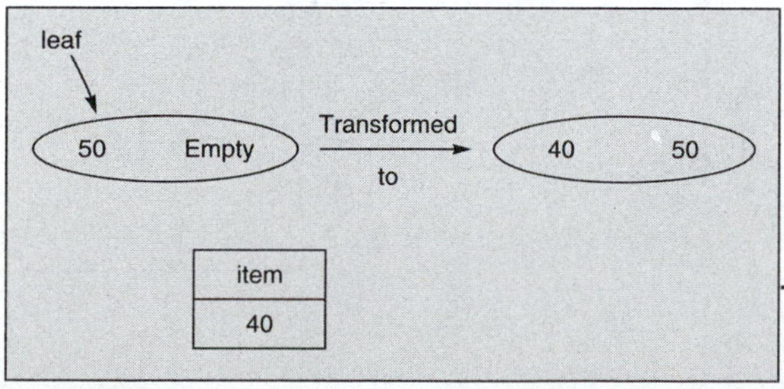

leaf
No room in **leaf**, so it must split
40 50
item
35

leaf
50 Empty
Transformed to
40 50
item
40

```
    parent = makeTreeNode();
    tree->parent = parent;
    parent->firstChild = tree;
    t = parent;
  }
  else
    parent = tree->parent;

  // Make sibling node with empty flags and NULL children
  sibling = makeTreeNode();
  sibling->parent = parent;

  // Determine which of the three key values is the middle one in terms
  // of value and assign it to middle.  Put/leave the smallest one in the
  // current node (tree), put the largest one into the new node (sibling).
  if (precedes(data, tree->firstInfo))
  {
    middle = tree->firstInfo;
    tree->firstInfo = data;
    sibling->firstInfo = tree->secondInfo;
    tree->secondInfo = (BaseData) NULL;
  }
  else
    if (precedes(data, tree->secondInfo))
    {
```

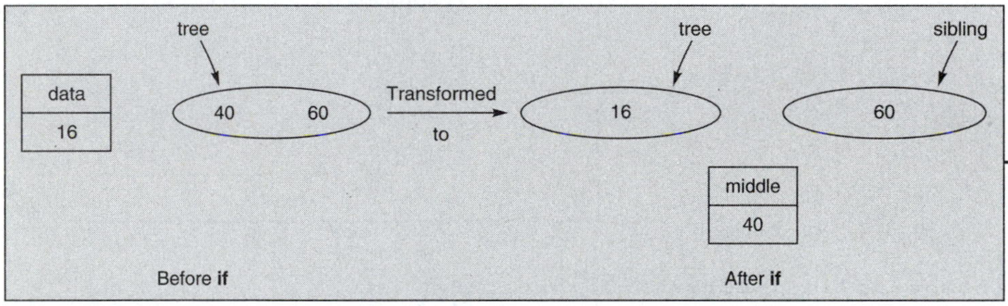

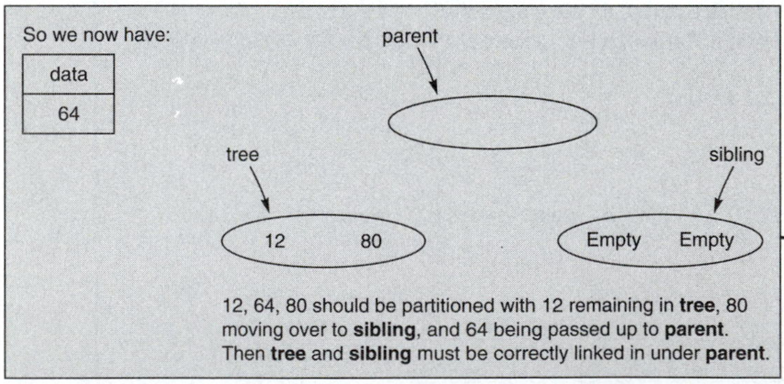

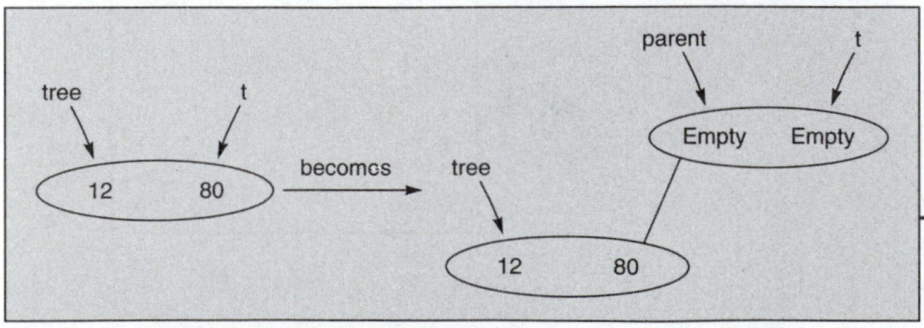

```
      middle = data;
      sibling->firstInfo = tree->secondInfo;
      tree->secondInfo = (BaseData) NULL;
    }
    else
    {
      sibling->firstInfo = data;
      middle = tree->secondInfo;
      tree->secondInfo = (BaseData) NULL;
    }

  // If this is an interior node, four children must be taken care of (the
  // fourth is branch).  Put/leave the two smallest (according to precedes
  // relation) children (subtrees) as the first two children of the old
  // node (tree), and put the two largest as the first two children of the
  // new node (sibling).  In addition, update the parent pointers of the
  // children to point to the appropriate parent nodes.

  if (addBranch)
  {
    key = branch->firstInfo;
    if (precedes(key, tree->firstChild->firstInfo))
    {
      sibling->secondChild = tree->thirdChild;
      sibling->firstChild = tree->secondChild;
      tree->thirdChild = NULL;
      tree->secondChild = tree->firstChild;
      tree->firstChild = branch;
      sibling->secondChild->parent = sibling;
      sibling->firstChild->parent = sibling;
      tree->firstChild->parent = tree;
    }
    else
      if (precedes(key, tree->secondChild->firstInfo))
      {
        sibling->secondChild = tree->thirdChild;
        sibling->firstChild = tree->secondChild;
        tree->thirdChild = NULL;
        tree->secondChild = branch;
        sibling->secondChild->parent = sibling;
        sibling->firstChild->parent = sibling;
        tree->secondChild->parent = tree;
      }
      else
        if (precedes(key, tree->thirdChild->firstInfo))
```

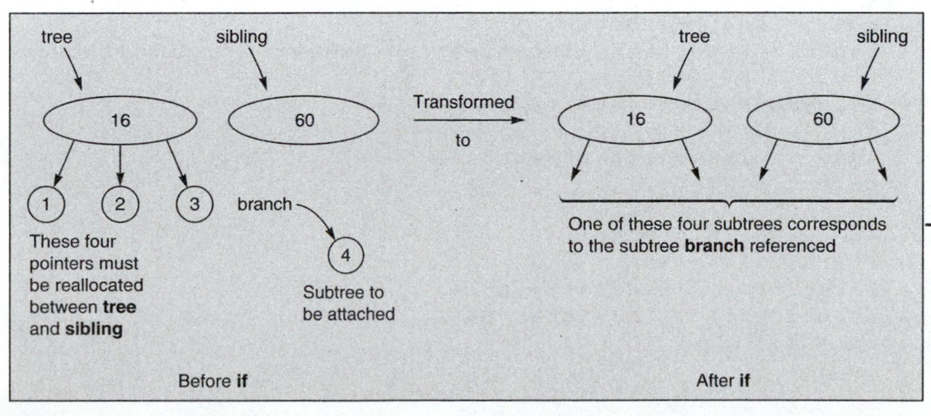

```
      {
        sibling->secondChild = tree->thirdChild;
        sibling->firstChild = branch;
        tree->thirdChild = NULL;
        sibling->secondChild->parent = sibling;
        sibling->firstChild->parent = sibling;
      }
      else
      {
        sibling->secondChild = branch;
        sibling->firstChild = tree->thirdChild;
        tree->thirdChild = NULL;
        sibling->secondChild->parent = sibling;
        sibling->firstChild->parent = sibling;
      }
  }  // if (addBranch)

  // Now "promote" middle up to the tree's parent node and determine whether
  // that node must be split.  If middle will fit, arrange the parent node
  // accordingly and return.  If not, then make a recursive call to split with
  // the parent node as tree, the sibling node as branch, and middle as data.

  if ((int) (parent->firstInfo) == NULL)   // Then firstInfo is empty flag
  {
    parent->firstInfo = middle;
    parent->firstChild = tree;
    parent->secondChild = sibling;
    return;
  }
  if ((int) (parent->secondInfo) != NULL)
  {
    split(t, parent, sibling, middle, TRUE);
    return;
  }
  if (precedes(parent->firstInfo, middle))
  {
    parent->secondInfo = middle;
    parent->thirdChild = sibling;
    return;
  }
  parent->secondInfo = parent->firstInfo;
  parent->firstInfo = middle;
  parent->thirdChild = parent->secondChild;
  parent->secondChild = sibling;
} // end of split function


template <class BaseData>
TwoThreeNode<BaseData> *TwoThreeTree<BaseData>::makeTreeNode()
{
  TwoThreeNode<BaseData> *p;

  p = new TwoThreeNode<BaseData>;
  p->parent = NULL;
  p->firstChild = NULL;
  p->secondChild = NULL;
  p->thirdChild = NULL;
  p->firstInfo = (BaseData) NULL;
  p->secondInfo = (BaseData) NULL;
  return(p);
}
```

Exercises 8.3

1. Repeat Exercise 7.3.1 for a 2-3 tree.
2. Repeat Exercise 7.3.2 for a 2-3 tree.
3. Repeat Exercise 7.3.3 for a 2-3 tree.
4. What is the percentage of informational fields wasted by storing empty flags for each of the final 2-3 trees from Exercises 8.3.1, 8.3.2, and 8.3.3?
5. What is the relationship of the distribution of data items in the nodes of a 2-3 tree to the order of their arrival for insertion in the tree? Explain your answer.
6. Develop a quasi-traversal algorithm for the data in a 2-3 tree. This algorithm should apply a function parameter **processNode** to all items in the tree that follow a specified lower bound and precede a specified upper bound. Code your algorithm as a C++ function to be added to the **TwoThreeTree** class.
7. Develop a remove algorithm for a target node in a 2-3 tree. Code your algorithm as a C++ function to be added to the **TwoThreeTree** class.
8. Could the definition of a 2-3 tree be extended to a 3-4 tree in which each node had up to three informational fields and four subtrees? If so, provide such a definition. What would be the advantages of using this new structure to implement an ordered list? What would be the drawbacks?

8.4 Application: The Union-Find Problem

As a final example of the wide variability of tree applications and implementations, we return to the union-find ADT, which was first introduced in Section 2.4. For reference in the discussion that follows, the public interface to the **UnionFind** class is presented here:

```
// Universe is a finite range of non-negative integers.
template <class Universe>
class UnionFind
{
  public:

// -----------------------------------------------------------------------
// Interface for UnionFind constructor
// GIVEN:     An uninitialized UnionFind object;
//            loElement -- the least element in the UnionFind universe;
//            hiElement -- the greatest element in the UnionFind universe.
// RETURN:    A UnionFind object initialized to collection of
//            disjoint sets in which each member of the universe is a
//            member of a one-element set, that is, a partition of
//            the universe into sets with only one element each.

    UnionFind(Universe loElement, Universe hiElement);

// -----------------------------------------------------------------------
// Interface for UnionFind destructor
// GIVEN:     A previously constructed UnionFind partition object.
// RETURN:    UnionFind object deallocated, with contents now unreliable.

    ~UnionFind();

// -----------------------------------------------------------------------
// Interface for ufFind operation
// GIVEN:     A previously constructed UnionFind partition object;
//            x, y -- two elements of the universe (between loElement and
//                    hiElement) from which the UnionFind object was constructed.
// RETURN as value of function:
//            TRUE if x and y are members of the same set in the
//            UnionFind object; FALSE otherwise.
```

```
    BOOLEAN ufFind(Universe x, Universe y);

// ---------------------------------------------------------------------------
// Interface for ufUnion operation
// GIVEN:     A previously constructed UnionFind partition object;
//            x, y -- two elements of the universe (between loElement and
//                    hiElement) from which the UnionFind object was constructed.
// RETURN:    The union of the sets containing x and y in the partition
//            is formed.  If the union is different from the original
//            sets containing x and y, the union is added to the partition
//            and the original sets removed.
// RETURN as value of function: void

    void ufUnion(Universe x, Universe y);
};
```

Because the **UnionFind** constructor assumes that the universe is an integer type with designated non-negative values **loElement** and **hiElement**, we can associate each element in the **UnionFind** universe with the index value of an **Array** object using the **Array** class defined in Section 2.1. The sets in the **UnionFind** partition may be viewed as a collection of trees whose node values correspond to **Universe** elements and in which each tree is identified by the value in its root. Because we only have two operations—**ufUnion** and **ufFind**—to consider, we can choose an implementation for these trees that is expressly tailored to optimize efficiency for this application. The implementation used is a simple one—a pointer to an **Array** object called **parent** that is indexed by the range from **loElement** to **hiElement**. Given a **Universe** element **e**, **(*parent)[e]** stores the array index corresponding to the parent of **e** in the tree containing **e.** If **e** is the root of the tree, **(*parent)[e]** stores the flagging value -1. We can choose -1 as this flagging value because of our assumption that the **Universe** class contains only non-negative values.

The C++ code necessary to implement the **UnionFind** operations according to this representation is quite simple. We must first add to the class definition a private data member to store the **parent** array.

```
// Universe is a finite range of non-negative integers.
template <class Universe>
class UnionFind
{
  private:
    Array<Universe,Universe> *parent;

    :  // Other class members defined as before
};
```

The four **UnionFind** operations can then be implemented as follows.

```
// Implementation of the UnionFind constructor
template <class Universe>
UnionFind<Universe>::UnionFind(Universe loElement, Universe hiElement)
{
  Universe i;

  parent = new Array<Universe,Universe>(loElement,hiElement);  // Allocate array
  for (i = loElement; i <= hiElement; ++i)     // Initially all elements are
    (*parent)[i] = -1;                         // roots of one-element trees
}
```

```
// Implementation of UnionFind destructor
template <class Universe>
UnionFind<Universe>::~UnionFind()
{
  delete parent;
}

// Implementation of ufFind operation
template <class Universe>
BOOLEAN UnionFind<Universe>::ufFind(Universe x, Universe y)
{
  Universe j, k;

  j = x;
  k = y;
  while ((*parent)[j] != -1)        // Find root of tree containing x
    j = (*parent)[j];
  while ((*parent)[k] != -1)        // Find root of tree containing y
    k = (*parent)[k];
  if (j == k)                       // Are these roots the same?
    return(TRUE);
  else
    return(FALSE);
}


// Implementation of ufUnion operation
template <class Universe>
void UnionFind<Universe>::ufUnion(Universe x, Universe y)
{
  Universe j,k;

  j = x;
  k = y;
  while ((*parent)[j] != -1)        // Find root of tree containing x
    j = (*parent)[j];
  while ((*parent)[k] != -1)        // Find root of tree containing y
    k = (*parent)[k];
  if (j != k)                       // If not in same tree, then attach tree
    (*parent)[k] = j;               // rooted at k as child of tree rooted at j
}
```

Example 8.5 shows this correspondence between the union-find partition, the representation of each set in the partition by a tree, and the **parent** array used to implement the tree.

Example 8.5

Suppose that the union-find universe consists of the eight integers 1, 2, 3, 4, 5, 6, 7, 8. Trace the status of a **UnionFind** object for the following sequence of **ufUnion** operations. Assume that **p.ufUnion(x,y)** results in the root of the tree containing **y** becoming a child of the root of the tree containing **x**. Assume also that if **x** is the root of a tree, then **(*parent)[x]** = −1.

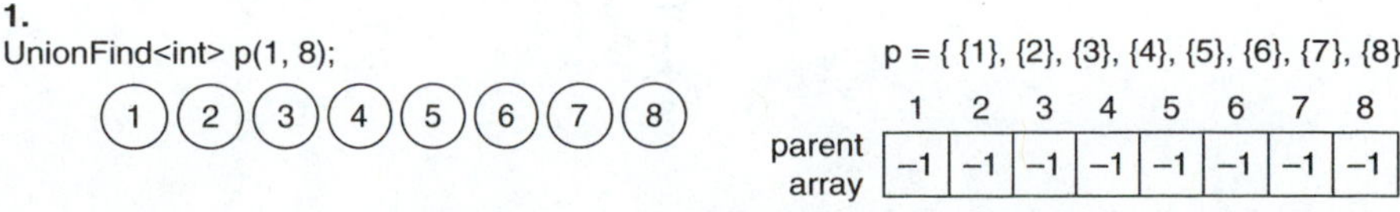

2.
p.ufUnion(1, 4);

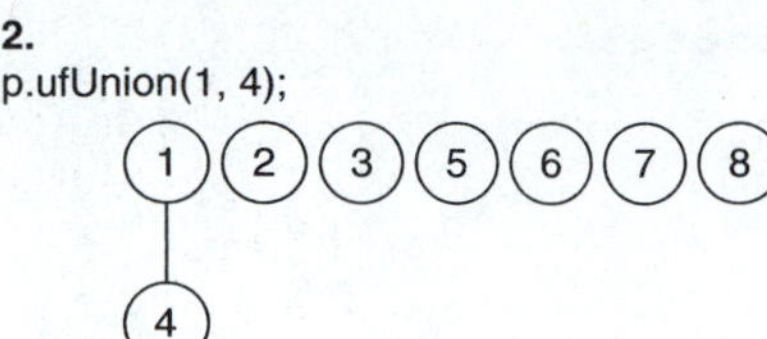

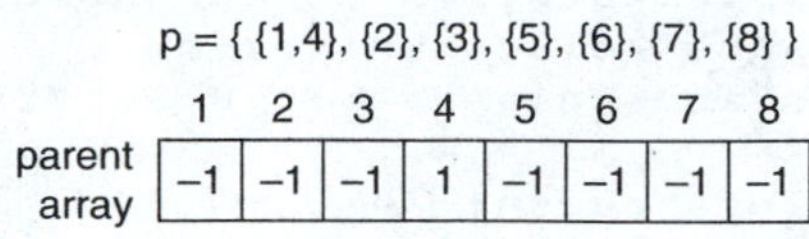

p = { {1,4}, {2}, {3}, {5}, {6}, {7}, {8} }

	1	2	3	4	5	6	7	8
parent array	–1	–1	–1	1	–1	–1	–1	–1

3.
p.ufUnion(5, 6);

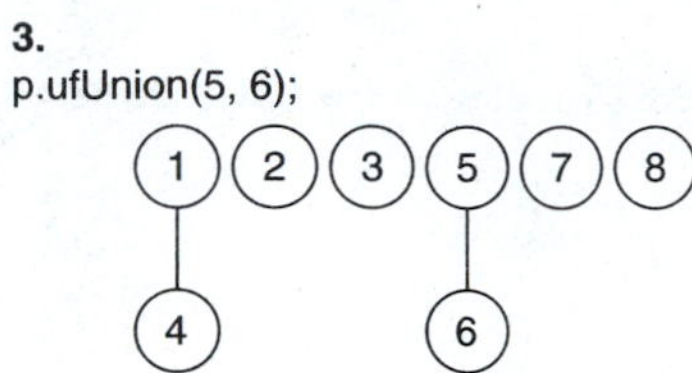

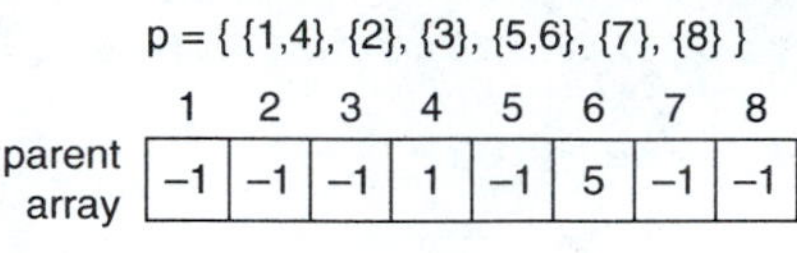

p = { {1,4}, {2}, {3}, {5,6}, {7}, {8} }

	1	2	3	4	5	6	7	8
parent array	–1	–1	–1	1	–1	5	–1	–1

4.
p.ufUnion(2, 8);

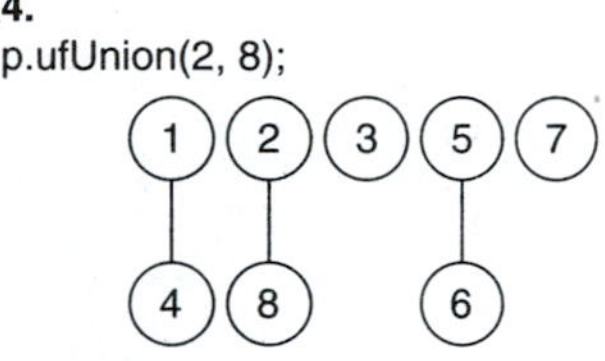

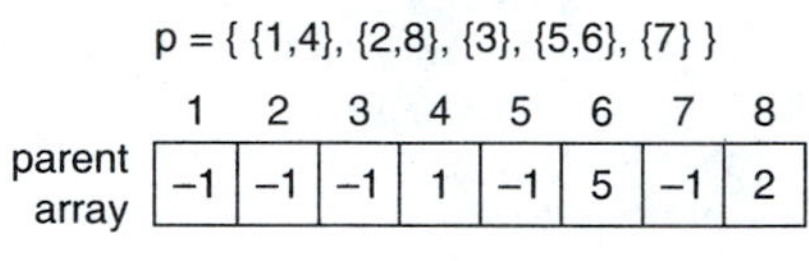

p = { {1,4}, {2,8}, {3}, {5,6}, {7} }

	1	2	3	4	5	6	7	8
parent array	–1	–1	–1	1	–1	5	–1	2

5.
p.ufUnion(1, 8);

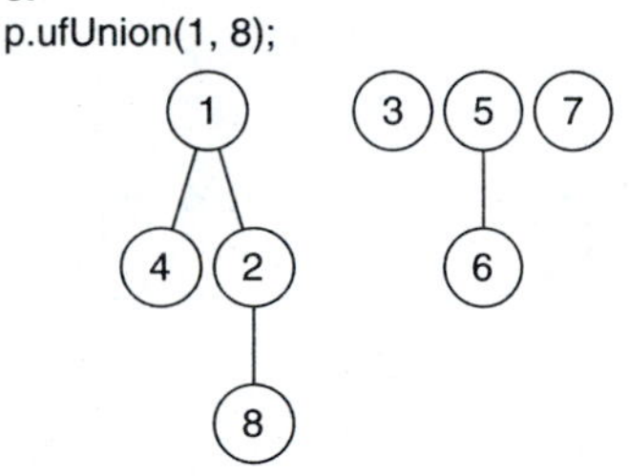

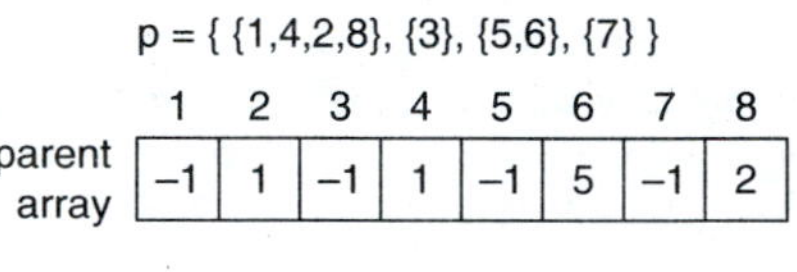

p = { {1,4,2,8}, {3}, {5,6}, {7} }

	1	2	3	4	5	6	7	8
parent array	–1	1	–1	1	–1	5	–1	2

6.
p.ufUnion(1, 3);

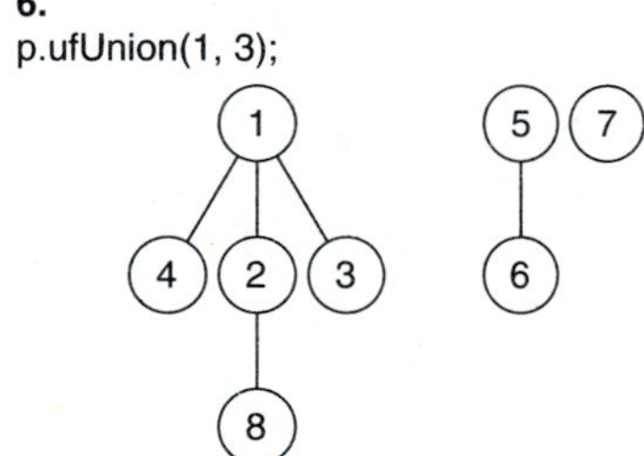

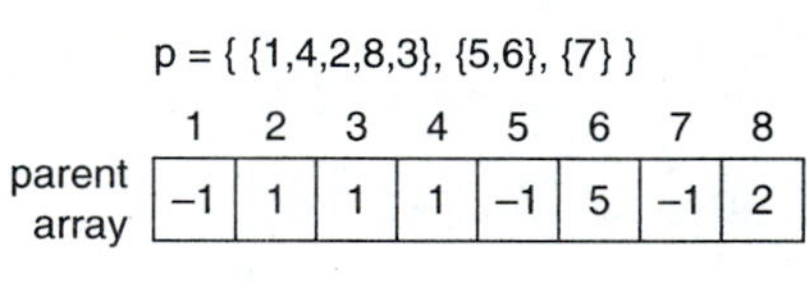

p = { {1,4,2,8,3}, {5,6}, {7} }

	1	2	3	4	5	6	7	8
parent array	–1	1	1	1	–1	5	–1	2

7.
p.ufUnion(6, 2);

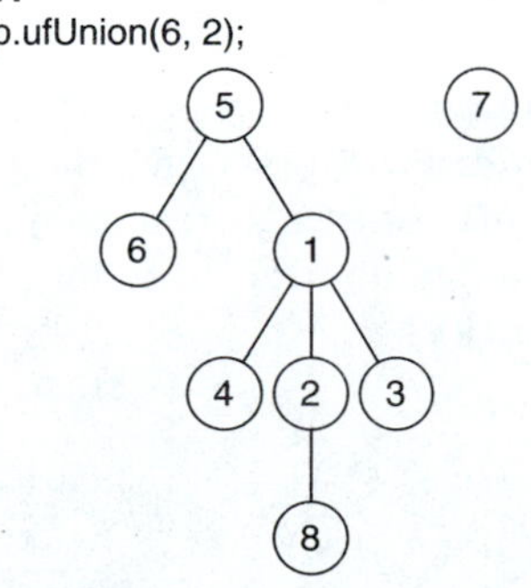

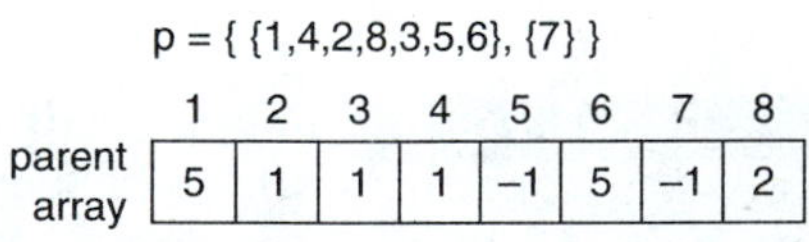

p = { {1,4,2,8,3,5,6}, {7} }

	1	2	3	4	5	6	7	8
parent array	5	1	1	1	–1	5	–1	2

Efficiency of the **ufUnion** and **ufFind** Operations

In both the **ufFind** and **ufUnion** functions, to determine if **x** and **y** are in the same set, we must climb paths from **x** and **y** to the roots of their respective trees and then check whether these roots are the same. Hence, the efficiency of both algorithms is proportional to the depth of the trees that are used to represent sets. This depth, in turn, is quite dependent on how we choose to attach one tree as the subtree of another when unions are formed. For instance, in operation 7 of Example 8.5, when performing **p.ufUnion(6,2)**, the resulting tree would have been more efficient if the tree rooted at 5 had been attached to the tree rooted at 1 to form:

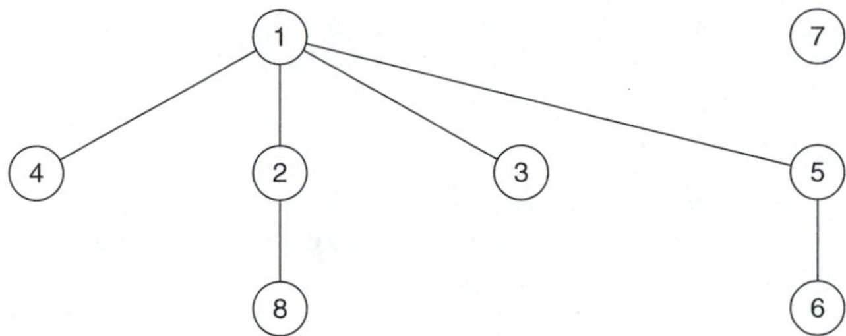

The worst case search efficiency would then have been 3 instead of 4. In the exercises at the end of this section, you will verify by example that when the **ufUnion** operation is performed without any consideration of the depth of the two trees that are unioned, then the efficiency of the **ufUnion** and **ufFind** operations for a universe of N elements can deteriorate to $O(N)$.

Improving the Efficiency of Union-Find Trees by Weight-Balancing

The preceding discussion implies that an "intelligent" choice made in the **ufUnion** algorithm can improve significantly the efficiency of **ufFind** and other **ufUnion** operations that may follow. "Intelligent" here means that we should select the "smaller" of the two trees being joined and attach that as a subtree to the "bigger" tree's root. Of course, we must define precisely what is meant by "smaller" and "bigger," and we want to be sure that this definition does not involve a great deal of computational effort. Otherwise, the expense of choosing which tree to attach may outweigh any gain derived from the more efficient structure that results. One strategy that is often used is to maintain a count of the number of nodes in each tree. Thus, the array of parent pointers would become an array of structs, each containing a parent pointer and a counter. For those array indices that correspond to a root, the counter would indicate the number of nodes in the tree rooted at that index. The counter field in other indices would be undefined. In the **ufUnion** operation, we would choose the tree with fewer nodes as the one to attach to the root of the other. Note that in operation 7 of Example 8.5 this would have resulted in the rooting of the tree at 1 instead of 5.

The technique described above is called *weight-balancing,* with the weight of a tree corresponding to the number of nodes in the tree. Although weight-balancing clearly should enhance the efficiency of the union-find implementation, the question arises whether it does so significantly. The answer is yes, as the following argument shows.

Suppose that we have N elements in our universe. Each time a set in the union-find partition is unioned with another set, the path length necessary to find each

Figure 8.11
Effect of **ufUnion** operation on path lengths to find nodes.

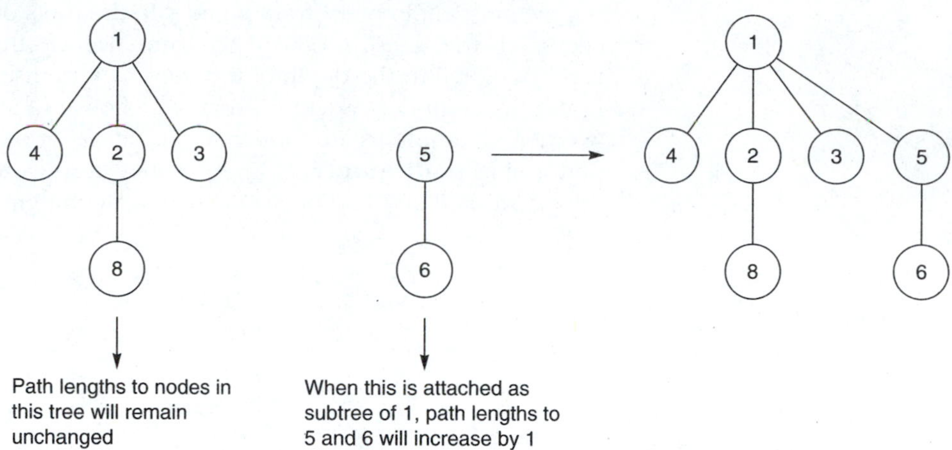
1
4
2
3
8
5
6
1
4
2
3
5
8
6
Path lengths to nodes in this tree will remain unchanged
When this is attached as subtree of 1, path lengths to 5 and 6 will increase by 1

of the elements in the set being attached will increase by one. This phenomenon is illustrated in Figure 8.11. Hence, the question reduces to finding a limit on the number of times a set containing a particular element **x** may be attached to another set in a **ufUnion** operation. *When weight-balancing is used,* each **ufUnion** operation will at least double the size of the set that is being attached. Hence, the maximum number of times **x** could be involved in a **ufUnion** operation, *as a member of the set being attached,* before it is in a set containing all N elements of the universe is $\log_2(N)$. Figure 8.12 illustrates such a series of occurrences. Since each of these unions could add at most 1 to the path length from **x** to the root, we conclude that $\log_2(N)$ is the worst case efficiency for the **ufUnion** and **ufFind** operations when weight-balancing is used.

Improving the Efficiency of Union-Find Trees by Path Compression

Yet another strategy for improving the efficiency of the union-find operations is known as *path compression.* By this scheme, whenever we locate the root of the tree containing an element **x** during a union or find operation, all the nodes along the path from **x** to its root are adjusted to have their parent pointer aimed at the root. For instance, if we were to call **p.ufFind(8,3)** after performing the union in

Figure 8.12
With weight-balancing, each union with **x** in the set being attached will at least double the size of the set containing **x**.

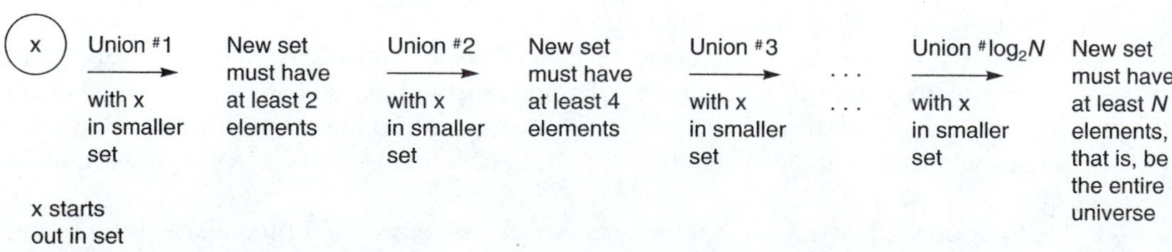
x
Union #1
with x in smaller set
New set must have at least 2 elements
Union #2
with x in smaller set
New set must have at least 4 elements
Union #3
with x in smaller set
. . .
. . .
Union #log$_2N$
with x in smaller set
New set must have at least N elements, that is, be the entire universe
x starts out in set by itself

Figure 8.13
Trees from operation 7 of Example 8.5 after **p.ufFind(8,3)** with path compression. The nodes along the path from 8 to 5 and along the path from 3 to 5 become children of 5.

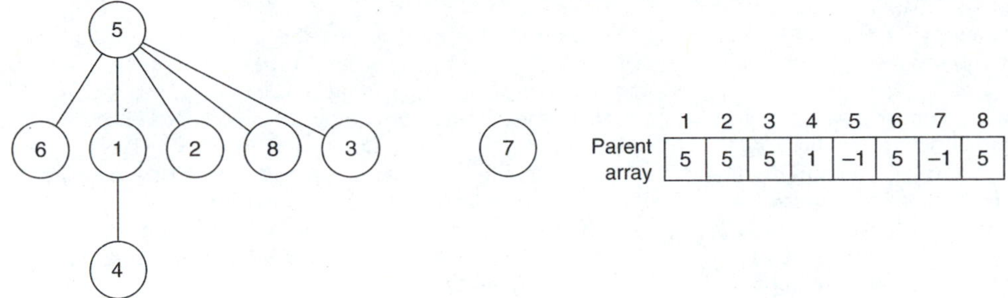

operation 7 of Example 8.5, we would have the partition picture of Figure 8.13. Notice from this figure that the paths for future **ufUnion** and **ufFind** operations have been shortened considerably from what they were in Example 8.5.

Unfortunately, there is a cost to pay when this technique is used. To adjust the parent pointers of all the nodes along the path from **x** to its root, we must first traverse the path to locate the root and then traverse the path again, this time adjusting all the parent pointers to reference the now-known root. The hope is that this double traversal done once will pay off in much shorter paths and therefore greater efficiency in future operations. The efficiency of this method is very difficult to analyze formally and is dependent on a large number of operations being performed so that, in the average case, we are able to benefit from these early double traversals. R. E. Tarjan ("Efficiency of a Good but Not Linear Set Union Algorithm," *Journal of the ACM*, 22, April 1975, pp. 215–225) has shown that the following interesting result holds when weight-balancing and path compression are combined:

> If M **ufUnion** and/or **ufFind** operations are performed in sequence, where M exceeds N, the number of elements in the universe, then the worst case efficiency of this sequence of operations is bounded by $O(M \times S(N))$.

Here $S(N)$ is a function of N, which grows so slowly that, for any reasonable value of N that can be represented on a modern computer, $S(N)$ will be less than 4. The definition of $S(N)$ itself is beyond the scope of this text. However, the significance of the result is that, for all practical purposes, the combination of weight-balancing and path compression enhances the efficiency of M union-find operations to $O(M)$ instead of the $O(M \log_2 N)$, which we might encounter with weight-balancing alone.

A RELEVANT ISSUE Computer Security and Tree-Structured File Systems

One of the prime concerns when developing operating systems for multiuser computers is to ensure that a user cannot, in an unauthorized fashion, access system files or the files of other users. A convenient data structure to implement such a file directory system is a general tree such as pictured in Figure 8.14.

Each interior node of the tree can be viewed as a directory containing various system information about those files or subdirectories that are its descendants. Leaf nodes in the tree are the actual files. Hence, in the diagram, files can be broken down into system files and user files. System files consist of the Pascal Development Tools, the C++ Development Tools, and the Text Editor. User directories are called Vera, David, and Martha. One of the very convenient features of such a system is that it allows the user to extend this tree structure as deeply as desired. For instance, in the given tree directory structure, we see that user Vera has created subdirectories for files related to Payroll and Inventory. David and Martha could have similarly partitioned subdirectories to organize their work.

In addition to offering users the convenience of being able to appropriately group their files into subdirectories, such a file system offers a very natural solution to the problem of file security. Since each individual user is, in effect, the root of a miniature subordinate file system, a user has free access to every node in his or her subtree. That is, the user is viewed as the owner of every node in the subtree. To jump outside of this subtree of naturally owned files and directories requires that special permissions be given to the user by other users or by the operating system itself. Hence, the tree structure offers convenience as well as a means of carefully monitoring the integrity of the file system.

AT&T's UNIX operating system, developed at Bell Laboratories in the early 1970s, was one of the first to use such a tree-structured directory system. The widespread popularity of UNIX today and the adoption of this scheme by a significant number of other operating systems is evidence of the attractive way in which it combines user convenience with system security. However, this is not to say that such systems are completely free of security problems. Once the security of such a system is slightly compromised, the tree structure lends itself to a cascade of far-reaching security breaks. An entertaining account of such a security incident is presented by Clifford Stoll in *The Cuckoo's Egg* (Doubleday, New York, 1989).

Figure 8.14
File directory system represented as a general tree with leaf nodes as files and interior nodes as directories.

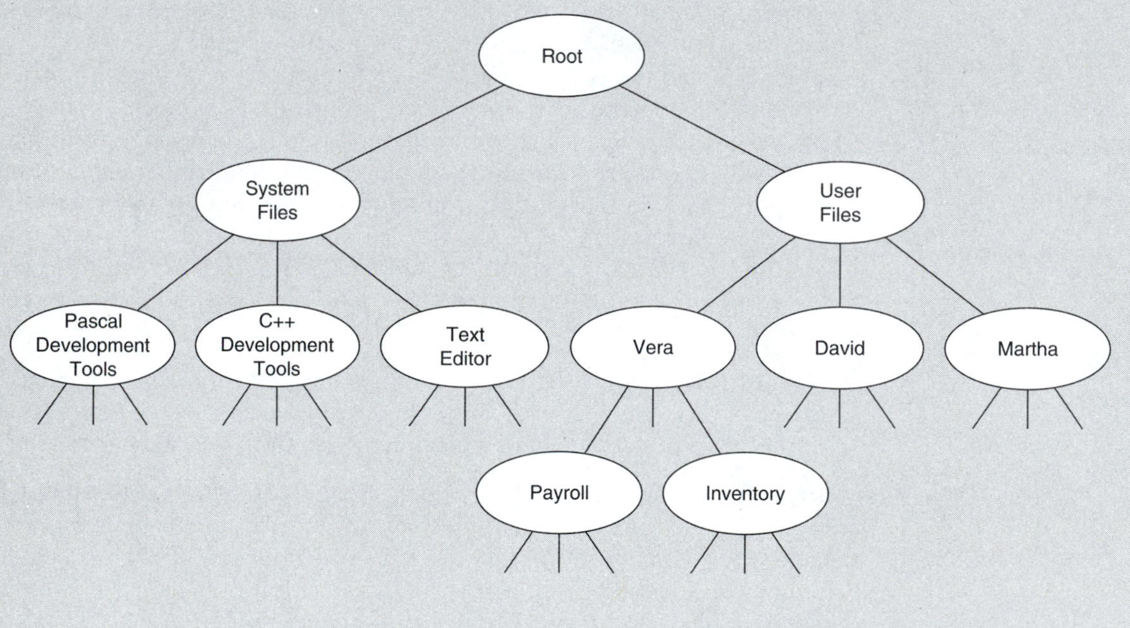

Exercises 8.4

1. Suppose we have a universe given by the set {1, 2, 3, 4, 5, 6, 7, 8, 9, 10}. Via diagrams, trace the union-find trees that would develop for the following sequence of operations if no weight-balancing or path compression is used.

```
UnionFind<int> p(1, 10);
p.ufUnion(9, 1);
p.ufUnion(5, 2);
p.ufUnion(5, 1);
p.ufUnion(7, 3);
p.ufUnion(8, 1);
p.ufUnion(1, 10);
p.ufUnion(1, 4);
p.ufUnion(6, 3);
p.ufUnion(9, 10);
```

2. Repeat Exercise 8.4.1 under the assumption that only weight-balancing is used.
3. Repeat Exercise 8.4.1 under the assumption that only path compression is used.
4. Repeat Exercise 8.4.1 under the assumption that both weight-balancing and path compression are used.
5. Provide a tree-based implementation of the **UnionFind** class that uses C++'s built-in arrays instead of using the **Array** class developed in Section 2.1.
6. Develop C++ code for **ufFind** and **ufUnion** under the assumption that only weight-balancing is used.
7. Develop C++ code for **ufFind** and **ufUnion** under the assumption that only path compression is used.
8. Develop C++ code for **ufFind** and **ufUnion** under the assumption that both path compression and weight-balancing are used.
9. Show by an example that the worst case for the Union and Find operations deteriorates to $O(N)$ when neither path compression nor weight-balancing is used.
10. Weight-balancing seems to double the space required for the union-find structure, because both counters and a parent pointer must be allocated for each index. Develop a scheme that achieves weight-balancing without doubling the space requirements.
11. Implement **ufFind** and **ufUnion** for a strategy that parallels weight-balancing but uses the depth of a tree as a guide for the **ufUnion** operation instead of number of nodes. Recall that the depth of a tree is the maximal level at which a node occurs in the tree.
12. What changes to the implementation of the **UnionFind** operations given in this section would have to be made to accommodate a Universe which is a finite range of characters or an **enum** type?

Chapter Summary

In Chapter 7 we discussed several ways in which the binary tree can be used to organize information. In this chapter we examine techniques for implementing more general trees, ones wherein a node may have an unrestricted number of children. The first such method, discussed in Section 8.2, uses a binary tree to implement any general tree. This discussion led to two derived classes, **TopDownTree** and **BottomUpTree,** that differ in the fashion in which nodes are added to the general tree. In Section 8.3 we consider 2-3 trees as a way to improve on the efficiency of the height-balanced approach described in Section 7.6, though with the potential risk of having more wasted space than occurs with such binary trees. We conclude the chapter by using general trees to implement the union-find ADT of Section 2.4 and include a discussion of the techniques of weight-balancing and path compression to improve the efficiency of the union-find operations.

Key Terms

BottomUpTree class	path compression	2-3 tree	weight-balancing
general tree	**TopDownTree** class	union-find problem	

Programming Problems/Projects

1. In Problems 11, 12, or 13 of Chapter 6 you wrote a recursive descent parser for a context-free grammar. Now extend that parser so that it builds a parse tree for valid expressions.
2. In Problem 5 of Chapter 7 you wrote a program that allows you to empirically compare the search efficiency of ordered binary search trees and height-balanced search trees. Extend that program by having it also build 2-3 trees for the data sets and then reporting the average search efficiency for this new structure. For 2-3 trees, your program should also report on the average amount of informational fields that are wasted by storing the empty flag. Expand the report you wrote for Problem 5 of Chapter 7 to include an analysis of 2-3 tree performance in comparison with the other two methods.
3. Wing-and-a-Prayer Airlines is expanding their record-keeping database. This database may now be pictured hierarchically as

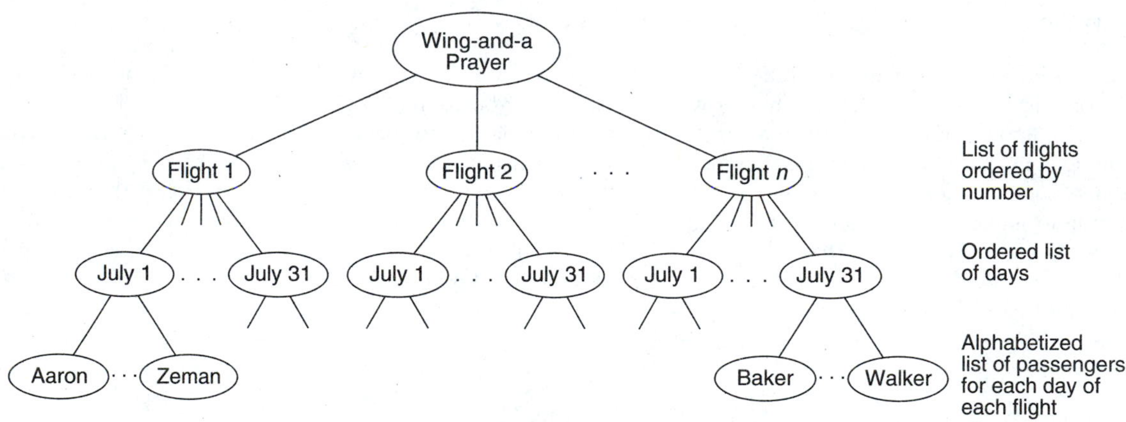

   Write a program to maintain this database. Your program should process requests to add, delete, or list the following:

   - Specified flight number
   - Specified day of the month (for a given flight number)
   - Specified passenger or all passengers (for a given flight number and day of the month).

4. Many statistical analysis packages support a cross-tabulation command designed to explore the relationship between statistical variables. A cross-tabulation between two variables produces a two-dimensional table containing a frequency count for each possible ordered pair of values of the two variables. However, these statistical packages typically allow this type of analysis to proceed even further than merely exploring two variables. For instance, in a legal-system database, we might be interested in cross-tabulating a defendant's age with the judge before whom the defendant stood trial. We may then wish to cross-tabulate this result with the sex of the defendant. Sex in this case is called the control variable. We would output a cross-tabulation table for both possible values of sex. Note that this type of output is not limited to just one control variable. There may be an arbitrary number of control variables and tables to cycle through. Moreover, the variables have an arbitrary number of observations and are all in arbitrary order. Yet for each variable, the list of possible values is always printed out in smallest-to-largest order.

The general tree structure that emerges for handling cross-tabulations is

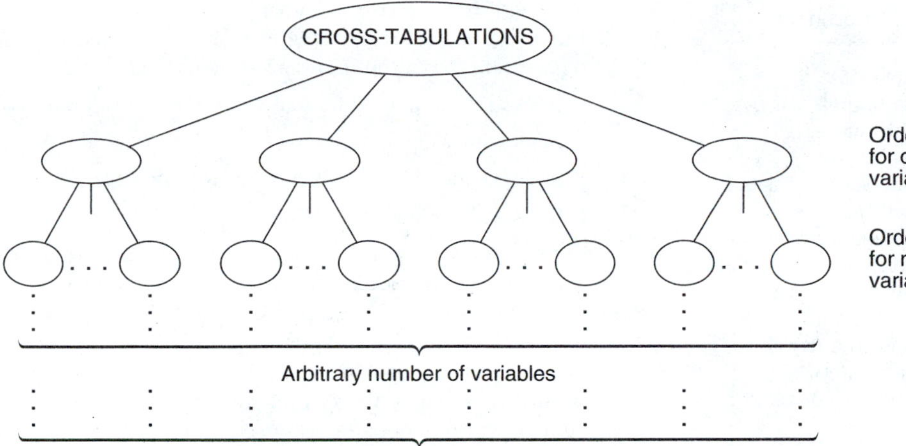

Write a program to handle the task of producing statistical cross-tabulations.

5. Write a program to print the nodes of a tree level by level; that is, all level-0 nodes, followed by all level-1 nodes, followed by all level-2 nodes, and so on. (*Hint:* This program will afford an excellent opportunity to practice using a queue in addition to a tree.)
6. Operating systems often use general trees as the data structure on which their file directory system is based. Leaf nodes in such a system represent actual files or empty directories. Interior nodes represent nonempty directories. For instance, consider the following situation:

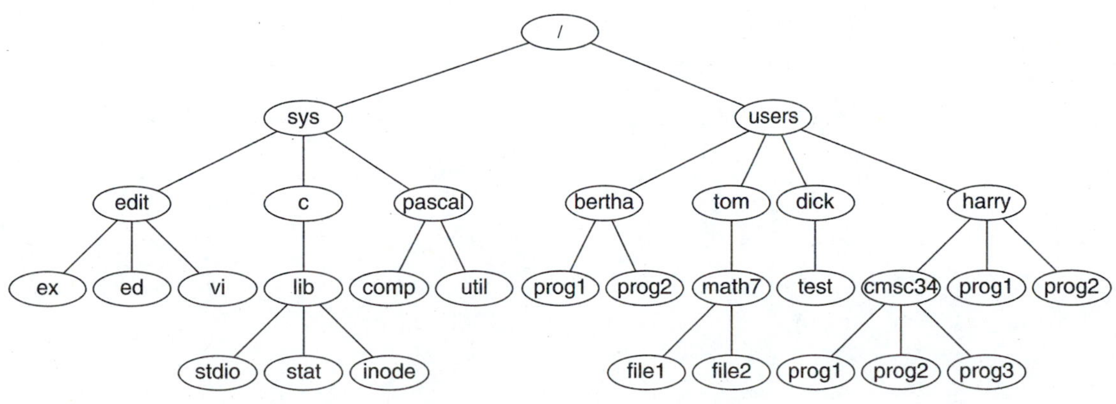

A directory entry is specified by the name of its path. A *pathname* consists of tree node names separated by slashes. Such a pathname is absolute if it starts at the root; that is, if it starts with a slash. It is relative to the current directory if it does not start with a slash.

In this assignment, you are to write a command processor that will allow a user to manipulate files within such a directory structure. The commands accepted by your processor will be in the form of numbers associated with particular operations and pathnames, as shown in the following table:

Number	Operation	Pathname
1	Change directory	Absolute pathname, relative pathname, or ".." for parent
2	Make a new directory	Absolute or relative pathname
3	Make a new file	Absolute or relative pathname
4	Remove a file	Absolute or relative pathname
5	Remove a directory, but only if it is empty	Absolute or relative pathname
6	Remove a directory and, recursively, everything below it	Absolute or relative pathname
7	Print directory entries in alphabetical order	Absolute or relative pathname
8	Recursively print directory entries in alphabetical order	Absolute or relative pathname
9	Print current directory name	
10	Quit processing commands	

Since even intelligent tree-walking users can easily get lost, your command processor should be prepared to trap errors of the following variety:

- Specifying a nonexistent pathname
- Specifying a pathname that is a file when it should be a directory
- Specifying a pathname that is a directory when it should be a file.

Upon detecting such an error, have your command processor print an appropriate error message and then return to accept the next user command.

7. In Section 8.4 several strategies were considered for implementing the union-find data structure via trees:

- Trees without any additional efficiency considerations
- Trees with weight-balancing
- Trees balanced by depth (see Exercise 8.4.11)
- Trees with path compression.

Develop a program that implements each of these individual strategies in addition to the combinations of weight-balancing with path compression and depth-balancing with path compression. Your program should also count the number of operations executed by **ufUnion** and **ufFind** for each of these implementations. Finally, have your program generate a long sequence of random calls to **ufFind** and/or **ufUnion.** For each of the methods implemented, your program should report the average efficiency and the worst case. Use the results of your program to develop a written report in which you compare all of these strategies, reaching conclusions about their relative effectiveness for particular sequences of operations. Does your program empirically verify the result of Tarjan, which we cited in Section 8.4?

8. If you have access to a collection of graphics routines, develop a C++ function that graphically displays the contents of a general tree. Test your function in a main program that allows a user to enter a tree in top-down or bottom-up fashion and then displays the tree on the graphics screen.

CHAPTER 9

Graphs and Networks

As for that famous network of Vulcan, which enclosed Mars and Venus, and caused that unextinguishable laugh in heaven, since the gods themselves could not discern it, we shall not pry into it.

Sir Thomas Browne, *The Garden of Cyrus*

Chapter Outline:

9.1 Basic Concepts of Graphs and Networks

A key characteristic of a tree is the hierarchical organization of its nodes resulting from the requirement that, except for the root node (which has no parent), every node must have exactly one parent node. Also, since the relationship between a parent node and a child node is expressed solely by pointers from parent to child, this hierarchical relationship is traditionally a one-way relationship. That is, there is no information within a child node that allows us to ascend directly to its parent. In many information storage applications, such a one-way relationship is not sufficient.

Consider, for instance, the relationship between students and courses at a university. Because a student typically enrolls in several courses, each student could be viewed as a parent node whose children are the courses he or she is taking. On the other hand, because each course normally enrolls several students,

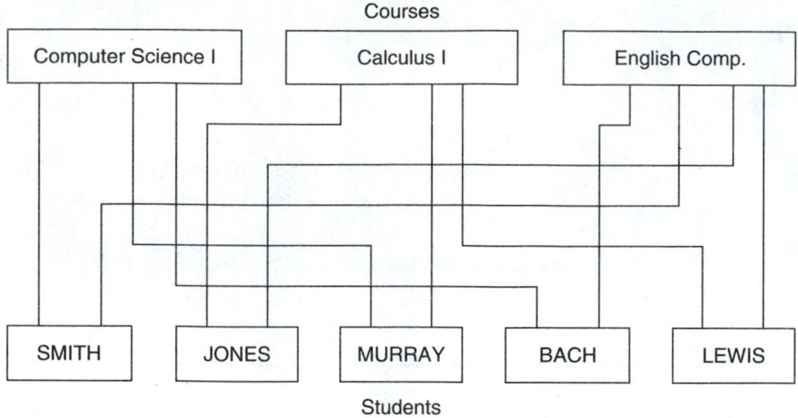

Figure 9.1
Bidirectional relationship between students and courses.

a given course could justifiably be viewed as a parent node whose children are the students enrolled. Because it is likely that the information retrieval requirements of the university will sometimes require moving from a course node to a related student node or vice versa, the information storage needs of any application doing such retrievals would be more effectively served by means of a data structure that admits a nonhierarchical, bidirectional relationship between courses and students instead of using two trees. The data structure that supports this type of bidirectional relationship is called a *graph*. In Figure 9.1 we show a graph that represents some student-course relationships of the type just described. In this figure the rectangles containing the names of a student or a course make up what are known as the *nodes* of the graph. The lines connecting various student and course rectangles are known as *edges*.

Using this example as a model, we define a *graph* as a structure comprised of two sets of objects, a set of *nodes* (or *vertices*) and a set of *edges*. Furthermore, with each edge we can associate two nodes (not necessarily distinct) called the *endpoints* of the edge. We say the endpoints are *directly connected* by the edge. A *loop* is an edge whose endpoints consist of the same node. An example of a graph with a loop is shown in Figure 9.2.

Another example of a graph can be seen from a collection of cities and an airline's routes between them. Each city is a node of the graph, and two cities are related (that is, directly connected by an edge) if the airline has a route between them. Such a relationship is not hierarchical because routes between cities will normally exist in both directions. An example of such a graph is shown in Figure 9.3. In this graph, the routes between cities have been assigned a numerical value

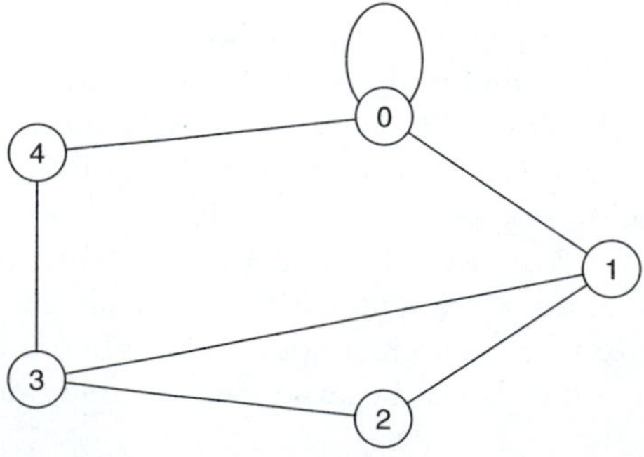

Figure 9.2
An example of a graph with nodes 0, 1, 2, 3, 4; edges between nodes 0 and 1, 1 and 2, 1 and 3, 2 and 3, 3 and 4, 4 and 0; and a loop at node 0.

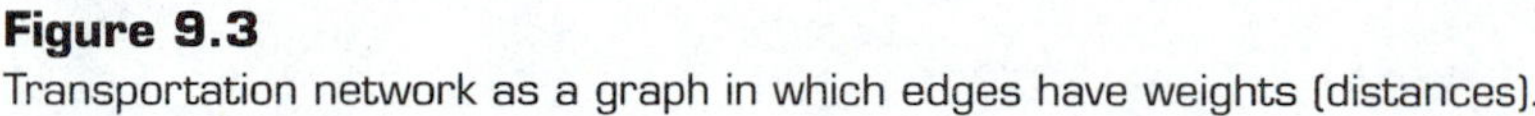

Figure 9.3
Transportation network as a graph in which edges have weights (distances).

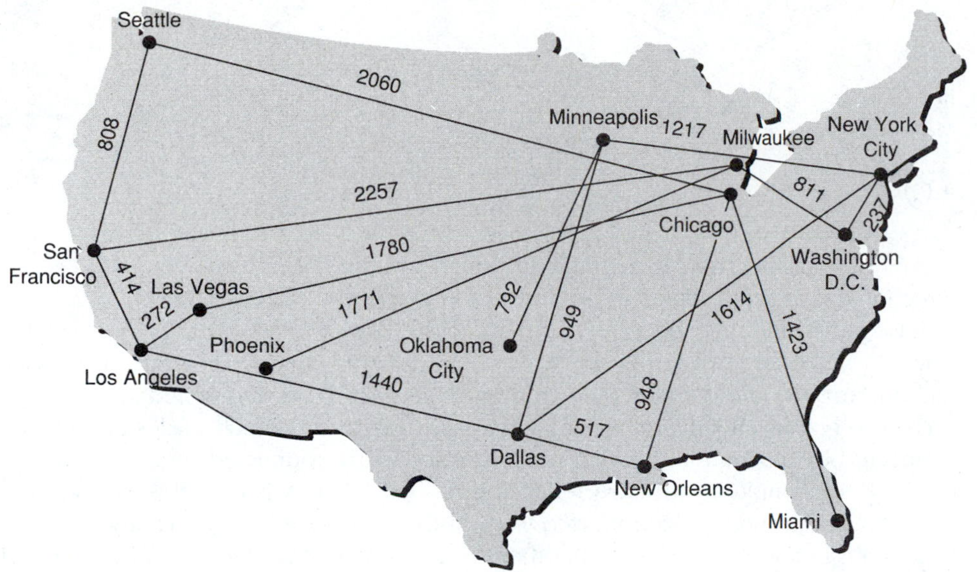

that represents the distance between cities for that route. A graph in which each edge has an associated numerical value (or *weight*) is called a *network*.

In this chapter, after some further discussion of the basic concepts and terminology of graphs, we will define graphs and networks as ADTs, examine ways of implementing them, and explore some of the many algorithms that are derived from their fundamental operations. We will also indicate how such algorithms find application in many diverse areas, including artificial intelligence, communications, transportation, the analysis of programming languages, and the scheduling of projects.

In a sense, graphs are the most general data structures we will discuss. Why? Because the relationships between items in a graph are completely arbitrary. With lists, queues, and stacks, the relationships between data items were linear; with trees, they were hierarchical; but, with graphs, any data item is potentially connected to any other. Even though the situation did not arise in Figure 9.1, the formal definition of a graph does not rule out the possibility of an edge connecting two courses or connecting two students. It is merely the nature of a course-student relationship that prevents the user from establishing a course-to-course edge or a student-to-student edge. In other applications, such as the transportation network pictured in Figure 9.3, it may be entirely feasible for any node in the graph to have an edge connecting it to any other node.

Because of the intrinsic generality of graphs, additional terminology is often needed to describe precisely some particular relationships underlying a given graph. In a *directed graph* (or *digraph*) each edge establishes a directional orientation between its endpoints. Terminology such as "the edge from node A to node B" or "the edge AB" is used to describe this orientation. In digraphs the edges are known as *directed edges,* or more commonly, *arcs,* and are represented pictorially with arrows. In the directed graph of Figure 9.4, AB is an arc but there is no arc BA. There are also arcs from B to C, C to D, and D to E. The digraph of Figure 9.4 can be looked on as expressing the alphabetical order relationship between the letters. In this text, we denote an arc from node x to node y by $x \rightarrow y$.

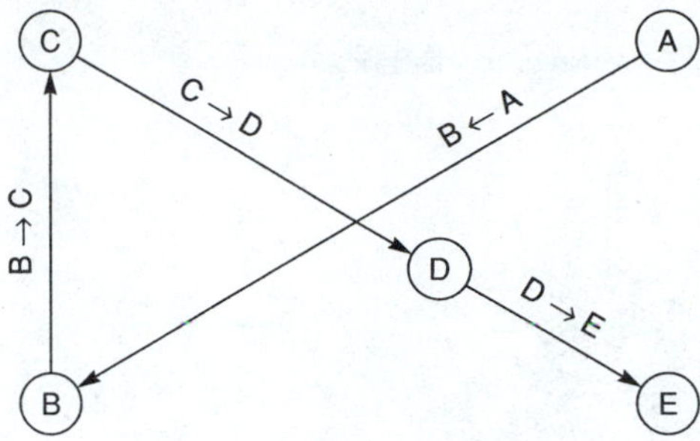

Figure 9.4
A directed graph.

An *undirected graph* is a graph in which an edge between two nodes is not directionally oriented. Thus, in an undirected graph, the edge from node A to node G (also called the *edge between A and G* or the *edge AG*) is the same as the edge from G to A (edge between G and A, or GA). Undirected graphs typically are drawn without arrows on the edges. The graph in Figure 9.5 is an undirected graph.

To use graphs effectively, we sometimes need to know which nodes are directly connected by an edge and which nodes are indirectly connected by a sequence of edges. For example, in the directed graph in Figure 9.4, A is directly connected to B, whereas B is indirectly connected to E via the arcs B → C, C → D, and D → E. In a digraph, therefore, we say that there is a *directed path of length n* from node I to node J if and only if there is a sequence of nodes $I_0, I_1, I_2, \ldots, I_n$, where $I_0 = I$ and $I_n = J$, such that for $k = 1, \ldots, n$, node I_{k-1} is directly connected to I_k via an arc. In Figure 9.4, there is no directed path from node E to node A, but there is a directed path of length 4 from node A to E.

A digraph is said to be *strongly connected* if, for any nodes I and J in the graph, there is a directed path from I to J *and* a directed path from J to I. A digraph is said to be *weakly connected* if, for any two nodes I and J, there is a directed path from I to J *or* from J to I. The digraph in Figure 9.4 is weakly connected, but it is not strongly connected because there is no directed path from E to C (or from E to D, or B to A, etc.). The digraph shown in Figure 9.6 is strongly connected. Clearly, any digraph that is strongly connected is also weakly connected.

The *outdegree* of a node in a digraph refers to the number of arcs extending from the node, whereas the *indegree* of a node is the number of arcs entering the node. In Figure 9.6, the indegree of node D is 2 and its outdegree is 1. The indegree and the outdegree of node B are 1 and 2, respectively. When a directed graph is applied to some data processing tasks, the indegree and the outdegree of a node sometimes indicate its relative importance in the data processing activity. A node whose outdegree is 0 largely acts as a depository of information and hence is called a *sink node;* on the other hand, a node whose indegree is 0 largely acts as a source of information and consequently is called a *source node.* In Figure 9.7 we use a

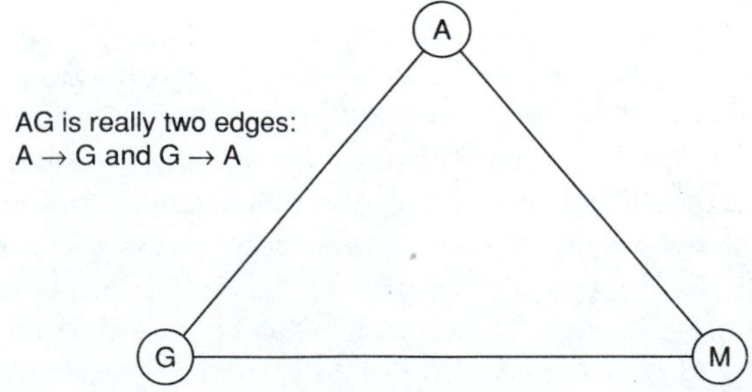

Figure 9.5
An undirected graph.

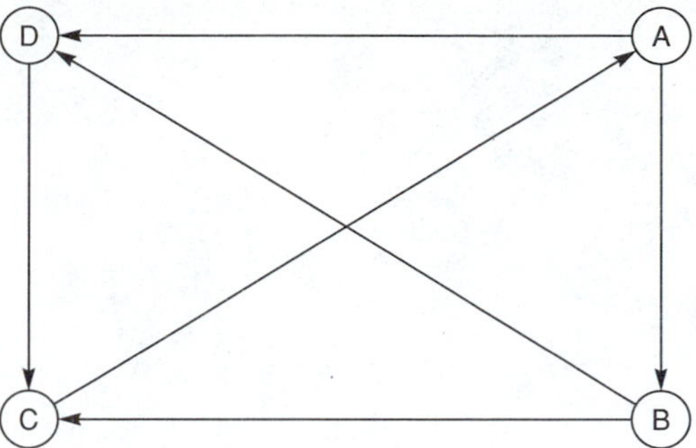

Figure 9.6
A strongly connected graph. For any nodes I and J in the graph there is a directed path from I to J and a directed path from J to I.

digraph to illustrate the fundamental input-to-output operation common to all data processing activity.

A *cycle* in a directed graph is a directed path of length at least 1 that originates and terminates at the same node in the graph. In Figure 9.6, D→C→A→D is a cycle of length 3. An *acyclic graph* is one having no cycles.

The concepts and terms discussed in the preceding paragraphs for digraphs can generally be extended to analogous concepts for undirected graphs. For example, we can define an undirected path (or simply a path) between two nodes to be a sequence of edges that directly or indirectly connects the two nodes. In Figure 9.5 there is a path between any two nodes. Although the concept of indegree and outdegree cannot apply to a node in an undirected graph, we can define the *degree* of a node to be the number of edges connected directly to the node; if the node is the endpoint of a loop, however, we count the loop as two edges. In Figure 9.5, the degree of each node is 2.

Because a network is a graph, all of the terminology we have defined for graphs applies to networks as well. For instance, a directed path between nodes I and J in a network may be thought of as a sequence of edges

$$I(= I_0) \rightarrow I_1 \rightarrow I_2 \rightarrow I_{n-1} \rightarrow I_n(= J)$$

However, since each edge $I_{k-1} \rightarrow I_k$ now has a numerical weight associated with it, we can define the *total path weight* between I and J as the sum:

$$\sum_{k=1}^{n} \text{edgeweight}(I_{k-1} \rightarrow I_k)$$

Therefore, in Figure 9.3, the total path weight of the path

San Francisco→Los Angeles→Las Vegas→Chicago

is $414 + 272 + 1780 = 2466$.

Many network problems revolve around finding paths that satisfy some specified criteria relative to their total weight. Many of these problems have been solved by

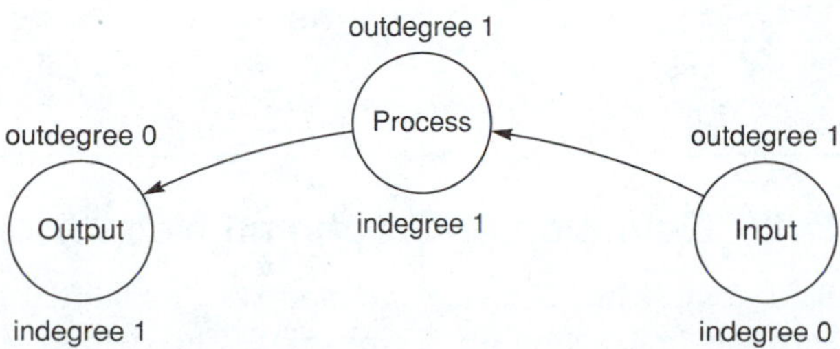

Figure 9.7
Indegrees and outdegrees of nodes.

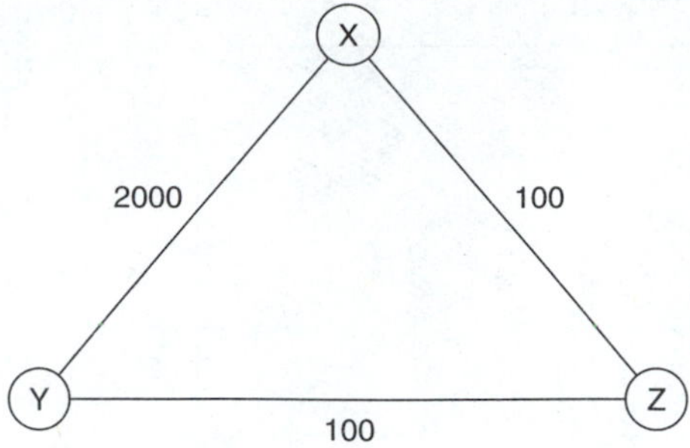

Figure 9.8
A network showing that edge weight does not necessarily correspond to Euclidean distance between nodes.

classic algorithms whose originators have often used the term *length* synonymously with weight. Although we do not object to such usage and, indeed, will often employ it in the remainder of this chapter, you should realize that *length* taken in this context does not necessarily mean Euclidean geometric distance between nodes. Euclidean distance is only one interpretation that an application may give to edge weight. Other applications may interpret edge weights as monetary cost, time units, and so forth. This potential for confusion arises because we often visualize the notion of a network as data points (nodes) connected by straight lines (edges). Hence, the network pictured in Figure 9.8 is perfectly valid even though the numeric labels on the edges make no sense in the context of Euclidean geometry.

Exercises 9.1

1. Is a general tree a graph? Is a graph a general tree? Justify your answers to both of these questions.
2. Consider the directed graph shown here:

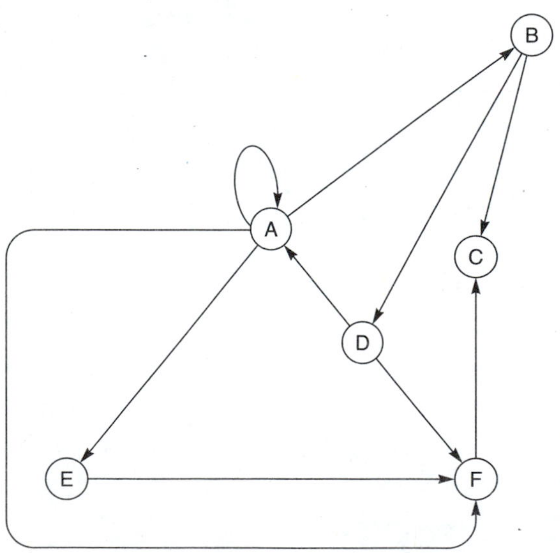

   a. Is this graph weakly connected?
   b. Is it strongly connected?
   c. What are the outdegrees of each node in the graph?
   d. What are the indegrees of each node in the graph?
   e. Does the graph have any sink nodes or source nodes? If so, what are they?
3. The *total degree* of a node in a digraph is the sum of that node's indegrees and outdegrees. Show that the sum of the total degrees of all the nodes in a digraph is an even number. What can you say about the number of nodes in a digraph with a total degree that is odd?
4. What is the maximum number of (nonloop) edges that can be present in a graph with four nodes, assuming only one edge joins a given pair of points? Suppose the graph has five nodes? Six nodes? Conjecture as to the maximum number of such edges that can be present in a graph with N nodes and prove your conjecture. A graph that contains the maximum number of such edges is said to be a *complete graph*.

9.2 Definition of Graph and Network ADTs

Since a network is merely a graph with additional numeric information, it makes sense to first define the Graph ADT. The definition of the Network ADT is then presented as a natural extension of the Graph ADT.

The Graph ADT

Definition: A *Graph* is a structure comprised of two sets of objects: a set of *nodes* (or *vertices*) and a set of *edges*. A node (or vertex) is a data element of the graph in that it stores a data value; an edge indicates a direct relationship between two nodes. If an edge exists between two nodes, we say the nodes are *adjacent,* or that one node is adjacent to another. Assuming each node of the graph stores data of type Basedata, the following operations are provided for the Graph ADT.

`Construct Operation (First Form)`
Precondition: An uninitialized Graph object.
Postcondition: The Graph object is initialized to an empty Graph.

`Construct Operation (Copy Constructor)`
Preconditions: An uninitialized Graph object;
initgraph—a Graph object that was previously constructed.
Postcondition: The Graph object is initialized to *initgraph*.

`Destroy Operation`
Precondition: A Graph object that currently exists.
Postcondition: All storage allocated to the Graph object is deallocated, that is, returned to an available space pool for allocation to other objects.

`Assign Operation`
Preconditions: A previously constructed Graph object;
source—a second Graph object that uses the same Basedata type.
Postcondition: The contents of *source* have been copied to the Graph object that owns the operation.

`Empty Operation`
Precondition: A Graph object.
Postcondition: If no nodes can be removed from the Graph, the operation returns the value TRUE; otherwise it returns the value FALSE.

`Full Operation`
Precondition: A Graph object.
Postcondition: If no nodes can be added to the Graph, the operation returns the value TRUE; otherwise it returns the value FALSE.

`AddNode Operation`
Precondition: A Graph object;
value—a value of type Basedata, which is to become the value of a new node in the Graph.
Postcondition: The Graph with a node containing *value* added to it. The node is not connected to any other node, including itself.

`AddEdge Operation`
Precondition: A nonempty Graph object;
value1 and *value2*—values of two nodes in the Graph.
Postcondition: The Graph with an edge added between the nodes with values *value1* and *value2*. If the edge existed prior to applying the operation, the Graph will remain unchanged.

`Edge Operation`
Precondition: A nonempty Graph object;
value1 and *value2*—values of two nodes in the Graph.

Postcondition: The operation will return the value TRUE if there is an edge between the nodes with values *value1* and *value2;* otherwise it will return the value FALSE.

`RemoveEdge` Operation

Precondition: A nonempty Graph object;
value1 and *value2*—values of two nodes in the Graph.

Postcondition: If there is an edge between the nodes with values *value1* and *value2,* it is removed; otherwise the Graph will remain unchanged.

`RemoveNode` Operation

Precondition: A nonempty Graph object;
value—the value of a node in the Graph.

Postcondition: If there are no edges between the given node and other nodes in the Graph, the node is removed; otherwise the Graph will remain unchanged.

`DepthFirstTraversal` Operation

Precondition: A nonempty Graph object;
start—the value of the node at which the traversal is to start;
processnode—a function that determines the process applied to each Graph node.

Postcondition: The Graph object will be modified so that each node that can be reached from *start* will be affected by *processnode.* The order in which nodes are affected is, first, *start* itself is affected; then, recursively, the first node adjacent to *start* and all nodes adjacent to that first node are affected; then, recursively, the second node adjacent to *start* and all nodes adjacent to that second node are affected; and so on, until *processnode* is applied to the last node adjacent to *start* and, recursively, to all nodes adjacent to that last node. The function *processnode* is not applied to any node more than once.

`BreadthFirstTraversal` Operation

Precondition: A nonempty Graph object;
start—the value of the node at which the traversal is to start;
processnode—a function that determines the process applied to each graph node.

Postcondition: The graph object will be modified so that each node that can be reached from *start* will be affected by *processnode.* The order in which nodes are affected is, first, *start* itself is affected; then, all nodes adjacent to *start* are affected; then, nodes adjacent to nodes affected in the previous step are affected; and so on, until *processnode* has been applied to all nodes that can be reached from *start.* The function *processnode* is not applied to any node more than once.

Before extending our formal definition of the Graph ADT to that of a Network, we should identify a point of potential ambiguity in the definition of the depth-first and breadth-first traversal operations. In particular, neither of these operations establishes a *unique* order in which nodes will be visited from the *start* node parameter for these operations. This lack of uniqueness is due to the potential variety of ways in which the phrase "first node adjacent to" can be interpreted in these definitions. The following examples will clarify these operations and how they can result in different orders of traversal from the *start* parameter.

Example 9.1

Consider a depth-first traversal from start node A in the graph of Figure 9.6. The essential strategy of a depth-first traversal dictates that a given path starting at A be explored as deeply as possible before another path is probed. If we assume that B is the first node adjacent to A, then the traversal will proceed from A to B. If we then assume that C is the first node adjacent to B, the traversal will continue from B to C. From C, it is not possible to visit any nodes that have not already been visited. Hence, we will backtrack to B and, from there, continue the traversal to D. Hence, the overall order in which nodes would be visited by a depth-first traversal under the assumptions of this example are

A B C D

However, as the next example will show, if we change our interpretation of "first node adjacent to," then we arrive at a different depth-first traversal from the same *start* node.

Example 9.2

Consider the order in which nodes would be visited in a depth-first traversal starting at A under the assumption that D is the first node adjacent to A. Now the traversal will proceed initially from A to D. From D, we can proceed only to C. No new nodes can be visited from C, so we backtrack to D. Again, no new nodes can be visited from D, so we backtrack to A, from where B can now be visited. The overall order in which nodes are visited by a depth-first traversal under the assumption of this example is

A D C B

The difference in the order of visited nodes in the depth-first traversals of this example and that of Example 9.1 is an indication that the underlying implementation of the Graph ADT may affect a depth-first traversal, particularly in situations where there is not a well-defined ordering among graph nodes.

Example 9.3

Indicate the order that nodes would be visited in a breadth-first traversal starting at node B in the graph of Figure 9.6. Assume that C is the first node adjacent to B.

Since the breadth-first strategy does not probe one path as deeply as possible but rather fans out to all nodes adjacent to a given node, we would proceed from B to C and then to D, the next node adjacent to B. Since all nodes adjacent to B have been exhausted, we would fan out from C, the first node we visited from B. This takes us to A by the edge C $\rightarrow$ A, completing the traversal in the overall order:

B C D A

The Network ADT

The definition of the Network ADT requires only slight modifications of the Graph ADT definition. These modifications merely reflect that a network is a graph in which the edges carry a numerical weight.

Definition: A *Network* is a graph in which each edge has an associated positive numerical weight whose type we shall identify as Weighttype. The operations associated with the Network ADT are specified in terms of the following pre- and postconditions.

`Construct Operation (First Form)`

Precondition: An uninitialized Network object.
Postcondition: The Network object is initialized to an empty Network.

`Construct Operation (Copy Constructor)`

Preconditions: An uninitialized Network object;
initnet—a Network object that was previously constructed.
Postcondition: The Network object is initialized to *initnet*.

`Destroy Operation`

Precondition: A Network object that currently exists.
Postcondition: All storage allocated to the Network object is deallocated, that is, returned to an available space pool for allocation to other objects.

`Assign Operation`

Preconditions: A previously constructed Network object;
source—a second Network object that uses the same Basedata type and Weighttype.
Postconditions: The contents of *source* have been copied to the Network object that owns the operation.

`Empty Operation`

Precondition: A Network object.
Postcondition: If no nodes can be removed from the Network, the operation returns the value TRUE; otherwise it returns the value FALSE.

`Full Operation`

Precondition: A Network object.
Postcondition: If no nodes can be added to the Network, the operation returns the value TRUE; otherwise it returns the value FALSE.

`AddNode Operation`

Precondition: A Network object;
value—a value of type Basedata, which is to become the value of a new node in the Network.
Postcondition: The Network with a node containing *value* added to it. The node is not connected to any other node, including itself.

`AddEdge Operation`

Precondition: A nonempty Network object;
value1 and *value2*—values of two nodes in the Network;
weight—a positive number of type Weighttype, representing the weight of an edge to be added between the nodes with values *value1* and *value2*.
Postcondition: The Network with an edge of the specified weight added between the nodes with values *value1* and *value2*. If the edge existed prior to applying the operation, the weight of that edge will be changed to *weight*.

`EdgeWeight Operation`

Precondition: A nonempty Network object;
value1 and *value2*—values of two nodes in the Network.
Postcondition: The operation will return the weight of the edge between the nodes with values *value1* and *value2 if such an edge exists;* otherwise it will return the value 0.

`RemoveEdge` Operation

Precondition: A nonempty Network object;
value1 and *value2*—values of two nodes in the Network.

Postcondition: If there is an edge between the nodes with values *value1* and *value2,* it is removed; otherwise the Network will remain unchanged.

`RemoveNode` Operation

Precondition: A nonempty Network object;
value—the value of a node in the Network.

Postcondition: If there are no edges between the given node and other nodes in the Network, the node is removed; otherwise the Network will remain unchanged.

`DepthFirstTraversal` Operation

Precondition: A nonempty Network object;
start—the value of the node at which the traversal is to start;
processnode—a function that determines the process applied to each Network node.

Postcondition: The Network object will be modified so that each node that can be reached from *start* will be affected by *processnode.* The order in which nodes are affected is, first, *start* itself is affected; then, recursively, the first node adjacent to *start* and all nodes adjacent to that first node are affected; then, recursively, the second node adjacent to *start* and all nodes adjacent to that second node are affected; and so on, until *processnode* is applied to the last node adjacent to *start* and, recursively, to all nodes adjacent to that last node. The function *processnode* is not applied to any node more than once.

`BreadthFirstTraversal` Operation

Precondition: A nonempty Network object;
start—the value of the node at which the traversal is to start;
processnode—a function that determines the process applied to each Network node.

Postcondition: The Network object will be modified so that each node that can be reached from *start* will be affected by *processnode.* The order in which nodes are affected is, first, *start* itself is affected; then, all nodes adjacent to *start* are affected; then, nodes adjacent to nodes affected in the previous step are affected; and so on, until *processnode* has been applied to all nodes that can be reached from *start.* The function *processnode* is not applied to any node more than once.

Exercises 9.2

1. Redo Example 9.3 under the assumption that D is the first node connected to B.
2. Provide the order in which nodes would be visited in a depth-first traversal starting at D in the graph of Figure 9.6. State any assumptions you made in arriving at your answer.
3. Provide the order that nodes would be visited in a breadth-first traversal starting at D in the graph of Figure 9.6. State any assumptions you made in arriving at your answer.
4. Provide the order in which nodes would be visited in a depth-first traversal starting at A in the graph given in Exercise 9.1.2. State any assumptions you made in arriving at your answer.
5. Provide the order that nodes would be visited in a breadth-first traversal starting at A in the graph given

in Exercise 9.1.2. State any assumptions you made in arriving at your answer.

6. Give an algorithm that uses the operations provided with the Graph ADT to compute the indegree and outdegree of a node.
7. Does the AddEdge operation for the Graph ADT correctly add an edge between nodes with values *value1* and *value2* if the associated graph is an undirected graph? If not, explain why and specify pre- and postconditions for such an operation, which we shall call AddUndirected-Edge.
8. Consider the following diagraph. How many paths of length 3 are there from A to B?

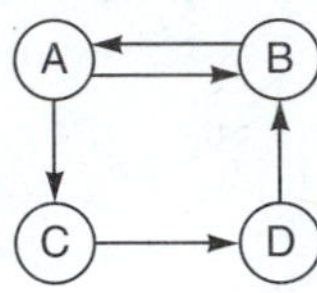

9.3 Implementations of the Graph and Network ADTs

In considering how to implement the Graph ADT and the Network ADT, we are first faced with the tasks of implementing the graph's or network's nodes and its edges (plus edge weights in the case of a network). At the same time, as we observed in Examples 9.1, 9.2, and 9.3 and in Exercise 9.2.3, the order in which nodes are visited in the depth-first or breadth-first traversals depends on the order in which one chooses from among the several nodes adjacent to a given node. Hence, to implement these traversal operations we need a way of specifying such an ordering. For the sake of simplicity, we once again use an assumption we relied on in our discussion of sets in Chapter 2—that the values of the nodes of the graph or network shall come from a finite subrange of some enumerated data type **BaseData**, with **firstValue** being the least value in this subrange and **lastValue** being the greatest value in this range.

Our approach for implementing the nodes of the graph/network is simply to keep a Boolean-valued array indexed between **firstValue** and **lastValue.** This requires the use of the Array ADT defined in Chapter 2. The presence of a node in the graph/network with an associated **value** can be indicated by assigning TRUE to the element of this Boolean array with index **value**; otherwise this element of the array will be FALSE. This is illustrated in Figure 9.9.

Adjacency List Implementation of the Edges of a Graph

We now consider two approaches for implementing the edges of a graph. Our first approach will be to maintain an array, indexed over the range **firstValue** to **lastValue,** of (pointers to) lists storing values of type **BaseData.** Each such list is known as an *adjacency list.* The presence of a value **dest,** in the adjacency list associated with array index **src,** indicates the presence of a directed edge from the node with value **src** to the node with value **dest.** This is illustrated in Figure 9.10. Adjacency lists can also be used to implement a network, but here the nodes in each list must be augmented to include the weight of the edge being represented. This is shown in Figure 9.11.

Figure 9.9
Representation of the nodes currently in a graph capable of storing values in the range A . . . F. Only nodes with the values 'A', 'C', and 'D' are currently in the graph.

A	B	C	D	E	F
TRUE	FALSE	TRUE	TRUE	FALSE	FALSE

Figure 9.10
Adjacency list representation of the graph from Figure 9.6.

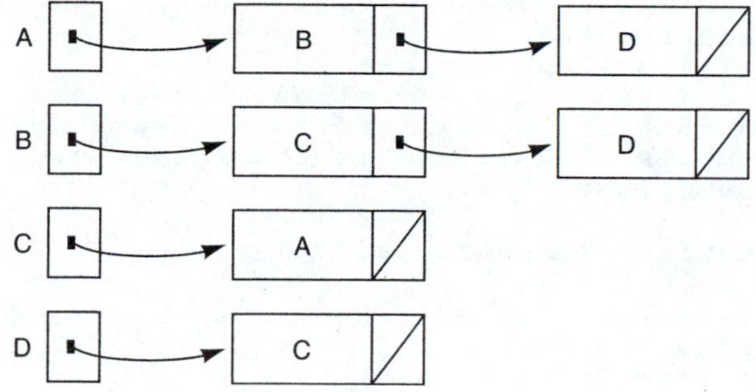

Figure 9.11
A network and a representation of its edges with adjacency lists.

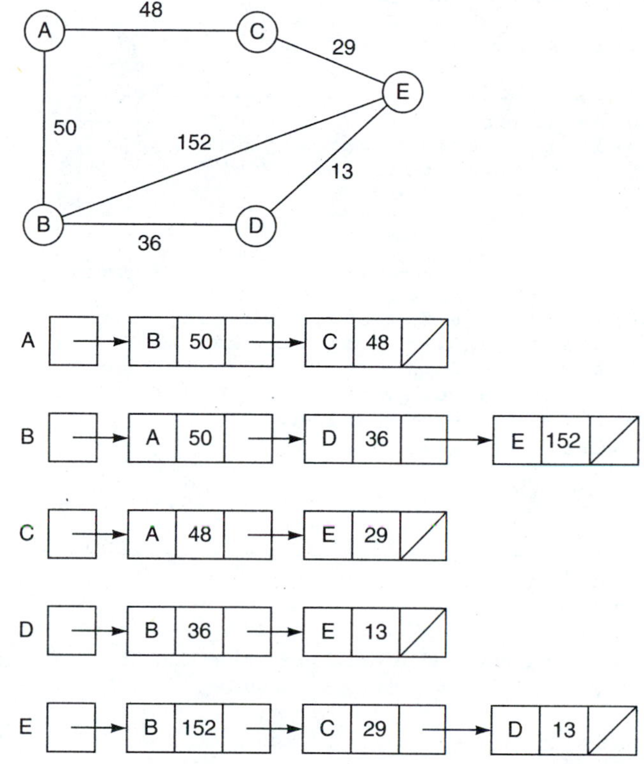

With this foundation in mind, we now give a C++ specification for the Graph ADT:

```
// HEADER  : graph.h
// PURPOSE : This file provides the definition for the Graph ADT.

// BaseData is a finite collection of consecutively enumerated values
// such as integers, characters, or values of an enum type.
template <class BaseData>
class Graph
{
  protected:
    BaseData firstValue, lastValue;
    Array<BaseData, BOOLEAN> *nodes;          // Storage for graph nodes
    Array<BaseData, List<BaseData>*> *edges; // Storage for graph edges using
                                             // adjacency lists

  public:
```

```
//------------------------------------------------------------
// Interface for Graph constructor
// GIVEN:    An uninitialized Graph object;
//           firstValue and lastValue -- values of type BaseData.
// RETURN:   The Graph object is initialized to an empty Graph, but capable
//           of storing nodes with values in the range between
//           firstValue and lastValue.

   Graph(BaseData firstValue, BaseData lastValue);

//------------------------------------------------------------
// Interface for Graph copy constructor
// GIVEN:    An uninitialized Graph object;
//           initgraph -- a Graph object that was previously constructed.
// RETURN:   The Graph object is initialized with the node values and
//           number of nodes of initgraph.

   Graph(Graph<BaseData> &initgraph);

//------------------------------------------------------------
// Interface for Graph destructor
// GIVEN:    A previously allocated Graph object.
// RETURN:   Graph object deallocated.

   ~Graph();

//----------------------------------------------------------------
// Interface for Graph assign = operator
// GIVEN:    A previously constructed Graph object;
//           source -- a second Graph object that must have been constructed with
//                     the same BaseData type as the owner of the assign operator.
// RETURN:   The contents of source have been copied to the Graph
//           object that owns the operation.
// RETURN as value of function: void

   void operator = (const Graph<BaseData> &source);

//------------------------------------------------------------
// Interface for empty operation
// GIVEN:    A Graph object.
// RETURN as value of function:
//           If no nodes can be removed from the Graph, return the
//           value TRUE; otherwise return FALSE.

   void empty();

//------------------------------------------------------------
// Interface for full operation
// GIVEN:    A Graph object.
// RETURN as value of function:
//           If no nodes can be added to the Graph, return the
//           value TRUE; otherwise return FALSE.

   void full();

//------------------------------------------------------------
// Interface for addNode operation
// GIVEN:    A Graph object;
//           value -- having type BaseData.
// RETURN:   The Graph object with a node containing value added to it; the
//           node is not connected to any other node, including to itself.
// RETURN as value of function: void

   void addNode(BaseData value);
```

```
//--------------------------------------------------------------
// Interface for addEdge operation
// GIVEN:     A nonempty Graph object;
//            value1 and value2 -- values of two nodes in the Graph.
// RETURN:    The graph will have an edge added between the nodes
//            with value1 and value2. If such an edge already exists
//            the graph will remain unchanged.
// RETURN as value of function: void

   void addEdge(BaseData value1, BaseData value2);

//--------------------------------------------------------------
// Interface for edge operation
// GIVEN:     A nonempty Graph object;
//            value1 and value2 -- values of two nodes in the Graph.
// RETURN as value of function:
//            TRUE if there is an edge between the nodes
//            with values value1 and value2; FALSE otherwise.

   BOOLEAN edge(BaseData value1, BaseData value2);

//--------------------------------------------------------------
// Interface for removeEdge operation
// GIVEN:     A nonempty Graph object;
//            value1 and value2 -- values of two nodes in the Graph.
// RETURN:    If there is an edge between the nodes with values
//            value1 and value2, it is removed; otherwise the Graph
//            will remain unchanged.
// RETURN as value of function: void

   void removeEdge(BaseData value1, BaseData value2);

//--------------------------------------------------------------
// Interface for removeNode operation
// GIVEN:     A nonempty Graph object;
//            value -- the value of a node in the Graph.
// RETURN:    If there are no edges between the node with value
//            and other nodes in the Graph, the node is removed;
//            otherwise the Graph will remain unchanged.
// RETURN as value of function: void

   void removeNode(BaseData value1);

//--------------------------------------------------------------
// Interface for depthFirstTraversal operation
// GIVEN:     A Graph object;
//            start -- the value of a node at which the traversal is
//                    to start;
//            processNode -- a function for processing node values:
//                  GIVEN:  value -- the value of a Graph node.
//                  RETURN: The given node processed in some manner.
//                  RETURN as value of function: void
// RETURN:    The Graph object will be modified so that each node
//            that can be reached from start will be affected by
//            processNode. The order in which nodes are affected
//            is, first, start itself is affected; then,
//            recursively, the first node adjacent to start and
//            all nodes adjacent to that first node are affected;
//            then, recursively, the second node adjacent to start
//            and all nodes adjacent to that second node are
//            affected; and so on, until processNode is applied to
```

```
//            the last node adjacent to start and, recursively, to
//            all nodes adjacent to that last node. The function
//            processNode is not applied to any node more than once.
// RETURN as value of function: void

    void depthFirstTraversal(BaseData &start,
                             void (*processNode)(BaseData &value));

//-------------------------------------------------------------------
// Interface for breadthFirstTraversal operation
// GIVEN:     A Graph object;
//            start -- the value of a node at which the traversal is to start;
//            processNode -- a function for processing node values:
//                  GIVEN:  value -- the value of a Graph node.
//                  RETURN: The given node processed in some manner.
//                  RETURN as value of function: void
// RETURN:    The Graph object will be modified so that each node that can be
//            reached from start will be affected by processNode.  The order
//            in which nodes are affected is, first, start itself is affected;
//            then, all nodes adjacent to start are affected; then, nodes
//            adjacent to nodes affected in the previous step are affected;
//            and so on, until processNode has been applied to all nodes that
//            can be reached from start. The function processNode is not
//            applied to any node more than once.
// RETURN as value of function: void

    void breadthFirstTraversal(BaseData &start,
                               void (*processNode) (BaseData &value));
};
```

Adjacency Matrix Implementation of Graphs and Networks

An alternative to using an adjacency list is to use an *adjacency matrix*. This approach for implementing the edges of a graph or network is once again based on an array that is indexed over the range **firstValue** to **lastValue,** but instead of being an array of pointers to lists it is an array of (pointers to) other arrays (or a matrix), each of which is also indexed over the range **firstValue** to **lastValue.** For graphs, these arrays can have a base type of BOOLEAN, in which case a value of TRUE in component **dest** of the array associated with array index **src** indicates the presence of a directed edge from the node with value **src** to the node with value **dest;** a value of FALSE for this component signifies the absence of such an edge. This is illustrated in Figure 9.12. For networks, the base type can be a numeric type, say **WeightType**, that gives the weight associated with an edge from the node with value **src** to the node with value **dest**. We show this in Figure 9.13.

Rather than implement an adjacency matrix directly in the implementation of a graph or network, we shall assume instead the existence of a Matrix ADT defined as follows:

	A	B	C	D
A	FALSE	TRUE	FALSE	TRUE
B	FALSE	FALSE	TRUE	TRUE
C	TRUE	FALSE	FALSE	FALSE
D	FALSE	FALSE	TRUE	FALSE

Figure 9.12
Adjacency matrix implementation of the graph from Figure 9.6. A value TRUE in the matrix entry at row **i** and column **j** indicates the presence of an edge from node **i** to node **j.** A value FALSE indicates the absence of such an edge.

Figure 9.13

Matrix implementation of the network from Figure 9.3. Only nonzero weights are shown.

	NYC	Wash	Miam	Milw	Chi	NOrl	Mpls	OklC	Dals	LVeg	Phex	StL	SFran	LA
NYC		237					1,217		1,614					
Wash	237			811										
Miam					1,423									
Milw		811									1,771		2,257	
Chi			1,423			948				1,780		2,060		
NOrl					948				517					
Mpls	1,217							792	949					
OklC							792							
Dals	1,614					517	949							1,440
LVeg					1,780									272
Phex				1,771										
StL					2,060								808	
SFran				2,257								808		414
LA									1,440	272			414	

Definition: The *Matrix* ADT is an association between a pair of index ranges and a collection of similarly typed data items. Each index range is a finite collection of consecutively enumerated values such as integers or characters. The association between an index range pair (i,j) and the data item allows us to designate the datum as the value in the *ith row* and *jth column* of the matrix. The operations that can be performed on a matrix are:

Construct Operation (First Form)

Preconditions: An uninitialized Matrix object.

Postconditions: The Matrix object has been allocated sufficient storage to store its associated data items, though no specific values have been stored in the Matrix.

Construct Operation (Copy Constructor)

Preconditions: An uninitialized Matrix object;
initmatrix—a Matrix object that was previously constructed.

Postconditions: The Matrix object is initialized to *initmatrix*.

Destroy Operation

Preconditions: A Matrix object that has been previously constructed.

Postconditions: All storage allocated to the Matrix object is deallocated, that is, returned to an available space pool for allocation to other objects.

Assign Operation

Preconditions: A previously constructed Matrix object;
source—a second Matrix object that uses the same data type as the owner of the operation.

Postconditions: The contents of *source* have been copied to the matrix object that owns the operation.

Retrieve Operation

Preconditions: A Matrix object that has been previously created;
i—a valid index from the row indices;
j—a valid index from the column indices.

Postconditions: The value associated with the pair (i, j) in the Matrix object is returned.

Assign operation

Preconditions: A Matrix object that has been previously created;
i—a valid index from the row indices;
j—a valid index from the column indices;
val—a specified value for a matrix datum.

Postconditions: The Matrix object has *val* associated with the pair (i, j). We say that "*val* is stored at row *i* and column *j* in the Matrix object."

In Exercise 2.1.6 you were asked to provide pre- and postconditions such as we have just furnished, and were asked to provide a complete C++ implementation of the Matrix ADT. You were also advised to overload the index operator [] twice, once for the row index and once for the column index. In this case a client program could access a location in a matrix **m** by using the notation **m[row][col]**.

Assuming the availability of such a Matrix ADT, we now show a possible protected portion of a C++ specification for the Graph ADT that uses an adjacency matrix.

```
// HEADER  : graph.h
// PURPOSE : This file provides the definition for the Graph ADT.

// BaseData is a finite collection of consecutively enumerated values
// such as integers, characters, or values of an enum type.
template <class BaseData>
class Graph
{
  protected:
    BaseData firstValue, lastValue;
    Array<BaseData, BOOLEAN> *nodes;               // Storage for graph nodes
    Matrix<BaseData, BaseData, BOOLEAN> *edges // Storage for graph edges using
                                               // an adjacency matrix
  public:
    as before
};
```

Similarly, a C++ implementation for the Network ADT based on an adjacency matrix for implementing its edges would begin as follows:

```
// HEADER  : network.h
// PURPOSE : This file provides the definition for the Network ADT.

//  BaseData is a finite collection of consecutively enumerated values such as
//  integers, characters, or values of an enum type; WeightType is a numeric type.
template <class BaseData, class WeightType>
class Network
{
  protected:
    BaseData firstValue, lastValue;
    Array<BaseData, BOOLEAN> *nodes;                  // Storage for network nodes
    Matrix<BaseData, BaseData, WeightType> *edges // Storage for network edges
                                                  // using an adjacency matrix
  public:
    analogous to that of graphs
};
```

Such an implementation of the transportation network from Figure 9.3 is given in Figure 9.13. Note that, since this network does not have a digraph as its underlying graph structure, the data are mirrored across the diagonal of the adjacency matrix.

Implementation of the Depth-First Traversal Operation

The **depthFirstTraversal** operation from a specified **start** node may be implemented by using an auxiliary Boolean array **visited** that is indexed from **firstValue** to **lastValue.** This **visited** array is used to mark those nodes that have already been visited at any given stage of the traversal. Initially, all entries in this array must be set to FALSE. The actual traversal is then accomplished by calling recursively on a subordinate function **searchFrom** that continues to probe along paths that can be reached from nodes adjacent to the start node, marking as TRUE each node that is visited to ensure that no node is visited twice. Since **searchFrom** is being used solely to facilitate the implementation of **depthFirstTraversal,** it should be specified as a **protected** operation of Graph. We now give implementations of both functions that are independent of the method used to implement the edges. In our discussion of the efficiency of our implementation, however, we consider situations in which these implementations might be improved by choosing adjacency lists over an adjacency matrix.

```
template <class BaseData>
void Graph<BaseData>::searchFrom(BaseData &start,
                                 void (*processNode)(BaseData &value),
                                 Array<BaseData,BOOLEAN> visited)
{
  BaseData k;

  processNode(start);
  visited[start] = TRUE;
  for (k = firstValue; k <= lastValue; ++k)
    if ((!visited[k]) && edge(start, k))
      searchFrom(k, processNode, visited);
}

template <class BaseData>
void Graph<BaseData>::
  depthFirstTraversal(BaseData &start, void (*processNode)(BaseData &value))
{
  Array<BaseData,BOOLEAN> visited(firstValue, lastValue);
  BaseData k;

  for(k = firstValue; k <= lastValue; ++k)
    visited[k] = FALSE;
  searchFrom(start, processNode, visited);
}
```

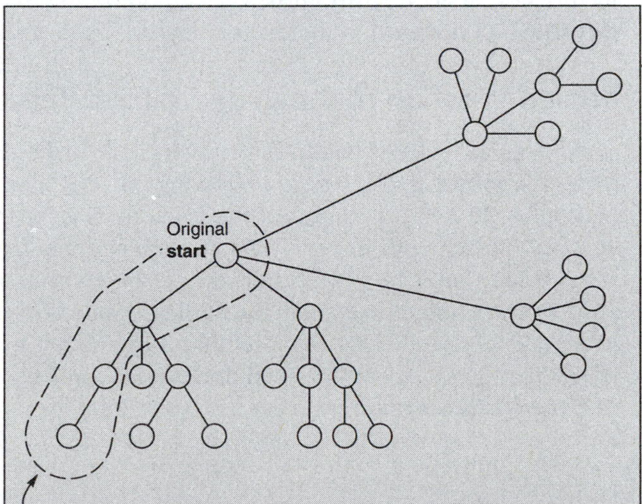

The recursive call will successively pass in as **start** graph nodes along this path, ensuring that this path is completely probed before any other nodes adjacent to the original **start** are visited.

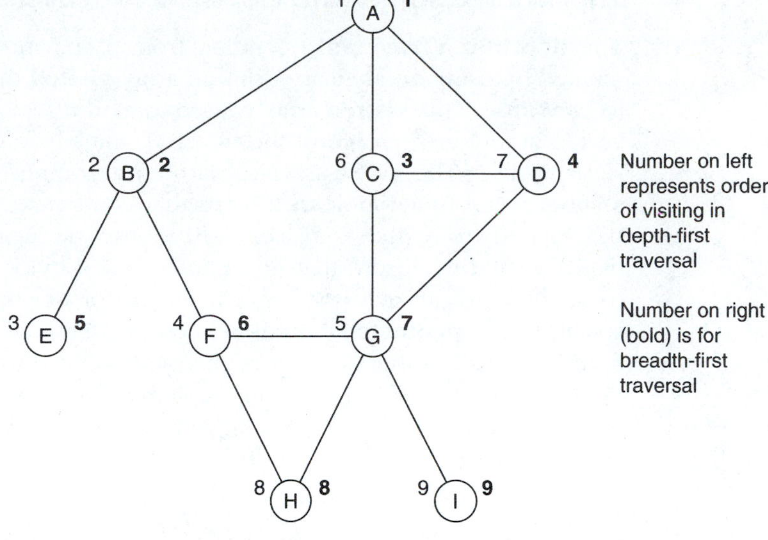

Figure 9.14
Difference in order of visiting nodes in depth-first and breadth-first traversals from A, assuming adjacency ordering is alphabetic.

Efficiency Analysis of This Implementation of DepthFirstTraversal

Although the preceding algorithm presents a clear statement of the depth-first logic, it may be quite inefficient for a graph with a large number of nodes because the recursive call in the subordinate function **searchFrom** could potentially be invoked *NumberOfNodes* times, where $NumberOfNodes = 1 + lastValue - firstValue$. You will devise a graph that generates this worst-case scenario in the exercises at the end of the section. Each time the recursive call is made, we will iterate *NumberOfNodes* times through the loop in function **searchFrom.** Hence, in the worst case, $O(NumberOfNodes^2)$ operations will be performed. If adjacency lists are used to implement the graph, the structure of these lists can be used to eliminate performing operations on nodes that are not connected to the **start** node in function **searchFrom.** You will explore developing such an implementation of **depthFirstTraversal** in the exercises at the end of the section.

Implementation of the Breadth-First Traversal Operation

The essence of the breadth-first traversal is to begin exploration of many paths from the **start** node before following any of them more deeply. Figure 9.14 highlights the fan-out nature of the breadth-first traversal compared to the probing strategy of the depth-first traversal. To achieve this fanning out, nodes adjacent to a visited node must be put on hold while we continue to visit nodes adjacent to the current **start** node. In general, the earlier a node is visited, the earlier nodes adjacent to it will be visited. This suggests that a queue is the natural data structure to hold nodes that are adjacent to visited nodes. Hence, the following C++ implementation of **breadthFirstTraversal** relies on operations from the Queue ADT of Chapter 4.

```
template <class BaseData>
void Graph<BaseData>::
  breadthFirstTraversal(BaseData &start, void (*processNode)(BaseData &value))
{
  Array<BaseData, BOOLEAN> nodeInQueue(firstValue, lastValue);
```

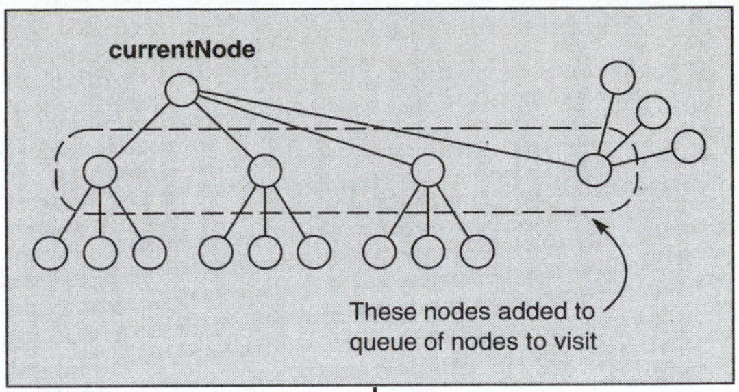

```
  BaseData k, currentNode;
  Queue<BaseData> nodesToVisit;

  for (k = firstValue; k <= lastValue; ++k)
    nodeInQueue[k] = FALSE;
  nodesToVisit.enqueue(start);
  nodeInQueue[start] = TRUE;
  while (!nodesToVisit.empty())
  {
    currentNode = nodesToVisit.front();
    nodesToVisit.dequeue();
    processNode(currentNode);
    for (k = firstValue; k <= lastValue; ++k)
      if ((!nodeInQueue[k]) && edge(currentNode,k))
      {
        nodesToVisit.enqueue(k);
        nodeInQueue[k] = TRUE;
      }
  }
}
```

Efficiency Analysis of This Implementation of BreadthFirstTraversal

This analysis is similar to the one we carried out for **depthFirstTraversal.** If it is possible to reach every node from the original **start** node, then every node will be put on the **nodesToVisit** queue. After being examined and dequeued, all nodes are checked for adjacency to the **currentNode**—a check involving $O\ (NumberOfNodes)$ operations, whereas before $NumberOfNodes = 1 + lastValue - firstValue$. Hence, the overall efficiency of the algorithm for this implementation is $O\ (NumberOfNodes^2)$. As with **depthFirstTraversal,** this efficiency can be improved for many graphs by direct use of an adjacency-list implementation of the graph. You will explore this improvement in the following exercises.

Exercises 9.3

1. If you did not do so in Chapter 2, provide a complete implementation of the Matrix ADT. Include in your implementation the overloading of the index operator [] as suggested in this section.
2. Complete the implementations for the Graph ADT and the Network ADT. Assume the following:
   - **a.** An adjacency matrix is used to implement the edges of the graph or network.
   - **b.** Adjacency lists are used to implement the edges of the graph or network.
3. What are the time efficiencies of the **edge, addEdge,** and **removeEdge** operations for a **Graph** or **Network** if
   - **a.** an adjacency matrix is used to implement the edges?
   - **b.** adjacency lists are used to implement the edges?
4. When the values of the nodes do not come from a finite collection of consecutively enumerated values, or when the values come from such a collection type but do not span an entire subrange of the collection, we can still use adjacency lists or an adjacency matrix for representing the edges, but we can no longer establish a one-to-one correspondence between values of type Basedata and a graph's nodes, since there will be data values without an associated node. For example, in Figure 9.6, if instead of using as node values the characters A, B, C, and D we wanted to use the characters B, C, M, and N, then it would be inefficient to use the subrange 'B'... 'N', since this would set up the data structures representing our graph to accommodate up to 13 nodes instead of just the four we need. One possibility is to use the following set of declarations:

```
Array<int, BaseData> *nodes;
Matrix<int, int, BOOLEAN> *edges;
int numNodes;
```

Here **edges** is a pointer to an adjacency matrix. The constructor operation for the Graph would accept a maximal size for the Graph as a parameter and then create appropriately sized ***nodes** and ***edges** structures. Through calls to **addNode** we would then make the following assignment of values to **nodes** for the Graph:

```
*nodes[1]  := 'B';
*nodes[2]  := 'C';
*nodes[3]  := 'M';
*nodes[4]  := 'N';
```

Finally, in order to move smoothly between our representations for nodes and edges, we can define a (protected) function:

```
int getNode(BaseData &value);
```

that maps a value to the node associated with that value. Provide a complete C++ implementation of the Graph and Network ADTs that is based on this more general set of node values.

5. Given the implementation of **depthFirstTraversal** appearing in this section, provide an example of a graph that leads to the worst case efficiency of $O(NumberOfNodes^2)$. Then provide another graph for which this worst case efficiency would not be realized.
6. Assuming an adjacency-list implementation of a graph, write a **depthFirstTraversal** that takes advantage of this implementation to avoid the $O(NumberOfNodes^2)$ worst case efficiency of an adjacency-matrix implementation. What is the worst case efficiency of your new implementation of **depthFirstTraversal?** Are there graphs for which the worst case efficiency of your new implementation will be worse than that for the adjacency-matrix implementation? Identify general conditions under which the adjacency-list strategy seems to provide a more efficient implementation for **depthFirstTraversal.**
7. Repeat Exercise 9.3.6 for the **breadthFirstTraversal** operation.
8. Write a function that will apply a **processNode** operation to all nodes in a graph, not just those nodes that can be reached from a given **start** node.
9. A graph that is not strongly connected is composed of disjoint subgraphs that are strongly connected. Each subgraph is called a *connected component* of the original graph. Write a function that takes as input a Graph object **g** and returns a count of the number of connected components in **g.** Analyze the time efficiency of your function.
10. Write a function that receives a Graph object **g** and a designated value for a **start** node and then determines whether or not the graph contains a cycle that begins and ends at this node. Analyze the time efficiency of your function.
11. Write a function that will count the number of edges in a graph
    a. assuming an adjacency matrix implementation.
    b. assuming an adjacency list implementation.
    Analyze the time efficiency of each of these functions.
12. Write a function that uses the operations provided with the **Graph** class to compute the indegree and outdegree of a node whose value is passed as a parameter to the function.
13. In Exercise 9.2.7 you specified pre- and postconditions for a **Graph** operation to correctly add an edge between nodes with values **value1** and **value2** if the associated graph is an undirected graph. Now implement this operation as a member function of the **Graph** class.

9.4 Path Algorithms

Shortest Path Algorithms

In a transportation network such as that shown in Figure 9.3, a typical question is how to find the shortest distance between two nodes in the network. This question can be asked from two perspectives. First, given two nodes in the network—a *start* node and a *destination* node—we may ask for the shortest path from *start* to *destination*. Second, we could ask to find the shortest path between all pairs of nodes in the network. An efficient algorithm to answer the first question was first discovered by E. W. Dijkstra. For further reading on this, see Dijkstra's work, "A Note on Two Problems in Connection with Graphs," (*Numerische Mathematik,* 1, pp. 269–272). Although the second question could certainly be answered by iterating pairs of nodes through Dijkstra's algorithm, a more efficient method of answering this was devised by R. W. Floyd. (More on this can be found in *Communications of the ACM,* 1962 Algorithm 97: "Shortest Path," 5, p. 345.)

Dijkstra's Algorithm to Find the Shortest Path between Two Nodes

Given a small network such as that in Figure 9.15, a careful examination reveals that the shortest path from node 0 to node 2 is not the direct edge connecting these nodes, but rather the path 0→1→2. That is, starting at node 0, it requires less total edge weight to reach node 2 by going through node 1 than it does to follow the edge directly linking 0 and 2. This is not surprising if you recall the caution about edge weights we mentioned at the end of Section 9.1: Edge weights are *not* necessarily Euclidean distances. Hence, if we visualize edge weights as the lengths of straight lines between nodes, we may possibly observe the "phenomenon" where the sum of two sides of a triangle has a smaller total edge weight than the third side. Indeed, this phenomenon is at the core of Dijkstra's algorithm to determine the shortest distance between two nodes.

In discussing Dijkstra's algorithm, we shall make the same assumptions about the **BaseData** data type for networks as we did for graphs in Section 9.3. That is, the values of the nodes are from a finite collection of consecutively enumerated values with identifiable limits **firstValue** and **lastValue.** Given such a collection of nodes, Dijkstra's algorithm requires three arrays in addition to a suitable implementation of the network. These three arrays are identified as follows:

```
Array<BaseData,WeightType> distance(firstValue,lastValue);
Array<BaseData,BaseData> path(firstValue,lastValue);
Array<BaseData,BOOLEAN> included(firstValue,lastValue);
```

Identifying one node as the **start** node, the algorithm finds the shortest distance from **start** to other nodes in the network until the shortest distance to the **destination** node is known. At the conclusion of the algorithm, the shortest distance from **start** to **destination** is stored in **distance[destination]** while **path[j]** contains the immediate predecessor of node **j** on the path determining the shortest distance. While the algorithm is in progress, **distance[j]** and **path[j]** are being continually updated until **included[j]** is switched from FALSE to TRUE. Once this switch occurs, it is known definitely that **distance[j]** contains the shortest distance from **start** to **j.** The algorithm progresses until the **destination** node has been so included, hence giving the shortest distance from **start** to **destination.** The algorithm may be easily extended to give us the shortest distance from **start** to every other node in the network.

Given a **start** node in a network, the algorithm may be divided into two phases: an *initialization phase* followed by an *iteration phase* in which nodes are included one by one in the set of nodes for which the shortest distance from **start** is known.

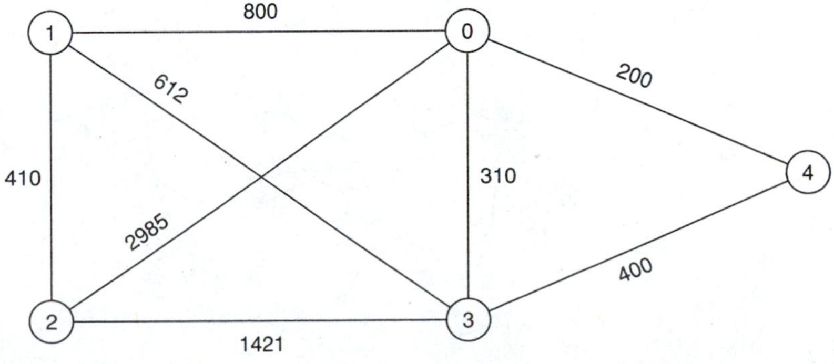

Figure 9.15
Network with edge weights. Note that the shortest path from node 0 to node 2 is not the direct edge 0→2, but rather the path 0→1→2.

During the initialization phase, the following steps must occur:

1. Initialize **included[start]** to TRUE, and **included[j]** to FALSE for all other **j.**
2. Initialize the **distance** array via the rule

$$\text{distance[j]} = \begin{cases} 0 & \text{if } j = \text{start} \\ \text{edgeWeight(start, j)} & \text{if edgeWeight(start, j) != 0} \\ \infty & \text{if j is not connected to start by a direct edge; that is, if edgeWeight(start, j)} = 0 \end{cases}$$

3. Initialize the **path** array via the rule

$$\text{path[j]} = \begin{cases} \text{start} & \text{if edgeWeight(start, j) != 0} \\ \text{undefined} & \text{otherwise} \end{cases}$$

Given this initialization, the iteration phase may be expressed in pseudocode as follows:

```
do
  Find the node j having minimal distance among those nodes not yet included;
  Mark node j as now included;
  for each node r not yet included
    if r is connected by an edge to j
       if (distance[j] + edgeWeight(j,r) < distance[r])
       distance[r] = distance[j] + edgeWeight(j,r);
      path[r] = j;
while destination node is not included
```

The crucial part of the algorithm occurs within the innermost **if** of the **for** loop. Figure 9.16 provides a pictorial representation of the logic involved here. The encircled nodes represent those nodes already included prior to a given iteration of the **do-while** loop. The node **j** in Figure 9.16 represents the node found in the first step of the **do-while** loop; **r** represents another arbitrary node that has not yet been included. The lines emanating from **start** represent the paths corresponding to the current entries in the **distance** array. For nodes within the circle—that is, those already included—these paths are guaranteed to be the shortest distance paths. If **j** is the node having the minimal entry in **distance** among those not yet included,

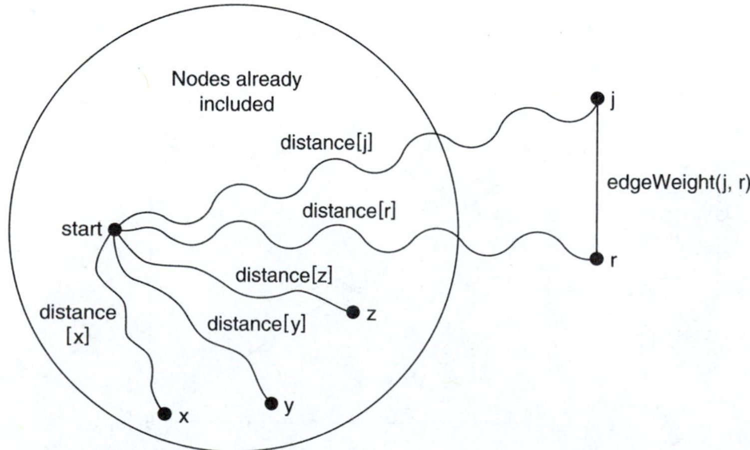

Figure 9.16
do-while loop logic in shortest path (Dijkstra's) algorithm.

we will add **j** to the circle of included nodes and check to see if **j**'s connections to other nodes in the network that are not yet included may result in a newly found shorter path to such nodes.

Referring to Figure 9.16 again, the sum of two sides of a triangle

```
distance[j] + edgeWeight(j, r)
```

may in fact be shorter than the third side, **distance[r].** As we hinted earlier, this geometric contradiction is possible because these are not true straight-sided triangles, but "triangles" whose sides may be very complicated paths through a network.

It is also apparent from Figure 9.16 why Dijkstra's algorithm works. As the node **j** in this figure is found to have the minimal **distance** entry from among all those nodes not yet included, we may now include it among the nodes whose minimal distance from the **start** node is *absolutely* known. Why? Consider any other path **p** from **start** to **j** that contains nodes not yet included at the time **j** is included. Let **x** be the first such nonincluded node on the path **p.** Then clearly, as the first nonincluded node on the path **p,** the node **x** must be adjacent to an included node. However, as Figure 9.17 indicates, the criterion that dictated the choice of **j** as an included node ensures that

```
distance[j] ≤  Total edge weight up to node x on the path p
            ≤  Total edge weight of path p
```

This inequality demonstrates that once **j** is included there exists no other path **p** to **j** through a nonincluded node that can yield a shorter overall distance. Hence, we have verified our claim that including a node guarantees our having found a path of shortest possible distance to that node.

Example 9.4

To be sure you understand Dijkstra's algorithm before you attempt to implement it, trace it through the network of Figure 9.15 with **firstValue** = 0, **lastValue** = 4, and **start** = **firstValue.** Initially we would have

```
distance[0] = 0      path[0] undefined
distance[1] = 800    path[1] = 0
distance[2] = 2985   path[2] = 0
```

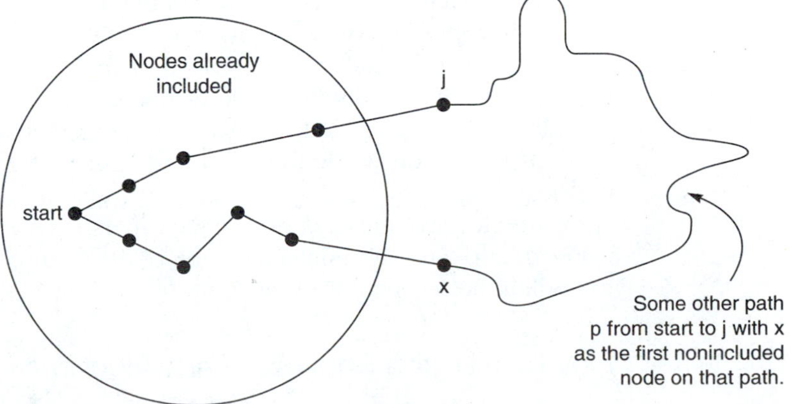

Figure 9.17
Guaranteeing the minimality of **distance** to **j** once it is included.

```
distance[3] = 310      path[3] = 0
distance[4] = 200      path[4] = 0
```

in accordance with steps 2 and 3 of the initialization phase. According to the iteration phase of the algorithm, we would then do the following, in order:

1. Include node 4; no changes in **distance** on **path** are needed

```
distance[0] = 0        path[0] undefined
distance[1] = 800      path[1] = 0
distance[2] = 2985     path[2] = 0
distance[3] = 310      path[3] = 0
distance[4] = 200      path[4] = 0
```

2. Include node 3; update **distance** and **path** to

```
distance[0] = 0        path[0] undefined
distance[1] = 800      path[1] = 0
distance[2] = 1731     path[2] = 3
distance[3] = 310      path[3] = 0
distance[4] = 200      path[4] = 0
```

(Note that it is shorter to go from node 0 to node 3 to node 2 than to follow the edge directly connecting node 0 to node 2.)

3. Include node 1; update **distance** and **path** to

```
distance[0] = 0        path[0] undefined
distance[1] = 800      path[1] = 0
distance[2] = 1210     path[2] = 1
distance[3] = 310      path[3] = 0
distance[4] = 200      path[4] = 0
```

(Now we find that traveling from node 0 to node 1 to node 2 is even better than the path determined in step 2.)

4. Finally node 2 is included with no changes made in **distance** or **path.**

Efficiency of Dijkstra's Algorithm

If we assume an implementation of the **edgeWeight** operation that is $O(1)$, then an inspection of the iterative control structure in our statement of Dijkstra's algorithm implies a worst case $O(\mathit{NumberOfNodes}^2)$ efficiency for the algorithm, where $\mathit{NumberOfNodes} = 1 + \mathit{lastValue} - \mathit{firstValue}$. The reason is that the steps to find the minimal distance among nodes not yet included and then to update the **distance** array are both $O(\mathit{NumberOfNodes})$ and they are nested sequentially inside the outer **do-while** loop, which is also $O(\mathit{NumberOfNodes})$. We shall see in the next chapter that for sparse networks, that is, those with relatively few edges compared to the number of nodes, we can achieve a somewhat better efficiency by using an adjacency-list implementation of the network and a priority queue to assist in finding the minimal distance.

Floyd's All-Pairs Shortest Path Algorithm

Dijkstra's algorithm is appropriate for finding the shortest distance between two specified nodes in a graph. However, if we want to use an iteration of Dijkstra's algorithm to find the shortest distance between every possible pair of nodes in the network, we would have to nest Dijkstra's $O(NumberOfNodes^2)$ algorithm in another $O(NumberOfNodes^2)$ looping structure—one for each ordered pair of nodes in the graph. The resulting efficiency would be $O(NumberOfNodes^4)$. Floyd's algorithm is designed specifically to find the shortest distance between all pairs of nodes in a network, allowing it to compute all of these shortest paths in $O(NumberOfNodes^3)$ run time. However, it remains inferior to Dijkstra's algorithm for finding the shortest distance between a single pair of nodes. Depending on the pair of nodes, it could require $O(NumberOfNodes^3)$ time to do a single-pair computation.

The essence of Floyd's algorithm is to use information from the network to compute a sequence of values for a matrix that has rows and columns indexed from **firstValue** to **lastValue.** We will call this matrix the *distance matrix*. At the *k*th stage of Floyd's algorithm (where **firstValue** ≤ **k** ≤ **lastValue**), the value **distance[i][j]** is computed to contain the distance of the shortest path satisfying the two following criteria:

1. The path must start at node **i** and end at node **j.**
2. Internal nodes on the path (that is, excluding the **start** and **end** nodes) must come from the set of nodes between **firstValue** and **k** inclusive.

Provided that such a succession of matrix values can be computed, we are guaranteed that, at the **lastValue** stage of the algorithm, **distance[i][j]** will contain the length of the shortest path from node **i** to node **j** because, by satisfying the second criterion, it contains the length of the shortest path whose internal nodes are selected from the set of all possible nodes.

Hence, we must merely ensure that the **distance** matrix satisfying the two criteria above can be computed. Floyd discovered a surprisingly easy algorithm to do this. During an initialization phase of Floyd's algorithm, each entry of the **distance** matrix is defined by the following rule:

$$\text{distance[i][j]} = \begin{cases} 0 & \text{if } i = j \\ \text{edgeWeight(i,j)} & \text{if the network contains an edge from node } i \text{ to } j \\ \infty & \text{otherwise} \end{cases}$$

Then, the following iterative step recomputes the **distance** matrix through a succession of triply nested loops.

```
for (k = firstValue; k <= lastValue; ++k)
  for (i = firstValue; i <= lastValue; ++i)
    for (j = firstValue; j <= lastValue; ++j)
      distance[i][j] = minimum(distance[i][j], distance[i][k] + distance[k][j])
```

To see why this computation of the **distance** matrix will satisfy the two criteria we have established as goals, consider the situation pictured in Figure 9.18, where the solid-line path from node **i** to node **j** represents the path of shortest length between those two nodes at the (**k** − 1)st stage of Floyd's algorithm. At the **k**th stage of the algorithm, we compare the solid-line path from node **i** to node **j** with the path formed by joining the dashed-line path from node **i** to node **k** with the dotted-line path from node **k** to node **j.** If the joining of these two paths results in a path from node **i** to node **j** whose overall length is less than the length of the solid-line path, we can adjust **distance[i][j]** since, at the **k**th stage of the algorithm, we allow node **k** to be an internal node on the shortest path.

The $O(NumberOfNodes^3)$ efficiency of Floyd's algorithm can be deduced immediately from its three-deep nested loop structure. We also see why Floyd's

Figure 9.18
Computation of **distance[i][j]** at *k*th stage of Floyd's algorithm.

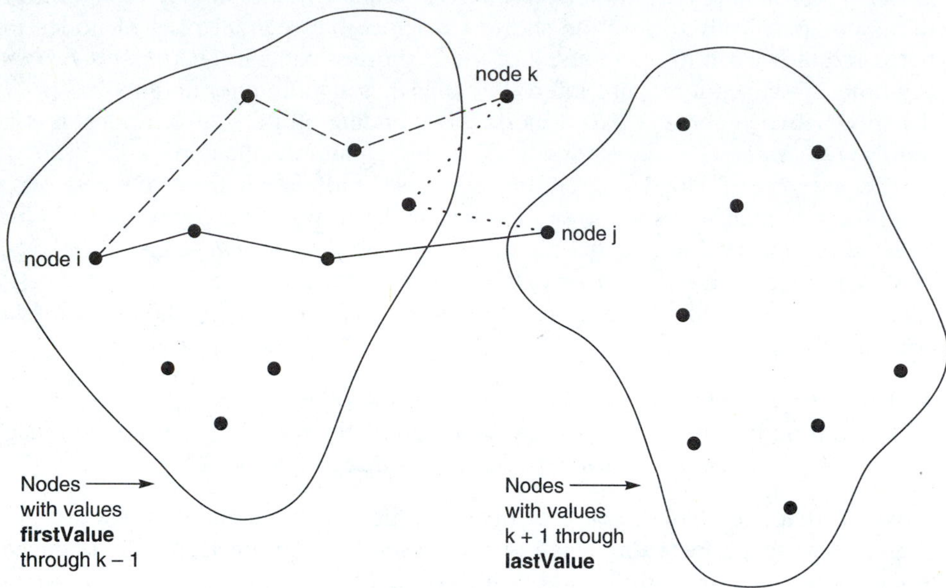

algorithm cannot be used efficiently to answer the single-pair shortest path question. The algorithm has no way of guaranteeing that it has found the shortest path between a specified pair of nodes until it checks whether **lastValue** should be part of that path, and it cannot perform this check without iterating through $O(NumberOfNodes^3)$ operations.

Example 9.5

To be sure that you understand Floyd's algorithm before you attempt to implement it in the exercises, trace through the contents of the **distance** matrix for the directed network of Figure 9.19.

1. During the initialization phase, the **distance** matrix would be set to the following values:

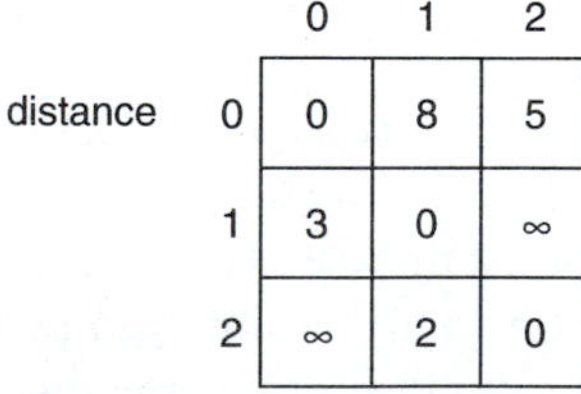

distance	0	1	2
0	0	8	5
1	3	0	∞
2	∞	2	0

Figure 9.19
Network for tracing Floyd's algorithm in Example 9.5.

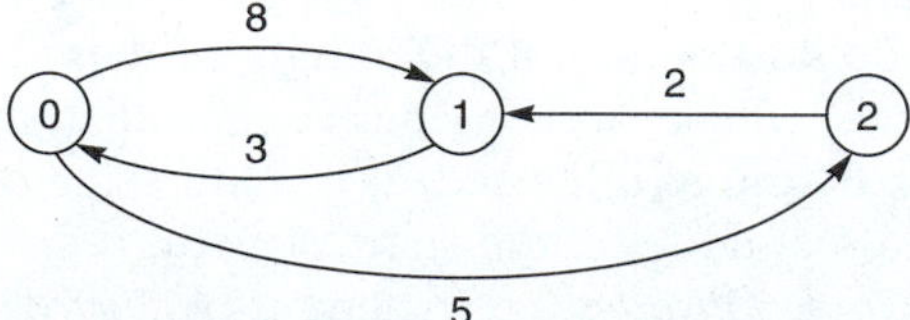

2. During the first iteration of the algorithm, we would determine whether any **distance** values from step 1 can be decreased by using a path that has node 0 as an interior node. Since the path

1 ⟶ 0 ⟶ 2
Length 3 Length 5

is certainly less than ∞ presently in **distance[1][2],** the **distance** matrix is updated to

distance	0	1	2
0	0	8	5
1	3	0	8
2	∞	2	0

3. In the second iteration, we seek paths that are shorter than those we currently have and that contain 1 as an interior node. The path

2 ⟶ 1 ⟶ 0
Length 2 Length 3

yields such a smaller value for **distance[2][0].** Hence, the matrix becomes

distance	0	1	2
0	0	8	5
1	3	0	8
2	5	2	0

4. The final iteration considers paths with node 2 as an interior node. In this case, we note that the path

0 ⟶ 2 ⟶ 1
Length 5 Length 2

is shorter than the direct edge 0→1 whose value is currently recorded in **distance[0][1].** Hence, the **distance** matrix is determined to be

distance	0	1	2
0	0	7	5
1	3	0	8
2	5	2	0

Transitive Closure and Warshall's Algorithm

In our previous discussion we were interested in finding the shortest path between given nodes in a graph. Sometimes, however, we might only be interested in discerning whether any path exists between two nodes and not what the shortest path is. One way to determine the existence of a path between two nodes of a graph **g** is to augment the edge structure of **g** by adding an edge directly between two nodes in **g** if there is a path between those nodes. The graph that results is known as the *transitive closure* of **g.** In this section we give an algorithm for converting a graph to its transitive closure. This algorithm is an adaptation of an algorithm formulated by Stephen Warshall in 1962 (S. Warshall, "A Theorem on Boolean Matrices," *Journal of the ACM,* 9(1), 1962, pp. 11-12). In outline form, our algorithm is as follows

```
do
  choose a node n of the graph;
  do
    choose a node m of the graph;
    if there is an edge from m to n
      do
        choose a node p of the graph;
        if there is an edge from n to p
          add an edge from m to p
      while all nodes p of the graph have not yet been examined
  while all nodes m of the graph have not yet been examined
while all nodes n of the graph have not yet been examined
```

The key observation behind Warshall's algorithm is that one can eventually derive the transitive closure of a graph by looking only at nodes **n** that are at the center of paths of length 2, and then adding an edge between the first and third nodes of this path, bypassing the center node. Once this edge is added, it has the potential to be part of another path of length 2 that may come up later if one or both of its edges are chosen as a new value for **n.** This approach certainly seems nonintuitive and may lead one to inquire why it works. (An "intuitive" approach might lead one to systematically select each node in the graph, examine paths that run through the node, and then make direct connections to the endpoints of each edge in this path.) Although we do not formally prove that Warshall's algorithm produces the transitive closure of graph **g,** we can develop some further understanding of how and why the algorithm works by considering the following simple graph **g** consisting of a path of length 3:

$$n_1 \rightarrow n_2 \rightarrow n_3 \rightarrow n_4$$

One of the edges that will appear in the transitive closure of **g** is the edge $\mathbf{n}_1 \rightarrow \mathbf{n}_4$. A complete discussion of how the edge would be produced would mean considering the 24 different ways that three nodes among $\mathbf{n}_1$ through $\mathbf{n}_4$ could be selected in the nested loop structure of Warshall's algorithm. Instead, we consider only the case in which the nodes are selected in the order $\mathbf{n}_1$, $\mathbf{n}_2$, $\mathbf{n}_3$, $\mathbf{n}_4$. In so doing, we will be examining a case in which the edges that have to be added for $\mathbf{n}_1$ will not be added at the time that $\mathbf{n}_1$ is selected in the outer control loop of Warshall's algorithm (which again seems the intuitive place to add them), but later, when $\mathbf{n}_2$ and $\mathbf{n}_3$ are selected.

When $\mathbf{n} = \mathbf{n}_1$, no edges are added to the graph because $\mathbf{n}_1$ is not the center of a path of length 2.

$$n_1 \rightarrow n_2 \rightarrow n_3 \rightarrow n_4$$
$$\uparrow$$
$$n$$

On the other hand, when $\mathbf{n} = \mathbf{n}_2$, the edge $\mathbf{n}_1 \rightarrow \mathbf{n}_3$ will be added:

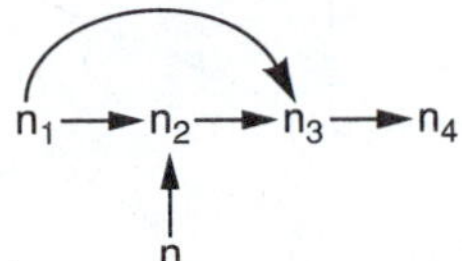

When $\mathbf{n} = \mathbf{n}_3$, the algorithm takes advantage of this newly added edge to determine that $\mathbf{n}_3$ is the center node of the path $\mathbf{n}_1 \rightarrow \mathbf{n}_3 \rightarrow \mathbf{n}_4$, so the path $\mathbf{n}_1 \rightarrow \mathbf{n}_4$ is added to the graph (later, edge $\mathbf{n}_2 \rightarrow \mathbf{n}_4$ will also be added):

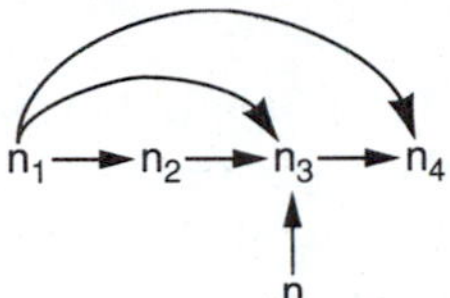

With this overview for Warshall's algorithm behind us, we now give a complete algorithm in C++, incorporating into it the operations of the Graph ADT and our previous assumptions about the nodes' values coming from a subrange of an ordinal type.

```
//--------------------------------------------------------------
// Interface and implementation for an operation to find the
// transitive closure of a Graph object:
// GIVEN:     A Graph object
// RETURN as value of function:
//            A pointer to a Graph object that is the transitive closure
//            of the Graph object that owns the operation

Graph<BaseData> *findTransitiveClosure()
{
  BaseData  m, n, p;
  Graph *tc;

  // Initially, give tc the same node and edge structure as the Graph object
  // by using the Graph copy constructor

  tc = new Graph<BaseData>(*this);

  //Now start adding edges to the transitive closure

  for (n = firstValue; n <= lastValue; ++n)
    for (m = firstValue; m <= lastValue; ++m)
      if (tc->edge(m, n))
        for (p = firstValue; p <= lastValue; ++p)
         if (tc->edge(n, p))
           tc->addEdge(m, p);
  return(tc);
}
```

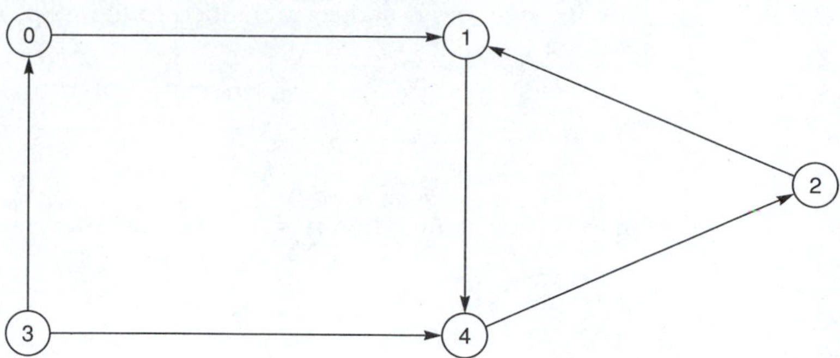

Figure 9.20
Graph for Example 9.6.

Example 9.6

Find the transitive closure of the graph of Figure 9.20.

Following Warshall's algorithm, we first include all edges from the original graph in the transitive closure. Now, starting with **n** = 0 and continuing on through 1, 2, 3, and 4, we seek in the current transitive closure paths of length 2 centered about node **n:**

1. For **n** = 0, there is one path of length 2 centered about node 0, the path 3→0→1; hence, we add the path 3→1 to the transitive closure.
2. For **n** = 1 we have the following paths of length 2 centered about node 1: 0→1→4, 2→1→4, and 3→1→4. Consequently, we add the edges 0→4, 2→4, and 3→4 to the transitive closure, though in the case of edge 3→4 nothing new is being added because the edge was already in the transitive closure by virtue of its being one of the edges of the graph.
3. For **n** = 2, there are two paths of length 2 centered at node 2: 4→2→1 and 4→2→4; hence, we add edges 4→1 and 4→4 to the transitive closure.
4. For **n** = 3 there are no paths of length 2 centered about node 3.
5. For **n** = 4 we have eight paths of length 2 centered about node 4: 0→4→1, 0→4→2, 1→4→1, 1→4→2, 2→4→1, 2→4→2, 3→4→1, and 3→4→2. Consequently, we add the edges 0→1, 0→2, 1→1, 1→2, 2→1, 2→2, 3→1, and 3→2 to the transitive closure, though the only edges added that were not in the transitive closure already are the edges 0→2, 1→1, 1→2, 2→2, and 3→2. The transitive closure is shown in Figure 9.21.

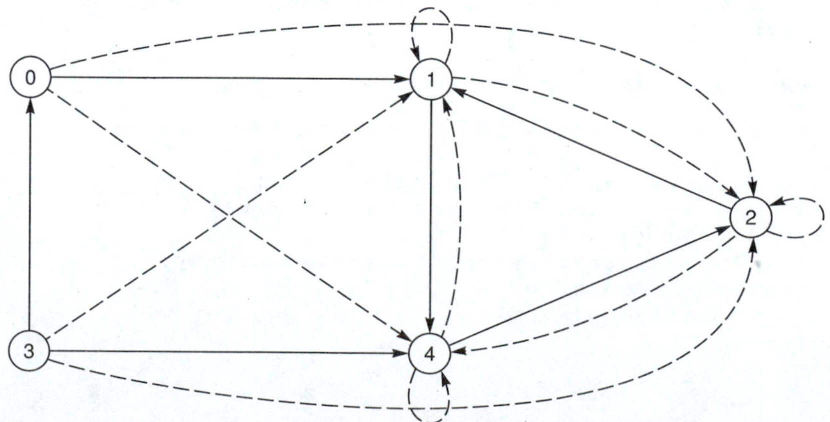

Figure 9.21
Transitive closure of the graph in Figure 9.20. The dashed arcs indicate those added to the graph to arrive at its transitive closure.

Warshall's Algorithm as a Special Case of Floyd's Algorithm

The alert reader may have noticed some similarities between our discussion of Warshall's algorithm, with its search for paths of length 2 centered about a node **n,** and our discussion of Floyd's algorithm and its concern with nodes **k,** which are interior to paths between other pairs of nodes. In fact, these similarities are more than just coincidental. Suppose we are given a directed graph **g.** Now let **g**′ be the directed network that has the same node structure as **g** and in which each pair of nodes is connected by an arc in each direction. Furthermore, for each arc **e** of **g**′, we shall assign it a weight of 0 if there is a corresponding arc in **g** and a weight of 1 otherwise. Now given a pair of nodes **i** and **j** of **g,** the arc **i→j** will be in the transitive closure of **g** if the shortest path between **i** and **j** in **g**′ is 0. Furthermore, if we represent the edges of **g** with an adjacency matrix, then the determination of the correct Boolean value for the entry in row **i,** column **j** of the transitive closure of **g** corresponds to the calculation of the value of **distance[i][j]** in Floyd's algorithm. Consequently, assuming the edges of **g** and its transitive closure **tc** are represented with adjacency matrices, an alternative implementation of **findTransitiveClosure** could have been given by

```
//---------------------------------------------------------------
// Interface and implementation for an operation to find the
// transitive closure of a Graph object:
// GIVEN:     A Graph object that uses an adjacency matrix
//            to represent its edges
// RETURN as value of function:
//            A pointer to a Graph object that is the transitive closure
//            of the Graph object that owns the operation

Graph<BaseData> *findTransitiveClosure()
{
  BaseData  i, j, k;
  Graph *tc;

  // Initially, give tc the same node and edge structure as the graph object
  // by using the Graph copy constructor

  tc = new Graph<BaseData>(*this);

  // Now start adding edges to the transitive closure

  for (k = firstValue; k <= lastValue; ++k)
    for (i = firstValue; i <= lastValue; ++i)
      for (j = firstValue; j <= lastValue; ++j)
        if ((tc->(*edges)[i][k]) && (tc->(*edges)[k][j]))
          tc->(*edges)[i][j]) = TRUE;
  return(tc);
}
```

We should point out that it is the triple **for** loop of this function that is traditionally referred to as Warshall's algorithm. The algorithm we gave earlier offers an overall improvement in run-time efficiency by making the execution of the third **for** loop conditional and dependent on the initial number of edges in the graph. Moreover, this earlier algorithm for calculating the transitive closure used only operations from the Graph ADT and hence does not depend on the method used to represent the graph's edges.

We consider issues related to the efficiency of Warshall's algorithms in Exercise 9.4.13.

Exercises 9.4

1. Trace the contents of the **distance, path,** and **included** arrays as Dijkstra's shortest path algorithm is applied to the transportation network of Figure 9.3. Use Phoenix as the **start** node and Chicago as the **destination** node.
2. Repeat Exercise 9.4.1. with Milwaukee as the **start** node and Oklahoma City as the **destination** node.
3. Only a skeletal form of Dijkstra's shortest path algorithm was presented in this section. Expand this skeletal version of the algorithm to a complete C++ implementation.
4. Modify your answer to Exercise 9.4.3. so that the C++ function you developed in that exercise finds the shortest path from a designated **start** node to all other nodes in the network. How does this modification affect the time efficiency of the algorithm?
5. Suppose that the transportation network of Figure 9.3 is restricted to the nodes Chicago, New Orleans, Dallas, Las Vegas, and Los Angeles and the edges that exist between them. Define an appropriate ordering for these nodes and then trace the contents of the **distance** matrix in Floyd's all-pairs shortest path algorithm for this five-node network.
6. Repeat Exercise 9.4.5 for the following network:

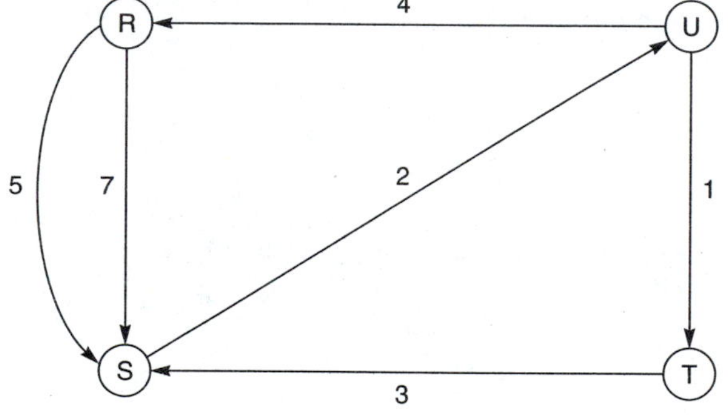

7. Only a skeletal form of Floyd's all-pairs shortest path algorithm was presented in this section. Extend it to a compete C++ implementation.
8. Modify your C++ function of Exercise 9.4.7 so that the nodes on each path are retrievable, as well as the lengths of the paths.
9. Trace the contents of the data structures involved in your algorithm from Exercise 9.4.8 when it is executed on the network of Exercise 9.4.5. Your trace should indicate how your recording of nodes on each path progresses as well as your recording of the lengths of these paths.
10. Repeat Exercise 9.4.9 for the network shown in Exercise 9.4.6.
11. Using the underlying graph structure for the network of Exercise 9.4.5 and assuming that an edge between two nodes indicates the existence of an arc in each direction between the nodes, find the transitive closure of this graph.
12. Repeat Exercise 9.4.11 for the network shown in Exercise 9.4.6.
13. Analyze the efficiency of both versions of Warshall's algorithm. What effect does the density of the edges have on these efficiencies? In the case of a graph with relatively few edges, discuss the potential tradeoffs in space-time efficiency for the first algorithm if adjacency lists were used to represent the edges of the graph.

9.5 Minimum Spanning Trees

A problem different in nature from those of the previous section is often faced by the designers of communications networks. Because of the high speed at which electronic communications travel, the length of a communications path between two nodes in such a network may not be a terribly critical issue. However, construction of the network itself can be a very expensive proposition, involving the installation of costly, high-speed data links between network nodes. Hence, a more crucial question for the designers of such networks is to minimize the cost of network construction, not to find the shortest path between any two nodes. That is, being able to link all nodes in the network for the least possible cost is a much more vital question than being able to link any two nodes in the most economical fashion.

A *minimum spanning tree* is a subnetwork constructed from a larger network to address this question. In particular, given an original undirected network in which there is a path between any two nodes, the edges for the minimum spanning tree are chosen in such a way that two properties result:

1. Every node in the network must be included in the spanning tree.
2. The total edge weight of the spanning tree is the minimum possible that will allow the existence of a path between any two nodes in the tree.

Two algorithms exist for the construction of minimum spanning trees. The first, described by R. C. Prim in his article "Shortest Connection Network and Some Generalizations," (*Bell System Technical Journal,* 36, pp. 1389–1401, 1957) is effective for *dense* networks, that is, networks that have relatively few edges missing from the maximum number they can have.

The second, originated by J. B. Kruskal in his article "On the Shortest Spanning Tree of a Graph and the Traveling Salesman Problem," (*Proceedings of the AMS,* 7(1), pp. 48–50, 1956), is designed for *sparse* networks; that is, for networks that have relatively few edges with respect to the maximum numbers of edges they can have. To simplify our discussion of both of these algorithms, we again assume that the data type **BaseData** is a subrange of a finite collection of consecutively enumerated values with an identifiable **firstValue** and **lastValue.**

Prim's Algorithm

Prim's algorithm parallels Dijkstra's shortest path algorithm (Section 9.4) in that it divides network nodes into two sets: *included* and *nonincluded* nodes. A node is included when we decide which edge will connect it into the minimum spanning tree. As in Dijkstra's algorithm, we include nodes (and corresponding edges) one at a time until all nodes have been included. In C++, Prim's algorithm may be stated as follows:

```
// EdgeStruct is a structure for storing edges needed by the following
// implementation of Prim's algorithm.
struct EdgeStruct
{
   BaseData node1, node2;
};

//------------------------------------------------------------
// Interface and implementation for an operation to find a minimum
// spanning tree of a Network object using Prim's algorithm:
// GIVEN:     A Network object that has all nodes from firstValue to
//            lastValue inclusive
// RETURN as value of function:
//            A pointer to a Network object that is a minimum spanning
//            tree of the Network object that owns the operation

Network<BaseData,WeightType> *minimumSpanningTree()
{
   Array<BaseData,BOOLEAN> included(firstValue,lastValue);
   BaseData k;
   EdgeStruct e;
   Network<BaseData,WeightType> *mst;

   mst = new Network<BaseData,WeightType>(firstValue,lastValue);

   // Begin by including any node in the MST. Here firstValue is chosen.

   mst->addNode(firstValue);
   included[firstValue] = TRUE;
   for (k = firstValue+1; k <= lastValue, ++k)
     included[k] = FALSE;
```

```
    // Next enter a loop in which a different node is included on each
    // iteration. Since the loop is executed lastValue-firstValue times,
    // all nodes are included on exit from the loop.

    for (k = firstValue; k <= lastValue-1; ++k)
    {
      e = findMinimum();         // Call on a function to return the endpoints
                                 // of an edge e of minimum weight connecting
                                 // a nonincluded node to an included node
      mst->addNode(e.node1);
      mst->addNode(e.node2);
      included[e.node1] = TRUE;
      included[e.node2] = TRUE;
      mst->addEdge(e.node1,e.node2,edgeWeight(e.node1,e.node2));

      // The next edge must be added since the network's edges are
      // assumed to be undirected

      mst->addEdge(e.node2,e.node1,edgeWeight(e.node2,e.node1));
    }
    return(mst);
}
```

0
1
2
3
600
430
400
360
120
440

The first time through the loop **findMinimum** would return the edge connecting 0 and 2, then 1 and 2, and finally 1 and 3

The function **findMinimum,** which you will develop in the exercises, is critical to understanding how Prim's algorithm works. To illustrate, we will trace it on a small network.

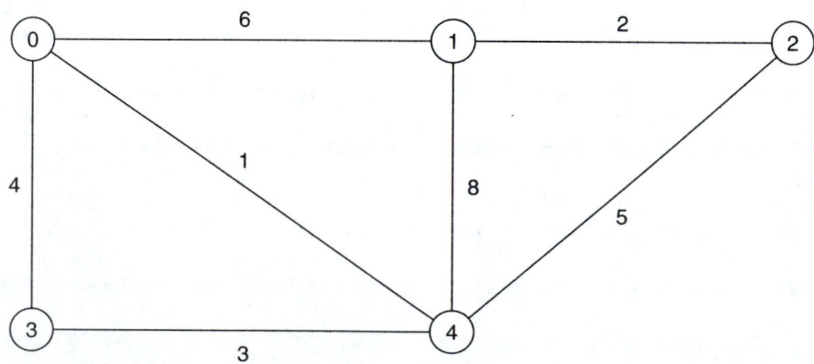

Figure 9.22
Network for Examples 9.7 and 9.8.

Example 9.7

Consider the network in Figure 9.22. Trace the order in which edges would be added to its minimum spanning tree.

1. After the initialization of the **included** array, only node 0 is included.
2. On the first pass through the construction loop, **findMinimum** would select the edge connecting nodes 0 and 4. Hence, the current state of **mst** would be:

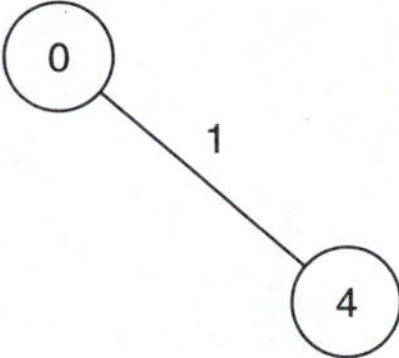

3. On the second iteration of the construction loop, **findMinimum** would select the edge connecting nodes 3 and 4. Hence, **mst** is updated to:

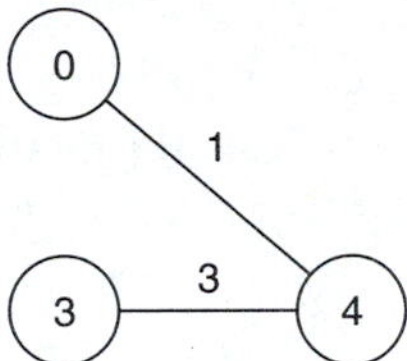

4. On the next iteration, the edge connecting nodes 2 and 4 is selected, expanding **mst** to:

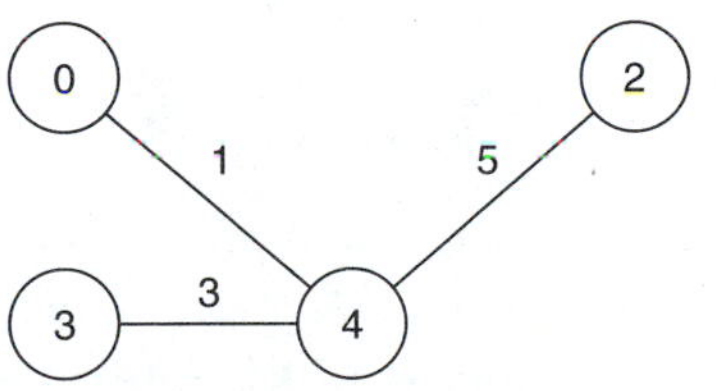

5. On the final iteration, the edge connecting nodes 1 and 2 is chosen, yielding a final **mst** of the form:

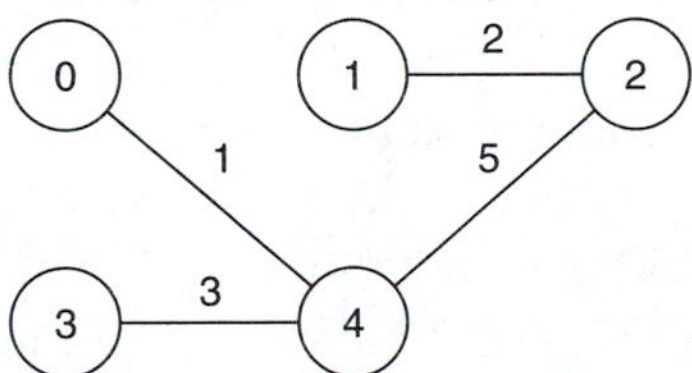

You should verify that this final **mst** satisfies the two minimum spanning tree properties established at the beginning of this section.

It is obvious that if the original network has a path between any two nodes, the subnetwork constructed by Prim's method will also have a path between any two nodes, and thus be a spanning tree. It is perhaps not as obvious that Prim's method will produce a spanning tree with the minimum total edge weight. The following argument indicates why this indeed must be so. Let M be a spanning tree for the

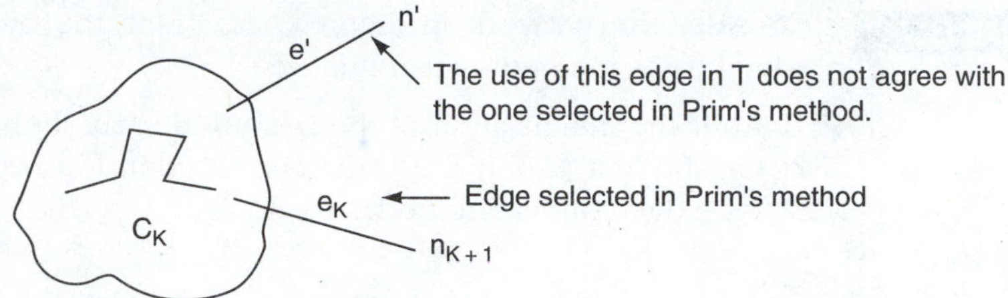
n'
e'
The use of this edge in T does not agree with the one selected in Prim's method.
e_K
Edge selected in Prim's method
C_K
n_{K+1}
M and T agree on the choices of nodes and edges within the set of nodes C_K

Figure 9.23
Edge e_K identifies the first edge chosen by Prim's method that is not also in T.

network N obtained by Prim's method, and let T be any minimum spanning tree for N. Note that the total edge weight for T cannot exceed that for M since T's total edge weight is assumed to be minimal. Define a sequence of sets of vertices in the following fashion:

C_1 = { the single vertex at which Prim's method started the construction of M}

$C_{i+1} = C_i \cup \{n_{i+1}\}$, where n_{i+1} is the node "included" on the *ith* iteration of Prim's algorithm as a result of the **findMinimum** function returning the edge e_i. The node n_{i+1} is one end node for e_i, with the other end node being a node in C_i. Clearly we have

$$C_1 \subseteq C_2 \subseteq C_3 \subseteq \ldots \subseteq C_p = V, \text{ the set of all vertices in the network.}$$

Let us assume now that M and T have the nodes of C_K and the edges $e_1, \ldots, e_{K-1}$ in common but disagree on the set C_{K+1}, with M using the node n_{K+1} and edge e_K, while T uses node n′ and edge e′ to connect the nodes in C_K to those in $V - C_K$. This difference between M and T is shown in Figure 9.23.

By the minimal edge weight criterion governing the selection of edges between included and non-included nodes in Prim's algorithm, we see that

$$\text{edgeWeight}(e_K) \leq \text{edgeWeight}(e')$$

In fact we must have $\text{EdgeWeight}(e_K) = \text{EdgeWeight}(e')$. Otherwise, as indicated in Figure 9.24, replacing the edge e′ in T by the edge e_K yields a spanning tree T′ (Why is T′ a spanning tree?) whose total edge weight is less than that of T, contradicting that T is a minimum spanning tree.

Note now, however, that if at the *Kth* iteration of Prim's algorithm in our construction of M, we had selected edge e′ instead of edge e_K (which is possible since both have the same edge weight), and included node n′ rather than node n_{K+1}, then M and T could have been made to agree on the nodes of C_{K+1}, and the edges $e_1, \ldots, e_{K-1}, e'$. By successive applications of this logic we can thus find a spanning tree M via Prim's algorithm whose nodes and edges precisely match those of T. Consequently, Prim's method will always generate a minimum spanning tree.

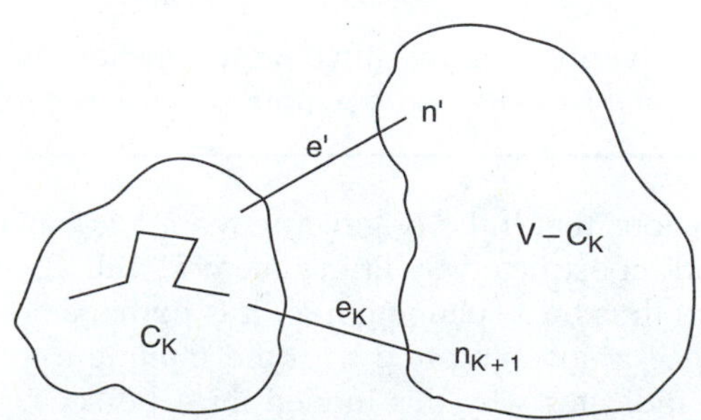
n'
e'
$V - C_K$
e_K
C_K
n_{K+1}

Figure 9.24
If the edge weight of e_K is less than that of e′, then replacing e′ by e_K in T connects vertices in C_K and $V - C_K$ using less total edge weight than T does.

Efficiency of Prim's Algorithm

In the exercises at the end of this section, you will develop an implementation of the **findMinimum** function (called by Prim's algorithm) that is $O(NumberOfNodes)$ in its run time, where $NumberOfNodes = 1 + lastValue - firstValue$. Given such a function, it is trivial to conclude that Prim's algorithm itself is $O(NumberOfNodes^2)$. Notice that the efficiency of Prim's algorithm is not dependent on the number of edges in the graph, only the number of nodes. This makes it the algorithm of choice for networks that are dense with edges. For sparse networks, we turn our attention to Kruskal's alternative algorithm for constructing a network's minimum spanning tree.

Kruskal's Algorithm

Kruskal's algorithm initially views the nodes of the network as existing in a union-find partition (Section 2.4) in which each set in the partition contains exactly one node. That is, the nodes of the network initially exist as members of a union-find partition after a union-find object is first created. Next, the edges of the network are arranged in a priority queue according to their respective edge weight. Edges are removed from this priority queue in the order dictated by increasing edge weights. When an edge is removed from the priority queue, the **ufFind** operation is performed on the two nodes connected by the edge. If **ufFind** indicates these two nodes are members of disjoint sets in the partition, then a **ufUnion** operation is performed on the two nodes and the edge is added to the minimum spanning tree that is being constructed. If **ufFind** indicates that the two nodes are already members of the same set in the partition, then the edge is discarded with no **ufUnion** operation being performed. Why? The fact that the two edges are already in the same set of the union-find partition means that we have already found a path between them composed of edges whose individual weights are less than or equal to the weight of the edge currently being examined. To include the current node in the minimum spanning tree at the expense of removing a node that was previously included would link the nodes in this partition set in a fashion that might not yield the minimal total edge weight—contradicting the defining property of the minimum spanning tree. This concept is highlighted in Figure 9.25. The following example clarifies the process of selecting edges in Kruskal's algorithm.

Example 9.8

Trace the order of edge selection as Kruskal's algorithm executes on the network of Figure 9.22.

1. Initially create a priority queue of edges and the partition formed by the constructor operation for the Union-Find ADT.

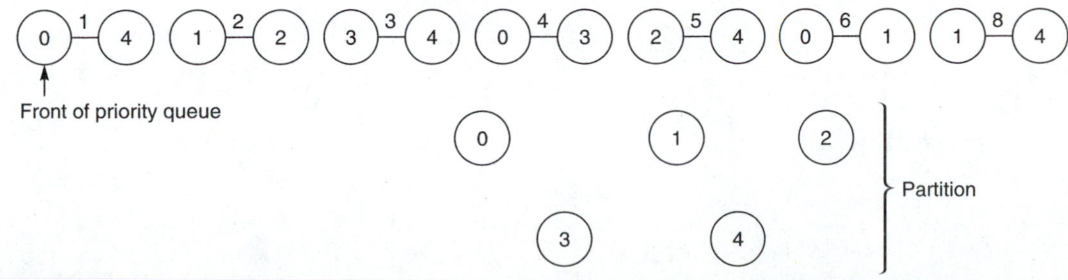

Figure 9.25
Consideration of an edge removed from the priority queue of Kruskal's algorithm.

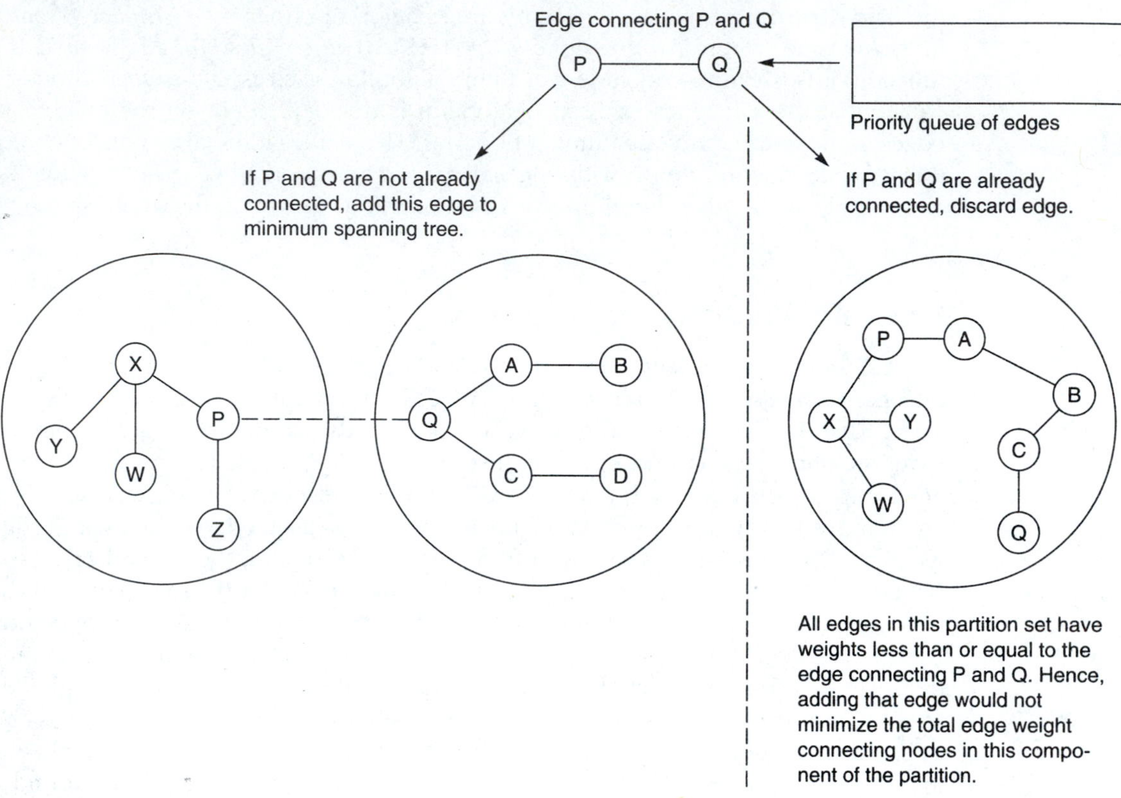
Edge connecting P and Q
P
Q
Priority queue of edges
If P and Q are not already connected, add this edge to minimum spanning tree.
If P and Q are already connected, discard edge.
X
Y
W
P
Z
Q
A
B
C
D
P
A
B
X
Y
C
W
Q
All edges in this partition set have weights less than or equal to the edge connecting P and Q. Hence, adding that edge would not minimize the total edge weight connecting nodes in this component of the partition.

2. Successively remove edges from the priority queue, and apply the **ufFind** operation to the nodes connected by each such edge.
   a. Remove

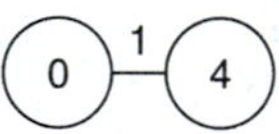
0
1
4

from the priority queue; **ufFind** returns FALSE, so the partition (and consequently the minimum spanning tree under construction) becomes

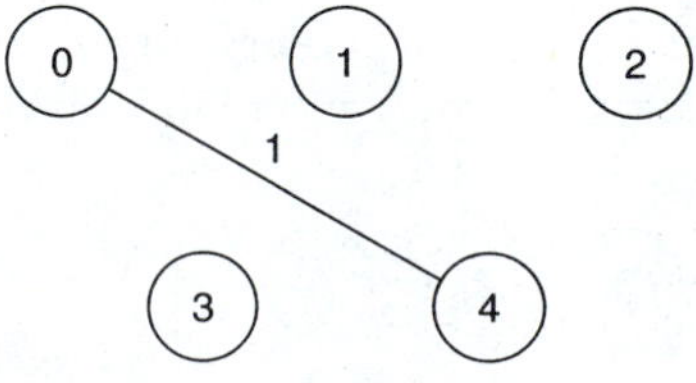
0
1
2
1
3
4

   b. Remove

from the priority queue; **ufFind** returns FALSE, so the partition becomes

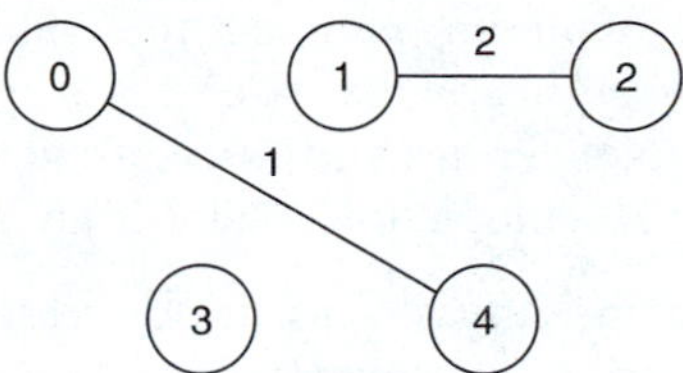

c. Remove

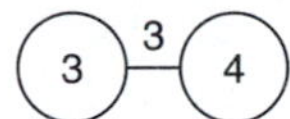

from the priority queue; **ufFind** returns FALSE, so the partition becomes

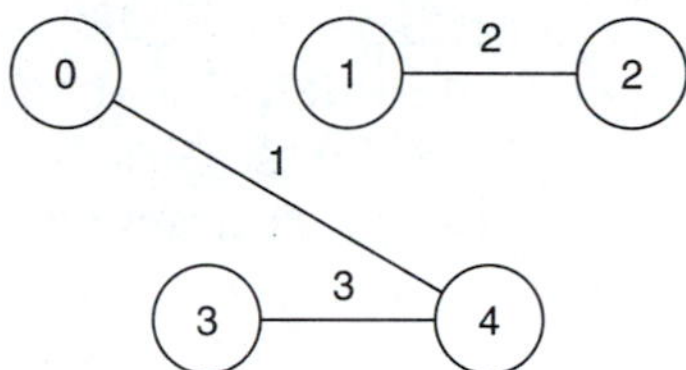

d. Remove

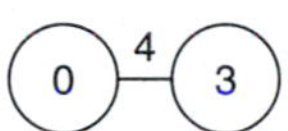

from the priority queue; **ufFind** returns TRUE, so discard this edge.

e. Remove

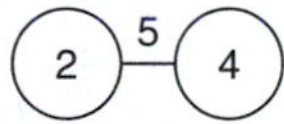

from the priority queue; **ufFind** returns FALSE, so the partition becomes

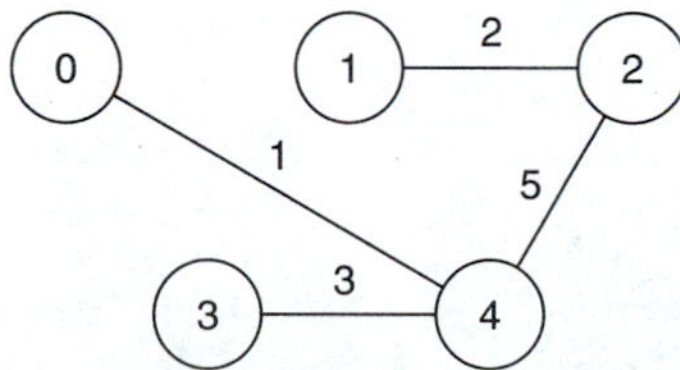

The construction of the minimum spanning tree is complete.

In comparing the selection of edges by Prim's algorithm and Kruskal's algorithms (Examples 9.7 and 9.8, respectively), we make the following observations and pose some questions.

1. Prim's and Kruskal's algorithms do not select edges in the same order.
2. Both algorithms terminate when *NumberOfNodes* − 1 edges are selected. This implies that a minimum spanning tree will always contain *NumberOfNodes* − 1 edges. Why must this be the case?
3. In these examples, Prim's and Kruskal's algorithms arrive at the same minimum spanning tree on completion. Will this always be the case?

You will explore the answers to these questions and develop a complete C++ implementation of Kruskal's algorithm in the exercises at the end of this section. We now turn our attention toward analyzing the efficiency of Kruskal's algorithm.

Efficiency of Kruskal's Algorithm

The efficiency of Kruskal's algorithm depends on the efficiency of the implementations we choose for the priority queue and union-find ADTs. In this regard, recall from Section 7.4 that a priority queue implemented by a heap provides $O(\log_2 n)$ efficiency for the **enqueue** and **dequeue** operations. Also recall from Section 8.4 that a union-find structure implemented by weight-balanced trees yields $O(\log_2 n)$ time efficiency for both the **ufFind** and **ufUnion** operations. In the argument that follows, we assume these efficiencies for the priority queue and union-find operations. We will also assume that an adjacency-list implementation is used for the network; this allows us to go through all edges in $O(NumberOfEdges)$ time.

Under these assumptions, the initial formation of the priority queue of edges will require $O(NumberOfEdges \times \log_2(NumberOfEdges))$ time. During the second phase of Kruskal's algorithm, when each edge is removed from the priority queue and one or two union-find operations are performed on the nodes that it connects, we also have an $O(NumberOfEdges \times \log_2(NumberOfEdges))$ efficiency. Here the rationale is that, potentially, each edge must be removed from the priority queue—an $O(\log_2(NumberOfEdges))$ operation for each edge. Then, each of the one or two union-find operations that follow for that edge are also $O(\log_2(NumberOfEdges))$. Hence, the algorithm can be broken into two phases, each of which is $O(NumberOfEdges \times \log_2(NumberOfEdges))$ in its efficiency—resulting in an overall $O(NumberOfEdges \times \log_2(NumberOfEdges))$ efficiency. Note that, as we claimed at the beginning of this section, this efficiency will make Kruskal's algorithm faster than Prim's for sparse networks with relatively few edges.

A RELEVANT ISSUE The Traveling Salesperson Problem

A well-known problem of classical graph theory, which is easy to state but difficult to solve, is the *traveling salesperson problem*. The problem essentially tries to minimize the round-trip cost of visiting once and only once every city on the business route of the salesperson. This problem was first proposed by the Irish mathematician Sir William Rowan Hamilton (1805–1865).

The problem can be viewed as a network such as that shown in Figure 9.3. The cities to be visited are the nodes in the network, and the weighted edges are the distances between the cities. The minimum spanning tree algorithm discussed in the text is not the solution to this problem, but it can be adapted to yield the solution in the following way:

1. Set the total cost of traveling to 0.
2. Select a home node (home city of the salesperson), and designate it **x**.
3. Find an unused node that minimizes the sum of the edge weight connecting it to **x** plus the total cost. Then add this edge weight to the total cost.
4. Designate the node found in step 3 as the new home node; that is, as node **x**.
5. Repeat steps 3 and 4 until all nodes are visited and the salesperson arrives home; that is, until **x** is the home node chosen in step 4.

Although this algorithm solves the traveling salesperson's problem, it is slow because of the extensive computation involved in step 3. When the number of cities on the salesperson's tour is moderately large (even as large as 20), the solution is annoyingly slow, but nothing better is known that will guarantee finding a solution to the problem. Prototypes of this classical algorithm find frequent application in the design of computer operating systems. For instance, suppose we have a collection of processes all waiting to access a popular disk file. The operating system designer is concerned with scheduling these processes in a fashion that minimizes the total disk access time. By viewing each process P_i as a network node, and the edge weight connecting node P_i to node P_j as the disk access time required if process P_j immediately follows process P_i in the scheduling, the solution to this operating system problem is essentially the traveling salesperson problem. A complicating factor is that the slowness of the algorithm cited earlier may make it impractical to incorporate it into an interactive operating system. The complexity of the traveling salesperson problem places it in a class of problems known as *NP-complete problems.* This theoretical class of problems has the following interesting property. If we can even find for any one such problem a solution that has a polynomial time efficiency, then we will automatically have polynomial time solutions to all other problems in this class and an even larger theoretical class of problems known as NP problems. A thorough discussion of NP and NP-complete problems may be found in *Theory of Computation: Formal Languages, Automata, and Complexity* by J. Glenn Brookshear, Benjamin Cummings, 1989.

Exercises 9.5

1. In the style of Examples 9.7 and 9.8, trace both Prim's and Kruskal's algorithms for constructing minimum spanning trees from the following network:

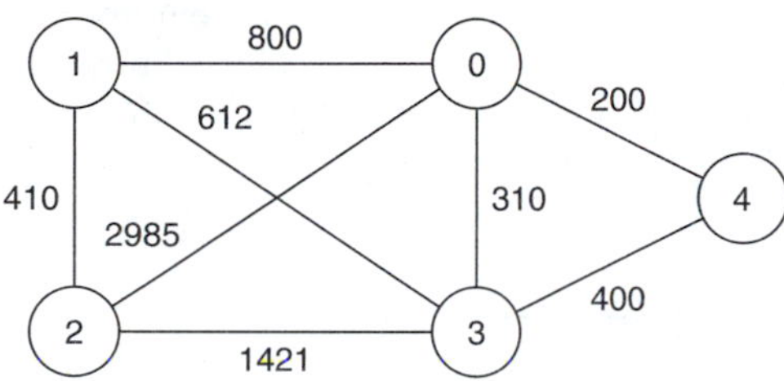

2. In the style of Examples 9.7 and 9.8, trace both Prim's and Kruskal's algorithm for constructing minimum spanning trees from the following network:

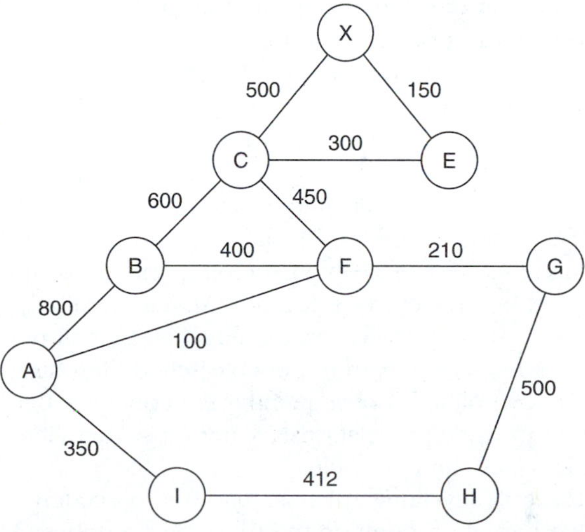

3. Complete Prim's version of the minimum spanning tree algorithm by writing the **findMinimum** function that is called in the second **for** loop of that algorithm. Recall that this function must find the edge of minimum weight that connects a *nonincluded* node to an *included* node. Be sure that your algorithm is $O(NumberOfNodes)$. (*Hint:* If necessary, introduce auxiliary data structures and update them as the algorithm executes.)

4. Suppose that we change the specification for the **findMinimum** function in Prim's version of the minimum spanning tree algorithm to the following: Find the edge of minimum weight that connects a *nonincluded* node to the node that was most recently *included.* Show by an example that the algorithm may now fail to construct a minimum spanning tree.

5. Write a C++ function **minimumSpanningTree** to completely implement Kruskal's algorithm. Assume an adjacency list implementation of networks to ensure $O(NumberOfEdges \times \log_2(NumberOfEdges))$ efficiency.

6. How would an adjacency-matrix implementation of the network affect the run-time efficiency of the function you wrote for Kruskal's algorithm in Exercise 9.5.4?

7. In our observations following Examples 9.7 and 9.8, we stated that a minimum spanning tree will always contain *NumberOfNodes* − *1* edges. Provide a logical argument to prove this claim. (*Hint:* Use a proof by contradiction.)

8. Given a network N, is there necessarily a unique minimum spanning tree for the network? If not, provide an example of a network that has two different minimum spanning trees.

9. In our observations following Examples 9.7 and 9.8, we stated that Prim's and Kruskal's algorithms arrived at the same minimum spanning tree for the network of Figure 9.22. Will this always be the case? If not, provide an example in which the two algorithms arrive at different minimum spanning trees.

10. Is the following statement true or false?: "In any network with three or more nodes and no two edges having equal weights, the two edges that have the smallest weights among all edges will always be part of the minimum spanning tree." If false, provide a counterexample.
11. Is the following statement true or false?: "In any network with four or more nodes and no two edges having equal weights, the three edges with the smallest weights among all edges will always be part of the minimum spanning tree." If false, provide a counterexample.
12. Is it possible for a minimum spanning tree to contain a cycle? Justify your answer.
13. In our tracing of Kruskal's algorithm in Example 9.8, we were able to stop removing edges from the priority queue before it became empty. Construct an example in which Kruskal's algorithm would have to examine all the edges in the priority queue before completing construction of the minimum spanning tree.
14. Use mathematical analysis to estimate the point at which the sparseness of a network dictates the use of Kruskal's algorithm instead of Prim's. That is, the maximal edge density that a network can have is *NumberNodes*^{2} edges—a network in which every node has edges connecting it to every node. The adjacency matrix for such a network would have only nonzero entries, and Prim's algorithm will clearly be more efficient than Kruskal's. What is the crossover point in the ratio of edges to nodes that makes Kruskal's algorithm more efficient than Prim's?
15. You are constructing a communications network of computers at more than 1000 remote sites. You wish to minimize construction costs for the network while, at the same time, making it possible for any computer to get a message to or from any other computer. In theory, it is possible to directly link any two computers, and you have a cost estimate for each such possible link. From these cost estimates, you must write a program that extracts the minimum spanning tree with respect to total cost. Which algorithm should you use to find the minimum spanning tree? Why?
16. In our "proof" that Prim's method yielded a minimum spanning tree (see page 418) we asserted that replacing the edge e' in the minimum spanning tree T by the edge e_K yields a spanning tree T'; that is, it yielded a subnetwork that contains all the nodes of the original network and whose edges allow the existence of a path between any two of these nodes. Provide a proof of this assertion.
17. The precondition for the function **minimumSpanningTree** that is developed on page 415 states that the Network object must have nodes for all values between **firstValue** and **lastValue** inclusive. How would the code for this function have to change if this precondition were removed, that is, if we allowed nodes in the Network object to be a proper subset of the set of all nodes between firstValue and lastValue inclusive?

9.6 Topological Ordering

One area in which directed graphs find frequent application is in establishing precedence relations among activities to be scheduled. For instance, consider the directed graph of Figure 9.26. This graph indicates a prerequisite structure among courses in a computer science curriculum. A directed edge from node x to node y is to be interpreted as meaning that course x is a prerequisite for course y. Analogous directed graphs can be developed to portray scheduling patterns for large projects that can be broken down into subordinate activities. Such graphs can even be used to coordinate the execution of a main program's subordinate modules on a computer with multiple processors.

We can make three important observations about directed graphs that reflect such scheduling patterns. First, we note that it makes no sense for such a graph to contain a cycle. That is, if we had a path such as $x \rightarrow y \rightarrow z \rightarrow x$ in such a graph, it would imply that activity x must be completed before activity y could be started. Similarly, y must be completed before z could be started. However, the edge $z \rightarrow x$ will not allow us to start x before z is completed. We have an impossible scheduling task; none of the tasks in the cycle can be completed. Consequently, we conclude that directed graphs that portray a feasible precedence relationship among subactivities in a large project must be acyclic, that is, contain no cycles.

A second observation about directed acyclic graphs is that the precedence relationships in such a graph define a partial ordering on the set of graph nodes. A *partial ordering* on a set S is a relation $<$ with the following three properties:

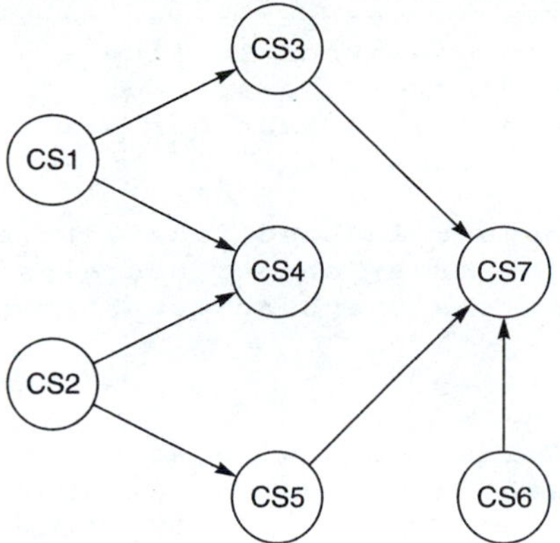

Figure 9.26
Course prerequisites in a computer science (CS) curriculum.

1. Irreflexivity: For each element s in S, $s \not< s$.
2. Asymmetry: For elements s and t in S, if $s < t$, then $t \not< s$.
3. Transitivity: For elements r, s, and t in S, if $r < s$, and $s < t$, then $r < t$.

You should verify that, in a directed acyclic graph with nodes belonging to a set S, the relationship defined by

$$s < t \text{ if and only if there is a path from } s \text{ to } t$$

satisfies the irreflexivity, asymmetry, and transitivity properties. Hence, we can conclude that the nodes in a directed acyclic graph form a partially ordered set.

Our third observation about directed acyclic graphs is related to the scheduling problems they often depict. For such problems, it is important that we be able to specify a linear sequence of graph nodes corresponding to the order in which subactivities may be completed, one after the other, and still comply with all of the precedence relationships in the graph. Such a linear ordering is called a *topological ordering* of the graph nodes. For example, in Figure 9.26, the sequence

CS1 CS2 CS3 CS4 CS5 CS6 CS7

is such a topological ordering. Notice that topological orderings are not unique for a given graph. You should verify that

CS2 CS1 CS5 CS4 CS3 CS6 CS7

and

CS6 CS2 CS5 CS1 CS4 CS3 CS7

are also topological orderings for the graph of Figure 9.26.

We now turn our attention to developing an algorithm that will find a topological ordering of the nodes for a given directed acyclic graph. Recall from Section 9.1 the notion of the *indegree* of a graph node—the number of edges entering a node. Clearly, a topological ordering can begin with any node that has an indegree of zero. Hence, we begin by adding all such nodes to a queue. As a node is removed from the queue of nodes with indegree 0, we record it as the next node in the topological ordering. We also subtract one from the indegree of all nodes connected by an edge from the removed node. If this subtraction results in nodes having an adjusted indegree of zero, these nodes are then added to the queue. Why? Because all predecessors of these nodes have been recorded previously in the topological ordering, the activities corresponding to these nodes can now be completed.

In the complete **topologicalOrder** algorithm that follows, we assume that type **BaseData** is a subrange of some finite collection of consecutively enumerated values with well-defined **firstValue** and **lastValue** values.

```
//------------------------------------------------------------------
// Interface and implementation for an operation to find a
// topological ordering for a directed acyclic graph
// GIVEN:    A directed, acyclic Graph object that has all nodes from
//           firstValue to lastValue inclusive.
// RETURN as value of function:
//           A pointer to an Array object indexed from 1 to number of nodes
//           in the Graph object.  The Array object contains a topological
//           ordering of the nodes in the Graph object that owns the operation.

Array<int,BaseData> *topologicalOrder();
{
  Queue<BaseData> zeroq;         // Holds nodes with adjusted indegree zero
  Array<BaseData,int> indeg(firstValue,lastvalue);    // Stores adjusted
                                                      // indegree of node
  Array<int,BaseData> *t;  // Pointer to the topological ordering
  BaseData node, tnode;
  int orderCount;

  t = new Array<BaseData,BaseData>(1, lastValue - firstValue + 1);

  // Call a function that computes the indegree of each node in the Graph object.
  // The indegree of node is stored at index node of the indeg Array.

  computeInitialIndegree(indeg);

  // Add nodes with indegree 0 to the queue zeroq

  for (node = firstValue; node <= lastValue; ++node)
    if (indeg[node] == 0)
      zeroq.enqueue(node);

  // Now move nodes from zeroq to topological order array and check
  // if additional nodes have an adjusted indegree of zero.

  orderCount = 0;
  while (!zeroq.empty())
  {
    tnode = zeroq.front();
    zeroq.dequeue();
    (*t)[++orderCount] = tnode;
    for (node = firstValue; node <= lastValue; ++node)
      if (edge(tnode, node))
      {
        --indeg[node];
        if (indeg[node] == 0)
          zeroq.enqueue(node);
      }
  }
  return(t);
}
```

If there are no other edges directed at **node**, all of **node's** predecessors have been processed. So **node** may be placed on **zeroq**.
node
tnode

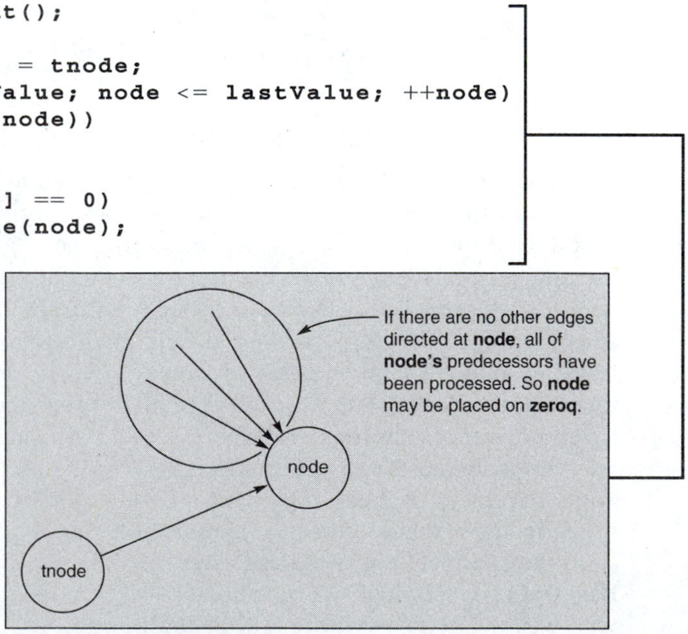

Efficiency of the Topological Order Algorithm

The version of the topological order algorithm just presented makes no assumptions about the implementation of the graph to which it is applied. Hence, the overall efficiency of the nested **while** structure within the function is $O(NumberOfNodes^2)$, where $NumberOfNodes = 1 + lastValue - firstValue$. The **computeInitialIndegree** function would also be $O(NumberOfNodes^2)$ if the implementation of the graph does not provide an effective way to process edges. In the exercises at the end of this section, you will explore several different topological order algorithms that enhance this efficiency for graphs with specific properties and implementations.

A RELEVANT ISSUE Critical Path Analysis, PERT, and CPM

In the late 1950s techniques based on directed networks were developed to assist managers of large-scale projects in planning, scheduling, and coordinating the numerous and interrelated activities of these projects. A project's activity is represented in a network by an edge, with the weight of the edge designating an estimated time for completing the activity. A node of the network, on the other hand, represents an event, that is, the completion of all activities that must be finished before any activity emanating from the node can commence.

The network at the right represents roughly the activities involved in building a small house. The events are labeled 0 through 10, with node 0 representing the starting time for the project and node 10 representing the completion time for the project. The dashed edges, marked dummy, are used to establish precedence relationships only and do not represent real activities of the project. They have an associated weight of 0. If we associate the following completion times with each activity: prepare lot — 3; lay foundation — 4 ; erect external frame — 10; erect roof — 3; install plumbing — 9; install electrical wiring — 7; exterior walls — 7 ; cover roof — 2; interior walls, floor, and ceiling — 5; finish exterior — 5; and finish interior — 8; then an examination of the network will show that there is one path in the network, 0→1→2→3→5→8→9→10, such that any delay in the completion of an activity along this path will delay the whole project (the duration of which this path also tells us is 39). Paths such as this are known as *critical paths*. Possessed with a knowledge of a project's critical paths, a project manager can analyze it to determine where the greatest attention should be focused to keep the project on schedule; to predict what effects, if any, a delay in the completion of a given activity will have on the completion time of the entire project; and to locate activities where an improvement in performance would have to occur in order to improve the project's completion time.

Two well-known techniques that use such a critical path analysis are PERT (Program Evaluation and Review Technique) and CPM (Critical Path Method). In PERT, three estimates are used for the completion time of each activity—a most likely estimate, an optimistic estimate, and a pessimistic estimate. This trio is then used to calculate an expected time and a variance for each activity. These times and variances in turn allow one to calculate an expected completion time and variance for the project, which are used to give a probability that a scheduled completion time can be met. PERT is often

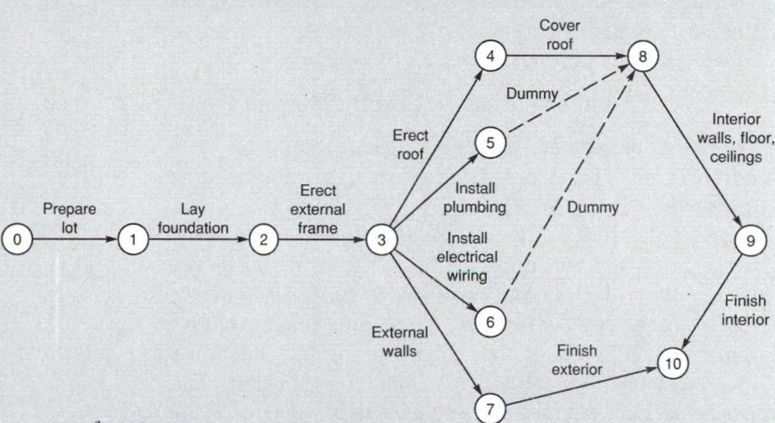

used for evaluating schedules for research and development projects, where the completion times of activities are not well known. It was originally developed for the *Polaris* missile project.

CPM, on the other hand, assumes that the completion times of a project's activities are well known. A time versus cost relationship is established for each activity and a critical path analysis applied to the CPM's network to determine a time-cost trade-off for each activity so that a scheduled completion time can be met at a minimum cost. CPM is especially appropriate for construction and maintenance projects, where experience allows activity times to be estimated with a high degree of certainty.

Although originally developed independently, the techniques of PERT and CPM are now merged into a single method of analysis often referred to as a *PERT-type analysis*. An overview of the PERT-CPM techniques can be found in Hillier and Lieberman, *Introduction to Operations Research* (2nd Ed.), Holden-Day, San Francisco, 1974, pp. 229–241.

Exercises 9.6

1. Trace the states of the topological order array **t** and the queue **zeroq** as the function **topologicalOrder** would execute on the directed acyclic graph in Figure 9.26. Assume the following enumeration of graph nodes:

   CS1 CS2 CS3 CS4 CS5 CS6 CS7

2. Repeat Exercise 9.6.1 except now assume the following enumeration of graph nodes:

   CS7 CS6 CS5 CS4 CS3 CS2 CS1

3. Provide a logical, written argument that all graph nodes will eventually pass through the queue **zeroq** in function **topologicalOrder.** (*Hint:* Your argument should use the precondition you are given regarding the graph.)
4. What behavior will function **topologicalOrder** display if the graph contains a cycle?
5. Explain how the behavior you described in Exercise 9.6.4 could be used to detect the existence of a cycle in a graph. Write a function that operates on a directed graph **g** and returns TRUE if **g** contains a cycle and FALSE otherwise.
6. Provide a written rationale supporting the claim made in this section that the nodes in a directed acyclic graph form a partially ordered set under the relation

   $s < t$ if and only if there is a path from s to t

   Your rationale must contain logical arguments that demonstrate this relation is irreflexive, asymmetric, and transitive.
7. Suppose that function **topologicalOrder** is implemented for a graph whose edges are represented by adjacency lists. Rewrite the internal code of the function to access these adjacency lists directly. How does this alternative implementation affect the efficiency of the algorithm? Provide a big-O analysis of the resulting efficiency. Under what circumstances would this new version of the algorithm be more efficient than the version given in this section? Under what circumstances would it be less efficient?
8. For this exercise, work under the assumption that a directed acyclic graph **g** has exactly one node with indegree zero. (Clearly, if more than one such node exists, we can add an artificial node that is a predecessor of all and only those nodes that have indegree 0 and satisfy this assumption with the augmented graph.) Consider a modified depth-first traversal operation that doesn't apply the **processNode** function to the **start** node until after it returns from the recursively called traversals of nodes adjacent to the **start** node. Suppose that **processNode** merely prints the value of the **start** node.

   a. What will be the order in which values of nodes are printed by this modified depth-first traversal if it is called with the following directed graph using CS0 as the original start node?

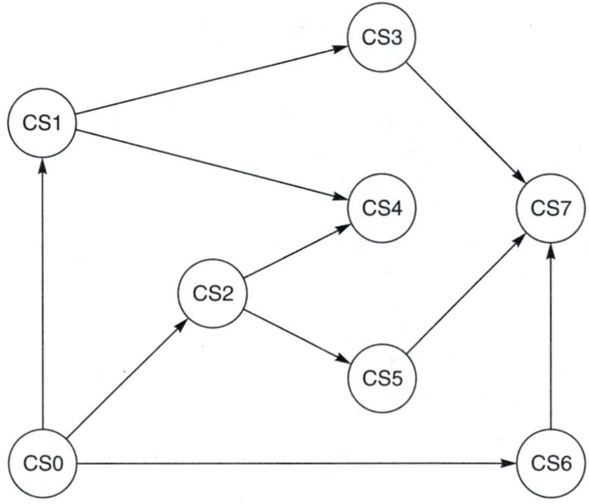

   b. What is the relationship between the order in which nodes are printed by this modified depth-first traversal and the linear arrangement of nodes in a topological ordering?

   c. Will the relationship you observed in part **b** always hold? If so, use it to develop an alternative version of function **topologicalOrder.**

   d. Analyze the efficiency of the **topologicalOrder** function you developed in part **c.** How is this efficiency contingent upon whether an adjacency matrix or adjacency lists are used to implement the graph?

Chapter Summary

In many information storage applications the hierarchical organization brought by trees is insufficient and a data structure that allows for two-way relationships among data entities is needed. In this chapter we introduce the concepts of a graph and a network (or weighted graph). Because relationships between items in a graph are completely arbitrary (as opposed to the linear relationships of lists, stacks, and queues, or the hierarchical relationships of trees), they represent the most general data structure we discuss in this book. We begin by introducing the basic concepts and terminology of graphs and networks in Section 9.1 and move on to a redefinition of both as abstract data types in Section 9.2. Examples of depth-first and breadth-first traversals are shown.

Implementations of graphs and networks are taken up in Section 9.3, with adjacency lists and the adjacency matrix being discussed as ways to represent the edges of a graph or a network. To avoid weighing down our discussion with cumbersome implementation details, we assume for the rest of the chapter that the values of the nodes of our graphs span exactly a subrange of a finite collection of consecutively enumerated values. This allows us to assign an ordering to the nodes based on the ordering of the values in the subrange. Such an ordering is necessary for providing algorithms for depth-first and breadth-first traversals.

Section 9.4 deals with path algorithms. Shortest path algorithms deal with how to find the shortest distance between two nodes in a network. Dijkstra's algorithm allows us to find the shortest distance between two specified nodes of a network, but does not extend efficiently to find the shortest distance between every possible pair of nodes in the network. Floyd's algorithm on the other hand deals effectively with the all-pairs shortest path problem but remains inferior to Dijkstra for finding the shortest path between a single pair of nodes.

For some applications it is not the shortest path between two nodes that is of interest, but merely the existence of a path between two nodes. One way to expedite answering queries about the existence of a path between two nodes of a graph is to augment the edge structure of the graph by adding an edge directly between two of its nodes if there is a path between those nodes. The resulting graph is known as the transitive closure of the given graph. Warshall's algorithm for finding the transitive closure of a graph is given and later shown to be a special case of Floyd's algorithm.

A problem different in nature from those of Section 9.4 is that of finding a minimum spanning tree for a network, that is, a subnetwork of a given network such that the total of all the edge weights of the subnetwork is minimal and yet all nodes of the original network are included in the subnetwork and any two nodes in the subnetwork have a path between them that is within this subnetwork. Algorithms by Prim and Kruskal are given for finding a minimum spanning tree. Kruskal's algorithm views the nodes of a network as existing in a union-find partition of single node sets, hence allowing us to use the operations of the Union-Find ADT from Section 2.4.

We conclude the chapter with a discussion of topological ordering in Section 9.6.

Key Terms

adjacency lists	digraph	Kruskal's algorithm	partial ordering
adjacency matrix	Dijkstra's algorithm	length	Prim's algorithm
adjacent	directed path	loop	strongly connected
arc	edges	matrix	topological ordering
breadth-first traversal	edge weight	minimum spanning tree	total path weight
cycle	Floyd's algorithm	network	transitive closure
degree	graph	nodes	Warshall's algorithm
depth-first traversal	indegree	outdegree	weakly connected

Programming Problems and Projects

1. Write a program that provides an implementation of the transportation network in Figure 9.3 and then uses that implementation to allow a user to find the shortest path (and its length) between two cities input by the user.

2. Write a program which provides an implementation of the transportation network in Figure 9.3 and then uses that implementation to find the shortest paths (and their lengths) between all pairs of cities.

3. Write a program that provides an implementation of the network in Figure 9.3 and then uses that implementation to find a minimal spanning tree of the network.

4. Recall that a directed graph is said to be *strongly connected* if for any two nodes A and B there is a path from A to B and one from B to A. Write a program that provides an implementation of the following graph and then uses that implementation to detect whether the graph is strongly connected. If your program determines that the graph is not strongly connected, it should report those pairs of nodes that are not connected by a path. What is the time efficiency of your algorithm?

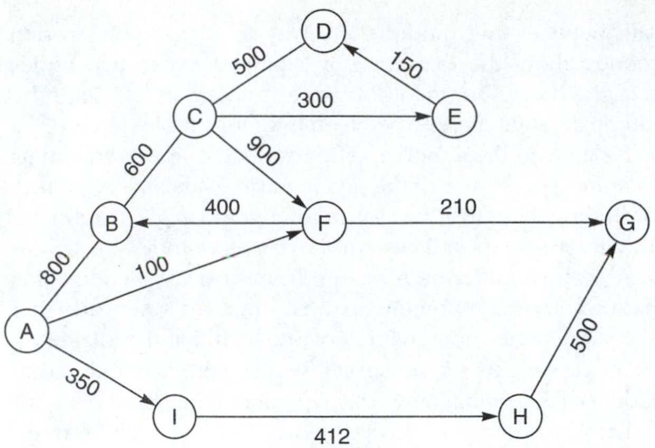

5. The Bay Area Brawlers professional football team is considering building a new stadium. The entire process of building the stadium has been broken down into a series of subtasks as specified in the following diagram:

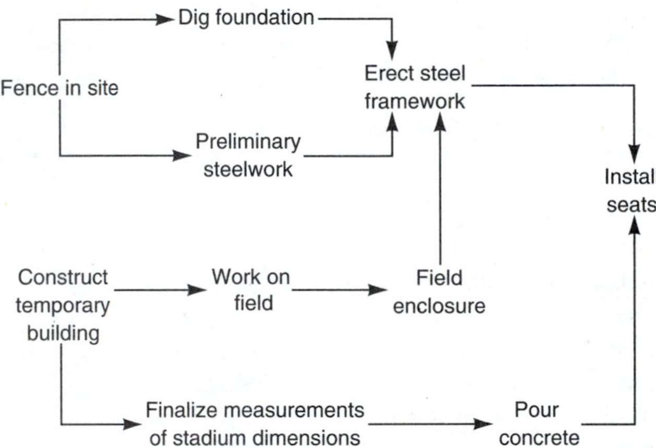

One subtask preceding another in this graph means that the first subtask must be completed before the second can be started. Write a program that will topologically order the subtasks in this graph. Note that this ordering represents a possible ordering in which the subtasks could be performed by the workers.

6. Many language compilers allow separate compilation of external modules that can be linked to form a complete executable program. Write a program that allows a user to enter a graph of dependency relationships between separately compiled modules; for example, see the following graph. The user should then be able to enter one module's identifier—representing a module in which edits were made and therefore had to be recompiled. Your program should then output an ordering of all other modules that need to be recompiled because of the changes made by the user in the input module. This ordering should represent a sequence in which the dependent modules could be recompiled.

Graph of dependency relationships between externally compiled modules. An edge from one module to another indicates that the compilation of the latter is dependent upon the former.

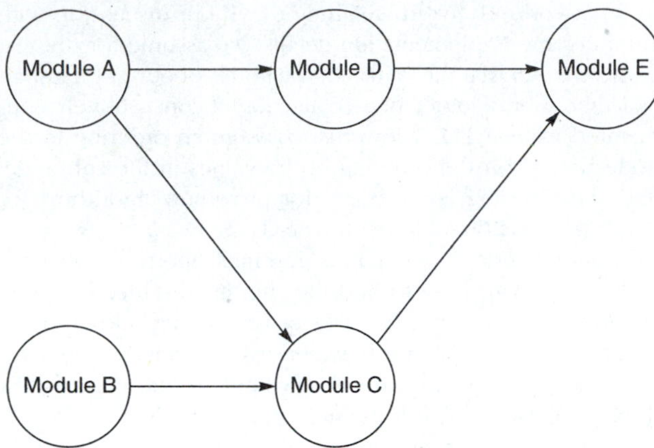

7. Implement a function that operates on a directed graph and indicates whether or not the graph contains a cycle. What is the time efficiency of your algorithm?

8. Write a function that randomly generates a specified number of points within the rectangular boundaries of the Euclidean plane. Your function should then randomly generate weighted edges connecting these points. The weight of an edge is merely the Euclidian distance between points. The number of edges generated should be user-specified and should ensure that the resulting network is strongly connected.

Given this network, develop separate functions that find its minimal spanning tree by Prim's and Kruskal's algorithms. Your functions should also count the number of operations performed by each algorithm. Write out these counts at the completion of both algorithms.

Now use the resulting program to experiment with the relationship between the sparseness of a graph (that is, the ratio of nodes to edges) and the corresponding efficiency of Prim's and Kruskal's algorithms. Do your experimental results confirm your answer to Exercise 9.5.14?

9. Write a program that includes an implementation of both of the topological sort algorithms discussed in Section 9.6 (that is, the one for which C++ code is given and the one you deduced in Exercise 9.6.7 of that section). Then augment each of the implemented algorithms by maintaining counters that keep track of the number of operations performed by these algorithms. Use the counters to empirically compare the performance of the two algorithms for a variety of directed acyclic graphs. Write a report in which you summarize the conclusions that you reach from this empirical testing of the algorithms. Under which condition does one algorithm tend to outperform the other? Provide an explanation of such differences in performance.

CHAPTER 10

Search Techniques for Conceptual Graphs and Networks

Attempt the end, and never stand to doubt; Nothing's so hard, but search will find it out.
Robert Herrick

Chapter Outline:

In the last chapter we examined some ways of finding paths through a graph or network. For instance, Dijkstra's algorithm finds a path from a designated start node to a goal node in a fashion that ensures the shortest possible path. In this chapter, we pursue the problem of finding paths from a start node to a goal node. However, we will add some variations to this general theme.

First, we will not always require that the path we find be the shortest path from the start node to the goal node; we hope that we may be able to find a path from the start to the goal *faster* if we settle for any path rather than the shortest one. That is, we will switch the emphasis from how long it takes to traverse the path found by our algorithm to how long it takes our algorithm to find a path.

Second, though we will still be searching through graphs and networks in theory, such graphs and networks will be viewed as purely conceptual search structures—structures that may never exist entirely as data in computer memory. Both of these adaptations on the path-finding motif are motivated by the existence of abstract graphs and networks so large that no implementation will squeeze them into a reasonable amount of space. Consider, for instance, the conceptual graph that underlies a game of strategy such as chess. A designated start node in such a graph is a representation of the initial state of a chessboard. That node is adjacent to each possible chessboard configuration that could be realized by the first player making one move. Each configuration attainable by the first player's move is similarly adjacent to each possible configuration achieved by the opponent's first countermove. This interpretation of adjacent nodes in a graph extends for second moves, third moves, and so forth as indicated in Figure 10.1. The number of possible paths in such a graph is estimated to be on the order of 10^{120}. Clearly, one cannot store a graph of this size in memory, though it is certainly possible to develop

Figure 10.1
Graph of game states in a chess game.

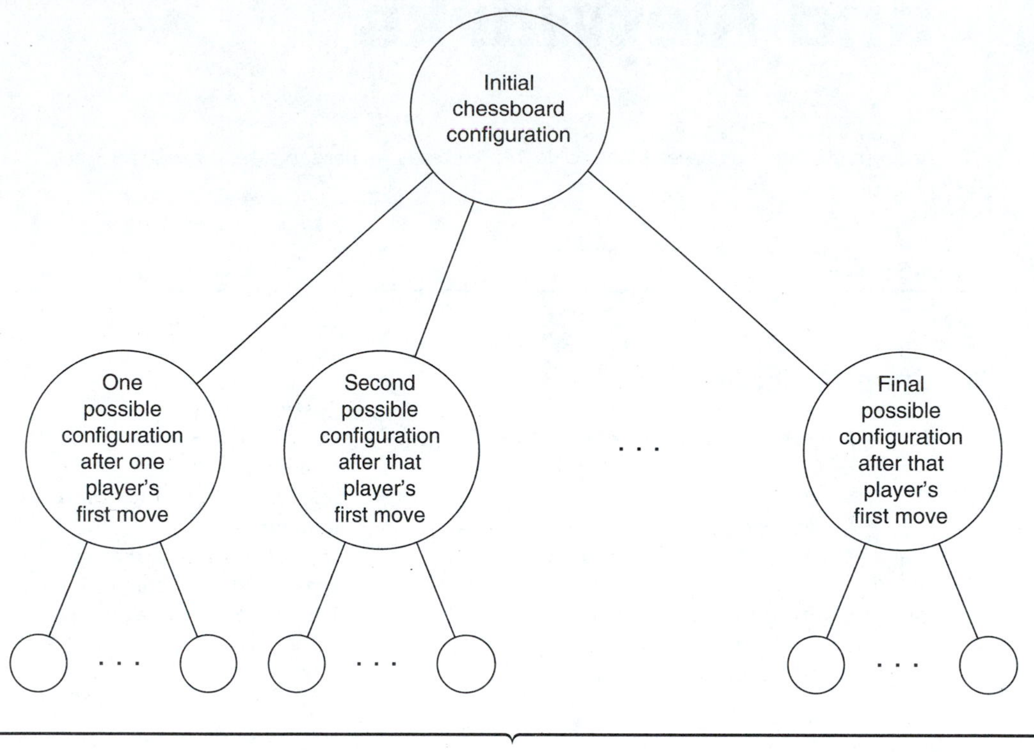

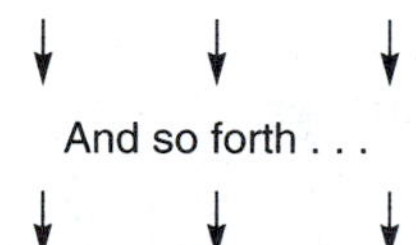

an algorithm for computing all nodes "adjacent" to a given game state. It is also clear that if we seek a path from the starting configuration of the chessboard to a goal state—that is, a winning configuration for a designated player—we are not necessarily concerned with the shortest such path. We would be happy merely to find a winning path as opposed to beating our opponent in the smallest possible number of moves.

Such is the framework from which we approach graph and network search algorithms. The methods we describe are often applied in such areas as artificial intelligence and natural language processing. In Section 10.1 we develop a brute-force technique that blindly generates paths radiating from the start node until the goal node is encountered. Though suitable for some types of problems, this method has a time efficiency that is exponential and hence is often not practical. In Section 10.2 we study ways of refining the technique from Section 10.1 in the hope of making such search algorithms polynomial instead of exponential in their run time. Finally, in Section 10.3, we look at the application of such techniques in the area of strategic game playing—one of the first endeavors in which computers were able to demonstrate "intelligent" behavior.

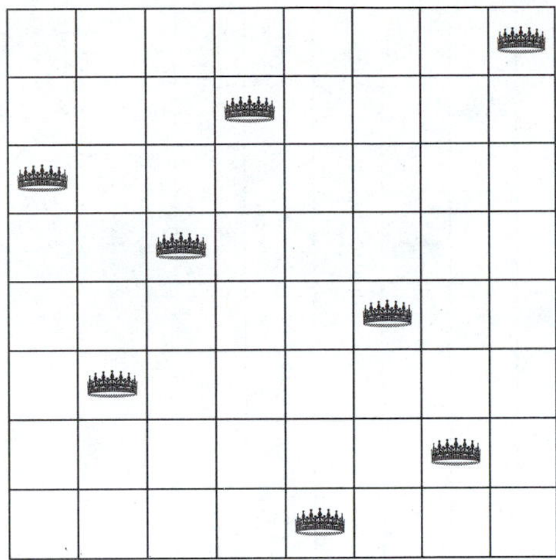

Figure 10.2
One successful Eight Queens configuration; no queen has access to any other.

10.1 Recursive Brute-Force Searches of Conceptual Graphs and Networks

As an example of a problem that can be attacked by the so-called brute-force strategy, we will consider a question that has long intrigued chess fanatics. The *Eight Queens problem* requires that we determine the various ways in which eight queens could be configured on a chessboard so that none of them could access any other queen. (The rules of chess allow a queen to move an arbitrary number of squares in a horizontal, vertical, or diagonal fashion.) Figure 10.2 illustrates one such configuration.

The logic we propose for solving this problem involves trial-and-error backtracking of the sort you might use to find a path out of a maze. You must explore numerous paths before you find the appropriate one. After exploring a given path and determining that it can lead only to a dead-end, you must retrace the points on the path in reverse order—backtrack—until you reach a point at which you can try an appropriate new path. This concept of trial-and-error backtracking is illustrated in Figure 10.3. Retracing points that have been visited previously in reverse order allows recursion to come into play.

Applying backtracking logic to the Eight Queens problem, we could attempt to find a "path" to a configuration by successively trying to place a queen in each column of a chessboard until we reach a dead-end: a column in which the placement of queens in prior columns makes it impossible to place the queen being moved. This situation is pictured in Figure 10.4. When we reach this dead end, we must

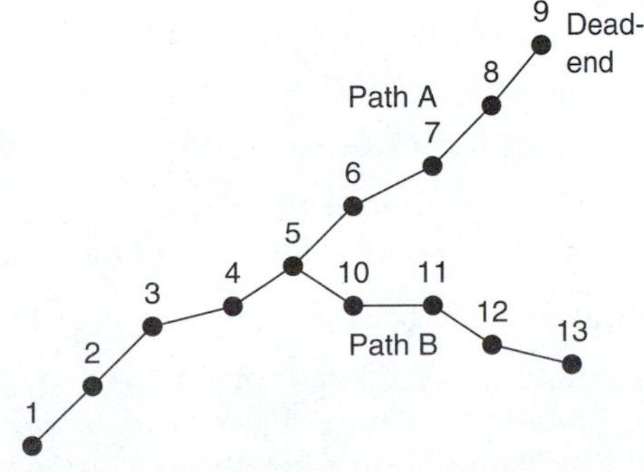

Figure 10.3
The backtracking problem as illustrated by a maze solution. After reaching a dead-end for path A, you must retrace steps 9 through 5 before you can try path B.

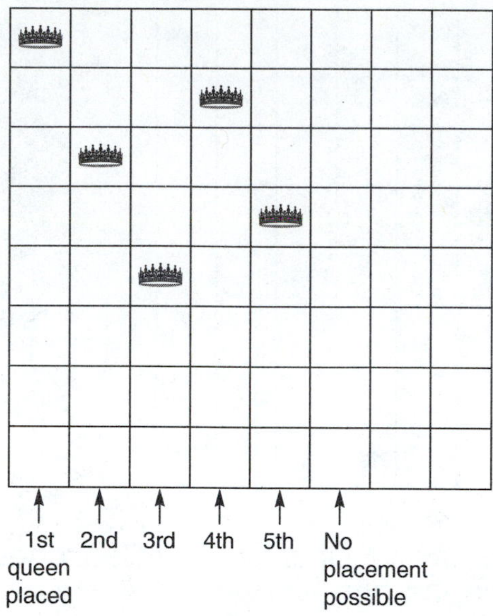

Figure 10.4
Dead-end in queen placement. Given the previous five placements, a queen cannot be placed in the sixth column. You must backtrack and attempt to reposition the queen in column 5. If that fails, you must backtrack to column 4, and so on.

backtrack one column (to column 5 in the case of Figure 10.4) and attempt to find a new placement for the queen in this column. If placement in the previous column is impossible, we must backtrack yet another column to attempt the new placement. This backtracking through previous columns continues until we are finally able to reposition a queen. At that point, we can begin a new path by again attempting to position queens on a column-by-column basis until another dead-end is reached or until a successful configuration is developed.

Rather than develop an algorithm specifically to solve the Eight Queens problem, we will extend our perspective to generating an algorithm for solving a general class of problems that could all be viewed analogously to the maze situation previously described. We will then discuss how the general algorithm could be used in the specific context of the Eight Queens problem and allow you to explore similar questions in the exercises and problems. Our general algorithm will require the following *Path* abstract data type.

Definition: A *Path* is a sequence of adjacent nodes (states) in a conceptual graph or network. In a nonempty path, the first node in the sequence is called the *start* node and the last node is called the *final* node. Assuming each node of the path stores data of type *Pathdata,* the following operations are provided for the *Path* ADT. (We assume that the type Pathdata includes a special value NULL for signaling a special condition, and a Boolean-valued function *IsNull* that returns TRUE if a value of type Pathdata is NULL, and FALSE otherwise. We also assume an object of type Pathdata is initialized to Null when it is created.)

`Construct Operation (First Form)`

Precondition: An uninitialized Path object.
Postcondition: The Path object is initialized to an empty Path.

`Construct Operation (Copy Constructor)`

Preconditions: An uninitialized Path object;
initpath — a Path object that was previously constructed.
Postconditions: The Path object is initialized to *initpath*.

`Destroy Operation`

Precondition: A Path object that currently exists.
Postcondition: All storage allocated to the Path object is deallocated, that is, returned to an available space pool for allocation to other objects.

`Assign Operation`

Preconditions: A previously constructed Path object;
source — a second Path object that uses the same Pathdata as the owner of the operation.
Postconditions: The contents of *source* have been copied to the Path object that owns the operation.

`FirstNode Operation`

Precondition: A nonempty Path object.
Postcondition: Returns the data of type Pathdata in the first node in the path.

`FinalNode Operation`

Precondition: A nonempty Path object.
Postcondition: Returns the data of type Pathdata in the final node in the Path.

`Extend Operation`

Precondition: A Path object;
data — a value of type Pathdata.
Postcondition: The Path object is extended by adding as a node adjacent to the final node one containing *data*. The added node becomes the final node of the Path.

`Contract Operation`

Precondition: A nonempty Path object.
Postcondition: The Path object with its final node removed.

`Length Operation`

Precondition: A Path object.
Postcondition: Returns the length of the Path object. The length is the number of nodes in the path minus 1—that is, the number of edges.

`GetSuccessor Operation`

Precondition: A nonempty Path object;
successor — a value of type Pathdata, whose value is either NULL, or that of a node adjacent to the final node on the Path.
Postcondition: If *successor* is NULL on entry to GetSuccessor, then *successor* is returned as the first node adjacent to the final node on the Path; otherwise *successor* is returned as the next node adjacent to the final node on the Path. Here "first" and "next" imply that we have a method for generating in sequence nodes adjacent to the final node in the Path. The operation will return the value TRUE if an adjacent node could be generated and FALSE otherwise.

`GoalReached Operation`

Precondition: A nonempty Path object.
Postcondition: Returns TRUE if the Path object represents a path to a goal state in the conceptual graph or network being explored; FALSE otherwise.

Implementation of the Path ADT

An implementation of the Path operations for a particular conceptual graph is fully realized as a derived class from an abstract base class we call **Path**. This parent **Path** class will provide all operations given in the preceding definition except **goalReached** and **getSuccessor**, which are defined as pure virtual functions. By using this approach we allow the parent **Path** class to provide those operations common to all different kinds of paths while allowing the implementor to employ whatever data structures are needed to efficiently represent the **getSuccessor** and **goalReached** operations. The **Path** class itself will use the interface that follows. Notice that this interface establishes **Path** as a derived class from the **List** class developed in Chapter 3. This derivation makes it easy to implement the nonvirtual functions in the **Path** class using **List** operations—a task that you will complete in the derivations. Deriving the **Path** class from the **List** class also makes sense on an abstract level since as we saw in Chapter 9, in the context of graphs and networks (whether they are real or conceptual) a path in a graph or network is often specified as a sequence of nodes.

```
// HEADER   : path.h
// PURPOSE : This file provides the definition for the path ADT.

// PathData is either a C++ built-in type, or a C++ class that has
// an assignment operation that overloads the "=" operator.  It also
// admits a special value "NULL" and a BOOLEAN-valued function isNull
// that returns TRUE if a value of type PathData is NULL, and FALSE otherwise.

template <class PathData>
class Path : public List<PathData>
{
  public:
//-------------------------------------------------------------------------------
// Interface for Path constructor
// GIVEN:  An uninitialized Path object.
// RETURN: The Path object is initialized to an empty path.

    Path();

//-------------------------------------------------------------------------------
// Interface for Path copy constructor
// GIVEN:     An uninitialized Path object;
//            initpath -- a Path object that was previously constructed.
// RETURN:    Path object initialized with the node values and
//            number of nodes of initpath.

    Path(Path<PathData> &initpath);

//-------------------------------------------------------------------------------
// Interface for Path destructor
// GIVEN:     A previously allocated Path object.
// RETURN:    All storage allocated to the Path object is deallocated, that is,
//            returned to an available space pool for allocation to other objects.

    ~Path();

//-------------------------------------------------------------------------------
// Interface for Path assign = operator
```

```
// GIVEN:     A previously constructed Path object;
//            source -- a second Path object that must have been
//                      constructed with the same PathData type
//                      as the owner of the assign operator.
// RETURN:    The contents of source have been copied to the Path
//            object that owns the operation.
// RETURN as value of function: void

    void operator = (const Path<PathData> &source);

//-------------------------------------------------------------------------------
// Interface for firstNode operation
// GIVEN:     A nonempty Path object.
// RETURN as value of function:
//            The data of type PathData in the first node in the Path.

    PathData firstNode();

//-------------------------------------------------------------------------------
// Interface for finalNode operation
// GIVEN:     A nonempty Path object.
// RETURN as value of function:
//            The data of type PathData in the final node in the Path.

    PathData finalNode();

//-------------------------------------------------------------------------------
// Interface for extend operation
// GIVEN:     A Path object;
//            data -- a value of type PathData.
// RETURN:    The Path object is extended by adding as a node
//            adjacent to the final node one containing data.  The
//            added node becomes the final node of the Path.
// RETURN as value of function: void

    void extend(const PathData &data);

//-------------------------------------------------------------------------------
// Interface for contract operation
// GIVEN:     A  nonempty Path object.
// RETURN:    The Path with its final node removed.
// RETURN as value of function: void

    void contract();

//-------------------------------------------------------------------------------
// Interface for length operation
// GIVEN:     A  Path object.
// RETURN as value of function:
//            The length of the Path. The length is the number of nodes
//            in the Path minus 1 -- that is, the number of edges.

    int length();

//-------------------------------------------------------------------------------
// Interface for getSuccessor operation
// GIVEN:     A nonempty Path object;
//            successor -- reference to a value of a node in the Path
//                         object, where the value being referenced is
//                         either NULL, or that of a node adjacent to the
//                         final node on the Path.
```

```
// RETURN:    If the value referenced by successor is NULL on
//            entry to getSuccessor, then successor will refer to
//            the value of the first node adjacent to the final
//            node on the Path; otherwise successor will refer to
//            the value of the next node adjacent to the final node
//            on the Path.  Here "first" and "next" imply that we
//            have a method for generating in sequence nodes adjacent
//            to the final node in the Path.
// RETURN as value of function:
//            The value TRUE if an adjacent node could be generated
//            and FALSE otherwise.

   virtual BOOLEAN getSuccessor(PathData &successor) = 0;

//-----------------------------------------------------------------
// Interface for goalReached operation
// GIVEN:     A  nonempty Path object.
// RETURN as value of function:
//            TRUE if the Path represents a path to a goal state in the
//            conceptual graph or network being explored; FALSE otherwise.

   virtual BOOLEAN goalReached() = 0;
};
```

Example 10.1

Let us consider how some of the Path operations might be implemented and used in the conceptual search graph underlying the Eight Queens problem. In this problem, a node in the graph being explored for a solution might contain as its data an ordered pair (**row,col**), where **row** and **col** are chessboard coordinates for the placement of a queen. A path **p** could then be represented by a sequence of these ordered pairs, such as

$$\mathbf{p} = ((3, 1)\ (6, 2)\ (4, 3)\ (2, 4))$$

This path **p** is the partial path of the first four nodes in the successful configuration of Figure 10.2. The **firstNode** and **finalNode** operations on **p** would return (3,1) and (2,4), respectively. The **length** operation would return 3. An invocation of **extend**((8,5)) would modify **p** to

$$\mathbf{p} = ((3, 1)\ (6, 2)\ (4, 3)\ (2, 4)\ (8, 5))$$

while **contract** would reduce **p** to the path

$$\mathbf{p} = ((3, 1)\ (6, 2)\ (4, 3))$$

The **goalReached** operation would return FALSE since these four placements do not constitute a complete Eight Queens configuration.

Finally, the result of the **getSuccessor** operation is dependent on the fashion in which we generate the nodes adjacent to the final node of the path currently under exploration. For instance, if we were extending the path

$$\mathbf{p} = ((3, 1)\ (6, 2)\ (4, 3)\ (2, 4))$$

into the fifth column, then there are two valid nodes adjacent to the final node on this path—(5,5) and (5,8). *Valid* here means that an extension of the path by such a node must preserve the property that no queen can access any other queen. Two successive invocations of the **getSuccessor** operation would return these two adjacent nodes. There is no specific requirement with respect to the order in which the adjacent nodes would be returned. For instance, (5,5) could be returned from the first invocation (when the value referenced by the parameter **successor** is NULL), and (5,8) could be returned from the second invocation (when **successor** is passed in as a reference to the value (5,5)). The implementor of the **getSuccessor** operation is free to determine the order of generation of adjacent nodes; the only requirement is that successive invocations of **getSuccessor** must eventually return all possible adjacent nodes.

The following C++ code represents one possible implementation of **getSuccessor** for the Eight Queens problem. This implementation must be done by a special class **QueensPath** that is derived from the **Path** class, with the pure virtual functions from **Path** being defined in **QueensPath** in a manner particularly suited to the Eight Queens problem. We assume that the template **PathData** will be replaced by a class **QueensData** that uses the following interface:

```
class QueensData
{
  protected:
    int row, col;    // Integer values indicating a row and column on a
                     // chessboard
  public:

//------------------------------------------------------------------------------
// Interface for constructor operation, first form
// GIVEN:    An uninitialized QueensData object.
// RETURN:   The QueensData object is initialized to a special value NULL.

    QueensData();

//------------------------------------------------------------------------------
// Interface for constructor operation, second form
// GIVEN:    A nonempty QueensData object;
//           row and col -- integer values.
// RETURN    The QueensData object is initialized to the given values
//           row and col, respectively.

    QueensData(int row, int col);

//------------------------------------------------------------------------------
// Interface for QueensData copy constructor
// GIVEN:    An uninitialized QueensData object;
//           initqueen -- a QueensData object that was previously constructed.
// RETURN:   The QueensData object is initialized with the value of initqueen.

    QueensData(QueensData &initqueen);

//------------------------------------------------------------------------------
// Interface for destructor operation
// GIVEN:    A QueensData object.
// RETURN:   All storage allocated to the QueensData object is deallocated.

    ~QueensData();

//------------------------------------------------------------------------------
// Interface for QueensData assign = operator
// GIVEN:    An uninitialized QueensData object;
//           source -- a QueensData object that was previously constructed.
// RETURN:   The contents of source have been copied to the QueensData
//           object that owns the operation.
```

```
// RETURN as value of function: void

    void operator = (const QueensData &source);

//-------------------------------------------------------------------------------
// Interface for setValue operation
// GIVEN:     A QueensData object;
//            newrow and newcol -- integer values.
// RETURN:    The QueensData object with new row and column values
//            given by newrow and newcol, respectively.
// RETURN as value of function: void.

    void setValue(int newrow, int newcol);

//-------------------------------------------------------------------------------
// Interface for setRow operation
// GIVEN:     A QueensData object;
//            newrow -- an integer value.
// RETURN:    The QueensData object with new row value given by newrow.
// RETURN as value of function: void.

    void setRow(int newrow);

//-------------------------------------------------------------------------------
// Interface for setColumn operation
// GIVEN:     A QueensData object;
//            newcol -- an integer value.
// RETURN:    The QueensData object with new column value given by newcol.
// RETURN as value of function: void.

    void setColumn(int newcol);

//-------------------------------------------------------------------------------
// Interface for setNull operation
// GIVEN:     A QueensData object.
// RETURN:    The QueensData object whose value has been set to a
//            special NULL value.
// RETURN as value of function: void.

    void setNull();

//-------------------------------------------------------------------------------
// Interface for currentRow operation
// GIVEN:     A QueensData object.
// RETURN as value of function:
//            The current row value of the object.

    int currentRow();

//-------------------------------------------------------------------------------
// Interface for currentColumn operation
// GIVEN:     A QueensData object.
// RETURN as value of function:
//            The current column value of the object.

    int currentColumn();

//-------------------------------------------------------------------------------
// Interface for isNull operation
// GIVEN:     A QueensData object.
// RETURN as value of function:
```

```
//            TRUE if the current value of the object is the
//            special value NULL; FALSE otherwise.

    BOOLEAN isNull();
};
```

The interface for the **QueensPath** class, which uses the **QueensData** class just specified, may be defined by:

```
#include "path.h"
#include "queensdata.h"

class QueensPath: public Path<QueensData>
{
  private:

//-------------------------------------------------------------------------------
// Interface for (private) conflict operation
// GIVEN:     A QueensPath object;
//            successor -- a value of type QueensData, whose value
//                         is potentially that of a node adjacent to the final
//                         node on the QueensPath object.
// RETURN as value of function:
//            FALSE if the candidate for the adjacent node does not
//            cause a conflict with any other queen placement existing
//            on the path. If the candidate for the adjacent node
//            causes a conflict, TRUE is returned.

    BOOLEAN conflict(const QueensData &successor);

  public:

//-------------------------------------------------------------------------------
// The interfaces for the getSuccessor and GoalReached operations
// are the same as those for the Path class.

    queensPath();
    ~queensPath();
    BOOLEAN getSuccessor(QueensData &successor);
    BOOLEAN goalReached();
};
```

A possible implementation for the **getSuccessor** function for the **QueensPath** class could now be:

```
BOOLEAN QueensPath::getSuccessor(QueensData &successor)
{
  QueensData  returnNode;      // Placeholder for the value returned
                               // by finalNode

  if (successor.isNull())      // Start with first row
    successor.setRow(1);
  else                         // Continue with next row
    successor.setRow(successor.currentRow()+1);
  returnNode = finalNode();
```

```
  successor.setColumn(returnNode.currentColumn()+1); // Probe into the
                                                     // next column
  while ((conflict(successor) && (successor.currentRow() <= 8)))
    successor.setRow(successor.currentRow()+1);
  if (successor.currentRow() != 9) // Only 8 rows on a chessboard; if
    return(TRUE);                  // currentRow gets to 9 there are
  else                             // no more successors
    return(FALSE);
}
```

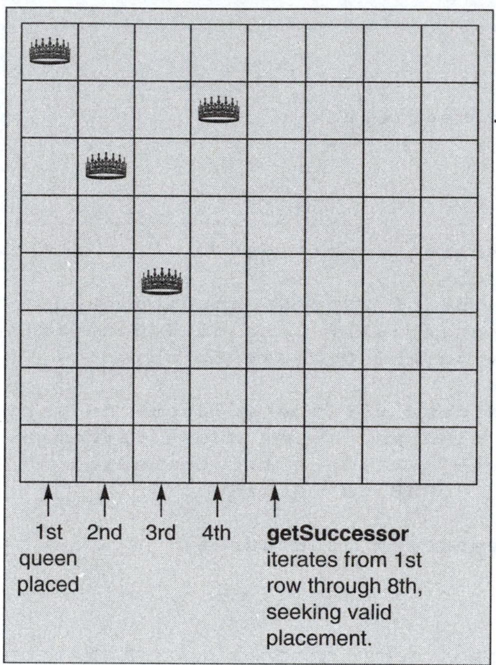
1st queen placed
2nd
3rd
4th
getSuccessor iterates from 1st row through 8th, seeking valid placement.

Using the **Path** class, we are now ready to describe a generalized search algorithm that could be used to probe a conceptual graph or network seeking a path to a particular goal node. The algorithm relies on two functions—**findPath** and **findPathAux**. **findPath** is a front-end function that prepares a one-node path containing the **start** node for **findPathAux**—the workhorse portion of the algorithm. **findPathAux** takes the path it is given and then uses the **getSuccessor** operation to iterate through nodes adjacent to the final node on the given path. For each adjacent node, it adds the node to the given path (via the **extend** operation) and then recursively calls itself with this new path, hoping to extend it even further—perhaps all the way to a goal state. The strategy used by **findPathAux** is to extend recursively one path as far as it will go—to a goal state or a dead-end state. In this respect, the algorithm resembles the depth-first traversal we introduced in the last chapter. If the goal state is reached, we are done and the resulting path can be returned. If a dead-end is reached, the path that was extended and probed deeper must be contracted and the next adjacent node added to it, so that we may probe this alternative path. A formal statement of this recursive probing appears in the following two functions.

```
//-------------------------------------------------------------------------
// Interface for findPathAux function
// GIVEN:     p -- a pointer to a Path object;
//            found -- a reference to a BOOLEAN value indicating whether the
//                     Path p has reached a goal state (TRUE) or not (FALSE).
// RETURN:    The Path p extended (through recursive calls) as far as it
//            will go.  If the path extends to a goal state, found will
//            be set to TRUE; otherwise the path will reach a dead-end
//            state and found will be set to FALSE.
// RETURN as value of function: void

    template class<PathData>
    void findPathAux(Path<PathData> *p, BOOLEAN &found);

//-------------------------------------------------------------------------
// Interface for findPath function
// GIVEN:     start -- a value for a start node from which exploration
//                     towards a goal is to start;
//            p -- a pointer to an empty Path object that has been
//                 constructed and is derived from the abstract Path class.
// RETURN:    If a path from the start node to a goal can be found, the
//            pointer to p now references that path.  If no such path
//            exists, the path referenced by p is an unreliable dead end
//            path that was encountered during the search.
// RETURN as value of function:
//            TRUE if a path was found to a goal state in the conceptual
//            graph or network being explored; FALSE if no such path was found.

    template class<PathData>
    BOOLEAN findPath(const PathData &start, Path<PathData> *p);
```

We now give the implementations of the **findPathAux** and **findPath** functions.

```
template class<PathData>
void findPathAux(Path<PathData> *p, BOOLEAN &found)
{
  BOOLEAN successorExists;
  PathData successor;              // Will be NULL on creation

  successorExists = p->getSuccessor(successor);
  while (!found && successorExists)
  {
    p->extend(successor);
    if (p->goalReached())
      found = TRUE;
    else
    {
      // Try findPathAux again with this extended path; if a goal state is not
      // found, back up to the path originally passed in and try another
      // successor (if there is one) to the (current) final node on p.
      findPathAux(p,found);
      if (!found)
      {
        p->contract();
        successorExists = p->getSuccessor(successor);
      }
    }
  }
}
```

```
BOOLEAN findPath(PathData start, Path<PathData> *p);
{
  BOOLEAN found = FALSE;

  p->extend(start);
  findPathAux(p, found);
  return(found);
}
```

Example 10.2

Partially trace the **findPath** and **findPathAux** functions for the Eight Queens problem, assuming that the **start** node is (1,1). Assume also that the **getSuccessor** operation generates adjacent nodes by placing queens in the next column. Within the next column, adjacent nodes are generated from first row to last (eighth) row, as the implementation in Example 10.1 suggested. The function **getSuccessor** only produces a successor node if this node is not in conflict with queen placements in prior columns.

A convenient way to trace such an algorithm is to use a graphic called a *search tree*. A partial search tree for this example appears in Figure 10.5. A given node within the search tree contains two items of information—the node added to the path currently being probed and a counter indicating the order in which nodes are received from **getSuccessor** for deeper exploration. The various paths are arranged from left to right descending from the **start** node, corresponding to the order in which they are explored. This implies that the order in which nodes are generated by **getSuccessor** corresponds to a preorder traversal of the search tree. A path reaching the goal occurs when we reach a node at level 7 of the search tree, that is, a branch with eight nodes and seven edges. Note that such search trees are conceptual trees only—just as the graph being explored in this type of problem is an intangible graph that never exists as a complete data structure in memory. They are analogous to the tree of recursive calls we used in Chapter 6 to analyze the efficiency of recursive algorithms. You should attempt to fill the partial tree in Figure 10.5. However, be forewarned that actual completion of the search tree—tracing all paths explored before the goal state is reached—may take a while!

Efficiency Analysis of the FindPath Algorithm

In the preceding example, we remarked that the search tree corresponds to the tree of recursive calls made to the **findPathAux** algorithm. For the Eight Queens problem, each call to the **findPathAux** operation potentially results in eight new probes generated by placing the queen in each row of the next column. Although many of these probes are never produced as valid probes by **getSuccessor** because they generate a conflict with queens placed in prior columns, a brute-force approach to implementing the **getSuccessor** operation must still consider a queen placement in each of the eight rows before deciding that placement in certain rows is not valid. Hence, an upper bound on the number of operations performed by the **findPath** algorithm for the Eight Queens problem is 8^7—eight possible row placements to consider for each of the seven columns in which we must place a queen through a recursive extension of the current path. In general, the brute-force strategy described here is bounded by an $O(N^M)$ efficiency, where N is an upper bound on the number of possible extensions that **getSuccessor** will consider for each attempt to extend a path one node deeper, and M is the maximal depth to which we must probe

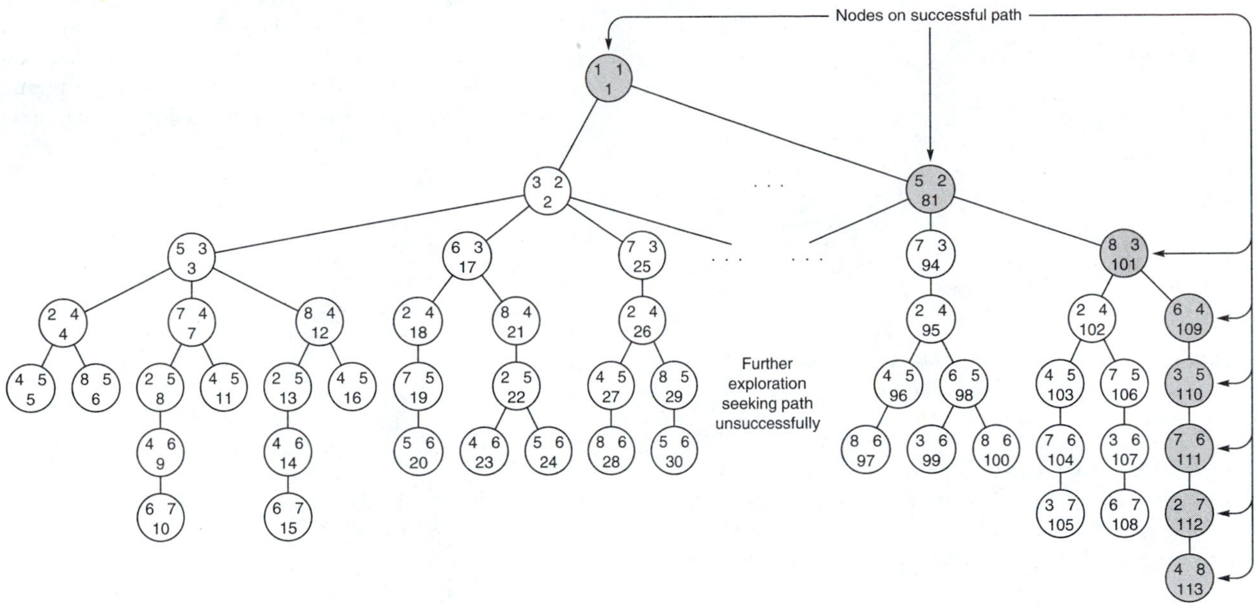

Figure 10.5
Partial search tree for Eight Queens placement. Within each circle, top numbers indicate row and column of queen placement and bottom number indicates order in which nodes (board positions) are explored.

before reaching a goal node or concluding a goal cannot be reached. Clearly, this brute-force approach generates algorithms whose time efficiencies are exponential; and thus it can only be used to solve problems of relatively small magnitude.

Exercises 10.1

1. Complete the implementation of the abstract **Path** class by implementing each of its nonvirtual functions. This is done most easily by calling on operations inherited from the **List** class, from which **Path** is derived.
2. Complete the implementation of a solution for the Eight Queens problem begun in Example 10.1 by providing first specific C++ implementations for the **QueensData** class. Now implement each of the operations of **QueensPath**, including the **conflict** function, which was invoked by **getSuccessor** in Example 10.1. Analyze the time efficiency of your **conflict** function.
3. Complete the partial search tree for the Eight Queens problem in Figure 10.5. Assume that the **getSuccessor** function of Example 10.1 is used. That is, assume a **getSuccessor** implementation that generates viable placements in ascending row number order.
4. Develop the search tree for the Eight Queens problem if the initial queen placement is in row 4 of column 1 instead of row 1. Assume that the **getSuccessor** function of Example 10.1 is used.
5. Repeat Exercise 10.1.4, except now assume that the **getSuccessor** function will begin by attempting a queen placement in the eighth row (instead of the first) and then work its way up to the first row. That is, it will generate viable placements in *descending* row number order.
6. The logic of the **findPathAux** function in concert with the **getSuccessor** function of Example 10.1 achieves a generalized nested looping control structure that enables us to control the depth to which an iteration is nested at program run time. In the Eight Queens problem this nesting depth is eight for a conventional chessboard, but notice that loops were not nested eight deep in our function. Rather, our function could handle the nesting of iterative constructs to the level demanded by the **goalReached** function. Keep in mind this generalized nested looping as you try to predict the output produced by the following C++ function:

```
int tough (int b, int c, int d)
{
  int k;
  if (b <= c)
  {
    cout << d << endl;
```

```
        for (k = b; k <= c; ++k)
            tough(b+1, c, k);
    }
}

void main()
{
    tough(1, 4, 12);
{
```

7. A maze could be viewed as an ADT, the information portion of which can be represented by a matrix of data of the form

```
struct
{
    BOOLEAN   northBlocked, eastBlocked,
              southBlocked, westBlocked;
}
```

At each square in the matrix, the Boolean fields are set to indicate whether or not we can proceed in the suggested direction. Implement, as a derived class from the **Path** class, a class **MazePath** for the problem of finding an exit from a maze of the above form. Analyze the efficiency of the **findPath** function for the implementation you develop.

8. (Knight's Tour Problem) Another classic chess problem that can be solved by trial-and-error backtracking is known as the Knight's Tour. Given a chessboard with a knight initially placed at coordinates x_0, y_0, specify a series of moves for the knight that will result in each board location being visited exactly once. From a given square on the chessboard, a knight may move to any one of the eight numbered squares in the following diagram:

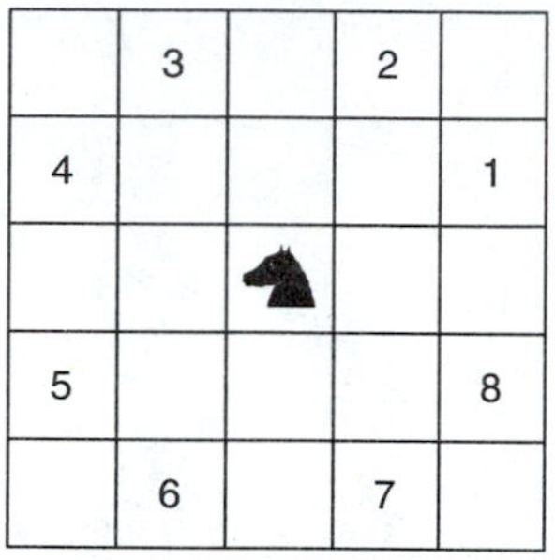

	3		2	
4				1
5				8
	6		7	

Derive from the **Path** class a class **KnightsPath** for the Knight's Tour problem. Analyze the efficiency of the **findPath** function for your implementation.

9. How would the **findPath** and **findPathAux** functions have to be modified to find all possible paths from the **start** node to a **goal** instead of just one path?

10.2 Guiding the Search of Conceptual Graphs and Networks

The recursive brute-force search method of the last section is severely limited by its exponential efficiency. It can only be applied to problems whose search space is sufficiently small. In this section, we examine methods of "guiding" graph and network searches in the hope of bringing their efficiency into the realm of polynomial time. Our method for doing this involves following the path that is most likely to lead to a goal. To determine this "most likely" criterion, we need a function that can be applied to a path and quickly return an estimate of the distance remaining from that path's final node to a goal node. Such a function, often called a *heuristic,* should guide us to a solution as quickly as possible. Heuristics are similar to the rules of thumb that humans use to help themselves solve problems. For instance, when playing chess, a human does not mentally play through all possible scenarios, looking for a final state in which she wins. Instead, she will look at the current state of the board, mentally generate the relevant successor states, and evaluate them quickly using a heuristic to decide where to move next. Unfortunately, heuristics are not guaranteed to succeed. Following a bad rule of thumb can lead to your quickly being defeated in a game of chess or to your pursuing paths that lead to dead-ends in other types of search endeavors. The same is true of computerizable heuristics. Often they cannot provide a mathematical guarantee of reducing a search's efficiency from exponential to polynomial time. However, in practice, a good heuristic can often produce this result. The determination of a good heuristic is usually a matter of time-consuming experimentation with a variety of methods.

Best-First Search Algorithm

A priority queue provides the key to the heuristic search algorithm we will develop, which is known as the *best-first search* algorithm for reasons that will soon be clear. We will use this priority queue to store paths created by extending prior paths with adjacent nodes returned from the **getSuccessor** operation. The arrangement of paths within the priority queue will give the path that appears to be closest to reaching a goal state (according to the heuristic) the highest priority. That is, given that the heuristic returns an estimate of "distance" from the current final node on a path to a goal node, the priority queue will be arranged so that the item with the smallest heuristic value is the first to be removed. Using this priority queue, the algorithm to perform a search guided by the heuristic function can be stated in the following skeletal terms:

```
Initialize a path to contain solely the start node;
Add this path to the priority queue of paths;
while ((a goal has not been reached) and
      (the priority queue is not empty))
{
  Remove the first path on the priority queue as the current path;
  while ((a goal has not been reached) and
        (there are nodes adjacent to current path))
  {
    Get such an adjacent node using the getSuccessor operation;
    Form a new path by extending the current path with the node obtained;
    if (this new path leads to a goal state)
      A complete path to goal has been found;
    else
      Add this new path to the priority queue;
  }
}
```

Before proceeding to detailed C++ code for this algorithm, you should be made aware of one potential problem. Remember that underneath this algorithm a conceptual graph is being searched. That conceptual graph may have cycles in it. If so, it would be possible to return to a node whose successors had already been generated via the **getSuccessor** operation. In turn, that would lead to infinite looping, where we just continue to generate paths reaching the same node over and over again. Each path would be longer than the previous one because it would contain one or more repetitions of a cycle embedded in it. However, relative to our heuristic, which estimates the distance from the path's final node to the goal, the path may continually appear to be a wise choice.

Example 10.3

To illustrate the complication just described, consider the network pictured in Figure 10.6. Suppose that we are starting at node B in this network and wish to find a path to node C. Suppose also that we use the following heuristic to estimate the distance from the final node on a path **p** to the goal node:

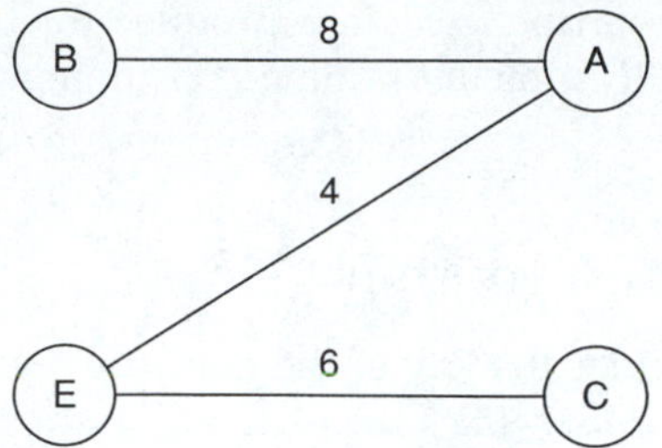

Figure 10.6
Network to illustrate possibility of infinite looping in Example 10.3.

heuristic(p) = Absolute value of the difference between the ordinal values of the letters that label the goal node and the final node on the path

For instance, the heuristic value of the path B→A with goal node C is 2, since the ordinal distance between A and C is 2. Granted, this may not be a good heuristic, but in practice not all heuristics that are tried will be good initially. We use this one merely to illustrate the dilemma that can occur with the algorithm as stated. If we now trace execution of the preceding algorithm to find a path from B to C, we have the infinite iteration described next.

Initially, the priority queue appears as the single path

(B)

We then generate successors of B, which in this case leads only to the path B→A. Hence, the priority queue becomes

(B→A)

This path is then removed from the priority queue, and the **getSuccessor** operation returns two nodes adjacent to A, namely, B and E. Thus, there are two paths to add to the priority queue: B→A→B and B→A→E. The heuristic arranges the priority queue as

(B→A→B, B→A→E)

The path B→A→B is removed from the queue, and the infinite looping emerges.

The process of generating the successors of the last node on a path is called *expanding* that node. The cure for the predicament illustrated by Example 10.3 is to keep a set of nodes that have been expanded at any given time in the algorithm's execution. This set is called the set of *closed nodes*. The nodes that occur as final nodes on paths in the priority queue are the *open nodes*. The open nodes are primed to be expanded when they are removed from the priority queue. If **getSuccessor** produces a node on the closed list, we discard it instead of extending the current path by it, because further exploration from a closed node can seldom reveal any substantive new path to a goal. (To see whether further exploration from a closed node could *ever* find a useful path, consider Exercises 10.2.10 and 10.2.11 at the end of this section.)

Using our previously defined operations for the **Path**, **PriorityQueue**, and **Set** classes, we can now provide a complete implementation of the **findPath** function for a heuristically guided search. The function receives a heuristic function, which is then passed to the priority queue **enqueue** operation. We assume that a lower valued heuristic is "better," since it suggests that we are closer to a goal and that the priority queue is thus implemented to dequeue the item of lowest priority.

```
//--------------------------------------------------------------------------
// Interface for findPath function (best-first search)
// GIVEN:    start -- a value for a start node from which exploration
//                    towards a goal is to start;
//           h -- a heuristic function h that, given a Path q, returns
//                an estimate of the distance from the final node on q
//                to the goal node;
//           p -- a pointer to an empty Path object p that has been constructed
//                and is derived from the abstract Path class.
// RETURN:   If a path from the start node to the goal can be found, the
//           pointer to p now references that path.  If no such path
//           exists, the path referenced by p is an unreliable path.
// RETURN as value of function:
//           TRUE if a path was found to a goal state in the conceptual graph
//           or network being explored;  FALSE if no such path was found.

// Assume that PathType is a class derived from the abstract Path class
// and with an appropriate implementation of the getSuccessor operation.
// Assume that PathData is the data type associated with a node on a
// path of type PathType.  PathData must have an assignment operation
// that overloads the "=" operator.

// Unlike the findPath function from Section 10.1, here we must template
// the class to which a path belongs as PathType.  The reason for this
// is that we call on new to allocate such a path, and new cannot be
// called with an abstract class such as the Path class defined in
// Section 10.1.

template <class PathType, class PathData>
BOOLEAN  findPath(const PathData &start, float (*h)(const PathType &q),
                  PathType *&p)
{
  Set<PathData> closed;
  PriorityQueue<*PathType> open;
  PathType *current, *newPathToExplore;
  PathData successor;
  BOOLEAN successorExists;
  BOOLEAN found = FALSE;

  newPathToExplore = new PathType;
  newPathToExplore->extend(start); // Put path containing only start node
  open.enqueue(newPathToExplore);  // on the open queue
  while (!found && !open.empty())
  {
    current = open.front();         // Obtain pointer to path at front
                                    // of open queue, then ...
    open.dequeue();                 // Remove a path from queue
    // Prepare to expand new current path
    if (!closed[current->finalnode()])    // Only expand nodes that
                                          // are not already closed
    {
      if (current->goalReached())          // Check if goal reached
      {
        found = TRUE;
        p = current;
      }
```

```
      else      // If not, extend current path
      {
        successor.setNull();
        successorExists = current->getSuccessor(successor);
        while (successorExists)
        {
          if (!closed[successor])
          {
            newPathToExplore = new PathType;
            *newPathToExplore = *current;   // Use PathType's = oper.
            newPathToExplore->extend(successor);
            open.enqueue(newPathToExplore);
          }
          successorExists = current->getSuccessor(successor);
        }
        closed.add(current->finalNode());   // Node just expanded now closed
        delete current;
      }
    }  // if (!closed[current->finalNode()])
  }   // outer while loop
  return(found)
}  // function findPath
```

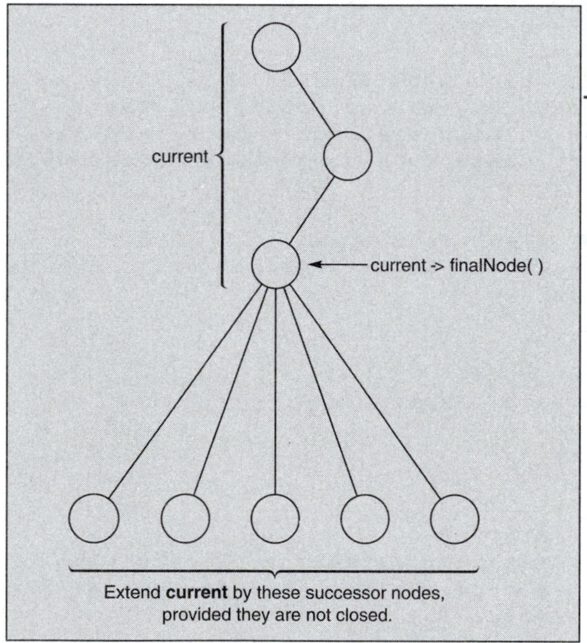
current
current -> finalNode( )
Extend **current** by these successor nodes,
provided they are not closed.

To illustrate the execution of the best-first search algorithm, consider the network in Figure 10.7. The following examples discuss the search trees that result from employing a best-first search strategy on this network for various choices of start and goal nodes and heuristic functions.

Example 10.4 Suppose that we use the heuristic function of Example 10.3 (absolute value of the difference between the ordinal numbers of the letters labeling the goal node and the final node on the path) to search for a path from Q to N in Figure 10.7. Figure 10.8 illustrates the search tree that results from the best-first search algorithm. Compare

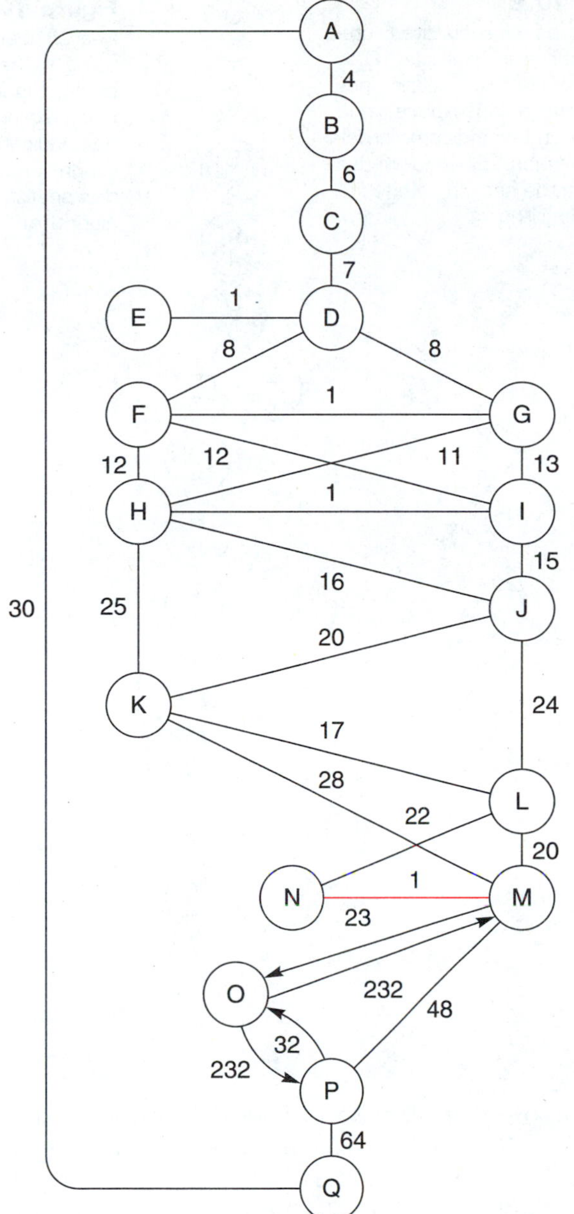

Figure 10.7
Network to explore by best-first search. Edges without arrows are assumed to have the same edgeweight in each direction.

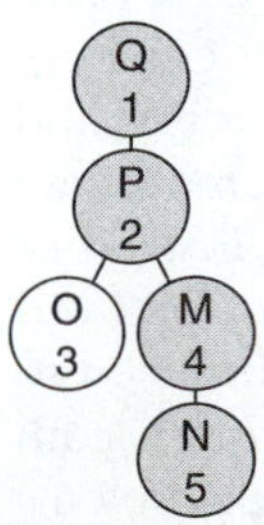

Figure 10.8
Search tree for best-first algorithm in Example 10.4. Within each circle, top letter indicates node being explored and bottom number indicates order of exploration. Shaded nodes comprise the search path found by the algorithm.

this to the search tree in Figure 10.9. This latter tree results from an unguided recursive search in which successors of a node were generated in alphabetical order of node labels. Note that in the search tree of Figure 10.9, 15 nodes must be examined and removed from the queue of open nodes before the goal node is reached. The search tree of Figure 10.8 indicates that only five nodes must be examined and dequeued before reaching the goal when guided by the heuristic. This is an indication of how the best-first search can speed the execution of the search.

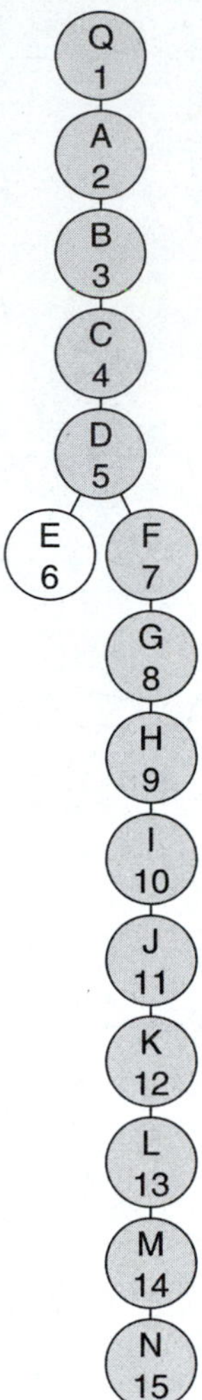

Figure 10.9
Search tree for recursive brute-force search in Example 10.4. Within circle, top letter indicates node being explored and bottom number indicates order of exploration. Shaded nodes comprise the search path found by the algorithm.

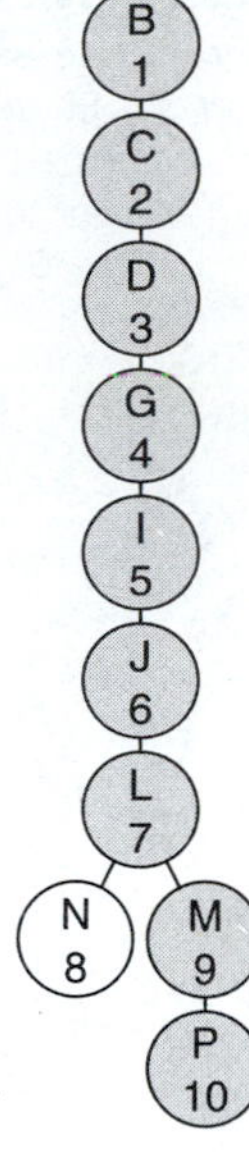

Figure 10.10
Search tree for Example 10.5 using h_1 heuristic. Within each circle, top letter indicates node being explored and bottom number indicates order of exploration. Shaded nodes comprise the search path found by the algorithm.

Example 10.5

Suppose that we wish to find a path from node B to node P in the network of Figure 10.7. In this example, we will experiment with different heuristic functions to guide us to the goal. The first heuristic, which we designate h_1, is the same heuristic used in Example 10.4. The second heuristic, h_2, we define as

$$h_2(p) = h_1(p) + p.length()$$

That is, the second heuristic is taken to be the sum of the first heuristic and the length of the path already traversed. The reason for doing this is to give equal weight to the two criteria of finding a path quickly and of finding the shortest path. The path length portion of the sum gives weight to the shortness of path criterion, and the h_1 portion contributes to finding a path quickly. The search trees for h_1 and h_2 are presented in Figures 10.10 and 10.11, respectively. These figures demonstrate the cost paid in execution time for attempting to find the shortest path instead of merely any path. In Figure 10.10, only 10 nodes must be examined and removed from the open queue before a path is found. In Figure 10.11, the weight given to shortness of path leads to 69 nodes being examined and dequeued before a path is found. In the exercises at the end of this section and the programming problems

Figure 10.11
Search tree for Example 10.5 using h_2 heuristic. Within each circle, top letter indicates node being explored and bottom number indicates order of exploration. Shaded nodes comprise the search path found by the algorithm.

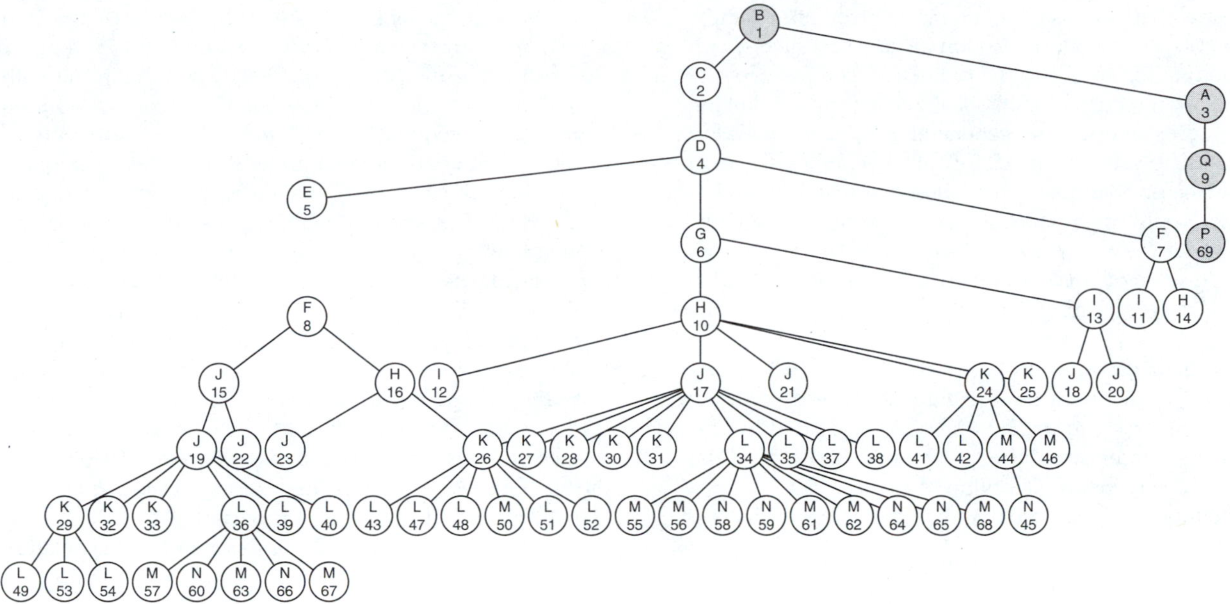

and projects at the end of the chapter, you will explore how a relatively small adjustment on the best-first algorithm presented here can lead to an alternative version of Dijkstra's shortest path algorithm.

Analysis of Best-First Search Algorithm

The two preceding examples illustrate the great degree of control the heuristic exercises over the best-first search algorithm. In the worst case, when the heuristic is bad and guides the search astray, the efficiency of the search algorithm is no better than the exponential efficiency of the recursive brute-force search technique developed in Section 10.1. However, a good heuristic can dramatically improve the efficiency of the search algorithm. In complex search spaces, such as those arising in artificial intelligence applications, much experimentation must usually be done before an effective heuristic is found.

Exercises 10.2

1. Suppose that we replace the priority queue in the best-first search algorithm with a stack. Describe the search strategy that results.
2. Suppose that we replace the priority queue in the best-first search algorithm with an ordinary queue. Describe the search strategy that results.
3. In implementing the priority queue for the best-first search algorithm, a path's heuristic value could be stored in the priority queue along with the path itself, or this heuristic value could be computed whenever it is needed. Discuss the trade-offs between these two alternatives.
4. In this section we defined an open node as one that is the final node of a path on the priority queue during execution of the best-first algorithm. Is it possible for a node to be an open node on more than one path in the priority queue, or does the set of closed nodes rule out this possibility? Explain.

5. By developing a search tree similar to that in Figure 10.8 (see Example 10.4), trace the execution of the best-first search algorithm as it attempts to find a path from node Q to node M in the network from Figure 10.7. Assume that we use the heuristic given in Example 10.3. How does the execution of the best-first search algorithm for this set of parameters compare to the brute-force recursive method of Section 10.1, assuming that successor nodes are generated in alphabetical order?
6. Discuss how the Path ADT could be implemented to allow the priority queue in the best-first search algorithm to store only open nodes instead of the complete paths ending at the open nodes. Incorporate the ideas from your discussion into a version of the best-first search that is more space efficient than the one given in the text.
7. Is the heuristic function given in Example 10.3 always effective for the network of Figure 10.7? If not, construct an example where the best-first search guided by this heuristic would actually explore more nodes than the brute-force recursive algorithm of Section 10.1.
8. In Example 10.5 suppose we adjust the heuristic function h_2 to be

$$h_2(p) = w * h_1(p) + p.length()$$

where w is a constant "weight" factor intended to weight the h_1 heuristic more than the path length in the hope of finding a path more quickly. By developing search trees for several values of w, trace the execution of the best-first algorithm in seeking a path from node B to node P. Can you find a value for w that results in fewer open nodes than we found in Example 10.5? Does this choice of w still find the shortest path, or have you weighted execution speed too heavily in finding a path?
9. Suppose we use the best-first search algorithm with a heuristic function that is the length of a path; that is, we use the length of the path already constructed instead of an estimate of distance to the goal as a guide for ordering the priority queue. By weighting the path length so heavily, does the best-first search algorithm now guarantee that we will find the shortest path from the start node to the goal node? If not, find an example in which the heuristic is taken to be path length and in which the shortest path still is not found by the algorithm.
10. Modify the best-first search algorithm so that by choosing the heuristic function to be path length instead of an estimate of distance to the goal, it will now find the shortest path from the start node to the goal node. (*Hint:* Consider your answer to Exercise 10.2.9 before you start the modifications for this exercise.) What is the time efficiency of your new algorithm? How does this compare to the implementation of Dijkstra's shortest path algorithm developed in Section 9.4? Under what circumstances would you use this new implementation of the shortest path algorithm instead of that developed in Section 9.4? Why?
11. In the discussion following Example 10.3, we said that exploration from a closed node can seldom reveal any substantive new paths to a goal. Under what circumstances might you want to reopen a closed node for further exploration? Why? In what sense would you be revealing a substantive new path to the goal that was not apparent when the node was originally closed?

10.3 Search Trees in Games of Strategy— The Minimax Algorithm

Grundy's game matches two opponents who are presented initially with one stack of seven pennies on a table in front of them. On a given move, a player must divide one of the stacks of pennies currently on the table into two *unequal* stacks. The player who is unable to find a stack that can be divided into two unequal stacks loses the game. Figure 10.12 illustrates a complete search tree for Grundy's game. (Search trees specific to games are often called *game trees.*) The alternating moves of the opposing players, identified by the names MAX and MIN, are indicated by square and circular tree nodes, respectively. Square nodes represent game states at which MAX is choosing a move, and circular nodes represent MIN's moves. The reason for this particular choice of names will soon become apparent. Because MIN moves first in Figure 10.12, the even levels of the tree have circular nodes, while the odd levels have only square nodes.

From the game tree in Figure 10.12, note that it is always possible for MAX to win if she moves second—regardless of MIN's initial move. This is apparent because we have a representation of the entire game in a compact tree that can be completely traversed to scan all possible outcomes. More challenging games

Figure 10.12
A complete search tree for Grundy's game, beginning with seven pennies.

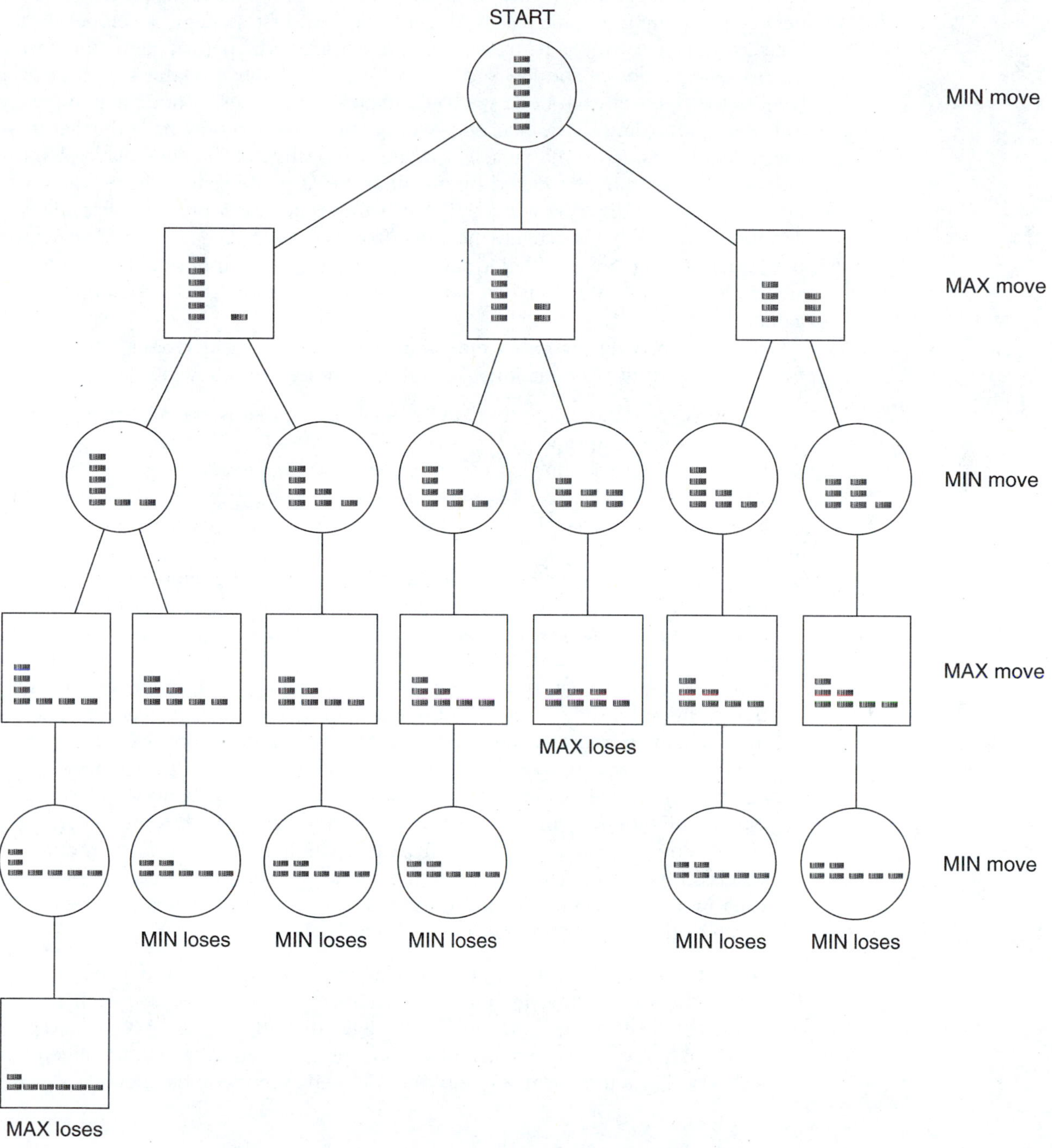

of strategy do not allow a representation and traversal of a complete game tree. Space limitations usually rule out the former, and time limitations make the latter practically impossible.

When playing games of strategy, humans rarely search an entire game tree. Rather, we have heuristic rules, similar to those introduced in the last section, that guide us intuitively toward making smart moves from a given game state. Of course, sometimes the moves aren't smart enough, and we lose. But that shouldn't surprise us—it's the nature of heuristics to be imperfect. One of the differences, however, between searching a game tree and using the best-first strategy developed in the last section is that with game trees we can only dictate the path at alternating levels. In the search trees of the last section, we were in control of the search at each level of the tree—at each node we could choose the successor node that appeared to be best according to the heuristic. With game trees, we only have this luxury at alternating levels. If we put ourselves in the perspective of the MAX player, we can only choose the moves dictated by our heuristic at game states where it is MAX's move. At levels of the tree where it is MIN's move, we must presume that MIN will choose the move that is actually the worst from MAX's perspective. In other words, our game-playing strategy should take into account the supposition that MIN will always try to force MAX into the worst possible situation at a given point in the game.

The game-playing algorithm emerging from these considerations is called the *minimax algorithm*. The minimax algorithm assumes the following:

1. We are playing the game from MAX's perspective; that is, we are attempting to develop a winning strategy for MAX.
2. We have a heuristic function (often called a *static evaluator* in game-playing contexts) that is given a game state and returns a number corresponding to that game state. The larger the number returned, the better the state is from MAX's perspective.
3. Time and space constraints will not allow a search of the entire game tree that descends from a particular state. Instead we search only to a specified depth from a particular game state. In the vernacular of game-playing programs, the levels that we search are called *plies*. Thus, a four-ply search would search the game tree four levels beyond the current game state. On reaching the ply limit, four in this case, the search would be cut off and the static evaluator called on to obtain an approximate characterization of the state. The deeper the ply to which we can carry out a game-playing search, the better our game playing strategy should be. Why? Because a deeper ply allows us to get closer to searching the entire game tree below our current state. As the game nears its end, this means that we may actually reach winning or losing states in our search efforts. In the early stages of the game, we hope that a deeper ply will result in a more accurate heuristic value. Hence, our goal will always be to search to the deepest possible ply in the time allowed.

To illustrate the concepts behind the minimax algorithm, consider the game of Fifteen. In this game, opposing players alternatively choose digits between 1 and 9 with the goal of selecting a combination of digits that adds up to 15. Once a digit is chosen, it may not be chosen again by either player. Hence, to win at Fifteen you must choose digits that include one of the following eight combinations:

```
1 5 9          2 6 7
1 6 8          3 4 8
2 4 9          3 5 7
2 5 8          4 5 6
```

This game could be represented by two sets of digits—those currently chosen by MAX and MIN, respectively. We suggest the following heuristic to guide MAX's moves. Remember, the larger the heuristic's value, the better the game state supposedly will be for MAX.

$$h(s) = \begin{cases} +\infty & \text{if game state s is a win for MAX} \\ -\infty & \text{if game state s is a loss for MAX} \\ & \text{Otherwise, using s, compute the following difference: (the number of winning combinations that remain open for MAX) } - \text{ (the number of winning combinations that remain open for MIN)} \end{cases}$$

For example, if game state s were ({5}, {2}), where the first and second sets represent the chosen digits of MAX and MIN, respectively, then $h(s)$ would be 1, since five winning combinations are still possible for MAX and four are possible for MIN.

The essence of the minimax algorithm is to explore the game tree descending from the present state to leaf levels if the ply limit will allow. If the ply limit is reached before a leaf level is encountered, then we explore to the ply limit and apply the heuristic to approximate the worth of a state. As we descend through levels of the tree, we must distinguish from those levels at which MAX is choosing a move and those levels at which MIN is making a move. At a game state where MAX is making a move, we should choose the successor state of maximum value because the heuristic is designed to produce larger values for states that are better from MAX's perspective. Because we assume that MIN will try to force MAX into the least advantageous states, a game state from which MIN is making a choice should be guided by the perspective that MIN will choose the minimum move among all possible successor states. To summarize, the minimax value of a game state s, dependent on the ply limit to which we will search, can be defined by the following rule:

$$\text{MINIMAX(s,plylimit)} = \begin{cases} & \text{The maximum of MINIMAX applied, with plylimit reduced by one, to each successor state of s if s is a maximizing node, that is, a node at which MAX is selecting a move.} \\ & \text{The minimum of MINIMAX applied, with plylimit reduced by one, to each successor state of s if s is a minimizing node, that is, a node at which MIN is selecting a move.} \\ h(s) & \text{if game state s occurs at a depth whose level has reached the ply limit, that is, if plylimit has been reduced to zero.} \\ h(s) & \text{if game state s is a leaf in the overall game tree, that is, s is a win, lose, or draw state for MAX.} \end{cases}$$

Example 10.6 Compute MINIMAX(s,2) in the game of Fifteen, where s is the state given by s = ({4, 5}, {6, 9}) and h is the heuristic defined at the top of this page.

Figure 10.13 highlights the work involved in this computation. We must descend from the current state to each of the possible choices that could be made by MAX:

Figure 10.13
Computation of minimax value for game state ({4, 5}, {6, 9}) with ply limit 2. Values inside circles and squares indicate number that is selected.

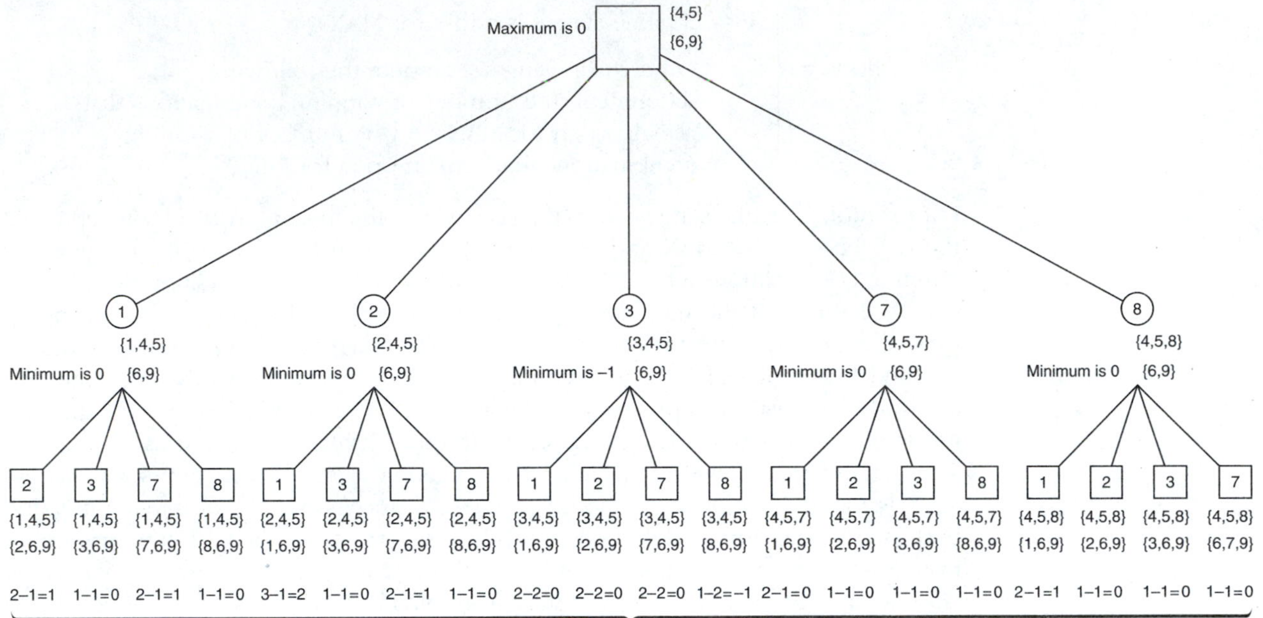

1, 2, 3, 7, or 8. For each of these choices, we must descend to each of the four options that MIN has. At this level, we have reached the ply limit. Hence, the heuristic *h* would be invoked at this level. Because this level represents a move made by MIN, the minimum value according to the heuristic would be returned to the prior level. In Figure 10.13, the minimum values 0, 0, −1, 0, and 0 are returned to ply level 1 from ply level 2. At ply level 0, we select the maximum of these five returned minimums. Therefore, the minimax value of *s* would evaluate to 0. This implies that, according to this particular heuristic, choices of 1, 2, 7, or 8 are all equally likely to optimize MAX's chances of winning. Remember, these choices are predicated on the heuristic *h* that we use and the ply limit to which time allows us to search. Searching to a deeper ply limit or changing the heuristic may well change the minimax value and hence the move that MAX selects.

Example 10.7

Consider the hypothetical partial game tree in Figure 10.14. Suppose that MAX is choosing a move from game state A. Use the minimax algorithm to determine MAX's best move. Assume that time considerations allow a ply limit of 3 and the numbers at the leaf levels of the tree in Figure 10.14 represent the values of the heuristic function at this level.

Because MAX is choosing a move at the nodes labeled E through K, we would seek to find the maximal value of the successors of each of these nodes. Hence, the values 7, 8, 3, 0, 6, 8, and 9 would be recursively returned to nodes E, F, G, H, I, J, and K, respectively. Since the nodes labeled B, C, and D are nodes at which MIN is selecting a move, their minimax values are the minimums of (7, 8, 3),

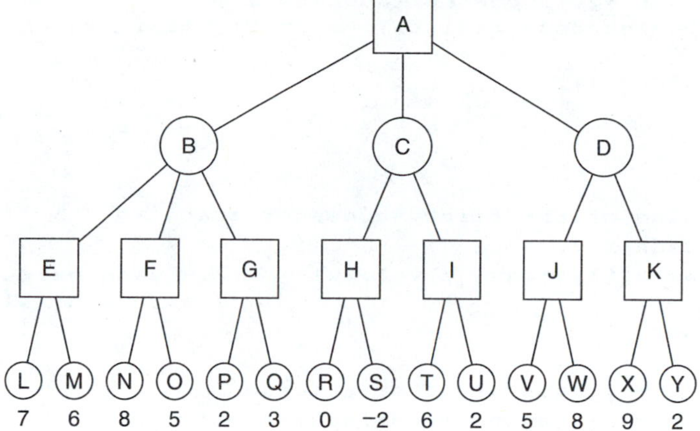

Figure 10.14
Partial game tree for Example 10.7.

(0,6), and (8, 9), respectively. That is, the minimax value of B is 3; the minimax value of C is 0; and the minimax value of D is 8. At node A, MAX would now choose the maximum among 3, 0, and 8. Hence, MAX would choose to move to D, whose minimax value is 8. Note this essentially implies that, if MAX moves to D, it can be guaranteed a position two levels deeper with a heuristic value of 8—even if MIN plays to its optimal strategy according to the heuristic being used.

In a C++ implementation of the minimax algorithm, the **Path** class may be conveniently used to represent the state of a game. This state may be regarded as the sequence of moves that has occurred in the game. Using a path to represent that sequence, the minimax algorithm is given by the following C++ code.

```
//------------------------------------------------------------------------
// Interface for the minimax algorithm
// GIVEN:   s -- a pointer to a path representing the present state of the game;
//          h -- a heuristic function (static evaluator) that can
//                 be applied to a game state;
//          max -- a BOOLEAN indicating whether it is MAX's move (TRUE)
//                   or MIN's move (FALSE);
//          ply -- an integer representing the ply limit for the search.
// RETURN:  move -- contains the move selected by the minimax
//                    algorithm
// RETURN   as value of function:
//               The minimax value of the move selected by the algorithm

// Assume that PathData is a C++ class that appropriately represents a
// move in the game.  PathData must have an assignment operation that
// overloads the "=" operator

template class<PathData>
float minimax(Path<PathData> *s, float (*h)(Path<PathData> s),
              BOOLEAN max, int ply, PathData &move)
{
  BOOLEAN   successorExists;
  PathData successor, x;        //successor is NULL on creation
  float newvalue, value;
```

```
  successorExists = s->getSuccessor(successor);
  if ((ply == 0) || !successorExists)     // Ply limit reached or leaf level
  {
    move = s->finalNode();
    return(h(s));
  }
  else
  {
    // Find the value of the first successor state
    s->extend(successor);
    value = minimax(s, h, !max, ply-1, x);    // x used merely to fill
                                              // parameter slot
    move = successor;
    s->contract();
    // Now compare to values of other successors
    successorExists = s->getSuccessor(successor);
    while (successorExists)
    {
      s->extend(successor);
      newvalue = minimax(s, h, !max, ply-1, x); // x fills parameter slot
      if (max)   // MAX or MIN node?
        if (newvalue > value)
        {
          move = successor;
          value = newvalue;
        }
      else
        if (newvalue < value)
        {
          move = successor;
          value = newvalue;
        }
      s->contract();
      successor Exists = s-> getSuccessor(successor);
    }
    return(value);
  }
}
```

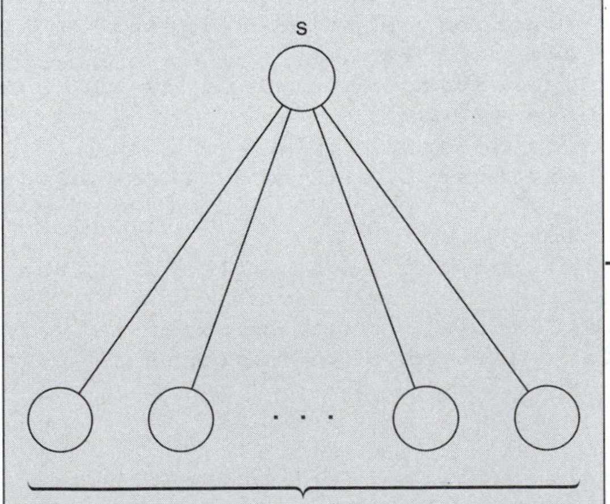

while loop iterates through successors of s, storing max/min in **value** and associated successor in **move**.

Analysis of the Minimax Technique

A higher level program would call on **minimax** and use the **move** parameter that **minimax** returns as a basis for selecting the next move in a game of strategy. Our analysis of **minimax** is based on its usage in this context. If we were to call on it and expect its recommendation for a move from a given state of the game, how long would we have to wait for a response? This is typical of the way game programs are used in computer chess tournaments, for instance. A limit is placed on the time the computer has to select each move in the game.

This time efficiency depends on two factors—the ply limit to which we are willing to carry out our analysis and the average number of successor moves possible from a given state. If n represents this average number of moves, then the generalized iteration caused by the recursive calls in **minimax** results in a time efficiency of n^{ply} for one external call to the algorithm. The goal in using **minimax** to play a game of strategy is to push the ply limit to the deepest possible value allowed by the time limits. The deeper the ply limit, the better the chance of being able to search all the way to leaf nodes in the overall game tree or, at least, of getting a more accurate estimate from the heuristic when it is finally invoked.

Refinements to the minimax algorithm allow certain subtrees to be skipped during the process of checking for the maximum or minimum of all states that succeed a given state. You will explore one of these techniques, called *alpha-beta pruning,* in the exercises for this section and in the problems at the end of the chapter.

A RELEVANT ISSUE Computer Chess

More than any other game of strategy, chess has attracted the attention of many computer scientists. Computer chess tournaments are quite commonplace, and, in 1968, British chess master David Levy issued a challenge that no computer chess program would be able to beat him in a best-of-seven match. Artificial intelligence experts Donald Michie, Seymour Papert, and John McCarthy raised the money to cover Levy's challenge, and in 1978 the match took place between Levy and Chess 4.7—a program developed by David Slate and Larry Atkin of Northwestern University. Although Chess 4.7 was trounced, winning only one game in the match, the publicity surrounding the event served to arouse a new crop of chess programs in the 1980s.

The early part of the 1980s was the era of the Cray Blitz program. Developed by Cray Research of Wisconsin and Minnesota, the Blitz program was powered by the fastest supercomputer of the decade and went four years without being defeated by another program. Unfortunately, it actually fared worse against David Levy than its Chess 4.7 predecessor. Levy walloped the Blitz program 4 to 0 in a $5000 rematch of his earlier human-computer confrontation.

The year 1985 marked the end of the Blitz's domination of the computer chess world; in the North American Computer Chess Championship, the Blitz was defeated by the Hitech program developed by Hans Berliner of Carnegie-Mellon University. The Hitech program was the first chess program to take real advantage of parallel processing. The program ran on a Sun minicomputer augmented by 64 microprocessors—one for each square of the chessboard. This configuration allowed Hitech to process 200,000 game states per second—a number doubling the state processing speed of the Cray Blitz but still paling when faced with the 10^{120} possible game states in chess.

Hitech in turn was overtaken by a chess-playing machine known as Deep Thought: A combination of software and specialized hardware, Deep Thought was developed by Feng-hsiung Hsu, Thomas Anantharaman, Murray Campbell, and Andreas Nowatzyk while they were doctoral students at Carnegie-Mellon. Its main hardware components were two processors, each capable of searching 500,000 positions per second. In January, 1988, Deep Thought defeated U.S. Grandmaster Brent Larson, a former contender for the world title, in a major tournament held in Long Beach, California (in fact, Deep Thought tied for first place in the tournament with Grandmaster Anthonly Miles). In March, 1991, it became the first computer to compete in a round-robin tournament for grandmasters and placed seventh out of eight participants in the IBM Cup, held in Hanover, Germany.

The human versus computer chess battle promises to heat up as we approach the end of the century. It is widely regarded among chess players that chess programs cannot capture the imagination required to win at the highest levels of competition. World champion Gary Kasparov, who defeated Deep Thought in a match in late 1989, maintained that "human creativity and imagination (in particular *his* creativity and imagination) will truly triumph over silicon and wires." (Quote taken from the article "A Grandmaster Chess Machine," by Hsu, Anantharaman, Campbell and Nowatzyk, which appeared in *Scientific American*, 263:4, October 1990, pp. 44–52). In May, 1994, however, in the Intel Grand Prix, the Pentium Chess Genius Program (the current microcomputer chess champion written by Richard Lang of Cambridge) defeated Kasparov in a game of "blitz chess." In blitz chess players are given much less time to determine their moves than in regular chess. Nevertheless, Kasparov's defeat did not go unnoticed. Raymond Keene, chess correspondent of the *London Times* who was serving as master of ceremonies, observed that "after the defeat, the champion's (Kasparov) demeanour changed. His handshake [which prior to the game had been firm and vigorous] had become flaccid and nervous."

Exercises 10.3

1. In the game of Nim, two players alternate in selecting one, two, or three pennies from a pile of five pennies. The person who forces his or her opponent to select the final penny is the winner. Construct a complete search tree for this game. Can one of the players be assured a win if he or she makes the appropriate moves? Which player? Construct a fail-safe heuristic to guide this player's moves.
2. Develop a heuristic for a more general game of Nim (see Exercise 10.3.1), in which the pile initially contains n pennies, the players are free to choose 1, 2, 3, . . . , m pennies on a given move.
3. Compute MINIMAX(s,2) in the game of Fifteen, where s is ({2, 8}, {4, 6}). Use the heuristic **h** employed in Example 10.6. Does the computed minimax value guarantee that MAX will choose 5 as its next move and consequently win the game?
4. Develop a heuristic for the game of tic-tac-toe. Then use your heuristic to compute the minimax value of the following game state to a ply level of 2. Assume that MAX marks its moves with X and is to make the next move from this state. What move does your heuristic dictate for MAX?

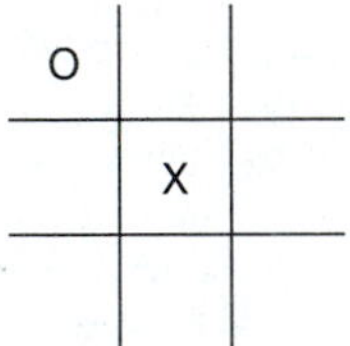

5. Try the heuristic you developed for Exercise 10.3.4 to compute the minimax value of the following state to a ply level of 2. Does your heuristic dictate that MIN must move to block MAX's win?

O		X
X	X	
O		

6. Consider the following game tree. Suppose that MAX is to choose one of the three possible moves at level 1 of this tree. Apply the minimax algorithm to a ply level of 3 to determine MAX's move and its minimax value. The numbers at the leaves of the tree indicate values returned by the heuristic function.

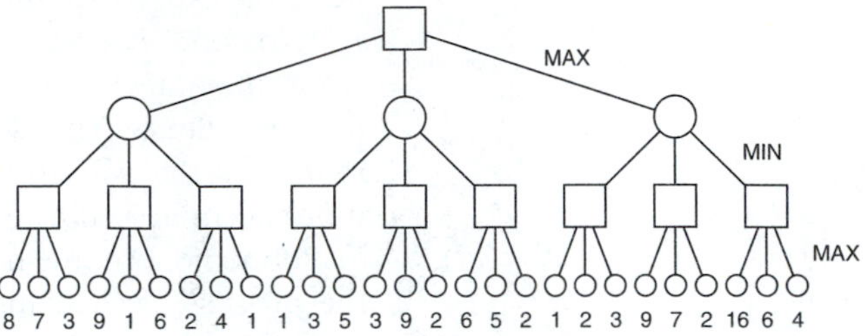

7. Consider the following game. Suppose that MAX is to choose one of the three possible moves at level 1 of this tree. Apply the minimax algorithm to a ply level of 3 to determine MAX's move and its minimax value. The numbers at the leaves of the tree indicate values returned by the heuristic function.

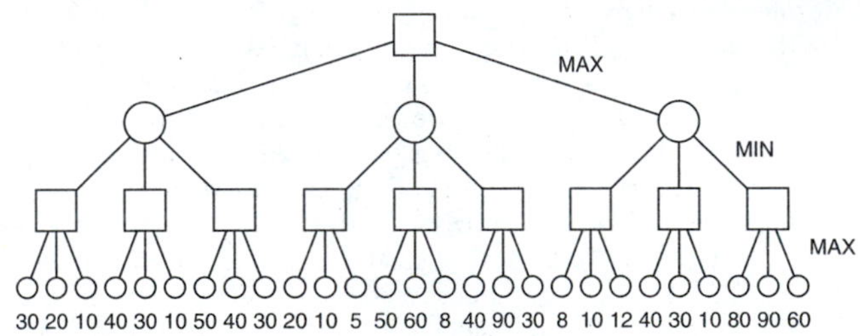

8. Suppose that you are MAX and that your opponent has been paid by gamblers to purposely lose. Hence your opponent is always choosing the worst possible move among the options open to her. How will the minimax algorithm perform under these circumstances? How would you adjust the minimax algorithm to allow you to defeat your opponent as rapidly as possible?
9. (Alpha-Beta Pruning) A technique known as *alpha-beta pruning* can reduce the number of nodes that must be explored when the minimax algorithm is invoked for a particular ply limit. When using this technique, two values, designated *alpha* and *beta* by convention, are maintained at each level of the game tree as it is being searched. During the search, the alpha value for a MAX node (that is, a node at which MAX is choosing a move) is maintained to be the maximum of the values that have been returned from exploration of successor nodes. Similarly, at a MIN node, the beta

value is maintained to be the minimum of the values that have been returned from exploration of successor nodes. With these definitions of alpha and beta values, note that generation of successor nodes can be discontinued below any MIN node having a beta value less than or equal to the alpha value of its MAX node ancestor. Why? Further generation of successors will only serve to decrease the beta value at the MIN node, and we already know that MAX, at the prior level, has found an alternative better (from MAX's perspective) than the beta value of this MIN node. Hence, MAX would never want to choose a move to this MIN state; thus it is a waste of time to explore it further. Similar reasoning dictates that generation of successor nodes can be discontinued below any MAX node having an alpha value greater than or equal to the beta value of its MIN node ancestor. Apply alpha-beta pruning to the game trees in Exercises 10.3.6 and 10.3.7. How many tree nodes can be avoided in each case because of the cutoff? Finally, modify the minimax algorithm presented in the text to take alpha-beta pruning into account.

Chapter Summary

In Chapter 9 we examined ways of finding paths through a graph or network. In this chapter we have pursued further the problem of finding paths from a start node to a goal node, but we have not required that the path we find be the shortest path from the start node to the goal node as we did in Dijkstra's algorithm. Rather, we have sought to expedite the search for a path between two nodes by settling for any path rather than the shortest one. Second, though we have been searching through graphs and networks in theory, such graphs and networks have been viewed as purely conceptual search structures—structures that might never exist entirely as data in computer memory. Both of these adaptations on the path-finding motif have been motivated by the existence of abstract graphs and networks so large that no implementation will squeeze them into a reasonable amount of space.

In Section 10.1 we apply a brute-force technique involving backtracking logic that blindly generates paths radiating from the start node until the goal node is encountered. The technique is illustrated using the search graph underlying the Eight Queens problem. Though suitable for some types of problems, the method of this first section has an exponential time efficiency and is thus often not practical.

In Section 10.2 we have refined the technique from Section 10.1 in the hope of making the run time of such search algorithms polynomial instead of exponential. The method we use, known as the best-first search algorithm, involves applying a heuristic function that quickly calculates an estimate of the distance remaining from a given path's final node to the goal node. This value is then used to select a path that is most likely to lead to a goal.

Finally, in Section 10.3, we apply heuristic search techniques, in particular the minimax algorithm, in the area of strategic game playing—one of the first endeavors in which computers were able to demonstrate "intelligent" behavior.

Keywords

alpha-beta pruning	Fifteen game	heuristic	ply limit
best-first search	game trees	minimax algorithm	search tree
Eight Queens problem	Grundy's game	path ply	static evaluator

Programming Problems/Projects

1. Implement a program that determines the number of possible Eight Queens configurations existing on a standard chessboard.
2. In Exercise 10.1.8 you were introduced to the Knight's Tour problem. Implement a program that searches for a knight's tour using the recursive brute-force strategy of Section 10.1. What is the time efficiency of this algorithm? Does your program find a solution to the knight's tour in a reasonable amount of time for an 8 by 8 chessboard? If not, what is the maximum board size for which your program is able to find a knight's tour solution on your computer?
3. Develop a heuristic to guide the choice of the knight chess piece as it searches for a valid knight's tour (see Problem 2). Develop a program that uses this heuristic in a best-first search for the Knight's Tour problem. Compare the performance of this program to the program you wrote for Problem 2. Is there a measurable increase in efficiency? If not, try adjusting the heuristic. Write up the results of your experimentation in a formal report.
4. In Exercise 10.1.7, you developed a Maze ADT. Now implement that ADT in a program that randomly generates mazes and then uses a recursive brute-force strategy to find a path through the maze. Experiment with the program to determine the types of mazes that the program is able to solve in a reasonable amount of time.

5. Retain the random maze generator you developed for Problem 4, but now develop one or more heuristics to find paths through the mazes generated. Using a best-first search that employs these heuristics, experiment with the heuristics you formulate. Write up the results of your experimentation to summarize the strengths and weaknesses of each heuristic. Include empirical evidence from runs of your program to substantiate your written conclusions.

6. In Problem 1 of Chapter 9 you implemented Dijkstra's shortest path algorithm using the Network ADT operations introduced in that chapter. Now modify that program to use the version of the shortest path algorithm that you formulated in your answer to Exercise 10.2.10. Which program (the one from Problem 1 of Chapter 9 or the new one) runs faster on the network of Figure 9.3? Can you find a network that reverses these results; that is, will the program that is slower on the network of Figure 9.3 run faster on your new network? If so, to what do you attribute this difference in performance? Develop some general criteria for the type of networks likely to be processed faster by each of these programs.

7. Develop a program that performs a best-first search for a path from the start node to the goal node in the network of Figure 10.7. Use your program to experiment with a variety of heuristics that guide the selection of nodes on this path. Include in your experimentation heuristics that weigh both the path length (that is, distance already covered) along with an estimate of the distance remaining to the goal node. Write up the results of your experimentation, including a discussion of which heuristics find the goal nodes fastest, which find the shortest path, and which produce a desirable blend of usually finding the shortest path in the least amount of time.

8. In Exercise 10.3.2 we described a generalized form of the game of Nim. Write a program that pits a computer against a human opponent in this game. The computer's moves should be guided by the minimax algorithm. Experiment with various heuristics and ply limits in this program. What heuristics seem to produce the best results in a reasonable amount of time?

9. Generalize the game of Fifteen described in Section 10.3 to a game in which two opponents alternately select different digits from among 1, 2, . . . , m, attempting to collect a combination of digits adding up to some specified n. Develop heuristics for this game and then implement those heuristics in a program that enables a computer to play a human opponent. In a written report, discuss the success (or lack thereof) of your program. What heuristics are most likely to lead to computer wins?

10. Write a computer program to play tic-tac-toe against a human opponent. Use the minimax algorithm with a variety of heuristics and ply limits. In a written report, discuss the level of tic-tac-toe expertise your program is able to attain. This report should include empirical evidence indicating the success your program has in defeating human opponents. Note that one way of viewing the game of tic-tac-toe is to assign the digits from 1 to 9 to board positions in the following pattern:

4	9	2
3	5	7
8	1	6

Then observe that playing tic-tac-toe is equivalent to playing the game of Fifteen as described in Section 10.3.

11. Modify any of the programs you developed for Problems 8, 9, or 10 to include the alpha-beta pruning technique described in Exercise 10.3.9. Given the time limits you establish for selecting a move in these games, to what extent does the alpha-beta technique allow you to search to a deeper ply? To what extent does this deeper search allow your program to play the game better?

12. Many of us have worked a sliding tile puzzle. In such a puzzle, there are 8 (or 15) numbered tiles in a 3 by 3 (or 4 by 4) grid. One grid position is unoccupied by a tile, so that tiles adjacent to that position can be moved into it. The object of the game is to manipulate the puzzle from its initial configuration into a specified final configuration. For instance, a series of moves to proceed from the following initial configuration (with X marking an unoccupied position) to the goal represents one possible way of "solving" the puzzle.

Initial Configuration

1	2	3
4	5	6
7	8	X

→

Goal

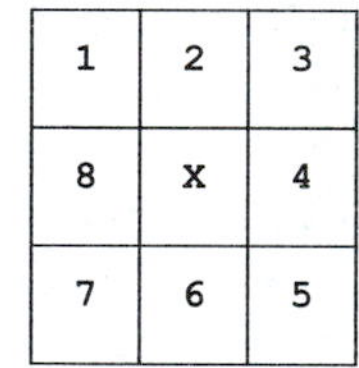

1	2	3
8	X	4
7	6	5

Develop a program that accepts an initial puzzle configuration and a goal arrangement for the tiles. Using a variety of heuristics, have your program search for a path to a particular goal using the best-first search strategy. Write up the results of experimenting with your program. This report should include a discussion of which heuristics proved most effective, whether the time limit you imposed on the computer's selection of a move allowed a 4 by 4 puzzle to be solved, and whether the heuristics you developed solved the puzzle with a path that included the minimum possible number of moves (as opposed to merely solving the puzzle by finding any path).

CHAPTER 11 Additional Search Strategies

He who would search for pearls must dive below.
John Dryden

Chapter Outline:

We have thus far studied a variety of structures and algorithms for maintaining and retrieving data items in an ordered fashion according to a precedence relation between the items. For instance, a linked list with sequential search capability is easy to implement and applicable to short lists, but limited in many practical situations by its $O(n)$ search efficiency. An array with binary search capability offers a much faster $O(\log_2 n)$ search efficiency but also has limitations. Foremost among these limitations are the need to maintain the array in physically contiguous order and the need to maintain a count of the number of records in the array. Both of these limitations are particularly restrictive for volatile arrays—that is, arrays in which additions and deletions are frequently made.

In Chapter 7 a binary search tree emerged as offering the best of both worlds. Additions and deletions can be done on a binary search tree by merely manipulating pointers instead of moving data, and an $O(\log_2 n)$ search efficiency can be achieved if the tree remains nearly full. Unfortunately, to guarantee that the tree remains nearly full and thus ensure the $O(\log_2 n)$ efficiency, height-balancing (see Section 7.6) is required. The complications involved in implementing this technique frequently dictate that it not be used. Essentially, you must weigh the significant cost in development time to implement a height-balanced tree against the risk that the order in which data arrive for insertion may cause search efficiency to deteriorate from $O(\log_2 n)$ to $O(n)$. If data items arrive in a relatively random order, then taking the risk may well be the prudent choice. In Chapter 8, a 2-3 tree was introduced as a means of maintaining data items arranged by a precedence relation. Although this technique guarantees $O(\log_2 n)$ search efficiency and $O(1)$ data interchanges for adds and deletes, it can be relatively inefficient in its use of space because many data records within the tree are potentially filled with an empty flag.

In this chapter we look at additional strategies for implementing retrieve, add, and remove operations on an ordered list. We begin with a lengthy section that further develops the idea of using trees to facilitate searching; in it we consider the advantages gained by moving from 2-3 trees to 2-3-4 trees and then from 2-3-4 trees to red-black trees. We conclude the section with a discussion of splay trees, which do not yield a worst case performance as efficient as that obtained from various balanced trees, but nevertheless, compare favorably with balanced trees when the efficiency of their operations is analyzed over sequences of such operations. They also employ simpler restructuring algorithms to achieve this level of performance. Should you wish to do so, Section 11.1 may be skipped without affecting your understanding of later sections.

The efficiency of all the search techniques considered up to this point and in Section 11.1 depends on the number of items in the data structure being searched. In Section 11.2 we study another search strategy called *hashing*. Its efficiency is contingent on the amount of storage you are willing to waste. Hashing can achieve phenomenally fast search times, regardless of how much data you have, provided that you can afford to keep a relatively large amount of unused space available. On the surface, the drawback to hashing would appear to be its inability to provide a means of traversing the data items in order. However, we find in Section 11.3 that combining hashing with linked lists allows us to overcome this deficiency. We also use Section 11.3 to see how variations on hashing can be used to implement the search operation for the String ADT.

We close the chapter by exploring some of the special considerations that enter into searching for data stored in a disk file instead of main memory. These considerations lead to a variety of search schemes, all of which employ some variations of a data structure known as an *index*.

11.1 Additional Tree-Based Search Techniques

2-3-4 Trees

We begin this section by generalizing 2-3 trees one more degree to allow for nodes with four children. Known as a *2-3-4 tree,* this type of tree offers an advantage over 2-3 trees in that insertions and deletions can be performed using one pass from the tree's root to a leaf, instead of requiring a root-to-leaf pass followed by a pass from the leaf back to the root. On the other hand, the overall storage requirements for a 2-3-4 tree increase because each node now has to accommodate three data fields and four pointer fields, not all of which will be used necessarily in each node in the tree; this means a potentially greater waste of storage than you have with 2-3 trees. It turns out, however, that a 2-3-4 tree can also be represented as a binary tree (known as a *red-black tree*), allowing us to allocate space more efficiently than in 2-3-4 trees while still retaining the simplicity of a single root-to-leaf pass for data insertion and deletion. We discuss red-black trees later in this section.

Formally, we can define a 2-3-4 tree as follows.

Definition: A *2-3-4 tree* consists of a general tree and a precedence relationship with the following properties:

1. Every node in the 2-3-4 tree has room for three informational fields. We call these fields **firstInfo**, **secondInfo**, and **thirdInfo**. Typically each such field represents a data record.
2. Every node in the 2-3-4 tree has room for four pointers to other nodes. We call these pointers **firstChild**, **secondChild**, **thirdChild**, and **fourthChild**.
3. Every node in the 2-3-4 tree has one of the following arrangements of data:
   a. **firstInfo** with active data, and **secondInfo** and **thirdInfo** with a special empty flag, which indicates that those fields have no active data. Such a node is called a *2-node*.
   b. The data in **firstInfo** preceding that in **secondInfo** according to the precedence relationship for the tree, and **thirdInfo** with the empty flag. Such a node is called a *3-node*.
   c. The data in **firstInfo** preceding that in **secondInfo** according to the precedence relationship and the data in **secondInfo** preceding that of **thirdInfo**. Such a node is called a *4-node*.
4. In any given nonleaf node:
   a. If the node is a 2-node, then all data in the subtree referenced by **firstChild** must precede **firstInfo**, and all data in the subtree referenced by **fourthChild** must follow **firstInfo** according to the precedence relationship for the tree. Note our convention here that the two subtrees of a 2-node are referenced by the **firstChild** and **fourthChild** pointer, respectively. We will see later that this is done to minimize data movement.
   b. If the node is a 3-node, then all data in the subtree referenced by **firstChild** must precede **firstInfo**; all data in the subtree referenced by **secondChild** must precede **secondInfo** and follow **firstInfo**; and all data in the subtree referenced by **fourthChild** must follow **secondInfo**. Note the convention that the three subtrees of a 3-node are referenced by the **first-**, **second-**, and **fourthChild** pointers in the node.
   c. If the node is a 4-node, then all data in the subtree referenced by **firstChild** must precede **firstInfo**; all data in the subtree referenced by **secondChild** must precede **secondInfo** and follow **firstInfo**; all data in the subtree referenced by **thirdChild** must precede **thirdInfo** and follow **secondInfo**; and all data in the subtree referenced by **fourthChild** must follow **thirdInfo**.

We can picture the structure of a 2-3-4 node as follows:

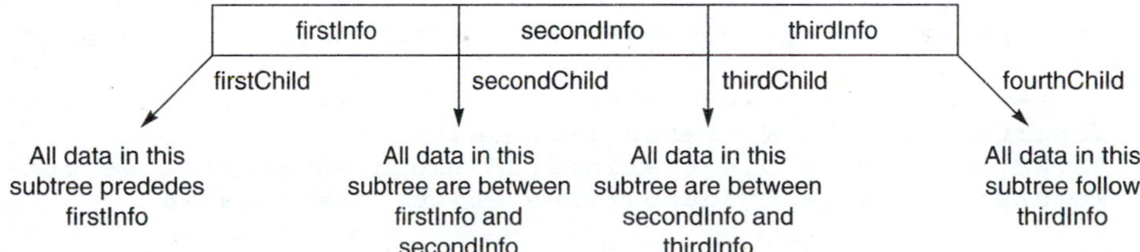

An example of a 2-3-4 tree with integer data fields is given in Figure 11.1. A public interface for a 2-3-4 tree class would appear very similar to the one we developed for 2-3 trees in Chapter 8.

Figure 11.1
Example of a 2-3-4 tree.

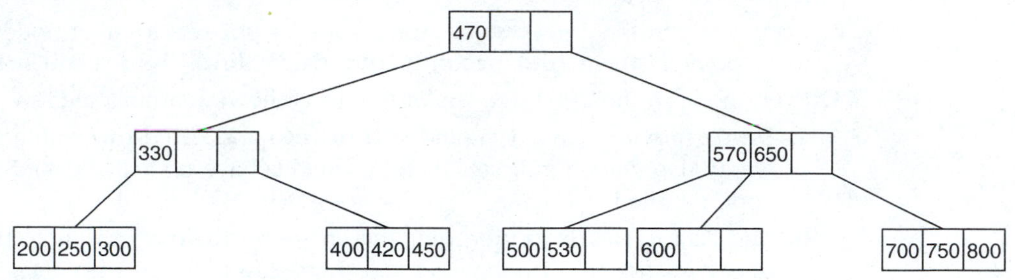


```
// BaseData is either a C++ built-in type, or a C++ class that has
// an assignment operation that overloads the "=" operator and an equality
// test that overloads the "==" operator.

template <class BaseData>
class TwoThreeFourTree
{
  public:
// -------------------------------------------------------------------------
// Interface for TwoThreeFourTree constructor
// GIVEN:    An uninitialized TwoThreeFourTree object;
//           precedes -- a function to compare BaseData values:
//             GIVEN:    x and y -- values to compare
//             RETURN as value of function:
//                       TRUE    if x precedes y,
//                       FALSE   if x and y are equal, or
//                               if y precedes x
// RETURN:   The TwoThreeFourTree object is initialized to the empty tree
//           with precedes establishing the hierarchical ordering of the
//           tree.

    TwoThreeFourTree(BOOLEAN (*precedes)(const BaseData &x, const BaseData &y));

// -------------------------------------------------------------------------
// Interface for TwoThreeFourTree copy constructor
// GIVEN:     An uninitialized TwoThreeFourTree object;
//            inittree -- a TwoThreeFourTree object that was previously
//                        constructed.
// RETURN:    The TwoThreeFourTree object is initialized with the node values
//            and number of nodes of inittree.

    TwoThreeFourTree(TwoThreeFourTree<BaseData> &inittree);

// -------------------------------------------------------------------------
// Interface for TwoThreeFourTree destructor
// GIVEN:     A previously allocated TwoThreeFourTree object
// RETURN:    The TwoThreeFourTree object deallocated

    ~TwoThreeFourTree();

// -------------------------------------------------------------------------
// Interface for TwoThreeFourTree assign = operator
// GIVEN:     A previously constructed TwoThreeFourTree object;
//            source -- a second TwoThreeFourTree object that must have
//                      been constructed with the same BaseData type as
//                      the owner of the assign operator.
```

```
// RETURN:   The contents of source have been copied to the
//           TwoThreeFourTree object that owns the operation.
// RETURN as value of function: void

    void operator = (const TwoThreeFourTree<BaseData> &source);

// --------------------------------------------------------------------
// Interface for add operation
// GIVEN:   A TwoThreeFourTree object;
//          item -- a value of type BaseData.
// RETURN:  item is added to the TwoThreeFourTree object in a fashion that
//          retains the ordering of the tree according to its precedes
//          relation.
// RETURN as value of function:
//           TRUE if item could be added to the TwoThreeFourTree;
//           FALSE if item was not added because it was already in
//           the tree.

    BOOLEAN add(const BaseData &item);

// --------------------------------------------------------------------
// Interface for search operation
// GIVEN:   A TwoThreeFourTree object;
//          target -- a value of type BaseData containing, perhaps in
//                    a special key field, a value to be searched for
//                    according to the equality test for the tree.
// RETURN:  item -- a value of type BaseData. If target can be found
//                  in the tree, item contains the entire contents of
//                  the tree node (key value and all associated data)
//                  that matches target.
// RETURN as value of function:
//           TRUE if target could be found in the TwoThreeFourTree;
//           FALSE if target is not in the tree.

    BOOLEAN search(const BaseData &target, BaseData &item);
};
```

Search Algorithm for 2-3-4 Trees The search algorithm for 2-3-4 trees is similar to those for ordered binary trees and 2-3 trees. We start at the root of the tree. A comparison of the target item to the informational fields indicates whether the target is in the current node or, based on the relationship of the target to **firstInfo**, **secondInfo**, and **thirdInfo**, which child pointer to follow. For instance, to find 600 in the tree of Figure 11.1:

1. Compare 600 to the value in **firstInfo**: 470. Since 600 follows 470 and since **secondInfo** is empty, we follow the **fourthChild** pointer from the root.
2. From the level-1 node containing 570 and 650, we follow the **secondChild** pointer because 600 is between 570 and 650.
3. At level 2 we find the target in the **firstInfo** field.

Suppose now that instead of 600 the search value was 610. Then our search would proceed as in steps 1 and 2, except that at the level-2 node, a comparison of 600 and 610 would show that 610 did not precede 600. On finding that **secondInfo** is empty, we begin a search of the subtree reached from the **fourthChild** pointer of the level-2 node. Since this is NULL, however, our search now terminates unsuccessfully.

Similar to our development of the **search** operation for 2-3 trees, the implementation of the **search** operation for 2-3-4 trees requires a constructor that initializes a **root** pointer for the tree to NULL and then assigns the **precedes** parameter of the constructor to a protected **precedes** function. This **precedes** member function is used thereafter to search and establish the hierarchical ordering of the tree.

```
// Establish the node class for 2-3-4 tree
template <class BaseData>
class TwoThreeFourNode
{
  public:
    BaseData firstInfo, secondInfo, thirdInfo;     // The data in the nodes
    TwoThreeFourNode *firstChild, *secondChild, *thirdChild, *fourthChild;
};

template <class BaseData>
class TwoThreeFourTree
{
  protected:
    TwoThreeFourNode<BaseData> *root;
    BOOLEAN (*precedes)(const BaseData &x, const BaseData &y);
   :
   :  // Other public class members defined as before
};

// Implementation of the TwoThreeFourTree constructor
template <class BaseData>
TwoThreeFourTree<BaseData>::
   TwoThreeFourTree(BOOLEAN (*precedes)(const BaseData &x, const BaseData &y))
{
  root = NULL;
  this->precedes = precedes;
}
```

The **search** function itself merely passes the **root** pointer for the tree to an auxiliary recursive workhorse, the **privSearch** function, which must be declared as a private member of the **TwoThreeFourTree** class.

```
template <class BaseData>
class TwoThreeFourTree
{
  private:

// ------------------------------------------------------------------------
// Interface for privSearch function
// GIVEN:     rt -- a pointer to root of TwoThreeFourTree;
//            target -- a value of type BaseData containing, perhaps in
//                      a special key field, a value to be searched for
//                      according to the equality test for the tree.
// RETURN:    item -- a value of type BaseData. If target can be found in the tree,
//                    item contains the entire contents of the tree node (key
//                    value and all associated data) that matches target.
//                    If target is not found, item is unreliable.
// RETURN as value of function:
//            TRUE if target could be found in the TwoThreeFourTree;
//            FALSE if target is not in the tree.

     BOOLEAN privSearch(TwoThreeFourNode<BaseData> *rt,
                        const BaseData &target, BaseData &item);
    :
    :  // Other class members defined as before

};

// Implementation of search and privSearch operations
```

```
template <class BaseData>
BOOLEAN TwoThreeFourTree<BaseData>::search(const BaseData &target, BaseData &item)

{
  // Just pass the root pointer to the recursive workhorse
  return(privSearch(root, target, item));
}

template <class BaseData>
BOOLEAN TwoThreeFourTree<BaseData>::privSearch(TwoThreeFourNode<BaseData> *rt,
                                               const BaseData &target,
                                               BaseData &item)

{
  if (rt == NULL)                      // target will not be in empty tree
    return(FALSE);
  if (target == rt->firstInfo)         // Check firstInfo's data
  {
    item = rt->firstInfo;
    return(TRUE);
  }
  if (precedes(target, rt->firstInfo))  // Recursively search 1st subtree
    return(privSearch(rt->firstChild, target, item));
  // If reach this point, target must follow rt->firstInfo,
  // so check to see if secondInfo is empty flag (that is, NULL)
  if (((int)(rt->secondInfo)) != NULL)
  {                                       // Then rt references a 3- or 4-node,
    if (target == rt->secondInfo)         // Check secondInfo's data
    {
      item = rt->secondInfo;
      return(TRUE);
    }
    if (precedes(target, rt->secondInfo))
      // Recursively search 2nd subtree of a 3- or 4-node
      return (privSearch(rt->secondChild, target, item));
    if (((int)(rt->thirdInfo)) != NULL)
    {                                     // Then rt references a 4-node,
      if (target == rt->thirdInfo)        // Check thirdInfo's data
      {
        item = rt->thirdInfo;
        return(TRUE);
      }
      if (precedes(target, rt->thirdInfo))
        // Recursively search 3rd subtree of a 4-node
        return (privSearch(rt->thirdChild, target, item));
      else  // Recursively search 4th subtree of a 4-node
        return (privSearch(rt->fourthChild, target, item));
    }
    else   // Recursively search third subtree of a 3-node, as referenced
      return (privSearch(rt->fourthChild, target, item)); // by fourthChild
  }
  else // Recursively search second subtree of a 2-node, as referenced
    return (privSearch(rt->fourthChild, target, item)); // by fourthChild
}
```

Search Efficiency for 2-3-4 Trees Suppose we had a 2-3-4 tree of height h, all of whose nodes are 2-nodes. Such a tree could hold a maximum of $2^{h+1} - 1$ data items. Similarly, if the tree contained only 4-nodes, the tree could hold a maximum of $4^{h+1} - 1$ data items. Thus, given a 2-3-4 tree storing N data items in a mixture of 2-, 3-, and 4-nodes, the height of the tree will be between $\log_4(N + 1) - 1$ and $\log_2(N + 1) - 1$. Consequently, searching in a 2-3-4 tree storing N data items will involve visiting no more than $\log_2(N + 1) - 1$ nodes, so 2-3-4 searching is $O(\log_2 N)$.

Add Algorithm for 2-3-4 Trees As noted in the opening remarks about 2-3-4 trees, one of their merits is that they allow insertions to be made with their structure preserved in one pass from the root to a leaf. The key insight permitting this is that, in the process of searching for the proper place to insert a data item, we "split" any 4-nodes we find along the way; that is, we form two additional 2-nodes and pass the data in **secondInfo** of the node being split to its parent. The newly formed 2-nodes are attached to the parent node via the proper child pointers and the value passed back to this parent is inserted in its proper place in the information fields. If the 4-node encountered is the tree's root, we handle the situation differently, creating two new nodes to be attached to the root.

Two other observations should be made:

1. Because we do this splitting as we are searching for a place to attach the node, the parent of a 4-node will always be a 2- or 3-node (and hence capable of holding the value being passed up to it from the 4-node). Also, because we make the split before advancing further in the tree, there will always be a leaf node available to hold the new data.
2. The manner in which 4-nodes are split and reattached to the tree allows it to remain "balanced," assuring that searches, as well as insertions and deletions, can be done in $O(\log_2 N)$ time.

Let us now examine the different situations that must be considered for splitting nodes and illustrate how they are handled.

A. The node to be split is the root of the 2-3-4 tree.

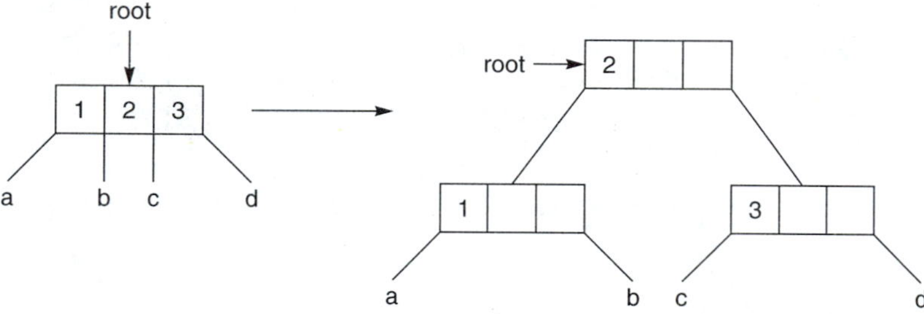

B. The parent of the node to be split is a 2-node. There are two subcases:

1. The 4-node is accessed by the **firstChild** pointer of the parent.

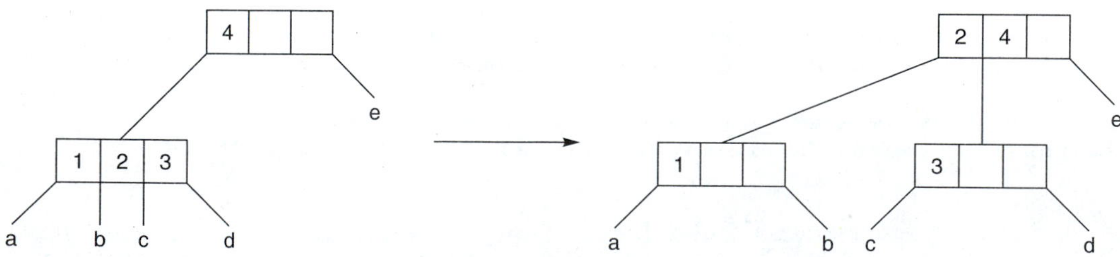

2. The 4-node is accessed by the **fourthChild** pointer of the parent.

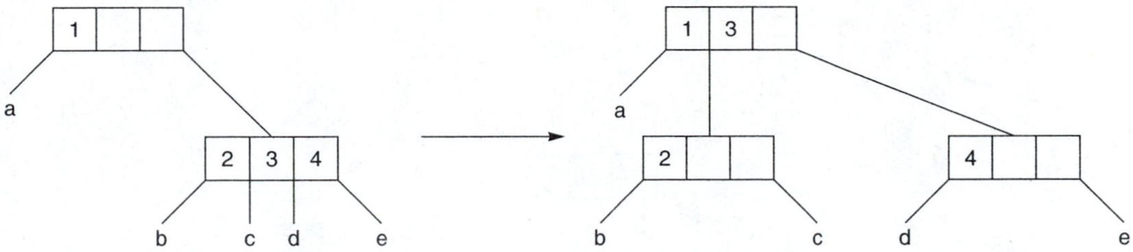

C. The parent of the node to be split is a 3-node. There are three subcases:

1. The 4-node is accessed by the **firstChild** pointer of the parent.

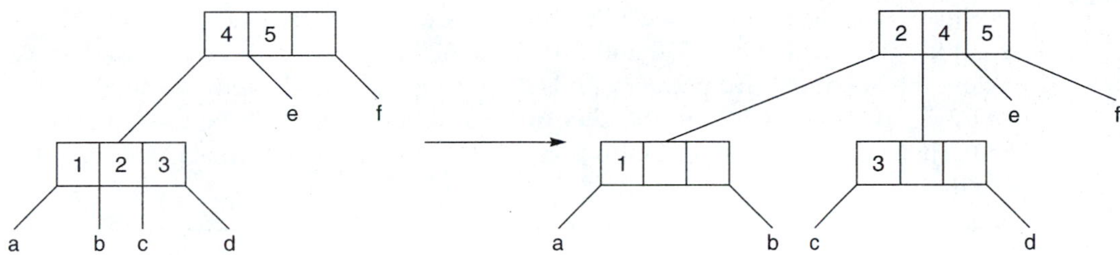

2. The 4-node is accessed by the **secondChild** pointer of the parent.

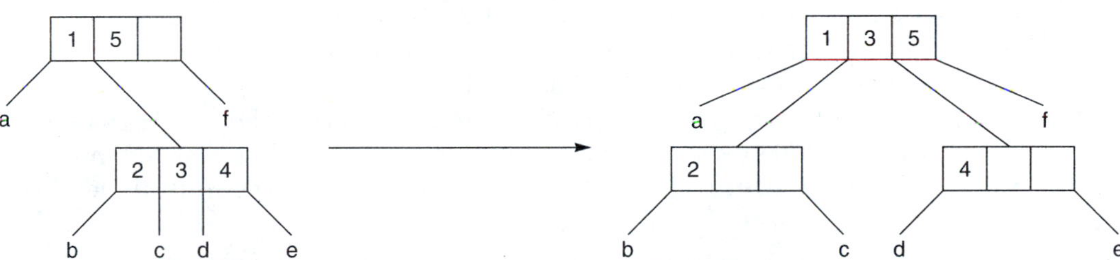

3. The 4-node is accessed by the **fourthChild** pointer of the parent.

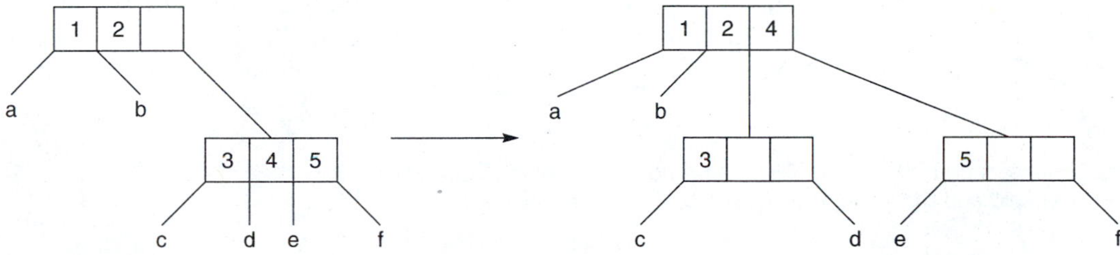

We now consider a few examples to show how these splittings work together.

Figure 11.2
Tree of Figure 11.1 after insertion of the value 620; no 4-nodes had to be split.

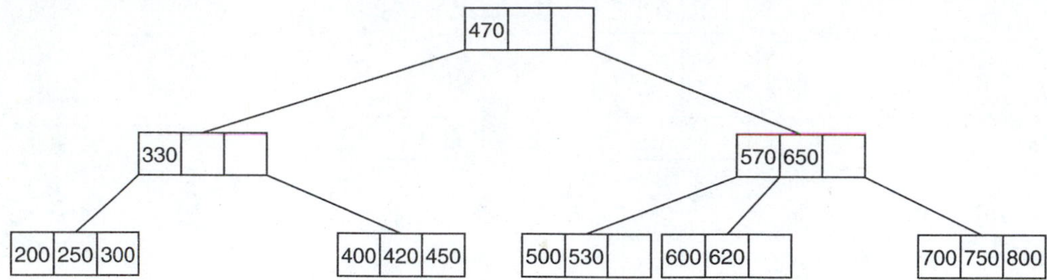

Example 11.1

Insert 620 as a data item in the tree of Figure 11.1.

Since 620 follows the value of the root node of our tree, 470, we advance to the node with data values 570 and 650. Since 620 is between these two values, we follow the **secondChild** pointer of this node to the leaf node with the single value 600. We now insert 620 into the **secondInfo** field of this node because it follows 600. The resulting tree appears in Figure 11.2. No nodes had to be split for this insertion.

Example 11.2

Add 790 to the 2-3-4 tree of Figure 11.2.

Our search proceeds as in Example 11.1, but this time at the level-1 node containing the values 570 and 650, we follow the **fourthChild** pointer since 790 follows 650. The next node we encounter is a 4-node. Since its parent is a 3-node, we are in the situation of case C.3. Splitting the node as described there, we obtain the tree in Figure 11.3. We now follow the **fourthChild** of the level-1 node with data values 570, 650, and 750 to the level-2 leaf node with value 800 and insert the value 790 in the **firstInfo** field, with 800 being moved to the **secondInfo** field. The resulting tree is shown in Figure 11.4.

Example 11.3

Add 270 to the 2-3-4 tree of Figure 11.4.

Because 270 precedes 470, our search takes us to the 2-node at level 1 containing the value 330. We then follow the **firstChild** pointer to the 4-node with values 200, 250, and 300. Since its parent is a 2-node, we are in the situation of case B.1.

Figure 11.3
Tree of Figure 11.2 prior to the insertion of the value 790. The 4-node with values 700, 750, and 800 in the Figure 11.2 tree was split and the value 750 passed to the parent node.

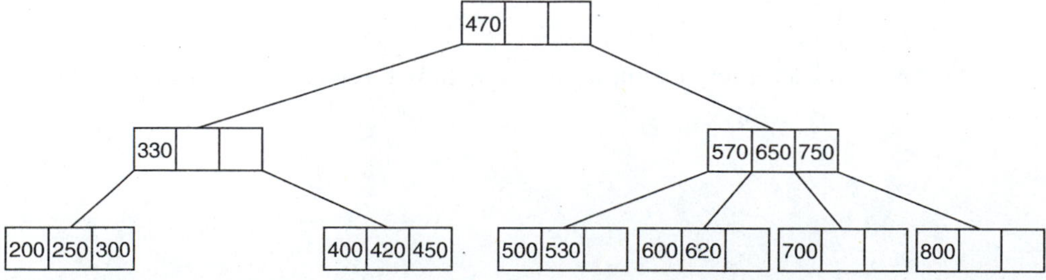

Figure 11.4
Tree of Figure 11.3 after insertion of the value 790. The value 800 was shifted from the **firstInfo** field to the **secondInfo** field and 790 inserted as the **firstInfo** value.

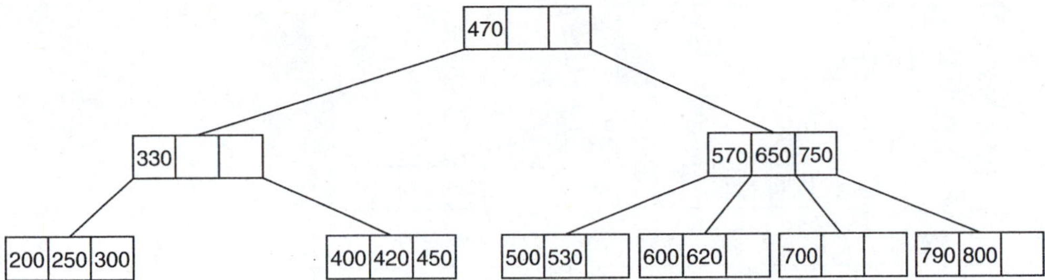

Splitting the node as described there, we obtain the tree in Figure 11.5. We now follow the **secondChild** of the level-1 node with data values 250 and 330 to the level-2 leaf node with value 300 and insert the value 270 in the **firstInfo** field, shifting 300 to the **secondInfo** field. The resulting tree is shown in Figure 11.6.

Figure 11.5
Tree of Figure 11.4 during insertion of the value 270. The 4-node with values 200, 250, and 300 in the Figure 11.4 tree was split and the value 250 was inserted in the parent node after the value 330 was shifted to the **secondInfo** field.

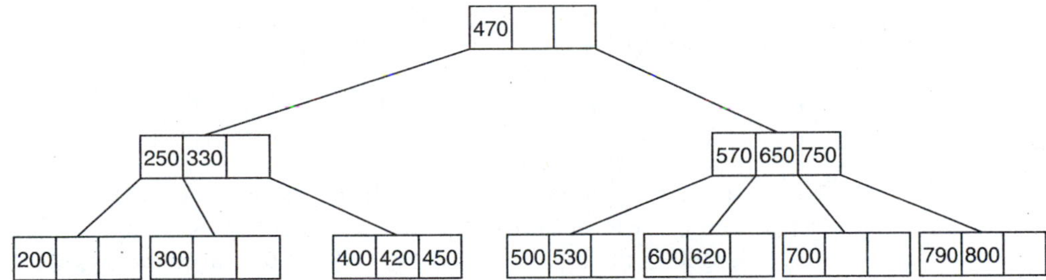

Figure 11.6
Tree of Figure 11.5 after insertion of the value 270. The value 300 was shifted from the **firstInfo** field to the **secondInfo** field and 270 inserted as the **firstInfo** value.

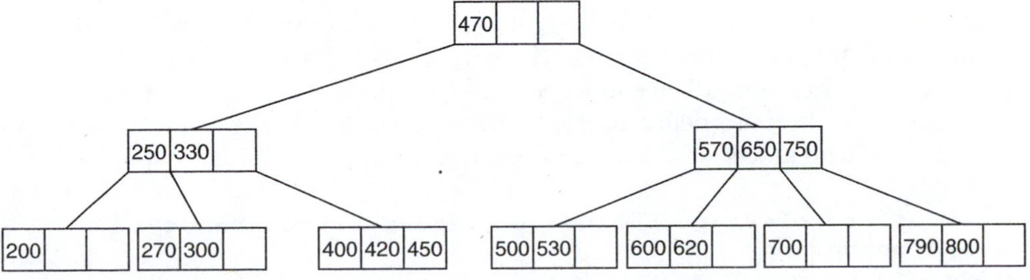

Figure 11.7
Tree of Figure 11.6 during insertion of the value 480. The 4-node with values 570, 650, and 750 in the Figure 11.6 tree was split and the value 650 inserted into the parent node (here the root of the tree) in the **secondInfo** field.

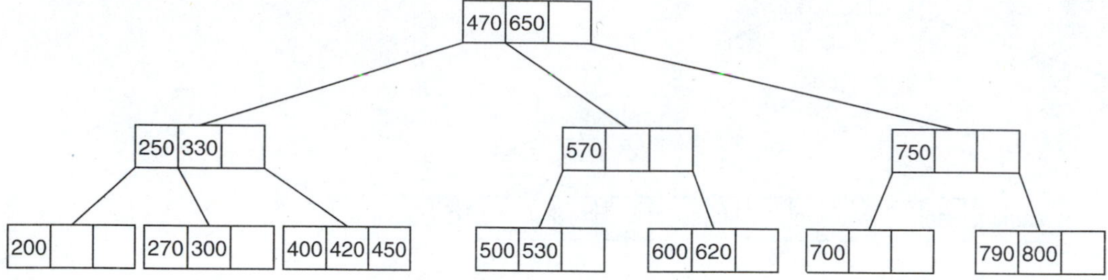

Figure 11.8
Tree of Figure 11.7 after insertion of the value 480. The values 500 and 530 were shifted from the **firstInfo** field and **secondInfo** field, respectively, to the **secondInfo** field and **thirdInfo** field, and 480 was inserted as the **firstInfo** value.

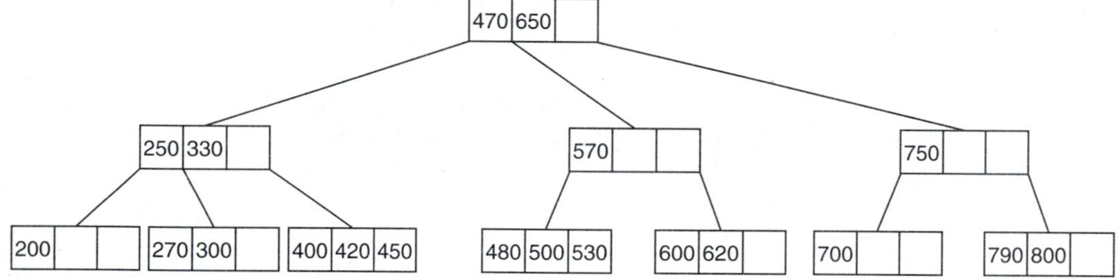

Example 11.4

Add 480 to the 2-3-4 tree of Figure 11.6.

This time at level 1 we encounter a 4-node with the values 570, 650, and 750. Since its parent is a 2-node, we are in the situation of case B.2. Splitting the node as described there, we obtain the tree in Figure 11.7. We now follow the **firstChild** of the level-1 node with data value 570 to the level-2 leaf node with values 500 and 530 and insert the value 480 in the **firstInfo** field, moving 500 to the **secondInfo** field and 530 to the **thirdInfo** field. The resulting tree is shown in Figure 11.8.

The following implementation of the **add** function for the **TwoThreeFourTree** class considers all the possibilities illustrated in Examples 11.1 through 11.4. The details of splitting a node are deferred to subordinate private functions **splitRoot**, **splitChildOf2**, and **splitChildOf3**. The specifications for these splitting functions, as well as other subordinate functions used by **add**, are given in the following expansion of the class definition for **TwoThreeFourTree**. The implementation of the subordinate functions is left for the exercises.

```
// Expansion of TwoThreeFourTree class to include private functions used
// in implementing the add operation
template <class BaseData>
class TwoThreeFourTree
{
  private:
```

```
// ----------------------------------------------------------------------
// Interface for splitRoot function
// GIVEN:    t -- a non-NULL pointer to a 2-3-4 tree node with
//                active data items.
// RETURN:   splitRoot will create two new 2-3-4 nodes and use
//           these to split the initial node into three nodes,
//           each with one active data item.  t will be returned
//           as a pointer to the root of a 2-3-4 subtree and will
//           have two children.

   void splitRoot(TwoThreeFourNode<BaseData> *&t);
```

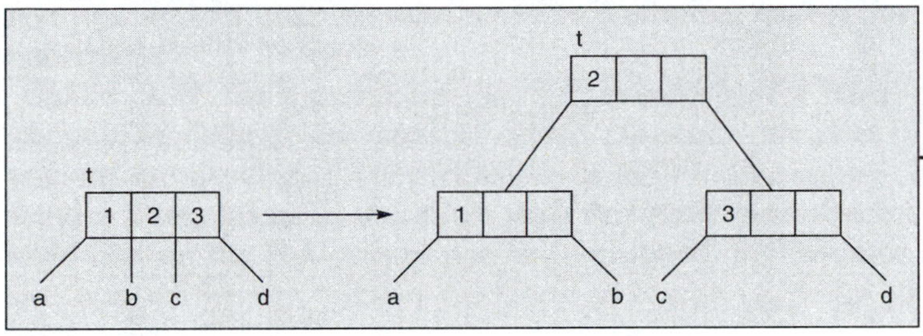

```
// ----------------------------------------------------------------------
// Interface for splitChildOf2 function
// GIVEN:    tree -- a pointer to a 2-3-4 tree 4-node (which stores
//                   three data values) and whose parent node, accessible
//                   through the pointer parent, has one data value.
// RETURN:   splitChildOf2 will split the node pointed to by tree into
//           two nodes, each of which will have one data value.  The
//           middle value will be promoted to the parent node.  Upon
//           return, tree will reference the same node as parent.

    void splitChildOf2(TwoThreeFourNode<BaseData> *&tree,
                       TwoThreeFourNode<BaseData> *parent);
```

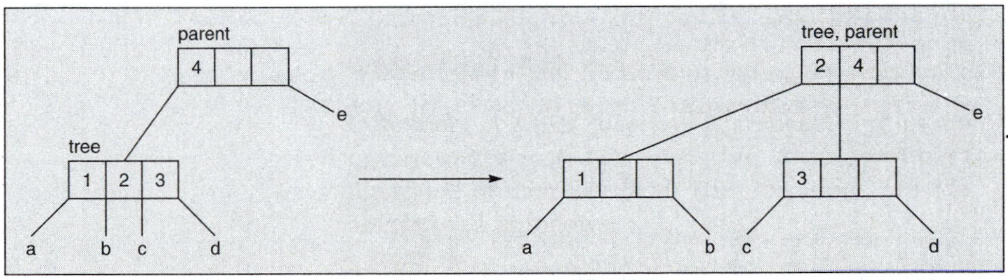

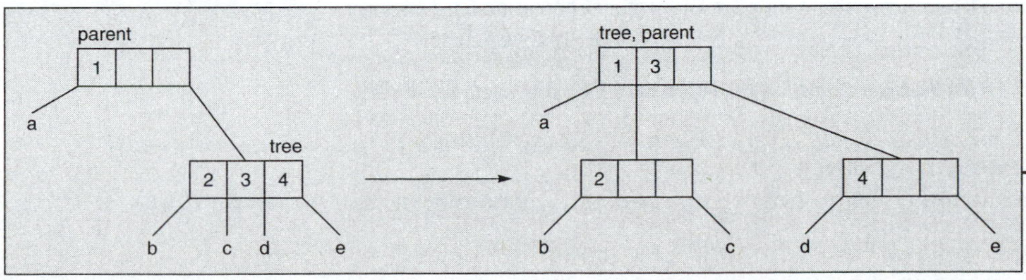

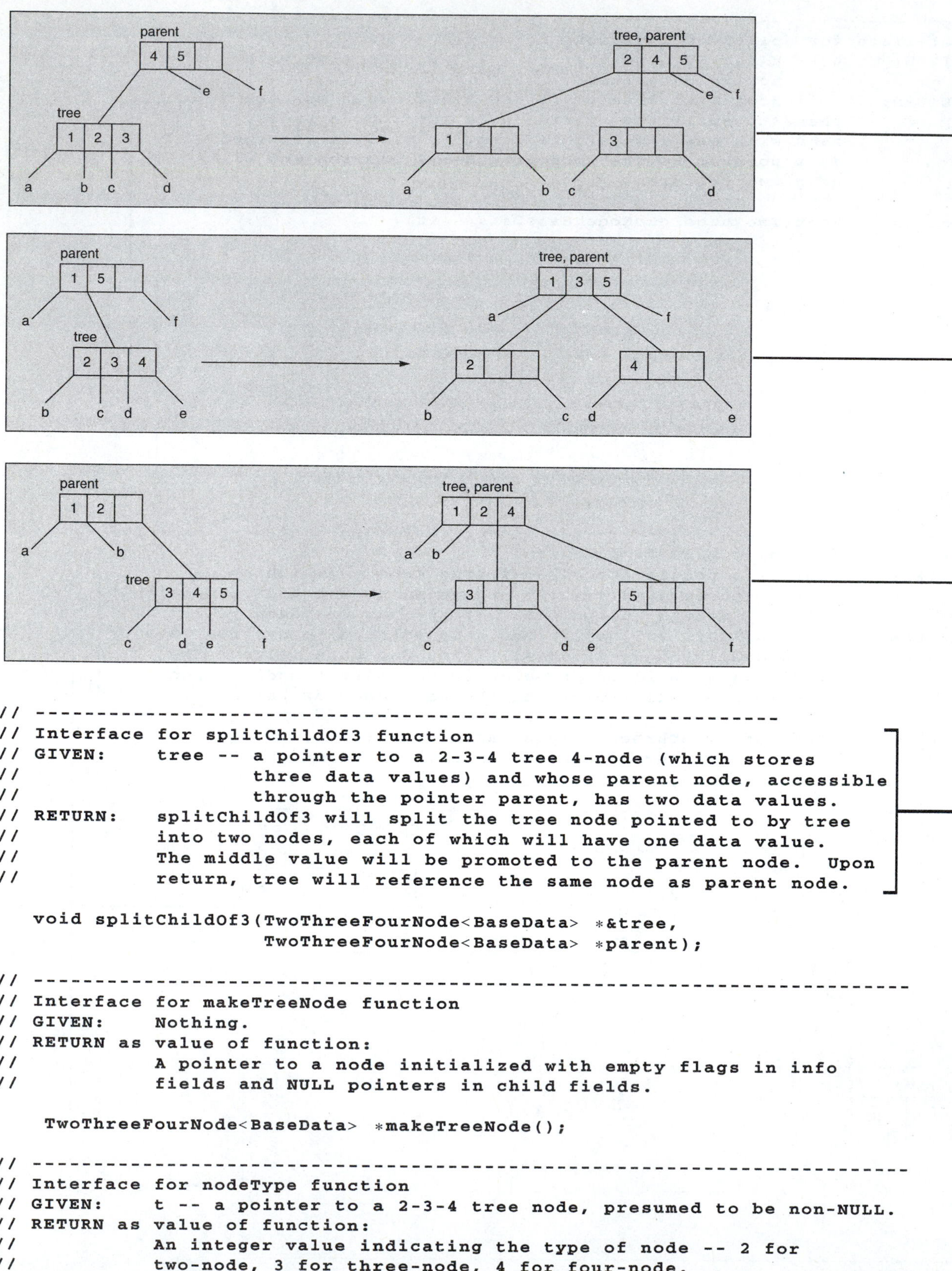


```
// ----------------------------------------------------------
// Interface for splitChildOf3 function
// GIVEN:    tree -- a pointer to a 2-3-4 tree 4-node (which stores
//                   three data values) and whose parent node, accessible
//                   through the pointer parent, has two data values.
// RETURN:   splitChildOf3 will split the tree node pointed to by tree
//           into two nodes, each of which will have one data value.
//           The middle value will be promoted to the parent node.  Upon
//           return, tree will reference the same node as parent node.

   void splitChildOf3(TwoThreeFourNode<BaseData> *&tree,
                      TwoThreeFourNode<BaseData> *parent);

// ------------------------------------------------------------------
// Interface for makeTreeNode function
// GIVEN:    Nothing.
// RETURN as value of function:
//           A pointer to a node initialized with empty flags in info
//           fields and NULL pointers in child fields.

    TwoThreeFourNode<BaseData> *makeTreeNode();

// ------------------------------------------------------------------
// Interface for nodeType function
// GIVEN:    t -- a pointer to a 2-3-4 tree node, presumed to be non-NULL.
// RETURN as value of function:
//           An integer value indicating the type of node -- 2 for
//           two-node, 3 for three-node, 4 for four-node.
```

```
    int nodeType(TwoThreeFourNode<BaseData> *t);

// ------------------------------------------------------------------------
// Interface for insertData function
// GIVEN:     t -- a pointer to a non-NULL 2-3-4 tree node.  Node referenced
//                by t is assumed to have values in one or two data fields;
//            newData -- a value to be inserted into the 2-3-4 tree node
//                       pointed to by t. It is assumed that newData is not
//                       already in the node.
// RETURN:    The node referenced by t will have newData inserted into a data
//            field of this node at an appropriate Info field, possibly
//            requiring that existing records be moved to make room.
// RETURN as value of function: void

    void insertData(TwoThreeFourNode<BaseData> *t, const BaseData &newData);

// ------------------------------------------------------------------------
// Interface for leafNode function
// GIVEN:     t -- a pointer to a 2-3-4 tree node.
// RETURN as value of function:
//            TRUE if the node is a leaf node; FALSE otherwise.

    BOOLEAN leafNode(TwoThreeFourNode<BaseData> *t);

// ------------------------------------------------------------------------
// Interface for whichChild function
// GIVEN:     t -- a pointer to a non-NULL 2-3-4 tree node;
//            data -- a value to be compared to the data items stored in
//                    node t.
// RETURN as value of function:
//            An integer value indicating whether the given data value
//            occurs in the current node or not. If a match, return the
//            value -1; if not, return the value 0 if the current node
//            is a leaf, otherwise return a value indicating which child
//            to follow to the appropriate next node where the data value
//            may occur. Here 1 implies firstChild, 2 implies secondChild,
//            3 implies thirdChild, 4 implies fourthChild.

    int whichChild(TwoThreeFourNode<BaseData> *t, const BaseData &data);
    :
    : // Other class members defined as before
};

// Implementation of add operation, given the preceding subordinate functions
template <class BaseData>
BOOLEAN TwoThreeFourTree<BaseData>::add(const BaseData &item)
{
  TwoThreeFourNode<BaseData> *p, *prev;
  int w;

  if (root == NULL)
  {
    root = makeTreeNode();
    root->firstInfo = item;
    return(TRUE);
  }
  if (nodeType(root) == 4)
    splitRoot(root);
  p = root;
  prev = NULL;    // prev is parent of p
  while (TRUE)    // Iterate until return exits loop
  {
```

```
    if (nodeType(p) == 4)
      if (nodeType(prev) == 2)
        splitChildOf2(p, prev);
      else
        splitChildOf3(p, prev);
    // After return from split function, p has been reset to its parent
    w = whichChild(p, item);
    switch (w)
    {
      case -1:          // item is already in the tree
        return(FALSE);
      case 0:           // p is a leaf node
        insertData(p, item);
        return(TRUE);
      case 1:           // Follow firstChild
        prev = p;
        p = p->firstChild;
        break;
      case 2:           // Follow secondChild
        prev = p;
        p = p->secondChild;
        break;
      case 3:           // Follow thirdChild
        prev = p;
        p = p->thirdChild;
        break;
      case 4:           // Follow fourthChild
        prev = p;
        p = p->fourthChild;
    }
  }  // while
}
```

Efficiency of Add for a 2-3-4 Tree For a 2-3-4 tree with N data elements, the **add** operation requires $O(\log_2 N)$ comparisons and splittings to reach the leaf where a new element can be added. Since the splittings themselves are $O(1)$, the efficiency of the **add** operation for a 2-3-4 tree is $O(\log_2 N)$.

Red-Black Trees

In our initial remarks on 2-3-4 trees we indicated that it was possible to represent any 2-3-4 tree with a binary tree known as a *red-black tree*. Such a representation will give us the worst case search efficiency of balanced search trees along with the economical storage utilization of binary trees. The price we pay for this is minimal: two additional Boolean fields, which we call **leftBlack** and **rightBlack,** to tell us if the child pointers of our binary tree node are being used (1) to represent child pointers from a 2-3-4 node or (2) to map a 2-3-4 node structure to its binary tree representation. Pointers used in the first sense are known as "black" pointers, and those used to map 2-3-4 nodes into binary tree nodes are known as "red" pointers.

In the following discussion on mapping 2-3-4 trees into a binary tree structure, we assume the following class definitions for a red-black tree and its associated nodes:

```
// BaseData is either a C++ built-in type, or a C++ class that has an
// assignment operation that overloads the "=" operator and an equality
// test that overloads the "==" operator.

template <class BaseData>
class RedBlackNode
```

```
{
  public:
    BaseData info;      // The data in the node
    RedBlackNode *leftChild, *rightChild;
    BOOLEAN leftBlack, rightBlack;
};

template <class BaseData>
class RedBlackTree
{
  protected:
    RedBlackNode<BaseData> *root;
    BOOLEAN (*precedes)(const BaseData &x, const BaseData &y);

  public:
// ------------------------------------------------------------------------
// Interface for RedBlackTree constructor
// GIVEN:   An uninitialized RedBlackTree object;
//          precedes -- a function to compare BaseData values:
//            GIVEN:   x and y -- values to compare
//            RETURN as value of function:
//                       TRUE    if x precedes y,
//                       FALSE   if x and y are equal, or
//                               if y precedes x
// RETURN:  The RedBlackTree object is initialized to the empty tree with
//          precedes establishing the hierarchical ordering of the tree.

    RedBlackTree(BOOLEAN (*precedes)(const BaseData &x, const BaseData &y));

// ------------------------------------------------------------------------
// Interface for RedBlackTree copy constructor
// GIVEN:    An uninitialized RedBlackTree object;
//           inittree -- RedBlackTree object that was previously
//                       constructed.
// RETURN:   The RedBlackTree object is initialized with the node values
//           and number of nodes of inittree.

    RedBlackTree(RedBlackTree<BaseData> &inittree);

// ------------------------------------------------------------------------
//  Interface for RedBlackTree destructor
//  GIVEN:    A previously allocated RedBlackTree object.
//  RETURN:   The RedBlackTree object deallocated.

     ~RedBlackTree() ;

// ------------------------------------------------------------------------
// Interface for RedBlackTree assign = operator
// GIVEN:   A previously constructed RedBlackTree object;
//          source -- a second RedBlackTree object that must have
//                    been constructed with the same BaseData type as
//                    the owner of the assign operator.
// RETURN:  The contents of source have been copied to the
//          RedBlackTree object that owns the operation.
// RETURN as value of function: void

    void operator = (const RedBlackTree<BaseData> &source);

// ------------------------------------------------------------------------
// Interface for add operation
// GIVEN:   A RedBlackTree object;
//          item -- a value of type BaseData.
```

```
// RETURN:   item is added to the RedBlackTree in a fashion that retains
//           the ordering of the tree according to its precedes relation.
// RETURN as value of function:
//            TRUE if item could be added to the RedBlackTree;
//            FALSE if item was not added because it was already in the tree.

    BOOLEAN add(const BaseData &item);

// ------------------------------------------------------------------------
// Interface for search operation
// GIVEN:    A RedBlackTree object;
//           target -- a value of type BaseData containing, perhaps in
//                     a special key field, a value to be searched for according
//                     to the equality test underlying the tree.
// RETURN:   If target can be found in the tree, item contains the entire contents
//           of the tree node (key value and all associated data)
//           that matches target.
// RETURN as value of function:
//            TRUE if target could be found in the RedBlackTree;
//            FALSE if target is not in the tree.

    BOOLEAN search(const BaseData &target, BaseData &item);
};
```

We consider separately the cases of 2-nodes, 3-nodes, and 4-nodes:

1. A 2-node, **p**, can be represented by a node **q** of type **RedBlackNode** that will have both of its color fields black (indicated in the following illustration by a solid line), **q→info** = **p→firstInfo, q→leftChild** = **p→firstChild,** and **q→rightChild** = **p→fourthChild.**

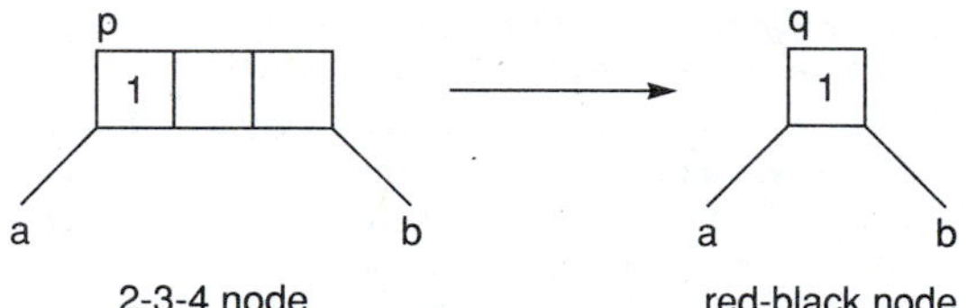

2. A 3-node, **p,** is represented by two nodes of type **RedBlackNode, q1** and **q2,** connected by a red pointer (represented in the following diagram by a broken line). This representation can be done in either of two ways. In the first form, known as a "left 3-node" (because the left child pointer uses a red link), we have
   - For **q1: q1→info** = **p→firstInfo, q1→leftChild** = **p→firstChild, q1→rightChild** = **p→secondChild, q1→leftBlack** = **TRUE,** and **q1→rightBlack** = **TRUE.**
   - For **q2: q2→info** = **p→secondInfo, q2→leftChild** = **q1, q2→rightChild** = **p→fourthChild, q2→leftBlack** = **FALSE,** and **q2→rightBlack** = **TRUE.**

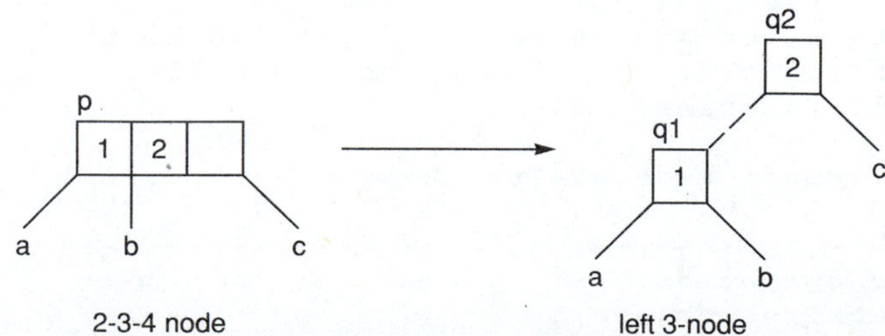

Alternatively, we have the following representation, known as a "right 3-node" because the right child pointer uses a red link:

- For **q1: q1→info** = **p→secondInfo, q1→leftChild** = **p→secondChild, q1→rightChild** = **p→fourthChild, q1→leftBlack** = **TRUE,** and **q1→rightBlack** = **TRUE.**
- For **q2: q2→info** = **p→firstInfo, q2→leftChild** = **p→firstChild, q2→rightChild** = **q1, q2→leftBlack** = **TRUE,** and **q2→rightBlack** = **FALSE.**

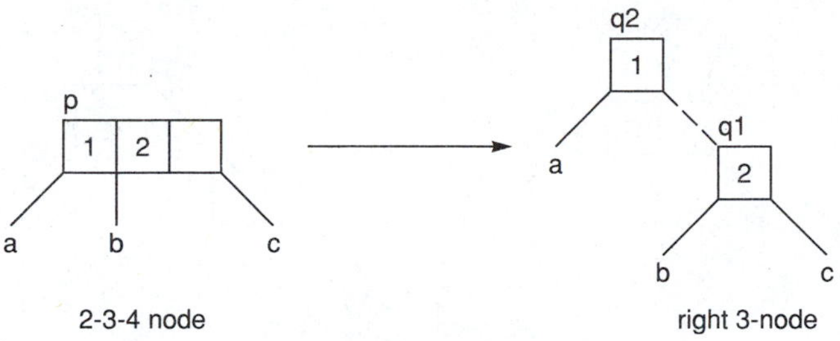

3. A 4-node, **p**, is represented by three nodes of type **RedBlackNode, q1, q2,** and **q3**, as follows:

- For **q1: q1→info** = **p→firstInfo, q1→leftChild** = **p→firstChild, q1→rightChild** = **p→secondChild, q1→leftBlack** = **TRUE,** and **q1→rightBlack** = **TRUE**.
- For **q2: q2→info** = **p→secondInfo, q2→leftChild** = **q1, q2→rightChild** = **q3, q2→leftBlack** = **FALSE,** and **q2→rightBlack** = **FALSE.**
- For **q3: q3→info** = **p→thirdInfo, q3→leftChild** = **p→thirdChild, q3→rightChild** = **p→fourthChild, q3→leftBlack** = **TRUE,** and **q3→rightBlack** = **TRUE.**

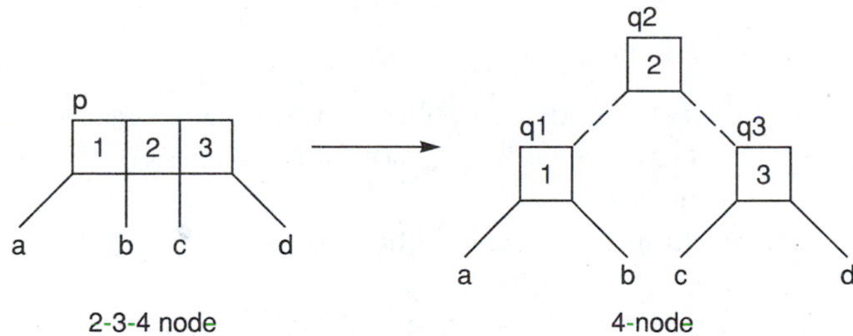

Search Algorithm for Red-Black Trees Since a red-black tree is a binary search tree, searches can be carried out using the same algorithm that was used for a binary tree search—the colors of the pointers never come into play.

Add Algorithm for Red-Black Trees A red-black tree is a representation of a 2-3-4 tree. Consequently, we can use the same fundamental algorithm to insert nodes into this tree that we used for adding nodes to a 2-3-4 tree. In particular, the splitting algorithms used for the insertion of a node into a 2-3-4 tree will be used here; we need only reformulate the algorithms in terms of left and right children and colors instead of **firstChild**, **secondChild**, and so on. As we shall see, in some cases, splitting a 4-node in a red-black tree is simpler than in 2-3-4 trees, involving nothing more than changing the colors of at most 3 links. To illustrate, let us review, pictorially, the different types of splits used in adding a node to a 2-3-4 tree and reformulate the before and after pictures of the splits in terms of red-black nodes in order to describe what must be done solely in red-black terms.

A. Splitting a root, **t**, which is a 4-node: In the case of a 2-3-4 node, we would represent the splitting as

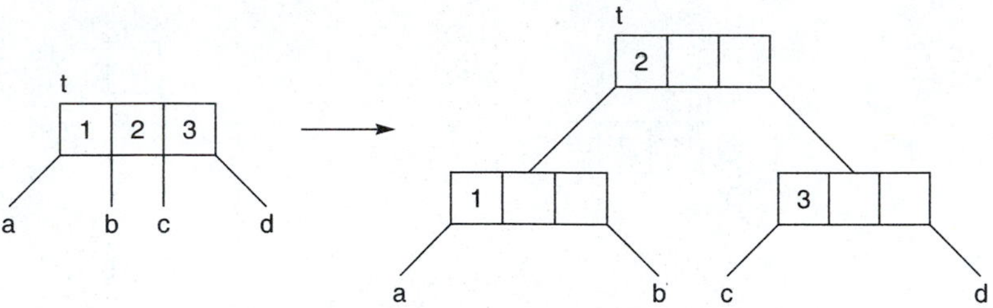

If we reformulate this diagram in terms of a red-black representation of the nodes, we get

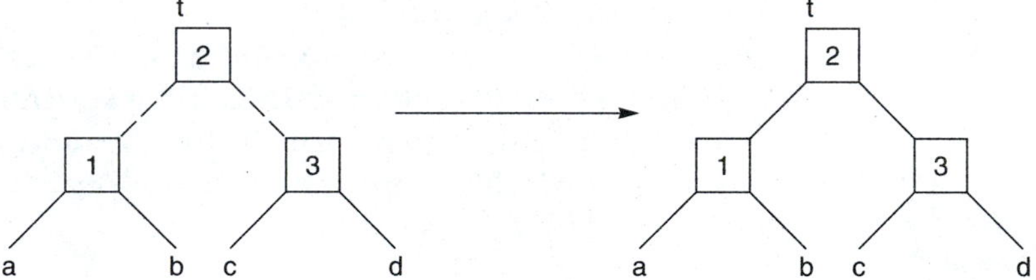

This shows us that splitting a red-black representation of a 4-node referenced by **t** involves nothing more than a change of colors (from red to black) of the pointers of **t**.

B. Splitting a 4-node, **t**, whose parent is a 2-node. Here we consider two subcases.

1. The 4-node is a first child of the 2-node. In the 2-3-4 case we represent the splitting as

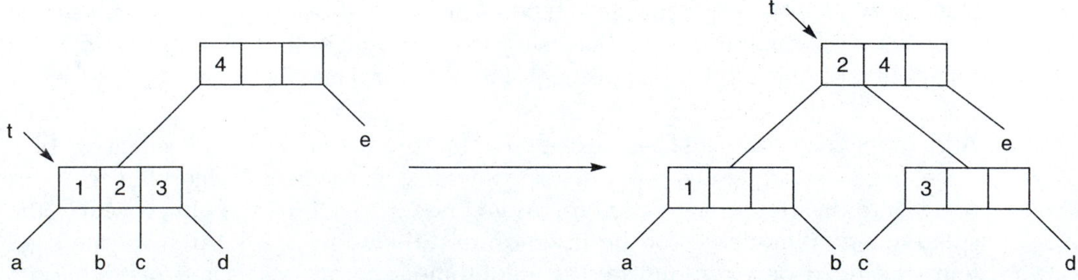

In terms of a red-black reformulation, this diagram becomes

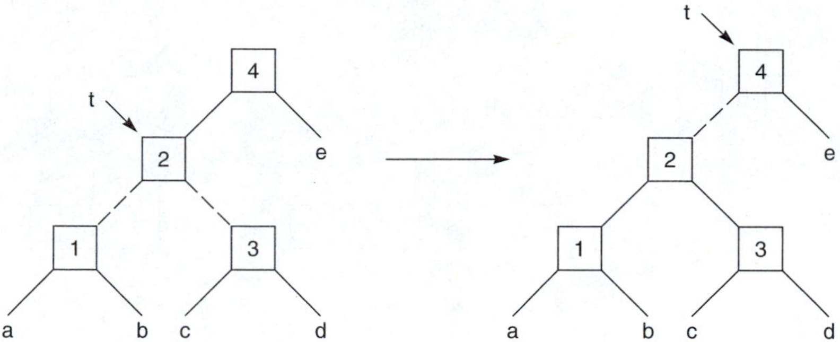

Here again, the only changes required were changes in the colors of the pointers of **t** and the left child of the parent of **t**; the pointer values themselves remain unaltered.

2. The 4-node is a fourth child of the 2-node. In the 2-3-4 case we represent the splitting as

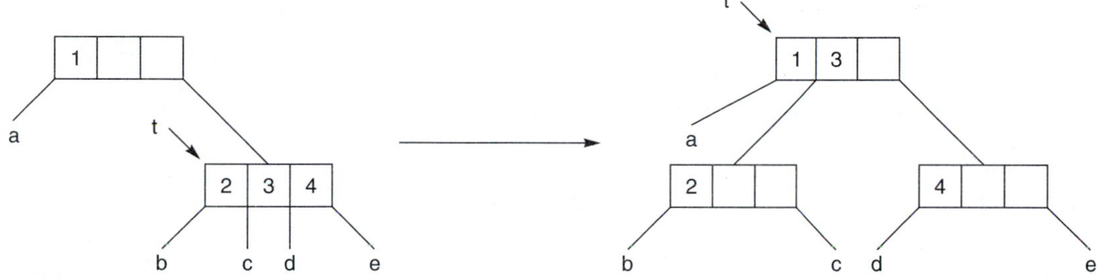

In terms of a red-black reformulation, this diagram becomes

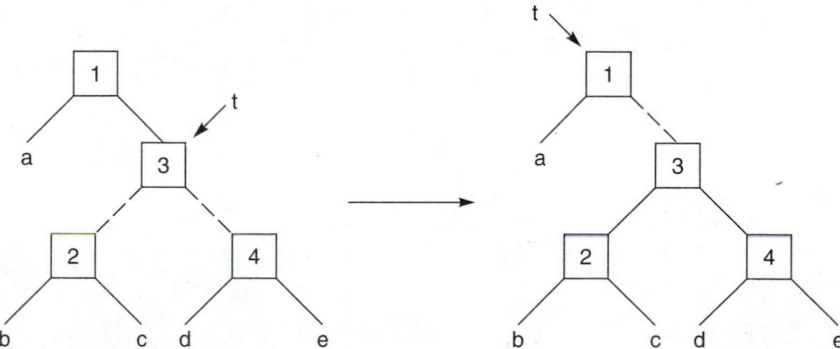

Again the only changes required were changes in the colors of the pointers of **t** and the right child of the parent of **t**.

C. Splitting a 4-node whose parent is a 3-node. Once more we have several subcases to consider.

1. The 4-node is the first child of the 3-node:
In the 2-3-4 case we represent the splitting as

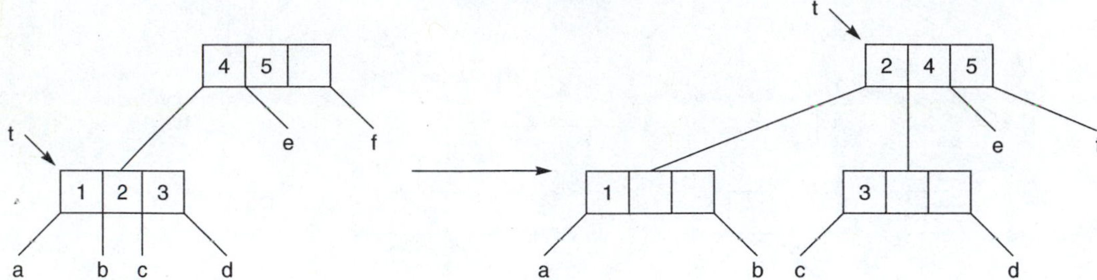

In terms of a red-black reformulation, we have two additional cases to consider. First we have the case where the 3-node is a left 3-node:

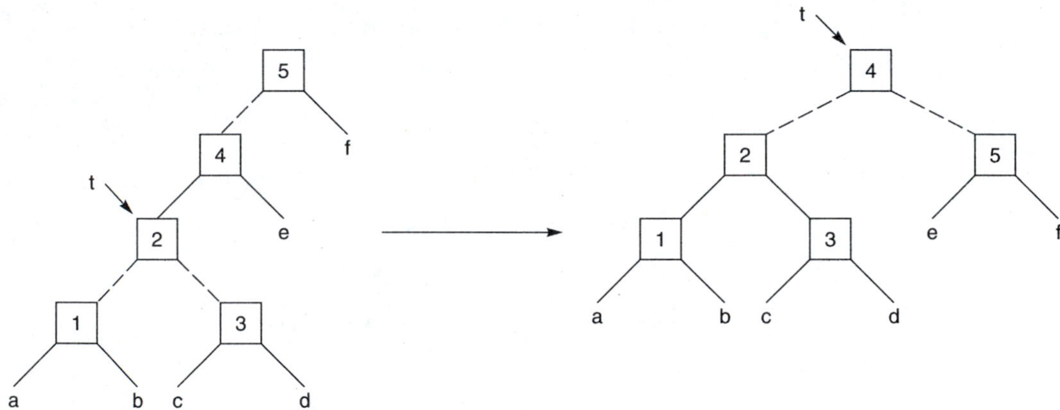

On the other hand, if the 3-node is represented using a right 3-node, the splitting would look like this:

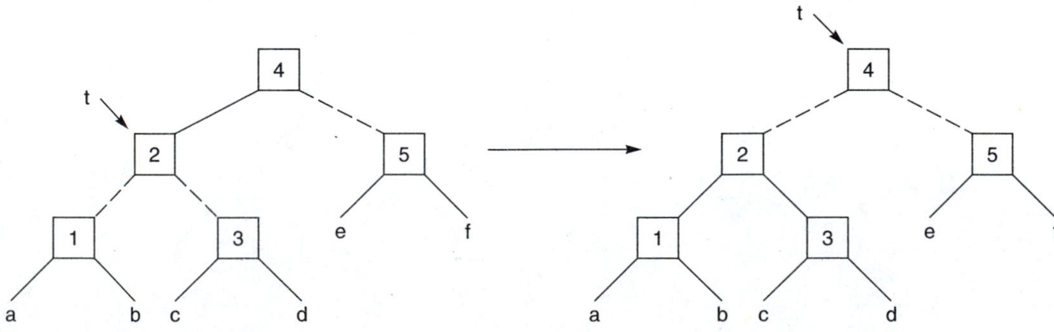

2. The 4-node is the second child of the 3-node. In the 2-3-4 case we represent the splitting as

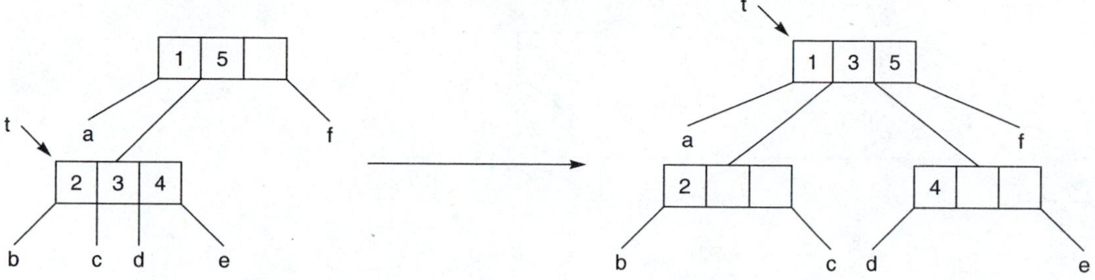

In terms of a red-black reformulation, we have two cases to consider. First we have the case where a left 3-node is used:

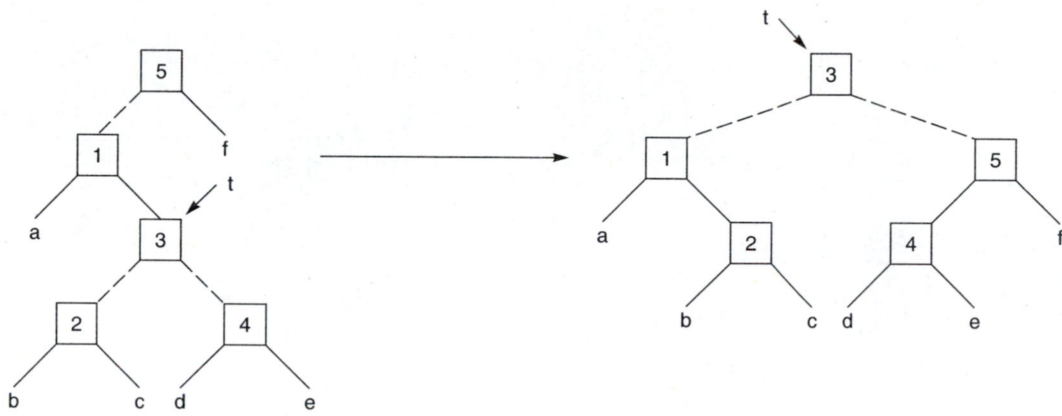

On the other hand, for a right 3-node the splitting would look like

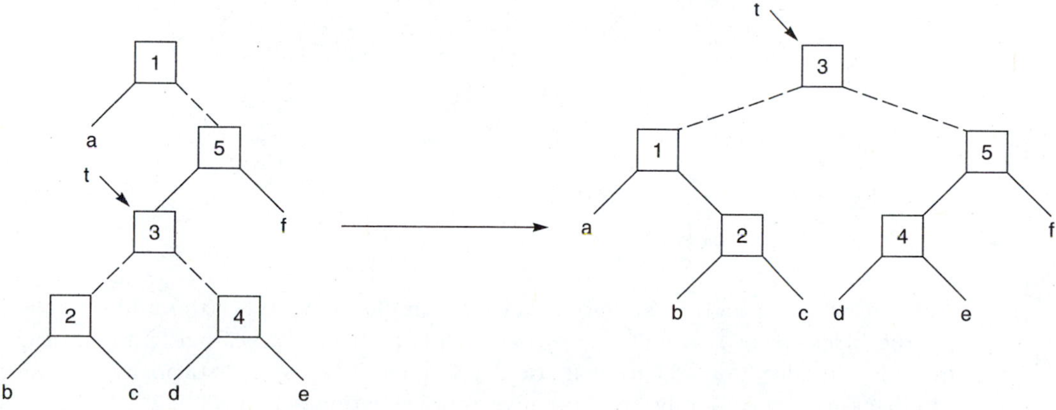

3. The 4-node is the fourth child of the 3-node. In the 2-3-4 case we represent the splitting as

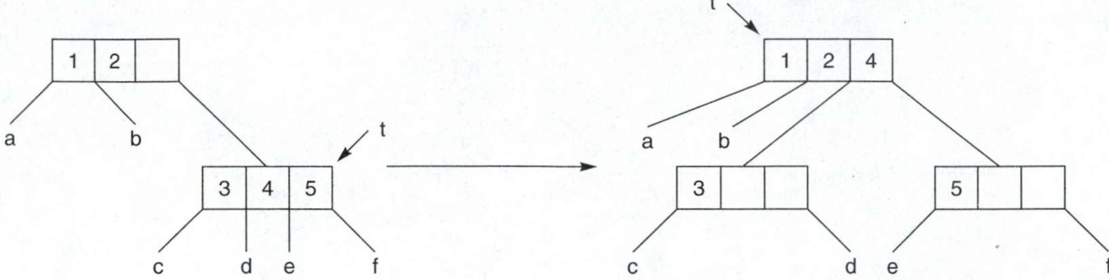

In terms of a red-black reformulation, we again have two cases to consider. In the case where the 3-node is represented using a left 3-node, we have

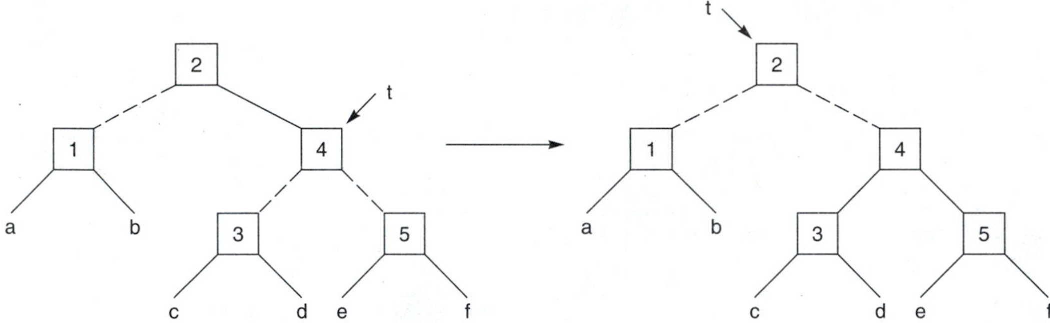

In this case only a change of some color indicators is required. On the other hand, if the 3-node is represented using a right 3-node, the splitting would look like

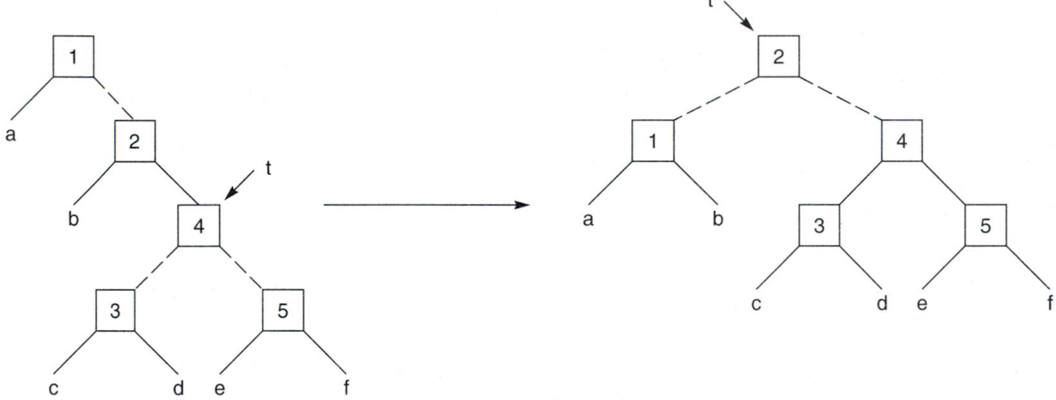

We now give a high-level algorithm for the implementation of the **add** operation for red-black-trees. You will notice that, at this high level, the logic for red-black-trees is virtually identical to that for 2-3-4 trees. This is not surprising because red-black-trees are merely an alternative representation scheme for 2-3-4 trees. As with our description of the **add** algorithm for 2-3-4 trees, we defer many details of the algorithm to a suite of private subordinate functions that are left for you to complete in the exercises. With the exception of the **advancePointers** function documented below, the specifications for the other subordinate functions would not change from what they were in the **TwoThreeFourTree** class. Note, however, that the **nodeType** function must now act in concert with the **advancePointers** function. Hence, it will have to distinguish right 3-nodes from left 3-nodes. The **advancePointers** function will then use the information returned by **nodeType** to move the **prev** and **p** pointers to the appropriate next tree nodes, taking into account complications caused by the mapping of a 2-3-4 node to a cluster of red-black nodes.

```
template <class BaseData>
class RedBlackTree
{
  private:
    // Internal auxiliary functions that, with the exception of advancePointers,
    // play the same roles that they did in the TwoThreeFourTree class

    void splitRoot(RedBlackNode<BaseData> *&t);
    void splitChildOf2(RedBlackNode<BaseData> *&tree,
                       RedBlackNode<BaseData> *parent);
    void splitChildOf3(RedBlackNode<BaseData> *&tree,
                       RedBlackNode<BaseData> *parent);
    RedBlackNode<BaseData> *makeTreeNode();
    int nodeType(RedBlackNode<BaseData> *t);
    void insertData(RedBlackNode<BaseData> *t, const BaseData &newData);
    BOOLEAN leafNode(RedBlackNode<BaseData> *t);
    int whichChild(RedBlackNode<BaseData> *t, const BaseData &data);

// -----------------------------------------------------------------------
// Interface for advancePointers function
// GIVEN:   current and previous --  pointers to tree nodes that will be
//                                   advanced;
//          next -- an integer indicator of which pointer to follow next,
//                  from a 2-3-4 tree perspective.  1 implies first child,
//                  2 second child, 3 third child, and 4 fourth child.
// RETURN:  The previous pointer points at what was the current node and the
//          current pointer points at the child indicated by the next
//          parameter.

    void advancePointers(RedBlackNode<BaseData> *&current,
                         RedBlackNode<BaseData> *&previous, int next);
    :
    : // All other class members defined as before
};

// Implementation of add operation, given the preceding subordinate functions
template <class BaseData>
BOOLEAN RedBlackTree<BaseData>::add(const BaseData &item)
{
  RedBlackNode<BaseData> *p, *prev;
  int w;

  if (root == NULL)            // Need to create a tree node
  {
    root = makeTreeNode();
    root->info = item;
    return(TRUE);
  }
  if (nodeType(root) == 4)     // Assume nodeType returns 4 for a 4-node
    splitRoot(root);
  p = root;
  prev = NULL;                 // prev is parent of p
  while (TRUE)                 // Iterate until return exits loop
```

```
// Descend in tree looking for a match with item or for a leaf where item
// can be inserted. Any 4-node encountered along the way is split in a
// manner dependent on the structure of its parent.
{
  if (nodeType(p) == 4)        // Assume nodeType returns 4 for 4-node
    if (nodeType(prev) == 2)   // Assume nodeType returns 2 for 2-node
      splitChildOf2(p, prev);
    else
      splitChildOf3(p, prev);
```

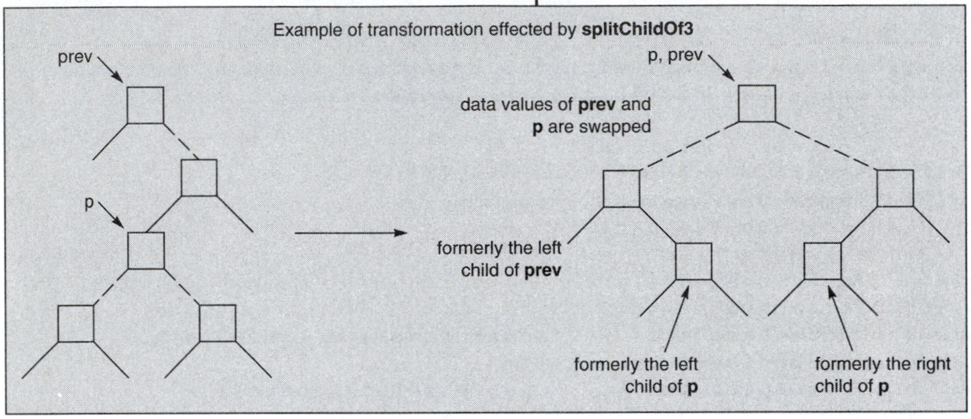

Example of transformation effected by **splitChildOf3**

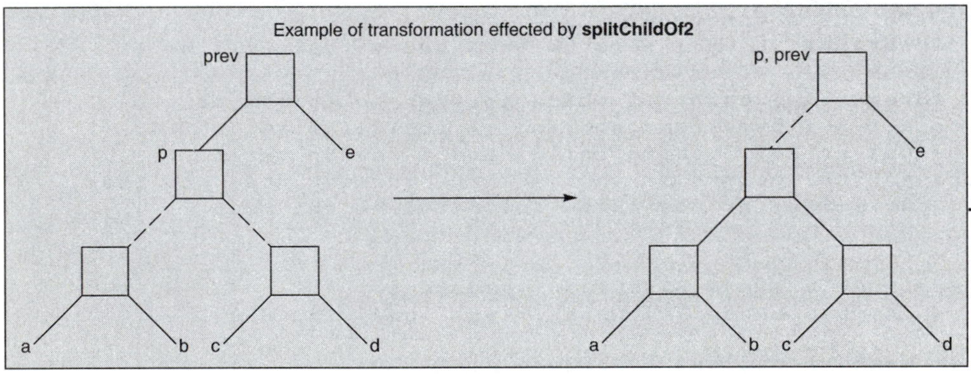

Example of transformation effected by **splitChildOf2**

```
  // After return from split function, p has been reset to its parent.
  // Assume that the following call to whichChild behaves as in the
  // earlier TwoThreeFourTree class; that is, return -1 for item
  // already in the node, 0 for a leaf node, 1 if first child pointer
  // is to be followed, 2 for a second child pointer, 3 for third child
  // pointer, and 4 for fourth child pointer.

  w = whichChild(p, item);
  switch (w)
  {
    case -1:         // item is already in the tree
      return(FALSE);
    case 0:          // p is a leaf node
      insertData(p, item);
      return(TRUE);
    case 1:          // Follow first child
    case 2:          // Follow second child
    case 3:          // Follow third child
    case 4:          // Follow fourth child
```

See the illustration at the top of page 491

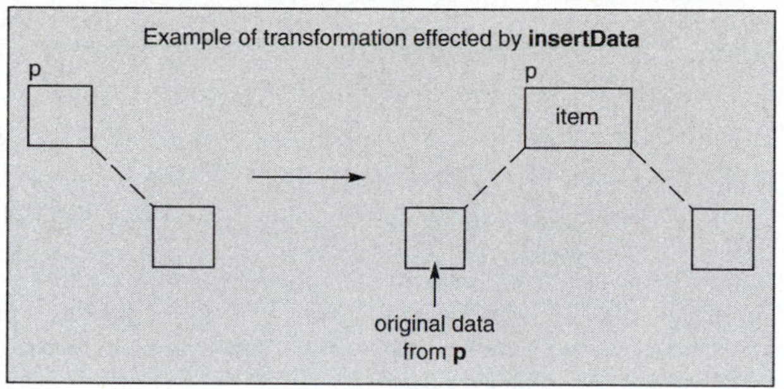


```
            advancePointers(p, prev, w);
        }  // switch
    }  // while
}
```

Efficiency of Search and Add Operations for Red-Black Trees Since red-black trees are simply binary tree representations of 2-3-4 trees, the search and add operations will have $O(\log_2 N)$ efficiency for a tree storing N data items.

Splay Trees

In our analyses of binary search tree operations—in particular searching and insertion—we determined that the use of balancing techniques can reduce the worst case times for these operations from $O(n)$ to $O(\log_2 n)$ for a tree with n data items. This reduction comes at a price, of course. First, the restructuring algorithms used to keep the trees balanced are somewhat complex. Second, additional storage is required in each node to accommodate the structure of the balanced trees, be it balance factors for AVL trees, multiple information and pointer fields for 2-3 and 2-3-4 trees, or pointer color information for red-black trees.

In this section we describe another type of binary search tree in which a **search, add,** or **remove** operation is carried out in exactly the same manner as for ordinary binary search trees, but in which these operations are followed by *splays*, which are sequences of rotations (called *splay rotations*) about nodes located between a given node and the tree's root. Their purpose is to move this given node—typically, one just accessed or one just inserted—to the root of the tree. At the same time the tree is restructured along the path from the root to the given node in such a way that, not only does the tree remain a binary search tree, but some of the nodes along this path may be moved closer to the root.

As we shall see, splay trees exchange the comparatively complex readjustments needed to maintain height-balanced binary search trees for simpler rotations. Although they may leave the tree with an overall structure that is suboptimal for carrying out efficient search and insertion operations, splay rotations readjust portions of the tree to improve the efficiency of future operations in those regions.

The rationale behind splay trees is that, in situations where a sequence of tree operations exhibits a phenomenon known as *locality of reference*, the time spent performing a splay rotation will be compensated for by improved performance in future operations involving the same data element. Locality of reference is exhibited when the references to data elements in a sequence of operations seem to favor a small subset of the data elements being referenced. Moreover, membership in this favored set may change gradually as one advances through the sequence of operations. In performing a splay after accessing or inserting a data element, one is anticipating that this same element will be frequently referenced in the near future. If that is the case, the additional time taken to move the element to the root and readjust the tree will in the long run become less detrimental because of the improved future access times. Thus, over an entire sequence of operations, the self-adjusting structure of the splay tree produces an overall efficient performance.

In our discussion of splay rotations and insertions into splay trees, we assume the following class definitions:

```
// BaseData is either a C++ built-in type, or a C++ class that has an
// assignment operation that overloads the "=" operator and an equality
// test that overloads the "==" operator.

template <class BaseData>
class SplayNode
{
  public:
    BaseData info;     // The data in the nodes
    SplayNode *leftChild, *rightChild, *parent;
};

template <class BaseData>
class SplayTree
{
  protected:
    SplayNode<BaseData> *root;
    BOOLEAN (*precedes)(const BaseData &x, const BaseData &y);

  public:
// -----------------------------------------------------------------------
// Interface for SplayTree constructor
// GIVEN:   An uninitialized SplayTree object;
//          precedes -- a function to compare BaseData values:
//            GIVEN:   x and y -- values to compare
//            RETURN as value of function:
//                     TRUE   if x precedes y,
//                     FALSE  if x and y are equal, or
//                            if y precedes x
// RETURN:  The SplayTree object is initialized to the empty tree with
//          precedes establishing the hierarchical ordering of the tree.

    SplayTree(BOOLEAN (*precedes)(const BaseData &x, const BaseData &y));

// -----------------------------------------------------------------------
// Interface for SplayTree copy constructor
// GIVEN:    An uninitialized SplayTree object;
//           inittree -- a SplayTree object that was previously constructed.
// RETURN:   The SplayTree object initialized with the node values and number
//           of nodes of inittree.

    SplayTree(SplayTree<BaseData> &inittree);

// -----------------------------------------------------------------------
// Interface for SplayTree destructor
// GIVEN:    A previously allocated SplayTree object.
// RETURN:   The SplayTree object deallocated.

    ~SplayTree();

// -----------------------------------------------------------------------
// Interface for SplayTree assign = operator
// GIVEN:    A previously constructed SplayTree object;
```

```
//             source -- a second SplayTree object that must have been
//                       constructed with the same BaseData type as the
//                       owner of the assign operator.
// RETURN:     The contents of source have been copied to the SplayTree
//             object that owns the operation.
// RETURN as value of function: void

   void operator = (const SplayTree<BaseData> &source);

// ------------------------------------------------------------------------
// Interface for add operation
// GIVEN:      A SplayTree object;
//             item -- a value of type BaseData.
// RETURN:     item is added to the SplayTree in a fashion that retains the
//             ordering of the tree according to its precedes relation
// RETURN as value of function:
//             TRUE if item could be added to the SplayTree;
//             FALSE if item was not added because it was already in the tree.

   BOOLEAN add(const BaseData &item);

// ------------------------------------------------------------------------
// Interface for search operation
// GIVEN:      A SplayTree object;
//             target -- a value of type BaseData containing, perhaps in a
//                       special key field, a value to be searched for
//                       according to the precedes relationship underlying
//                       the tree.
// RETURN:     item -- a value of type BaseData. If target can be found in the
//                     tree, item contains the entire contents of the tree node
//                     (key value and all associated data) that matches target.
// RETURN as value of function:
//             TRUE if target could be found in the SplayTree;
//             FALSE if target is not in the tree.

   BOOLEAN search(const BaseData &target, BaseData &item);
};
```

The inclusion of the **parent** pointer in a splay node will assist us in readjusting the tree along the path backward from a given node to the tree's root.

We describe six types of splay rotations, each of which is designed to move a given node, **t**, to the root of a particular subtree. Successive rotations will then enable **t** to be advanced to the root of the entire splay tree.

A. The first type of splay rotation, known as an *L rotation*, is used when node **t** is a left child of the root of the splay tree; it makes **t** the root.

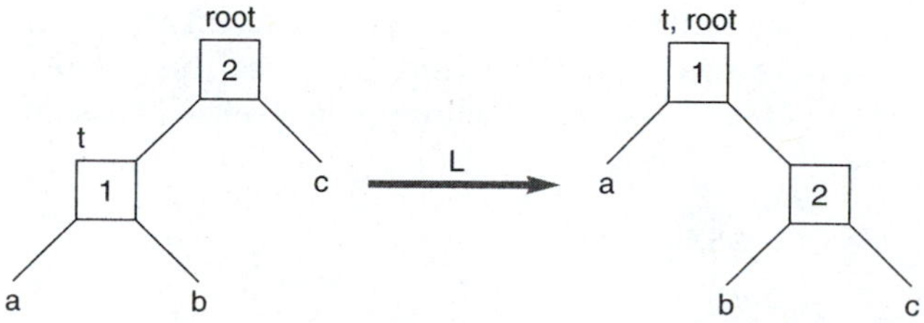

In our implementation, the L rotation will be performed via the following sequence of pointer transfers:

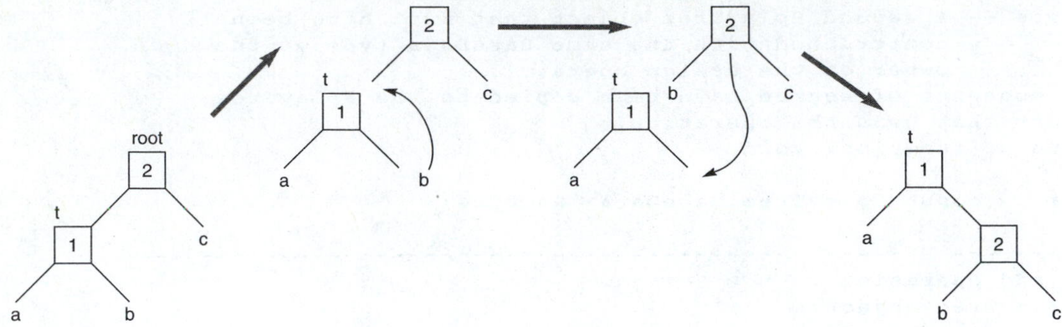

B. Symmetric to the L rotation is the *R rotation*, which moves the right child of the tree's root so that it becomes the new root.

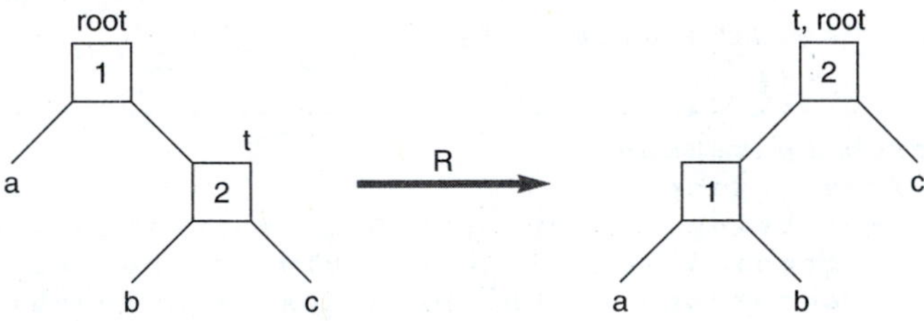

Its implementation is similar to that of the L rotation:

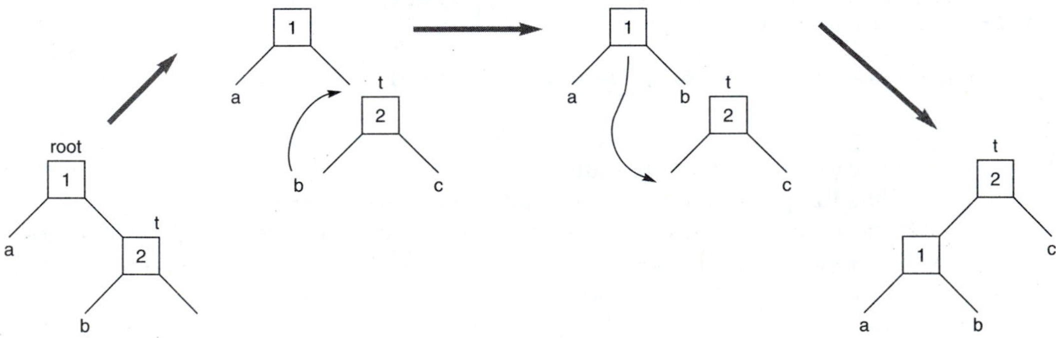

C. The next rotation is the first of the double rotations. All are intended to move a given node **t** two levels higher in the tree. The rotation we show here is known as an *LL rotation* because the given node is the left child of the left child of the node whose position it will assume.

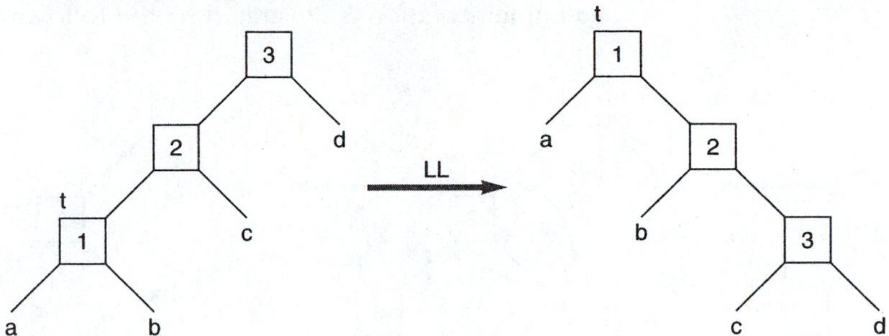

Its implementation will be carried out via the following sequence of pointer transfers:

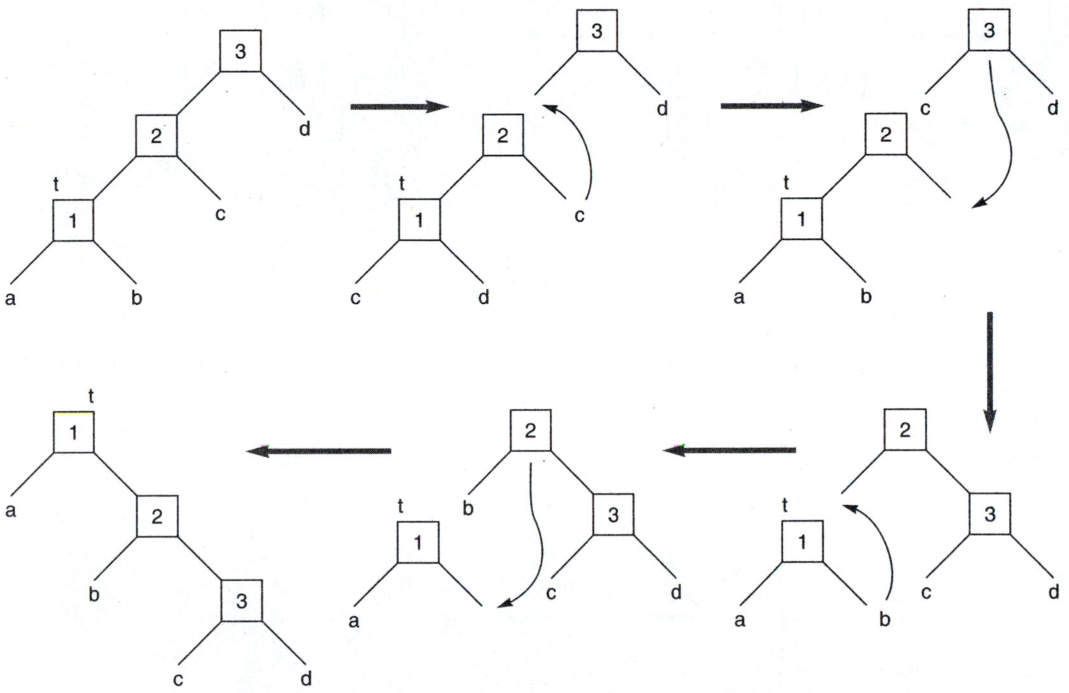

D. Symmetric to the LL rotation is the *RR rotation*.

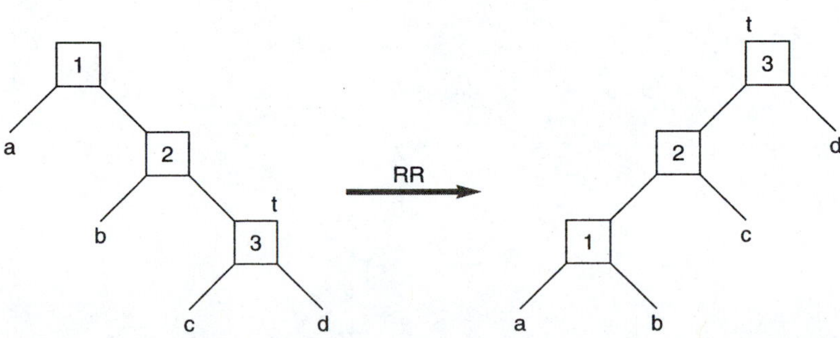

Its implementation is illustrated by the following diagram:

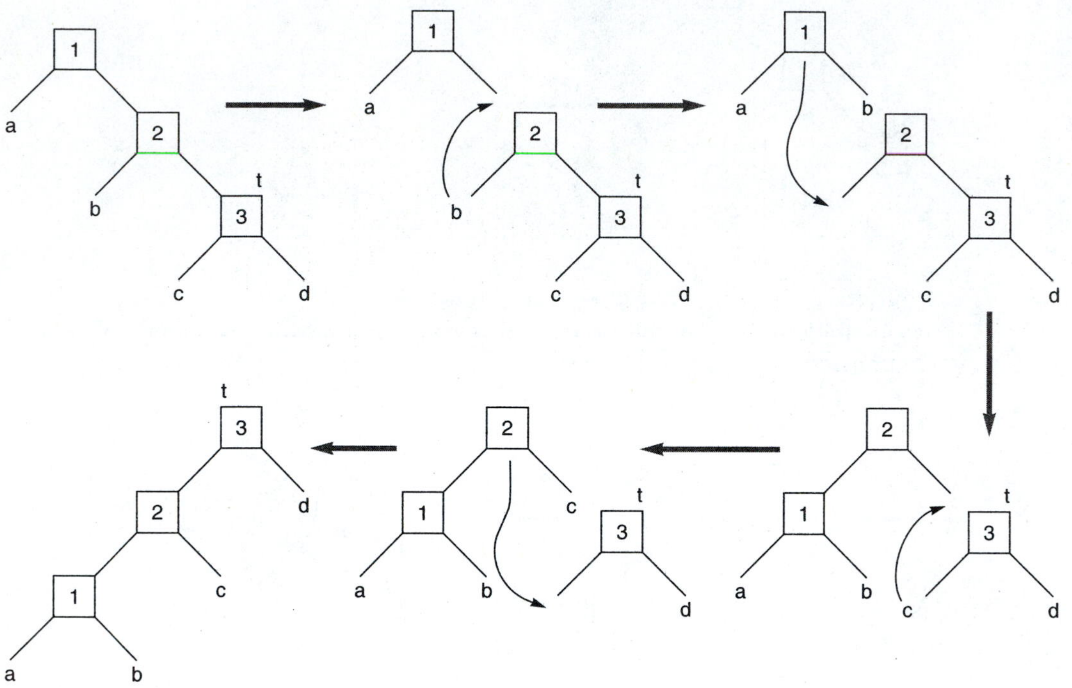

E. Our next rotation is the first of the two "zig-zag" rotations, and is labeled the *LR rotation*.

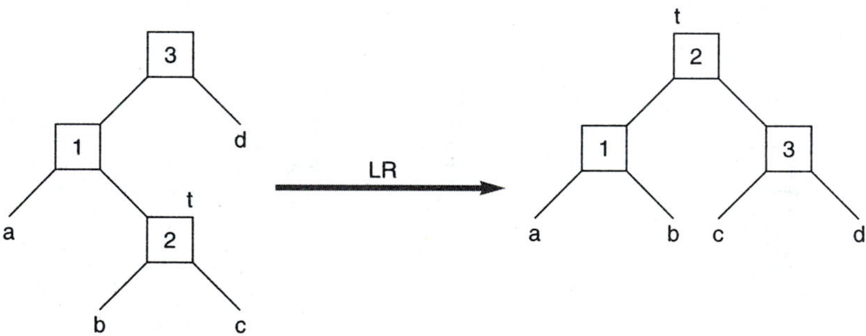

Its implementation, more complex than the others, can be illustrated as follows:

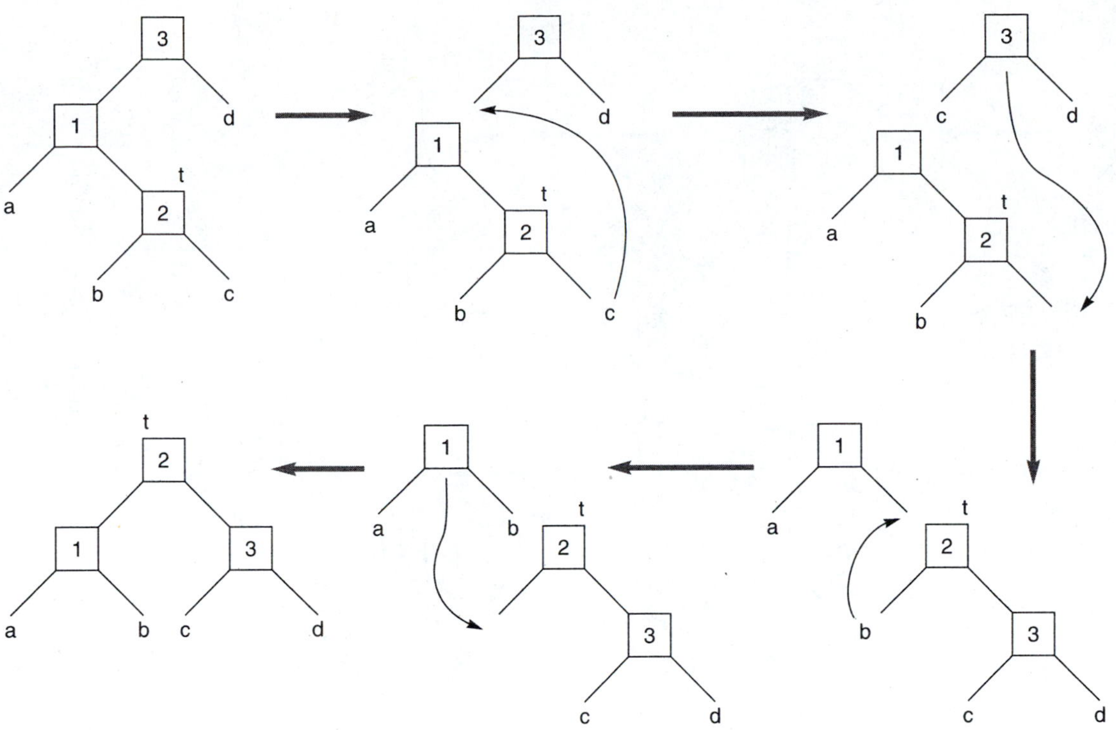

F. Our last rotation is the second of the "zig-zag" rotations, the *RL rotation*.

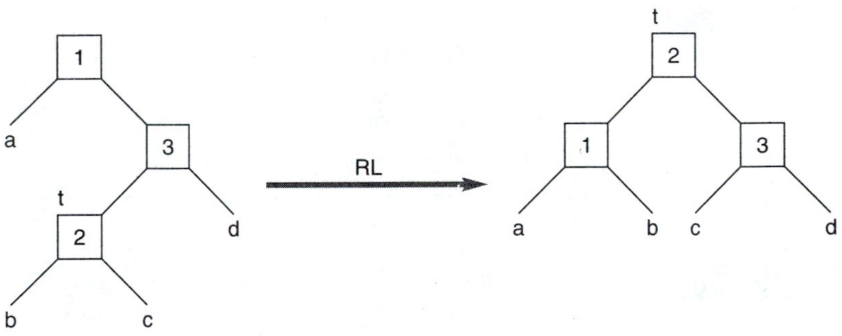

Its implementation is, of course, similar to that of the LR rotation:

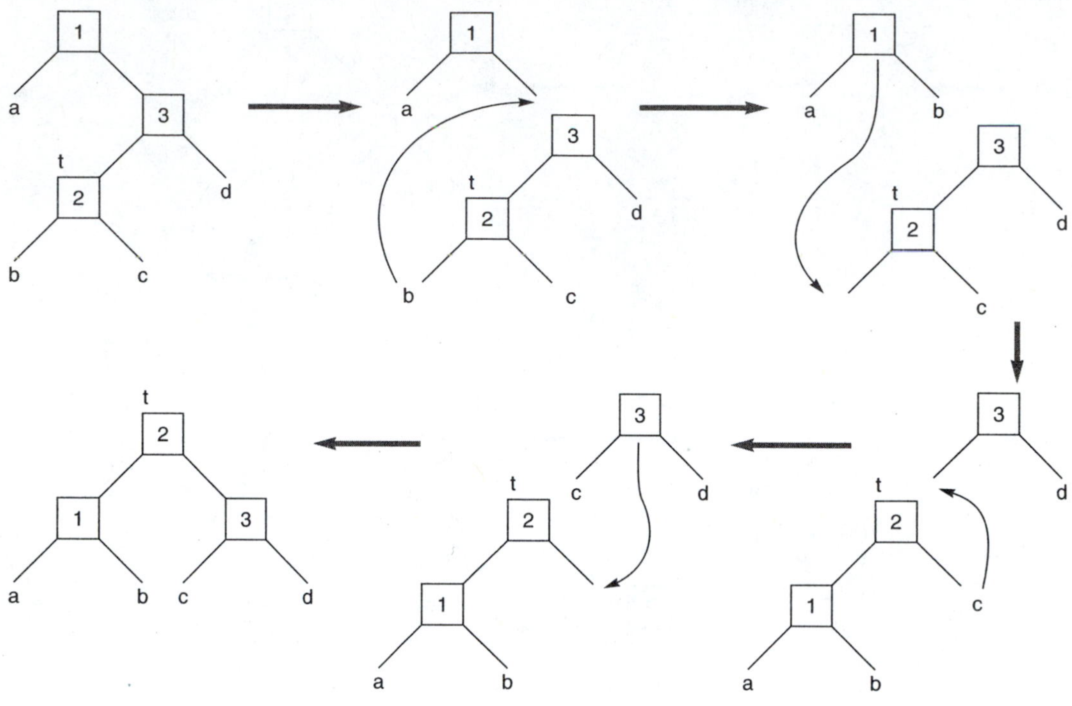

Before proceeding to the algorithms for searching a splay tree or inserting a node in one, we illustrate the behavior of a splay with some examples.

Example 11.5

Insert the value 55 into the splay tree of Figure 11.9.

Following the usual algorithm for inserting a value in a binary search tree, we insert the value in node **t** as shown in Figure 11.10. Performing an LR rotation at **t**, we obtain the tree of Figure 11.11. Executing an R rotation at **t** will then move 55 to the root, completing our splay and giving us the tree of Figure 11.12.

Example 11.6

Insert the value 90 into the splay tree of Figure 11.12.

Again following the algorithm for inserting a value in a binary search tree, we insert the value 90 into node **t** as shown in Figure 11.13. Executing an RL rotation at **t**, we obtain the tree of Figure 11.14. Following this with an RR rotation will move **t** to the root of the tree. The final tree is shown in Figure 11.15.

Figure 11.9
Tree used for illustrating splay rotations in Example 11.5. The value 55 will be inserted into this splay tree.

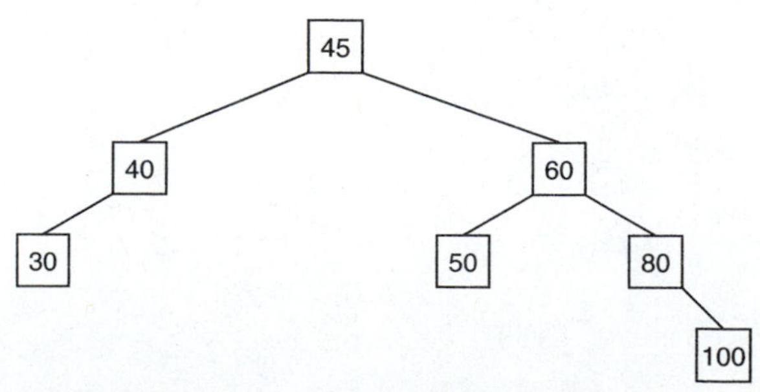

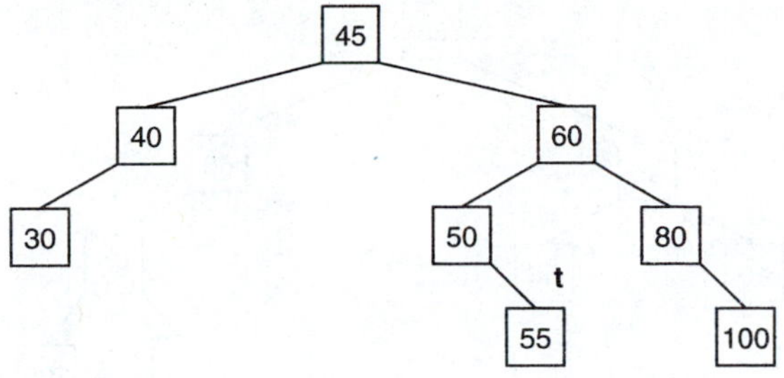

Figure 11.10
Splay tree of Figure 11.9 with the value 55 inserted into node **t**. The splay rotations have not yet been performed.

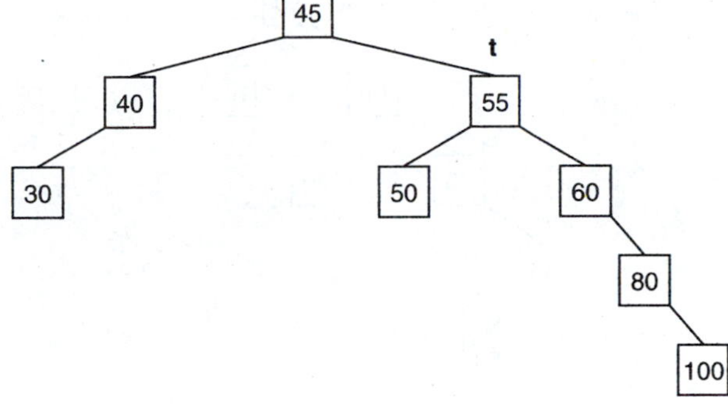

Figure 11.11
Splay tree of Figure 11.10 following an LR rotation at node **t**.

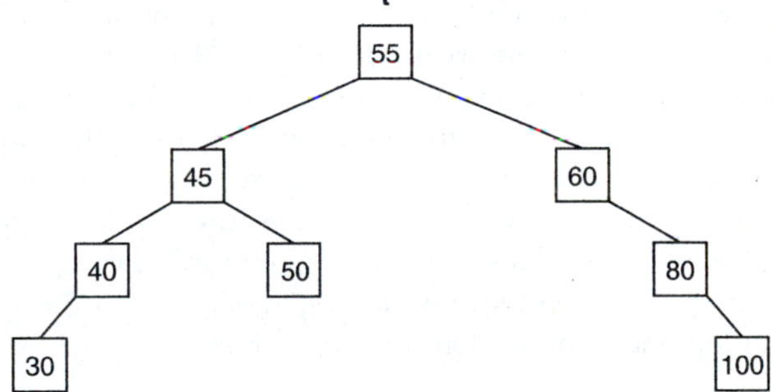

Figure 11.12
Splay tree of Figure 11.11 following an R rotation at node **t**, which made **t** the new root of the tree.

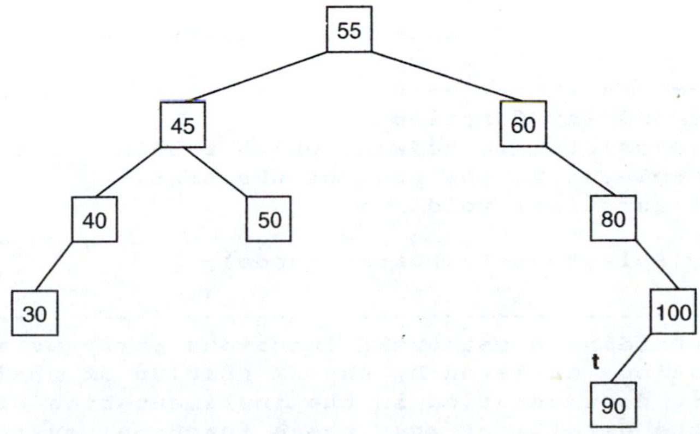

Figure 11.13
Splay tree of Figure 11.12 with the value 90 inserted into the tree at node **t**. The splay rotations have not yet been performed.

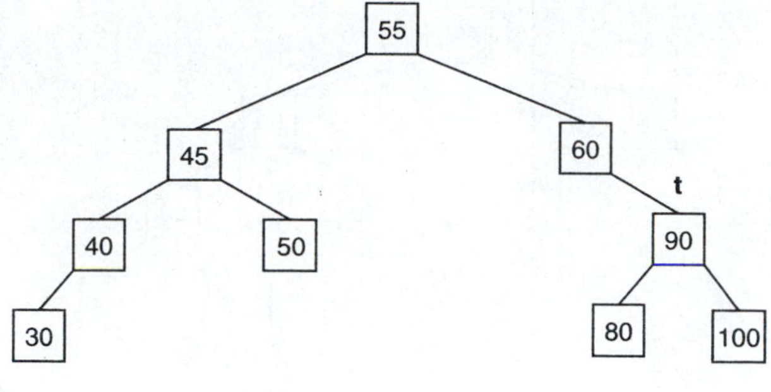

Figure 11.14
Splay tree of Figure 11.13 following an RL rotation at node **t**.

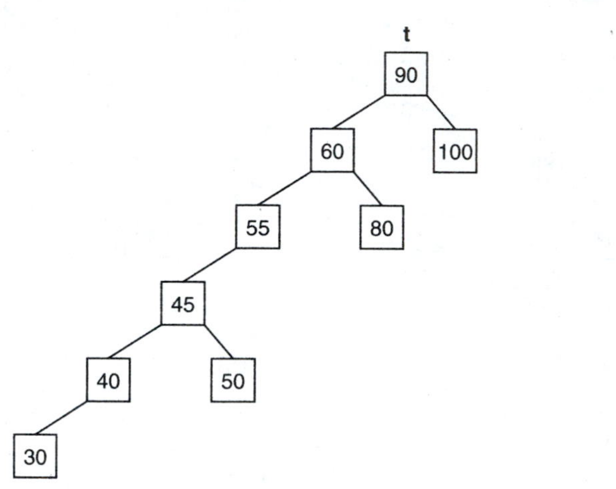

Figure 11.15
Splay tree of Figure 11.14 following an RR rotation at node **t**, which made **t** the new root of the tree.

We now give C++ code for implementing a splay tree, as well as the code for the **add** and **search** operations. Most of the work for the **add** and **search** operations is done in subordinate private functions **privAdd** and **privSearch**. Each of these subordinate functions in turn calls the private function **performSplay** whenever a node is found or inserted into the tree. The **performSplay** function invokes an appropriate subordinate function for each of the six possible rotations. These subsidiary functions are named in an obvious fashion, with their respective actions indicated by graphic documentation in the code for **performSplay**. Their implementations are left for the exercises.

```
// Additional private functions declared for the SplayTree class
template <class BaseData>
class SplayTree
{
  private:                          // Internal auxiliary functions

// ------------------------------------------------------------------
// Interface for performSplay function
// GIVEN:    node -- a pointer to node at which a splay is to be performed.
// RETURN:   node is splayed to the root of the tree.
// RETURN as value of function: void

     void performSplay(SplayNode<BaseData> *node);

//-----------------------------------------------------------------
// Each of the six subordinate performXX functions performs a particular
// type of splay rotation, as keyed by the XX portion of their name.
// Consult the graphic documentation in the implementation of
// performSplay for the details of what these functions must do.
```

```
    void performL(SplayNode<BaseData> *node, SplayNode<BaseData> *p);
    void performR(SplayNode<BaseData> *node, SplayNode<BaseData> *p);
    void performLL(SplayNode<BaseData> *node, SplayNode<BaseData> *p,
                   SplayNode<BaseData> *gp);
    void performLR(SplayNode<BaseData> *node, SplayNode<BaseData> *p,
                   SplayNode<BaseData> *gp);
    void performRL(SplayNode<BaseData> *node, SplayNode<BaseData> *p,
                   SplayNode<BaseData> *gp);
    void performRR(SplayNode<BaseData> *node, SplayNode<BaseData> *p,
                   SplayNode<BaseData> *gp);

// ----------------------------------------------------------------------
// Interface for privSearch function
// GIVEN:     t -- a pointer to root of SplayTree;
//            target -- a value of type BaseData containing, perhaps in a
//                      special key field, a value to be searched for
//                      according to the precedes relationship underlying
//                      the tree.
// RETURN:    item -- a value of type BaseData. If target can be found
//                    in the tree, item contains the entire contents of
//                    the tree node (key value and all associated data)
//                    that matches target;
//            where -- a pointer that references the node where target was found.
//            If target is not found, item and where are unreliable.
// RETURN as value of function:
//            TRUE if target could be found in the SplayTree;
//            FALSE if target is not in the tree.

    BOOLEAN privSearch(SplayNode<BaseData> *t, const BaseData &target,
                       BaseData &item, SplayNode<BaseData> *&where);

// ----------------------------------------------------------------------
// Interface for privAdd function
// GIVEN:     t -- a pointer to current node of SplayTree;
//            par -- a pointer to the parent of t; will be NULL if t is
//                   root of entire tree;
//            item -- a value of type BaseData to be added according
//                    to the precedes relationship underlying the tree.
// RETURN:    If item is not already in the tree referenced by t, the tree is
//            recursively searched for the spot to add item;  item is then
//            inserted in the tree and where is returned as a pointer to the
//            newly created tree node with item in it.  If item is already
//            in the tree, the tree is left unaltered, and where is
//            unreliable.
// RETURN as value of function:
//            TRUE if item could be added to the SplayTree;
//            FALSE otherwise.

    BOOLEAN privAdd(SplayNode<BaseData> *&t, SplayNode<BaseData> *par,
                    const BaseData &item, SplayNode<BaseData> *&where);

    : // All other class members as specified before

};

// Implementation of the SplayTree constructor
template <class BaseData>
SplayTree<BaseData>::
SplayTree(BOOLEAN (*precedes)(const BaseData &x, const BaseData &y))
```

```
{
  root = NULL;
  this->precedes = precedes;
}


// Implementation of performSplay, which, in turn, is called for each
// successful add or search operation
template <class BaseData>
void SplayTree<BaseData>::performSplay(SplayNode<BaseData> *node)
{
  BOOLEAN done;

  SplayNode<BaseData> *gp, *p;

  while (node != root)
  {
    p = node->parent;
    gp = p->parent;
    if (gp == NULL)  // p is root of SplayTree.  Depending on where node is
                     // with respect to p, a left or right rotation is needed.
      if (node == p->leftChild)   // Perform L rotation
        performL(node, p);
      else                        // Perform R rotation
        performR(node, p);
    else             // gp not NULL, so double rotation is needed
      if (p == gp->leftChild)
        if (node == p->leftChild)  // Perform LL rotation
          performLL(node, p, gp);
        else                       // Perform LR rotation
```

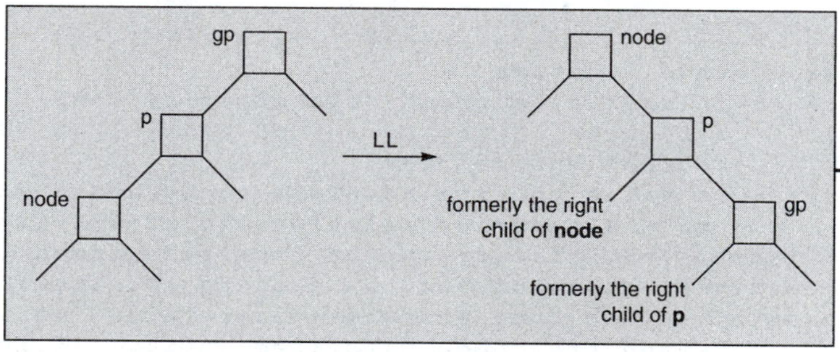

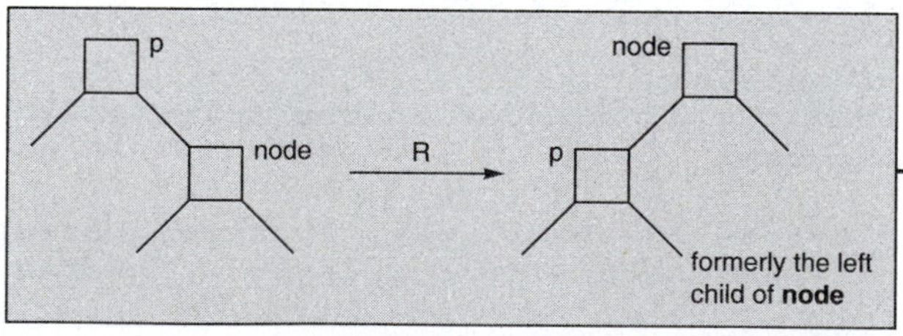

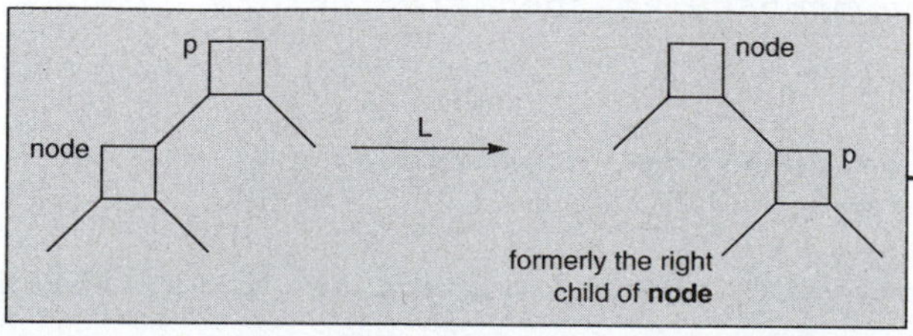

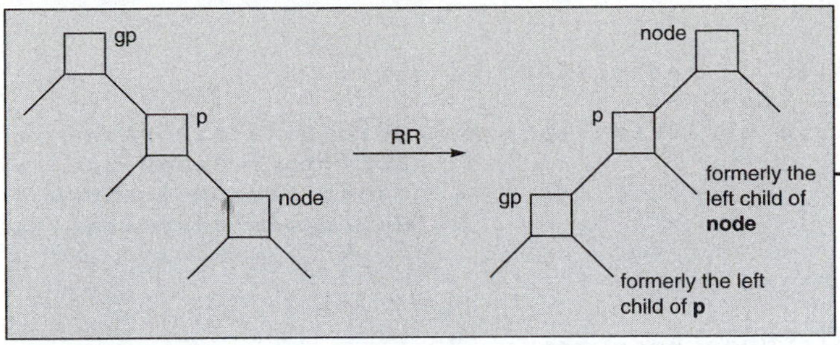

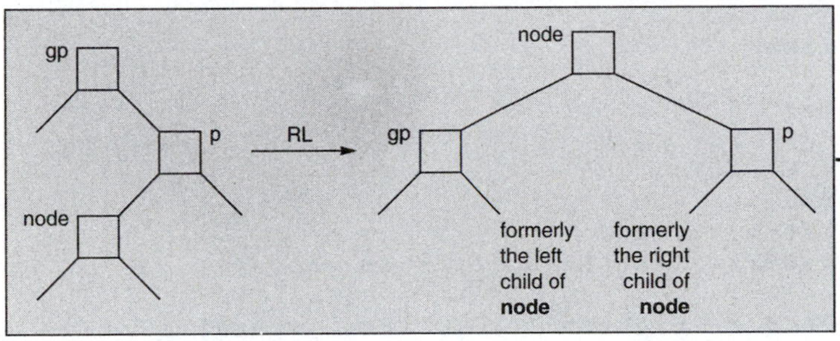

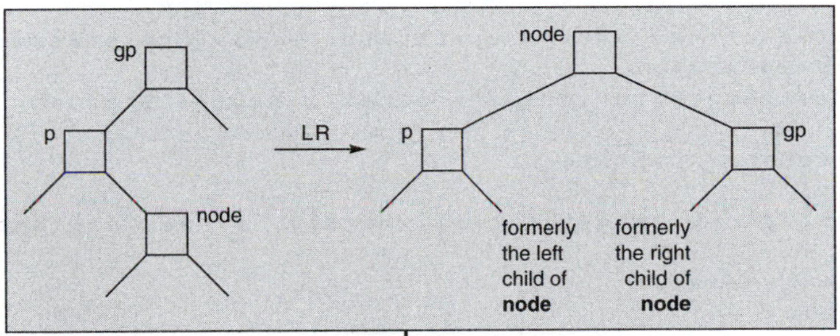

```
        performLR(node, p, gp);
    else            // p is right child of gp
      if (node == p->leftChild)  // Perform RL rotation
        performRL(node, p, gp);
      else                       // Perform RR rotation
        performRR(node, p, gp);
  }
}

// Implementation of add operation -- via the subordinate privAdd function
template <class BaseData>
BOOLEAN SplayTree<BaseData>::add(const BaseData &item)
{
  SplayNode<BaseData> *where;

  if (privAdd(root, NULL, item, where))  // Perform splay upon success
  {
    performSplay(where);
    return(TRUE);
  }
  else
    return(FALSE);
```

```
}

// Implementation of the privAdd function
template <class BaseData>
BOOLEAN SplayTree<BaseData>::privAdd(SplayNode<BaseData> *&t,
                                      SplayNode<BaseData> *par,
                                      const BaseData &item,
                                      SplayNode<BaseData> *&where)
{
  if (t == NULL)
  {
    t = new SplayNode<BaseData>;
    t->leftChild = NULL;
    t->rightChild = NULL;
    t->parent = par;
    t->info = item;
    where = t;
    return(TRUE);
  }
  if (target == t->info)
    return(FALSE);
  if (precedes(item, t->info))
    return(privAdd(t->leftChild, t, item where));
  else
    return(privAdd(t->rightChild, t, item, where));
}


// Implementation of the search operation -- via the privSearch function
template <class BaseData>
BOOLEAN SplayTree<BaseData>::search(const BaseData &target, BaseData &item)
{
  SplayNode<BaseData> *where;

  if (privSearch(root, target, item, where))  // Perform splay if success
  {
    performSplay(where);
    return(TRUE);
  }
  else
    return(FALSE);
}

// Implementation of the privSearch function
template <class BaseData>
BOOLEAN SplayTree<BaseData>::privSearch(SplayNode<BaseData> *t,
                                        const BaseData &target, BaseData &item,
                                        SplayNode<BaseData> *&where)
{
  if (t == NULL)
    return(FALSE);
  if (target == t->info)
  {
    item = t->info;
    where = t;
    return(TRUE);
  }
  if (precedes(target, t->info))
    return(privSearch(t->leftChild, target, item, where));
  else
    return(privSearch(t->rightChild, target, item, where));
}
```

Analysis of Splay Trees Since the rationale behind a splay tree is that it performs a "localized" restructuring designed to improve the efficiency of future operations in the tree rather than improve the worst case time per operation, it is important to analyze its efficiency with respect to sequences of operations. Using a method known as *amortized complexity*, Sleator and Tarjan show that splay trees are as efficient as balanced trees when total running time for a sequence of operations is the measure of interest (see D. D. Sleator, and R. E. Tarjan, "Self-Adjusting Binary Search Trees," *Journal of the ACM*, 32, July 1985, pp. 652–686).

Exercises 11.1

1. Repeat Exercise 7.3.1 for 2-3-4 trees.
2. Repeat Exercise 7.3.2 for 2-3-4 trees.
3. Repeat Exercise 7.3.3 for 2-3-4 trees.
4. Complete the development of functions for 2-3-4 trees by writing **splitRoot**, **splitChildOf2**, **splitChildOf3**, **nodeType**, **insertData**, **leafNode**, and **whichChild**. Recall that detailed specifications of these functions were given in our discussion of the **add** algorithm for 2-3-4 trees.
5. Write a C++ function to remove an item from a 2-3-4 tree.
6. Repeat Exercise 7.3.1 for red-black trees.
7. Repeat Exercise 7.3.2 for red-black trees.
8. Repeat Exercise 7.3.3 for red-black trees.
9. Complete the development of functions for red-black trees by writing **splitRoot**, **splitChildOf2**, **splitChildOf3**, **nodeType**, **insertData**, **leafNode**, **whichChild**, and **advancePointers**. Specifications for these functions were given in our discussion of the **add** algorithm for red-black trees.
10. Write a C++ function to remove an item from a red-black tree.
11. If, instead of using **leftBlack** and **rightBlack** members for red-black nodes, we use a member to represent the color of the pointer from the parent of a node (if any) to the node, we need only use one color member in a node. Write the corresponding **add** function for this alternative representation of red-black trees.
12. Repeat Exercise 7.3.1 for splay trees.
13. Repeat Exercise 7.3.2 for splay trees.
14. Repeat Exercise 7.3.3 for splay trees.
15. Find a sequence of insertions that will lead to the splay tree in Figure 11.9.
16. Complete the development of the **performSplay** function by writing the subordinate functions **performL**, **performR**, **performLL**, **performLR**, **performRL**, and **performRR** that carry out the six possible splay rotations.
17. Write a C++ function to remove an item from a splay tree.

11.2 Density-Dependent Search Techniques

In an ideal data-processing world, all identifying keys such as product codes, Social Security numbers, and so on would start at 0 and follow in sequence thereafter. Then, in any given sequence of data items, we would merely store the key and its associated data at the position that matched the key. The search efficiency for any key in such a sequence would be one access to the sequence. Unfortunately, in the real world users desire keys that consist of more meaningful characters, such as names, addresses, region codes, and so on. For instance, it may be that in an inventory-control application, product codes are numbered in sequence beginning with 10,000 instead of 0. A moment's reflection should indicate that this is still a highly desirable situation since, given a key, we need merely locate the key at position (**keyValue** – 10000) in the sequence, and we still have a search efficiency of 1. What we have done here is to define what is known as a key-to-address transformation, or *hashing function*. The idea behind a hashing function is that it acts on a given key in such a way as to return the relative position in the sequence at which we expect to find the key.

Most hashing functions are not as straightforward as the preceding one and present some additional complications. Suppose we use the following hashing function:

hash(keyValue) = keyValue % 4

Then the set of keys 3, 5, 8, and 10 will be scattered as illustrated here:

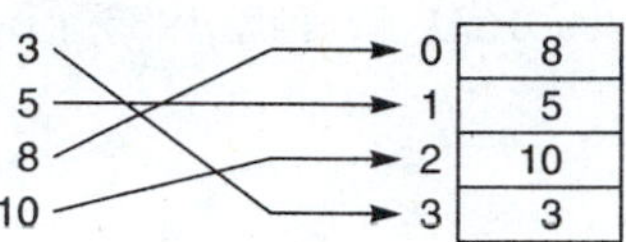

However, if we happen to have 3, 4, 8, and 10 as keys instead of 3, 5, 8, and 10, a problem arises: 4 and 8 hash to the same position. They are said to be *synonyms*, and the result is termed a *collision*. In this situation, there is a collision at position 0, as shown in the following illustration.

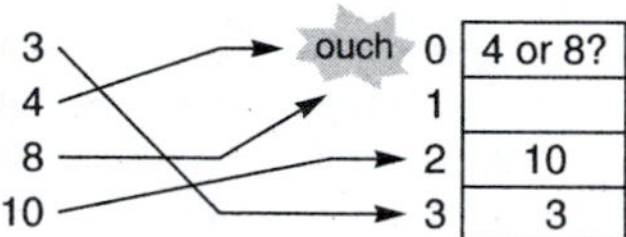

Clearly, one of the goals of the hashing functions we develop should be to reduce the number of collisions as much as possible.

The Construction of Hashing Functions

The business of developing hashing functions can be quite intriguing. The essential idea is to build a mathematical black box that will take a key value as input and issue as output the position in the sequence where that key value should be located. (To facilitate using the integer remainder operation in computing such positions, we will assume that positions in the sequence are numbered starting with 0 instead of 1.) This position should have a minimal probability of colliding with the position that would be produced for any different key. In addition, the black box we create must ensure that a given key will always produce the same position as output. You should begin to note a similarity between some of the properties possessed by a good hashing function and a good *random number generator* such as that used in our simulation of users sharing a resource in an operating system environment (Section 4.4). Indeed, data access by means of a hashing function is sometimes called *randomized storage*, and the first type of hashing function we discuss makes direct use of a random number generator.

Method 1: Use of a Random Number Generator Many high-level languages provide a random number generator to produce random sequences of real or integer values. If one is not provided, you may easily write one using a method such as that described in Appendix A. (For readable discussions of other methods of random number generation see Chapter 7 of *Numerical Recipes* by William H. Press, Brian P. Flannery, Saul A. Teukolsky, and William T. Vetterling, Cambridge, England: Cambridge University Press, 1986.) Typically, these methods rely on having a static seed variable to start the process of generating random numbers. Computations done on this seed produce the random number. At the same time, the computations alter the value of the seed so that the next time the random number generator is called, a different random number will almost surely be produced.

In typical applications of random number generation, you need merely initialize the seed to some arbitrary value to start the random sequence. Once the seed is supplied, the random sequence is completely determined. If you have access to a system procedure that returns the current time, day, month, and year, this procedure can be called to initialize the seed in a fashion that ensures there is only a very small likelihood of generating the same random sequence twice.

How does all of this relate to hashing? For a hashing application, we must slightly alter the definition of our random number generator so that the seed is supplied as a value parameter. Then we supply the values of search keys as the seeds. The nature of the random number algorithm ensures the following:

- Each time the same key is passed to the function, the same random value will be returned.
- It is unlikely that two different keys will yield the same random value.

The random number that is correspondingly produced can then be appropriately multiplied, truncated, and shifted to produce a hash value within the range of valid positions.

Method 2: Folding In situations where the key to be positioned is not a pure integer, some preliminary work may be required to translate it into a usable form. Take, for instance, the case of a Social Security number such as 387-58-1505. Viewed as one integer, this would cause overflow on many machines. By a method known as *shift folding*, however, this Social Security number would be viewed as three separate numbers to be added: 387 + 58 + 1505, producing the result 1950. This result could be regarded as either the hash position itself or, more likely, as a pure integer that could be further acted on by Method 1 or 4 to produce a final hash position in the desired range.

Another often-used folding technique is called *boundary folding*. The idea behind boundary folding is that, at the boundaries between the numbers making up the key under consideration, every other number is reversed before being accumulated into the total. Applying this method to our Social Security number example, we would have 387 + 85 (58 reversed) + 1505, yielding a result of 1977. Clearly, the two methods do not differ by much, and a choice between them must often be made on the basis of experimentation to determine which will produce more scattered results for a given application.

Regardless of whether shift or boundary folding is used, one of the great advantages of the folding method is its ability to transform noninteger keys into an integer suitable for further hashing action. For keys such as names, which contain alphabetic characters, the type of folding just illustrated may be done by translating characters into their ASCII (or other appropriate) codes.

Method 3: Digit or Character Extraction In certain situations, a given key value may contain specific characters that are likely to bias any hash value arising from the key. The idea in *digit* or *character extraction* is to remove such digits or characters before using the result as a final hash value or passing it on to be further transformed by another method. For instance, a company may choose to identify the various products it manufactures by using a nine-character code that always contains either an A or a B in the first position and either a 1 or a 0 in the fourth position, with the rest of the characters in the code tending to occur in less predictable fashion. Character extraction would remove the biased first and fourth characters, leaving a seven-character result to pass on for further processing.

Method 4: Division Remainder Technique All hashing presupposes a given range of positions that can be valid outputs of the hash function. In the remainder of this section, we assume the existence of a variable, **tableSize**, which is set to the number of locations available in the hash table. That is, the function should produce values between 0 and **tableSize** − 1. It should then be evident that

hash(keyValue) = keyValue % tableSize

is a valid hashing function for the integer **keyValue**.

To begin examining criteria for choosing an appropriate **tableSize**, we load the keys 41, 58, 12, 92, 50, and 91 into a table with **tableSize** = 15. Table 11.1 shows the results. In this table, NULLs are used to denote empty positions. However, if we keep **tableSize** the same and try to load the keys 10, 20, 30, 40, 50, 60, and 70, we have many collisions, as shown in Table 11.2. With this choice of **tableSize**, a different set of keys causes disastrous results even though the table seemingly has plenty of room available. On the other hand, if we choose **tableSize** to be 11, we have a table with considerably less room but no collisions. Table 11.3 indicates the hashing positions when the same set of keys is acted on by 11 instead of by 15.

Although these examples are far from conclusive, they suggest that choosing a prime number for **tableSize** may produce a more desirable hashing function. You will continue to explore this question in the exercises for this section. Also, in Section 11.3 we will investigate more deeply the issue of how to choose **tableSize** to produce an optimal hashing function for keys that are strings. Apart from considerations of whether or not **tableSize** should be prime, it is clear that the nature of a particular application may dictate against the choice of certain **tableSize** values. For instance, in a situation where the rightmost digits of key values happen to follow certain recurring patterns, it would be unwise to choose a power of 10 for **tableSize**. (Why?)

Despite such **tableSize** cautions, no hashing function can preclude the possibility of collisions; it can only make them less likely. You should be able to imagine quickly a key value that will produce a collision for the hashing function used in determining the arrangement of Table 11.3. Notice that, as the table becomes more full, the probability that collisions will occur increases. Hence, when using hashing as a search strategy, one must be willing to waste some positions in the table; otherwise search efficiency will drastically deteriorate. How much space to waste is an interesting question that we discuss later in this section. Further, since no hashing function can eliminate collisions, we must be prepared to handle them when they occur.

The Keyed Collection ADT

Before discussing collision-processing strategies, we should put hashing into the context of abstract data types. Because hashing scatters keys within the search table, hashing is not *by itself* an appropriate implementation technique for an ADT that includes a traversal operation in which all items are processed in order according to a precedence relation. The randomized placement of keys by a good hashing function is directly opposed to such an ordered traversal. Consequently,

TABLE 11.1
Table with **tableSize** 15 loaded using a division remainder hashing function.

Position	Key
0	NULL
1	91
2	92
3	NULL
4	NULL
5	50
6	NULL
7	NULL
8	NULL
9	NULL
10	NULL
11	41
12	12
13	58
14	NULL

TABLE 11.2
Table from Table 11.1, loaded with other values and having several collisions.

Position	Key	
0	30	← 60 (collision)
1	NULL	
2	NULL	
3	NULL	
4	NULL	
5	20	← 50 (collision)
6	NULL	
7	NULL	
8	NULL	
9	NULL	
10	10	← 40 ← 70 (collision)
11	NULL	
12	NULL	
13	NULL	
14	NULL	

TABLE 11.3
Table with same keys as Table 11.2 but with **tableSize** 11. No collision results.

Position	Key
0	NULL
1	NULL
2	NULL
3	NULL
4	70
5	60
6	50
7	40
8	30
9	20
10	10

we will define a new ADT—the keyed collection—that is more directly suited to an implementation by hashing.

Definition: A *keyed collection* is an unordered group of records, each of which has one field designated as a *key field.* Records within the collection are identified by the value of their key field. The operations provided on this collection of records are defined as follows:

`Construct Operation (First Form)`

Preconditions: An uninitialized keyed collection object.
Postconditions: The keyed collection object is initialized to an empty keyed collection.

`Construct Operation (Copy Constructor)`

Preconditions: An uninitialized keyed collection object;
initkc — a keyed collection object that was previously constructed.
Postconditions: The keyed collection object is initialized to *initkc.*

Destroy Operation

Preconditions: A previously constructed keyed collection.
Postconditions: All storage associated with the keyed collection is deallocated. The keyed collection object itself is in an unreliable state.

Assign Operation

Preconditions: A previously constructed keyed collection object;
source—a second keyed collection object that uses the same data type as the owner of the operation.
Postconditions: The contents of source have been copied to the keyed collection object that owns the operation.

Add Operation

Preconditions: A keyed collection object;
item—a record with a key value and other associated data to be added to the keyed collection.
Postconditions: If the key value of *item* is not already in the keyed collection, its record is added to the keyed collection and a flagging TRUE value is returned as an indication of the successful addition to the table. If *item*'s key value is already in the keyed collection, a flagging FALSE value is returned, and the keyed collection is left unaltered.

Retrieve Operation

Preconditions: A keyed collection object;
target — a key value to be searched for in the keyed collection.
Postconditions: If *target* can be found in the keyed collection, the data associated with it is returned in *item*, and a flagging TRUE value is returned to indicate a successful search. Otherwise a flagging FALSE value is returned, and the contents of *item* are unreliable.

Remove Operation

Preconditions: A keyed collection object;
target — a key value to be deleted from the keyed collection.
Postconditions: If *target* can be found in the keyed collection, the record associated with it is deleted, and a flagging TRUE value is returned to indicate a successful search. Otherwise a flagging FALSE value is returned, and the keyed collection is left unaltered.

Recasting this conceptual ADT definition into a C++ class interface, we have:

```
// KeyData is either a C++ built-in type, or a C++ class that has an
// assignment operation that overloads the "=" operator and an equality
// test that overloads the "==" operator.  OtherData is either a C++
// built-in type, or a C++ class that has an assignment operation that
// overloads the "=" operator.

template <class KeyData, class OtherData>
class KCRec                        // Records within the keyed collection
{
  public:
    KeyData key;
    OtherData data;
};
```

```
template <class KeyData, class OtherData>
class KeyedCollection       // The keyed collection itself
{
  public:

// ----------------------------------------------------------------------
// Interface for KeyedCollection constructor
// GIVEN:   An uninitialized KeyedCollection object;
//          maxSize -- an integer representing the maximum size for the
//                     collection.
// RETURN:  The KeyedCollection object is initialized to the empty
//          KeyedCollection with maxSize establishing the maximum size
//          to which the collection can grow.

    KeyedCollection(int maxSize);

// ----------------------------------------------------------------------
// Interface for KeyedCollection copy constructor
// GIVEN:    An uninitialized KeyedCollection object;
//           initkc -- a KeyedCollection object that was previously
//                     constructed.
// RETURN:   The KeyedCollection object is initialized with the same records
//           that are in initkc.

    KeyedCollection(KeyedCollection<KeyData, OtherData> &initkc);

// ----------------------------------------------------------------------
// Interface for KeyedCollection destructor
// GIVEN:    A previously initialized KeyedCollection object.
// RETURN:   All storage associated with the KeyedCollection is deallocated.
//
    ~KeyedCollection();

// ----------------------------------------------------------------------
// Interface for KeyedCollection assign = operator
// GIVEN:    A previously constructed KeyedCollection object;
//           source -- a second KeyedCollection object that must have been
//                     constructed with the same KeyData and OtherData types
//                     as the owner of the assign operator.
// RETURN:   The contents of source have been copied to the KeyedCollection
//           object that owns the operation.
// RETURN as value of function:  void

    void operator = (const KeyedCollection<KeyData, OtherData> &source);

// ----------------------------------------------------------------------
// Interface for add operation
// GIVEN:    A KeyedCollection object;
//           item -- a record of type KCRec.
// RETURN:   item is added to the KeyedCollection object provided it is
//           not already in the collection and provided the size of the
//           collection will not exceed the maximum size of the collection.
//           If item is already in the collection or adding item would
//           force the collection to exceed its maximum size, then the
//           KeyedCollection is left unchanged.
// RETURN as value of function:
//           TRUE if item could be added to the KeyedCollection;
//           FALSE if item was not added.

    BOOLEAN add(const KCRec<KeyData, OtherData> &item);
```

```
// ----------------------------------------------------------------------
// Interface for retrieve operation
// GIVEN:    A KeyedCollection object;
//           target -- a value of type KeyData containing the key value
//                     to be searched for in the KeyedCollection.
// RETURN:   item -- a value of type OtherData. If target can be found
//                   in the KeyedCollection, item contains the OtherData
//                   in the record whose key field matches target. If target
//                   cannot be found in the KeyedCollection, then item is
//                   unreliable.
// RETURN as value of function:
//           TRUE if target could be found in the KeyedCollection;
//           FALSE if target is not in the collection.

   BOOLEAN retrieve(const KeyData &target, OtherData &item);

// ----------------------------------------------------------------------
// Interface for remove operation
// GIVEN:    A KeyedCollection object;
//           target -- a value of type KeyData containing the key value
//                     to be deleted from the KeyedCollection.
// RETURN:   If target can be found in the KeyedCollection, it and its
//           associated data are deleted; if target cannot be found,
//           the KeyedCollection is left unaltered.
// RETURN as value of function:
//           TRUE if target and its associated data could be deleted from the
//           KeyedCollection; FALSE if target is not in the collection.

   BOOLEAN remove(const KeyData &target);
};
```

The keyed collection is an appropriate ADT for information retrieval systems in which individual records must be accessed frequently (and quickly) but the entire collection of records must never be processed sequentially. It should be evident that hashing is potentially an ideal way to implement a keyed collection—once we resolve what to do with the problem of collisions.

Collision Processing—Implementation of a Keyed Collection by Hashing

The essential problem in collision processing is to develop an algorithm that will position a key in a table when the position dictated by the hashing function itself is already occupied. Ideally, this algorithm should minimize the possibility of future collisions; that is, the problem key should be located at a position that is not likely to be the hashed position of a future key.

However, the nature of hashing makes this latter criterion difficult to meet with any degree of certainty, since a good hashing function does not allow prediction of where future keys are likely to be placed. We will discuss five methods of collision processing: linear, quadratic, rehashing, linked, and buckets. In all of the methods it is necessary to detect when a given table position is not occupied. To signify this, we use a NULL value to distinguish unoccupied positions. As you read, give some thought to the question of how the **remove** operation could be accomplished in a keyed collection implemented by one of these hashing methods. In particular, will the use of NULL as an empty flag suffice to denote positions that have never

TABLE 11.4
Insertion with linear collision processing.

	First insert hash(18) = 4	Second insert hash(31) = 3	Third insert hash(67) = 4	Fourth insert hash(36) = 1	Fifth insert hash(19) = 5	Sixth insert hash(34) = 6
0	NULL	NULL	NULL	NULL	NULL	34
1	NULL	NULL	NULL	36	36	36
2	NULL	NULL	NULL	NULL	NULL	NULL
3	NULL	31	31	31	31	31
4	18	18	18	18	18	18
5	NULL	NULL	67	67	67	67
6	NULL	NULL	NULL	NULL	19	19

been occupied *and* positions previously occupied but now vacant? This question is explored in the exercises and programming problems in this chapter.

Linear Collision Processing The linear method of resolving collisions is the simplest to implement (and, unfortunately, the least efficient). *Linear collision processing* requires that, when a collision occurs, we proceed down the table in sequential order until a vacant position is found. The key causing the collision is then placed at this first vacant position. If we come to the physical end of our table in the attempt to place the problem key, we merely wrap around to the top of the table and continue looking for a vacant position. For instance, suppose we use the hashing function

hash(keyValue) = keyValue % tableSize

with **tableSize** = 7 and attempt to insert the keys 18, 31, 67, 36, 19, and 34. The sequence of tables in Table 11.4 shows the results of these insertions. When a collision occurs at the third insert, it is processed by the linear method; 67 is thus loaded into position 5.

Example 11.7 Suppose that a hashing implementation of a keyed collection has been loaded with data using the linear collision processing strategy illustrated in Table 11.4. Write an implementation of the constructor and **retrieve** operations *under the assumption that no* **remove** *operations will be performed on the collection.*

```
// The following private members must be added to a hash table implementation
// of the KeyedCollection class.
template <class KeyData, class OtherData>
class KeyedCollection
{
  private:
    int tableSize;                           // Size of hash table
    Array<int, KCRec<KeyData, OtherData>>    // Array of records in the collection
    int hash(KeyData key);               // Hashing function, assumed to return
                                         // a value between 0 and tableSize - 1
    :
    :  // public class members defined as before
};
```

```
// Implementation of the constructor
template <class KeyData, class OtherData>
KeyedCollection<KeyData, OtherData>::KeyedCollection(int maxSize)
{
  int k;

  tableSize = maxSize;              // Establish tableSize
  kc = new Array <int, KCRec<KeyData, OtherData>>(0, maxSize - 1);
  for (k = 0; k < maxSize; ++k)     // Empty flag in each location
    (*kc)[k].key = (KeyData) NULL;
}


template <class KeyData, class OtherData>
BOOLEAN KeyedCollection<KeyData, OtherData>::
  retrieve(const KeyData &target, OtherData &item)
{
  int k, j;

  k = hash(target);         // Original hash position
  j = k;                    // j will advance through table
  do
    if (target == (*kc)[j].key)
    {
      item = (*kc)[j].data;
      return(TRUE);
    }
    else
      j = (j + 1) % tableSize;
  while ((((int)((*kc)[j].key)) != NULL) && (j != k));
  // If we don't exit the previous loop by the embedded return, then
  // target is not in the table.
  return(FALSE);
}
```

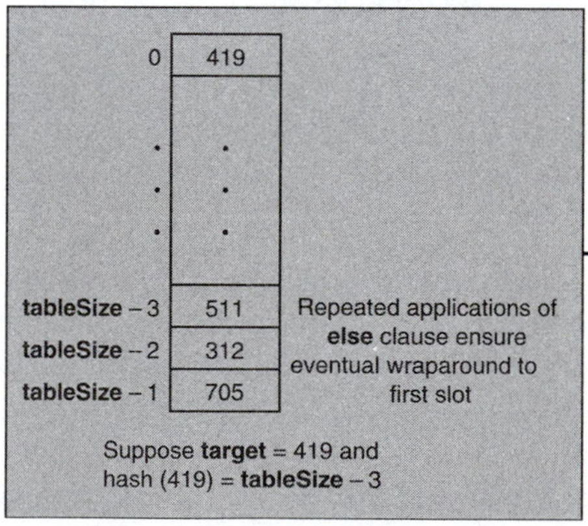

0	419
.	.
.	.
.	.
tableSize – 3	511
tableSize – 2	312
tableSize – 1	705

Repeated applications of **else** clause ensure eventual wraparound to first slot

Suppose **target** = 419 and hash (419) = **tableSize** – 3

Several remarks are in order concerning the function in Example 11.7. First, we emphasize that the function as it stands would not necessarily handle keyed collection processing in which it was necessary to process deletions. You will explore the problem of deletions from a keyed collection maintained by hashing in greater detail in the exercises and programming problems.

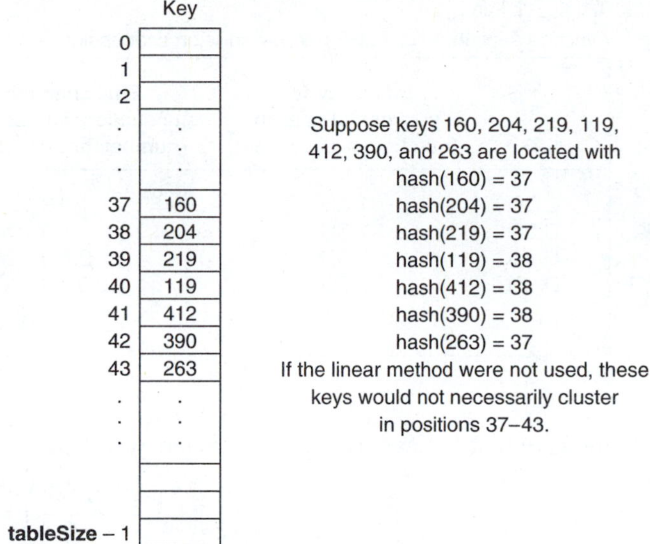
Key
0
1
2
37 160
38 204
39 219
40 119
41 412
42 390
43 263
tableSize – 1
Suppose keys 160, 204, 219, 119,
412, 390, and 263 are located with
hash(160) = 37
hash(204) = 37
hash(219) = 37
hash(119) = 38
hash(412) = 38
hash(390) = 38
hash(263) = 37
If the linear method were not used, these
keys would not necessarily cluster
in positions 37–43.

Figure 11.16
Clustering due to linear collision processing. As the primary clusters from locations 37 and 38 merge, the value 263 is located even farther from the initial hash point than dictated by just the collisions at location 37.

Second, note that the linear method is not without its flaws. In particular, it is prone to a problem of *clustering* (or more precisely, *primary clustering*). Clustering occurs when a collision resolution strategy relocates keys that have a collision at the same initial hashing position to the same region (known as a *cluster*) within the storage space. This usually leads to further collisions with relocated values and further relocations until everything gets resolved. With linear resolution the clustering problem becomes compounded because as one cluster expands it can run into another cluster, immediately creating a larger cluster. This one big cluster ultimately causes collision resolutions from both initial hashing points to be drawn out longer than they would otherwise be. The occurrence of such clustering phenomena brought on by linear collision resolution is shown in Figure 11.16.

Efficiency Considerations for Linear Hashing A final point to note about the linear hashing method is its search efficiency. Knuth has shown that the average number of table accesses for a successful search using the linear method is

$$\left(\frac{1}{2}\right)\left(1 + \frac{1}{1 - D}\right)$$

where

$$D = \frac{\text{Number of currently active records}}{\text{tableSize}}$$

(See Donald E. Knuth, *Searching and Sorting*, Vol. 3 of *The Art of Computer Programming*, Menlo Park, CA: Addison-Wesley, 1973.) An interesting fact about this search efficiency is that it is not solely dependent on the number of records currently in the table, but rather on the *density ratio (D)*—the ratio of the number of records currently in the table to the total record space available. In other words, no matter how many records there are, a highly efficient result can be obtained if one is willing to waste enough vacant records. This is what is meant by a *density-dependent search technique*. In the case of searching for a key that cannot be found, Knuth's results

TABLE 11.5
Average search efficiency for linear collision procession.

D	Efficiency for successful search (number of accesses)	Efficiency for unsuccessful search (number of accesses)
0.10	1.06	1.18
0.50	1.50	2.50
0.75	2.50	8.50
0.90	5.50	50.50

indicate that the average search efficiency will be

$$\left(\frac{1}{2}\right)\left(1 + \frac{1}{(1-D)^2}\right)$$

Table 11.5 illustrates the effectiveness of linear collision resolution by showing the computed efficiencies for a few strategic values of D.

Quadratic, Rehashing, and Double Hashing Methods of Collision Processing

Both the quadratic and rehashing collision-processing methods attempt to correct the problems of primary clustering caused by linear collision resolution. The *quadratic method* examines locations whose distance (excluding the effects of any wraparound) from the initial collision point increases as the square of the number of previous locations tried. Thus, suppose that a key value initially hashes to position K and a collision results. Then, on its first attempt to resolve the collision, the quadratic algorithm attempts to place the key at position $K + 1^2$. Then, if a second attempt is necessary to resolve the collision, position $K + 2^2$ is probed. In general, the Rth attempt to resolve the collision probes position $K + R^2$. Each of these values may have to be adjusted, however, if it extends beyond the upper limit of the hash table and needs to be wrapped around to the table's lower end. By leaving increasingly larger gaps between successive relocation positions, quadratic collision processing prevents formation of the contiguous relocation regions that characterize primary clustering. Figure 11.17 illustrates this type of dispersal. At this point you should verify that if the hashing function

hash(keyValue) = keyValue % tableSize

is used with **tableSize** equal to 7, then the quadratic method will locate keys 17, 73, 32, and 80 in positions 3, 4, 5, and 0 respectively.

Although quadratic collision resolution effectively eliminates primary clustering, there is another problem, known as *secondary clustering*, that arises. Note that any two values having a collision at a given location, say K, will subsequently examine the same sequence of alternative locations—$K + 1^2, K + 2^2, K + 3^2, \ldots$—until the collision is resolved. Such a sequence of locations, which is examined by a key that has a collision at location K, is known as a *secondary cluster*. Though not as deleterious to the effectiveness of collision processing as primary clusters (although they may intersect, secondary clusters cannot merge to form larger secondary clusters), secondary clustering can generate undesirably long sequences of additional collisions before a resolution is attained.

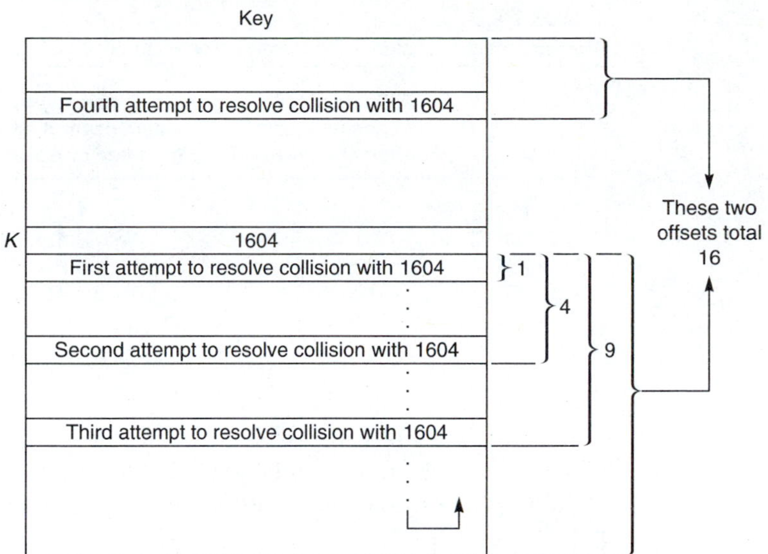

Figure 11.17
Quadratic collision processing.

If we want to avoid secondary clustering, it is necessary to generate different sequences of collision resolution locations for each value that becomes involved in a collision at a given location. Under a collision processing method known as *rehashing*, additional hashing functions are applied to a given key each time a collision occurs. If a collision results from the first hashing function, a second is applied, then a third, and so on, until the key can be successfully placed. If the key exhausts the entire sequence of hashing functions, we could (perhaps prematurely) declare the hash table to be full or resort to linear collision processing from the final hash position. Ideally, the rehashing sequences for each key would have a random pattern that is independent of that of any other key so that no primary or secondary clustering would occur. Unfortunately, this approach appears to be difficult to implement in general, but there is a rehashing scheme, known as *double hashing*, that has been shown by empirical studies to provide behavior that is almost as good (see page 523 of Knuth, *Sorting and Searching*, cited earlier in this section).

The idea behind double hashing is to define a second hashing function, r, that for a given key K, calculates an integer, $r(K)$, that is relatively prime to **tableSize**. If h is the original hash function, then the entire sequence of table locations to be examined, where L_i is the ith location in the sequence, is given by

$$L_i(K) = (h(K) + i \times r(K))\ \%\ \textbf{tableSize} \quad i = 0, 1, \ldots$$

Efficiency Considerations for the Quadratic, Rehashing, and Double Hashing Methods Knuth's results (see *Searching and Sorting*, cited earlier in this section) demonstrate the effectiveness of the rehashing and quadratic methods versus the linear method. For the quadratic method, average search efficiencies improve to

$$1 - \log_e(1 - D) - \frac{D}{2}$$

for the successful case and

$$\frac{1}{1 - D} - D - \log_e(1 - D)$$

TABLE 11.6
Average search efficiency for quadratic collision processing.

D	Efficiency for successful search (number of accesses)	Efficiency for unsuccessful search (number of accesses)
0.10	1.05	1.11
0.50	1.44	2.19
0.75	2.01	4.64
0.90	2.85	11.40

for an unsuccessful search, where D is the density ratio defined earlier in this section and e is the base for the natural logarithm function. Compare the numbers presented in Table 11.6 for quadratic collision processing to those for the linear method given in Table 11.5.

You may have surmised that the increased efficiency of the quadratic method entails at least some drawbacks. First, the computation of a position to be probed when a collision occurs is somewhat more obscure than it was with the linear method. We leave it for you to verify that the position for the ith probe after an initial ($i = 0$) unsuccessful hash to position K is given by

$$(K + i^2) \ \% \ \textbf{tableSize} \quad i = 0, 1, \ldots$$

A more significant problem, however, is that the quadratic method seemingly offers no guarantee that we will try every position in the table before concluding that a given key cannot be inserted. With the linear method, the only way that the insertion could fail is for every position in the table to be occupied. The linear nature of the search, although inefficient, ensured that every position would be checked. However, with the quadratic method applied to the **tableSize** in Figure 11.18, you can confirm that an initial hash to position 4 will lead to future probing of positions 3, 4, and 7 only; it will never check positions 0, 1, 2, 5, or 6.

Fortunately, a satisfactory answer to the question of what portion of a table will be probed by the quadratic algorithm was provided by Radke for values of **tableSize** that are prime numbers satisfying certain conditions. Radke's results and their application to the quadratic algorithm are explored in the exercises at the end of the section. (If you wish to read Radke's results, see C. E. Radke, "The Use of Quadratic Residue Research," *Communications of the ACM*, 13, February 1970, pp. 103–105.)

Figure 11.18
Quadratic probing after initial hash to 3.

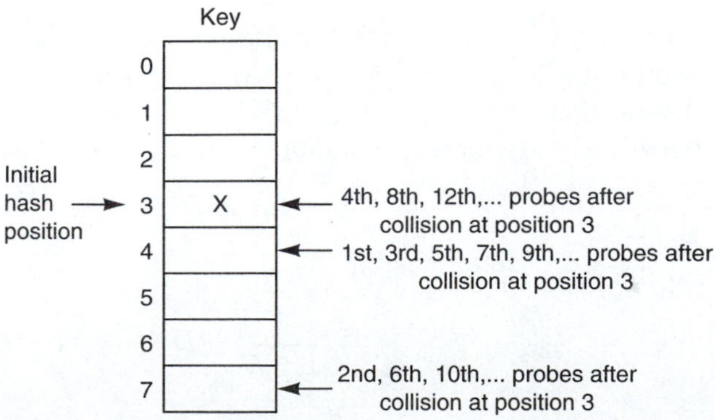

TABLE 11.7
Average search efficiency for collision processing using double hashing, or rehashing.

D	Efficiency for successful search (number of accesses)	Efficiency for unsuccessful search (number of accesses)
0.10	1.05	1.11
0.50	1.39	2.00
0.75	1.84	4.00
0.90	2.56	10.00

For rehashing with a random sequence of rehashed locations for each key we get efficiencies on the order of

$$-\frac{1}{D}\log_e(1 - D)$$

for the successful case and

$$\frac{1}{1 - D}$$

for an unsuccessful search. As we noted in our discussion of double hashing, empirical tests indicate that its performances compare favorably with these results. Compare the numbers presented in Table 11.7 for double hashing and (ideal) random rehashing to those in Tables 11.5 and 11.6. Finally, we point out that choosing r in the double hashing scheme so that its values are relatively prime to **tableSize** ensures that all entries of the table will be tried before determining that a particular key is not in the table or that it cannot be inserted.

Linked Method of Collision Processing The logic of this method completely eliminates the possibility that one collision begets another. It requires that a storage area be divided into two regions: a *prime hash area* and an *overflow area*. Each storage location requires a **link** field in addition to the **key** and **data** fields. The

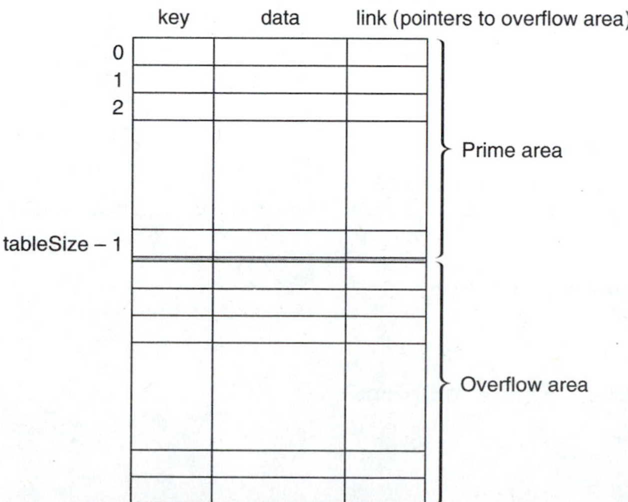

Figure 11.19
Storage allocation for linked collision processing.

Figure 11.20
Loading keys with (**keyValue** % 7) and linked collision procession.

	Key	Link
0	NULL	NULL
1	22	7
2	NULL	NULL
3	31	NULL
4	67	9
5	NULL	NULL
6	NULL	NULL
7	36	8
8	29	NULL
9	60	NULL
10	NULL	NULL
11	NULL	NULL
12	NULL	NULL
13	NULL	NULL
14	NULL	NULL
15	NULL	NULL
16	NULL	NULL

constant **tableSize** is applicable to the prime hash area only. This storage concept is illustrated in Figure 11.19.

Initially, the hashing function translates keys into the prime hashing area. If a collision occurs, the key and its associated data are inserted into a linked list with its initial node in the prime area and all following nodes in the overflow area. Figure 11.20 shows how this method would load the keys 22, 31, 67, 36, 29, and 60 for **tableSize** = 7 and hashing function

hash(keyValue) = keyValue % tableSize

Example 11.8

Suppose that a hashing implementation of a keyed collection has been loaded with data using the linked collision processing strategy illustrated in Figures 11.19 and 11.20. Write an implementation of the first constructor and **retrieve** operations *under the assumption that no* **remove** *operations will be performed on the collection.*

```
template <class KeyData, class OtherData> // Keyed collection data record
class KCRec
{
  public:
    KeyData key;
    OtherData data;
};


template <class KeyData, class OtherData>
class KCLinkRec          // Add a link field for linked collision processing
{
  public:
    KCRec<KeyData, OtherData> kcr;
    int link;
};

template <class KeyData, class OtherData>
class KeyedCollection
{
  private:
```

```
    int tableSize, overflowSize;          // Prime area and overflow area size
    Array<int, KCLinkRec<KeyData, OtherData>> *kc;  // Array of records with links
    int hash (KeyData key);              // Hashing function, assumed to return
                                         // a value between 0 and tableSize - 1
    :
    :  // Other public members defined as before

};

template <class KeyData, class OtherData>
KeyedCollection<KeyData, OtherData>::KeyedCollection(int maxSize)
{
  int k;

  tableSize = maxSize;     // Establish size of prime hash area

  // In this implementation, we make the size of the overflow area equal
  // to the size of the prime hash area.

  overflowSize = maxSize;
  kc = new Array<int, KCLinkRec<KeyData, OtherData>>(0, 2*maxSize-1);
  for (k = 0; k < 2*maxSize; ++k)
  {
    (*kc)[k].kcr.key = (KeyData) NULL;
    (*kc)[k].link = NULL;
  }
}


template <class KeyData, class OtherData>
BOOLEAN KeyedCollection<KeyData, OtherData>::
  retrieve(const KeyData &target, OtherData& item)
{
  int k;

  k = hash(target);
  do
  {
    if (target == (*kc)[k].kcr.key)
    {
      item = (*kc)[k].kcr.data;
      return(TRUE);
    }
    else
      k = (*kc)[k].link;
  }
  while (k != NULL);
  // If we don't exit the previous loop by the embedded return, then target
  // is not in the table.
  return(FALSE);
}
```

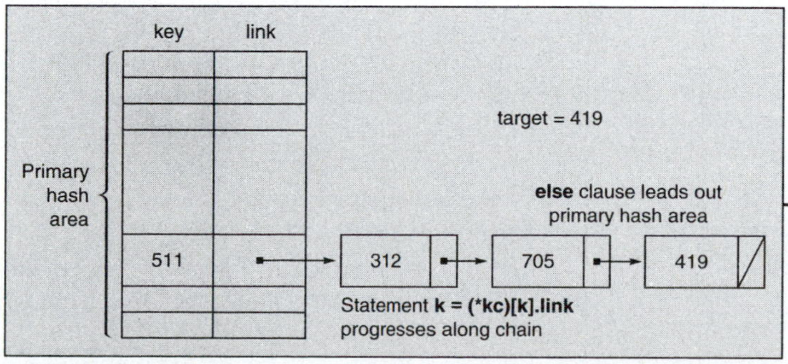

TABLE 11.8
Average search efficiency for the linked method showing densities greater than 1.

D	Efficiency for successful search (number of accesses)	Efficiency for unsuccessful search (number of accesses)
2	2	2
5	3.5	5
10	6	10
20	11	20

Efficiency Considerations for Linked Hashing Knuth's efficiency results for the linked hashing method depend on a density factor D computed using the **tableSize** in the prime hashing area only. Hence, unlike the other hashing methods we have discussed, the linked method allows a density factor greater than 1. For example, if the **tableSize** for the primary hash area is 200 and the overflow area contains space for 300 additional records, then 400 active records will yield a density factor of 2. Given this variation, average search efficiencies for the successful and unsuccessful cases are $1 + (D/2)$ and D, respectively. Table 11.8, which shows computations of this search efficiency for selected values of D, should be compared to the corresponding results for the linear, quadratic, and rehashing methods, which were presented in Tables 11.5, 11.6, and 11.7, respectively.

Figure 11.21
Storage allocation for bucket hashing.

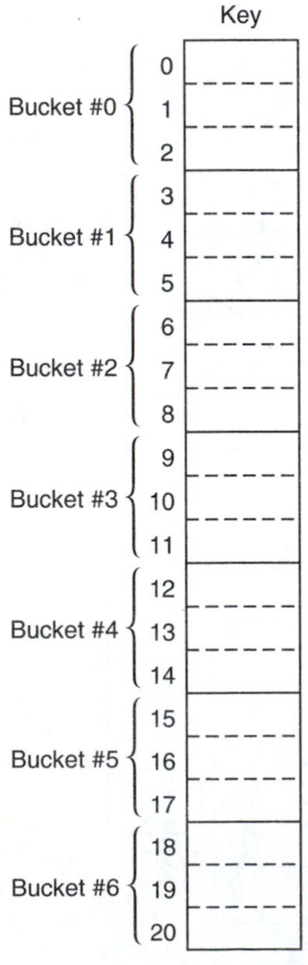

Bucket Hashing In the bucket hashing strategy for collision processing, the hashing function transforms a given key to a physically contiguous region of locations within the table to be searched. This contiguous region is called a *bucket*. Thus, instead of hashing to the *K*th location, a key would hash to the *K*th bucket of locations. The number of locations contained in this bucket would depend on the bucket size (we assume that all buckets in a given table are the same size). Figure 11.21 illustrates this concept for a list with seven buckets and a bucket size of 3.

Having hashed to a bucket, the **target** must then be compared sequentially to all of the keys in that bucket. On the surface, it would seem that this strategy could do no better than duplicate the efficiency of the linked hash method discussed earlier. Indeed, because a sequential search is conducted in both cases after the initial hash is made, the average number of table accesses for a successful or unsuccessful search cannot be improved by using buckets. Moreover, provisions for linking to some sort of overflow area must still be made in case a series of collisions consumes all of the space in a given bucket.

What then could be a possible advantage of using buckets? If the table to be searched resides entirely in main memory, there is no advantage. However, if the table resides in a disk file, the bucket method will allow us to take advantage of some of the physical characteristics of the storage medium itself. To illustrate this, let us assume a one-surface disk divided into concentric *tracks* and pie-shaped *sectors* as indicated in Figure 11.22.

There are two ways in which the bucket hashing strategy may take advantage of the organization of the data on the disk. First, when records in a contiguous random-

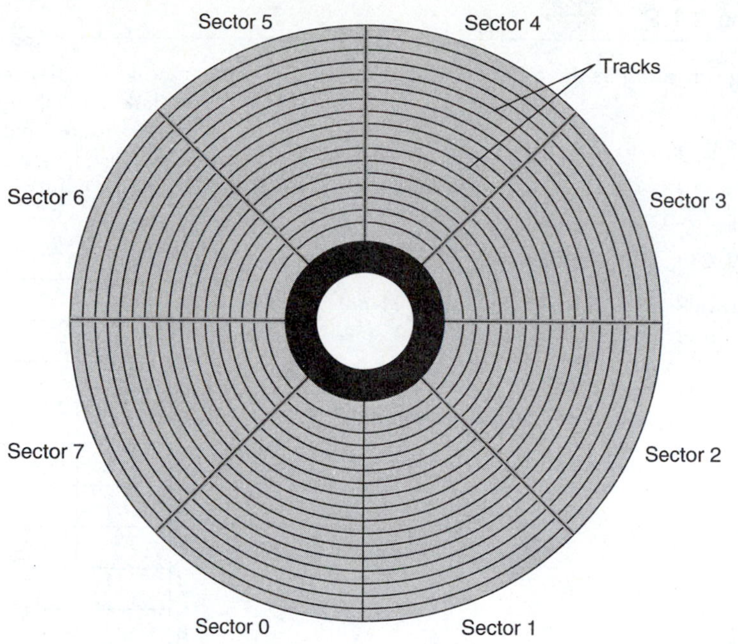

Figure 11.22
One-surface disk.

access file are stored on a disk, they are generally located in relative record number order along one track, then along an adjacent track, and so on. The movement of the read-write head between tracks is generally the cause of the most significant delays in obtaining data from a disk. The farther the movement, the greater the delay. Hence, if our knowledge of the machine in question allows us to make a bucket coincide with a track on the disk, then hashing to the beginning of a bucket and proceeding from there using a sequential search within the bucket (that is, the track) will greatly reduce head movement. A linked hashing strategy, on the other hand, could cause considerable movement of the read-write head between tracks on the disk, thereby slowing program execution. This consideration is an excellent example of how one must examine more than just the number of table accesses when measuring the efficiency of a program involving disk files.

A second advantage in using the bucket hashing algorithm when disk files are being searched is related to the way in which records are transferred between the disk and main memory. Frequently, programming languages create the illusion that each record accessed requires a separate disk access. However, records are frequently blocked—that is, positioned in contiguous regions on a track of the disk—so that a fixed number of them are brought into main memory when a record in that block is requested. This means that, if the record requested happens to be part of the block presently in main memory, a program statement that requests a record may not even require a disk access but only a different viewing window applied to the block already in main memory. Since main memory manipulations are orders of magnitude faster than the rate of data transfer to and from a disk, positioning buckets to coincide with a disk block will necessitate only one disk access each time an entire bucket is sequentially searched. Here again, the more scattered nature of a purely linked hashing algorithm would not allow this disk-oriented efficiency consideration to be taken into account.

Exercises 11.2

1. Assume a hashing function has the following characteristics:

Keys 459 and 333 hash to 0.

Key 632 hashes to 1.

Key 1090 hashes to 2.

Keys 1982, 379, 238, and 3411 hash to 9.

Assume that insertions into a hash table of size 11 are performed in the order 1982, 3411, 333, 632, 1090, 459, 379, and 238.

a. Indicate the position of the keys if the linear method is used to resolve collisions.

Index	key
0	
1	
2	
3	
4	
5	
6	
7	
8	
9	
10	

b. Indicate the position of the keys if the quadratic method is used to resolve collisions.

Index	key
0	
1	
2	
3	
4	
5	
6	
7	
8	
9	
10	

c. Indicate the position of the keys and the contents of the link fields if the chaining (that is, linked) method is used to resolve collisions. Assume that the first record used in the overflow area is index 11, then 12, then 13, and so on.

Prime area

Index	key	link
0		
1		
2		
3		
4		
5		
6		
7		
8		
9		
10		

Overflow area

Index	key	link
11		
12		
13		
14		
15		
16		
17		
18		
19		
20		
21		

2. Repeat Exercise 11.2.1 with the order of insertion of keys reversed.

3. a. Given the arrival of integer keys in the order 67, 19, 4, 58, 38, 55, and 86 and **tableSize** = 9 with

hash(keyValue) = keyValue % tableSize

trace the insertion steps for linear processing of collisions.

Index	key
0	NULL
1	NULL
2	NULL
3	NULL
4	NULL
5	NULL
6	NULL
7	NULL
8	NULL

b. Given the arrival of integer keys in the order 32, 62, 34, 77, 6, 46, and 107 and **tableSize** = 15 with

hash(keyValue) = keyValue % tableSize

trace the insertion steps for quadratic processing of collisions.

Index	key
0	NULL
1	NULL
2	NULL
3	NULL
4	NULL
5	NULL
6	NULL
7	NULL
8	NULL
9	NULL
10	NULL
11	NULL
12	NULL
13	NULL
14	NULL

c. Given the arrival of integer keys in the order 5, 3, 16, 27, 14, 25, and 4 and **tableSize** = 11 with initial hashing function

$$\textbf{hash}_1\textbf{(keyValue)} = \textbf{keyValue \% tableSize}$$

trace the insertion steps of the rehashing collision-processing method where the secondary hashing function is

$$\textbf{hash}_2\textbf{(keyValue)} = (5 \times \textbf{keyValue) \% tableSize}$$

Assume that, if the secondary hashing function is not successful in locating a position for the key, linear collision processing is used from the address indicated by the secondary hashing function. Comment on the effectiveness of rehashing with this particular secondary hashing function. Can you think of a better one?

Index	key
0	NULL
1	NULL
2	NULL
3	NULL
4	NULL
5	NULL
6	NULL
7	NULL
8	NULL
9	NULL
10	NULL

d. Given the arrival of integer keys in the order 6, 21, 9, 20, 88, 42, 7, 51, and 72 and **tableSize** = 11 with initial hashing function

$$\textbf{hash}_1\textbf{(keyValue)} = \textbf{keyValue \% tableSize}$$

trace the insertion steps using the double hashing collision-processing method with the second hashing function defined by

$$\textbf{hash}_2\textbf{(keyValue)} = \textbf{(keyValue/tableSize) \% tableSize}$$

If hash_2 evaluates to zero, set it to 1 instead. Then, since **tableSize** = 11 is a prime number, the values of $\textbf{hash}_2$ are automatically relatively prime to **tableSize**.

4. What search strategy would you use for each of the following applications? Justify your choices of strategy in a short essay.

a. The information to be maintained is the card catalog of a library. Frequent additions to and deletions from this catalog are made by the library. Additionally, users frequently search for the data associated with a given book's key. However, the library rarely prints an ordered listing of all its holdings; ordering the data is therefore not to be considered a high priority.

b. You are writing a program that maintains the lists of passengers on flights for an airline company. Passengers are frequently added to these lists. Moreover, passengers quite often cancel flight plans and must be removed from a list. You are also told that the airline frequently wants alphabetized listings of the passengers on a given flight and often needs to search for a particular passenger by name when inquiries are received from individuals.

c. You are writing a program that will access a large customer database and build up counts for the numbers of customers from each of the 50 states (plus the District of Columbia). To do this you will use a collection of records consisting of the two-character state abbreviation and an integer representing the count of customers from that state. For each customer you read in from the database, you must find the customer's home state in your collection and increase the corresponding count field. At the end, you must print the counts in order, alphabetized by the two-character state abbreviation.

5. Write a complete implementation for the keyed collection ADT using hashing with linear collision processing. Unlike Example 11.7, make sure that your implementation correctly processes removals.

6. Write a complete implementation for the keyed collection ADT using hashing with rehashing by separate hash functions to resolve collisions. Make sure that your implementation allows for removal of keys from the collection.

7. Write a complete implementation for the keyed collection ADT using double hashing to resolve collisions. Make sure that your implementation allows for removal of keys from the collection.

8. Write a complete implementation for the keyed collection ADT using hashing with linked collision processing. Unlike Example 11.8, make sure that your implementation correctly processes removals.

9. In Section 11.2 we mentioned a result by Radke that answered the question of how many array slots would be probed by the quadratic hashing algorithm for certain values of **tableSize**. In particular, Radke showed that if **tableSize** is a prime number of the form $4m + 3$ for some integer m, then half of the array slots would be probed by the sequence

$$K,\ K + 1^2,\ K + 2^2,\ K + 3^2, \ldots$$

where K is the original hash position. Radke also showed that the other half would be probed by the sequence

$$K - 1^2,\ K - 2^2,\ K - 3^2, \ldots$$

Use Radke's result to write a complete implementation for the keyed collection ADT using hashing with quadratic collision processing. Make sure that your implementation correctly processes deletions and does not prematurely declare a hash table to be full when the **add** operation is invoked.

10. Explain how hashing could be used to implement a variation of a keyed collection in which keys were not unique. For example, we might have several people identified by the same name.

11.3 Applications of Hashing

Ordered Lists

Our discussion of hashing in Section 11.2 introduced a new ADT, the keyed collection, with an eye toward hashing as an implementation technique. The limitation of a keyed collection is that arrangement of data in order is not a required operation.

Hashing is an implementation technique for a keyed collection that can virtually guarantee $O(1)$ efficiency for the **add**, **remove**, and **retrieve** operations—regardless of the amount of data in the collection. With this kind of performance, it seems natural to ask whether we can extend hashing to provide an implementation of an ordered list, that is, to allow list traversals in order by key value. Although the requirement that a good hashing function scatter keys seems directly at odds with ordered traversals, there are strategies that can be used to allow hashing and ordering of data to coexist. One such strategy is simply to sort the data in the hash table *logically* when an ordered list is needed. Here sorting the data *logically* means that an array of pointers into the hash table would be sorted instead of physically rearranging data items within the hash table. This would allow us to traverse the data in order while at the same time maintaining the positions of data within the hash table. Such a *pointer sort* strategy has the drawback of not maintaining the list in order but actually performing a potentially costly sort algorithm each time an ordering is requested. Clearly, this strategy is not wise if such an ordering is to be requested frequently. However, it is appropriate if requests for ordered lists come only at a relatively few, regularly scheduled intervals. In such situations, the time required to perform a pointer sort will not normally be a negative factor from a user's perspective.

In situations where requests for ordering would come frequently enough to make maintaining the list in order (as opposed to sorting) a necessity, we could follow a strategy that would combine the search speed of hashing with the advantages offered by a linked list. This combination uses hashing to search for an individual record but adds link fields to each record so that a linked list for each desired ordering can be woven through the collection of hashed records. Implementing this combination of hashing and linked list entails the following considerations with respect to the ordered list operations:

- *Adding an element to an ordered list.* In effect, the hashing/collision-processing algorithm will provide us with an available node to store data. That is, instead of using C++'s built-in **new** operator to get an available node, we use the hashing algorithm itself to find an empty slot in the hash table. Each linked list involved will then have to be traversed to link the node into each ordering in the appropriate logical location.

- *Retrieving an element from an ordered list.* There is no problem here because the hash algorithm should find the desired record quickly.
- *Removing an element from an ordered list.* Hashing can be used to find the record to be deleted; then the link field will be adjusted appropriately. Here a doubly linked list could prove to be particularly valuable. (Why?)
- *Traversing the list in order.* There is no problem here because the linked lists constantly maintain the appropriate orderings.

The Rabin-Karp String Search Algorithm

Recall, from the definition of the **String** class (Section 2.3), the **search** operation:

```
//---------------------------------------------------------------------------
// Interface for search operation
// GIVEN:     A previously constructed String object that is considered the
//            master string to be searched for a substring;
//            sub -- a String to search for in the master string;
//            start -- a character position in the master string. The master
//                     string is to be searched from this position onward.
// RETURN as value of function:
//            The position of the first occurrence of sub in the master
//            string, beginning at position start or after.  Zero is
//            returned if sub is not found in the master string.

    int search(const String &sub, int start);
```

The String ADT as we defined it in Section 2.3 assumed that the positions of characters in a string started at position 1, unlike a traditional C array that starts indexing at 0. Because of this assumption, returning a 0 value for an unsuccessful search caused no ambiguity.

In the worst case, the straightforward implementation of this algorithm, presented in Section 2.3, can deteriorate to $O(Length(Master) \times Length(Sub))$ efficiency. A variation on hashing, however, can virtually guarantee an efficiency of $O(Length(Master) + Length(Sub))$ for this same operation. This adaptation of hashing to string searching requires the notion of a *perfect* hashing function for strings.

A Perfect Hashing Function for Strings

We will assume that our strings are drawn from an alphabet with C possible characters. Then we can easily define a function Index that maps each character to a different integer in the range from 0 to $C - 1$. Now suppose that we have a string S of length N. Then, via the Index function, the characters of S can be viewed as the digits of a number in the base-C number system. Hence, corresponding to S, we have the number

$$\text{Index}(S_1) \times C^{N-1} + \text{Index}(S_2) \times C^{N-2} + \cdots + \text{Index}(S_{N-1}) \times C^1 + \text{Index}(S_N) \times C^0$$

where S_i represents the ith character in the string S. Note that this number is uniquely associated with this string; no other string drawn from the same C characters can have this as its number. We will designate the number associated with a string in this fashion as Number(S). The uniqueness property cited earlier implies that, for strings S and T with $S \neq T$, we have Number(S) $\neq$ Number(T). Given a hash table of infinite size, we thus have a perfect hash function for strings from this particular alphabet of C characters. Namely, Number(S) will give us an address for S that no other string could claim.

Example 11.9

Consider strings drawn from uppercase alphabetic characters with an Index function that maps A to 0, B to 1, C to 2, and so forth. Compute Number("ZETA").

Since $C = 26$ for strings under consideration, and since the characters 'Z', 'E', 'T', and 'A' are mapped to the numbers 25, 4, 19, and 0, respectively, we have

$$\begin{aligned}\text{Number ("ZETA")} &= (25) \times 26^3 + (4) \times 26^2 + (19) \times 26^1 + (0) \times 26^0 \\ &= 442{,}598\end{aligned}$$

Limitations to Perfection Unfortunately, computers are not machines with infinite resources. Hence, the perfect hashing function just described is not realizable on any machine. First, we cannot declare a hash table of infinite size. Second, the computation of Number(S) would quickly cause integer overflow on strings of reasonable size. So a compromise must be reached. Instead of working with an infinite table, we declare a hash table of a particular **tableSize**, designed to fit within the limits of our application. To map a string to a particular location in this table, we compute

$$\text{Number}(S) \ \% \ \text{tableSize}$$

Even this computation, however, is not without its problems. First, note that Number(S) is a polynomial in powers of C. To compute this efficiently, we can use an algorithm known as *Horner's method*. This algorithm views the definition of Number(S) for a string of length 4,

$$\text{Index}(S_1) \times C^3 + \text{Index}(S_2) \times C^2 + \text{Index}(S_3) \times C^1 + \text{Index}(S_4) \times C^0$$

as the equivalent expression:

$$(((((\text{Index}(S_1) \times C) + \text{Index}(S_2))) \times C) + \text{Index}(S_3))) \times C) + \text{Index}(S_4)$$

In general, after initializing Number(S) to Index(S_1), Horner's method reduces the computation of Number(S) to a loop involving $N - 1$ multiplications (by C) and $N - 1$ additions (of the Index corresponding to the next character in the string). This is illustrated in the following iterative control structure;

```
Number(S) = Index(S1);
for k running from 2 to Length(S)
  Number(S) = Number(S) * C + Index(Sk);
```

Example 11.10

To evaluate Number("ZETA") by Horner's method, we would perform the following computations:

$$\underbrace{25 * 26}$$
$$\underbrace{650 + 4}$$
$$\underbrace{654 * 26}$$
$$\underbrace{17004 + 19}$$
$$\underbrace{17023 * 26}$$
$$\underbrace{442598 + 0}$$
$$442598$$

Figure 11.23
Substrings of length 3 of KOKOMO as the sole occupants of a large hash table.

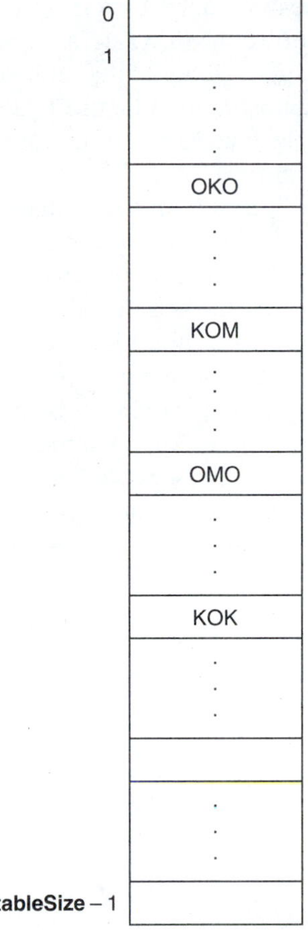

Although Horner's method provides an $O(Length(S))$ algorithm for the computation of Number(S), it will not by itself solve the problem of overflow in the computation of the hash function value, Number(S) % **tableSize**. The computation of Number(S) may overflow before the remainder operation is performed. To remedy this, note that we may take the remainder of dividing Number(S) by **tableSize** after each iteration of the loop in Horner's algorithm to arrive at the computation of Number(S) % **tableSize**. That is, we modify Horner's algorithm so that it becomes

```
Number(S) = Index(S1 );
for k running from 2 to Length(S)
   Number(S) = (Number(S) * C + Index(Sk )) % tableSize;
```

Now Number(S) will always be less than **tableSize** as we iterate the loop. Hence the expression

$$\text{Number}(S) \times C + \text{Index}(S_I)$$

will be less than

$$\textbf{tableSize} \times C + C = (\textbf{tableSize} + 1) \times C$$

So choosing **tableSize** small enough to ensure that (**tableSize** + 1) × C will not overflow guarantees that no overflow will occur in the iterative computation of our hash function value.

The choice of **tableSize** should also be made to minimize the chance that two different strings will hash to the same position. In this regard, we want to be sure that the effect of each term in the expression for Number(S),

$$\text{Index}(S_1) \times C^{N-1} + \text{Index}(S_2) \times C^{N-2} + \cdots + \text{Index}(S_{N-1}) \times C^1 + \text{Index}(S_N) \times C^0$$

is not canceled when we take the remainder of dividing by **tableSize**. Such cancellation will occur if the remainder of dividing by the **tableSize** operation reduces a nonzero term to zero; that is, if the term is a nonzero multiple of **tableSize**. We can guarantee that this won't happen if **tableSize** is chosen to be a prime number larger than C. Since C will usually be relatively small, this criterion should be easy to satisfy.

In summary, here is the recommended compromise to the perfect hashing function for strings.

1. Choose **tableSize** to be a prime number that is (a) larger than C, (b) small enough to ensure that (**tableSize** + 1) × C will not cause overflow on your machine, and (c) within the range of a hash table size that your application will allow.
2. Then compute the "compromised" value of Number(S) by a Horner's algorithm loop that takes the remainder of dividing by **tableSize** in each iteration. Hereafter we will refer to this value as CompNumber(S).

Example 11.11

You have an application in which the keys being hashed are composed of uppercase letters and spaces, so C is 27. The application is running on a 16-bit computer, which implies an integer overflow point of 32,767. Hence, **tableSize** should be chosen to be a prime number larger than 27 and small enough to ensure that (**tableSize** + 1) × 27 ≤ 32, 767.

The Rabin-Karp Algorithm We are now ready to attack the string search problem that initiated our discussion. Suppose that we wish to search the Master string KOKOMO for the Sub string KOM. Then KOM must be compared against all the three-character substrings of KOKOMO: KOK, OKO, KOM, and OMO. If any of these comparisons returns a successful match, then the search succeeds; otherwise it fails. The Rabin-Karp algorithm suggests that we imagine KOK, OKO, KOM, and OMO as the only four strings stored in an exceptionally large hash table determined by the hashing function CompNumber(S). This concept is illustrated in Figure 11.23. How large can this table be? Since it is a conceptual table that is never allocated in computer memory, it must meet only the preceding criteria of 1(a) and 1(b); that is, **tableSize** must be larger than C (the number of characters in the alphabet for our strings) and small enough to insure that (**tableSize** + 1) × C will not cause overflow. To determine whether or not Sub is contained in Master, we must merely determine whether or not Sub is contained in the conceptual hash table of Figure 11.23. But this is the same as determining whether or not CompNumber(Sub) equals the CompNumber of any of the substrings of Master that are "contained" in this table. Since **tableSize** can be chosen extremely large, we ignore, for the time being, the remote possibility that CompNumber(Sub) could equal the CompNumber of another one of the substrings of Master. That is, because of the large **tableSize** and relatively small number of strings stored in it, the possibility of a hashing collision is so small that we temporarily pretend it cannot happen. Hence, the Rabin-Karp string search algorithm can be formalized as follows:

```
// Implementation of Rabin-Karp string search algorithm.  We assume that
// tableSize and C have been defined appropriately via const int declarations and
// that index and compNumber functions have been implemented as per the
// prior discussion

int String::search(const String &sub, int start)
{
  int target, candidate, position, lm, ls;
  BOOLEAN found;

  ls = sub.length();                              // Length of substring
  lm = length();                                  // Length of master string
  target = sub.compNumber();                      // Substring's compNumber
  candidate = substring(start,ls).compNumber();   // compNumber of part of
                                                  // master beginning at start
  position = start;
  found = FALSE;
  while ((position <= lm - ls + 1) && !found)
    if (target == candidate)
      found = TRUE;
    else
      candidate = substring(++position,ls).compNumber(); // Next compNumber in
                                                         // master string
  if (found)
    return(position);
  else
    return(0);
}
```

Analysis of the Rabin-Karp Algorithm Clearly the **while** loop in the Rabin-Karp algorithm is $O(Length(Master))$. The repeated computations of CompNumber nested within the loop are each $O(Length(Sub))$ under the assumption that Horner's algorithm is used. However, under the special circumstances of the string search, we may achieve a more efficient computation of CompNumber within the **while** loop. In particular, note that, from one iteration of this loop to the next, the substring whose CompNumber is being computed shifts only by one character. Hence much of the computation of **candidate** from one iteration of the loop can be used again in the next iteration. For instance, if **ls** is used to denote the length of the string **sub, candidate** will be

$$(\text{Index}(\text{Master}_K) \times C^{ls-1} + \text{Index}(\text{Master}_{K+1}) \times C^{ls-2} + \cdots + \text{Index}(\text{Master}_{K+ls-1}) \times C^0) \;\%\; \textbf{tableSize}$$

on the Kth pass through the loop and, on the $(K + 1)$st pass,

$$(\text{Index}(\text{Master}_{K+1}) \times C^{ls-1} + \text{Index}(\text{Master}_{K+2}) \times C^{ls-2} + \cdots + \text{Index}(\text{Master}_{K+ls}) \times C^0) \;\%\; \textbf{tableSize}$$

Note that the latter value of **candidate** may be computed from the former by

$$\textbf{candidate} = (\textbf{candidate} \times C - \text{Index}(\text{Master}_K) \times C^{ls} + \text{Index}(\text{Master}_{K+ls})) \;\%\; \textbf{tableSize}$$

To avoid problems with the remainder operation when $(\textbf{candidate} \times C - \text{Index}(\text{Master}_K) \times C^{ls} + \text{Index}(\text{Master}_{K+ls}))$ is negative, we must add a **tableSize** $\times C$ term:

$$\textbf{candidate} = (\textbf{candidate} \times C - \text{Index}(\text{Master}_K) \times C^{ls} + \textbf{tableSize} \times C + \text{Index}(\text{Master}_{K+ls})) \;\%\; \textbf{tableSize}$$

Thus, we can obtain a better algorithm by computing C^{ls} prior to the **while** loop and using the more efficient computation of **candidate** presented above. This refined version of the Rabin-Karp algorithm is incorporated into the following:

```
// Refinement of Rabin-Karp string search algorithm.  Again assume that
// tableSize and C have been defined appropriately via const int declarations
// and that index and compNumber functions have been implemented as per the
// prior discussion.

int String::search(const String &sub, int start)
{
  int target, candidate, position, cpower, lm, ls, i;
  BOOLEAN found;


  ls = sub.length();                            // Length of substring
  lm = length();                                // Length of master string
  target = sub.compNumber();                    // Substring's compNumber
  candidate = substring(start,ls).compNumber(); // compNumber of part of
                                                // master beginning at start
                                                // Now compNumber is only called
                                                // outside the while loop

  // Next compute C to the ls power.
  cpower = 1;
  for (i = 1; i <= ls; ++i)
    cpower = (cpower * C) % tableSize;
  position = start;
  found = FALSE;
  while ((position <= lm - ls +1) && !found)
    if (target == candidate)
      found = TRUE;
    else
```

```
      {
        // Character at position is given by (*this)[position]
        candidate = (candidate*C - index((*this)[position])* cpower +
                     tableSize*C + index((*this)[position+ls])) % tableSize;
        ++position;
      }
    if (found)
      return(position);
    else
      return(0);
}
```

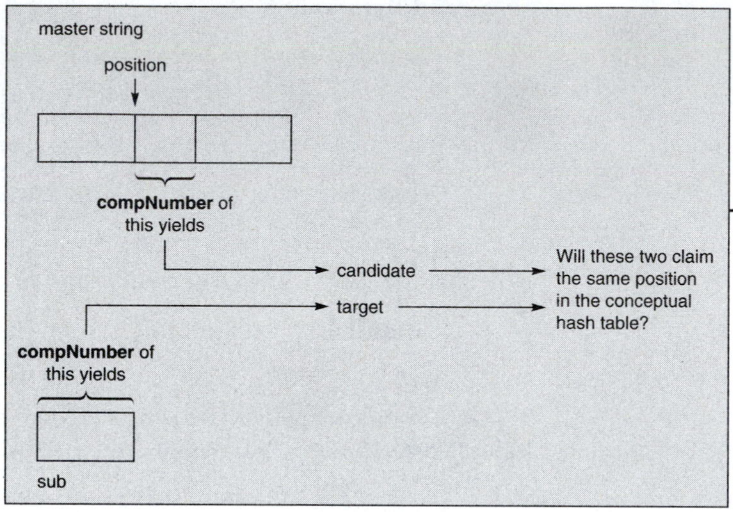

master string
position
compNumber of this yields
candidate
target
Will these two claim the same position in the conceptual hash table?
compNumber of this yields
sub

With these modifications, the **while** loop will have *O*(*Length*(*Master*)) efficiency. Because CompNumber(Sub) and CompNumber(Master) are computed before the loop, the entire procedure will have *O*(*Length*(*Sub*) + *Length*(*Master*)) efficiency.

The only problem that remains is that the present implementation of the Rabin-Karp algorithm could fail under the *highly improbable* occurrence that CompNumber(Sub) equals the CompNumber of one of Master's substrings even though the two strings are not identical. The modifications necessary to handle this possibility are left for the exercises.

Exercises 11.3

1. Suppose that we combine hashing with a linked list in the fashion described in Section 11.3 so that all ordered list operations can be performed efficiently. Which of the variations on a linked-list structure described in Section 3.4 would be most effective in this context? Why?
2. In Exercise 3.1.1 you defined an ordered list ADT. Now write a complete implementation of this ADT that uses hashing combined with a pointer sort to achieve the traversal operation.
3. In Exercise 3.1.1 you defined an ordered list ADT. Now write a complete implementation of this ADT that uses hashing combined with a linked list to achieve the traversal operation.
4. Suppose that we are drawing strings from the set of uppercase letters and the space character. Compute Number("ZEBRA").
5. You are working on a 16-bit computer with strings drawn from the set of uppercase letters and the space character. What should the **tableSize** be for the Rabin-Karp algorithm? Given this choice, compute CompNumber("ZEBRA").
6. What would be the effect of choosing **tableSize** equal to *C* in the computation of a string's CompNumber?
7. Complete the Rabin-Karp string search algorithm presented in this section by adding code to handle the remote possibility that a substring of the Master string and Sub will have the same CompNumber even when they are not identical as strings.
8. The Rabin-Karp algorithm can also be modified to search for patterns in two-dimensional tables. Suppose that we have a large matrix of 1's and 0's representing a graphic image. A 1 indicates that the screen dot (pixel) corresponding to that position in the matrix should be black; a 0 indicates white. We want to determine whether a certain subimage, represented as a smaller two-dimensional array of 1's and 0's is contained in this larger image. Write a variation of the Rabin-Karp algorithm that will search the larger image for an occurrence of the smaller image.

9. When searching strings for a particular pattern, it is often convenient to allow certain characters to count as *wildcards*. A wildcard character matches any other character. Suppose that * were designated as a wildcard character. Then a wildcard string search for "M*T" in "METAMATHEMATICS" would turn up both "MET" and "MAT" (twice) as matches. Modify the Rabin-Karp algorithm to accept wildcard characters in the Sub string.

Exercises 10 through 12 apply to the sparse matrix ADT that was introduced in Exercises 6 and 7 of Section 2.1. Recall that the sparse matrix problem attempts to answer the following question: Given a matrix with a high percentage of a certain uniform value, say 0, how can we implement this matrix in a space-efficient fashion without completely sacrificing processing speed? One strategy for implementing the sparse matrix ADT would simply create a list of the (row, column) pairs of indices corresponding to nontrivial (that is, nonzero) values in the matrix. Along with each (row, column) pair, we maintain the nontrivial value stored at that position of the matrix. Thus, determining the value of the data at a conceptual row/column location is simply a matter of searching this list.

Hashing allows us to search for a row/column coordinate in the list in a very efficient fashion. Moreover, since the order of the data in the list is not important for this application, the scattered nature of hashed storage does not present any obstacle at all. The following figure illustrates how a hash table could be used as the implementation underlying a sparse table.

10. Write a complete C++ implementation for the sparse matrix ADT using the hashing technique described above.
11. Suppose that we have a $3{,}000 \times 4{,}000$ matrix of real values that contain no more than 15% nonzero values. Suppose also that we wish to resolve any request to retrieve or assign a value in an average of three probes into an underlying hash table implementation. How large would you declare the hash table? Provide a rationale for your choice of size.
12. You are considering hashing as an implementation technique for a sparse matrix of floats. The following are parameters that will influence your deliberations.

    R = the number of bytes to store a float

    I = the number of bytes to store an integer (such as a row or column coordinate)

    P = the percentage of matrix locations that store a nontrivial value

    N = the average number of hash table probes you are willing to tolerate for resolving collisions

    In terms of the other parameters, what must P be before the hashing implementation actually becomes more space efficient than the standard row major implementation of the matrix? Assume linear collision processing is used. What if quadratic collision processing is used? Linked collision processing?

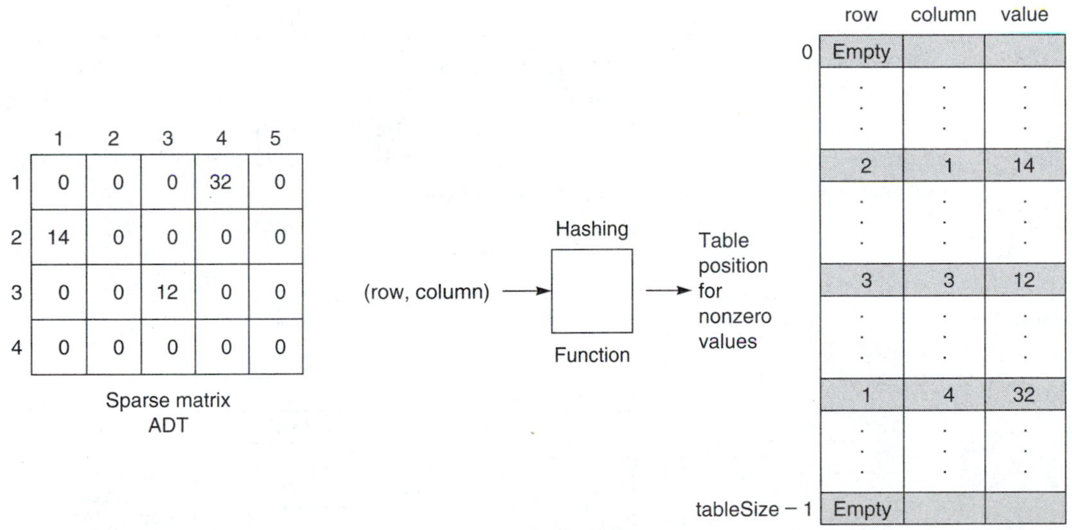

	1	2	3	4	5
1	0	0	0	32	0
2	14	0	0	0	0
3	0	0	12	0	0
4	0	0	0	0	0

Sparse matrix ADT

(row, column) → Hashing Function → Table position for nonzero values

	row	column	value
0	Empty		
	⋮	⋮	⋮
	2	1	14
	⋮	⋮	⋮
	3	3	12
	⋮	⋮	⋮
	1	4	32
	⋮	⋮	⋮
tableSize − 1	Empty		

11.4 Indexed Search Techniques

All the search strategies we have studied up to this point could be applied to data structures implemented in main memory or on a random access disk. However, with the exception of bucket hashing, none of the methods we have studied takes into account physical characteristics of actual disk storage in an attempt to enhance their efficiency. In practice, because retrieval of data from a disk file is orders of magnitude slower than retrieval from main memory, we often cannot afford to ignore these special characteristics of disk files if we want reasonable response time for our searching efforts. The indexing schemes we discuss in this section are primarily directed toward file-oriented applications and will thus take into account the operational properties of this storage medium. We encourage you to reread the discussion of bucket hashing at the end of Section 11.2 for a short analysis of file storage considerations.

The idea behind the use of an index is analogous to the way in which we routinely use an address book to find a person we are seeking. That is, if we are looking for a person, we do not simply knock on the doors of numerous houses until we find the one where that person lives. Instead, we apply a search strategy to an address book. There we use the name of the person as a key to find a pointer—that is, an address—that swiftly leads us to where the person can be found. Only one actual "house access" must be made, even though our search strategy may require numerous accesses into the address book index.

In a computer system, records (or more precisely blocks) could play the role of houses in the search scenario just described. Data records on disk are (when compared to main memory) terribly slow and awkward creatures to access. One reason for this is that a large amount of data must often be moved from disk to main memory when a record is accessed. Because of this, we must revise the conceptual picture we have of the general setup for an indexed search so that our sequence of keys is no longer parallel to the actual data the keys are logically associated with but rather is parallel to a sequence of pointers that will lead us to the actual data. This revised picture is presented in Figure 11.24.

The general strategy of an indexed search is to use the key to search the index efficiently, find the relative record position of the associated data, and then make only one access into the actual data. Because the parallel sequences of keys and relative record positions require much less storage than the data itself, the entire index can frequently be loaded and permanently held in main memory, necessitating only one disk access for each record being sought. For larger indices, it is still true that large blocks of keys and associated pointers may be manipulated in main memory, thereby greatly enhancing search efficiency.

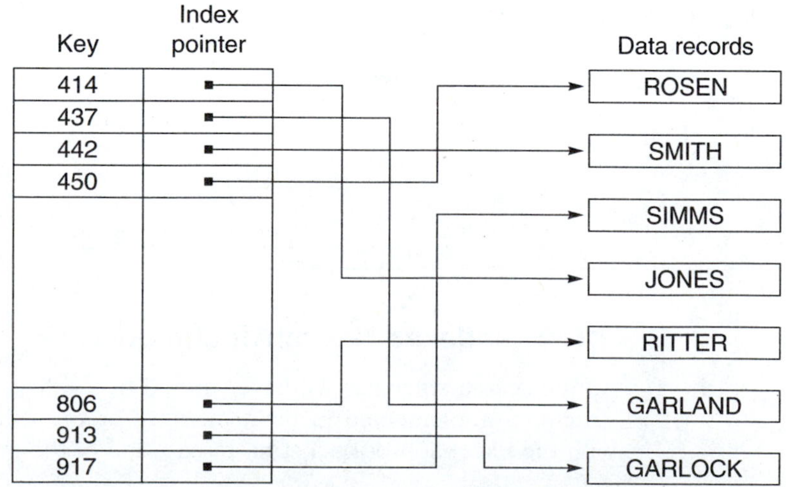

Figure 11.24
General setup for an indexed search.

Indexed Sequential Search Technique

The *indexed sequential search* technique is also commonly recognized by the acronym ISAM, which stands for *Indexed Sequential Access Method*. This technique involves carefully weighing the disk-dependent factors of blocking and track size to build a partial index.

The partial index, unlike some other index structures we will study, does not reduce to one the number of probes that must be made into the actual data. To continue the analogy between searching for data and searching for a person, the indexed sequential strategy is somewhat like an address book that would lead us to the street on which a person lives but leave it to us to check each house on that street. The ISAM method correspondingly leads us to an appropriate region (often a track or a cylinder containing multiple tracks within a disk pack), leaving it for us to search sequentially within that region.

As an example, let us suppose that we can conveniently fit the partial index, or directory, pictured in Figure 11.25 into main memory and that the organization of our disk file allows six records per track. This directory contains the highest

Figure 11.25
One-level indexed sequential file.

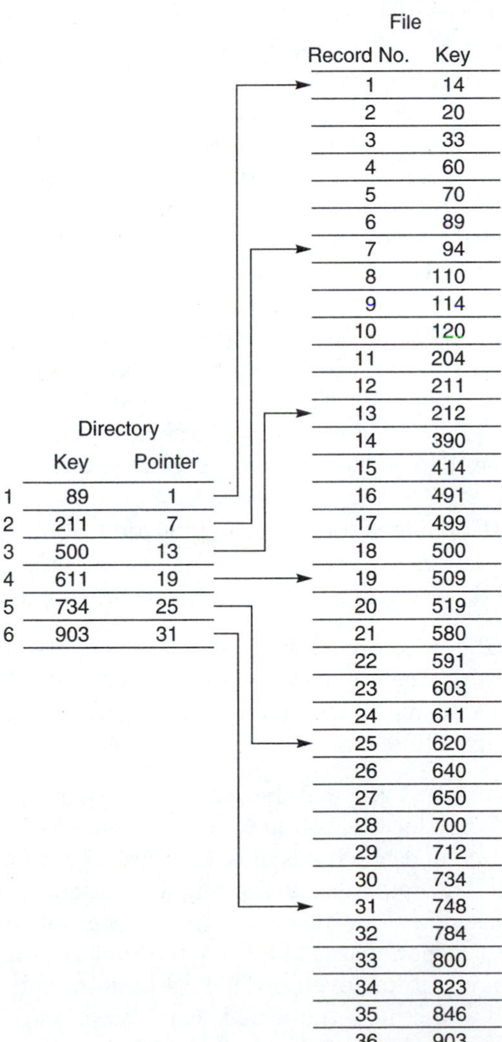

key value in each six-record track along with a pointer indicating where that track begins. Here our pointers are simply relative record numbers; in practice they could well be more disk dependent. The strategy to conduct an indexed sequential search is as follows:

1. Search the main memory directory for a key that is greater than or equal to the **target.**
2. Then follow the corresponding pointer out to the disk and there search sequentially until a match (success) or the high key within that particular region (failure) is found.

For the data given in Figure 11.25, this technique would mean that the 36-record file would require no more than six main memory index accesses plus six disk accesses, all of which are located in the same track.

For larger files, it may be advantageous to have more than one level of these directory structures. Consider, for instance, the two-level directory structure for a file with 216 records given in Figure 11.26. Here we suppose that storage restrictions allow the entire primary directory to be kept in main memory, the secondary directory to be brought in from a disk file in blocks of six key–pointer pairs each, and the actual data records to be stored six per track. The primary directory divides the file into regions of 36 records each. The key in the primary directory represents the highest valued key in a given 36-record region, but the pointer leads us into the subdirectory instead of the actual file. We therefore search the primary directory for a key greater than or equal to the target we are seeking. Once this is done, we follow the primary directory pointer into the secondary directory. Beginning at the position indicated by the primary directory's pointer, we again search for a key greater than or equal to the target. Notice that fetching one block of six key–pointer pairs from the subdirectory has necessitated one disk access in our hypothetical situation. In return for this single disk access, we are able to subdivide the 36-record region determined by the primary directory into six 6-record regions, each of which will lie entirely on one track by the time we get out to the actual disk file. Following the subdirectory's pointer to the file, we end up with a fairly short sequential search on the storage medium itself. In this example, the maximum number of disk accesses required to find any record would be seven, and six of those would be isolated on one track of the disk.

Efficiency Considerations for the Indexed Sequential Search It should be clear from the preceding discussion that the search efficiency of the indexed sequential technique depends on a variety of factors, including

- To what degree the directory structures are able to subdivide the actual file
- To what degree the directory structures are able to reside in main memory
- The relationship of data records to physical characteristics of the disk such as blocking factors, track size, cylinder size, and so on.

It should also be clear that the indexed sequential method may not be ideal for a highly volatile file. This is true because, as implicitly indicated in Figures 11.25 and 11.26, the actual data records must be physically stored in increasing (or decreasing) key order. The requirement for physical ordering is obviously not conducive to frequent insertions and deletions. In practice, the solution to this problem is that each file subregion that is ultimately the subject of a sequential search is equipped with a pointer to an overflow area. Insertions are located in this overflow area and linked to the main sequential search area. As the overflow area builds up, the search efficiency tends to deteriorate. In some applications this deterioration can

Figure 11.26
Two-level directory structure.

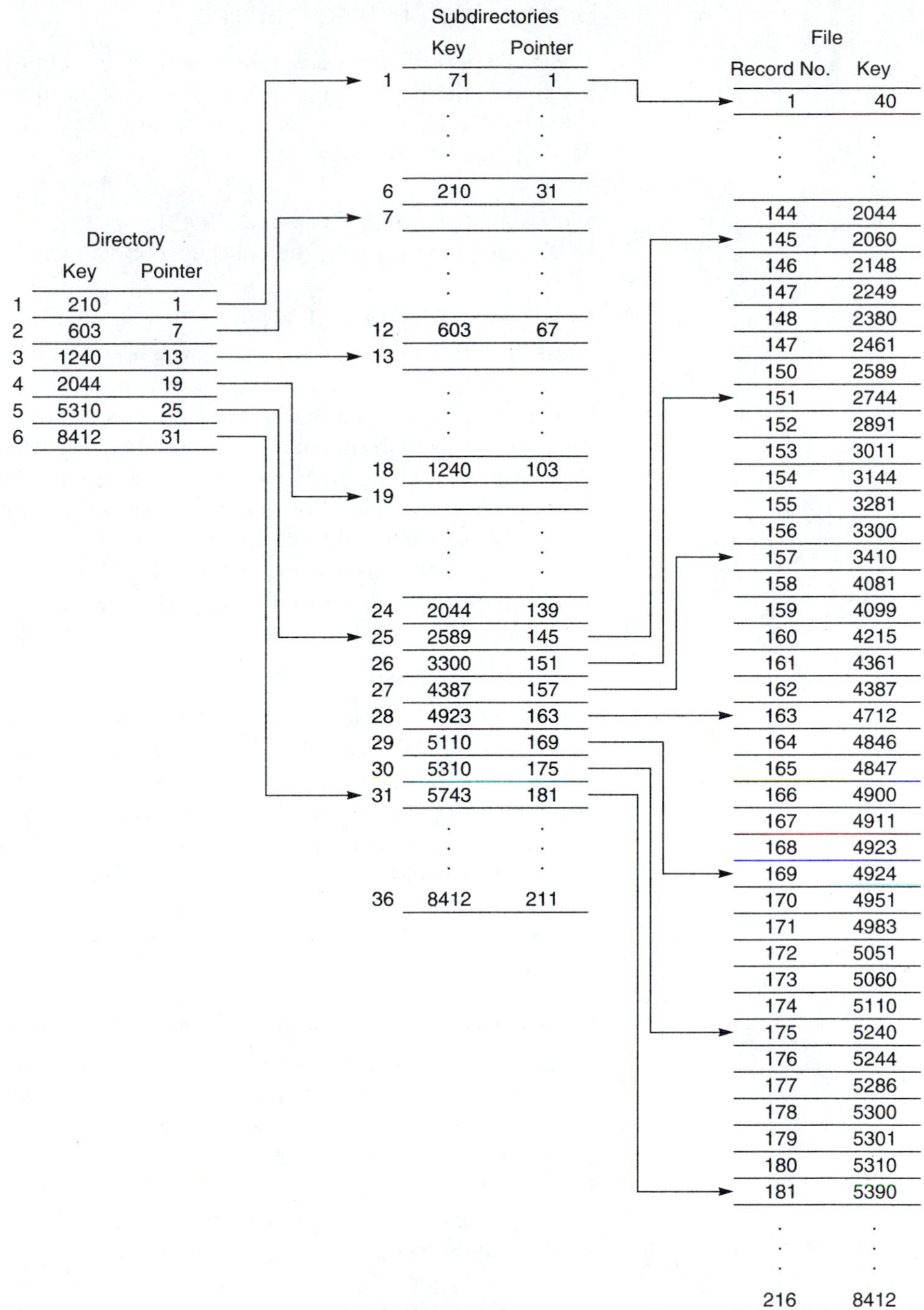

be so severe that data-processing personnel have been known to refer to the ISAM technique as the *Intrinsically Slow Access Method*.

The way to avoid deterioration is to periodically reorganize the file into a new file with no overflow. However, such reorganization cannot be done dynamically. It requires going through the file in key sequential order and copying it to a new one. Along the way the indices must be rebuilt, of course. These types of maintenance problems involved with the ISAM structure have led to the development of several more dynamic indexing schemes.

Binary Search Tree Indexing

The concept of a binary search tree was covered in Chapter 7. The only twist added when the binary search tree plays the role of an index is that each node of the tree contains a key and a pointer to the record associated with that key in some larger data aggregate. The advantages of using a binary search tree as an index structure include

- A potential search efficiency of $O(\log_2 n)$
- The ability to traverse the collection of data values indexed by the tree in key order
- Dynamic insertion and deletion capabilities.

These qualities make the binary search tree the ideal index structure for situations in which the entire tree can fit in main memory. However, if the data collection is so large that the tree index must itself be stored on disk, the efficiency of the structure is less than optimal. This is true because each node of the index may lie in a different disk block and hence require a separate disk access. For example, with 50,000 keys a search of a binary tree index could require 16 disk accesses. To solve this problem, we would like to cluster the nodes along a given search path into one, or at least relatively few, disk blocks. The *B-tree* index structure is a variation on the tree index that accomplishes this.

B-Tree Indexing

We begin this discussion of B-trees with a reminder that one index entry is nothing more than a pair consisting of a key and a pointer. Moreover, we have assumed that both the key and the pointer are integers, and we continue to operate under this assumption during our discussion of B-trees. In a B-tree a given tree node will contain many such key–pointer pairs because a B-tree node will in fact coincide with one disk block. The idea behind a B-tree is that we will somehow group related key–pointer pairs in the search algorithm into a few strategic B-tree nodes, that is, disk blocks. At this point, we make a formal definition; later, we'll clarify this definition via some examples.

Definition A *B-tree of order n* is a structure with the following properties:

1. Every node in the B-tree has sufficient room to store $n - 1$ key–pointer pairs.
2. Additionally, every node has room for n pointers to other nodes in the B-tree (as distinguished from the pointers within key–pointer pairs, which point to the position of a key in the file).
3. Every node except the root must have at least $(n - 1)/2$ (integer division) key–pointer pairs stored in it.
4. All terminal nodes are on the same level.
5. If a nonterminal node has m key–pointer pairs stored in it, then it must contain $m + 1$ non-NULL pointers to other B-tree nodes.
6. For each B-tree node, we require that the key value in key–pointer pair KP_{i-1} be less than the key value in key–pointer pair KP_i, that all key–pointer pairs in the node pointed to by pointer P_{i-1} contain keys that are less than the key in KP_i, and that all key–pointer pairs in the node pointed to by pointer P_i contain key values that are greater than the key in KP_i.

According to property 5 of the definition, we can think of a B-tree node as a list

$$P_0,\ KP_1,\ P_1,\ KP_2,\ P_2,\ KP_3, \ldots, P_{m-1},\ KP_m,\ P_m$$

where P_i represents the ith pointer to another B-tree node and KP_i represents the *i*th key–pointer pair. Note that a B-tree node will always contain one more pointer to another B-tree node than it does key–pointer pairs. If you keep this picture in mind, the sixth property of our definition makes sense. Figure 11.27 illustrates how this rather involved definition applies to a B-tree node with three key–pointer pairs.

As a further illustration of this definition, a complete B-tree of order 6 serving as an index structure for the 36-record file of Figure 11.25 appears in Figure 11.28. (In this figure, the slash between numbers denotes a key–pointer pair; ⊦ denotes a NULL pointer.) Carefully verify that all six defining properties are satisfied.

The choice of order 6 for Figure 11.28 was made only for the purposes of making the figure fit on a page of text. In practice, the order chosen would be the maximum number of B-tree pointers and key–pointer pairs that we could fit into one disk block. That is, the choice should be made to force a disk block to coincide with a B-tree node.

Efficiency Considerations for B-Tree Indexing Let us now consider what is involved in searching a B-tree for a given key. Within the current node (starting at the root), we must search sequentially through the key values in the node until we come to a match, a key value that is greater than the one being sought, or the end of the key values in that particular node. If a match is not made within a particular B-tree node, we have a pointer to follow to an appropriate follow-up node. Again, you should verify this algorithm for several of the keys appearing at various levels of Figure 11.28. The sequential search on keys within a given node may at first seem unappealing. However, it is important to remember that each B-tree node is a disk block that is loaded entirely into main memory. Hence, it may be possible to search sequentially on hundreds of keys within a node in the time it would take to load one new node from disk. Our main concern is to minimize disk accesses, and here we have achieved a worst-case search for our 36-entry file in three disk accesses. What, then, in general is the search efficiency for a B-tree index? It should be clear from the nature of the structure that the maximum number of disk accesses for any particular key will simply be the number of levels in the tree. Thus, the efficiency question really amounts to knowing the maximum number of levels that the six defining criteria will allow for a B-tree containing n key–pointer pairs; this number is the worst-case search efficiency. To determine this number, we use the minimum number of nodes that must be present on any given level. Let L be the smallest integer greater than or equal to $K/2$, where K is the order of the B-tree in question. Then

Level 0 contains at least 1 node.
Level 1 contains at least 2 nodes.
Level 2 contains at least $2L$ nodes.
Level 3 contains at least $2L^2$ nodes.
⋮
Level m contains at least $2L^{m-1}$ nodes.

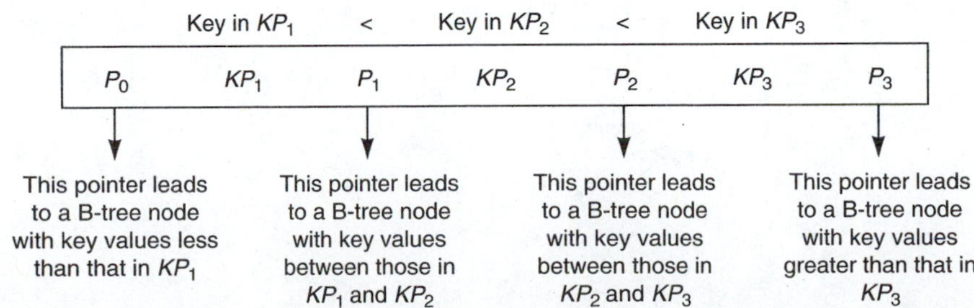

Figure 11.27
Example of a B-tree node with three key–pointer pairs.

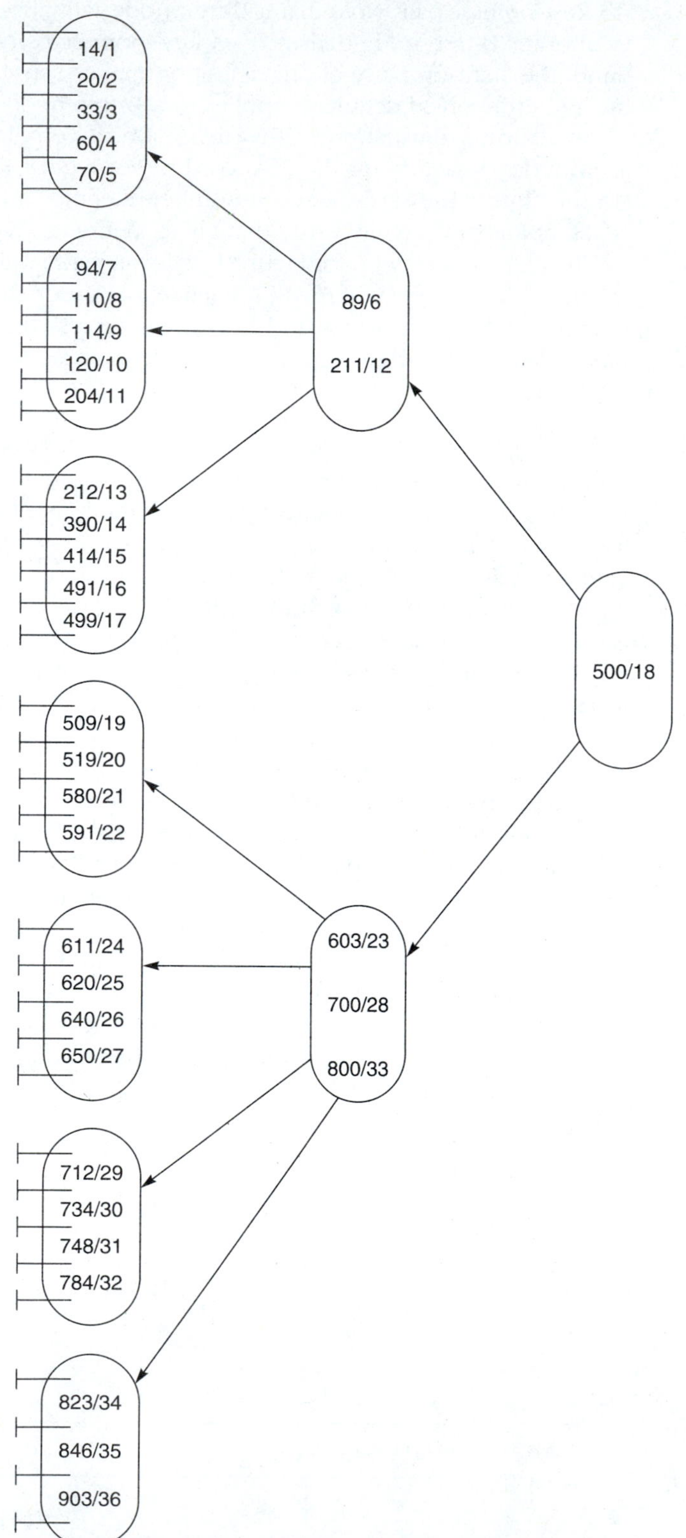

Figure 11.28
B-tree index of order 6 for file in Figure 11.25.

An argument due to Knuth (see *Searching and Sorting,* cited in Section 11.1) uses this progression to show that the maximum number of levels (and thus the worst-case search efficiency) for n key–pointer pairs is

$$\log_K \frac{n+1}{2}$$

Thus, a B-tree search has an $O(\log_K n)$ efficiency where n is the number of records and K is the order of the B-tree. Note that this can be considerably better than an $O(\log_2 n)$ search efficiency. As an example, the index for a file of 50,000 records, which would require on the order of 16 disk accesses using a binary tree structure, could be searched with three disk accesses using a B-tree of order 250. Note that, given typical block sizes for files, the choice of order 250 for this example is not at all unrealistic.

Unlike ISAM, the B-tree index can dynamically handle insertions and deletions without a resulting deterioration in search efficiency. We next discuss how B-tree insertions are handled; making deletions is left for an exercise. The essential idea behind a B-tree insertion is that we must first determine which bottom-level node should contain the key–pointer pair to be inserted. For instance, suppose that we want to insert the key 742 into the B-tree of Figure 11.28. By allowing this key to walk down the B-tree from the root to the bottom level, we could quickly determine that this key belongs in the node presently containing

712/29
734/30
748/31
784/32

Since, by the definition of a B-tree of order 6, this node is not presently full, no further disk accesses are necessary to perform the insertion. We merely need to determine the next available record space in the actual data file (37 in this case) and then add the key–pointer pair 742/37 to this terminal node, resulting in a node containing in order,

712/29
734/30
742/37
748/31
784/32

A slightly more difficult situation arises when we find that the key–pointer pair we wish to add should be inserted into a bottom-level node that is already full. For instance, this would occur if we attempted to add the key 112 to the B-tree of Figure 11.28. We would load the actual data for this key into file position 38 (given the addition already made in the preceding paragraph) and then determine that the key–pointer pair 112/38 belongs in the bottom-level node containing

94/7
110/8
114/9
120/10
204/11

The stipulation that any B-tree node except the root have at least $(6 - 1)/2 = 2$ key–pointer pairs allows us to split this node, creating one new node with two key–pointer pairs and one with three key–pointer pairs. We also have to move one of the key–pointer pairs up to the parent of the present node. The resulting B-tree is given in Figure 11.29.

Although it does not happen in this particular example, note that it is entirely possible that the moving of a key–pointer pair up to a parent node that is already full would necessitate a split of this parent node using the same procedure. Indeed, it is possible that key–pointer pairs could be passed all the way up to the root and cause a split of the root; this is how a new level of the tree would be introduced. A split of the root would force the creation of a new root which would only have one key–pointer pair and two pointers to other B-tree nodes. At the root level, however, this is still a sufficient number of pointers to retain the B-tree structure. Because the insertion algorithm for a B-tree requires checking whether a given node is full and if so, moving back up to a parent node, it is convenient to allow space within a node to store both of the following:

- A count of the number of key–pointer pairs in the node
- A back pointer to the node's parent.

Trie Indexing

In the indexing applications we have discussed so far, the keys involved have been integers. In practice, however, we must be prepared to deal with keys of different types. Perhaps the worst case is that of keys that are variable-length character strings. *Trie indexing* has developed as a means of retrieving keys in this worst case. (The term is derived from the four middle letters of *retrieve* but is usually pronounced "try.")

Let us suppose that the strings in the following list represent a set of keys. Each string may be thought of as a last name followed by initials and a delimiting character, here denoted by $.

ADAMS BT$
COOPER CC$
COOPER PJ$
COWANS DC$
MAGUIRE WH$
MCGUIRE AL$
MEMINGER DD$
SEFTON SD$
SPAN KD$
SPAN LA$
SPANNER DW$
ZARDA JM$
ZARDA PW$

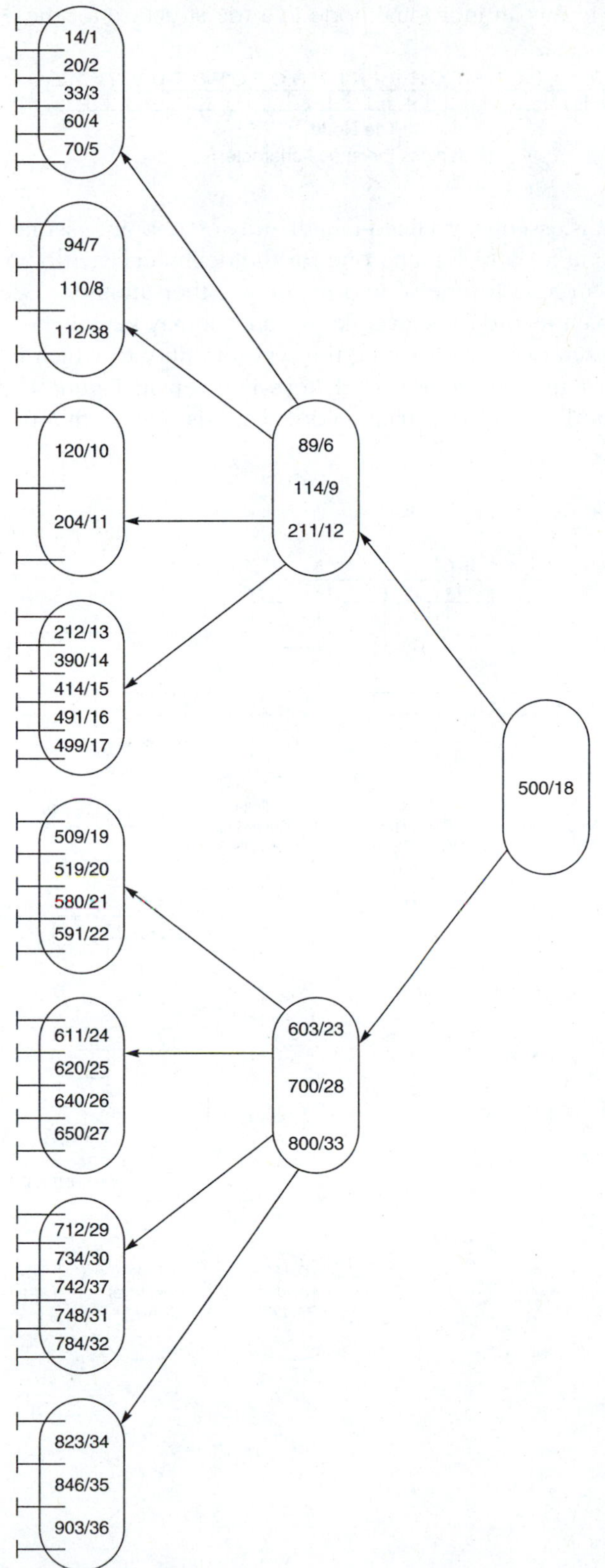

Figure 11.29
B-tree of Figure 11.28 after insertion of 742/37 and 112/38.

Here is an individual node in a trie structure for these keys:

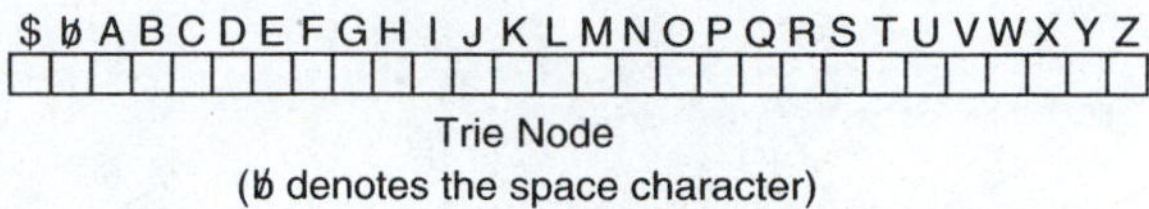

Trie Node
(ƀ denotes the space character)

It is essentially a fixed-length array of 28 pointers: one for each letter of the alphabet, one for a blank, and one for the delimiter. Each pointer within one of these nodes can lead to one of two entities—either another node within the trie or the actual data record for a given key. Hence it may be convenient to embed a Boolean flag in each pointer indicating the type of entity to which it is pointing. The trie structure for the preceding list of keys is given in Figure 11.30. In this figure, pointers to nodes labeled as data records lead us outside the trie structure itself.

Figure 11.30
Trie index structure.

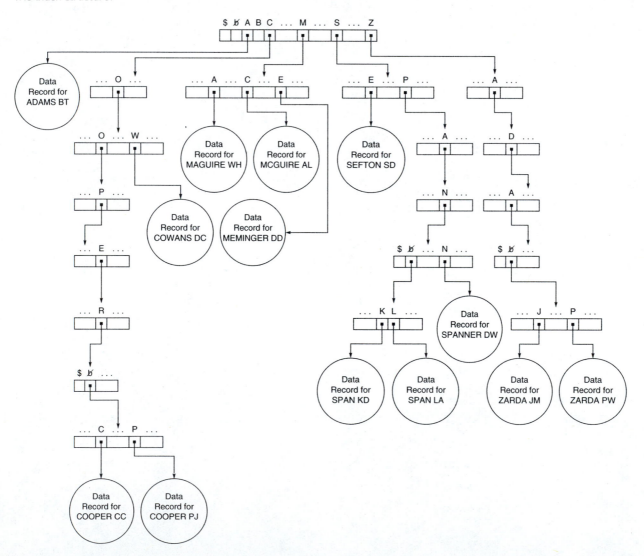

The logic behind a trie structure may best be seen by tracing through an example. The search algorithm involves examining the target key on a character-by-character basis (see Figure 11.30). Let us begin by considering the easy case of finding the data record for ADAMS BT$. In this case, we look at A, the first character in the key, and follow the A pointer in the root node to its destination. We know that its destination will be either another node within the trie structure or an actual data record. If it were a node within the trie, it would be a node on the search path for all keys that begin with A. In this case, there is only one key in our list that begins with A, so the A pointer in the root node leads us directly to the actual data record for ADAMS BT$. On the other hand, the search path to find the key COOPER CC$ in the trie is somewhat longer. We follow the C pointer from the root node down a level to a node shared by all keys starting with C. From there, the O pointer is followed to a trie node shared by all keys that start with CO. The process continues down level by level, following the O pointer to a trie node shared by all keys starting with COO, the P pointer to a node for all keys starting with COOP, the E pointer to a node for all keys starting with COOPE, the R pointer to a node for all keys starting with COOPER, and the blank pointer to a node shared by all keys starting with COOPER followed by a blank. Notice that, as each character is read in, we must continue following these pointers from trie node to trie node (instead of from trie node to actual data record) until we finally reach a point where the next character to be read will uniquely define the key. At this point, the key in question no longer needs to share its pointer with other keys that match it on an initial substring, so the pointer may now lead to an actual data record. This is what happens in our example when we read in the next C to form the uniquely defined substring COOPER C.

Efficiency Consideration for Trie Indexing The search efficiency for the trie index is quite easily determined. The worst case occurs when a key is not uniquely defined until its last character is read in. In this case, we may have as many disk accesses as there are characters in the key before we finally locate the actual data record. You may have observed, however, that there is another efficiency consideration to take into account when using the trie method. This is the amount of wasted storage in the trie nodes. In our example using a short list of keys, only a small percentage of the available pointers are ever used. In practice, however, a trie would be used only for an extremely large file, such as the list represented by a phone book with names as keys. In such a situation, a much larger number of character combinations occurs, and the resulting trie structure is correspondingly much less sparse.

A final point to consider about trie indexes is their ability to handle insertions and deletions dynamically. Here we discuss insertions; deletions are left as an exercise. Insertions may be broken down into two cases. For both we must begin by reading the key to be inserted, character by character, and following the appropriate search path in the trie until we come to either of the following:

- A trie node that has a vacant pointer in the character position corresponding to the current character of the insertion key
- An actual data record for a key different from the one being inserted.

The first case is illustrated by trying to insert the key COLLINS RT$ into the trie of Figure 11.30: We follow the search path pointers until we come to the trie node shared by all keys starting with CO. At this point, the L pointer is NULL. The insertion is completed by merely aiming the presently NULL L pointer to a data record for the key COLLINS RT\$. The second case is illustrated by trying to insert the key COOPER PA\$ into the trie of Figure 11.30. Here, following the search path of the trie eventually leads us to the data record for the key COOPER PJ\$. The dynamic solution is to get a new trie node, aim the P pointer presently leading to the data record for COOPER PJ\$ to this new trie node, and use the A and J pointers in the new trie node to lead us to data records for COOPER PA\$ and COOPER PJ\$, respectively. Both the COLLINS RT\$ and COOPER PA\$ insertions are shown with the resulting trie in Figure 11.31.

Figure 11.31

Trie of Figure 11.30 after insertions of COLLINS RT\$ and COOPER PA\$.

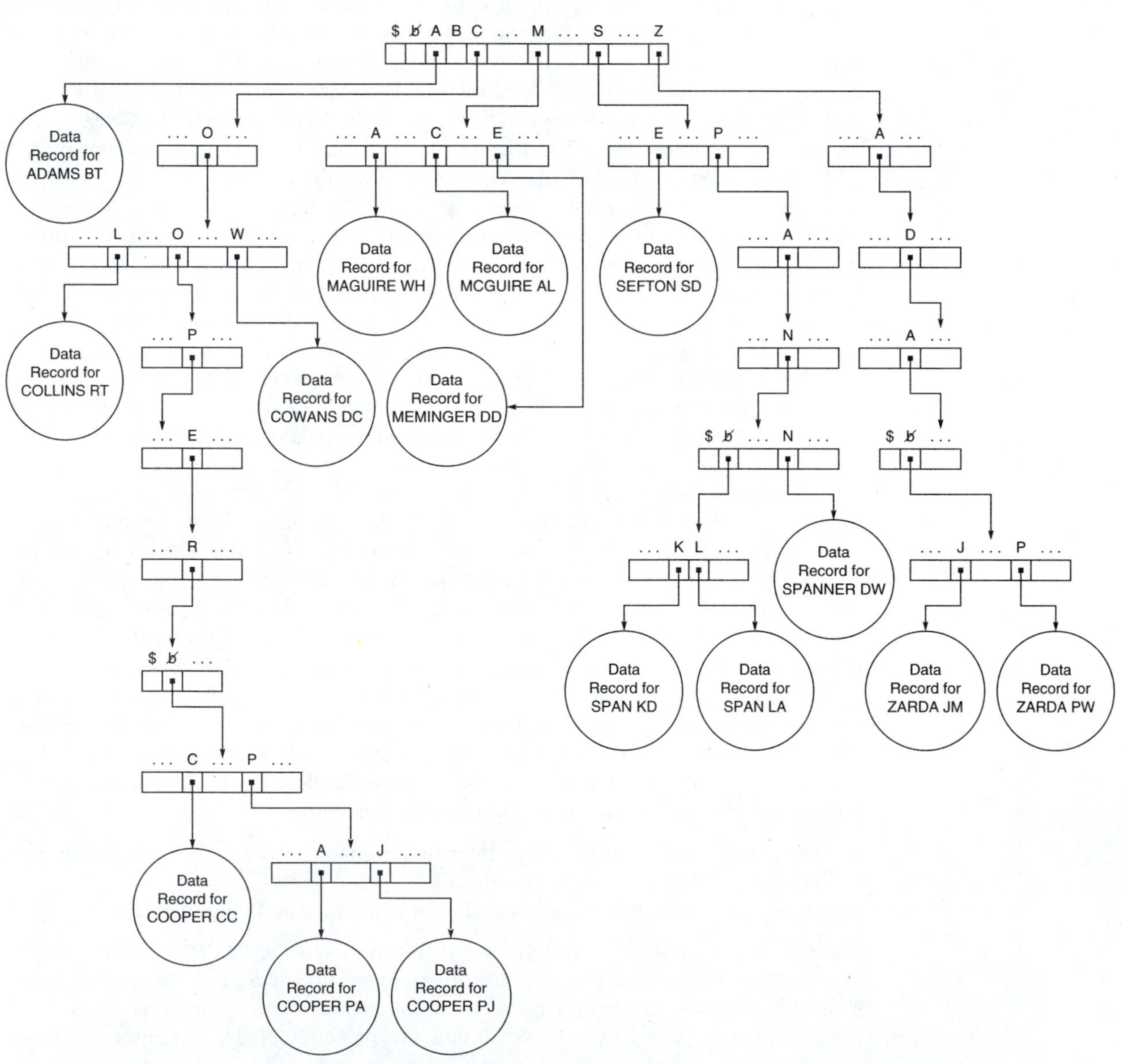

Exercises 11.4

1. **a.** Suppose that the records associated with keys 810, 430, 602, 946, 289, 106, and 732 are stored in positions 1, 2, 3, 4, 5, 6, and 7 of a file, respectively. Draw a B-tree index of order 8 for this file.

   b. Suppose the key 538 then arrives for insertion in position 8. Redraw your B-tree of order 8 after this insertion.

2. Suppose that the following strings arrive for insertion into a trie index:

   CARTER
   HERNANDEZ
   HERMAN
   HERMANSKI
   HERSCHEL
   HALL
   CARSON
   CARSWELL
   CARSEN

   a. Draw the trie index.

   b. Draw the index after CARSWELL and HERMANSKI have been deleted.

3. Discuss a key deletion strategy for B-trees. Write a function that implements your strategy.

4. Discuss a key deletion strategy for trie indexes. Write a function to implement your strategy.

5. Carefully read your system reference material concerning the specifics of how disk file records are blocked. Then explain how this knowledge would influence your decisions in the construction of

   a. An ISAM index structure

   b. A B-tree index structure

   c. A trie index structure

   d. A bucket hashing structure

6. All the search strategies we have discussed assume a key that is uniquely valued. That is, no two records have the same value for their key field. In practice this will not always be the case; we may have duplicate keys. For instance, a list of personnel records may contain two records for different people with the same name. Discuss how each of the search strategies we have covered would have to be modified to perform a duplicate key search. What effect would these modifications have on the performance of the algorithm?

7. Write a C++ implementation of an ordered list ADT, assuming that the data in the list are stored in a random access disk file using the indexed sequential access method as a means of efficiently processing these data.

8. Repeat Exercise 7 but use a B-tree index instead of the indexed sequential access method.

9. Repeat Exercise 7 but use a trie index instead of the indexed sequential access method.

A RELEVANT ISSUE Relational Database Management Systems

A *database* is a collection of related files. For example, the registrar's system at a large university may contain a file of professor records, a file of class records, and a file of student records. These files do not exist in isolation because records in one file are related to one or more records in the other files. For instance, each professor teaches classes and advises students. Each class has many students enrolled and may have many sections, each of which is taught by a different professor. Each student takes several classes. Software that allows users to conveniently manage all of the files in a database and make queries of them is called a *database management system* (DBMS). For instance, in a database management system, a user may make a query such as "During what hours of the day is Mary Jones in class?" Although this information may not be a part of Mary Jones' record in the student file directly, the DBMS will be able to consult the student file to determine what classes Mary Jones is enrolled in and, from there, move to the file of course records to determine the times at which these classes meet. Hence, the user's query is answered because of the ability of the DBMS to associate records in one file with those in another.

Many models have been proposed for DBMS, but the *relational model* appears to be emerging as the winner. The relational model was originated in 1970 by E. F. Codd ("A Relational Model of Data for Large Shared Data Banks," *Communications of the Association of Computing Machinery*, 13, June 1970). The most appealing characteristic of Codd's model is its simplicity. In the relational model, files are typically called relations. A relation is simply a table of rows and columns. Each column corresponds to a field in a record (though it is called an *attribute* in relational terminology), and each row corresponds to a record (though it is called a *tuple* in relational terminology). Codd then defines a collection of operations on relations that allow the construction of new conceptual relations based on queries made by the user. Hence, if the user requests to see the courses taken by each student, the DBMS constructs the following relation.

Name	Course
Emerson, I	BOT422 A
Emerson, I	MAT444 B
Emerson, I	PHI309 A
Emerson, I	CPS110 B
Kupper, D	MAT111 C
Kupper, D	MAT111 C
Smart, B	PHI723 B
Smart, B	PSY388 A
Smart, B	ZOO910 A
Smart, B	CPS310 B
Smart, B	ENG222 B
Smart, B	MAT311 A

Note that Codd's relational example is data abstraction at its purest. There is no hint provided by Codd as to how these relations and the operations on them are to be implemented. For instance, in the conceptual student/course relation above, each student's name appears many times. This does not imply that these names would be stored redundantly in the database. It is left to the implement to decide how to present to the user this image of relations consisting of rows and columns of data while at the same time providing performance that does not cripple a system from a time or space perspective. Although Codd defined his relational model in 1970, it was not until the latter portion of the 1980s that hardware and software technology combined to make it a practical tool. Many of the information retrieval techniques presented in this chapter have played instrumental roles in moving Codd's relational database model from a purely theoretical existence to a high degree of functionality.

Chapter Summary

In this chapter we examine additional strategies for searching for items, for adding items to, and for deleting items from a collection of values. In Section 11.1 we look at three more types of trees that can be used to facilitate searching: 2-3-4, red-black, and splay trees. Two-three-four trees offer an advantage over the 2-3 trees discussed in Chapter 8 in that insertions and deletions can be performed using one pass from the tree's root to a leaf, rather than requiring a root-to-leaf pass followed by a pass from the leaf back to the root. On the other hand, the overall storage requirements for a 2-3-4 tree will increase because each node has to accommodate three data fields and four pointer fields. A red-black tree offers a way to implement a 2-3-4 tree as a binary tree, allowing us to allocate space more efficiently than in 2-3-4 trees while still retaining the simplicity of a single root-to-leaf pass for data insertion and deletion. Splay trees provide an alternative to balanced trees for carrying out searching operations. Although they may not always yield as efficient a worst case search performance as the various balanced trees, they compare favorably when their efficiency is analyzed over sequences of searches. An advantage is that they employ simpler restructuring algorithms than the balanced trees to achieve this level of performance.

The efficiency of all the search techniques considered up to this point and in Section 11.1 depends on the number of items in the list being searched. In Section 11.2 we study another search strategy, called hashing, whose efficiency is measured in terms of the amount of storage you are willing to waste. Hashing can achieve phenomenally fast search times regardless of how much data you have, provided that you can afford to keep a relatively large amount of unused list space available. On the surface, hashing makes it impossible to go through a sequence of values in order without augmenting the basic method. In our discussion we describe different ways of constructing hashing functions: a random number generator, folding, digit or character extraction, and division remainder. Because hashing scatters keys within a search table, it is not by itself an appropriate implementation technique for an ordered list. We therefore define a new ADT—the keyed collection—that does not require an ordering among its elements or a traversal operation for processing these elements in order. In Section 11.3, however, we look at an adaptation of hashing to ordered traversals using a combination of linked lists and hashing.

The keyed collection ADT is suited to an implementation by hashing that can virtually guarantee $O(1)$ efficiency for the add, remove, and retrieve operations—regardless of the amount of data in the collection. We conclude Section 11.2 with a discussion of the various collision-processing methods that such an implementation may employ: the linear, quadratic, rehashing, linked, and bucket collision-processing methods.

In Section 11.3 hashing is applied, via the Rabin-Karp algorithm and Horner's method, to the search operation for the string ADT.

We close the chapter by exploring some of the special considerations that enter into searching for data stored in a disk file instead of main memory. These considerations lead to a variety of search schemes, all of which employ some variations of a data structure known as an index. Indexed sequential search and tree indexing (especially B-tree indexing) are effective when the search keys are of a fixed size, such as integer data. Indexed sequential searching can be effective in situations where the data being stored are relatively stable, but its performance can deteriorate rapidly if it must handle frequent insertions or deletions. B-tree indexing provides a way to handle insertions and deletions dynamically without a resulting deterioration in search efficiency. Perhaps the worst search keys are variable-length character strings. Trie indexing has developed as a means of retrieving keys in this worst case.

Keywords

B-tree
binary tree index
boundary folding
bucket hashing
character extraction
clustering
collision processing
density-dependent search
density ratio
digit extraction
double hashing
folding
hashing
Horner's method
index
indexed sequential search
key field
keyed collection
linear collision processing
linked hashing
locality of reference
overflow area
primary cluster
prime hash area
quadratic collision processing
Rabin-Karp algorithm
red-black tree
rehashing
secondary hashing
sectors
shift folding
splay
splay rotations
tracks
trie indexing
2-3-4 tree

Programming Problems/Projects

1. Wing-and-a-Prayer Airlines has the records of all its customers stored in the following form:

- Last name
- First name
- Address
- Arbitrarily long list of flights on which reservations have been booked

Using a trie index, write a search-and-retrieval program that will allow input of a customer's last name (and, if necessary, the first name and address to resolve conflicts created by matching last names) and then output all flights on which that customer has booked reservations.

2. SuperScout Inc. is a nationwide scouting service for college football talent to which the Bay Area Brawlers professional team subscribes. As the pool of college talent increases in size, SuperScout has found that its old record-keeping system has deteriorated considerably in its ability to quickly locate the scouting record associated with a given player in its file. Rewrite the scouting record system using a trie to look up the record location of the data associated with a given player's name.

3. Using a large collection of randomly generated keys, write a series of programs that will test various hashing functions you develop. In particular, your programs should report statistics on the number of collisions generated by each hashing function. This information could be valuable in guiding future decisions about which hashing functions and techniques are most effective for your particular system.

4. Repeat Problem 3 but test different collision-processing strategies instead of different hashing functions.

5. Consider a student data record that consists of

- Student identification number
- Student name
- State of residence
- Sex

Choose an index structure to process a file with such records. Then write a program to maintain such a file in a fashion that allows retrieval and traversal of records by both the identification number and name fields.

6. Suppose that data records for a phone book file consist of a key field containing both name and address, and a field containing the phone number for that key. Devise an appropriate index for such a file. Then write a program that calls for input of (a) a complete key or (b) if a complete key is not available, as much of the initial portion of a key as the inquirer is able to provide. In the case of situation (a), your program should output the phone number corresponding to the unique key. In the case of situation (b), have your program output all keys (and their phone numbers) that match the provided initial portion.

7. Consider the following problem faced in the development of a compiler. The source program contains many character-string symbols such as variable names, procedure names, and so on. Each of these character-string symbols has associated with it various attributes such as memory location, data type, and so on. However, it would be too time-consuming and awkward for a compiler to manipulate character strings. Instead, each string should be identified with an integer that is viewed as an equivalent to the string for the purpose of compiler manipulation. In addition to serving as a compact equivalent form of a string symbol within the source program, this integer can also serve as a direct pointer into a table of attributes for that symbol. Devise such a transformation that associates a string with an integer, and in turn serves as a pointer into a table of attributes. Test the structure(s) you develop by using them in a program that scans a source program written in a language such as C++. You will, in effect, have written the symbol table modules for a compiler.

8. Write a spelling-check program. Such a program must scan a file of text, looking up each word it finds in a dictionary of correctly spelled words. When a word cannot be found in the dictionary, the program should convey this fact to its user, giving the user the opportunity to take one of the following steps:

- Change the spelling of the word in the text file.
- Add the word to the dictionary so it will not be reported as incorrectly spelled in the future.

Since the dictionary for such a program will be searched frequently and is likely to become quite large, an efficient search algorithm is an absolute necessity. One possibility in this regard is to use a trie index with pointers into a large string workspace instead of the pointers to data records. Test your program with a text file and a dictionary large enough to handle all the possibilities your algorithm and data structure may encounter.

9. If you did one of the problems from Chapter 3 that involved maintaining an ordered list, redo that problem using hashing combined with linked lists as an implementation technique. When finished, write a report in which you empirically compare the performance of your two implementations.

10. If you did one of the problems from Chapter 2 that involved maintaining a sparse matrix, redo that problem using hashing of row and column indices as an implementation technique. When finished, write a report in which you empirically compare the performance of your two implementations.

11. If you did one of the problems in Chapter 2 that involved an implementation of the string search operation, redo that problem using the Rabin-Karp algorithm. When finished, write a report in which you empirically compare the performance of your two algorithms.

12. Implement in a test program the wildcard version of the Rabin-Karp algorithm you formulated in your answer to Exercise 9 of Section 11.3.

13. Implement in a test program the two-dimensional version of the Rabin-Karp algorithm you formulated in your answer to Exercise 8 of Section 11.3.

14. If you did one of the problems from Chapter 3 that involved maintaining an ordered list, redo that problem using 2-3-4, red-black, or splay trees. When finished, write a report in which you empirically compare the performance of your two implementations.

CHAPTER 12 Sorting—Revisited and Extended

We shall now proceed to construct the socialist order.
Lenin

Chapter Outline:

We have already covered a wide variety of sorting algorithms— selection, insertion, radix, quick, merge, and heap sorts. Often we presented a sorting algorithm because it happened to provide an excellent illustration of another topic such as big-O analysis or recursion. In this chapter, we focus only on sorting. In Section 12.1, we present an overview of the methods already covered. We demonstrate that no sorting method based on making comparisons can improve on the $O(n \log_2 n)$ performance that we have been able to achieve with the heap, merge, and quick sort algorithms.

In Section 12.2, we shift our attention from *internal sorting,* that is, sorting data within main memory, to *external sorting,* that is, sorting data stored in sequentially accessible secondary memory such as disk and tape files. The methods used for external sorting often involve a combination of a main memory algorithm, such as quick sort, with a variation on the merge logic that we introduced in Section 6.3.

12.1 Internal Sorting Algorithms—A Theoretical Bound on Efficiency

The criteria we use to evaluate sorting algorithms are the same used to evaluate any algorithm—time and space efficiency. Table 12.1 presents a concise summary of what we have already learned about sorting, with references to the chapter in which a particular method was studied. The question of particular interest at this point in our study of sorting is whether any sorting algorithm can better the $O(n \log_2 n)$ efficiency of the heap, merge, and quick sorts. Radix sort is excluded from consideration for two reasons:

1. The disadvantages cited in the comments column of Table 12.1 dictate a choice other than radix sort in most applications.

TABLE 12.1
Summary of sorting methods we have studied.

Sorting method	Chapter	Number of comparisons relative to the number of data items being sorted (n)	Space requirement	Additional comments
Binary tree	7	Between $O(n^2)$ and $O(n \log_2 n)$ depending on original data and whether tree is height-balanced	Pointers for tree and possible stack space for recursive traversals	
Heap	7	$O(n \log_2 n)$	No additional overhead	
Insertion	1	$O(n^2)$	No additional overhead	Loop check allows early exit as soon as item is correctly placed
Merge	6	$O(n \log_2 n)$	Requires duplicate array and stack space for recursion	Since only requires sequential access, can be used for linked lists and sequential files
Radix	4	$O(n)$ but with a large constant of proportionality	Minimal extra storage if queues are allocated dynamically	Large constant of proportionality often makes it slower than $O(n \log_2 n)$ algorithms; highly dependent on type of data being sorted and machine representations of that data, so a difficult method to generalize
Quick	6	$O(n \log_2 n)$ on the average but $O(n^2)$ for worst case	Stack space for recursion	Variations on choosing pivot can make worst case almost impossible to generate
Selection	1	$O(n^2)$	No additional overhead	Only $O(n)$ data interchanges
Shell	1	Between $O(n(\log_2 n)^2)$ and $O(n^{1.5})$ depending on increments used	No additional overhead	

2. Radix sort is different from other sorting algorithms in that it is not based on making comparisons between values in the array being sorted. Instead it works by iteratively categorizing *individual* values and then appending categories until the entire array is sorted.

We claim that *no sort based on comparisons between array values can be more efficient than* $O(n \log_2 n)$.

To prove this claim, we need to introduce the notion of a decision tree for comparison-based sorting algorithms. Such a tree is illustrated in Figure 12.1 for a three-element insertion sort algorithm. To interpret such a tree, assume that array indices start at 1 and observe that all interior nodes represent comparisons made between elements of the array **x** relative to the original position of these elements in the array. Hence, at the root of the tree, we compare the original **x[1]** to the original **x[2]**. If the former precedes or equals the latter, then we follow the

Figure 12.1
Decision tree for three-element insertion sort; x[k] represents item *originally* in kth array index.

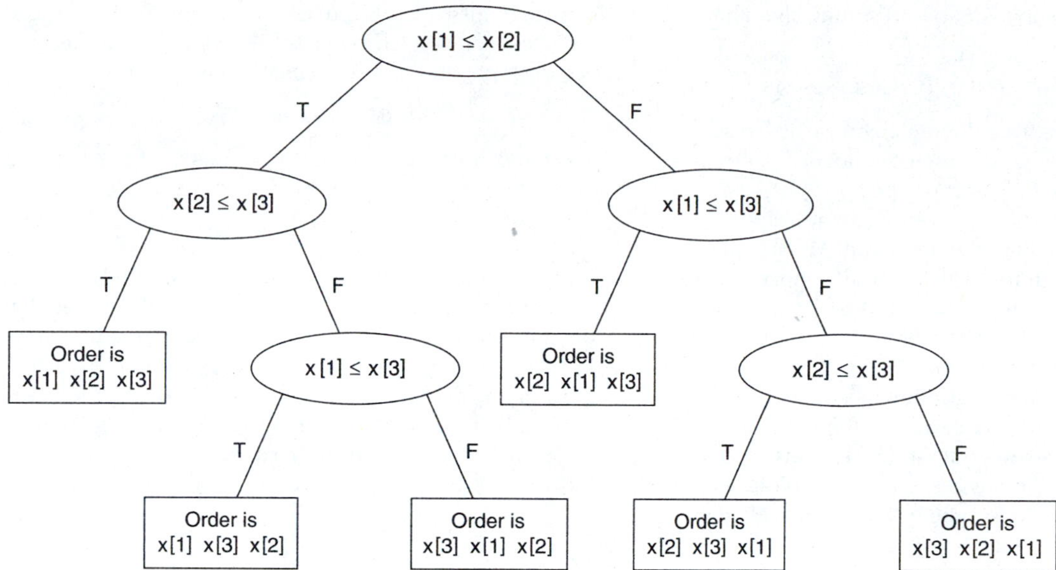

true (T) branch and compare the original **x[2]** to the original **x[3]**; otherwise we follow the false (F) branch and compare the original **x[1]** (which would now be in the second array position) to the original **x[3]**. When we reach a leaf node of the tree, we have made sufficient comparisons to determine the sorted order of the array. Consequently, there are six leaf nodes in the tree of Figure 12.1, corresponding to the six possible arrangements of data in a three-element array.

Although it may not be easy to do manually, it is evident that such a decision tree can be constructed for any comparison-based sorting algorithm applied to an n-element array. In this general case, there must be $n!$ leaf nodes in the decision tree, because there are $n!$ possible arrangements of data in the array. From our work with binary trees in Chapter 7 we know that, even if it is full, a binary tree with $n!$ leaf nodes must contain at least $\log_2(n!)$ levels. This implies that the sort efficiency for any comparison-based algorithm must be at least $O(\log_2(n!))$ because potentially all comparisons corresponding to the longest path in the decision tree must be made. However, in the exercises at the end of this section, you will prove the following inequality:

$$n! \geq (n/2)^{n/2}$$

Hence, $\log_2(n!) \geq \log_2((n/2)^{n/2}) = (n/2)\log_2(n/2)$. This last inequality implies that the number of comparisons must indeed be $O(n \log_2 n)$, and the proof of our claim is complete.

This result establishes a lower bound for the efficiency of all comparison-based sorting algorithms. Such an algorithm simply cannot handle all cases in time faster than $O(n \log_2 n)$—it is logically impossible. So, if you hoped to make a name for yourself in computer science by discovering a comparison-based sorting algorithm that is an order of magnitude faster than those already known, it is a hopeless endeavor!

Exercises 12.1

1. Prove the inequality used in our proof of the lower bound on the efficiency of comparison-based sorting algorithms; that is,

   $n! \geq (n/2)^{n/2}$ (Hint: Use induction.)

2. Produce a decision tree for a three-element selection sort. Does it have more, less, or the same number of nodes as the corresponding tree for insertion sort?
3. Construct a decision tree for a seven-element heap sort.
4. Show that we cannot find the minimum or maximum element in an array with fewer than $O(n)$ comparisons.
5. Suppose that we alter the specifications for a sorting algorithm as follows. The algorithm is to produce an array of sorted *distinct* elements. If the original array contains duplicates, the new algorithm must remove those duplicates from the final sorted array. Is the lower bound for the efficiency of this new algorithm less than, equal to, or greater than the lower bound we established for ordinary sorting? Justify your claim with a proof analogous to that presented for ordinary sorting.
6. A sorting method is said to be *stable* if two data items of matching value are guaranteed *not* to be rearranged with respect to each other as the algorithm progresses. For example, in the four-element array

   $60 \quad 42_1 \quad 80 \quad 42_2$

   a stable sorting method would guarantee a final ordering of

   $42_1 \quad 42_2 \quad 60 \quad 80$

   Classify each of the sorting algorithms in Table 12.1 as to their stability. For the binary tree method, assume that the data are loaded into the binary tree by reading array indices 1 through n; then the data are written back into the array by doing an inorder traversal of the tree. (To see why stability may be important, consider Programming Problem 1 at the end of this chapter.)

12.2 External Sorting

The sorting algorithms we have studied so far assume that the data being sorted is randomly accessible. That is, we may access the kth data item without going through the first $k - 1$ entries. Such access is typical of arrays that are stored in main memory. However, data on permanent storage devices such as disk and tape are frequently accessible only in a sequential fashion. In this section, we turn our attention to sorting data that are organized sequentially. Algorithms that sort data maintained in a sequentially accessible structure (which we call a *stream*) are called *external sorting* algorithms—as opposed to the *internal sorting* algorithms that operate within the confines of main memory.

The **merge** function that we developed as a subordinate algorithm to the **msRecursive** function in Section 6.3 is noteworthy because it requires only sequential access to each of the arrays being merged. This feature makes merging an essential ingredient of virtually all external sorting algorithms. In broad terms, these algorithms take a sequentially accessible data stream and partition it into *runs*—sequentially accessible substructures that are sorted. These runs are then merged into larger runs, with this process continuing until we are left with just one large run containing all records in the original data stream.

To more formally describe external sorting algorithms, we require the definition of a sequentially accessible data stream as an abstract data type. It should be apparent how the operations described below can be mapped to the file and tape processing commands of your favorite programming language.

Definition: A *data stream* is a sequence of homogenous records (of type *Streamdata*) that can be accessed only by starting at the first record in the sequence and then reading the second record, third record, and so forth. A *run* is a subsequence of a stream arranged in order according to a specified precedence relationship *precedes* between records. The operations on a stream are defined in the following pre- and postconditions. Note that these operations indicate that a given stream may either be read from (the stream is in "read" mode) or written to (the stream is in "write" mode). Implicit in this definition is the notion of a *current record* in the stream, which we will interpret to be the record (if there is one) whose value will be returned by the next *get* operation, or the record after which a record will be placed by a *put* operation. Also implicit in this definition is the notion of an *end-of-stream marker,* which indicates when the end of a stream has been reached.

`Construct Operation (First Form)`

Preconditions: An uninitialized Stream object.

Postconditions: The Stream object is initialized as an empty stream, in write mode, and ready to be written to via the Put operation.

`Construct Operation (Copy Constructor)`

Preconditions: An uninitialized Stream object;
initstream—a Stream object that was previously constructed.

Postconditions: The Stream object is initialized with the values of *initstream* and is placed in read mode with its "current record" being the first record in the Stream.

`Destroy Operation`

Preconditions: A Stream object that currently exists.

Postconditions: All storage allocated to the Stream object and its records is deallocated.

`SetMode Operation`

Preconditions: A Stream object previously created and possibly acted on by other operations;
mode—either the character 'r' (for read) or 'w' (for write), indicating the mode into which the Stream is to be set.

Postconditions: If mode = 'r', the Stream is placed in read mode. The Stream object may not be written to again unless the mode is reset to 'w'. If mode = 'w' the Stream is placed in write mode and is reinitialized to an empty stream. The Stream object may not be read from again unless it is (re)set to 'r'. Setting an empty Stream to read mode will result in the end of the Stream having been reached.

`EndOfStream Operation`

Preconditions: A Stream object in read mode.

Postconditions: Returns TRUE if the current record in the Stream has reached the end of the Stream; returns FALSE otherwise.

`Get Operation`

Preconditions: A Stream object in read ('r') mode.

Postconditions: Returns the record in the Stream that follows the one returned by the most recent invocation of Get or, if following a call to set the mode of the Stream to read, returns the first record in the Stream. If a previous Get returned the last record in the Stream, the operation will succeed, although the value returned will be unreliable—the end of the Stream will have been reached. After reaching the end of the Stream, a subsequent call to Get without resetting the Stream will be treated as an error. The function Get always leaves the Stream in read mode.

Put Operation

Preconditions: A Stream object in write mode, possibly having been acted on by previous invocations of Put;
record—a value of type Streamdata to append to as the last record of the Stream.

Postconditions: The Stream object with a copy of *record* appended to the end of the Stream. The Stream remains in write mode.

A C++ interface for the Stream ADT, using records represented via the template class **StreamData,** can be defined as follows:

```
// StreamData is either a C++ built-in type, or a C++ class that has
// an assignment operation that overloads the ''=" operator.
template <class StreamData>
class Stream
{
  protected:
   // data structure(s) for representing the organization of
   // records in the stream;


  public:
//----------------------------------------------------------------
// Interface for Stream constructor
// GIVEN:   An uninitialized Stream object.
// RETURN:  The Stream object initialized as an empty Stream, in
//          write mode, and ready to be written to via the put operation.

     Stream();

//----------------------------------------------------------------
// Interface for Stream copy constructor
// GIVEN:    An uninitialized Stream object;
//           initstream -- a Stream object that was previously
//                         constructed.
// RETURN:   The Stream object is initialized with the values
//           of initstream and is placed in read mode with its "current
//           record" being the first record in the Stream.

     Stream(Stream<StreamData> &initstream);

//----------------------------------------------------------------
// Interface for Stream destructor
// GIVEN:   A previously allocated Stream object.
// RETURN:  All storage allocated to the Stream object and its
//          records is deallocated.

     ~Stream();

//----------------------------------------------------------------
// Interface for setMode operation
// GIVEN:   A Stream object previously created and possibly acted
//          on by other operations;
//          mode -- either the character 'r' (for read) or 'w' (for
//                  write), indicating the mode into which the Stream is
//                          to be set.
```

```
// RETURN:   If mode = 'r', the Stream is placed in read mode and the
//           first record is made the current record. The Stream
//           object may not be written to again unless the mode is
//           reset to 'w'. If mode = 'w' the Stream is placed in
//           write mode and is reinitialized to an empty Stream.
//           The Stream object may be not read from again unless it
//           is (re)set to 'r'.
// RETURN as value of function: void

    void setMode(char mode);

// --------------------------------------------------------------------
// Interface for endOfStream operation
// GIVEN:     A Stream object in read mode.
// RETURN as value of function:
//            TRUE if the current record in the Stream is at the end
//            of stream marker; returns FALSE otherwise.

    BOOLEAN endOfStream();

// --------------------------------------------------------------------
// Interface for get operation
// GIVEN:     A Stream object in read mode.
// RETURN as value of function:
//            Returns the record of type StreamData in the Stream
//            that follows the one returned by the most recent
//            invocation of get or, if following a call to set the
//            mode of the Stream to read, returns the
//            first record in the Stream. If the Stream is at the
//            end-of-stream marker when a get is issued, the operation
//            will succeed, although the value returned will be
//            unreliable; a subsequent call to get without resetting
//            the Stream will be treated as an error. The function get
//            always leaves the Stream in read mode.

    StreamData get();

// --------------------------------------------------------------------
// Interface for put function
// GIVEN:     A Stream object in write mode, possibly having been
//            acted on by previous invocations of put;
//            record -- a value of type StreamData to append to the
//                      end of the Stream.
// RETURN:    The Stream object with a copy of record appended to the
//            end of the Stream.  The Stream remains in write mode.
// RETURN as value of function:  void

    void put(const StreamData &record);
};
```

Example 12.1

To illustrate the use of streams, consider the following function, **mergeRuns**, which merges runs beginning with the most recently accessed records on streams **in1** and **in2.** The run resulting from merging these two runs is written to stream **out,** which we assume to have been previously created. The internal logic of the function follows closely that of the **merge** function we developed in conjunction with the merge sort algorithm in Section 6.3. The particular interface we have chosen for this function is designed so the function may be strategically called in the external sorting algorithms we will soon discuss.

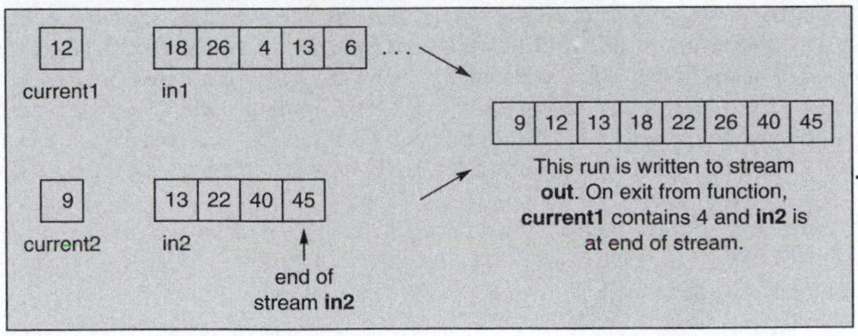

```
// Interface for mergeRuns function
// GIVEN:     in1 and in2 -- two streams, each of which is in read mode;
//            current1 and current2 -- contain the last datum read from
//                                        in1 and in2 respectively;
//            precedes -- a function to compare StreamData values
//              GIVEN: a and b -- values of type StreamData to compare.
//              RETURN as value of function:
//                       TRUE if a precedes b according to some ordering
//                       relation for values of type StreamData; FALSE
//                       otherwise.
//            out -- a (reference to) a stream in write mode; the stream
//                   will be altered by mergeRuns.
// RETURN:    The stream out will have appended to it the run formed
//            by merging the runs in in1 and in2 that begin at their
//            respective current records.  If an end of stream has
//            been reached for either of in1 or in2, the run in the
//            other will be copied to out.
// RETURN as value of function: void

template <class StreamData>
void mergeRuns(Stream<StreamData> &in1, Stream<StreamData> &in2,
               StreamData &current1, StreamData &current2,
               BOOLEAN (*precedes) (const StreamData &a, const Streamdata &b),
               Stream<StreamData> &out)

{
  BOOLEAN done1, done2;          // Used to signal end of run in in1 and in2
  StreamData prev1, prev2;       // Retain record last written from in1 and in2

  done1 = in1.endOfStream();
  done2 = in2.endOfStream();
  while((!done1) && (!done2))
  // Choose first among two current records
  {
    if (precedes(current1, current2))
    {
      prev1 = current1;
      out.put(current1);
      current1 = in1.get();
      if (in1.endOfStream())
        done1 = TRUE;
      else
        done1 = precedes(current1,prev1);
    }
    else
    {
      prev2 = current2;
```

```
        out.put(current2);
        current2 = in2.get();
        if (in2.endOfStream())
         done2 = TRUE;
        else
         done2 = precedes(current2, prev2);
      }
   }
   if (done1)    // Flush the rest of the run that remains on one stream
     while (!done2)
     {
        prev2 = current2;
        out.put(current2);
        current2 = in2.get();
        if (in2.endOfStream())
          done2 = TRUE;
        else
          done2 = precedes(current2, prev2);
     }
   else       // Flush the rest of the run on the other stream
     while (!done1)
     {
        prev1 = current1;
        out.put(current1);
        current1 = in1.get();
        if (in1.endOfStream())
          done1 = TRUE;
        else
          done1 = precedes(current1, prev1);
     }
}
```

We will now use the **mergeRuns** function of Example 12.1 in developing two external sorting algorithms: the n-way merge sort and the n-stream polyphase merge sort. We will discuss both algorithms for the case in which $n = 2$ and leave their generalizations for you to ponder in the exercises.

The Two-Way Merge Sort

Both of the external sorting algorithms we will consider assume that we have streams with embedded runs. In the extreme case, the size of these embedded runs could be as small as 1. However, more typically, the runs are larger, having been put on the stream by loading a large amount of data into main memory, sorting it by invocation of an efficient internal sorting algorithm, and then writing the sorted data out to a stream. The external sorting algorithms work regardless of the size of the runs on the initial streams; however, they become more efficient with larger runs. We will use m to designate the size of runs on the initial input streams; this value will then be factored into our efficiency analyses of the external sorting algorithms.

The two-way merge sort requires four streams—two with the original data split between them, arranged in runs of size m; and two scratch streams. One of these streams will be returned as the value of the function. Figure 12.2 depicts this situation for a stream originally containing 25 items. Using an appropriate internal sorting algorithm with size $m = 2$ (an unrealistically small value for m, but convenient for illustration), these original data are split over two streams **s1** and **s2**. The runs of size (at least) 2 on **s1** and **s2** are then merged, via repeated calls to **mergeRuns,** producing streams **s3** and **s4**—each with runs of size (at least) 4. We now cascade back and forth between **s3, s4** and **s1, s2**—each time producing runs that increase the size of the previous runs. Eventually we are left with just one large run on one of the streams. This is the stream we must return as the sorted stream. The version of the two-way merge sort presented next assumes that the original data stream has already been split into two streams. The real work of the function **twoWayMergeSort** is done in the subordinate function **mergeStreams,** which we give first. Here the merging of all runs from two input streams onto two output streams is accomplished. The function **twoWayMergeSort** merely must control the back-and-forth cascading of **mergeStreams** until we are left with one long run, which is then copied onto the stream to be returned.

Figure 12.2
Two-way merging where the original data stream is split into two streams s1 and s2.

Original Stream: (14, 2, 57, 6, 3, 28, 45, 1, 30, 4, 9, 31, 23, 35, 12, 8, 11, 13, 19, 18, 21, 5, 37, 89, 77)

↓ Use internal sort to produce runs of size m = 2

s1: ((2, 14), (3, 28), (4, 30), (23, 35), (11, 13), (5, 21))

constitutes one run

s2: ((6, 57), (1, 45), (9, 31), (8, 12), (18, 19), (37, 89), (77))

s3:

s4:

↓ Merge runs on s1 and s2 to produce longer runs on s3 and s4

s1:

s2:

s3: ((2, 6, 14, 57), (4, 9, 30, 31), (11, 13, 77))

s4: ((1, 3, 28, 45), (8, 12, 18, 19, 23, 35, 37, 89), (5, 21))

↓ Merge runs on s3 and s4 to produce longer runs on s1 and s2

s1: ((1, 2, 3, 6, 14, 28, 45, 57), (5, 11, 13, 21, 77))

s2: ((4, 8, 9, 12, 18, 19, 23, 30, 31, 35, 37, 89))

s3:

s4:

↓ Merge runs on s1 and s2 to produce longer runs on s3 and s4

s1:

s2:

s3: ((1, 2, 3, 4, 6, 8, 9, 12, 14, 18, 19, 23, 28, 30, 31, 35, 37, 45, 57, 89))

s4: ((5, 11, 13, 21, 77))

↓ Merge runs on s3 and s4 to produce sorted file on s1

s1: (1, 2, 3, 4, 5, 6, 8, 9, 11, 12, 13, 14, 18, 19, 21, 23, 28, 30, 31, 35, 37, 45, 57, 77, 89)

s2:

s3:

s4:

```
// Interface for function mergeStreams
// GIVEN:     s1 and s2 -- streams, each containing a number of runs.
//                         The streams will be altered by the
//                         mergeStreams function.
//            precedes -- a function to compare StreamData values.
//              GIVEN: a and b -- values of type StreamData to compare.
//              RETURN as value of function:
//                        TRUE if a precedes b according to some ordering
//                        relation for values of type StreamData, FALSE
//                        otherwise.
//            s3 and s4 -- streams each of which will be altered by
//                         mergeStreams.
// RETURN:    s3 will contain runs from merging the 1st, 3rd, 5th,...
//            runs on s1 and s2.  s4 will contain runs from merging
//            the 2nd, 4th, 6th,... runs on s1 and s2.
// RETURN as value of function:
//            The number of runs on each of s1 and s2.  If the two
//            streams do not have the same number of runs, the number
//            for the stream with more runs is returned.

template <class StreamData>
int mergeStreams (Stream<StreamData> &s1, Stream<StreamData> &s2,
                  BOOLEAN (*precedes) (const StreamData &a, const StreamData &b),
                  Stream<StreamData> &s3, Stream<StreamData> &s4)
{
StreamData current1, current2; // Hold the values of the current
                               // records in s1 and s2 respectively
  int numberOfRuns = 0;

  s1.setMode('r');
  s2.setMode('r');
  current1 = s1.get();
  current2 = s2.get();
  s3.setMode('w');
  s4.setMode('w');
  while (!s1.endOfStream() || !s2.endOfStream())  // More data on one
  {                                               // of the streams?
    ++numberOfRuns;

    // Call function mergeRuns from Example 12.1
    mergeRuns(s1, s2, current1, current2, precedes, s3);
    if (!s1.endOfStream() || !s2.endOfStream())
    {
      ++numberOfRuns;
      mergeRuns (s1, s2, current1, current2, precedes, s4);
    }
  }
  return (numberOfRuns);
}

// Interface for function twoWayMergeSort
// GIVEN:     s1 and s2--two streams, each containing a number of runs.
//                       Ideally, the number of runs on the two streams
//                       will differ by at most one, although this is
//                       not necessary for the algorithm to work
//                       correctly. The streams s1 and s2 will be altered
//                       by the twoWayMergeSort function.
//            precedes -- a function to compare StreamData values.
//              GIVEN: a and b -- values of type StreamData to compare.
//              RETURN as value of function:
```

```
//                          TRUE if a precedes b according to some ordering
//                          relation for values of type StreamData, FALSE
//                          otherwise.
// RETURN as value of function:
//              A stream containing the data originally on s1 and s2,
//              but sorted according to the precedes function.

template <class StreamData>
Stream<StreamData> twoWayMergeSort(Stream<StreamData> &s1,
                                   Stream<StreamData> &s2,
                                   BOOLEAN (*precedes)(const StreamData &a,
                                                       const StreamData &b))
{
  int count;                      // Used to determine which streams to merge
  int numberOfRuns;
  Stream<StreamData> s3, s4;      // Scratch streams

  count = 0;
  do
  {
    ++count;
    // Use odd-even test on count to flip-flop between merging
    // s1 and s2 (odd count) or s3 and s4 (even count)
    if ((count % 2) != 0)
      numberOfRuns = mergeStreams(s1, s2, precedes, s3, s4);
    else
      numberOfRuns = mergeStreams(s3, s4, precedes, s1, s2);
  }
  while (numberOfRuns > 1);

  if ((count % 2) != 0)    // Did s1 or s3 end up with the sorted list?
    return (s3);
  else
    return (s1);
}
```

Analysis of the Two-Way Merge Sort

The **mergeStreams** function is clearly *O(NumberofRecs),* where *NumberOfRecs* is the number of records in the original stream. Observe that, because the number of runs is halved on each iteration of the **do-while** loop in twoWayMergeSort, this loop is $O(\log_2(\textit{maximum of number of runs in original } \mathbf{s1} \textit{ and } \mathbf{s2}))$. Under the assumption that **s1** and **s2** are created by producing runs equal in size to M (the maximum number of values that we can sort internally at one time), it then follows that the **do-while** loop in twoWayMergeSort is $O(\log_2(\textit{NumberofRecs}/M))$. Hence, the overall efficiency of the two-way merge is $O(\textit{NumberOfRecs} \times \log_2(\textit{NumberOfRecs}/M))$. Of course, this does not take into account the cost of originally producing the runs on **s1** and **s2**. You will analyze the price paid for this factor in the exercises. The exercises will also allow you to explore how much the algorithm increases in efficiency if more than two input streams are provided initially (so that the algorithm becomes an *N*-way merge instead of a two-way merge).

Two-Stream Polyphase Merge Sort

The two-way merge sort required four streams to sort one stream. This is a considerable price to pay in resources—particularly if a separate tape drive must be allocated for each stream. The polyphase merge algorithm represents an attempt to reduce this resource cost. It only requires one scratch stream in addition to the two streams with embedded runs that are provided as input to the algorithm. Figure 12.3 highlights the essence of the algorithm. The same original stream of 25 values used in Figure 12.2 is distributed in runs of size $m = 2$ over streams **s1** and **s2**. Stream **s1** contains five runs and **s2** contains eight runs. This choice for distributing runs over the two input streams works nicely for reasons that will soon become apparent. The first five runs on **s1** and **s2** are merged, producing five runs on **s3** and leaving three runs on **s2**. Then the first three runs on **s2** and **s3** are merged, producing three larger runs on **s1** and leaving two runs on stream **s3**. Now we

Figure 12.3
Polyphase merging with two input streams.

↓ Use internal sort to produce runs of size m = 2, that yield 5 runs on s1 and 8 runs, including two empty runs, on s2

s1: ((2, 14), (3, 28), (4, 30), (23, 35), (11, 13))

each constitutes one run

s2: ((6, 57), (1, 45), (9, 31), (8, 12), (18, 19), (5, 21), (37, 89), (77)( ), ( ))

s3:

↓ Merge 5 runs from each stream onto s3

s1:

s2: ((77), ( ), ( ))

s3: ((2, 6, 14, 57), (1, 3, 28, 45), (4, 9, 30, 31), (8, 12, 18, 19, 23, 35), (5, 11, 13, 21, 37, 89))

↓ Merge 3 runs from each stream onto s1

s1: ((2, 6, 14, 57, 77), (1, 3, 28, 45), (4, 9, 30, 31))

s2:

s3: ((8, 12, 18, 19, 23, 35), (5, 11, 13, 21, 37, 89))

↓ Merge 2 runs from each stream onto s2

s1: ((4, 9, 30, 31))

s2: ((2, 6, 8, 12, 14, 18, 19, 23, 35, 57, 77), (1, 3, 5, 11, 13, 21, 28, 37, 45, 89))

s3:

↓ Merge 1 runs from each stream onto s3

s1:

s2: ((1, 3, 5, 11, 13, 21, 28, 37, 45, 89))

s3: ((2, 4, 6, 8, 9, 12, 14, 18, 19, 23, 30, 31, 35, 57, 77))

↓ Merge 1 runs from each stream onto s1

s1: (1, 2, 3, 4, 5, 6, 8, 9, 11, 12, 13, 14, 18, 19, 21, 23, 28, 30, 31, 35, 37, 45, 57, 77, 89)

s2:

s3:

A RELEVANT ISSUE Virtual Memory Systems and External Sorting

The more sophisticated operating systems of today will often allow a user to apply an internal sorting algorithm to an entire file through what is known as *virtual memory*. In such systems, a programmer is able to view main memory as virtually limitless. That is, such systems give the programmer "infinite" main memory. Given this perspective, the programmer can sort a relatively large file by loading it into a virtually infinite array, applying an internal sorting algorithm to it, and then writing the array back to permanent storage in a file.

Does this mean that external sorting algorithms are, or soon will be, obsolete? They will not be completely obsolete for two reasons. First, such "infinite" memory systems are not really infinite. They are limited by the memory address size of the computer. For instance, on a computer with a 32-bit address architecture, this memory address size is $2^{32} - 1$, or 2,147,483,647. Such a computer can access that many bytes of virtual memory. If a file does not fit in that many bytes, then it cannot be loaded in virtual memory and cannot have an internal sorting algorithm applied to it. Although there are techniques to push this maximum memory address to higher limits, all computers have such a limit. A file that surpasses the limit simply cannot be loaded all at once into virtual memory.

The second argument against using a large amount of virtual memory to sort a data stream internally centers around the "virtual" portion of virtual memory. Virtual memory is not true main memory. Rather, it is memory divided into pages—some of which actually reside in main memory while others reside on disk storage. When you write a program that accesses a virtual-memory page not presently in main memory, the operating system must execute a *paging algorithm*—an algorithm responsible for bringing into main memory the page your program requests and deciding which page presently in main memory should be swapped out to disk storage to make room for the new page.

Paging is the hidden price you pay for the programming convenience offered by virtual memory systems. Any internal sorting algorithm applied to a virtually infinite array will cause paging to occur. Since paging represents a disk access, it will take longer than a pure memory access, which does not generate a page swap. The key to the efficiency of a virtual internal sorting algorithm is whether the algorithm forces an excessive amount of paging to occur. That is, does the algorithm frequently require the operating system to fetch back from disk storage a page just recently swapped out? If so, an $O(n \log_2 n)$ sorting algorithm may well take longer than a theoretically based estimate would predict. Such an estimate will not include the paging costs.

What is the cure for this problem? Consult local system references to determine the paging algorithm your system uses and then try to tailor the sorting algorithm you choose to take advantage of this information. Or, resort to an external sorting algorithm that allows you to have more direct control over the paging that occurs.

merge runs from **s3** and **s1** onto **s2**, and so forth, until we finish with just one run which, in this example, is produced on **s1**.

We will not delve into a detailed efficiency analysis of the polyphase merge sort because it is quite complex. The interested reader is referred to Knuth (*The Art of Computer Programming: Searching and Sorting*) for these particulars. However, note the following interesting facts about the polyphase algorithm. First, the distribution of runs on the initial two input tapes is determined by the famous Fibonacci sequence—the same sequence that arose in our discussion of interpolative search strategies in Chapter 1 (Exercise 1.3.6). Recall that this sequence has the property that each member of the sequence is the sum of the two preceding members, with the first two members initialized to one. In the polyphase merge algorithm, runs should be distributed on the original input streams in a way that ensures that the number of runs on **s1** and **s2** are successive members of the Fibonacci sequence. (If necessary, one of the streams may be padded with empty runs to guarantee this.) Second, a careful comparison of Figures 12.2 and 12.3 indicates that, on the same set of data, the two-way merge sort will require four iterations of merging input streams whereas the two-stream polyphase merge will require five. This is evidence that the polyphase merge will be somewhat less efficient in time—a fact that should not be surprising given its greater efficiency in terms of resources.

Exercises 12.2

1. Provide C++ implementations for all the operations of the Stream ADT.
2. In keeping with our objective of defining ADT operations with optimal functional cohesion, we specified separate Get and EndOfStream operations. Suppose instead we specify just one function, again called Get, which accepts a reference parameter *record* of type Streamdata that will receive the value of the current record in the stream. This function Get will return a Boolean value—TRUE if the stream was currently not at the end-of-stream marker, and FALSE otherwise. Provide a C++ implementation for this operation.
3. Rewrite the **mergeRuns** function of Example 12.1 using the **get** function you developed for Exercise 12.2.2 instead of **get** and **endOfStream** operations of the original definition of the **Stream** class.
4. Complete the efficiency analysis for sorting a stream using a two-way merge sort by determining the cost of initially producing runs of size M from a stream with *NumberOfRecs* records. In practice, is this cost likely to be more or less than the cost of actually performing the two-way merge sort? Remember that, since streams usually exist on secondary storage devices, accessing the next record in a stream could well be an order of magnitude slower than accessing an item in a main memory array.
5. It can be argued that the **twoWayMergeSort** function should not be allowed to alter either of its given input streams **s1** and **s2**.
   a. Assuming the existence of an **assign** operation (possibly overloading the "=" operator),

```
assign (const Stream<StreamData> &s)
```

   that allows a **Stream** object to be assigned the values of another **Stream** object **s**, rewrite the **twoWayMergeSort** function so the original values of **s1** and **s2** are preserved.
   b. Implement the **assign** operation described in part **a.**
6. Write an **nWayMergeSort** function that receives **n** input streams (instead of two) and uses **n** scratch streams. Assume that you can declare an array of streams for this purpose. This is not an unrealistic assumption since the implementation of a stream or file variable in an actual programming language typically does not associate the entire stream with the variable. Rather, the stream variable is only a pointer to the memory address of the current record for that stream. How does the expansion of this algorithm to encompass **n** input streams instead of two affect the algorithm's efficiency?
7. Write an implementation of the two-stream polyphase merge sort algorithm.
8. The two-stream polyphase merge sort can be generalized to an n-stream algorithm that receives n input streams, each containing an appropriate number of runs, and still requires only one scratch stream. How should runs be distributed over the input streams for this more general form of the algorithm? (*Hint:* Think about ways of generalizing the Fibonacci sequence.) Illustrate how the method would work by tracing a three-stream polyphase merge sort for the list of keys in Figure 12.3.

Chapter Summary

In this chapter we focus only on sorting. In Section 12.1, we give an overview of the methods already covered and demonstrate that no sorting method based on making comparisons can improve on the $O(n \log_2 n)$ performance that we were able to achieve with the heap, merge, and quick sort algorithms.

In Section 12.2, we shift our attention from internal sorting, that is, sorting data within main memory, to external sorting, which is sorting data stored on sequentially accessible secondary memory such as disk and tape files. The two methods we present for external sorting rely on the **merge** function developed as a subordinate algorithm to the merge sort in Section 6.3. Both algorithms take a sequentially accessible data stream and partition it into runs—sequentially accessible substructures that are sorted. These runs are then merged into larger runs, with this process continuing until we are left with just one large run containing all records in the original data stream. The two-way merge sort requires four streams—two with the original data split between them, arranged in runs of some minimal size m and two scratch streams. One of these streams will return the sorted data. The two-stream polyphase merge algorithm reduces this resource cost by requiring one scratch stream in addition to the two streams with embedded runs that are provided as input to the algorithm. The price paid for the increased efficiency in resource cost of the polyphase algorithm is a more costly run-time efficiency.

Keywords

external sorting	run	two-stream polyphase merge sort	two-way merge sort
internal sorting	stream		

Programming Problems/Projects

1. Consider a sequence of records, each containing four fields:
   - name
   - month_of_birth
   - day_of_birth
   - year_of_birth

   Write a program to sort this sequence in oldest-to-youngest order. People with the same birth date should be arranged alphabetically. One strategy you could employ would be to concatenate strategically the four fields into one, and then just sort that one field. Another strategy would be to sort the sequence four times, each time by a different field. (Think carefully about which field to sort first.) Which of the strategies would require that you choose a stable sorting algorithm?
2. In Table 12.1, the quick sort function is identified as an $O(n \log_2 n)$ algorithm that can occasionally degenerate to $O(n^2)$. Write a program in which you throw a large number of random data sets at quick sort. Use this program to estimate empirically the percentage of time that quick sort will degenerate to its worst case efficiency.
3. Develop a program to sort external data files using the two-way merge sort algorithm. Your program should allow the user to input m, the size of the initial runs produced by an internal sorting algorithm. Insert timing statements into your program so that you can experiment to determine which value of m produces the fastest execution time. In a short essay, relate your experimental findings to the answer you gave for Exercise 12.2.1.
4. Develop a program to sort external data files using the two-stream polyphase merge algorithm. Your program should allow the user to input m, the size of the initial runs produced by an internal sorting algorithm. Race this program against the program that you (or a classmate) developed for Problem 3. Write up the results of your experimental race between these two algorithms. Your write-up should address the question of what execution-time price was paid for the more efficient use of resources achieved by the polyphase algorithm.
5. Pivotal to the execution-time efficiency of both the two-way merge sort and the polyphase merge sort is the size m of the runs given to the initial input streams. The larger these runs are, the more efficient the external sorting algorithm becomes. In Section 12.2 we assumed that the runs would be produced by invoking an internal sorting algorithm on an array of size m, which is loaded by getting the next m items from the original data stream. Consider the following alternative strategy, known as *replacement selection,* for producing these runs using an internal array with room for m values.

   Instead of getting a block of m values from the original stream and sorting these m values, use the array to provide a modified implementation of a priority queue that can accommodate up to m items at a time. Begin by loading m values from the original input stream into this priority queue. Then access and remove the first item in the priority queue and put it out to the run that is currently being produced. There is now room to bring another item into the priority queue from the original input stream; so do this. If the item brought in precedes the item that was just accessed and dequeued, then "mark" it so that it will not move to the front of the priority queue and, hence, not be removed with the next invocation of the **front** and **dequeue** operations for the priority queue. (Think about the need for this marking. Its necessity explains why the priority queue used in the replacement selection algorithm to create runs is a slightly modified priority queue.) If the item that is brought in does not precede the item that has previously been accessed and dequeued, then it may be enqueued in the normal fashion. Continue accessing and dequeueing unmarked items and bringing in additional items from the original stream until the marking of items dictates that a new run must be started.

   Given an internal array of size m, implement the replacement selection strategy to create runs in the streams initially fed to the two-way merge sort or the polyphase merge sort. Incorporate this implementation into the program you developed for Problem 3 or 4 above. Execute a series of experimental tests to determine the average size of a run produced in terms of m, the internal array size used for the modified priority queue. By running your new program against the program you developed previously for Problem 3 or 4, determine the effect of the replacement selection strategy on the actual execution time of the overall sorting algorithm. Write up the results of your experimentation in a report.
6. Use a high-level language to create a program that will complete the following steps. Artificially create a stream s of 1000 randomly chosen names. Read into a separate stream $s1$ all those names from s whose last names begin with A through G. Sort this stream with an internal sorting algorithm such as heap sort, and store this sorted stream in another stream *large*. Now read into $s1$ all those names from s whose names begin with H through N; sort it, and append it to the end of *large*. Repeat this process until all names from s are exhausted. The stream *large* will be the sorted version of the original stream s. Observe the execution time of your program. Provide a general efficiency analysis of this external sorting method in terms of the size of the streams s and $s1$.

CHAPTER 13

Memory Management Techniques

A government that is big enough to give you all you want is big enough to take it all away.
Barry Goldwater

Chapter Outline:

In this chapter we examine methods for allocating memory to applications that need it and for effectively reclaiming this memory when the application explicitly or implicitly declares it is no longer needed. In Section 13.1, we introduce the Memory ADT as an abstraction for the computer storage systems whose management is the focus of this chapter. We use the example of memory allocation among users in a time-sharing environment to illustrate how memory resources can be managed when users are requesting blocks of memory of varying sizes. The discussion of Section 13.1 will also indicate how the allocation of variably sized blocks complicates the problem of *garbage collection*—the rather colorful term applied to algorithms that effectively recover memory from users who no longer need it.

In Section 13.2, we pursue the example of a multiuser, time-sharing environment to illustrate three variations of memory management strategies identified by the common term *buddy systems*. The three buddy systems we explore are the binary, Fibonacci, and boundary tag systems. All of these methods are designed to allow fast garbage collection with a minimum of wasted space.

Finally, in Section 13.3, we switch from the example of allocating memory among users in a time-sharing environment to the problem faced by the implementors of programming languages that provide a pointer type—extending the memory management techniques discussed in Sections 13.1 and 13.2 to handle one additional complication—the potential to have multiple pointer references to a particular data node. The techniques that encompass this complication are specific to an area of memory management often referred to as *heap management*. The use of the term *heap* in this context is somewhat unfortunate since it bears no relationship to our earlier discussion of the Heap ADT in Section 7.4.

13.1 Memory Allocation and the Fragmentation Problem

Perhaps the most precious commodity in a multiuser, time-sharing environment is memory. The designers and implementors of operating systems must have as their overriding goal a distribution scheme that ensures that each user gets their requested amount of this resource, but no more. Moreover, as a user finishes with a block of memory, it should be immediately reclaimed by the operating system so that it may be reallocated to other users. This is similar to what we have been doing in some of our C++ implementations of ADTs when we request storage for various objects via the **new** operation and when we release the storage via the **delete** operation. To emphasize these similarities, we are going to treat memory systems such as this as an instance of a more abstract Memory ADT. More precisely, we will use the Memory ADT as the foundation for special subclasses to which are deferred such decisions as what the unit of storage is to be, the structure of the pool of available storage from which these units are allocated and to which they are returned, and how this available storage is maintained. In our ADT we use the operation names **allocate** and **reclaim** instead of our preferred choices of **new** and **delete** because overriding **new** and **delete** as C++ member functions would require that we digress more than is warranted at this point in order to introduce the necessary C++ concepts. The interested reader is referred to Johnsonbaugh, R. and Kalin, M. *Object-Oriented Programming in C++* (Englewood Cliffs, NJ: Prentice-Hall, 1995, pp. 320–325).

Definition: The *Memory* ADT is an abstraction of a computer storage system such as main memory, disk storage, or tape storage. It is comprised of contiguous *units* of storage, each of which has associated with it a unique value known as its *address*. We assume that the unit is of type *UnitType*, its address is of type *AddressType*, and that AddressType admits a special value NULL.

Construct Operation

Precondition: An uninitialized Memory object;
size—a nonnegative integer indicating the maximal number of units of storage available for allocation.

Postcondition: The Memory object is initialized to permit requests to allocate storage via the Allocate operation and to reclaim storage via the Reclaim operation.

Destroy Operation

Precondition: A Memory object that currently exists.

Postcondition: All storage allocated to the Memory object and its records is rendered inaccessible.

Allocate Operation

Precondition: A Memory object that was previously created;
size—a nonnegative integer indicating the number of units of contiguous storage of type UnitType desired.

Postcondition: If the Memory object currently has a block of units of at least the desired size available, this block is allocated and a reference (of type AddressType) to the first unit in the block allocated is returned.

Reclaim Operation

Precondition: A Memory object;
address—of type AddressType, that references the first unit of a previously allocated block of storage.

Postcondition: The block of storage is reclaimed by the Memory object and made available for reallocation via the Allocate operation.

Based on this definition, a skeleton for a C++ specification for the Memory ADT might be:

```
// memory.h

// UnitType is the unit of storage that will be managed by the Memory
// class; AddressType is a type representing the address associated
// with a unit of type UnitType.  We assume AddressType admits a
// special value NULL.

template<class UnitType, class AddressType>
class Memory
{
  public:

//------------------------------------------------------------------------
// Since Memory itself uses no data structures, but rather defers
// this to its derived classes, no constructors or destructors are needed.

//------------------------------------------------------------------------
// Interface for allocate operation
// GIVEN:    A Memory object previously created;
//           size -- a nonnegative integer indicating the number of
//                   units of contiguous storage desired.
// RETURN as value of function:
//           If the Memory object currently has a block of units of at
//           least the desired size available, this block is allocated
//           and a reference (of type AddressType) to the first unit in
//           the block allocated is returned; if no memory is available
//           the  NULL value is returned.

    AddressType virtual allocate(int size) = 0;

//------------------------------------------------------------------------
// Interface for reclaim operation
// GIVEN:    A Memory object that was previously created;
//           address -- a value of type AddressType, that references
//                      the first unit of a previously allocated block
//                      of storage.
// RETURN:   The block of storage is reclaimed by the Memory object and
//           made available for reallocation via the allocate operation.
// RETURN as value of function: void

    void virtual reclaim(AddressType &address) = 0;
};
```

To help you acquire a feeling for what is involved in memory management, we begin with the relatively simple task of allocating and reclaiming single units of storage of type **UnitType**. Although you may argue that this is unnecessary because C++ provides its **new** and **delete** operations on pointers for just this purpose, there are several reasons why we should implement them ourselves:

1. The techniques we use in our example provide a foundation for understanding some of the more involved techniques that will come up later.
2. We are using C++ only as a language for specifying our ADTs and indicating how they may be implemented. Even though pointers are implemented in many languages (including Pascal, Modula-2, and Ada), they are not implemented in all languages, including some that are still widely used (such as

FORTRAN, COBOL, and BASIC). Thus, it is important for you to have an idea of how they might be implemented in the event that you want to use them while working in a language that does not support them directly. It is important to realize that, just because the language does not have pointers, you need not completely avoid data structures that require pointers—you merely have to provide your own implementation.

3. Even in languages that provide pointers, you may run into situations where the implementation is not suitable for your application. For instance, even though Pascal does support pointers, you cannot display the values of a pointer with a **write** or **writeln** statement (these are Pascal's output operations). Often it would be useful to see the value, especially when you have a bug in a program that you suspect may be caused by a pointer having an improperly assigned value. By implementing your own pointers you can provide them with additional features suitable for debugging purposes, and then easily switch back to the language's implementation of bona fide Pascal pointers once you are convinced that your program is working properly.
4. Situations can arise in which memory-resident pointers will be insufficient for your needs. For example, if you need to map a pointer-dependent data structure such as a linked list onto a random access file, you would not be able to use a programming language's implementation of memory-resident pointer variables. Recall also that when we studied hashing in Chapter 11 we explored a situation, collision resolution through linking, in which supplied pointer variables would not meet our needs.

Hence, an understanding of what lies below the abstract-level pointer variables is likely to be valuable regardless of your future endeavors in computer science.

Example 13.1

We specify and implement a subclass, **BlockMemory,** of the class **Memory** that manages storage (allocated from the computer's main memory) for a storage system that uses units of storage of type **UnitType** but in which only a single unit is to be allocated on a given call to **allocate.** Our approach to solving this problem will be to use an Array object whose components are of type **UnitType** and to link each unit of available memory into an *available space* list whose nodes use part of the storage in each block to store the location of the next available block. When a request is made for memory, we merely retrieve from the available space list the block at the head of the list.

```
#include "memory.h"
#define NULL -1
template<class UnitType, class AddressType>
class BlockMemory:  Memory<UnitType, AddressType>
{
  protected:
    struct FreeNode  // Represents a block of storage that holds a
                     // UnitType of data, but in which the last sizeOf(int)
                     // bytes are used as a link to another block in an
                     // array
    {
      char bytes[sizeOf(UnitType)-sizeOf(int)];
      int link;
    };

    FreeNode* blocks; // Will reference the first element in an array
                      // of FreeNodes
```

```
    int avail;          // Index of the head of available space list
    int maxBlocks;      // Stores maximal number of units available for allocation

    int calIndex(AddressType address)    // Private function for converting
                                         // a block address to the array
                                         // index for a block
    {
      return((address - (AddressType) &blocks[0]) / sizeof(UnitType));
    }

    AddressType calAddress(int index)    // Private function for converting
                                         // array index for a block to a block
                                         // address
    {
      return(((sizeof(UnitType) * index) + (AddressType) blocks));
    }

  public:
//-----------------------------------------------------------------------
// Interface for BlockMemory constructor
// GIVEN:    An uninitialized BlockMemory object;
//           size -- a nonnegative integer indicating the maximal number
//                   of units of storage available for allocation.
// RETURN:   The BlockMemory object is initialized to permit requests to
//           allocate storage via the allocate operation and to deallocate
//           storage via the reclaim operation.

    BlockMemory(int maxSize);

//-----------------------------------------------------------------------
// Interface for BlockMemory destructor
// GIVEN:    A BlockMemory object that currently exists.
// RETURN:   All storage allocated to the BlockMemory object
//           is rendered inaccessible.

    ~BlockMemory();

//-----------------------------------------------------------------------
// Interface for allocate operator
// GIVEN:    A BlockMemory object that was previously created;
//           size -- a nonnegative integer indicating the number of units
//                   of contiguous storage desired.  As used in the class
//                   BlockMemory, size will always be 1, but has been left
//                   as a parameter to be consistent with the memory class.
// RETURN as value of function:
//           If the BlockMemory object currently has a block available, this
//           block is allocated and a reference (of type AddressType) to
//           the block allocated is returned; if no memory is available
//           the NULL value is returned.

    AddressType allocate(int size);

//-----------------------------------------------------------------------
// Interface for reclaim operator
// GIVEN:    A BlockMemory object that was previously created;
//           address -- a reference to a value of type AddressType. The address
//                      referenced is that of a previously allocated block of
//                      storage.
// RETURN:   The block of storage is reclaimed by the BlockMemory object and
//           made available for reallocation via the allocate operation.
// RETURN as value of function: void

    void reclaim (AddressType &address);
};
```

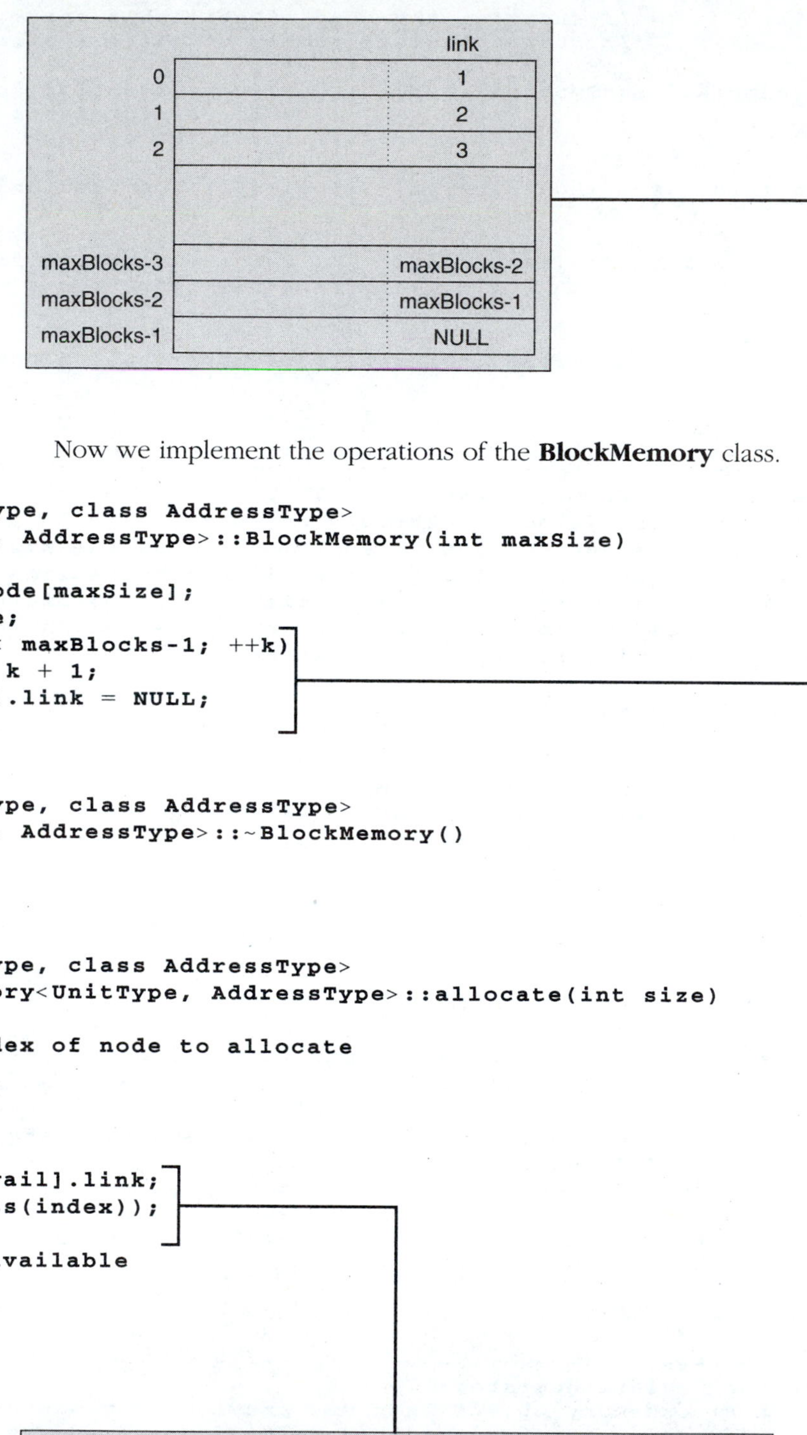

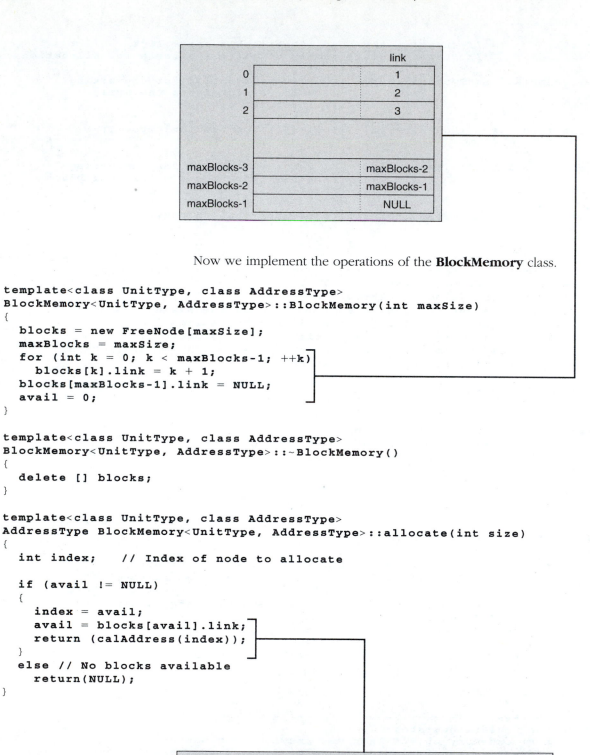

Now we implement the operations of the **BlockMemory** class.

```
template<class UnitType, class AddressType>
BlockMemory<UnitType, AddressType>::BlockMemory(int maxSize)
{
  blocks = new FreeNode[maxSize];
  maxBlocks = maxSize;
  for (int k = 0; k < maxBlocks-1; ++k)
    blocks[k].link = k + 1;
  blocks[maxBlocks-1].link = NULL;
  avail = 0;
}

template<class UnitType, class AddressType>
BlockMemory<UnitType, AddressType>::~BlockMemory()
{
  delete [] blocks;
}

template<class UnitType, class AddressType>
AddressType BlockMemory<UnitType, AddressType>::allocate(int size)
{
  int index;    // Index of node to allocate

  if (avail != NULL)
  {
    index = avail;
    avail = blocks[avail].link;
    return (calAddress(index));
  }
  else // No blocks available
    return(NULL);
}
```

avail

This pointer altered

address of this block is returned

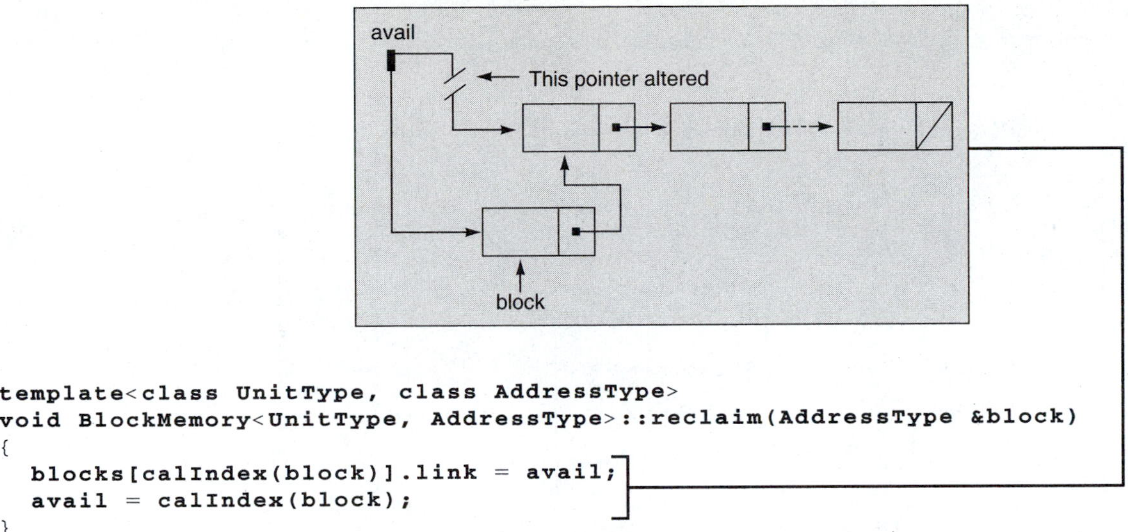


```
template<class UnitType, class AddressType>
void BlockMemory<UnitType, AddressType>::reclaim(AddressType &block)
{
  blocks[calIndex(block)].link = avail;
  avail = calIndex(block);
}
```

As an example of the complications that can arise as memory is subjected to **allocate–reclaim–**(re)**allocate** cycles, consider the sequence of user requests for memory presented in Figure 13.1. This figure illustrates what is known as the *fragmentation problem.* That is, as memory is allocated to users and then returned, the resulting overall pattern of available memory contains relatively small, disconnected fragments of available space. The problem with this fragmented pattern is that we cannot honor a user request for a contiguous memory area exceeding the size of the largest available memory block, even though overall we may have more than enough memory to grant the request. This dilemma is illustrated by the 10K request in the final memory snapshot of Figure 13.1.

One solution to this fragmentation problem would be to move all used memory blocks down (or up) in memory, resulting in just one large free block whose size is equal to the sum of the sizes of all the original smaller free blocks. This strategy is called *compaction* (or "burping memory") and is not acceptable from an operating system perspective because operating systems must be extremely time-efficient in their responses to users. The compaction process would require stopping all user activity while memory is reorganized by moving large amounts of data. Compaction would therefore inevitably result in periodic and time-consuming interruptions in service.

Another approach to solving this problem would be to generalize the approach we used in Example 13.1 and link each block of available memory into an *available space* list whose nodes use storage in each block to store the size of the block as well as a pointer to the next available block. For instance, the free blocks pictured in the last memory snapshot of Figure 13.1 could be linked into an available list by allocating two words in each block to store the size of the block and a pointer to the next available block (see Figure 13.2).

Now when a request is made for memory we could search the available space list for a block whose size satisfies the request. This search could employ one of two algorithms:

1. A *first-fit* algorithm, in which the available space list is searched until we find the first block whose size meets or exceeds the request.

Figure 13.1
The fragmentation problem on a multiuser system. In snapshot VIII, a 10K request could not be met even though a total of 15K is unused.

I: 64K words, FREE, 16K words, A, 0K words — User A allocated memory
II: 64K words, FREE, 24K words, B, 16K words, A, 0K words — User B allocated memory
III: 64K words, FREE, 38K words, C, 24K words, B, 16K words, A, 0K words — User C allocated memory
IV: 64K, FREE, 38K, C, 24K, FREE, 16K, A, 0K — User B finished
V: 64K, 44K, D, 38K, C, 24K, FREE, 16K, A, 0K — User D allocated memory
VI: 64K, FREE, 63K, E, 44K, D, 38K, C, 24K, FREE, 16K, A, 0K — User E allocated memory
VII: 64K, FREE, 63K, E, 44K, FREE, 38K, C, 24K, FREE, 16K, A, 0K — User D finished
VIII: 64K, FREE, 63K, E, 44K, FREE, 38K, C, 24K, FREE, 16K, A, 0K — What if next request is 2K? 10K?

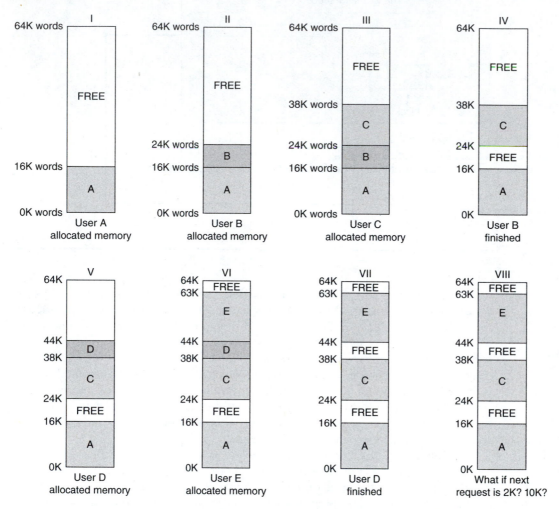

2. A *best-fit* algorithm, in which the available space list is searched for the block whose size surpasses the request by the least amount.

Having identified the block to allocate to the user, next it would be wise to determine whether or not the user actually requires the entire block. If not, it could

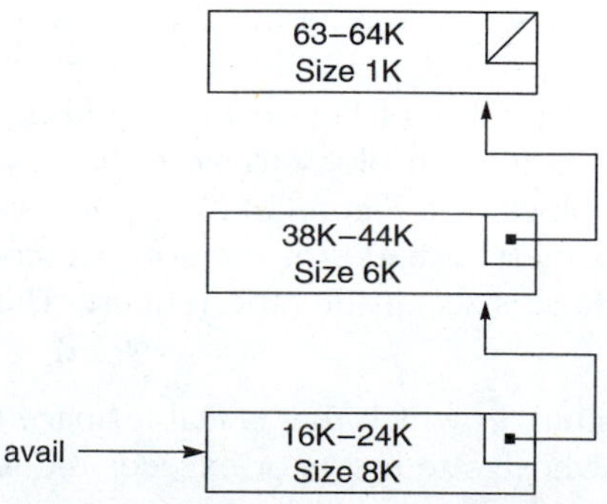

Figure 13.2
Available space list derived from snapshot VIII of Figure 13.1.

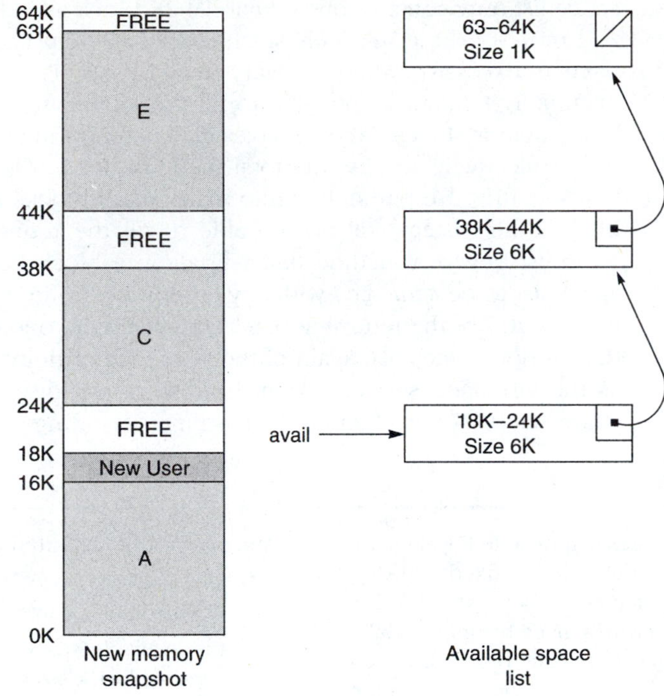

Figure 13.3 Honoring a 2K request from the available space list of Figure 13.2.

be split, giving the user what she requested and keeping what remains of the block in the available space list. This strategy, applied to the available space list of Figure 13.2 for a request of 2K memory, yields the result displayed in Figure 13.3.

Unfortunately, this scheme will lead to another problem when it comes time to collect the memory blocks no longer needed by users. Consider, for instance, what happens if the 2K memory block allocated in Figure 13.3 is returned by its user before any other changes are made in the available space list. The new available

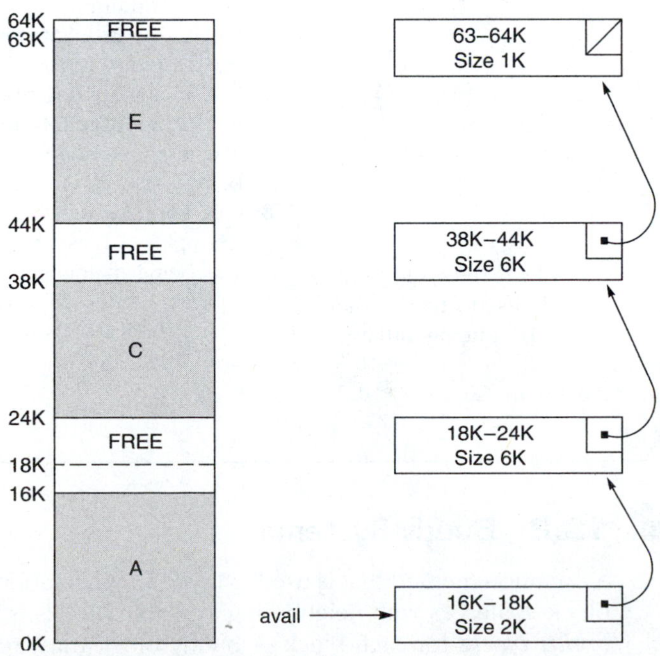

Figure 13.4 Available space list after returning the 2K block.

space list now contains one additional 2K block as indicated in Figure 13.4. As more and more of these relatively small blocks are returned, the available space list will have an excessive number of very small blocks. This is not desirable because it will eventually become impossible to fill the legitimate request of a user needing one large memory block. We will have small neighboring blocks, the sum of whose sizes may collectively surpass the total memory needed by the large request; however, because they are partitioned into many small blocks instead of relatively few large blocks, the system will not be able to fill the request. To remedy this problem, we must devise a method that will allow a block being returned to the available space list to be *coalesced* with any other block(s) in the list that is (are) the physical neighbor(s) of the returning block. Interestingly, one of the solutions we are about to describe makes use again of the sequence of numbers from mathematics known as the Fibonacci sequence, which arose in our discussions of interpolative search strategies (Chapter 1) and polyphase merge sorting (Chapter 12).

Exercises 13.1

1. In the operating system routines responsible for file management, users are typically allocated a fixed-size disk block, such as 512 bytes, each time they extend a file. Hence, the blocks associated with a given file might not be contiguous on the disk surface; but linked blocks scattered over the entire disk. Which form of storage allocation would be most appropriate for the file management portion of an operating system: the implementation of Example 13.1, the first-fit strategy, or the best-fit strategy? Why?
2. Given a memory region of 128K words, trace the blocks allocated to users and the status of the list of available blocks for the following sequence of user requests:

   User 1 requests 47K

   User 2 requests 39K

   User 3 requests 4K

   User 4 requests 34K

   User 1 finishes

   User 5 requests 6K

   User 4 finishes

   User 6 requests 18K

   User 7 requests 32K

   User 8 requests 30K

   Assume that the list of available blocks is traversed from the available block at the lowest address to that at the highest address. Assume also that the best-fit algorithm is used.
3. How is your tracing of the scenario in Exercise 13.1.2 affected if
   a. the first-fit algorithm is used?
   b. the available space list is maintained in order of *descending* block sizes and the first-fit algorithm is used?
   c. the available space list is maintained in order of *ascending* block sizes and the first-fit algorithm is used?
4. Will the best-fit algorithm always manage memory more space efficiently than the first-fit algorithm? If yes, explain why; otherwise, provide a sequence of user requests for which the first-fit algorithm would perform better from a space perspective.
5. Specify the additional data that must be maintained to implement the compaction strategy mentioned at the beginning of this section. Then supply full declarations for these data and use these declarations to implement a compaction algorithm. Analyze the time efficiency of your algorithm.
6. Extend the **BlockMemory** class of Example 13.1 to manage memory nodes of varying size units by using the first-fit strategy described in Section 13.1.
7. Extend the **BlockMemory** class of Example 13.1 to manage memory nodes of varying size units by using the best-fit strategy described in Section 13.1.
8. Our implementation of the **BlockMemory** subclass of Example 13.1 assumed that the list of available blocks was being maintained in main memory. Define another subclass of the **Memory** class, **DiskMemory,** that assumes the list of available units is being maintained on a disk drive.

■ 13.2 Buddy Systems

A common method that is used to avoid fragmentation and to ensure that a returning block coalesces with neighboring available blocks is that of designating one or two *buddy blocks* for each block. A buddy block must reside next to its corresponding block in memory. When a block is ready to be returned, we check the available space list for its buddy. If the buddy is also available, we coalesce the two before returning them as one block to available space. This is not quite as easy as it seems. To determine the buddy of a given block, it is necessary to impose certain restrictions on block sizes and/or to store a fair amount of bookkeeping data in each block. We will examine three buddy schemes:

1. Binary buddies
2. Fibonacci buddies
3. Boundary tag buddies.

These schemes differ in the data structures used for their implementation. After stating the general algorithms in skeletal pseudocode, we provide a more detailed discussion of these data structures.

```
//------------------------------------------------------------------------
// Interface for allocate operation (buddy system implementation)
// GIVEN:     A Memory object that was previously created;
//            size -- a nonnegative integer indicating the number of
//                    units of contiguous storage desired.
// RETURN as value of function:
//            If the Memory object currently has available a block of
//            units of at least the desired size, the block that meets
//            the request with the least amount of waste is allocated
//            and a reference (of type AddressType) to the first unit
//            in the block allocated is returned; if no memory is available
//            the NULL value is returned.

AddressType allocate(int size)
{
  call a search function to search the available space list and find
       a block that surpasses the size requested with the least possible
       amount of excess;

  if (no such block can be found)
    invoke an insufficientMemory exception handler;
  else
    if (the block found cannot be split into buddies, one of which
        would satisfy the size requested)
      return the address of the block found by the search function;
    else
    // The buddy system being used allows splitting
    {
      split the block into two buddies;
      return one buddy to appropriate available block list(s);
      return the address of the other buddy;
    }

}
```

The *search* function called on to find a block in this function would be dependent on the data structure used by a particular buddy system to store available blocks. Whether a block, once found, can be further split is determined by the restrictions the given buddy system imposes on block sizes.

A similar skeletal pseudocode algorithm for the **reclaim** operation that returns memory blocks to the available space list is presented here in recursive form. The recursion expresses the fact that, once a returning block has been coalesced with its buddy on the left or right, we have a larger block that may itself be a candidate for coalescing with another buddy.

```
void reclaim(AddressType &block)
{
  //  Begin by recursively coalescing the block with its buddies
  coalesce (block);           //  See following coalesce function

  // Upon return from coalesce, block may well be pointing to a much
  // larger block than it was before.  The final step is now to attach
  // this potentially larger block to the available space structure
  attach(block);
}

//----------------------------------------------------------------------
// Interface for coalesce function
// GIVEN:     block -- the address of an unallocated memory block.
// RETURN:    Will return with block now pointing to a potentially larger
//            block formed by coalescing the original block with its
//            buddies on the left and/or right.
// RETURN as value of function: void

void coalesce(AddressType &block)
{
  // The call to checkBuddies represents a call to a function that will
  // determine whether buddies of a block exist in the available space
  // structure.  If a left buddy of block is available, then its address
  // is returned in lbuddy. Otherwise, lbuddy is returned as NULL.  A similar
  // convention is followed for a right buddy and its address rbuddy.

  checkBuddies(block, lbuddy, rbuddy);

  // If both lbuddy and rbuddy come back as NULL, both of the conditional
  // tests that follow will fail and an immediate return will result.
  // Otherwise, coalescing must occur on left and/or right.

  if (rbuddy != NULL)
  {
    remove rbuddy from avail structure;
    change appropriate members of block to coalesce block with rbuddy;
    // These members are dependent on buddy system being used

    coalesce(block);
    // Recursively attempt to coalesce the new, larger block with its buddies
  }
  if (lbuddy != NULL)
  {
    remove lbuddy from available space structure;
    change appropriate members of lbuddy to coalesce block with lbuddy;
    //  These members are dependent on buddy system being used

    set block to lbuddy;    // block now references larger block
    coalesce(block);
    //  Recursively attempt to coalesce the new, larger block with its buddies
  }
}
```

We now explain in more detail the methodology of each of the three previously cited buddy systems. From the generic functions **allocate** and **reclaim** that we have given, it is clear that a detailed exposition must describe both the data structure used to store available blocks and the bookkeeping data that must be stored within and about each memory block. This bookkeeping data might include, for example, the size of the block, a flag to indicate whether or not it is free, and so on.

Binary Buddy System

The logic of the *binary buddy system* method requires that all blocks be of size 2^i for some i. Whenever a block is split, the resulting two buddies must be of equal size. That is, if a block of size 2^i is split, then the resulting buddies will each be of size 2^{i-1}. As an example, let us suppose that we have 2^{16} (64K) words of memory to manage and that we wish to allocate no blocks smaller than 2^{10} (1K) words. Then, at any given time, we could potentially have free blocks of size 2 raised to the 10th, 11th, 12th, 13th, 14th, 15th, and 16th powers. The available space structure in this case will consist of a doubly linked list of free blocks for each of the seven potential block sizes. Hence, we would need head pointers as follows:

`avail[0]` → head of list for blocks of size 2^{10}
`avail[1]` → head of list for blocks of size 2^{11}
`avail[2]` → head of list for blocks of size 2^{12}
.
.
.
`avail[6]` → head of list for blocks of size 2^{16}

Each block would need to contain the following bookkeeping information:

- A Boolean flag to indicate whether or not it is free
- An integer member to store its size
- **left** and **right** links used when it is a node in an **avail** list.

An illustration of such a node is given in Figure 13.5.

Initially, all 2^{16} words of memory would be viewed as one free block; that is, **avail[6]** would point to the beginning of memory and all other **avail** pointers would be NULL. Now let us suppose that a sequence of user requests came in the following order:

a. Request for memory block of size 2^{14}
b. Request for memory block of size 2^{13}
c. Request for memory block of size 2^{14}
d. Request for memory block of size 2^{14}
e. Block from request **a** no longer needed
f. Block from request **b** no longer needed.

The dynamic processing of these requests can best be described pictorially. In Figure 13.6, we use tree diagrams to represent the splitting and coalescing that

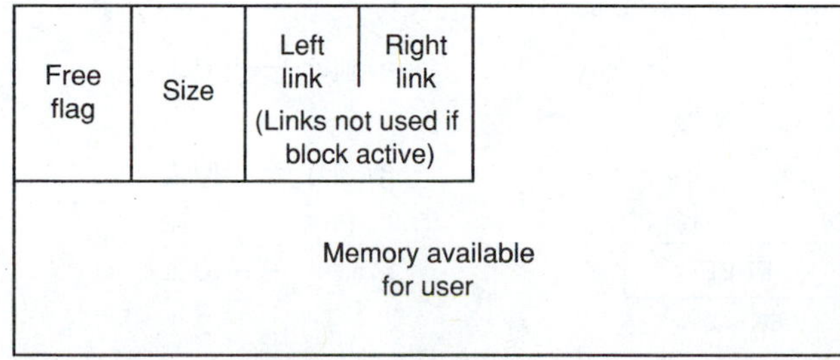

Figure 13.5
Bookkeeping information in block for binary buddy system.

Figure 13.6
Processing requests using the binary buddy system.

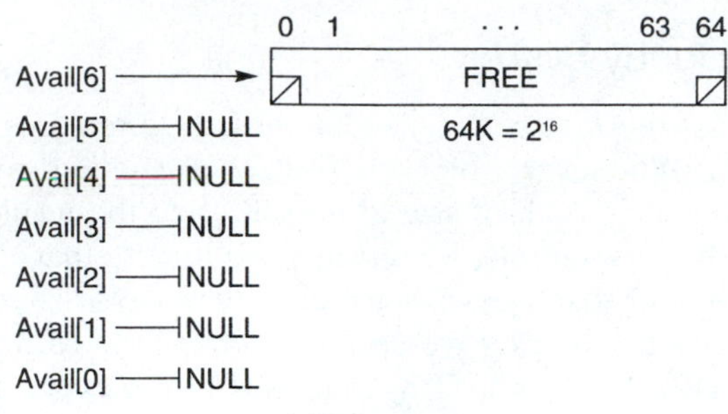

Initial status

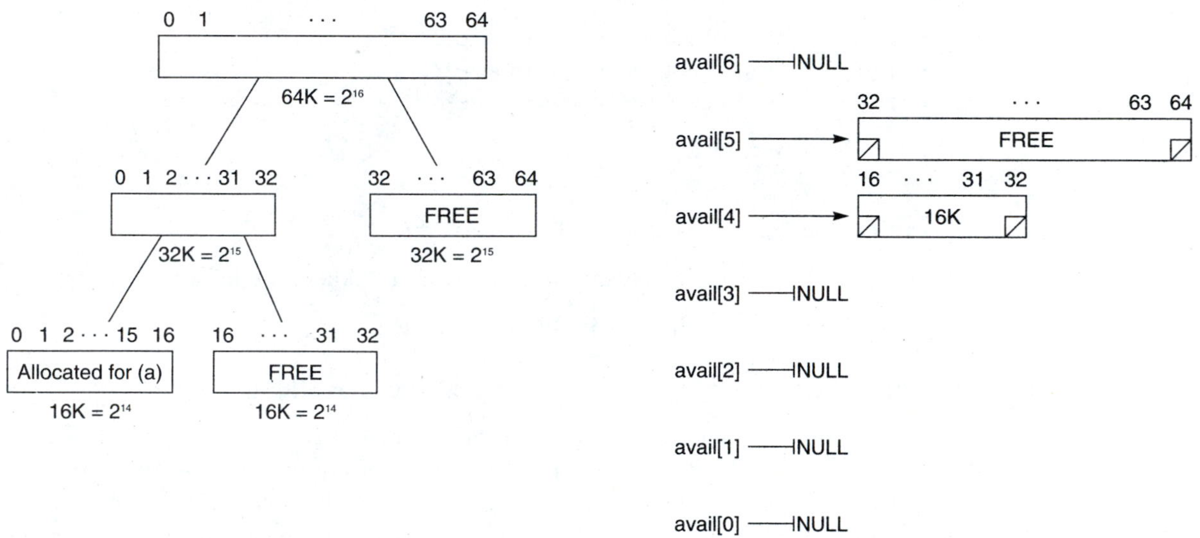

Request (a) process—allocate block of size 2^{14}

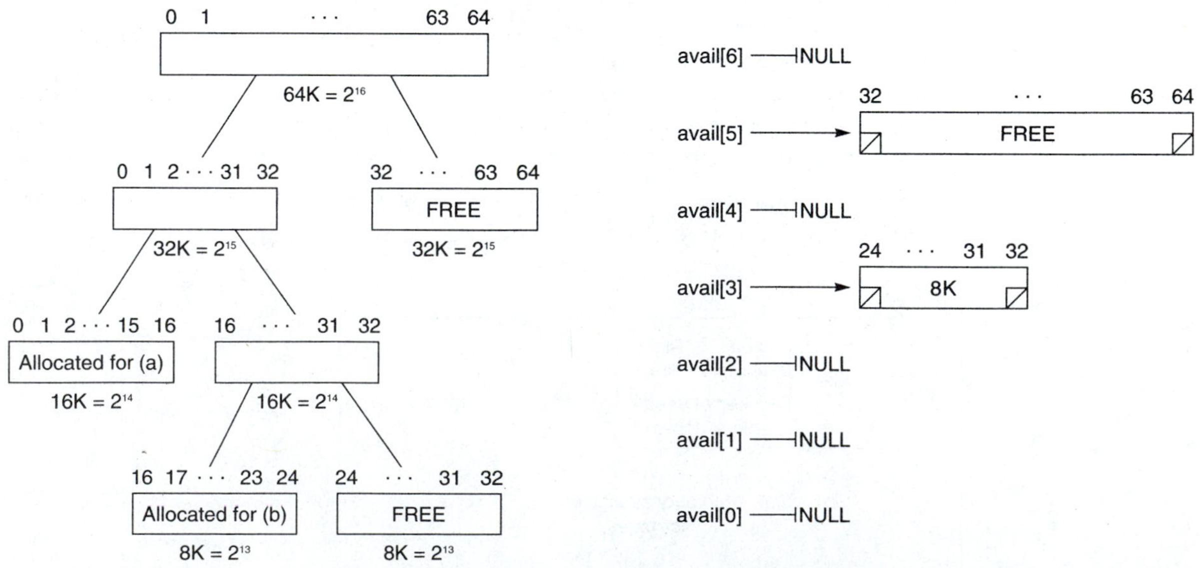

Request (b) process—allocate block of size 2^{13}

Figure 13.6
(continued)

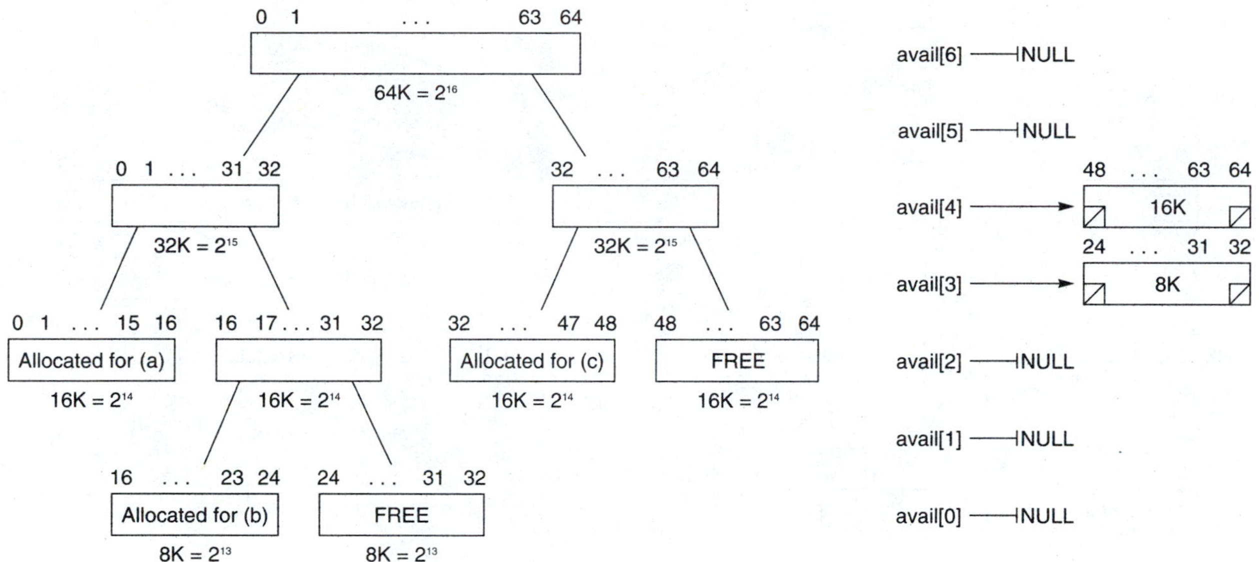

Request (c) processed—allocate block of size 2^{14}

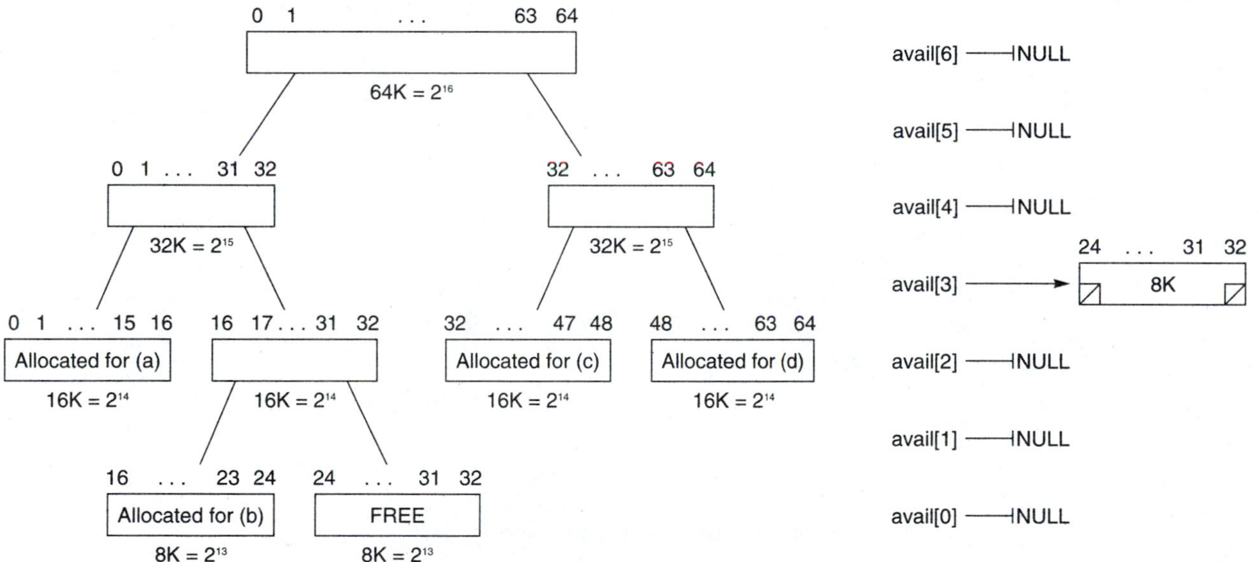

Request (d) processed—allocate block of size 2^{14}

would occur as requests **a** through **f** are processed. Memory addresses in this figure are given as 0, 1, 2, . . . , 62, and 63; i represents the beginning of the $(i + 1)$st K memory block (of which there are 64 in all).

Three comments are needed to explain more fully the actions highlighted in Figure 13.6. First, the reason for coalescing is that one available block of size $2n$ is always preferred over two available blocks of size n. The whole is greater than the sum of its parts. This is why, in returning the block from request **b** in Figure 13.6,

Figure 13.6
(*continued*)

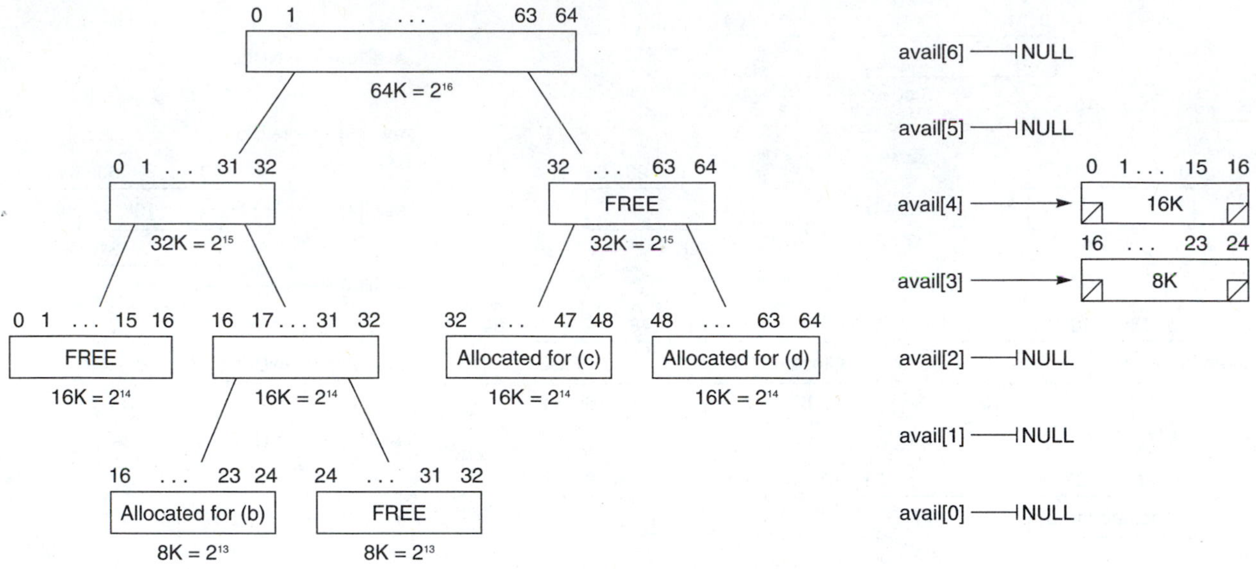

Block from (a) returned—no coalescing occurs

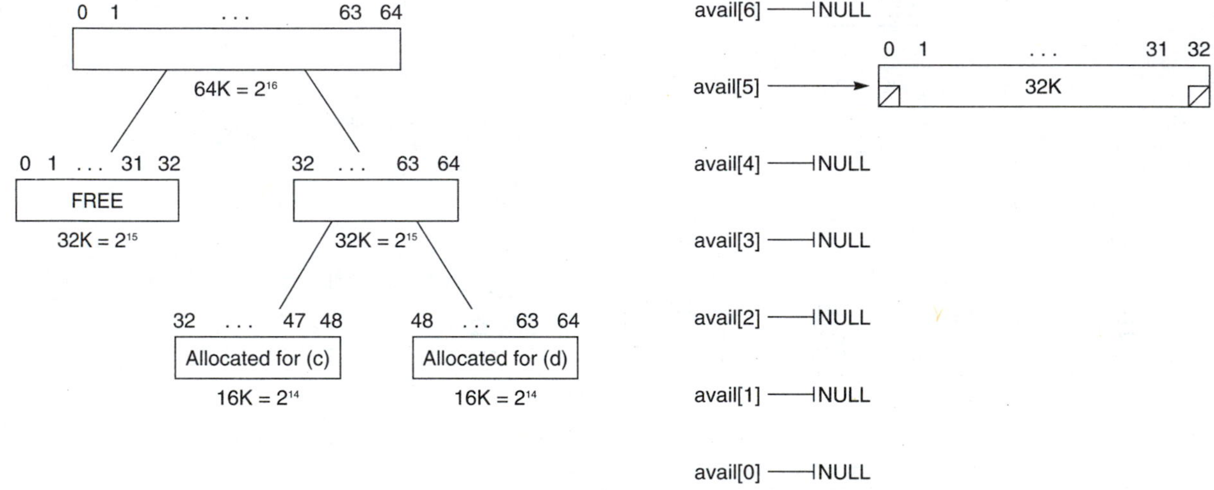

Block from (b) returned—coalescing occurs (twice)

we coalesce two 8K blocks into a 16K block and then immediately take advantage of an available 16K left buddy to coalesce further into a 32K block.

Second, the binary splitting scheme means that, when a block is to be returned, the address of its buddy can be immediately determined. For instance, the block of size 2^{14} (16K), which begins at address 0 (relative to 1K blocks), has a right buddy of the same size that begins at address 16 (relative to 1K blocks). The location of this block's buddy is purely a function of the block's own size and location. In absolute terms, a block of size 2^i with starting address $n \times 2^i$ will have a right buddy with starting address $(n + 1) \times 2^i$ if n is even, and a left buddy starting at address $(n - 1) \times 2^i$ if n is odd. This means that, as a block is being returned, a simple computation allows us to find its buddy, whose free flag is then checked to determine whether or not coalescing is possible. Notice that, in a binary buddy system, a given block has either a left or a right buddy but not both.

Third, if the buddy of the block to be returned is free, the doubly linked nature of the available block lists becomes crucial because we have essentially jumped into the middle of an available space list in accessing the buddy of the block to be returned. Without the double linking, we would not have the back pointer necessary to remove this buddy from the available list of which it is presently a part. Of course, once a returning block has been coalesced with its buddy, we have a new returning block that can recursively undergo further coalescing as indicated in our generic **coalesce** function.

Fibonacci Buddy System

Let us start with a consideration of Fibonacci systems by analyzing the binary buddy system. Contradictory as this may seem, the rationale consists of defining the relationships between block sizes that must exist in a buddy system of this type. Examining the sequence of possible block sizes in the binary system,

$$2^1, 2^2, 2^3, \ldots, 2^{10}, 2^{11}, \ldots$$

we notice that every member of the sequence except the first is the result of adding the previous member to itself. Since any block size (except the smallest possible) can result from coalescing two smaller blocks, it becomes clear that any sequence of possible block sizes for a buddy system of this variety must have the property that any size element within the sequence is the sum of two preceding members of the sequence. In the binary buddy system, this sum is always obtained by adding the size of the immediately prior member of the sequence to itself. However, the binary system is a special case; all that is really required is that any size can be represented as the sum of two smaller sizes.

Perhaps the most famous sequence of numbers having this property is the Fibonacci sequence. The ith member of the Fibonacci sequence can be recursively defined as

$$\begin{aligned} F_1 &= 1 \\ F_2 &= 1 \\ F_i &= F_{i-1} + F_{i-2} \qquad \text{for } i > 2 \end{aligned}$$

Hence, the initial members of the Fibonacci sequence are

$$1, 1, 2, 3, 5, 8, 13, 21, 34, \ldots$$

Suppose, for instance, that we were managing 21K memory using Fibonacci block sizes and were faced with the following requests for storage:

a. Request for 7K
b. Request for 7K
c. Request for 2K
d. 7K from request **c** no longer needed
e. 2K from request **a** no longer needed
f. 7K from request **f** no longer needed.

Figure 13.7 illustrates the allocation, reclamation, and resulting coalescing that would occur as these requests were processed. Naturally, some additional overhead (beyond that required for the binary buddy system) is required when the Fibonacci

Figure 13.7
Processing requests using the Fibonacci buddy system. Circled digits represent left buddy counts.

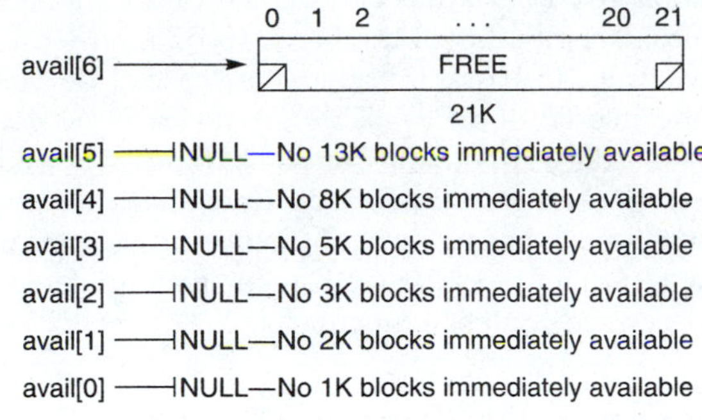

Initial state of memory—21K free

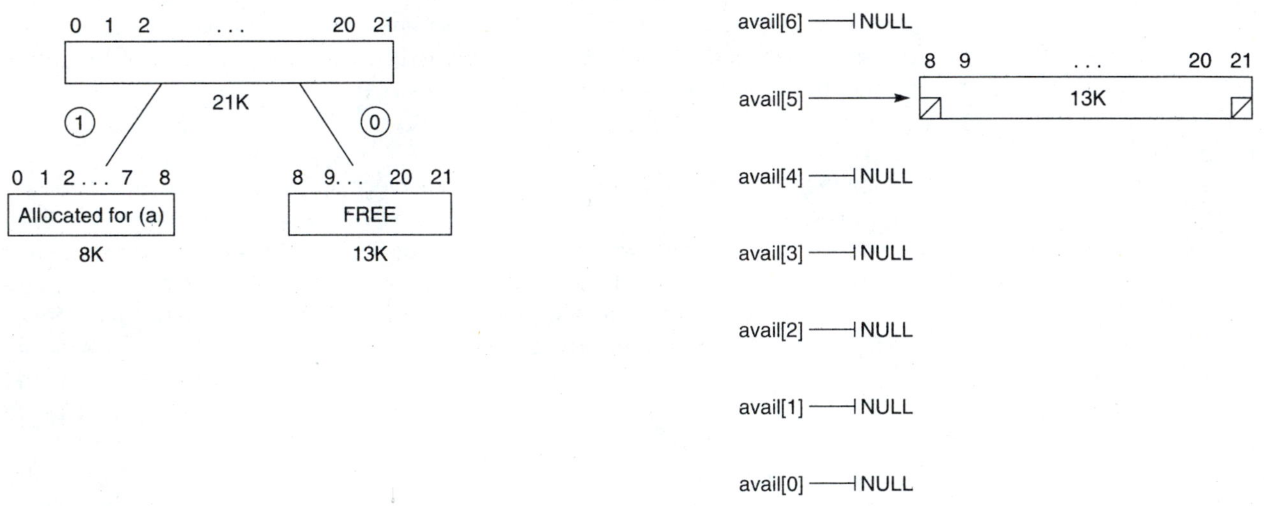

Request (a) processed—8K allocated for 7K request

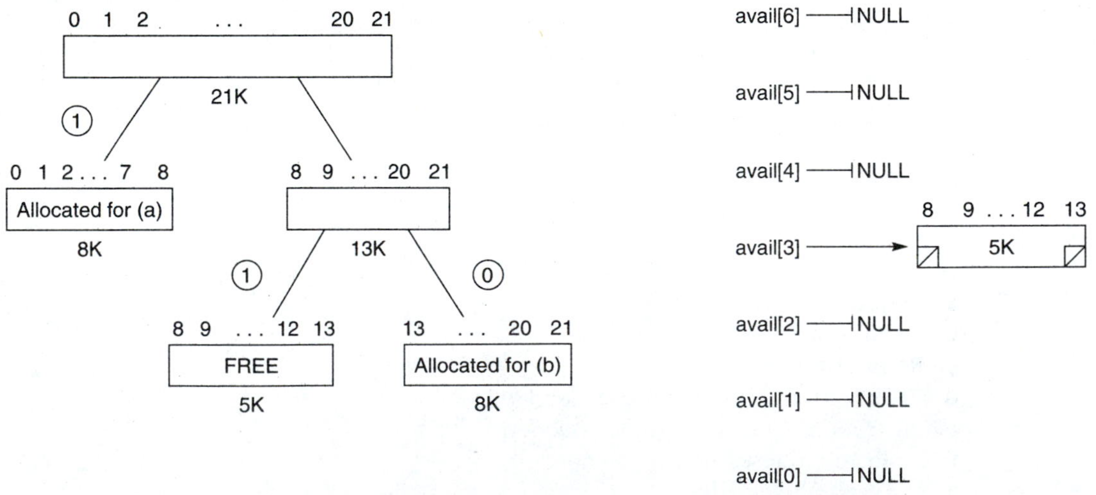

Request (b) processed—8K allocated for 7K request

Figure 13.7
(continued)

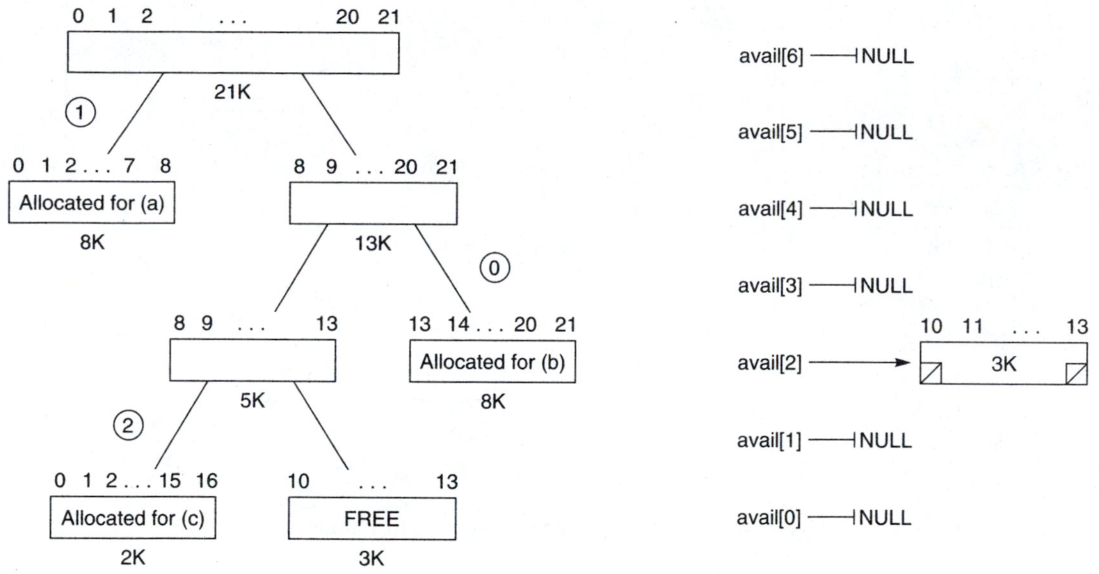

Request (c) processed—2K allocated for 2K request

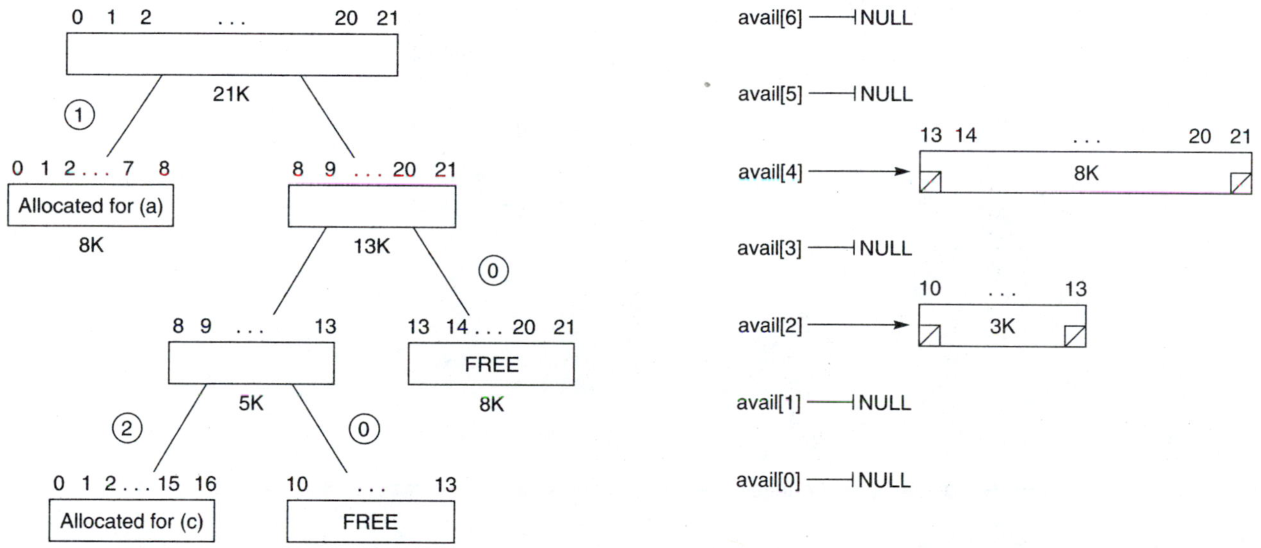

Request (d) processed—memory for (b) released, no coalescing occurs

buddy system is used. First, depending on the implementation scheme, it might be necessary to store the Fibonacci numbers themselves in an array to allow quick access to data necessary to allocate, split, and coalesce blocks. The alternative would be to recompute the sequence each time it is needed. Second, unlike the binary system, it is not clear from a block's size and location whether it is the left buddy or the right buddy of another block. Consequently, it becomes necessary to store some additional bookkeeping data within each block, in the form of a left buddy count as indicated in Figure 13.8. The left buddy count maintains a record of how deeply a given block is nested as the left buddy of other blocks. In Figure 13.7, the

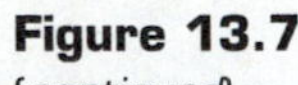

Figure 13.7
(continued)

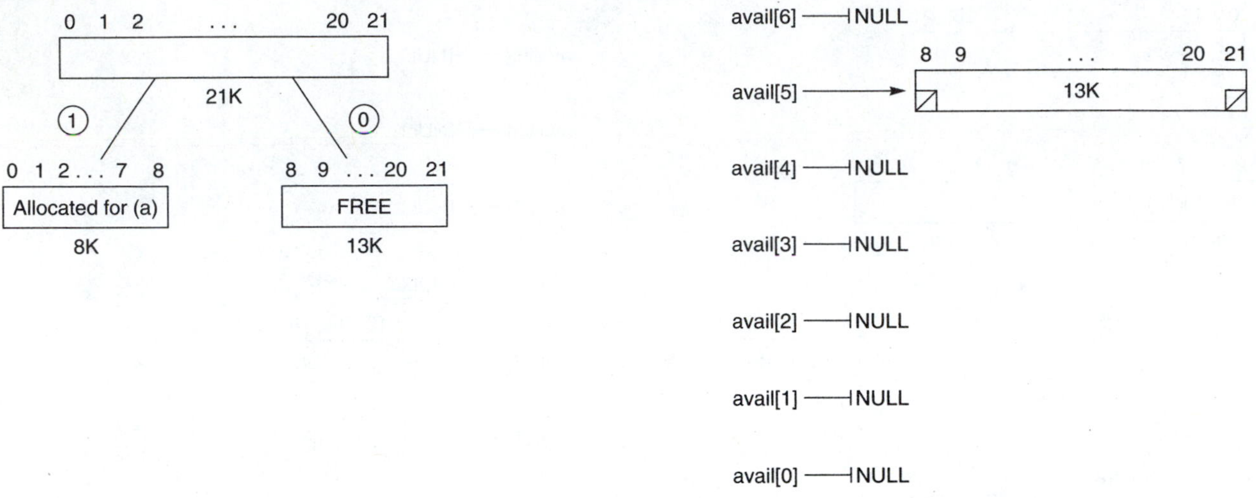

Request (e) process—memory for (c) released, coalescing occurs up to 13K block

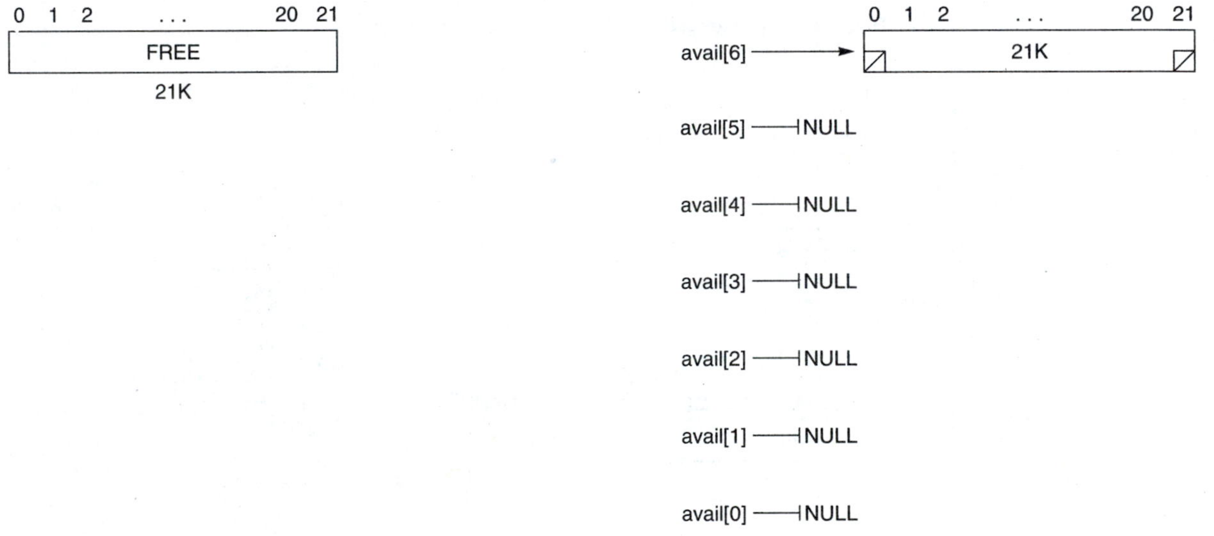

Request (f) processed—memory for (a) released, coalescing occurs—one free 21K block results

Figure 13.8
Bookkeeping information in block for Fibonacci buddy system.

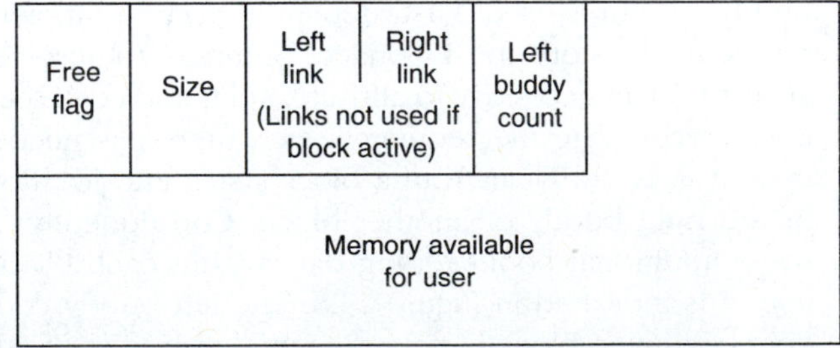

left buddy count is indicated by the circled digit appearing above each block. The algorithm for maintaining this left buddy count involves these steps.

1. As a block is split, the resulting left buddy has its left buddy count increased by one. The resulting right buddy has its left buddy count set to zero.
2. As coalescing occurs, the left buddy must always have its left buddy count decreased by one.

Given the increase in overhead involved in the Fibonacci system, it is certainly a valid question to ask whether or not it offers any advantage over the binary system. Its primary advantage is that it allows for a greater variety of possible block sizes in a given amount of memory than its binary counterpart. For instance, in 64K words of memory, the Fibonacci system would allow block sizes of 1K, 2K, 3K, 5K, 8K, 13K, 21K, 34K, and 55K; nine sizes in all. Clearly, a greater variety of sizes allows us to allocate memory in a way that minimizes the difference between what the user actually needs and what our block sizes force us to give.

In fact, if one uses a more generalized kth Fibonacci sequence defined by

$$F_j = 1 \qquad \text{for } j = 1, 2, \ldots, k$$
$$F_j = F_{j-1} + F_{j-k} \qquad \text{for } j > k$$

then it can be readily seen that, the larger k becomes, the finer our partitioning of block sizes will be. (Notice that by this definition the binary buddy system is in fact generated by the first Fibonacci sequence.) Of course, with each increase in k comes a corresponding increase in the overhead of bookkeeping information that must be balanced against the greater selection of block sizes.

For a more theoretical discussion of which k may be appropriate to choose in a given situation, see J. A. Hinds, "A Design for the Buddy System with Arbitrary Sequences of Buddy Sizes," Technical Report No. 74 (Buffalo, NY: State University of New York at Buffalo, 1973).

Boundary Tag Buddies

Both the binary and Fibonacci systems have the disadvantage of not allowing an arbitrary selection of block sizes, thereby forcing the waste of some memory each time a user's request does not precisely match one of the specified block sizes. The *boundary tag buddy system* overcomes this drawback but only at the expense of requiring even more bookkeeping data than either of the other methods.

The reason that the binary and Fibonacci schemes limit us to a finite number of block sizes and splitting possibilities is that, without such a limitation, it would be impossible to determine where a block's buddy begins. For instance, suppose that we were using the Fibonacci buddy system and were about to return a block of size 13K whose left buddy count was found to be zero. Because of the limitations on the sizes into which a block may be split under the Fibonacci method, we know that this block must have a left buddy of size 8K with which it could possibly coalesce. Using the starting address of the block to be returned and the fact that its left buddy has size 8K, the starting address of the left buddy can be obtained.

The problem of determining the size and starting location of a returning block's buddy is less complicated if the returning buddy has a right buddy instead of a left buddy. The distinction between finding the size and starting location of right and left buddies in the binary and Fibonacci systems can be seen in Figures 13.9 and 13.10. As highlighted in Figure 13.9, in a block with a right buddy, the starting location and size of the returning block would tell us the starting address of the right buddy. Then, provided we have stored the bookkeeping information for that right

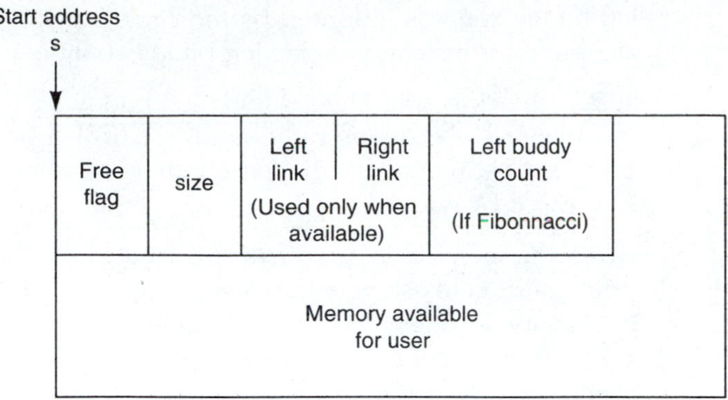

Figure 13.9
Determining size and start address of a right Fibonacci or binary buddy.

buddy precisely at its starting location, the size field and free flag are immediately available for our inspection. Here, the bookkeeping information for the right buddy can be accessed at memory address ($s + size$).

As shown in Figure 13.10, the bookkeeping information for this block's left buddy can be accessed at one of the following memory addresses:

- ($s - size$) for binary buddy system
- (s − Fibonacci number preceding *size*) for Fibonacci buddy system

Figures 13.9 and 13.10 should make it apparent that if we are willing to store duplicate copies of a block's size and free flag at its right boundary as well as its left boundary, then the problem of determining the starting address of a left buddy does not require prior knowledge of what its size must be. Its size can be found by checking the bookkeeping information along the right boundary. The effect of this concept is that sizes can be chosen arbitrarily to meet a user's specific request. No longer is it necessary to allocate 13K to meet an 11K request because the available choices of block sizes demand it. This is the primary motivation behind the boundary tag buddy system. A block and the bookkeeping information within it appear as shown in Figure 13.11.

The boundary tag technique has advantages and disadvantages that you must carefully consider before choosing it to use in a particular context. The major

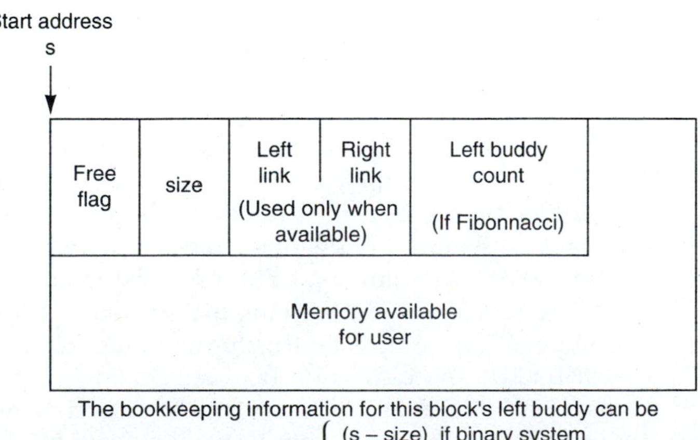

Figure 13.10
Determining size and start address of a left Fibonacci or binary buddy.

Figure 13.11
Block and bookkeeping information for boundary tag method.

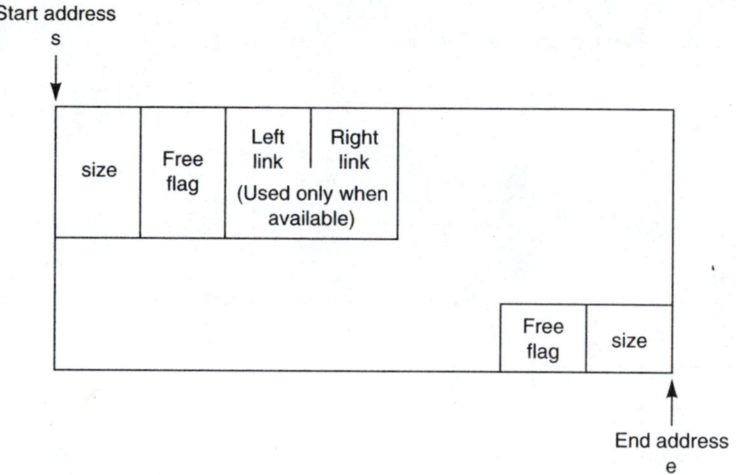

advantage is that it allows a user's request to be granted precisely, with no excess memory being allocated and therefore wasted. The logic of the method also implies that a given block is not a left or right buddy per se. Rather, any block except one starting or ending at a memory boundary has both a left and a right buddy with which it could coalesce. The primary disadvantages of the boundary tag method are the additional bookkeeping information that must be stored and maintained within each block and the fact that the available space structure now must be stored as one long doubly linked list instead of as a sequence of doubly linked lists for each of the respective block sizes allowed. This second disadvantage means that, in determining whether a user's request can be met, the boundary tag method requires a sequential search of a single available space list, clearly a slower process than that required for either the binary or Fibonacci schemes.

Trace the actions diagrammed in Figure 13.12, highlighting the allocation and deallocation of memory as the following requests are processed:

a. Initially all memory, 64K, is free
b. User requests 7K
c. User requests 9K
d. User requests 4k
e. Memory requested in request **c** is no longer needed
f. Memory requested in request **b** is no longer needed
g. Memory requested in request **d** is no longer needed.

The three memory management methods discussed in this section provide an excellent illustration of the application of data structures at the operating system level. Notice in particular that all three methods require the use of one or more doubly linked lists to store available memory blocks. The elegance of this relatively simple data structure allows us to delete a given block from the middle of an available list without having to traverse the entire list to find a back pointer as we would be forced to do with a singly linked list. In the next section, we examine memory management from the perspective of the developer of a programming language. In particular, we consider the implementation of a completely general pointer system for such a language. Although the techniques we have described in Sections 13.1 and 13.2 are applicable in this context, one further complication is also introduced—the referencing of a single memory area by multiple pointers.

Figure 13.12
Processing requests using boundary tag buddy system.

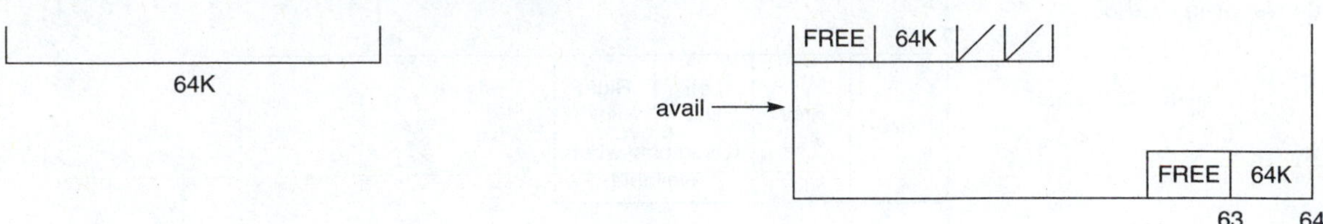

Initial state of memory—64K free

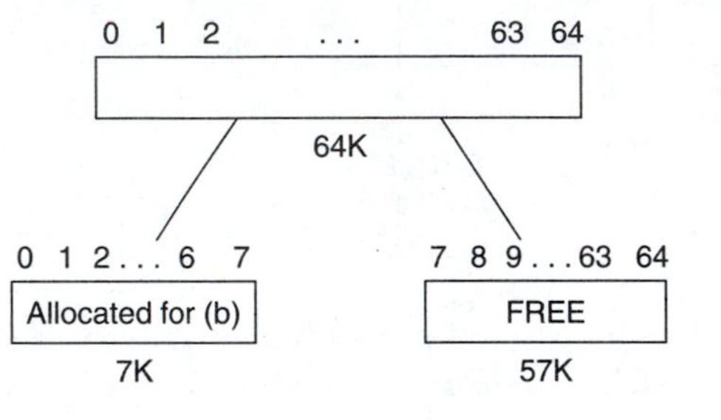

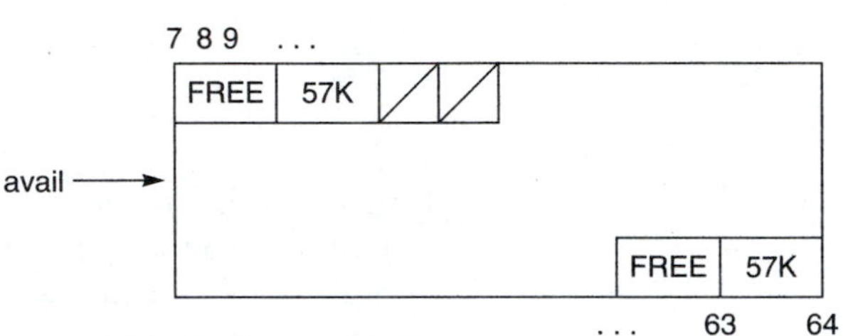

Request (b) for 7K processed

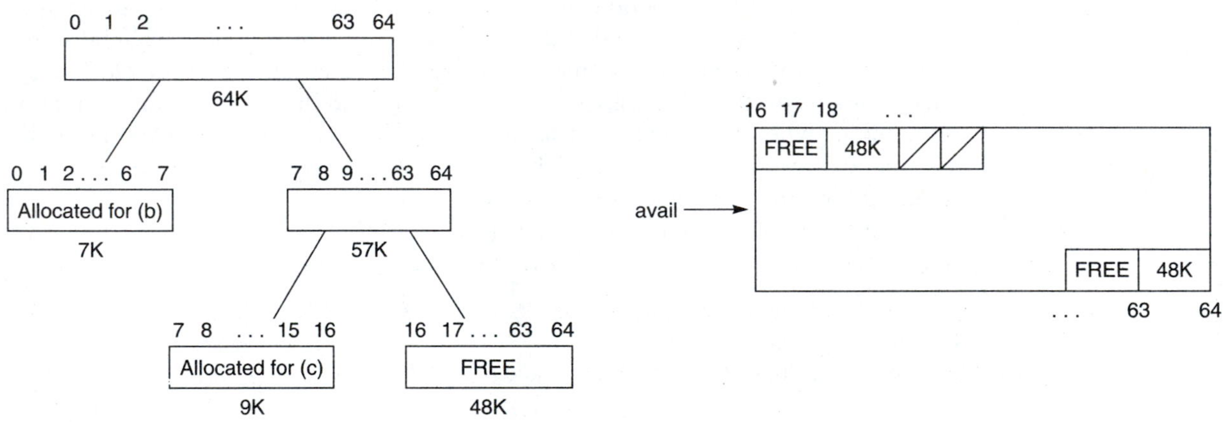

Request (c) for 9K processed

(figure continues on next page)

Exercises 13.2

1. Suppose you have a 128K memory and receive the following sequence of requests from users for memory allocation or reclamation:

   User A requests 32K
   User B requests 19K
   User C requests 6K
   User D requests 22K
   User B finishes
   User E requests 12K
   User C finishes
   User F requests 13K
   User D finishes
   User E finishes
   User A finishes
   User F finishes.

   Use the binary buddy system to trace the status of available and allocated memory blocks as these requests are

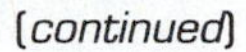
Figure 13.12
(*continued*)

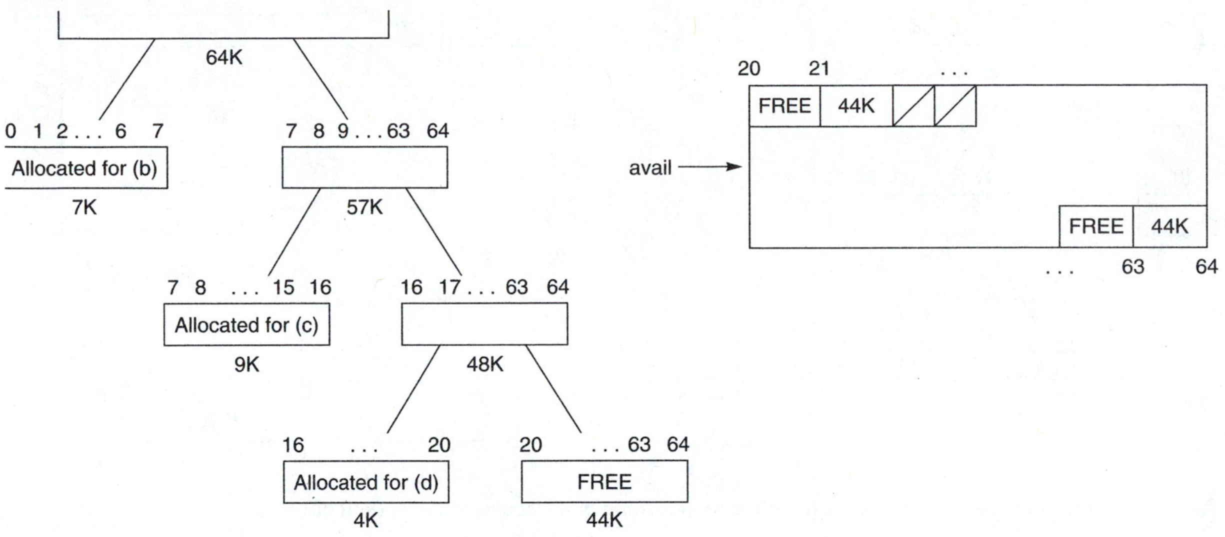

Request (d) for 4K processed

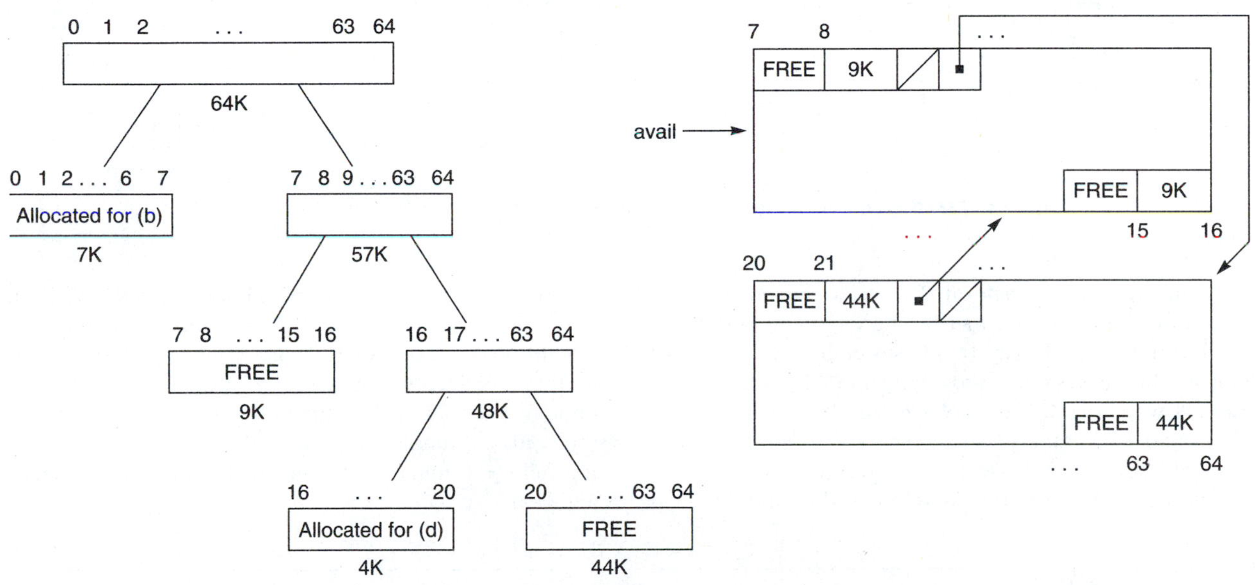

(e) Processed—memory for (c) released, no coalescing occurs

(figure continues on next page)

processed. Of the memory allocated by the system, what percentage is not actually needed by the user?

2. Repeat Exercise 13.2.1 for the standard Fibonacci buddy system. Treat the difference between 128 and the Fibonacci number preceding 128 as the size of a block that cannot be further subdivided.
3. Repeat Exercise 13.2.1 for a Fibonacci buddy system using the general Fibonacci sequence with $k = 3$. Treat the difference between 128 and the Fibonacci number preceding 128 as the size of a block that cannot be further subdivided.
4. Repeat Exercise 13.2.1 for the boundary tag buddy system. Assume a best-fit algorithm is used to search the list of available blocks. Do this again under the assumption that a first-fit algorithm is used to search the list of available blocks.
5. The Fibonacci buddy system allows a finer degree of block sizes than the binary buddy system. You have

Figure 13.12
(continued)

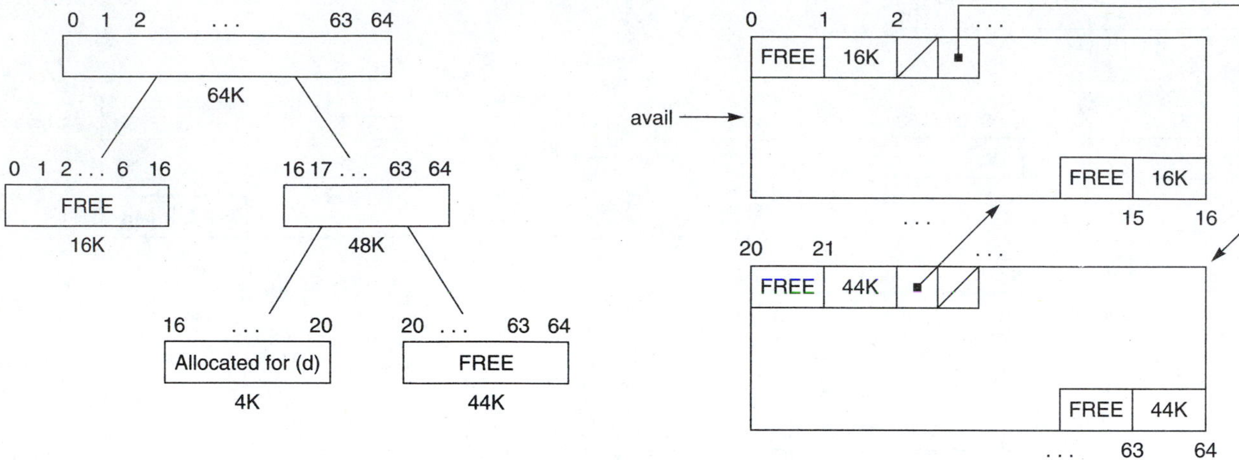

(f) Processed—memory for (b) released, returning block coalesces with right buddy

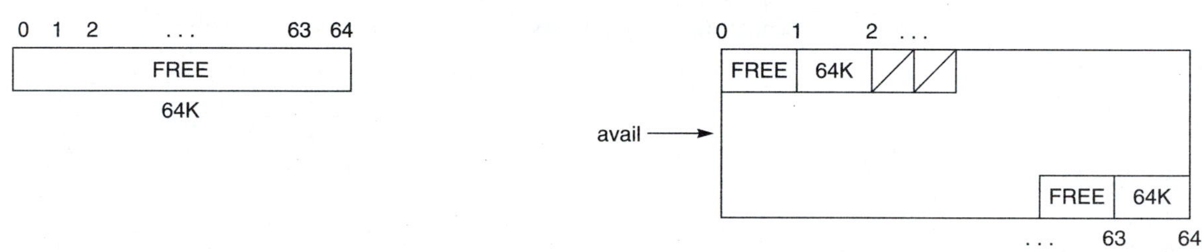

(g) Processed—memory for (d) released, coalescing occurs on both sides

512K memory at your disposal. Devise a sequence of user requests that could be met by the Fibonacci buddy system but not by the binary buddy system.

6. A Fibonacci buddy system based on the third Fibonacci sequence allows a finer degree of block sizes than one based on the standard Fibonacci sequence. You have 1000K memory at your disposal. Devise a sequence of requests that could be met by a buddy system based on the third Fibonacci sequence but not by a buddy system based on the standard (that is, the second) Fibonacci sequence.
7. The **allocate** and **reclaim** algorithms described in this section are given in skeletal C++ code, which is general enough to apply to all of the buddy systems discussed in the section. Complete this skeletal C++ code by providing full C++ implementations for the binary, Fibonacci, and boundary tag systems.

A RELEVANT ISSUE Computer Viruses: Corrupting the Memory Resource

It is becoming increasingly evident that operating system software must not only manage memory efficiently for well-intentioned users, but must also provide security against corruption of the memory resource by malicious users whose intent is to spread viruses. According to John McAfee and Colin Haynes (*Computer Viruses, Worms, Data Diddlers, Killer Programs, and Other Threats to Your System,* New York: St. Martin's Press, 1989), a virus is a program created to infect other programs with copies of itself. Having achieved this, it may do nothing other than continue spreading itself within the infected system and systems networked to that system. More malicious viruses may destroy valuable data as they spread.

Self-replicating programs have long intrigued computer scientists. As early as the 1960s, researchers at the Massachusetts Institute of Technology, AT&T's Bell Laboratories, and Xerox Corporation's research center in Palo Alto entertained themselves by engaging in so-called "Core Wars." In these contests, the programmers developed self-replicating programs that infected and devoured the programs of opponents. The winner was the player whose program rendered all other players' programs to a state of total inoperability.

From such harmless beginnings, self-replicating programs have grown to a very serious hazard, particularly to networked computing. Perhaps the most famous incident involving such a virus was the Internet virus created by Cornell graduate student Robert Morris, Jr., in November 1988. This virus took advantage of a loophole in operating system soft ware to spread itself to a variety of computers on the Internet. Having infected a computer, the Internet virus replicated itself on the host system until so many resources were consumed by the virus that other users were totally ignored by the system. Although not malicious in the sense of destroying data, Morris's virus did force numerous computer centers to shut down and to reboot an estimated 42,000 machines. The resulting loss in human and machine time is estimated by McAfee and Cohen to have a monetary value of more than $98 million!

13.3 Heap Management for Programming Languages

Thus far we have examined memory allocation from the perspective of an operating system designer who must meet the requests of users for memory blocks of various sizes. Let us now work from the perspective of a programming language implementor who must manage the memory nodes associated with pointers in the language. Such memory management is often termed *dynamic memory management* or *heap management*. The former term derives from the fact that this management of the memory resource takes place as your program runs, not at compilation time. To understand the origin of the latter term, we must examine the configuration of memory when your program is loaded into it from an external file. As indicated in Figure 13.13, there are memory costs that must be paid in addition to the storage space required for the object code of your program. In particular, memory must have room to accommodate the following:

- Various operating system requirements
- A stack used by the operating system for subroutine processing (as explained in Chapter 6)
- The object code of your program, that is, the machine-language version of your program's instructions
- Static data areas, that is, the globally declared arrays and other variables used by your program.

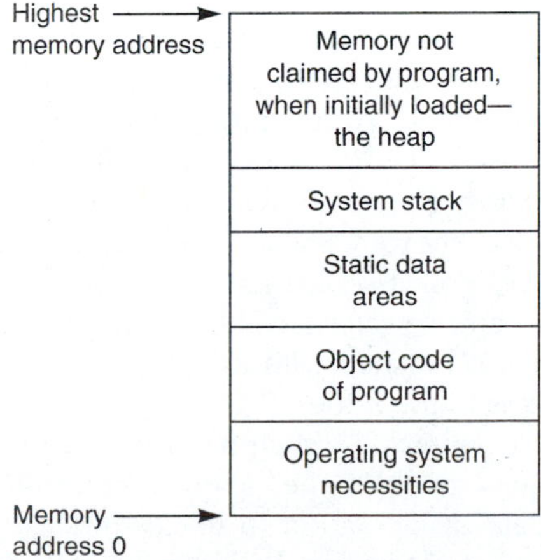

Figure 13.13
Computer memory configuration for typical program.

Notice that the four memory components listed will generally not consume all of the available computer memory. What is left over is called the *heap*. (Do not confuse this use of the term *heap* with the Heap ADT discussed in Chapter 7.) It is in the heap area that memory associated with pointer-based variables is allocated.

What are the similarities and differences between the heap management required of a programming language implementor and the memory management issues that we have already discussed from an operating system perspective? Like an operating system, a heap management system must often allocate nodes of different sizes. The reason is that different pointer variables within the same program in languages such as C++ and Pascal may be associated with structures having dissimilar size requirements. That is, the pointer variable **p** could reference a structure requiring 18 bytes, whereas another pointer variable **q** could point at a structure consuming 1800 bytes. Hence, the techniques already discussed for managing nodes of various sizes apply to general heap management just as they do in an operating system environment.

What sets heap management apart are the complexities arising from the possibility of a node in the heap being referenced by more than one pointer. Consider, for instance, the following C++ code:

```
int *p, *q;
   .
   .
   .
p = new int;
*p = 14;
q = p;
cout << *q;
```

Certainly, there is nothing wrong with this code, and it is evident that the **cout** instruction will produce 14 as its output. However, suppose that we now append the following two instructions to the preceding code:

```
delete p;
cout << *q;
```

What should the second **cout** instruction produce? Is the call to **delete** even valid? That is, should we be allowed to return a node to available space when it is still referenced by another pointer? Though C++ will allow such (unwise) usage of **delete,** other languages (for example, some versions of Pascal) will flag the call to **delete** as a run-time error.

These questions revolve around the issue of how much explicit responsibility is placed on the programmer to control the return of nodes to available space. Granting the programmer completely explicit control would dictate that the call to **delete p** in the above coding should actually return the node to available space despite its also being referenced by the pointer **q**, an approach that assumes that the programmer always knows what she is doing no matter how unorthodox it may be. A lesser degree of explicit programmer control would be to use the call to **delete p** to indicate that the node referenced by **p** can be returned to available space when the pointer **q** is also finished with it, that is, when all pointers in addition to **p** no longer need access to the node.

There are even languages, such as Lisp and SNOBOL, that make the return of nodes to available space in the heap completely implicit—they do not provide a programmer-callable operation to release nodes. To illustrate how such implicit garbage collection might be invoked, consider the following code:

```
int *p, *r;
   .
   .
   .
p = new int;
r = new int;
p = r;
```

In a language that requires the programmer to explicitly return nodes to the heap, the assignment statement **p** = **r** will render the portion of the heap originally referenced by **p** inaccessible for future use, even though it is no longer used by the program. The implementation of a language in which garbage is collected implicitly would detect the inaccessibility of this node and return it to an available heap without an explicit request to do so by the programmer.

We will discuss two methods for garbage collection, *reference counting* and *marking*. Both methods take into account the complexities associated with multiple pointers referencing a node in the heap. The first of these strategies is simpler and more efficient but has loopholes that make it inappropriate in some contexts. We should emphasize that both strategies augment the space management algorithms already discussed in the first two sections of this chapter and that neither strategy is needed in a language where control over returning nodes to the heap is under the total, explicit control of the programmer. In the latter case, we simply obey the programmer's dictate. The operator **delete** means precisely that—regardless of how many other pointers may be referencing the node.

Reference Counting

This strategy merely retains in each node a reference count **(refCount)** member that is used by the heap management system to keep track of the number of pointers that reference a given node. This concept is highlighted in Figure 13.14. As indicated in this figure, an invocation of **delete p** cannot restore a node to available space if **refCount** is more than 1; that is, if pointers other than **p** currently reference the node. Instead, **p.refCount** is merely reduced to 1. The assignment statement **q** = **r** in Figure 13.14 must reduce by 1 the **refCount** member in the node originally referenced by **q** and increase by 1 the **refCount** member in the node referenced by **r**. Since **refCount** in the node originally referenced by both **p** and **q** is now zero, it is this assignment statement that actually restores the node to available space, not the earlier invocation of **delete p.** Table 13.1 summarizes the effect of **new** and **delete** when the reference counting technique is used.

Although relatively simple to implement, the reference counting strategy just described has the serious drawback that it will not correctly return to available space any nodes that are linked in a circular structure. Convince yourself that the circular list consisting of one node in Figure 13.15 can *never* be returned to available space when reference counting is used. This implies that, ideally, reference counting should be employed only for applications in which you know beforehand that circular structures will not be created in the heap.

Marking

Marking has arisen as a more comprehensive garbage collection strategy than reference counting. It avoids the flaws of reference counting and circular lists. The marking technique dictates that we do no actual garbage collection until we apparently run out of heap. When this occurs, the following three steps are invoked:

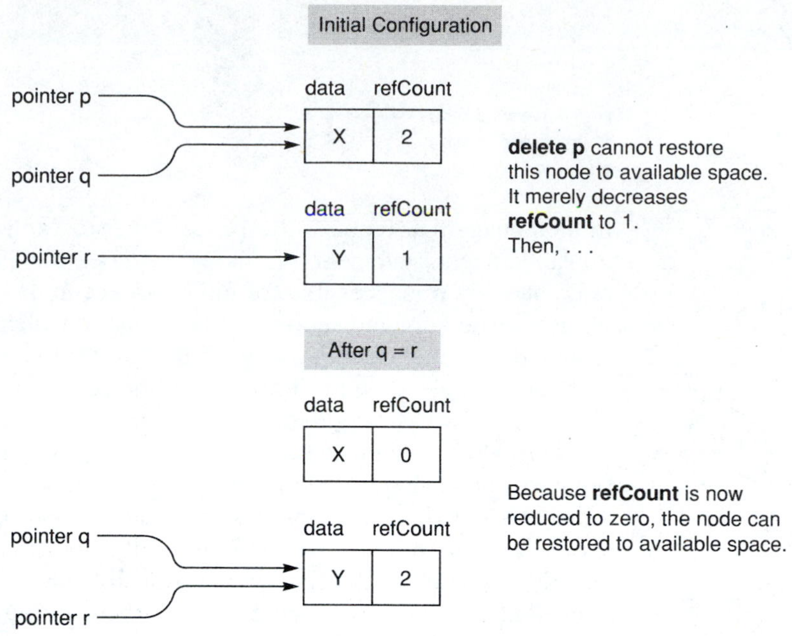

Figure 13.14
Using a hidden reference counter to determine when a node can safely be returned to available space. From the initial configuration, **delete p** followed by a **q** = **r** assignment reduces **refCount** to zero.

1. All heap nodes are initially marked as available.
2. Then each heap node reachable through an active pointer is marked as in use.
3. Those nodes that remain marked as available after step 2 are then linked into an appropriate, available space structure.

Because all nodes in the heap will be visited at least once during this marking phase, this technique is clearly *O(NumberOfNodes)* in its time efficiency. However, unlike the compaction strategy cited in Section 13.1, this strategy necessitates no movement of data and hence will require substantially less time than compaction.

It is the second step of the marking phase that requires more discussion. The symbol tables maintained by the programming language will provide us with a record of each active pointer variable. Given such an active pointer variable **p**, we view the heap node referenced by **p** as a graph node. The non-NULL pointers

TABLE 13.1
Effect of pointer operations on available space pool when reference counting is used.

Operation	Effect on refCount and available space
p = new data	Reduce by 1 **refCount** in the node previously referenced by **p.** If this **refCount** is now zero, return the node to available space. Finally, establish **p**'s new pointer value, and set its **refCount** to 1.
delete p	Reduce **p→refCount** by 1. If **refCount** is now zero, it may actually be returned to available space.
Pointer assignment *q = r*	Reduce by 1 **refCount** in the node previously referenced by **q.** If this **refCount** is now zero, return it to available space. Finally, increase by 1 **refCount** in the node referenced by **r.**

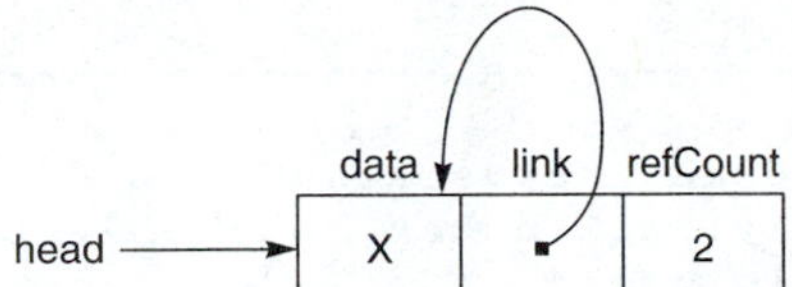

Figure 13.15
A data structure for which the reference count technique will render a node inaccessible for future use.

embedded in this graph node lead us to other graph nodes (that is, heap nodes) adjacent to the node referenced by **p**. For instance, in Figure 13.16, if the programmer had developed a binary tree referenced by the pointer variable **p**, then the nodes B and F would be adjacent to A, nodes C and D would be adjacent to B, and node E would be adjacent to D under this graph interpretation of nodes in the heap. To mark the nodes reachable through **p** as being in use, we could generate a depth-first traversal of the graph starting at the node referenced by **p**. As a node is visited in this traversal we mark it as *in use*. We would have to call this depth-first traversal for each active pointer to complete step 2 of the mark-and-collection process.

To implement this depth-first traversal, we must first make some assumptions about the structure of the heap nodes being visited. Clearly a heap node will contain some user data and, quite possibly, some pointers to other heap nodes that are maintained by the programmer. From the perspective of the programming language implementor, we are not interested at all in the user's data. The pointers in the heap node can be viewed as an array of pointers. Additionally, we will need to add a Boolean **inUse** member to indicate whether or not a heap node is currently reachable through an active pointer. These considerations give rise to the following heap node structure:

```
struct HeapNode
{
  UnitType data;
  HeapNode *ptrs[numberPtrs];
  BOOLEAN inUse;
}
```

The following C++ algorithm, which is called for each active pointer variable, will then accomplish step 2 of the marking phase via a depth-first traversal of all heap nodes reachable through the current pointer.

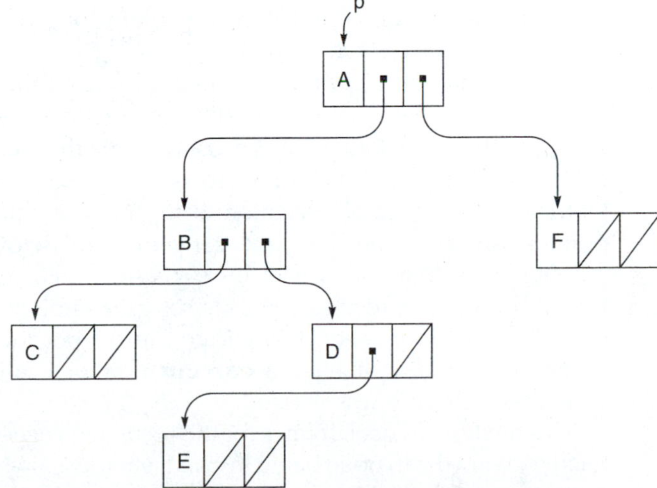

Figure 13.16
Nodes reachable through the pointer **p** may be obtained by a depth-first traversal starting at A; that is, A, B, C, D, E, F.

```
//---------------------------------------------------------------
// Interface for markInUse function
// GIVEN:      current -- a pointer to an active heap node.
// RETURN:     current and (recursively) all nodes reachable through
//             it will be marked as "in use."
// RETURN as value of function: void

void markInUse(HeapNode *current);
{
  if ((current != NULL) && (!current->inUse))
  {
    current->inUse = TRUE;
    for (int k = 0; k < numberPtrs; ++k)
      markInUse((current->ptrs)[k]);
  }
}
```

The marking technique for garbage collection, implemented by this version of the **markInUse** function, eliminates the circular structure loophole inherent in reference counting. However, this particular implementation of **markInUse** has a potential subtle flaw of its own. In practice, **markInUse** is only called when we are running short on space. However, the recursive implementation of this algorithm may require a relatively large amount of stack space—you will analyze how much stack space for the worst possible scenario in the exercises. Hence, the algorithm we must execute to recover space might not be able to execute because of insufficient space to accommodate its run-time stack!

We need a nonrecursive version of the **markInUse** function that does not require a run-time stack. Fortunately, a nonrecursive version was discovered simultaneously by Deutsch and Bobrow (L. P. Deutsch and D. G. Bobrow, "An Efficient Incremental Automatic Garbage Collector," *Communications of the ACM,* 9:9, 1966, pp. 522–526) and by Schorr and Waite (H. Schorr and W. M. Waite, "An Efficient, Machine-Independent Procedure for Garbage Collection in Various List Structures," *Communications of the ACM,* 10:8, 1967, pp. 501–506). This nonrecursive version of the algorithm is reminiscent of the threading method we used in Section 7.5 to avoid the use of recursion in tree traversals. Essentially, we use the pointers within the heap nodes to embed the information that would be stored in the recursive stack. This embedding must be a temporary situation because it actually changes the contents of the heap nodes that are in use. The original contents of these nodes must be restored on completion of marking or we will corrupt the data structures that the user has created in the heap.

Figure 13.17
Status of system stack when node containing E in Figure 13.16 is being marked as **current** node by recursive implementation. At each level, there may be additional pointers to process in the **current** node.

current references node containing E with two NULL pointers to process
current references node containing D with second pointer next to process
current references node containing B with no more pointers to process
current references node containing A with second pointer next to process

To illustrate the algorithm, we begin by carefully analyzing the contents of the run-time stack that would be used by the recursive version of the algorithm. Figure 13.17 illustrates a portion of the contents of this stack that would exist when the node containing E in Figure 13.16 is being marked as in use. Figure 13.17 tells us that, at this stage of execution of the recursive algorithm, the topmost **current** pointer is referencing the node containing E. Below this topmost stack frame is another stack frame in which the **current** pointer references the node containing D and the loop of recursive calls is set to resume at the second pointer within the node. Similar information is replicated in deeper level stack frames with the stack frame at the bottom having a **current** pointer leading to the heap node through which the structure was entered.

This analysis of stack frames for the recursive version of the algorithm implies that, relative to any heap node being marked, we must always have two information items: a pointer to the node that preceded this node and an indication of which pointer within the node is being followed as we descend deeper into the structure. The latter

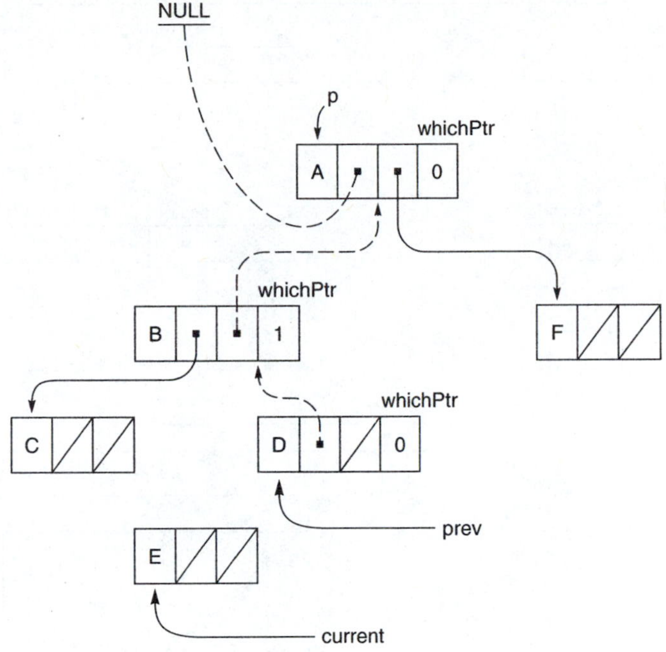

Figure 13.18
Status of internal pointers when node containing E is being marked as **current** node by nonrecursive implementation.

item we can store in an integer member **whichPtr,** which now must be included in each heap node. The former item we will store temporarily in the pointer we have followed to descend deeper into the structure. Some fairly tricky coding involving a temporary variable can then be used to restore this pointer to its original contents. Figure 13.18 indicates how the stack contents of Figure 13.17 can be embedded in the pointers of the structure being marked. In this figure, the dashed pointers indicate the return path to ascend in the structure being marked; the **whichPtr** value indicates the array index of the pointer that has been altered temporarily to store this path of ascent. The details of the nonrecursive marking algorithm are provided in the following C++ code:

```
struct HeapNode
{
  UnitType data;
  HeapNode *ptrs[numberPtrs];
  BOOLEAN inUse;
  int whichPtr;   // Additional member needed for nonrecursive version
}

//----------------------------------------------------------------------
// Interface for markInUse function (nonrecursive version)
// GIVEN:     current -- a reference to an active heap node.
// RETURN:    current and all nodes reachable through
//            it will be marked as "in use."
// RETURN as value of function: void

void markInUse(HeapNode *current)
{
  HeapNode *prev, *temp;
  BOOLEAN descend;

  prev = NULL;
  descend = TRUE;   // To indicate we are descending from current node

  do
  {
```

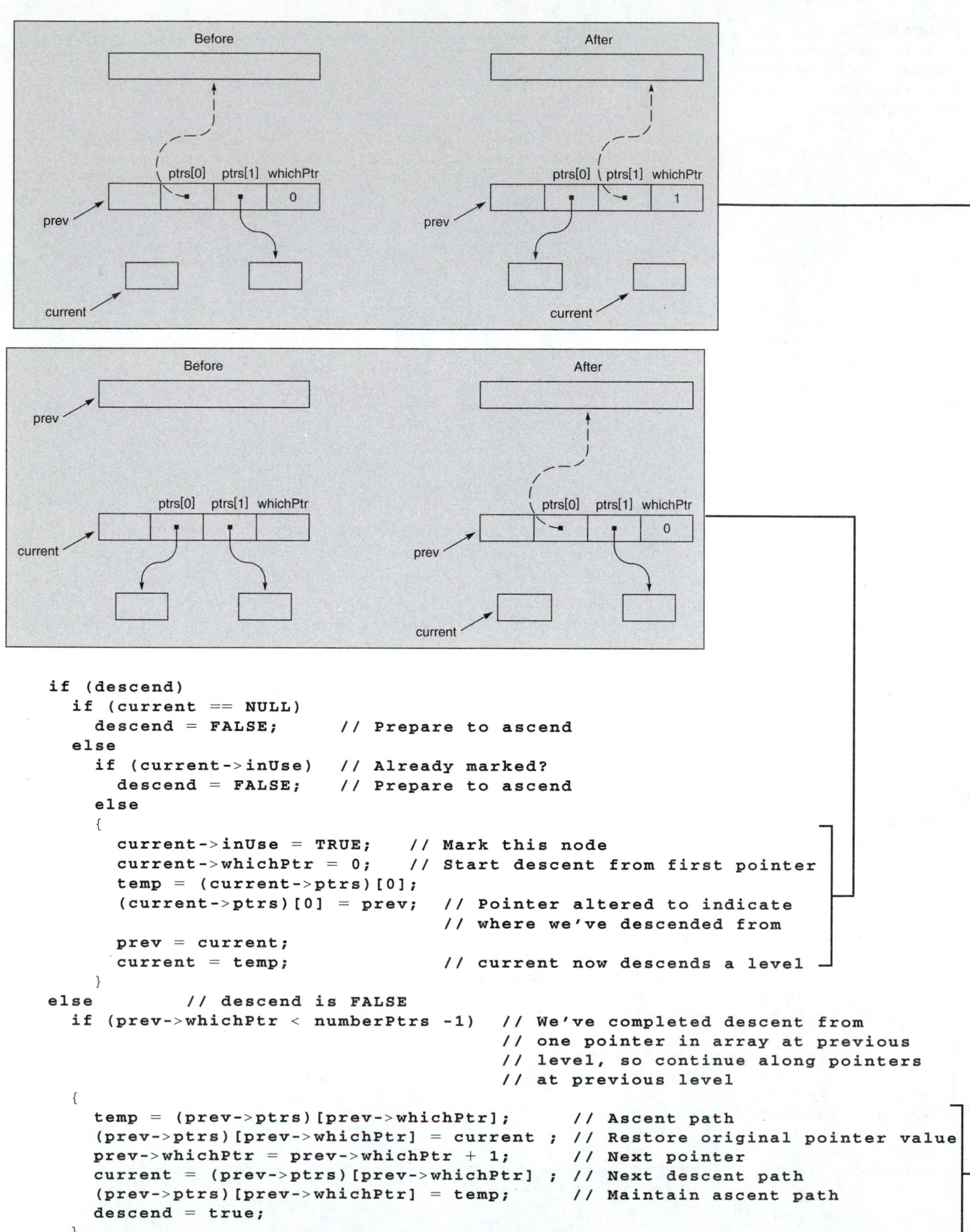


```
if (descend)
  if (current == NULL)
    descend = FALSE;       // Prepare to ascend
  else
    if (current->inUse)    // Already marked?
      descend = FALSE;     // Prepare to ascend
    else
    {
      current->inUse = TRUE;     // Mark this node
      current->whichPtr = 0;     // Start descent from first pointer
      temp = (current->ptrs)[0];
      (current->ptrs)[0] = prev;   // Pointer altered to indicate
                                   // where we've descended from
      prev = current;
      current = temp;              // current now descends a level
    }
else          // descend is FALSE
  if (prev->whichPtr < numberPtrs -1)   // We've completed descent from
                                        // one pointer in array at previous
                                        // level, so continue along pointers
                                        // at previous level
  {
    temp = (prev->ptrs)[prev->whichPtr];       // Ascent path
    (prev->ptrs)[prev->whichPtr] = current ;   // Restore original pointer value
    prev->whichPtr = prev->whichPtr + 1;       // Next pointer
    current = (prev->ptrs)[prev->whichPtr] ;   // Next descent path
    (prev->ptrs)[prev->whichPtr] = temp;       // Maintain ascent path
    descend = true;
  }
```

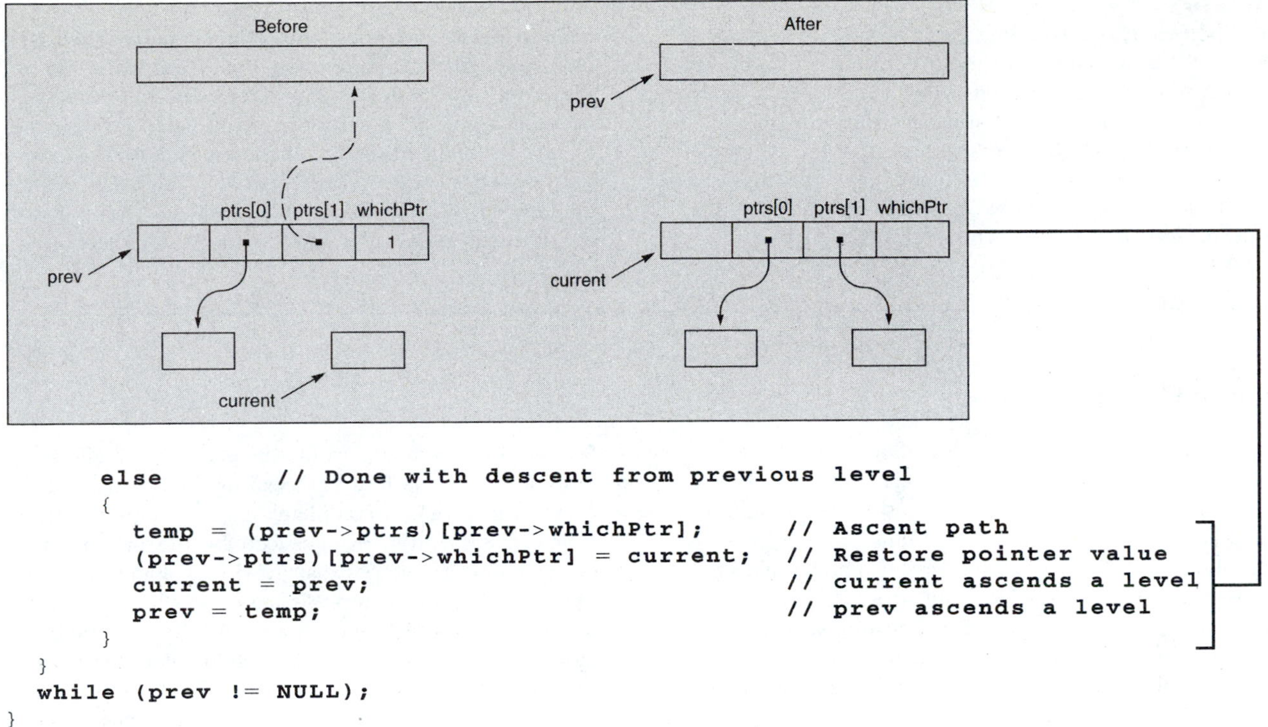


```
        else          // Done with descent from previous level
        {
            temp = (prev->ptrs)[prev->whichPtr];      // Ascent path
            (prev->ptrs)[prev->whichPtr] = current;   // Restore pointer value
            current = prev;                           // current ascends a level
            prev = temp;                              // prev ascends a level
        }
    }
    while (prev != NULL);
}
```

Exercises 13.3

1. In a brief essay, explain why the one-node circular list in Figure 13.15 can never be returned to available space when reference counting is used for garbage collection.
2. Consider the structure referenced by the pointer variable **p** in the following figure. By a series of pictures that show the settings for **current, prev,** and pointers internal to the structure, trace how these pointers change as each node reachable through **p** is marked by the nonrecursive implementation of **markInUse.**

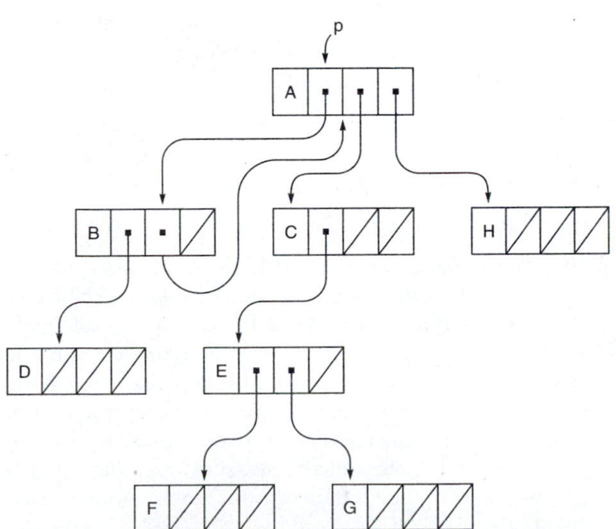

3. What is the maximal size to which the run-time stack could grow in the recursive version of function **markInUse**? What kind of structure in the heap generates this maximal-size stack? Does this maximal size provide a rational for using a nonrecursive version of the algorithm? Explain why or why not.
4. Consider the following algorithm.

```
int *p, *q;
.
.
.
p = new int;
q = p;
*q = 14;
cout << *q << endl;
delete p;
cout << *q << endl;
p = new int;
*p = 16;
cout << *p << endl;
delete p;
cout << *q << endl;
```

What do you predict the output will be from this algorithm? Explain why in a short essay. Then implement the algorithm in your version of C++ and execute it. Do any discrepancies arise from what you predicted? If so, try to explain them.

5. In a short essay, explain why the nonrecursive version of the **markInUse** algorithm should *not* be used on nodes in a heap that stores data structures shared concurrently by several users in a time-sharing environment.
6. Another strategy for heap management is known as the *mark-and-release* method. This technique views the heap as a stack in which the **new** operation always allocates a node on top of the stack. The **reclaim** operation is replaced by two operations—**mark** and **release.** The **mark** operation marks the current top of the heap/stack. The **release** operation restores to available space all heap/stack nodes down to the topmost mark. Develop C++ implementations of the **allocate, mark,** and **release** operations for this method of heap management. In an essay, discuss the benefits and drawbacks of this method compared to the other techniques you have studied in this section.

Chapter Summary

This chapter examined methods for allocating memory to applications needing it and for later reclaiming the memory when no longer needed. Section 13.1 used the example of memory allocation among users in a time-sharing environment to illustrate how memory resources could be managed when users request blocks of varying sizes. The best-fit and first-fit strategies were described for allocating such variably sized blocks of memory, and compaction and coalescing were discussed as alternative methods for effectively recovering memory that is no longer needed.

In Section 13.2, we used the example of a multiuser, time-sharing environment again to illustrate three variations of memory management strategies identified by the term *buddy systems:* the binary, Fibonacci, and boundary tag systems. All of these methods are designed to allow fast garbage collection with a minimum of wasted space.

Section 13.3 switched from the example of allocating memory among users in a time-sharing environment to the problem of providing a completely general implementation of pointers. This problem, as faced by the implementors of programming languages that provide a pointer type, requires extending the memory management techniques discussed in Sections 13.1 and 13.2 to handle one additional complication—the potential of multiple pointer references to a particular data node. The techniques that encompass this complication are specific to an area of memory management often referred to as *heap management.* Two methods for garbage collection, reference counting and marking, were discussed. Both methods take into account the complexities associated with multiple pointers possibly referencing a node in the heap.

Keywords

best-fit searching
binary buddy system
boundary tag buddy system
coalescing
compaction
dynamic memory management
Fibonacci buddy system
first-fit searching
fragmentation
garbage collection
heap
heap management
marking
reference counting

Programming Problems/Projects

1. Try to determine as much as you can about the heap management techniques used by an implementor of your favorite programming language. Do this by writing a series of short programs, similar to the algorithm of Exercise 13.3.4, designed specifically to exercise the heap management implementation. Write up the results of your experimentation in a report in which you state your conclusions about how heap management is conducted by your programming language. Justify each of your conclusions by citing the results from running one or more of your test programs.
2. In Section 13.2, we described three memory management schemes that might be used by an operating system: binary buddy, Fibonacci buddy, and boundary tag buddies. Write a program in which random numbers are used to simulate users requesting and then returning memory. Interface this program with each of the three memory management schemes presented in Section 13.2 and accumulate statistics regarding various measures of space efficiency for each of these three methods.

3. Write a program in which random numbers are used to simulate users requesting and then returning memory. Interface your program with an implementation of a memory management system in which a best-fit algorithm is used. Repeat this process, but use a first-fit algorithm. Accumulate statistics on the effectiveness of each algorithm and write up your conclusions, backed by empirical evidence from your runs, in a formal report.

4. Provide a complete implementation for dynamic memory management that uses the reference counting strategy for heap management. Then test your implementation with a variety of pointer-based programs (which you developed earlier for this course and, possibly, for other courses and applications).

5. Repeat Problem 4, but use a marking strategy to implement the dynamic memory management.

APPENDIX A

Random Numbers: Generation and Use in Events Based on Probabilities

The discussion of computer simulation in Chapter 4 cited the use of random numbers in determining the occurrence of a particular event. There are really two issues involved here:

- How to generate a sequence of random numbers
- How to use that sequence to simulate the occurrence (or nonoccurrence) of a particular event

For the discussion that follows, a sequence of random numbers is a sequence of real numbers $x_1, x_2, x_3, \ldots$ such that:

1. For each x_i, $0 \leq x_i < 1$.
2. The x_i are not biased toward any particular subinterval of the reals between 0 and 1. That is, members of the sequence should be evenly distributed between 0 and 1.
3. It should not be possible to predict the value of x_i from prior members of the sequence. That is, members of the sequence occur in an unpredictable fashion.

Random numbers generated by computer are often called pseudo-random. The origin of this latter term is due to the fact that sequences of such computer-generated numbers appear to be random even though there is a fixed mathematical formula underlying their generation. If you know the formula, you can in principle compute the sequence—hence, it is not truly unpredictable. However, if you merely observe the sequence without knowledge of the formula, the sequence appears to satisfy the three properties of randomness cited above.

Generating a Sequence of Random Numbers

C and C++ offer a built-in random number generator called **rand.** The formula on which it is based requires a *seed* number to begin its computation. The **rand** function uses this seed to determine a random integer between 0 and a built-in constant called RAND_MAX. The seed is altered as part of this evaluation, so that the next time rand is called a new random value will be produced. Note, however, that the initial value of the seed will completely determine the random sequence that is produced by **rand.** Hence C must also offer some way of "randomizing" the initial value of the seed; otherwise the same random sequence will always be produced. Randomizing the seed is done by calling the **srand** function. **srand** takes an unsigned **int** argument and uses it to initially set the seed value. One way of making sure that this initial seed is chosen arbitrarily is to use C's **time** function, as illustrated in the following example.

```
// Example using rand, RAND_MAX, srand, and
// time to produce 10 random floats in the
// range 0.0 <= x < 1.0

#include <stdlib.h>     // Needed for rand,
                        // srand, and RAND_MAX
#include <iostream.h>
#include <time.h>       // Needed for the time
                        // function
void main()
{
  int i;
  time_t t;  // time_t is an integer type for
             // argument to the time function

  // The time is supplied as seed by srand
  srand((unsigned) time(&t));
  cout << "Ten randoms between 0 and 1"
       << endl << endl;
  for (i=0; i<10; i++)
    // By dividing rand's value by RAND_MAX,
    // we insure a value between 0 and 1
    cout << (float) rand() / (float) RAND_MAX
         << endl;
}
```

Given that we now have a technique for generating sequences of random values between 0 and 1, the discussion in the next section will focus on how to use such values in the simulation of various events.

Using Random Numbers to Simulate Events According to Probabilities

Here we describe three situations in which the generation of a random number may be used to simulate the occurrence of an event in a simulation. Our description here is intended only to be brief and prescriptive in nature. An explanation of the theory underlying these and other applications of random number generation in simulation is given in *Modern Statistical Systems and GPSS Simulation* by Zaven Karian and Edward Dudewicz (New York, NY: Computer Science Press, 1991).

Situation 1 An event occurs with a certain probability p. For example, in a given time unit of a simulation, there is a probability of 0.40 that a car will arrive in a queue waiting at a toll booth.

In this situation, generate a random number X. If X is less than p, declare that the event in question occurred; otherwise, declare that it did not occur. In the previous example, if X is less than 0.40, we process the event of a car's arrival; otherwise our simulation proceeds as if no car arrived.

Situation 2 The occurrence of an event is associated with a value, and that value is distributed uniformly over some interval $[a, b)$. Here the term *uniformly* means that the value associated with the event shows no bias to any portion of the interval $[a, b)$.

For instance, you must generate the time of day at which an event occurs, based on a 24-hour clock. The event is no more likely to occur at one time than another. Thus, you wish to generate a value in the interval [0, 24).

In this situation, generate a random number $X, 0 \leq X < 1$. Then convert X to the desired value by the formula

$$a + (b - a)X$$

In our 24-hour clock example, if you generate a random value $X = 0.8125$, the formula above would convert it to 19.5, indicating a 7:30 PM time of occurrence.

A restricted case of this second situation occurs when the values to be generated are integers that are uniformly distributed over the range of integers given by Lo, Lo + 1, Lo + 2, . . . , Hi − 1, Hi. For instance, you are rolling a die and hence must generate an integer value uniformly distributed over the range 1, 2, 3, 4, 5, 6, that is, Lo = 1 and Hi = 6. In this situation, create the integer you want by generating a real number in the interval [Lo, Hi + 1) and then truncating this real to produce an integer. For instance, a random value $X = 0.24$ would yield a die's value of 2, according to the following evaluation:

$$1 + (7 - 1)(0.24)$$

Evaluates to

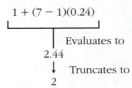

2.44

↓ Truncates to

2

Situation 3 The occurrence of an event is associated with a value, and the value is *normally* distributed, with mean μ and standard deviation σ. We assume here a familiarity with the notion of a bell-shaped normal distribution and its associated mean and standard deviation. Such a distribution is used to model a variety of events in which values tend to aggregate around a middle value, known as the mean. For instance, test scores may be normally distributed around a mean of 70 with a standard deviation of 10, or temperature readings (in Fahrenheit) may be normally distributed around a mean of 60 with a standard deviation of 15. For a precise definition of the normal distribution, consult any introductory statistics text.

In such a situation, the normally distributed value may be approximated by generating 12 random numbers X_1, X_2, X_3, . . . , X_{12} and then using them in the following formula:

$$\mu + \sigma \left(\left(\sum_{i=1}^{12} X_i \right) - 6 \right)$$

For instance, to generate a normally distributed temperature with mean 60 and standard deviation 15:

1. Generate 12 random values between 0 and 1 and form their sum. Suppose that this sum turns out to be 5.5.
2. Subtract 6 from the sum in step 1, obtaining −0.5.
3. Multiply the value in step 2 by the standard deviation 15, obtaining −7.5.
4. Add the result of step 3 to the mean 60, yielding a generated temperature of 52.5.

A justification of why the formula described above approximates a normally distributed variable is due to a famous theorem of statistics called the Central Limit Theorem. If you are interested in finding out more about this theorem, see Chapter 4 of the Karian and Dudewicz text cited earlier in this Appendix.

APPENDIX B Explicit Solutions of Recurrence Relations

In Chapter 6 we cited explicit solutions to certain recurrence relations that were necessary to analyze the efficiency of the recursive algorithms studied in that chapter. In this Appendix, we give an overview of some general methods for finding explicit solutions to recurrence relations. The explicit solutions to recurrence relations cited in Chapter 6 represent specific cases of these general methods. The theoretical basis for these general methods is not presented here. A presentation of the theory underlying the methods may be found in *Applied Discrete Structures for Computer Science* by Alan Doerr and Kenneth Lavasseur (New York, NY: Macmillan, 1989).

Before discussing these general methods, some definitions are needed. We shall use E to represent a recurrence relation

$$E(N) = f(E(K_1),\ E(K_2), \ldots,\ E(K_n),\ g(N)) \qquad \text{(B.1)}$$

where all $K_i < N$. This equation implies that the evaluation of the recurrence relation E for the nonnegative integer N is defined in terms of the function f of $m+1$ arguments. Substituted for the first m of these arguments are the results of prior evaluations of E, that is, evaluations of E for nonnegative integers smaller than N. Substituted for the last argument of f is the result of evaluating some explicit function g at N. Initially, this formula for $E(N)$ appears complicated, because it is stated in full generality. An example should help clarify matters.

Suppose f is a function of two arguments X and Y, defined by $f(X,\ Y) = X + Y$. Then if $K_1 = N - 1$ and $g(N) = 1$, the recurrence relation expressed by (B.1) is

$$E(N) = E(N-1) + 1$$

This should be recognized as one of the particular recurrence relations we cited in Chapter 6.

Types of recurrence relations for which general methods of finding explicit solutions are known include a variety of situations in which f is a linear function.

Explicit solution to (B.1) when f is a linear function, $K_1 = N - 1, K_2 = N - 2, \ldots, K_m = N - m$, $g(N) = 0$.

In this case, Equation (B.1) takes the form

$$E(N) = c_1E(N-1) + c_2E(N-2) + \cdots + c_mE(N-m) \qquad \text{(B.2)}$$

where $c_1,\ c_2, \ldots,\ c_m$ are constants, Equation (B.2) is called an *mth-order linear homogeneous recurrence relation*. The term *homogeneous* denotes that the function g is identically zero. Doerr and Lavasseur show that the general solution of such a recurrence relation may be obtained by

1. Finding all roots of the equation
$$x^m - c_1x^{m-1} - c_2x^{m-2} - \cdots - c_{m-1}x - c_m = 0 \qquad \text{(B.3)}$$
where the c_i come from (B.2). Equation (B.3) is called the *characteristic equation* of (B.2).
2. If equation (B.3) has m distinct roots $x_1,\ x_2,\ \ldots,\ x_n$, then the explicit solution of (B.2) is of the form
$$E(N) = d_1x_1^N + d_2x_2^N + \cdots + d_mx_m^N$$
where the d_i must be determined.
3. To determine the coefficients d_i, use the m initial conditions for the recurrence relation. These initial conditions specify the values of $E(1),\ E(2), \ldots, E(m)$.

Again, the notation can become imposing, so an example should help to clarify. If we have the recurrence relation

$$E(N) = 2E(N-1) \qquad \text{with initial condition } E(1) = 1$$

then the method tells us to find a solution of the characteristic equation

$$x - 2 = 0$$

Clearly a solution to this is $x = 2$. Hence, all explicit solutions of the recurrence relation

$$E(N) = 2E(N-1)$$

will be of the form

$$E(N) = d_1 2^N$$

Since the given initial condition is $E(1) = 1$, d_1 must be $\frac{1}{2}$. Hence for the initial condition $E(1) = 1$, we have the specific explicit solution

$$E(N) = (\tfrac{1}{2})2^N = 2^{N-1}$$

A complication in obtaining general solutions for linear homogeneous recurrence relations occurs when the corresponding characteristic equation has roots of multiplicity greater than 1. We omit discussion of the general solution for this more complicated case; it is covered in Doerr and

Lavasseur.

Explicit solution to (B.1) when f is a linear function, $K_1 = N - 1, K_2 = N - 2, \ldots, K_n = N - m$, $g(N) \neq 0$.

In such a case, equation (B.1) takes the form

$$E(N) = c_1E(N-1) + c_2E(N-2) + \cdots + c_mE(N-m) + g(N) \tag{B.4}$$

The appearance of the nonzero $g(N)$ function causes this type of recurrence relation to be called an *mth-order linear nonhomogeneous recurrence relation.* The method for solving such a nonhomogeneous recurrence relation is

1. First find the general explicit solution of the corresponding homogeneous recurrence relation—that is, the recurrence relation with $g(N) = 0$.
2. Then, often by taking an educated guess, find one particular solution of (B.4).
3. Obtain the general solution to (B.4) by adding the general solution obtained in step 1 and the particular solution from step 2.
4. Use the initial conditions to find the values of the constants in the general solution of step 3.

For example, to solve the nonhomogeneous recurrence relation

$$E(N) = 2E(N-1) + 1 \qquad \text{initial condition } E(1) = 1$$

we would first obtain the general solution

$$E(N) = d_1 2^N$$

to the corresponding homogeneous equation. Observation also reveals that $E(N) = -1$ is one particular solution to the original nonhomogeneous relation. Hence, the general solution to the nonhomogeneous relation is

$$E(N) = d_1 2^N - 1$$

Since $E(1) = 1$, d_1 must be 1, yielding a solution

$$E(N) = 2^N - 1$$

for the specified initial conditions. You should recognize this explicit solution as the one we used in analyzing the efficiency of the Towers of Hanoi algorithm in Chapter 6.

Explicit solution to (B.1) when f is of the form $f(X, Y) = aX + Y$, $K_1 = N/b$ (integer division) for an integer $b > 1$, $g(N) = N^r$ for some integer $r \geq 0$, with initial condition $E(1) = c$.

This form of recurrence relation occurs in many divide-and-conquer algorithms, where the work involved in computing for input of size N may be recursively expressed as the amount of work done in computing for input of size N/b. Our analyses in Chapter 6 often have $b = 2$.

The assumptions for this case mean that the recurrence relation we are trying to solve appears as

$$E(N) = aE(N/b) + N^r \qquad E(1) = c \tag{B.5}$$

Doerr and Lavasseur show that an explicit solution to this recurrence relation is given by

$$E(N) = cN^{\log_b a} + \begin{cases} \dfrac{a^{\log_b N} - b^{r\log_b N}}{\dfrac{a}{b^r} - 1} & \text{if } a \neq b^r \\ N^r \log_b N & \text{if } a = b^r \end{cases} \tag{B.6}$$

For instance, if $E(N) = E(N/2) + 1$ with $E(1) = 1$ (as it was for the binary search), then the formula for $a = b^r$ in (B.6) tells us that

$$E(N) = 1 + \log_2 N$$

In a broader context, (B.6) implies the following:

- $E(N)$ is $O(N^{\log_b a})$ if $a > b^r$.
- $E(N)$ is $O(b^{r\log_b N}) = O(N^r)$ if $a < b^r$.
- $E(N)$ is $O(N^r \log_b N)$ if $a = b^r$.

APPENDIX

Review of the C Programming Language

This appendix presents those features of the C programming language with which we assume a familiarity on your part. If you have not programmed in C prior to reading this book, Appendix C should be read in conjunction with the introduction to C++ presented in Chapter 1. Together, they will provide you with a background in C adequate for reading the algorithms in this book and for developing the C++ programs and functions that are specified in the exercises and programming problems. However, this appendix should not be construed as a comprehensive treatment of the C programming language. Reading the appendix will not turn you into a true C "hacker" who is able to manipulate those features of C that take advantage of the hardware on which it runs. Instead, our goal here is only to establish the foundation in C necessary for our coverage of algorithms and data structures in C++. If you're interested in a more thorough coverage of all features of the C language, we suggest you read a textbook on C, such as *Applications Programming in ANSI C* (second edition) by Richard Johnsonbaugh and Martin Kalin (Macmillan, 1993).

Simple Data Types The text uses three simple data types that are built into C—**char, float, int.** Variables of these types can store individual characters, real-valued numbers, and integers respectively. Additionally, using C's **enum** keyword, Chapter 1 defines a BOOLEAN data type capable of storing the logical values TRUE and FALSE. We have used the BOOLEAN data type in situations where many C programmers would instead use an **int** with the value zero corresponding to "false" and a non-zero value corresponding to "true."

Expressions & Assignment Statements

- Relational and Logical Operators in Expressions

C Symbol	Meaning
<	less than
>	greater than
<=	less than or equal to
>=	greater than or equal to
==	equal to
!=	not equal
!	logical NOT
&&	logical AND
||	logical OR

- Assignment Statements and Arithmetic Operations

```
int a,b,c;
float x,y,z;
:

a = b + c;    // a assigned the value of b
              // plus c
a = b - c;    // a assigned the value of b
              // minus c
a = b * c;    // a assigned the value of b
              // times c
a = b / c;    // a assigned the integer-
              // valued, truncated quotient
              // of b divided by c
x = y / z;    // x assigned the real-valued
              // quotient of y divided by z
x = (float) a / (float) b;  // This
              // illustrates what C calls
              // "type-casting." The integer
              // values a and b are converted
              // to floats before the division
              // is done, so a real-valued
              // quotient without truncation is
              // computed and stored in x
a = b % c;    // a is assigned the integer
              // remainder obtained when b
              // is divided by c
```

- Combination assignment operators

Combination operator	Equivalent using conventional operators
`a += b;`	`a = a + b;`
`a *= a + b;`	`a = a * (a + b);`
`++i;`	`i = i + 1;`
`--i;`	`i = i - 1;`

`j = ++i;`	`i = i + 1; // followed by`
	`j = i;`

`j = i++;`	`j = i;     // followed by`
	`i = i + 1;`

Control structure statements:

- **if** statement

General syntax:

```
if (conditional expression)
  statement;
```

Example:

```
if (temp > 32)
  cout << "Above freezing" << endl;
cout << "Fahrenheit temperature is "
     << temp << endl;
```

Example (illustrating use of curly braces to group several simple statements into one compound statement):

```
if (temp <= 32)
{
  cout << "Freezing or below" << endl;
  cout << "Good weather for skiing" << endl;
}
cout << "Fahrenheit temperature is "
     << temp << endl;
```

- **if-else** statement

General syntax:

```
if (conditional expression)
  statement-1;
else
  statement-2;
```

Example:

```
if (x < y)
  min = x;
else
  min = y;
cout << "Minimum value " << min << "\n";
```

- **while** statement (pretest loop)

General syntax:

```
while (conditional expression)
  loop-body-statement;
```

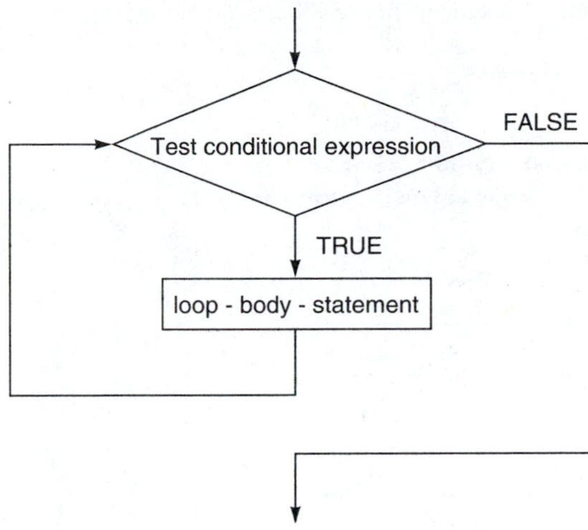

Example (form sum of integers from 1 to 10):

```
i = 1;
sum = 0;
while (i <= 10)
{
  sum += i;
  ++i;
}
```

- **for** statement

General syntax:

```
for (expression1; expression2; expression3)
  loop-body-statement;
```

In the above representation *expression1* consists of statements (separated by commas) to be executed prior to execution of the loop. *expression2* determines the exit condition for the loop; the loop continues to execute as long as *expression2* is TRUE (non-zero). *expression3* consists of statements to be executed after the loop-body statement is executed and prior to the next iteration of the loop. Thus, the above **for** construct is equivalent to the following **while** construct:

```
expression1-statements;
while (expression2)
{
  loop-body-statement;
  expression3-statements;
}
```

Example (compute $n! = n \times (n-1) \times \cdots \times 2 \times 1$*):*

```
for (factorial = n, i = n - 1; i >= 1; --i)
  factorial *= i;   // Note combination
                    // *= operator
```

- **do-while** statement (posttest loop)

General syntax:

```
do
  loop-body-statement;
while (conditional expression);
```

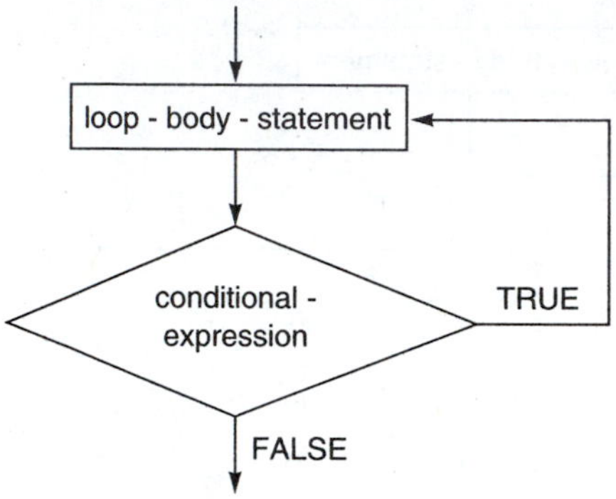

Example (form sum of integers from 1 to 10):

```
sum = 0;
i = 10;
do
{
  sum += i;
  --i;
}
while (i > 0);
```

- **break** statement—causes exit from the innermost enclosing loop or **switch** statement (use with **switch** follows)

- **switch** statement—multiway decision-making when **break** is used with **switch**

General syntax:

```
switch (integer expression)
{
  case constant-1:
    statements-1

  case constant-2:
    statements-2
  :
  case constant-n:
    statements-n
  default:          // optional for use when
                    // all previous cases fail
    statements
}
```

Example:

```
switch (score)
{
  case 9:
  case 10:
    ++aGrades;    // Increment A grade counter
                  // for 9 or 10. Then
    break;        // execute break statement
                  // to avoid drifting into
                  // statements for the cases
                  // that follow
  case 8:
    ++bGrades;    // Score of 8 is a B
    break;
  case 7:
    ++cGrades;    // Score of 7 is a C
    break;
  default:
    ++fails;      // All else fails
};
```

Program structure A C program consists of one or more functions, including the special function **main.** Functions are described in detail in Chapter 1.

Arrays in traditional C (different from the Array class developed in Chapter 2) Arrays in traditional C allow access to their components in a variety of ways. If your background is in a language like Pascal, you will probably be most comfortable with the Pascal-like index operator [ ] used by C. One detail to be aware of is that all array indexing in C starts at index zero. That is, the first component of an array is always at index zero. For instance, the following main program declares an array of **int**s with five elements—a[0], a[1], a[2], a[3], a[4]. The program then initializes each array component to the square of its index and calls on a function to return the sum of the components.

```
// Sum the entries in an array referenced by
// Pascal-like indices
#include <iostream.h>

const int size = 5;

void main()
{
  int a[size];       // a is declared to be
                     // array with 5 elements
  int i;
  for (i = 0; i < size; ++i)
    a[i] = i * i;    // [] operator accesses
                     // ith component
  cout << sum (a, size) << endl;
                     // function is called
                     // to accumulate sum of
                     // array components
```

```
}

// The function below does the summing.  The
// argument b[] establishes an int array
// parameter that is automatically passed by
// reference.  Arrays are always passed by
// reference in C.  The empty pair of index
// brackets [] indicates that an int array
// of any size may be passed in for the b[]
// argument.

int sum(int b[], int n)
{
  int i, s = 0;
  for (i = 0; i < n; ++i)
    s += b[i];
  return(s);
}
```

Pointers Pointers are widely used in C programs. The asterisk (*) is used both to declare pointer variables as in

```
int *x;   // declares x to be a pointer to
          // an integer
```

and to dereference them

```
*x = 14;       // assigns the value 14 to the
               // location pointed to by x above
cout << *x;    // displays the value of the
               // integer pointed to by x
```

Complementing the use of pointers is the reference operator, **&**, which means "return the address of . . . " It is often used to assign values to pointers.
Example:

```
int *x, y = 14;    // x points to an integer and
                   // y is an integer variable
                   // initialized to 14
x = &y;            // x is assigned the address
                   // associated with the
                   // variable y
cout << *x;        // the value displayed will
                   // be that of the variable y,
                   // that is, 14
```

Structures A structure (or **struct**) is a collection of nonhomogeneously typed members that are accessed by means of their names. The declaration

```
struct nodestruct
{
  int data;
  nodestruct *link;
} node, *nodeptr;
```

illustrates the syntax for declaring a variable **node** having a structured type **nodestruct** with two members, an integer **data** and a pointer **link** to a **nodestruct** structure; the variable **nodeptr** is a pointer to such a structure. Members of structures are selected using the dot operator, **.**, as shown below

```
node.data = 14;
```

Here 14 will be assigned as the value of the **data** member of **node.**

When accessing members via a pointer, cumbersome notation such as

```
(*nodeptr).link
```

can be replaced by the cleaner syntax

```
nodeptr->link
```

In C, an array is essentially a pointer to the zeroth index of the array. This allows access to array components via pointer notation as well as the bracket index [ ] operator. For example, the following two versions of the **sum** function each take advantage, in different ways, of this equivalence between an array and a pointer to a contiguous block of memory locations.

```
// Pointer Version 1
int sum(int b[], int n)
{
  int s = 0;
  int *p;      // p is a pointer to an integer

  // p starts out at the address of the
  // initial location in array b and is then
  // incremented through all array locations
  // up to and including index [n-1].  When
  // p has been incremented to the address
  // of b[n], we leave the loop.
  for (p = b; p < &b[n]; ++p)
    s += *p;            // Increase s by what
                        // p is referencing
  return(s);
}

// Pointer Version 2
int sum(int b[], int n)
{
  int  i, s = 0;
  for (i = 0; i < n; ++i)
    s += *(b + i);
    // (b + i) will be the address of the
    // ith component of the array b.
    // Dereference that address and add
    // the resulting value to s
  return(s);
}
```

APPENDIX D

Input and Output—the IOStream Library

As is the case in C, in C++ input and output operations are not part of the language's definition, but instead are implemented as part of a standard library of C++ functions. Here we describe one such library, the IO stream library *iostream*. Any program that uses this library for its IO operations must include its header file *iostream.h* using the include statement

```
#include <iostream.h>
```

The basic idea behind the IO stream operations is to provide functions that allow the programmer to convert typed data values—ints, floats, chars, strings (char*), and so forth—into a sequence of bytes and conversely. Such sequences of bytes are known as *streams*. This back-and-forth conversion between a program's data and a stream is carried out by three classes: a class **istream** for managing input, a class **ostream** for managing output, and a class **iostream** that is derived from istream and ostream for bidirectional IO. In addition four stream objects are predefined:

cin an object of class istream, for handling standard input;
cout an object of class ostream, for handling standard output;
cerr an object of class ostream for managing unbuffered output to standard error. Unbuffered output means the output is sent immediately.
clog an object of class ostream, for managing buffered output to standard error. Buffered output is held in a buffer and not sent until the buffer is full or until it is explicitly "flushed."

Output The fundamental output operation is the *insertion* operation (for inserting a value into an output stream) which uses the operator symbol "<<" (this overrides the "left shift" bit manipulation operator of C). This operator has been overloaded several additional times to allow values of the built-in data types of C++ to be converted to a sequence of characters and inserted into an output stream. You may also overload it to perform a similar conversion for objects of class types you have defined.

As an example of the use of the insertion operator, suppose the variable **i** is of type **int** and currently stores the value 5, while the variable **s** is of type **char*** and points to the string "world". When compiled and executed the sequence of statements

```
cout << "Hello ";
cout << s;
cout << "\nThe value of the variable i is: ";
cout << i;
```

will produce as output

```
Hello world
The value of the variable i is: 5
```

Fortunately the insertion operation returns as a value a reference to its left operand. This means the ungainly style above (that is, using one invocation of the insertion operator per value) can be avoided by concatenating insertions as follows:

```
cout << "Hello " << s;
cout << "\nThe value of i is: " << i;
```

or even

```
cout << "Hello " << s
     << "\nThe value of i is: " << i;
```

The operator << uses a left-to-right associativity and permits the use of parentheses where necessary.

For character values, an alternative to using the insertion operator is to use the member function **put,** whose interface is

```
ostream& put(char)
```

For a character variable c, the statements

```
cout << c;
```

and

```
cout.put(c);
```

are equivalent.

End-of-line Insertion In an earlier example we used C's "newline" designator '\n' to insert a line break between "Hello world" and the output that followed. This is one of two ways in which an end-of-line marker can be inserted into an output stream. The other is to use the stream manipulator **endl,** which in addition to inserting the newline character into the output stream also flushes the output buffer. This causes the buffer's contents to be written even if the buffer is not yet full.

Using **endl,** we could rewrite our earlier output code as:

```
cout << "Hello " << s << endl;
cout << "The value of i is: " << i << endl;
```

Input The fundamental input operation is the *extraction* operation (for extracting a value from the input stream), which is invoked by the operator ">>". This operator overrides the "right shift" operator of C and as is the case with the insertion operator is pre-defined for built-in data types and char* but can be overloaded for user-defined types. The extraction operator works by reading characters from an input stream and converting the characters to values of the appropriate type. It also returns a reference to its left operand and thus can be concatenated.

For example, if the variable **x** is of type **int,** then the statement

```
cin >> x;
```

will extract a sequence of characters from standard input, convert them to the appropriate integer, and assign the value of this integer to x.

Values in the input stream are separated by white space (blanks, tabs, and newlines). The white space characters are not treated as characters, even when being read into a character or string variable. A user who does not want to skip over white space can use the **istream** member function **get,** whose interface is

```
istream& get(char &c).
```

This function extracts a character from the input stream and stores it in the variable associated with the formal parameter **c.** Alternatively, one can use the function **get()** which returns the character read as its value. When an end-of-file on the stream is encountered **get** returns EOF, an end-of-file value defined in *iostream.h*. There is also an **istream** member function **eof** that returns 0 (false) if end-of-file has not been encountered, and 1 (true) when it has been encountered. We note in addition that the extraction operation will return the value 0 when end-of-file has been encountered, providing us with yet a third way of monitoring for this condition.

The **istream** class also provides a member function **getline** that can be used when a user wishes to read an entire string that includes white space. The interface for **getline** is

```
getline(char *buffer, int limit,
        char delimiter);
```

which will extract a block of up to **limit**-1 characters and place them in a character array addressed by means of the character array associated with the formal parameter **buffer. getline** will append the null character ('\0') to **buffer.** Also, if either the end-of-file or the delimiting character is encountered, then fewer than **limit**-1 characters will be placed within **buffer.** The default delimiter is the newline; the delimiter is not placed within **buffer.**

File Input and Output Support for working with disk files in C++ is provided by one of three file stream classes: **ifstream** for input only files, **ofstream** for output only files, and **fstream** for bidirectional files. In order to be able to use these classes, the user must include the *fstream.h* header file in addition to the *iostream.h* header file:

```
#include <iostream.h>
#include <fstream.h>
```

Prior to accessing a file stream in a C++ program a user must:

1. Declare a file stream object from an appropriate file stream class. For example:

```
ifstream inFile;
ofstream outFile;
fstream  inoutFile;
```

2. Associate the file stream object with a particular disk file via the open function. For example the statements

```
inFile.open("InputFile.dat");
outFile.open("OutputFile.dat");
inoutFile.open
       ("InOutFile.dat",ios::in | ios::out);
```

would associate the file stream objects declared above with the files *InputFile.dat, OutputFile.dat,* and *InOutFile.dat* that exist (or will be created) on some disk. Rather than specify the names of the files explicitly, a user can also use a char* variable that references the name of the file.

We note that since **ifstream, ofstream** and **fstream** are classes their constructor operations permit an association with a disk file to be made at the time a file stream object is declared; thus we could have combined steps 1 and 2 above into:

```
ifstream inFile("InputFile.dat");
ofstream outFile("OutputFile.dat");
fstream inoutFile
        ("InOutFile.dat",ios::in | ios::out);
```

You will observe that the **open** function for the **fstream** object (or the **fstream** constructor) used an additional argument designating a file *open mode,* which in this case allowed the file to be opened for both input and output. Among the open mode designators for **fstream** objects are:

ios::in	open for input (reading)
ios::out	open for output (writing)
ios::trunc	discard the file's contents if it exists (also the default action for ios::out)
ios::app	append output to the end of the file
ios::nocreate	open fails if file does not exist
ios::noreplace	open fails if file exists

Our example shows that the bitwise or operator | can be used to affect combinations of modes.

A file is disassociated from a file stream object with the member function **close( ).** For example,

```
inFile.close();
```

would be used to disassociate the file stream **inFile** from the disk file "InputFile.dat" with which it was associated by the previous call to **open.**

By default, file stream objects are all IO stream objects, whence they have available to them all of the operators and member functions of those classes, including the **get** and **put** functions and the insertion (<<) and extraction (>>) operators. The incorporation of these functions and operators into file-directed IO is straightforward.

We conclude by noting that in this brief appendix we have only scratched the surface concerning the power of the IO stream library, giving only enough details so you can understand its use in our sample code. We recommend to you Chapter 7 of *Object-Oriented Programming in C++* by Richard Johnsonbaugh and Martin Kalin (Prentice Hall, Englewood Cliffs, NJ, 1995) for a fuller discussion of these issues.

APPENDIX E Hints and Solutions to Selected Exercises

Chapter 1

Section 1.1

1.
```
template <class ElementType>
void Invert (ElementType ar[], int size)
{
  int j = size-1;
  for (int i=0; i<(size/2); i++)
  {
    swap (ar[i], ar[j--]);
  }
}
```

3.
```
template <class ElementType>
void accumulate (ElementType source[], int size,
                 int (*Operation)(const int &initial,
                                  const int &value), int &total)
{
  if (size > 0)
  {
    total = source[0];
    for (int i=1; i<size;i++)
      total = Operation(total, source[i]);
  }
  else total = 0;
}
```

Section 1.2

1. Selection Sort:

18	90	40	9	3	92	6
3	90	40	9	18	92	6
3	6	40	9	18	92	90
3	6	9	40	18	92	90
3	6	9	18	40	92	90
3	6	9	18	40	92	90
3	6	9	18	40	90	92

3.
```
template <class ElementType>
  void sort(ElementType ar[], int numvals,
            BOOLEAN (*precedes)(const ElementType &x,
                                const ElementType &y))
{
  int j,k,save;
  BOOLEAN done;
  for (k=1; k<numvals; k++)
```

```
    {
        j = k-1; done = FALSE; save = ar[k];
        while (j>=0 && !done)
        {
            if (Precedes(ar[j], save)) done = TRUE;
            else ar[j+1] = ar[j--];
        }
        ar[++j] = save;
    }
}
```

5. **a.** N^2 **b.** $N \log_2 N$ **c.** $N \log_2 N$

7. **a.** $n^3 \log_2 n$. **b.** 4^n **c.** n^4

9. Insertion sort is stable. Selection sort as presented in the text is not stable.

Consider the array

18 13_1 6 12 13_2 9

Section 1.3

1. 23 probes; 23 microseconds.

3. The search is sequential, which is O(N).

5.
```
template <class ElementType>
void Split (ElementType ar[], ElementType target, int &spl,
            int lo, int hi)
{
  if (target < int (ar[lo])) spl = lo;
  else
  {
    if (target > int (ar[hi])) spl = hi;
    else
      spl = lo + int(((hi - lo) * (int (target) - ar[lo])) /
            (int(ar[hi]) - int (ar[lo])));
  }
}
```

Section 1.4

1.

60	12	90	30	64	8	6
6	12	8	30	64	90	60
6	8	12	30	60	64	90

5. The advantage of using increments of relatively prime values lies in the fact that the increments will not divide evenly into each other; all the segments are therefore distinct.

7. The best case data set would have the data already in order. In the worst case data set none of the data would be partially sorted at all; that is, each segment would initially be in descending instead of ascending order.

9. Insertion sort: 28 comparisons.
Shell Sort (diminishing increments = / 2 (integer division)): 22 comparisons
Shell Sort (diminishing increments = 5,3,1) : 20 comparisons.

11. In each case write an initial loop to determine the first member of the sequence that surpasses **numvals.** Then, to compute the diminishing sequence, interactively execute:

a. eledist = (eledist/2) + 1;

b. eledist = eledist/2;

c. On alternate iterations, divide by 2 or divide by 2 and add 1

d. eledist = eledist/3;

Chapter 2

Section 2.1

1. The term "information hiding" describes the ability of a package to meet the specifications of an abstract data type in a self-contained fashion, allowing use of the package without having to know how it achieves the implementation.

The user of the array class has no knowledge of how the values of the array are stored, manipulated, or retrieved. For example, she does not have to worry about the 0-based arrays that are used in C++, nor does she have to worry about how the array class makes sure that the array indices accessed are not out of range.

3.
```
C++ function
void main()
{
  // Will read in uppercase characters only.
  // Could easily be changed to read in lowercase.
  Array<char, int> ar('A', 'Z');
  char i;
  ifstream in;
  for (int a = 'A'; a<= 'Z'; a++)
  {
    ar[a] = 0; // init. counters
  }
  in.open ("datafile.dat", ios::nocreate);
  char b;
  while (in.get(b))
  {
    ar[b]++;    // read in character from file
    in.get(b); // read in '\n' character
  }
  in.close();
}
```

5.
```
struct salInfo
{
  int numEmployees;
  float salary;
};

void main()
{
  Array<char, salInfo> ar('A', 'H');
  ifstream in;
  for (char a = 'A'; a<= 'H'; a++)
  {
    ar[a].salary = 0;
    ar[a].numEmployees = 0; // init. counters
  }
  in.open ("data3.dat", ios::nocreate);
  char dept;
  float sal;
  while (in >> dept)
  {
    ar[dept].numEmployees++;
    in >> sal;
    ar[dept].salary+=sal;  // read in salaries from file
  }
  float highSal = 0;
  char highDept;  // dept w/ highest salary
  for (char q = 'A'; q <= 'H'; q++)
  if (ar[q].salary > highSal)
  {
     highSal = ar[q].salary;
     highDept = q;
  }
  int mostEmp = 0;
  char mostDept;  // dept w/ most employees
  for (q = 'A'; q <= 'H'; q++)
  if (ar[q].numEmployees > mostEmp)
  {
     mostEmp = ar[q].numEmployees;
     mostDept = q;
  }
 in.close();
}
```

7. C++ implementation for Sparse array:

```
template <class IndexType, class BaseData>
class Sparse
{
  private:
    struct Data
    {
      IndexType position;
      BaseData value;
    };
    int maxNumValues;
    BaseData ADeflt;
    Data *arrayData;
    IndexType loIndex, hiIndex;
    BOOLEAN outOfRange(IndexType i);

  public:
    Sparse(IndexType lo, IndexType hi, BaseData deflt);
    ~Sparse();
    BaseData retrieve(IndexType i);
    void assign(IndexType i, BaseData val);
};
```

Here are constructor and retrieve operations.

```
template <class IndexType, class BaseData>
Sparse<IndexType, BaseData>::Sparse(IndexType lo, IndexType hi, BaseData deflt)
{
  maxNumValues = 20; // stores the max # of "non-default"
  // values that the sparse array can store
  ADeflt = deflt;
  arrayData = new Data[maxNumValues];
  assert(arrayData != 0);
  loIndex = lo;
  hiIndex = hi;
  for (IndexType q = 0; q <= maxNumValues; q++)
     arrayData[q].position = -1; // init. arrayData
}


template <class IndexType, class BaseData>
BaseData Sparse<IndexType, BaseData>::retrieve(IndexType i)
{
  assert(!outOfRange(i));
  for (IndexType z = 0; z < maxNumValues; z++)
    if (arrayData[z].position == i)
      return (arrayData[z].value);
  return(ADeflt); // value not in array; return default
}
```

Section 2.2

1. Only the following two changes need to be made:

```
1-->  replace the lessThanFloat function with the following:
BOOLEAN greaterThanFloat (const char&x, const char& y)
{
  if (x > y) return(TRUE);
  else return(FALSE);
}

2-->  call on the SortArray constructor as follows:
SortArray <int, float> x(100, 103, greaterThanFloat);
```

3. The advantage is that a single SortArray object can use more than one "precedes" function; that is, it can sort its data in more than one way.

```
template <class IndexType, class BaseData>
class SortArray: public Array<IndexType, BaseData>
{
  protected:
    BOOLEAN (*compare) (const BaseData&x, const BaseData&y);
    void segmentedInsertionSort(int numvals, int k);
    void swap(BaseData &x, BaseData& y);

  public:
    SortArray(IndexType lo, IndexType hi);
    void sort (int numvals,
               BOOLEAN (*precedes)(const BaseData& x, const BaseData& y));
};

template <class IndexType, class BaseData>
SortArray<IndexType, BaseData>::SortArray(IndexType lo, IndexType hi):
 Array<IndexType, BaseData>(lo, hi)
 {
  // do nothing
 }

template <class IndexType, class BaseData>
void SortArray<IndexType, BaseData>::segmentedInsertionSort(int numvals, int k)
{
  int j, m;
  BOOLEAN done;
  for (m = k; m < numvals; ++m)
  {
    j = m;
    done = FALSE;
    while ((j>=k) && !done)
      if (compare(arrayData[j], arrayData[j-k]))
      {
        swap(arrayData[j], arrayData[j-k]);
        j-= k;
      }
      else
        done = TRUE;
  }
}

template <class IndexType, class BaseData>
void SortArray<IndexType, BaseData>::sort(int numvals,
               BOOLEAN (*precedes)(const BaseData &x, const BaseData &y))
{
  compare = precedes;
  int eleDist;
  eleDist = numvals / 2;
  while (eleDist > 0)
  {
    segmentedInsertionSort(numvals, eleDist);
    eleDist /= 2;
  }
}

void main()
{
  SortArray<int, float> x(100, 103);
  x[100] = 3.2;
  x[101] = 7.8;
  x[102] = 2.1;
  x[103] = 19.4;
  x.sort(4, lessThanFloat);
  x.sort(4, greaterThanFloat);
}
```

5. Definition:

The Searchable Array ADT is an array on which we can search for a particular target value. The operations performed on a Sortable array are:

Search Operation:

Preconditions: A Searchable array object that has previously been constructed. Beginning with the first index of the array, numvals consecutive locations in the array have been assigned well-defined values. Target is the key value that is to be searched for. Compare is a function that compares values of type Target.

Postconditions: If the key value Target is found, TRUE is returned, and the variable Location contains the location in the array that contains Target if TRUE is returned; otherwise FALSE is returned and Locations's value is unreliable.

C++ Interface:

```
#include "array.h"

template <class IndexType, class BaseData>
class SearchArray: public Array<IndexType, BaseData>
{
  protected:
    BOOLEAN (*precedes)(BaseData x,  BaseData y);
    int (*split)(int lo, int hi);

  public:
    SearchArray(IndexType lo, IndexType hi);
    BOOLEAN search(int numvals, BaseData target,
                   BOOLEAN (*compare)(BaseData x,  BaseData y),
                   int (*split)(int lo, int hi), int& location);
};

template <class IndexType, class BaseData>
BOOLEAN SearchArray<IndexType, BaseData>::search(int numvals, BaseData target,
                   BOOLEAN (*compare)(BaseData x,  BaseData y),
                   int (*split)(int lo, int hi), int& location)
{
  split = split;
  precedes = compare;
  int h, l, guess;
  BOOLEAN found;
  h = numvals - 1;
  l = 0;
  found = FALSE;
  while (!found && (l <= h))
  {
    guess = split (l, h);
    if ((arrayData[guess] == target))
    {
      location = guess+ loIndex;
      found = TRUE;
    }
    else
      if (compare(arrayData[guess], target))
        l = guess + 1;
      else
        h = guess - 1;
  }
  return(found);
}

void main()
{
  SearchArray<int, float> x(100, 103);
  x[100] = 3.2;
  x[101] = 7.8;
  x[102] = 2.1;
  x[103] = 19.4;
```

```
    int location;
    if (x.search (4, 3.2, comp, spl, location))
      cout << location << endl;
  }
```

Section 2.3

1.
```
// Interface for Copy Constructor
Array(const Array<IndexType,BaseData> & initArray);

// Implementation of Copy Constructor
template <class IndexType, class BaseData>
Array<IndexType, BaseData>::Array(const Array<IndexType,BaseData> & initArray)
{
  loIndex = initArray.loIndex;
  hiIndex = initArray.hiIndex;
  arrayData = new BaseData[hiIndex-loIndex+1];
  assert(arrayData != 0);
  for (IndexType i = loIndex;i <= hiIndex;i++)
    arrayData[i] = initArray.arrayData[i];
}
```

3.
```
class String : public Array<int, char>
{
  protected:
    int maxL;
  public:
    as given in text;
};
```

Here are the second constructor, concatenate, and remove operations:

```
  String::String (int maxLength, char* initstr) : Array<int, char>(1, maxLength)
  {
    maxL = maxLength;
    int c = 0;
    int currentLength = 0;// just a counter
    (*this)[1] = '\0';
    while (initstr[c] != '\0')
    {
      ++currentLength;
      (*this)[currentLength] = initstr[c];
      (*this)[currentLength+1] = '\0'; // increase "currentLength"
      ++c;
    }
  }

void String::concatenate(const String &t)
{
  int j = t.length() + length();
  if (j > maxL)
  {
    cout << "j too long, truncating...";
    j = maxL;
  }
  int temp = length();
  for (int q = length()+1; q <= j; q++)
    (*this)[q] = t[q-temp];
  (*this)[j+1]= '\0';
}

void String::remove(int start, int number)
{
  if (start > maxL)
    cout << start << " out of range!";
  else
  {
    int j = start + number;
    if (j > maxL)
```

```
      {
        cout << "j too big, truncating...";
        j = maxL;
      }
      String tempcopy(maxL);
      for (int a = 1; a <= length(); a++)
        tempcopy[a] = (*this)[a];
      for (int q = start; q <= length()-(j-start); q++)
        (*this)[q] = tempcopy[q + (j-start)];
      int jtemp = length();
      jtemp -= (j-start);
     (*this)[jtemp] = '\0';
   }
 }
```

5. In the first implementation, the calls to length do not add appreciably to the time efficiency, since the length function only has to return currentLength, an O(1) operation.

   In the second implementation, the calls to length do add appreciably to the time efficiency because if the array has maximum length N, the length function might have to check every value in the array before it finds the '\O' terminating value. In other words, the length function will have a Big-O efficiency of O(N), where N is the maximum array size, which is much worse than the previous O(1) big-O efficiency of the length function.

7. The algorithm is most efficient in the unsuccessful case if Align[P] is close to 0, and is most efficient for the successful case if Align[P] is close to P - 1.

13. Strategy: create a dynamic array of size N and store N in a global variable called currMaxSize. When currSize reaches N-1 , copy the contents of the old array into a new dynamic array of size 2N, and destroy the old array, using a function called createBiggerArray.
    Example of Function:

```
void String::concatenate(const String &t)
{
  int j = t.currentLength+ currentLength;
  if (j > currMax Size)
  {
    createBiggerArray();  // create an array of double size
    currMaxSize *= 2;
  }
  for (int q = currentLength+1; q <= j; q++)
    (*this)[q] = t[q-currentLength];
  currentLength = j;
}
```

Section 2.4

1. Here are the copy constructor and intersection operator &&

```
template <class Universe>
  Set<Universe>::Set(Set<Universe> &initSet)
  {
    this->loElement = initSet.loElement;
    cout << loElement;
    this->hiElement = initSet.hiElement;
    cout << hiElement;
    elements = new Array<Universe, BOOLEAN>(loElement, hiElement);
    for (Universe element = loElement; element <= hiElement; element++)
      (*elements)[element] = (*initSet.elements)[element];
    }

  template <class Universe>
  Set<Universe> Set<Universe>::operator && (const Set<Universe> &t)
  {
    Set<Universe> temp(this->loElement, this->hiElement);
    if ((loElement!=t.loElement)  (hiElement !=t.hiElement))
    {
      cout <<"invalid && operation:sets have different lo & hi values!";
      return(*this);
    }
    else
```

```
    {
      for (Universe element = loElement; element <= hiElement; element++)
        if (((*this)[element])&&(t[element]))
          (*temp.elements)[element] = TRUE;
        else
          (*temp.elements)[element] = FALSE;
      return(temp);
    }
  }
```

3. The empty function would become O(1), since we now only need to check to see if the number of element equals 0. The operator `==` operation would become more efficient in certain cases, since we could check to see if the two sets have the same number of elements before we begin checking each individual elements. The <= operator would also sometimes be more efficient, because if the set t had fewer elements than the owner set, we could immediately exit the function. The add and remove operations would become slightly less efficient, and the `&&`, `||`, and `-` operators all become more inefficient, because they must keep track of the number of elements being inserted into the owner set.
5. Store the strings in an array of strings. Then, in the Boolean array, a TRUE at index **i** would indicate that the strings at index i in the array of string is in the set. A FALSE indicates that the string is not in the set.
7.

```
template <class Universe>
class UnionFind
{
  private:
    Array <Universe, Universe>*  ufArray;
    Universe loEl, hiEl;
  public:
    // as given in text;
};
```

Here are the constructor and ufUnion operation

```
template <class Universe>
UnionFind<Universe>::UnionFind(Universe loElement, Universe hiElement)
{
  loEl = loElement;
  hiEl = hiElement;
  ufArray = new Array<Universe, Universe> (loEl, hiEl);
  for (Universe i = loEl; i <= hiEl; i++)
    (*ufArray)[i] = i;
}

template <class Universe>
void UnionFind<Universe>:: ufUnion(Universe x, Universe y)
{
  Universe temp = (*ufArray)[y];
  (*ufArray)[y] = (*ufArray)[x];
  for (Universe i = loEl; i <= hiEl; i++)
    if ((*ufArray)[i] == temp)
      (*ufArray)[i] = (*ufArray)[x];
}
```

9.

```
void main()
{
  Set<char> s1('A', 'Z');
  BOOLEAN finished = FALSE;
  int input;
  char ch;
  while (!finished)
  {
    cout << "Enter 1 to add, 2 to remove, 3 to exit" << endl;
    cin >> input;
    cout << endl;
    switch (input)
    {
      case 1:
        cout << "Enter the letter to be added" << endl;
```

```
          cin >> ch;
          s1.add (ch);
          break;
        case 2:
          cout << "Enter the letter to be removed" << endl;
          cin >> ch;
          s1.remove(ch);
          break;
        case 3:
          finished = TRUE;
          break;
      }
    }
    for (char j = 'A'; j <= 'Z'; j++)
      if (s1[j])
        cout << char(j) << endl;
}
```

Chapter 3

Section 3.1

1. Except for Insert and Replace, all other operations would have the same pre- and postconditions as their unordered List counterparts.

Insert Operation:

Preconditions: A list object, possibly empty; item, having type BaseData, which is to become the value of a new node in the list; precedes, a function which accepts two values of type BaseData and returns TRUE if the first precedes the second, and FALSE otherwise.

Postconditions: The list with item inserted in a new node such that the list is still ordered according to the ordering relationship established by Precedes. If the list is empty, or if item precedes all other nodes, it becomes the first node in the list.

Replace Operation:

Preconditions: A nonempty list object; item, having type BaseData; and the Precedes function

Postconditions: The current node is deleted, and item is inserted in the list in such a way that the list maintains its ordering relationship.

3.
```
template <class BaseData>
void processAllItems(List<BaseData> &l)
{
  int start = l.current();
  l.first();
  for (int i = 1; i <= l.count(); i++)
  {
     processItem(l.examine());
     if (i != l.count()) l.next();
  }
  l.makeCurrent(start);
}
```

5. *makeCurrent Operation:*

GIVEN: a List object containing nodes of type BaseData; a value newpos of type BaseData that specifies the data value of the new node; and a function "condition" that accepts two values of type BaseData as parameters and returns a boolean value.

TASK: Starting with the first node, evaluate condition for the value of the node and newpos. The first node for which condition returns true becomes the new current node. If condition is never true, then the old current node remains the current node.

RETURN: The list object with its (possibly) new current value.

7.
```
template <class BaseData>
float sum(List<BaseData> &l)
{
  int currPos = l.current();
```

```
    float temp = 0;
    l.first();
    if (l.count())
      for (int i = 1; i <=l.count(); i++)
      {
        temp += l.examine();
        if (i != l.count()) l.next();
      }
    l.makeCurrent(currPos);
    return (temp);
  }
```

Section 3.2

1. Here are the C++ implementations of the examine, remove, makeCurrent operations:

```
template <class BaseData>
class List
{
  protected:
    int maxSizeList;                     // Some appropriately sized integer
    Array<int, BaseData> *listArray;     // Storage for list data
    int numNodes;                        // Store current size of list
    int currentNode;                     // Store index to current node
};

template <class BaseData>
BaseData List<BaseData>::examine()
{
  BaseData x;
  if (numNodes)
    x = ((*this->listArray)[currentNode]);
  return(x);
}

template <class BaseData>
void List<BaseData>::makeCurrent(int position)
{
  if ((position < 1) || (position > numNodes))
    currentNode = 0;
  else
    currentNode = position;
}

template <class BaseData>
void List<BaseData>::remove()
{
  if (numNodes)                                    // List is not empty
  {
    for(int k=currentNode; k <= numNodes-1; ++k)
      (*this->listArray)[k] = (*this->listArray)[k+1];
    if (currentNode == numNodes)
      currentNode --;
    numNodes--;
  }
}
```

3a.
```
#include "list.h"
template <class BaseData>
class OList:public List<BaseData>
{
  public:
    OList(BOOLEAN (*precedes)(BaseData x, BaseData y));
    void OInsert(BaseData item, BOOLEAN (*precedes)(BaseData x, BaseData y));
    void OReplace(BaseData item, BOOLEAN (*precedes)(BaseData x, BaseData y));
};

template <class BaseData>
```

```
void OList<BaseData>::OInsert(BaseData item,
   BOOLEAN (*precedes)(BaseData x, BaseData y))
{
  if (numNodes)
  {
    first();
    while ((currentNode < numNodes) && (!precedes (item, examine())))
      next();
    if (currentNode == numNodes)
    {
       last();
       if (!precedes(item, examine()))
         insertAfter(item);
       else insertBefore(item);
    }
    else insertBefore(item);
  }
  else
  {
    insertAfter(item);
  }
}
```

3c. Because Binary Search might select a matching value in a position different from the first appearance of the value in the array, while MakeCurrent always selects the first appearance of the value in the array.

5. The following are O(1) operations: List, ~List, first, next, current, count, replace, and examine. The following are O(N) operations: last, makeCurrent, prev, insertAfter.

7. Broccoli Corn Lima Beans Peas Spinach

9. A search for an item in an ordered array is $O(\log_2 n)$, but in a pointer-linked list the search must be sequential ($O(n)$). However, the data manipulation required for Adds and Deletes in an ordered array is ($O(n)$). An addition or deletion requires a lot of data shifting. In the linked list, however, only pointers are manipulated. Therefore, the linked list is good for a volatile database, whereas an ordered array is better for a stable database.

Section 3.3

1. When a linked list is implemented using a dummy header, operations that involve empty lists are made easier. Further, the header can be used to store information about the list.

3.
```
template<class BaseData>
class List
{
  protected:

   ListNode *head,         // pointer to head of list; will be NULL if
                           // the list is empty
            *currentNode,  // pointer to current node in list
            *previous;     // pointer to node immediately preceding
                           // currentNode; will be NULL if currentNode
                           // points to the first node in the list or
                           // if the list is empty
   int numNodes;           // gives the number of nodes currently in
                           // the list
   int currentPos;         // gives the position in the list
                           // of currentNode
};
```

Here are insertBefore, remove, and constructor.

```
template <class BaseData>
void List<BaseData>::insertBefore(BaseData item)
{
  ListNode  *p;
  p = new ListNode;
  p->listData = item;  // assumes BaseData has an
                       // assignment operator that
                       // overloads the "=" symbol
  if (numNodes)
```

```
    {
      p->link = currentNode;
      previous->link = p;
      ++numNodes;
      currentNode = p;
    }
    else
    {
      p->link = head->link;
      head->link = p;
      previous = head;
      previous->link = p;
      ++numNodes;
      currentNode = p;
    }
  }

  template <class BaseData>
  void List<BaseData>::remove()
  {
    ListNode *p, *temp;
    p = currentNode;
    if (previous)
    {
      previous->link = currentNode->link;
      if (currentNode->link != NULL)
        currentNode = currentNode -> link;
      else
      {
        currentNode = previous;
        temp = head;
        while (temp->link != currentNode)
          temp = temp->link;
        previous = temp;
      }
    delete p;
    --numNodes;
    }
    else
      cout << "empty list!";
  }

  template <class BaseData>
  List<BaseData>::List()
  {
    previous = NULL;
    ListNode *p;
    p = new ListNode;
    p->link = NULL;
    p->listData = 0;
    head = p;
    numNodes = 0;
    currentPos = 0;
  }
```

Section 3.4

3. When string2 is assigned to string1, no new copy is made of the 'COFFEE' string. Instead, the pointer for string2 is directed to the same location as the pointer for string1. When string1 changes, it is possible with this implementation that string2 also changes. So the output given would be 'TEA' and not the 'COFFEE' that we would expect.

5. Place a copy of **t,** rather than **t** itself, into string **s.** Use the = operator. The cost in efficiency is that string T is traversed in operator = ($O(N)$) to copy it.

Section 3.5

3a. We must assume that the data in the **Universe** can be sorted in some sort of lexicographic order (e.g. numerical or alphabetical).

5a.
```
struct Element
{
  String city(80);
  Element *nextEl;
};

void main()
{
  Set<Element> s;
}
```

5b.
```
Array<int, Element*> partition(1, maxCities);
```

7. The sets in the union-field problem are disjoint, so each element is unique and it is not necessary to compare every element of one set against every element of another set. The elements must be located ($O(N)$ comparisons) and the links established to join the two sets containing them (an $O(1)$ operation).

Chapter 4

Section 4.1

1.
```
#include "queue.h"

template <class BaseData>
void substitute(Queue<BaseData> &q, const BaseData &oldvalue,
                const BaseData &newvalue)
{
  BaseData temp;
  if (!q.empty())
  {
    temp = q.front();
    q.dequeue();
    q.enqueue(-1);
    while (temp != -1)
    {
      if (temp == oldvalue)
        q.enqueue(newvalue);
      else
        q.enqueue(temp);
      temp = q.front();
      q.dequeue();
    }
  }
}
```

3a.
```
template <class BaseData>
void substitute(Queue<Basedata> &q, const BaseData &oldvalue,
                const BaseData &newvalue)
{
  BaseData temp;
  if (!q.empty())
  {
    temp = q.dequeue();
    q.enqueue(-1);
    while (temp != -1)
    {
      if (temp == oldvalue)
        q.enqueue(newvalue);
      else
        q.enqueue(temp);
      temp = q.dequeue();
    }
  }
}
```

3c. One example of an inelegant situation is the following: you want to examine the data value at the front of the queue but do not want to dequeue the node.

Section 4.2

1. Here are the front and enqueue operations

```
#include "list.h"
template <class BaseData>
BaseData Queue<BaseData>::front()
{
  first();
  return(examine());
}

template <class BaseData>
void Queue<BaseData>::enqueue(BaseData item)
{
  last();
  insertAfter(item);
}
```

3. `frontInd = 1; readInd = maxQueueSize;`
5. The Rear pointer is necessary since `q.front = q.rear->link`.

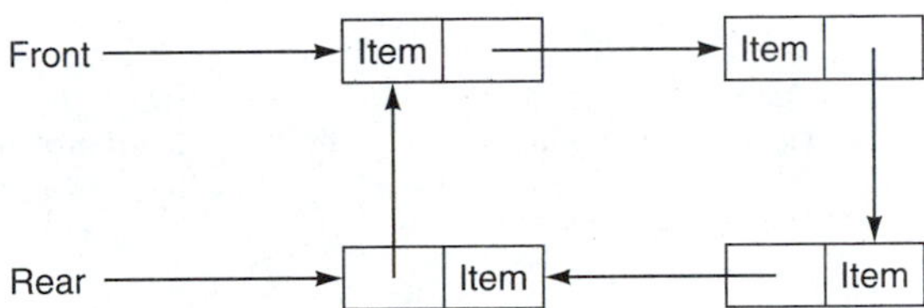

7. If a count is maintained of the number of elements in a circular queue, the constructor operation can be implemented by simply setting the count to 0, the empty operation can be implemented by testing whether the count is 0, and the full operation can be implemented by testing whether the count is equal to MaxQueueSize.
9. Here are the constructor, dequeue, and front operations:

```
template <class BaseData>
Queue<BaseData>::Queue(int size)
{
  maxQueueSize = size;
  frontInd = 1;
  rearInd = maxQueueSize;
  nodes = new Array<int, BaseData>(1, maxQueueSize);
}

template <class BaseData>
void Queue<BaseData>::dequeue()
{
  assert (!empty());
  frontInd = (frontInd%maxQueueSize) + 1;
}

template <class BaseData>
void Queue<BaseData>::enqueue(BaseData item)
{
  assert (!full());
  rearInd = (rearInd % maxQueueSize) + 1;
  (*nodes)[rearInd] = item;
}
```

11.

Operation	**Problem 4.2**				
	6	**7**	**8**	**9**	**10**
`Queue()`	$O(1)$	$O(1)$	$O(1)$	$O(1)$	$O(1)$
`~Queue()`	$O(1)$	$O(1)$	$O(1)$	$O(1)$	$O(N)$
`empty()`	$O(1)$	$O(1)$	$O(1)$	$O(1)$	$O(1)$
`full()`	$O(1)$	$O(1)$	$O(1)$	$O(1)$	$O(?)$
`enqueue`	$O(1)$	$O(1)$	$O(N)$	$O(1)$	$O(N)$
`dequeue`	$O(1)$	$O(1)$	$O(1)$	$O(1)$	$O(1)$

Problem 4.2.8 enqueue has a time efficiency of O(N) since all elements in the array may be shifted to the first N elements of the array.
Problem 4.2.10: ~Queue has a time efficiency of O(N) since all elements in Q must be returned to the available memory.
full has an unpredictable time efficiency since exception handling of dynamic memory is environment dependent. Newer versions of C++ have exception handling facilities.
enqueue has a time efficiency of O(N) since the entire linked list must be traversed to find the rear of the queue.

Section 4.3

1. 1st Pass: **DigitSublist**

Digit	Sublist
0	
1	9021
2	1142
3	
4	94
5	
6	3216 416 3316
7	
8	9438
9	

2nd Pass: **DigitSublist**

Digit	Sublist
0	
1	3216 416 3316
2	9021
3	9438
4	1142
5	
6	
7	
8	
9	94

3rd Pass: **DigitSublist**

Digit	Sublist	
0	9021	94
1	1142	
2	3216	
3	3316	
4	416	9438
5		
6		
7		
8		
9	94	

4th Pass: **DigitSublist**

Digit	Sublist
0	94 416
1	1142
2	
3	3216 3316
4	
5	
6	
7	
8	
9	9021 9438

3. Rather than test the Master List at each digit to find if there are values at that digit level, it is better to search the Master List once to find the largest digit, which can be done during the first pass through RadixSort.

5. Since the length of each sublist is variable, a linked list implementation is preferable.

7. No. The resulting algorithm is $O(n^2/4)$, which is still $O(n^2)$, although with a smaller constant of proportionality.

9. RadixSort is inflexible for data of varying size. If a set of real numbers could be preprocessed to be presented to RadixSort in a uniform formant (i.e., of uniform length to the right of the decimal point, and possibly with the decimal point removed), the list could be sorted by RadixSort just as any other list of strings of digits.

Section 4.4

1.

Time Slice	Ready Queue	Blocked Queue	Signal	Pause	Current Process
1	A(6)*				A(6)
2	B(4),A(5)				B(4)
3	A(5),B(3)			Y	A(5)
4	B(3),C(6),A(4)				B(3)
5	A(4),B(2)	C(6)		Y	C(6)
6	A(4),B(2)	C(6)			A(4)
7	B(2),A(3)	C(6),B(2)		Y	B(2)
8	A(3)	C(6),B(2)		Y	A(3)
9	A(3),C(4)	C(6),B(2)	Y		A(2)
10	C(4),A(2)	B(2)			C(6)

*The number in parentheses represents the remaining time slices available to that process.

3. Instead of using a boolean variable for the semaphore, use an integer variable that keeps track of the number of resources that are available for allocation from the pool. When the number available reaches 0 and a request is made, the requesting process must be enqueued.

Section 4.5

1. dequeue() is very efficient. Removal of an item merely involves increasing the pointer to the front of the queue (O(1)). enqueue(), however, requires first a search to locate the position for insertion of the new element (average search is N/2 elements) and then shifting the preceding or succeeding elements of the array to the left or right, respectively. The average shift is N/2 elements, depending on which shift direction would require the least data movement.
3. You can use a linked list to great advantage when implementing a priority queue. Whenever an item arrives to be inserted into a given priority level, the rear pointer for that priority gives us an immediately accessible pointer to the node after which the item is to be inserted. This avoids a costly sequential search for the insertion point. If a dummy header is included at the beginning, the empty conditions for any given priority are as shown:

Condition	**Priority**
Front = Rear1	For priority 1, the highest priority
Rear1 = Rear2	For priority 2
Rear(n − 1) = Rear n	For priority n

7. Option #1 unaffected

   Option #2 unaffected

   Option #3 unaffected

   Option #4 unaffected

   Option #5 Since the items in the subordinate queues maintained in this implementation must evaluate to the same priority value, the classic problem of round-off error will surely surface. Priorities could be considered equal if they fall within a determined tolerance. A second method would be for the item with an evaluated priority to take on the closest "known" priority. This could be inconsistant if the finite number of priority values are separated by different interval sizes along the real number line.

Chapter 5

Section 5.1

1. In a stack structure, the first item in is the last item out. The most recent addition to the stack is always at the top of the stack.
3. When a function call is made, the return address, local variables, and parameters are stored in a struct of type StackData. This struct is called an activation struct. The struct is pushed onto the run-time stack. When the subroutine is terminated, the top activation struct is popped off the top of the run-time stack and control is returned to the return address stored in that struct.

Section 5.2

1.
```
template <class BaseData>
class Stack: private List<BaseData>
{
  public: // as per description in text
};
```

   Here are constructor and pop:

```
template <class BaseData>
Stack<BaseData>::Stack():List<BaseData>()
{}

template <class BaseData>
void Stack<BaseData>::pop()
{
  assert (!empty());
  last();
  remove();
}
```

3.
```
template <class BaseData>
class Stack
{
  protected:
```

```
  struct stackNode
  {
    BaseData data;
    stackNode* link;
  };
  stackNode *Stk;

  public: // as per description in text
};
```

Here are constructor and pop

```
template <class BaseData>
Stack<BaseData>::Stack()
{
  stk = NULL;
}

template <class BaseData>
void Stack<BaseData>::pop()
{
  stackNode* tempS;
  if (stk)
  {
    tempS = stk;
    stk = stk->link;
    tempS->link = NULL;
    delete tempS;
  }
}
```

5.
```
template <class expressionType>
int balancedParanthesis (expressionType expression)
{
  Stack <token> s;
  BOOLEAN goodExpression, finished;
  expressionType* position;
  initialize(position);
  goodExpression = TRUE;
  finished = FALSE;
  while (!finished)
  {
    if (endOfExpression (expression, position))
      finished = TRUE;
    else if (rightParanthesis(token))
    {
      if (s.empty())
      {
        goodExpression = FALSE;
        finished = TRUE;
      }
      else
      {
        token = s.top();
        s.pop;
      }
    }
  }
  if (goodExpression && s.empty())
    return(TRUE);
  else return(FALSE);
}
```

Section 5.3

1. Postfix notation: ABCD − PR − / * +
   Prefix notation: +A * B/ − CD − PR

3. The stacks would vary as follows:

Operator Stack	Postfix Queue
#	P
#+	P
#+(	P
#+(	PQ
#+(−	PQF
#+(−	PQF−
#+	PQF−
#+/	PQF−Y/+

5. The stacks would vary as follows:

Operator Stack	Postfix Queue
#	P
#*	P
#*(	P
#*(	PQ
#*(/	PQ
#*(/	PQY
#*	PQY/
#*+	PQY/
#*+	PQY/A
#*+−	PQY/A
#*+−	PQY/AB
#*+−+	PQY/ABD
#**	PQY/ABD+
#**	PQY/ABD+Y
	PQY/ABD+Y**

7. When the infix priority of a given operator is greater than the stack priority of another given operator, the operator with the lower stack priority has a lesser overall algebraic priority. In the normal system we use, the + and − have a low stack priority when compared with the infix priority of the * or the /. Similarly, when the stack priority of a given operator is high, it will be performed before other "incoming" operators.

9. The comparison between stack and infix operators determines how long an operator must wait on the stack before being popped. To correctly evaluate 3^2^3 , 2^3 must be computed first, and then 3 raised to that power. In 3^2^3, the first symbol must have a higher priority than the second ^ or the expression will be incorrectly evaluated as (3^2)^3. Therefore, for the operator ^ , the infix priority must be lower than the stack priority for the same operator, so that the ^ on the stack will not be popped prematurely.

13. In the parseToPost routine, the unary operators must be pushed onto the Operator Stack when they are new tokens. Whenever the new token is a binary operator, all unary operators on top of the operator stack are popped off the stack and enqueued to Postfix before the priority of the binary operator is compared with the operators on the operator stack. The parseToPost routine uses the local function "Negation" that returns a value of true if the token passed in to it is the "−" token and a value of false otherwise. In the special case where the "−" token is used as unary negation rather than binary subtraction, the token is replaced with a special constant token called the "NegateToken." The constant "NULLtoken" is also used to initialize the variable "PrevToken." The "−" token is determined to be the unary operator if it is immediately preceded by nothing or by an operator.

    In the evaluate routine, the unary operators are applied to the element on top of the value stack. A new function "unaryOperator" is passed into the evaluate function.

Chapter 6

Section 6.1

1. The advantage to passing the split function in to the search operation instead of the constructor is that one can now use different split functions for different searches in the same SearchArray class, since to search using a different split function one only needs to pass in that different split function to the search function. The disadvantage is that if we only want to use a single split function in our class, we will have to pass the same function in over and over again in our search calls, while previously we would only have to pass in in once, to the constructor.

3.

Return	M	N	Function Evaluation
1	0	1	2
3	1	0	2
2	0		2
3	1	1	3
2	0		3
3	1	2	4
2	1		4
0	1	3	5

5. First define a function:

```
template <class ElementType>
void insertValue (Array<int, ElementType> &a, int n, ElementType item,
                  BOOLEAN (*precedes)(ElementType x, ElementType y));
```

This function inserts the value item into the array a of n values, where the values are already sorted according to the precedes relationship.

For the function sort:

```
if (numVals > 1)
{
  sort(a, numVals -1 , precedes);
  insertValue(a, numVals -1, a[numVals], precedes);
}
```

9.

```
void reverse(String s, String &r)
{
  String t(80);
  String v(80);
  if (s.length() > 1)
  {
    t = s.substring(2, s.length() - 1);
    reverse(t,r);
    v = t.substring(1,1);
    s.concatenate(r);
  }
  else
    r = s;
}
```

Section 6.2

1. The value output from the array would vary as follows:

lo	hi	array
1	7	60 12 90 30 64 8 6
1	4	6 12 8 30
2	4	12 8 30
2	2	8
4	4	30
6	7	64 90
7	7	90

3. When the data are already in order.
5. When the data are in order or when there is a small data set.
7. The best-case behavior of QuickSort consists of a randomly distributed data set and a pivot that always divides the set evenly into two. This results in an $O(n \log_2 n)$ sort. The worst case is a completely sorted data set, for which the pivots chosen distribute the dubarrays unevenly into sets of 0 and $n - 1$ elements for an ascending sort and into sets of $n - 1$ and 0 elements for a descending sort. This will be $O(n^2)$.
9.

Sort	Stability
insertion	stable
selection	stable
radix	stable
shell	unstable
quick	unstable

shell sort example:

array								**k**
18	13(1)	10	6	11	12	13(2)	19	
6	11	10	13(2)	13(1)	12	18	19	3
6	10	10	12	13(2)	13(1)	18	19	1

quick sort example:

array				**lo**	**hi**	**pivot**
60	42(1)	80	42(2)	1	4	60
42(2)	42(1)	60	80	1	2	42(2)
42(2)	42(1)	60	80	2	2	42(1)
42(2)	42(1)	60	80	4	4	80

Section 6.3

1. The output values would be

lo	**hi**	**array**
1	7	60 12 90 30 64 8 6
1	4	60 12 90 30
1	2	60 12
1	1	60
2	2	12
3	4	90 30
3	3	90
4	4	30
5	7	64 8 6

and so on.

3. There is no data set that can cause the efficiency of the Merge Sort to deteriorate. Its efficiency is always $O(n \cdot \log n)$.

5. **a.** Insertion Sort appropriate: iterative, not recursive efficiency approaches $O(n)$ as the array approaches sorted.

b. Selection Sort inappropriate: $O(n^2)$ cannot be improved

c. Shell Sort appropriate: iterative, not recursive efficiency $= O(n^{1.5})$

d. Quick Sort inappropriate: recursive algorithm efficiency approaches $O(n^2)$ as the array approaches sorted.

e. Radix Sort inappropriate: uses additional space

f. Merge Sort inappropriate: recursive algorithm uses additional space

Section 6.4

1a.

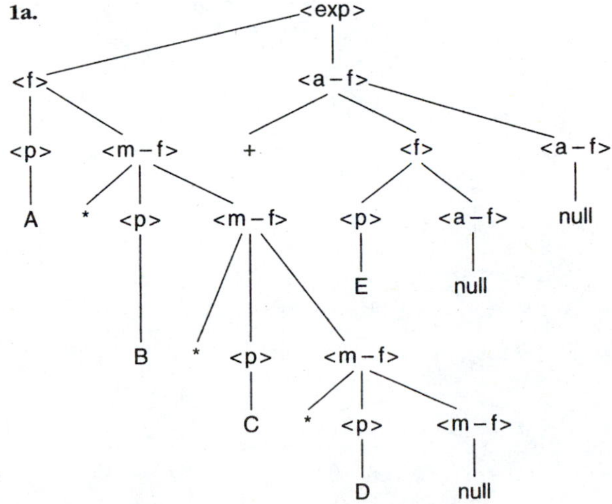

3a. yes

3b. (parse tree for expression of **1a)**

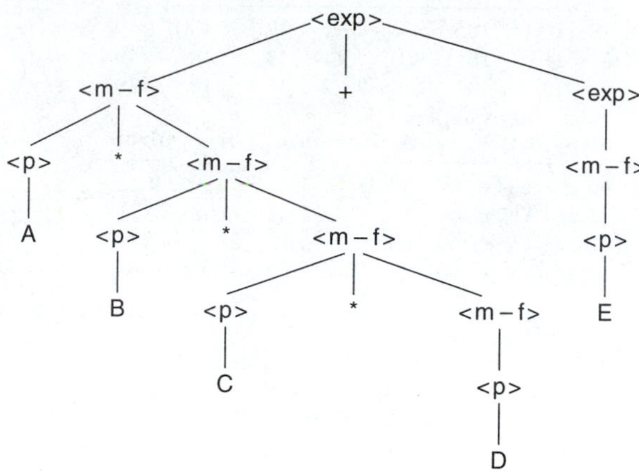

3d. Grammar of exercise 3 has right to left associativity for + and ∗. Example 6.8 has left to right associativity for + and ∗.

5.
```
<if-statement> -> if <condition>
                  then <statement>
               -> if <condition>
                  then <statement>
                  else <statement>
```

we assume **<statement>** is also defined.

Since two different parse trees may be derived from this grammar, this grammar is ambiguous.

(1) let **<s> = <statement>**, **<c> = <condition>**, and **<ifs> = <ifstatement>**

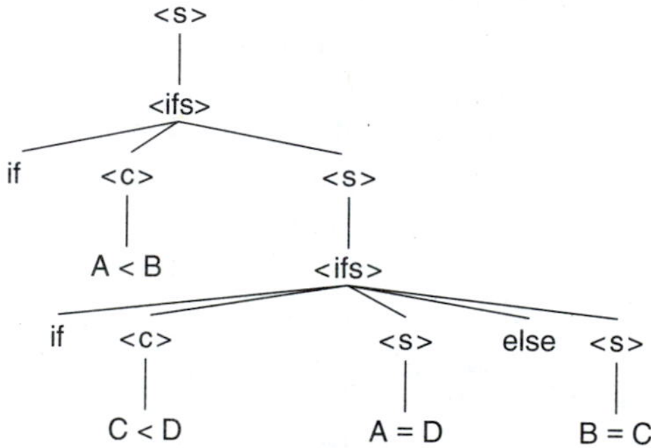

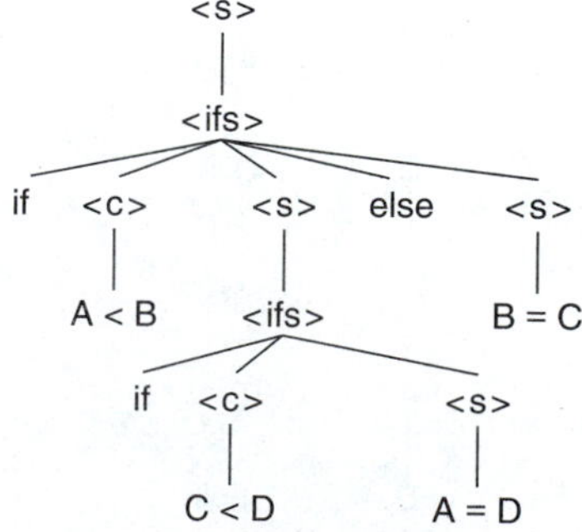

(2) C interpretation corresponds to parse tree (1).

Chapter 7

Section 7.1

1. A ∗ B − (C + D) ∗ (P/Q)

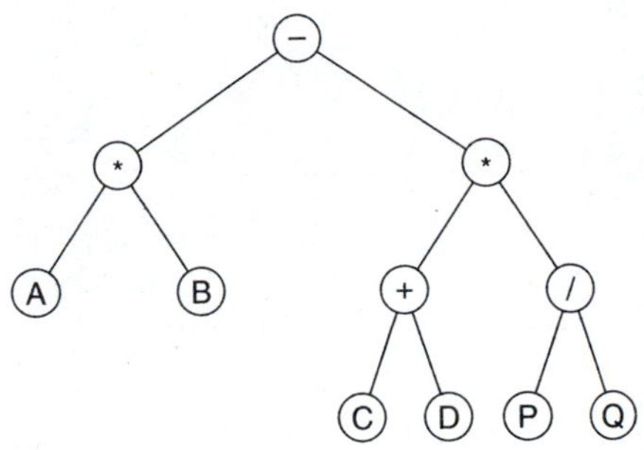

3.
```
struct Student
{
  String name (80);
  int credits;
  float gradePoints;
}

void printData (Student &stu)
{
  cout << name << endl;
  cout << (gradePoints / credits) << endl;
}

studentTree.inorderTrav(printData);
```

5. **a.** This binary tree is a heap.

b. The node containing 19 has a right subtree with a node containing 35. The node containing 36 has a left sub-tree with a node containing 39. In a heap, no descendent of a node may contain data greater than the node's data.

c. This binary tree is a heap.

7.

binary-to-heap	The data in any given node of the tree are greater than or equal to the data in its left and right subtrees.
binary-to-ordered	The data value in each node of the tree is greater than all of the data in that node's left subtree and less than or equal to all the data in the right subtree.
binary-to-expression	The relationship of binary operator to its two operands.

Section 7.2

1b.

Location	Data	Left Child	Right Child
1	C	3	NULL
2	R	NULL	3
3	G	NULL	NULL
4	F	NULL	NULL
5	X	9	4
6	Y	NULL	NULL
7	B	6	5
8	A	7	1
9	J	NULL	NULL

Root = 8 Avail = 2

3. Values will appear on separate lines and without commas in actual output.
OOPS, OOPS, OOPS, K, OOPS, I, OOPS, OOPS, OOPS, J, H, G, C, OOPS, OOPS, E, OOPS, OOPS, D, B, A

7.

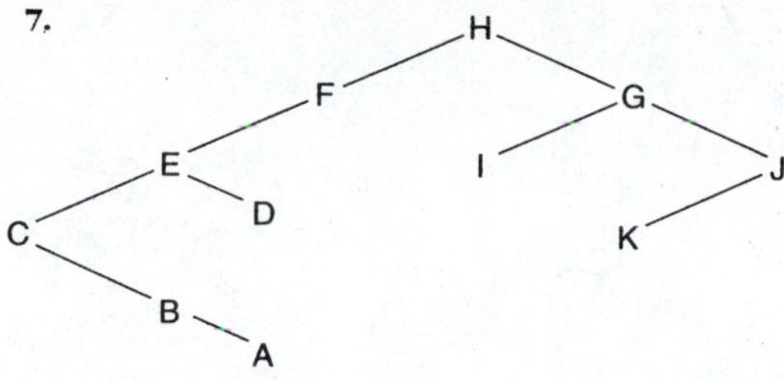

9. A, B, E, J, NULL, NULL, NULL, K, NULL, NULL, NULL, L, NULL, NULL, NULL, NULL, NULL, C, F, NULL, NULL, NULL, G, NULL, NULL, NULL, H, NULL, NULL, NULL, D, NULL, NULL, I, NULL, M, O, NULL, NULL, NULL, NULL, NULL, N, NULL, NULL, NULL

Section 7.3

1. The resulting tree is not very full. Its big-O efficiency would be $O(n)$.

100
90
80
70
60
50
40
30
20
10

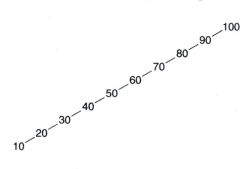

3. In terms of fullness, the tree here is better than the tree in Exercise 1. But since constants are not considered significant with large values of n, its big-O performance remains $O(n)$.

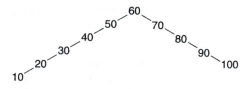

60
50 70
40 80
30 90
20 100
10

5. With any of these three implementations, the insertion of a node is relatively easy. To find the correct position in a single-linked list, two pointers have to be used: one to keep track of the previous node and the other to keep track of current node. In a doubly linked list and in a binary tree, this situation is avoided. However, in a doubly linked list, the entire list has to be sequentially searched to find the correct node. In a binary tree, the search is potentially equivalent to a binary search.

13. Complications arise when trying to retrieve all nodes with a particular value since the entire tree must be traversed.

Section 7.4

1. Final tree:

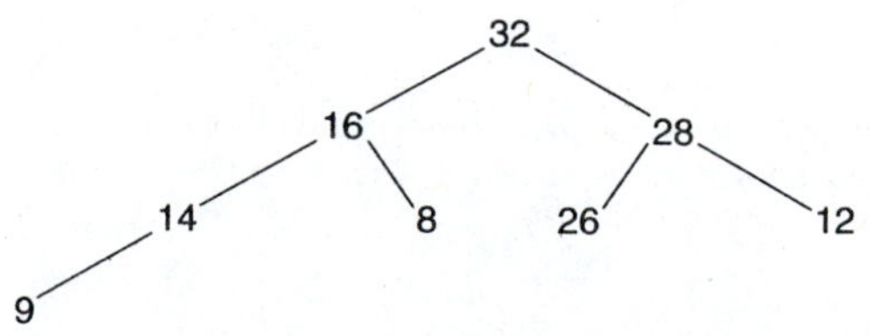

3. 67, 64, 12, 61, 42, 6, 4, 55, 55, 32

7.

Phase I:	1	8	6	7	3	2
	1	8	6	7	3	2
	8	7	6	1	3	2
Phase II:	7	3	6	1	2	8
	6	3	2	1	7	8
	3	1	2	6	7	8
	2	1	3	6	7	8
	1	2	3	6	7	8

9. Heap sort is $O(n \log_2 n)$ regardless of the data being sorted.

Section 7.5

1a.

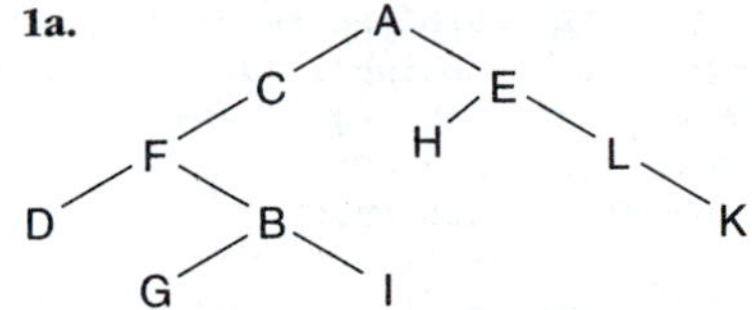

3. To thread a tree for postorder traversal, the threads of the rightmost nodes would have to point back to the header, but the header would also have to be pointed to by the left-most nodes. So when the header was reached by traversing the threads, you would not know if you had really traversed all the nodes.

9. If the tree is very sparse and is very large and recursion is used, then the system stack will quickly overflow with the large number of recursive calls generated while the tree is being traversed in order. By avoiding recursion, we can avoid the memory problems caused by the large buildup of recursive calls.

Section 7.6

1. This tree is balanced but not full.

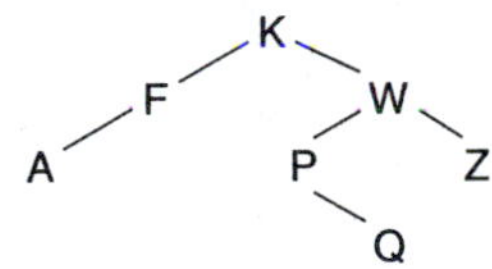

3.

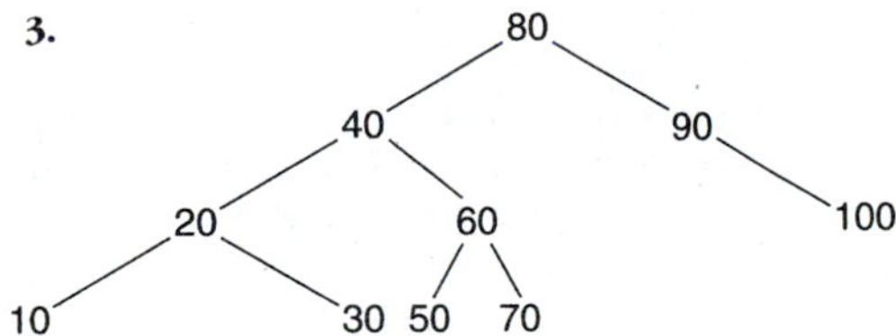

Chapter 8

Section 8.1

1. 12, 6, 3, 17, 64, 25, 8, 49, 36, 16, 40, 63, 93, 78, 4, 9, 13, 97, 84, 18, 2, 6, 44, 19, 1

3. An inorder traversal of a binary tree requires that you recursively visit all nodes in the left subtree, process the root node, and then recursively visit all nodes in the right subtree. Any node in a general tree may have more than two children, and therefore the terms *left* subtree and *right* subtree lose their meaning; thus, a general tree cannot be processed by an inorder traversal.

5. Use a global variable to keep count of the nodes visited. Have processNode increase the count each time it is invoked by postOrderAux.

Section 8.2

1. `root-> info is P.  root->firstChild is "Q".  root->sibling = NULL;`

```
"Q"->firstChild is "T".   "Q"->sibling is "A".
"T"->firstChild is NULL.  "T"->sibling is "U".
"U"->firstChild is NULL.  "U"->sibling is "V".
"V"->firstChild is "C".   "V"->sibling is "W".
"C"->firstChild is NULL.  "C"->sibling is "D".
"D"->firstChild is NULL.  "D"->sibling is "E".
"E"->firstChild is "M".   "E"->sibling is NULL.
"M"->firstChild is NULL.  "M"->sibling is "N".
"O"->firstChild and O->sibling are NULL.
"W"->firstChild and O->sibling are NULL.
"A"->firstChild is "G".   "A"->sibling is "B".
"G"->firstChild is NULL.  "G"->sibling is NULL.
"B"->firstChild is "H".   "B"->sibling is "X".
"H"->firstChild is NULL.  "H"->sibling is "I".
"I"->firstChild is NULL.  "I"->sibling is "J".
"J"->firstChild is NULL.  "J"->sibling is NULL.
"X"->firstChild is "K".   "X"->sibling is NULL.
"K"->firstChild is NULL.  "K"->sibling is "L".
"L"->firstChild is NULL.  "L"->sibling is NULL.
```

3. Postorder traversal of the general tree: T, U, C, D, M, N, O, E, V, W, Q, G, A, H, I, J, B, K, L, X, P
Postorder traversal of the general tree using binary implementaion: O, N, M, E, D, C, W, V, U, T, G, J, I, H, L, K, X, B, A, Q, P

Section 8.3

1.

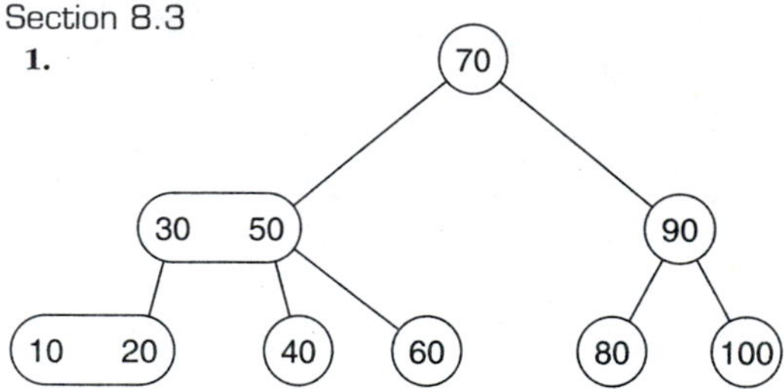

5. The order in which data arrive does not affect the distribution of data in a 2-3 tree, since insertion maintains a tree with all of its leaves on the same level. A new level is added by sprouting a new root rather than adding a leaf at a deeper level.

Section 8.4

1. Final configuration:
P = {{7, 3, 6}, {8, 5, 2, 9, 1, 10, 4}}

Parent	1	2	3	4	5	6	7	8	9	10
Array	9	5	7	8	8	7	0	0	5	8

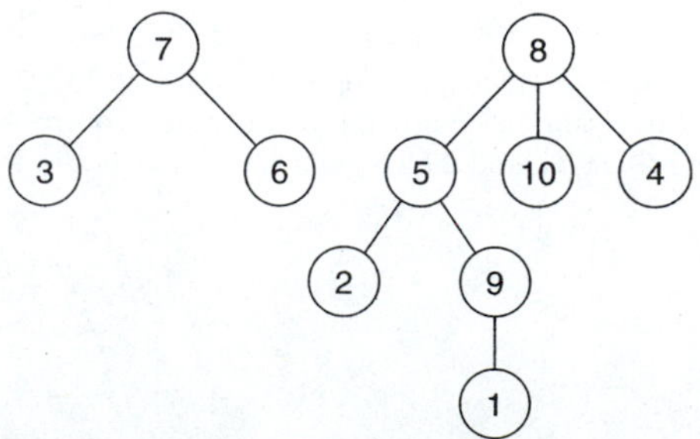

3. Final configuration:

P = {{7, 3, 6}, {8, 5, 2, 9, 1, 10, 4}}

Parent	1	2	3	4	5	6	7	8	9	10
Array	8	5	7	8	8	7	0	0	8	8

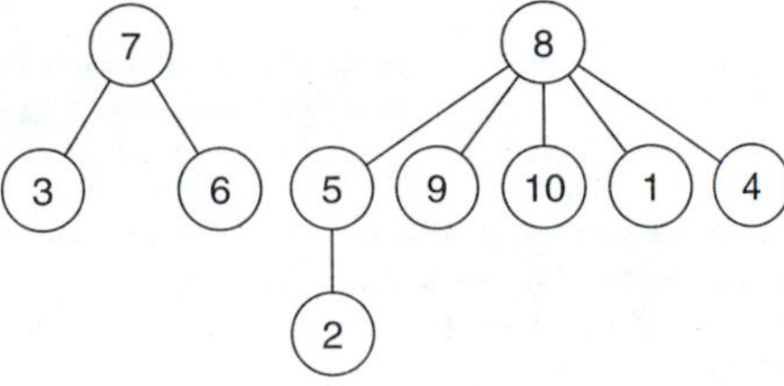

9. Consider the following example:

```
UnionFind<int> p (1, 5);
ufUnion(1,2);
ufUnion(2,3);
ufUnion(3,4);
ufUnion(4,5);
```

Chapter 9

Section 9.1

1. A nonempty general tree is a graph since it is a set of nodes connected by parent/child relationships, which are depicted as edges. Each edge has two end-points: the parent node and the child node. A graph, however, is not necessarily a general tree. A graph, for example, may have a loop or a cycle, which a tree may not have.

3. Since each edge in a graph has two endpoints, each edge contributes two degrees to the sum of the total degrees of all the nodes in a digraph. Therefore, the sum must be even. The number of nodes in a digraph that has an odd total degree must be even.

Section 9.2

1. B D C A

3. D C A B

5. A B D C. Assume that B is the first node adjacent to A.

7. The **addEdge** operation does not correctly add an edge between nodes with values **value1** and **value2** if the graph is an undirected graph. In an undirected graph, an edge between two nodes is not directionally oriented. The edge from the node with **value1** to the node with **value2** is the same as the edge from the node with **value2** to the node with **value1.** The **addEdge** operation gives an edge from the node with **value1** to the node with **value2** but does not establish an edge from the node with **value2** to the node with **value1.** Function **addUndirectedEdge** needs to call **addEdge** twice—first with the parameters (node with **value1**, node with **value2**), and then with the parameters (node with **value2,** node with **value1**).

Section 9.3

1. Use the Array class from Chapter 2 and this Matrix class will work:

```
#include "array.h"

template <class RowType, class ColType, class BaseData>
class Matrix
{
  public:
    Matrix(RowType loRow, RowType hiRow, ColType loCol,ColType hiCol);
    // copy constructor
    Matrix (const Matrix<RowType, ColType, BaseData> & initMatrix);
    ~Matrix();
    Array<ColType, BaseData> &operator [] (RowType row);
    void operator = (const Matrix<RowType, ColType, BaseData> & initMatrix);
```

```
  private:
    Array<RowType, Array<ColType, BaseData>*>* arrayData;
    RowType loRowIndex, hiRowIndex;
    ColType loColIndex, hiColIndex;
    BOOLEAN outOfRange(RowType row);
};

template <class RowType, class ColType, class BaseData>
Matrix<RowType,ColType, BaseData>::Matrix(RowType loRow, RowType hiRow,
                                          ColType loCol, ColType hiCol)
{
  arrayData = new Array<RowType, Array<ColType, BaseData>*> (loRow, hiRow);
  for (int i = loRow; i <= hiRow; i++)
    (*arrayData)[i] = new Array <ColType, BaseData>(loCol, hiCol);
  assert(arrayData != 0);
  loRowIndex =loRow;
  hiRowIndex =hiRow;
  loColIndex =loCol;
  hiColIndex =hiCol;
}

template <class RowType,class ColType, class BaseData>
Array<ColType,BaseData>& Matrix<RowType,ColType,BaseData>::operator[](RowType row)
{
  assert(!outOfRange(row));
  return ((*(*arrayData)[row]));
}
```

3. **a.** *O*(1)

b. *O*(NumberofNodes) (worst case)

5. The worst-case efficiency is realized when every node in the graph is connected (directly or indirectly) to the start node. In that case, the recursive call in the subordinate procedure SearchFrom will be involved for each connected node, totaling NumberofNodes times.

9.
```
template <class BaseData>
void Graph<BaseData>::connectedComponent(int &n)
{
  Array<BaseData, BOOLEAN> visited(firstValue, lastValue);
  n = 0;
  for (BaseData i = firstNode; i <= lastNode; i++)
     visited[i] = FALSE;
  for (i = firstNode; i <= lastNode; i++)
    if (!visited[i])
    {
      n++;
      searchFrom(i, processNode, visited);
    }
}
```

11.
```
template <class BaseData>
void Graph<BaseData>::countEdges(int &numEdges)
{
  BaseData j,k;
  numEdges = 0;
  for (j = firstNode; j <= lastNode; j++)
     for (k = firstNode; k <= lastNode; k++)
        if (edge (j,k)) numEdges++;
}
```

Section 9.4

1. Final structures:

	Distance	Path	Included
NYC	2819	WASH	True
WASH	2582	MILW	True
MIAM	∞	?	False
MILW	1771	PHEX	True
CHI	6494	LVEG	True
NORL	4950	DALS	False
MPLS	5382	DALS	False

OKLC	∞	?	False
DALS	4433	NYC	True
LVEG	4714	LA	True
PHEX	0	?	True
STL	4836	SRAN	False
SFRAN	4028	MILW	True
LA	4442	SRAN	True

5. Final structure:

	CHI	NORL	DALS	LVEG	LA
CHI	0	948	1465	1780	2052
NORL	948	0	517	2229	1957
DALS	1465	517	0	1712	1440
LVEG	1780	5559	1712	0	272
LA	2052	1957	1440	272	0

11.

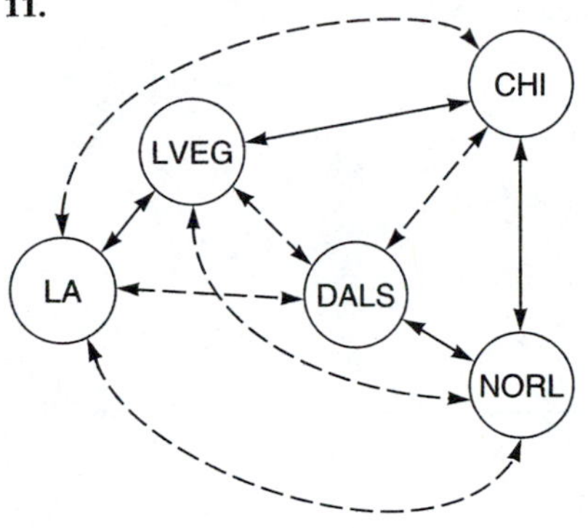

- Solid lines indicate the original edges of the underlying graph.
- Dotted lines indicate edges added in the transitive closure of the graph.

Section 9.5

1. Prim's algorithm: Final MST

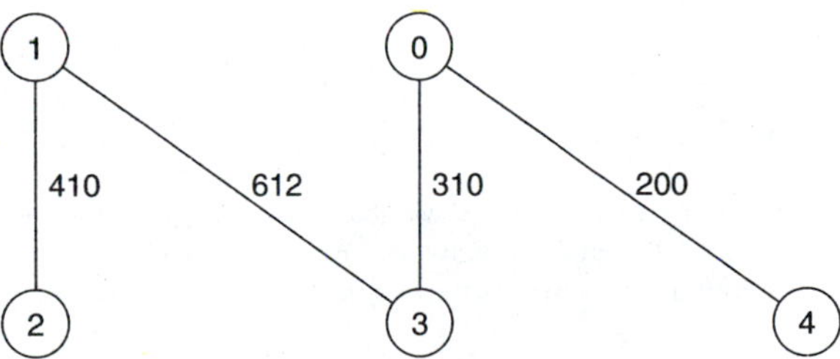

Kruskal's algorithm: Final MST

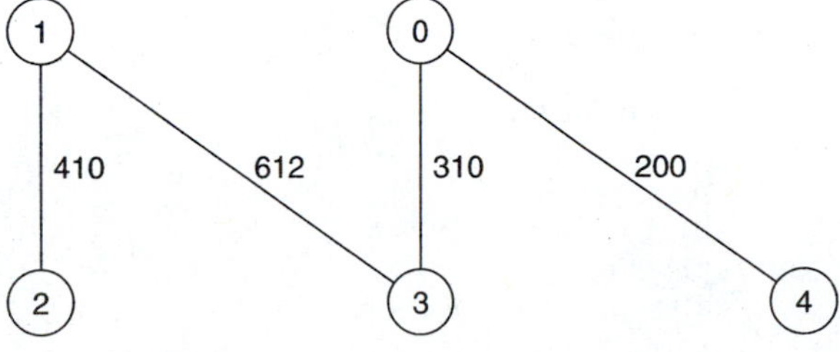

7. In a minimal spanning tree there is only one edge connecting any two nodes. If the number of edges is greater than or equal to the number of nodes, then some node is connected by more than one path, thus creating a cycle. This contradicts the definition of a minimal spanning tree, since we may remove one of the edges in the cycle and hence have a spanning tree of lesser total edge weight.

11. False. For this network

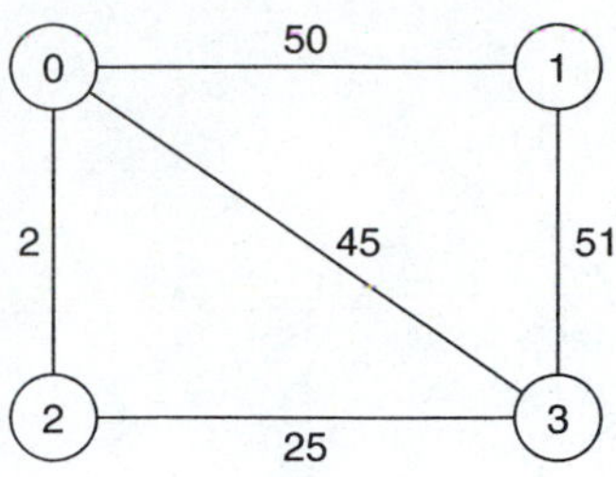

the minimal spanning tree would be

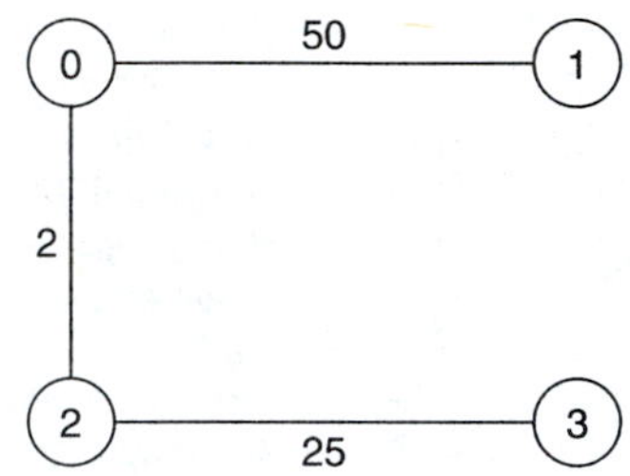

13.

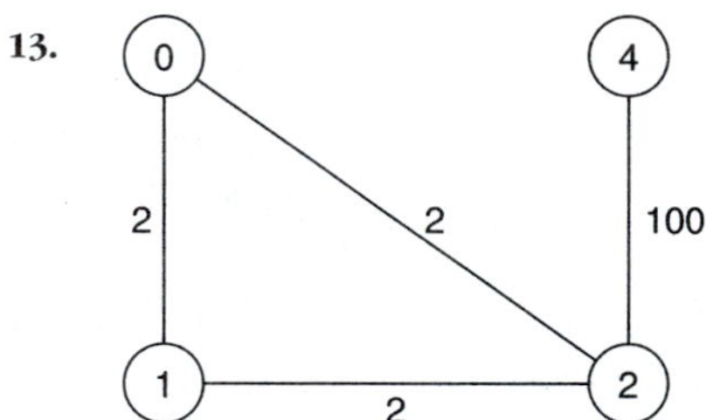

15. Since a cost estimate (a weighted edge) is given for each direct link between any two computers for all 1000 sites, the network can be considered dense: it has a maximum number of edges. Prim's algorithm is the most effective for this type of network.

Section 9.6

1. Initialize zeroQ: zeroQ = 1,2,6.

Loop: dequeue from zeroQ and reduce indegree of all nodes connected to the dequeued item by one. Add any connected nodes of indegree zero to zeroQ.

Loop iteration:

(1) zeroQ = 2, 3, 6
[1] = 1

(2) zeroQ = 6, 3, 4, 5
[1] = 1, t[2] = 2

(3) zeroQ = 3, 4, 5
[1] = 1, t[2] = 2, t[3] = 6

(4) zeroQ = 4, 5
t[1] = 1, t[2] = 2, t[3] = 6, t[4] = 3

(5) zeroQ = 5
t[1] = 1, t[2] = 2, t[3] = 6, t[4] = 3, t[5] = 4.

(6) zeroQ = 7
t[1] = 1, t[2] = 2, t[3] = 6, t[4] = 3, t[5] = 4, t[6] = 5

(7) zeroQ = empty
t[1] = 1, t[2] = 2, t[3] = 6, t[4] = 3, t[5] = 4, t[6] = 5, t[7] = 7.

3. Since the graph is acyclic, there must exist one or more nodes in the graph of indegree zero. When these nodes are processed (removed from zeroQ), they may be considered as having been removed from the graph, along with the edges connected to their successor nodes. As edges are removed, the indegree of the successor nodes is reduced. When all the predecessors of a node have been removed (placed on zeroQ), the node will have an indegree of zero, and thus will be placed on the zeroQ. Once a node is on zeroQ, it has no predecessor nodes, so no other node will have an edge leading to it (i.e., it cannot be resubmitted to zeroQ). Thus all the nodes of a directed acyclic graph will be placed on zeroQ once.

Chapter 10

Section 10.1

5.

order	row	column
1	4	1
2	8	2
3	5	3
4	3	4
5	6	5
6	1	5
7	7	6
8	2	7
9	6	8

7. The maze ADT can be implemented similarly to the eight queens problem. The only significant difference is the omission of testing the diagonal direction as a possible blocked path.

9. Rather than stopping when a path is found, the algorithm continues traversing the problem until all possible paths have been attempted.

Section 10.2

1. A depth-first strategy results. The Stack ADT has no way of using any completed heuristic value to organize its elements.

3. The trade-offs are the time it takes to compute the heuristic value every time it is needed versus the memory space required to store the heuristic value in the priority queue.

7. The heuristic function is always effective.

9. The path from A to E chosen by the heuristic function of path weight will be A→B→C→D→E instead of the shorter path A→D→E.

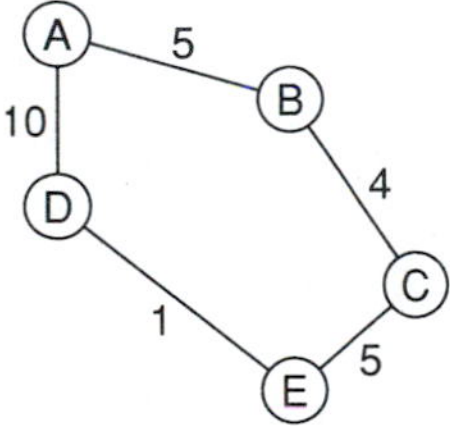

Chapter 11

Section 11.1

3.

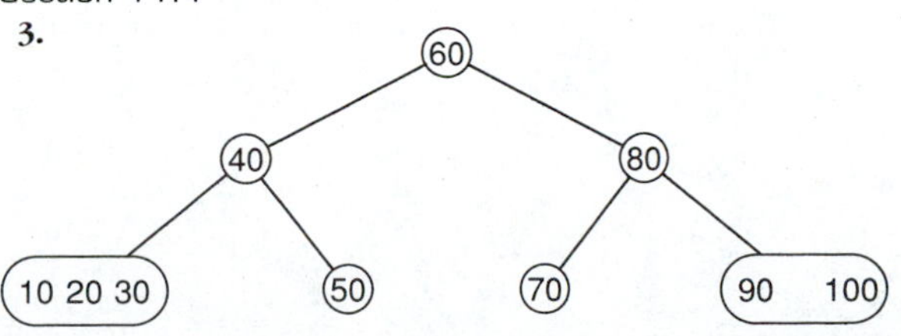

7.

13.

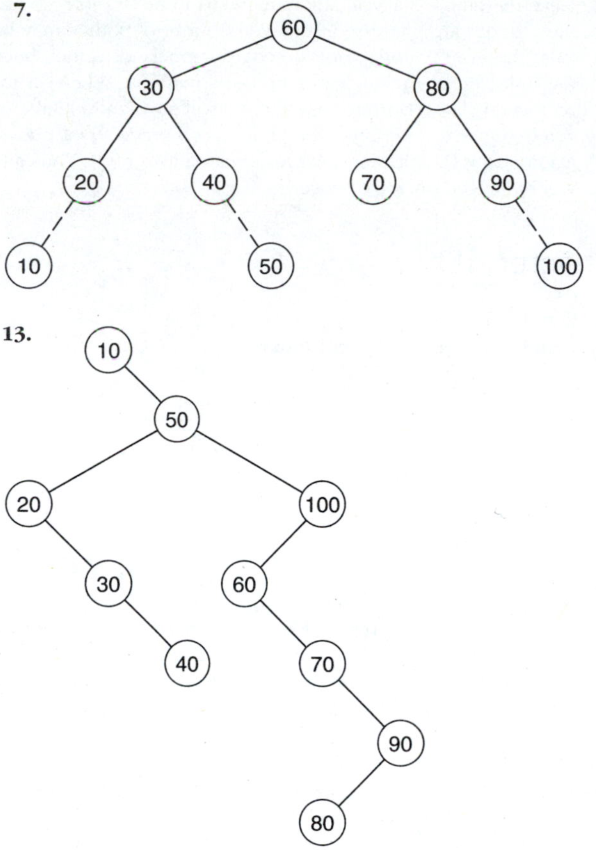

Section 11.2

1. a.

Index	Key
0	333
1	632
2	1090
3	459
4	379
5	238
6	
7	
8	
9	1982
10	3411

b.

Index	Key
0	333
1	632
2	1090
3	238
4	459
5	
6	
7	379
8	
9	1982
10	3411

c.

Index	Key	Link	Index	Key	Link
0	333	13	11	3411	14
1	632	0	12	459	0
2	1090	0	13	379	15
3			14	238	0
4			15		
5			16		
6			17		
7			18		
8			19		
9	1982	12	20		
10			21		

3. a.

Position	Key
0	0
1	19
2	38
3	55
4	67
5	4
6	58
7	86
8	0

b.

Position	Key
0	0
1	46
2	32
3	62
4	34
5	0
6	77
7	6
8	0
9	0
10	0

c.

Position	Key
0	0
1	0
2	0
3	4
4	16
5	5
6	27
7	14
8	25
9	20
10	0
11	107
12	0
13	0
14	0

d.

Position	Key
0	20
1	7
2	42
3	51
4	0
5	72
6	6
7	88
8	0
9	9
10	21

Section 11.3

1. The doubly linked list is the best choice for implementing linked lists with hashing. When the order of the list is disturbed during a change of a key field or during a deletion of an item in the list, the linked list must be rebuilt. If a doubly linked list is not used, the list would have to be traversed to find the predecessor node in the linked list. The doubly linked list makes rebuilding lists more efficient.
5. With **tableSize** 29, **compNumber** is 19.
9. Compute a lower bound CompNum using MAT and an upper bound CompNum using MZT. Select strings with CompNumbers between these two values and check known characters.
11. The table size would be approximately 6,000,000 elements since this would give a density of .50. Using the rehashing method we could then achieve the desired 3 probe average.

Section 11.4

1. **a.**

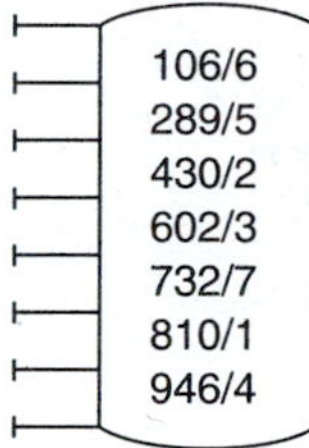

b.

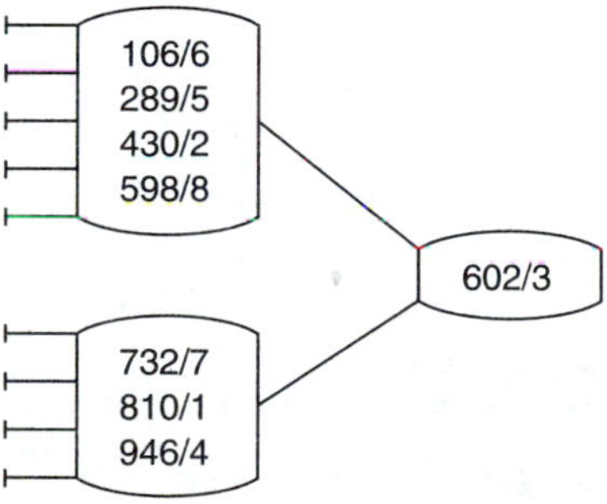

Chapter 12

Section 12.1

1. Using induction, at the induction step we determine that $(n + 1)! = (n + 1)n! > (n + 1)(n/2)^{n/2}$. Using calculus, one can show that the function $f(n) = (n+1)(n/2)n/2 - [(n+1)/2]^{(n+1)/2}$ is positive and increasing; hence $(n + 1)(n/2)^{n/2} > [(n + 1)/2]^{(n+1)/2}$, completing the induction step.
5. Using a decision tree analysis as in the text, we determine that an algorithm to produce an array of sorted distinct elements would require $\log_2(n!)$ comparisons to sort the elements and another $n - 1$ comparisons among adjacent values to remove duplicate values. Thus, a lower bound for this algorithm is $(n/2)\log_2(n/2) + (n - 1)$. Since, however, $n \log_2 n$ dominates n for large values of n, the lower bound is asymptotically equal to the lower bound established for ordinary sorting.

Section 12.2

1.
```
#include "list.h"

template <class streamData>
class Stream
{
  protected:
```

```
    // for illustration of a "concrete" implementation of
    // the stream class, we will use a list of characters
    // as an example of a sequence of homogenous records
    // that may be accessed only by starting at the first
    // record of the sequence...
    // however, the actual data structures implemented in
    // this section do not have to be lists --
    // they could be anything that could represent the
    // organization of records in the stream
    List<char> l;
    char currMode; // could be "r" or "w"
  public:
    as given in text
};
```

Here are the setMode and get operations

```
template <class streamData>
void Stream<streamData>::setMode(char mode)
{
  if ((mode == 'w') || (mode == 'W'))
  {
    l.last();
    for (int i = l.count(); i >=1; i--)
      l.remove();
    l.first();
    currMode = 'w';
  }
  else
    if ((mode == 'r') || (mode == 'R'))
    {
      currMode = 'r';
      l.first();
    }
    else
    {
      cout << "invalid mode!" << endl;
    }
}

template <class streamData>
streamData Stream<streamData>::get()
{
  if (currMode == 'r')
  {
    streamData temp = l.examine();
    if (l.count() != l.current())
      l.next() ;
    return (temp);
  }
  else
  {
    cout << "not in r mode!" << endl;
    return streamData(NULL);
  }
}
```

5a.
```
template <class StreamData>
Stream<streamData> twowaymergeSort(const Stream<StreamData> &s1,
                                   const Stream<StreamData> &s2,
                                   BOOLEAN (*precedes)(const StreamData &a,
                                   const StreamData &b)

{
  int count;
  int numberofruns;
  Stream<StreamData> temp1, temp2, s3, s4;
  count = 0;
  temp1 = s1; // s1 and s2 will not be modified
  temp2 = s2;
```

```
    do
    {
      ++count;
      if ((count % 2) != 0)
        numberofruns = mergestreams(temp1, temp2, precedes, s3, s4);
      else
        numberofruns = mergestreams(s3, s4, precedes, temp1, temp2);
    }
    while (numberofruns > 1);
    if ((count % 2) != 0)
      return s3;
    else
      return temp1;
}
```

Chapter 13

Section 13.1

1. The implementation of Example 13.1 or first-fit seems most appropriate for file management using fixed size disk blocks, since it is already set up to allocate and reclaim fixed-size units of storage.

5. Relocation information must be maintained to identify those data values, such as addresses of instruction operands, that would have to be changed to perform correctly if they are moved during the compaction.

Section 13.2

1. Ratios of unused storage after each event: 0/32, 13/32, 15/32, 25/104, 12/72, 16/88, 14/80, 17/96, 7/64, 3/48, 3/16, 0

3. Ratios of unused storage after each event: 7/39, 9/60, 11/68, 44/123, 42/102, 51/123, 49/115, 49/128, 16/73, 7/52, 0/13, 0

Section 13.3

3. *O*(SizeOfHeap); linked list

Index